W9-BSP-329

FOR REFERENCE

Do Not Take From This Room

The Oxford Companion to American Theatre

The Oxford Companion to
AMERICAN THEATRE

SECOND EDITION

GERALD BORDMAN

New York   OXFORD UNIVERSITY PRESS   Oxford
1992

Oxford University Press

Oxford   New York   Toronto
Delhi   Bombay   Calcutta   Madras   Karachi
Petaling Jaya   Singapore   Hong Kong   Tokyo
Nairobi   Dar es Salaam   Cape Town
Melbourne   Auckland
and associated companies in
Berlin   Ibadan

Copyright © 1984, 1992 by Oxford University Press, Inc.

Published by Oxford University Press, Inc.,
200 Madison Avenue, New York, New York 10016

Oxford is a registered trademark of Oxford University Press

All rights reserved. No part of this publication may be reproduced,
stored in a retrieval system, or transmitted, in any form or by any means,
electronic, mechanical, photocopying, recording, or otherwise,
without the prior permission of Oxford University Press.

Library of Congress Cataloging-in-Publication Data
Bordman, Gerald Martin.
The Oxford companion to American theatre / Gerald Bordman.—2nd ed.
p.   cm.
ISBN 0-19-507246-4
1. Theater—United States—Dictionaries.
2. Theater—United States—Biography—Dictionaries.   I. Title.
PN2220.B6   1992
792'.0973—dc20   91-16720

2   4   6   8   9   7   5   3   1
Printed in the United States of America
on acid-free paper

Memorial Library
Mars Hill College
Mars Hill, N. C.

Preface to the Second Edition

Seven years have elapsed since the first edition of this *Companion*. When we studied under the great folklorist MacEdward Leach, he pointed out that the numbers three and seven were frequent figures in older Western storytelling and suggested that they need not always be taken literally. Three he suggested was a code word for "several"; seven for "many." Yet seven years are not many in the two hundred-odd years of our American theatre, especially at a time when the theatre, or certainly Broadway, seems to offer less and less in the face of technological competition. Nonetheless, there have been changes. New talents and new plays have appeared to brighten the scene. So there is a need for addition and revision. Space considerations dictated that the new be accommodated at the expense of some older entries that we hope will not be seriously missed.

The principal criticism which several judicious reviewers levelled at the first edition was that we slighted a number of important figures and organizations of contemporary significance. We had hoped that our comments in the original Preface would have forestalled such criticism, but they did not. We therefore asked four major American drama critics to suggest some additional entries. Surprisingly, only two names—Joseph Chaikin (and his Open Theatre) and Mabou Mines—appeared on all four lists. We added all suggestions found on two or more lists. Even so, we were left with the feeling that our initial choices were on target. Of course, we have also added entries for other significant figures, groups, and plays which have appeared since our first writing and the end of 1990. We trust most readers will find the selection satisfactory.

The same space considerations that forced us to delete a few older entries preclude our thanking individually the many people who wrote with helpful ideas or kindly pointed out errors in the first edition. They know who they are; their thoughtfulness has not gone unappreciated.

Kirk's Mills, Pa.   G.B.
September 1991

R 792.0973
098b

1995

Preface

"Companion" is such a likable word, connoting something or someone so welcoming and comfortable, that it has been a special pleasure to bring it hand in hand with two more words that have long suggested admirable qualities and good times, "American" and "Theatre." We can only hope, then, that this *Oxford Companion to American Theatre* will prove delightful, useful company, whether habitually or for particular occasions. Perhaps focusing first on "Companion" is slightly unfair, since the real emphasis here might rather be on "American." After all, for many years theatre lovers have had recourse to the *Oxford Companion to the Theatre*, a basic reference book designed to cover theatre the world over. Both *Companions* cover some of the same matter and readers are urged to compare entries since often material has been approached differently.

An important difference is the inclusion here of entries for plays themselves—several hundred of them. We trust that no American play of major importance has been omitted, but our aim has not been merely to offer plays of enduring aesthetic or historical significance. Rather, we have attempted to give a broad picture of the popular American stage, so we have included as many commercially successful plays as practicable, regardless of the fact that they now may be totally forgotten or have no claim to permanence. To this end, we have offered entries for all non-musical American plays (except for some farce-comedies that straddled the fence between straight play and musical) which achieved a New York run of 100 or more performances before the end of the 1908–09 season, a run indicative in those years of substantial contemporary appeal. Thereafter, as longer runs became more common, the numbers were raised, so that, as an instance, between mid-1909 and 1920 a play had to survive 200 performances to be given an entry. Because hit musicals have almost always run considerably longer than non-musicals we employed even more demanding figures for their inclusion. Of course, numerous plays with shorter runs have been included when they are deemed to have some special interest. (In early years many shows were booked in New York

for only limited runs prior to a national tour, and this, too, has been considered.) In play entries, the number of performances is the one assigned by the *Best Plays* series. Although different sources give different figures, the numbers rarely disagree by more than a handful of performances. Students of particular plays of course might want to go back to primary sources to determine the precise count. For plays before 1894 we have used several sources to determine length of run, but primarily Odell's *Annals of the New York Stage*. We have listed producers only where it was deemed to be of interest. In play entries, PP represents Pulitzer Prize, while NYDCCA stands for New York Drama Critics Circle Award. In the latter case only winners of the over-all best play category, established in the 1962–63 season, are acknowledged from that season on.

We have also included a number of foreign plays which had long careers on American stages or which influenced American theatre significantly. Here, however, our choice has been a little arbitrary and the form of the entry is different.

We believe that we have discussed all the giants among our actors, authors, producers, and other theatrical notables. Below this top level we have, of necessity, again had to be a bit arbitrary, but we hope that we have included more than a representative cross section, covering not only all aspects of the theatre, but all years and, where possible, all important theatrical centers. Two difficulties did arise. Among certain artists, especially designers and directors, facts were dismayingly hard to secure as one went back in time, so that a few deserving figures may have been denied an entry for lack of sufficient information. Moreover, material is often equally hard to unearth for figures who were important away from New York, especially in the 19th century. Such towering artists as Boston's Mrs. Vincent or William Warren might present no problem but many other cities had permanent stock companies whose leading figures now appear to be little more than names mentioned in old theatrical memoirs. We can only hope that local theatrical historians will fill in these gaps so that in future editions of this *Companion* such now shadowy figures will once again stand in the limelight.

We have tried, albeit not at the same length or depth, to look at more than legitimate theatre. Minstrelsy, vaudeville, circuses, wild west shows, tent shows, and other instances of live theatre have been allotted as much treatment as space permitted. Film careers of figures and plays have been mentioned only briefly, if at all. Fuller information on these can be found in the *Oxford Companion to Film* and elsewhere.

Phyllis Hartnoll, in the preface to the first edition of the *Oxford Companion to the Theatre,* noted, "the difficulty has been to decide what to omit." In two particular areas our omissions may distress some dedicated contemporary playgoers: the first, a number of figures and plays admired by off-Broadway or by more venturesome regional critics and audiences; the second, a number of rising young talents. In the first case, we believe that these off-Broadway or regional favorites do not yet belong to the theatrical mainstream. In the second, we have no doubt that if the newcomers realize their early promise they will command entries in the future. In both cases a few, admittedly very few, representative entries have been included.

Several lesser matters. When dates are given they are those that apply to New York City unless the entry makes clear otherwise. Dates are sometimes open to question. Unfortunately, especially for some early people, birth and occasionally death dates are uncertain or unknown. Where sources give conflicting dates and we could not resolve the problem we placed a question mark after the date given. In a few instances we have fallen back on indicating the epoch during which a figure flourished.

As in other *Companions* the length of an entry is not necessarily an indication of the subject's importance. For only a few of the most salient figures have we attempted to offer a more or less complete history. Instead, we have endeavored to examine the highlights of a figure's career and say something about the essence of his or her art. Thus, an actor or actress might be listed as a cast member in a play's entry without any mention of that play in the performer's entry. A ◆ following a name in an entry indicates the existence of an individual entry for that figure or work. We have tried, wherever possible, to bring this *Companion* up to mid-1983, although we have also included, however sadly, later death dates.

The list of people and organizations we have to acknowledge is long. Particular thanks must go to the library staff at Millersville University in Millersville, Pennsylvania. The library has a surprising range of materials for a theatrical historian and a staff that is exceptional both in knowledgeability and courtesy. Geraldine Duclow, Elaine Ibo, and Laura Simms of the Theatre Collection of the Free Library of Philadelphia have been unstintingly helpful as has Louis Rackow, librarian for The Players. Mary Henderson and her associates at the Theatre Collection of the Museum of the City of New York, Brigitte Kueppers at the Shubert Archive, and the staff of the Harvard Theatre Collection have all contributed to making our work easier and more pleasant. So have the excellent Lancaster County Library, San Francisco Library, and Paul Bailey and his associates at the Theatre Arts Library of the University of Texas. We have used, too, the collection of the Library of the Performing Arts at New York's Lincoln Center. We are especially grateful to Mr. Rackow, as well as to Stanley Green and Paul Myers for carefully examining our long list of projected entries and making suggestions about names we had omitted. We would also like to express gratitude to Helen Armstead-Johnson, Hobart Berolzheimer, Sam Brylawski, Claudia Cassidy, Richard Coe, Stuart Tipton Cooke, Herbert G. Goldman, Jacques Kelly, Miles Kreuger, William Torbert Leonard, Nedda Harrigan Logan, George McKinnon, Raymond Mander and Joe Mitchenson, Marc Miller, Marilyn Moorcroft, Pamela Nicely, Frederick Nolan, Megan Rosenfeld, John R. Rothgeb, Wayne Silka, Richard Stoddard, Glenna Syse, Douglas Watt, and Bernard Weiner, as well as to the press representatives who so kindly and promptly sent us the information we requested about their organizations.

Those who know us know we can be pesty and exasperating, so our heartfelt thanks must go to those at Oxford University Press who have responded with patience and thoughtfulness to our telephone calls, our irate letters, and all the other annoyances we seem to contrive—to our imperturbable, impeccable typist, Joellyn Ausanka; to counselor Leona Capeless; and, most of all, to the skipper who keeps us on an even keel every time we would list dangerously to starboard, our editor Sheldon Meyer.

Yellow Wood Farm   G.B
Kirk's Mills, Pennsylvania
June 1984

The Oxford Companion
to American Theatre

A

AARONS, ALEX[ANDER] A. (1891–1943) The son of Alfred E. Aarons,♦ he was born in Philadelphia and originally decided not to follow in his father's footsteps, trying the clothing business instead. His love of theatre proved irresistible, so in 1919 he produced *La La Lucille,* the first of his many associations with George Gershwin.♦ After several more ventures he joined forces with Vinton Freedley♦ in 1923. Together they produced such shows as *Lady, Be Good!♦* (1924), *Tip-Toes♦* (1925), *Oh, Kay!♦* (1926), *Funny Face♦* (1927), *Here's Howe* (1928), *Hold Everything!♦* (1928), *Spring Is Here* (1929), and *Girl Crazy♦* (1930). In 1927 they built the Alvin Theatre as a showcase for their musicals. Several of their productions in the early 1930s were failures, and this, coupled with problems arising from the Depression, lost them their theatre in 1932. A year later they dissolved their partnership, and Aarons retired from active production.

AARONS, ALFRED E. (1865–1936) After beginning his career as a theatrical call boy in his native Philadelphia, he moved to New York to become manager of the Standard Theatre and of Koster and Bial's.♦ He next turned his hand to composing and inserted songs such as "Rag Time Liz" into Broadway musicals. Soon he was producing musicals for which he wrote the principal score, including *Mam'selle 'Awkins* (1900) and *The Military Maid* (1900). Both shows starred his wife, Josephine Hall. In 1901 he produced Ivan Caryll's♦ *The Ladies' Paradise,* not at a regular Broadway theatre but at the Metropolitan Opera House. His later mountings included *His Honor the Mayor* (1906), *Magnolia* (1923), *Tell Me More* (1925), and *$25 an Hour* (1933).

ABARBANELL, LINA (1880–1963) Trained as an opera singer in her native Germany, she came to America in 1905. For a time she performed in German-language productions at the Irving Place Theatre, then made her Metropolitan Opera debut as Gretel. By 1906 she was fluent in English and was awarded the leading role in the operetta *The Student King.* A petite woman, with dark hair and high cheekbones, she was admired primarily for her singing. Later she was assigned the lead in the first touring company of *The Merry Widow.*♦ Her biggest success came when she was starred in *Madame Sherry♦* (1910). She also played heroines in *Miss Princess* (1912), *The Geisha* (1913), *The Red Canary* (1913), and *Flora Bella* (1916), her last important assignment. Thereafter she assumed secondary roles both in musicals and in straight plays. Retiring from the stage, she spent her last active years on Dwight Deere Wiman's♦ staff.

ABBEY, HENRY [EDWIN] (1846–96) Characterized by Odell♦ as "a restless genius of far-reaching vision and managerial astuteness," he was born in Akron, Ohio, where his father was a clockmaker and jeweler. A practice of the time was to sell theatre tickets at jewelry stores, so he received his first taste of the theatre business when he went to work for his father. He became a ticketseller at the Akron Opera House and within two years was managing the auditorium. From there he moved to Buffalo and then to Boston to manage the Park Theatre. In 1876, with financial backing from Charlotte Crabtree,♦ he assumed the reins of the Park Theatre in New York City. Shortly afterward he also took over Booth's and Wallack's. He quickly brought great players under his aegis, including Edwin Booth,♦ E. A. Sothern,♦ Otis Skinner,♦ William H. Crane,♦ and Stuart Robson,♦ initiating with *Our Boarding House♦* the long popular pairing of the last two. He was equally instrumental in bringing to America many great foreign companies and performers, notably Bernhardt,♦ Salvini,♦ and Lillie Langtry.♦ His interests were not confined to the legitimate stage. For several seasons he ran the Metropolitan Opera and imported such distinguished musical artists as Adelina Patti and Josef Hofmann. In 1893 he built Abbey's Theatre on Broadway, bringing over Irving♦ and Terry♦ to open the house. His early death cut short a remarkable career, although his growing interest in musical affairs makes moot just what his future importance to the American theatre might have been. Some sources give his middle name as Eugene.

Abbey Theatre [the Irish Players of], THE The great Irish theatre company founded by Miss

E. F. Horniman in 1903 helped spread the fame of plays by Lady Gregory, Yeats, and, most of all, Synge and O'Casey. ♦ It was relatively new plays by the first three of these playwrights that the company offered when it initially played in America in 1911. One of the works, *The Playboy of the Western World* by Synge, precipitated riots by hooligans offended at some of the depictions of Irish life. In New York, vegetables (including, of course, potatoes) and asafoetida balls were hurled at the stage; in Philadelphia, the company and the rioters were arrested. The turmoil continued when the troupe appeared on a second visit in 1913. Both the plays and the acting received a mixed reception. When the company returned for several visits in the 1930s the plays were no longer unfamiliar and many of them had become accepted as modern classics. By then the ensemble playing was much admired. Among the best known of the performers were Arthur Sinclair, Sara Allgood, and Barry Fitzgerald.

ABBOTT, Emma (1850–91) The daughter of a Concord, N.H., innkeeper, she studied singing in Europe and performed at Covent Garden before returning to America to found the Abbott English Opera Company in 1879. She toured the country with her ensemble until her early death, singing not only many roles now confined to opera houses but leading roles in French opéra bouffe, Gilbert♦ and Sullivan♦ operettas, and a few contemporary American comic operas as well. She was said to have an excellent voice but a somewhat mannered delivery. Her popularity was enhanced by her clever self-publicizing. She claimed she was so poor as a child that she walked barefoot to her debut. She also professed to be as shocked as many in her audience by the "immorality" of some of the works in which she sang, but concluded that the tights in which she dressed for trouser roles were "worn modestly" and that her heroine in *La Traviata* "tried to be good." Her death came after she caught cold while performing in a drafty theatre in Ogden, Utah.

ABBOTT, George [Francis] (b. 1887) Born in Forestville, N.Y., he studied with Professor George Pierce Baker♦ in the famous 47 Workshop.♦ An early play of his was mounted by the Harvard Dramatic Club♦ in 1913 and another effort briefly in Boston that same year. In 1913 he also made his acting debut in New York in *The Misleading Lady,* then continued to perform until the mid-1920s. Thereafter his onstage appearances were rare, although in 1955 he played Mr. Antrobus in an important revival of *The Skin of Our Teeth.* ♦ Apart

from helping to rewrite *Lightnin'*♦ in 1918, he did not resume serious play-writing until 1925, when he collaborated with James Gleason♦ on *The Fall Guy*♦ and with Winchell Smith♦ on *A Holy Terror.* After enjoying a minor success with *Love 'Em and Leave 'Em* (1926), written with J. V. A. Weaver, he scored a huge hit with *Broadway*♦ (1926), which he wrote with Philip Dunning and which he also staged. His lean, taut direction, followed by his forceful staging in the same season of another hit, *Chicago,* ♦ established him as a master of swift-paced melodrama. That reputation was consolidated when he collaborated on and directed two more popular pieces, *Four Walls* (1927), written with Dana Burnett, and *Coquette*♦ (1927), written with Ann Preston Bridgers. A series of failures followed, suggesting Hollywood had pre-empted melodrama from Broadway, so he turned again to farce, triumphing with his staging of *Twentieth Century*♦ (1932). He followed this with such hits as *Three Men on a Horse*♦ (1935), which he wrote with John Cecil Holm; *Boy Meets Girl*♦ (1935); *Brother Rat*♦ (1936); *Room Service*♦ (1937); and *What a Life*♦ (1938). Meanwhile he also turned his talents to directing, and sometimes writing, musical comedy, at first working often with Richard Rodgers♦ and Lorenz Hart.♦ He staged, among others, *Jumbo*♦ (1935), *On Your Toes*♦ (1936), *The Boys from Syracuse*♦ (1938), *Too Many Girls* (1939), *Pal Joey*♦ (1940), *On the Town*♦ (1944), *High Button Shoes* (1947), *Where's Charley?*♦ (1948), *Call Me Madam*♦ (1950), *A Tree Grows in Brooklyn*♦ (1951), *Wonderful Town*♦ (1953), *The Pajama Game*♦ (1954), *Damn Yankees*♦ (1955), *Fiorello!*♦ (1959), and *A Funny Thing Happened on the Way to the Forum*♦ (1962). Between 1932, with *Twentieth Century,* and a 1954 revival of *On Your Toes,* he produced many of the shows he wrote or directed. He was librettist and director of the failed musical *Music Is* (1976), then at the age of ninety-five coproduced and staged yet another revival of *On Your Toes* in 1983. In 1987 he directed a revival of *Broadway,* but the mounting was a quick failure.

Exceptional in his ability to keep his shows moving, while never seeming heavy-handed or forced, he was a strict, somewhat formal disciplinarian. Lehman Engel♦ wrote of him, "He always wore a necktie and never removed his jacket at rehearsal. What he said was positive and absolute."

Autobiography: *Mister Abbott,* New York, 1963.

Abe Lincoln in Illinois, a play in three acts by Robert E. Sherwood.♦ Produced by the Playwrights'

Company♦ at the Plymouth Theatre. October 15, 1938. 472 performances. PP.

In the log schoolhouse of Mentor Graham (Frank Andrews), Abe Lincoln (Raymond Massey♦) is dismayed to learn that sectionalism prevented everyone from applauding Webster's plea for "Liberty and Union." But for the moment Lincoln must put that concern behind him. His fiancée Ann Rutledge (Adele Longmire) dies, and he marries Mary Todd (Muriel Kirkland), whose fiercely possessive, shrewish nature foreshadows her eventual madness. He then runs for Senator from Illinois against the pro-slavery Stephen Douglas (Albert Phillips). Before long, Lincoln is a presidential candidate, but somehow his victory at the polls gives him no cause for elation. Mary's behavior and the country's divisive sectionalism have both grown worse. As he leaves for Washington, he tells those who have come to see him off of an ancient Eastern potentate who ordered his wise men to sum up all that was "true and appropriate" in a single sentence. That sentence was "And this too shall pass." He hopes such fatalism is not the only answer.

The first production of the newly formed Playwrights' Company, the play was extolled by most critics. Richard Watts, Jr.,♦ of the *Herald Tribune* called it "Not only the finest of modern stage biographies, but a lovely, eloquent, endearing tribute to all that is best in the spirit of democracy." Massey headed the cast of the film version, while the play itself was revived in 1963 by the Phoenix Theatre.♦

Abie's Irish Rose, a comedy in three acts by Anne Nichols.♦ Produced by Miss Nichols at the Fulton Theatre. May 23, 1922. 2,327 performances.

Because of their fathers' strong religious prejudices, Abie Levy (Robert B. Williams) and Rose Mary Murphy (Marie Carroll) have been secretly married by a Methodist minister. Pretending they are still single, Abie introduces his bride to his father as Jewish Rosie Murpheski. Solomon Levy (Alfred Wiseman) arranges for his son and Rosie to be wed by a rabbi. Rose Mary invites her father (John Cope) to the ceremony, telling him her fiancé's name is Michael Magee. Her father appears along with his friend, Father Whalen (Harry Bradley). Mr. Murphy's arrival elicits the true story and an explosion of ill-feeling. Only the rabbi and priest are understanding. To appease Murphy, Father Whalen weds the couple for a third time. Matters are satisfactorily resolved a year later when Rose Mary has what Solomon calls "twinses": Patrick Joseph Murphy Levy and Rebecca Levy. The grandchildren

reconcile the grandfathers. Throughout battles and reconciliations a character named Mrs. Cohen (Mathilde Cottrelly♦) chatters on about her operation.

Miss Nichols based her play, originally called *Marriage in Triplicate,* on complaints of a friend who found himself in the hero's predicament. Most reviews were kind, if unenthusiastic. However, some of the sharper critics such as Benchley,♦ Broun,♦ and Nathan♦ were scathing. At first playgoers were unenthusiastic, too. When Miss Nichols depleted her own funds she turned to a notorious gangster, Arnold Rothstein, and to Leblang's Ticket Office♦ for help. Rothstein underwrote losses until the play caught on. The comedy eventually established a new Broadway long-run record, as did many of its road companies. One modern critic, Howard Taubman, in his retrospective assessment of the play, observed, "Its plot is childish, its characters puerile, and even its ear for Jewish and Irish dialects monstrously false."

ABORN, Milton (1864–1933) Born in Marysville, Calif., he began his career as a stage manager and actor, and for several years worked with B. F. Keith♦ in Boston. At the turn of the century he joined with his brother Sargent (1867?–1956) to produce popular-priced productions of favorite musicals. Within a few years they had no fewer than six companies touring the country. Milton supervised the artistic end; Sargent, the financial side. The brothers split in the early 1920s. Milton opened a school of opera and operetta. In 1922 Sargent took over the A. W. Tams Music Library, later merging it with the Witmark Music Library. The Tams-Witmark Music Library remains a principal source for licensing musicals for production. As late as the 1929–30 season Milton presented a repertory of operettas on Broadway, many of which have never been presented there since.

Accent on Youth, a comedy in three acts by Samson Raphaelson.♦ Produced by Crosby Gaige♦ at the Plymouth Theatre. December 25, 1934. 229 performances.

Steven Gaye (Nicholas Hannen), a successful middle-aged playwright, has written a play about a middle-aged man in love with a young girl. The actors hired for the work are unhappy with it until Gaye's young secretary, Linda Brown (Constance Cummings), shows them its virtues. By then, however, Gaye has decided to throw over the play and sail for Europe. Linda now must convince him to remain, and she succeeds after promising to assume the leading role herself. During the run she falls in love with her leading man, Dickie Reynolds (Theodore Newton), and marries him. Left alone, Gaye finds himself unable to write more plays. Suddenly Linda arrives, announcing she is disillusioned with her handsome but vacuous husband. Linda and Gaye realize that despite differences in age they are in love. That thought awakens Gaye's little muse, so he begins to dictate a new play to Linda: "Act One . . . Scene One . . . A penthouse apartment in New York City . . . change that—The Bedroom of a Castle in Spain."

Although the play competed with three other Christmas night openings, it drew most of the first-string critics, who divided on the merits of the work. Brooks Atkinson♦ took a middle ground, finding it too long and contrived, but "lightly good-humored and pleasantly insane." It remained a favorite in summer stock for many years.

Across the Continent; or, Scenes from New York Life and the Pacific Railroad, a melodrama in four acts by James J. McCloskey♦ (revised by Oliver Doud Byron♦). Produced at Wood's Museum. March 13, 1871. 42 performances.

In the depths of New York's most fetid slum, Five Points, a bedraggled widow (Lizzie Safford) begs callous, greedy barroom owner John Adderly (Charles Waverly) for pennies to feed her starving children. Her husband has spent his last cent at Adderly's gin mill. When Adderly refuses, she curses him and his heirs, then goes out in the snow to die. Twenty years pass. Adderly has framed a good-hearted gambler, Joe Ferris or "The Ferrit" (Byron), unaware that the noble Joe is the widow's son. Adderly is also attempting to destroy a rich merchant, Thomas Goodwin (Joseph Sefton), at the same time he is seeking to marry Goodwin's daughter Louise (Annie Firmin). Joe escapes from prison, entraps Adderly, and sees him go to jail. Five more years pass. Joe has renounced the city and gambling and taken a job as stationmaster for the Union Pacific in Indian territory. The Goodwins detrain at the station on their way to visit a ranch. Adderly, who in turn has escaped from jail, has goaded the Indians into attacking the station. As the raid begins Joe desperately telegraphs for a trainload of soldiers. The men at the station hold off the attack until the "Train comes on . . . and stops, and soldiers from the train fire at the Chief and Adderly, both of whom fall. Louise rushes into Joe's arms."

Although the work was dismissed by most critics with terms such as "claptrap," "rubbish," and "purely sensational," Byron's tour de force and the clever employment of such newsworthy features as telegraphy and the then equally new Union Pacific Railroad gave the piece a special excitement for audiences. McCloskey had originally written the work in the 1860s as *New York in 1837; or, The Overland Route,* perhaps inspired by the success of Tom Taylor's♦ *The Overland Route.* Byron bought the rights, and his redaction gave him a vehicle for many seasons.

Acting Company, THE Founded in 1972 by John Houseman♦ and Margot Henley, it was an offshoot of special productions mounted by students of the drama division of the Juilliard School and was originally known as the City Center Acting Company. Since that time the company has toured the country, sometimes playing in regular legitimate houses but emphasizing university theatres and art centers. Thus it serves not merely as a training ground for young performers, but as a practical seminar for students of the theatre. Its repertory consists primarily of classics, interspersed with new plays of interest. While it has met with success in its interpretations of Shakespeare, Marlowe, Sheridan, Shaw, and others, its most popular work has proved to be the musical *The Robber Bridegroom* (1975). Zelda Fichandler is slated to take over as artistic director in 1991.

Actors' Equity Association Founded December 22, 1912, following the dissolution of the Actors' Society of America,♦ it had its constitution and bylaws formalized on May 26, 1913. Francis Wilson♦ was elected its first president. Curiously, it was the older group which provided a name for the newer one. In 1910 the Actors' Society president Thomas Wise♦ had remarked, "The motto of the Actors' Society is 'equity.' It is their desire to establish an equitable contract, equitable for the actor and equitable for the management." The need for "equity" arose from the gross abuse of performers by many callous managements. Actors often had been stranded far from home, had been forced to rehearse for weeks without pay, and frequently had been given little other consideration. The growth of the Theatrical Trust♦ had only aggravated matters. Making but small headway, the actors struck in August 1919, closing virtually all Broadway shows. Performers held a number of benefits to draw financial support, and the public, looking on the actors as friends and aware of the indignities they had suffered, responded wholeheartedly. George M. Cohan,♦ himself a beloved performer, and the Producing Managers' Association♦ organized a rival organization, the

Actors' Fidelity Association, enlisting many distinguished, more established performers into their camp. But numbers told, so Equity prevailed. With the coming of the New Deal and its support of organized labor, Equity sometimes grew brazen and destructive. For example, its refusal to allow Eva Le Gallienne♦ and her Civic Repertory♦ to offer Sunday performances probably doomed that fine group. In more recent years the minimums and bonds demanded by this and other unions have been a factor in stifling production, shrinking the road, and forcing musicals to perform in auditoriums that are really too large for live performances, although the avarice of producers has played no small part in this last absurdity.

Actors' Fidelity Association, see *Actors' Equity Association*

Actors' Fund of America This organization assists needy performers and others who have worked professionally in the theatre. In 1881 Harrison Grey Fiske♦ and his *Dramatic Mirror*♦ began to campaign for a fund modeled on England's Actors' Benevolent Fund. Beginning with a benefit on March 13, 1882, by M. B. Curtis in his starring vehicle, *Sam'l of Posen,*♦ special performances were given all across the country to help establish the charity. The act of incorporation was passed into law by the New York state legislature on June 8, 1882. Lester Wallack♦ was elected the first president. The organization quickly became pre-eminent among theatrical charities, aiding in many quiet ways as well as establishing a home (now in Englewood, N.J.) for retirees and opening special cemetery plots. A line of distinguished theatrical figures succeeded Wallack as president: Henry C. Miner♦ (1884–85), Albert M. Palmer♦ (1885–97), Louis Aldrich♦ (1897–1901), Al Hayman♦ (1901–04), Daniel Frohman♦ (1904–41), Walter Vincent (1941–59), Vinton Freedley♦ (1959–69), Louis A. Lotito♦ (1969–80), Nedda Harrigan Logan (1980–1989), and Tom Dillon (1989–   ).

Actors' Order of Friendship A fraternal order for performers chartered in Philadelphia in 1849, its first lodge was called the Shakespeare Lodge. In 1888 a New York City branch, the Edwin Forrest Lodge, was established by Louis Aldrich,♦ John Drew,♦ and Otis Skinner,♦ among others. While the Philadelphia branch was active in providing comradeship and charity for nearly half a century, the order eventually gave way to the more efficient and richer Actors' Fund of America. ♦

Actors' Society of America An organization formed in 1895, partially in reaction to the practices of the Theatrical Trust,♦ it attempted to regulate and, wherever possible, to standardize contractual obligations between performers and producers. Led by Louis Aldrich,♦ the group had only minimal influence, and declined in membership after Aldrich's death in 1901. An attempt was made to incorporate it into the Actors' Fund of America,♦ but when that failed the group was dissolved in 1912.

Actors Studio, Inc., THE A workshop for professional actors, it was founded in 1947 by Cheryl Crawford,♦ Elia Kazan,♦ and Robert Lewis.♦ Membership is by invitation and is limited. Auditions customarily precede invitations. In 1948 Lee Strasberg♦ joined the group and soon became its prime mover. With Strasberg at the helm the studio evolved into the leading proponent of "method" acting, a school of performing which encouraged actors to respond as much to their own deepest feelings as to the requirements of the text or dramatic effectiveness. The style of acting developed into a major force in contemporary theatre. Among its proponents were Geraldine Page♦ and Kim Stanley.♦ Hollywood stars such as Marilyn Monroe, Paul Newman, and Joanne Woodward sometimes came East to study with the group. In the late 1950s and early 1960s the studio established special units for playwrights, for directors, and for production. This last unit mounted several noteworthy offerings, including a fine 1963 revival of *Strange Interlude.* ♦ In 1982, shortly after Strasberg's death, Ellen Burstyn♦ and Al Pacino were appointed directors. Frank Corsaro took over in 1988.

Actors' Theatre, see *Equity Players*

Actors Theatre of Louisville (Kentucky) A professional resident theatre founded by Richard Block and Ewel Cornett in 1964, it began to achieve major recognition after Jon Jory became its producing director in 1969. Although the company offers a repertory that includes many classic plays and a Classics in Context Festival, it has become best known for its promotion of new native work. The annual Humana Festival of New American Plays, which now incorporates its former one-act play festival, Shorts, has made the company a leading advocate of contemporary play-writing. Among dramas to receive trial productions there were *Crimes of the Heart,* ♦ *Getting Out,* ♦ and *The Gin Game.* ♦ The troupe has performed on numerous international stages, but at home works in two playhouses: the 637-seat Pamela Brown Auditorium and the 180-seat Victor Jory Theatre.

Actor's Workshop, THE Founded in 1952 by two professors from San Francisco State College, Herbert Blau and Jules Irving, it rapidly became the city's leading regional theatre. The use of the singular in the name was a conscious decision since it was the founders' intention to offer "a place where each individual could pursue his craft." After two years in a loft and a highly praised mounting of Lorca's *Blood Wedding,* the troupe moved to an abandoned warehouse. A year later it took over the Marines' Memorial Theatre. Although the company presented classics such as *Hedda Gabler* and *The Playboy of the Western World,* it was best known for its interpretation of modern avant-garde and politically oriented works. Among its noteworthy productions were *Mother Courage, The Caucasian Chalk Circle, The Birthday Party,* and *Waiting for Godot.*◆ It gave performances at the Brussels and Seattle World's Fairs and initiated a workshop for prisoners at San Quentin. After Blau and Irving left in 1965 to head the new theatre at Lincoln Center,◆ it fell apart, despite sporadic attempts to keep it going.

Adam and Eva, a comedy in three acts by Guy Bolton◆ and George Middleton.◆ Produced by F. Ray Comstock◆ and Morris Gest◆ at the Longacre Theatre. September 13, 1919. 312 performances.

James King (Berton Churchill), who has made a fortune in rubber, is fed up with his extravagant family, who seem inclined to live beyond even his very ample means. He longs to flee from them. When Adam Smith (Otto Kruger◆), manager of King's Brazilian estates, pays him a visit and says he longs for noise, people, and outstretched arms, King hits upon the expedient of changing places for a year with Adam, although he warns the younger man he'll find not outstretched arms but outstretched hands. Taking over with authority, Adam quickly requires the Kings to live within their allowances. Furious, they threaten to hock their jewelry to pay for their high life, so Adam arranges to have all their jewels "stolen." Sensing that the two men who are courting King's unmarried daughter, Eva (Ruth Shepley), are fortune hunters, Adam goes a step further. He announces that King has lost his entire fortune and that the family will have to roll up its sleeves and find gainful employment. To his surprise, they do, even running a successful chicken farm in New Jersey. Eva realizes she is falling in love with Adam. When she discovers that he was the

"burglar," she keeps her silence. King returns to find a changed family. Adam and Eva prepare to wed, but not before Eva has offered Adam a token of her love—an apple.

Coming after the hiatus created by the bitter Actors' Equity◆ strike, it was eagerly embraced by Broadway. Burns Mantle◆ called it "a characteristic comedy of American home life." For years it remained a stock and little theatre favorite.

ADAMS, EDWIN (1834–77) Born in Medford, Mass., he made his debut in Boston in 1853 in *The Hunchback.*◆ He then worked in Baltimore, Philadelphia, and with amateur groups in New York, serving some of his apprenticeship under Joseph Jefferson◆ and E. A. Sothern.◆ His first important New York appearance was in 1862, playing Clifford in Kate Bateman's◆ production of *The Hunchback.* With her company he also essayed Charles Surface in *The School for Scandal* and Macduff in *Macbeth.*◆ He began to tour on his own as a star in 1864—he jokingly called himself a "war star"—but met with ill luck when he was booked to open at Ford's Theatre◆ in Washington. Lincoln's assassination there two nights before his opening put a temporary halt to his tour. His playing caught the eye of Edwin Booth,◆ who selected Adams to play opposite him at the opening of Booth's Theatre in 1869. Adams played Mercutio to Booth's Romeo, following it with Iago to Booth's Othello. The *Times* savaged his performance as Iago, stating, "It is certainly Mr. Adams' worst interpretation. He is utterly deficient in subtlety and guile." On June 21 of the same year Adams gave his first New York performance as the man who returns home after being written off as dead, Enoch Arden, the role with which he is most identified. Although he afterwards tried other roles, mostly in contemporary light comedies and melodramas, he returned to *Enoch Arden* regularly. His last performance was as Iago in San Francisco, playing opposite John McCullough.◆ Sothern gave a number of benefits to provide for young Adams's widow. Jefferson characterized Adams's success as "well-earned," continuing, "The animation of his face, the grace of his person, and, above all, the melody of his voice, well fitted him for the stage. While he could not fairly be called a great artist, he was something often more highly prized—a born actor, a child of nature if not of art, swayed by warm impulse rather than premeditation."

ADAMS, FRANK R. (1884–1963) Briefly prolific as a librettist and lyricist, he began writing shows while a student at the University of Chicago. In 1904, although still in school, he collaborated with Will M. Hough,♦ a fellow student, on the songs for a Chicago musical, *His Highness the Bey.* The composer was Joe Howard.♦ Over the next several seasons the trio offered Chicago some of its most successful musical comedies, including *The Isle of Bong Bong* (1905); *The Umpire*♦ (1905); *The Girl Question* (1906); *The Time, the Place and the Girl*♦ (1906), which established a long-run record for the city; *The Land of Nod* (1907); *Honeymoon Trail* (1908); *A Stubborn Cinderella* (1908); *The Prince of Tonight* (1909); *The Golden Girl* (1909); *The Flirting Princess* (1909); *The Goddess of Liberty* (1909); and *Miss Nobody from Starland* (1910). Although several of these shows toured successfully after their Chicago runs, none was successful in New York. Thereafter Adams spent most of his time as a journalist, novelist, and early Hollywood screenwriter, only rarely returning to the theatre. His last show was *Princess April* (1924).

ADAMS, John Jay (1798?–1839) A New Yorker who apparently had enjoyed some success as a businessman, he abandoned his mercantile interests to make his debut as Hamlet in 1822. His repertory also included such standard roles as Othello and Rolla (*Pizarro*♦). Apart from a two-year retirement beginning in 1824, he continued to perform until drink and general dissipation brought about his early death. Despite the brevity of his career his Hamlet was recalled as one of the finest of his era.

ADAMS, Lee (b. 1924) Born in Mansfield, Ohio, the lyricist studied journalism at Ohio State University and at Columbia before teaming with composer Charles Strouse♦ to write revues for the summer circuit. Ben Bagley♦ brought their songs to off-Broadway in his *Shoestring Revues*♦ and in *The Littlest Revue* (1956). Their reputation was firmly established by their songs for *Bye Bye Birdie*♦ (1960), although two years later their excellent songs could not save *All American* (1962). A black, musicalized *Golden Boy*♦ (1964), for which they provided words and music, ran over a year, largely on the strength of Sammy Davis, Jr.'s♦ appeal. Their 1966 effort, *It's a Bird It's a Plane It's SUPERMAN,* delighted many, but failed commercially. Adams and Strouse's longest running musical was *Applause* (1970), another show whose extended New York stand could be attributed in good measure to a star—in this case, Lauren Bacall.♦ Two later shows, *A Broadway Musical* (1978) and *Bring Back Birdie* (1980), had only the briefest stays.

ADAMS, Maude [née Kiskadden] (1872–1953) One of the most beloved of all American actresses, she was first carried onstage by her actress mother, Annie Adams. Annie Adams had been a performer in a Mormon stock company in Salt Lake City, where she married James Kiskadden and where her daughter was born. Her husband proving a poor provider, Annie Adams soon resumed her career and encouraged her daughter to follow in her footsteps. Adopting her mother's maiden name, Maude Adams played in small theatres in California before settling in San Francisco. She won her first important notices at the age of five as Little Schneider in *Fritz, Our Cousin German.* ♦ Young David Belasco♦ was a member of the cast. A few years later, Charles Frohman♦ witnessed one of her performances and told her mother she might make a good actress if she could rid herself of her western accent. She moved East in a play called *The Paymaster,* making her New York debut in 1888, then came to the attention of E. H. Sothern,♦ who cast her as Jessie Deane in *Lord Chumley.* She also played for Charles Hoyt♦ in *A Midnight Bell.* In 1890 she played in both *All the Comforts of Home* and in Belasco and H. C. deMille's♦ *Men and Women.* ♦ The part of Dora in the latter play had been created especially for her at the request of its producer Charles Frohman, who had by now reconsidered his earlier rejection. Within a year Frohman had paired her with John Drew,♦ beginning with *The Masked Ball* and continuing until *Rosemary* in 1896. For some time Frohman had been urging James M. Barrie♦ to dramatize his novel *The Little Minister.* Watching Miss Adams in *Rosemary,* Barrie realized he had found his Lady Babbie, so he agreed. The play opened at the Empire Theatre♦ in 1897, with Miss Adams starred for the first time. In 1899 she essayed a highly praised Juliet opposite William Faversham's♦ Romeo. She was the original American Phoebe in *Quality Street* (1901). On November 6, 1905, she first played the role written with her in mind and with which she always was identified thereafter, the title part in Barrie's *Peter Pan.* ♦ An unhappy William Winter♦ called it "a tolerable performance, in a vein of grotesquerie, pleasantry, impulse and vim," but most critics agreed with another colleague who said the star was "true to the fairy idea, true to the child nature, lovely, sweet, and wholesome. She combines all the delicate sprightliness and the gentle, wistful pathos necessary to the role." After briefly portraying Viola in *Twelfth Night* (1908), she scored again in yet another Barrie play, as Maggie in *What Every Woman Knows.* A major disappointment was her failure in the title role of Rostand's♦ *Chantecler* (1911), which had opened to much ballyhoo and a huge advance sale. Her last important new role was Miss Thing in Barrie's *A Kiss for Cinderella* (1916). Once coming under Frohman's aegis, she never left him. But after his death in 1915 her relations with his firm began to deteriorate. When matters came to a head in 1918, she announced her retirement, although she was still unquestionably one of the theatre's most popular stars. Over the years many important playwrights, Philip Barry♦ for example, wrote plays with her in mind, hoping to lure her back to the stage. She resisted many offers, returning only twice. During the 1931–32 season she toured as Portia in *The Merchant of Venice,* but refused to bring the play into New York. In the summer of 1934 she played Maria in *Twelfth Night* in summer stock.

Unlike many stars, Maude Adams shunned the limelight. Away from the theatre she was the most private of people, and for much of her later life lived quietly with a woman friend. But she was generous and high-principled. She sometimes raised salaries of fellow players out of her own pay and gave thoughtful gifts to kind stagehands. Once, when a theatre owner doubled the cost of gallery tickets because he knew her name would guarantee a sold-out house, she made him refund the difference before she would perform.

"Graceful as a kitten," she had a small, pointed nose, straight, pale hair, and gray-green eyes. The noted Chicago drama critic Amy Leslie♦ wrote of her, "She is direct and graceful and alive with the finer, more soulful emotions, so that she sighs and melts and droops with supine pleasantness. She is brightly intelligent and reads . . . with much charming intuition and feeling."

Biography: *Maude Adams, An Intimate Portrait,* Phyllis Robbins, New York, 1956.

ADDAMS, Augustus A. (d. 1851) No precise records survive to show when or where this star-crossed performer was born, although in or near Boston is generally accepted. Even the theatre in which he first performed is open to dispute, but it was apparently either the Tremont or the Boston Theatre, in 1828. He first called real attention to himself when he played William Tell in Philadelphia in 1831. He made his New York debut on April 2, 1835, as Damon in *Damon and Pythias.* Two nights later he offered his Othello. Remarking on his performance, the drama critic of the *Knickerbocker Magazine* wrote, "This young American actor bids fair to attain distinguished rank as a native trage-

dian. Physically, he is liberally endowed. His frame is well-knit, and his port commanding. His features, too, are full of expression, and susceptible, in an eminent degree, of sudden and powerful change. His voice also is deep and full. His personation of Othello was the best we have witnessed since we saw Forrest—whom Mr. Addams as an actor greatly resembles . . ." During the same and ensuing seasons he won acclaim as Lear, Shylock, Jaffier, Virginius, Hamlet, Rolla, and Macbeth. In 1835 Robert T. Conrad♦ wrote the play *The Noble Yeoman* for him, but its first night was cancelled when Addams was too drunk to perform, and a delayed premiere was botched because he was still inebriated. Conrad later turned the play over to Forrest,♦ who scored a tremendous hit in it under the title *Jack Cade.*♦ Addams's last New York performance was in 1848 as Carwin in *Thérèse.* Thereafter, unreliability stemming from his alcoholism hurt his career and kept him off major stages. T. Allston Brown♦ noted, "Had he let drink alone he would have become the greatest actor ever seen in this country."

Adding Machine, The, a tragedy in seven scenes by Elmer Rice.♦ Produced by the Theatre Guild♦ at the Garrick Theatre. March 19, 1923. 72 performances.

On the 25th anniversary of his employment by The Firm, Mr. Zero (Dudley Digges♦) is told by The Boss (Irving Dillon) that modern adding machines have replaced him. In blind fury, Mr. Zero kills his employer. Mrs. Zero (Helen Westley♦), Mr. Zero's harridan wife, offers him no consolation. He is tried and executed, after which he wanders through a graveyard and the Elysian Fields, rejecting the company of those who would lure him from his narrow but purposeful ways. His only comforter becomes Daisy Diana Dorothea Devore (Margaret Wycherly♦), his onetime co-worker, who has killed herself to be with him. In Heaven, Mr. Zero briefly finds satisfaction operating a gigantic adding machine, until he is ordered to return to earth. He refuses to go back until he learns that he has been doing just that for many incarnations and will continue to do so until he is a totally crushed soul doomed to "sit in the gallery of a coal mine and operate the super-hyper-adding machine with the great toe of his right foot."

Many of New York's most perceptive critics agreed with John Corbin,♦ who wrote that *The Adding Machine* was "the best and fairest example of the newer expressionism in the theatre, that it has yet experienced." Along with a fine cast and the superb direction of Philip Moeller,♦ the original production offered Lee Simonson's♦ imaginative sets. The bars and railings in the courtroom set were distorted, Mr. Zero's fury was suggested by large numbers whirling across the stage, and in Heaven there was that huge adding machine which Mr. Zero could walk on. This last piece nearly prevented the show from being seen, when an internal union disagreement erupted over whether it was a set or a prop. For all its excellence, *The Adding Machine* had only a modest Broadway run. Nevertheless it remained popular for years with college and experimental theatres. More so than even his trail-blazing *On Trial,*♦ the play established Rice as a major playwright.

ADE, GEORGE (1866–1944) An American humorist most popular in his own day for what he called his "Fables in Slang," he was born in Kentland, Ind., and was also active in journalism and as a librettist and playwright. His first theatrical plunge was as librettist for *The Night of the Fourth* (1901), a failure. Success came with his libretto for *The Sultan of Sulu*♦ (1902), which started the rage for musicals about Americans abruptly transplanted to exotic places. His libretto for *Peggy from Paris* (1903) was also well received. In the same season he turned his hand to straight plays, offering with great success *The County Chairman,*♦ centering on a warm-hearted, ethical politician. In 1904 *The College Widow,*♦ in which a college president's daughter prevents a football hero from switching campuses, was a major hit and added a new expression to the language. A few weeks later his libretto for *The Shogun* gave Ade two successes on Broadway at once. None of his later straight plays was quite as successful, although *Just Out of College* (1905), in which a young man uses his prospective father-in-law's money to set up a rival pickle factory, and *Father and the Boys* (1908), in which an aging father determines to prove he is young at heart, were by no means failures. He had rather more success with his librettos for *The Fair Co-ed* (1909) and *The Old Town* (1910).

Ade was a master at employing contemporary vernacular, especially the slang of the youth of his day. His comedy was always wholesome and not a little innocent. However, his heavy reliance on quickly forgotten slang and his uncritical views of life make his plays seem puzzling and naïve to a more cynical era.

ADLER, JACOB P. (1855–1926) The pre-eminent figure of the Yiddish-American theatre, Adler turned to acting in his Russian homeland after dabbling in business and working briefly as one of the few Jews in the Russian civil service. When edicts directed at Jews made performing difficult in Russia, Adler immigrated to London, then came to America in 1887. His attempts to establish a theatre in Chicago failed, and after a brief, unsatisfactory stay in New York he returned to London. Two years later he was back in New York heralded as "Greater Than Salvini." His first appearance was in the title role of a comedy called *The Beggar of Odessa*. Both Adler and the play were poorly received, although the play had been popular with Yiddish audiences elsewhere. Nor did his appearance in *Under the Protection of Sir Moses Montefiore* prove more propitious. Adler's luck changed when he played *The Russian Soldier,* and his reputation grew when he followed that work with *La Juive,* in which he played Eleazar. For several months he toured with Boris Thomashefsky.♦ Professional rivalry, a personal scandal, and Adler's distaste for the operettas Thomashefsky included in his repertory soon drove the men apart. Adler was determined to offer a loftier theatre. To that end he took over the Union Theatre, established the Independent Yiddish Art Company, and commissioned a play from Jacob Gordin,♦ the best of the Yiddish playwrights. The result was *The Yiddish King Lear* (1892). This was not a Yiddish translation of Shakespeare but a free use of the story. The hero was Dovid Moishele, a rich merchant, whose daughters were viciously selfish housewives. "Shenkt a neduve der Yiddisher Kenig Lear" (Alms for the Yiddish King Lear), Moishele pleads at the curtain. The role remained an important part of Adler's repertory for the rest of his career. Another successful Gordin play followed, *The Wild Man,* in which a self-important father destroys his children. In 1901 Adler brought out a Yiddish translation of *The Merchant of Venice.*♦ So impressive was his Shylock that it was brought to Broadway in 1903 and 1905, with Adler performing in Yiddish, his fellow actors in English. Gordin's last play, *Elisha ben Avuya,* after an initial failure in 1909, gave Adler another lifelong success, as did Tolstoy's *The Living Corpse*. A stroke in 1920 forced Adler to retire.

Despite an often scandalous private life and some questionable business practices, Adler was adored by his special public. An emotional rapport between actor and playgoer enlivened Yiddish performances long after American performances and audiences had become far more restrained. When Dovid Moishele was denied a bowl of soup by one of his monstrous daughters, a voice from the gallery rang out, "Leave those rotten children of yours and come home with me. My wife is a good cook. She'll fix you up." Aware that Adler is German for eagle, his followers saw in the actor's piercing glance, his strong profile, and his commanding presence a natural and appropriate symbol personified.

Biography: *Bright Star of Exile,* Lulla Rosenfeld, New York, 1977.

ADLER, LUTHER (1903–84) The son of Jacob Adler,♦ he was born in New York, where he made his earliest appearance in Yiddish theatre, then acted with the Provincetown Players.♦ His Broadway debut was as Leon Kantor, the young violinist with a self-sacrificing mother, in *Humoresque* (1923). He later played Sam, the law student, in *Street Scene*♦ (1929). Afterwards he joined the Group Theatre,♦ appearing with it in the minor role of Don Fernando in *Night Over Taos* (1932) and as the vicious, ambitious Sam Ginsburg in *Success Story.* In 1933 he played Julian Vardaman, the radical professor, opposite Katharine Cornell♦ in *Alien Corn,* and the following season played Dr. Gordon, the steadfast, middle-aged physician, in *Men in White.*♦ He created the part of Moe Axelrod, the crippled war veteran, in *Awake and Sing!*♦ (1935). His most important role may well have been Joe Bonaparte, who abandons a promising career as a violinist to make money as a fighter, in *Golden Boy*♦ (1937). Many of his later assignments were as replacements to original stars, such as Joseph Schildkraut♦ in *Uncle Harry*♦ and Zero Mostel♦ in *Fiddler on the Roof.*♦

ADLER, RICHARD (b. 1921) The New York-born composer-lyricist, son of Clarence Adler, a concert pianist and music teacher, rejected his father's interest in classical music, preferring to study at the University of North Carolina with the intention of becoming a writer. An interest in song-writing soon surfaced, but Adler had little success until he met up with Jerry Ross (1926–55), another composer and lyricist. Their work impressed Frank Loesser,♦ who signed them to an exclusive contract. In 1953 they wrote many of the songs for *John Murray Anderson's Almanac.* The scores for two major hits followed, *The Pajama Game*♦ (1954) and *Damn Yankees*♦ (1955). The team's songs were melodic, adventurous, and witty. After Ross's death, Adler's luck turned sour again, although his songs for *Kwamina* (1961) and *Music Is* (1976) were highly praised. He also wrote the score for *A Mother's Kisses* (1968), which folded out of town. In 1973 Adler co-produced a commendable but unsuccessful

revival of *The Pajama Game*♦ and three years later produced Richard Rodgers's♦ failed *Rex.*

Autobiography: *You Gotta Have Heart,* New York, 1990.

ADLER, STELLA (b. 1902) The daughter of Jacob Adler,♦ she first performed with her father in Yiddish Theatre, and for many years moved back and forth between Broadway and Yiddish playhouses. Her best Broadway part may have been that of Bessie Berger, the dominating mother in *Awake and Sing!*♦ (1935). She directed a number of plays, and for many years ran the Stella Adler Conservatory of Acting, which she founded in 1949.

Adonis, a "burlesque nightmare" in two acts by William F. Gill. Music culled from various sources. Produced by E. E. Rice♦ at the Bijou Theatre. September 4, 1884. 603 performances.

The sculptress Talamea (Lillie Grubb) creates a statue of Adonis so beautiful that she falls in love with it and, helped by the goddess Artea (Louise V. Essing), brings it to life. Unfortunately, she has sold the statue to the Duchess (Jennie Reiffarth), who is equally taken by the living, wickedly winking beauty, and who insists that Adonis (Henry E. Dixey♦) is hers. The villainous Marquis de Baccarat (Herbert Gresham♦), determined to marry the Duchess for her money, attempts to dissuade her. Adonis is unmoved by all the attention. He would prefer to play the field, so he runs away to the country, where he promptly falls in love with a simple country girl, Rosetta (Amelia Summerville). The sculptress, the goddess, the Duchess, and the villain pursue him there and in the end make life so hectic for him that Adonis begs the goddess to turn him back into stone. She does.

The music, as Gill wrote, was by "Beethoven—Audran—Suppé—Sir Arthur Sullivan—Planquette—Offenbach—Mozart—Haydn—Dave Braham—[John] Eller—and many more too vastly numerous to individualize, particularize or plagiarize." Sullivan provided the evening's most popular musical moment when "A Most Susceptible Chancellor" became "A Most Susceptible Statue." Gill's text and Rice's production offered not merely an adroit spoof of the Pygmalion-Galatea legend, but of contemporary dramatic and musical theatre mannerisms as well. Thus, the constant rejection of Rosetta by her father was a travesty of a famous scene in the then popular *Hazel Kirke.*♦ Nevertheless, it was young Dixey's brilliant tour de force which won the most applause and was the chief attraction. The public flocked to the theatre in such numbers that

Adonis enjoyed the longest run in Broadway history up to its time. Dixey played it off and on for twenty years.

Adrea, a play in five acts by David Belasco♦ and John Luther Long.♦ Produced by Belasco at the Belasco Theatre. January 11, 1905. 123 performances.

Adrea (Mrs. Leslie Carter♦), a 5th-century princess on an Adriatic isle, has been passed over in the line of inheritance because she is blind. As a result she is deserted by her betrothed, Kaeso (Charles A. Stevenson), who marries her sister Julia (Edith Crane) instead. The wicked Julia, however, tricks Adrea into marrying the court jester, Minus the Echo (J. Harry Benrimo♦), by telling her the groom is Kaeso. Adrea learns of Kaeso's disloyalty and Julia's treachery when she regains her sight and becomes queen. She kills Kaeso but then blinds herself again and puts Kaeso's son by Julia on the throne.

Professor Sculley Bradley has compared *Adrea* with Belasco and Long's collaboration of two years before, *The Darling of the Gods,* ♦ noting that both "are romantic tragedies in each of which a beautiful high-born woman, in revolt against the outrages of society and fate, gives all for love and counts the world well lost. Both of these plays present a never-never world, while their language, though passionate and often poetic, is so highly stylized as to intensify the sense of unreality."

Although Mrs. Carter's most memorable moment was her bell-ringing scene in *The Heart of Maryland,* ♦ many critics felt Adrea was her finest performance. Apart from some revivals which immediately followed, it marked her last association with Belasco, as it did for Long.

Adulateur, The, a satire by Mercy Otis Warren,♦ published in 1773 but apparently never acted, it was described on its title page as "a Tragedy, As it is now acted in Upper Servia." It ridiculed the hypocrisies of Governor Thomas Hutchinson of Massachusetts, who pretended to favor the colonists while actually working against them. In the play Hutchinson was personified as Rapatio, and his sycophantic brother, Foster, as Meagre. Rapatio attempts to undermine the plans for freedom of Brutus, Cassius, Junius, and Portius (read James Otis (Mrs. Warren's brother), John Adams, Samuel Adams, and John Hancock). In his last soliloquy, Rapatio recognizes the baseness and hollowness of his actions and wails, "I dare not meet my naked heart alone." Despite its

never being acted, the play was widely circulated and read by an appreciative audience.

After the Fall, a play in two acts by Arthur Miller. ♦ Produced by the Repertory Theatre of Lincoln Center♦ at the ANTA Washington Square Theatre. January 23, 1964. 208 performances.

Quentin (Jason Robards, Jr.♦) is a middle-aged lawyer who attempts to bring his life into focus by examining his past. Clearly the women in his life have been pivotal. They were his troubled Mother (Virginia Kaye), his first wife, Louise (Mariclare Costello), who valued her independence above all, and his prospective third wife, Holga (Salome Jens), still scarred by her life in Nazi Germany. But most of all there was his second wife, Maggie (Barbara Loden), a beautiful but insecure actress who ultimately committed suicide.

Many critics saw the play as an autobiographical shriving, with the main action centered on Miller's failed marriage to actress Marilyn Monroe. The play was the first production of this repertory theatre, but was mounted at a specially constructed theatre pending the completion of the Vivian Beaumont Theatre in Lincoln Center. It was one of the group's few successes.

Ah Sin, a play by Bret Harte and Mark Twain. Produced by Augustin Daly♦ at the Fifth Avenue Theatre. ♦ July 31, 1877. 35 performances.

Broderick (Edmund K. Collier), a "Knave through circumstances over which he ought to have control," attacks Uncle Billy Plunkett (P. A. Anderson), "the Champion Liar of Calaveras," leaving him for dead and attributing the attack to York (Henry Crisp), "the Gentleman Miner and Owner of the '40 Mill.' " Just as a lynch mob is about to hang York, the wily Ah Sin (Charles T. Parsloe♦) solves the crime by connecting an incriminating coat to Broderick.

The play, developed about a character in Harte's poem "Plain Language from Truthful James," was a failure, but is remembered because of the speech Mark Twain, dressed in white, gave at the end. Many critics claimed the speech was better than anything in the play. Sensing a poor reception, Mark Twain began by wryly telling the audience that the play was "intended rather for instruction than amusement" and suggesting, as an example, that "For the instruction of the young we have introduced a game of poker." The program stated that the title role had been written expressly for Parsloe, and his performance of the part established his popularity for several seasons as a delineator of Chinese.

Ah, Wilderness!, a comedy in four acts by Eugene O'Neill.♦ Produced by the Theatre Guild♦ at the Guild Theatre. October 2, 1933. 289 performances.

In "a large small-town in Connecticut," almost the whole Miller family is preparing to celebrate July 4th, although to their teenage son, Richard (Elisha Cook, Jr.), they are all slaves of the capitalistic system and the holiday is "a stupid farce." If young Richard's misguided political enthusiasms merely amuse his tolerant father, Nat (George M. Cohan♦), another of his passions, reading, seriously concerns his mother, Essie (Marjorie Marquis). Politics, poetry, and prose are scarcely enough to claim all of Richard's youthful ardor. The real love of his life is Muriel McComber (Ruth Gilbert), to whom Richard has been sending letters filled with the same ardent poetry that so worries his mother. It worries Muriel's father (Richard Sterling) too. He demands that Richard no longer see his daughter, and if Richard disobeys he'll remove his advertisements from Nat's paper. In adolescent desperation Richard heads for a local bar, where he meets up with "a typical college 'tart'" and gets hopelessly drunk. Luckily his family is understanding and forgiving. Even Muriel would like to continue their romance, so Richard promises he will write and remain loyal when he leaves for Yale in the fall.

George Jean Nathan,♦ to whom O'Neill dedicated the play, proclaimed it "the tenderest and most amusing comedy of boyhood in the American Drama," while Burns Mantle♦ noted, "It goes back in the American theatre scene to such homely old hits as 'The Old Homestead' and 'Shore Acres,' and was inspired by much the same desire to translate to the stage truthfully and pleasantly a comedy of American home life peopled by recognizable native characters." A revival in 1988 garnered favorable notices, but attracted few playgoers. O'Neill's only comedy, in tandem with *Long Day's Journey into Night*♦ it dramatized the playwright's recollections of his Connecticut boyhood. In *Ah, Wilderness!* these recollections were affectionate and affirmative; in the later play they were drenched in corrosive bitterness. The comedy became the source of the musical *Take Me Along* with book by Joseph Stein♦ and Robert Russell, and lyrics and music by Robert Merrill. It was produced by David Merrick♦ at the Shubert Theatre, October 22, 1959, and ran for 448 performances. Walter Pidgeon was Nat; Robert Morse,♦ Richard; Una Merkel, Essie; and

Jackie Gleason♦ the boozy Uncle Sid. Although the adaptation was remarkably faithful, only the title song enjoyed much popularity. A 1985 revival failed.

AIKEN, George L. (1830–76) Born in Boston, he made his first stage appearance in *Six Degrees of Crime* in Providence, R.I., in 1848. While never an important actor, he seems, unlike many of his colleagues, to have been constantly employed and often was assigned major roles, although in second string companies. His play *Helos the Helot* (1852) won one of the many prizes given at the time to encourage native drama. Of his plays that followed most were mounted either at the Bowery♦ or at Barnum's American Museum,♦ a testimony to their melodramatic nature. Numbered among them were *Ups and Downs of New York Life* (1857), *The Doom of Deville* (1859), *Harry Blake* (1860), an adaptation of Wilkie Collins's *The Woman in White* (1861), and *The Earl's Daughter* (1861). Aiken's importance to the American theatre rests on one work, his adaptation of Harriet Beecher Stowe's *Uncle Tom's Cabin.*♦ His was not the first adaptation, but it was the one that caught the public's fancy. Aiken made the dramatization at the request of his cousin, George C. Howard, who ran the Troy (New York) Museum. Howard wanted the piece as a vehicle for his wife, who was to play Topsy, and his daughter, Cordelia,♦ who was to play Little Eva. Aiken is said to have completed his writing in a single week. The version was an instant success, establishing an amazing run of 100 consecutive performances. Brought to New York at the insistence of G. L. Fox,♦ Mrs. Howard's brother, the play established an up-till-then unequaled record of more than 300 performances.

Ain't Misbehavin', a revue in two acts with music by Thomas "Fats" Waller. Produced by the Shubert Organization♦ and others at the Longacre Theatre. May 9, 1978. 1,604 performances.

This was a musical retrospective using the songs written, with various lyricists, by the black composer-entertainer Waller (1904–43). Only a few of the songs had been created for Broadway, most notably the title number, which had first been sung in the 1929 revue *Hot Chocolates*. A 1988 revival, with the original performers, was well received. Several retrospective revues also enjoyed popularity at this time, including *Eubie* (1978), which featured the work of Eubie Blake,♦ and *Sophisticated Ladies* (1981), which used Duke Ellington melodies.

AKINS, Zoë (1886–1958) She was born in Humansville, Mo. Her first play produced professionally was *The Magical City* (1916), a one-acter. Many critics saw great promise in *Papa* (1919), her comedy about a father who attempts to save his faltering fortune by marrying off his daughters; but her reputation was established by the success of *Déclassée*◆ (1919), spotlighting the downfall of a woman who abandons home and husband. To some extent she coasted through the 1920s on the renown of that one work, meeting varying success with such plays as *Footloose* (1920), a rewriting of an old play, *Forget-Me-Not; Daddy's Gone A-Hunting* (1921), which depicted the consequences of a man's desertion of his family; *The Varying Shore* (1921), the history of a courtesan told in flashbacks in reverse chronological order; *The Texas Nightingale* (also known as *Greatness*) (1922), a story of the troubled life of an opera singer; *A Royal Fandango* (1923), in which a promiscuous princess is brought to her senses; and a series of adaptations of foreign plays: *The Moon-Flower* (1924), *First Love* (1926), *The Crown Prince* (1927), *The Love Duel* (1929), and *South of Siam* (1929). A bawdy comedy about gold-digging ex-Follies girls, *The Greeks Had a Word for It* (1930), was a huge success. She won a Pulitzer Prize◆ for her dramatization of Edith Wharton's *The Old Maid*◆ (1935). Thereafter, however, her adaptations and such original plays as *O Evening Star* (1936), recounting the last hurrah of a fading musical comedy favorite, and *Mrs. January and Mr. X* (1944), describing the romance of a flighty widow and an ex-President, met largely with indifference. While many of her early plays shocked audiences by their candor, changing moral codes have dulled their sharpness. Nevertheless, her works can be perceived as urbane, with a superior flare for dramatic situations.

Alabama, a play in four acts by Augustus Thomas.◆ Produced by A. M. Palmer◆ at the Madison Square Theatre.◆ April 1, 1891. 37 performances.

A quarter-century after the Civil War, Colonel Preston (J. H. Stoddart◆) is still an unrepentant Confederate, still advocating slavery and condemning the North for destroying his way of life. When the hated Northern-owned railroads come to set tracks along his property, Preston at first fails to recognize that the engineer is his son, Captain Davenport (Maurice Barrymore◆), who had gone off as a young man to fight for the Union and who had not been home since. Davenport puts his father's failing estate in order and frees his old sweetheart (May Brookyn) and her son (Henry Woodruff◆) from the clutches of a villainous brother-in-law (Walden Ramsay).

Thomas's plot, though it confronted still festering sectional differences, was secondary to his studies of various homespun types such as Squire Tucker, "a large baby of fifty . . . tied for life to the apron strings of his mother." As a result the *Dramatic Mirror*◆ suggested that the play "would seem to point to the speedy realization of Mr. [William Dean] Howells' prediction that the future American drama will be 'a prolongation of character sketches.' " The play was produced in what was perceived as a highly realistic manner, even to sending magnolia perfume wafting through the theatre during a scene in a magnolia grove.

Previous commitments forced Palmer to take it on the road while it was still drawing large houses. At first the road was unreceptive. Poor business on tour, coming after a succession of New York failures, forced Palmer to relinquish the Madison Square Theatre and ended his career as one of New York's most distinguished producers. Ironically, the play eventually caught on with hinterland audiences and remained popular for more than a decade.

ALBAUGH, John W., Sr. (1837–1909) A leading 19th-century theatre owner and manager, he was born in Baltimore and began his professional career there as an actor while still in his teens. For several seasons he was a member of the stock company at the Holliday Street Theatre,◆ then toured with his wife Mary, who was the sister of Maggie Mitchell.◆ He turned to theatre management in the 1860s, running playhouses in St. Louis, Albany, and Washington, D.C. In 1879 he took over the Holliday Street Theatre and a year later added Washington's National Theatre◆ to his growing chain. He continued to enlarge his holdings and began building playhouses as well, including the theatre that later became Washington's Belasco. He retired a year before his death. His son, John, Jr. (1867–1910), was a popular performer.

ALBEE, Edward [Franklin, III] (b. 1928) The adopted grandson of the vaudeville magnate, he was born in Washington, D.C. After an unhappy childhood, which included being enrolled and removed from a number of schools, Albee entered Trinity College. He remained there only a year and a half, leaving to assume a series of odd jobs that ranged from Western Union delivery boy to salesclerk. When early attempts at writing poetry were unrewarding he turned to play-writing at the suggestion of Thornton Wilder.◆ His first play, *Zoo*

Story, ◆ centering on a young vagrant with a death wish, was initially produced in Germany in 1959, then in America a year later. In *The Sandbox* (1960), he tells how an exasperated Mommy and Daddy leave Grandma on a beach to await the coming of Death in the guise of a young boy. *The American Dream* ◆ (1961) in which parents kill their disappointing child, and *The Death of Bessie Smith* (1961), a dramatization of the singer's last hours, were well received. His study of a troubled marriage, *Who's Afraid of Virginia Woolf* ◆ (1962), won the New York Drama Critics Circle Award. ◆ The next year saw his adaptation of Carson McCullers's *The Ballad of the Sad Café* reach Broadway. Critics and audiences alike were baffled by *Tiny Alice* ◆ (1964), in which the richest woman in the world seduces and destroys a Catholic lay brother. In 1966 his dramatization of a novel, *Malcolm,* and his libretto for *Breakfast at Tiffany's* were unfavorably received, but *A Delicate Balance,* ◆ an examination of the interaction of love, fear, and madness, had a modest run. Another adaptation, *Everything in the Garden,* failed a year later, as did a story of a family's deathbed quarrels, *All Over,* in 1971. Despite some critical praise, *Seascape* (1975), in which a couple encounter two disturbing humanoid figures on a beach, had a short run. Nor did the strange visitor who consoles a dying woman in *The Lady from Dubuque* (1980) please playgoers. *The Man Who Had Three Arms* (1983), a tirade by a man whose early renown was freakish, received devastating notices. Albee's other short plays, mostly early, include *Fam and Yam, Quotations from Chairman Mao Tse-Tung, Counting the Ways,* and *Listening.* Beginning in 1967 Albee co-produced several plays both on and off Broadway.

Albee's plays have dealt with his unique miasma of fantasy and reality, and his figures' inability to come to terms with this sometimes frightening combination. His later plays, however literate and thoughtful, have lacked the theatricality of his first efforts, so whether Albee eventually will fulfill the exciting promise of his early work seems doubtful. His bent has been largely confrontational and philosophic, unlike Tennessee Williams's ◆ more romantic approach, but beneath the work of both playwrights lies a disturbed sexuality.

Biography: *Edward Albee,* Ruby Cohn, Minneapolis, 1969.

ALBEE, E[DWARD] F[RANKLIN] (1857–1930) The scion of an old and wealthy Maine family, he ran away from home to join a circus, serving first as a common roustabout and then as principal ticket-seller. In 1885, on a visit to Boston, he stumbled on a shabby variety house being managed by B. F. Keith. ◆ Business was poor, especially as a result of the success of *The Mikado* ◆ playing nearby. He persuaded Keith to mount a shortened version of the operetta, present it as part of the variety bill four times a day, and charge cut-rate prices. Albee himself stood outside the theatre urging passersby to accept the bargain. They did. Under Albee's guidance Keith quickly began to expand his chain, buying and restoring old theatres in New England, then building his first new house in Philadelphia. Within a short time, Albee was effectively running the Keith circuit, with Keith remaining loftily behind the scenes. For a while Albee succeeded in monopolizing booking arrangements and on several occasions broke performers' attempts to form unions, at one point establishing an in-house union. By vaudeville's heyday in the first quarter of the 20th century, the Keith chain dominated Eastern vaudeville. Albee was forced out a year before his death by Joseph P. Kennedy, who merged the then faltering Keith and Orpheum circuits into a motion picture theatre chain.

ALBERT, EDDIE [né EDWARD ALBERT HEIMBERGER] (b. 1908) A native of Rock Island, Ill., he made a successful Broadway debut as Bing Edwards, the secretly married school athlete, in *Brother Rat* ◆ (1936). Later he was Leo David, the befuddled writer, in *Room Service* ◆ (1937), and the leading man in *The Boys from Syracuse* ◆ (1938) and *Miss Liberty* (1949). He also replaced Robert Preston ◆ in *The Music Man* ◆ and Jason Robards ◆ in the 1983 revival of *You Can't Take It with You.* ◆ He has been popular in both films and television.

ALBERT [BROWN], ERNEST (1857–1946) The Brooklyn-born set designer was a prize-winning student at the Brooklyn Institute School of Design before beginning an apprenticeship in 1877 under Harley Merry, who created scenery for New York's Park Theatre and Union Square Theatre. ◆ In 1880 he moved to St. Louis where he formed the firm of Noxon, Albert and Toomey. The company also established branches in Chicago and Cedar Rapids, and became one of middle America's major set designers. He settled in Chicago five years later, heading the new firm of Albert, Grover, and Burridge. In 1894 he returned to New York, where he worked primarily for Klaw ◆ and Erlanger ◆ and for Charles Frohman. ◆ Among the many productions which displayed his work were *An American Beauty* (1896), *The Idol's Eye* (1897), *The Reverend*

Griffith Davenport♦ (1899), *Ben Hur*♦ (1899), *Sapho* (1900), *The Casino Girl* (1900), *The Climbers*♦ (1901), *The Little Duchess* (1901), *The Virginian*♦ (1904), and *George Washington, Jr.* (1906). Many critics considered his spectacular sets for *Ben Hur* the high point in his career, one noting, "Nothing approaching it in pictorial display and mechanical ingenuity has ever before been seen in the country." These included the setting for the famous chariot race in the Colosseum, the Grove of Daphne at Antioch, and the Fountain of Castalia. After 1909 he devoted himself largely to painting. One of his fortes both as a painter and set designer was autumn and winter scenery, and one of his rare later returns to the theatre, his winter landscape for the "Flirting in St. Moritz" number in the Hippodrome's♦ *Hip Hip Hooray!* (1915), was advertised as the largest watercolor ever contrived for the American stage, being 243 feet wide and 70 feet high.

ALBINI, HERBERT Considered by some the best of the vaudeville magicians, he played mostly on Western circuits. Legend has it that the English-born Albini was the crucial witness in the court hearings when John Considine was accused of shooting a policeman. In gratitude Considine gave him virtual carte blanche on the Sullivan-Considine♦ circuit. No small part of Albini's success was his effective use of his audience, which he badgered and insulted in his high, rasping voice all the while he was astonishing them with his tricks. Heavy drinking eventually put an end to his career.

ALDREDGE, THEONI V[ACHLIOTIS] (b. 1932) The Greek-born costume designer first gained fame for her work with the Goodman Memorial Theatre♦ in Chicago. Later she designed clothes for many of the New York Shakespeare Festival♦ revivals, as well as for such diverse hits as *Sweet Bird of Youth*♦ (1959), *Mary, Mary*♦ (1961), *Who's Afraid of Virginia Woolf?*♦ (1962), *Any Wednesday*♦ (1964), *Cactus Flower*♦ (1965), *Little Murders*♦ (1967), *A Chorus Line*♦ (1975), *42nd Street*♦ (1980), *Woman of the Year* (1981), *Dreamgirls*♦ (1981), *La Cage aux Folles*♦ (1983), *The Rink* (1984), and *Blithe Spirit* (1987).

ALDRICH, LOUIS [né LYON] (1843–1901) Born in a village called Ohio State Line, he made his first appearance, as a child prodigy, in 1855 at the Cleveland Academy of Music playing the title role in *Richard III.*♦ Using such stage names as Master Moses and the Ohio Roscius he toured the Midwest

playing Macbeth, Shylock, and similar parts. For five years, beginning in 1858, he toured the West and then Australia and New Zealand with the Marsh Juvenile Troupe.♦ After a brief stint in San Francisco, he came east to perform with the stock company at the Boston Theatre, and in 1873 accepted Mrs. John Drew's♦ offer to be leading man at her celebrated Arch Street Theatre♦ in Philadelphia. He moved to New York the next year as leading man for the company at Wood's Museum. His role as the Parson in *The Danites*♦ (1877) brought him widespread fame, and he played it nearly 600 times in the following two seasons. Another brilliant success followed when he produced and starred in Bartley Campbell's♦ *My Partner*♦ (1879). He made a fortune touring with this play for six years, then enhanced his popularity when he produced and starred as Shoulders, the boozy, vengeful swamp rat, in *The Kaffir Diamond* (1888) and as Col. Hawkins, the rugged Arizona newspaperman on a visit to New York, in *The Editor* (1890), although neither play was especially profitable. While appearing in Syracuse in the latter play, he sustained serious injuries in the Leland Hotel fire, injuries that for a while seemingly affected his mental stability. His playing was erratic thereafter. However, his personal problems did not prevent him from serving from 1897 until his death as president of the Actors' Fund.♦ He is generally credited with establishing that organization's home for aging actors. A heavyset man, often gruff and blustering on stage, in private he was quiet, dependable, and much admired.

ALDRICH, RICHARD S. (1902–86) Born in Boston, he served as president of the Harvard Dramatic Club♦ and shortly after graduation founded an early summer stock group, the Jitney Players. In 1926 he became general manager of the American Laboratory Theatre,♦ and two years later co-produced his first New York show, *La Gringa.* For several seasons he was co-producer, often uncredited, with Kenneth MacGowan♦ of several more shows. In 1933 he joined forces with Alfred de Liagre, Jr.,♦ and, after several failures, found success with *Petticoat Fever* (1935). A solo venture, *Aged 26*, folded quickly. With Richard Myers♦ he co-produced two more well-received plays, *Margin for Error*♦ (1939), and *My Dear Children* (1940). Aldrich married Gertrude Lawrence♦ in 1940, and on his return from war service produced a successful revival of *Pygmalion*♦ (1945) for her. Between 1946 and 1948 he helped bring American audiences the Old Vic,♦ the Habimah Players, and a company from the Dublin

Gate Theatre. *Goodbye, My Fancy*♦ (1948), *The Moon Is Blue*♦ (1951), and *The Love of Four Colonels* (1953) were all postwar successes of his, as were highly praised revivals of *Caesar and Cleopatra*♦ (1949) and *The Devil's Disciple*♦ (1951). For many years he operated the Cape Playhouse in Dennis, Mass., and also ran the National Theatre♦ in Washington in conjunction with Myers.

ALDRIDGE, IRA [FREDERICK] (1804?–67) He was often called the first great black American actor, although he did virtually none of his performing in America. Believed to have been born in Africa, (although some sources say New York and give the year as late as 1807), he is said to have accepted menial jobs at New York theatres while performing leading roles in *Romeo and Juliet*♦ and *Pizarro*♦ with a small Negro ensemble. Prejudice and the practice of having Negroes played by whites in blackface denied him opportunities at major theatres. Dissatisfied, he left America permanently in 1826, settling in England, but playing across the Continent.

ALFRED, WILLIAM, see *Hogan's Goat*

Alias Jimmy Valentine, a play in four acts by Paul Armstrong.♦ Produced by Liebler♦ and Co., at Wallack's Theatre. January 21, 1910. 155 performances.

Lee Randall (H. B. Warner♦) is a trusted bank employee, engaged to Rose Lane (Laurette Taylor♦). What neither Rose nor his employers know is that he was once a professional safecracker and is an escaped convict. Detective Doyle (Frank Monroe) knows, but he lacks the proof that will allow him to arrest Randall. He dogs Randall's footsteps in hope of evidence. When Rose's young niece, Kitty (Alma Sedley), is accidentally locked in the bank's vault, Randall is caught in a dilemma. Deciding the youngster's life is worth more than his freedom, he jimmies open the vault. He then walks toward the detective to give himself up, but Doyle turns away and walks out of his life.

A fast-moving, if transparent melodrama, based on O. Henry's *A Retrieved Reformation,* the show toured for many seasons and was revived on Broadway in 1921. Armstrong is reputed to have written it at the suggestion of the producers and to have completed it over a single weekend. Liebler and George Tyler♦ accepted it at once. According to the same story, the show was on the boards at its Chicago premiere just two weeks later.

Alien Corn, a play in three acts by Sidney Howard. ♦ Produced by Katharine Cornell♦ at the Belasco Theatre. February 20, 1933. 98 performances.

Although Elsa Brandt (Miss Cornell) is a superb young pianist, she is forced to drudge for a living as a teacher in a dreary school in order to support her crippled father (Siegfried Rumann) and make ends meet. At the outbreak of World War I her parents, an opera diva and a violinist, had been in America and were interned as aliens. Her mother had died during the flu epidemic, and her father, attempting to commit suicide, had irreparably smashed his playing arm. Elsa is courted by two young men: Julian Vardaman (Luther Adler♦), a radical English teacher, and Harry Conway (James Rennie♦), a suave, rich married man who wants Elsa for a mistress. After she rejects them both, Julian kills himself. The ramifications of the scandal that will probably ensue allow Elsa to decide her future. When the investigating policeman asks if this is her home, she replies, "No. Vienna."

Howard's story was replete with the coincidences and foreshadowings that were the stock in trade of older melodrama. For example, early on Julian brandishes his gun and talks of shooting practice, in a moment not unlike that in *Hedda Gabler.* But for all his melodramatic devices, Howard's writing was subdued, giving the play a modern, civilized air. Nevertheless it was largely on the strength of Katharine Cornell's luminous performance that the play found its small audience.

Alison's House, a drama in three acts by Susan Glaspell. ♦ Produced at the Civic Repertory Theatre,♦ December 1, 1930. 41 performances. PP.

Alison Stanhope was a spinster who lived in a room in her brother's house and who wrote poetry, which was not published until after her death. Her poetry gave her a posthumous fame. Now, eighteen years after her death, her brother (Donald Cameron) is selling the home. The family has gathered to claim keepsakes. Even Mr. Stanhope's daughter Elsa (Eva Le Gallienne♦) appears, although she has been ostracized by the family for running off with a married man. The excitement proves too much for another of Mr. Stanhope's spinster sisters, Agatha (Alma Kruger), who tries to burn down the house lest her sister's dark secret be discovered, but who dies from a heart attack. The secret is finally revealed. Alison, like Elsa years later, was in love with a married man. Unlike her niece, she sublimated her yearnings by writing poetry about her romance. The family agrees in the end to release these poems.

The basic story was suggested by the life of Emily Dickinson, but Miss Glaspell set her version in her native Iowa. The play was indifferently received by the critics, who found it too literary. It was given only 25 performances in the regular repertory season, when, unexpectedly, it was awarded the Pulitzer Prize.♦ The Shuberts♦ hastily agreed to move the play uptown, but it lasted only two weeks more.

All God's Chillun Got Wings, a play in two acts by Eugene O'Neill.♦ Produced at the Provincetown Playhouse.♦ May 15, 1924. 43 performances.

Although Jim Harris (Paul Robeson♦), who is black, and Ella Downey (Mary Blair), who is white, have known each other since childhood, Ella drifts away from their relationship as her awareness of racial prejudice grows. But Jim still loves Ella passionately. Ella takes up with a local ruffian and has a child by him, only to have him desert her and the child die. In desperation she marries Jim. Her racial prejudices continue to bedevil her, finally driving her over the brink of sanity. Dealing with her problems causes Jim to fail his bar exams, but he remains loving and devoted. In her dementia Ella becomes like a child. Yet she retains enough basic sense to recognize she has hurt Jim. She begs forgiveness and asks him to play marbles with her. "I'll play right up to the gates of Heaven with you!" Jim responds.

Critics were sharply divided on the play's merits. Heywood Broun♦ dismissed it in the *World* as "a very tiresome play," while in the *Telegram-Mail* Robert Welsh predicted that it was "likely to take a permanent place in the American theatre."

Many found this serious, understanding treatment of miscegenation offensive. No one was surprised when the Ku Klux Klan issued threats to O'Neill, who replied that he had written not a "race problem play" but "a study of two principal characters, and their tragic struggle for happiness." However, attempts at repression came from less expected sources. Disturbed by rumors that a black man kisses a white girl on stage, the New York City license commissioner threatened to shut down the theatre if the play was produced, and just before the first performance began police served an injunction forbidding the use of child actors in the play. The players got around these problems by reading from the manuscript and cutting the children's minor roles. Furious at this evasion, District Attorney Joab H. Banton promised to bring charges of obscenity and he did—against a later O'Neill play, *Desire Under the Elms.*♦

All My Sons, a drama in three acts by Arthur Miller.♦ Produced by Harold Clurman,♦ Elia Kazan,♦ and others at the Coronet Theatre. January 29, 1947. 328 performances. NYDCCA.

Joe Keller (Ed Begley) is a manufacturer who has sold defective airplane parts to the government. As a result a number of young pilots have lost their lives in plane crashes. However, Keller has let his partner take the lion's share of the blame. Joe's son, Larry, has been engaged to Ann Deever (Lois Wheeler), his partner's daughter, but Larry, a pilot, has been reported missing. A letter arrives from him, written before he disappeared. Larry has learned from the papers what his father has done. He is so ashamed that he has decided never to return from his next mission. Chris (Arthur Kennedy♦), Keller's other son, shows the letter to his father, who recognizes that he has not only prompted his son's death but has killed the other pilots as well. He understands that in Larry's eyes "they were all my sons." Keller shoots himself.

Critics for some of the more conservative papers held reservations about this pat, cliché-ridden play, Howard Barnes writing in the *Herald Tribune* that the piece displayed "more indignation than craftsmanship . . . the offering merely stammers to a climax." Louis Kronenberger,♦ writing in the more liberal *PM,* felt the play allowed Miller "to stand easily first among our new generation of playwrights." A 1987 revival was a failure.

All the Way Home, a play in three acts by Tad Mosel.♦ Produced at the Belasco Theatre. November 30, 1960. 334 performances. PP, NYDCCA.

Although Jay Follet (Arthur Hill♦) is a country boy and relatively indifferent to religion, he has made a happy marriage with his devoutly Catholic, city-bred wife, Mary (Colleen Dewhurst♦). Their life with their young son Rufus (John Megna) is all the richer for their many visits to their extended family. However, Jay is disturbed by Mary's refusal to explain to Rufus that she is pregnant. He goes off to visit his dying father and is killed in an auto accident. Mary is left to question her religious beliefs and to prepare Rufus for the new baby.

"Though hardly a play," Louis Kronenberger♦ noted, "it often proved vividly playable." Based on James Agee's novel *A Death in the Family,* its winning of both top drama awards suggested the weakness of American play-writing at the time. Most of the better plays of the 1960–61 season were foreign: *Becket, The Hostage, Rhinoceros,* and *A Taste of Honey.* Nevertheless, the same season brought forth such fine, original domestic works as *Big Fish, Little Fish* and *Mary, Mary.* ♦

Allegro, a musical in two acts. Book and lyrics by Oscar Hammerstein II.♦ Music by Richard Rodgers.♦ Produced by the Theatre Guild♦ at the Majestic Theatre. October 10, 1947. 315 performances.

Joseph Taylor, Jr. (John Battles) is born in a typical American town in 1905. He is given a typical American upbringing by his typical American parents, who, when he begins to date pretty Jenny (Roberta Jonay), take comfort in the fact that "A Fellow Needs a Girl." When Joe goes off to college and medical school Jenny agrees to wait for him. Joe is not totally faithful, acting on his date's hint that "So Far" they have nothing to remember. But at least he remembers Jenny, so after graduation they are married. However, Jenny is the pushy kind, demanding Joe do something more than remain a small-town doctor. She pushes him right into a big-city medical practice, where everything moves at a pace best described as "Allegro," and where his loyal, affectionate nurse, Emily (Lisa Kirk), seeing how unhappy yet unrebellious Joe is, can only lament, "The Gentleman Is a Dope." After he discovers that Jenny has been unfaithful, he gives up his large practice and returns to his small-town roots.

A sentimental chronicle, its action was commented on by a singing chorus stationed on one side of the stage. The most venturesome departure from tradition by Rodgers and Hammerstein, it was also their first commercial failure. Coming after *Oklahoma!*♦ and *Carousel,*♦ it consolidated their reputation as musical theatre experimenters, but was their last truly off-beat musical.

ALLEN, FRED [né JOHN FLORENCE SULLIVAN] (1894–1956) Born in Cambridge, Mass., the baggy-eyed, deadpan comedian with a marked nasal delivery was most widely known for his successful radio comedy program, but for many years was a favorite both in vaudeville and on Broadway. Called "Vaudeville's Voltaire," he was one of its few genuine wits, although he began his career simply as a juggler. Realizing that his juggling left much to be desired, he inserted jokes to cover up his inadequacies. In one of his best remembered routines, he had a sign lowered before he appeared on stage. The sign read: "Mr. Allen is quite deaf—If you care to laugh and applaud please do so loudly." After a joke he then walked to the footlights, cupped his hand to his ear, and waited for the response. His Broadway appear-

ances were in *The Passing Show of 1922,* ♦ *Vogues of 1924, Polly* (1929), *The Little Show*♦ (1929), and *Three's a Crowd* (1930). It was in *The Little Show* that he was one of the performers in George S. Kaufman's♦ famous sketch "The Still Alarm."

Autobiography: *Much Ado About Me,* Boston, 1956.

ALLEN, VIOLA (1867–1948) The daughter of actors, she was born in Huntsville, Ala., and made her first New York appearance in 1882 as Annie Russell's♦ replacement in the title part of *Esmeralda.* ♦ In the following seasons she played important roles opposite John McCullough,♦ W. E. Sheridan,♦ and Tommaso Salvini.♦ In 1889 she won plaudits when she was cast as Gertrude Ellingham in *Shenandoah,*♦ but a previous commitment forced her to withdraw after five weeks to perform opposite Joseph Jefferson♦ and W. J. Florence♦ in *The Rivals.* Her Lydia Languish showed her as adept in comedy as she was in tragedy and melodrama. She joined Charles Frohman's♦ celebrated stock company at the Empire Theatre♦ in 1893 and might have remained there indefinitely had not Elisabeth Marbury♦ shown her Hall Caine's♦ dramatization of his novel *The Christian.* ♦ Frohman dismissed the work as trash and refused to produce it, but Miss Allen felt it had merit. George C. Tyler♦ mounted it in 1898, with Miss Allen, starred for the first time, playing Glory Quayle, the strong-headed, worldly girl converted by her clergyman lover. It became her most famous role. Between appearances in contemporary plays such as *In the Palace of the King*♦ (1900), Caine's *The Eternal City* (1902), and Clyde Fitch's♦ *The Toast of the Town* (1905), she successfully essayed such Shakespearean roles as Viola, Hermione, Perdita, Cymbeline, and Rosalind. Thereafter she appeared largely in plays of little significance, relying on her acting and appeal to lure audiences. In 1915–16 she spent a season touring as Lady Macbeth opposite J. K. Hackett.♦ In March 1916 she portrayed Mistress Ford in *The Merry Wives of Windsor,* her last New York appearance. When another play in which she starred failed out of town, she retired. Lewis C. Strang♦ wrote of the wide-eyed, round-faced, somewhat sad-miened beauty, "Miss Allen acts mentally rather than emotionally. Her conception of a part is always intelligent, comprehensive, and logical. One catches her meaning instantly."

ALLEN, WOODY, see *Play It Again, Sam*

Alley Theatre, THE Founded as an amateur group in Houston, Texas, in 1947 by Mr. and Mrs. Robert Altfeld and by Nina Vance, who rapidly assumed sole leadership, the company began producing plays a year later. In 1949 it moved to an abandoned fan factory and began using professional actors. To overcome continuing financial problems the company became fully professional in 1954 and started hiring stars to bolster receipts. With increasing recognition and substantial grants, it constructed a new complex of two theatres, one with a thrust stage and seating nearly 800, the other arena-style and holding just under 300. The auditoriums were opened in 1968. Repertory leaned heavily toward popular modern plays but recently has begun to emphasize classics and original musicals.

ALSWANG, RALPH (1916–79) The Chicago-born designer studied at the Goodman Theatre,♦ Chicago Art Institute, and under Robert Edmond Jones.♦ He was first represented on Broadway with sets for *Comes the Revelation* (1942). His later designs were seen in such shows as *Winged Victory*♦ (1943), *Home of the Brave* (1945), *Strange Bedfellows* (1948), Louis Calhern's♦ *King Lear*♦ (1950), *The Rainmaker*♦ (1954), *Time Limit!* (1956), *The Tunnel of Love* (1957), *Sunrise at Campobello*♦ (1958), and his last work, an off-Broadway revival of *The Lesson* (1978). On a few occasions he co-produced plays and sometimes directed and costumed them as well. In 1970 he worked with the architects of the new Uris Theatre in designing that house. Unlike several of his contemporaries whose work was so strikingly original or poetic that it instantly called attention to itself, Alswang was content to create quietly comfortable backgrounds. He excelled at homey, realistic designs. Critics sometimes passed over his work entirely in their reviews or acknowledged it much the way Lewis Nichols did in his notice for *Home of the Brave,* when he observed merely "the settings—good ones—are by Ralph Alswang."

ALTON [HART], ROBERT (1897–1957) Born in Bennington, Vt., he began his career as a chorus boy in *Take It from Me* (1919). He moved up in the ranks by assisting other choreographers, then struck out on his own with his dances for *Hold Your Horses* (1933). His choreography was seen in such successful musicals as *Ziegfeld Follies of 1934,* ♦ *Life Begins at 8:40* (1934), *Anything Goes*♦ (1934), *Ziegfeld Follies of 1936, Leave It to Me!*♦ (1938), *One for the Money* (1939), *Du Barry Was a Lady*♦ (1939), *Two for the Show* (1940), *Panama Hattie*♦ (1940), *Pal Joey*♦ (1940), *Son's o' Fun* (1941), *By Jupiter*♦ (1942), *Ziegfeld Follies of 1943,* and *Early to Bed* (1943). He also served as director for *Early to Bed,* the 1952 revival of *Pal Joey,* and for his last show, *The Vamp* (1955). Brooks Atkinson♦ hailed his work in the original *Pal Joey* as "wry and wistful." Alton is given much of the credit for breaking up the regimented platoons of dancers that had dominated Broadway in the 1920s. He split his choruses into smaller groups and often allowed his dancers brief solos.

Amadeus Peter Shaffer's♦ version of the Mozart-Salieri story, told from Salieri's point of view, was done in London in 1979 and first offered to Broadway in December 1980. It ran just short of three years. Ian McKellen was the original American Salieri and Tim Curry, Mozart.

AMBERG, GUSTAV (1844–1921) Within two years of his coming to America from his native Prague during the Civil War, he was managing German-language theatres in Detroit and Cincinnati. In 1879, along with Mathilde Cottrelly♦ and Heinrich Conried, he refurbished the historic old Bowery Theatre,♦ renamed it the Thalia, and presented there what one historian has called "the most brilliant sequence of stars and plays ever given here in German." His repertory included not merely the classics and new German plays, but translations of successful American shows. He gave the American premieres of many contemporary Berlin and Viennese operettas, some of which were later successfully translated into English. Among the great German performers he presented were Marie Geistinger, Antonie Janisch, Adolf Sonnenthal, Emil Thomas, August Junkermann, Heinrich Bötel, Ernst Possart, Ludwig Barnay, and Gertrud Giers. In 1888 he built the Amberg Theatre (later the Irving Place), but a succession of poor seasons cost him the house in 1891. He was retained briefly as manager. His last active years were spent working for the Shuberts. ♦

American Academy of Dramatic Arts The oldest ongoing American school of acting, it was founded in 1884 as the Lyceum Theatre School for Acting by Franklin Haven Sargent after Harvard, where he was a member of the faculty, rejected his plea to open a drama school there. Steele MacKaye,♦ Lawrence Barrett,♦ Charles♦ and Daniel Frohman,♦ and David Belasco♦ were among its early associates. At first the curriculum was based on the conservative theories of François Delsarte, which were soon displaced, and the school pioneered in its student productions of Ibsen, ♦ Strindberg, ♦ and Maeterlinck. ♦ For a time it used the name New York School of Acting. The theories of its second director, Charles Jehlinger, were similar to those of Stanislavsky. ♦ Francis Fuller and then George Cuttingham succeeded Jehlinger. In 1974 the school opened a West Coast branch in Pasadena, with Michael Thomas as director. Among the school's famous graduates are Lauren Bacall, ♦ Anne Bancroft, ♦ Hume Cronyn, ♦ Clare Eames, ♦ Grace George, ♦ Ruth Gordon, ♦ Doris Keane, ♦ Jason Robards, Jr., ♦ Edward G. Robinson, ♦ Rosalind Russell, ♦ Spencer Tracy, ♦ and Margaret Wycherly. ♦

American Buffalo, a play in two acts by David Mamet. ♦ Produced at the Ethel Barrymore Theatre. February 16, 1977. 135 performances. NYDCCA.

Don Dubrow (Kenneth McMillan), the owner of a junkshop, his "gofer," Bobby (John Savage), and his friend Walter "Teach" Cole (Robert Duvall) plan to rob a customer they believe to have a valuable coin collection. Instead, they get to fighting and Cole, in a fury, goes on a rampage and wrecks the shop. The burglary never takes place.

Despite some objectionable language, the play told its simple story well. It has been revived on several occasions.

American Company, THE The most famous and long-lived troupe of traveling professional actors in our early history was headed initially by David Douglass ♦; his wife, the former Mrs. Hallam ♦; and his stepson, Lewis Hallam, Jr. ♦ The name, prompted to some extent by growing anti-British sentiments of the day, seems to have been used first in 1763 while the company was touring Virginia and the Carolinas. Constant travel was necessary when the company was formed not only because no American city could yet sustain a full season of theatricals, but because puritanical movements frequently succeeded in closing playhouses for intervals. Although under Douglass the company continued to move about regularly, Douglass supervised the building of several important early American playhouses, including New York's John Street Theatre ♦ where the troupe eventually was based. After Douglass's departure, Hallam and John Henry ♦ led the company until Henry was replaced by John Hodgkinson. ♦ In 1796 Hodgkinson sold half his interest to his supporter, William Dunlap, ♦ hoping to dominate and discourage Hallam. Instead, shortly after the company moved to the new Park

Theatre ♦ in 1798, Dunlap bought out both his associates. By this time the troupe was known affectionately and officially as the Old American Company. The name remained until 1805, when Dunlap went bankrupt and Thomas Abthorpe Cooper ♦ assumed the reins at the Park.

During its forty-plus years virtually every important performer in America appeared with the troupe at one time or another. Most of its repertory consisted of the popular English pieces of the era, but to the company goes credit for being the first professional ensemble to mount native drama when it presented Thomas Godfrey's ♦ *The Prince of Parthia* ♦ in Philadelphia on April 20, 1767.

American Conservatory Theatre Popularly known as ACT, the company was founded in Pittsburgh in 1964 by William Ball, ♦ who remained its general director until 1986. The company moved in 1965 to Stanford University, then a year later took up residence at the Geary Theatre in San Francisco, its home ever since. For a time, beginning in 1968, it added a second San Francisco house, the small Marines' Memorial Theatre. Since the earthquake the company has been using various venues while the Geary is being repaired. Offering a full season in true repertory fashion (that is, different plays every night or two), the troupe mounts seven or eight major works a year, ranging from Greek classics to the latest European successes. In more recent seasons, especially under Ball's successor, Edward Hastings, the policy has been to bring out at least one new American play per season and to hold a "Plays in Progress" workshop. Among its most acclaimed productions have been superior revivals of *The Taming of the Shrew,* ♦ *Cyrano de Bergerac,* ♦ *Saint Joan;* ♦ and *Burn This.*

American Dramatic Authors Society, see *Dramatists Guild*

American Dramatic Fund Association Established in New York in 1848 and patterned to a large extent after Philadelphia's General Theatrical Fund, ♦ which it eventually absorbed, its purpose was "To raise by subscription from the members thereof, by voluntary donations and bequests from members and others—by Public Donors and Theatrical Benefits—a stock or fund for making a provision, by way of annuity, for aged and decrepit Members, and such provision for the Nominees' Widows and Orphaned Children of Members and also for Funeral Expenses." In essence the Association combined characteristics of a fraternal organization and life insurance group. One irony of the arrangement was that often the most needy were denied benefits because their subscriptions had lapsed. This, coupled with poor management, eventually led to cries for a sounder, more compassionately constructed charity, pleas answered with the founding of the Actors' Fund of America. ♦

American Dramatists Club, see *Society of American Dramatists and Composers*

American Dream, The, a play in one act by Edward Albee. ♦ Produced at the York Playhouse. January 24, 1961. 370 performances.

Mommy (Jane Hoffman) is a domineering middle-class wife, and Daddy (John C. Becher) is a henpecked, acquiescent husband, whose only son (Ben Piazza) fails to live up to the dream they have of his becoming a typical American young man. In despair and fury they kill the boy.

Although on its surface the play seemed a detached, intellectualized exercise, it proved effective theatre. Much of Albee's dialogue seemed surrealistic, as when Mommy asks a newly arrived guest, "Won't you take off your dress?"

American Guild of Variety Artists AGVA, as it is often designated, began as a voluntary professional association in 1938 and was organized into a traditional labor union the next year. Its aim was to protect the rights of performers in such fields as vaudeville, burlesque, rodeos, and touring carnivals. As such it was successor to such weaker groups as the American Federation of Actors, the Actors National Protective Union (both vaudeville-oriented), and the Burlesque Artists Association. With the decline of vaudeville, burlesque, and other genres from which it initially drew its membership it has moved in recent years to represent performers in night clubs, casinos, concert arenas, ice shows, and other such outlets.

American Laboratory Theatre, see *Boleslawski, Richard*

American Museum, THE Originally opened in Chambers Street in 1810 by John Scudder, it found, even in its early history, that its lecture room was given over frequently to variety performers, and entertainment quickly vied with the regular exhibits for popularity. The idea that it was a museum and the entertainment, "moral lectures," allowed many otherwise puritanical citizens to patronize the establishment. The Museum was moved several times and

was housed at Broadway and Ann Street when P. T. Barnum♦ took charge in 1842. Although Barnum never changed the institution's name, it quickly became accepted simply as Barnum's Museum. Barnum also retained the practice of presenting variety acts, but added evenings of minstrelsy and drama as well. For the most part the plays he mounted were claptrap popular melodramas or classics, frequently in curious productions. Thus the Bateman♦ sisters, child prodigies, appeared playing principal Shakespearean roles. In mid-1850 Barnum remodeled the lecture room into a full-fledged theatre seating nearly 3000. The opening attraction at the renovated auditorium was *The Drunkard,* ♦ which ran over 100 performances, setting a long-run record for the time. The theatre and museum were destroyed by fire in July 1865. Barnum quickly opened a new combination playhouse and museum, only to sell it a year later. The newer building was also destroyed by fire, in 1868.

Apart from the somewhat freakish success of *The Drunkard* and olio appearances by the likes of Tom Thumb,♦ the theatre of the American Museum contributed little to the course of drama in New York. Yet, possibly because of Barnum's name, it continues to be remembered as "one of the most celebrated playhouses in the city's history."

American National Theatre and Academy Chartered by Congress in 1935, it was to provide a "people's" self-supporting national theatre. The word "self-supporting" allowed Congress to refuse financial assistance. The commercial theatre, bucking the Depression, displayed little interest in supporting the undertaking. Enthusiasm or distaste for the concurrent Federal Theatre Project♦ also held back development. After World War II the organization was reorganized with a new board that included representatives from all important facets of the theatre. However, for several seasons its work consisted largely of offering encouragement and advice. In 1950 it purchased the Guild Theatre, renamed it the ANTA, and began to produce a series of revivals and new plays, starting with *The Tower Beyond Tragedy.* ♦ Although several of the mountings, notably a brilliant revival of *Twentieth Century*♦ and *Mrs. McThing,* were successful, the series soon petered out. In 1963, while the Vivian Beaumont Theatre at Lincoln Center♦ was under construction, ANTA built a temporary theatre on Washington Square for use by the company that was planned as the Center's repertory ensemble. With time ANTA simply leased its theatre to commercial productions, while retaining offices in the house.

However, with growing financial difficulties and some sense of purposelessness, the theatre was sold in 1981. Working with the Denver Center, in 1984 it established the National Theatre Conservatory in the Colorado city. The Conservatory is a performing arts school which, at long last, is supposed to act as "the final 'A' in ANTA." ANTA West was established as a West Coast branch, while in 1990 principal offices began the move from New York to Washington.

American Place Theatre Founded in 1963 by Wynn Handman and Sidney Lanier to promote new American plays, it was originally housed at St. Clement's Church, where its first production was Robert Lowell's *The Old Glory*. In 1971 it moved to a new 299-seat auditorium with a thrust stage. This bunker-like playhouse was constructed in the bowels of a new building on the Avenue of the Americas and was made possible by an ordinance allowing tax benefits to developers whose high rises included public amenities. Remaining loyal to its original aims, it has offered works by such growing native talents as Ed Bullins, Ronald Ribman, Sam Shepard,♦ and Joyce Carol Oates. The group also promoted a special project to encourage women dramatists. but this has since been spun off as a separate entity called "The Women's Project." In recent years the theatre has turned over its stage to such players as Eric Bogosian and Bill Irwin, who frequently perform their own material and who often are perceived as essentially soloists.

American Play Company An important source for licensing plays for stock or amateur productions, it flourished in the first decades of the 20th century when it served as exclusive agent for such playwrights as Paul Armstrong,♦ Hall Caine,♦ Clyde Fitch,♦ Arthur Wing Pinero,♦ Channing Pollock,♦ and Mark Twain.♦ The noted authors' agent, Elisabeth Marbury,♦ was its president; Edgar Selwyn,♦ its vice president; Roi Cooper Megrue,♦ secretary; and Arch Selwyn,♦ treasurer. It was eventually absorbed by Samuel French, Inc.♦

American Repertory Theatre Created in 1946 with Cheryl Crawford,♦ Eva Le Gallienne,♦ and Margaret Webster♦ as directors, the company stated its purpose was to "be for the drama what a library is for literature or a symphony orchestra for music." Besides Misses Le Gallienne and Webster, its roster of distinguished performers included Philip Bourneuf, Walter Hampden,♦ Victor Jory, and Ernest Truex.♦ It was hoped that with time the

organization might develop into the New York equivalent of London's Old Vic♦ or Paris's Comédie Française.♦ The schedule for the first season offered *King Henry VIII, What Every Woman Knows, John Gabriel Borkman, Androcles and the Lion, Pound on Demand, Yellow Jack,* and *Alice in Wonderland*. The company was housed in an old theatre on Columbus Circle, far from the theatrical center, and disbanded at the end of its first season, which had elicited a disappointing response from both critics and public.

American Shakespeare Festival Theatre and Academy Conceived in 1950 by Lawrence Langner,♦ it was later incorporated in Connecticut as a non-profit organization. A theatre, loosely suggested by surviving drawings of Shakespeare's Globe, but fully enclosed and employing the finest modern conveniences and equipment, was opened in 1955 on a site along the Housatonic River near Stratford. The house opened with *Julius Caesar,*♦ and over the next twenty or so years numerous other Shakespearean works were staged. Beginning in 1959 special spring performances for students were initiated. As interest and the quality of production waned, non-Shakespearean plays were added to the programs. The name of the organization was shortened in 1972 to the American Shakespeare Theatre. The theatre saw fewer and fewer productions, most critical and public failures. Bankruptcy followed. In 1988 the property was reincorporated as the non-profit American Festival Theatre. The group hopes to repair the playhouse and to reopen as a local art center in 1993.

American Society for Theatre Research Founded in 1956 and incorporated in 1967 as a tax-exempt organization under New Jersey law, its purpose is "to serve the needs of theatre historians in the practice of their profession, and to foster the increase of knowledge of the theatre in America." It publishes the *ASTR Newsletter,* the *Theatre Survey,* and books of special interest in its field.

American Society of Composers, Authors and Publishers Founded in 1914 by Victor Herbert♦ and a number of other distinguished writers and publishers, and known popularly as ASCAP, it was designed to protect and license performing rights of musical compositions. A rival group, Broadcast Music, Inc., or BMI, was founded in 1940. Virtually all major composers and lyricists of the American stage have been members of these associations; neither group deals in dramatic rights.

American Theatre, see *Theatre Communications Group*

American Theatre Critics Association Founded in 1974 by some of the most distinguished of American drama critics, it has among its stated purposes: 1) "To make possible greater communication among American theatre critics"; 2) "To encourage absolute freedom of expression in theatre and theatre criticism"; 3) "To advance standards of theatre by advancing standards of theatre criticism"; and 4) "To increase public awareness of the theatre as a vital national resource." The ATCA annually recommends a Tony Award♦ to be given to an outstanding regional theatre. Affiliated with the Association Internationale des Critiques de Théâtre, it played an important role in the release of two South African actors from imprisonment.

American Theatre Wing This organization was established in 1939 at the behest of Rachel Crothers♦ and other theatrical women, many of whom had been active in the earlier Stage Women's War Relief.♦ Shortly thereafter it established the Stage Door Canteen,♦ which entertained servicemen during World War II. After the war it organized important seminars on all aspects of the theatre, enlisting the best talents to lead the seminars. It has made numerous scholarship grants. In 1974 it sponsored F.A.C.T., the First American Congress of Theatre. Playgoers know it best for its Antoinette Perry (Tony♦) Awards, named for a former director.

American Wars in American Drama, see *Wars in American Drama*

America's Lost Plays First published by Princeton University Press in the early 1940s, under the general editorship of Barrett H. Clark,♦ this was a series in twenty volumes. Most volumes dealt with the work of a single playwright such as William Dunlap,♦ James A. Herne,♦ or Bronson Howard,♦ but several volumes offered works by more than one writer. With few exceptions the plays included had never before been published. The research was accomplished with the aid of the Rockefeller Foundation under the auspices of the Dramatists' Guild♦ of the Authors' League of America. The set has been republished by Indiana University Press.

AMES, ROBERT (1889–1931) Born in Hartford, Conn., he served an apprenticeship with stock companies in New England before catching New York's attention opposite Ruth Chatterton♦ in *Come Out of the Kitchen*♦ (1916). The boyish-looking Ames was best known as Billy Wade, the high-principled hero of Rachel Crothers's♦ *Nice People*♦ (1921); the unprincipled central figure of *The Hero*♦ (1921); the pathetically overreaching husband of *It's a Boy!* (1922); and the black sheep, Ben, in *Icebound*♦ (1923).

AMES, WINTHROP (1870–1937) The scion of a wealthy New England family, he was born in North Easton, Mass., and decided on a career in art and architecture after graduating from Harvard. However, he soon found his major interest was the stage. He leased Boston's famous Castle Square Theatre in 1904, and for several seasons ran a stock company which changed bills weekly. After a protracted tour of European playhouses, he returned to America and was appointed manager of the ambitious New Theatre♦ in New York, where he mounted a series of notable productions, mostly of the classics. For a number of reasons, the theatre was a failure, so Ames built two more centrally located and smaller houses, the Little Theatre in 1912 and the Booth in 1913. In 1914 Ames offered a $10,000 prize for the best new American drama. The winning play, selected from 1,875 entries, was Alice Brown's *Children of the Earth,* but when Ames produced it, it failed. Among his most memorable productions were *The Affairs of Anatol* (1912), *The Pigeon* (1912), *Prunella* (1913), *A Pair of Silk Stockings* (1914), *Pierrot the Prodigal* (1916), *The Green Goddess* (1921), *Will Shakespeare* (1923), *Beggar on Horseback*♦ (1924), *Minick* (1924), *Old English* (1924), *White Wings*♦ (1926), and *Escape* (1927). During the 1920s, when Gilbert♦ and Sullivan's♦ popularity had waned, he rekindled interest with gorgeously mounted revivals of *Iolanthe, The Mikado,* ♦ and *The Pirates of Penzance.* ♦

Ames directed a number of the plays he produced and was considered by many critics to be a leading director of his day. A dignified, reticent man, he was in his demeanor and other respects remarkably different from most of his contemporary rivals. He retired in 1932. When he died, it was discovered that he had given not merely his time, his talent, and his love to the theatre, but his great fortune as well. He died virtually broke.

ANDERS, GLENN (1890–1981) Born in Los Angeles, he began his career with a hometown stock company in 1910. He then moved to vaudeville, but left it after a short time to play more stock in Richmond and in New York. In 1912 he toured with E. H. Sothern♦ and Julia Marlowe.♦ After his first important New York appearance in 1919 in *Just Around the Corner*, the handsome, versatile actor quickly became one of the theatre's busiest, most sought-after performers. Among his notable roles were Andy Lowry, the heroine's excitable brother, in *Hell-Bent fer Heaven*◆ (1924); Joe, the farmhand who fathers the heroine's child, in *They Knew What They Wanted*◆ (1924); Lewis Dodd, the bohemian who makes a wrong marriage, in *The Constant Nymph* (1926); Edmund Darrell, who chooses a career to escape the clutches of a possessive woman, in *Strange Interlude*◆ (1928); Reuben Light, who makes a god of modern technology, in *Dynamo*◆ (1929); Pat Farley, the heroine's suicidal beau, in *Hotel Universe*◆ (1930); Victor Hallam, whose wife saves him from his domineering mother, in *Another Language*◆ (1932); Bill Blake, the alcoholic lawyer, in *Skylark* (1939); Alexander Craig, the amused observer of other people's problems, in *Soldier's Wife* (1944); and Carleton Fitzgerald, the effeminate director, in *Light Up the Sky*◆ (1948).

Writing of his performance in *They Knew What They Wanted*, Stark Young◆ noted in part, "Glenn Anders steps well out ahead of his past achievements. He understands exactly the kind of shiftless integrity in such a character . . . Mr. Anders brings to the part his singular gift for casual naturalness in his readings and inflections and for a varied tempo in his cues."

ANDERSON, John Murray (1886–1954) Coming to New York from his native Newfoundland, he started his career as a ballroom dancer. Before long he was serving as compère in cabaret revues and shortly thereafter began staging his own productions at Paul Slavin's Palais Royal. With Slavin's financial backing he produced the first *Greenwich Village Follies*◆ in 1919. Further editions followed every year through 1924. He also produced and directed several other highly praised revues, notably *What's in a Name* (1920) and *John Murray Anderson's Almanac* (1929 and 1953). He served as lyricist for *What's in a Name* and all his *Follies* except the last, to which he contributed sketches. Among the many musicals he directed were the *Music Box Revue*◆ (1924), *Dearest Enemy*◆ (1925), *Ziegfeld Follies of 1934,*◆ *Life Begins at 8:40* (1934), *Jumbo*◆ (1935), *Ziegfeld Follies of 1936, One for the Money* (1939), *Two for the Show* (1940), *Ziegfeld Follies of 1943, Three To Make Ready* (1946), and *New Faces of 1952.*◆

Robert Baral has observed in his study, *Revue,* "John Murray Anderson achieved ravishing stage effects by stressing Simplicity and Taste, which on occasion rivalled Ziegfeld's opulence. Even burlap became exotic when he sprayed it with paint." Anderson subtly created movement by coordinating color and design, and by experimenting with such innovations as revolving stages and treadmills.

Autobiography: *Out Without My Rubbers,* New York, 1954.

ANDERSON, Judith [née Frances Margaret Anderson-Anderson] (b. 1898) Coming to New York after gaining her earliest theatrical experience in her native Australia, she played with the stock company at the 14th Street Theatre, then toured with William Gillette◆ in *Dear Brutus* in 1920. After more stock work in Boston and Albany, she returned to New York in 1923. She first called attention to herself with her performance as the clawing Elsie Van Zile in *Cobra* (1924). Following a return tour of Australia, she won further recognition as the spoiled, unstable Antoinette Lyle in *Behold the Bridegroom*◆ (1927). She succeeded Lynn Fontanne◆ as Nina Leeds in *Strange Interlude*◆ (1928) and toured with the drama. After playing the Unknown One in *As You Desire Me* (1931), she toured as Lavinia Mannon in *Mourning Becomes Electra*◆ (1931). She enjoyed a *succès d'estime* as the Woman in *Come of Age* (1934), and a year later played Delia Lovell, who raises her sister's illegitimate child, in *The Old Maid.*◆ In 1936 she was Gertrude opposite John Gielgud's◆ Hamlet. Her Clytemnestra in *A Tower Beyond Tragedy*◆ (1940, N.Y. 1950), Lady Macbeth in 1941, and Olga in *The Three Sisters* (1942) further enhanced her reputation. Her greatest performance was probably in *Medea* (1947). Writing in *Theatre Arts,* Rosamund Gilder◆ observed, "Her Medea is pure evil, dark, dangerous, cruel, raging, ruthless. From beginning to end she maintains an almost incredible intensity, yet she varies her moods so constantly, she moves with such skill through explored regions of pain and despair that she can hold her audience in suspense throughout the evening." In 1953 she was Gertrude, the domineering mother, in *In the Summer House,*◆ and in a 1982 revival of *Medea* portrayed the nurse. One critic described the dark, hard-faced actress as a "diminutive woman, burning with passion, [who] gave heroic performances."

ANDERSON, Mary [Antoinette] (1859–1940) Born in Sacramento, Calif., but raised in Louisville, she determined to become an actress after watching Edwin Adams◆ perform. She was encouraged by Charlotte Cushman◆ and George Vandenhoff,◆ so she made her hometown debut at the age of sixteen as Juliet. After seasons in Louisville, St. Louis, and

San Francisco, she first appeared in New York as Pauline in *The Lady of Lyons* in 1877. Hailed as a promising but unfinished performer, she went on to play Juliet, Lizzie in *Evadne,* the title part of *Meg Merrilies,* and Parthenia in *Ingomar.* When critics attacked her Julia in *The Hunchback,* several important playwrights, including Dion Boucicault, ♦ wrote her warm, encouraging letters. She was considered by many the most beautiful actress on the stage, and her good looks and fervor instantly won over the public, if not the critics. By 1882 she had taken on, among others, the title role in *Ion* and of Galatea in W. S. Gilbert's *Pygmalion and Galatea.* The following year she left for England, where she spent the next several seasons. She returned to America in 1885, a mature actress, offering Rosalind; Clarice in W. S. Gilbert's *Comedy and Tragedy* (a part written expressly for her); and Juliet. Later she was the first actress to double in the parts of Hermione and Perdita in *The Winter's Tale.* In 1889, at the height of her fame, she announced she would marry and retire from the stage. To the surprise and disappointment of her many admirers, she kept her word. She did, however, help with the successful dramatization of *The Garden of Allah* (1911).

To convey something of her radiant good looks to its readers, the *Herald* described her as "Tall, willowy and young, a fresh, fair face, short and rounded, a small finely chiselled mouth, large, almond shaped eyes of dark gray or blue, hair of a light brown, a long white throat." Odell ♦ remembered her voice as a rich contralto. Her fellow performers, like the critics, were sharply divided about her acting. Modjeska ♦ was profuse in her praise, but Otis Skinner ♦ insisted she became a serious artist only after her return from England. On her retirement, William Winter ♦ wrote, "She filled the scene with her presence, and she filled the hearts of her audience with a refreshing sense of delightful, ennobling conviction of possible loveliness and majesty of the human soul." Few performers were so affectionately remembered.

Autobiography: *A Few Memories,* New York, 1896.

ANDERSON, [James] Maxwell (1888–1959) Born in Atlantic, Penna., and educated at the University of North Dakota and at Stanford, he became a playwright only after careers as a schoolteacher and a journalist. His first produced play, *The White Desert* (1923), a study of the tragic consequences of marital jealousy, was a failure. Success followed when he collaborated with Laurence Stallings on a story of American soldiers in World War I France,

What Price Glory? ♦ (1924). After several other less satisfactory collaborations with Stallings, he again found acclaim with his picture of white-collar married life, *Saturday's Children* ♦ (1927). His first attempt to dramatize the Sacco-Vanzetti case, *Gods of the Lightning* (1928), written with Harold Hickerson, won little attention, but later in the same season his examination of a mercurial, unstable flapper, *Gypsy* (1929), won some high praise. He turned to blank-verse drama for his recounting of the Elizabeth-Essex story, *Elizabeth the Queen* ♦ (1930). Its success prompted him to write many of his subsequent dramas in similar blank verse, making him the only major 20th-century American playwright to do so. *Night Over Taos* (1932) told of Spanish resistance to American advances in early 19th-century New Mexico. A series of highly lauded plays followed, consolidating his reputation: *Both Your Houses* ♦ (1933), a Pulitzer-Prize ♦-winning political satire; *Mary of Scotland* ♦ (1933), centering on Mary Stuart; *Valley Forge* (1934), dealing with Washington's struggles in the Revolutionary War; *Winterset* ♦ (1935), another play based on Sacco and Vanzetti and the first work to win the New York Drama Critics Circle Award ♦; *Wingless Victory* (1936), a story of a doomed interracial marriage; and *High Tor* ♦ (1937), a fantasy about one man's attempt to escape modern civilization. His 1937 verse play about the Mayerling incident, *The Masque of Kings,* failed, but was followed by his fantasy about a couple who return to their youth to reconsider their lives, *The Star Wagon* (1937), and his book and lyrics for *Knickerbocker Holiday* ♦ (1938), which included his words to "September Song." More verse plays followed: *Key Largo* ♦ (1939), dealing with the Spanish Civil War; *Journey to Jerusalem* (1940), a story of the young Jesus; and *Candle in the Wind* (1941), an anti-war play. The last two works were coolly received, although *Candle in the Wind* was a modest success. *The Eve of St. Mark* (1942) depicted a family farm during the war. But after the drubbings handed *Storm Operation* (1944), centering on the North African campaign, and *Truckline Cafe* (1946), telling of an ex-soldier's search for his unfaithful, shamed wife, he issued an intemperate diatribe calling the critics "a sort of Jukes family of journalism" and adding, "It is an insult to our theatre that there should be so many incompetents and irresponsibles among them." His next play, *Joan of Lorraine* (1946), succeeded largely on the appeal of Ingrid Bergman ♦ in the title role. His gifts returned in style with his story of Anne Boleyn, *Anne of the Thousand Days* ♦ (1948). He offered the book and lyrics for *Lost in the Stars* ♦

(1949) and his version of the Xanthippe-Socrates legend in *Barefoot in Athens* (1951) before adapting William March's novel about a vicious child, *The Bad Seed* (1954). In 1938 he was one of the founding members of the Playwrights' Company. ◆

John Mason Brown ◆ recalled him as "a great, shy bear of a man, rich in humility and conscience, haunted by a high vision of tragedy, a better dramatist than poet, needing actors to lift his verse into poetry but bravely trying to bring back the music of language to a tone-deaf stage."

Biography: *The Life of Maxwell Anderson,* Alfred S. Shivers, New York, 1983.

ANDERSON, ROBERT [WOODRUFF] (b. 1917) Born in New York and educated at Harvard, he won the National Theatre Conference's ◆ prize for his 1944 play *Come Marching Home.* His first Broadway success was *Tea and Sympathy* ◆ (1953), a story of a shy student and his headmaster's understanding wife. The only other work of his to achieve a long run was his bill of one-acters, *You Know I Can't Hear You When the Water's Running* ◆ (1967), although he enjoyed modest runs with three others: *All Summer Long* (1954), depicting a family's attempt to save its endangered house; *Silent Night, Lonely Night* (1959), a romance between two strangers who meet at an inn on Christmas Eve; and *I Never Sang for My Father* (1968), telling of a middle-aged man's attempts at reconciliation with his aging father. On the strength of *Tea and Sympathy* he was made a member of the Playwrights' Company, ◆ but his early promise was never realized.

André, a tragedy in five acts by William Dunlap. ◆ Produced by the Old American Company ◆ at the Park Theatre. ◆ March 30, 1798. 3 performances.

Major André (John Hodgkinson ◆) has been captured and condemned to die for being a British spy. His friends, including patriotic Americans, admire him enough to attempt to save him. First among these friends is Bland (Thomas Abthorpe Cooper ◆), whom André once had released from a British prison. Bland's mother (Mrs. Melmoth ◆) also has good reason to plead André's cause, for the British are holding her husband as hostage against the Major's safety. André's English sweetheart, Honora (Mrs. Johnson), comes from England to plead for clemency. Their efforts are in vain. As he goes to his execution André remarks:

> But I think your country has mistook
> Her interests. Believe me, but for this I should
> Not willingly have drawn a sword against her.

While the play was well constructed, the poetry of its blank verse was pedestrian and derivative. In an era when ill feelings against England remained strong, Dunlap's attempt to be even-handed in his characterizations disturbed some playgoers. The first night was also beset with problems. The set painter, Ciceri, ◆ had not finished his work, but Hodgkinson ordered the play to begin anyway. Ciceri walked off in a huff. Moreover, Cooper displayed a trait for which he was to become notorious. He did not learn his lines and had to ask the prompter for help. Five years after its premiere Dunlap revived the work and presented it as a musical extravaganza, *The Glory of Columbia.*

ANDRÉ, MAJOR JOHN (1751–80) A British spy in the Revolutionary War, his winning personality endeared him to many of his enemies, and his execution aroused much disapproval, even among loyal Americans. His story was dramatized several times, including versions by William Dunlap ◆ and Clyde Fitch. ◆ His brief stay in America also saw him engaged in theatricals, although the claim that he was "America's first pageant creator" is somewhat exaggerated. In 1778 he did, however, design and build the scenery and design the costumes for a performance of General Burgoyne's play, *Meschianza.* William Dunlap states that André also designed scenery for other New York productions. John Durang ◆ described one of André's drops that remained at the John Street Theatre ◆ long after André's death: "It was a landscape, presenting a distant champagne country and a winding rivulet, extending from the front of the picture to the extreme distance. In the foreground and center was a gentle cascade—the water exquisitely executed—overshadowed by a group of majestic forest trees. The perspective was excellently preserved; the foliage, verdure and general coloring artistically toned and glazed . . . André's name was inscribed on the back of it in large black letters."

ANDREWS, JULIE [née JULIA ELIZABETH WELLS] (b. 1935) The attractive English performer came to New York's attention playing the leading lady, Polly, in *The Boy Friend* (1954). She created the roles of Eliza Doolittle in *My Fair Lady* ◆ (1956), in which she introduced "I Could Have Danced All Night," and of Guinevere in *Camelot* ◆ (1960). She brought to these roles, as Stanley Green ◆ has noted, an "air of patrician innocence and her cool, clear voice." Her later career has been in films and television.

Androboros, a "Biographical Farce" in three acts by Robert Hunter. Established as the first American play to be printed, it has left no records of any performance. Hunter published the work in 1714 as an oblique attack on his adversary, the colonial administrator Francis Nicholson. Hunter depicted Nicholson as Androboros (Man Eater), a militaristic hothead determined to war against the Mulomachians (the French). Androboros persuades an all-too-docile senate to pass a resolution praising his bravery. When asked to explain its action, the senate suggests it praised Androboros before the battle, since there might be no reason to afterwards. The play also attacked the officials of Trinity Church, who opposed Hunter after his refusal to grant land to the parish. The title page claimed the book was printed in Moronopolis (City of Morons).

Hunter (d. 1734) was governor of New York and New Jersey from 1710 to 1719 and later served as governor in Jamaica from 1729 until his death. He was an author of some contemporary repute, his works having been singled out for praise by Jonathan Swift.

Angel Street Patrick Hamilton's English thriller about a man's attempt to drive his wife insane was first done in London as *Gas Light* in 1939. Under its American title it opened two nights before Pearl Harbor. Concern about our entry into World War II hurt business initially, but trade soon perked, and the show chalked up 1,295 performances, making it the longest-run foreign drama in Broadway history. Judith Evelyn♦ and Vincent Price played the wife and husband, while Leo G. Carroll♦ was the helpful detective. Most Americans remember the film version, *Gaslight,* with Ingrid Bergman♦ and Charles Boyer.♦

ANGLIN, MARGARET (1876–1958) Born in Ottawa, where her father was Speaker of the Canadian House of Commons and her brother later the country's Chief Justice, she came to New York to train at the Empire Dramatic School, which Charles Frohman♦ ran in conjunction with his Empire Theatre.♦ Impressed by her work, Frohman offered her the part of Madeleine West in *Shenandoah,*♦ in which she made her first New York appearance in 1894. She then toured with James O'Neill♦ and with E. H. Sothern,♦ performing in such varied pieces as *The Count of Monte Cristo,*♦ *Lord Chumley,* and *Hamlet.*♦ She won plaudits in 1898 for her performance when she appeared as Roxane opposite Richard Mansfield's♦ Cyrano. In the following year she returned to the Frohman fold, assuming numer-

ous roles under his aegis, most notably Mrs. Dane, the foredoomed woman with a past, in *Mrs. Dane's Defense* (1900) and the wrongly suspected Dora in *Diplomacy♦* (1901). However, she felt most of Frohman's offerings were too insubstantial, so in 1903 she joined forces with Henry Miller,♦ and the two toured together in a repertory that included *The Devil's Disciple♦* and *Camille.♦* She gave one of her most memorable portrayals when she played opposite Miller as Ruth Jordan, the traditional New Englander who finds love with a rough-hewn Westerner, in *The Great Divide♦* (1906). She enjoyed long runs in *The Awakening of Helen Richie* (1909) and *Green Stockings* (1911). In the teens she turned her attention to revivals, appearing in the principal woman's roles in *As You Like It,*♦ *Twelfth Night,*♦ *The Taming of the Shrew,*♦ *Antony and Cleopatra,*♦ and *Lady Windermere's Fan.* She also essayed a number of classic Greek roles, mounting some of the first important professional productions of the school, including *Antigone, Electra, Hippolytus,* and *Medea.* She then scored a major hit as Vivian Hunt, the long-suffering, faithful wife in *The Woman of Bronze* (1920). In the spring of 1921 she gave a special performance as Clytemnestra in *Iphigenia in Aulis* and then played Joan in *The Trial of Joan of Arc.* Her last New York appearance was as the impoverished but resourceful Lady Mary Crabbe in *Fresh Fields* (1936), although she played several of her old roles in summer stock thereafter.

Of her Katherine, Walter Prichard Eaton♦ wrote, "She herself is the best Shrew since Ada Rehan . . . She is brilliantly vitriolic, edged like a saber, and she is properly and convincingly subdued, but only after a tussle that kindles the blood. She is not so regal and magnificent as Miss Rehan, but, unless our memory is at fault, she possesses a certain tart humanity the elder actress lacked."

Biography: *Margaret Anglin, A Stage Life,* John Le Vay, Toronto, 1989.

Animal Acts in Vaudeville While earlier circuses regularly featured splendidly trained animals, usually larger beasts such as horses, elephants, or bears, acts displaying trained smaller animals did not become voguish until the mid-19th century. The rage for dog dramas♦ coincided with the beginnings of variety or vaudeville in the 1860s, and when canine plays lost their appeal trainers and animals alike continued to find a welcome in olios. One favorite of the time was Parker's Megatherian Dog Circus, not really a circus but rather an elaborate variety turn. Although dogs remained by far the most common feature, other animals were utilized. Often these acts were chosen to open a bill, so that latecomers could not disturb more sensitive performers or prevent audiences from hearing lyrics or dialogue. One of the most famous was Coin's Dogs, which presented a miniature village scene without a human in sight. Other popular dog acts included Charles Henry's Peter, Cecil and Van, Mlle. Fogardus (who mixed dogs with cockatoos), J. W. Hampton (who combined dogs and geese), Harry W. Parker (whose act also offered cats), Mac Penningill, Col. Magnus Schultz, and Ed Vinton and Buster. Nelson's Boxing Cats was among the most celebrated feline turns. Loyal and Pierrot, and Mlle. Lucille and Cockie were bird acts. Mlle. Eichbrette and Belle Hathaway both presented trained monkeys. Possibly the most famous of all was Fink's Mules, which included monkeys, dogs, and a stereotypical blackface or black clown, as well as mules, and which, coming relatively late to vaudeville stages, had been preceded by Cliff Berzac, who delighted audiences with his trick mule, and Professor Matthews with his goats. Lockhart's Elephants, Powers' Elephants, Strassel's Wonder Seal, and Woodward's Educated Seals represented more circus-like acts at home on vaudeville stages. Similarly, Annette Carver and Emile Gautier were riders, as much an attraction as their horses. Acts of mixed animals included Gautier's Toy Shop, Haverman's Animals, and Prof. Leonidas.

Animal Kingdom, The, a comedy in three acts by Philip Barry.♦ Produced by Gilbert Miller♦ and Leslie Howard♦ at the Broadhurst Theatre. January 12, 1932. 183 performances.

Tom Collier (Howard) has summoned his father (Fredrick Forrester), his friend Owen Arthur (G. Albert Smith), and Cecelia Henry (Lora Baxter) to his home. Mr. Collier thinks it might have something to do with the lady friend Tom has been seeing for many years. Embarrassed by this indiscretion, Cecelia confesses that Tom is to announce his intention to marry her. Owen insists Tom and Cecelia have not one thing in common. His father's slip forces Tom to tell Cecelia about Daisy Sage (Frances Fuller). Cecelia's reaction is chilly. When Tom visits Daisy to tell her of his plans, Daisy is pained but understanding. But, studying a picture of Cecelia, Daisy warns Tom, "Look out for that chin." After the marriage, Cecelia becomes possessive and intrusive. She forces Tom to fire his houseman (William Gargan), whom she doesn't like, and interferes in his business affairs. When she doesn't get her way she has convenient headaches or even locks the door against her husband. Taking his

houseman, whom he has rehired, with him, Tom leaves Cecelia. He tells his houseman, "I'm going back to my wife." Of course, he means Daisy.

In his preface to Barry's collected plays, Brendan Gill wrote that *The Animal Kingdom* "is a comedy simple in theme and economic in plot. Barry argues that a man may be more truly married to his mistress than to his wife, and in that case an adulterous relation is more honorable than monogamy. The point is proved without a line or gesture too many, and the dialogue is at once the wittiest and most natural-seeming that Barry had yet achieved."

Anna Christie, a drama in four acts by Eugene O'Neill.♦ Produced by Arthur Hopkins♦ at the Vanderbilt Theatre. November 2, 1921. 177 performances. PP.

At Johnny-the-Priest's waterfront saloon, where Chris Christopherson (George Marion♦) whiles away the hours he is not on his coal barge, a letter arrives for him from his daughter, Anna (Pauline Lord♦), announcing she is coming back to New York. Chris has not seen her since she was a youngster, for his wife and Anna went to live with relatives on a farm in Minnesota, and after his wife's death, as Chris explains, "Ay tank it's better Anna live on farm, den she don't know dat ole davil sea, she don't know fader like me." When Anna appears, however, it is obvious to everyone but Chris that Anna has known devils of her own. She was seduced by her cousin when she was sixteen, and, running away to St. Paul, became a prostitute. Since Chris is about to sail out on his barge again, Anna reluctantly agrees to join him. At first the sea seems to regenerate Anna, "like I'd found something I'd missed and been looking for." Then her father's barge rescues some sailors from a sinking. One of the sailors is a powerful, rough man, Mat Burke (Frank Shannon). Mat soon falls in love with Anna and asks her to marry him. In time Anna falls for Mat, but concludes she is not good enough for him. She tells Mat and her father of her history. The men go out, get drunk, and sign on a ship that will take them to Africa. Before they leave, however, they are reconciled with Anna. She promises to await their return and "make a regular place for you to come back to." Chris is uncertain of what that means. "Only dat ole davil sea, she know!" he responds.

Burns Mantle♦ called *Anna Christie* "one of the big dramas of the day, soundly human, impressively true in characterization and, in its bigger moments, intensely dramatic." O'Neill had originally written the play as *Chris Christopherson*. It failed in tryout,

even though Anna was played by Lynn Fontanne. ◆
At the time of *Anna Christie*'s New York premiere
O'Neill stated that it had been given the finest
production ever received by any of his plays, but he
later developed reservations about the drama itself,
claiming that the writing had been "too easy" and
that he had "deliberately employed all the Broadway tricks which I had learned in my stage training."
While the play may, indeed, have been somewhat
more commercially slanted than many other O'Neill
plays, it has remained eminently theatrical, has
enjoyed a number of successful revivals, been
turned into a Garbo film, and was made into a
musical, *New Girl in Town*. The musical had a book
by George Abbott ◆ and songs by Robert Merrill.
With Gwen Verdon ◆ as Anna, it opened at the 46th
Street Theatre on May 14, 1957, and ran 431
performances. However, the last major revival of
the play, with Liv Ullmann as star, failed in 1977.

Anna Lucasta, a drama in three acts by Philip
Yordan. Produced at the Mansfield Theatre. August
30, 1944. 957 performances.

Anna Lucasta (Hilda Simms) has been thrown out
of her Pennsylvania home and has become a
prostitute in Brooklyn waterfront dives. She tries to
give up this life by returning home and rehabilitating
herself. She falls in love with Rudolph (Earle
Hyman), a young boy from the South. They marry,
but then her past is exposed. Anna flees, returning
to her old Brooklyn haunts. Rudolph follows her
there and assures her that the past means nothing to
him.

Many critics saw *Anna Lucasta* as a latter-day
Anna Christie. ◆ Although the basic story is similar,
O'Neill had concentrated on his three principal
characters, while the effectiveness of Yordan's
drama came from richly drawn minor figures. The
Chicago-born Yordan (b. 1914) has been a successful
film writer, and this is his only Broadway success.
He originally conceived the principals as Poles, but
when he failed to find a producer, he gave the play
to the American Negro Theatre Company to mount.
It was their production that was brought to Broadway.

Annals of the New York Stage This virtually complete
record of the New York stage from its beginnings
until mid-1894, written by George C. D. Odell, ◆
was published by the Columbia University Press in
15 volumes between 1927 and 1948. The books are
distinguished not merely for their completeness, but
for their accuracy and readability as well. Odell
wrote with an obvious affection for the period he

was covering, viewing, wherever possible, a theatre
season from the eyes of its contemporaries. The set
was republished in 1970 by AMS Press.

Anne of the Thousand Days, a drama in two acts by
Maxwell Anderson. ◆ Produced by the Playwrights'
Company ◆ and Leland Hayward ◆ at the Shubert
Theatre. December 8, 1948. 288 performances.

Henry VIII (Rex Harrison ◆) is tired of both his
wife, Queen Catherine, and his mistress, Mary
Boleyn. He lusts after Mary's younger sister, Anne
(Joyce Redman), so he decides he will divorce
Catherine and marry Anne, even if he must split
with the Church of Rome to do so. At first,
however, his most stubborn opponent is not the
Church, but Anne herself. She would marry Percy,
Earl of Northumberland (Robert Duke). The determined Henry callously forces Percy to marry someone else. Percy dies shortly after the marriage, and
though Anne blames Henry for his death she
nevertheless finds herself falling in love with the
king. The marriage begins happily enough. Only
when Anne gives birth to a daughter does Henry's
love sour. Deciding another queen would more
likely give him a male heir, Henry confronts Anne
with the choice of exile or death. So that her baby,
Elizabeth, may someday sit on the English throne,
Anne elects to die. When she is dead Henry realizes
that his feelings for her still run deep. "It would have
been easier," he muses, "to forget you living than to
forget you dead."

Critics were divided about the merits of the blank-
verse drama. The majority sided with the *Sun,* which
hailed it as "a robust and vivid play." That New
York's critics liked it at all surprised many, for on
tryout *Anne of the Thousand Days* had been written
off as a hopeless failure.

Annie, a musical comedy in two acts. Book by
Thomas Meehan. Lyrics by Martin Charnin. ◆ Music
by Charles Strouse. ◆ Produced by Mike Nichols ◆
and others at the Alvin Theatre. April 21, 1977.
2,377 performances.

In the midst of the Depression little Annie
(Andrea McArdle) has been left at an orphanage by
parents who promise to return but never do. Still,
she hopes "Maybe" they will someday. Until then,
her dorm-mates agree, "It's the Hard Knock Life."
The orphanage is run by a harridan spinster, Miss
Hannigan (Dorothy Loudon), who makes life so
miserable for Annie that the little girl tries to
escape. "Tomorrow," she is sure, will now be better.
Just as she is returned, a secretary to rich Oliver
Warbucks (Reid Shelton) comes looking for a waif

who can spend Christmas at the Warbucks home. Annie is selected. Warbucks takes an instant liking to Annie and invites her to live with him. He also takes her to Washington, where she meets the President, and he advertises on radio to find her real parents. After the program the orphans proclaim, "You're Never Fully Dressed Without a Smile." The advertisements bring a deluge of claimants, all frauds. When the FBI learns that Annie's real parents are dead, Daddy Warbucks adopts her, along with another waif she has befriended—a dog named Sandy.

The show, which was first done at the Goodspeed Opera House,♦ was suggested by Harold Gray's famous comic strip, "Little Orphan Annie." Critics, recognizing <i>Annie</i>'s obvious appeal to children, attempted to examine the musical on two levels. Thus Douglas Watt♦ of the <i>Daily News</i> characterized it as "a kiddie show for adults," but refused to recommend it to anyone over eleven. Martin Gottfried in the <i>Post</i> condemned it for its "greasepaint sentimentality," "mawkishness," "cheap nostalgia," and "unabashed corniness," only to conclude, "the damn thing works." "Tomorrow" was the last Broadway show song for many years to achieve widespread popularity.

Annie Get Your Gun, a musical comedy in two acts. Book by Herbert♦ and Dorothy Fields.♦ Music and lyrics by Irving Berlin.♦ Produced by Rodgers♦ and Hammerstein♦ at the Imperial Theatre. May 16, 1946. 1,147 performances.

Annie Oakley (Ethel Merman♦) is a poor but happy country girl who boasts "I Got the Sun in the Morning." She is also an infallible shot, an asset which lands her in Buffalo Bill's Wild West Show. After all, she is merely "Doin' What Comes Natur'lly." She falls in love with a rival sharpshooter, Frank Butler (Ray Middleton), but when he tells her "The Girl That I Marry" must be a dainty thing she can only lament, "You Can't Get a Man with a Gun." Her one consolation is "There's No Business Like Show Business." All she and Frank can seem to agree on is that when other folk talk about love "They Say It's Wonderful." A shooting match is arranged between her and Frank, and Sitting Bull (Harry Bellaver) takes her aside to counsel that she can win her man only by losing the match. Although she tells Frank "Anything You Can Do (I Can Do Better)," she loses the match.

Not all of New York's critics were enthusiastic about <i>Annie Get Your Gun.</i> Lewis Funke, writing in the <i>Times,</i> hailed Ethel Merman but thought that the libretto left her "working in something of a void"

and that Berlin's score contained nothing to match his older hits. Time proved doubters wrong. Not only was the musical a smash hit on Broadway, but Mary Martin♦ had equal success with the road company. The show remains a revival favorite, while "There's No Business Like Show Business" has become a theatrical anthem. Jerome Kern♦ was scheduled to compose the score, but died before he could begin work.

Anniversary Waltz, a comedy in three acts by Jerome Chodorov♦ and Joseph Fields.♦ Produced at the Broadhurst Theatre. April 7, 1954. 615 performances.

In an unguarded moment Bud and Alice Walters (Macdonald Carey and Kitty Carlisle♦) reveal to their children that they had had premarital sex. When the children broadcast the news the ensuing brouhahas nearly break up a happy marriage.

Branded by Louis Kronenberger♦ as "the season's high in tasteless hackwork," the play provided enough mildly salacious escapism to overcome generally cool notices.

Another Language, a play in three acts by Rose Franken. Produced at the Booth Theatre. April 25, 1932. 348 performances.

Mrs. Hallam (Margaret Wycherly♦) has dominated her four sons. Only Stella (Dorothy Stickney), the wife of the youngest son Victor (Glenn Anders♦), has the courage to object to this domination. Her battle requires her to use many ploys, such as insisting that the family's traditional Tuesday night dinners not always take place at mama's. But she brings matters to a head when she has an affair with Mrs. Hallam's oldest grandson and her own nephew, Jerry (John Beal). Disclosure of the affair sets off a furious confrontation, but at the same time succeeds in revealing to Victor how blindly clannish he has been. At least he and Jerry will no longer be under Mrs. Hallam's thumb.

Gilbert Gabriel of the <i>American</i> found the play "steadfastly authentic . . . constantly wise and interesting." Opening with no advance sale, the play turned into a hit with good reviews and fine word-of-mouth.

The Texas-born Mrs. Franken [née Rose Lewin] (1894–1988) was also the author of <i>Claudia</i>♦ (1941) as well as such less successful plays as <i>Outrageous Fortune</i> (1943) and <i>Soldier's Wife</i> (1944).

Another Part of the Forest, a play in three acts by Lillian Hellman.♦ Produced by Kermit Bloomgarden♦ at the Fulton Theatre. November 20, 1946. 182 performances.

Marcus Hubbard (Percy Waram) made his fortune during the Civil War by blockade-running and extortion. Apparently he was also paid to lead Union troops to a massacre of Confederate soldiers, although this was never proven. Now, it turns out, his children are as ruthless and grasping as he. His eldest son, Ben (Leo Genn), does not hesitate to blackmail him to get his hands on the Hubbard money. What neither Marcus nor Ben takes into account is Marcus's favorite, his unloving daughter Regina (Patricia Neal), who is content to wait until her time comes. And she is sure it will.

This chilling look at the earlier history of the same family Miss Hellman had portrayed so brilliantly in her 1939 hit *The Little Foxes♦* won general critical approval but failed to find a large audience.

ANOUILH, JEAN (1910–87) Often called the leading French playwright of his day, the dramatist observed both the lighter and darker sides of life with an essentially rueful wit. Unfortunately he was not always well served by his American translators and producers. Among the American mountings of his work were *Antigone* (1946), *Ring Around the Moon* (1950), *Mademoiselle Colombe* (1954), *Thieves' Carnival* (1955), *The Lark* (1955), *Waltz of the Toreadors* (1957), *The Fighting Cock* (1959), and *Becket* (1960).

ANSPACHER, LOUIS K[AUFMAN] (1878–1947) A Cincinnatian who studied at New York's City College and at Columbia Law School, he was primarily known as a lecturer. He spent some time as a young man acting, and between 1904 with his *Tristan and Isolde* and *The Rhapsody* in 1930 saw over a dozen of his plays produced. However, he is likely to be remembered for a single work, his study of an incorrigibly vicious and self-centered wife, *The Unchastened Woman♦* (1915).

ANTA, see *American National Theatre and Academy*

Antony and Cleopatra Shakespeare's tragedy has had a fitful record in America. New Orleans saw it in 1838 with Ellen Tree♦ and William Hield. Its first New York presentation seems to have come surprisingly late, not until George Vandenhoff♦ and Mrs. Bland assumed the title roles in 1846. Infrequent subsequent mountings included those featuring Edward Eddy♦ and Mme. Ponisi♦ in 1859 and Joseph Wheelock and Agnes Booth♦ in 1877. Spectacle was as important to these mountings as was drama.

Interest flared in the play in the late 19th and early 20th century. For an 1889 revival headed by Kyrle Bellew♦ and Mrs. Brown-Potter,♦ the critics twitted another sort of spectacle, the spectacle of two performers unsuited for their roles, and gave only cursory praise to Goatcher's♦ lavish settings. In 1909 the New Theatre♦ opened with a physically sumptuous production of the play and with the Marlowe♦-Sothern♦ team giving their lushly poetic readings. Later notable 20th-century revivals have been Katharine Cornell's♦ 1947 production with Godfrey Tearle as her leading man and the Laurence Olivier♦-Vivien Leigh presentation in 1951.

Any Wednesday, a comedy in two acts by Muriel Resnik. Produced at the Music Box Theatre. February 18, 1964. 982 performances.

John Cleves (Don Porter) is an arrogant, lecherous, hopelessly spoiled business tycoon who, every Wednesday, meets with his oddball mistress, Ellen Gordon (Sandy Dennis♦). Naturally his loyal wife, Dorothy (Rosemary Murphy), knows nothing about his affair. She continues to pamper his childishness, letting him go first in every silly game they play and ignoring mistakes he makes. When Cass Henderson (Gene Hackman), a lowly employee he treats like dirt, discovers that Cleves writes off Ellen as a tax deduction, the cat is out of the bag. Cleves's puerile, petulant reaction alienates both his wife and his mistress. He realizes that if he cheats at any game from now on, that game will be solitaire.

Henry Hewes,♦ the critic for the *Saturday Review,* dismissed the play as "slight" but "amusing." Most critics concurred. Yet *Any Wednesday* represented the sort of trivial, if slick comedy that often keeps theatres lit and profitable between more ambitious plays. Coming to New York with little praise and advance sale, the play proved one of the "sleepers" that make for legend on Broadway.

Anything Goes, a musical comedy in two acts. Book by Guy Bolton,♦ P. G. Wodehouse,♦ Howard Lindsay,♦ and Russel Crouse.♦ Lyrics and music by Cole Porter.♦ Produced by Vinton Freedley♦ at the Alvin Theatre. November 21, 1934. 420 performances.

Reno Sweeney (Ethel Merman♦), an evangelist turned bar hostess, gets such a kick out of Billy Crocker (William Gaxton♦) that she boards a Europe-bound liner to dissuade him from pursuing Hope Harcourt (Bettina Hall♦). Although Billy dreams of Hope all through the night, Hope is determined to marry an English peer. Crocker has boarded without a ticket, so is forced to adopt a number of disguises. Also aboard is a wistful little man, the Reverend Dr. Moon (Victor Moore♦), whom J. Edgar Hoover has branded "Public Enemy 13." Moon's ambition is to rise to the top of Hoover's list. With a minister and former evangelist as passengers the captain hopes to cheer his Depression-ridden travelers with a revival meeting. Reno obliges with a rousing anthem directed at the archangel Gabriel. On landing, Hope discovers she has become an heiress. She drops her Englishman and consents to marry Billy. The Englishman turns his attention to Reno, while Moon, learning he has been judged harmless and dropped from the FBI list, walks away muttering nasty things about Hoover.

Principal songs: All Through the Night · Anything Goes · Blow, Gabriel, Blow · I Get a Kick Out of You · You're the Top

Praised by Brooks Atkinson♦ as "a thundering good song and dance show," with time this work came to be perceived as the quintessential American musical of the 1930s—brassy, lighthearted, contemporary, and more or less topical. Its comedy was inserted for comedy's sake, its songs were lively and its dances livelier. Porter's score was considered his best before *Kiss Me, Kate*♦ (1948). A disaster almost scuttled the show. Bolton and Wodehouse's original libretto dealt with a shipwreck, but just before the musical went into rehearsal the *Morro Castle* sank with a huge loss of life. Bolton and Wodehouse were out of the country, so Freedley enlisted Lindsay to write a new story. Lindsay asked Crouse to join him, thus initiating one of Broadway's more successful partnerships. A heavily rewritten 1987 revival succeeded in New York, but failed on tour.

APA, see *Association of Producing Artists*

Apple Blossoms, an operetta in a prologue and two acts. Book and lyrics by William Le Baron. Music by Victor Jacobi and Fritz Kreisler. Produced by Charles Dillingham♦ at the Globe Theatre. October 7, 1919. 256 performances.

Nancy Dodge (Wilda Bennett♦) thinks she loves Dickie Stewart (Percival Knight), while Philip Campbell (John Charles Thomas♦) is sure he loves Anne Merton (Florence Shirley). But when Nancy and Philip are pressed into marriage by their families they agree to wed with the understanding that after the marriage each is free to go his or her own way. They soon resume their old flirtations only to find at a masked ball that they have come to love each other. Dickie and Anne, old flames, also decide to marry.

Principal songs: Little Girls, Goodbye · Who Can Tell? · You Are Free

The musical gave a handsome leg up to the careers of its chief dancers, Fred♦ and Adele Astaire. ♦ Much of Kreisler's contribution to its score was later used in his 1932 Viennese operetta *Sissy,* while his melody for "Who Can Tell?" was given yet a third set of lyrics in 1936 and became popular as "Stars in Your Eyes." Kreisler was, of course, better known as a violinist.

ARBUCKLE, MACLYN (1863–1931) Born in San Antonio, Texas, he gave up a burgeoning law career to try his hand at acting. After making his debut in 1888 in Shreveport, La., he spent several seasons touring, playing mostly in smaller cities. His first New York appearance was not until 1900, and he did not really call attention to himself until the following year, when he appeared as the Earl of Rockingham in *Under Two Flags.* ♦ Later in 1901 he portrayed Antonio in *The Merchant of Venice.* ♦ He found his true métier in 1903 when he was cast as the folksy-wise George Washington Skipper in *Skipper and Co., Wall Street,* then created his most memorable role several months later as Jim Hackler in *The County Chairman.* ♦ Playing Hackler kept him busy for the next four seasons. Thereafter he met with varying degrees of success depicting similar home-spun characters in *The Round Up*♦ (1907), *The Circus Man* (1909), and *The New Henrietta* (1915). In 1919 he headed a road company of *The Better 'Ole.* Before retiring, the pudgy, friendly miened actor participated in two all-star revivals mounted by The Players,♦ playing Anthony Absolute in *The Rivals* in 1923 and Stingo in *She Stoops To Conquer* in 1924.

Arch Street Theatre (Philadelphia) Built by a syndicate financed from New York but lead locally by W. B. Wood,♦ it was based on designs by John Haviland, one of the leading architects of his day, and opened in 1828 as a rival to the Chestnut Street Theatre♦ and Walnut Street Theatre.♦ At first it was unsuccessful, but after William Forrest, brother of Edwin Forrest,♦ took over its management in 1830 it quickly became one of the city's major playhouses. Most of Edwin Forrest's best vehicles were played there when he was in his prime, and several were given their premieres at the theatre. William Burton♦ took over the house in the 1840s, giving it some of its greatest hits, including *A Glance at Philadelphia,* his localized version of Benjamin A.

Baker's♦ *A Glance at New York.* ♦ After Burton left, William Wheatley♦ ran the house. The theatre's heyday is generally considered to have begun in 1861, when Mrs. John Drew♦ assumed the reins and quickly established one of the greatest of all American stock companies. The house remained under her control for thirty-one years. During the administrations of Forrest, Burton, and Mrs. Drew virtually every great performer in America appeared on its stage at one time or another. The decline of the playhouse commenced with Mrs. Drew's withdrawal in 1892. Another stock company failed, so under Charles E. Blaney♦ the theatre initiated a policy of popular melodramas. In later years the theatre offered musical comedy stock companies, Yiddish plays, and burlesque. It was demolished in 1936.

Arena Stage (Washington, D.C.) Founded in 1950 by Zelda Fichandler and Edward Mangum, the company gave its first performances in an old film house, then moved to a converted brewery. In 1961 it moved to a new complex where, over the years, it established three playhouses—the Arena Stage, its principal auditorium; the Kreeger; and a small basement semi-cabaret, the Old Vat. Its repertory has balanced classics with new plays, among them premieres of several works which later moved to Broadway, including *The Great White Hope,* ♦ *Indians,* and *Moonchildren.* ♦ The company toured the Soviet Union under State Department aegis in 1973, and later performed in Hong Kong. It was the first regional theatre to receive a Tony Award♦ for services to its community. Mrs. Fichandler, after guiding the company for forty years, announced she would leave in mid-1991.

Arena-style Theatre (Theatre-in-the-Round) Although some hailed the proliferation after World War II of arena-style playhouses, in which audiences surround the stage, as a revolutionary departure, others saw it as the extension of the more open, thrust-stage playhouses that had characterized many Elizabethan and Jacobean theatres before the proscenium-style auditoriums took over at the time of the Restoration. Still others saw such staging merely as an adaptation of standard circus practice to the presentation of more traditional drama. Advocacy of such staging had arisen earlier. Surprisingly, none of the great artists, such as Mrs. Fiske♦ and Sarah Bernhardt,♦ who were forced by their rejection of the Trust♦ to perform in circus tents at the turn of the century, apparently carried the opportunity to its logical conclusion, preferring to convert the tents into something resembling proscenium auditoriums. In this they were following the practice of most tent shows♦ that were long popular in American backwaters. But by the 1920s progressive designers such as Robert Edmond Jones♦ were toying with the idea, which began to achieve worldwide testing a decade later. A major American experimenter was Professor Glenn Hughes of the University of Washington. In 1932 he converted the penthouse of an old hotel into a theatre-in-the-round seating sixty patrons. His success was such that by 1935 his "Penthouse Theatre" had moved to larger quarters in a lodge near the campus, and in 1940 he built a more permanent, somewhat elliptically shaped arena theatre on campus. By that time other cities ranging in size from St. Paul to Lewistown, Montana, had tried similar enterprises with varying success. World War II temporarily halted the spread of the movement, but with peace, arena stages began to appear in many places. Some of the first were the summer stock♦ tents, cheaper and easier to erect than standard playhouses. Regional theatres were also in the vanguard, with Margo Jones's♦ Theatre 47 in Dallas, Washington's Arena Stage,♦ and New York's Circle in the Square♦ among the most noteworthy. The vogue for arena-style theatre, besides answering the need for more economical theatres and productions, reflected the move away from restrictive theatrical realism. To some extent, by bringing audiences closer to players, it also helped these younger microphone-trained performers to project better, although with the construction of many larger arena theatres (often on the sites of more successful summer tents), microphones and amplification became as commonplace as in large proscenium houses.

Arizona, a play in four acts by Augustus Thomas. ♦ Produced by Kirk LaShelle♦ and Fred Hamlin at the Herald Square Theatre. September 10, 1900. 140 performances.

Captain Hodgman (Walter Hale) of the 11th Cavalry, for all his charm and good looks, is an immoral scoundrel. He has fathered an illegitimate child by Lena Kellar (Adora Andrews) and tries to seduce Estrella Bonham (Jane Kennark), his colonel's wife. Lieutenant Denton (Vincent Serrano) discovers that Estrella plans to elope with Hodgman, to whom she has given her jewels. He talks her out of her plan and recovers the jewels, but Col. Bonham (Edwin Holt), discovering Denton with the jewels, accuses him of theft. Denton renounces his commission, but remains near at hand to be with his fiancée, Bonita Canby (Eleanor Robson♦), Estrella's sister. When Hodgman is shot, Denton is suspected. To exculpate the devoted Denton, Estrella must confess her attempted infidelity. She tells Bonham she now truly loves him. At first he is icy, but sensing how much his own rigid behavior had led Estrella to seek affection elsewhere, he picks up a rose which Estrella has dropped on the floor and thrusts it in his shirt.

Bernard Sobel, in *The Theatre Handbook,* branded *Arizona* as "an example par excellence of well constructed melodrama of the type popular at the turn of the century." The play was successfully revived several times, and made into an unsuccessful musical, *The Love Call* (1927). But its importance lies far more in its direct and indirect influences than in any contemporary excellence. The play is generally credited with starting the rage for "Westerns" in the American theatre. Booked at the failing Herald Square Theatre, which the young Shubert♦ brothers had taken over as their first New York base, its success allowed them to start their climb to theatrical heights.

ARLEN, HAROLD [né HYMAN ARLUCK] (1905–86) Born in Buffalo, he began his career by writing songs for cabaret productions and by interpolating songs in Broadway revues. His first success, "Get Happy," came in an otherwise undistinguished show, *9:15 Revue* (1930). Thereafter he composed most or all of the music for the *Earl Carroll Vanities♦* (1930); *You Said It* (1931); *Life Begins at 8:40* (1934), which offered "Let's Take a Walk Around the Block"; *Hooray for What!* (1937), recalled for "Down with Love"; *Bloomer Girl♦* (1944), from which came "Right as the Rain"; *St. Louis Woman* (1946), whose score included "Come Rain or Come Shine"; *House of Flowers♦* (1954), remembered for "A Sleeping Bee" and the title song; *Jamaica* (1957); and *Saratoga* (1959). One of his most famous songs, "I Gotta Right To Sing the Blues," was interpolated in the 1932 edition of the *Vanities.* His music leaned heavily on commercialized jazz forms, especially blues, and other black musical mannerisms.

Biography: *Happy with the Blues,* Edward Jablonski, New York, 1961.

ARLISS, GEORGE [né AUGUSTUS GEORGE ARLISS-ANDREWS] (1868–1946) After making his American debut in 1901 opposite Mrs. Patrick Campbell♦ as Cayley Drummle in *The Second Mrs. Tanqueray* and playing a season of repertory with her, he was enlisted by David Belasco♦ to portray the villainous Zakkuri in *The Darling of the Gods♦* (1902). He

then came under the management of Harrison Grey Fiske♦ and appeared with Mrs. Fiske♦ as the Marquis of Steyne in *Becky Sharp♦* (1904), Raoul Berton in *Leah Kleschna♦* (1904), Judge Brack in *Hedda Gabler* (1904), Sir Cates-Darby in *The New York Idea♦* (1906), and Ulric Brendel in *Rosmersholm* (1907). He next played the title role in *The Devil* (1908) and the following year acted the absent-minded inventor, the title role in *Septimus.* In 1911 he essayed one of his greatest interpretations, the title part in *Disraeli,* a role he played across the country for four years. This was followed by the leading figure in *Paganini* (1916), a revival of Barrie's♦ *The Professor's Love Story* (1917), and the principal role in *Hamilton* (1918). He toured as a member of the all-star cast of *Out There* (1918) before assuming another of his most famous roles, the malevolent Rajah in *The Green Goddess* (1921). Alexander Woollcott♦ wrote of his performance, "With his countenance at once gentle and diabolic, with his cat-like tread and with his uneasy but sinister hands, he seems to have been roaming our stage all his days in wistful quest of a play about a rajah with . . . an evil heart." He returned to Broadway in 1924 to play the dogged eighty-year-old Sylvanus Heythorp in John Galsworthy's♦ *Old English.* In 1928 he offered his Shylock to New York and following a tour in the role retired from the theatre. He also had a notable career in films.

Ward Morehouse♦ described him as "a thin-faced, smallish man, inclined to sinister roles, a creative and intellectual actor who invariably gave a lesson in acting to fellow members of his trade." His piercing eyes and seductive voice quietly underscored his sardonic humor and the essential humanity of even his blackest figures.

Autobiography: *Up the Years from Bloomsbury,* Boston, 1927.

ARMSTRONG, PAUL (1869–1915) Born in Kidder, Mo., he began his writing career as a journalist, providing sporting news under the name Right Cross. When he turned to play-writing he often wrote plays to order, frequently producing a completed script in three or four days. Many of his plays were claptrap melodramas created for second-rate touring companies, but others were written for New York and several received respectful attention. Significantly, his biggest hits seemed to be either adaptations of good stories or collaborations. *Salomy Jane,♦* derived from Bret Harte's *Salomy Jane's Kiss,* was a 1907 success. In 1909, his comedy *Going Some,* written with Rex Beach, delighted playgoers with its story of two imposters at a race.

Armstrong's most notable play was *Alias Jimmy Valentine*♦ (1910), a tale of a reformed crook. With Wilson Mizner♦ he wrote two popular dramas, *The Deep Purple* (1911), an early realistic treatment of the underworld, and *The Greyhound* (1912), a tough-fibered play about a transatlantic cardsharp. Among his other plays were *The Superstition of Sue* (1904), *The Heir to the Hoorah* (1905), *Via Wireless* (1908) written with Winchell Smith,♦ *Society and the Bulldog* (1909), *The Escape* (1913), *The Bludgeon* (1914), and *The Heart of a Thief* (1914). Although Armstrong's plays usually had a hard veneer, H. L. Mencken♦ remembered him as "a very sentimental man [who] often shed tears at his own dinner table over the sufferings of the heroines of his plays."

ARONSON, BORIS (1900–1980) After studying art and set design in his native Kiev, in Moscow, and in Berlin, he came to New York in 1923 and soon found employment designing sets for the Unser Theatre in the Bronx and for Maurice Schwartz's♦ Yiddish Art Theatre.♦ By 1927 he was also providing sets for Eva LeGallienne's♦ Civic Repertory Theatre.♦ He moved rapidly into the commercial theatre where his work was seen in such shows as *Walk a Little Faster* (1932), *Three Men on a Horse*♦ (1935), *Awake and Sing!*♦ (1935), *The Gentle People*♦ (1939), *Cabin in the Sky*♦ (1940), *Detective Story*♦ (1949), *I Am a Camera*♦ (1951), *Bus Stop*♦ (1955), *A View from the Bridge*♦ (1955), *The Diary of Anne Frank*♦ (1955), *Fiddler on the Roof*♦ (1964), *Cabaret*♦ (1966), *Company*♦ (1970), *A Little Night Music*♦ (1973), and *Pacific Overtures*♦ (1976). When plays required them, he designed excellent realistic settings, but his forte was highly stylized, often symbolic settings such as those he conceived for *J.B.*♦ (1958) and for such failures as the futuristic *Sweet Bye and Bye* (1946) and *Orpheus Descending* (1957). His stylization, free placement of form, and use of bright colors were heavily influenced by his admiration of Marc Chagall. He was also one of the first to employ projections against neutral backgrounds to effect changes of mood and place.

ARONSON, RUDOLPH (1856?–1920) The New York-born entrepreneur conceived and built the Casino Theatre,♦ which opened in 1882 as the first playhouse designed specifically for Broadway musicals. Initially with John A. McCaull♦ and later alone, he produced many important turn-of-the-century Continental operettas, giving Americans their first opportunity to hear in English works that were among the reigning hits of their era—some of which have remained popular ever since. He introduced most of Johann Strauss's♦ best works, including *The Queen's Lace Handkerchief* (1882), *Prince Methusalem* (1883), *Die Fledermaus* (1885), *The Gypsy Baron* (1886), and *Vienna Life* (1901). However, his biggest success came with a now forgotten work, Edward Jakobowski's *Erminie*♦ (1886). An accomplished musician, he also composed and orchestrated the scores for several comic operas, notably *The Rainmaker of Syria* (1893). Aronson eventually lost both the Casino and his producing organization, but to the end remained filled with grand plans, including an "American Palace of Art," a sort of Lincoln or Kennedy Center, a half-century ahead of its time.

Autobiography: *Theatrical and Musical Memoirs,* New York, 1913.

Around the World in Eighty Days In the late summer of 1875 Jules Verne's popular 1873 novel became the source of two competing extravaganzas, which mingled Verne's tale of Phileas Fogg with elaborate settings, trick scenery, lavish ballets, and a variety of musical numbers. The more successful of the two was mounted at the Academy of Music by the Kiralfy♦ brothers. It was revived regularly until the mid-1890s and was second in popularity among such musical extravaganzas only to *The Black Crook.*♦ In 1946 Orson Welles♦ mounted his own version, with music by Cole Porter.♦ Welles filled his entertainment with magic stunts, circus performers, and such clever scenic bits as a miniature train wreck, and he assumed the role of the villainous Dick Fix. However, the musical was short-lived.

Arrah na Pogue; or, The Wicklow Wedding, a play in four acts by Dion Boucicault.♦ Produced at Niblo's Garden.♦ July 12, 1865. 68 performances.

Arrah Meelish (Josephine Orton), a simple peasant girl, offers to shelter the fugitive, Beamish McCoul (W. E. Sheridan♦), when he appears at her cottage. McCoul's presence is discovered by the treacherous informer, Michael Feeney (W. Scallan). Feeny divulges the secret on the eve of Arrah's wedding to Shaun the Post (T. H. Glenney), hinting that more than anti-British sentiments prompted Arrah's actions. Shaun is not deceived. To save Arrah's life and reputation Shaun claims that he had urged Arrah to hide the man. In the end Arrah, Shaun, and McCoul all manage to escape official wrath, and Arrah and Shaun are wed.

The play was filled with what critics of the day liked to call "sensations," such as Shaun's false confession and his later escape by climbing down a growth of ivy. Although the *Times* suggested, "It lacks the heartiness of the 'Colleen Bawn,' the contrasts of the 'Octoroon' and the enthusiasm of 'Jessie Brown,' " the public adored the play. It was revived regularly for the remainder of the century. Boucicault himself, who played the role at its London premiere, later frequently assumed the role of Shaun.

Arsenic and Old Lace, a comedy in three acts by Joseph Kesselring. Produced by Howard Lindsay♦ and Russel Crouse♦ at the Fulton Theatre. January 10, 1941. 1,444 performances.

Abby Brewster (Josephine Hull♦) and her sister Martha (Jean Adair) are two nice, sweet old ladies who murder nice, sweet, lonely old men. Their method is simple. They invite the old men home and offer them a drink of their special elderberry wine, which has been laced with a little arsenic. Of course, burying their victims might be a problem. Luckily, their brother is crazy, too. Teddy (John Alexander), a heavy-set man with big teeth and a large mustache, wears a pince-nez. Teddy never walks up a flight of stairs. Yelling "Charge," he bolts up them, since, after all, the stairs are San Juan Hill. Teddy Brewster, in short, thinks he is Teddy Roosevelt, so the graves he digs in the Brewster cellar are really excavations for the Panama Canal. Their nephew Mortimer (Allyn Joslyn) is thrown for a loss when he learns of their activities. Complications set in when another Brewster nephew, Jonathan (Boris Karloff), arrives, accompanied by strange Dr. Einstein (Edgar Stehli). Jonathan is a criminal on the run, and he, too, is a murderer. In fact, the body of his latest victim is outside in the rumbleseat of his car, and he is determined to hide it in his aunts' home. Mortimer as next of kin arranges to commit the entire family to a mental institution, but the sisters have a surprise for him. He's not truly next of kin; merely an adopted child. Relieved to learn that he is a bastard, Mortimer departs. Left alone with the man from the mental home, the sisters sweetly offer him a glass of their elderberry wine.

Richard Lockridge of the *Sun* described the play as "a noisy, preposterous, incoherent joy," adding, "You wouldn't believe that homocidal mania could be such great fun." Legend has it that the play, originally called *Bodies in Our Cellar,* was conceived as a serious thriller and that Lindsay and Crouse were responsible for turning it into a comedy. A 1986 revival received mixed notices, but toured profitably because of the television names in the cast. Joseph Otto Kesselring (1902–67) was a New York-born teacher, actor, author, and playwright. This was his only success.

ARTEF Its acronym derived from the Yiddish for Workers' Theater Group, it was founded in 1925 as a dramatic studio under the auspices of *Freiheit,* the Yiddish Communist daily, to produce plays on "a sound social basis." The group flourished through most of the 1930s, mounting both Yiddish classics and modern Yiddish propaganda plays, usually in that formally stylized, almost balletic manner known as agitprop. Few of the actors were professional. Most shows were cast from theatrically interested laborers. The group disbanded in 1937, but sputtered back to life at intervals thereafter. Many Broadway critics visited their productions at one time or another, and often reviewed them favorably. Bernard Sobel wrote in the *Daily News* that they displayed "a refinement of inflection, perfect esprit de corps, a joyous bawdiness . . . conscious intellectualization . . . laughter, freshness and sustained emotional elevation."

ARTHUR [SMITH], JOSEPH (1848–1906) One of the most successful turn-of-the-century melodramatists, he was born in Centerville, Ind., the son of a clergyman. He served as a newspaper reporter and foreign correspondent before turning to the theatre. Even here unprofitable attempts at acting and producing preceded the discovery of his true métier. Despite his wide travels most of his best plays were set in his native state, but it was neither his settings nor plots that accounted for his sometimes huge successes. Rather, like Dion Boucicault,♦ he had a special gift for contriving unusual, sensational, and memorable scenes. *The Still Alarm♦* (1887) featured a scene in a fire house in which firemen slide down the pole and prepare the fire engine, horses and all, while in *Blue Jeans♦* (1890) an unconscious man is placed on a belt moving ever closer to a whirling buzz saw. Among his other plays were a comedy, *A Cold Day When We Get Left* (1885); *The Corncracker* (1893), dealing with family members long separated; *The Cherry Pickers♦* (1896), a military melodrama set in India; and *The Salt of the Earth* (1898), in which a country boy overcomes all variety of wicked machinations to rise in politics and win his sweetheart's hand. A shrewd businessman, Arthur died wealthy. At the time of his death no fewer than a dozen touring companies were presenting his plays.

ARTHUR, JULIA [née IDA LEWIS] (1869–1950) She left her native Canada, where she had participated in amateur theatricals, to spend several seasons playing important Shakespearean roles in Daniel E. Bandmann's♦ touring company. Her first New York appearance was under A. M. Palmer's♦ aegis as Queen Fortunetta in *The Black Masque* in 1891. In the next season she played Lady Windermere in the first American production of *Lady Windermere's Fan,* and shortly thereafter portrayed the heroine in *Mercedes,* a much heralded play that nevertheless proved a disappointment. She went to England, where she joined Henry Irving's Lyceum Company and toured with that troupe when it made an American visit. She was granted stardom when she played the title role in *A Lady of Quality* (1897). In 1899 she toured in repertory, offering her Parthenia in *Ingomar,*♦ Rosalind in *As You Like It,*♦ and Galatea in *Pygmalion and Galatea.* Later in the year, after playing Josephine in *More Than Queen,* she temporarily retired, not returning to the stage until 1914, when she gave special performances in Boston and Baltimore. New York applauded her again as the Woman in *The Eternal Magdalene* (1915). Two years later she performed the title role in *Seremonda,* directing the tragedy as well. She was selected to be a member of the all-star cast of *Out There* (1918). During 1920–21 she played Lady Cheveley in *An Ideal Husband* and Lady Macbeth. After touring in 1924 in the title role of *Saint Joan*♦ she retired permanently. A small, dark-haired, large-eyed beauty, she was said to have brought her singular hauteur and dignity to all the roles she played.

Artists and Models A series of revues mounted by the Shuberts♦ in 1923, 1924, 1925, 1927, and 1930. Unlike the more lavishly dressed extravagant annual revues of this period, these shows emphasized nude or nearly nude girls and a lower order of comedy, thus mirroring more closely the style of the *Earl Carroll Vanities.*♦ A 1943 version credited Lou Walters, the night-club owner, as producer.

As Husbands Go, a comedy in three acts by Rachel Crothers.♦ Produced by John Golden♦ at the John Golden Theatre. March 5, 1931. 148 performances.

Lucile Lingard (Lily Cahill) and Emmie Sykes (Catherine Doucet), two nice little ladies from Dubuque, have had a fling in Paris, and both have found new loves. That might be all right for Emmie, who is a widow, but Lucile is a married woman. Still, she promises Ronald Derbyshire (Geoffrey Wardell), a young, successful English novelist, that when she returns to America she will ask her husband for a divorce. When Lucile does return home she finds it

difficult to broach the subject. Moreover, Charles Lingard (Jay Fassett) has complicated matters by inviting his young nephew Wilbur (Buddy Proctor) to live with them. After several weeks, Ronald arrives in Dubuque, hoping to bring the affair to a head. All he succeeds in actually doing is making Lucile fall out of love with him, and himself no longer want Lucile.

"A light, truthfully observing domestic comedy . . . an honest, amusingly human study of character," was Burns Mantle's♦ assessment of the play.

As Thousands Cheer, a musical revue in two acts. Sketches by Moss Hart. ♦ Lyrics and music by Irving Berlin. ♦ Produced by Sam H. Harris♦ at the Music Box Theatre. September 30, 1933. 400 performances.

A revue cleverly tied together by the device of pretending that each song and skit was derived from a headline in one imaginary newspaper. Thus, the headlines "HEAT WAVE HITS NEW YORK" and "UNKNOWN NEGRO LYNCHED BY FRENZIED MOB" provided cues for Ethel Waters's♦ two great numbers, "Heat Wave" and "Supper Time." The latter song was an early attempt to inject serious social comment into a basically light-hearted evening. The first act finale, coming to life from the cover of the paper's rotogravure section, celebrated a turn-of-the-century "Easter Parade," with Marilyn Miller♦ and Clifton Webb♦ leading the paraders. Sketches poked fun at famous people. Miss Miller impersonated Barbara Hutton; Miss Waters, Josephine Baker; Webb, Mahatma Gandhi on a hunger strike and John D. Rockefeller rejecting the gift of Rockefeller Center; while Helen Broderick♦ spoofed Aimee Semple McPherson.

Other principal songs: How's Chances? · Harlem on My Mind · Lonely Heart · Not for All the Rice in China

Brooks Atkinson♦ of the *Times* called the revue "a superb panorama of entertainment." Although the production was often as lavish as the opulent extravaganzas of earlier decades, the lavishness in this case was always secondary to the content, and the show took its place among the new generation of more thoughtful revues.

As You Like It Shakespeare's sylvan comedy was first offered at the John St. Theatre♦ in 1786 and later was selected to open the Park Theatre. ♦ Its richly panoplied, highly moral romanticism gave it immense appeal to all the changing approaches and attitudes of the Victorian era, especially so in the last half of the 19th century, when scarcely a season passed without a major presentation. According to William Winter,♦ many of these mountings, notably in the troubled times of the Civil War and Reconstruction, leaned heavily on the darker, sadder aspects of the work, although Daly's♦ biographer-brother recalled that in the producer's 1869 offering, "The sing-song of Mrs. Scott-Siddons was like the carol of a bird in the forest of Arden." Twenty years later his restudied version, with Ada Rehan♦ as Rosalind, discarded "Every tone and every tint of melancholy." Other great 19th-century Rosalinds included Adelaide Neilson♦ and Julia Marlowe.♦ With the growing public cynicism that followed World War II major revivals became less frequent, although the comedy retained its popularity with collegiate and, later, with festival groups. Probably the most famous and successful of later 20th-century Rosalinds was Katharine Hepburn♦ in an archly traditional Theatre Guild♦ revival in 1950.

ASCAP, see *American Society of Composers, Authors and Publishers*

ASHTON, HERBERT, JR., see *Brothers*

Association for the Promotion and Protection of an Independent Stage in the United States, THE Founded either in 1897 or 1898, the organization was established by Mrs. Fiske,♦ Richard Mansfield,♦ Helena Modjeska,♦ James O'Neill,♦ Francis Wilson,♦ and other theatrical figures who had been shabbily treated by the growing Theatrical Syndicate or Trust.♦ Members agreed to try to play only in houses not allied with the Trust, to give fiery curtain speeches and interviews assailing the growing monopoly, and to alert the public in every other way to the menace. The power of the Trust and the cynical defection of Mansfield undermined the group.

Association of Producing Artists Popularly known as APA, it was founded by Ellis Rabb in 1960 and gave its first performances in Bermuda. After serving briefly as the acting company at Princeton's McCarter Theatre, it moved first to the Fred Miller Theatre in Milwaukee, then to the Folksbiene Playhouse in New York. It later became the resident company at the University of Michigan at Ann Arbor. In 1964 it joined the Phoenix Theatre♦ at its small off-Broadway♦ house, where it won applause for its productions of *The Tavern,♦ Right You Are If You Think You Are, The Lower Depths,* and *Scapin.* Depleted funds forced it to return to Michigan,

where its mounting of *You Can't Take It with You*♦ was so successful that it was brought to Broadway in 1965. The company spent several seasons at the Lyceum♦ in New York, including in its repertory *The School for Scandal, Pantagleize, The Cherry Orchard* (staged by Eva Le Gallienne♦ and starring Uta Hagen♦), and a rousingly successful 1967 revival of *The Show-Off,♦* with Helen Hayes.♦ Although a subsequent tour of the George Kelly♦ play helped fill the company's coffers, internal differences, including the departure of Rosemary Harris,♦ its finest regular, hurt the troupe, and after several failures it was, for all practical purposes, left in limbo.

Association of Theatrical Press Agents and Managers [ATPAM] Formed in 1938 by the merger of several older unions, it represents both press agents and advance agents as well as both company and house managers.

ASTAIRE, ADELE, see *Astaire, Fred*

ASTAIRE, FRED [né FREDERICK AUSTERLITZ] (1899–1987) With his sister Adele (1898–1981), they comprised the pre-eminent Broadway dance team of the 1920s. They were born in Omaha and achieved recognition in vaudeville before making their Broadway debut in *Over the Top* (1917). There followed appearances in *The Passing Show of 1918,♦ Apple Blossoms♦* (1919), and *The Love Letter* (1921). They became virtual stars in two 1922 shows, *For Goodness Sake* and *The Bunch and Judy,* then, after a season in London, earned lasting recognition as the stars of *Lady, Be Good!♦* (1924). Among the songs they sang in the show, together or alone, were "Fascinating Rhythm" and "Hang On to Me." Another success, *Funny Face♦* (1927), followed, with one or both of the Astaires introducing the title song, "He Loves and She Loves," " 'S Wonderful," and "The Babbitt and the Bromide." *Smiles* (1930) was a failure, but left Fred Astaire with "Say, Young Man of Manhattan." Their last joint success was *The Band Wagon♦* (1931), in which they sang and danced "Hoops" and "I Love Louisa." When the revue closed, Miss Astaire retired, so her brother appeared alone in what proved to be his last Broadway show, *Gay Divorce♦* (1932). The musical gave him the chance to introduce one final great song, "Night and Day." The rest of his career was spent in Hollywood, where his early films with Ginger Rogers at RKO and his later work at Paramount and especially MGM made him one of filmdom's greatest stars.

Although neither Fred nor Adele was especially good-looking, they were both slim, agile dancers, whose routines were characterized by a streamlined stylishness and a delightfully impish wit. Writing of their work in *Smiles,* the *Boston Evening Transcript*'s famous critic, Henry Taylor Parker,♦ observed, "They are quite unsentimental. Whether they speak, dance or would sing, their touch is light, dry, sophisticated." Until her departure, Adele Astaire was generally considered the better of the two, universally praised not only for her dancing but for her brilliant gifts as a comedienne, gifts many critics compared to Beatrice Lillie's.♦ The pair's trademark was a run-around, in which they described ever widening arcs until, before their audience realized it, they had danced themselves off stage.

Autobiography (Fred): *Steps in Time,* New York, 1959.

ASTON, ANTHONY (*fl.* first half of 18th century) A vagabond player, he generally is considered to have been the first professional actor to appear on an American stage. In an autobiographical preface to his play, *The Fool's Opera,* Aston wrote, "You are to know me, as a Gentleman, Lawyer, Poet, Actor, Soldier, Sailor, Exciseman, Publican; in *England, Scotland, Ireland, New York, East* and *West Jersey, Maryland, Virginia* (on both sides *Chesapeek*), *North* and *South Carolina, South Florida, Bahama's, Jamaica, Hispaniola,* and often a Coaster by all the same." He then adds, "Well, we arriv'd in *Charlestown,* full of Lice, Shame, Poverty, Nakedness and Hunger:—I turn'd *Player* and *Poet,* and wrote one Play on the Subject of the Country." Aston goes on to tell of visiting New York and "acting, writing, courting, fighting that Winter." No records survive of precisely what roles and plays Aston offered, nor exactly where or when. Most scholars, despite the player's bravado, take him at his word and suggest that he was in America in 1703 and 1704.

Biography: *Anthony Aston, Stroller and Adventurer,* by Watson Nicholson, South Haven, Mich., 1920.

Astor Place Riots The most serious disorders ever connected with the American theatre, they occurred in 1849, although their origins can be traced back to 1826 when their two central figures, Edwin Forrest♦ and the English actor, William Charles Macready,♦ both made debuts in New York. From the beginning both men, but especially the vain, jealous Forrest, perceived themselves as rivals, even though their styles were distinct and each attracted a somewhat different audience. Forrest's thunder and lightning acting appealed principally to the gallery and the pits, while Macready's more severe, formal methods pleased the boxes. When Forrest played London in 1845 he met with a cold reception, which he blamed on Macready. Early in 1846 both men were playing Edinburgh, and Forrest attended a Macready performance, sitting conspicuously in a box and hissing audibly. On Macready's 1849 visit to America, the English actor announced that he would perform *Macbeth*♦ at the Astor Place theatre on May 7. Forrest promptly announced that he would play the same role on the same night at the Bowery Theatre.♦ Many of Forrest's loyalists attended Macready's performance and created such a ruckus that the evening was a fiasco. Actors were pelted with rotten food, chairs were thrown on stage, and asafoetida thrown from the gallery. Macready wanted to cancel the rest of his New York engagement. A group of prominent citizens, led by Washington Irving,♦ petitioned him to reconsider, so he agreed to appear again on May 10. While he was performing a large horde of rabble, led by one E. Z. C. Judson, gathered to attack not only the theatre, but the homes of many of the men who had signed the petition to Macready. Judson, who wrote under the name Ned Buntline, was a founder of the Know-Nothing party and a notorious agitator. When the troublemakers approached the Astor Place theatre they found it guarded by the police and the militia. Rather than retreat, the mob, armed with stones and clubs, assaulted their better-armed opponents. In the ensuing melee, twenty-two were killed and at least thirty-six more injured, many seriously. Apart from a handful of radicals, most New Yorkers applauded Mayor Woodhull's firm handling of the rioters. Judson was later sentenced to a year's imprisonment for instigating the incident, but suspicion was widespread at the time and has remained that the real instigator was none other than Forrest.

Albeit the whole ugly affair may have begun as a personal rivalry between two men, it quickly involved other issues. America had many Anglophiles, especially among the upper classes, but others still viewed England, thirty-odd years after the War of 1812, with suspicion or enmity. Class distinctions also exacerbated the problem, as did seemingly simple aesthetic disagreements, although these were in no small part interwoven into the class differences.

The Astor Place theatre never recovered from the incident, closing three years later. Nor did the Bowery remain a prime house, beginning its descent into a house of blue-collar melodrama just two years later. Many students also date the start of Forrest's decline in popularity and vigor from this time, even if he remained an idol of the gallery gods for some while.

ATKINSON, [Justin] Brooks (1894–1984) Born in Melrose, Mass., and educated at Harvard, he taught briefly at Dartmouth, then entered the newspaper world as a reporter for the Springfield (Mass.) *Daily News.* In 1919 he joined the *Boston Evening Transcript* as an assistant drama critic, but soon moved to the New York *Times.* He became its drama critic in 1924, a post he held, except for a stint as war correspondent (1941–46), until 1960. As such he became the best known and most important of New York's reviewers. His writing was gracious and gentlemanly, and his views generally tolerant, except for a strong prejudice against older musicals after the advent of *Oklahoma!*♦ and the "musical play." He also wrote several excellent books on the theatre, including *Broadway Scrapbook* (1947), *Broadway* (1970), and *The Lively Years: 1920–1973* (1974).

Typical of his style was the opening of his review of a 1952 revival of *Summer and Smoke.* ♦ "Nothing has happened for quite a long time," he observed, "as admirable as the new production at the Circle in the Square—in Sheridan Square, to be precise. Tennessee Williams' 'Summer and Smoke' opened there last evening in a sensitive, highly personal performance. When it was put on at the Music Box in 1948 it looked a little detached, perhaps because the production was too intricate or because the theatre was too large."

ATTERIDGE, Harold R. (1886–1938) Born in Lake Forest, Ill., he graduated from the University of Chicago and tried his hand at librettos at the suggestion of his friends, Frank R. Adams♦ and Will Hough. ♦ His first musical was *A Winning Miss* (1905); his second, *The Girl in the Kimono* (1907). Moving to New York, he quickly became the Shuberts'♦ in-house librettist, creating over 40 musicals to order for the producers, beginning with *Vera Violetta* (1911), which he wrote in collaboration with Leonard Liebling. Alone or with associates he turned out librettos for, among others, all the *Passing Shows*♦ from 1912 to 1924, *The Honeymoon Express* (1913), *Sinbad* (1918), *Bombo* (1921), *Make It Snappy* (1922), *The Dream Girl* (1924), *Big Boy* (1925), *Ziegfeld Follies of 1927,* ♦ and *Everybody's Welcome* (1931). Many of his librettos were constructed as vehicles for particular stars, especially Al Jolson. ♦ For the most part unimaginative and trite,

they nevertheless were professionally competent and satisfied audiences if not critics.

ATWILL, Lionel (1885–1946) After a long career in his native England, he came to America in 1915 to tour with Lillie Langtry. ♦ In 1917 he produced and starred in *The Lodger,* a mystery play. Several quick failures followed before he won attention in 1918 playing the leading male roles opposite Alla Nazimova♦ in Arthur Hopkins's♦ revivals of *The Wild Duck, Hedda Gabler,* and *A Doll's House.* He scored another success as the politician, Clive Cooper, in *Tiger! Tiger!* (1918), a play he toured in until late 1920, when he essayed another successful role, that of the sadly beset pantomimist, the title part in *Deburau.* Two more bittersweet title roles followed, *The Grand Duke* (1921) and *The Comedian* (1923). In 1924 he played the put-upon inventor, Anton Rogatsky, in *The Outsider.* In a change of pace the following year he played Caesar opposite the Cleopatra of Helen Hayes. ♦ Thereafter he appeared mostly in failures until he left to spend his last years in films. Atwill was a fine character actor with a curiously quizzical, doleful face and an elegant playing style.

Auctioneer, The, a play in three acts by David Belasco,♦ Charles Klein,♦ and Lee Arthur. Produced by Belasco at the Bijou Theatre. September 23, 1901. 105 performances.

Simon Levi (David Warfield♦) is a good-hearted, struggling auctioneer on Hester Street who suddenly inherits a small fortune. Only with reluctance does he leave his beloved old haunts, but he understands that his wife and most especially his adopted daughter long to move up in the world. His daughter loves a young, but somewhat naïve stock broker, who persuades Simon to let him invest Simon's money for him. The stocks tumble and Simon is reduced to peddling toys until the stocks suddenly recover.

For Warfield, who had heretofore been known largely as a dialect comedian, the play began his long, profitable association with Belasco and his career as a serious dramatic star. Several critics complained that the evening offered too much Warfield, but agreed at the same time that without him the show would have been worthless. Warfield was able to employ his comic talents to great advantage in the auction and peddling scenes. However, his high moment was the close of the first act in which he took a poignant farewell of his Hester Street home and friends.

AUDIN [or ODIN], MONSIEUR (*fl.* late 18th century) Little is known about the personal life of this artist, who, except for Charles Ciceri,♦ was probably the finest set designer of his day. His most productive years seem to have been spent in Charleston. In his monograph on Ciceri, Edwin Duerr noted of Audin, "Working there with his son, with Belzons who could paint a sublime display of an erupting volcano, with Oliphant and Schultz, he succeeded in bringing to his southern stages some of the most varied and opulent of eighteenth century American theatrical scenes. Elaborate French pantomimes were beautifully colored and costumed; processions were splendidly mounted and arranged; melodramas maneuvered before wild backgrounds; and many views of Charleston itself, the Exchange, Wharves, Race-Track, etc., were transplanted to the proscenium—all under the supervision of Audin." He was famous for transcribing well-known paintings to the stage, such as Hogarth's drawing of the gate of Calais for a 1793 mounting of *The Surrender of Calais.* In *The Charleston Stage in the XVIII Century,* Eola Willis suggests he may have pioneered in dimming lights to effect scene changes. It is unclear whether the Audin who later worked under Ciceri at the Park Theatre♦ in 1798 was the father or son.

AUGUSTA, MLLE. (1806–1901) A French ballerina, she made a sensational debut in 1836 and for a few seasons was the rage of New York. She danced in a number of the spectacles that were mounted at the time, but mostly in regular ballets that were occasionally offered as part of the varied, long bills common until the mid-century legitimate theatre. Her most celebrated role was in *La Bayadère.* After her vogue she remained in the country, giving dancing lessons when not appearing on the bills of early variety theatres.

Auntie Mame, a comedy in two acts by Jerome Lawrence♦ and Robert E. Lee.♦ Produced at the Broadhurst Theatre. October 31, 1956. 639 performances.

Auntie Mame (Rosalind Russell♦), an irrepressible scatterbrain, finds she must take under her wing her young orphaned nephew, Patrick Dennis (Jan Handzlik as Patrick, the boy; Robert Higgins as Patrick, the young man). Her often indulgent, free-thinking ideas of how to raise a youngster bring her into confrontation with the authorities and sometimes even with her friends. But in the end her guidance proves more than satisfactory. Patrick grows up to be a stable man, marries and brings his own son to visit Mame, who promptly hustles the boy off to Europe. Told she must have him back by Labor Day, she remarks that Labor Day is sometime in November.

Based on the novel by Patrick Dennis, the play was more a series of entertaining vignettes than a sustained, well-plotted story. Louis Kronenberger♦ observed, "The adaptors, doubtless wisely, went in for a kind of scene-a-minute technique. Their slapdash method, if wholly uncreative, did manage to make speed a kind of substitute for wit." After Miss Russell left the cast, Bea Lillie♦ assumed the role, and later played it in London. The show was turned into the successful musical comedy *Mame,* which opened at the Winter Garden♦ on May 24, 1966, and ran for 1,508 performances. Its book was by Lawrence♦ and Lee, and its songs by Jerry Herman. ♦ His most popular offering was the title number. Angela Lansbury♦ was Mame, as she was in the 1983 revival.

Authors League of America, see *Dramatists Guild*

Avon Comedy Four A vaudeville act assembled shortly before World War I by Max Hart, it remained for years one of the most popular turns in two-a-day. From the start Joe Smith and Charlie Dale were part of the act, the other two performers changing with some frequency. Their routine most often was a "school act," in which a harassed teacher was hounded by ignorant or impish students. After vaudeville's heyday Smith and Dale continued as a double, usually playing their famous Dr. Kronkeit dialogue, in which neither doctor nor patient is quite able to communicate with the other.

Awake and Sing!, a drama in three acts by Clifford Odets.♦ Produced by the Group Theatre♦ at the Belasco Theatre. February 19, 1935. 184 performances.

The Bergers, a lower-middle-class Jewish family in the Bronx, are a miserable lot. The mother, Bessie (Stella Adler♦), is shrill and selfish; the father, Myron (Art Smith), a drudging ne'er-do-well. Their unmarried daughter, Hennie (Phoebe Brand), is pregnant with an unwanted child. If there is any hope for redemption it rests with the Berger son, Ralph (Jules, later John, Garfield♦), a bitter but ambitious young man, and his grandfather, Jacob (Morris Carnovsky♦), who long ago found his consolation in philosophy. Seeing only one way out for Ralph, Jacob quietly makes him the beneficiary of his $3000 life insurance policy, then "accidentally" falls from the roof of their tenement. His death allows Hennie to run away with Moe Axelrod

(Luther Adler♦), a crippled war veteran who offers her financial security. It also liberates Ralph: "Did Jake die for us to fight for nickels? No! 'Awake and sing,' he said . . . I saw he was dead and I was born!" He resolves to become a left-wing agitator.

In the uneasy climate of the Depression, John Mason Brown♦ considered the play "a well-balanced, meticulously observed, always interesting and ultimately quite moving drama." A number of critics saw something Chekhovian in the play, ignoring Chekhov's gift of understatement. Odets had first written the work a year earlier as *I Got the Blues,* but not until the electrifying reception of *Waiting for Lefty*♦ was it seriously considered for production.

AXELROD, GEORGE, see *Seven Year Itch, The*

AYERS, LEMUEL (1915–55) A New Yorker, he studied at Princeton and the University of Iowa before being chosen by Leonard Sillman♦ to design sets for 1939 revivals of *Journey's End* and *They Knew What They Wanted.*♦ Major recognition came with his costume designs for the Maurice Evans♦-Judith Anderson♦ *Macbeth*♦ (1941). His settings were subsequently seen in, among others, *Angel Street*♦ (1941); *The Pirate*♦ (1942); *Harriet*♦ (1943);

Oklahoma!♦ (1943); *Song of Norway*♦ (1944); *Bloomer Girl*♦ (1944); *Cyrano de Bergerac*♦ (1946); *Inside U.S.A.* (1948); *Kiss Me, Kate*♦ (1948) and *Out of This World* (1950), both of which he co-produced; *Kismet*♦ (1953); and *The Pajama Game*♦ (1954). He sometimes designed costumes for these shows as well. Ayers was a master at creating a sense of vast spaciousness within a proscenium frame. His stylized settings for *Oklahoma!* and his richly beautiful settings for *Out of This World* were noteworthy examples of this gift. One critic suggested that despite Cole Porter's♦ superb score and Charlotte Greenwood's♦ memorable performance, Ayers's settings were the "real star" of *Out of This World.*

AZENBERG, EMANUEL (b. 1934) The New York native studied at N.Y.U. Alone or with others (frequently the Shubert♦ Organization) he has produced such shows as *The Lion in Winter*♦ (1966), *Ain't Supposed to Die a Natural Death*♦ (1971), *The Sunshine Boys*♦ (1972)—and all subsequent Neil Simon♦ works, *Ain't Misbehavin'*♦ (1978 and the revival in 1988), *Children of a Lesser God*♦ (1980), *The Real Thing* (1984), *Sunday in the Park with George*♦ (1984), and *Jerome Robbins' Broadway* (1989).

B

Babes in Arms, a musical comedy in two acts. Book by Richard Rodgers♦ and Lorenz Hart.♦ Lyrics by Hart. Music by Rodgers. Produced by Dwight Deere Wiman♦ at the Shubert Theatre. April 14, 1937. 289 performances.

Threatened with assignment to a work farm, the children of traveling vaudevillians band together to mount a musical revue. The show wins critical acclaim but loses money, so the children are sent to the farm. They are rescued when a French aviator, on a transatlantic flight, makes an emergency landing on their farm and comes to their aid.

Principal songs: Babes in Arms · I Wish I Were in Love Again · Johnny One Note · The Lady Is a Tramp · My Funny Valentine · Where or When

Hailed by John Mason Brown♦ as "joyous and delectable," the musical's major claim to fame, apart from its large list of great songs, was the many young talents to which it gave a leg up: Dan Dailey (from its chorus), Alfred Drake,♦ Mitzi Green, Ray Heatherton, Wynn Murray, and Robert Rounseville.

Babes in Toyland, a musical extravaganza in three acts. Book and lyrics by Glen MacDonough.♦ Music by Victor Herbert.♦ Produced by Fred R. Hamlin and Julian Mitchell♦ at the Majestic Theatre. October 13, 1903. 192 performances.

When Jane (Mabel Barrison) and Alan (William Norris) are shipwrecked through the machinations of their wicked Uncle Barnaby (George W. Denham), they find themselves in Toyland. Barnaby pursues them there and, while courting Contrary Mary, contrives with the equally wicked Toymaker (Dore Davidson) to do away with them. But all his nefarious plots are foiled with the help of Mary, Jack and Jill, Bo Peep, the Widow Piper and her son Tom Tom, and a host of other Mother Goose figures, as well as by tree spirits, fairies, life-size dolls, and talking flowers. In the end Barnaby is brought to justice in Toyland's court.

Principal songs: I Can't Do the Sum · March of the Toys · Toyland

At a time when most musicals had only a few sets, the production was exceptionally lavish. Among the settings were Barnaby's farm, the spectacle of the shipwreck, Mary's garden, the Spider's forest, the floral palace of the Moth Queen, the Toymaker's workshop (filled with giant toys), and the Toyland Palace of Justice.

The *Dramatic Mirror*♦ exclaimed of the show, "It will prove a perfect dream of delight to the children, and will recall the happy days of childhood to those who are facing the stern realities of life." Of Herbert's music, Henry Finck wrote in the *Evening Post,* "Every bar is melodious, while some of the incidental and melodramatic music betrays Mr. Herbert's position among the leading American composers."

Baby Mine, a comedy in three acts by Margaret Mayo.♦ Produced by William A. Brady♦ at Daly's Theatre. August 23, 1910. 287 performances.

Zoie Hardy (Marguerite Clark♦) is a compulsive fibber, so when she refuses to acknowledge that she dined in a restaurant with an unidentified man—who, if the truth were known, was actually her husband's best friend, Jimmy Jinks (Walter Jones)—her exasperated husband Albert (Ernest Glendinning) packs his bag and leaves. Jimmy suggests that the best way to win back Albert would be for Zoie to have a baby—and quickly. He offers to find her one, but in his enthusiasm rounds up three infants. Albert is totally flustered and confused until the mothers of the tots appear to reclaim them. He ought to be angry, yet he realizes the lengths Zoie will go to show how much she loves him.

Welcomed by the *Times* as "one of the funniest farces this town has ever seen," the comedy was the source of Jerome Kern's♦ 1918 musical *Rock-a-Bye Baby.*

BACALL, Lauren [née Betty Joan Perske] (b. 1924) Described by Stanley Green♦ as a "smokey-voiced actress of angular intensity," she was born in New York and studied at the American Academy of Dramatic Arts♦ before making her New York debut as a walk-on in *Johnny 2 × 4* (1942). That same year she played the ingenue in *Franklin Street,* which folded during its tryout. After nearly twenty years in Hollywood, she returned to New York to play Charlie, the callous philanderer whose punishment is to return to earth as a woman, in *Goodbye, Charlie* (1959). In 1965 she played

Stephanie, a dentist's secretary who wins her boss after obligingly posing as his wife, in *Cactus Flower.* ♦ Her most successful role was Margo Channing, the fading film star, in the musical *Applause* (1970), for which she won a Tony Award. ♦ In 1981 she portrayed Tess Harding, the high-powered lady newscaster, in another musical, *Woman of the Year.* She was married to Humphrey Bogart and later to Jason Robards, Jr. ♦

Autobiography: *By Myself,* New York, 1978.

BACKUS, CHARLES (1831?–83) Born in Rochester, N.Y., the son of a doctor and the grandson of the first president of Hamilton College, he shocked his family, who had decided on a literary career for him, by leaving school and seeking employment as an actor. While looking for work he supported himself as a bookseller, but soon made his debut in Cleveland in 1851 as Jerry Clip in *The Widow's Victim.* Shortly thereafter he moved to San Francisco, where he joined the minstrel troupe of Thomas Maguire. ♦ He organized his own Backus Minstrels in 1854. For the next ten years, except for a brief hiatus in 1860, he led his minstrels not merely in San Francisco, but in several extended world tours. In 1864 he organized the San Francisco Minstrels ♦ with William H. Bernard, Billy Birch, ♦ and Dave Wambold. A year later the troupe moved to New York, remaining there for many seasons as that city's last permanent bastion of traditional minstrelsy.

The *Dramatic Mirror* ♦ wrote of the huge, homely farceur, "His were not the hackneyed jokes of the common end man . . . Had Backus adopted the legitimate drama as a field for exercise of his talents, he would have been beyond doubt one of the greatest comedians of his day." He performed celebrated spoofs of Shakespearean plays as well as many original skits. In one of the most famous, "Pleasant Companions," he portrayed an inmate of an asylum who thought he was a mad dog and who walked about barking at and biting other inmates.

BACON, FRANK (1864–1922) Born in Marysville, Calif., he spent time as a journalist and photographer before making his stage debut in San Jose, Calif., in 1890 as Sample Switchell in *Ten Nights in a Barroom.* ♦ He remained in stock in San Jose for seventeen years, running a small farm to supplement his income. Moving East after the 1906 earthquake, he spent three years touring as Sam Graham in *The Fortune Hunter.* ♦ New York appearances followed in *Stop, Thief* (1912), *The Miracle Man* (1914), *The Cinderella Man* (1916), and *Barbara* (1917). His

crowning moment came when he created the role of the boozy, easygoing spinner of tall tales, Lightnin' Bill Jones, in *Lightnin',* ♦ a play which he wrote in collaboration with Winchell Smith. ♦ The play established a New York long-run record for its time. Bacon played the role over two thousand times and was touring with it when he died. Many critics saw his Lightnin' Bill as a latter-day Rip Van Winkle and compared him, in both the style and quality of his acting, to Joseph Jefferson ♦ in the earlier play. Bacon acknowledged that his rough-hewn but warm characterization was, in fact, modeled on Jefferson's.

BAGLEY, BEN[JAMIN JAMES] (b. 1933) Coming to New York from his native Vermont while still in his teens, he worked in a series of odd jobs before producing *The Shoestring Revue* ♦ (1955), *The Littlest Revue* (1956), *Shoestring '57,* and *The Decline and Fall of the Entire World as Seen Through the Eyes of Cole Porter* (1965). These revues were among the most consistently witty ever done in New York, and gave an important boost to such talents as Chita Rivera, ♦ Bea Arthur, and a superb, sadly shortlived comedienne, Dorothy Greener. Turning to recording with his Painted Smiles label, he released an excellent "Revisited" series, putting on disks the often neglected songs of major Broadway composers and lyricists.

BAILEY, PEARL [MAE] (1918–90) A native of Newport News, Va., the black singing comedienne, whose unique style was marked by an informal, broken delivery and sometimes slurred pronunciation, appeared in *St. Louis Woman* (1946); *Arms and the Girl* (1950), in which she stopped the show with "There Must Be Somethin' Better Than Love"; *Bless You All* (1950); and *House of Flowers* ♦ (1954). She scored her greatest success when she headed an all-black company of *Hello, Dolly!* ♦ in 1967 and in later revivals.

Autobiographies: *The Raw Pearl,* New York, 1968, and *Talking to Myself,* New York, 1971.

BAINTER, FAY (1891–1968) After performing as a child actress in stock in her hometown of Los Angeles, she made her New York debut in a musical, *The Rose of Panama* (1912), appeared in *The Bridal Path* (1913), and then toured with Mrs. Fiske ♦ in *Mrs. Bumpstead-Leigh* ♦ (1914). She returned to stock in Albany and Toledo, until she first called attention to herself in New York as the patriotic Ruth Sherwood in *Arms and the Girl* (1916) and as Mary Temple, the name given a statue come to life, in *The Willow Tree* (1917). In 1918 she returned to musicals to play Aline in *The Kiss Burglar,* then essayed her most famous role, Ming Toy, the spunky young girl who would escape her strict Oriental past, in *East Is West*♦ (1918). As one of the most sought-after and busiest actresses of the 1920s, her notable appearances included Elspeth in Victor Herbert's♦ *The Dream Girl* (1924); Pauli Arndt in the anti-war play *The Enemy*♦ (1925); Louise in a revival of the old melodrama *The Two Orphans*♦ (1926); Julia Sterrol in Noel Coward's♦ *Fallen Angels* (1927); Kate Hardcastle in *She Stoops To Conquer* (1928); and Mrs. Sullen in *The Beaux' Stratagem* (1928). In the early thirties she played important roles in more revivals, among them Kalonika in *Lysistrata* (1930) and Lady Mary Lasenby in *The Admirable Crichton* (1931). After briefly returning to musical comedy to play the female lead, Mimi, in a road company of *Gay Divorce*♦ (1933), she accepted her last important Broadway assignment, Fran Dodsworth in *Dodsworth*♦ (1934). She spent ten years in Hollywood before she returned to New York as Margaret Brennan in *The Next Half Hour* (1945). Thereafter she appeared primarily in summer stock, although she spent much of the 1957–58 season touring as Mary Tyrone in *Long Day's Journey into Night.*♦ She has been characterized as a "charming, demure" actress whose performances displayed "technical perfection."

BAKER, BELLE [née BELLA BECKER] (1895–1957) Born on New York's Lower East Side, she first appeared on stage playing a boy in Jacob Adler's♦ production of *The Homecoming.* Singing in Yiddish productions, she came to the attention of vaudeville agents and was soon playing major vaudeville houses. Although she made her Broadway debut in a minor part in *Vera Violetta* (1911), her only important musical comedy appearance was as star of the short-lived *Betsy* (1926), in which she introduced Irving Berlin's♦ "Blue Skies." She remained primarily a star vaudeville attraction, helping popularize such songs as "My Yiddische Mama," a song long identified with her friend Sophie Tucker♦; "All of Me"; "Put It On, Take It Off, Wrap It Up and Take It Home"; and "Cohen Owes Me $97." The short, dark, plump entertainer with a deep, resonant voice made one of her last appearances at the Palace♦ special bill in 1950.

BAKER, BENJAMIN A. (1818–90) Two years after making his stage debut in 1837 in Natchez, Miss., where he played small roles opposite Junius Brutus Booth,♦ he came back to his native New York to join William Mitchell♦ at the Olympic as actor and prompter. On occasion he helped Mitchell write burlesques. His most famous play, which was written for his own benefit performance, was *A Glance at New York in 1848.*♦ The play was a huge success, establishing a vogue for such local dramas, and Baker quickly churned out sequels such as *New York As It Is* (1848), *Three Years After* (1849), and *Mose in China* (1850). After several years of running theatres in Washington and San Francisco, he returned to New York in 1856 to manage Edwin Booth's♦ company. Although he continued to write burlesques and some musical comedy librettos, he spent most of his remaining years as a theatre manager. He was also active as an officer of the Actors' Fund.♦

BAKER, GEORGE M. (1832–90) Probably his era's most prolific and successful writer of plays for amateurs, he penned his first comedy, *Wanted a Male Cook,* as a lark for an amateur group in which he performed. At least seventy-nine of his plays were published, with titles ranging from *Above the Clouds, Among the Breakers, Better Than Gold,* and *The Freedom of the Press* to *Rebecca's Triumph, The Tempter,* and *We're All Teetotalers.* To supplement his income he often toured in his own *Too Late for the Train,* which was advertised as a "Dialogue for 2 males, introducing songs and recitations."

BAKER, GEORGE PIERCE (1866–1935) Born in Providence, R.I., he graduated from Harvard in 1887. He returned to teach there in 1905, sponsoring the Harvard Dramatic Club♦ when it was founded in 1908 and initiating his soon celebrated 47 Workshop,♦ a laboratory for playwrights whose alumni number among the greatest writers of the first half of the 20th century, including George Abbott,♦ Philip Barry,♦ S. N. Behrman,♦ Sidney Howard,♦ Eugene O'Neill,♦ and Edward Sheldon.♦ In 1925 Baker moved to Yale, where he continued to teach the technique and history of drama, chaired the Department of Drama, and directed the University Theatre. Among his works are *The Development of Shakespeare as a Dramatist* (1907), *Some Unpublished Correspondence of David Garrick* (1907), *Dramatic Technique* (1919), and *Modern American Plays* (1920).

Biography: *George Pierce Baker and the American Theatre,* Wisner Payne Kinne, Cambridge, Mass., 1954.

BALANCHINE, GEORGE [né GYORGI MELITONO- VITCH BALANCHIVADZE] (1904–83) Born in St. Petersburg, he worked with Diaghilev and Colonel de Basil and also choreographed several London revues before coming to America and settling in New York, where he founded the School for American Ballet and organized the New York City Ballet Company. Probably the greatest of 20th-century choreographers, he was to his field what Picasso and Stravinsky were to theirs, brilliant, significant revolutionaries. In his best work he moved away from traditional ballet story-telling and, while retaining the basic dance idioms, attempted to abstract the essence of the music around which he often created his masterpieces. His pioneering work was rarely in evidence in his superb Broadway contributions, which nonetheless displayed what ballet historian Robert Lawrence called a "crispness of phrasing, musicality of movement, and feeling for absolute design." His first Broadway assignment was the *Ziegfeld Follies of 1936.*♦ In the same year he created the first ballet conceived as an integral dramatic part of a musical with "Slaughter on 10th Avenue"♦ in *On Your Toes.*♦ He later choreographed *Babes in Arms*♦ (1937), *I Married an Angel*♦ (1938), *The Boys from Syracuse*♦ (1938), *Keep Off the Grass* (1940), *Louisiana Purchase*♦ (1940), *Cabin in the Sky*♦ (1940), *The Lady Comes Across* (1942), *Rosalinda* (1942), *What's Up* (1943), *Dream with Music* (1944), *Song of Norway*♦ (1944), *Mr. Strauss Goes to Boston* (1945), *The Chocolate Soldier* (1947), *Where's Charley?*♦ (1948), and *Courtin' Time* (1951). In 1942 he staged an elephant ballet for the Ringling Brothers circus, and in the 1950s devised dances for some productions at the American Shakespeare Festival.♦

Biography: *Balanchine,* Bernard Taper, New York, 1974.

BALDERSTON, JOHN, see *Berkeley Square*

Baldwin Theatre (San Francisco) Built on Market Street in 1875 by the celebrated San Francisco gambler and entrepreneur, Elias Jackson "Lucky" Baldwin, as Baldwin's Academy of Music, it quickly became the principal rival to the California Theatre.♦ The older house remained the home of a distinguished resident ensemble, while the Baldwin emphasized touring stars and attractions. Sumner Bugbee was the architect. In 1878 Baldwin built a magnificent hotel which encompassed the playhouse and occupied the rest of the block. Virtually all the great touring performers of the day appeared in their best-known vehicles at the house. Thomas Maguire♦ and young Charles Frohman♦ were

among its managers. Both hotel and theatre were destroyed by fire in 1898.

BALL, WILLIAM (b. 1931) Born in Chicago, he studied acting, directing, and design at the Carnegie Institute of Technology. He toured for two years as assistant designer and actor in Margaret Webster's♦ company, then joined the Oregon Shakespeare Festival♦ in 1950. From 1950 to 1953 he was also associated with the Pittsburgh Playhouse.♦ Over the next several years he appeared with the Antioch Shakespeare Festival, San Diego Shakespeare Festival, Arena Stage,♦ Actor's Workshop,♦ American Shakespeare Festival,♦ the New York City Opera, and the Circle in the Square♦ both as an actor of leading parts and as a director. In 1964 he founded the American Conservatory Theatre,♦ and his career was tied almost totally to this organization until his resignation in 1986.

BALLARD, LUCINDA [née GOLDSBOROUGH] (b. 1906) Born in New Orleans, she studied at the Art Students' League in New York and also in France. Her first Broadway costume designs were for *As You Like It*♦ (1937). Among other shows for which she created costumes were *The Three Sisters* (1939), *Morning's at Seven*♦ (1939), *I Remember Mama*♦ (1944), *The Glass Menagerie*♦ (1945), *Show Boat*♦ (1946), *Annie Get Your Gun*♦ (1946), *Happy Birthday*♦ (1946), *Another Part of the Forest*♦ (1946), *Silk Stockings* (1955), *The Dark at the Top of the Stairs*♦ (1957), *J.B.*♦ (1958), and *The Sound of Music*♦ (1959). Her designs have won numerous awards. During World War II she created the murals for New York's Stage Door Canteen.♦

Ballet in American Theatre Ballet has been a feature of regular American theatre, as distinguished from a totally separate ballet theatre with great ballet companies, virtually from the start. Indeed, because we could not support whole ballet ensembles, ballet first appeared as an ornament in the ballad operas of the late 18th and early 19th century or as divertissements on the extended bills that were common before the Civil War. Occasionally, great ballerinas such as Fanny Elssler♦ were able to present entire evenings of dance, but even celebrated artists such as Celine Celeste♦ were required to perform in spoken drama to supplement their dancing. Spectacle ballets, largely decorative and with little narrative connected to any play, became the rage about the time of the Civil War, most notably in *The Black Crook*♦ (1866), and remained popular well into the 20th century. Examples of this style remained a staple in the work of Marilyn Miller♦ in the 1920s, and on a more intimate, artful scale in revues such as the *Greenwich Village Follies.*♦ At about the same time, however, some more avant-garde revues began offering examples of more progressive, modern dance, although it was not until the 1930s with the work of George Balanchine♦ in such shows as *On Your Toes*♦ and *I Married an Angel,*♦ and the 1940s with Agnes de Mille's♦ ballets for *Oklahoma!*♦ and *Carousel*♦ that contemporary ballet began to be woven carefully into the fabric of the modern musical, often telling part of the musical's story in choreographic terms. As a rule these ballets, however excellent, have been too short to offer in regular ballet evenings, albeit several have achieved fame. The most notable is probably "Slaughter on Tenth Avenue"♦ from *On Your Toes,* which undoubtedly owes its celebrity as much to Richard Rodgers's♦ fine and well-known music for it as it does to Balanchine's choreography. Another memorable example was Jerome Robbins's♦ comic gem, the "Mack Sennett Ballet"♦ from *High Button Shoes.* Many critics and playgoers would also cite Robbins's "The Small House of Uncle Thomas" from *The King and I.*♦ Yet in many minds it was Miss de Mille's works which more than any initiated the vogue for ballet in musicals. Her work tended to be less razor sharp or striking than Balanchine's, less humor-filled than Robbins's. At heart, though often dramatic and helping to forward the story, her ballets were sentimental and it was this trait which gave them such immediacy to large audiences. For a time, the vogue threatened to get out of hand, with ballets and, for a while, specifically "dream" ballets being inserted in many musicals that had no real place for them. To some extent this problem was answered by Robbins in *West Side Story,*♦ where the dance not only advanced the story but was an integral part of the very construction and tempo of the show. This answer moved a step further in recent years with the decline of great composers and librettists. Thus, such choreographers as Robbins, Gower Champion,♦ Bob Fosse,♦ and Michael Bennett♦ have come to the fore not merely to create dances, but to conceive and direct whole musicals. A good example would be *A Chorus Line,*♦ which began as a workshop project with Bennett.

Baltimore (Maryland) Although Baltimore was the scene of occasional theatricals in the early 18th century, it long played second fiddle to Annapolis, which called itself "The Athens of America" and where Douglass,♦ Hallam,♦ and the American Company♦ performed regularly. Thomas Wall♦ and Adam Lindsay♦ built Baltimore's first important playhouse in 1781 on East Baltimore Street and opened it in January of the following year. In 1794 Thomas Wignell♦ and Alexander Reinagle♦ erected the Holliday Street Theatre,♦ which with several rebuildings remained a major playhouse throughout the 19th century. One of its later managers was John T. Ford,♦ who also built Ford's Theatre there. In the 20th century the city served as a relatively important touring and tryout town, although by the Depression the only surviving active playhouse was Ford's. The theatre was demolished in 1964, and the city had no regular legitimate theatre until the opening of the Morris Mechanic in 1967. But now with both the Mechanic and Center Stage♦ regularly lit and with the Lyric Opera House hosting larger touring productions, the city is once again a lively theatre town.

BANCROFT, ANNE [née ANNA MARIA LUISA ITALIANO] (b. 1931) Born in the Bronx, she studied at both the American Academy of Dramatic Arts♦ and the Actors Studio.♦ She won a Tony Award♦ for her first Broadway role, Gittel Mosca, the Jewish girl who falls in love with a Midwestern lawyer, in *Two for the Seesaw*♦ (1958). Of her performance Brooks Atkinson♦ wrote, "She explodes with gestures that are natural, she modulates the part with vocal inflections that are both funny and authentic, and she creates a gallant character who rings true." A year later her performance as Annie Sullivan, Helen Keller's devoted teacher, in *The Miracle Worker*♦ earned her both another Tony and a New York Drama Critics Circle♦ Award. In 1963 she played Mother Courage in *Mother Courage and Her Children,* and two years later portrayed the Prioress in *The Devils.* At the Vivian Beaumont she appeared as Regina in *The Little Foxes*♦ (1967) and Anne in *A Cry of Players* (1968). After several years in Hollywood, she returned to New York to play the title role in *Golda* (1977), a theatricalized biography of the Israeli political figure, then portrayed Stephanie Abrahams, a Jacqueline du Pré-like musician whose career is destroyed by a crippling disease, in *Duet for One* (1981).

Band Wagon, *The,* a revue in two acts. Sketches by George S. Kaufman♦ and Howard Dietz.♦ Lyrics by Dietz. Music by Arthur Schwartz.♦ Produced by Max Gordon♦ at the New Amsterdam Theatre.♦ June 3, 1931. 260 performances.
    Principal songs: Confession · Dancing in the

Dark · High and Low · I Love Louisa · New Sun in the Sky

Brooks Atkinson♦ wrote, "Mr. Schwartz's lively melodies, the gay dancing of the Astaires, and the colorful merriment of the background and staging begin a new era in the artistry of the American revue." The revue was, indeed, one of the first successfully to abandon the often heavy-handed opulence of the Ziegfeld♦ era. Its designer, Albert R. Johnson,♦ and director, Hassard Short,♦ made effective use of revolving stages to speed the action, and it was the first show to discard footlights in favor of lighting from the balcony. Among the high points, apart from the great songs, were its opening, where the arriving audience found the curtain up and, on stage, the chorus pretending to be another audience taking its seats and singing "It Better Be Good"; a ballet, "The Beggar Waltz," in which Fred Astaire♦ played a beggar who dreams he dances with a great ballerina (Tilly Losch); and a skit, "The Pride of the Claghornes," which satirized Southern mores. A stellar cast also included Frank Morgan,♦ Helen Broderick,♦ and Adele Astaire.♦ For the Astaires it marked their last appearance together. After the show closed, Adele retired.

BANDMANN, Daniel [Edward] (1840–1905) The intense, fiery tragedian was born in Germany, where he began acting while quite young. He was in his late teens when he debuted at German-speaking theatres in New York. His first essay at English theatricals was his highly praised Shylock, given at Niblo's♦ in 1863. Over the next quarter of a century he regularly toured the country. Among his best-known roles were Hamlet, Richelieu, and Narcisse, in the German play of the same name. He became a rancher in Montana around 1890, thereafter returning to the stage only rarely. In 1886 he published *An Actor's Tour; or, Seventy Thousand Miles with Shakespeare.*

Banker's Daughter, The, a play in five acts by Bronson Howard.♦ Produced by Sheridan Shook and A. M. Palmer♦ at the Union Square Theatre.♦ November 30, 1878. 137 performances.

Lilian Westbrook (Sara Jewett) scoffs at her friend Florence St. Vincent (Maud Harrison), who has announced she will marry a man old enough to be her father. Lilian loves young Harold Routledge (Walden Ramsay), although she is annoyed at his jealousy of her flirtation with Count de Carojac (M. V. Lingham). However, when her own father is threatened with bankruptcy she throws over Routledge to marry a much older, richer man. "Aunt Fanny," she confesses to her loving aunt (Mrs.

E. J. Phillips), "Mr. Strebelow is to be my husband. Oh, Aunt Fanny, my heart is broken!" Seven years pass. Lilian's life now revolves about her young daughter, but she still secretly loves Routledge, and is still seen regularly by both Routledge and the Count. The Count has never forgiven Routledge for being the love of Lilian's life. When the men have an open falling-out, a duel is held in which the Count mortally wounds Routledge. Overcome emotionally, Lilian blurts out to Strebelow (C. P. Thorne, Jr.♦) that she had never loved him but has been nevertheless a dutiful wife. Blaming himself for not understanding his wife, Strebelow leaves her. More years pass. Lilian comes to realize that she loves Strebelow. Their little daughter's letters, sometimes dictated by Lilian, bring about a reconciliation.

In his history of the work, *Autobiography of a Play,* Howard noted that the play initially had been done as *Lilian's Last Love* at Hooley's Theatre in Chicago in 1873. A. R. Cazauran,♦ Palmer's "reconstructor," helped rewrite the piece for its New York presentation, discarding its original unhappy conclusion. It was later performed in London as *The Old Love and the New.* Despite its contrived ending, the play was immensely popular with both critics and playgoers. It was frequently revived, and remained a favorite of stock companies until World War I.

BANKHEAD, Tallulah (1903–68) Born in Huntsville, Ala., she used her family's influence (her uncle was a U.S. Senator) to land a walk-on part in her first Broadway show, *Squab Farm* (1918). After a brief fling in films she replaced Constance Binney as Penelope in *39 East* (1919), then played Rose de Brissac in *Footloose* (1920). In 1921 she played Hallie Livingston, a determined flapper, in *Nice People♦* and the rebellious Phyllis Nolan in *Everyday* (the latter her third Rachel Crothers♦ play). When that play quickly closed, she replaced another actress as the loyal secretary, Mary Hubbard, in *Danger,* and in rapid order replaced yet another performer as the will-thwarting Blanche Ingram in *Her Temporary Husband.* Following a short run as the crippled, restless Rufus Rand in *The Exciters* (1922), she left for England where, for the next eleven years, she played increasingly important roles. Her return to America as the jilted bride, Mary Clay, in *Forsaking All Others* (1933) was unpropitious. Nor was her luck better as the fatally ill Judith Traherne in *Dark Victory* (1934). Her appearances as Sadie Thompson in a revival of *Rain♦* (1935) and as the cheated-on wife, Monica Grey, in *Something Gay* (1935) were short-lived. She finally enjoyed a modest success as the emotional actress Muriel Flood in George Kelly's♦ *Reflected Glory* (1936). A major fiasco was her revival of *Antony and Cleopatra*♦ (1937). In 1939, however, she triumphed as Regina Giddens in *The Little Foxes.* ♦ But her luck ran out again when she played the slatternly housewife, Mae Wilenski, in Clifford Odets's♦ *Clash by Night* (1941). The next season she appeared in one of her best roles, the sibyl-like servant Sabina in *The Skin of Our Teeth*♦ (1942). She then played the actress Sophie Wing in Philip Barry's *Foolish Notion* (1945). From 1946 through 1950 she essayed her most popular role, Amanda Prynne, in a free-slugging revival of *Private Lives,* ♦ stopping only briefly to assume the role of the Queen in *The Eagle Has Two Heads* (1947). Only her performance as the mother determined to legitimatize her children kept *Dear Charles* (1954) alive, but even her portrayal of a prankish society doyen could not save *Midgie Purvis* (1961). Her last Broadway appearance was as a typical Tennessee Williams♦ lady in his *The Milk Train Doesn't Stop Here Anymore* (1964). In her last years, when major Broadway success eluded her, she appeared regularly on radio, calling everyone "dahling" in her deep baritone voice and behaving seemingly like a parody of herself.

Miss Bankhead's performances occasioned some of the wittiest criticism ever elicited. Most famous was John Mason Brown's♦ dismissal of her Shakespearean queen: "Tallulah Bankhead barged down the Nile as Cleopatra and sank. As the serpent of the Nile she proves to be no more dangerous than a garter snake." When she appeared in *Eugenia,* a 1957 theatricalization of Henry James's *The Europeans,* Louis Kronenberger♦ concluded, "Only Mae West as Snow White could have seemed more unsuited to the part." The distinguished Boston critic Elliot Norton,♦ on the other hand, recalled of her acting in *The Little Foxes,* "Miss Bankhead was as coldly and classically handsome as a Greek sculpture, but her Regina was a woman, not a statue; a woman driven by Furies, driven and driving . . . cold, calculating and calmly cruel, yet absolutely true and fascinating . . . Her laughter was a silver ripple on ice, the glint of a glacier. Her wrath . . . was the rumbling of thunder with flashes of lightning."

Autobiography: *Tallulah,* New York, 1952.

BANNISTER, NATHANIEL, see *Wars in American Drama*

Barbara Frietchie, a play in four acts by Clyde Fitch. ♦ Produced by Charles Frohman♦ at the Criterion Theatre. October 23, 1899. 83 performances.

Almost all the citizens of Frederick are Confederate sympathizers, so they condemn their neighbor, young Barbara Frietchie (Julia Marlowe♦), for accepting the attentions of a Yankee, Capt. Trumbull (J. H. Gilmour). Many had hoped she would marry the boy next door, Jack Negly (Arnold Daly♦), but Barbara dismisses him as a coward who won't fight for either side. Her brother Arthur (Lionel Adams) suddenly appears. He has been wounded at Gettysburg and asks her to hide him in the house from Yankee search parties. Just at this moment, Trumbull appears. He pretends not to have seen Arthur, and when a search party arrives he sends them away. Though Barbara is loyal to the Confederacy, she loves Trumbull enough to accept his offer of marriage. The wedding is interrupted by the arrival of Confederate troops. When a Southern sharpshooter attempts to shoot Trumbull, Barbara shoots the Southerner's gun from his hand. But she offers him refuge in her house, where Trumbull is also brought in wounded. Negly learns Trumbull is there and would betray him, but Barbara dissuades him. "You have broken my heart," he sobs, to which Barbara replies, "Forgive me—by not breaking mine." For all her ministrations, Trumbull dies. Just then the victorious Confederates march through town. All the houses display Confederate flags except the Frietchies'. Barbara stands on the porch defiantly brandishing the stars and stripes. Negly goes to shoot her, but Stonewall Jackson, passing by, admires her bravery and orders that anyone molesting her be shot in turn. Nevertheless, Negly does shoot her. His own father, Col. Negly (W. J. Le Moyne), orders Jackson's command carried out.

In his *History of the American Drama,* Quinn♦ has noted, "Fitch was vigorously criticized for falsification of history, and rather feebly defended himself on the grounds that Barbara Frietchie was ninety-six years old and bedridden when Stonewall Jackson went through Fredericksburg. But Whittier's heroine, rightly or wrongly, had become established as the real Barbara, and it was dangerous to experiment, since it distracted the attention of the critics from the play itself. For, while false to fact and legend, it is true to the spirit of the time, from the social if not from the military point of view." It was also true to the theatrical spirit of the time which wanted more romance than realism in its war plays. The drama was revived successfully several times and in 1926 was made into the popular operetta, *My Maryland.* The show, produced by the

Shuberts,♦ had a book and lyrics by Dorothy Donnelly♦ and music by Sigmund Romberg.♦ Evelyn Herbert♦ was its Barbara. After a record-breaking 40-week tryout in Philadelphia, it opened on September 12, 1927, at the Jolson Theatre, running 312 performances. Its major song hits were "Silver Moon," "Won't You Marry Me?," and "Your Land and My Land."

Barefoot in the Park, a comedy in three acts by Neil Simon.♦ Produced by Saint Subber at the Biltmore Theatre. October 23, 1963. 1,530 performances.

When, after a glorious six-day honeymoon at the Plaza, Corie (Elizabeth Ashley) and Paul Bratter (Robert Redford) move into their dilapidated walk-up—six flights up, in fact—their first visitors are Corie's mother, Mrs. Banks (Mildred Natwick♦), and their eccentric gourmet lothario neighbor, Victor Velasco (Kurt Kasznar). Corie unwittingly invites both her mother and Mr. Velasco to dinner on the same night, and when the oven does not work, Mr. Velasco takes them to a wild Albanian restaurant on Staten Island. Everyone has a good time except Paul, whom Corie accuses of being so prim and proper that he would prefer to sleep with his tie on. Corie decides she wants a divorce. But when her mother comes in wearing a man's bathrobe after a night with Mr. Velasco, and after Paul has gotten drunk and danced barefoot in the park, Corie realizes she loves Paul and his sane, quiet ways.

Henry Hewes observed that the play "was nothing more than a minor quarrel between two young newlyweds spiced with their amusing responses to the sort of physical discomforts New Yorkers find themselves so illogically putting up with." As director, Mike Nichols had fun with inventing any number of comic entrances after the principals had supposedly climbed many stairs. Coming after the success of *Come Blow Your Horn,* the play confirmed Neil Simon's mastery of one-liners, although his gift for genuine comic complications left something to be desired.

BARKER, JAMES NELSON (1784–1858) The son of a prominent Philadelphia family—his father was later to be mayor—he based his first, unfinished play, *The Spanish Rover* (1804) on Cervantes, and then turned his hand to a masque, *America* (1805), which was never performed or published. He met a measure of success with *Tears and Smiles*♦ (1807), which contrasted French society airs with American simplicity. At the suggestion of the first Joseph Jefferson♦ he added the character of Nathaniel Yank, which he modeled after that of Jonathan in

The Contrast.♦ His next play, *The Embargo; or, What News?* (1808), provoked riots at Philadelphia's "Old Drury," the Chestnut Street Theatre,♦ with its support of the Embargo Acts and pro-administration bias. A play with music, *The Indian Princess; or, La Belle Sauvage*♦ (1808), recounted the legend of Pocahontas with a happy ending. It was thus the first "Indian play" written by an American and produced. Billed as a melodrama, a sign of growing French influence in the American theatre, it was successfully mounted in several cities, and became the first American play to be presented in London, where it was offered as *Pocahontas.* A theatricalization of Scott, *Marmion; or, The Battle of Flodden Field* (1812), was initially presented as being by an English dramatist "in order to avoid the neglect usually accorded to native playwrights," but no falling off of receipts followed the revelation of Barker's authorship. During the War of 1812 Barker became captain of an artillery regiment. His next play, *The Armourer's Escape; or, Three Years at Nootka Sound* (1817), was based on the real-life adventures of John Jewitt, who played himself at its premiere. In the same year, Barker also wrote a light comedy, *How To Try a Lover,* which was put into rehearsal, then dropped. It was not performed publicly until 1836, when it was acted as *A Court of Love.* Barker temporarily set aside play-writing when he was elected mayor of Philadelphia in 1819. However, he returned to the theatre in 1824 with his last and best play, *Superstition; or, The Fanatic Father,*♦ an attack on Puritan excesses. Thereafter, Barker devoted himself to public service, becoming Collector of the Port from 1829 to 1838 and from then until his death Controller of the United States Treasury.

Alexander Cowrie has written in *Literary History of the United States,* "Without being fanatically nationalistic, he staunchly did his part in building a native tradition in the drama. Compared with [Royall] Tyler, he seems more earnest but less of an artist. Compared with [William] Dunlap, he seems less significant by reason of the latter's more voluminous production and more intense devotion to the cause of the drama."

Biography: *James Nelson Barker,* Paul H. Musser, Philadelphia, 1929.

BARKER, RICHARD (1834?–1903) Almost nothing is known about the private life of this Englishman who became the leading director of musicals in America in the late 19th century. He first came to New York as part of D'Oyly Carte's♦ staff in 1879. Although he continued to work closely with D'Oyly Carte in

England until his death, he soon was the director of choice of such celebrated musical stars as De Wolf Hopper,♦ James T. Powers,♦ Lillian Russell,♦ and Francis Wilson.♦ In 1895 alone he staged *The 20th Century Girl, Aladdin, Jr., Fleur de Lis, Princess Bonnie, The Chieftain,* and *A Stag Party.* On occasion he staged non-musicals, most notably assisting Lawrence Barrett♦ in mounting William Young's♦ *Ganelon* (1889). In their reminiscenses his stars speak of his dictatorial, martinet attitudes and of his affected anti-Americanism, but rarely of the particular skills that made him so respected. However, Powers does recall Barker's staging of a West End musical as "a work of art—every movement of the one hundred trained ballet-children made a picture never to be forgotten. The old masters would have been fascinated and inspired by his fairy scenes."

BARNABEE, HENRY CLAY (1833–1917) Although he quit school in his native Portsmouth, N.H., to work as a dry-goods clerk, performing in occasional amateur theatricals and concerts convinced him his future lay in music and theatre. He made his professional debut in recital at the Music Hall in Boston in 1865. His fame as a soloist and as a performer in musical theatre remained largely local until 1879, when he became one of the original members of the Boston Ideal Opera Company.♦ He stayed with the Bostonians, as they were later called, for their quarter-century history, serving as their principal comedian. While he was hailed for such interpretations as Sir Joseph Porter (in *H.M.S. Pinafore*), Bunthorne (in *Patience*), Izzet Pasha (in *Fatinitza*), Dulcamara (in *The Elixir of Love*), and Lord Allcash (in *Fra Diavolo*), his greatest role was the Sheriff of Nottingham in *Robin Hood.*♦ He created the role in the original 1891 production and played it some 2000 times. The horse-faced performer was appreciated for his rare combination of fine bass-baritone singing and humor, one Kansas City critic noting, "At all times he is a gentleman, and nothing in his quiet and Jeffersonian wit is ever vulgar or out of place."

Autobiography: *My Wanderings,* Boston, 1913.

BARNARD, CHARLES, see *County Fair, The*

BARNES, CHARLOTTE [MARY SANFORD] (1818–63) The daughter of John♦ and Mary Barnes♦ of the Park Theatre,♦ she made her debut there as a child of four in 1822. Returning to the stage in 1834 as a young adult, she played Angela in *The Castle Spectre,* first at Boston's Tremont Theatre and then in New York. In the following seasons she was applauded for her interpretations of Juliet, Jane Shore, Evadne, Desdemona, and Lady Teazle. After playing in London she returned to America, married Edmond S. Connor, and acted with him when he managed Philadelphia's Arch Street Theatre.♦ She translated several French melodramas and wrote several plays based on popular novels or legends. Notable among the last were *Octavia Bragaldi* (1837), a blank-verse tragedy set in Italy but actually recounting a famous Kentucky scandal in which a wife prevailed upon her husband to murder her seducer, then killed herself when her husband was sentenced to death; *La Fitte* (1840), now lost but which, despite its curious spelling, depicted the famous buccaneer; and *The Forest Princess* (1844), one more version of the Pocahontas legend.

BARNES, CLIVE [ALEXANDER] (b. 1927) London-born and Oxford-educated, he was a drama and dance critic for several English periodicals before becoming dance critic for the New York *Times* in 1965. In 1967 he became the paper's drama critic and a decade later switched to the *Post.* He is often considered the major newspaper critic easiest to please.

BARNES, JOHN (1761–1841) and his wife, MARY (1780?–1864) Coming from England, where she had played at Drury Lane and he at the Haymarket, they made their American debut at the Park Theatre♦ in 1816, and, apart from a return to England between 1822 and 1824, remained at the playhouse until their retirements. Mrs. Barnes made her debut first, playing Juliet. The *Evening Post* noted, "She was precisely just, and so exactly entered into the nature of the part that we unhesitatingly ascribed to her deep study and the most distinct conception. She *did* and looked Juliet better than we have ever seen it played on this stage, if what we have seen heretofore can be called playing." When her husband made his debut five nights later as Sir Peter Teazle the same critic commented, "His person and voice are well calculated for the characters he fills. His judgment was fully displayed, by making Sir Peter what we have long wished to see him, a gentleman." From the start Mrs. Barnes was considered the better, more versatile performer. Among her roles were Desdemona, Jane Shore, Belvidera, Amy Robsart, Lady Teazle, and Aladdin. Her husband was best at comedy and for the most part confined himself to supporting roles. Mrs. Barnes played only occasionally after 1833, but her husband continued to perform until shortly before his death.

BARNET, R[OBERT] A[YERS] (1853–1933) A leading figure in Boston's popular musical theatre at the turn of the century, he was born in New York but educated in the Hub. Although his father's friendship with several famous actors early on exposed him to the theatre, he elected a career in business and for many years contented himself with amateur theatricals. However, in 1890 a paramilitary group, the First Corps of Cadets, asked him to write and stage a musical to aid their drive for funds for their armory. The success of *Injured Innocents* launched both Barnet and the Cadets on a long professional career. Many of the musicals he created for the Cadets were so successful that they were recast and enjoyed extended runs in New York and on tour. His biggest hits were *1492* (1893), *Tabasco* (1894), *Excelsior, Jr.* (1895), and *Miss Simplicity* (1902).

BARNUM, P[HINEAS] T[AYLOR] (1810–91) The colorful, Connecticut-born showman is best remembered as a circus impresario and for his statement that "a sucker" is born every minute. After failing in several enterprises he made a large profit in 1835 by touring a troupe of freaks and curiosities, headed by Joyce Heth, a Negress whom Barnum claimed was 160 years old and had been George Washington's nurse. When she died a year later, she was proved to be in her sixties. Undeterred by this exposure, Barnum continued to tour a similar troupe until 1839. In 1842 he purchased the American Museum, ♦ which he quickly turned into one of New York City's most celebrated showplaces. There he continued to offer exhibits of both dead and live curiosities, while he enlarged the Museum's theatre, which soon rivaled the Bowery Theatre ♦ as a home to popular melodrama and farce. He attained international renown when he toured Europe with his famous dwarf, Charles Stratton, whom he billed as General Tom Thumb. ♦ Within a few seasons he was also bringing European artists to America, most notably orchestrating Jenny Lind's sensational 1850–52 tour. In 1871 he organized his traveling circus, which he advertised as "the greatest show on earth." Ten years later he combined his show with that of his major competitor, James A. Bailey. Their circus's leading attraction was Jumbo, the largest elephant in captivity, purchased by Barnum for $10,000 from England's Royal Zoological Gardens.

Barnum is generally conceded to have been the first American master of ballyhoo. He used any method that occurred to him to publicize his shows, from hyperbolic and sometimes fraudulent statements to keeping an elephant in a farm field near principal railroad lines and promoting his circus by having a man in Oriental costume plow the field with elephant power whenever a train passed.

Barnum wrote several books, including his autobiography (1854, and later editions), *The Humbugs of the World* (1865), and *Struggles and Triumphs* (1869).

Biography: *Barnum,* Morris R. Werner, New York, 1923.

Barnum's Museum, see *American Museum*

BARR, RICHARD [né BAER] (1917–89) Born in Washington, D.C., and educated at Princeton, he began his career as an actor with the Mercury Theatre ♦ and later served as a director of plays for the New York City Center. ♦ Subsequently he became active as a producer, usually working in conjunction with one or more other producers. Among the notable productions with which he has been associated have been *At Home with Ethel Waters* (1953), Ruth Draper's ♦ 1954 and 1956 solo appearances, *The Zoo Story* ♦ (1960), *The American Dream* ♦ (1961), *Who's Afraid of Virginia Woolf?* ♦ (1962), *Tiny Alice* ♦ (1964), *A Delicate Balance* ♦ (1966), and *The Boys in the Band* ♦ (1968).

BARRAS, CHARLES M., see *Black Crook, The*

BARRATT, WATSON (1884–1962) Born in Salt Lake City, he took work with the Shuberts ♦ in 1918 and thereafter became virtually their house set designer. Although he remained active until the early 1950s, his heyday was in the 1920s when he created sets for such Shubert productions as *Blossom Time* ♦ (1921) and *The Student Prince* ♦ (1924), as well as for their Winter Garden ♦ revues. He also served with the St. Louis Municipal Outdoor Opera Company. ♦

BARRETT, GEORGE [HORTON] (1794–1860) The son of actors in Dunlap's ♦ company at the Park Theatre, ♦ he made his debut in 1798 as "a boy" in *The Stranger.* ♦ Although he played several minor roles in Boston, he did not again perform in New York until he acted Young Norval in 1806. Schooling and some additional touring followed before Barrett returned to New York in 1822 to offer a brief season of repertory in which he portrayed many of the popular comic figures of the era (Charles Surface, etc.). In the summer of 1824 his performances at the Chatham Garden summer theatre led to one contemporary critic hailing him as "a comedian of the First

Class," and established him as a reigning favorite. His most popular representations included, besides Surface, Sir Andrew Aguecheek, Captain Absolute, and Puff. In 1826 he became the principal director at the Bowery, where he continued to act, and later served in both capacities at the Tremont in Boston and at Burton's and the Broadway Theatre. His last appearances were in 1855. Barrett's public posture, as elegant as his acting, soon won him the affectionate nickname "Gentleman George."

MRS. BARRETT [née ANNE JANE HENRY] (1801–57), his wife, made her debut as a dancer at Boston's Federal Street Theatre,♦ using the name Miss Stockwell. She later performed as Mrs. Drummond before marrying Barrett. Her career was marred for a time by a bout with alcoholism, but Fanny Kemble♦ pronounced her "a faultless piece of mortality in outward loveliness," while Walter Leman♦ recalled, "She was the petted idol of the Boston public; of rare excellence in her art, it would be hard to say what she played best, she played everything so well."

BARRETT, LAWRENCE [PATRICK] (1838–91) The self-educated son of a poor tailor, he was born in Paterson, N.J., but raised in Detroit. His family's real name was generally believed to be Brannigan, but Barrett was persistent in denying this. He made his debut in Detroit in 1853 as Murad in *The French Spy*. Three years later he made his New York debut at the Chambers Street Theatre playing Sir Thomas Clifford in *The Hunchback*.♦ In short order he played Fazio, The Stranger, Ingomar, and Claude Melnotte, before moving to Burton's Theatre, where he remained until the house failed. During the 1862–63 season he appeared at the Winter Garden, playing with Edwin Booth♦ in *Hamlet*♦ and taking over Richard III after Booth left to be near his dying wife. He supported Booth again the following season before leaving to serve as a captain in the Union army. After the war he joined John McCullough♦ in managing San Francisco's California Theatre. In 1870 he returned to New York, where he played in support of Booth at that actor's new theatre. Because Booth refused to play on Saturday nights, Barrett was able to mount plays with himself as star. But it was only after Booth's season had ended and Barrett took over the house that he won fame as James Harebell, the mad poet, in W. G. Wills's *The Man o' Airlie* (1871). In 1875 his Cassius earned him additional laurels. He also met with personal success touring during the 1877–78 season in two works by William Dean Howells,♦ playing the mistrusted painter Bartlett in *A Counter-*

feit Presentment and the tragic jester in *Yorick's Love*. The latter he played in New York in 1880. For many, however, his crowning achievement came in 1883 when he reached back to an all-but-forgotten past to revive *Francesca da Rimini*. ♦ William Winter♦ called the actor's Lanciotto a performance of "terrible beauty." Another success was his revival in 1887 of Mary Russell Mitford's *Rienzi*. Later that year he joined Booth in several important Shakespearean revivals, beginning with *Julius Caesar,*♦ and continuing with *Othello*♦ (in which the men alternated as hero or villain) and *The Merchant of Venice.* ♦ Barrett took charge of the plays' direction and production. Until shortly before his death, Barrett continued his partnership with Booth and mounted one more praised work, William Young's♦ *Ganelon* (1889). His last performance, which he was unable to finish, was as de Mauprat opposite Booth's famous Richelieu.

The same sense of history that prompted him to revive neglected works may have induced him to become a theatrical historian as well. Among his writings are *Edwin Forrest* (1881) and *Edwin Booth and His Contemporaries* (1886).

Most scholars agree with Odell,♦ who called Barrett "our most farsighted and ambitious, if not our greatest tragedian," citing his willingness to go beyond the standard repertory and the excellent taste of his acting and mountings. "His features," Otis Skinner♦ recalled, "were attractive; a good nose, wide mobile mouth, deep-set and burning eyes, and a broad and thoughtful forehead. It might have been the face of a monk." There is also agreement that Barrett's voice was "deep and guttural" and "of unusual range," but disagreement over whether he was "diminutive" (San Francisco *Dramatic Chronicle*), "of medium height" (Skinner), or "tall" (*Oxford Companion to the Theatre*).

Biography: *Lawrence Barrett, A Professional Sketch,* Elwyn A. Barron, Chicago, 1889.

BARRETT, WILSON (1846–1904) The noted English actor-manager and playwright made several tours of the United States, in which he performed his most celebrated roles. His American debut came in 1886 in *Claudian,* but his most famous part in American eyes was unquestionably as Wilfred Denver—who comes to America after being falsely accused of murder and here makes a second fortune—in *The Silver King,* which had been written expressly for him and which he first played here in 1889. In 1895 he staged the world premiere of his own play, *The Sign of the Cross,* at the Grand Opera House in St. Louis, assuming the principal role of Marcus Superbus. This role, along with that of Denver, were the two for which he remained best known. Easterners, however, never saw him play the latter part, since he relinquished it to Charles Dalton soon after the opening, in order to return to England.

Barretts of Wimpole Street, The A play by Rudolf Besier dealing with the courtship of Elizabeth Barrett by her fellow poet Robert Browning, it was produced by Katharine Cornell♦ at the Empire Theatre♦ on February 9, 1931, and ran for 372 performances. Brian Aherne♦ was Browning and Charles Waldron♦ was Elizabeth's father. It gave Miss Cornell her most famous role. The often acid Dorothy Parker♦ wrote in her *New Yorker* review, "Miss Katharine Cornell is a completely lovely Elizabeth Barrett—far lovelier than the original, I fear. It is little wonder that Miss Cornell is so worshipped; she has that thing we need, and we so seldom have, in our actresses; she has romance . . . she has glamour." After its New York run it was taken first on a twenty-week "short" tour, then on a longer tour during the 1933–34 season, at a time when few shows played anything but major cities. On Christmas night the production was supposed to open in Seattle, but the company's train, delayed by washouts, did not arrive until 11:15. When she was advised that the entire audience was still waiting, Miss Cornell agreed to perform. The curtain rose after one in the morning and did not come down finally until nearly four.

BARRIE, James M[atthew] (1860–1937) The English playwright who hid a barbed wit and slightly mocking view of life beneath often cloyingly sentimental surfaces was first represented in America by *The Professor's Love Story* (1892) and *Walker, London* (1894). He was long associated by American playgoers with producer Charles Frohman♦ and actress Maude Adams,♦ an association that began with *The Little Minister* (1897). His subsequent successes included *Quality Street* (1901) with Miss Adams; *The Admirable Crichton* (1903), which starred William Gillette♦; *Peter Pan♦* (1905), Miss Adams's most famous part; *Alice Sit-by-the-Fire* (1905), which starred Ethel Barrymore♦ and included John Barrymore♦ in the cast; *What Every Woman Knows* (1908), in which Miss Adams played opposite Richard Bennett♦; *A Kiss for Cinderella* (1916), again with Miss Adams; *Dear Brutus* (1918), whose cast included Gillette and Helen Hayes♦; and *Mary Rose* (1920). Miss Barrymore toured in vaudeville for many years with his playlet *The Twelve-Pound Look,* while Miss Hayes later appeared in

another short play, *The Old Lady Shows Her Medals.* Indeed, Miss Hayes eventually became one of Barrie's leading advocates, appearing in revivals of several of his works, especially *What Every Woman Knows,* her curious blend of saccharine and iron precisely matching his.

BARRIÈRE, Henry P. (1783?–1826) A confectioner who took over management of Chatham Garden in 1819, he sought to lure patrons to his simple entertainments and fine ice cream by means of unusual, amusingly discursive advertisements which often included such succinct notices as "Admission free for those that have *consciences,* none for *dandies.*" In 1824 he opened a theatre on the grounds. It immediately became the city's most popular summer playhouse and resort, extended its season, and was able to mix serious drama with farce and musical plays. Its heyday, however, was brief, for when Barrière died suddenly in 1826, his successors were unable to maintain its popularity.

BARROW, Julia Bennett (1824?–?) She left the Haymarket company in London to make her American debut in 1851 as Lady Teazle. She was an instant success, with the *Albion* describing her as "a blonde, extremely pretty and prepossessing in her air and manner; her figure is slight, and her movements are easy and graceful. Her voice is rather high pitched." Although she later played a well-received Viola, many of her best roles were in now forgotten contemporary comedies. She was also adept at more serious impersonations. Indeed, among her last roles before moving to Boston were the principal woman's roles in *Richard III♦* and *The Marble Heart,* ♦ playing opposite John Wilkes Booth. ♦ For many years she ran Boston's Howard Atheneum♦ to great acclaim, before apparently returning to England.

BARRY, Philip [Jerome Quinn] (1896–1949) Born in Rochester, N.Y., he was the son of an immigrant Irish father who had become a successful businessman; his mother was of old Philadelphia Irish-Catholic stock. His father died when he was a year old. Young Barry was a frail child with defective eyesight, yet despite his myopia he became an avid reader. He also became a precocious wit. He entered Yale in 1914, plunging eagerly into campus literary activities. His studies were interrupted by America's entry into World War I. Rejected by all the military services, he secured a position in the Communications Office of the State Department and was posted to London, where he became a life-long Anglophile. After the war he returned to Yale. In his senior year his play *Autonomy* won a prize offered by the school dramatic society. One reviewer described it as "a political satire which depends rather on the lines and upon contemporary hits than upon any dramatic situation." Over strident family objections, Barry decided to enroll in George Pierce Baker's◆ famed 47 Workshop◆ at Harvard. He was able to do so since his father had no time before his death to change his will to include his youngest son, and the law thus automatically guaranteed Barry a share equal to his brothers' and sister's. Barry later used this incident as the story for his 1924 play *The Youngest.* A play called *The Jilts*—in which a businessman attempts an artistic career—was submitted to several managements but turned down. Barry then submitted it to the Belmont Repertoire Company competition, where it won the Herndon Prize. Richard Herndon◆ himself agreed to produce it in 1923, changing the title to *You and I.*◆ Its success was the first of many on Broadway for Barry. Underlying the charm and razor-sharp wit of both *You and I* and *The Youngest* was a deep-seated disenchantment with life. This malaise began to seep to the surface in Barry's third Broadway play, *In a Garden* (1925), whose dramatist hero sets up his wife for an affair to test a theory. Barry moved even farther away from traditional high comedy with *White Wings*◆ (1926), a semi-fantasy about a proud turn-of-the-century street cleaner who rebels against the menace of the automobile. It was a quick failure. A curious Biblical piece, *John* (1927), dealing with John the Baptist, also had a short run, but later in the same year Barry reverted to high comedy and had a major success with *Paris Bound,*◆ a look at infidelity among the rich. *Cock Robin* (1928), a mystery written as a lark in collaboration with Elmer Rice,◆ barely made the grade. On the other hand, another civilized drawing room piece, *Holiday*◆ (1928), in which the hero elects to be hedonistic while young, was hugely applauded. Barry's next play, *Hotel Universe*◆ (1930), was another fantasy in the guise of more standard work. It centered on a group of seemingly successful people whose lives cross in France. Many critics admired it, but playgoers stayed away.

With *Tomorrow and Tomorrow*◆ (1931), in which a woman must choose between her husband and the father of her child, and *The Animal Kingdom*◆ (1932), in which a man must choose between his wife and his mistress, Barry gave audiences what they wanted and was rewarded with long runs. Deeply saddened by the death of his baby daughter, Barry took darker turns in his next plays. *The Joyous*

Season (1934), written in the hope that it would lure Maude Adams◆ back to the theatre, in the end starred Lillian Gish.◆ The play belied its title with a somewhat somber story of a nun's attempt to rejuvenate her family spiritually. *Bright Star* (1935), a story of misguided ambition and tragic, misdirected love, was even gloomier. *Spring Dance* (1936) was Barry's hasty adaptation of a collegiate play by other writers. A fourth failure in a row, *Here Come the Clowns* (1938), represented Barry at his most serious and most experimental. The story presented a confrontation between an old stagehand and God. Critics found Barry too profound and too obscure.

Returning to the sort of play the theatre expected of him, Barry enjoyed his greatest success with *The Philadelphia Story*◆ (1939), the saga of a free-wheeling socialite. The rest of his career was anticlimactic. *Liberty Jones* (1941), an allegory about the problems destroying Liberty and her rescue by a Navy man, seemed to critics "pretty well muddled." *Without Love* (1942), toying with an attempt at a platonic marriage, survived four months largely on Katharine Hepburn's◆ drawing power. Similarly it was the appeal of Tallulah Bankhead◆ which allowed *Foolish Notion* (1945) a modest run. The play was a drawing-room comedy interrupted by the fantasies of its principals. Few critics approved his adaptation of Jean Pierre Aumont's *My Name Is Aquilon* (1949). After Barry's death, Robert Sherwood◆ put finishing touches on the incomplete *Second Threshold* (1951). A story of a disillusioned old man and his attempt to establish a relationship with his daughter, it was another failure.

Joseph Wood Krutch◆ expressed a commonly held view of Barry's accomplishment when he observed, "In his writing he seemed to be a somewhat divided personality . . . The result is that the impression produced by an attempt to consider his work as a whole is somewhat blurred and that, therefore, he seems less fit than [S. N.] Behrman to stand as our ablest exponent of the comic spirit." Nevertheless many other critics consider Barry our finest creator of high comedy. Certainly his strange interplay of wit and despair gives his best works a dramatic tension and meaningfulness unique to our theatre.

Biography: *Philip Barry,* Joseph P. Roppolo, New York, 1965.

BARRY, THOMAS (1798–1876) Coming to America in 1826 from England, where he had performed a highly praised Hotspur to Macready's◆ Henry IV, he made his debut at the Park Theatre◆ as The Stranger. He was a handsome, well-voiced actor but often criticized for his exaggerated mannerisms. Although he continued to act, increasingly in supporting roles, he found a major niche as a director, theatre manager, and occasionally as an author of such melodrama as *The Battle of Mexico*. He became the principal stage manager, as directors were then called, at the Park until he took over Boston's Tremont Theatre in 1833, running the latter house until 1839. He then returned to New York to act as manager first at the Bowery♦ and later again at the Park. From 1848 to 1851 he ran Boston's National Theatre and subsequently ran the Broadway in New York, the new Boston Theatre, and houses in Cincinnati and Chicago. He retired in 1870. Walter Leman♦ recalled, "Though an estimable man, [he] had . . . a chilly and far-away manner that appeared anything but pleasant, even to those who knew him best; and was always in the habit of expressing by a short, spasmodic laugh—something between the grunt which a pugilist would utter if hit below the belt, and the sharp bark of a dog—his opinion of anything not in accord with his taste or judgment."

BARRY, Tom, see *Courage*

BARRYMORE, Ethel (1879–1959) Born in Philadelphia, daughter of Maurice♦ and Georgiana Drew Barrymore,♦ she made her stage debut in 1894 playing opposite her grandmother, Mrs. Drew,♦ in *The Rivals*. After performing with her uncle, John Drew,♦ in *The Bauble Shop* later the same year, she assumed a number of other minor roles before sailing for London to play with William Gillette♦ in *Secret Service*♦ and to act with Sir Henry Irving's♦ great company at the Lyceum. She returned to America in 1898. In 1901 Charles Frohman,♦ recognizing her growing talent, awarded her star billing as Madame Trentoni in *Captain Jinks of the Horse Marines.*♦ Although in the next few seasons she briefly attempted Nora in *A Doll's House* (1905) and won applause as an older woman, Mrs. Grey, in *Alice Sit-by-the-Fire* (1905), most of her assignments were in the polite, well-made importations that Frohman favored. More substantial roles came her way when she played the falsely accused servant, Mrs. Jones, in Galsworthy's♦ *The Silver Box* (1907) and the title part in Maugham's♦ *Lady Frederick* (1908). In 1910 she played Zoe Blundell, whose marriage is destroyed by illness, in Pinero's♦ *Mid-Channel*, after which Frohman revived the same author's *Trelawny of the Wells* so that she might portray Rose. About this time she began filling in periods between plays with vaudeville tours in which

she starred in short or abbreviated dramas, most famous of which was Barrie's♦ *The Twelve-Pound Look*. She enjoyed one of her longest runs as the motherly business woman of *Our Mrs. McChesney* (1915), then turned to her own favorite role, Marguerite Gautier in Edward Sheldon's♦ redaction of *The Lady of the Camellias* (1917). She scored a major success as the self-destructive Lady Helen Haden in *Déclassée*♦ (1919), only to come a cropper with her interpretation of Juliet (1922). Further revivals saw her play Paula in *The Second Mrs. Tanqueray* (1924), Ophelia, and Portia (1925). In 1926 she created one of her most memorable parts as Maugham's *The Constant Wife*, which she played until she assumed the role of Sister Gracia in *The Kingdom of God* (1928) at the opening of a New York theatre named in her honor. For the next decade success eluded her, albeit she gained some attention playing a 101-year-old grandmother in *Whiteoaks* (1938). Her finest achievement may well have been the compassionate schoolmarm, Miss Moffat, in *The Corn Is Green* (1940). Her last two shows, *Embezzled Heaven* (1944) and *The Joyous Season* (1945), the latter offered only on tour, were failures.

John Mason Brown♦ remembered "the fluttering eyes, the throaty voice, and the imperious beauty, lending her special alchemy to Somerset Maugham's *The Constant Wife*," but many playgoers will recall her most fondly for the famous line she always delivered at the end of her curtain calls: "That's all there is, there isn't any more!"

Autobiography: *Memories,* New York, 1955.

BARRYMORE, Georgiana [Emma] Drew (1856–93) The daughter of Mrs. John Drew,♦ wife of Maurice Barrymore,♦ and mother of Lionel,♦ Ethel,♦ and John,♦ she made her debut at her mother's Arch Street Theatre♦ in Philadelphia in 1872 in *The Ladies' Battle*. She continued under her mother's tutelage for several seasons before moving to New York, where she first appeared for Augustin Daly♦ in 1876 as a replacement in the role of Mary Standish in *Pique*.♦ There had been some suspicion that her favorable notices in Philadelphia were prompted by critics' affection for Mrs. Drew, but her New York reviews immediately won her recognition as a young actress of great promise. She continued for a while with Daly, playing such roles as Grace, the comic Irish maid, in a revival of *Divorce*♦ and Maria in *The School for Scandal*. Her career was then interrupted by the coming of her children, but she returned to the stage to play Eureka Grubb, the outspoken miner's daughter, in her husband's play,

Nadjezda (1884), performing opposite him and Helena Modjeska. ◆ The tall, supple actress, with large blue eyes, which became a Barrymore family trademark, then appeared as Madge Heskitt, the wronged wife, in *Jack* (1887). The *Journal* said of her performance, "Her intelligence, naïveté and personal graces, combined with the power of clear musical utterance, took a strong hold on popular appreciation." Later portrayals included Lady Frank Brooks, the other woman, in *On Probation* (1889); Mrs. Hilary, the coquettish widow, in *The Senator* ◆ (1890); Mrs. Rippendale, the impudent adventuress, in *Balloon;* and the title role of Mrs. Wakefield in *The Woman of the World* (these last two plays in an 1890 double bill). She next joined Charles Frohman's ◆ Comedians to play the comically jealous wife in *Mr. Wilkinson's Widows* ◆ (1891); the ludicrously sentimental Lucretia Plunkett in *Settled Out of Court* (1892); and Mrs. Briscoe, the neglected wife, in the farce *The Sportsman* (1893). Her promising career was cut short by her early death.

BARRYMORE, JOHN [SIDNEY BLYTHE] (1882–1942) The younger son of Maurice ◆ and Georgiana Drew Barrymore, ◆ he was born in Philadelphia and made his stage debut in Chicago in 1903 as Max in *Magda,* then made his New York debut in the same year as Corley in *Glad of It.* Supporting roles followed in *The Dictator* ◆ (1904), *Yvette* (1904), *Sunday* (1905), *Alice Sit-by-the-Fire* (1905), and *Miss Civilization* (1906). For several seasons he played supporting roles before replacing the leading man in *The Boys of Company B* (1907), following that with the major role of Lord Meadows in *Toddles* (1908). Later the same year he turned leading man in musical comedy, playing Mac, the sculptor, in *A Stubborn Cinderella.* In September 1909 he began a two-year engagement as Nat Duncan, the city slicker determined to win a rich hick, in *The Fortune Hunter.* ◆ After a number of failures or modest successes he played Julian Rolfe in Michael Morton's ◆ study of Russian prostitution, *The Yellow Ticket* (1914), and Chick Hewes in Willard Mack's ◆ melodramatic *Kick In* ◆ (1914). With his assumption of the part of William Falder, the cruelly imprisoned clerk in Galsworthy's ◆ *Justice* (1916), he abandoned more superficially theatrical roles and revealed surprising depth. His reputation grew with his portrayal of Peter Ibbetson, a man who attempts to transcend time, in the play named after the character (1917), and of Fedor Vasilyevich Protosov in *Redemption* (1918), a translation of Tolstoy's *The Living Corpse.* A major success, *The Jest* (1919), found him playing the put-upon hero Ginnetto to his brother Lionel's ◆

villainous Neri. In the 1920s he played only three roles, two of which are generally acknowledged as the pinnacles of his career: in 1920 Richard III and in 1923 Hamlet, which established a New York long run for the play at the time. After many years in Hollywood he returned to Broadway briefly in a feeble comedy, *My Dear Children* (1939).

Looking back, John Mason Brown ◆ reminisced, "Although I have sat before many Hamlets, some better read and more solidly conceived, John Barrymore, with his slim, proud figure, the lean Russian wolfhound aquilinity of his profile, and the princely beauty of his full face, continues for me to be the embodiment of the Dane. His Hamlet had a withering wit. It had scorn at its command; passion, too. Though undisciplined, it crackled with the lightning of personality." There seems little disagreement that had he possessed the dedication and determination, he would have been the greatest actor of his generation. After 1925, however, the hedonistic actor dissipated his talents. His antics were satirized in the character of the gadabout matinee idol Anthony Cavendish in *The Royal Family* ◆ (1927).

Biography: *Good Night, Sweet Prince,* Gene Fowler, New York, 1944.

BARRYMORE, LIONEL (1878–1954) The elder son of Maurice ◆ and Georgiana Drew Barrymore, ◆ he made his debut in his native Philadelphia in 1893 playing Thomas to the Mrs. Malaprop of his grandmother, Mrs. John Drew. ◆ A year later he appeared with her again when making his New York debut in *The Road to Ruin.* Other early appearances were in *The Bachelor's Baby* (1895), *Mary Pennington, Spinster* (1896), *Squire Kate* (1896), *Cumberland '61* (1897), *Uncle Dick* (1898), and *Honorable John Grigsby* (1898). His colleagues' growing respect for his abilities prompted James A. Hearne ◆ to write a small role for him in *Sag Harbor,* but he made his first real hit as Giuseppe, the organ grinder, in *The Mummy and the Humming Bird* (1902). He scored as "The Kid," a prize fighter who would marry into society, in *The Other Girl* ◆ (1903). In 1905 he won applause playing the title role in Barrie's ◆ *Pantaloon.* He also toured in vaudeville in a sketch called "The Still Voice." Only a few short-lived roles followed before he played the malicious Col. Ibbetson opposite the Peter Ibbetson of his brother John ◆ in 1917. Many believe his finest performance was as Milt Shanks, a Northerner suspected of Southern sympathies during the Civil War, in *The Copperhead* ◆ (1918). In 1919 he was reunited with John, playing the villain Neri in *The*

Jest. After his portrayal of the cruel judge Mouzon in *The Letter of the Law* (1920), he turned with great hopes to *Macbeth*♦ (1921), but found little favor with it. He had a modest success as Achille Cortelon, the radical politician destroyed by his wife, in *The Claw* (1921) and as Tito Beppi, a modern-day Pagliacci, in *Laugh, Clown, Laugh!* (1923). When a series of failures followed in 1925, he left Broadway permanently for the West Coast.

John Corbin,♦ the New York *Times* critic, wrote of his Neri, "Barrymore illumines it with a touch of genius. Malicious bully though the huge mercenary is, he is yet comprehensibly, deliciously human. An audience that is inwardly terrified at him, almost stunned by his ferocity, can yet laugh at his burly exhibitions of rage and strength, and his no less vigorous and picturesque oaths, with no dramatic letdown. Indeed, the effect is rather to intensify illusion." While Lionel may not have had quite the range or depth of his brother, he was a great actor who scarcely realized his potential. If dissipation kept John Barrymore from the stage, disinclination kept Lionel from it. He preferred the easy money of Hollywood, which allowed him to devote more time to his real loves, painting and music. A crippling illness, which later confined him to a wheelchair, precluded any return to the stage, even had he been so inclined.

Autobiography: *We Barrymores,* New York, 1951.

BARRYMORE, Maurice [né Herbert Blythe] (1849–1905) Born in India, he studied law in London and won some fame as an amateur boxer before turning to the stage. After a few London appearances and an American debut in Boston in *Under the Gaslight,*♦ he came to New York where in 1875 he first appeared for Augustin Daly♦ as Bob Ruggles in *The Big Bonanza,*♦ replacing John Drew,♦ whose niece Georgiana♦ he later married. He was an immediate success and in quick succession played Talbot Champeys in *Our Boys,* Laertes and Aumerle opposite Edwin Booth,♦ Raymond Lessing in *Pique,*♦ and Sir Frederick Blout in *Money.* Moving to Wallack's, he portrayed, among others, Charles in *London Assurance*♦ and Capt. Molineux in *The Shaughraun.*♦ In 1882 he joined Helena Modjeska♦ as her leading man, acting Orlando, Romeo, Sebastian, Armand, and roles in many now forgotten contemporary pieces. He moved to A. M. Palmer's♦ company in 1888, where his parts included Wilding in *Captain Swift* and Captain Davenport in *Alabama.*♦ His greatest role is generally considered to be Rawdon Crawley in *Becky Sharp*♦ (1899), in which he played opposite Mrs. Fiske.♦ In his last active years, his erratic behavior, stemming from the paresis that ultimately killed him, caused producers to shun him, so he turned to vaudeville. Barrymore also wrote several plays, including *Blood Will Tell* (never produced in America), *Nadjezda* (1884), *The Robber of the Rhine* (1892), and *Roaring Dick & Co.* (1896). He later sued Sardou,♦ claiming the playwright had stolen the plot of *Nadjezda* for *Tosca,* but failed to prevent *Tosca*'s American premiere.

A fellow performer once described him as "a tall man, dark and pale, with cool Northern grey eyes . . . He was lightly built, but of a round-muscled, strong shouldered powerful lightness." The *Evening Sun* observed, "As *Rawdon Crawley* he was superb. In looks, speech and manner he might have stepped directly out of Thackeray's pages. His performance was a blending of sterling manliness and the gentlest pathos."

Biography: *Good Times/Great Times,* James Kotsilibas-Davis, Garden City, 1977.

Barter Theatre In 1932, in the depths of the Depression, Robert Porterfield conceived the idea of establishing a theatre where impecunious playgoers could pay for tickets with foodstuffs in lieu of cash. A year later he opened his playhouse in Abingdon, Virginia. The group has flourished ever since, although most playgoers now pay for their seats in the customary way. However, a children's theatre still encourages youthful audiences to barter for tickets. Over the years the company has operated two theatres in Abingdon, performed at the Fairfax Theatre at George Mason University, and regularly toured the region. The repertory ranges from classics to modern plays. In 1946 the Barter Theatre became the official state theatre of Virginia, the first such honor accorded an acting company. For many years the theatre offered the Barter Theatre of Virginia Award, presented to a notable actor or actress and providing the recipient with a ham, an acre of land in Abingdon, and the right to choose two young performers for the company's intern program. Rex Partington assumed the directorship after Porterfield's death in 1972.

BARTON, James (1890–1962) Born in Gloucester, N.J., he was carried on stage at the age of two by his actor parents, and made his vaudeville debut at the age of four. For many years he played the Midwest and the South in stock and repertory before making his New York debut in *The Passing Show of 1919.*♦ Appearances followed in *The Last Waltz* (1921), *The Rose of Stamboul* (1922), *Dew Drop Inn* (1923),

Passing Show of 1924, Artists and Models♦ (1925), *No Foolin'* (1926), as Skid in a touring company of *Burlesque*♦ (1927), and in *Sweet and Low* (1930). Between stage roles he was popular in vaudeville. In 1934 he succeeded Henry Hull♦ as Jeeter Lester in *Tobacco Road,* ♦ a part he played for over five years. After several failures he distinguished himself as Hickey in *The Iceman Cometh*♦ (1946). In 1951 he returned to musicals to play Ben Rumson in *Paint Your Wagon.* His last Broadway appearance was as Pat in *The Sin of Pat Muldoon* (1957). Gravel-voiced, and with a fighter's punched-in face, he was most famous for his drunk routine, which he managed to insert in practically all his appearances.

Basic Training of Pavlo Hummel, The, a play in two parts by David Rabe.♦ Produced by Joseph Papp♦ and the New York Shakespeare Festival♦ at the Public Theatre. May 20, 1971. 363 performances.

A hand grenade thrown in a Vietnam brothel ends the life of an American soldier, Pavlo Hummel (William Atherton). Flashing back, Pavlo is seen joining the army, eager to be a soldier and a hero. His gaucheries and his patently tall stories make him a butt of ridicule, but he is undeterred. His black sergeant, Tower (Joe Fields), represents the military establishment, which turns him into a benumbed orderly, while Ardell (Albert Hall), acting as an involved Greek chorus, comforts him and explains the often baffling world to him. At the end of the play his coffin sits alone on the stage.

Hailed by Clive Barnes♦ of the *Times* as introducing "a new and authentic voice to our theatre," the play was the first in Rabe's trilogy on the war, the other plays being *Sticks and Bones*♦ and *Streamers.*♦ It employed the cinematic technique of short, quickly changing scenes to portray an unmitigated, often ugly, picture of war. As such it was a far cry from many more romantic earlier war plays.

Bat, The, a mystery drama in three acts by Mary Roberts Rinehart♦ and Avery Hopwood.♦ Produced by Wagenhals♦ and Kemper♦ at the Morosco Theatre. August 23, 1920. 867 performances.

An elderly spinster, Cornelia Van Gorder (Effie Ellsler♦) rents the summer home of a banker who reportedly has been killed, but who, it turns out, may have absconded after hiding stolen bank funds in the house. When a number of people are said to be after the money, Miss Van Gorder hires a detective to solve the mystery. Miss Van Gorder and her guests are beset by sundry frightening occurrences, even murder, until it is discovered that the detective is not the man he seems to be.

The play was based on Mrs. Rinehart's story "The Circular Staircase." For many contemporary playgoers May Vokes's comic performance as the easily terrified maid was the high point of the evening. When the play closed it was the second longest running show in Broadway history. Long popular in stock and amateur theatres, the play was revived in 1953 with Lucile Watson as Miss Van Gorder and Zasu Pitts as the maid. Curiously, when Alexander Woollcott♦ reviewed the original production for the *Times,* a production he found "thoroughly interesting," he suggested Miss Watson would have made the ideal Miss Van Gorder.

BATEMAN, H[EZEKIAH] L[INTHICUM] (1812–75) After making his stage debut in his native Baltimore in 1832, he continued acting for many years. However, when his daughters Kate♦ and Ellen proved to be child prodigies, he gave up acting to take over their management. Thereafter he acted only on rare occasions, usually in support of his daughters or in one of his wife's plays. He himself wrote several plays for Kate, including *Rosa Gregorio; or, the Corsican Vendetta* (1862). In 1863 he produced *Leah, the Forsaken*♦ in conjunction with Augustin Daly,♦ giving Kate her most famous role. His production of *La Grande Duchesse de Gérolstein*♦ (1867) began the long rage in America for French opéra bouffe,♦ and for two more years he continued mounting the operettas. In 1871 he and his wife followed Kate to London, where both remained the rest of their lives. His wife MRS. BATEMAN [née SIDNEY FRANCES COWELL] (1823–81), a New Yorker, also started her career as a performer, but was best known for her play-writing. Her finest play was one of her first, *Self*♦ (1856), a study of a girl with cruel, greedy parents. Among her later plays were *Geraldine; or, Love's Victory* (1858), a complicated tragedy of family feuds in the time of Edward I, and *Evangeline* (1860), a play written to allow Kate Bateman to portray the popular figure of Canadian and American legend.

Autobiography (Mrs. Bateman): *Reminiscences*

BATEMAN, KATE (1842–1917) The daughter of H. L. Bateman♦ the producer and his playwright wife, she was born in Baltimore and made her debut in 1846 in Louisville in *Babes in the Woods*. With her sister Ellen she then toured, as a child prodigy, in the leading roles of *Richard III*♦ (Kate was Richmond; Ellen, Richard) and other classics as well as in dramas written especially for them. In 1860 she won applause as an ingenue playing the title role of *Evangeline,* a play written by her mother. Her performance as Julia in *The Hunchback*◆ in 1862 raised her to star status. The next year she first essayed what became her most famous role, the title part of the Jewess deserted by her Christian lover in *Leah, the Forsaken.* ◆ Of her portrayal of Leah, the *Albion* wrote, "Its merits are strength, impetuosity and pathos. Its profound defect is its lack of emotional abandon." She won praise for her Pauline in *The Lady of Lyons*◆ (1866) and for her interpretation as the falsely accused and imprisoned heroine of *Mary Warner* (1869). Shortly after the latter she left for London, where she spent the remainder of her career.

BATES, BLANCHE (1873–1941) The daughter of a theatre manager and an actress, she was born in Portland, Ore., and made her debut in San Francisco in 1894 as Mrs. Willoughby in *The Picture,* and then spent several seasons there in T. D. Frawley's stock company. She made her New York debut in 1897 as Bianca in *The Taming of the Shrew*◆ with Augustin Daly's◆ company, later playing such roles as Celia in *As You Like It*◆ and Lady Sneerwell in *The School for Scandal.* She first called real attention to herself as Hannah Jacobs in *The Children of the Ghetto* (1899). Coming under David Belasco's◆ management, she played briefly as the flirtatious model Cora in *Naughty Anthony* (1900), then won wide acclaim as Cho-Cho-San in *Madame Butterfly.*◆ In 1901 she played Cigarette, the Foreign Legion camp follower, in *Under Two Flags.*◆ A year later she scored as Yo-San, another forlorn Oriental, in *The Darling of the Gods.*◆ Appearances in Chicago as Hedda in *Hedda Gabler* (1904) and Katherine in *The Taming of the Shrew* (1904) were followed by her return to New York as the Girl, who finds freedom and love running a bar, in *The Girl of the Golden West*◆ (1905), which she played for the next several seasons. In 1908 she played Anna, the wife who destroys the evidence against her embezzling husband, in *The Fighting Hope.*◆ Her last appearance under Belasco was as Roxanna Clayton, who cannot rid herself of a philandering mate, in *Nobody's Widow*◆ (1910). For the next several years she appeared in plays such as a revival of *Diplomacy*◆ (1914), *Getting Together* (1918), and *Medea*◆ (1919). Between legitimate assignments she often played in vaudeville. She achieved another success as the liberated Nancy Fair in *The Famous Mrs. Fair*◆ (1919). In 1923 she was Karen Aldcroft in a play about wife-switching, *The Changelings,* and two years later played Maisie Partridge, the domineering mother, in *Mrs. Partridge Presents.* After performing in repertory on the West Coast, she

temporarily retired. She came out of retirement in 1933 to tour as Maud Mockridge, the dinner guest, in *Dangerous Corner.* Her last New York appearance was in 1933 as Lena, a small role in *The Lake.*

When she appeared in *The Darling of the Gods,* the *Times* wrote of the "dark, animated" performer: "The acting of Miss Blanche Bates has, all along, shown a sweet wildness of impulse, a freedom of abandonment, a delightful impetuosity of feeling. In the performance she is, if possible, more unconventional than ever . . . spontaneous, graceful, alert with vigor and free from all restraint of self-consciousness and finical prudery."

Battle, The, a play in four acts by Cleveland Moffett. Produced by Liebler and Co.◆ at the Savoy Theatre. December 21, 1908. 144 performances.

John J. Haggleton (Wilton Lackaye◆), a multimillionaire, determines to prove to his son Phillip (H. B. Warner◆) that a man's abilities, not his background, determine his success in life. Haggleton goes to live in a tenement with only a few dollars to his name and starts a new enterprise which soon succeeds. His son still resents some past actions of the man, but when a crazed socialist attempts to shoot Haggleton, Phillip jumps in front of his father and is seriously wounded. A reconciliation follows.

In an era of muckraking, the play was unusual in its defense of capitalism and capitalists.

BAY, HOWARD (1912–86) Born in Centralia, Wash., he studied in a variety of fine schools before first winning public recognition with his set designs for Federal Theatre◆ productions, including *Power* and *One Third of a Nation.* He soon became one of Broadway's busiest designers, creating the sets for eleven shows in 1944 alone. Among the notable works for which he conceived the sets have been *The Little Foxes*◆ (1939), *The Corn Is Green* (1940), *The Patriots*◆ (1943), *One Touch of Venus*◆ (1943), *Carmen Jones*◆ (1943), *Deep Are the Roots*◆ (1945), *Up in Central Park*◆ (1945), revivals of *Show Boat*◆ (1946, 1954 and 1960), *Come Back, Little Sheba*◆ (1950), *The Music Man*◆ (1957), and *Man of La Mancha*◆ (1965). He also directed shows, including *As the Girls Go* (1949) and *There Are Crimes and Crimes* (1951). His work has won two Tony Awards◆ among others. Besides teaching at several universities, he has published *Stage Design* (1975).

It is hard to characterize Bay's work, other than remark on its virtually universal excellence. He himself consciously resisted being identified with any particular school. Howard Taubman of the

Times praised his work for *Man of La Mancha* as "sparing in its furniture and props [but] rich in illusion."

BAYES, NORA [née DORA GOLDBERG] (1880–1928) The earliest history of the famous vaudevillian is clouded by uncertainty. Some sources give her real name as Leonora or even Eleanor Goldberg, while her birthplace, generally stated as Milwaukee, is occasionally said to be Chicago or Los Angeles. She made her vaudeville debut in Chicago in 1899 and her Broadway stage debut two years later in *The Rogers Brothers in Washington*. In 1902 she popularized "Down Where the Wurzberger Flows," and her career progressed slowly but steadily thereafter. Major recognition came in 1908 when she left Al Fields, her old partner and manager, to marry and team with Jack Norworth.♦ In the same year she introduced their "Shine On Harvest Moon" in the *Follies*. The couple's act had one of the most famous of all vaudeville billings:

NORA BAYES
Assisted and Admired by Jack Norworth

She appeared in the [*Ziegfeld*] *Follies*♦ *of 1909,* then in 1910 with Norworth in *The Jolly Bachelors,* in which she introduced "Has Anybody Here Seen Kelly?" Other stage appearances included *Little Miss Fix-It* (1911), for which she wrote many of the songs, *Roly Poly* (1912), *Maid in America* (1915), *The Cohan Revue* (1917), *Ladies First* (1918), *Her Family Tree* (1920), *Snapshots of 1921,* and *Queen o' Hearts* (1922). Among the many other songs with which she was associated were "Take Me Out to the Ball Game," "Over There," "Just Like a Gypsy," and "Japanese Sandman." Douglas Gilbert has written of the tiny, big-voiced performer, "Nora Bayes was the American Guilbert, mistress of gesture, poise, delivery and facial work. No one could outrival her in dramatizing a song."

BEACH, LEWIS, see *Goose Hangs High, The*

Bear and the Cub, The, a play, presumably by an American, which became a *cause célèbre* in 1665. One Edward Martin accused Cornelius Watkinson, Philip Howard, and William Darby of acting "a play commonly called the Bear and the Cub" in Accomac County, Virginia, on August 27 of that year. The men were ordered to appear in court "in the habiliments which they had acted in" and to repeat their performance. Martin's charge of public wickedness was dismissed and he was ordered to pay court costs. Nothing is known about the play itself, but,

for want of more complete early records, Watkinson, Howard, and Darby must be considered the earliest American actors, although they were almost certainly amateurs.

BEATON, CECIL (1904–80) The noted English designer and photographer created costumes and sometimes sets for such productions as the 1946 revival of *Lady Windermere's Fan, The Grass Harp* (1952), and *Quadrille* (1954), but is remembered most for his sumptuous period costumes for *My Fair Lady*♦ (1956).

Beau Brummell, a play in four acts by Clyde Fitch.♦ Presented by A. M. Palmer♦ and Richard Mansfield♦ at the Madison Square Theatre.♦ May 19, 1890. 150 performances.

Beau Brummell (Mansfield), vain, effete, and supercilious, cares only about the pleasures of life. He is totally irresponsible, telling his valet, Mortimer (W. J. Ferguson), to hide his bills where he "would not see them," so that he might "think that they are paid." Only his gambling debts are honored. To replenish his funds he plans to marry Mariana Vincent (Agnes Miller), daughter of a rich London merchant, unaware that his own nephew Reginald (F. W. Lander) is courting her and has her affections. Brummell's haughtiness extends even to the Prince of Wales (D. H. Harkins), who at first is amused by the man's presumption. But when, on leaving a ball, Brummell snaps at the Prince, "I shall have to order my carriage. Wales, will you ring the bell?," he finally alienates the future king. Realizing the damage he has done to himself, he sends the Prince an expensive gift, only to have it publicly returned. He is further confounded to overhear Mariana and Reginald exchange endearments. Head high, he determines to leave London. Time passes. Aging and impoverished, and befriended only by his loyal valet, he sits in his French rooms by the light of a single candle and entertains his old companions, now merely phantoms of his mind, at a regal, if imaginary, supper.

The play, originally spelled *Beau Brummel,* was Fitch's first major play, although Mansfield attempted to take credit for it. Fitch replied, "The idea of a play on Beau Brummel is, I believe, Mr. William Winter's. The execution of that play—Mr. Winter claims it has been an execution in more ways than one—some of the business, and the great bulk of the dialogue is mine. The artistic touch, some of the lines in the comedy, not the most important ones, and the genius that has made it a success are Mr. Mansfield's." Certainly many critics held that it was Mansfield's finest delineation, and he kept it in his repertory until his death. Arnold Daly♦ later performed it successfully.

Beaucaire, a comedy in five acts by Booth Tarkington♦ and Evelyn Greenleaf Sutherland.♦ Produced by Richard Mansfield♦ at the Herald Square Theatre. December 2, 1901. 64 performances.

Because his escapades have forced him into hiding, the Duc d'Orleans (Mansfield) has disguised himself as a French barber, Monsieur Beaucaire, in Bath, England. Yet even his somewhat precarious position cannot restrain the fun-loving nobleman from further adventure. When he catches the Duke of Winterset (Joseph Weaver) cheating at cards, he threatens to expose him if the Duke refuses to introduce him into society as a French gentleman. His charm and breeding make him instantly welcome, and he successfully courts Lady Mary Carlisle (Lettice Fairfax). But his newfound friends reject him savagely when they are given to understand he is merely a barber. He returns as the rightful Duc and courteously puts them in their places.

This comic attack on society's often absurd distinctions was based on Tarkington's novelette *Monsieur Beaucaire.* Mansfield, convinced by the failure of his *Monsieur de Jadot* that Americans were embarrassed by their inability to pronounce "monsieur" correctly, insisted on the shortened title. The success of the production helped the young Shubert brothers♦ start their first New York theatre on a firm footing. Mansfield kept the play in his repertory until his death. It was later made into a popular operetta by André Messager.

Beautiful People, The, a fantastic comedy in two acts by William Saroyan.♦ Produced by Saroyan at the Lyceum Theatre.♦ April 21, 1941. 120 performances.

The Websters are an unconventional clan, living in a decaying San Francisco mansion. Jonah (Curtis Cooksey), the father, is a deeply pious man who forges the signature of the former occupant of the house on annuity checks to make ends meet. His son Owen (Eugene Loring) writes one-word novels, and his daughter Agnes (Betsy Blair) talks to mice, whom she believes bring flowers into the house to spell her name. When one of her mice runs away, Owen climbs a church steeple to recover it. The family is regularly visited by equally unconventional friends, whom they entertain with a cornet concert by another brother three thousand miles away.

Eventually, even that brother, Harold (Don Freeman), returns for a visit.

Unable to find backers for his play, Saroyan not only produced it with his own money but directed it as well. As did most of his plays, the work sharply divided the critics. Richard Lockridge of the *Sun* dismissed it as "downright foolish," while six of his colleagues voted it the best play of the season.

BECK, Martin (1865–1940) Details of his early years are uncertain. He emigrated from Germany while still a young man and soon became manager of a Chicago beer garden, where he induced the owner to build a stage and offer variety acts, and where he earned the nickname "Two Beers Beck." In the 1890s he joined the young Orpheum circuit,♦ bought into the group, and around 1906 became head of its New York office. In 1913 he opened the Palace Theatre♦ in New York and quickly made it vaudeville's mecca, although Edward Albee♦ soon wrested control of the house from him. Profiting from his experience, he later built the Martin Beck Theatre, the first major legitimate playhouse west of Eighth Avenue and the only legitimate theatre with no mortgage. He also dabbled in producing and was the first man to bring the modern D'Oyly Carte♦ company to America.

BECKETT, Samuel [Barclay] (1906–90) Irish dramatist whose absurdist, usually actionless, and fundamentally philosophic plays have delighted a coterie of intellectuals and experimental playgoers, is best remembered for his *Waiting for Godot*♦ (1956). *Godot* enjoyed a long run on Broadway in large measure because of the performance of Bert Lahr,♦ a musical comedy clown. However, for the most part Beckett has found success not in mainstream playhouses but off-Broadway♦ and at more adventuresome regional theatres. Among his best-known works are *Endgame* (1958), *Krapp's Last Tape* (1960), and *Happy Days* (1961). He lived in Paris after 1937.

Becky Sharp, a play in four acts by Langdon Mitchell.♦ Produced by Mrs. Fiske♦ at the Fifth Avenue Theatre.♦ September 12, 1899. 116 performances.

The adventurous, unprincipled Becky (Mrs. Fiske) rises from nothing into a life of luxury by secretly marrying Rawdon Crawley (Maurice Barrymore♦) at the same time she accepts money from the Marquis of Steyne (Tyrone Power♦). When the two men confront each other, Becky seems doomed. But, ever resourceful, she begins to wheedle a new life from the fatuous Joseph Sedley (William F. Owen) and young Sir Pitt Crawley (Robert V. Ferguson).

The play, derived from Thackeray's *Vanity Fair,* gave Mrs. Fiske one of her greatest successes, despite the efforts of the Theatrical Syndicate♦ to keep it off the boards. She revived it on several occasions over the next twenty years. The Players♦ produced it in 1929.

BEDFORD, BRIAN [ANTHONY] (b. 1935) The English actor first called attention to himself in two importations: *Five Finger Exercise* (1958) and the double bill of *The Private Ear* and *The Public Eye* (1963). Subsequently he won acclaim in a 1969 revival of *Private Lives,* ♦ in numerous Shakespearean roles with the Stratford (Canada) Festival, and touring in the leading roles of *Equus*♦ and *Deathtrap.* ♦ He typifies the many outstanding performers who have never quite found major stardom in New York.

BEECHER, JANET [née MEYSENBURG] (1884–1955) An actress who for over twenty years played leading roles without ever achieving stature as a major star, she was born in Jefferson City, Mo., and was raised in Chicago, where her father was German vice-consul. Among her notable parts were Helen Heyer, who wins her man in a raffle, in *The Lottery Man*♦ (1909); Helen Arany, the uncomplaining wife of a temperamental genius, in *The Concert* (1910); Laura Bartlett, the outgoing wife of a stay-at-home husband, in *Fair and Warmer*♦ (1915); Margaret Fairfield, who is caught between an old love and a new one, in *A Bill of Divorcement* (1921); and Mary Colebrook, the widow who remains loyal to her illegitimate son, in *Courage*♦ (1928). After spending the 1930s in films she scored one final success as Catherine Apley, wife of *The Late George Apley*♦ (1944).

Beggar on Horseback, a play in two acts by George S. Kaufman♦ and Marc Connelly.♦ Produced by Winthrop Ames♦ at the Broadhurst Theatre. February 12, 1924. 224 performances.

Neil McRae (Roland Young♦) is a talented serious composer who barely makes a living doing hack orchestrations. He is so impractical that his neighbors, Cynthia Mason (Kay Johnson) and Dr. Albert Rice (Richard Barbee), must look after him without seeming to do so. Gladys Cady (Ann Carpenter), daughter of a rich widget manufacturer from Neil's hometown, is determined to marry Neil. Mr. Cady (George W. Barbier) encourages the match, offering to take Neil into the widget business. It will even be all right for Neil to compose popular songs on the side, so long as the songs make a million dollars. After the Cadys leave, Neil takes a sleeping pill Dr. Rice has given him. He dreams of marriage to Gladys, whose wedding bouquet is made of banknotes, of their home where six butlers announce every caller and where he must fill out requisition forms to obtain a pencil. His new life drives him to murder his in-laws. At his trial "Judge" Cady, proclaiming "This thing of using the imagination has got to stop," sentences Neil to work in an art factory, mass-producing masterpieces. When he wakes from his dream Neil decides to marry Cynthia instead of Gladys.

Ames had given Kaufman and Connelly a copy of a German play, Paul Apel's *Hans Sonnenstössers Höllenfahrt,* and asked them to adapt it. For all practical purposes, the finished work was a new play, but it fell in with the vogue for Expressionism. ♦ Alexander Woollcott♦ wrote in the preface to the published play that it represents "the distaste that can be inspired by the viewpoint, the complacency and the very idiocy of Rotarian America. It is a small and facetious disturbance in the rear of the Church of the Gospel of Success."

BEHMAN, LOUIS C., see *Hyde and Behman*

Behold the Bridegroom, a play in three acts by George Kelly.♦ Produced at the Cort Theatre. December 26, 1927. 88 performances.

Antoinette Lyle (Judith Anderson♦) returns home suddenly from Europe. She is bored and lonely. Her friends suggest she marry Gehring Fitler (Lester Vail), who long has courted her, but she rejects him as an alcoholic ne'er-do-well. In fact, she rejects all her rich suitors. Then she meets a handsome, reserved businessman, Spencer Train (John Marston), "the first man that ever held me cheap," and realizes not only that she is in love, but that her life until then has been a waste. She has been, she recognizes, "The notorious Tony Lyle— that ridiculed every sincerity and thought it smart to say and do the meanest and most embarrassing thing to everybody on every occasion." Train, however, displays no special interest in Tony. She languishes, beset by an affliction as much spiritual as physical. When Mr. Lyle (Thurston Hall♦) asks Train to see Antoinette, she accepts that she is not ready for her "bridegroom" nor the singular redemption he might offer.

The play which competed with ten other openings on the busiest first night in Broadway's history, baffled many critics and playgoers with its vague, somewhat mystical ending. Its fine dialogue, honesty, and inexorability make it, nonetheless, as close as Kelly ever came to writing high tragedy.

BEHRMAN, S[AMUEL] N[ATHANIEL] (1893–1973) Born in Worcester, Mass., he studied at Clark University before enrolling in Professor George P. Baker's♦ 47 Workshop♦ at Harvard. Later he did graduate work at Columbia under Brander Matthews♦ and St. John Ervine. Stints followed as book reviewer, play reader, and press agent before he teamed with Kenyon Nicholson♦ to write *Bedside Manner* (1924) and *A Night's Work* (1927), and with Owen Davis♦ to write *The Man Who Forgot* (1926), none of which reached New York. He scored with his first solo effort, *The Second Man*♦ (1927), a play about a novelist torn between two women. A week later he suffered failure with another collaboration with Nicholson, *Love Is Like That,* a tale of the love of a young socialite for an exiled prince. *Serena Blandish* (1929), based on Enid Bagnold's novel, told of a wide-eyed innocent in Mayfair, while *Meteor* (1929) centered on a ruthless businessman. *Brief Moment*♦ (1931) examined the difficult romance of a rich young man and a night-club singer. His best work was *Biography*♦ (1932), which focused on a much-courted portrait painter. Somewhat less successful were *Rain from Heaven* (1934), about an English lady and her houseparty guests, and *End of Summer*♦ (1936), about the disillusioning romance of a millionairess and a young radical. In 1937 he adapted Jean Giraudoux's♦ *Amphitryon 38* for the Lunts,♦ but in the following year came a cropper with *Wine of Choice,* in which several rich men band together to discourage their protégée from marrying a communist. Many of those who do not consider *Biography* his best play select *No Time for Comedy*♦ (1939), which centered on a successful writer of comedies who longs to do a serious work. Curiously, Behrman's next play, *The Talley Method* (1941), failed when it took a serious look at a cold, narrow doctor and his family. Returning to comedy, and to the Lunts, he scored a popular success with *The Pirate*♦ (1942), his freewheeling adaptation of Ludwig Fulda's play about a mountebank and the wife of a pirate-turned-politician. A second comic adaptation, from Franz Werfel, won favor as *Jacobowsky and the Colonel* (1944), a saga of a Jewish refugee and an anti-Semitic Polish colonel together fleeing the Nazis. But another attempt at serious drama failed with *Dunnigan's Daughter* (1945), in which a long-suffering wife finally leaves her greedy, ambitious

husband. *Jane* (1947), based on a Somerset Maugham♦ story, failed, while an adaptation of Marcel Achard's *Auprès de Ma Blonde* as *I Know My Love* (1949) ran largely on the appeal of the Lunts. *Let Me Hear the Melody* (1951), suggested by the life of F. Scott Fitzgerald, closed on tryout, as did another adaptation, *The Foreign Language.* With Joshua Logan♦ he wrote the libretto for the long-run musical *Fanny*♦ (1954). In 1958 he offered *The Cold Wind and the Warm,* a semi-autobiographical look at Jewish life in his hometown at the turn of the century, and in 1962 wrote *Lord Pengo,* which was loosely based on his biography of the famous art dealer Duveen. His last play, which he called a "serious comedy," was *But for Whom Charlie* (1964), which depicted the exploitation of a selfless philanthropist.

Like those of his closest rival in the field of high comedy, Philip Barry,♦ Behrman's writings were marked by a distinctive dichotomy. But whereas Barry's best work drew strength from his interweaving of wit and despair, Behrman's sometimes profited and sometimes was hurt by his unique mixture of brilliant, high social comedy and increasingly strong political (leftish) colorings. Joseph Wood Krutch♦ observed in *Literary History of the United States,* "Faced with the problem of writing comedy in an atmosphere which many are ready to say makes comedy either impossible or impertinent, he thus invented something which might not improperly be called the comedy of illumination . . . Behrman's wit enables him to make discussion really illuminating and hence to write comedies which are neither merely didactic nor merely trivial."

Autobiography: *People in a Diary,* Boston, 1972.

BELASCO, DAVID (1853–1931) He was born in San Francisco to parents of Portuguese-Jewish origin. His family's name had once been Velasco, and his father had played in London pantomimes. While he was still very young the family moved briefly to Victoria. Details of this period are obscure, but the boy apparently came under the tutelage of a Father McGuire. Although he soon ran away from home, he retained an affection for the priest and later claimed his affectation of wearing a clerical collar to be in his honor. He may have made his acting debut in 1864 playing the young Duke of York opposite Charles Kean's Richard III. At the age of twelve he wrote his first play, *Jim Black; or, The Regulator's Revenge.* By 1873 he was a call boy at the Metropolitan Theatre in San Francisco. Continuing to act as well, he performed with John McCullough,♦ Edwin Booth,♦ and other leading players. A year later in

Virginia City, Nevada, he met Dion Boucicault,♦ from whom he learned much about acting, directing, and play-writing. Returning to San Francisco, he became an assistant stage manager for Thomas Maguire♦ and then managed the Baldwin Theatre♦ for James A. Herne.♦ Some of his earliest plays, such as *La Belle Russe,* a tale of female treachery, and *The Stranglers of Paris,* which William Winter♦ called "a repulsive sensation melodrama" and Belasco himself later dismissed as "buncombe," were first mounted at the Baldwin in 1881. In 1882 he came to New York, where he served as stage manager of the Madison Square Theatre♦ for two years, went back to San Francisco, then returned to New York in 1886 as stage manager for Daniel Frohman♦ at the Lyceum.♦ While in that capacity, he also wrote a number of plays with Henry C. de Mille,♦ including, *The Wife♦* (1887), recounting a husband's forgiveness of his wife's fickleness; *Lord Chumley* (1888), centering on an English eccentric; *The Charity Ball♦* (1889), whose central figure was a self-sacrificing clergyman; and *Men and Women♦* (1890), revolving around a bank scandal. In 1888 he staged Sophocles' *Electra* for the American Academy of Dramatic Arts♦ in a mounting years ahead of its time in its stark simplicity. Thereafter his luck seemingly ran out until Charles Frohman♦ asked him to write a play to open the Empire Theatre.♦ The result was a collaboration with Franklin Fyles,♦ *The Girl I Left Behind Me♦* (1893), whose love story was set against a background of soldiers and Indians. He firmly established himself as a playwright, producer, and director with *The Heart of Maryland♦* (1895), a Civil War romance. His adaptation from the French, *Zaza* (1899), and *Naughty Anthony* (1900), a slight farce, followed. After the latter play opened he recognized that it did not amount to a full evening's entertainment, so he created a double bill by adapting John Luther Long's♦ tale of a tragic love affair between a Japanese girl and an American sailor, *Madame Butterfly♦* (1900). A succession of hits ensued: *Du Barry♦* (1901), retelling the rise and fall of a king's mistress; *The Auctioneer♦* (1901), written with Charles Klein♦ and Lee Arthur and recounting the ups and downs of a New York Lower East Side peddler; *The Darling of the Gods♦* (1902), written with Long and describing the plight of a Japanese princess tricked into betraying her lover; *Sweet Kitty Bellairs♦* (1903), based on a novel and depicting the intrigues of an Irish charmer; *Adrea♦* (1905), a tragedy of a blind princess, written with Long; *The Girl of the Golden West♦* (1905), a barmaid's romance with an outlaw; *The Rose of the Rancho♦* (1906), a study of an American take-over of Spanish lands, written with Richard Walton Tully♦; *A Grand Army Man♦* (1907), contrasting an old veteran and his dishonest adopted son, written with Pauline Phelps and Marion Short; *The Return of Peter Grimm♦* (1911), in which the hero returns from the dead; *The Son-Daughter* (1919), in which a Chinese girl, sold into marriage, murders her husband; and *Kiki* (1921), spotlighting an ambitious chorus girl, which Belasco adapted freely from the French. Among the many plays which he produced but which he had little or no hand in writing were *The Music Master♦* (1904), *The Fighting Hope♦* (1908), *The Easiest Way♦* (1909), *The Woman♦* (1911), *The Boomerang♦* (1915), *Polly with a Past♦* (1917), *Tiger Rose♦* (1917), *Daddies♦* (1918), and *Lulu Belle♦* (1926). In 1901 he leased the Republic Theatre, renaming it the Belasco; but in 1906 he built his own house. At first he called it the Stuyvesant, but later gave it his own name.

Belasco was obsessed with realism on stage, in one play re-creating a Child's restaurant in which fresh coffee was brewed and pancakes made. Although many critics felt his determined "arch-realism" of setting masked a lack of artistic seriousness, Walter Prichard Eaton♦ attempted a balanced assessment when he wrote in *The American Stage of To-day,* "What Mr. Belasco has done has been to write pieces for the play-house, not criticisms of life. Well aware that such pieces to be successful or to satisfy his own standards must, however, superficially resemble life, he has bent his mind to devise them with all possible air of probability and with all possible fidelity of pictorial setting. Especially in the latter respect he has succeeded as no other man of our time has." Many of his better plays, as well as those of fellow authors which he mounted, retain a theatrical effectiveness and might well succeed in an open-minded theatre that does not largely reject its past.

His off-stage life was in some ways as extravagant and carefully staged as his plays. One favorite trick was a temper tantrum in which he would stamp on his own watch, smashing it into uselessness. Close associates knew he kept a stock of cheap, second-hand watches for just such occasions.

Biography: *The Bishop of Broadway,* Craig Timberlake, New York, 1954.

BEL GEDDES, Barbara (b. 1922) She was born in New York and made her debut as a walk-on in summer stock in 1940. The next year she came to Broadway as Dottie Coburn, a fledgling actress, in *Out of the Frying Pan,* then toured for the USO as the over-imaginative Judy in *Junior Miss.♦* After appearing in several failures, she began to earn attention as Cynthia Brown, the daughter who encourages her father to have an affair, in *Little Darling* (1942), and followed that with Alice, the co-ed turned detective, in *Nine Girls* (1943) and Wilhemina in *Mrs. January and Mr. X* (1944). She first won important recognition as Genevra Langdon, the sympathetic younger daughter, in *Deep Are the Roots*♦ (1945). She scored a major success as Patty O'Neill, the naïve actress, in *The Moon Is Blue*♦ (1951). Turning again to more serious roles, she portrayed the suicidal Rose Pemberton in *The Living Room* (1954) and Maggie, the unloved wife, in *Cat on a Hot Tin Roof*♦ (1955). Mary, the American chorus girl courted by a Grand Duke, in *The Sleeping Prince* (1956) and the lonely Katherine Johnson in *Silent Night, Lonely Night* (1959) followed. Her biggest hit came as the contrary heroine of *Mary, Mary*♦ (1961). She later replaced Anne Jackson in *Luv,* then played Jenny, the bored housewife-turned-prostitute, in *Everything in the Garden* (1967) and Katy Cooper, the loyal wife of a philandering professor, in *Finishing Touches*♦ (1973).

A strapping blonde, her performance in *Deep Are the Roots* was praised by Lewis Nichols in the *Times* as having "grace and tenderness and an honesty which breathes life into the part," while Brooks Atkinson♦ later wrote in the same paper that her acting in *Mary, Mary* had "an agreeably light touch; her quirk of pausing for quick intakes of breath in the midst of phrases, whether a habit or not, seems felicitous." She is the daughter of Norman Bel Geddes.

BEL GEDDES, NORMAN [né NORMAN MELANCTON GEDDES] (1893–1958) Born in Adrian, Mich., he studied at art schools in Cleveland and Chicago. His first designs were for *Nju* at Los Angeles' Little Theatre in 1916. Coming to New York under the auspices of Otto Kahn, he created the sets for several Metropolitan Opera productions before turning to Broadway, where his work was seen in, among others, a revival of *Erminie*♦ (1920), *The Truth About Blades* (1921), *The Rivals* (1922), *The School for Scandal* (1923), Reinhardt's♦ *The Miracle* (1924), *Lady, Be Good!*♦ (1924), *Jeanne d'Arc* (1925), *Ziegfeld Follies of 1925*♦ (actually sets created for the failed *The Comic Supplement* and brought over for a revised edition of the 1924 *Follies*), *Julius Caesar*♦ and *The Five O'Clock Girl* (1927), *The Patriot* (1928), *Fifty Million Frenchmen*♦ (1929), *Lysistrata* (1930), *Hamlet*♦ (1931), *Flying Colors* (1932), *Dead End*♦ (1935), *Iron Men*

(1936), *The Eternal Road* and *Siege* (1937), *It Happened on Ice* (1940), and *Seven Lively Arts* (1944). Although not an architect, he designed several theatres.

Bel Geddes's interests were so broad that he eventually drifted away from the theatre, but in his earliest days he pioneered in abandoning the proscenium and foresaw the vogue for arena stages. He was an ardent modernist, so his 1920s' musical sets were masterpieces of art deco. However, his most famous theatrical achievements were his settings for *The Miracle, Hamlet,* and *Dead End.* Writing of the first, the *Times's* John Corbin♦ observed, "The cathedral into which the Century Theatre has been transformed . . . is indescribably rich in color, unimaginably atmospheric in its lofty, aerial spaces." *Hamlet,* which he staged with Raymond Massey♦ in the lead, made ingenious use of stairways and rostrums to suggest the various settings. He was the father of Barbara Bel Geddes. ♦

Autobiography: *Miracle in the Evening,* Garden City, 1960.

Bell, Book and Candle, a comedy in three acts by John van Druten.♦ Produced at the Ethel Barrymore Theatre. November 14, 1950. 233 performances.

Gillian Holroyd (Lilli Palmer) is a witch who is certain that through her black arts she can get anything she wants. One thing she badly wants is the publisher in the neighboring apartment, Shep Henderson (Rex Harrison♦). He promptly knocks on her door and falls in love with her. In no time they are set to be married. To please Shep, Gillian conjures up an author he has been trying to land. The happy arrangement is spoiled when Gillian fights with her brother and aunt, who are also witches, and they spill the beans to Shep. To keep Shep she gives up witchery.

The play, which the *Times* described as "completely enchanting . . . a wonderfully suave and impish fancy," gave promise of having a long run, but when Harrison and Miss Palmer left the cast, the producer was unable to find suitable replacements, so closed the show while it was still doing good business. Later, road companies toured successfully with Rosalind Russell♦ and Dennis Price, and with Joan Bennett and Zachary Scott, starring.

BELL, DIGBY [VALENTINE] (1851–1917) Although the Milwaukee-born performer studied in Europe to become a concert singer, he made his mark as a comedian. Long associated with John McCaull's♦ productions, he first starred in the musical *Jupiter*

(1892). Later he was the leading comedian in Lillian Russell's♦ company, appearing opposite her in such shows as *Princess Nicotine* and *The Grand Duchess.* ♦ Much of his later career was in straight plays or vaudeville.

Bell for Adano, A, a drama in three acts by Paul Osburn. ♦ Produced by Leland Hayward♦ at the Cort Theatre. December 6, 1944. 296 performances.

Major Victor Joppolo (Fredric March♦), an Italian-American, arrives in Adano to head the Allied Military Government in that city. He is sympathetic to the needs of the Sicilians, but his commanding officer, who is stationed far away, is not. When the commander orders that carts not be allowed to impede modern traffic in the village, Joppolo ignores the order. His behavior is reported, and he is ordered transferred, but not before he has gotten the villagers one of the things they most want—a new bell to replace one the Fascists melted down to make arms. Just as he is leaving the new bell sounds for the first time. "It shakes the whole damned building," Joppolo proudly tells his sergeant.

With the war still raging, a realistic treatment of its brutalities was out of the question. In a sense, this play, based on John Hersey's novel, looked back to the romantic war plays of earlier times. Thus while the play was unquestionably timely, it was also sentimental and idealistic.

Bella Union (San Francisco) Opened on Portsmouth Square as a combination gambling house, saloon, and variety theatre in October 1849, its first attraction was a minstrel show. The tenor of the establishment was set on opening night when one of the performers was shot and killed in an altercation that followed the show, but this very roughness remained part of the house's singular appeal. A San Francisco historian has noted, "What [audiences] wanted from the Bella Union—comfort, liquor, handsome women, entertainment without ornament—they could get nowhere else. There were rivals . . . but none of them offered such continuously satisfying entertainment as the 'Belly' Union. Here alone could be had any penetrating criticism of the drawing-room moralities and 'company' manners of the age . . . the free and easy atmosphere, the laugh-and-grow-fat attitude, the pungent ribaldry of the Bella Union could be had elsewhere only in duplicate of the original." Gambling was abolished in 1856, and the house became known as a "melodeon," a local term for a vaudeville theatre. Rebuilt after several fires, the original building was

demolished in 1868, and the proprietor, Samuel Tetlow, opened a new theatre on its site. It remained active until 1895, when it was converted into a museum. The structure was destroyed in the earthquake and fire of 1906. Among the important performers who began to learn their trade there were Edward Harrigan♦ and Charlotte Crabtree. ♦

BELLAMY, RALPH (b. 1904) The Chicago-born actor made his debut in a 1922 production of *The Shepherd of the Hills* on the Chautauqua Circuit and after many seasons in stock first appeared on Broadway in *Town Boy* (1929). A long career followed in films before he returned to New York to create the role of Michael Frame, who helps re-educate a young Nazi, in *Tomorrow the World*♦ (1943). He next scored major successes as Grant Matthews, the presidential candidate, in *State of the Union*♦ (1945) and as Detective McLeod, the dedicated but excessively harsh policeman, in *Detective Story*♦ (1949). His last appearance was generally regarded as his finest achievement, portraying Franklin Roosevelt in *Sunrise at Campobello*♦ (1958). He won a Tony Award♦ for this interpretation, which prompted Louis Kronenberger♦ to observe, "In Ralph Bellamy's extraordinarily effective impersonation of Roosevelt—in his coping with wheelchairs and crutches and braces, in his conversion of the humiliating into the heroic—there was no trace of either virtuosity or tear-jerking vaudevillism; there was a sense of characterization and indeed of character."

Belle of New York, The, a musical comedy in two acts. Book and lyrics by Hugh Morton. ♦ Music by Gustave Kerker. ♦ Produced by George Lederer♦ at the Casino Theatre. ♦ September 28, 1897. 56 performances.

Violet Gray (Edna May♦), a Salvation Army lass, takes it upon herself to reform the spendthrift ways of Harry Brown (Harry Davenport), who has been cast out by his hypocritical, crusading father, Ichabod (Dan Daly♦). So grateful is Ichabod that he is prepared to break his son's engagement to another girl, Cora (Ada Dare), and force him to marry Violet. Realizing that Harry and Cora are very much in love, Violet purposely alienates Ichabod by singing a risqué ditty.

Principal songs: The Purity Brigade · She Is the Belle of New York · They All Follow Me

Although the musical's run in New York was brief, it was taken to London, where it became the first American musical to achieve real success, compiling 674 performances in the West End. It was also mounted with great success on the Continent. While there have been a number of important and profitable European revivals, the musical has never been given a major rehearing in America, unless a 1921 rewriting, *The Whirl of New York,* is so classified.

BELLEW, [Harold] Kyrle (1855–1911) After spending time in the Royal Navy and appearing on English and Australian stages, he came to America in 1885 and made his debut with Wallack's◆ company as Hubert Hastings in *In His Power.* He continued with the troupe, playing classic roles such as Captain Absolute and parts in popular melodramas of the day such as Lt. Kingsley in *Harbour Lights* and the title role in an adaptation of *Tom Jones.* For several years in the 1890s he toured as leading man to Mrs. J. Brown-Potter,◆ a rich woman determined to make her mark as an actress. Once again his assignments moved from contemporary parts to classics such as Antony and Romeo. He retired from the stage and spent several years in Australia, where he is reputed to have made a modest fortune. In 1901 he returned to America and the stage to assume the title role in a swashbuckler, *A Gentleman of France,*◆ playing opposite Eleanor Robson.◆ The next year he portrayed Charles Surface in *The School for Scandal.* In 1903 he again was partnered with Miss Robson, performing Romeo to her Juliet. After that production closed he scored a major success in the title role of *Raffles.*◆ His Chevalier de Vaudrey was praised in an all-star revival of *The Two Orphans*◆ (1904). Miss Robson was Kate Hardcastle to his Marlow in a 1905 mounting of *She Stoops To Conquer.* His greatest success came as Richard Voysin in Henri Bernstein's *The Thief* (1907). His last two performances were in failures, *The Builder of Bridges* (1909) and *The Scandal* (1910).

A critic in *Harper's Weekly* wrote of him, "He poses and struts, yet one has to confess that his poses are graceful, and his struttings recall a pleasurable memory of days gone by. His voice is not strong, but is sweet of tone and falls pleasantly upon the ear, and his enunciation is sufficiently, though not convincingly, clear. The impression he makes today [1902] is quite the same as that upon which he seemed to us to rely so many years ago, and which is best described by the adjective 'pulchritudinous.'" His pictures suggest that in after-years he bore a resemblance to a later President, Warren G. Harding.

Ben Hur, a melodrama in a prologue and six acts by William Young.◆ Produced by Klaw◆ and Erlanger◆ at the Broadway Theatre. November 29, 1899. 194 performances.

After a prologue recounting the legend of the three wise men, the story centers on Ben Hur (Edward Morgan), a good-natured Roman Jew who is betrayed into servitude on a galley by his treacherous friend Messala (William S. Hart◆). Later freed by a man whose life he saved, Hur is given a good education and eventually leaves for Antioch, where his father's old servant Simonides (Henry Lee) has carefully husbanded the Hur fortune. Learning that his false friend Messala has entered a chariot race, Hur enters his own name, too. Bets carefully placed by Hur and Simonides prompt Messala to stake his whole fortune on the race. Messala attempts to panic Hur's horses, but Hur interlocks his wheels with Messala's, who is thrown and crippled. Hur wins the race. Messala is later murdered, and Hur becomes a devout Christian.

General Lew Wallace, whose popular novel was the source of the play, had originally refused offers from Lawrence Barrett,◆ Tommaso Salvini,◆ and the Kiralfy Brothers◆ to dramatize the play. The production that Klaw and Erlanger mounted was one of the most extravagant ever seen on Broadway. Besides twenty-two speaking principals, there were eighty in the chorus and over a hundred supers. The chariot race, using real horses (part of the time on treadmills), was as spectacular as theatrical design of the period could make it. The more serious critics were displeased, Walter Prichard Eaton◆ dismissing it as "a thing of bombastic rhetoric, inflated scenery, pasteboard piety, and mechanical excitement." The play was presented by innumerable touring companies, some of dubious quality, and was regularly revived successfully in major houses as late as 1916, when films began to offer a superior medium for spectacle and such theatrical mountings came to seem ludicrous by comparison. The story itself was used in two spectacular films.

BEN-AMI, Jacob [né Shtchirin] (1890–1977) Coming to America in 1912 from Russia, he soon joined Maurice Schwartz's◆ famous theatre at Irving Place, but found his purist ideals clashed with Schwartz's more pragmatic approach. In 1918 he came to the attention of Arthur Hopkins,◆ who encouraged him to improve his English and perform on Broadway. His first English-speaking role was as Peter Krumback in *Samson and Delilah* (1920). Thereafter he moved back and forth between American and Yiddish theatres. He played and directed for the Theatre Guild◆ and supported Eva Le Gallienne◆

at her Civic Repertory Theatre♦ (including Trigorin in *The Sea Gull* and Epihodov in *The Cherry Orchard*), as well as assuming important roles in other Broadway shows. He established a number of Yiddish theatre groups, dedicated to mountings of Yiddish classics and Yiddish translations of important works in other languages. Called "the knight of the Yiddish intelligentsia," he was praised by Stark Young♦ as "the most profoundly natural actor we have."

BENCHLEY, ROBERT [CHARLES] (1889–1945) Once described by Helen Hayes♦ as "an enchanting toad of a man," the American humorist was born in Worcester, Mass., and educated at Harvard. He served as drama critic for *Life* (1920–29) and *The New Yorker* (1929–39), where his frequently iconoclastic reviews were leavened with common sense and wit. Examining a new Eugene O'Neill♦ play, he wrote, "Let us stop all this scowling talk about 'the inevitability of Greek tragedy' and 'O'Neill's masterly grasp of the eternal verities' and let us admit that the reason why we sat for six hours straining to hear each line through the ten-watt acoustics of the Guild Theatre was because *Mourning Becomes Electra* is filled with good, old-fashioned, spine-curling melodrama." Having to write weekly single-line summaries of each Broadway show, he once summed up *Abie's Irish Rose,*♦ which he hated, as "Hebrews 13:8." A look at the Bible revealed the reference was to the line "Jesus Christ, the same yesterday, and today, and forever." He also contributed sketches to *The 49ers* (1922) and *The Music Box Revue, 1923–24,*♦ and collaborated with Fred Thompson on the libretto to *Smarty* (1927), which was rewritten without him as *Funny Face.*♦ In the *Music Box Revue* he also performed his famous skit, "The Treasurer's Report."

Biography: *Robert Benchley: His Life and Good Times,* Babette Rosmond, Garden City, 1970.

Benefits These became an American theatrical tradition early on as a means for actors to supplement their often meager salaries. Guest performers were customarily allowed benefits at the end of their visit, while regular members of a troupe had theirs at season's end. They were also offered occasionally to authors and others associated with the theatre. As a rule, the beneficiary was allowed a portion of the gross on a particular night, that portion growing in relation to his or her importance to the company. He or she was also allowed to plan the program. The seats allotted were usually handed over to the beneficiary, who became responsible for selling

them. However worthy the practice in theory, it was employed so frequently that it became a nuisance. With the coming of the Actors' Fund♦ and the growth of unions, benefits were carefully regulated and greatly reduced in number, with the revenues usually accruing to the union or fund. In recent years they have all but disappeared, except for specially organized galas.

In postwar theatre the term "benefit" was also applied to the block sale of huge numbers of seats for a particular performance of a show to a charitable group who would then resell the seats for the group's profit. As a result, for a time so many performances of a potential hit were sold out in advance that individual playgoers had difficulty obtaining seats at the box office. The practice has largely disappeared in recent seasons.

BENNETT, JAMES GORDON (1795–1872) The publisher of the New York *Herald* was a figure in the first major controversy over theatrical newspaper advertising. In the fall of 1865, when his *Herald* was probably New York's most important paper and certainly carried more theatrical advertisements than any other city paper, he refused to accept P. T. Barnum's♦ advertisements after an argument over a property transaction. With Max Maretzek, who was disturbed by the paper's harsh criticism of his opera company, Barnum persuaded all the other theatrical advertisers to remove their announcements from the paper. The boycott persisted for much of the season, until both sides realized they were suffering.

Papers sometimes had refused to carry advertisements for specific shows, usually basing their refusal on moral grounds, but had customarily printed letters protesting their action. A few later boycotts occurred, most notably when the Shuberts♦ removed all advertisements from the New York *Times* over their displeasure with the *Times* critic Alexander Woollcott.♦ In retaliation the *Times* refused to review plays at Shubert houses. As a rule, however, these boycotts ended quickly.

BENNETT [DI FIGLIA], MICHAEL (1943–87) Born in Buffalo, he made his debut as a dancer in *Subways Are for Sleeping* (1961). After dancing in several other musicals he was the choreographer for *A Joyful Noise* (1966), which was a failure, as was the next show for which he did dances, *Henry, Sweet Henry* (1967). In the following year, however, his work for the hit show *Promises, Promises*♦ won him widespread recognition. After choreographing *Coco* (1969), he worked closely with Harold Prince♦ and

Stephen Sondheim♦ to bring to fruition their idea of conceptualized musical comedy in *Company*♦ (1970) and *Follies*♦ (1971), serving as co-director of the latter. He moved closer to totally controlling the conception of his musicals when he served as librettist, director, and choreographer for *Seesaw* (1973). Over the next several years he slowly developed another musical, interviewing dancers to learn their life stories and trying out his ideas in innumerable workshop performances. The result was *A Chorus Line*♦ (1973), his major triumph. A similar attempt failed with *Ballroom* (1979). In 1981 he scored another major success with *Dreamgirls*. ♦ Frank Rich♦ wrote of his work in this show, "He keeps 'Dreamgirls' in constant motion—in every conceivable direction—to perfect his special brand of cinematic stage effects (montage, dissolve, wipe) . . . Throughout the show, Mr. Bennett uses shadows and klieg lights, background and foreground action, spotlighted figures and eerie silhouettes, to maintain the constant tension."

Biography: *One Singular Sensation,* Kevin Kelly, New York, 1990.

BENNETT, RICHARD (1873–1944) Born in Deacon's Mills, Ind., he made his debut in Chicago in 1891 as Tombstone Jake in *The Limited Mail,* and then played the role in New York later that year. For the next several seasons he toured in popular plays of the day and spent some time in stock. He returned to New York as a replacement in the musical *A Round of Pleasure* (1897), then appeared in a series of plays under Charles Frohman's♦ aegis. He first scored heavily as the rich man's son, Jefferson Ryder, in the muckraking *The Lion and the Mouse*♦ (1905). In 1906 he scored again as Lennard Willmore, who lies about his social position, in *The Hypocrites.* Further success followed when he became the first American John Shand, playing opposite Maude Adams♦ in *What Every Woman Knows* (1908). After some time in London and a brief return to stock, he played Jack Doogan, the ingratiating jewel thief, in *Stop, Thief* (1912), then had a modest success as George Dupont, the man victimized by hereditary venereal disease, in *Damaged Goods* (1913), which he co-produced. After the failure of his translation of Eugene Brieux's *Maternity* (1915), in which he played Julian, whose stance on childbearing is hypocritical and self-serving, he took to the road in several plays, most notably as Chick Hewes in *Kick In.*♦ A series of failures ensued before he had another long run as Peter Marchmont, who learns the secret of invisibility, in *The Unknown Purple*♦ (1918). His next success was

as the doomed Robert Mayo in *Beyond the Horizon*♦ (1920). In 1921 he played Andrew Lane, the good brother, in *The Hero,* ♦ then turned to the title role of the tragic clown in *He Who Gets Slapped* (1922). A season as Tony, the barkeep who inherits an English title, in *The Dancers* (1923), was followed by one of his most memorable interpretations, as Tony, the aging grape-grower, in *They Knew What They Wanted*♦ (1924). His next success came four years later as Jack Jarnegan, the cynical film director, in *Jarnegan.* In 1932 he toured as Cyrano de Bergerac, then made his last Broadway appearance as Judge Gaunt in *Winterset*♦ (1935).

His screen actress daughter Joan Bennett described him as "a handsome, virile man with blue-gray eyes, a determined chin, a firm and generous mouth, and a magnificent speaking voice." An intellectual performer, he bore much of the credit for bringing a number of important plays to New York, including *Beyond the Horizon* and Channing Pollock's♦ *The Fool,*♦ although he played in the latter only during its tryout. While his readings were sometimes criticized as too deliberate, Woollcott♦ hailed his Robert Mayo as a performance of "fine eloquence, imagination and finesse."

Biography: *The Bennett Playbill,* Joan Bennett and Lois Kibbee, New York, 1970.

BENNETT, ROBERT RUSSELL (1894–1981) The leading orchestrator of his day, he was born into a musical family and learned harmony, counterpoint, and composition under Carl Busch. He migrated to New York from his native Kansas City in 1916, and took work as a copyist with Schirmer, Inc. His first orchestrations were heard in *Hitchy Koo, 1919.* Among the shows he orchestrated were *Rose-Marie*♦ (1924), *Show Boat*♦ (1927), *Of Thee I Sing*♦ (1931), *Music in the Air* (1932), *Anything Goes*♦ (1934), *Oklahoma!*♦ (1943), *Annie Get Your Gun*♦ (1946), *Kiss Me, Kate*♦ (1948), *South Pacific*♦ (1949), *The King and I*♦ (1951), *My Fair Lady*♦ (1956), *The Sound of Music*♦ (1959), and *Camelot*♦ (1960), the two Lerner♦ and Lowe♦ works in collaboration with Philip J. Lang. Bennett's rich, well-balanced orchestrations established the Broadway musical "sound" for the forties, fifties, and much of the sixties. In all he is said to have scored nearly 300 musicals, although this count may include non-Broadway work.

BENNETT, WILDA (1894–1967) Born in Asbury Park, N.J., she made her debut as Conscience in *Everywoman* (1911), but was best known as a leading lady in musicals. Her most noteworthy successes were *The Only Girl* (1914), in which she introduced "When You're Away"; *Apple Blossoms*♦ (1919), in which she sang "You Are Free"; and the 1921 edition of the *Music Box Revue,*♦ in which she introduced "Say It with Music."

BENRIMO, J[OSEPH] HARRY (1874–1942) A theatrical jack-of-all-trades who often employed only his surname, he made his debut in his native San Francisco in 1892, playing there until 1897, when his performance as Hop Kee, the pipe-bowl vendor, in *The First Born* was seen by David Belasco,♦ who brought him east to re-create the role in New York. For the next two decades he appeared in important supporting roles in such plays as *The Conquerors*♦ (1898), *Lord and Lady Algy* (1899), *In the Palace of the King*♦ (1900), *Adrea*♦ (1905), *The Girl of the Golden West*♦ (1905), *The Rose of the Rancho*♦ (1906), *Beethoven* (1910), and *Maggie Pepper* (1911). In 1912, in collaboration with George C. Hazelton, Jr., he wrote the enormously popular *The Yellow Jacket,*♦ purportedly based on several classic Chinese dramas. He claimed to have made a study of Chinese theatre during his years in San Francisco. This was followed in 1915 by *Taking Chances,* which he and Agnes Morgan translated freely from a Continental comedy. In 1917 he collaborated with Harrison Rhodes on "a fantasy of Japan," *The Willow Tree.* Early on he proved his skill as a director, staging not only all of his own plays but many others, especially for the Shuberts.♦ After spending much of the 1920s in London, he returned to direct *Creoles* (1927), *The Well of Romance* (1930), and *The Right to Happiness* (1931). All three failed and he retired from the stage.

BENT, MARION, see *Rooney, Pat*

BENTLEY, ERIC [RUSSELL] (b. 1916) An English-born, versatile man of the theatre, he served as drama critic for *New Republic* from 1952 to 1956, wrote plays—and translated those of Bertolt Brecht♦ and others—and has been the author of numerous books on theatre, including many anthologies.

BERG, GERTRUDE [EDELSTEIN] (1899–1966) A stereotypical plump, homey Jewish mother, the New Yorker adapted her radio character of Molly Goldberg into a starring vehicle, *Me and Molly* (1948). Later she played Mrs. Jacoby, who falls in love with a rich Japanese, in *A Majority of One*♦ (1959) and Libby Hirsch, who employs psychoanalysis to help her family, in *Dear Me, the Sky is Falling* (1963).

BERGHOF, HERBERT (1909–90) Born in Vienna, he studied at the Vienna State Academy of Dramatic Art and with Max Reinhardt,♦ then spent many years performing in Austria and Germany. He first appeared before New York audiences in 1941. Although he played, among others, important roles in Ibsen♦ revivals of the late 1940s and early 1950s and in 1956 directed the Broadway production of *Waiting for Godot,*♦ he was best known as a leading teacher of acting. He taught at several noted institutions before founding his own studio in 1946, which he directed with his wife, Uta Hagen.♦

BERGMAN, INGRID (1915–82) The wholesome-looking, blonde Swedish actress made her New York debut as Julie in a 1940 revival of *Liliom.*♦ In the following year she toured California in the title role of *Anna Christie.*♦ After a highly successful career in films she returned to the stage in the title role of Maxwell Anderson's♦ *Joan of Lorraine* (1946). In 1967 she portrayed Deborah Harford, the loving mother of a weak son, in Eugene O'Neill's♦ *More Stately Mansions.* Her last appearances were in revivals, playing Lady Cicely in *Captain Brassbound's Conversion* (1972) and Constance Middleton in Maugham's♦ *The Constant Wife* (1975).

BERGNER, ELISABETH (1900–1986) The famed Viennese-born actress came to America as a refugee and first appeared as the unwed mother Gemma Jones in *Escape Me Never* (1935). After some years in London, she returned to New York where she had her biggest success as Sally, whose husband tries to poison her, in *The Two Mrs. Carrolls*♦ (1943). While playing the role, she successfully directed a comedy, *The Overtons* (1945). In 1946 she was *The Duchess of Malfi,* acting opposite Canada Lee.♦ Her last American appearance was touring as Mrs. Patrick Campbell♦ in *Dear Liar* in the early sixties.

BERKELEY, BUSBY [né WILLIAM BERKELEY ENOS] (1895–1976) Although best known for the mammoth precision dance routines he created in Warner Bros. films in the 1930s, he was briefly an important figure on Broadway. He came to New York from his native Los Angeles after touring in *The Man Who Came Back* (1917). For his New York debut he was a replacement in the role of Madame Lucy, the dress designer, in the original *Irene*♦ (1919). After several years directing stock in New England and Canada he returned to Broadway as choreographer for *Holka Polka* (1925). His dances were later seen in *The Wild Rose* (1926); *Lady Do* (1927); *A Connecticut*

Yankee♦ (1927); *The White Eagle* (1927); *Present Arms* (1928), in which he also played a supporting role; *Earl Carroll Vanities*♦ (1928); *Good Boy* (1928); *Rainbow* (1928); *Hello, Daddy* (1928); *Pleasure Bound* (1929); *A Night in Venice* (1929); *Broadway Nights* (1929); *The Street Singer* (1929), which he also directed and produced; *9:15 Revue* (1930); *International Revue* (1930); and *Sweet and Low* (1930). While his Broadway routines featured the popular precision routines of the day, they were marked as well by an imaginative irreverence that sent dancers scampering over furniture and props. In 1970 he supervised the successful revival of *No, No, Nanette.* ♦

Berkeley Square, a drama in three acts by John Lloyd Balderston. Produced by Gilbert Miller♦ and Leslie Howard♦ at the Lyceum Theatre.♦ November 4, 1929. 229 performances.

In 1784 a young American, Peter Standish, comes to London to marry Kate Pettigrew (Valerie Taylor). In 1928 his descendant, also named Peter Standish (Howard), has read all of his ancestor's diaries and correspondence and believes he knows the older man so well that he could exchange places with him, which he promptly does. But transported to the 18th century, things do not progress as smoothly for Standish as he had hoped. He is constantly making gaffes and giving away his special knowledge. For example, he knows what is in a gift box before it is opened and carelessly blurts out the secret. Most urgently, it is not the sharp-tongued Kate with whom he falls in love but her sister Helen (Margalo Gillmore♦). His upsetting behavior forces him to return to the 20th century. There, from a tombstone, he learns that Helen died shortly after the original Peter resumed his rightful role. He tells his 20th-century sweetheart that he has decided to remain a bachelor, so she leaves as he slowly reads the inscription he has copied from the grave.

Heywood Broun,♦ writing in the *Telegram,* called the work "easily the finest play now to be seen in New York," while Burns Mantle,♦ in his *Best Plays,*♦ observed, "It is neither fantasy nor straight drama, but an artful combination of the two. To speak of it as fantastic drama is to appear to ignore its finer qualities, its delicate and most appealing spiritual realities." The Philadelphia-born Balderston (1889–1954), who claimed descent from Betsy Ross, went to England as a journalist after failing to graduate from Columbia College. He wrote several successful plays while overseas, including a dramatization of *Dracula,* presented in New York in 1927. His *Red Planet* was produced in 1932. The idea for

Berkeley Square came from Henry James's unfinished *A Sense of the Past.* Balderston's last years were spent writing horror films in Hollywood.

BERLIN, IRVING [né ISRAEL BALINE] (1888–1989) Emigrating from Russia while still a boy, he took a job at sixteen as a singing waiter and began composing songs, publishing his first one, "Marie from Sunny Italy," in 1907. He soon was interpolating songs in Broadway shows and even sang some of his own melodies in the revue *Up and Down Broadway* (1910). The next year he won world-wide recognition with "Alexander's Ragtime Band." His first complete score was for *Watch Your Step*♦ (1914), which included "Simple Melody." *Stop! Look! Listen!* (1915) offered "I Love a Piano" and "The Girl on the Magazine Cover." Neither *The Century Girl* (1916), which he wrote in collaboration with Victor Herbert,♦ nor *The Cohan Revue of 1918,* which he wrote with George M. Cohan,♦ produced major songs, but his all-soldier show *Yip, Yip, Yaphank* (1918) produced "Oh, How I Hate To Get Up in the Morning" and "Mandy." He toured with the show and introduced the former song. His score for the *Ziegfeld Follies of 1919*♦ included "A Pretty Girl Is Like a Melody"♦ and "You'd Be Surprised," while that for the 1920 edition offered "Tell Me, Little Gypsy." In 1921, in partnership with Sam Harris,♦ he built the Music Box Theatre and initiated his own series of brilliant *Music Box Revues.* ♦ Out of its four editions came "Say It with Music," "Everybody Step," "Lady of the Evening," "What'll I Do?", and "All Alone." After abandoning the series, he composed the scores for a Marx Brothers♦ romp, *The Cocoanuts* (1925), and the *Ziegfeld Follies of 1927. Face the Music* (1932), a superb spoof of corruption, introduced "Let's Have Another Cup O' Coffee" and "Soft Lights and Sweet Music," and was followed by a masterful revue, *As Thousands Cheer*♦ (1933), from whose score came "Easter Parade" and "Heat Wave." "It's a Lovely Day Tomorrow" was the hit of another political satire, *Louisiana Purchase* (1940), which he co-produced. When World War II broke out Berlin again wrote an all-soldier show, *This Is the Army*♦ (1942), and again toured with it, singing "Oh, How I Hate To Get Up in the Morning." New songs included "I Left My Heart at the Stage Door Canteen" and "This Is the Army, Mr. Jones." In 1946, after the death of Jerome Kern,♦ who was to do its score, Berlin hastily composed the music for what proved to be his biggest hit, *Annie Get Your Gun.* ♦ Among its many popular songs were "Doin'

What Comes Natur'lly," "The Girl That I Marry," "I Got the Sun in the Morning," "There's No Business Like Show Business," "They Say It's Wonderful," and "You Can't Get a Man with a Gun." He next wrote and co-produced a musical about the arrival of the Statue of Liberty in America, *Miss Liberty* (1949), but the show was beset by a dismal book which dragged his fine score down with it. His last two musicals took light-hearted but jaundiced looks at politics. *Call Me Madam*◆ (1950), suggested by the career of the Washington hostess-turned-ambassador, Pearl Mesta, and starring Ethel Merman,◆ was a hit. "You're Just in Love," "It's a Lovely Day Today," "Marrying for Love," and "They Like Ike" were its most popular songs. In 1962 *Mr. President* closed his career on a down note.

Berlin was rarely the innovator that his rivals Kern, George Gershwin,◆ and Richard Rodgers◆ were. More than any of theirs his music changed with and took direction from the popular forms of the moment. Some accused him of consciously over-simple writing, both in his melodies and lyrics. But his uncanny melodic ear and his gift for expressing basic feelings succinctly made him probably the most popular composer of his era. Kern said, "Irving Berlin has no *place* in American music, he *is* American music."

Biography: *As Thousands Cheer: The Life of Irving Berlin,* Laurence Bergreen, New York, 1990.

BERNARD, BARNEY (1877–1924) A short, balding, mustachioed man with very slightly crossed eyes, he was born in Rochester, N.Y., and began his career as a Jewish dialect comedian in vaudeville. He played in San Francisco for many years, then found growing renown in a variety of productions. His greatest success came as Abe Potash in the *Potash and Perlmutter*◆ series, but he died at the height of his popularity.

BERNARD, BAYLE, see *Bernard, John*

BERNARD, JOHN (1756–1828) The English low comedian was an established favorite at Covent Garden by the time Thomas Wignell◆ signed him in 1797 to appear with the company at Philadelphia's Chestnut Street Theatre,◆ although a plague in that city forced him to make his American debut in New York. He became a leading artist in Philadelphia from later that year until 1803, when he joined the ensemble at Boston's Federal Street Theatre.◆ In 1806 he was appointed manager of the theatre; in 1810 he left the post to become one of the earliest major performers to make an extended tour of all American theatrical cities. He returned to Boston in 1816 and gave his final performance shortly before sailing for England in 1819. Although his repertory included such classic roles as Sir Peter Teazle, Puff, and Gratiano, he was most admired for his playing of comic parts in now forgotten plays, such as Nipperkin in *The Rival Soldiers* and Sheva in *The Jew.* Of this last the *Boston Weekly Magazine* noted, "Throughout his performance of this truly interesting character, we recognized his undiminished excellence in those powers of the pathetic and humourous united, which we have already noted as his most striking peculiarity as a comedian." After his death his *Retrospections of the Stage* was edited by his Boston-born son, WILLIAM BAYLE BERNARD (1807–75), who became a well-known London drama critic and playwright. Many of his early works had American settings and enjoyed some popularity in this country as well as in England. These included *Casco Bay* (1832), *The Kentuckian*◆ (1833), *The Nervous Man* (1833), and a version for Hackett◆ of *Rip Van Winkle* (1834).

BERNARD, SAM [né BARNETT] (1863–1927) The English-born comedian was brought to America while still a child. His first professional appearance was in vaudeville in the notorious Five Points section of New York. From 1885 to 1896 he toured in vaudeville, both in America and in England, and also accepted roles in several plays, in almost all cases portraying a German or Jewish immigrant. His playing came to the attention of two other great dialect comedians, Joe Weber◆ and Lew Fields,◆ who signed him on to the company at their new Music Hall. There the short, stocky, balding performer appeared in the team's celebrated travesties such as *The Geezer* (1896); *The Glad Hand; or, Secret Servants* (1897); and *Pousse Cafe* (1897). On leaving Weber and Fields he assumed his first starring role as Hermann Engel, the central figure in *The Marquis of Michigan* (1898). Similar roles followed in *A Dangerous Maid* (1898), *The Man in the Moon* (1899), *The Casino Girl* (1900), and *The Belle of Bohemia* (1900). He was reunited briefly with Weber and Fields in *Hoity Toity* (1901), then appeared in *The Silver Slipper* (1902). He scored a major success as Mr. Hoggenheimer in *The Girl from Kay's* (1903), and after playing in *The Rollicking Girl* (1905) he was starred in a vehicle written around that role in *The Rich Mr. Hoggenheimer* (1906). More dialect roles came in *Nearly a Hero* (1906), *The Girl and the Wizard* (1909), *He Came from Milwaukee* (1910), *All for the Ladies* (1912), *The Modiste Shop* (1913), *The Belle of Bond Street*

(1914), and *The Century Girl* (1916). In 1918 he portrayed Henry Block in *Friendly Enemies,*♦ a play about anti-German sentiments. He returned to musicals in *As You Were* (1920) and the *Music Box Revue 1921–1922,*♦ then wrote much of the material as well as starred in *Nifties of 1923*. His last show was a modernized version of *The Rich Mr. Hoggenheimer,* presented as *Piggy* (1927).

BERNEY, WILLIAM, see *Dark of the Moon*

BERNHARDT, SARAH [née BERNARD] (1844–1923) The great French actress had only recently made her front-page departure from the Comédie-Française and embarked on a career as an independent star when she made her American debut at Booth's Theatre on November 8, 1880. Wisely, she chose for her first appearance the role many American critics came to consider her best part, the doomed actress, the title role in *Adrienne Lecouvreur*. While she was no beauty, her frizzy red-gold hair, her thin, pale face with its sharp eyes, and her slim, almost frail body were not unattractive. She had a voice variously described as like a "golden bell" and the "silver sound of running water." Her notoriety was such that she had been guaranteed $1000 a performance plus all traveling expenses, so that when her sell-out tour was over she had earned over $156,000 for a series of performances that grossed the producer, Henry E. Abbey,♦ $553,000. Including her first visit and her last, in 1916, she toured America nine times. The most unusual tour was that which covered the 1905–06 season. Defying the Theatrical Syndicate or Trust,♦ whose terms she refused to accept, she was forced, like Mrs. Fiske♦ and others before her, to play in tents and oddly assorted makeshift playhouses. Except on rare occasions in later years, she always performed in French. From the start most American critics considered her best in emotional roles and much weaker in truly tragic parts. The *Herald* observed, "In depicting human suffering she seems to absolutely control every organ of her body—her cheek blanches, tears come at her bidding . . . but where her lines call for the grand and imposing effects of concentrated passion . . . Mlle Bernhardt lacked breadth, force and passion." Among her most celebrated vehicles were *Frou-Frou, Phèdre, Ernani, La Dame aux Camélias, Jeanne d'Arc, L'Aiglon,* and *La Tosca*.

Autobiography: *Memories of My Life,* New York, 1923.

BERNSTEIN, ALINE [née FRANKAU] (1881–1955) The New York-born designer originally intended to become a portrait painter. When her interest in costume design surfaced, she worked with Irene and Alice Lewisohn, then designed costumes as well as some sets for the Neighborhood Playhouse's♦ productions of *The Little Clay Cart* and *The Grand Street Follies* (both 1924). Her later designs were seen in such notable plays as *Ned McCobb's Daughter*♦ (1926), the revivals of the Civic Repertory Theatre,♦ *Tomorrow and Tomorrow*♦ (1931), *Reunion in Vienna*♦ (1931), *The Children's Hour*♦ (1934), *The Male Animal*♦ (1940), *Harriet*♦ (1943), and *The Happy Time*♦ (1950). In 1937 she was one of the founders of the Museum of Costume Art,♦ which was eventually absorbed by the Metropolitan Museum of Art. Helen Hayes♦ recalled a costume she designed for Miss Hayes's 1925 appearance in *Caesar and Cleopatra*♦ as "hand-dyed blue tafetta appliques on cloth of gold in the form of little feathers like the wings of ibis. It was a work of art." Thomas Wolfe, with whom she had a prolonged affair, wrote about her as Esther Jack in *The Web and the Rock*.

Biography: *Aline,* Carole Klein, New York, 1979.

BERNSTEIN, LEONARD (1918–90) Born in Lawrence, Mass., and educated at Harvard and the Curtis Institute of Music, he had earned recognition as a symphonic conductor and composer of the ballet "Fancy Free," about three sailors on the town in wartime New York, before adapting that ballet into a musical comedy. The new work was called *On the Town*♦ (1944) and included such memorable songs as "Lucky To Be Me" and "New York, New York." In 1950 he wrote music for *Peter Pan,*♦ then scored a major success with *Wonderful Town*♦ (1953), recalled for "Ohio," "A Quiet Girl," and "Wrong Note Rag." In 1956 his score for the operetta *Candide*♦ included "Glitter and Be Gay" and the now famous overture. Another musical, *West Side Story*♦ (1957), marked a complete change of venue and tone and offered "Maria," "Something's Coming," and "Tonight." He suffered a quick failure with *1600 Pennsylvania Avenue* (1976). The musical theatre historian Stanley Green♦ noted, "Bernstein has shown a certain eclecticism in his work for the theatre that has made it less of an individual expression than highly technical, remarkably effective music with each score sounding almost as if it were the work of a different man." Away from the legitimate stage, Bernstein served an extended tenure as conductor of the New York Philharmonic and directed many other internationally famous orchestras. His compositions covered a wide range, including opera and a Mass.

Biography: *Bernstein,* Joan Peyser, New York, 1987.

Bertha, the Sewing Machine Girl, a melodrama in four acts by Theodore Kremer.♦ Produced at the American Theatre. August 13, 1906. 9 performances.

Bertha Sloane (Edith Browning) and her blind sister Jessie (Leona Francis) come to New York, where Bertha hopes to claim their late father's estate and also earn enough money in a sweatshop to help cure her sister's blindness. Harold Cutting (W. A. Tully), whose father murdered Bertha's father for his money, is determined to thwart the girl, as is Olive Roberts (Rose Tiffany), Harold's fiancée. Together they chloroform Bertha and dump her in a lake. Tom Jennings (W. L. Gibson), who has fallen in love with Bertha, and Mrs. Katzenkopf (Ada St. Alva), the sisters' kind landlady, rescue her. Later Harold and Olive tie Bertha on a belt that is moving into the huge wheels of a machine, and when Tom and Mrs. Katzenkopf again rescue her, the villains frame Bertha for a policeman's murder. Bertha defends herself in court and wrests a confession from Harold.

Several different plays with the same title toured at this time. All were loosely based on a serial which had run in the late 1860s in the *New York Weekly.* Indeed, a version by Charles Foster, in which the heroine was called Bertha Bascome and in which her agonies, while equally harrowing, were not always the same as in Kremer's dramatization, began touring as early as 1871. Kremer's later version seems to have been by far the most popular, although neither it nor any other redaction enjoyed much success with more sophisticated playgoers.

BEST, EDNA (1900–74) An English actress at once winsome and biting, she first appeared in America in the 1920s in *These Charming People* (1925) and *The Constant Nymph* (1926). However, it was not until late in her career that she again distinguished herself, often in failures. Among these plays were the double bill of *The Browning Version* and *Harlequinade* (1949); *Jane* (1952), in which she played the title role; *The Ladies of the Corridor* (1953); *Mademoiselle Colombe* (1954); and *Quadrille* (1954). She was the wife of actor Herbert Marshall.

Best Little Whorehouse in Texas, The, a musical comedy in two acts. Book by Larry L. King and Peter Masterson. Lyrics and music by Carol Hall. Produced at the Entermedia Theatre. April 17, 1978. 1,576 performances.

For decades The Chicken Ranch, where clients could pay in produce, has been a perfectly respectable brothel. Currently operated by Miss Mona Stangley (Carlin Glynn), who keeps her girls strictly in line, it numbers among its friends Sheriff Dodd (Henderson Forsythe) as well as notable politicians and football players. But "Watchdog" Thorpe (Clint Allmon), a self-glorifying regional television preacher, takes aim against the establishment and before long another fine old Texas tradition bites the dust.

Based on a real incident, the musical was so well received at its off-Broadway premiere that it was immediately hustled to Broadway. Reasonably good, if raunchy, fun, the show offered the added attraction of a country-and-western style score to lure visiting firemen. Tommy Tune's♦ inventive staging was also an asset.

Best Man, The, a play in three acts by Gore Vidal.♦ Produced by the Playwrights' Company♦ at the Morosco Theatre. March 31, 1960. 520 performances.

The leading contenders in a battle for the presidential nomination are William Russell (Melvyn Douglas♦), a gentlemanly liberal of the old school, and Joseph Cantwell (Frank Lovejoy), a calculating, unscrupulous Senator. Cantwell obtains a damaging psychiatric analysis once made of Russell and releases it to the press. A feisty ex-President, Arthur Hockstadter (Lee Tracy♦), tells Cantwell, "It's not that I mind your being a bastard . . . It's your being such a *stupid* bastard, I object to." Hockstadter leaves the Cantwell camp and joins Russell, whom he urges to make public Cantwell's history of homosexuality. Russell refuses, withdraws from the race, and throws his support to a third candidate.

A wittily written, shrewdly observed comedy, it was peopled with figures playgoers recognized as thinly disguised modern political celebrities: Russell was not unlike Adlai Stevenson; Cantwell, Senator Joseph McCarthy; and Hockstadter, Harry Truman.

Best Plays A series begun in 1920 by Burns Mantle,♦ the full title of the first volume was *The Best Plays of 1919–20 and the Year Book of the Drama in America.* Each year a new edition contains extended excerpts from ten selected plays, plus a general review of the season and vital statistics on all of the season's productions including casts and brief synopses of plots. In 1933 Mantle, in collaboration with

Garrison P. Sherwood, issued a single volume called *Best Plays of 1909–1919,* and some years later issued another volume entitled *Best Plays of 1899– 1909.* After Mantle's death the editorship was assumed in succession by John Chapman,♦ Louis Kronenberger,♦ Henry Hewes, and Otis L. Guernsey, Jr.♦ Since the 1985–86 edition Jeffrey Sweet has collaborated with Guernsey. In 1955 Chapman and Sherwood issued a special volume called *Best Plays of 1894–1899.* The publication of this volume, coupled with Odell's♦ *Annals of the New York Stage,* ♦ meant that a complete record was in print of every major theatrical production mounted in New York City. The two sets are invaluable to both theatre-lovers and scholars.

BEVAN, Donald, see *Stalag 17*

Beyond the Horizon, a tragedy in three acts by Eugene O'Neill.♦ Produced by John D. Williams♦ at the Morosco Theatre. February 2, 1920. 111 performances. PP.

Robert Mayo (Richard Bennett♦) has grown up on his family's New England farm dreaming of mysterious, faraway places. He is anything but the "husky, sun-bronzed, handsome" natural-born farmer that his brother Andrew (Edward Arnold) is. Robert finally hopes to fulfill his dreams by sailing on his Uncle Dick's ship. Both Robert and Andrew are in love with Ruth Atkins (Helen MacKellar). The day before Robert is to sail, Ruth persuades him to marry her. Andrew sails in his stead. Three years pass. Robert has made a mess of both the farm and his marriage. His only passion is his sickly young daughter Mary (Elfin Finn). His wife and his mother (Mary Jeffery) belittle him and hold Andrew up to him as an example. Robert retorts that Andrew's letters show he has learned nothing from his travels. When Andrew does return, Robert proves correct, for his experiences have made Andrew hard and unloving. He cruelly tells Ruth, who realizes too late that she really loved him, he had forgotten about her long ago. He goes back to sea, and another five years pass. Mary dies, Ruth grows apathetic, and, with Robert dying of consumption, the farm is in ruins. Andrew returns. Robert asks Andrew to move his bed so that "I can watch the rim of the hills and dream of what is waiting beyond." He urges Andrew to marry Ruth after he dies and save the farm. Andrew berates Ruth for her behavior and confesses that he had always loved his brother "better'n anybody in the world." He demands that

Ruth tell Robert she truly loves him and will do what he wants. Ruth at first refuses, but when she finally agrees it is too late. Robert is dead. "God damn you!" Andrew yells at her. "You never told him!"

No major producer wanted to mount the play, but Williams, pressed by Bennett, finally agreed to give it at a special matinee. The response was so overwhelming that more matinees were offered, and on March 9 the play began a regular run at the Little Theatre. "By that time," Burns Mantle♦ wrote shortly afterwards, "there were many who were willing to accept this first long play from Eugene O'Neill's pen as representing the closest approach any native author has yet made to *the* great American play." For no small number of students of the theatre this stark, unyielding work marks the beginnings of modern American drama. However, one modern critic, Howard Taubman, has noted, "In the light of today's uncompromising freshness of language and unsparing probing of character, it is tame . . . What impressed people eager for a new voice to lead the American theatre out of its wilderness of mediocrity now strikes us as essentially sentimental . . . a reversion to romanticism; it had a sophomoric ring; it was rhetorical rather than true." Others would reply that O'Neill's very romanticism coupled with his bleak outlook was a major source of his strength.

Bianca Visconti; or, The Heart Overtasked, a tragedy in five acts by Nathaniel Parker Willis. ♦ Produced by Edmund Simpson♦ at the Park Theatre.♦ August 24, 1837. In repertory.

Although their families have long been enemies, Bianca Visconti (Josephine Clifton♦) marries Francesco Sforza (J. K. Mason), a 15th-century Duke of Milan. He is a high-minded, ambitious man, but cold and unloving. Nevertheless, Bianca loyally defends his every action. The Viscontis and the other noble houses are jealous of the Duke's power, so plot to assassinate him. Bianca overhears the scheme and arranges to substitute her loving, playful page Giulio (Charles Mestayer). Only after Giulio's death does she learn he was really her brother. The shock drives her insane, and she dies of a broken heart.

Awarded one of the many prizes given at the time to encourage native drama, Willis saw the play as a defense of democracy against the forces of aristocracy. However unsympathetic the character of the Duke may seem to modern readers, he was perceived by Willis as an idealist fighting against these forces.

Big Bonanza, The, a comedy in four acts by Augustin Daly.♦ Produced by Daly at the Fifth Avenue Theatre.♦ February 17, 1875. 137 performances.

Lucretia Cawallader (Annie Graham) is a stuffy, domineering wife, annoyed by a husband who "insists on doing what he calls enjoying his own home." She is especially worried since her daughter Eugenia (Fanny Davenport♦) is returning home from school and is of marriageable age. When she learns that her daughter was escorted from the station by a shabbily dressed young man, she is horrified. Her distress is interrupted by the arrival of her husband's cousin, Professor Agassiz Cawallader (James Lewis♦). Lucretia's warning to her husband Jonathan (Charles Fisher♦) not to argue with his cousin goes unheeded. After disputing the merits of their respective occupations, Jonathan gives the Professor $30,000 and bets him that he cannot invest it successfully for a month. The Professor's problems learning the ways and odd terms of the market are compounded by the arrival of his wife's nephew Bob (John Drew♦), a generous, amiable young man fresh from the mines out west. In the end Agassiz's buying and selling come to naught, but he learns to his relief that Jonathan's clerk disobeyed his instructions and he has lost nothing. At the same time, Jonathan and Lucretia discover that Bob was the shabbily dressed young man who helped Eugenia at the station. They agree to let their daughter marry him.

Daly based his play on Gustav von Moser's German comedy *Ultimo.* Its success relieved him of financial difficulties at his new theatre. The play itself succeeded despite largely negative reviews. William Winter♦ wrote that the piece "has no claim to consideration. The dialogue drivels through four acts of hopeless commonplace in which there is not one spark of wit, not one bright thought, not even a gleam of smartness. The play can hardly be said to have a plot." Although Winter was correct about the story never quite realizing its early promises, audiences disagreed about its wit. Because of loose copyright laws several competing versions of von Moser's play were also mounted. Daly's was by far the most successful, and was revived profitably as late as 1899.

Big River: The Adventures of Huckleberry Finn, a musical in two acts. Book by William Hauptman. Lyrics and music by Roger Miller. Produced at the Eugene O'Neill Theatre. April 25, 1985. 1005 performances.

Huck (Daniel H. Jenkins) and a runaway slave, Jim (Ron Richardson), sail the Mississippi on their raft, meeting such figures as The King (Bob Gunton), The Duke (Rene Auberjonois), and Tom Sawyer (John Short), much as they do in Mark Twain's classic.

Coming at the end of a season filled with musical disappointments and disasters, the show received a warmer welcome than it might have otherwise. But it drew family audiences and remains popular in stock and in schools.

Billboard The theatrical trade sheet was first published in Cincinnati in 1894. Begun as a monthly, it became a weekly in 1900. With increasing competition from New York-based publications, it soon began to emphasize amateur theatre, carnivals, and circuses. In recent decades its main concern has been the popular music field. For many years, starting in 1920, it published an annual *Billboard Index of the Legitimate Stage.*

Biloxi Blues, a comedy in two acts by Neil Simon.♦ Produced by Emanuel Azenberg♦ and others at the Neil Simon Theatre. March 28, 1985. 524 performances.

Eugene Jerome (Matthew Broderick) is still determined to become a writer, although Uncle Sam has different, if temporary, plans for him. Drafted into the army he resolutely continues to hone his writing skills by keeping a notebook commenting on his fellow draftees and his army life. He also resolves to stay alive and to lose his virginity. He succeeds, despite the comic contretemps his notes and his young lusts create.

The second in Simon's semi-autobiographical trilogy, falling between *Brighton Beach Memoirs*♦ and *Broadway Bound*♦, it was a hit, if slightly less popular than the others.

BINGHAM, AMELIA [SMILEY] (1869–1927) Born in Hicksville, Ohio, and educated at Ohio Wesleyan, she elected a theatrical career despite the vigorous opposition of her deeply religious family. Her earliest appearance was on the West Coast, playing in a company headed by McKee Rankin.♦ She came to New York in 1892 to play in a series of melodramas including *The Struggle of Life, The Power of Gold,* and *A Man Among Men.* Her first important role came opposite Robert Hilliard♦ in a failure called *The Mummy* (1896). Thereafter she played for several seasons for Charles Frohman♦ in such plays as *His Excellency the Governor* (1899) and *Hearts Are Trumps* (1900). In late 1900 she determined to become New York's first important actress-manager since Laura Keene.♦ To that end she leased the Bijou Theatre and enjoyed a major success with her first production, Clyde Fitch's♦ *The Climbers*♦ (1901), in which she played the compassionate Mrs. Sterling. Her subsequent productions were more or less failures, although *The Frisky Mrs. Johnson* (1903) had a modest run largely because of the publicity that followed her highly vocal battle with the critics who panned it. After that she played in stock until she returned in *The Lilac Room* in 1907. Another battle with the critics ensued, but this time the publicity was no help, and after a fight with the play's authors as well, the production closed in its first week. For several seasons thereafter she toured successfully in vaudeville, performing "Big Moments from Great Plays." From 1913 through 1916 she played in *The New Henrietta,* a modernization of Bronson Howard's♦ 1887 hit. Her last appearance was in a supporting role in *The Pearl of Great Price* (1926).

Biography, a comedy in three acts by S. N. Behrman.♦ Produced by the Theatre Guild♦ at the Guild Theatre. December 12, 1932. 267 performances.

Marion Froude (Ina Claire♦) is a celebrated artist who has had many lovers all over the world but no husbands. One of her earliest loves, Leander Nolan (Jay Fassett), now a successful lawyer and running for Senator, comes to have his portrait painted. He tells Marion that he is engaged to be married to the daughter of the publisher who is promoting his campaign. At the same time, Richard Kurt (Earle Larimore♦), a radical young editor, appears with an offer to publish Marion's autobiography. Although at first she finds Kurt "bumptious and unsufferable," she quickly develops a fondness for him. When Nolan learns that Marion has agreed to write her life history he is furious, for he knows it will ruin his chances of election. But the behavior of his prospective father-in-law and his fiancée makes him wonder if he really doesn't still love Marion. Kurt also falls for Marion. Marion recognizes that she would be happy neither with Nolan, who has grown too conservative, nor with Kurt, who is hopelessly hate-filled. She destroys her manuscript. Receiving an offer to paint some Hollywood celebrities, she tells her maid to pack. She will resume her wayfaring, wayward existence.

Although *Time* dismissed the work as "a play which is not of more importance than the over-stuffed situation with which it is concerned," most critics agreed with Robert Garland of the *World-Telegram* who noted, "The Theatre Guild has gotten around to a play worthy of the high position it occupies in the history of the modern American theatre . . . adult and provocative . . . an evening of rare playgoing felicity." It remains Behrman's finest work.

BIRCH, [WILLIAM] BILLY (1831–97) Born in Utica, N.Y., he was only thirteen when he began his life-long career in minstrelsy by appearing as part of an amateur performance in nearby New Hartford. Two years later he turned professional, joining the Raymond Minstrels at Stamford, Conn. For eighteen years he moved across the country playing with a variety of blackface ensembles and expanding both his skills and reputation. The height of his career came when he co-founded the San Francisco Minstrels♦ in 1864. Although he occasionally left the troupe to form other bands, he returned to it regularly all through its long history. His last appearance was in 1890 with William Henry Rice's World's Fair Minstrels. A heavy-set but agile and lively comedian, he was called "one of the most original performers in the business, on the bone end." Audiences long recalled his clowning as Zeb Doolittle, a burglar trying to rob sleepwalkers without waking them, in the skit "Pleasant Companions."

BIRCH, PATRICIA (b. 1934?) A native of Scarsdale, N.Y., she studied with such prominent dancers as Martha Graham and Merce Cunningham before first performing on Broadway in the chorus of *Goldilocks* (1958). She turned to choreography with her work for *You're a Good Man, Charlie Brown*♦ (1967). Her dances were subsequently seen in such shows as *A Little Night Music*♦ (1973), the 1974 revival of *Candide,*♦ *Pacific Overtures* (1976), and *They're Playing Our Song*♦ (1979). Although she remains active, her subsequent work for Broadway has been in short-lived works.

BIRD, ROBERT MONTGOMERY (1806–54) Born into a well-to-do New Castle, Del., family, he was four when his father died, whereupon he was shipped off to a wealthy uncle who enrolled him in a school run by a vicious martinet. He remained there, unhappy, until he was fourteen when he was reunited with his mother in Philadelphia. There he attended German-town Academy and then the medical school at the University of Pennsylvania. He had often written poetry, but while at medical school or soon thereafter turned to play-writing, finishing three plays in short order. *News of the Night; or, A Trip to Niagara,* a farce set in Philadelphia, in which two nieces deceive their miserly guardian, displayed strong influences of Plautus, Terence, and Ben Jonson; *The Cowled Lover* employed a Romeo and Juliet motif, albeit the lovers were murdered by the heroine's father; and *Caridorf; or, The Avenger* was a Gothic horror piece set in Vienna. A fourth, unfinished play, *'Twas All for the Best; or, 'Tis a Notion,* was a comedy of manners reminiscent of Congreve. None of these plays was produced in his lifetime. A year later he wrote *The City Looking Glass: A Philadelphia Comedy,* which held up its mirror to metropolitan low life. It too was not produced. In 1830 he submitted *Pelopidas; or, The Fall of the Polemarchs* to one of Edwin Forrest's♦ play-writing contests. The play, taken from Plutarch's account of the Theban revolt against the Spartans, won first prize. But Forrest refused to produce it, contending it lacked sufficient dramatic incidents. The actor was far more receptive to the author's next play, *The Gladiator*♦ (1831), recounting a slave insurrection. It was an immediate success and remained one of Forrest's most popular offerings. In 1832 Forrest produced his *Oralloossa,*♦ concerned with the assassination of Pizarro, and two years later mounted his best play, *The Broker of Bogota,*♦ in which a trusting father is betrayed by his children. Bird also revised *Metamora*♦ for the actor, but shortly thereafter had a falling out with him, when Forrest refused to pay several thousand dollars due him. Discouraged, he abandoned the theatre and turned to writing novels, one of which, *Nick of the Woods; or, The Jibbenainosay,*♦ was dramatized by Louisa Medina in 1838 and long remained a stage favorite. From 1841 to 1843 he taught at the Philadelphia Medical College, and then became an editor of the staunchly Whig Philadelphia *North American and United States Gazette.*

Quinn♦ has written: "Had he lived in a time when the American playwright received fair treatment, it is not easy to put a limit to his possible achievements. For he had a rare sense of dramatic effect, a power to visualize historic scenes and characters, to seize the spirit of the past out of the mass of facts and, in a few lines, to fuse those facts into life."

Biography: *The Life and Dramatic Works of Robert Montgomery Bird,* Clement E. Foust, New York, 1919.

Bird of Paradise, The, a play in three acts by Richard Walton Tully.♦ Produced by Oliver Morosco♦ at Daly's Theatre. January 8, 1912. 112 performances.

On a languid Hawaiian island, a promising young American scientist, Paul Wilson (Lewis S. Stone), falls in love with a beautiful if superstitious native princess, Luana (Laurette Taylor♦). They marry, but the marriage destroys all of Wilson's drive and ambition. Neither an attempt by fellow Americans to foment a revolution which would make Luana queen nor a move back to civilization seems to help. When Kilauea, long dormant, suddenly begins to rumble, Luana reads it as a sign that the gods are angry with her and demand a human sacrifice. To appease the gods and to give her husband a chance to fulfill his early promise she throws herself into the crater.

Although the play opened in New York to largely favorable notices, the producer's disagreements with several theatre owners cut short its Broadway run. On the road, however, its several companies turned it into one of the biggest money-makers of its era. In 1930 it was made into an unsuccessful operetta, *Luana.*

Bitter Sweet Noel Coward's♦ operetta was presented in America by Florenz Ziegfeld♦ at the Ziegfeld Theatre♦ on November 5, 1929, just short of four months after its London premiere. Its story centered on a great lady whose niece must choose between marrying for love or position. The lady recounts her own similar history to help her niece make the proper selection. British singing actress Evelyn Laye was starred. Although the musical was well received, its short run of 157 performances can be attributed to the onset of the Depression. In retrospect the show can be seen as virtually the last in the school of traditional operetta. Among its many successful songs were "I'll See You Again" and "Zigeuner."

Black Crook, The, a melodramatic musical spectacle in four acts. Book by Charles M. Barras. Lyrics by numerous contributors. Original music by Thomas Baker (with much borrowing and continual interpolating). Produced by William Wheatley♦ and Henry C. Jarrett♦ at Niblo's Garden.♦ September 12, 1866. 475 performances.

The "Arch Fiend" Zamiel (E. B. Holmes) induces Hertzog (C. H. Morton), the Black Crook, to deliver a human soul into his power once a year on New Year's Eve. Hoping to snare the painter Rudolf (G. C. Boniface♦), who has been unjustly imprisoned, Hertzog frees him and promises to lead him to a large cache of gold. On his way to the treasure Rudolf saves a dove's life. The dove is really Stalacta (Annie Kemp Bowler), Queen of the Golden Realm. She warns him of his danger, removes him to fairyland, and helps him win Amina (Rose Morton).

Principal songs: March of the Amazons · You Naughty, Naughty Men (G. Bicknell/T. Kennick)

Allegedly mounted at a cost of $50,000, the musical was the most successful Broadway play up to its time and the first to run for over a year. It has generally been believed that the production came about when a French ballet troupe, scheduled to perform at the Academy of Music, was deprived of a stage after the theatre burned down. The troupe was hastily combined with a dramatic company about to present Barras's metaphysical melodrama. A 1954 musical, *The Girl in Pink Tights,* retold the tale. Recent research by Stanley Green,♦ however, has called this story into question. No small part of the musical's fame came from its long line of choryphees (chorus girls) in what were euphemistically called pink tights, but were actually flesh colored. Companies quickly sprang up all across the country, and the spectacle was revived regularly throughout the rest of the century. Christopher Morley and Agnes de Mille♦ staged a popular reconstruction in 1929. Barras (1826–73) was a Philadelphia-born actor-playwright. Most of his works were written-to-order vehicles for contemporary favorites. Clara Morris♦ paints a vivid picture of him in her autobiography.

Blackbirds A series of revues, with black casts, produced by Lew Leslie♦ both in London and New York. Of the four American editions, in 1928, 1930, 1933, and 1939, only the first was a success. Its cast included Bill Robinson♦ and Adelaide Hall. Robinson sang and danced "Doin' the New Low-Down," but the most memorable numbers were "Diga Diga Doo," sung by Miss Hall, and "I Can't Give You Anything But Love," sung by Aida Ward, Willard McLean, and Miss Hall. The Eubie Blake♦ standard, "Memories of You," came from the failed 1930 edition, where it was sung by Minto Cato. The shows, relatively simple in mounting, emphasized song and dance. What little comedy there was represented the stereotypical black humor of the era.

BLACKMER, SIDNEY (1895–1973) Born in Salisbury, N.C., he studied law before turning to the stage. He made his first New York appearance as a Young Man in *The Morris Dance* in 1917, then played several other supporting roles prior to serving in World War I. Upon his return he replaced Henry Hull♦ as the leading man in *39 East.* Thereafter the tall, dark-haired, classic-featured actor was a most sought-after leading man, but although he had the principal male role in nearly twenty plays over the next decade, he was never in a major hit. Among his highly praised performances were Aaron Winterfield, the mountaineer who

inherits a fortune, in *The Mountain Man* (1921); Eugene Thorne, the loyal illegitimate son, in *The Love Child* (1922); Tony Blunt, the explorer, in *Quarantine* (1924); and Janos, the virtuous forester, in Belasco's♦ *Mima* (1928). Following a long career in films he came back to Broadway, where once again he was awarded good roles in mediocre plays. His luck changed dramatically in 1950 when he portrayed the failed, alcoholic Doc in *Come Back, Little Sheba.*♦ He won a Tony Award♦ for this performance. His last Broadway appearance was as Paul Cleary, the accused's attorney, in *A Case of Libel* (1963).

Blacks in American Theatre and Drama Despite the number of blacks in America during much of the colonial era, their lack of social position and the concomitant prejudices denied them any place in the earliest American theatre. Similarly, because virtually all dramatic entertainment during these years was of English origin and only infrequently depicted blacks, they were rarely presented as characters in plays Americans of the time saw. The most notable exception was, of course, Othello, who was always performed by a white actor. Later Thomas Southern's *Oroonoko,* reputedly based on the real story of an African prince sold into slavery during the time of Charles II, was briefly popular. In 1769 the John Street Theatre♦ saw the American premiere of Isaac Bickerstaffe and Charles Dibdin's comic opera *The Padlock,* which had first been presented the year before at Drury Lane and which introduced the comically drunk, profane character of Mungo, who nonetheless suggested the plight and bitterness of his race at the hands of cruel or thoughtless whites:

> Night and day 'tis the same;
> My pain is deir game;
> Me wish to de Lord me was dead!
> Whate'er's to be done
> Poor black must run.

This duality of the illiterate, shiftless yet sometimes shifty buffoon and of the shamefully downtrodden appeared frequently in characterizations of blacks for the next hundred or more years, although it was the comic stereotype that prevailed. Lewis Hallam, Jr.,♦ was the first American Mungo. The popularity of Defoe's *Robinson Crusoe* led to numerous stage versions, such as *Robinson Crusoe and Harlequin Friday* (1786) and *The Bold Buccaneers; or, The Discovery of Robinson Crusoe* (1817), which offered a similarly clowning Friday.

In recent years it has been suggested that Raccoon, a character in the first American comic opera,

The Disappointment (1767), was meant to represent a black, but this is debatable. However, minor black characters did begin to appear in American plays at this time. The figure of Ralpho in *The Candidates,* a play written before 1770 but possibly never mounted, could well be the first black depicted in American drama.

Inevitably, as the free black community grew in the North some blacks took to the stage. In the 1820s an actor named James Hewlett♦ apparently headed a small company in New York that performed such works as *Richard III* and *Othello.* The first black actor of distinction, Ira Aldridge,♦ served behind the scenes with some white companies and acted with black troupes, but, unable to find work commensurate with his abilities, spent most of his career in Europe.

As a rule only white men played blacks. Actresses, out of prejudice or vanity, long demurred, and even Edwin Forrest,♦ failing to convince any leading lady to play in blackface opposite him in *The Tailor in Distress* (1823), drafted a black washerwoman for the role.

The stereotyped black was given widespread popularity by T. D. Rice♦ in the 1830s. His great song and dance turn, "Jim Crow," besides reinforcing the standard stage picture of the black, presaged the imminent rise of the minstrel show♦ and was a harbinger of the importance of blacks and black music to our lyric stage. So was the dancing of William Henry Lane,♦ a black who performed as Master Juba, and who helped evolve the Irish jig into contemporary black stepping.

Within a few years of the rise of minstrelsy, the growing abolition sentiment in the North spawned a number of protest dramas. By far the most famous and effective was the dramatization of Harriet Beecher Stowe's *Uncle Tom's Cabin,♦* which from 1852 on was for many years the most successful contemporary American play. Although in retrospect its characterizations betray much of the condescension toward blacks long patent, it was a cogent argument for freedom, if not real equality, for slaves. Not all attempts were successful, and even the dramatization of Mrs. Stowe's *Dred* found only small audiences. Another extremely popular work of the time, Dion Boucicault's♦ *The Octoroon,♦* took an equivocal stance, depicting slavery and the Southern viewpoint with some approbation, but decrying the plight of an innocent half-breed.

In the very late 1870s and in the 1880s Edward Harrigan's♦ portraits of blacks were among the best-known and most interesting on the American stage. Although all of Harrigan's figures verged on caricatures—and these included his Germans, Italians, Jews, and fellow Irishmen—they were all drawn with a compassion and depth of understanding unique for the day. Thus, one of his most famous figures was Mrs. Welcome Allup or Rebecca Allup, a sassy but wise maid, who was always played in blackface by Harrigan's great partner, Tony Hart. ♦ Indeed, Harrigan created a whole society of memorable black figures.

As Harrigan's career was closing, blacks began to develop a theatre of their own, largely musical. After the Civil War blacks had organized their own minstrel troupes and later turned to writing black musicals, patterned after contemporary white musicals and originally offered only in theatres catering to blacks. When black ragtime entered our musical mainstream these black songs began to be heard by highly receptive white audiences, and before long black shows, both written and performed by blacks, were mounted in regular theatres. The first of these was presented by E. E. Rice♦ as an afterpiece of a summer bill on the roof of the Casino Theatre♦ in 1898. Called *The Origin of the Cake Walk,* it was more popularly known by its subtitle, *Clorindy.* ♦ However, the most popular black musical comedies were those starring Bert Williams♦ and his partner George Walker. They included *In Dahomey♦* (1903), *Abyssinia* (1906), and *Bandanna Land* (1908). The Johnson♦ brothers, Will Marion Cook,♦ and Paul Dunbar♦ were among the leading writers. In 1910 Williams joined the *Ziegfeld Follies,♦* becoming the first black entertainer to receive equal billing with whites in a Broadway show.

The vogue for these black musicals quickly passed, and not until the 1920s did blacks truly begin to make a mark on Broadway. Eugene O'Neill♦ had employed black figures in some of his early one-act plays, but his *Emperor Jones♦* (1920), with Charles Gilpin♦ playing the memorable title role, created the first important black figure in original American dramatic literature. He later wrote an interesting study of an interracial marriage, *All God's Chillun Got Wings♦* (1924). Other important black plays of the era, all written by whites, included *In Abraham's Bosom♦* (1926) and *Porgy♦* (1927). Whatever their authorship, these plays allowed theatregoers to see the fine black actors of the day—Charles Gilpin, Paul Robeson,♦ Rose McClendon♦—in significant roles. But the idea that blacks could receive an open welcome and logical casting in black roles was not yet prevalent. Thus many black characters in contemporary plays were performed by whites in blackface, one of the most notable being Lenore Ulric,♦ who assumed the title part of the black prostitute in *Lulu Belle*♦ (1926).

The 1920s also saw a revival of interest in black musicals, sparked by the runaway success of *Shuffle Along*♦ (1921), whose songs were written by the black team of Noble Sissle and Eubie Blake.♦ But these musicals still trafficked in stereotypes that had been a theatrical stock in trade for two centuries and in plots very like those employed in the Williams and Walker shows. Many, like the *Blackbirds*♦ series, were plotless revues. A few musicals written by whites, such as *Deep River* (1926), *Show Boat*♦ (1927), and *Great Day* (1929) attempted to look at the black predicament with fresh eyes, though even *Show Boat* used a white actress to portray one of its leading black figures. But the lyric for that musical's "Ol' Man River" expressed sentiments not unlike those of Mungo's 160 years before.

The 1930s saw a number of prominent black actors and entertainers play roles on Broadway but usually in all-black productions or in specialty numbers. Ethel Waters♦ was a major song-and-dance figure but she starred mainly in revues with white casts, where her numbers could be separated from the rest of the show—in *As Thousands Cheer*♦ (1933) she sang the moving "Supper Time," about a black mother whose husband was lynched, as well as the exuberant "Heat Wave." Only in *Cabin in the Sky*♦ (1940) did she have a role in a plotted musical, this time with an all-black cast. Twice in her later career—in *Mamba's Daughters* (1939) and *The Member of the Wedding*♦ (1950)—she gave memorable performances in dramas. Bill Robinson♦ was the most famous black song-and-dance man of the period, but he was relegated to the all-black *Blackbirds* revues, and later to an ineffectual Gilbert♦ and Sullivan♦ parody, *The Hot Mikado* (1939).

Many of the period's experimental operas and musicals made use of all-black casts. The Virgil Thomson–Gertrude Stein♦ opera *Four Saints in Three Acts*♦ (1934), in a controversial production, featured a cellophane set and a cast of black singers recruited from New York black churches. *Porgy and Bess*♦ (1935)—George Gershwin's♦ lyric and compassionate "folk opera" based upon *Porgy*♦—attracted only small audiences at first on Broadway and was only really recognized as the classic it is in its 1942 revival and in subsequent Broadway productions in the 1950s and 1970s. Later musicals, also written by whites, such as *Cabin in the Sky,* with Vernon Duke's♦ memorable songs, and *Carmen Jones,*♦ which Oscar Ham-

merstein II♦ derived from Bizet's *Carmen,* attempted new perspectives.

The period also saw the production of a large number of protest plays, many concerned with the conditions of blacks; the Federal Theater Project♦ and its offshoots were especially active. Many of these plays were too strident for most playgoers' tastes. *Stevedore* (1934) told of a black longshoreman framed for a crime he didn't commit. John Wesley's *They Shall Not Die* (1934), produced by the still respected Theatre Guild♦ depicted the Scottsboro Trial, a *cause célèbre* of the period wherein the Communist Party defended Alabama black youths accused of rape. The black poet Langston Hughes wrote a dozen plays of various types and lengths during the decade. *Mulatto*♦ (1935), describing the plight of half-castes, with Rose McClendon♦ as the black mistress of a white plantation owner, had a long run, while *Do You Want To Be Free?* (1938) ran on weekends for many weeks at the Harlem Suitcase Theater. By far the most successful black-acted, albeit white-written play of the era was *The Green Pastures*♦ (1930). Away from Broadway, in Harlem, the Lafayette Theatre♦ featured black casts in black-related plays.

The Federal Theater sponsored a Negro Theatre group, one of whose principal figures was the director John Houseman,♦ who was also involved with Orson Welles♦ in the Mercury Theater,♦ which produced a version of *Macbeth* set in Haiti, with a mixed white and black cast. From this base Houseman and Welles later produced the most distinguished black drama of the period, *Native Son*♦ (1941), Richard Wright's adaptation of his novel, with Canada Lee♦ in the central role of Bigger Thomas. The outstanding black actor of the time, Paul Robeson,♦ was outside America during much of the 1930s but returned as Othello (1943), with José Ferrer♦ and Uta Hagen.♦

World War II helped create greater interest in the problems of black America. The dramas continued to be written largely by whites and tended to be protest plays, albeit with more balance and less radical rhetoric. One such play, *Deep Are the Roots*♦ (1945), enjoyed a long run. One "black" hit, *Anna Lucasta*♦ (1944), was written by a white about white people but was cast with blacks when no producer would mount it with a white cast. During this decade several producers attempted to cast blacks in roles that did not specifically call for them, such as one of the policemen in *Detective Story*♦ (1948).

Broadway musicals such as *Finian's Rainbow*♦ (1947) and *South Pacific*♦ (1949) dealt with racial prejudice. Kurt Weill's♦ *Lost in the Stars* (1949) adapted Alan Paton's novel of South African blacks and starred Todd Duncan,♦ the original Porgy in *Porgy and Bess.* Much more significant, however, were the efforts of white songwriter Harold Arlen,♦ who wrote several musicals featuring black casts and calling in the talents of major black performers— Pearl Bailey, Juanita Hall, Lena Horne, and Diahann Carroll. Starting with two specialty numbers for Dooley Wilson in *Bloomer Girl♦* (1944), Arlen created shows about black life with appropriate jazz-derived music. *St. Louis Woman* (1946) deals with a high-stepping black society in St. Louis around a racetrack in 1898 and features "Come Rain or Come Shine," Arlen's great torch song. *House of Flowers♦* (1954), with a book by Truman Capote, describes a trade war between two brothels on a West Indian isle and had Arlen's most exquisite score. Later musicals included a 1964 adaptation of Odets's♦ famous *Golden Boy,♦* with Sammy Davis, Jr., as the prizefighter, and *Purlie* (1970), which Ossie Davis adapted from *Purlie Victorious♦* (1961), about a Southern preacher's encounter with rednecks. Black entertainers now had the chance to star in interracial casts, such as Leslie Uggams did in *Hallelujah, Baby!* (1967) and Diahann Carroll as a black model in an interracial romance in Richard Rodgers♦ *No Strings* (1962).

The emergence of black playwrights on Broadway gathered momentum in the 1950s with such plays as Louis Peterson's *Take a Giant Step* (1953), a failure, and Lorraine Hansberry's *Raisin in the Sun♦* (1959), a success. Other notable plays written by blacks included Martin Duberman's *In White America* (1963)—mounted off-Broadway♦—actually a stitching together of black writings by a white playwright, and James Baldwin's "inflammatory" *Blues for Mister Charlie* (1964). During this time blacks not only occasionally played roles that were not specifically Negro in character, but even some that were specifically white. An example of the former was Diana Sands in *The Owl and the Pussycat♦* (1964); the most heralded example of the latter was Canada Lee as de Bosola in *The Duchess of Malfi* (1946), a role he played in white makeup. Joseph Papp's♦ New York Shakespeare Festival♦ gave blacks a chance to play other classic roles, notably James Earl Jones♦ in *King Lear.* Jones also played Othello (1982) on Broadway opposite Christopher Plummer♦ but gave his most powerful performance in *The Great White Hope♦* (1968), in which he portrayed the black boxing champion Jack Johnson.

The civil-rights revolution of the 1960s gave great impetus to an increased black presence on every level of the theatre, particularly off-Broadway. There was a whole new wave of protest plays, this time all written by blacks, including those like Leroi Jones's (later Imamu Amiri Baraka) *The Slave* and *The Toilet* (1965) and Ed Bullins's *The Taking of Miss Jamie,* which represented direct physical assaults on whites on stage. Jones's *The Dutchman* (1964), about a white slut seducing and then killing a middle-class black on a subway, is his most effective play. A more positive black response, however, was the foundation off-Broadway in the 1960s of the Negro Ensemble Company,♦ sponsoring plays written by blacks and played by black casts. This company has continued in existence and has on occasion sent its plays to Broadway. Among its important works have been James A. Walker's *The River Niger* (1972) and two Pulitzer Prize♦ winners, Charles Gordone's *No Place To Be Somebody♦* (1969) and Charles Fuller's *A Soldier's Play♦* (1982).

In the last half of the 1980s, August Wilson♦ emerged as an important new dramatist. His plays, which have garnered numerous awards, include *Ma Rainey's Black Bottom♦* (1984), *Fences♦* (1987), *Joe Turner's Come and Gone♦* (1988), and *The Piano Lesson♦* (1990).

In recent seasons a number of musicals with all or largely black casts and often featuring material written by blacks have been long-run successes. *The Wiz♦* (1975) is a "soul" version of *The Wizard of Oz♦; For Colored Girls Who Have Considered Suicide/When the Rainbow Is Enuf* (1976), Ntozake Shange's poetic dance drama in support of black women; and *Dreamgirls♦* (1981), a re-creation of the world of Motown Records and the rise of its most famous group, The Supremes. Three shows have been homages to black performers and musicians whose work has been "anthologized" in songs and dances: Fats Waller in *Ain't Misbehavin'♦* (1978); Eubie Blake in *Eubie!* (1978); and Duke Ellington in *Sophisticated Ladies* (1981), which featured Mercer Ellington, Duke's son, conducting the Ellington orchestra on stage. *Black and Blue* (1989), initially mounted in Paris, looked back affectionately at the heyday of jazz and blues.

One interesting sidelight is that one of the longest non-musical runs in off-Broadway history was attained by Jean Genet's♦ *The Blacks* (1961), which exposed the underlying resentments and rages of blacks after centuries of oppression by the white world. Much black theatre to date has focused on protest and propaganda. But as blacks attain more of an equal place in the theatre, on Broadway and off, black drama is likely to take on the more universal concerns shown by the dramas of other minority groups.

BLAKE, [JAMES HUBERT] EUBIE (1883–1983) The Baltimore-born composer and his partner Noble Sissle (1889–1975) spent 1915–19 with the famous black conductor James Reese Europe. After Europe's murder, the pair enjoyed success as a vaudeville act which shunned traditional black stereotypes. In 1921 they wrote the songs for *Shuffle Along,* ♦ the most popular black musical up to its time. Among the show's hits were "I'm Just Wild About Harry" and "Love Will Find a Way." More of their songs were heard in *Elsie* (1923) and *The Chocolate Dandies* (1924). With Andy Razaf, Blake wrote the songs for *Blackbirds of 1930,* ♦ a score that included "Memories of You." Blake was reunited with Sissle on two failed attempts to recapture the appeal of their first hit: *Shuffle Along of 1933* and *Shuffle Along of 1952.* A revival of ragtime in the 1970s brought Blake renewed attention as a pianist, and in 1978 a retrospective revue, *Eubie!,* further rekindled his popularity as a performer and raconteur.

Biography: *Eubie Blake,* Al Rose, New York, 1979.

BLAKE, WILLIAM RUFUS (1802–63) After playing the Prince of Wales in *Richard III* ♦ with a band of strolling players who visited his hometown of Halifax, Nova Scotia, in 1817, he decided to make acting his career. He first appeared in New York in 1824 as Frederick in *The Poor Gentleman.* His trim figure and good looks prompted managers to cast him as romantic leads, although early on he exhibited a comic flair. With age and increasing corpulence he was able to concentrate on comic parts. Among his prime interpretations were Sir Peter Teazle, Mr. Hardcastle, Malvolio, Sampson Legend, and Sir Anthony Absolute, but he also scored heavily in many contemporary, now forgotten works. He was often first comedian in the greatest companies of the time including Burton's ♦ and Wallack's. ♦ A good businessman, he at one time or another managed the Bowery, ♦ Franklin, Olympic, and Broadway theatres, as well as Philadelphia's Walnut Street Theatre ♦ and Boston's Tremont. A contemporary critic wrote of his performance in the long popular *The Heir at Law* that the actor "is a glorious Lord Duberly—one charm of his acting consists in bringing all the vulgarity of the 'old chandler' out in broad relief, and yet preserving his representation from being coarse—a great stroke of art." Writing in more general terms, Joseph Jefferson ♦ observed,

"He was a superior actor, with the disadvantage of small eyes, a fat, inexpressive face, and heavy and unwieldy figure. There must be something in the spirit of an actor that is extremely powerful to delight an audience when he is hampered like this. Without seeming to change his face or alter the stolid look from his eyes, Mr. Blake conveyed his meaning with the most perfect effect. He was delicate and minute in his manner, which contrasted oddly with his ponderous form."

BLANEY, CHARLES E[DWARD] (1866–1944) Born in Columbus, Ohio, he began his career as an actor but soon switched to play-writing and became a prolific author of melodramas, tear-jerkers, and farce-comedies. The titles of some of his plays suggest their nature: *The Curse of Drink, For His Brother's Crime, King of the Opium Ring,* and *More To Be Pitied Than Scorned.* Many of these plays were written for the Stair ♦ and Havlin circuit, while others were created for a chain of theatres—often playhouses fallen on hard times such as Philadelphia's Arch Street Theatre ♦—which Blaney ran. The coming of films destroyed his market.

BLAU, HERBERT, see *Actor's Workshop*

BLEDSOE, JULES (1898–1943) The black performer was born in Waco, Texas. On Broadway he was the original Abraham McCranie, the rebellious half-breed, in *In Abraham's Bosom* ♦ (1926) and also won praise for his performance in the musical *Deep River* (1926). However, he is best remembered as the first Joe in *Show Boat* ♦ (1927), in which he introduced "Ol' Man River." ♦

BLINN, HOLBROOK (1872–1928) Remembered by Ward Morehouse ♦ as "a steadying and inspirational influence . . . an actor of extraordinary finesse and charm," he made his debut in his native San Francisco as a child in an 1878 production of *The Streets of New York.* ♦ His first New York appearance was as Corporal Ferry in *The New South* (1893). After some years of playing increasingly important roles both in New York and London, he made his mark as Napoleon in *The Duchess of Dantzic* (1903, London; 1905, New York), a musical version of Sardou's ♦ *Madame Sans-Gêne.* A failure as the leading man in *Man and His Angel* (1906), which he also directed, was followed by a major supporting role opposite Eleanor Robson ♦ in *Salomy Jane* ♦ (1907). His star rose in 1908 when he joined Mrs. Fiske ♦ to play Jim Platt, the jailbird-lover, in *Salvation Nell.* ♦ In 1910 he played Karsten

Bernick to her Lona in *Pillars of Society,* and later the same year was her leading man in *The Green Cockatoo* and *Hannele.* His first starring role was the ruthless politician Michael Regan, a corrupt man reformed by a loving wife, in *The Boss*♦ (1911). When the Princess Theatre♦ opened in 1913, he was active in promoting its program of experimental plays, acting in and staging many of them. Leaving that theatre, he starred in and directed several failures, before winning applause for his Lord Illington opposite Margaret Anglin♦ in a 1916 revival of *A Woman of No Importance.* The next season he was Georges Duval in a multi-star revival of *The Lady of the Camellias.* His Orrin Palmer in the war play *Getting Together* (1918) was succeeded by his Louis XIV in *Molière* (1919), with Henry Miller♦ in the title role. In 1919 he also portrayed Henry Winthrop, an enlightened conservative, in *The Challenge,* after which he replaced Henry Miller as Jeffrey Fair in *The Famous Mrs. Fair.*♦ He also succeeded Miller as president of the Actors' Fidelity League.♦ His colorful performance as Pancho Lopez (read Pancho Villa) earned a long run for *The Bad Man* (1920). He played another bandit, Don José, in *The Dove* (1925), then turned to sophisticated comedy as Sandor Turai in *The Play's the Thing* (1926). At the time of his death he was rumored to be considering the formation of a repertory company.

BLITZSTEIN, MARC (1905–64) The Philadelphia-born composer created a furor on Broadway with his propaganda musical *The Cradle Will Rock*♦ (1937), which was performed despite strenuous efforts to stop it. Blitzstein himself played the piano at the hurriedly moved performance. In 1949 his opera *Regina,* based on *The Little Foxes,*♦ was performed in a Broadway house. His major claim to fame, however, may be his brilliant translation of the Bertolt Brecht♦–Kurt Weill♦ work *The Threepenny Opera*♦ (1954), which ran for 2,611 performances off-Broadway. *Juno* (1959), his musicalization of *Juno and the Paycock,* for which Joseph Stein♦ wrote the libretto, was a quick failure.

Biography: *Mark the Music: The Life and Work of Marc Blitzstein,* Eric A. Gordon, New York, 1990.

Blockade, *The,* a play by General John Burgoyne which ridiculed American soldiers, was presented in Boston in 1775 while the British occupied the city. When the British left, a burlesque called *The Blockheads,* often attributed to Mercy Otis Warren,♦ was produced as a response in 1776. The burlesque was a dialogue between redcoats and

sympathetic refugees after Howe's unsuccessful attempt to take Dorchester Heights.

BLOODGOOD, CLARA [neé STEVENS] (1870–1907) A young, socially prominent New Yorker, she determined to try her luck on stage and surprised many with her fine acting and purposeful professionalism. Under the aegis of Charles Frohman♦ she made her debut in *The Conquerors*♦ (1898), then appeared for him in *Catherine* (1898), *Phroso* (1898), and *Miss Hobbs* (1899). She won such good notices as the caustic-tongued Miss Godesby in *The Climbers*♦ (1901) that its author, Clyde Fitch,♦ decided to write a play for her. While he was writing it she appeared briefly in his *The Way of the World* (1901). Her performance as the tormented Jinny Austin in the specially written *The Girl with the Green Eyes*♦ (1902) was enthusiastically hailed. Another Fitch play for her, *The Coronet of the Duchess* (1904), was a quick failure, but her reputation was reassured when she played Violet Robinson in the first American production of Shaw's♦ *Man and Superman*♦ (1905). In 1907 she appeared as Becky Warder, the pathological liar, in Fitch's *The Truth.* The play opened to unkind notices in New York and soon closed, but Fitch and Frohman urged her to take it on the road, where it garnered better reviews and better business. Meanwhile the drama had become a major hit in London with Marie Tempest♦ in the Bloodgood part. While playing in Baltimore, Miss Bloodgood committed suicide in her hotel room. Fitch thereafter strenuously denied a widely circulated rumor that her suicide had been prompted by his dedicating the published text to Miss Tempest.

Bloomer Girl, a musical comedy in two acts. Book by Sig Herzig and Fred Saidy. Lyrics by E. Y. Harburg.♦ Music by Harold Arlen.♦ Produced by John C. Wilson♦ and others at the Shubert Theatre. October 5, 1944. 654 performances.

Evelina Applegate (Celeste Holm♦), the rebellious daughter of an upstate New York hoopskirt manufacturer, not only refuses to marry the man her father has selected for her but joins her aunt, Dolly Bloomer (Margaret Douglass), in promoting bloomers instead of hoopskirts. Although she is against slavery, she weds Southern slave-owner Jeff Calhoun (David Brooks).

Principal songs: The Eagle and Me · Evelina · Right as the Rain

One of the earliest "new wave" musicals to follow in the wake of *Oklahoma!,*♦ it featured the look back at a bygone America, and marvelous Agnes de

Mille♦ ballets (especially one in which the women await their men's return from the war), much as the Rodgers♦ and Hammerstein♦ operetta had.

BLOOMGARDEN, KERMIT (1904–76) The Brooklyn-born producer served as a public accountant and general manager to Herman Shumlin♦ before embarking on his own producing career. His first venture, *Heavenly Express* (1940), was a failure, but his second try, *Deep Are the Roots♦* (1945), succeeded. Among his important productions were *Another Part of the Forest* (1946), *Command Decision♦* (1947), *Death of a Salesman♦* (1949), *The Autumn Garden* (1951), *The Crucible♦* (1953), *The Diary of Anne Frank♦* (1955), *The Most Happy Fella♦* (1956), *Look Homeward, Angel♦* (1957), *The Music Man♦* (1957), *Toys in the Attic♦* (1960), *Hot l Baltimore♦* (1973), and *Equus♦* (1974).

BLOSSOM, HENRY [MARTYN], JR. (1866–1919) After attending private schools in St. Louis, he rejected college to enter his father's insurance company. He soon turned to writing novels, one of which he dramatized successfully as *Checkers* (1903), a horse-racing yarn. Thereafter his work was largely confined to librettos for musicals, most often to scores by Victor Herbert♦. Among his best were *The Yankee Consul* (1903), *Mlle. Modiste♦* (1905), *The Red Mill♦* (1906), *The Only Girl* (1914), *The Princess Pat* (1915), *Eileen* (1917), and *The Velvet Lady* (1919). Although most librettos of the period were loosely structured fripperies, Blossom's work had a colloquial charm and cohesiveness rare at the time. He was certainly the best librettist Herbert ever had.

Blossom Time, an operetta in three acts. Book and lyrics by Dorothy Donnelly.♦ Music by Sigmund Romberg,♦ based on themes of Franz Schubert. Produced by the Messrs. Shubert♦ at the Ambassador Theatre. September 29, 1921. 592 performances.

Kitzi (Frances Halliday), Fritzi (Dorothy Whitmore), and Mitzi Kranz (Olga Cook) are three eligible Viennese young ladies. Franz Schubert (Bertram Peacock) falls in love with Mitzi. So does Baron Franz Schober (Howard Marsh♦). The men's similar initials cause a misunderstanding which prompts Mitzi to favor the Baron. Heartbroken, Schubert dies.

The operetta was a drastic rewriting of the German operetta *Das Dreimäderlhaus,* which was popular in England as *Lilac Time* and in France as *Chanson d'Amour.* Its tremendous popularity

prompted a rash of operettas purporting to be biographical and employing themes by other composers. *Blossom Time* toured incessantly until World War II, often in such shabby mountings that "a road company of *Blossom Time*" became a term of derision.

Blue Jeans, a play in four acts by Joseph Arthur.♦ Produced at the 14th Street Theatre. October 6, 1890. 176 performances.

When Perry Bascom (Robert Hilliard♦), a rich young man who is running for Congress in Indiana, marries Sue Eudaly (Judith Berolde), the marriage so infuriates Sue's old suitor, Ben Boone (George Fawcett♦), that he runs against Bascom and wins. But Sue turns out to be an adventuress and bigamist, so Bascom divorces her and marries June (Jennie Yeamans), a waif from the county poorhouse. Sue, believing that Bascom cannot prove her first marriage, threatens to bring him to trial as a bigamist. She also tells Boone that Bascom is all that stands in the way of their marrying. Boone lures Bascom and June to a sawmill, where he locks June in a small office and, after knocking out Bascom, places him on a belt that is moving toward a huge, spinning buzz saw. June breaks down the door in time to rescue her husband, who later succeeds in finding Sue's other husband.

The scene in which the unconscious hero moves ever closer to the whirling saw was the sensation of the play and became one of the most famous and imitated moments in American melodrama. The play remained a popular favorite for several decades.

Blue Mouse, The, a comedy in three acts by Clyde Fitch.♦ Produced at the Lyric Theatre. November 30, 1908. 232 performances.

Knowing that his boss Mr. Lewellyn (Harry Conor♦), the president of the railroad, is an inveterate skirt-chaser, Augustus Rollett (Jameson Lee Finney) persuades a popular cabaret star, Paulette Divine (Mabel Barrison), who is known as "The Blue Mouse," to pretend to be his wife and let his boss have a brief flirtation with her. Augustus banks on this leading to a promotion. What he does not bank on are appearances by Mrs. Lewellyn (Zelda Sears♦), his own wife (Jane Laurel), and several other friends and relatives, all of whom arrive at inconvenient moments and misconstrue the situation.

Fitch freely adapted and Americanized a German play by Alexander Engel and Julius Horst. The comedy was later the source of the 1919 musical *The Little Blue Devil.*

BMI, see *ASCAP*

BOCK, [JERROLD LEWIS] JERRY (b. 1928) Born in New Haven, Conn., he began to write songs for shows at high school and at the University of Wisconsin. Thereafter he wrote for Sid Caesar♦ and Imogene Coca's television shows and for summer camp revues. With lyricist Larry Holofcener he composed several songs for the Broadway revue *Catch a Star* (1955), and then created the score for Sammy Davis, Jr.'s♦ vehicle, *Mr. Wonderful* (1956). Popular numbers from the show, with lyrics by Holofcener and George Weiss, were "Too Close for Comfort" and the title song. Shortly afterwards he teamed with lyricist Sheldon Harnick♦ to write *The Body Beautiful* (1958); the Pulitzer Prize♦ winner *Fiorello!*♦ (1959), whose best songs were " 'Til Tomorrow" and "A Little Tin Box"; *Tenderloin* (1960); *She Loves Me*♦ (1963); and *Fiddler on the Roof*♦ (1964). The long-run *Fiddler* produced such widely sung songs as "Matchmaker, Matchmaker," "Sunrise, Sunset," and "To Life." In 1966 they did the songs for *The Apple Tree* and in 1970 for *The Rothschilds.* Bock's music was noteworthy not only for its melodicism but for its sense of place and time.

Bohemian Girl, The An English opera by Michael William Balfe, it was first played in America at the Park Theatre♦ on November 25, 1844, and told of a young girl kidnapped by gypsies. Along with Balfe's *The Enchantress* (1846) and William Vincent Wallace's *Maritana* (1848) it held regular stages for several decades at a time when theatres devoted exclusively to opera did not exist. *The Bohemian Girl* accustomed audiences to a type of musical theatre that ultimately made them receptive to the operettas of a later era and it was retained in the repertory of such comic opera troupes as the Boston Ideal Opera Company.♦ Its most famous song was "I Dreamt That I Dwelt in Marble Halls." A modern version, done as *Gypsy Blonde* in 1934, failed.

BOKER, GEORGE HENRY (1823–90) Born into a comfortable Philadelphia family, he was educated at Princeton and prepared for a career in law, but elected to travel and write instead. After publishing a volume of poetry, he turned to drama. His first play, *Calaynos,* a tale of Spanish-Moorish animosities, was published in 1848, produced successfully in London without authorization in 1849, and mounted by James E. Murdoch♦ in Philadelphia's Walnut Street Theatre♦ in 1851. His next play, *Anne Boleyn* (1850), was considered for production by Charlotte Cushman,♦ who later decided against it. In the same year his comedy in verse, *The Betrothal,* in which the heroine is saved from an unwanted marriage to a wicked merchant, was played successfully in several cities. Another comedy, this time in prose, *The World a Mask* (1851), had a brief run at the Walnut. It was a social satire set in London. The theatre next accepted his blank-verse comedy, *The Widow's Marriage* (1852), but dropped its plans when it could not find a suitable actress to play the central figure of a foolish widow tricked into behaving sensibly. His two most distinguished plays followed. *Leonor de Guzman*♦ (1853) told of the tragic rivalry between the heroine and Queen Maria of Castile. It was first played by Julia Dean♦ at the Walnut and later in New York. *Francesca da Rimini*♦ (1855), based on the Paolo and Francesca story in Dante's *Inferno,* was only a modest success at its first hearing but won great popularity in later revivals. Boker's last produced play was a melodrama, *The Bankrupt* (1855). Shortly thereafter he wrote the unproduced *Königsmark* (1857, published 1868), a story of intrigue in 17th-century Hanover. Not until Lawrence Barrett's acclaimed revival of *Francesca da Rimini* in 1882 did Boker again take up play-writing, but his last two plays, *Nydia* and *Glaucus,* both derived from Bulwer-Lytton's♦ *Last Days of Pompeii,* were never produced. He continued to write poetry and served as Minister to Turkey (1871–75), and Minister to Russia (1875–78).

One of his modern editors, Richard Moody, has observed, "American audiences of the nineteenth century had an insatiable taste for romantic tragedy, as is clearly demonstrated by the repeated performances of *Hamlet, Othello, Macbeth* and *Lear,* but only George Henry Boker, among the native and foreign dramatists, produced an original romantic tragedy of notable quality for them."

Biography: *George Henry Boker: Poet and Patriot,* Edward S. Bradley, Philadelphia, 1927.

BOLAND, MARY (1885–1965) The Philadelphia-born comedienne made her debut in Detroit in 1901 in *A Social Highwayman.* Over the next several years she played seasons with various stock companies and also toured in *Sky Farm.* Her New York debut came as Dorothy Nelson in *Strongheart* (1905), a role in which she continued for two years. She was at this time a young performer of notable beauty and charm. After acting the role in London she returned to portray Dorothy Osgood opposite Dustin Farnum♦ in *The Ranger* (1907). A season performing with Francis Wilson♦ in *When Knights Were Bold* (1907), a dream play in which she was saucy Lady Rowena Eggington, was followed by her succeeding Billie Burke♦ as leading lady to John Drew♦ for Charles Frohman. ♦ With the comedian she played in *Jack Straw* (1908), *Inconstant George* (1909), *Smith* (1910), *A Single Man* (1911), *The Perplexed Husband* (1912), *Much Ado About Nothing♦* (1913), *The Tyranny of Tears* (1913), *The Will* (1913), and *A Scrap of Paper* (1914). She then left Frohman to assume the roles of all the women who wore *My Lady's Dress* (1914). Her next success came when she took on the role of the stepmother, Mrs. Wheeler, in *Clarence♦* (1919), her first essay as the sort of fluttery grande dame that would become her trademark. Among her major assignments in the 1920s were Paula Ritter, the amateur theatre buff in *The Torch-Bearers♦* (1922); Gertrude Lennos, the inadvertent bigamist, in *Meet the Wife* (1923); and Susan Martin, whose plans to make her husband jealous backfire, in *Cradle Snatchers♦* (1925). One of her best performances was as the flighty matron Laura Merrick in *The Vinegar Tree* (1930). In 1932 she was the nouveau riche Mrs. Meshbesher in *Face the Music* and three years later the Queen in *Jubilee.* ♦ She returned from Hollywood to play Mrs. Malaprop in 1942. Her last New York appearance was as the domineering mother in *Lullaby* (1954).

BOLESLAWSKI, RICHARD (1889–1937) The Warsaw-born actor and director performed for many years with the Moscow Art Theatre♦ before immigrating to America in the early 1920s. He directed a number of Broadway productions, including *The White Eagle* (1927), *Ballyhoo* (1927), *The Three Musketeers♦* (1928), and *Mr. Moneypenny* (1928), but is best remembered as co-founder with Maria Ouspenskaya of the American Laboratory Theatre in 1925. The group worked in the tradition of the Moscow Art Players, so that each production was looked on as a "collective education." Among the company's productions were *Twelfth Night,* a dramatization of *The Scarlet Letter,* Thornton Wilder's♦ *The Trumpet Shall Sound,* and Lynn Riggs's♦ *Big Lake.* In later years he worked in films.

BOLGER, RAY[MOND WALLACE] (1904–87) Born in Dorchester, Mass., he made his professional debut in 1922 with a musical comedy stock company in Boston. After several years of touring with similar small troupes and appearing in vaudeville, he first came to Broadway in *The Merry World* (1926). A

Night in Paris and a tour in *The Passing Show of 1926♦* followed. He then returned to vaudeville before appearing in *Heads Up* (1929). His first important assignment was as principal dancer in *George White's Scandals of 1931.* ♦ He was one of the stars of *Life Begins at 8:40* (1934), in which he introduced "You're a Builder-Upper." A high point of his career was the role of Phil Nolan in *On Your Toes♦* (1936), which permitted him to sing "There's a Small Hotel" and dance "Slaughter on 10th Avenue." ♦ He next appeared in a failure, *Keep Off the Grass* (1940), then enjoyed a success with *By Jupiter.* ♦ The show closed so that he could spend the war entertaining troops. He won encores with "The Old Soft Shoe" in *Three To Make Ready* (1946), but his biggest hit was as Charley Wykeham in *Where's Charley?♦* (1948), a musical version of *Charley's Aunt.* ♦ His nightly show-stopper, "Once in Love with Amy," which he persuaded audiences to sing along with him, virtually became his theme song. His performance won him a Tony Award. ♦ His last appearances were in two failures: as Professor Fodorski in the collegiate musical *All American* (1962) and as Phineas Sharp in *Come Summer* (1969). For all his stage successes, he is unquestionably best remembered as the Scarecrow in the film *The Wizard of Oz.*

The nimble, loose-jointed performer was the best and most loyal "eccentric" dancer of his age. Of his performance in *Where's Charley?* David Ewen wrote: "In a ladies' room, in an athletic love scene with a vigorous man, while fussing around with an affected feminine air, Bolger always succeeded in being amusing without stooping to Varsity Show vulgarity or offending good taste."

BOLTON, GUY [REGINALD] (1884–1979) Born in England to American parents, he studied architecture, which he practiced briefly before turning to play-writing. Although he is best remembered as the librettist of innumerable successful musicals, he also has several important straight comedies among his credits. His works include *Hit-the-Trail Holliday♦* (1915), written with George Middleton♦ and George M. Cohan♦; *Very Good Eddie♦* (1915) with Philip Bartholomae; *Oh, Boy!♦* (1917) and *Leave It to Jane♦* (1917) with P. G. Wodehouse♦; *Polly with a Past♦* (1917), with Middleton; *Oh, Lady! Lady!!♦* (1918), with Wodehouse; *Adam and Eva♦* (1919), with Middleton; *Sally♦* (1920); *Polly Preferred* (1923); *Chicken Feed* (1923); *Lady, Be Good!♦* (1924), with Fred Thompson♦; *Tip-Toes♦* (1925), with Thompson; *The Ramblers* (1926), with Bert Kalmar♦ and Harry Ruby♦; *Oh, Kay!♦* (1926), with Wodehouse; *Rio Rita*♦ (1927) and *The Five O'Clock Girl* (1927), both with Thompson; *Simple Simon* (1930), with Ed Wynn♦; *Girl Crazy*♦ (1930), with Jack McGowan♦; *Anything Goes*♦ (1934), with Wodehouse; and *Follow the Girls*♦ (1944), with Thompson. His last Broadway show was *Anya* (1965), a musical version of his previously successful adaptation from the French, *Anastasia* (1954).

His main claim to fame may well be the literate, witty, and cohesive librettos he created for the Princess Theatre♦ shows between 1915 and 1918. Far advanced for their time, in combination with Wodehouse's brilliant lyrics and Kern's♦ superior melodies, they helped move an adolescent genre to maturity.

BONFANTI, MARIE (1852?–1921) The tiny, dark-haired ballerina was born in Milan, and began dancing professionally in Europe at the age of thirteen. Her reputation rapidly reached America, and she was signed as prima ballerina for the original production of *The Black Crook*♦ (1866). Its success assured her own fame. She played in it for its entire record-breaking run, then appeared in its failed successor, *The White Fawn* (1868). During the 1870s and 1880s she remained the leading dancer in many of the spectacles at Niblo's,♦ including several revivals of *The Black Crook*. Her style was traditional and unexceptional, but her grace and charm made her a special favorite. Augustin Daly♦ made her the featured dancer in his production of *Life* (1876). She also won applause in productions in Boston, San Francisco, and Chicago. After 1890 she rarely performed, although she remained active as a dance teacher.

BONIFACE, GEORGE C. (1833–1912) After making his theatrical debut in Baltimore in 1851, he first performed in his native New York opposite Charlotte Cushman♦ during her 1857 repertory season. The following year he appeared in repertory with the Wallacks♦ at the National Theatre. In 1859 he briefly co-managed the old Bowery Theatre,♦ all the while assuming leading roles in now forgotten plays. He soon switched allegiances to the competing New Bowery Theatre without surrendering his penchant for heroes of contemporary melodrama. One of his most celebrated roles was as Rudolf, the hero of the original *The Black Crook*♦ (1866). Trained in a fading school of uninhibited acting, he was on occasion criticized for not bending to the requirements of new techniques of writing and performing. Thus, when he played Pygmalion in Gilbert's *Pygmalion and Galatea* (1872) the *Times*

remarked, "Mr. Boniface does not rant in the part; but he mouths in a distressing fashion, the recollection of old-fashioned melodrama, played in an old-fashioned way, seeming to possess his soul to the exclusion of everything else." Nevertheless he was a popular, much sought-after performer, rarely out of work. Among his many appearances were *The Twelve Temptations*♦ (1870), *The Colleen Bawn*♦ (1871), *Les Miserables* (1871), *Kit, the Arkansas Traveller*♦ (1877), *The Streets of New York*♦ (1886), *Under Cover* (1888), *Sam'l of Posen*♦ (1894), and *The Climbers*♦ (1901). His last appearance was as James Telfer in a 1911 revival of *Trelawny of the Wells*. He had created the same role in the play's American premiere in 1898. His wife, who performed as Mrs. G. C. Boniface, his son George C. Boniface, Jr., and his daughter Stella were all well known on the stage.

BONSTELLE, JESSIE [neé LAURA JUSTINE BONE-STEELE] (1872–1932) Born in the small town of Greece, N.Y., she was encouraged by her mother to give public readings and act in amateur productions. Her professional debut was as the deserted wife in a touring company of *Bertha, the Sewing Machine Girl.*♦ She later took small parts under Augustin Daly,♦ then learned theatre management while working for the Shuberts.♦ After running her own stock companies in Rochester, Syracuse, and Northampton, Mass., she moved to Detroit, where she leased the Garrick Theatre and mounted plays there until 1910. She still sometimes returned to Broadway, in 1910 creating the role of Rhoda in *The Faith Healer.*♦ Summers she often moved the troupe to Buffalo for a short season. It was here that she helped young Katharine Cornell,♦ one of the first in a long line of promising performers she encouraged. Others she assisted early in their careers were Ann Harding, Melvyn Douglas,♦ William Powell, and Frank Morgan.♦ Her ability to pick promising performers earned her the appellation "Maker of Stars." In 1923 she briefly ran the Harlem Opera House in New York. Two years later she took over Detroit's Playhouse, later renaming it the Detroit Civic Theatre. Here she continued to produce plays and encourage young performers. Broadway producers respected her acumen and skill, often asking her to try out new plays for them.

Boomerang, The, a comedy in three acts by Winchell Smith♦ and Victor Mapes.♦ Produced by David Belasco♦ at the Belasco Theatre. August 10, 1915. 522 performances.

When Budd Woodbridge (Wallace Eddinger♦)

comes to Dr. Gerald Sumner (Arthur Byron♦) for treatment of a baffling ailment, the doctor concludes he is suffering from an acute case of jealousy, brought on by the many flirtations of his sweetheart Grace Tyler (Ruth Shepley). He suggests the cure is for Budd to make Grace jealous. To effect the cure Dr. Sumner assigns his new nurse, Virginia Xelva (Martha Hedman), to flirt publicly with the patient. Suddenly Dr. Sumner suffers the same symptoms. He realizes that he too is jealous because he is in love with Virginia.

A sunny, youthful, spirited play, its success was enhanced by the excellent performances of Byron and Miss Hedman, who subtly tilted their playing to the verge of caricature, and by Belasco's excellent production.

BOOTH, AGNES [née MARIAN AGNES LAND ROOKES] (1846–1910) Coming from her native Sydney, Australia, she made her first American appearance in San Francisco in 1858 as a child dancer. For several years thereafter she acted in small roles at Maguire's Opera House, using the name Agnes Land. Under the name Mrs. H. A. Perry, she made her Broadway debut in 1865 as Florence Trenchard in *Our American Cousin,* ♦ and several weeks later played Julie to Forrest's♦ Richelieu. She married Junius Brutus Booth, Jr., in 1867, thereafter appearing first under the name Mrs. J. B. Booth and finally as simply Agnes Booth. She won applause as the pathologically destructive Diane Bérard in *La Femme de Feu* (1874). Her acting prompted the *News* to praise her as "the most finished and effective emotional actress at present on the metropolitan stage." In the same season she also essayed well-received interpretations of Pauline, in *The Lady of Lyons,* ♦ and Juliet. In 1877 she offered her lauded Cleopatra. She surprised many with her excellent comic skills as the openly selfish Belinda Treherne in Gilbert's *Engaged* (1879) and the rattle-brained Mrs. Chetwyn in Bronson Howard's♦ *Young Mrs. Winthrop*♦ (1882). Joining A. M. Palmer♦ in 1885 when his ensemble was at its height, she won distinction as the deceived Mrs. Ralston in *Jim, the Penman*♦ (1886); Mrs. Seabrook, the woman with a secret, in *Captain Swift* (1888); the comic, uninhibited Joan Bryson, otherwise known as *Aunt Jack* (1889); the Marquise D'Alein, who must destroy her own reputation to save her son's marriage, in *Betrothed* (1891); and Audrey in *As You Like It*♦ (1891). After leaving Palmer in 1892, her star began to wane, to some extent because of poorly chosen vehicles but also because her robust acting style was seen as superannuated by the newer

naturalistic schools. Her last major appearance was in *L'Arlesienne* in 1897.

BOOTH, EDWIN [THOMAS] (1833–93) The second son of the elder Junius Brutus Booth♦ to become an actor, he was born in Belair, Maryland, and made his debut in 1849 at the Boston Museum♦ playing Tressel to his father's Richard III. He made an unobtrusive New York debut in 1850 as Wilford in *The Iron Chest,* but later garnered attention when he replaced his ailing father as Richard III. Shortly afterward he left to spend several seasons in California and the South Pacific, during which time his father died. It was on this tour that he mastered virtually all the roles for which he would be famous, notably Hamlet, Cardinal Richelieu, and Sir Giles Overreach. On his return to New York in 1857, he was billed as "the Hope of the living Drama." His season included not only *Hamlet,* ♦ *Richelieu,* ♦ and *A New Way To Pay Old Debts*, but also *King Lear,* ♦ *Romeo and Juliet,* ♦ *The Lady of Lyons,* ♦ and *Othello*♦ (in which he played Iago to Charles Fisher's♦ Moor), as well as several now forgotten works. Critics were unawed by his name or billing, the *Tribune* noting, "Mr. Booth is the most unequal actor we remember ever to have seen; and his fine, careful acting in one scene is no guaranty that he will not walk feebly through the next, and let it go by default." By 1862, when he became manager of the Winter Garden, his acting had improved, although many critics still complained about occasional unevenness. He mounted many highly praised Shakespearean productions at the house, including a *Julius Caesar*♦ in which he portrayed Brutus, Junius Brutus Booth, Jr., played Cassius, and John Wilkes Booth♦ played Marc Antony. The following night, November 26, 1864, he began a 100-performance run as Hamlet, the longest run the play had ever had until that time. Less than a month after the play closed, Booth went into temporary retirement on learning that his brother had assassinated President Lincoln. He returned to the stage in 1866. When the Winter Garden was destroyed by fire, he built his own theatre on the southeast corner of 23rd Street and Sixth Avenue, opening it on February 3, 1869, with *Romeo and Juliet*. His Juliet, Mary McVicker, later became his second wife. Unfortunately, the playhouse sat on the edge of the main theatre district. This, coupled with some poor financial management, forced Booth to declare bankruptcy and lose the theatre in 1873. He then toured the country and from 1880 to 1882 performed successfully in England and Germany. In London he played at Henry Irving's♦ Lyceum, where he and Irving alternated as Othello and Iago. On his return he formed noteworthy partnerships with Lawrence Barrett,♦ Helena Modjeska,♦ Madame Ristori,♦ and Tommaso Salvini.♦ In 1888 he gave his home on Gramercy Park to the newly organized Players,♦ though he retained an apartment there until his death. His last appearance was as Hamlet in 1891 at the Academy of Music in Brooklyn.

Booth's personal life was as plagued by tragedy as any of the characters he portrayed. His father and several other close family members died insane; both his first wife, Mary Devlin Booth, and his second died young; his brother's murder of Lincoln gave him his blackest moment; and financial and drinking problems often beset him. Quite possibly the daunting distractions of his private life determined his conservative approach to drama. Unlike Edwin Forrest,♦ he never sought to promote native plays; unlike Barrett, he never risked reviving obscure or neglected masterpieces. From early on he recognized that he had small ability in comic or in basically romantic plays. Tragedy was his forte, and he remained content with his reasonably large but relatively safe repertory.

Booth stood about five feet six inches tall. His black hair, dark complexion, brown eyes, and sad mouth gave him a slightly Latin or Semitic appearance. Of his acting in *Hamlet,* William Winter♦ wrote, "his impersonation of *Hamlet* was vital with all the old fire, and beautiful with new beauties of elaboration. Surely the stage, at least in our time, has never offered a more impressive and affecting combination than Mr. Booth's *Hamlet* of princely dignity, intellectual stateliness, glowing imagination, fine sensitiveness to all that is most sacred in human life and all that is most thrilling and sublime in the weird atmosphere of 'supernatural soliciting,' which enwraps the highest mood of the man of genius!"

A statue of Booth was erected in 1918 in Gramercy Park opposite the Players, making Booth one of the rare actors so honored.

Biography: *Prince of Players,* Eleanor Ruggles, New York, 1953.

BOOTH, John Wilkes (1839–65) The youngest and handsomest son of the elder Junius Brutus Booth,♦ he was born in Belair, Md., and made his debut in Baltimore in 1857 as Richmond in *Richard III.*♦ His New York debut came in 1862 when he assumed the lead in the same play. According to the *Herald,* he created "a veritable sensation . . . His face blackened and smeared with blood, he seemed Richard himself; and his combat with Richmond . . . was a masterpiece." With the outbreak of

the Civil War he played largely in the South but did cross the lines, ostensibly to act in the North although quite possibly to transmit secret messages. Among his parts were Hamlet, Marc Antony, and other then-standard romantic and tragic roles. Perhaps out of jealousy of his brother Edwin Booth,♦ he affected a style much closer to the old school of his father than to the newer, more tempered acting. One Cleveland theatre manager wrote of him that he "has more of the old man's power in one performance than Edwin can show in a year. He has the fire, the dash, the touch of *strangeness.*" How greatly his art would have developed was left unanswered by his death following his assassination of Lincoln. Booth shot Lincoln♦ while the President was watching a performance of *Our American Cousin*♦ from a box at Ford's Theatre♦ in Washington on April 14, 1865. Jumping from the box, he is said to have shouted, "Sic Semper Tyrannis!" But in his jump he caught his leg and was injured in the fall. Grabbing a horse that had been kept waiting in the alley by the theatre he eluded pursuers until he was caught on April 26 in a barn not far from Bowling Green, on the Richmond and Fredericksburg Railroad. He was shot but refused to leave the barn, and since he was known to be armed the building was set afire. Only after he was badly burned did he come out. He died shortly thereafter.

Biography: *The Man Who Killed Lincoln,* Phillip Van Doren Stern, New York, 1939.

BOOTH, Junius Brutus (1796–1852) Slated for the law in his native England, he elected to become an actor instead. He soon rose to play opposite Edmund Kean,♦ who was seen in many quarters as his rival. In 1821, however, Booth deserted his wife, wed Mary Ann Holmes, a Bow Street flower-seller, and came to America, where in Richmond he made his debut as Richard III. The role served for his New York debut later the same year. The critic for the *National Advocate* described him as "slender, and below middle size; youthful in appearance and rather handsome than otherwise. His countenance is open and expressive; his eye of that peculiar cast which is well adapted to display the workings of a distorted mind; his voice pleasing and capable of great modulation." Among his other famous roles were Hamlet, Sir Giles Overreach, Posthumus, Iago, and Cassius, as well as important parts in now neglected plays such as Payne's♦ *Brutus.*♦ Many critics suggested his interpretations were copied from Kean, but nonetheless they recognized his unique abilities and hailed him as the first powerful tragedian of the American stage. Early on he developed a habit of beginning quietly and saving his full force for the final impassioned scenes. At one time he played Oreste in Racine's *Andromaque* in French and claimed to have done Shylock in Hebrew, the last possibly reflecting his Jewish ancestry. As with all actors of his day, he toured regularly. His last performance was in New Orleans, and he died on a Mississippi steamboat while continuing that tour.

Because his first wife would not grant him a divorce until 1851, all his children but the first were born out of wedlock. His eldest son by his second marriage, Junius Brutus Booth, Jr. (1821–83), made his New York debut as Abder Khan in *Mazeppa* in 1843. Never the fine performer his father or brothers were, he played largely in supporting roles, although he had a moderately successful career as actor-manager, especially in California. He retired early to enter the hotel business.

Biography: *Booth Memorials: Passages, Incidents and Anecdotes in the Life of Junius Brutus Booth (the Elder),* Asia Booth Clarke, New York, 1866.

BOOTH, SHIRLEY [née THELMA BOOTH FORD] (b. 1907) A native New Yorker, she made her debut with the Poli Stock Company in Hartford, in 1919 in *The Cat and the Canary.* ♦ Her New York debut was as Nan Winchester in *Hell's Bells* (1925). A variety of roles followed before she made her mark as Mabel, a gambler's moll, in *Three Men on a Horse*♦ (1935). She won further popularity as Elizabeth Imbrie, the wisecracking photographer, in *The Philadelphia Story*♦ (1939) and as Ruth Sherwood, the would-be authoress, in *My Sister Eileen*♦ (1940). Turning to drama, she played Leona Richards, who tries to re-educate a young Nazi, in *Tomorrow the World*♦ (1943). She earned her first Tony Award♦ as Grace Woods, the back-talking secretary, in *Goodbye, My Fancy*♦ (1948). Her second Tony came for what many believe her finest performance, the slovenly Lola in *Come Back, Little Sheba*♦ (1950). The versatile, baby-voiced actress was hailed by Brooks Atkinson,♦ who noted, "She has the shuffle, the maddening garrulity and the rasping voice of the slattern, but withal she imparts to the role the warmth, generosity and valor of a loyal and affectionate woman." After playing the feisty Aunt Cissy in the musical *A Tree Grows in Brooklyn*♦ (1951), she garnered her third Tony as the lonely Leona Samish in *The Time of the Cuckoo*♦ (1952). She next scored personal success in two minor works, the musical *By the Beautiful Sea* (1954) and a comedy, *The Desk Set* (1955). Her last Broadway appearance was in a 1970 revival of *Hay Fever*.

BOOTHE [LUCE], [ANNA] CLARE (1903–87) A New Yorker who was briefly a child actress, she turned to play-writing after successfully serving as managing editor of the magazine *Vanity Fair* and writing books. Her first play, *O Pyramids* (1933), never reached Broadway, and her second, *Abide with Me* (1935), a story of a cruel dipsomaniac, was a quick failure. She won success with *The Women*♦ (1936), a witty, slashing comedy of female manners. A spoof of Hollywood's celebrated search for a Scarlett O'Hara, *Kiss the Boys Good-bye*♦ (1938), and *Margin for Error*♦ (1939), in which a Jewish policeman is assigned to guard a Nazi diplomat, also won favor. The wife of publisher Henry Luce, she later became active in conservative politics and served a stint as United States ambassador to Italy.

BORDONI, IRENE (1895–1953) The tiny Corsican-born singing comedienne, who was perceived as a latter-day Anna Held♦ because of her coyly naughty performing, first appeared in New York in *Broadway to Paris* (1912). Subsequently she played in *Miss Information* (1915) and the 1917 and 1918 editions of *Hitchy Koo*. Her heyday was in the 1920s, when she was starred by her husband E. Ray Goetz♦ in *As You Were* (1920); *The French Doll* (1922), in which she sang "Do It Again"; and *Paris* (1928), in which she introduced Cole Porter's♦ "Let's Do It." In 1938 she played in *Great Lady* and two years later sang Irving Berlin's♦ "It's a Lovely Day Tomorrow" in *Louisiana Purchase.* ♦ Her last major appearances came when she toured as Bloody Mary in *South Pacific*♦ in 1951. She also appeared in vaudeville and occasionally in straight plays.

BORETZ, ALLEN, see *Room Service*

BORGE, VICTOR (b. 1909) The Danish-born pianist and humorist was known to playgoers for his witty one-man show, *Comedy in Music* (1953), in which he entertained with his wry observations and often hilarious interpretations.

Born Yesterday, a comedy in three acts by Garson Kanin. ♦ Produced by Max Gordon♦ at the Lyceum Theatre. ♦ February 4, 1946. 1,642 performances.

Billie Dawn (Judy Holliday♦) is the "dumb-blonde" mistress of the crass but very rich junkman Harry Brock (Paul Douglas), who always lives "at the top of his voice." She is forever embarrassing him with her gaffes, so he hires a handsome young liberal writer, Paul Verrall (Gary Merrill), to tutor her. Brock's reward is to have Billie's eyes opened and to have her turn against him, accusing him of being "not couth." When he orders her to co-sign some important papers she refuses, so he slaps her. Billie signs the papers, packs her bags, and heads for the door, quietly asking Harry for just one favor before she leaves. He growlingly wants to know what that favor might be, and she asks softly, "Drop dead?" With Billie gone, Brock regrets his savagery, wondering if he couldn't get her back and then find "somebody to make her dumb again." Later Billie returns to get the rest of her things. She stuns Brock with the announcement that she has turned over to Paul incriminating papers which can send Brock to jail. Since Brock has long since put most of his property in her name, however, she offers a compromise. Paul will not publish the papers and she will sign back his property to him—but only a bit each year, for as long as he behaves.

Although, like so much Kanin-family writing, the play was a sermon on the virtues of liberalism, its bright lines, sharp character studies, and superb performances made it capital theatre. The performance of Miss Holliday was all the more remarkable since she was a relative unknown who had been cast hastily when the original star, Jean Arthur, quit during the tryout. A fine 1989 revival did disappointing business.

BOSCO, PHILIP [MICHAEL] (b. 1930) A native of Jersey City, he was graduated from Catholic University of America. He earned a Tony Award♦ nomination for his first Broadway assignment, Heracles in *The Rape of the Belt* (1960), but most of his subsequent career was with such groups as the Repertory Theatre of Lincoln Center,♦ the New York Shakespeare Festival,♦ and the Circle in the Square.♦ By the late 1970s and 1980s he was playing important leading roles with these groups: Mac the Knife (1977), Nat Miller in *Ah, Wilderness!*♦ (1983), Doc in *Come Back, Little Sheba*♦ (1984). He also did principal Shavian parts as Undershaft, Boss Mangan, the Waiter (in *You Never Can Tell*), and General Burgoyne. His years of loyalty to live theatre were rewarded when he was starred on Broadway as Saunders, the beleaguered impresario, in *Lend Me a Tenor* (1989). He afterwards was starred in the Circle in the Square's 1990 revival of *The Miser*.

BOSLEY, [THOMAS EDWARD] TOM (b. 1927) The portly, kind-faced performer was born in Chicago, where he made his acting debut. He later won notice in a number of off-Broadway productions, but is best remembered for his portrayal of Mayor La Guardia in *Fiorello!*♦ (1959). When several subse-

quent starring roles came to naught he carved out a successful career in television, particularly in *Happy Days*.

Boss, The, a play in four acts by Edward Sheldon. ♦ Produced by William A. Brady♦ at the Astor Theatre. January 30, 1911. 88 performances.

Michael R. Regan (Holbrook Blinn♦) is an ex-bartender turned contractor and political boss. By corrupt means he has secured the lucrative grain contracts that are at the heart of James Griswold's wealth. Knowing that Griswold (Henry Weaver) has used funds from banks of which Griswold is a director to promote the Griswold companies, Regan threatens to send the man to prison. Griswold assures Regan that what he did was legal, but Regan replies, "Tain't what you *do* that counts in this world. It's what folks *think* ye done!" He will spare Griswold—in fact, he will take him on as partner—if Griswold's daughter Emily (Emily Stevens♦) will marry him. To save her father, Emily agrees. But she tells Regan that she will not be a loving wife—"Everything will stop at the church door." Since Regan wants Emily only for the social position she will bring, he accepts her conditions. Emily's brother Donald (Howard Estabrook) organizes the workers against Regan. Archbishop Sullivan (Frank Sheridan), a boyhood friend of Regan's, sides with Donald. They succeed in destroying Regan, who would flee to Canada. But when Emily tells him to remain home and take his licking like a man, he realizes that she has come to love him, and he stays.

Although the play told an exciting story, at its best it was an incisive study of two people and their romance. Quinn♦ has written, "The attention of the audience is centered upon the relations of 'Regan' and his wife. They are strongly contrasted types and at first glance their union seems impossible. Yet Mr. Sheldon has indicated unobtrusively enough but surely with sufficient definiteness, the inherent attraction which the strength of 'Regan' had for 'Emily Griswold' and the way in which her pity and sympathy finally turned to something deeper."

Boston (Massachusetts) Although it was long one of the most important American theatrical centers, players found little welcome there in early times when puritanical influences were still strong. Not until 1792, with the opening of the New Exhibition Room (later called the Broad Alley Theatre), did the city have anything resembling a playhouse and even then the name suggested the subterfuge required. The first major playhouse in the city was the Federal Street Theatre♦ (1794), which long dominated local theatricals. The Haymarket, erected two years later, was never able to compete successfully and was razed in 1803. The first important opposition came from the Tremont, which opened in 1827 and remained active for a decade and a half. The leading mid-19th-century auditoriums were the Boston Museum♦ (1841) and the Howard Atheneum♦ (1846). In 1879 the Boston Ideal Opera Company♦ was founded and soon became the nation's leading light opera ensemble. While it regularly toured the country, Boston remained its base.

In the first half of the 20th century Boston was a major tryout and touring center while supporting such once famous local organizations as the Jewett Players and Mrs. Lyman Gale's Toy Theatre. Indeed, theatre flourished, albeit the city was infamous for the harshest theatrical censorship in the land. One reason Boston remained so vital was the excellence of its theatrical criticism as exemplified by the renown of Henry Taylor Parker♦ and Henry Austin Clapp.♦ Even today, when major live theatre has become sharply circumscribed, no small part of Boston's surviving theatrical vigor, though it supports only three regular legitimate theatres, has been the writing of Elliot Norton♦ of the *Herald-American,* now retired, and Kevin Kelly of the *Globe.*

Boston Ideal Opera Company The organization was founded in 1879 by Effie H. Ober specifically to mount an "ideal" production of *H.M.S. Pinafore*♦ for Boston. The production was so successful, establishing a long-run record for the city at the time, that other comic operas were quickly mounted and the troupe became a de facto repertory company. The company soon began touring and on its regular trips eventually covered every important city in the United States and Canada. After an internal dispute the management was assumed by the leading performers, and the group adopted the simpler name by which it had become popularly known, the Bostonians. Among the members were Henry Clay Barnabee,♦ Jessie Bartlett Davis,♦ W. H. MacDonald, Eugene Cowles,♦ Tom Karl, and other distinguished performers, who were joined for shorter periods by such fine players as Bertha Waltzinger and Camille D'Arville.♦ Their ensemble playing was of such high quality that they were recognized as the foremost group of their kind. The Montreal *Herald* noted, "The Bostonians have been together since the beginning of American lyric opera. It is not strange that they should be its best interpreters." Besides offering lighter operas, such as *Fra Diavolo, Martha,* or *The Elixir of Love,* as well as English and Continental operettas, the company made a determined effort to encourage American works. Their most famous American mounting was *Robin Hood*♦ (1891), but they also produced the earliest works of Victor Herbert,♦ among them *Prince Ananias* (1894) and *The Serenade* (1897). When one member, Alice Nielsen,♦ left the company to form her own troupe in 1898, taking with her several other important members, the troupe began to decline. It disbanded after the 1904–05 season.

Boston Museum [and Gallery of Fine Arts], THE Conceived by Moses Kimball, who had purchased the old New England Museum, it was opened on June 14, 1841. Its stock company gave its first performance on September 4, 1843, and thereafter remained one of the nation's finest ensembles. Its favorite performers were William Warren,♦ who first acted there in 1847, and Mrs. R. H. Vincent,♦ but at one time or another in its long career many great artists of the era appeared, either as members of the troupe or as guest stars. The subterfuge of housing a theatre in a museum was not uncommon, for it allowed many otherwise puritanical people to enjoy play-going. The theatre closed in 1893.

Both Your Houses, a play in three acts by Maxwell Anderson. ♦ Produced by the Theatre Guild♦ at the Royale Theatre. March 6, 1933. 120 performances. PP.

After Alan McClean (Sheppard Strudwick) was fired for exposing misappropriations at his school, his muckraking publisher father used the incident as a springboard to elect Alan to Congress. Advised that their freshman colleague is "Serious. Wears mail-order clothes. Reads Thomas Jefferson," the older Congressmen on the Appropriations Committee are alarmed. Their fears are quickly justified when Alan denounces the very contractors who supported his election bid and argues against money for a dam in his district. When he fails to defeat a carefully negotiated pork-barrel bill, he does an about-face and offers his own bill—which includes money for every congressman's request no matter how absurd. To his disgust the bill passes and he is hailed as a political genius.

This preachy, bitter, but powerfully written play, with perceptive portraits of a variety of Congressmen, was only a modest hit, and had already begun its post-Broadway tour when it was awarded the Pulitzer Prize. ♦ It was hastily returned to New York for a short additional run. Burns Mantle,♦ who called it "a propaganda play," noted that it was "so soundly based in reason and so substantially buttressed by provable facts, and withal so fair and forthright and entertaining in statement, that it inspired immediate favor with a thinking minority."

BOUCICAULT, AUBREY (1869–1913) The London-born son of Dion Boucicault,♦ he made his American stage debut in St. Louis in 1887 in *The Two Orphans.*♦ He appeared in many roles associated with his father, played in numerous musical comedies and in vaudeville, and portrayed Basanio opposite Nat Goodwin♦ in *The Merchant of Venice*♦ (1901), Paolo in Otis Skinner's♦ revival of *Francesca da Rimini*♦ (1901), and Clifford opposite Viola Allen♦ in *The Hunchback*♦ (1902). He was Charles II, lover of the heroine, in *Mistress Nell*♦ (1900) and Dandy, the heroine's falsely accused sweetheart, in *The Dawn of Tomorrow*♦ (1909). Shortly before his early death he had joined John Kellard's company as second lead.

BOUCICAULT, DION[YSIUS LARDNER] (1820?–90) Named for his parents' friend, Dr. Dionysius Lardner, who may have been his natural father and who was known to have taken a paternal interest in the boy, he left his native Dublin to study at the College School of London University, a boys' grammar school. The school's name afterwards led to erroneous stories about his studying civil engineering there and to the similarly false conclusion that these studies allowed him to devise the clever stage effects for which he became famous. He started acting and play-writing in 1836, making his London debut under the name Lee Moreton three years later. He soon dropped this name and, changing the spelling of his surname from Boursiquot, adopted the name he used thereafter. In 1841 he earned additional acclaim for his brilliant comedy *London Assurance.*♦ The late 1840s were spent in France, where his wife died under mysterious circumstances. Returning to England, he presumably married Agnes Robertson,♦ and then came to America in 1853, where he continued to act and write. He made his American acting debut in Boston in 1854 and two months afterwards gave his first New York performance as Sir Charles Coldstream in his own play, *Used Up.*

He is said to have written at least 200 plays, many of them during his stays here from 1853 to 1860 and from 1870 to 1890. Among these plays were *The Poor of New York*♦ (1857), adapted from the French and telling how an unscrupulous banker deprives a man and his family of their fortune (a work frequently revived as *The Streets of New York*); *Jessie Brown; or, The Relief of Lucknow*♦ (1858),

centering on an Indian uprising; *The Octoroon*♦ (1859), examining racial prejudices; *Dot* (1859), a dramatization of *The Cricket on the Hearth; Smike* (1859), a dramatization of *Nicholas Nickleby; Jeanie Deans* (1860), taken from *The Heart of Midlothian; The Colleen Bawn; or, The Brides of Garryowen*♦ (1860), based on Gerald Griffin's novel, *The Collegians; Arrah Na Pogue*♦ (1865), in which lovers help an Irish fugitive; *Rip Van Winkle*♦ (1866); *The O'Dowd* (1873), another Irish melodrama, as was *The Shaughraun*♦ (1874); and a Civil War play, *Belle Lamar* (1874). His last play of any importance, *The Jilt,* was mounted in San Francisco in 1885. After the opening of *The Poor of New York* he commented, "I can spin out these rough-and-tumble dramas as a hen lays eggs. It's a degrading occupation, but more money has been made out of guano than out of poetry." He also observed, "Sensation is what the public wants and you cannot give them too much of it." "Sensation scenes" were frequent in his works: the rescue from the burning building in *The Poor of New York,* the blazing ship in *The Octoroon,* and an underwater rescue in *The Colleen Bawn* are but three examples.

In the long run, his successful struggle to secure passage of a copyright law may have been as important to the development of American drama as his writings. Recalling indignities an author such as Robert Montgomery Bird♦ suffered at the hands of Edwin Forrest,♦ he and George Henry Boker♦ lobbied arduously until the Copyright Law of 1856 was passed.

Not only was Boucicault the most successful and popular playwright of his era, he also remained widely admired as an actor, especially in his Irish plays. His personal reputation was seriously hurt late in life when he repudiated his marriage to Agnes Robertson in order to marry another actress. She won overwhelming sympathy and insisted on retaining her married name, although her children had become technically illegitimate. Boucicault spent most of his last years teaching at a drama school established by A. M. Palmer♦ and serving as the producer's play doctor.

William Winter♦ wrote of his acting that it was "all intellect . . . but he knew the emotions by sight, and he mingled them as a chemist mingles chemicals; generally with success." That his best plays still have theatrical validity was demonstrated when the Phoenix Theatre♦ revived *The Octoroon* in 1961. Richard Watts, Jr.,♦ wrote in the *Post,* "Some of its theatrics do seem excessive to us now . . . but, on the whole, it is still a play of sturdy dramatic values and it deserves to be seen far more for its intrinsic merits than for its occasional sins of innocence against modern sophistication."

Biography: *Dion Boucicault,* Richard Fawkes, London, 1979.

Bought and Paid For, a play in four acts by George Broadhurst.♦ Produced by William A. Brady♦ at the Playhouse. September 26, 1911. 431 performances.

Although Virginia Blaine (Julia Dean♦), a young telephone operator, is uncertain that she really loves millionaire Robert Stafford (Charles Richman♦), she accepts his proposal of marriage. At first the marriage seems everything both could want, but Virginia soon learns that Stafford drinks too much and can be demanding when drunk. When she refuses his drunken caresses and locks herself in her room, he breaks down the door and tells her she cannot refuse him since she has been bought and paid for. Virginia announces she will not live with him until he promises to reform, but Stafford honestly replies there is no point in his making a promise he is not sure he can keep. The couple finally come to realize that they are loving and intelligent enough to work out their problems.

Several critics saw a similarity between this work and Eugene Walter's♦ earlier *Paid in Full,*♦ both of which made working-class heroines the central figures of problem plays. For many critics the highlight of the evening was the performance of Frank Craven♦ as the wiseacre shipping clerk James Gilley. His performance made him a star.

Bound East for Cardiff, a one-act play by Eugene O'Neill.♦ Produced by the Provincetown Players♦ at the Provincetown (Mass.) Playhouse.♦ July 28, 1916.

Yank (George Cram Cook♦), a seaman on the tramp steamer *S.S. Glencairn,* is critically injured in a fall. His buddies attempt to offer him solace; all the while they recognize that he is dying. Yank can only respond that "this sailor life ain't much to cry about leaving." In the end death comes to him as a vision of "a pretty lady dressed in black."

The play, originally written as *Children of the Sea,* was the second in a group of four known as *S.S. Glencairn.* The others are *The Moon of the Caribbees,*♦ *The Long Voyage Home,*♦ and *In the Zone.*♦ They represent O'Neill's finest writing before he successfully essayed longer dramas.

BOWERS, Mrs. D. P. [née ELIZABETH CROCKER] (1830–95) Born in Stamford, Conn., she appeared under her maiden name for her debut at the Park

Theatre♦ in 1846 as Amanthis in *The Child of Nature.* She married Bowers in 1847 and shortly thereafter moved to Philadelphia, where she and her husband were important members of the Walnut Street Theatre♦ company. Among her best received roles there were Juliet, Camille, Julia in *The Hunchback,*♦ and Pauline in *The Lady of Lyons.*♦ After her husband's death in 1857 she played in New York and on tour, then spent several seasons in England. Her star declined somewhat in later years, but she continued to play important supporting roles with major ensembles, most often as strong, regal characters. She was Emilia in the Booth♦-Salvini♦ *Othello*♦ (1886) and the Queen in their *Hamlet*♦ (1886). In 1893 she was the Duchess of Berwick in the first American performance of *Lady Windermere's Fan.*

BOWERS, ROBERT HOOD (1877–1941) A native of Chambersburg, Penn., he graduated from the Chicago Conservatory of Music, where he won several high awards, then began writing scores for Chicago musical comedies, including *Rubes and Roses* (1903), *The Paraders* (1903), and *The Maid and the Mummy* (1904). Moving to New York he composed the music for, among others, *The Vanderbilt Cup* (1906), *The Hoyden* (1907), *A Lonely Romeo* (1919), and *Oh, Ernest!* (1927). He also composed accompaniments for a number of dramas and comedies, including the original production of *The Scarecrow*♦ (1911). Between composing assignments he frequently conducted Broadway musicals.

Bowery Theatre Originally planned as the Bull's Head Theatre after a tavern on the site, it was opened in 1826 as the New York Theatre, Bowery. The name never took and it was always known simply as the Bowery Theatre. In its early years it was the major competition to the Park Theatre,♦ and was the New York home of Edwin Forrest.♦ The house burned and was rebuilt in 1828. Shortly afterwards Thomas Hamblin♦ took over management, emphasizing new plays, especially increasingly popular melodramas. Shortly before it burned again in 1836 the theatre witnessed the farewell of Thomas Abthorpe Cooper♦ and the first appearance of Charlotte Cushman♦ as Lady Macbeth. The rebuilt theatre suffered a third fire in 1838. By the time it was rebuilt in 1839 the theatre district had begun to move away and the area was changing. Ineluctably the house's fare became less lofty. Under a succession of managers, including Edward Eddy,♦ it gained fame as the home of roaring, all-stops-pulled melodrama and briefly, under George L.

Fox,♦ the home of pantomime. Although from the first the theatre attracted a less elite audience than the older Park, it was in this period that the playhouse's rambunctious clientele became a theatrical legend. The theatre was the last major auditorium in New York to retain a pit, which survived well into the 1860s. There and in the upper reaches filthy urchins sold fruit, nuts, and candy. The nut-shells, fruit stones, and rinds were often hurled on stage by the disgruntled ruffians who comprised a large segment of the playgoers, and verbal insults accompanied the trash. On happier occasions outspoken encouragement was offered to luckier performers, and they were often expected to depart from the text and drop the character they were portraying to engage in a dialogue with the audience. By 1879 the theatre, which was surrounded by immigrant tenements, was renamed the Thalia and offered plays in German and Yiddish. No attempt was made to rebuild it when it burned in 1929.

BOWLES, Jane, see *In the Summer House*

Boy Meets Girl, a comedy in three acts by Bella and Sam Spewack.♦ Produced by George Abbott♦ at the Cort Theatre. November 27, 1935. 669 performances.

Robert Law (Allyn Joslyn) and J. Carlyle Benson (Jerome Cowan) are two rambunctious, practical-joking screenwriters who simply cannot become serious when told they must devise a scenario to save fading cowboy star Larry Toms (Charles McClelland). "Even Wilkes-Barre doesn't want him, and they're still calling for Theda Bara." Law at heart is something of a dreamer while Benson is a nuts-and-bolts writer, convinced the only attractive story is boy meets girl, boy loses girl, boy gets girl. Yet it is not a boy-meets-girl story they finally devise. Learning that a pregnant studio waitress is about to give birth, Law and Benson obtain power of attorney and set about making the baby Toms's co-star. The baby's popularity saves Toms's career. But when Toms's lawyer wrests the power of attorney from the writers, the writers attempt to destroy baby's vogue by hiring a studio extra to claim he is the baby's real father. The waitress, Susie (Joyce Arling), had met the extra, Rodney (James MacColl), before and fallen for him, but now she is furious. She would run off with Toms. The baby, however, develops the measles and gives them to Toms, whose reaction is very uncharitable. Susie realizes she still loves Rodney. Only after she agrees to marry him does she learn he is really a titled

Englishman. Law and Benson see a great story in that—you know, boy meets girl . . . .

"An extraordinarily hilarious comedy," as Brooks Atkinson♦ observed, the play was not only a telling spoof of Hollywood in general, but a particularly adroit send-up of Ben Hecht♦ and Charles MacArthur♦ as well. The fine script was enhanced by Abbott's "madcap fooling at high speed," which filled the stage with all variety of Hollywood moguls, yes-men, players, midgets, and blaring trumpeters.

BOYER, Charles (1899–1978) The French actor, long a popular romantic leading man in films, came to the theatre only after his film career had faltered. He made his debut as Hoederer, the vicious Communist leader, in *Red Gloves* (1948), but scored a far greater success as Don Juan in Shaw's♦ *Don Juan in Hell* (1951). Subsequently, he was Philip Clair, a banker pursued by a determined actress, in *Kind Sir* (1953); Paul Delville, the married professor whom a Swedish beauty wants to father her child, in *The Marriage-Go-Round* (1958); Lord Pengo, a great art dealer, in the play of the same name (1962); and Gregor Antonescu, the financier whose empire is crumbling, in *Man and Boy* (1963).

Boys from Syracuse, The, a musical comedy in two acts. Book by George Abbott.♦ Lyrics by Lorenz Hart.♦ Music by Richard Rodgers.♦ Produced by Abbott at the Alvin Theatre. November 23, 1938. 235 performances.

The twins Antipholus of Ephesus (Ronald Graham) and Antipholus of Syracuse (Eddie Albert♦), who were separated when young, have taken on twin servants, both named Dromio (Teddy Hart and Jimmy Savo). When the pair from Syracuse come to Ephesus a comedy of errors ensues, in the course of which Adriana (Muriel Angelus) concludes that "Falling in Love with Love" is foolish, while Luciana (Marcy Wescott) and Antipholus tell each other "This Can't Be Love."

Unlike the later *Kiss Me, Kate,* ♦ which used much of its Shakespearean source, *The Boys from Syracuse* employed only a single line from *The Comedy of Errors,* which Savo popped out from the wings to alert audiences. Hailed as "the best musical in many a year" by *Time,* the musical was successfully revived off-Broadway during the 1962–63 season.

Boys in the Band, The, a play in two acts by Mart Crowley. Produced at the Theatre Four. April 14, 1968. 1000 performances.

Michael (Kenneth Nelson) is holding a birthday party for his friend Harold (Leonard Frey). Michael,

Harold, and all their friends are homosexuals, so no one is surprised when Michael's present to Harold is a fling with a handsome male hustler, Cowboy (Robert La Tourneaux). Drink loosens tongues, and exchanges quickly become bitchy. But the carefully controlled viciousness is shattered by the unwanted arrival of Michael's old school roommate Alan (Peter White). Alan is heterosexual, and Michael has always kept his own proclivities from him. Realizing the true situation, Alan turns hostile and belligerent, spoiling the evening for Michael. Hurt and a little baffled, Michael tells the last guest, "I don't understand any of it. I never did."

The play was one of a rash of works centering on homosexuality, which became one of the theatre's most overworked motifs of the period. While the subject offended a few playgoers, most audiences and critics simply accepted each offering on its own merits. Otis L. Guernsey, Jr.,♦ was able to discern at least some pattern to these plays when he observed, "The first act tends towards comedy; but then in the second act when the script must reveal the tension underneath the warp, there is an onslaught of bitterness leading to hysteria. Yet there was no emotion, no sympathy evoked by the second-act tears that had not already been evoked in the first-act laughter; that has been the weakness of the theater's treatment of this theme so far in the 1960s." Crowley (b. 1935) is a native of Vicksburg, Miss. This has been his only successful play.

BRACKENRIDGE, Hugh Henry (1748–1816) Brought to America from his native England while still a child, he subsequently studied theology at Princeton and served as a chaplain during the Revolutionary War. During this period he wrote and published two patriotic plays intended for amateur productions: *The Battle of Bunkers-Hill* (1776) and *The Death of General Montgomery* (1777). Both plays smack more of the pulpit or academe than of the stage. They carefully observe the dramatic unities so popular in literary theory of the day and are moved forward by speeches that seem like dignified sermons rather than lively dialogue. Following classical tradition, all real action occurs off stage. In later years Brackenridge won a reputation as a novelist.

BRADY, Alice (1892–1939) The daughter of William A. Brady,♦ she was born in New York and studied at the Boston Conservatory of Music with the intention of becoming an opera singer. Changing her mind, she made her stage debut in 1909 as a minor courtier in Robert Mantell's♦ mounting of *As You Like It.*♦ Thereafter she played Olga in the musical *The Balkan Princess* (1911) and Hebe, Lady Saphir, Kate, and Pitti-Sing in a 1912 series of Gilbert♦ and Sullivan♦ revivals. In later years she often interspersed dramatic roles with parts in other Savoyard productions. She played Meg in *Little Women* (1912); Alice Nelson, the wife who reclaims her straying husband, in *The Family Cupboard* (1913); the sentimental Beulah Randolph in *Things That Count* (1913); and Mary Horton, who would hide her past, in *Sinners*♦ (1915). She enjoyed an extended run as Jennie, the rich girl in love with a poor soldier, in *Forever After*♦ (1918). Her longer runs in the 1920s included Mamie, the hostage in *Zander the Great* (1923); the guilt-ridden Ina Bowman in *Bride of the Lamb* (1926); and Laura Sargent, the blackmailer, in *A Most Immoral Lady* (1928). Her last role generally was acknowledged her best: Lavinia Mannon in *Mourning Becomes Electra*♦ (1931). Brooks Atkinson♦ wrote, "Miss Brady . . . has one of the longest parts ever written. None of her neurotic dramatics in the past has prepared us for the demonic splendor of her Lavinia. She speaks in an ominous, full voice that only once or twice breaks into the splintery diffusion of artificial climaxes." She enjoyed a successful film career in the 1930s.

BRADY, William A[loysius] (1863–1950) After getting his theatrical start by bluffing his way into a small part in *The White Slave*♦ that Bartley Campbell♦ was producing in Brady's native San Francisco in 1882, he himself turned to producing in 1888. He soon found he was in trouble for presenting pirated works. Chastened when Dion Boucicault♦ forced him to buy the rights to *After Dark,* he toured with it, playing a major role himself, and soon added James J. Corbett♦ to the cast. He then mounted several vehicles written especially for Corbett. He also secured the Western rights to *Trilby,* even taking it to Australia. In 1896 he leased the Manhattan Theatre in New York and began to mount plays there. By far his most successful production was *Way Down East,*♦ which he tried out in Chicago and New England before bringing it to New York in 1898. A year later he married his second wife Grace George,♦ whose career thereafter was often intermixed with his. In 1911 he built the Playhouse. He also managed Wilton Lackaye,♦ Robert Mantell,♦ and Henry E. Dixey,♦ among other performers. His notable productions included *Baby Mine*♦ (1910), *The Boss*♦ (1911), *Bought and Paid For*♦ (1911), *Bunty Pulls the Strings* (1911), *Sinners*♦ (1915), *The Man*

Who Came Back♦ (1916), *Forever After*♦ (1918), *The Skin Game* (1920), *The Enchanted Cottage* (1923), and *Street Scene*♦ (1929).

Autobiography: *Showman,* New York, 1937.

BRADY, William A., Jr. (1900–35) The son of William A. Brady,♦ he was born in New York. In 1923 he directed *Chains* and *The Enchanted Cottage,* and a year later launched his producing career with *Nerves.* Entering into partnership with Dwight Deere Wiman,♦ they produced, among others, *Lucky Sam McCarver*♦ (1925), *Little Eyolf* (1926), *The Two Orphans*♦ (1926), *The Road to Rome*♦ (1927), *Women Go on Forever* (1927), *The Little Show*♦ (1929), and *The Second Little Show* (1930). After the partnership was dissolved he produced *Little Women* (1931) and several more, failed plays.

BRAHAM, David, (1838–1905) The London-born musician came to the United States while still a relatively young man. He worked for a time as a violinist with Tony Moore's Minstrels, then became Tony Pastor's♦ musical director. His heyday came when he doubled as musical director and composer for the shows written by his son-in-law Edward Harrigan.♦ Among his best-loved melodies were those for "The Babies on Our Block," "Little Widow Dunn," "Maggie Murphy's Home," "The Mulligan Guard," and "Paddy Duffy's Cart." After Harrigan's retirement he continued to compose with less success and to conduct orchestras at various New York playhouses.

BRANDO, Marlon, see *Streetcar Named Desire*

BRECHT, [Eugen] Bertolt [Friedrich] (1898–1956) The German Marxist playwright and librettist spent time in America as a refugee from Nazism. After he appeared before the House Un-American Activities Committee in 1947, he left for Zurich, and moved to East Germany in 1949. There he was given carte blanche and co-founded—and until his death co-directed—the Berliner Ensemble in East Berlin; producing his and other works. It earned renown in both Germanies and made its first appearance in London in 1956 but has yet to visit New York. American playgoers know Brecht best for his book and lyrics to *The Threepenny Opera.*♦ The work was one of several musicals he wrote with Kurt Weill♦ in his Berlin days. It was a failure when first presented here in 1933 but became immensely popular in the Marc Blitzstein♦ adaptation first offered in 1954. Among his other works done with some frequency on American stages, thanks to Eric Bentley's♦

translations and promotion efforts, are *Galileo, The Good Woman of Setzuan, The Caucasian Chalk Circle, Arturo Ui,* and *Mother Courage.* Many of these plays exemplified Brecht's concept of epic theatre which sometimes moved a story beyond the logical or expected unities of time and place, and which regularly imbued it with larger human and political meaning. His "alienation" technique was utilized to get his audiences to think, as opposed to conventional theatre technique which invited them to become totally emotionally involved. His enormous influence, from plays and critical works alike, is felt in theatre and film to this day.

BREESE, Edmund (1871–1936) Although he never achieved stardom, the Brooklyn-born actor was much sought after for over forty years. He made his debut in Eureka Springs, Ark., in 1895 and later supported James O'Neill♦ in *The Count of Monte Cristo*♦ and Robert Edeson♦ in *Strongheart.* His most famous roles were the Rockefeller-like millionaire, John Burkett Ryder, in *The Lion and the Mouse*♦ (1905) and Hiram Draper, who opposes his son's marriage to an English girl, in *So This Is London* (1922). In between he was Dickon, the Devil, in the first New York production of *The Scarecrow*♦ (1911) and John, the unhappily married brother, in *Why Marry?*♦ (1917). He was playing District Attorney Flint in *Night of January 16*♦ (1935) at the time of his death.

BRENNAN, Jay, see *Savoy, Bert*

Brewster's Millions, a play in four acts by Winchell Smith♦ and Byron Ongley. Produced at the New Amsterdam Theatre.♦ December 31, 1906. 163 performances.

Montgomery Brewster (Edward Abeles) is left one million dollars in the will of his grandfather, who died remorseful over neglecting his daughter, Brewster's mother. Monty's joy at his inheritance is at once compounded and confounded when he learns his uncle has also died and left him seven million dollars. But his uncle's will contains a hitch. The uncle hated his father—Monty's grandfather—and demands that Monty spend all of the grandfather's money at once, without revealing why and without giving any money to charity. Monty enlists a group of his friends to help on the spending spree, but complications arise because of the secrecy clause.

In this raucous farce, which was based on George Barr McCutcheon's story, Smith introduced a mysterious performer named George Spelvin,♦ who later reappeared in many of his plays whenever the real identity of a figure had to be kept secret. The name became something of a Smith trademark.

BRIAN, DONALD (1877–1948) He began singing publicly as a child in his native Newfoundland. After traveling with glee clubs and medicine shows and playing small parts on the road, he came to New York, where he made his debut in 1899 as Spangler in *On the Wabash*. His first musical role was Tom Schuyler in a touring company of *The Chaperones*. Parts in *The Supper Club, Florodora,*◆ and *The Belle of New York*◆ followed. In 1904 he came under George M. Cohan's◆ aegis, playing Henry Hapgood in *Little Johnny Jones*◆ and, two years later, Tom Bennett in *Forty-five Minutes from Broadway.*◆ His most famous assignment was as Prince Danilo in the original American production of *The Merry Widow*◆ (1907), in which he introduced "The Merry Widow Waltz" and "Maxim's." He then was starred as Freddy Smythe in *The Dollar Princess* (1909); the Marquis de Ravaillac in *The Siren* (1911); Jack Fleetwood in *The Marriage Market* (1913); Sandy Blair in *The Girl from Utah*◆ (1914), in which he introduced "They Didn't Believe Me"◆; the Grand Duke in *Sybil* (1916); André de Courcy in *Her Regiment* (1917); Robert Lambrissac in *The Girl Behind the Gun* (1918); Sonny in *Buddies* (1919); and Bumerli in a 1921 revival of *The Chocolate Soldier*. During the 1920s and early 1930s he also appeared in a number of straight plays, besides heading a road company of *No, No, Nanette.*◆ He played Danilo again in a 1932 revival of *The Merry Widow*. His last Broadway appearance was as William Graham, the father, in *Very Warm for May* (1939).

Although he was trained as a singer many critics claimed the wavy-haired, dimpled performer excelled as a dancer. "Light of voice and lighter of feet," the *Herald* said of his Danilo.

Briar Cliff; or, Scenes of the Revolution, a play in five acts by George P. Morris. Produced by Henry Wallack◆ at the Chatham Garden Theatre. June 15, 1826. In repertory.

Although Mary Jansen (Mrs. Waring) is a member of a loyalist family, she has fallen in love with Alfred Leslie (Mr. Duff◆), who has been fighting for independence and has been captured. Not even General Howe (Mr. Herbert) can change Leslie's sentiments. With the help of a sympathetic Englishman, Eugene Grant (Mr. Stevenson), Mary contrives Leslie's escape. He hides in the cave of Crazy Bet (Mrs. Duff◆) and also disguises himself as a preacher. Mary is kidnapped by a rival for her hand,

a British officer, Major Waldron (Mr. Durang). She is placed on a sloop in Long Island Sound, and when the sloop founders she is rescued by Indians. As the war ends she is reunited with Leslie, but the romance ends tragically when the disgruntled Waldron shoots her. She dies holding Leslie's hand.

Based on the novel *Whig and Tory,* the play was sometimes spelled *Brier Cliff* and often subtitled *A Picture of Former Times*. The dramatization apparently assumed playgoers were familiar with the original, since it is poorly motivated and makes illogical skips of plot. Nevertheless it is filled with colorful characters and interesting dialogue, offering intriguing glimpses of the period. One English soldier exclaims, "America! There's nothing here but mosquitoes, bats, savages, equality, sour crout, 'liberty' and bumble bees." It remained popular for many years, at one time or another being mounted at every New York theatre and in many theatres elsewhere.

George Pope Morris (1802–64), a journalist, novelist, and poet, was editor of the New York *Mirror* when the play was produced. He named his mansion Briarcliff.

BRICE, FANNY [née BORACH] (1891–1951) Born in New York, she first performed for customers in her parents' saloon. At thirteen she won an amateur night contest in Brooklyn. In 1909 her performance at a benefit, where she sang Irving Berlin's◆ "Sadie Salome" with a comic Jewish accent, landed her a part in the burlesque musical comedy *College Girls*. It was while touring with this troupe that she came to the attention of Florenz Ziegfeld,◆ who signed her for his *Follies of 1910*. She stopped the show with Berlin's "Goodby, Becky Cohen" and another song, "Lovie Joe." Thereafter she was an important performer in the *Ziegfeld Follies*◆ of 1911, 1916, 1917, 1920, 1921, and 1923, as well as in *Honeymoon Express* (1913), a road company of *Nobody Home*◆ (1915), the *Music Box Revue 1924–1925,*◆ *Fioretta* (1929), *Sweet and Low* (1930), and *Billy Rose's Crazy Quilt* (1931). She also appeared in the *Ziegfeld Follies* of 1934 and 1936, which were produced by the Shuberts◆ after Ziegfeld's death. Although she was a great comedienne and introduced such comic songs as "Second Hand Rose," "I'm an Indian," and "Old Wicked Willage of Wenice," Ziegfeld discovered she could be a moving torch singer as well. Some of her most memorable *Follies'* moments came when she introduced "My Man" and "Rose of Washington Square." In *Crazy Quilt,* produced by her husband Billy Rose,◆ she first sang "I Found a Million Dollar Baby." She initially played the mischievous brat Baby Snooks (a character she later popularized on radio) in the 1934 *Follies,* having done similar brats earlier.

Gilbert Seldes,♦ citing her "exceptional qualities of caricature and satire," described her famous comic Vamp, "in which she plays the crucial scene of all vampire stories . . . the hollow laughter, the haughty gesture, the pretended compassion, that famous defense of the vampire which here, however, ends with the magnificent line, 'I may be a bad woman, but I'm awful good company.' In this brief episode she does three things at once: recites a parody, imitates a moving picture vamp, and creates through these another, truly comic character." Her personal history, especially her marriage to gangster Nicky Arnstein, served as the basis for the 1964 musical *Funny Girl.* ♦

Biography: *The Fabulous Fanny,* Norman Katkov, New York, 1953.

BRIDGERS, ANN PRESTON, see *Coquette*

Brief Moment, a comedy in three acts by S. N. Behrman.♦ Produced by Katharine Cornell♦ and Guthrie McClintic♦ at the Belasco Theatre. November 9, 1931. 129 performances.

To the dismay of his friend Harold Sigrift (Alexander Woollcott♦), Roderick Deane (Robert Douglas), a rich, handsome young man, is determined to marry Abby Fane (Francine Larrimore♦), a nightclub singer. As Mrs. Deane, Abby quickly displays "layers of adaptive coloring" and becomes a popular society hostess. But she is also something of a coquette, so she cannot resist flirting with an old flame, Cass Worthing (Louis Calhern♦). Abby's behavior puzzles and disturbs Roderick, and they separate. In the end, however, they are reconciled, with Roderick accepting that he cannot resist "the eternal glamor of the illicit."

This brittle, literate comedy marked the debut of Cornell and her husband as producers of plays apart from Miss Cornell's vehicles. The part of Sigrift was written with Woollcott in mind, and he gave a capital performance, spending most of the evening wise-cracking as he lolled on a sofa.

Brigadoon, a musical play in two acts. Book and lyrics by Alan Jay Lerner.♦ Music by Frederick Loewe.♦ Produced by Cheryl Crawford♦ at the Ziegfeld Theatre.♦ March 13, 1947. 581 performances.

In Scotland, two American hunters, Tommy Albright (David Brooks) and Jess Douglass (George Keane), lose their way and stumble upon a village that seems to belong to another time, and where Charlie Dalrymple (Lee Sullivan), a kilted swain, rejoices that soon "I'll Go Home with Bonnie Jean." Tommy falls in love with Fiona MacLaren (Marion Bell), whom he invites for a walk through "The Heather on the Hill." Jeff has a fling with Meg Brockie (Pamela Britton). Before Charlie's wedding to Jean MacLaren (Virginia Bosler), Charlie bids her "Come to Me, Bend to Me," and Tommy acknowledges he feels "Almost Like Being in Love." Then the Americans learn that the village is bewitched, coming back to life for a day only once a century. They flee. But Tommy's love for Fiona is so strong that he returns to Scotland, where the village miraculously appears just long enough to embrace him.

Apart from George Jean Nathan,♦ who savagely attacked the work as unoriginal and dreary (in a personal vendetta, Lerner has stated), most critics were delighted with this sensitive handling of fantasy, although many felt the second act was not as good as the first. All praised Agnes de Mille's♦ ballets, especially the exciting Sword Dance. The play has remained a favorite in stock and dinner theatres and was revived on Broadway in 1980, with Martin Vidnovic as Tommy and Meg Bussert as Fiona.

Brighton Beach Memoirs, a play in two acts by Neil Simon. ♦ Produced at the Alvin Theatre. March 27, 1983. 1,299 performances. NYDCCA.

Eugene Jerome (Matthew Broderick) is an ambitious, somewhat starry-eyed teen-ager living with his extended Jewish family in a lower-middle-class home. His ambition is to be a writer. There are terrible tensions in the home. The father, Jack (Peter Michael Goetz), works as a cutter in the garment trade and his long, hard hours have wearied him. The mother, Kate (Elizabeth Franz), and her sister, Blanche (Joyce Van Patten), have harbored age-old angers which finally explode. Cousins in Europe are threatened by the Nazi advance. But Eugene also has some assets, such as an ability to see through life's short-range problems and view matters with a cutting wit. Most problems do, in fact, seem to work themselves out for the Jeromes and there is every reason to believe Eugene will realize his ambition.

An admittedly autobiographical work, the comedy was hailed by many critics as a move away from the wise-cracking formula plays that Simon had previously offered.

BRISSON, FREDERICK (1913–84) The Danish-born son of film actor Carl Brisson, he produced, alone or in conjunction with others, such shows as *The Pajama Game*♦ (1954), *Damn Yankees*♦ (1955), *The Pleasure of His Company*♦ (1958), *Five Finger Exercise* (1959), *The Caretaker* (1961), *Generation*♦ (1965), *Coco* (1969), and *Twigs* (1971). He was the husband of Rosalind Russell. ♦

Broadcast Music, see *ASCAP*

BROADHURST, GEORGE [HOWELLS] (1866–1952) Coming to America from England when he was twenty, he began his theatrical career by running theatres in Milwaukee, Baltimore, and San Francisco. The first play he wrote, *The Speculator* (1896), was a quick failure. Some comedies that followed had better luck, notably *The Wrong Mr. Wright* (1897), *What Happened to Jones* (1897), and *Why Smith Left Home* (1899), although, ironically, all were more successful in London than in New York. For the next several seasons he tried his hand at dramas, comedies, and musical comedy librettos before writing a tremendous hit, *The Man of the Hour*♦ (1906), a tale of a dedicated New York mayor who triumphs over a corrupt political machine. His next major success was *Bought and Paid For*♦ (1911), in which an arrogant self-made millionaire husband is humbled by the poor telephone operator he married. In *Today*♦ (1913) a husband discovers his wife in a brothel. *The Law of the Land*♦ (1914) recounted the justifiable homicide of a brutal husband by his wife. In 1919 the Shuberts♦ named their newest theatre after him, and he managed it in conjunction with them. He produced many of his own plays as well as those of other writers. He was once characterized as a playwright "who had a knack for the sort of melodrama that poses as a serious study of morals."

Broadway A street running north-south the length of Manhattan Island, it has given its name as a synonym for American theatre or at least for New York theatre. A "Playhouse on Broadway" was shown on a map as early as about 1735. Over the years many important legitimate theatres have, indeed, actually stood on Broadway, the newer ones being built further north as the city moved upward. Today the theatre district lies largely between Times Square and 53rd Street, with most theatres on Broadway itself film houses, while the legitimate theatres generally are clustered on side streets. When electric lights became prevalent the area became known as "The Great White Way." Since World War II the expression "off-Broadway" has been used to describe many small, often experimental theatres, most of which are situated away from the major playhouses and which some unions have allowed special lower pay scales. And later "off-off-Broadway" was devised to denote shoestring operations below even the level of "off-Broadway."

Broadway, a drama in three acts by Philip Dunning and George Abbott. ♦ Produced by Jed Harris♦ at the Broadhurst Theatre. September 16, 1926. 603 performances.

At the Paradise Night Club, Steve Crandall (Robert Glecker) kills another gangster. Crandall's girlfriend, "Billie" Moore (Sylvia Field), sees the body being carried out but Crandall persuades her to claim she has seen nothing, telling her it was a drunken, though important politician. A hoofer at the club, Roy Lane (Lee Tracy♦), also loves Billie. He reveals the truth about the murder. The dead gangster's girl kills Crandall, and Billie goes off with Roy.

Dunning (1891–1968), an actor and stage manager, originally wrote the play as *A Little White Guy*. First produced as *The Roaring Forties,* then as *Bright Lights,* the play was put into final form by Abbott at Harris's suggestion. Percy Hammond♦ of the *Herald-Tribune* called the mounting "the most completely acted and perfectly directed show I have seen in thirty years of professional playgoing." A 1987 revival, staged by Abbott, failed.

Broadway Bound, a comedy in two acts by Neil Simon. ♦ Produced by Emanuel Azenberg♦ at the Broadhurst Theatre. December 4, 1986. 756 performances.

Eugene Jerome (Jonathan Silverman) and his brother, Stanley (Jason Alexander), are pushing hard to become writers of comedy for radio, but their home life is often unfunny. Their father (Philip Sterling) is planning to desert their mother (Linda Lavin); their maternal grandfather (John Randolph) has become incontinent and refuses to live with his richer daughter (Phyllis Newman), a move that would go against his Trotskyite beliefs. Eugene is also courting a girl who is engaged to another man. Luckily, Eugene can see humor in all of this, even when things don't turn out in fairy tale fashion.

A strong first act, good character drawings, and Simon's gift for one-liners made this last of his semi-autobiographical trilogy a pleasant evening, despite second-act problems.

BRODERICK, HELEN (1891–1959) The Philadelphia-born comedienne, who was the daughter of an actor, made her debut in the chorus of Ziegfeld's♦

first *Follies*♦ in 1907. For the next decade she developed her caustic, wisecracking style while appearing in a few musicals, but mainly in vaudeville. She began to gain widespread recognition in the 1920s and is best remembered for her appearances in *Oh, Please!* (1926), *Fifty Million Frenchmen*♦ (1929), *The Band Wagon*♦ (1931), and *As Thousands Cheer*♦ (1933). Her last years were spent in films.

Broker of Bogota, The, a tragedy in five acts by Robert Montgomery Bird.♦ Produced by Edwin Forrest♦ at the Bowery Theatre.♦ February 12, 1834. In repertory.

Because he keeps bad company, Ramon (David Ingersoll) has been disinherited by his father, the honest, respected moneylender Batista Febro (Forrest). As a result the Viceroy of New Granada will not allow Ramon to marry his daughter Juana (Mrs. McClure). Ramon is goaded by the profligate Antonio De Cabarero (Henry Wallack♦) to rob his father and then claim that Batista himself staged the robbery. Batista is convicted. To compound his woes, his daughter Leonor (Mrs. Flynn) elopes with Fernando (H. Jones), the Viceroy's son. "The blows that bruise the body are not much," he wails, "when the heart is crushed." Juana, learning of Ramon's treachery, berates him. Filled with remorse, he commits suicide. Batista is exonerated but dies of a broken heart.

Although the tragedy's blank verse and general construction were Elizabethan, the play was well received and remained in Forrest's repertory for most of his career. No doubt Forrest's acting played a large part in its popularity, for the play was rarely revived after Forrest's death. Nevertheless, some of its appeal must stem from Bird's delineation of Batista Febro. Quinn♦ has written, "Certainly in the character of 'Febro,' with his middle-class mind, lifted into tragedy by his passionate love for his children and his betrayal by his oldest and best loved son, Bird drew one of the most living portraits in our dramatic history."

Brook, The; or, A Jolly Day at the Picnic This farce-comedy♦ was first offered to New York on May 12, 1879, at the San Francisco Minstrels' Hall. It was presented by the Salsbury Troubadors, whose leader, Nate Salsbury, had earlier written a similar piece called *Patchwork*, which he dropped as unsuitable after touring. The simple plot took a very small handful of performers on a picnic where they entertained with songs, dances, and other turns. The work proved so popular that it gave birth to the whole tradition of farce-comedy, which in turn led to the development of the American musical comedy. Coming as it did at the end of the same season that saw the premiere of *H.M.S. Pinafore*♦ and the first extended Harrigan♦ and Hart♦ vehicle, it marked the 1878–79 season as the real beginning of modern American musical theatre.

BROOK, PETER [STEPHEN PAUL] (b. 1925) The English director was born in London and educated at Oxford. He had established himself as a major West End director before staging the American musical *House of Flowers*♦ (1954). He next directed the Lunts♦ in their final appearance, *The Visit* (1958). He subsequently staged *The Fighting Cock* (1959) and *Irma La Douce* (1960). For many playgoers the high point of his career had been his work with the Royal Shakespeare Company's♦ production of a play known for short as *Marat/Sade* (1965). He brought fluid movement and powerful order to this strange, somewhat loose play about inmates in an insane asylum doing a play about the French Revolution. His direction of *The Physicists* (1964) and the Royal Shakespeare's *A Midsummer Night's Dream*♦ (1971) with its innovative setting of what appeared to be a modern black and white gymnasium, were less favorably received here. In 1980 his Centre Internationale de Créations Théâtrales was given the New York Drama Critics Circle Award♦ for its repertory.

Biography: *Peter Brook,* John C. Trewin, London, 1971.

BROOKE, CLIFFORD (1872–1951) Born in England, where he began his career as an actor, he came to America in the early years of the 20th century and for a time made a name for himself as a director. Among his notable assignments were *Within the Law*♦ (1912); *Peter Ibbetson* (1917), which starred John♦ and Lionel Barrymore♦; *Lombardi Ltd.*♦ (1917); and *East Is West*♦ (1918). He remained active on Broadway for the next twenty years, both as an actor and director, but rarely again enjoyed major success. His final years were spent as a performer in films.

Brother Rat, a comedy in three acts by John Monks, Jr., and Fred Finklehoffe. Produced by George Abbott♦ at the Biltmore Theatre. December 16, 1936. 575 performances.

Although Bing Edwards (Eddie Albert♦) is his military school's star pitcher, he is not certain that he will win the school's $200 award as its best athlete. He needs the money since he is, against school rules, secretly married. The day before the big game he learns his wife is pregnant. The news unnerves him and the well-meaning help offered by his friends, Billy (Frank Albertson) and Dan (José Ferrer♦), only makes matters worse. He loses the game, but discovers he has won $300 as the first father in the class.

A typical example of the high school and collegiate comedies that remained popular from the turn of the century until World War II, the play enjoyed Abbott's fast-paced direction and excellent performances by then unknown youngsters. The Brooklyn-born Monks (b. 1910) became a film writer, while Finklehoffe (1910–77), who was born in Springfield, Mass., later produced a number of Broadway shows including *The Heiress♦* (1947), *Affairs of State* (1950), and *Ankles Aweigh* (1955).

Brothers, a play in three acts by Herbert Ashton, Jr. Produced at the 48th Street Theatre. December 25, 1928. 255 performances.

To discover whether character is determined by environment or heredity, three doctors take orphaned identical twins and place one in an upperclass home and the other in the slums. Years later the slum-bred man, Eddie Connelly (Bert Lytell), is accused of murder. His lawyer is none other than his natural brother, Robert Naughton (also Lytell). Naughton, for all his wealth and breeding, turns out to be a scoundrel and a drug addict, but he has something of a conscience. He commits himself to a sanitarium and allows Eddie to take his place at home. Naughton dies at the hospital and Eddie marries Naughton's fiancée.

While the play has little literary or artistic merit, it was a solid piece of theatre and typified Broadway's often shallow, theatrical treatment of interesting contemporary medical and social problems. This treatment was not confined to so-called serious drama, but was also seen in comedies and musicals. Ashton was a minor actor, director, and playwright who was active in the 1920s and very early 1930s.

BROUGHAM, JOHN (1810–80) Educated at Trinity College in his native Dublin, he spent much of his college career participating in amateur theatricals. He made his professional debut in London in 1830, worked under the celebrated Madame Vestris,♦ and became manager of the Lyceum before sailing to America. He made his American debut at the Park Theatre♦ in 1842 in *His Last Legs*. In 1848 he joined William Burton♦ and later James Wallack,♦ acting with both men important comic roles such as Sir Lucius O'Trigger, Micawber, Captain Cuttle, and

Dazzle. Between 1850 and 1857 he also managed Brougham's Broadway Lyceum and the Bowery,♦ but the business side of theatre was not his forte. While acting and managing he nevertheless found time to write no fewer than 126 plays, including burlesques such as *Pocahontas♦* (1855) and *Much Ado about the Merchant of Venice* (1869); adaptations such as *Dombey and Son* (1848), a major hit; *Jane Eyre* (1849); and *Vanity Fair* (1849); Gothic melodramas such as *The Duke's Motto; or, I Am Here* (1863); tear-jerkers such as *The Dark Hour Before Dawn;* Irish plays such as *Take Care of Little Charlie* (1858); and social satire such as *The Game of Love♦* (1856). After spending the Civil War years in England he returned in 1865, acting at the Winter Garden and with Augustin Daly's♦ troupe. But his vogue had faded. He then ventured another unsuccessful attempt at management. His last appearance was in Boucicault's♦ *Felix O'Reilly* (1879).

He was one of the first to bring a bit of the action of his plays into the auditorium. In his popular *Row at the Lyceum♦* (1851), arriving playgoers found the cast still rehearsing. When the gaslights were lowered a Quaker in the audience jumped up and began to yell, "My wife! Come off that stage, thou miserable woman!" A fireman wrestled with the upset man, who got away and ran down the aisle. The Quaker was, of course, Brougham.

In his heyday he was one of the most popular of American performers, although his fellow actor Joseph Jefferson♦ regretted that he always "acted a part as though it were a joke." Other commentators, focusing more on his writings, were less critical. In 1890 Laurence Hutton♦ concluded, "If America has ever had an Aristophanes, John Brougham was his name," while a modern editor, Richard Moody, described him as "a mid-nineteenth-century combination of W. C. Fields and George S. Kaufman."

BROUN, HEYWOOD [CAMPBELL] (1888–1939) Born in Brooklyn and educated at Harvard, he worked as a reporter for several newspapers before becoming drama critic for the New York *World* (1921–28). He was also drama editor for *Vanity Fair* as well as a popular lecturer on theatre. He appeared in *Round the Town* (1924), and produced and appeared in *Shoot the Works* (1931), a revue designed to give some employment to out-of-work performers and writers. His criticism was marked by a refreshing directness and wit. Reviewing John Barrymore♦ in *Hamlet♦* he began, "John Barrymore is far and away the finest Hamlet we have ever seen. He excels all others we have known in grace, fire, wit, and clarity. This final quality should be stressed. Back in high school we remember being asked whether Hamlet was really mad. If we had seen Barrymore it would have been possible for us to tell the teacher, 'Don't be silly.' "

BROWN, ARVIN (b. 1940) Since 1967 the artistic director of the Long Wharf Theatre♦ in New Haven, Conn., he was born in Los Angeles and studied at Stanford, Harvard, the University of Bristol (England), and at the Yale School of Drama. ♦ He has directed both numerous classics and world premieres, as well as the American premieres of foreign plays. He has occasionally worked on Broadway and at the Circle in the Square. ♦ Unfortunately, though Broadway praised such mountings as his 1987 revival of *All My Sons*♦ and 1988 revival of *Ah, Wilderness!*♦, they were not commercial successes.

BROWN, DAVID PAUL (1795–1875) One of the many gentleman-playwrights who comprised the Philadelphia School of Dramatists, ♦ he intended to become a physician but, after the death of his favorite teacher, read for the law. He had a long, distinguished professional career in his native Philadelphia and served on the Pennsylvania Supreme Court. His private passion, however, was writing, and he wrote at least four elegant, if static plays: *Sertorious; or, The Roman Patriot* (1830); *The Prophet of St. Paul's* (1836); *The Trial;* and one farce, *Love and Honor; or, The Generous Soldier.* The last two plays seem never to have been performed.

BROWN, GILMOR (1887?–1960) A native of New Salem, N.D., he began his career as an actor in Western stock companies. For a time he joined Ben Greet's♦ traveling ensemble. In 1918 he founded the Pasadena Community Playhouse♦ and remained its head for thirty-one years. He also served as California state supervisor for the Federal Theatre Project♦ and as president of the National Theatre Conference. ♦
   Biography: *Gilmor Brown, Portrait of a Man—and an Idea,* Harriet L. Green, Pasadena, 1933.

BROWN, [JOSEPH EVANS] JOE E. (1892–1973) The comedian recalled for his wide-mouthed grin and rubber face was born in Holgate, Ohio, and became a circus performer at the age of seven. After many years in vaudeville he won praise, but never stardom, in such musicals as *Jim Jam Jems* (1920), *Greenwich Village Follies*♦ (1921), *Betty Lee* (1924), *Captain Jinks* (1925), and *Twinkle Twinkle* (1926).

His real fame came from his many film appearances, but Chicagoans will remember him as Elwood P. Dowd in the 1946 road company of *Harvey.* ♦ He later played New York in *Courtin' Time* (1951) and in a 1961 revival of *Show Boat.* ♦

BROWN, JOHN MASON (1900–69) A native of Louisville, he studied under Professor George P. Baker♦ at Harvard, then became an associate editor and drama critic of *Theatre Arts Monthly.* ♦ He left the magazine to become critic of the *Evening Post* in 1929, then moved to the *World-Telegram* in 1939. Following service in World War II, he was appointed drama critic for the *Saturday Review of Literature.* From 1925 to 1931 he was a lecturer at the American Laboratory Theatre, ♦ and he conducted courses at Harvard, Yale, Middlebury College, and elsewhere. Among his many books are *The Modern Theatre in Revolt* (1929), *Upstage: The American Theatre in Performance* (1930), *Letters from Greenroom Ghosts* (1934), *The Art of Playgoing* (1936), *Two on the Aisle* (1939), *Seeing Things* (1946), *Seeing More Things* (1948), *Dramatis Personae* (1963), and *The Worlds of Robert E. Sherwood* (1965). His style, often described as courtly or urbane, was suffused with an elegant humor, as in his recollection of his first exposure to theatre: "I have been stage-struck ever since, when eight, I was taken to Macauley's Theatre in Louisville, Kentucky, to see Robert B. Mantell play King Lear, one of the few parts, I realize now, that he was still young enough to act."
   Biography: *Speak for Yourself, John,* George Stevens, New York, 1974.

BROWN, LEW [né LOUIS BROWNSTEIN] (1893–1958) The Russian-born lyricist and occasional librettist came to America at the age of five. His first important collaborator was Albert Von Tilzer, for whom he wrote the lyrics to "I'm the Lonesomest Gal in Town," "Give Me the Moonlight, Give Me the Girl," and "I May Be Gone for a Long, Long Time," the last introduced in *Hitchy-Koo, 1917.* In 1922 he began his association with Ray Henderson. ♦ Their song "Georgette" was a hit in the *Greenwich Village Follies of 1922.* ♦ After B. G. De Sylva♦ joined the pair, the team composed the songs and sometimes collaborated on the books for a series of shows that have come to represent the quintessential musical comedies and revues of their day: *George White's Scandals*♦ *of 1925, 1926,* and *1928, Good News!*♦ (1927), *Manhattan Mary* (1927), *Hold Everything!*♦ (1928), *Follow Thru*♦ (1929), and *Flying High*♦ (1930). (Songs from these shows are listed in Henderson entry.)

Following De Sylva's departure they wrote *George White's Scandals of 1931, Hot-Cha!* (1932), and *Strike Me Pink* (1933). With other composers Brown wrote lyrics for *Calling All Stars* (1934) and *Yokel Boy* (1939).

BROWN, T[HOMAS] ALLSTON (1836–1918) Born in Newburyport, Mass., he began his career as an advertising agent for circuses and in 1860 managed Blondin, who was famous for crossing Niagara Gorge on a tightrope. From 1870 on, he ran a theatrical agency in New York. His clients included Dion Boucicault. ♦ In 1859 he founded a theatrical weekly, *The Tatler,* and from 1864 to 1870 was dramatic editor for the *New York Clipper.* ♦ He remained active as "the oldest theatrical manager in America" until his retirement in 1916. However, he probably will be best remembered as the author of two pioneering studies: *History of the American Stage: 1733–1870* (1870) and *History of the New York Stage: From the First Performance in 1732 to 1901* (1903). He was sometimes known as Colonel Brown.

BROWNE, JAMES S. (1791–1869) The English comedian made his American debut as Bob Acres in New York in 1838 and quickly established himself as "one of the best actors of light and eccentric comedy that ever trod the American stage." He was the first to play Robert Macaire in this country and was long identified with the role. Famous for his high living, he later became mentally unstable and died alone, ill and impoverished.

BROWNE, MAURICE (1881–1955) After fighting in the Boer War this sometime poet came to America and in 1919 founded the Chicago Little Theatre with his wife Ellen Van Volkenburg. He did much to promote the little theatre ♦ in America and is often called the father of the movement in this country, although a number of these successful troupes existed long before his arrival. He produced several shows in New York, including a highly praised but short-lived mounting of *Medea* (1920), with Miss Van Volkenburg in the title role. Returning to England, where he spent the rest of his career, he wrote a curiously embittered autobiography, *Too Late To Lament* (1955).

BROWNE, PORTER EMERSON (1879–1934) A native of Beverly, Mass., he worked as a journalist and novelist before turning playwright. He enjoyed a success with his first play, *A Fool There Was* ♦ (1909), based on Kipling's *The Vampire,* in which a

family man is destroyed by a femme fatale. *The Spendthrift* (1910) found a modest audience but it was followed by several failures: *Waste* (1910); *Chains* (1912), adapted from an English play; *Wild Oats* (1914); *A Girl of Today* (1915); *Rich Man, Poor Man* (1915); and *Don't Shoot* (1915). He scored a final success with his last play, *The Bad Man* (1920), which he based on his own novel and which told of a Mexican bandit who rids a charming woman of her troublesome husband by shooting him.

BROWN-POTTER, MRS. J. [née CORA URQUHART] (1857–1936) The daughter of a wealthy New Orleans man and the wife of an even wealthier New Yorker, she was a strikingly handsome woman celebrated for her elegance of dress. In the early 1880s she offered several amateur mountings in New York. She first acted professionally in London in 1887, returning to America later the same year to set up her own company. With Kyrle Bellew ♦ as her leading man, she offered herself in such roles as Juliet, Pauline (*The Lady of Lyons* ♦), Kate Hardcastle, Camille, and Cleopatra. Her reception varied from chilly to little more than kind, but she persisted for a number of years, even taking her troupe overseas. In later years she tried newer plays without major success. She returned to England to appear in vaudeville there, then retired. In 1933 she wrote her reminiscences, *The Age of Innocence and I.*

BRUSTEIN, ROBERT [SANFORD] (b. 1927) After studying at the High School of Music and Art in his native New York, he attended Amherst, Yale School of Drama, ♦ and Columbia. He acted with stock companies and on television before becoming drama critic for the *New Republic* from 1959 to 1968. His criticism won several awards. During his tenure he also taught drama at Vassar and Columbia. In 1965 he was appointed professor of Drama and English Literature at Yale, where he founded and served as artistic director for the Yale Repertory Theatre. The troupe quickly became one of the leading collegiate ensembles in America. In 1979 he left Yale for Harvard. Among his books are *The Theatre of Revolt* (1964), *Seasons of Discontent* (1966), *The Third Theatre* (1968), *Revolution as Theatre* (1970), *The Cultural Watch* (1975), *Critical Moments* (1980), *Making Scenes* (1981), and *Who Needs Theatre* (1987).

Brutus; or, the Fall of Tarquin, a tragedy in five acts by John Howard Payne. ♦ Produced by Edmund

Simpson♦ at the Park Theatre. ♦ March 15, 1819. In repertory.

Lucius Junius (James Pritchard), whose noble family has been deposed and murdered by the usurping Tarquins, escapes death by feigning idiocy and becoming the Tarquin court jester. The Tarquin queen, Tullia (Mrs. Barnes♦), sneeringly gives him another name, Brutus. But when Sextus, a Tarquin prince, rapes Lucretia (Miss Leesugg), a senator's wife, Brutus drops his disguise to lead the Romans against the usurpers. His son Titus (Simpson) sides with the enemy because of his love of Princess Tarquinia, so it falls to his father to sentence him to death.

> A few sad steps have brought thee to the brink
> Of that tremendous precipice whose depth
> No thought of man can fathom . . .

As Titus is led off Brutus cries, "Justice is satisfied and Rome is free!"

Payne compiled the play from seven older works on the subject, including Voltaire's *Brutus, A Tragedy* and English pieces by Nathaniel Lee, William Duncombe, Hugh Downman, and Richard Cumberland. The play was first presented in England with Edmund Kean♦ in the lead. Simpson was apparently unprepared for its American success and had booked other plays to follow quickly. But its success caused it to be brought back regularly in the repertory. Kean performed it on his American tour, and the play featured importantly in the repertories of Junius Brutus Booth,♦ Edwin Booth,♦ and James Wallack.♦

William Winter♦ called the play "a series of episodes in Roman history, rather than a single dramatic narrative," but considered it "valuable for its tumultous action, its splendid pictorial effects and its moments of pathos." However, a modern critic, Howard Taubman, has suggested that for modern audiences the play "is impossibly long, flamboyant and pretentious."

BRYANT, DAN [né DANIEL WEBSTER O'BRIEN] (1833–75) Born in Troy, N.Y., he joined the Sable Harmonists, a traveling minstrel entourage, in 1849, then made his New York debut with Charles White's Minstrels in 1851. A year later he moved to Wood's Minstrels and in 1855 to Campbell's Minstrels, which soon became Bryant and [Ben] Mallory's Campbell's Minstrels. With his brothers Jerry and Neil he established Bryant's Minstrels in 1856. The troupe quickly established itself as New York's leading minstrel ensemble and held that position

until Bryant's death. It was at Bryant's request for a "walk-around" in 1859 that Dan Emmett♦ wrote and introduced "Dixie."♦ Bryant was a versatile performer, popular in blackface entertainment as a singer and comic, but most of all for his dancing. His routine for "The Essence of Old Virginny" was billed as the "unequalled plantation dance," a billing critics and audiences supported. Only George Christy♦ rivaled him in popularity. But Bryant was also a fine actor and occasionally left the minstrel stage to perform an Irish play. Among his best roles were those in *Handy Andy* (which he first performed in 1863); *The Irish Immigrant* (1864), sometimes called *The Irish Emigrant;* Myles in *The Colleen Bawn♦* (1864); *Born to Good Luck* (1865); *Shamus O'Brien* (1866); and Shaun in *Arrah Na Pogue♦* (1867). The boyishly handsome performer was admired not only for his fine acting but for his "compelling personality."

Bryant's Minstrels, see *Bryant, Dan*

BRYNNER, YUL, see *King and I, The*

BUCHANAN, JACK (1891–1957) The reedy-voiced song-and-dance man, who to many Americans personified the suave, dapper Englishman, made his American debut in *Charlot's Revue♦* (1924). Subsequently he appeared in only three other musicals: *The Charlot Revue of 1926,* in which he introduced "A Cup of Coffee, a Sandwich and You"; *Wake Up and Dream* (1929); and *Between the Devil* (1937), in which he sang "By Myself." For what proved his final Broadway assignment he deserted the musical theatre to play Daniel Bachelet, the suspicious husband, in Sacha Guitry's comedy *Don't Listen, Ladies* (1948).

BUCHANAN, THOMPSON (1877–1937) After studying in the South and serving as a reporter, he became drama critic of the Louisville *Herald* for the 1902–03 season. Returning to his native New York he was on the staff of the *Evening Journal* until 1909. During his last years on the paper he wrote several plays which failed to reach New York, but scored a success with *A Woman's Way♦* (1909), which told how a wife wins back her husband from a more sophisticated rival. Following a series of failures, his *Life* (1914), which recounted the saving of an innocent man condemned to death, enjoyed a profitable run at the huge Manhattan Opera House. Neither *Let Us Divorce* nor *Our Daily Bread* reached New York, but *Civilian Clothes* (1919), an urbane comedy of an ex-soldier who humbles his snobbish wife by becoming her family's butler, won appreciative audiences. *The Sporting Thing To Do* (1923), *Pride* (1923), and *Bluffing Bluffers* (1924), the last written with John Meehan, were poorly received. *Sinner* (1927), a tale of a wildly inconstant wife tamed into submission, overcame a largely indifferent press to enjoy a modest run. His last plays, *Star of Bengal* (1929) and *As Good as New* (1930), were failures.

BUCK, [EDWARD EU]GENE (1885–1957) After leaving art school in his native Detroit, he designed covers for sheet music. He came to the attention of Florenz Ziegfeld♦ when Buck created an act for Lillian Lorraine. From 1912 on he wrote lyrics for many of the *Ziegfeld Follies,* ♦ his most famous song being "Hello, Frisco!" (music, Louis Hirsch♦). He also wrote lyrics for Victor Herbert,♦ Rudolf Friml,♦ and Jerome Kern.♦ More importantly, he became Ziegfeld's right-hand man, "in whom," Billie Burke♦ wrote, "Flo placed more confidence . . . than anyone else in his organization." While Ziegfeld had final say, Buck did much of the hiring except for principals and was in charge of rehearsals and tryout revisions. It is generally accepted that he selected songs. In 1927 he produced and directed *Yours Truly* and *Take the Air,* writing songs for the latter with Dave Stamper. He was president of ASCAP♦ from 1924 to 1941 as well as president of the Catholic Actors' Guild.

Buckley's Serenaders Sometimes known as Buckley's New Orleans Serenaders, the group was established in 1853, led by George Swayne Buckley, Frederick Buckley, and R. Bishop Buckley. The men had previously worked with the Congo Melodists in Boston and the New Orleans Operatic Serenaders. Their troupe, which offered traditional olios, parodies, and minstrel routines, was one of the earliest to make a complete transcontinental tour. They occasionally presented serious concerts of sacred music. George Swayne Buckley was one of the great minstrels and offered to beat George Christy♦ or any other rival "as a musician in bone playing, sentimental or comic singing, banjo playing, playing on a pair of kitchen bellows, and general delineator of the Ethiopian character." He also played the violin, metaphone, and a comb and popularized a minstrel favorite, "The Laughing Song." Another sometime member of the troupe, J. W. McAndrews, made famous "The Watermelon Man," using a song and dance, clothing, and even a cart and donkey he had purchased from a black fruit-seller. The troupe disbanded during the Civil

War, although attempts to revive it were made as late as 1870.

BUCKSTONE, J[OHN] B[ALDWIN] (1802–79) The English actor and playwright performed in America during the 1840–41 and 1841–42 seasons but with only middling success. However, many of his plays were long in the standard repertory, especially at more popular, less elite playhouses. These included such works as *A Kiss in the Dark, The Lottery Ticket, Single Life,* and *Weak Points.* Ireland♦ has noted, "In America . . . he had contributed to the stage more than one hundred and fifty [plays], scarcely any of which have proved failures, and most of them have had a long career of popularity, and remain among the best approved standard comedies, farces and melo-dramas of the day."

Budget, The (also known as *Madison's Budget*) Published by James Madison from 1898 to 1918, it was a standard source for jokes for vaudevillians, and sold for one dollar per issue. Madison himself had failed as a performer despite good material, so he made his living from this magazine and from selling other material to more successful players.

Buffalo Bill, see *Cody, William*

BUFMAN, ZEV (b. 1930) A native Israeli, he performed in his homeland and in America before turning producer. Much of his early producing was in California, but he later moved his base to Florida. He has sponsored touring versions of several Broadway plays. In New York he has co-produced such fine original works as *Your Own Thing* (1968) and *Jimmy Shine* (1968). However, in recent years he is best known as co-producer of major revivals, including *Peter Pan♦* (1979), *Oklahoma!♦* (1979), *Brigadoon♦* (1980), *West Side Story♦* (1980), *The Little Foxes♦* (1981), *Joseph and the Amazing Technicolor Dreamcoat* (1982), and *Private Lives♦* (1983).

BULWER-LYTTON, EDWARD, see *Lytton, Edward*

BUNCE, OLIVER BELL (1828–90) A New York-born writer, he enjoyed some slight success with the rural comedy *The Morning of Life* (1848), then met with quick failure when James W. Wallack♦ mounted his play about the recent Greek revolt, *Marco Bozzaris; or, The Grecian Hero* (1850). Wallack is also said to have accepted another play, *Fate; or, The Prophecy,* but never produced it, and it is apparently lost. Bunce's most important play was his last, *Love in*

'76♦ (1857), a drawing-room comedy with a Revolutionary War background. Later a consultant to publishers as well as a novelist, short story writer, and essayist, in 1872 he became editor of *Appleton's Journal,* a post he held for nine years. He often included his own theatrical criticism and reminiscences in the magazine, where he argued against the excesses of both the new realistic style of acting and writing and the old fustian schools.

BURGESS, NEIL (1846–1910) Born in Boston, he made his stage debut in variety with Spalding's Bell Ringers in 1865 and his New York debut as a solo artist in 1872 at Tony Pastor's,♦ where he was billed as an "Ethiopian Comedian." His first New York appearance as a female impersonator was in a Harrigan♦ and Hart♦ olio at their Theatre Comique in 1877 as "The Coming Woman." Two years later he earned widespread fame in the title role of *Widow Bedott,*♦ a role he played for the rest of his career. Two other great parts of his were Tryphena "Betsy" Puffy in *Vim; or, A Visit to Puffy Farm* (1882), which was enlarged from an 1879 vaudeville sketch, and Aunt Abby Prue in *The County Fair*♦ (1889). In 1891 he portrayed Lady Teazle in the first Lambs'♦ Gambol. The greatest female impersonator of his day, he was recalled by Odell♦ as "a big man, without the slightest trace of good looks, [who] could, without difficulty, seem the woman he was playing, whether making a pie in the kitchen, giving a piece of her mind to an interfering interloper or starting a young couple on the way to matrimony. Nothing of the effect, somewhat unpleasing, that one associates with the young 'female impersonator' of vaudeville inhered in Burgess's wholesome, jolly characterizations."

Buried Child, a play in two acts by Sam Shepard.♦ Originally produced at the Theatre de Lys. December 5, 1978. 152 performances. PP.

After several years in Los Angeles, Vince (Christopher McCann) returns to the Illinois farm of his grandparents, bringing with him his saxophone, his girl Shelley (Mary McDonnell), and a parcel of fond memories and hopes. He is quickly disillusioned. His grandmother, Hallie (Jacqueline Brooks), preaches morality but spends her evenings on the town with the local priest, Father Dewis (Bill Wiley). His dying, drunken grandfather, Dodge (Richard Hamilton), has murdered an unwanted child and wails, "I'm descended from a long line of corpses and there's not a living soul behind me." Vince must also confront his crazed father, Tilden (Tom Noonan), and brutal, crippled uncle, Bradley

(Jay Sanders). The visit leaves Vince to work out a new life in a spiritually bankrupt world.

Originally produced by San Francisco's Magic Theatre, the play was mounted off-off-Broadway before this off-Broadway engagement began.

BURK, JOHN DALY (1775?–1808) The writer was forced to flee Ireland after he was expelled from Dublin's Trinity College for his free-thinking religious and political stands. According to legend he adopted his middle name in gratitude to a Miss Daly who abetted his escape. Coming to Boston, he tried his hand unsuccessfully at editing a radical newspaper. Two weeks after the paper closed, his first play, *Bunker-Hill; or, The Death of General Warren* (1797), was presented at Boston's Haymarket Theatre. Although Warren was ostensibly the central figure, his role consisted of little but bombastic speeches in praise of America and against the British. The real interests were the staged battle scenes and the love story in which an American girl goes mad after her redcoat lover chooses duty above romance and is killed. Dismissed by critics as "a deplorable play," it was widely popular with audiences for its often fiery theatricality and was revived regularly. His best play, *Female Patriotism; or, The Death of Joan of Arc*♦ (1798), portrayed the maiden not as a religious visionary but as an ardent republican. It was performed in New York, where he had come to edit yet another paper, and was better received by the press than by the public. Arrested for sedition, he was forced to flee to Virginia and there wrote his last surviving play. *Bethlem Gabor, Lord of Transylvania; or, The Man-Hating Palatine* (1807) was a Gothic revenge tragedy with a happy ending, telling of Protestant struggles in the 17th century. Burk himself acted in the play. Four other plays are generally attributed to him: *The Death of General Montgomery in Storming the City of Quebec, The Fortunes of Nigel, The Innkeeper of Abbeville,* and *Which Do You Like Best, the Poor Man or the Lord?* The contentious Burk was killed by a Frenchman in a duel that arose after he abused Napoleon and called the French a "pack of rascals."

BURKE, [MARY WILLIAM ETHELBERT APPLETON] BILLIE (1885–1970) Born in Washington, D.C., she was raised in England, where her father was a well-known clown. She appeared in a number of English musical comedies and with Charles Hawtrey before coming to New York under contract to Charles Frohman♦ to play the naïve Beatrice Dupré opposite John Drew♦ in *My Wife* (1907). Successes followed as the newlywed Jacqueline in *Love*

Watches (1908); the charmingly conniving title role in *Mrs. Dot* (1910); Lily Parradell, the chorus girl who marries a peer, in *The "Mind-the-Paint" Girl* (1912); Lady Thomasine, who was raised by her father to be a boy, in *The Amazons* (1913); Norah Marsh, who wins the heart of the hard-bitten farmer she has married in desperation, in *The Land of Promise* (1914); and the iron-willed heroine, the title role in *Jerry* (1914). In the same year she married Florenz Ziegfeld♦ and a year later Frohman died. Thereafter she acted for various important producers. She played opposite Henry Miller♦ in a revival of *A Marriage of Convenience* (1918), then appeared as the heroine in Maugham's♦ *Caesar's Wife* (1919). Her next two roles were in Booth Tarkington♦ plays: as the kittenish spinster Isabel in *The Intimate Strangers* (1921), and as the night-club singer, the title role of *Rose Briar* (1922). For her husband she did her only American musical, *Annie Dear* (1924), a song-and-dance version of *Good Gracious Annabelle.*♦ In the 1930s she played *The Vinegar Tree* and *The Marquis* in California, and lent her name as producer to editions of the *Ziegfeld Follies,*♦ although the actual producers were the Shuberts.♦ Her last Broadway appearance was as the widow who is courted by a former President in *Mrs. January and Mr. X* (1944). She later performed in summer stock and in the road company of *The Solid Gold Cadillac.*♦ The dainty redhead with the quivering voice was hailed by John Corbin♦ of the *Times* as "a comedienne of matchless charm."

Autobiography: *With a Feather on My Nose,* with Cameron Shipp, New York, 1949.

BURKE, Charles (1822–54) Born in Philadelphia, he began his career as a child prodigy (not to be confused with Joseph Burke♦), but after a brief retirement returned to the stage as a polished comedian. He was acclaimed for his Rip Van Winkle and his Solon Shingle, the cracker-barrel Yankee in *The People's Lawyer,*♦ as well as for principal parts in many once popular but now forgotten comedies. He was also a consummate performer in burlesques, many of which he wrote himself. Among his burlesque roles were Iago in a spoof of *Othello;* Clod Meddlenot in *The Lady of the Lions,* a spoof of *The Lady of Lyons*♦ and its hero Claude Melnotte; MacGreedy, a take-off of Macready♦; Met-a-roarer, a mocking of Macready's foe Forrest♦; and *La Chiselle* in a burlesque of *La Giselle.* During the 1848–49 season he managed the Chatham Theatre. His death at age thirty-two deprived the theatre of one of its most promising and admired artists.

His half-brother, the most famous Joseph Jefferson,♦ insisted Burke's Rip Van Winkle was a masterful interpretation. He wrote, "Burke was subtle, incisive and refined . . . lithe and graceful. His face was plain, but wonderfully expressive. The versatility of this rare actor was remarkable, his pathos being quite as striking as his comedy." Laurence Hutton♦ observed that in Burke's hands Solon Shingle, until then a stock portrayal, "became the simple-minded, phenomenally shrewd old man from New England, with a soul which soared no higher than the financial value of a bar'l of apple-sass."

BURKE, Joseph (1818–1902) Master Burke, as he was popularly known, came to America in 1830 as a celebrated child prodigy. Not only did he offer his interpretations of Richard III, Shylock, Sir Giles Overreach, and other celebrated roles, but soloed on the violin and conducted orchestras. As such Ireland♦ stated he was "unapproached by any child who has trodden the American stage." In later years he was a distinguished violinist who gave solo concerts and also accompanied artists such as Jenny Lind.

Burlesque, a play in three acts by George Manker Watters and Arthur Hopkins.♦ Produced by Hopkins at the Plymouth Theatre. September 1, 1927. 372 performances.

Bonnie (Barbara Stanwyck) and Skid Johnson (Hal Skelly♦) are not only husband and wife but work together in a second-string burlesque company in which Skid is the leading comedian. Bonnie worries about Skid, who is a heavy drinker, takes hurtful pratfalls as part of his act, and has his eye on a cute showgirl who is about to leave for a Broadway musical. To make Skid jealous, Bonnie openly flirts with a rich rancher who has been buying tickets for their show every night. Skid is unconcerned. When an offer comes for Skid to appear in the same Broadway show as the chorus girl, he takes it. In no time he is having an affair with the showgirl, so Bonnie sues for divorce and agrees to marry the rancher. Just before the divorce becomes final, Bonnie comes to New York. Skid visits her, goes on a binge, and loses his job. A friend offers to produce a musical featuring Bonnie and Skid. Skid realizes he loves Bonnie, and Bonnie recognizes how much he still needs her.

Like *Broadway*♦ the season before, *Burlesque* was written by a new young playwright and revised by an experienced hand. Burns Mantle♦ saw the play as a "rough drama in the sense that it cross-sections life among the lowly and uncultured performers of the burlesque theatres, revealing them on good authority as they live and as they are, refining no more than their mental reactions and only occasionally softening the common speech of their kind." The play was revived in 1946 by Jean Dalrymple♦ with Bert Lahr♦ as Skid and Jean Parker as Bonnie, and with Hopkins once again directing. It ran for over a year. Watters (1891–1943) was born in Rochester, N.Y., into an old theatrical family. He managed a number of theatres and spent his last years writing films. This was his only produced play.

Burlesque in America Traditional burlesque, in the sense of a travesty or satire, came early to America and was well represented both in specific works, such as the 18th-century spoof of *The Blockade*♦ as *The Blockheads,* and in more extended manifestations such as the productions mounted in the 1840s by William Mitchell♦ at the Olympic. Notable later 19th-century examples might be John Brougham's♦ *Pocahontas*♦ and the musicals *Evangeline*♦ and *Adonis.* ♦

The modern burlesque, which is perceived as a much lower order of entertainment, filled with bump-and-grind strippers and raunchy clowning, began to develop in the last half of the 19th century. Coming on top of the sensation caused by a chorus line of girls in tights in *The Black Crook*♦ (1866), the arrival in 1868 of Lydia Thompson♦ and her "British Blondes" in their burlesques started the slow and at first subtle transition. Her burlesques were totally in the older tradition but the presence of a line of beautiful women in tights added a new and ultimately telling dimension. The decline of minstrelsy, oddly enough, was the next major factor. Michael Leavitt♦ ran an all-girl blackface company called Mme. Rentz's Female Minstrels, and when business waned he changed the nature and name of his troupe, dropping blackface, adding vaudeville turns not unlike the often suggestive comic bits of the time, and emphasizing his line of beautiful girls. Since his leading performer was Mabel Santley, he called his reconstituted troupe the Rentz-Santley show. Before long another star, May Howard, headed her own companies. The cleaning up of vaudeville by Tony Pastor♦ and later by Keith♦ shoved many less amenable players and producers into the ranks of burlesque and underscored the emerging difference. Many historians suggest that Sam T. Jack, who had worked with Leavitt and who incorporated risqué features of Western honky-tonk entertainments, initiated the more modern show in Chicago. His and other burlesque shows of the turn

of the century still assumed much of the form of period musical comedy or revue, to an extent to give the productions a certain legitimacy. During this period the two great circuits were formed. The Empire, or so-called Western, Circuit was first established as a loose confederacy of houses from such cities as Cincinnati, Louisville, Chicago, and Minneapolis in the early 1880s and officially incorporated in 1897. The Columbia, or Eastern, Wheel was established in 1902. Sam A. Scribner, its first president, attempted to de-emphasize the growing bawdy elements, but failed. While suggestive dress and even nudity were not unknown to the legitimate stage, the modern striptease began to come to the fore about the time of World War I and continued to grow in importance until burlesque was finally closed by police order in the 1930s and faded away on its own a decade or two later. The Minskys♦ and their greatest star, Gypsy Rose Lee,♦ exemplified burlesque at its modern apogee.

Miss Lee was one of the few strippers to move into legitimate theatre and make a mark there, but in its heyday burlesque proved a remarkable training ground for great comedians, among them Fanny Brice♦ and Bobby Clark.♦ A few leading clowns, such as Billy "Cheese 'n' Crackers" Hagen, were never able to transplant their art.

In 1979 the successful Broadway musical *Sugar Babies,* ♦ starring Mickey Rooney and Ann Miller, revived much of the old material for a nostalgic look back.

BURNETT, FRANCES HODGSON (1849–1924) The English-born authoress was often successful at dramatizing her works. Her first success, *Esmeralda*♦ (1881), was adapted from her short story and written in collaboration with William Gillette.♦ It recounted how a young girl determines to marry a man over the opposition of her domineering mother. Her most famous work, both as novel and play, was *Little Lord Fauntleroy* (1888). Neither *Phyllis* (1889) nor *The Showman's Daughter* (1891) reached New York, while *Love's Young Dream* (1892), her adaptation of Dickens's "Boots at the Holly Tree," was quickly withdrawn. Both *The First Gentleman of Europe* (1897), which she wrote with George Fleming, and *A Lady of Quality* (1897), which she adapted in collaboration with Stephen Townsend, enjoyed modest runs. *The Little Princess* (1903) was less well received, but Maude Adams♦ helped *The Pretty Sister of Jose* (1903) win audiences. Similarly, Eleanor Robson♦ earned *The Dawn of a Tomorrow*♦ (1909) a five-month run. It told of a girl named Glad who performs miracles and reforms burglars. Her last play, *Racketty-Packetty House* (1912), was written for children and employed films to help tell its tale. Mrs. Burnett's plays were always sentimental—at worst cloyingly so, at best, the sentimentality was successfully restrained.

BURNS, DAVID (1902–71) A native New Yorker, the pudgy, dour, often snarling comedian made his debut in 1921 and two years later first played in New York. From the early 1930s on he was a sought-after featured performer, who is remembered for his work in such shows as *The Man Who Came to Dinner*◆ (1939), *Make Mine Manhattan* (1948), *Out of This World* (1950), *A Funny Thing Happened on the Way to the Forum*◆ (1962), and *Hello, Dolly!*◆ (1964).

BURNSIDE, R[OBERT] H[UBBER THORNE] (1870–1952) The son of the manager of Glasgow's Gaiety Theatre, he began his career when he was carried on stage as a baby. Moving to London when he was twelve he served as call boy first to Edward Terry and then for Gilbert◆ and Sullivan◆ at London's Savoy Theatre, where he eventually became assistant to Richard Barker. ◆ He came to New York in 1894 to work with Lillian Russell◆ and the following year staged his first musical, the burlesque *Thrilby.* Between then and 1944, when he staged a revival of *Robin Hood,*◆ he directed some sixty other musicals, most notably the gigantic spectacles mounted at the Hippodrome◆ from 1909 to 1921. Besides serving as director, he wrote the librettos and/or lyrics for many shows, including some Hippodrome productions and the Montgomery and Stone vehicle, *Chin-Chin*◆ (1914), as well as Fred Stone's◆ vehicles after Dave Montgomery's death: *Jack o' Lantern* (1917), *Tip Top* (1920), and *Stepping Stones* (1923).

BURROWS, ABE [né ABRAM SOLMAN BOROWITZ] (1910–85) The New Yorker turned to the stage after writing for radio and television. His first venture was the highly successful *Guys and Dolls*◆ (1950), whose libretto he wrote in collaboration with Jo Swerling. His later hits were *Can-Can*◆ (1953); *Silk Stockings* (1955), written in collaboration with George S. Kaufman◆ and Leueen McGrath; *How To Succeed in Business Without Really Trying*◆ (1961); and *Cactus Flower*◆ (1965), a play adapted from the French. Alone or with others he also wrote *Make a Wish* (1951), *Three Wishes for Jamie* (1952), *Say, Darling* (1958), and *First Impressions* (1959). He served as director for many of these plays, as well as for others, and also often acted as play doctor.
Autobiography: *Honest Abe,* Boston, 1980.

BURSTYN, ELLEN [née EDNA RAE GILLOOLY] (b. 1932) Elected in 1982 to be the first woman president of Actors' Equity,◆ the wholesome, young-looking actress was born in Detroit. She studied acting in California and then in New York with Stella Adler◆ and Lee Strasberg.◆ Under the name Ellen McRae she made her Broadway debut in *Fair Game* (1957). Her major Broadway success has been Doris, the happily married wife who nonetheless keeps an annual tryst, in *Same Time, Next Year*◆ (1975). She won praise for her Masha in a 1977 Brooklyn revival of *The Three Sisters* and as the booklover in *84 Charing Cross Road* (1982).

BURTON, RICHARD [né JENKINS] (1925–84) The Welsh-born actor first came to America to play Richard in *The Lady's Not for Burning* (1950), and thereafter played the Musician in *Legend of Lovers* (1952) and Prince Albert in *Time Remembered* (1957). His best-known stage roles were King Arthur in the musical *Camelot*◆ (1960), for which he won the New York Drama Critics Circle Award,◆ and Hamlet in a production staged by John Gielgud◆ in 1964. In 1976 he was a replacement as Dr. Martin Dysart in *Equus,* ◆ and in 1981 he toured briefly in a revival of *Camelot.* His next role was Elyot Chase, playing opposite his sometime wife Elizabeth Taylor, in a 1983 revival of *Private Lives.* He was widely celebrated as a film actor, a celebrity which helped his stage career.

BURTON, WILLIAM E[VANS] (1804–60) The English-born actor had given up a career in publishing and turned to performing only a few years before coming to America in 1834. Making his debut at Philadelphia's Arch Street Theatre◆ as Dr. Ollapod in *The Poor Gentleman,* he was recognized for his comic talents. He made his first New York appearance in 1837, but maintained Philadelphia as his base for several years, acting and running theatres there. While retaining his Philadelphia interests, he came to New York in 1848 and turned Palmo's decaying opera house into Burton's Chambers Street Theatre, where he presented seasons mainly of old comedies, burlesques, and dramatizations of popular novels. His first season included two of his most famous portrayals: Captain Cuttle in *Dombey and Son* and Timothy Toodle, the husband beset by a wife who buys useless things at auctions, in *The Toodles.* ◆ Typical of his range were other hits of that season, from the burlesque *Lucy Did Sham Amour* to a mounting of Milton's *Comus.* In 1849 he offered another celebrated interpretation, that of Aminadab Sleek in *The Serious Family.* ◆ Over the years he also presented several Shakespearean revivals that were deemed among the best of the era: *The Winter's Tale* (1851), *Twelfth Night*♦ (1851), *A Midsummer Night's Dream*♦ (1854), and *The Tempest*♦ (1854). For all his excellences, Burton found himself unable to compete after Wallack's♦ great ensemble began performing in 1852. He relinquished his theatre at the end of the 1855–56 season, and while he continued to produce and act at other theatres, he never again enjoyed the success of his brief heyday.

Joseph Jefferson♦ recalled, "Burton's features were strong and heavy, and his figure was portly and ungainly." Of his acting Jefferson noted, not unkindly, "Burton colored highly, and laid on the effect with a liberal brush."

Biography: *William E. Burton, Actor, Author, Manager,* William Linn Keese, New York, 1885.

Bus Stop, a play in three acts by William Inge.♦ Produced by Robert Whitehead♦ and Roger L. Stevens♦ at the Music Box. March 2, 1955. 478 performances.

At a small-town Kansas restaurant and bus stop, run by a hardnosed woman called Grace (Elaine Stritch♦), a bus discharges its passengers during a blizzard. One of the riders is a strumpety night-club "chantoosie," Cherie (Kim Stanley♦). Another is an aggressive, randy cowboy, Bo Decker (Albert Salmi), who is determined to pester Cherie until he gets what he wants. At first Cherie would hide from Bo, but the long stopover forces her to change her tack. By the time the bus is ready to move on, Cherie has brought out Bo's tenderness and humility. When he tells her he is virgin enough for the two of them, Cherie responds, "Thass the sweetest, tenderest thing that was ever said to me." They board the bus together, their new-found romance applauded by the oddly assorted travelers who have shared their wait.

Another of Inge's treatments of modern sexuality, the play, Louis Kronenberger♦ noted, had "a rowdy, positive quality that is theatrically very useful to the largely static form, the largely Chekhovian mood of the play; it gives a sense of motion to what is becalmed, and of lustiness to what is basically sentimental." Although Miss Stanley won both the Donaldson Award♦ and *Variety's*♦ drama critic poll for her performance, the film version assigned her part to Marilyn Monroe, who gave it a more comic turn.

BUSH, [Benjamin] Frank[lyn] (1856?–1927) One of the first popular Jewish dialect comedians, he began his career as a youngster at the rowdy Grand

Duke Theatre on Water Street. Although he attempted Irish, Yankee, and other types with success, his Jewish clown remained his act most in demand. He performed his turn in grotesque makeup, and wearing a battered hat, long black coat, tattered pants, oversize spectacles, and an exaggeratedly long beard. Typical of his songs was one that began, "Oh, my name is Solomon Moses; I'm a bully Sheeny man." As part of the act he often inserted a tin-whistle solo, and customarily exited with an eccentric dance. He was long a main attraction at Tony Pastor's♦ and other leading vaudeville houses. In 1896 he toured briefly in the play *A Girl Wanted*. In later years, when a reaction set in against his brand of stereotypical caricature, he performed in a tuxedo, but his change of dress apparently failed to bring about any fundamental change of approach. As his humor was perceived as dated his star waned. On his retirement he boasted he had never missed a performance.

Business Before Pleasure, a comedy in three acts by Montague Glass♦ and Jules Eckert Goodman.♦ Produced by A. H. Woods♦ at the Eltinge Theatre. August 15, 1917. 357 performances.

Although their own business seems solid enough for the moment, Abe Potash (Barney Bernard♦) and Mawruss Perlmutter (Alexander Carr) see nothing wrong in adding to their profits by joining their many friends and associates who are going into "fillums." They quickly find they have leaped "out of the frying pan into the hot water." Before they write "The End" to their own adventures they have starred their own wives, Rosie (Mathilde Cottrelly♦) and Ruth (Lotte Kendall), in a flicker, had to deal with a siren named Rita Sismondi (Clara Joel), and gotten involved with shady bankers.

This tremendously successful sequel to *Potash and Perlmutter*♦ prompted one critic to note, "When the annals of the American drama are written it will perhaps be found that these plays of Yiddish life are the historical descendants of the Hoyt farces." Of course, the farces of Charles H. Hoyt♦ dealt largely with old-line Americans. The critic might better have pointed to the ethnic comedies of Edward Harrigan.♦

Butter and Egg Man, The, a comedy in three acts by George S. Kaufman. ♦ Produced by Crosby Gaige♦ at the Longacre Theatre. September 23, 1925. 243 performances.

Joe Lehman (Robert Middlemass) and Jack McClure (John A. Butler) are two shoestring Broadway producers with a problem. The gangster backer of their new play has been arrested moments before he could sign the check for the money they needed. Even Joe's wife Fanny (Lucille Webster) thinks so little of the play she refuses to help. In walks Peter Jones (Gregory Kelly♦), a yokel from Chillicothe, looking to invest his savings in a play, make a bundle, and return home to buy a hotel. His $20,000 buys 49 percent of the piece. The play opens out of town to dreadful reviews, so Lehman and McClure want to close it. Jones buys out the producers, repairs the play, and opens it in New York, where it is a smash hit. However, Jones is confronted with a lawsuit charging the play has been stolen. Without divulging the legal problem, Jones sells the play back to Lehman and McClure for a whopping profit, and returns home with his helpful sweetheart to build his hotel.

Kaufman's only important solo effort, the play was praised by Gilbert W. Gabriel of the *Sun* as "the wittiest and liveliest jamboree ever distilled from the atmosphere of Broadway." Malcolm Goldstein, Kaufman's biographer, has noted that the play's underlying theme—a not-too-bright young man spurred to success by a sharper woman—had been common to all Kaufman's earlier plays as well. The term "butter and egg man" was originated or popularized by night-club hostess Texas Guinan to suggest a hick from the sticks.

Butterflies Are Free, a play in two acts by Leonard Gershe. Produced at the Booth Theatre. October 21, 1969. 1,128 performances.

To escape his domineering mother, Don Baker (Keir Dullea) has taken his own apartment in New York. The decision is a brave one, since Don is totally blind. Before long Don is having an affair with a slightly kooky actress, Jill Tanner (Blythe Danner). But his mother (Eileen Heckart♦) will not leave Don alone. She and Jill are soon locked in battle, and for a while it seems that Mrs. Baker will scare Jill into leaving Don. Jill claims she simply does not want to be tied down to anyone. Don, however, recognizes it is his blindness that frightens her. He tells her she is leaving because she is "emotionally retarded . . . crippled. I'd rather be blind." Jill stays.

A small play with an essentially pathetic theme, it was hailed by Richard Watts, Jr.,♦ of the *Post* as "humourous, winning and quietly moving." The title came from Dickens's *Bleak House*. This was the only successful play by Gershe, who has been primarily a screenwriter.

BUTTERWORTH, Charles [Edward] (1896–1946) Born in South Bend, Ind., the comedian who specialized in shy, gawky, or professorial types spent several years in vaudeville before winning acclaim for his monologues in *Americana* (1926). He was later seen in, among others, *Good Boy* (1928), *Sweet Adeline*♦ (1929), and *Flying Colors* (1932). His last years were spent largely in films.

By Jupiter, a musical comedy in two acts. Book by Richard Rodgers♦ and Lorenz Hart.♦ Lyrics by Hart. Music by Rodgers. Produced by Dwight Deere Wiman♦ and Rodgers at the Shubert Theatre. June 3, 1942. 427 performances.

So long as Queen Hippolyta (Benay Venuta) of Pontus can retain her magic, strength-giving girdle, she and her Amazons will rule over their milksop husbands. The Greeks, led by Theseus (Ronald Graham) and Hercules (Ralph Dumke), invade Pontus, hoping to capture the girdle and elevate the hapless consort Sapiens (Ray Bolger♦) to the throne. Their swords fail them but their sexual prowess prevails. Theseus is awarded the hand of Hippolyta's sister Antiope (Constance Moore).

Principal songs: Careless Rhapsody · Everything I've Got · Nobody's Heart

Based on Julian F. Thompson's *The Warrior Husband,* the musical was Rodgers and Hart's final collaboration. When it was successfully revived off-Broadway in 1967, *Variety*♦ observed that it "is still a melodious laughrouser."

Bye Bye Birdie, a musical comedy in two acts. Book by Michael Stewart.♦ Lyrics by Lee Adams.♦ Music by Charles Strouse.♦ Produced at the Martin Beck Theatre. April 14, 1960. 607 performances.

When the popular rock star Conrad Birdie (Dick Gautier) is about to be drafted, his agent, Albert Peterson (Dick Van Dyke), arranges a coup he hopes will keep revenues coming in during Birdie's army stint and allow him to marry Rosie Grant (Chita Rivera♦). Birdie will go to a small American town and sing his latest song to a typical American teenager. Albert tells Conrad's unhappy fans, who have come to see him off at Penn Station, to "Put On a Happy Face." But that is something Albert's possessive mother, Mae (Kay Medford), cannot do, since if Albert succeeds she will lose him to Rosie. The group arrives in Sweet Apple, Ohio, where they have selected Kim McAfee (Susan Watson) as the girl Conrad will sing to. The decision makes no one happy. Conrad determines to go off for a night on the town, insisting he has "A Lot of Livin' To Do"; Kim's father (Paul Lynde) cannot understand what delights modern "Kids"; and Mae appears, precipitating a break between Rosie and Albert, who finally wins Rosie back after he has phoned and pleaded, "Baby, Talk to Me." In the end Kim returns to her old beau; Rosie and Albert are reconciled; and Birdie heads off to the army.

The first musical to pay real attention to the new rock 'n' roll craze, it was apparently suggested by the induction into military service of singing star Elvis Presley. The production was imaginatively staged by Gower Champion. ◆ Kenneth Tynan ◆ of the *New Yorker* found it "filled with a kind of affectionate freshness that we have seldom encountered." A sequel, *Bring Back Birdie,* failed in 1980.

BYRON, ARTHUR [WILLIAM] (1872–1943) The son of Oliver Doud Byron, ◆ he was born in Brooklyn and made his debut with his father's company in 1889. After playing with Sol Smith Russell ◆ and in San Francisco stock, he spent several seasons under Charles Frohman's ◆ aegis in support of John Drew. ◆ By 1902 he was playing leading roles such as the maligned suitor of the heroine in *The Stubbornness of Geraldine.* He was Maxine Elliott's ◆ vicious suitor in *Her Own Way* ◆ (1903); Gavin Dishart, the little minister in a 1904 revival of Barrie's ◆ play of the same name; John Ryder, the leading man, in a touring company of *The Lion and the Mouse* ◆ (1906); and Jerome Le Govain in *Samson* (1908). He was again Maxine Elliott's leading man in *The Inferior Sex* (1910), then toured with Maude Adams ◆ as John Shand in *What Every Woman Knows* (1911) and played opposite Mrs. Fiske ◆ in *The High Road* (1912). He scored a major success as Dr. Gerald Sumner, the young doctor who falls in love with his nurse, in *The Boomerang* ◆ (1915). Another long run came as The Friend to the absurdly jealous Husband in *Tea for Three* ◆ (1918). After a lengthy tour and brief New York stand as Comte de Larsac, the aging boulevardier, in *Transplanting Jean* (1921), he won applause as Dr. John Dillard, who gains the hand of a widow haunted by the memory of her first husband, in *The Ghost Between* (1921). His biggest hit was as Richard

Sones, who tames his irresponsible wife, in *Spring Cleaning* (1923). Somewhat less successful was *A Kiss in a Taxi* (1925), in which he played the sugar daddy, Leon Lambert. In a change of pace he was hailed as Martin Brady, the state's attorney, in *The Criminal Code* ◆ (1929). Another drama, *Five Star Final* ◆ (1930), allowed him to play the guilt-ridden editor, Randall. In 1936 he essayed Polonius to John Gielgud's Hamlet. Elected president of Actors' Equity ◆ in 1938, he made his last appearance as the militaristic King Zedekiah in *Jeremiah* (1939).

BYRON, JOSEPH (1844–1923) One of the leading photographers of the American stage, he was born in Nottingham, England, and came to this country in 1888. Three years later he began to photograph theatrical productions. Many of the most famous stage pictures of the early 20th century were his. His heirs continued to operate the firm until 1942.

BYRON, OLIVER DOUD (1842–1920) Born in Frederick, Md., he made his first appearance at the Holliday Street Theatre ◆ in Baltimore in 1856, playing with Joseph Jefferson ◆ in *Nicholas Nickleby.* For his earliest appearances he used the name Oliver B. Doud. In 1856 he joined the Richmond (Virginia) Theatre, playing alongside John Wilkes Booth. ◆ Afterwards he acted with companies in Washington, Pittsburgh, and New Orleans, and then became a member of Wallack's ◆ celebrated New York ensemble. At one time he alternated with Edwin Booth ◆ in the roles of Othello and Iago. Although he claimed to have originated the part of Richard Harre in *East Lynne,* ◆ Byron's principal claim to fame was his Joe Ferris in *Across the Continent* ◆ (1871), a part he played several thousand times over thirty years. Some critics ridiculed Byron's characterization as being unrealistically virtuous, but Odell ◆ remembered it as "a manly, wholesome, resourceful characterisation that pleased women and men alike." Byron retired from the stage in 1912 after costly and losing battles with the Theatrical Syndicate or Trust, ◆ to whom he refused to bow. His wife Kate and his son Arthur ◆ were both popular performers.

C

Cabaret, a musical in two acts. Book by Joe Masteroff. Lyrics by Fred Ebb.♦ Music by John Kander.♦ Produced by Harold Prince♦ and others at the Broadhurst Theatre. November 20, 1966. 1,165 performances.

At the sleazy Kit Kat Klub the effete Master of Ceremonies (Joel Grey♦) bids one and all "Will-kommen" to the tumultuous Berlin of the Weimar Republic, where Cliff Bradshaw (Bert Convy), a young American writer, strikes up a series of foredoomed relationships. One is with his landlady, Frau Schneider (Lotte Lenya♦), who lives in day-dreams of a probably imaginary past and who is courted by a Jewish boarder, Herr Schultz (Jack Gilford). Another is with Ernst Ludwig (Edward Winter), whose main preoccupation is smuggling in funds for the Nazis. However, Cliff becomes closest to Sally Bowles (Jill Haworth), an attractive English girl working as an entertainer in the club. He finds her "Perfectly Marvelous," but she can only view life as a "Cabaret," where hedonism and amorality prevail. Neither the times nor Sally's unstable charms provide an anchor for the romance, so Cliff elects to leave Germany,

A musical redaction of *I Am a Camera,* ♦ *Cabaret* employed the night club as a frame for the action and the club's M.C. as its Elizabethan prologue, Greek chorus, and contemporary colorist. Walter Kerr♦ noted in the *Times,* "Instead of putting the narrative first . . . it pops the painted clown and gartered girls directly into our faces, making them, in effect, a brilliantly glazed window . . . through which we can perceive the people and the emotional pattern of the plot." The musical was revived successfully in 1987. A film version starred Liza Minnelli.

Cabin in the Sky, a musical fantasy in two acts. Book by Lynn Root. Lyrics by John Latouche. ♦ Music by Vernon Duke.♦ Produced by Albert Lewis in association with Vinton Freedley♦ at the Martin Beck Theatre. October 25, 1940. 156 performances.

When the pious Petunia Jackson (Ethel Waters♦) prays to the Good Lord to spare the life of her troublesome husband, Little Joe (Dooley Wilson), the Good Lord allows Joe six months in which to redeem himself. He even sends The Lord's General (Todd Duncan♦) to help, but his move is countered by the appearance of Lucifer, Jr. (Rex Ingram). Just as it seems Joe has turned over a new leaf, he has an argument with Petunia and shoots her. They arrive at the Pearly Gates, where Petunia's loving pleas melt the Good Lord's heart, so Joe is permitted to enter along with her.

Principal songs: Cabin in the Sky · Honey in the Honeycomb · Takin' a Chance on Love

One of several adventurous musicals of the 1940–41 season, which included *Pal Joey*♦ and *Lady in the Dark,* ♦ the musical's relatively short run was probably attributable to its being perceived as a black show. But in its willingness to touch on fantasy (always a theatrical bugaboo), its superb Dunham♦ and Balanchine♦ dances, and its pervasive sense of restraint and tone, it was several steps ahead of its time. When it was revived in 1964 John McClain of the *Journal-American* observed, "The book by Lynn Root seems to have withstood the ravages of time wonderfully well . . . [*Cabin in the Sky*] is a small classic in our time."

CABOT, ELIOT (1899–1938) The darkly handsome leading man was born in Boston and educated at Harvard and at Cambridge (England). He made his debut as the youngster in *Six Characters in Search of an Author* (1922), but is best recalled as David, the defiant son, in *The Silver Cord*♦ (1926) and as the insolent, shiftless Michael in *Coquette*♦ (1927).

Cactus Flower An Americanization by Abe Burrows♦ of Pierre Barillet and Jean Pierre Gredy's Parisian hit, *Fleur de Cactus,* which told of a philandering bachelor dentist eventually subdued by his strong-willed nurse, it opened in New York in December 1965 and ran for 1,234 performances, the longest run to date of any Continental play on Broadway. Barry Nelson♦ and Lauren Bacall♦ were the leads.

CAESAR, [ISIDOR] IRVING (b. 1895) The New York-born lyricist came to the attention of Al Jolson♦ when he won a contest for new lyrics to Jolson's World War I tongue-twister, "Sister Susie's Sewing Shirts for Soldiers." The winning lyric was entitled "Brother Benny's Baking Buns for Belgians." A few seasons later he wrote the lyrics for one of Jolson's most memorable hits, "Swanee," with music by George Gershwin.◆ He wrote words to songs for several *Greenwich Village Follies,*◆ before creating the lyrics to "I Want To Be Happy" and "Tea for Two" to Vincent Youmans's◆ music for *No, No, Nanette.*◆ Youmans's and Caesar's "Sometimes I'm Happy" earned widespread popularity in *Hit the Deck!* (1926), although it was written for an earlier failure, *A Night Out* (1925). For the 1928 musical *Here's Howe* he wrote the lyric for "Crazy Rhythm," with music by Roger Wolfe Kahn. Among his other shows were *No Foolin'* (1926); *Yes, Yes, Yvette* (1927); *Americana* (1928); *Polly* (1929); *Ripples* (1930); *Nina Rosa* (1930); *The Wonder Bar* (1931), for which he also supplied the American libretto; *Melody* (1933); and *White Horse Inn* (1936). His last show was *My Dear Public* (1943), for which he served not only as lyricist but as co-librettist and producer. His lyrics were bright, often clever, and colloquial, but hardly distinguished.

CAESAR, [Isaac Sidney] Sid (b. 1922) The brash comedian, who excelled at aping different accents and types, was born in Yonkers, N. Y. Although best known for his work on television, especially for *The Show of Shows* (early 1950s), he was starred in two Broadway musicals, *Make Mine Manhattan* (1948) and *Little Me* (1962), in the latter playing all of the heroine's diverse lovers. His return in *Sid Caesar and Company* (1989), a slapped-together revue, was a quick failure.

Caesar and Cleopatra Originally presented at the New Amsterdam Theatre◆ in 1906 with Johnston Forbes-Robertson◆ and his wife, Gertrude Elliot, in the leading roles, Shaw's◆ work was perceived as an interesting, but uneven play made noteworthy by the brilliant scene in which the two principals first meet. The Theatre Guild◆ used the play to open its new playhouse in 1925, with Lionel Atwill◆ and Helen Hayes◆ as the rulers. It was a major success, although critics such as Stark Young◆ felt both the production and the stars missed the grandeur of Shaw's conception. The best later revival was that which featured Cedric Hardwicke and Lilli Palmer in 1949. Laurence Olivier◆ and Vivien Leigh performed the play, in a program alternating with Shakespeare's *Antony and Cleopatra,*◆ in 1951. The work also served as the basis of a failed musical, *Her First Roman* (1968).

Cage aux Folles, La, see *La Cage aux Folles*

Café La Mama, see *La Mama Experimental Theatre Club*

Caffe Cino a coffee house on Cornelia Street in New York's Greenwich Village. In 1959 its owner, Joe Cino, a would-be dancer, turned it into one of the earliest such establishments offering avant-garde theatricals. It flourished until Cino's suicide in 1967 and closed shortly thereafter. Lanford Wilson,◆ Marshall Mason, and Tom Eyen are artists once closely associated with it and who went on the renown on Broadway or off-Broadway. Ironically, for all its avant-garde reputation, the most famous work to be developed first on its tiny stage was the still frequently revived musical *Dames at Sea.* Ellen Stewart, duenna of the similar La Mama Experimental Theatre Club,◆ has said, "It was Joseph Cino who started off-off-Broadway."

CAHILL, Marie (1870–1933) A tiny, plump, feisty singer-comedienne, she made her debut in her hometown Brooklyn in *Kathleen Mavourneen,* then made her New York debut in 1888 in *C.O.D.* After appearing briefly in *McKenna's Flirtation*◆ and a revival of *A Tin Soldier* in 1889 she left for Europe, where she spent the next several seasons in Paris and London. She returned to assume a small role in *Excelsior, Jr.* (1895) and played the title part on tour. She earned remarkable notices as Lady Patty Larceny, forever seeking the perfect mate, in Victor Herbert's◆ short-lived *The Gold Bug* (1896), in which she stopped the show singing "When I First Began to Marry, Years Ago." After several other supporting roles, she won widespread attention introducing "Nancy Brown" in *The Wild Rose* (1902). Her most famous song was "Under the Bamboo Tree," which she first sang while playing the title role in *Sally in Our Alley* (1902). Star parts followed in *Nancy Brown* (1903), *It Happened in Nordland* (1904), *Moonshine* (1905), *Marrying Mary* (1906), *The Boys and Betty* (1908), *Judy Forgot* (1910), *The Opera Ball* (1912), and *Ninety in the Shade* (1915). Thereafter her career began to falter, although she remained popular in vaudeville. Her last appearances were in the revue *Merry-Go-Round* (1927) and as the gigolo-seeking Park Avenue matron, Mrs. Wentworth, in *The New Yorkers* (1930). During her career, the strong-willed actress often won notoriety by insisting on inserting her own interpolations. Her battles cost her several important roles.

Cahn's Guide Properly known as *Julius Cahn's Official Theatrical Guide,* it was long considered the authoritative source for information required by booking agents and producers who were taking shows on the road. State by state and city by city it provided details on all playhouses as well as town population figures, newspapers, hotels, and railroads. It was published from 1896 to 1920 when it was merged with the *Gus Hill Theatrical and Motion Picture Guide.*

CAINE, [THOMAS HENRY] HALL (1853–1931) The English novelist dramatized several of his own books. His most notable American success was *The Christian*♦ (1898), in which a strongheaded, worldly girl is brought to Christ by the personal ardor and religious fervor of a young clergyman. The play was presented in New York before it was offered to London. Among his other works were *The Land of the Midnight Sun* (1893), adapted by Edwin Barbour from *The Bondsman; The Manxman* (1894), adapted by Wilson Barrett♦; *The Eternal City* (1902); *The Prodigal Son* (1905); and *Margaret Schiller* (1916).

Cain's Warehouse Opened by John J. Cain in the late 1880s or early 1890s, it specialized in storing theatrical scenery of closed Broadway shows. The scenery was then rented to touring and stock companies. "Going to Cain's Warehouse" became a euphemism for closing a show. The warehouse itself closed in 1938 when the shrinking road and the decline of stock companies deprived it of its market.

Caius Marius, a tragedy in five acts by Richard Penn Smith.♦ Produced at the Arch Street Theatre♦ (Philadelphia). January 12, 1831. In repertory.

The rapid rise to power of the low-born Roman general, Caius Marius (Edwin Forrest♦), irks the patrician Sylla (Robert C. Maywood) and Metellus (Thomas Archer), both of whom had helped him but now perceive him as a rabblerouser and an ingrate. A battle for control ensues, couched in terms of a class struggle. At one point, when mobs endanger Sylla, Caius Marius offers him the sanctuary of his home. In the end, however, after Caius has slain Metellus and Sylla's army is at Rome's gates, Caius' beloved and loving slave girl, Martha (Mrs. Sharpe), prevents Caius' humiliating defeat by joining him in drinking a cup of poisoned wine. The dying, bitter general tells Sylla,

> I bequeath
> An abject world to thy unpitying care.
> Now unoppos'd, go drive thy chariot wheels
> Across the necks of slaves who will not groan.

A subplot details the doomed love of Caius Marius' son, Granius (Mr. Smith), for Metellus' daughter, Metella (Mrs. Rowbotham).

Many contemporary critics felt this blank-verse tragedy was Smith's best play, but the public was unresponsive, so after a few additional performances in New York, Boston, and possibly elsewhere, Forrest dropped the piece. It was apparently not revived until 1858, when F. B. Conway♦ headed the cast at Philadelphia's Walnut Street Theatre♦ in two performances mounted as a memorial to Smith. The text was lost for nearly a century. Rediscovered, it was published in 1968.

CALDARA, ORME (1875–1925) A virile leading man, he earned fame in such roles as the guilt-ridden Jack Payson in *The Round-Up*♦ (1907); Richard Gilder, who comes to love the girl who married him for revenge, in *Within the Law*♦ (1912); and Hugh Fullerton, the seducer, in *Common Clay*♦ (1915). Before tuberculosis led to his early retirement and death he played opposite Jane Cowl♦ in such dramas as *Lilac Time* (1917) and *Smilin' Through* (1919).

CALDWELL, ANNE (1867–1936) Born in Boston, she began her career as a singer and briefly turned her hand to composing before deciding to become a lyricist and librettist. She was first represented on Broadway in *Top o' the World* (1907), although songs she composed with her husband James O'Dea had been interpolated into *The Social Whirl* (1906). Growing recognition came when she served as co-librettist for Victor Herbert's♦ *The Lady of the Slipper* (1912) and as librettist and lyricist for *When Claudia Smiles* (1914). Her work on *Chin-Chin*♦ (1914) so delighted its star, Fred Stone,♦ that he employed her for all his remaining shows but his last: *Jack o' Lantern* (1917), which included her lyric for "Wait Till the Cows Come Home"; *Tip Top* (1920); *Stepping Stones* (1923); *Criss Cross* (1926); and *Three Cheers* (1928). Many of her other works were written in collaboration with Jerome Kern♦: *She's a Good Fellow* (1919); *The Night Boat* (1920), which offered " 'Left All Alone Again' Blues"; *Hitchy-Koo, 1920; Good Morning, Dearie* (1921), famous for "Ka-lu-a"; *The Bunch and Judy* (1922); *The City Chap* (1925), for which she wrote only the lyrics; and *Criss Cross* (1926). Her 1926 collaboration with Vincent Youmans,♦ *Oh, Please!,* left behind "I Know That You Know."

CALDWELL, JAMES H. (1793–1863) Coming to America from England in 1816, he made his acting debut that same year in Charleston, S.C., as Belcour in *The West Indian*. The role also served for his New York debut in 1828. Although he was an actor of some repute and continued performing until 1843, he was best known as a builder and manager of theatres. His first attempt at managing was in Columbus, Ky., but it soon ended in failure. Profiting from his experiences he erected theatres in Cincinnati, Mobile, Nashville, and St. Louis. However, he is best remembered for his work in New Orleans, where he managed the St. Philip Street Theatre and the American Theatre, in which he introduced the use of gaslighting, before erecting the St. Charles Theatre in 1835. The St. Charles was long the city's prime playhouse. A vivid picture of the man is drawn by Noah M. Ludlow♦ in his *Dramatic Life as I Found It.*

CALDWELL, Zoë [Ada] (b. 1933) The Australian-born actress, who is the wife of Robert Whitehead,♦ acted with the Royal Shakespeare Company♦ before coming to America. She has appeared with the Tyrone Guthrie Theatre♦ of Minneapolis and other regional theatres in a variety of roles. Her first Broadway appearance was as Sister Jean in *The Devils* (1965), but she is probably best remembered for her portrayal of the title roles in *The Prime of Miss Jean Brodie* (1968) and a 1982 revival of *Medea.* She won Tony Awards♦ for these last two performances, as well as one for best supporting actress when she portrayed Polly, the eccentric gossip columnist, in *Slapstick Tragedy* (1966). She later portrayed Lillian Hellman in a one-woman show, *Lillian* (1986).

CALHERN, Louis [né Carl Henry Vogt] (1895–1956) The lanky, suave actor made his debut while still a boy with Cecil Spooner's stock company in his native New York. He played stock in St. Louis for two seasons beginning in 1914, then toured with Margaret Anglin♦ before serving in World War I. In the early 1920s he replaced supporting players in *The White Peacock* and *The Czarina.* The first role he created on Broadway was the minor one of Eugene Poppin in *Roger Bloomer* (1923), which was followed by his portraying Joseph Murdoch in George M. Cohan's♦ *The Song and Dance Man* (1923). His first major assignment was as the untemptable Jack Race opposite Judith Anderson♦ in *The Cobra* (1924). In 1926 he played Morris Bliss, the house guest drafted as a lover, in Philip Barry's♦ *In a Garden* and Lovberg to Emily Stevens's♦ *Hedda Gabler.* Neither was successful and initiated a string of leading roles in failed plays, broken only

when he assumed the supporting role of Cass Worthing, the hero's rival, in *Brief Moment*♦ (1931). Long runs eluded him until he accepted the role of Father in a touring company of *Life with Father*♦ in 1941, and later played the same part in New York. Probably his best remembered role was the bigoted Colonel Tadeusz in *Jacobowsky and the Colonel* (1944). He won further laurels as Oliver Wendell Holmes in *The Magnificent Yankee* (1946). His last important roles were in two disparate revivals, as Sandor Turai in *The Play's the Thing* (1948) and as King Lear (1950). A final New York appearance came as the senilescent Pop in *The Wooden Dish* (1955). He also enjoyed a long career in films.

California Theatre (San Francisco) William Ralston, the head of San Francisco's Bank of California, was so impressed by the work of two fine performers, John McCullough♦ and Lawrence Barrett,♦ that he offered to build a theatre for them. The playhouse opened on Bush Street in 1869 and for many years was home for the finest company away from the East Coast. The house was designed by S. C. Bugbee and Son, and cost $150,000. Under various managements the theatre remained the city's leading playhouse until it was demolished in 1888. Another theatre, using the same name, was erected on the site and continued to flourish until it was destroyed in the 1906 earthquake and fire, but this second house, having to buck increasing competition, never enjoyed the prestige of the first.

Call Me Madam, a musical comedy in two acts. Book by Howard Lindsay♦ and Russel Crouse.♦ Lyrics and music by Irving Berlin.♦ Produced by Leland Hayward♦ at the Imperial Theatre. October 12, 1950. 644 performances.

Sally Adams (Ethel Merman♦) has been appointed ambassadress to Lichtenburg not because of any diplomatic skills, but rather because in Washington she was "The Hostess with the Mostes' on the Ball." At her new post she falls for Prime Minister Constantin (Paul Lukas), but insists on the idea of "Marrying for Love." Her assistant, Kenneth Gibson (Russell Nype), however, falls for Princess Maria (Galina Talva) and slyly suggests to the princess that they spend some time together since "It's a Lovely Day Today." When the local opposition makes things hot for Constantin, Sally is willing to retreat discreetly, although she suggests to him she would be "The Best Thing for You." She must also hold Kenneth's hand and make him aware that the pangs he feels stem from the fact that "You're

Just in Love." The opposition is foiled and both pairs of lovers can continue courting.

The musical, which proved to be Berlin's last success, was written as a send-up of the famous Washington hostess, Pearl Mesta, whom President Truman had made an ambassador.

Camelot, a musical in two acts. Book and lyrics by Alan Jay Lerner.♦ Music by Frederick Loewe.♦ Produced by Lerner, Loewe, and Moss Hart♦ at the Majestic Theatre. December 3, 1960. 873 performances.

A somewhat reluctant King Arthur (Richard Burton♦) awaits the arrival of his bride, Guinevere (Julie Andrews♦), an innocent young lady raised on bloody romances which have prompted her to look forward to a world where "kith will kill their kin for me." Her innocence disappears soon after the marriage when she falls in love with Lancelot (Robert Goulet). Their affair is betrayed by Mordred (Roddy McDowall), and the idyll of Camelot, that "one brief shining moment," is destroyed forever.

Principal songs: Camelot · If Ever I Would Leave You

The musical, based on T. H. White's *The Once and Future King,* was beset not only by the serious illnesses of both Lerner and Hart during the tryout, but by the unrealistically high expectations in the wake of *My Fair Lady.*♦ An advance sale of over $3,000,000 allowed *Camelot* to buck disappointed notices and to succeed both on Broadway and on the road. The musical was revived to more balanced reviews and good business on the road in the 1980–81 season, then taken back to New York. Richard Harris was King Arthur.

Camille [*La Dame aux Camélias*] This dramatization of Alexandre Dumas *fils's* novel was first acted in France in 1852 and brought to America the following year by Jean M. Davenport♦ in her own version, which she called *Camille; or, The Fate of a Coquette.* The story remains well known, largely because of the ongoing popularity of the opera *La Traviata,* which was based on the French original. A courtesan named Marguerite Gautier finds true love with young Armand Duval and prepares to give up her questionable ways. However, Duval's family is scandalized and his father persuades her to sacrifice her love for the sake of Armand's family. She leads Armand to believe she has been unfaithful, but the separation strains Marguerite beyond endurance. She dies in the arms of the forgiving Armand. The first great American Marguerite was Matilda

Heron,♦ who for many years had no rival in the part. Afterwards Clara Morris♦ was equally popular. The play was one of the triumphs of Sarah Bernhardt's♦ tours. As late as the early 1930s the work remained a favorite with playgoers, proving one of Eva Le Gallienne's♦ biggest successes at the Civic Repertory Theatre.♦ However, a major 1963 revival with Susan Strasberg was a quick failure.

CAMPBELL, BARTLEY [THOMAS] (1843–88) He began his career as a newspaperman on his hometown Pittsburgh *Post,* later moving to the Louisville *Courier Journal* and the Cincinnati *Enquirer.* In 1869 he founded the *Southern Monthly Magazine* in New Orleans. With the success of his first produced play, *Through Fire* (1871), a no-holds-barred melodrama centering on a man falsely accused of theft, he abandoned journalism and determined to support himself solely by his play-writing. Although, as a result, he is frequently called our first fully professional dramatist, he did often produce and direct plays as well. In 1872 he wrote a social comedy, *Peril; or, Love at Long Branch,* for E. L. Davenport♦ and that same year helped convert R. M. Hooley's♦ Chicago theatre from minstrelsy into a legitimate playhouse. Among the plays he wrote during his stay there were *Fate* (1873), in which an adventuress attempts to destroy a happy home; *Risks; or, Insure Your Life* (1873), recounting the melodramatic problems arising from a secret marriage as well as the comic exploits of an insurance agent trying to insure all the principals; *The Virginian* (1874), a love story framed in a pro-South view of the Civil War; *On the Rhine* (1875), "a military comedy" set in the Franco-Prussian war; *Gran Uaile* (1875), a story of the Irish Rebellion; and *My Foolish Wife* (1877), a comedy about a stage-struck matron. In 1875 he traveled to San Francisco with Hooley's troupe to play at Thomas Maguire's♦ Opera House. He immediately fell in love with the city and its ways, and befriended Bret Harte♦ and Joaquin Miller.♦ While there he wrote *Bulls and Bears,* a version of the same *Ultimo* which Augustin Daly♦ had presented as *The Big Bonanza.*♦ Not until an 1876 trip to London did he begin to put his Western affections on paper. The result was played in London as *How Women Love* and in a revised version in America as *The Vigilantes; or, the Heart of the Sierras* (1877). After a failed attempt to tell the story of a sculptor's troubled romance with a waif whom he makes his model, *Clio* (1878), he wrote his best and most famous play, *My Partner*♦ (1879), in which the hero is falsely accused of murdering his unprincipled partner. With the huge profits from the success he mounted his *The Galley Slave* ♦ (1879), in which a man allows himself to be condemned as a thief rather than compromise a woman's honor and later saves her from a bigamous marriage. *Siberia* ♦ (1882) dealt with Russians exiled after the assassination of Tsar Alexander II. *The White Slave* ♦ (1882) was seen by many as a rewriting of Dion Boucicault's ♦ *The Octoroon,* ♦ but was immensely successful. A number of other plays that Campbell wrote and produced at the same time failed, with losses outrunning the income from his hits. Unable to handle emotionally the financial problems that followed, he was committed to a mental institution, where he died two years later.

For a short while, from about 1875 to 1883, Campbell not only was the most successful American playwright but was hailed by many critics as the best the country had yet produced. Reaction quickly set in, and at his death Andrew C. Wheeler, ♦ writing as Nym Crinkle, noted, "He never quite reached the level of literary greatness, but he overshot the level of generous impulse—if impulse can have a level . . . Bartley never wrote a play that the hard sense of the public did not have to correct some of his emotional effusiveness." Nevertheless, his best plays remain eminently readable, and probably, if given a chance, eminently playable.

CAMPBELL, Mrs. Patrick [née Beatrice Stella Tanner] (1865–1940) The English actress famous for her wit and beauty, but best recalled for her correspondence with George Bernard Shaw, ♦ made her American debut in 1902 in the title role of *Magda.* On the tour she also offered what then were her two most celebrated roles, the title parts in *The Second Mrs. Tanqueray* and *The Notorious Mrs. Ebbsmith.* In all she made half a dozen visits to America, including a 1914 visit in which she appeared as Liza Doolittle in *Pygmalion,* ♦ a play Shaw had written for her and with which she was long identified. She was, of course, really too old to play the young flower vendor, but that proved only a small drawback. Her last appearance came in 1933. On first seeing her J. Rankin Towse ♦ wrote, "Her voice is a charming instrument, rich, soft, and musical, with sufficient volume, but no abnormal power or resonance; her eyes, large and dark and deep, often partly veiled, as in Orientals, by drooping lids, lighten finely, in her moments of excitement, and become wonderfully expressive and striking. Her great height, her graceful, sinuous figure, and her long arms make her poses singularly picturesque and her gestures uncommonly eloquent

and striking." However, for all her virtues, many agreed with another, unidentified critic, who observed, "Her appeal is essentially to the head and not to the heart . . . what she has best to offer is likely to remain 'caviare to the general.' "

Biography: *Mrs. Patrick Campbell,* Alan Dent, London, 1961.

Can-Can, a musical comedy in two acts. Book by Abe Burrows. ♦ Lyrics and music by Cole Porter. ♦ Produced by Cy Feuer ♦ and Ernest H. Martin ♦ at the Shubert Theatre. May 7, 1953. 892 performances.

A young, straitlaced judge, Aristide Forestier (Peter Cookson), is assigned to investigate stories of scandalous can-can dancing at a Montmartre café. He falls in love both with the dancing and with the café's proprietress, La Mome Pistache (Lilo), helps legalize the dance, and marries the lady. At the same time, one of the dancers, Claudine (Gwen Verdon ♦), has a duel fought over her by her two suitors.

Principal songs: Allez-vous-en · Can-Can · C'est Magnifique · I Love Paris · It's All Right with Me

Although the musical opened to indifferent notices and its French star was respectfully received, the real hit of the evening was the superb dancing and comic artistry of Gwen Verdon, in a role that had been substantially reduced during the tryout to assuage the star. Within a few months much of Porter's score had won recognition, adding to the play's box office appeal. A major revival in 1980 was unsuccessful.

Candida Arnold Daly ♦ first offered Shaw's ♦ play at a special matinee in 1903 with Dorothy Donnelly ♦ as Candida and himself as Marchbanks. The reception was such that additional matinees were given and then a four-month run followed. Curiously its good reception was largely the result of word of mouth, since many critics initially ignored the play. Its story of woman who must choose between a visionary and a practical socialist was less beset by matters of passing topical interest and had more of a genuine love story than virtually any other major Shaw play, and so has retained a loyal following and enjoyed more important revivals than other Shaw plays. Many of these revivals were led by Katharine Cornell, ♦ who first played the part in 1924 when she gave it its longest run to date, five months. She brilliantly juxtaposed the heroine's frailty and strength, giving a performance Stark Young ♦ found "so delicate and translucent and moving as we rarely see." Richard Bird was her first Marchbanks, but the role was assumed in her later revivals by such eventually more famous actors as Orson Welles,♦ Burgess Meredith,♦ and Marlon Brando.♦

Candide, a musical in two acts. Book by Lillian Hellman.♦ Lyrics by Richard Wilbur, John Latouche,♦ and Dorothy Parker.♦ Music by Leonard Bernstein.♦ Produced at the Martin Beck Theatre. December 1, 1956. 73 performances.

Tutored by the incorrigibly optimistic Doctor Pangloss (Max Adrian), who feels we live in "The Best of All Possible Worlds," young Candide (Robert Rounseville) marries Cunegonde (Barbara Cook♦) and prepares to enjoy life. Instead, war breaks out and Cunegonde is carried off. At one point she is forced to lead the life of a demimonde, striving to "Glitter and Be Gay" in a sordid world. Candide spends years traveling about the world searching for his bride, for success, and for understanding. When he finally discovers Cunegonde working as a scrubwoman, he takes her back to Westphalia, where they elect to retire and pray to God to "Make Our Garden Grow."

Louis Kronenberger♦ saw this musicalization of Voltaire's novella as "a medley of the brilliant, the uneven, the exciting, the earthbound, the adventurous and the imperfectly harmonized." Such tempered criticism discouraged all but the most dedicated playgoers. Not until Harold Prince♦ staged a drastically revised version in 1974 did the operetta win popular acceptance. The revival altered the book and opened up the action, taking it to all parts of the auditorium. Unlike the original, the 1974 production included no instantly recognizable names in the cast. In recent years major opera companies have added the work to their repertories. The Overture is the most famous piece from the work.

CANTOR, Arthur (b. 1920) Born in Boston and educated at Harvard, he served as a press representative before turning producer. Alone or with others he produced such plays as *The Tenth Man*♦ (1959), *All the Way Home*♦ (1960), *Gideon*♦ (1961), *A Thousand Clowns*♦ (1962), *In Praise of Love* (1974), *On Golden Pond*♦ (1979), and *Pack of Lies* (1985). During this time he continued his press work.

CANTOR, Eddie [né Isidore Itzkowitz] (1892–1964) The slim, jumpy, pop-eyed singer-comedian was born in New York and won an amateur night contest at Miner's Bowery Theatre when he was fourteen. A year later he first performed in professional vaudeville at the Clinton Music Hall. Thereafter he worked as a singing waiter when vaudeville

bookings were unavailable. In 1914 he went to England, where he played more vaudeville and made his legitimate debut in *Not Likely.* He returned to America to accept a part as a blackface chauffeur in the touring *Canary Cottage* (1916). While appearing in the musical he caught the eye of Florenz Ziegfeld,♦ who signed him to perform in the *Ziegfeld Follies of 1917,*♦ although he actually made his first appearance for Ziegfeld in the producer's cabaret atop the New Amsterdam Theatre.♦ Playing in blackface with an all-too-innocent leer, rolling his eyes, and finishing by prancing off waving a handkerchief, he scored a hit with "That's the Kind of Baby for Me." Further successful appearances followed in the 1918 and 1919 editions of the *Follies,* with his introducing Irving Berlin's♦ "You'd Be Surprised" in the latter; *Brevities* (1920); and *Make It Snappy* (1922). In the last revue he introduced his celebrated skit in which he played a mousy tailor whose customer demands a coat with a belt in the back. The "belt" the customer received was not the sort he expected. After a brief stint in the *Follies of 1923,* he returned to book musicals with *Kid Boots,* in which he introduced "Alabamy Bound," "Dinah," and "If You Knew Susie." In 1927 he returned to the fading *Follies,* then in 1929 had what should have been his biggest hit, *Whoopee,*♦ in which he sang "Makin' Whoopee." The show was closed by Ziegfeld, who at the time desperately needed funds, when Sam Goldwyn purchased the rights to film it. After many years in Hollywood, where he starred not only in films but in a popular radio show, Cantor made his final Broadway appearance in a musical version of *Three Men on a Horse,*♦ called *Banjo Eyes* (1941). His lone effort at producing, *Nellie Bly* (1946), closed quickly. Among the other songs with which he is associated are "Ida" and "Margie."

Autobiographies: *My Life Is in Your Hands,* New York, 1927, and *Take My Life,* New York, 1957.

CAPOTE, Truman, see *House of Flowers*

Captain Jinks of the Horse Marines, a comedy in three acts by Clyde Fitch.♦ Produced by Charles Frohman♦ at the Garrick Theatre. February 4, 1901. 168 performances.

When Aurelia Johnson of Trenton, N.J., returns to America as a world-famous prima donna, Mme. Trentoni (Ethel Barrymore♦), she wins over the newsmen and others at the dock with her beauty, grace, and charm—addressing them gaily as "darlings." She also enchants Captain Robert Carrolton Jinks (H. Reeves-Smith♦), who makes a written wager of $1000 with his friends that he can win her love. He quickly succeeds and not even the stormy disapproval of his snobbish mother, Mrs. Jinks (Mrs. Thomas Whiffen♦), can seemingly deter the young couple. But on the eve of her big concert, Mme. Trentoni is shown the wager. She is so distressed that she doubts she can perform that night. However, her American debut is a triumph, made all the sweeter when Jinks convinces her that what began as a cynical bet has blossomed into real affection.

Upset by Fitch's strenuous objections, Frohman cast Miss Barrymore with some trepidation—a trepidation shared by Miss Barrymore, who found the part "very taxing for so young and inexperienced an actress. There were comedy, pathos and dancing in it. I was more worried about the dancing than about anything else." The tryout was not a success, but New York reviews established the play as a major hit and launched Miss Barrymore's career as a star. In 1925 the comedy was turned into a popular musical comedy, *Captain Jinks,* with a book by Frank Mandel♦ and Laurence Schwab,♦ lyrics by B. G. DeSylva,♦ and music by Lewis E. Gensler and Stephen Jones. Featuring Louise Brown and J. Harold Murray♦ in the principal roles, it ran five months.

CARIOU, LEN (b. 1939) The Canadian-born actor had appeared in a wide variety of roles with the Stratford Shakespeare Festival (Ontario), the Chichester Festival (England), the Tyrone Guthrie Theatre♦ in Minneapolis, and Chicago's Goodman Memorial Theatre♦ before winning widespread recognition in the musical *Applause* (1970). Although he has made several returns to serious drama since then, he is best recalled for his work in two other musicals, *A Little Night Music♦* (1973) and *Sweeney Todd♦* (1979).

CARLE, RICHARD [né CHARLES NICHOLAS CARLETON] (1871–1941) A native of Somerville, Mass., the gawky, high-voiced comedian made his debut in New York in 1891 playing a minor role in *Niobe.* He won good notices as Worthington, the befuddled butler, in *A Mad Bargain* (1893) and again as Washington Strutt in *The Country Sport* later the same year. Important supporting roles followed in *Excelsior, Jr.* (1895), *The Lady Slavey* (1896), and *A Round of Pleasure* (1897). After essaying the part of Schossi Schmendrik in Zangwill's *Children of the Ghetto* (1899), he returned to musicals to play briefly in *The Greek Slave* before appearing in *Mam'selle 'Awkins* (1900), for which he provided the libretto. He also wrote several of the songs for *The*

Rogers Brothers in Central Park. Two seasons in London followed. On his return he performed in *The Ladies Paradise* (1901), then moved to Chicago which was becoming an important producing center for musicals. His first effort there was as Bonaparte Hunter, who is bested by a lady lion tamer, in *The Explorers* (1902); his second as the incompetent magician, Malzadoc, in *The Storks* (1902), for which he was co-librettist. He enjoyed a long run and tour as the dithering Professor Pettibone in *The Tenderfoot* (1903), for which he was librettist and lyricist. Although he nightly earned encores singing "My Alamo Love," New York critics assailed his humor as obvious and slightly salacious. This was to be a position they would long retain, although it scarcely hurt his popularity there or elsewhere. In 1905 he provided the book and lyrics for *The Mayor of Tokio,* in which he portrayed the leader of a troupe of stranded actors. He next starred as a flirtatious lawyer in his own adaptation of the London hit, *The Spring Chicken* (1906), stopping the show with "A Lemon in the Garden of Love." Further successes followed as the henpecked Leander Lamb in *Mary's Lamb* (1908); as Dr. Petypon, whose wife finds a grisette in his bedroom, in *The Girl from Montmartre* (1912); and as the jealous marquis in *The Doll Girl* (1913). When his popularity began to wane he turned to vaudeville, appearing in musicals only intermittently thereafter. His last Broadway assignment was as the mistress-flaunting Dr. Wentworth in *The New Yorkers* (1930).

CARLETON, HENRY GUY (1856–1910) Although best known as a humorist, the sometime inventor, who was born in Fort Union, N.M., made his first forays into play-writing with two serious works. The first, *Memnon* (1881), recalled the tragedy of a prophet of ancient Thebes. Meant for Booth♦ or McCullough,♦ it seems never to have been given a full mounting, although it was sometimes used by George Riddle, the elocutionist, in his public readings. Carleton's second play was *Victor Durand* (1884), in which a man is falsely imprisoned for murder but escapes to marry the murdered man's fiancée. It was the last successful new play produced by Lester Wallack.♦ *A Gilded Fool* (1892), which dealt with a seemingly unworldly young man who suddenly inherits a huge fortune, was written for Nat Goodwin♦ and proved popular. However, *Ye Earlie Trouble* (1892), a comedy; *The Lion's Mouth* (1893), a tragedy; and *Lem Kettle* (1894), another comedy, were unsuccessful. For John Drew♦ he wrote *Butterflies* (1894), in which Drew portrayed a playboy determined to lead a more useful life.

Another play for Drew, *That Imprudent Young Couple* (1895), which told of complications that ensue after a groom fails to mail his wife's letters announcing their marriage, was quickly dismissed, despite a cast that included Maude Adams,♦ Ethel Barrymore,♦ and Arthur Byron.♦ The failure of *Ambition* (1895) was followed by his last play, *Colinette* (1899), an adaptation from the French in which Julia Marlowe♦ scored a personal success. John Golden♦ recalled that Carleton insisted on personally reading his plays at first rehearsal despite a grotesque stammer, which led to agonizingly long, wasted hours.

CARLISLE, KITTY [née CATHARINE CONN] (b. 1915) A native of New Orleans and the wife of Moss Hart,♦ she played in such 1930s' musicals as *Champagne Sec, White Horse Inn, Three Waltzes,* and *Walk with Music,* but enjoyed her longest run as Alice Walters, the mother who dismays her children by admitting to premarital sex, in the comedy *Anniversary Waltz*♦ (1954).

Carmen Jones, a musical in two acts. Book and lyrics by Oscar Hammerstein II.♦ Music by Georges Bizet. Produced by Billy Rose♦ at the Broadway Theatre. December 2, 1943. 502 performances.

Carmen Jones (Muriel Smith) works in an old Southern cigarette factory that has turned to making parachutes for the duration of the war. When she is arrested by Joe (Luther Saxon), an army corporal, for creating a ruckus, she seduces him into letting her go. He quickly falls madly in love with her. But when she deserts him for the prizefighter, Husky Miller (Glenn Bryant), Joe kills her.

Principal songs: Beat Out Dat Rhythm on a Drum · Dat's Love

A modern, American version of *Carmen,* with a black cast, the show was turned into a major hit by Hammerstein's ingenious redaction, including his imaginative adaptation of the original lyrics, by Rose's astute publicity, and by wartime prosperity. Even the often bigoted, arch-conservative Col. Robert R. McCormick of the Chicago *Tribune* hailed it as more pertinent for contemporary audiences than the original opera.

CARMINATI [DE BRAMBILLA], TULLIO (1894–1971) Born in Dalmatia, he is recalled by playgoers primarily for two roles: Count di Ruvo, the charming philanderer who wins the heroine, in *Strictly Dishonorable*♦ (1929), and the composer in *Music in the Air*♦ (1932), in which he introduced "The Song Is You."

CARNCROSS, JOHN L. (1834–1911) Called "the father of modern minstrelsy," he received his training in his native Philadelphia under Sam S. Sanford,♦ who had built the city's first minstrel house and was its leading minstrel until his retirement in 1862. Carncross, best known for his fine tenor voice, left Sanford in 1860 to form a company with Sam Sharpley and E. F. Dixey. Two years later, when Sanford retired, he organized the Carncross and Dixey Minstrels, which remained the city's prime minstrel company until 1878, the occasion of Dixey's retirement. For the next 18 years he continued to lead Carncross's Minstrels. He retired in 1896. Although the minstrel-burlesque tradition continued under his guidance, he removed all suggestive material and emphasized the musical portion of the show. The result was that his entertainments were perceived as wholesome enough for the entire family. Among the many young minstrels whose careers he helped were Eddie Foy,♦ Chauncey Olcott,♦ Francis Wilson,♦ Lew Dockstader,♦ and Willis P. Sweatnam. In 1882 Frank Dumont joined the troupe and after Carncross's leaving turned it into Dumont's Minstrels,♦ which became the last important permanent minstrel ensemble in America and gave Philadelphia the longest continuing history of minstrelsy.

CARNEY, ART[HUR WILLIAM] (b. 1918) Born in Mount Vernon, N.Y., he was long famous as a television comedian before trying Broadway. His best known assignments were James Hyland, the shiftless father of a deformed child, in *The Rope Dancers* (1957); Frank Michaelson, father of a marriageable daughter, in *Take Her, She's Mine* (1961); and Felix Ungar, the meticulously fussy member of *The Odd Couple*♦ (1965).

CARNOVSKY, MORRIS (b. 1897) A native of St. Louis, he worked at several stock companies, including that run by Henry Jewett♦ in Boston, before making his New York debut in *The God of Vengeance* (1922). From 1924 through 1930 he was a member of the Theatre Guild's♦ acting company, and appeared with it in important supporting roles in such plays as *Marco Millions*♦ (1928), a 1929 revival of *Uncle Vanya,* in which he assumed the title role, *Hotel Universe*♦ (1930), and *Elizabeth the Queen*♦ (1930). After appearing in *Both Your Houses*♦ (1933), he joined the Group Theatre,♦ where he played such roles as Dr. Levine, the unhappy physician, in *Men in White*♦ (1933); Jacob, the self-sacrificing grandfather, in *Awake and Sing!*♦ (1935); Mr. Bonaparte, the father whose son refuses to become a violinist, in *Golden Boy*♦ (1937), and Ben

Stark, the dentist with a shrewish wife, in *Rocket to the Moon*♦ (1938). In later years his most distinguished performances came when he played Lear and Shylock with the American Shakespeare Festival. ♦ Elliott Norton ♦ called his 1967 interpretation of the latter role "a heroic performance . . . powerful, rich in understanding, proud to the very end, and infinitely moving." Although he rarely achieved stardom in a career that spanned over sixty years, he was kept busy regularly and just as regularly was admired for whatever sort of role he tackled, but he excelled as troubled, thoughtful men.

Carolina Playmakers This long-lived company was founded in 1918 at the University of North Carolina at Chapel Hill by Professor Frederick Henry Koch, who in 1910 had organized a similar group, the Dakota Playmakers, at the University of North Dakota. North Carolina proved a more fertile field for Professor Koch's ambition to develop a writing and producing company devoted primarily to fostering a drama of native material. The company regularly mounted seasons of new plays, including works by young Thomas Wolfe and Paul Green.♦ Many of the plays were published in the *Carolina Folk-Plays* series. In time, the group was hailed as "America's Folk Theatre." By the late 1970s it had abandoned its original program and had become a professional repertory company which presented native drama only on rare occasions.

Carousel, a musical play in a prelude and two acts. Book and lyrics by Oscar Hammerstein II.♦ Music by Richard Rodgers.♦ Produced by the Theatre Guild♦ at the Majestic Theatre. April 19, 1945. 890 performances.

When Billy Bigelow (John Raitt♦), a New England carnival barker, falls in love with Julie Jordan (Jan Clayton), he proves so shy that he can only convey his feelings by suggesting what might happen "If I Loved You." Nonetheless, by the time "June is Bustin' Out All Over," he wins Julie. Later he discovers she is pregnant, so he agrees to join the scowling Jigger Craigin (Murvyn Vye) in a robbery to earn extra money. The plan misfires, and Billy kills himself rather than be caught. Before a heavenly judge, he pleads for another chance to return to earth, to redeem himself and see his daughter. But when the daughter refuses his gift of a star he has stolen from the sky he slaps her and must return to purgatory. The widowed Julie and her child are left to continue alone in the world, in stark contrast to her old friend Carrie Pipperidge (Jean

Darling), who has made a prosperous marriage to the rich Mr. Snow (Eric Mattson). Julie's sole comforter, Nettie Fowler (Christine Johnson), assures her "You'll Never Walk Alone."

This lyrical retelling of Molnar's♦ *Liliom*♦ was hailed by Robert Coleman of the *Mirror* as "the product of taste, imagination and skill. It will bewitch your senses and race your theatrical pulses." Among its notable and venturesome moments were its opening ballet-pantomime ("Carousel Waltz"), which was choreographed by Agnes de Mille,♦ and Billy's eight-minute "Soliloquy." Now generally acknowledged to be the finest of the Rodgers and Hammerstein operettas, the musical has been revived regularly.

CARPENTER, Edward Childs (1872–1950) Born in Philadelphia, he became a newspaperman after leaving school and quickly rose to an editorial position. In 1903 he published his first novel and two years later collaborated with John Luther Long♦ on his first play, *The Dragon Fly,* telling of the Texan rebellion against Mexico. The play was produced in Philadelphia, but never reached New York. Over the next three decades, however, more than a dozen of his plays did reach New York. The most successful were *The Cinderella Man* (1916), in which a rich young lady falls in love with a starving artist; *The Bachelor Father* (1928), in which a man holds a reunion for all his illegitimate children; and *Whistling in the Dark* (1932), written with Laurence Gross and telling of a mystery writer who is kidnapped by gangsters and forced to plan an unsolvable crime. Whatever his shortcomings as a dramatist, he was highly respected for his integrity and was elected as president of both the Dramatists Guild♦ and the Society of American Dramatists and Composers.♦

CARR, Benjamin (1768?–1836) Coming to America in the 1790s from his native England, he was soon established in Philadelphia as a respected composer and music teacher. A good singer and adequate actor, he often performed in the plays for which he provided overtures, songs, and incidental music. His most important contribution to the theatre was his score for one of the best early American operettas, *The Archers* (1796). Dunlap♦ questioned the theatricality of his writing, noting that his "knowledge of music without the graces of action made him more acceptable to the scientific than to the vulgar auditor." Carr must have come to a similar conclusion, for early on he abandoned the theatre to devote his time to teaching.

Carrère and Hastings The noted architectural firm was founded by John Mervan Carrère (1858–1911) and Thomas Hastings (1860–1920). Besides designing such landmark buildings as the New York Public Library and the Frick mansion, they designed Abbey's (later Knickerbocker) Theatre (1893); the New (later Century) Theatre♦ (1909); and the Globe (later Lunt-Fontanne) Theatre (1910). Their work was characterized by classic elegance and spaciousness.

CARROLL, EARL (1893?–1948) He began his theatrical career as a program-seller in his native Pittsburgh. After several years as a seaman he settled in New York, where he took up lyric-writing. One of his earliest efforts, "Isle d'Amour," with music by Leo Edwards, was a hit of the *Ziegfeld Follies of 1913.*♦ He served as lyricist for *Pretty Mrs. Smith* (1914), *So Long, Letty* (1916), *Canary Cottage* (1916), *The Love Mill* (1918), and *Flora Bella* (1920). Turning his hand to producing, he suffered a number of failures with straight plays before finding success with his revue, *Earl Carroll Vanities of 1923.*♦ The show featured scantily clad girls and off-color humor, establishing the pattern for later editions. In 1923 he also produced the hugely successful *White Cargo.*♦ Among his other productions were *Laff That Off* (1925), *What Ann Brought Home* (1927), *Fioretta* (1929), *Earl Carroll Sketch Book* (1929 and 1935), and *Murder at the Vanities* (1933). He built two theatres, one in 1922 and the other in 1931, both of which he named for himself. He made headlines in 1926 when he was sent to prison for violating prohibition after allowing one of his showgirls to take a bath in a tub of champagne during a party he threw at his theatre for his principal backer, oilman William R. Edrington. Some sources list Carroll's birth as 1892.

Biography: *The Body Merchant,* Ken Murray, Pasadena, 1976.

CARROLL, LEO G. (1892–1972) The English-born actor, who excelled in portraying placid, distinguished types, first came to America in 1924 and appeared in such plays as *The Vortex* (1925), *The Constant Nymph* (1926), and *The Green Bay Tree* (1933). He also brought his skills to classic revivals and modern musicals. But he is best recalled for two later appearances: Detective-Inspector Rough, who nearly gives everything away by forgetting to take his hat, in *Angel Street*♦ (1941), and the title part of the Boston Brahmin in *The Late George Apley*♦ (1944).

CARTER, LINCOLN J. (1865–1926) A prolific author of blood-and-thunder melodramas, his plays were rarely presented in New York and then usually in minor playhouses. But his best plays remained popular with touring companies and were revived regularly until shortly before World War I. Among his works were *The Fast Mail* (1890), *Tornado* (1894), *The Heart of Chicago* (1898), *Under the Dome* (1898), *Remember the Maine* (1898), *Chattanooga* (1899), *Bedford's Hope* (1906), and *An American Ace* (1918).

CARTER, MRS. LESLIE [née CAROLINE LOUISE DUDLEY] (1862–1937) Born in Lexington, Ky., the fiery redhead turned to the stage after being snubbed by society following a sensational divorce case in which she was found guilty of adultery. She persuaded David Belasco♦ to give her the role of Kate Graydon, the central figure of *The Ugly Duckling* (1890). Belasco may have agreed as much because of her notoriety as because of her as yet latent acting talents. Nature aptly fitted her for the role, for though she was not beautiful, her slim, willowy figure, piercing green eyes, and expressive face were exceedingly attractive. Her acting, however, was criticized as too unrestrained, even if, like Belasco, the critics saw great promise in her. The play was a failure, but Belasco and Charles Frohman♦ confidently cast her for the title role in Audran's operetta, *Miss Helyett* (1891). Real success came when she played the determined Maryland Calvert in *The Heart of Maryland*♦ (1895). Her "sizzling" performances as the prostitute in the title part of *Zaza* (1899), followed by her courtesan in the title role of *Du Barry*♦ (1901), added to her popularity. In 1905 she gave what many considered her finest portrayal as the tragic heroine of *Adrea.*♦ William Winter,♦ who had long been critical of her overplaying, wrote of her Adrea, "No denotement in Mrs. Carter's acting of *Du Barry* had even remotely indicated such depth of tragical feeling and such power of dramatic expression as she revealed in the scene of the tempest, in pronouncing *Kaeso's* doom, and, above all, in the terrible, piteous, tragic self-conflict through which the Woman became the incarnation of Fate and the minister of death. Mrs. Carter has long been known for her exceptional facility of feminine blandishment, her absolute command of the enticing wiles of coquetry and the soft allurements of sensuous grace,—known, likewise, and rightly admired for the clarity and purity of her English speech, always delightful to hear: but observers studious to see and willing to be convinced had not supposed her to be an actor of tragedy."

Shortly thereafter she left Belasco after an argument over her second marriage. For many years she toured, primarily in revivals, before winning good notices as Lady Catherine in Somerset Maugham's♦ *The Circle* (1921). Later she toured as Mother Goddam in *The Shanghai Gesture.* ♦ Her last New York appearance was as Mrs. Hardcastle in a 1928 revival of *She Stoops To Conquer,* although she made several appearances on California stages before her retirement.

CARUS, EMMA (1879–1927) A chunky, blonde, blue-eyed singer with a big, deep voice, she emigrated from her native Germany while still a youngster. Her mother had sung in opera, but she had no interest in the field despite a careful musical training. She made her debut in American vaudeville in 1894 and for the next twenty years alternated between two-a-day and the legitimate stage. After a minor part in *Nell Go-In* (1899), she played important roles in, among others, *The Giddy Throng* (1900), *The Wild Rose* (1902), *The Medal and the Maid* (1904), *Woodland* (1904), [*Ziegfeld*] *Follies of 1907,*♦ *Up and Down Broadway* (1910), and *The Wife Hunters* (1911). After 1915 she confined her appearances to vaudeville, where she was always more at home. Her ability to sing in Dutch, Scotch, Irish, British, and Negro dialects led to her being billed as "The Human Dialect Cocktail." But she was most famous for her trick of jumping from a contralto to deep baritone voice. Although the famous Chicago critic, Amy Leslie,♦ admired her as "the only one of the bigtime singers who has a cultivated and genuine voice," a Kansas City critic addressed her penchant for forceful projection by admonishing her publicly, "Remember, you are in an enclosed building and not trying to be heard throughout the whole city, including the stockyards."

CARYLL, IVAN [né FELIX TILKIN or TILKEN] (1861–1921) After studying music in his native Liège, he moved briefly to Paris and then settled in London where, between 1886 and 1908, he composed a series of popular operettas. He arrived in America in 1910. His first American score was for *Marriage à la Carte* (1911), but he did not achieve major success until *The Pink Lady*♦ later the same season. His subsequent works were *Oh! Oh! Delphine* (1912), *The Little Cafe* (1913), *The Belle of Bond Street* (1914), *Chin-Chin*♦ (1914), *Papa's Darling* (1914), *Jack o' Lantern* (1917), *The Girl Behind the Gun* (1918), *The Canary* (1918), *Tip Top* (1920), *Kissing Time* (1920), and *The Hotel Mouse* (1922), the last

produced after his death. Best known among his songs are "My Beautiful Lady" from *The Pink Lady* and "Wait Till the Cows Come Home" from *Jack o' Lantern.*

"Casey at the Bat" A poem by Ernest Lawrence Thayer in which the mighty slugger strikes out at a crucial moment, it was introduced by De Wolf Hopper♦ at a performance in 1888 of either *The Lady or the Tiger* or *Prince Methusalem.* Neither musical had anything to do with baseball or even America. Thereafter Hopper managed to insert it into most of his other appearances, although in later years, when a consistency of style and tone was demanded, he generally saved his recitation for his curtain call.

Casino Theatre The first theatre built in America specifically for the presentation of popular musicals, it opened on October 12, 1882, with a performance of Strauss's *The Queen's Lace Handkerchief.* It was the brainchild of Rudolph Aronson,♦ who originally conceived it as a theatre with restaurants, gambling rooms, and New York's first roof garden playhouse. Designed by Francis Kimball and Thomas Wisebell in the Moorish style then in vogue, it stood at the southeast corner of Broadway and 39th Street, (the old Metropolitan Opera House was later erected on the northwest corner). For many of its early years it was home to a distinguished ensemble of singers and comedians, although for its first decade it presented only importations. In 1894, however, it offered the first American revue, *The Passing Show.* ♦ Its summer roof garden was the site of the premiere of *The Origin of the Cake Walk; or, Clorindy*♦ (1898), the first black musical to be offered to a white Broadway audience. The house's beautiful chorus line was so famous that a 1900 musical, called *The Casino Girl,* was based on the imaginary adventures of one of its young ladies. By the turn of the century, the stock company had been disbanded and the Casino, taken over by the young Shuberts,♦ was booked in the same way as other theatres. Among its hits were *Florodora*♦ (1900), *A Chinese Honeymoon* (1902), *Wildflower* (1923), *The Vagabond King*♦ (1925), and *The Desert Song*♦ (1926). It was demolished in 1930.

CASSIDY, CLAUDIA (b. 1905?) A native of Shawneetown, Ill., she studied at the University of Illinois before beginning to write on the arts for the Chicago *Journal of Commerce* in 1925. She moved to the Chicago *Sun* in 1941 and to the *Tribune* a year later, remaining there until her retirement in 1965. By far the most influential critic in the Midwest, she was often condemned for the severity of her judgments but insisted she was merely attempting to battle lowering standards in touring productions. *Variety*♦ noted, "She almost singlehandedly stopped the process of Broadway producers sending third-rate versions of New York hits on the road."

Caste An 1867 play by W. T. Robertson,♦ it told how an officer, who is a marquise's son, proves by his devotion to the instinctively well-bred daughter of a common drunkard that social class is no barrier to a happy marriage. The production of *Caste* led to one of the American theatre's most celebrated law cases. Lester Wallack♦ had expected to premiere the piece in New York as he had earlier Robertson works. Before he could open his season, W. J. Florence♦ brought out an unauthorized production. Wallack attempted to obtain an injunction, but Florence argued successfully that "in the absence of international copyright" he had done no wrong, since a quirk in the law allowed anyone who could memorize a play to produce it. Florence claimed he had done just that and was upheld. Wallack later had great success with the work and it was revived with some regularity until World War I.

CASTLE, Vernon [né Blythe] (1887–1918) Coming to America from his native England, he made his debut in *About Town* (1906), the first of seven Lew Fields♦ shows in which he danced and often served as Fields's stooge: *The Girl Behind the Counter* (1907), *The Mimic World* (1908), *The Midnight Sons* (1909), *Old Dutch* (1909), *The Summer Widowers* (1910), and *The Hen-Pecks* (1911). After he married Irene Foote (1893–1969), who danced in the chorus of the last two shows, they went to Paris, where they perfected their ballroom technique and became a dancing sensation. On their return they almost single-handedly initiated a rage for ballroom dancing in America, starting what was called "the dancing craze" and introducing or popularizing such dances as the tango, the Maxixe, the Castle Walk, and the Turkey Trot. Vernon appeared briefly in *The Lady of the Slipper* (1912), a Victor Herbert♦ musical Irene had walked out of during rehearsals, but they then danced as a team in *The Sunshine Girl* (1913) and in Irving Berlin's♦ ragtime musical, *Watch Your Step*♦ (1914). They were also applauded for their vaudeville appearances. While Vernon was training pilots for the war, Irene appeared alone in *Miss 1917*. After her husband was killed in a training accident, she retired from performing, although she helped later Broadway shows re-create period dances.

Autobiography (Irene): *Castles in the Air,* New York, 1958.

Cat and the Canary, The, a play in three acts by John Willard. Produced at the National Theatre. February 7, 1922. 349 performances.

At the reading of Ambrose West's will it is discovered that young Annabelle West (Florence Eldridge♦) is his sole heir—provided she remain of sound mind. Annabelle and her relatives learn the news at West's eerie castle on the Hudson, minutes before a stormy midnight. Their discomfort is aggravated by the spooky behavior of West's old voodoo-obsessed maid, "Mammy" Pleasant (Blanche Frederici), and by the arrival of Hendricks (Edmund Elton), a guard at a nearby insane asylum who is seeking an escaped homocidal maniac. Shortly, inexplicable screams are heard, a clutching claw appears from behind a sliding panel, and a corpse is seen, only to vanish mysteriously. In the end Annabelle's seemingly Milquetoast suitor, Paul Jones (Henry Hull♦), helps catch one of her relatives who, it turns out, was in league with Hendricks. Annabelle retains both her sanity and her inheritance.

Called "the prototype of a vast number of 'let's-scare-the-heroine-to-death' chillers," the play was long a favorite of stock and amateur troupes. The San Francisco-born John Clawson Willard (1885–1942) was an actor and dramatist. This was his only successful play, although half a dozen were produced.

Cat and the Fiddle, *The,* a musical in two acts. Book and lyrics by Otto Harbach.♦ Music by Jerome Kern.♦ Produced by Max Gordon♦ at the Globe Theatre. October 15, 1931. 395 performances.

In Brussels two young composers meet and fall in love. Unfortunately, their disparate goals soon drive them apart, for Victor Florescu (Georges Metaxa) aims at composing the loftiest music, while Shirley Sheridan (Bettina Hall♦) seeks merely to write popular songs. But the ardor of their affections triumphs over their separate ambitions.

Principal songs: The Night Was Made for Love · She Didn't Say "Yes" · Try To Forget

Although critics came down harshly on the book, with the *New Yorker* noting, "Mr. Harbach has really outdone himself in banality," Kern's lovely score saved the day. A device he had used timidly before, the extended musical lead-in, was employed from beginning to end, and orchestral passages underscored much of the action. The orchestra itself was small—only eighteen—but the musicians were so select that they were listed by name in the program.

Cat on a Hot Tin Roof, a play in three acts by Tennessee Williams. ◆ Produced by the Playwrights' Company◆ at the Morosco Theatre. March 24, 1955. 694 performances. PP, NYDCCA.

Margaret Pollitt (Barbara Bel Geddes◆) is a woman of strong passions and determination. At the moment what she most wants is the love of her detached, alcoholic husband, Brick (Ben Gazzara◆), an ex-football star. The family has assembled to celebrate the birthday of its patriarch, "Big Daddy" (Burl Ives), the richest cotton planter in the Mississippi Delta. The gathering exacerbates tensions and animosities, so in a fit of despair Maggie reveals to Brick that she has had an affair with his closest friend, Skipper, even though she knew Skipper was at heart a homosexual. The affair drove Skipper to drink and suicide. Big Daddy also assails Brick, making Brick see that his alcoholism stems from his refusal to help Skipper because he shared Skipper's homosexual tendencies. Infuriated, Brick reveals that Big Daddy is dying of cancer. Maggie knows that there is no will, and fearing that Big Daddy might disinherit Brick and her in favor of her brother-in-law and his family, she lies that she is pregnant. Throwing away Brick's liquor, she says, "We can make that lie come true. And then I'll bring you liquor, and we'll get drunk together, here, tonight, in this place that death has come into!"

The play was essentially another variation of Williams's favorite themes, Southern decadence and homosexuality. Nevertheless, it was, as Brooks Atkinson◆ observed, "a stunning drama . . . the work of a mature observer of men and women and a gifted craftsman." An excellent 1990 revival confirmed the drama's theatrical effectiveness.

***Cataract of the Ganges,* The** An equestrian melodrama by W. T. Moncrieff, it was presented at the Park Theatre◆ in 1824, a year after its Drury Lane premiere. The highlight of the complicated plot came when its heroine, Zamine, rode her horse to safety by leaping over the huge waterfall. However, from the start its spectacle and not its story was its main attraction. The *Mirror* noted, "it is, indeed, a succession of splendid and gorgeous scenes, which beam upon the dazzled eye with almost magical effect . . . the beautiful horses, arrayed in all the trappings of eastern magnificence—the long processions—the chariots . . . the crowds which throng the stage, glittering in such princely apparel—all pass

before the mind like a dazzling and glorious dream." The play remained a staple for fifty years, especially in houses such as the Bowery,◆ which catered to thrill-seeking playgoers. A major revival succeeded as late as 1873 with John Brougham◆ and Mrs. John Wood◆ in the cast.

CATLETT, WALTER (1889–1960) The bespectacled, cigar-chomping comedian who usually played rambunctious "wise-guys," was born in San Francisco and spent his earliest theatrical years with West Coast troupes. In the 1910s and 1920s he was notable in many Broadway musicals, especially *Sally*◆ (1920) and *Lady, Be Good!*◆ (1924), in which he introduced the title song. He later performed in films.

Cats An English musical in two acts, first presented in London in 1981, it set many of T. S. Eliot's◆ poems from *Old Possum's Book of Practical Cats* to music by Andrew Lloyd Webber. ◆ All the characters were cats and, although there was a slim plot about selecting a cat to ascend to heaven to be reborn, there was no spoken dialogue. Its most popular song was "Memory." The American production opened at the Winter Garden Theatre◆ on October 7, 1982, and was still running at press time. Trevor Nunn directed, while Gillian Lynne recreated her highly praised dances.

Caught in the Rain, a farce in three acts by William Collier◆ and Grant Stewart. Produced by Charles Frohman◆ at the Garrick Theatre. December 31, 1906. 161 performances.

Publicly, Dick Crawford (Collier), a Colorado mining man, is a grumpy woman-hater. Privately, he is an old softie. Caught in a downpour, he finds himself shoulder to shoulder with a beautiful girl who quickly captures his affections, but she disappears before he can learn her name. About the same time he recklessly promises a friend, Mr. Mason (John Saville), to marry his daughter to help him out of a financial problem. No sooner had he made his promise than he recalls the unknown girl and tries to back out. Even when he discovers that Mr. Mason's daughter, Muriel (Nanette Comstock), and the mysterious beauty are one and the same, his problems are not solved, for Muriel is upset by his fickleness. Of course, all ends happily.

Superb staging and playing turned this preposterous farce into a memorable hit. A 1920 musical, *Pitter Patter,* was based on the play. Stewart (1866–1929) was an English-born actor who also collaborated on several less successful plays.

CAWTHORN, Joseph (1867–1949) Born in New York, he made his debut there as a child performer at Robinson's Music Hall in 1872 and a year later played with Haverly's Minstrels. After several years in England he returned to play in vaudeville and to tour in *Little Nugget* (1883), then spent several seasons in stock. His performances in a touring company, *A Fool for Luck* (1895), led to a major role in a transcontinental company of *Excelsior, Jr.* (1896). The next year he appeared in New York in *Nature,* before touring again in *Miss Philadelphia.* His abilities as a dialect comedian first came to New York's attention when he played the leading comic role of Boris in Victor Herbert's◆ *The Fortune Teller*◆ (1898). With few exceptions, such as his drag performance in the title part of *Mother Goose* (1903), all subsequent roles of the small, round-faced, balding comedian were Dutch dialect parts. Among his notable portrayals were Aufpassen in Herbert's *The Singing Girl* (1899); Siegmund Lump in John Philip Sousa's◆ *The Free Lance* (1906); Baron Hugo Weybach in *The Hoyden* (1907); Louis Von Schloppenhauer in *The Slim Princess* (1911); Schlump in *The Sunshine Girl* (1913); the Mormon, Trimpel, in *The Girl from Utah*◆ (1914); Otto Spreckels in *Sybil* (1916); Timothy in *The Canary* (1918); and, his last Broadway appearance, Siegfried Peters in *Sunny*◆ (1925).

While playing Dr. Pill in Herbert's *Little Nemo* (1908) in New Haven, he was told to stall until a mishap was corrected backstage. The scene called for him to describe imaginary animals he had hunted. One water-dwelling, food-gobbling creature he invented he called a whiffenpoof. Yale students in the audience seized on the name and adopted it when they founded a singing society.

CAYVAN, Georgia (1858–1906) Born in Bath, Maine, this beautiful actress spent several years playing in Boston before succeeding Effie Ellsler◆ as Hazel Kirke in New York in 1881. She immediately became a prominent leading lady, portraying the heroine in such famous comedies or dramas as *The Professor*◆ (1881); *The White Slave*◆ (1882), in which she spoke the once famous lines, "Rags are royal raiment when worn for virtue's sake"; *Siberia*◆ (1883); *May Blossom*◆ (1884); *The Wife*◆ (1887); *The Charity Ball*◆ (1889); and *Squire Kate* (1892). An illness forced a premature retirement and led to her early death.

CAZAURAN, A[ugustus] R. (1820–89) Born in Bordeaux, and educated by Jesuit priests in France and Ireland, he became a reporter for the New York *Herald* shortly after his arrival in America. During the Civil War he was briefly imprisoned as a spy, but was released in time to take a post with the *Washington Chronicle,* for which he wrote a once famous eye-witness account of Lincoln's assassination. A. M. Palmer◆ hired him as a playreader, and came so to respect his talents that he made him his right-hand man. His ability to speak several languages, combined with his theatrical acumen, helped Cazauran to become the most celebrated adapter and play doctor of his time. Bronson Howard◆ credited the success of *The Banker's Daughter*◆ (1878) to his revisions. Among his many adaptations were *Miss Multon* (1876), *The Danchieffs* (1877), *The Mother's Secret* (1877), *The Man of Success* (1877), *A Celebrated Case* (1878), *Daniel Rochat* (1880), *Felicia* (1881), *Far from the Madding Crowd* (1882), *A Parisian Romance* (1883), and *The Fatal Letter* (1884).

CELESTE, La Petite (*fl.* 1840s) A young girl whose real name was said to be Williams, she first danced in Philadelphia in 1837, and three years later joined William Mitchell's◆ troupe at New York's Olympic Theatre. T. Allston Brown◆ has called her "the smallest child to dance with such perfection ever seen on the stage," but the assignments Mitchell awarded her suggest she also had some comic skills. By the early 1850s she had disappeared from programs. Her history, aside from her stage work, is obscure.

CELESTE, Mlle. [née Keppler] (1810–82) Brought from her native Paris to New York by Charles Gilfert,◆ then manager of the Bowery,◆ she made her debut there in 1827 dancing a *pas seul* on a large bill whose main offering was *The School for Scandal.* She attracted little notice, but continued to perform in small ballets along the Eastern seaboard until she returned to Europe in 1830. She came back in 1834 with the reputation of being both a fine actress and dancer, and caused a sensation in a double bill of the melodrama *The French Spy* and the ballet *La Bayadère.* Walter Leman◆ called her "the most profitable star of her day" and said she told him she had cleared over $100,000 from *The French Spy* alone. In plays such as *The Wizard Skiff, The Wept of Wish-ton Wish,* and *The Spirit Bride* she regularly played two or three different roles in the same night. Comparing her dancing with that of Mme. Augusta,◆ the New York *Mirror* observed, "There is more vivacity in Celeste, more taste, tenderness and delicacy in Augusta, who is very sparing of the whirligigs and some other affectations in which

Celeste delights to indulge." Celeste, of course, simply gave the ruder Bowery audiences what they wanted, prompting the New York *Herald* to accept her "wonderful tragic power amidst peanuts, cigar smoke, and scents of the varied kind. We never saw real pathos and peanuts so mixed up before." She remained in America until 1843, then made two brief returns, in 1851 when she won applause as the Indian Miami in *Green Bushes* and in 1865. By then, age and her refusal to develop fluent English took their toll, so her reception was far more restrained than it had been earlier.

Censorship in American Theatre Although the settlement of America coincided with the flourishing of both Jacobean and Restoration play-writing in England, the relatively small number of settlers and their general religious bent precluded the emergence of real theatre during the 17th century and much of the early 18th century. Certainly the New England Puritans, the Dutch in New Amsterdam, and the Quakers in Pennsylvania were all vehemently opposed to theatricals of any sort. Even in the somewhat liberal atmosphere of cavalier Virginia, what may have been the first American play, *The Bear and the Cub*◆ (1665), was performed at a court hearing after a public performance led to charges of licentiousness. The actors were acquitted, but the trial was the harbinger of nearly three centuries of court battles and other harassment of American theatre by authorities. In the late 18th century many colonies and later many states passed laws banning theatricals. However, by this time a number of cities had grown sufficiently populous that the demand for theatrical entertainments could no longer be ignored. Men such as David Douglass◆ were politic enough to persuade authorities to permit the erection of playhouses and the production of plays, although even where licenses were granted they were frequently precariously held and just as frequently revoked. Inevitably, as with any prohibition, not only were appetites whetted but means of circumvention were found. Plays were often advertised as "concerts," "lectures," or "dissertations."

No national office equivalent to that of the English Lord Chamberlain was ever established to censor plays in advance. Instead, censorship was left to theatrically important cities or, occasionally, to states. Actually very few localities ever resorted to advance censorship, the most notorious exception in the late 19th and early 20th century being Boston. But pervasive Victorian concepts of morality conditioned the writing and presentation of many plays as well as something so seemingly slight as the naming

of playhouses. For much of the 19th century, when opera never shared the opprobrium of drama, countless theatres were called opera houses, although they were given over primarily to the presentation of drama and rarely, if ever, offered real operas. Many theatres were also called "halls," and in a few major cities theatres often had additional space devoted to exhibitions and so were called "museums." The most famous of the latter were Barnum's American Museum◆ and the Boston Museum.◆ These appellations allowed many publicly prudish people to have the best of both worlds by attending the theatre and retaining their respectability.

Perhaps because most performers, writers, and producers seemed to share the moral consensus, there was little outright censorship in the 19th century. Men such as Augustin Daly◆ appeared to understand precisely how far they could go in handling what was deemed touchy subject matter. Moreover, most drama critics shared contemporary pruderies and were frequently quick to denounce the slightest overstepping of implicit limitations. Much of the outcry against theatre continued to come from the clergy, who often deplored all theatricals as a matter of principle, and from newspaper editors, who may have agreed with the narrow strictures of the day or who, more likely, were simply seeking to increase circulation with shrill attacks. *The Black Crook*◆ (1866), with its long line of girls in flesh-colored tights, and Ada Isaacs Menken's◆ *Mazeppa* (1861), in which she appeared to ride nude on a horse, typified productions which scandalized, while Daly's treatment of divorce in the play of the same name exemplified the use of subject matter which many thought should not be treated. It is to the credit of the better dramatists, producers, and critics of the day that they were able gradually to broaden the scope and depth of American play-writing in the face of the prevalent morality.

In the very late 19th century the coming of Ibsenite realism and Shavian farce, both of which, in their disparate ways, touched on many matters previously considered unbroachable, infuriated many conservative critics, playgoers, and lawmakers, so that by the early 20th century the hue and cry for censorship rose to heights unknown before. Throughout the first half of the 20th century, and sometimes later, overt censorship and repression led to frequent and often highly publicized battles between authorities, responding to puritanical wailings, and the theatre, which was determined to apply increasingly open standards of honesty and permissibility. One of the most famous cases concerned Clyde Fitch's♦ *Sapho* (1900), in which a courtesan begs to be seduced and is carried up a flight of stairs to her bedroom in the arms of her latest lover. Goaded by the outcries of clergy and of such yellow journalists as William Randolph Hearst, who wrote, "We expect the police to forbid on the stage what they would forbid in streets and low resorts," New York authorities closed the show and arrested its star, Olga Nethersole,♦ her leading man, and the manager of the theatre. They were acquitted in court. Among the other distinguished plays of the era to be closed or banned in New York or elsewhere were *Mrs. Warren's Profession, Monna Vanna,* and *The Easiest Way.* ♦ *Monna Vanna* was allowed to proceed after Mrs. Fiske♦ grudgingly capitulated to the demand for revisions, but *The Easiest Way* was not allowed to play Boston and several other cities.

After World War I, when films had lured away the lowest level of playgoers, and when the postwar perception of new freedom and enlightenment prompted playwrights and playgoers to demand a theatre more truly reflective of modern society, the battle intensified. Such fine American plays as *All God's Chillun Got Wings*♦ (1924), *Desire Under the Elms*♦ (1924), *The Firebrand*♦ (1924), *They Knew What They Wanted*♦ (1924), and *What Price Glory?* ♦ (1924) were all either forced to make revisions or were closed in New York or elsewhere. So were more patently tawdry but still theatrically interesting works as Mae West's♦ *Sex*♦ (1926), *The Shanghai Gesture*♦ (1926), and *Lulu Belle*♦ (1926). In 1927, responding to the agitation for censorship, New York City enacted the Wales padlock law, which not only enabled authorities to arrest the producer and actors in any offensive play, but to deprive the theatre housing the play of its license for one year. The law was not rescinded until 1967. However, the most extreme instances of censorship continued to come from Boston, and to a lesser extent from Chicago, both of which required submission of plays in advance. Thus, many of Eugene O'Neill's♦ works and, indeed, many of the productions of his producer, the Theatre Guild,♦ were not allowed to play Boston, so were booked into suburban theatres instead. *Strange Interlude*♦ (1928) was the most celebrated instance of this exclusion.

Almost inevitably the battle between conservative advocates of censorship and liberal proponents of freer speech took on a political coloring in the 1930s. While many of these confrontations remained local, some assumed a national scale because they involved the Federal Theatre Project♦, which had

been established and funded by Congress. Thus, the Department of State attempted to censor and finally was able to force the cancellation of the FTP's projected mounting of the anti-Mussolini play *Ethiopia*. Ultimately extremists on both sides prevailed, the FTP producing plays filled with increasingly left-wing propaganda and the ultra-conservatives in Congress responding by killing the whole Federal Theatre Project. However, moral considerations still figured heavily in censorship, so it was in this decade that New York's Mayor Fiorello LaGuardia finally succeeded in closing that city's burlesque houses, and Lillian Hellman's♦ *The Children's Hour*♦ (1934), with its whispered accusation of lesbianism, was banned in Boston and Chicago.

Censorship for military reasons became accepted during World War II, although strenuous objections were raised when the military frequently extended its grip and banned plays and performances on moral grounds. Nor were regular plays in regular theatres free from interference. The Shuberts♦ were threatened with invocation of the Wales law when they mounted a sleazy burlesque-style revue, but, more importantly, another serious study of lesbianism, *Trio* (1944), was closed when its playhouse was faced with loss of its license.

From the 1950s on, serious contretemps gradually faded, especially in New York, and those which did occur usually had a comic touch to them. For example, when *'Tis Pity She's a Whore,* John Ford's 300-year-old classic, was revived in New York the city refused to allow public billboards to display the last word, and the supposedly liberal New York *Times* refused to accept advertisements unless the word was omitted. Twenty years later there was little objection to the title *The Best Little Whorehouse in Texas,* ♦ except when the producer placed advertisements on buses using only the word "whorehouse." In the 1970s, Supreme Court decisions confirmed what had been time-honored practice when it agreed that local authorities were the ones with the right to censor entertainments. However, by this time the road had shrunk to the point where it was all but non-existent and censorship was invoked primarily against films and books. Self-appointed vigilantes and clergy, especially Southern fundamentalists and the Roman Catholic Church, still were able to prevent regional productions, but censorship had all but disappeared in New York.

Ironically, the abolition of the Wales padlock law and the virtual disappearance of the slightest theatrical censorship in New York coincided with the explosive freedoms and social turmoil of the 1960s, so that it was significant and not unexpected that the theatre burst forth with the greatest display of obscenity ever seen. Not only did the formerly unspeakable become commonplace, but the crassest nudity and the depiction of everything from bestiality to urination was offered, especially in the off-Broadway theatres, but on Broadway as well. By the early 1980s a reaction had begun to set in. Happily it has not taken the form of a return to public censorship, but rather of a realization on the part of many playwrights, directors, and producers that excesses have been self-defeating and that restraint and suggestion are usually more effective in making a point than careless vulgarity. Yet the theatre must go on living with the unsettling knowledge that there are those who would, for a number of reasons, still rejoice in the revival of censorship.

An interesting book on this subject, subtitled *A History of Censorship and Harassment in the United States,* is Abe Laufe's *Wicked Stage* (1978).

Center Stage The company was founded in Baltimore in 1963 by Edward J. Golden, who was shortly thereafter replaced by William Bushnell. Their artistic director was Douglas Seale. Following Bushnell's retirement and his replacement by Peter W. Culman, John Stix became artistic director, and was later succeeded by Stan Wojewodski, Jr. The company's first production was Schnitzler's *La Ronde,* and since then its schedule has included a wide, responsible selection of classics and new plays. Among the original offerings afterwards presented on Broadway were *Slow Dance on the Killing Ground, G. R. Point, Crimes of the Heart,*◆ and *Roza.* Since 1975 the company has operated in the old Loyola College complex, presenting its attractions in a 500-seat theatre with a semi-thrust stage.

CHAIKIN, Joseph (b. 1935) The Brooklyn-born actor and director studied at Drake University and with several distinguished acting teachers, including Herbert Berghof, before becoming a member of The Living Theatre.◆ He left that group to found The Open Theatre in 1963 and for the decade of its existence made it one of the nation's most admired avant-garde groups. To a large extent its philosophy was that the text was merely a starting point, with actors and director meant to develop freely from there. Yet Chaikin regularly evinced the remarkable ability to bring order out of potential chaos "in that undefined territory where playwright, director, actor, and audience interchange roles, abandon strictly logical texts, and go for soul-broke with improvised sound and unexplained silences." Performances in the loft and other stages the group employed were frequently by invitation only; more regular audiences were allowed in only intermittently. Among the group's mountings were *Viet Rock* and *The Serpent.* Chaikin continued to act and direct elsewhere until he suffered a stroke. Since then his work has been drastically curtailed. He published his ideas of theatre in *The Presence of the Actor* (1972).

CHAMPION, Gower (1920–80) Born in Geneva, Ill., he became a professional dancer while still in his early teens, and danced in *The Streets of Paris* (1939) and *Count Me In* (1942). His choreography was first seen in *Small Wonder* (1948), but he won much more attention later the same year when he directed and choreographed another revue, *Lend an Ear.* Hits which he afterwards both directed and choreographed included *Bye Bye Birdie*◆ (1960), *Carnival* (1961), *Hello, Dolly!*◆ (1964), *I Do! I Do!* (1966), *The Happy Time*◆ (1968), *Sugar* (1972), a revival of *Irene*◆ (1973), and *42nd Street*◆ (1980). His work had great style and wit, and often displayed a captivating period charm. His death was announced to a shocked cast at the end of the opening-night performance of *42nd Street.*

CHANEY, Stewart (1910–69) Born in Kansas City, Mo., he studied at Yale under Professor George P. Baker◆ before embarking on a career as set designer. His work was first seen on Broadway in *Kill That Story* (1934). Among the many other plays for which he designed sets, and sometimes costumes and lighting, were *The Old Maid*◆ (1935), *Having Wonderful Time*◆ (1937), *Life with Father*◆ (1939), *The Voice of the Turtle*◆ (1943), *Jacobowsky and the Colonel* (1944), *The Late George Apley*◆ (1944), and *The Moon Is Blue*◆ (1951). Of his cleverly conceived set for *The Voice of the Turtle* (1943), one of the earliest small-cast plays, Lewis Nichols wrote in the *Times,* "Stewart Chaney has fallen into the spirit of the occasion by constructing a splendid set showing a bedroom, sitting room and kitchen, all apparently of normal size, perfectly appointed. The cast could live there."

CHANFRAU, [Francis S.] Frank (1824–84) Born in a famous New York tenement known as "The Treehouse" or "Old Tree House," and largely self-educated, he left his hometown to work as a ship's carpenter in the West. When he returned to New York he took up amateur dramatics and shortly thereafter obtained work as a super at the Bowery Theatre.◆ His imitations of Edwin Forrest,◆ one of that theatre's great stars, caught the ear of the manager, who gave him small roles. Moving to

William Mitchell's♦ Olympic Theatre, he "created a sensation" as Jeremiah Clip in a revival of *The Widow's Victim,* in no small part again because of his mimic abilities. His performance so delighted the theatre's prompter, Benjamin A. Baker,♦ that when Baker decided to write a play to be performed at his own benefit he wrote the central role around Chanfrau's special talents. The play was *A Glance at New York in 1848*♦ and the leading character, Mose, a New York fireman. For nearly twenty years Chanfrau played little except Mose, both in the original play and in numerous sequels. Luckily, when he became too old to perform the youthful, athletic fire-fighter, two more excellent parts came his way. In 1865 he first appeared in the title role of *Sam,* an American who arrives in England in time to vanquish several villains. An even better character was the pioneer Kit Redding in *Kit, the Arkansas Traveller*♦ (1870). The two parts kept him in front of audiences until shortly before his death.

Otis Skinner♦ wrote of him, "Nearly everything about Chanfrau was big: voice, body, limbs, method. He must have been a very handsome man in his younger days." Although some contemporaries described him as smaller than Skinner recalled, they agreed about his good looks, noting in particular his striking dark eyes and dark, curly hair.

CHANNING, Carol [Elaine] (b. 1921) A tall, blonde comedienne whose voice runs the gamut from babyish squeals to baritone, she was born in Seattle and made her debut in the chorus of *No for an Answer* (1941). Later the same year she understudied Eve Arden in *Let's Face It.* After a brief appearance in *Proof Through the Night* (1942), she traveled the night-club circuit. Her fame was assured when she appeared in *Lend an Ear* (1948), where her superb comic talents flourished, most notably as a wildly energetic chorus girl in a spoof of 1920s' musicals. She consolidated her reputation when she essayed the role of Lorelei Lee in a musical version of *Gentleman Prefer Blondes*♦ (1949), in which she introduced "Diamonds Are a Girl's Best Friend" and "A Little Girl from Little Rock." Brooks Atkinson♦ noted, "She goes through the play like a dazed automaton—husky enough to kick in the teeth of any gentleman on the stage, but mincing coyly in high-heel shoes and looking out on a confused world through big, wide, starry eyes. There has never been anything like this before in human society." In 1954 she succeeded Rosalind Russell in *Wonderful Town,*♦ then appeared in the title role of *The Vamp* (1955) and in an intimate revue designed around her talents, *Show Girl*

(1961). Her greatest success was as the pushy Dolly Levi in *Hello, Dolly!*♦ (1964), in which she introduced the title song and in which she toured regularly for many seasons. She returned to the character of Lorelei Lee for *Lorelei* (1974), a revised version of *Gentlemen Prefer Blondes.* In 1986 she toured with Mary Martin♦ in *Legends,* a play which never reached New York.

CHANNING, Stockard [née Susan Stockard] (b. 1944) The New Yorker was educated at Harvard and made her acting debut in Boston in 1966. She came to Broadway in 1971 in the chorus of the musical *Two Gentlemen of Verona.* After performing for several seasons in California, she replaced the leading lady in *They're Playing Our Song.* Afterwards she appeared in a 1985 revival of *Joe Egg,* a 1986 revival of *The House of Blue Leaves,*♦ an off-Broadway presentation of the London hit, *Woman in Mind* (1988), and in *Six Degrees of Separation* (1990).

CHAPMAN, John [Arthur] (1900–1972) Born in Denver, the son of journalists, he studied at the University of Colorado and at Columbia. He began his newspaper career in 1917 on the Denver *Times* and joined the New York *Daily News* in 1920, becoming its drama editor in 1929 and its drama critic in 1943, a post he held until his retirement. He also served as Burns Mantle's♦ assistant on the *Best Plays*♦ and after Mantle's death edited the series from the 1947–48 volume through the 1951–52 edition. Thereafter for many years he edited a less successful series.

CHAPMAN, William B., Sr. (1764–1839) Generally considered the founder of the tradition of Ohio and Mississippi River show boats, he first acted in his native England before coming to America, where he made his debut at the Bowery Theatre♦ in 1828 playing Iago to Edwin Forrest's♦ Othello. After several seasons at the Park Theatre♦ he toured the West, concluding theatre could be brought to river towns by boat. With the aid of a Captain Brown he built "a large flatboat with a rude kind of house upon it." The house was, of course, his floating theatre. Because of navigational difficulties, after sailing down the Ohio and the Mississippi to New Orleans, Chapman would sell the boat for firewood and entrain north to build a new boat. After his death his widow maintained the tradition for several years before selling out to Sol Smith.♦

Chapman's son, William B. Chapman, Jr. (1799–1857), was long prominent as a comedian at the

Bowery, where he made his debut in 1827 as Billy Lackaday in *Smiles and Tears*. He later managed the Walnut Street Theatre♦ in Philadelphia, before spending his last years in San Francisco. Critics there called him the "best low comedian in the state," singling out for special praise his performances as Tony Lumpkin and the First Gravedigger.

Chapter Two, a comedy in two acts by Neil Simon. ♦ Produced at the Imperial Theatre. December 4, 1977. 857 performances.

"Chapter Two in the life of George Schneider" begins when he returns home from a trip abroad, a trip designed to distract him from his grief at the loss of his wife. George (Judd Hirsch) is a novelist and is looking for a researcher to help him with his new book. Mistaking her name and number for a suggested helper, he phones a divorced actress, Jennie Malone (Anita Gillette). Their relationship blossoms and before long they are married. Nevertheless, memories of his first wife obsess George, for a time even threatening the marriage. Finally he realizes how much he fears being happy with Jennie and starts to write a book about his experience.

Another in Simon's long line of observant, witty comedies, the play was said to be semi-autobiographical, written after Simon's remarriage following the death of his own first wife. It was also the second play written subsequent to his move to California, and while the two-apartment set remained throughout the play, the short, quickly moving scenes reflected cinematographic practices. A commentary on theatrical economics was offered when this play with a cast of four was booked into a large musical comedy theatre.

Charity Ball, The, a play in four acts by David Belasco♦ and Henry C. de Mille. ♦ Produced by Daniel Frohman♦ at the Lyceum Theatre. ♦ November 19, 1889. 200 performances.

John Van Buren (Herbert Kelcey♦), the rector of St. Mildred's, has kept his promise to the dying father of blind Phyllis Lee (Grace Henderson) to take her under his protection, unaware that his aggressive brother, Dick (Nelson Wheatcroft), once told the young woman he wanted to marry her and then despoiled her. But Dick is so determined to rise in Wall Street that he has thrown her over and proposed to Ann Cruger (Georgia Cayvan♦), whose father is a powerhouse on the Street. When John learns the truth he confronts Dick and forces him to marry Phyllis. In time John comes to recognize that he loves Ann as much as she has always loved him.

The third act, in which John learns about Phyllis

and confronts his brother, was considered one of the most powerful scenes in contemporary drama, and was in large measure responsible for the success of the play.

Charles the Second; or, The Merry Monarch, a comedy in three acts by John Howard Payne♦ and Washington Irving♦ [uncredited]. Produced by Stephen Price♦ and Edmund Simpson♦ at the Park Theatre. ♦ October 25, 1824. In repertory.

When his mistress, Lady Clara (Mrs. Clarke), accuses the Earl of Rochester (Mr. Stanley) of being "the chief cause of the king's irregularities," the Earl agrees to help reform Charles II (Simpson). He takes the King to a seaman's tavern run by old Captain Copp (Thomas Hilson♦). There he deserts the King, leaving him to fend for himself without any money. Copp threatens to have the King arrested, but the King escapes through a window. Realizing the Earl and the lady have had his best interests at heart, the King is forgiving and promises to mend his ways. He pays his debt to Copp and gives him a fine watch as well.

Written during Payne's long London sojourn, it was first mounted at Covent Garden in May 1824. Payne based his play on Alexandre Duval's *La Jeunesse de Henri V,* itself taken from earlier works. Much of Payne's original draft was hardly more than a literal translation. The main attraction of the evening, Captain Copp, was Irving's invention, as was the comic device of having Copp repeatedly start the risqué song he was never permitted to finish:

> In the time of the Rump,
> An old Admiral Trump,
>   With his broom swept the chops of the Channel;
> And his crew of Big Breeches
> Those Dutch sons of—

"Charleston" A song by Jimmy Johnson and Cecil Mack and a knee-twisting, high-kicking dance, it was introduced by Elisabeth Welch in the black musical *Runnin' Wild* (1923). It became the quintessential dance of the 1920s, leading to such imitations as the "Black Bottom" and the "Varsity Drag." As such it was one of the most significant songs to come out of the American theatre.

Charleston (South Carolina) One of the earliest important American theatrical centers, it saw its first play when *The Orphan* was presented on January 18, 1735. Just over a year later, on February 12, the Dock Street Theatre♦ opened to become the city's first regular playhouse. In after years David Douglass,♦ Thomas Wall,♦ Dennis Ryan,♦ the younger Hallam,♦ and John Henry♦ all performed in the city. By the end of the century several playhouses were active, and Alexandre Placide♦ was a dominant figure. In the early 19th century the city could boast of its own school of dramatists, including William Ioor, John Blake White, Isaac Harby, and, for a time, Mordecai Noah. ♦ After the Civil War the city's importance as a theatrical center waned quickly. Today it rarely plays host to major touring companies. However, since 1977 the American branch of the Spoleto festival has been held there annually. It has offered the American premieres of such works as Tennessee Williams's♦ *Crève-Coeur,* Arthur Miller's♦ *The American Clock,* and William Gibson's♦ *Monday After the Miracle.* Eola Willis's♦ *The Charleston Stage in the XVIII Century* (1933) remains the best study of the early years.

Charley's Aunt Brandon Thomas's 1892 London hit was offered with great success a year later to Americans. It told how a student, Lord Fancourt Babberley, disguises himself as the aunt of his college roommate in order to fill the need for a chaperone. The real aunt lives in Brazil, "where the nuts come from," and her unwonted appearance naturally leads to complications. Etienne Girardot♦ created the role of Babberley in America and was identified with it for decades afterwards. He also played it in a major 1906 revival. José Ferrer♦ led a popular 1940 revival. In 1948 it was turned into the long-running musical *Where's Charley?,* ♦ with Ray Bolger♦ playing the lead.

Charlot's Revue (also known as *Charlot's London Revue*). Compiled largely from the best material that had been offered by André Charlot in his West End revues, the 1924 musical marked the American debuts of Jack Buchanan, ♦ Gertrude Lawrence,♦ and Bea Lillie.♦ Equally important, its effective intimacy, both in its musical and comic numbers, was a major influence in sounding the death knell for gargantuan extravaganzas of the Ziegfeld♦ school. A number of earlier American revues, notably *The 49ers,* had embarked on a similar path, but the exceptional finish and widespread success of this English importation give it a special place in the evolution of American revue. Among its best numbers were "Limehouse Blues" and Miss Lillie's "March with Me."

CHASE, MARY COYLE (1907–81) Born in West Denver, Colo., she had a long career as a Denver newspaperwoman before writing her first play for the Federal Theatre Project.♦ The play was presented in 1936 in Denver, as *Me Third,* and a year later in New York as *Now You've Done It.* It was short-lived. A second play, *A Slip of a Girl* (1941), folded on tryout. But her next play not only won a Pulitzer Prize,♦ but remains one of the most beloved and often revived of American comedies. *Harvey*♦ (1944) was the story of an invisible rabbit and his boozy friend. A fourth play, *The Next Half Hour* (1945), failed. Helen Hayes♦ helped make a hit of *Mrs. McThing* (1952), telling of a snobbish woman brought to earth by a witch who substitutes a prissy brat for her roughneck son. In the same year *Bernadine* presented the world as viewed through teenagers' eyes and enjoyed a modest run. Her last play to reach New York was *Midgie Purvis* (1961), in which Tallulah Bankhead♦ played a rich matron who poses as a doddering crone.

CHATTERTON, RUTH (1893–1961) A petite beauty, noted for the "exquisite naturalness" of her acting, she was born in New York City and made her stage debut in Washington, D.C., in 1909. For the next several years she played in stock there, in Milwaukee, and in Worcester, Mass. Her first New York appearance was in a short-lived failure, *The Great Name* (1911). Coming under the aegis of Henry Miller, ♦ she won her earliest important notices as the daughter who reconciles her mother and father in *The Rainbow* (1912). She scored a major success as Judy Abbott, the orphan who marries her rich sponsor, in *Daddy Long-Legs*♦ (1914). Another well-received role was Olive Daingerfield, the daughter who must act as a servant when her impoverished family rents their mansion to a rich man, in *Come Out of the Kitchen*♦ (1916). After playing Judith Baldwin, who puts all her suitors to a test, in *Moonlight and Honeysuckle* (1919), she portrayed the titular heroine of James M. Barrie's♦ *Mary Rose* (1920). In 1922 she was Marthe Dellieres, a playwright's mistress, in *La Tendresse,* and followed this by playing Kay Faber in *The Changelings* (1923), a play about wifeswitching. An unsuccessful foray into musicals with *The Magnolia Lady* (1924), a lyric version of *Come Out of the Kitchen,* began a series of failures which ended only when she took the role of Irish Fenwick in a touring company of *The Green Hat* (1926). She spent most of the ensuing years in films, returning to the theatre intermittently though never with a major success. Her last New York appearance was as Irene in a 1951 City Center♦ revival of *Idiot's Delight.* ♦

CHAYEFSKY, [Sidney] Paddy (1923–81) The New York-born playwright attended City College before serving in World War II. He made a reputation in the early 1950s as a writer of low-key, sentimental, but realistic television dramas, often best remembered for their naturalistic dialogue. His first Broadway play, *Middle of the Night*♦ (1956), which recounted a May-December romance, was based on one of his television pieces. Some hint that he was to turn to a broader, more mystical canvas came with his second and most successful play, *The Tenth Man*♦ (1959), centering on an exorcism in a synagogue. His canvas was even grander, but his hand less sure, in *Gideon*♦ (1961), a dramatization of the Old Testament story. When he met with failure with *The Passion of Joseph D* (1964), a play about Stalin, and *The Latent Heterosexual* (1968), which never reached New York, he abandoned the theatre to write for films. At the time of his death he was said to be working on a play about Alger Hiss.

Cheating Cheaters, a play in four acts by Max Marcin.♦ Produced by A. H. Woods♦ at the Eltinge Theatre. August 9, 1916. 286 performances.

Nan Carey (Marjorie Rambeau♦) enlists a number of suave criminals to pose with her as the rich Brockton family, in order to win the friendship of the equally rich Palmer clan and then steal the Palmer jewels. To make her disguise all the more plausible she even arranges to borrow some very expensive jewels to wear. But just as the Brocktons are not really the Brocktons, so the Palmers are also criminal poseurs. The Palmers are determined to steal the Brockton jewels. Both groups worry most about a mysterious detective named Ferris, who has sent many of their former colleagues to prison. Ferris turns out to be none other than Nan, who is able to arrest more than half the cast by the final curtain.

It was one of the many skillfully contrived "crook plays" that delighted Broadway in this era.

CHEER, Miss [Margaret] (*fl.* 2nd half 18th century) Little is known about this actress, who for a brief period of time was a reigning favorite on American stages. She apparently made her debut with Douglass's♦ company in Charleston in 1764 and later moved with the troupe to Philadelphia and New York. Among the many roles for which she was applauded were her Portia, Ophelia, Juliet, and Cordelia, as well as Belvidera (*Venice Preserved*) and Sylvia (*The Recruiting Officer*). She is said to have married Lord Rosehill in Maryland in 1768 and appeared on the stage only infrequently thereafter.

However, *Burke's Peerage* gives the name of the Lord's wife as Catherine Cameron, which may have been Miss Cheer's real name. She returned later to England and did not play again in America until 1793, when she returned under the name of Mrs. Long. Her reception was cool and she soon retired permanently.

CHEKHOV, Anton [Pavlovich] (1860–1904) The great Russian playwright did not achieve American recognition until nearly twenty years after his death. The earliest performances of his works in the United States were generally given in Russian by small groups of émigré artists. Among these performers were Alla Nazimova,♦ who played in *The Seagull* in New York in 1905. A few tentative translations were made available to English-speaking ensembles and allowed such avant-garde companies as the Washington Square Players♦ to present his one-act *The Bear* in 1915 and *The Seagull* a year later. Almost all of these productions were failures since the plays were perceived as arty, gloomy tragedies instead of as dark comedies about a decaying bourgeoisie. The visits of the Moscow Art Theatre♦ during the 1922–23 and 1923–24 seasons, and the company's mounting of *The Three Sisters, The Cherry Orchard*, and *Uncle Vanya*, coupled with the virtually simultaneous availability of superior translations, brought about a real appreciation of the works. The Civic Repertory Theatre♦ offered *The Three Sisters, The Cherry Orchard*, and *The Seagull* between 1926 and 1929. Subsequent noteworthy revivals included the Lunts♦ in *The Seagull* (1938); Judith Anderson,♦ Katharine Cornell,♦ Ruth Gordon,♦ and Dennis King♦ in *The Three Sisters* (1942); *Uncle Vanya* by the visiting Old Vic♦ in 1946; and a series of off-Broadway revivals under David Ross in the 1950s. *Ivanov*, the playwright's first full-length work, is the most frequently revived of his less-known pieces.

CHENEY, Sheldon [Warren] (1886–1980) Born in Berkeley, Calif., he studied at the University of California and with Professor George Pierce Baker♦ at Harvard before founding *Theatre Arts Magazine*♦ in 1916, where he remained as editor until 1921. Among his books were *The New Movement in the Theatre* (1914), *The Art Theatre* (1917), *The Open-Air Theatre* (1918), *Stage Decoration* (1927), and *The Theatre—Three Thousand Years of Drama, Acting and Stagecraft* (1929).

Cherry Pickers, The, a play in four acts by Joseph Arthur.♦ Produced by Augustus Pitou♦ at the 14th

Street Theatre. October 12, 1896. 120 performances.

In the British-Afghan War, John Nazare (William Harcourt), a half-caste, is an officer in the Eleventh Hussars, a regiment popularly known as "The Cherry Pickers." His rival for the hand of the half-caste, Nourmallee (Roselle Knott), is his fellow officer, Col. Brough (Ralph Delmore). Brough trumps up a charge to arrest Nazare and ties him to the wall of a fort in range of Afghan bullets. When that fails and the Afghans are about to seize the fort, he turns Nazare over to an Afghan who has vowed to kill him. However, with Nourmallee's help John escapes, and the Afghan kills Brough.

Typical of the highly colored melodramas presented by Pitou on the road and at this relatively out-of-the-way, low-priced theatre, it nevertheless prompted Edward Dithmar♦ to note, " 'The Cherry Pickers' is an honestly made play, and though we do not look for original and progressive ideas from melodramatists, they are the fellows who now do the most wholesome work for the stage."

Cherry Sisters [Addie, Effie, Ellen, Jessie, and Lizzie] Five sisters from Indian Creek, Iowa, they first appeared in New York in 1896 under the aegis of the first Oscar Hammerstein.♦ Their performances in a series of skits were so grotesquely bad that audiences hooted and threw coins. Managers capitalized on the fun playgoers had berating the girls, and the act was soon headlined as a freak attraction. Although the sisters strenuously denied it, it was bruited about that protective netting was often in place when they performed. Critics argued over whether their atrocious acting was genuine or faked, but, again, the sisters claimed they were serious artists. The act was disbanded when Jessie died while on tour in 1903, but their short career remained one of vaudeville's more amusing legends. If a net was, in fact, installed it was not the first time. An obscure performer named Doc Landis had toured in vaudeville in the early 1870s playing his own condensed version of *Hamlet* with a long flowing beard, which he refused to shave off, and an unfeigned, but ludicrous sincerity. After the rougher audiences of his day pelted him with rotten vegetables, a transparent screen was placed before him during his turn.

Chestnut Street Theatre (Philadelphia) In 1791 Thomas Wignell♦ and Alexander Reinagle♦ convinced a group of Philadelphians to build a theatre to house the company Wignell had formed. Wignell's brother-in-law, John Inigo Richards, ob-

tained the plans of the Theatre Royal in Bath, England, and the new playhouse was erected from these designs. It was built in traditional shape, with three tiers of boxes making a horseshoe around the pits and was originally painted in pinks and reds. Seating capacity was said to be about 2000. It opened in 1793 but was immediately shut down by a yellow fever epidemic. The first regular season began in February 1794 with a double bill of *The Castle of Andulasia* and *Who's the Dupe?* At first called the New Theatre, it became the city's leading playhouse. In 1816 it was the first American theatre to be lit by gas. Many of the most important American plays of the early 19th century, including virtually all the major works by the Philadelphia school of dramatists,♦ received premieres there. After Wignell retired the elder William Warren♦ and William Wood♦ continued to run the house successfully. However, with the conversion of the Walnut Street Theatre♦ to legitimate purposes in 1811, and the erection of the Arch Street Theatre♦ in 1828, the playhouse began to fall on hard times. A small fire in 1820 had forced a temporary closing, and when the theatre burned to the ground in 1856 it was not rebuilt until 1863. Its final production was a stock revival of *The Second Mrs. Tanqueray* in 1913. Shortly thereafter the theatre was demolished.

CHEVALIER, Maurice (1888–1972) The French boulevardier of song, with his straw hat and his raffish, jaunty delivery, was an international favorite by the time he made his American debut for Florenz Ziegfeld♦ on the New Amsterdam Roof Garden in 1929. A year later he appeared at a regular legitimate theatre in a one-man show. He returned at intervals thereafter until shortly before his death, and not even accusations of collaboration with the enemy during World War II, which he strongly denied, could dampen his popularity. Among the songs associated with him were "Mimi" and "Louise." He was also popular in films in the early 1930s.

Autobiography: *I Remember It Well,* trans. by Cornelia Higginson, New York, 1970.

Chicago, a satirical comedy in a prologue and three acts by Maurine Watkins. Produced by Sam H. Harris♦ at the Music Box Theatre. December 30, 1926. 172 performances.

Roxie Hart (Francine Larrimore♦) shoots her married lover. With the help of Jake (Charles A. Bickford), a hard-nosed, cynical reporter, Mary Sunshine (Eda Heinemann), a sob-sister newswoman, and, most of all, Billy Flynn (Edward Ellis), Roxie's venal lawyer, her trial is turned into a three-ring circus. The attention the publicity brings turns Roxie's head, and she even lies that she is pregnant to obtain another front-page story. After her acquittal she announces she is going into vaudeville. But her press conference is broken up when the police bring in a new murderess, Machine-Gun-Rosie. Roxie obligingly poses with Rosie for one last photograph.

Born in Kentucky, Maurine Dallas Watkins (1901–69) was a Chicago newspaperwoman who had earlier worked at play-writing with Leo Ditrichstein.♦ She quit her job on the *Tribune* to study with Professor George P. Baker♦ at Yale, and the first draft of *Chicago* was submitted as a class assignment. The play was her only success.

A musical version with songs by John Kander♦ and Fred Ebb,♦ and book by Ebb and Bob Fosse,♦ began a 898-performance run at the 46th Street Theatre on June 3, 1975. Gwen Verdon♦ was Roxie; Jerry Orbach♦ was Billy Flynn; and Chita Rivera♦ was co-starred in the much enlarged role of Velma Kelly. The part of Mary Sunshine was played by a man in drag.

Chicago (Illinois) In his autobiography Joseph Jefferson♦ speaks of visiting Chicago in 1839 when he was still a young boy and when the city had a population of about 2000, yet he writes of the city's "new theaters" and recounts his experiences in one. These may have been wooden structures erected by two young actors—Harry Isherwood, brother-in-law to Jefferson's father, and Alexander McKenzie—who had first performed in the dining room of a hotel there two years before. The first major theatre built in Chicago was a wooden structure erected in 1847 by John B. Rice, who later abandoned the theatre to become one of the city's early mayors. However, Chicago did not become an important theatrical center until after reconstruction following the great 1871 fire. Among the leaders of its revived theatre were David Henderson♦ and James J. McVicker.♦ By the late 19th century Henderson was mounting musical spectacles that toured the country successfully, and in the first years of the new century the LaSalle and Princess Theatres were home to musical comedies—often written by Will Hough,♦ Frank Adams,♦ and Joseph Howard♦— that were hugely popular and played the Midwest, if not New York, to great acclaim. Some, such as *The Sultan of Sulu*♦ (1902), started the period rage for musical comedies about Americans stranded in exotic lands. Others, such as the long-running *The Time, the Place and the Girl*♦ (1907), trafficked in basically home-spun tales. Almost all had sweet,

relatively elementary songs closer to contemporary Tin Pan Alley♦ material than to the best new Broadway music. In the field of non-musicals Chicago was less creative. By the 1920s the city was the second most important theatrical center in the country, with over twenty theatres operating simultaneously at its peak. A number of great drama critics, including Burns Mantle,♦ Percy Hammond♦ (both of whom later migrated to New York), and Ashton Stevens♦ helped spark interest. Moreover, Chicago newspapers were leaders in giving women a chance at drama criticism. Amy Leslie♦ was a noted example, as was Claudia Cassidy♦ later. Miss Cassidy was famous for her often harsh notices, written to lament the tackiness of many touring companies. Some historians feel she was excessively and indiscriminately negative, thus playing an unfortunate role in Chicago's decline as a theatrical center, but Glenna Syse, a leading contemporary critic, has suggested the decline was caused by real estate interests who found more profitable use for land occupied by playhouses. Away from the mainstream, Chicago has given rise to a number of noteworthy enterprises, among them the Goodman Theatre.♦ In recent years, however, the city has not been a creative force or even as significant a touring stand as its size suggests it could be. Yet again it has given rise to many lively "off-Loop" organizations such as the Steppenwolf♦ and Wisdom Bridge theatres.

Children of a Lesser God, a play in two acts by Mark Medoff. Produced at the Longacre Theatre. March 30, 1980. 887 performances.

James Leeds (John Rubinstein♦) is an instructor at a school for the deaf. He is assigned the task of continuing to teach Sarah Norman (Phyllis Frelich). Sarah is much older than most students, but she is difficult, hostile, and has refused to learn to read lips or to try to speak. She uses only sign language. After a while James and Sarah fall in love. They marry, but the marriage soon falls apart because she fears James pities her and because she is afraid they might have a deaf child. All the pair can tell each other is, "I'll help you if you'll help me."

Otis L. Guernsey, Jr.,♦ called the play, which won a Tony Award♦ as the best of the season, "an outcry for a group which, it insists, speaks more eloquently for itself in signs than hearing people are able to manage with mere words." No small part of Miss Frelich's strength in the role of Sarah came from the fact that she herself was born deaf.

Medoff (b. 1940) was born in Mt. Carmel, Ill., and was educated at the University of Miami and at

Stanford. Earlier plays, *When You Comin' Back, Red Ryder?* (1973), in which a criminal bully destroys people's illusions, and *The Wager* (1974), in which a woman is seduced on a bet, were both off-Broadway successes.

Children's Hour, The, a drama in three acts by Lillian Hellman.♦ Produced by Herman Shumlin♦ at Maxine Elliott's Theatre. November 20, 1934. 691 performances.

At the Wright-Dobie School a class reading is interrupted by the late arrival of one of the young students, Mary Tilford (Florence McGee). Her excuse is that she went walking and stopped to pick some wildflowers for the teacher. But Karen Wright (Katherine Emery) recognizes the flowers as some thrown in the refuse that morning. Since Mary has a reputation for being a habitual liar, Karen decides to punish her by rescinding her privileges. Without meaning to, she also punishes her own associate, Martha Dobie (Anne Revere), when she announces her forthcoming marriage. The vengeful Mary returns home to whisper to her grandmother that Karen and Martha are lesbians. The rumor destroys the school, wrecks Karen's marriage plans, and drives Martha to suicide. When Mrs. Tilford, having learned the truth, comes to apologize, Karen refuses to accept her apologies.

The play, based loosely on a 19th-century incident in Scotland, was the sensation of the season. Percy Hammond♦ wrote in the *Herald Tribune* that it "will make your eyes start from their sockets as its agitating tale unfolds." The New York Drama Critics Circle Award♦ was established in no small measure because the Pulitzer Prize♦ was awarded to another play that year. A 1952 revival was only moderately successful; the whispered accusation, the death off stage, and the general restraint of the work having come to seem tame in comparison to later plays.

Chin-Chin, a musical in three acts. Book by Anne Caldwell♦ and R. H. Burnside.♦ Lyrics mostly by Miss Caldwell and James O'Dea. Music by Ivan Caryll.♦ Produced by Charles Dillingham♦ at the Globe Theatre. October 20, 1914. 295 performances.

The evil Abanazar (Charles T. Aldrich) would not only steal the magic golden lamp owned by Aladdin (Douglas Stevenson), he also would help its prospective buyer, the rich American Cornelius Bond (R. E. Graham), stop Aladdin from marrying Bond's daughter, Violet (Helen Falconer). But two canny slaves of the lamp, Chin Hop Hi (Fred Stone♦) and Chin Hop Lo (Dave Montgomery♦),

find magical ways of assuming many wonderful disguises and even of transporting Aladdin to exotic places in order to retain the lamp for him and assist in his winning Violet.

Principal songs: Goodbye Girls, I'm Through (lyric, John Golden♦) · Ragtime Temple Bells

The show was the biggest musical hit of its season (except for the annual Hippodrome♦ extravaganza), in large part because of the acrobatic and clean humor of Montgomery and Stone, which invariably mixed knowing wit with childlike fun.

CHODOROV, EDWARD (1904–88) The brother of Jerome Chodorov,♦ the playwright-director was born in New York and began his theatre career as an assistant stage-manager after attending Brown University. His first play, *Wonder Boy* (1931), told of a dentistry student who becomes a movie star without meaning to. It was a success on the road, but failed in New York. He had better luck with his second play, *Kind Lady* (1935), a dramatization of Hugh Walpole's *The Silver Mask,* in which a kindly matron is menaced by a sinister visitor. Two failures followed: *Cue for Passion* (1940) recounted the attempt of a wife to make her husband's murder seem a suicide, and *Those Endearing Young Charms* (1943) depicted the wiles a young girl employed to reform and win a caddish aviator. When no producer would accept his next play, *Decision* (1944), he was forced to underwrite much of its costs himself. The drama was a veiled warning against domestic fascism, in which a school principal who exposes a corrupt Senator is framed for rape and lynched. Opening to a divided press, it ran five months. *Common Ground* (1945), in which a captured U.S.O. troupe chooses death rather than help the Nazis, was poorly received. His biggest hit was a comedy, *Oh, Men! Oh, Women!*♦ (1953), which revolved around a psychoanalyst who discovers his fiancée is not a virgin. Thereafter, luck eluded him, and his last plays all closed out of town. Except for his first work, he directed all his own plays.

CHODOROV, JEROME (b. 1911) The brother of Edward Chodorov,♦ he was born in New York and began his career writing for films. In Hollywood he met Joseph Fields,♦ with whom he would regularly collaborate. Their first effort, *Schoolhouse on the Lot* (1938), was, like his brother Edward's first play, a spoof of Hollywood, and it, too, failed. Success came with *My Sister Eileen*♦ (1940), based on Ruth McKenny's autobiographical stories of two sisters seeking their fortunes in New York. Another adaptation, this time of Sally Benson's stories of an over-imaginative teenager, won widespread popularity as *Junior Miss*♦ (1941). After serving in World War II, he again collaborated with Fields, but *The French Touch* (1945), in which a Parisian actor outwits the Nazis, had only a short run. Their next play, *Pretty Penny* (1949), closed before coming to New York, but their book for *Wonderful Town*♦ (1953), a musical version of *My Sister Eileen,* helped that show achieve a long run. They had less success with the libretto for *The Girl in Pink Tights* (1954), a musical which told the story of the creation of *The Black Crook.*♦ *Anniversary Waltz*♦ (1954), in which two parents inadvertently admit to their children that they lived together before being married, enjoyed a long run despite disappointing reviews. Divided notices, however, led to a relatively short stay for *The Ponder Heart* (1956), their adaptation of Eudora Welty's story about an engaging man suspected of murdering his bride. In 1964 Chodorov alone wrote the book for *I Had a Ball,* and in later seasons updated librettos of *The Great Waltz* and *The Student Prince*♦ for West Coast productions. At various times in his career he also directed plays.

Chorus Lady, The, a play in four acts by James Forbes.♦ Produced by Henry B. Harris♦ at the Savoy Theatre. September 1, 1906. 315 performances.

To help support her family and gain a measure of independence, Patricia O'Brien (Rose Stahl♦) has gone into the theatre. When the touring burlesque company in which she is a chorus girl closes, she returns to the Long Island home of her parents, who work for Dan Mallory (Wilfred Lucas) at his stables. For some time Dan has been courting Pat, although at the moment his financial interests are in trouble and he has taken on a partner, Dick Crawford (Francis Byrne). Pat reluctantly agrees to help her irresponsible sister, Nora (Eva Dennison), obtain work in a chorus. Once in New York, however, Nora quickly finds herself in debt. Crawford lends her the money she needs to pay off her debts, but also gets her to forge her father's signature on her note and then attempts to blackmail her into having an affair. Pat learns of what has happened and goes to Crawford's apartment to confront him with his treachery. While she is there Dan and Mrs. O'Brien appear. Rather than hurt her sister, Pat makes it appear that she was having an affair with Crawford. Dan is furious until he recognizes the true situation. He buys out Crawford and convinces Pat to leave the theatre to marry him. She agrees, remarking, "Dan, we'll settle down like a couple of Reubens. Us an' the cows."

Originally a magazine story by Forbes, it was afterward turned into a vaudeville sketch for Miss Stahl. The sketch was so successful that Forbes next developed it into a full-length play for her. Walter Prichard Eaton♦ branded it a "character comedy" which he saw as "a play in which some one or more vivid and entertaining persons are allowed the run of the stage, making the most of their eccentricities and thus always conditioning the story to immediate theatrical demands."

Chorus Line, A, a musical performed without intermission. Book by James Kirkwood and Nicholas Dante. Lyrics by Edward Kleban. Music by Marvin Hamlisch.♦ Produced by the New York Shakespeare Festival♦ at the Public Theatre. April 15, 1975. (Moved to Broadway at the Shubert Theatre, July 25, 1975.) 6,137 performances. PP.

Zach (Robert LuPone), a director-choreographer, auditions youngsters for a chorus line in a forthcoming musical. Not content with collecting photographs and résumés, nor with watching them perform a few sample steps, Zach requests each applicant to tell a little about himself or herself. They do. The aspirants include his old girlfriend, Cassie (Donna McKechnie). With time he eliminates those he cannot use, then the rest unite in glittering top hats and tails to celebrate that they are "One."

Principal songs: One · What I Did for Love

The show was the brainchild of its own director and choreographer Michael Bennett,♦ who spent months in auditions and workshops recording histories not unlike those employed in the show. Although Walter Kerr♦ held serious reservations about the "ordinariness" of many of the histories Bennett used, condemning some as too self-pitying and even irrelevant, he admired the show's "lightning-stroke severity" and hailed the total accomplishment as "brilliant." In September, 1983 the musical became the longest run show in Broadway history.

Christian, The, a play in a prologue and four acts by Hall Caine.♦ Produced by Liebler and Co.♦ at the Knickerbocker Theatre. October 10, 1898. 160 performances.

John Storm (Edward J. Morgan) is a clergyman who proposes marriage to Glory Quayle (Viola Allen♦). Glory rejects him, preferring to go her own ambitious way. Her path takes her farther and farther from the road Storm would have her follow. At one point she sings in music halls. But wherever she goes John remains watchful, until she eventually joins him in his missionary work in the slums.

Based on Caine's novel, it was rejected by all major American and English producers until Elisabeth Marbury♦ gave a script to Miss Allen, who went to England to help Caine rewrite it. Its success consolidated both her stardom and the position of the year-old producing company. The play was sometimes performed in five acts.

CHRISTIANS, [MARGUERITA MARIA] MADY (1900–1951) The Viennese-born actress appeared in German-language productions in New York while still a youngster, then did not return to America until 1931. Although she played such roles as Gertrude to Maurice Evans's♦ Hamlet in 1938 and Sara Mueller, the exiled woman, in *Watch on the Rhine*♦ (1941), she is recalled primarily as the loving central figure in *I Remember Mama*♦ (1944).

CHRISTY, E[DWIN] P. (1815?–62) The famed minstrel worked for many years in New Orleans, where he frequented the Congo Square area in which blacks often provided impromptu entertainments. Moving to Buffalo in the late 1830s he organized a series of small traveling shows that could be seen as a precursor to later variety or vaudeville bills. The shows included jig dancing, magic acts, and blackface acts. He claimed to have founded Christy's Minstrels♦ in Buffalo in 1842 (his offer in 1849 of $500 to anyone who could prove he was not the first to have organized a minstrel troupe apparently found no takers), but this would mean his group predated the Virginia Minstrels,♦ generally conceded to be the first such band. However, he is usually acknowledged to have first perfected the accepted forms and traditions of the earliest style of minstrel shows. How many he actually composed of the numerous celebrated minstrel songs for which he took credit is moot, since it is known that he purchased songs from Stephen Foster and other writers, even originally publishing "Old Folks at Home" as his own. Worsening mental instability forced him to retire in 1854.

CHRISTY, GEORGE N. [né HARRINGTON] (1827–68) After making his debut as a jig dancer in Buffalo in 1839, he performed under the aegis of E. P. Christy,♦ whose surname he adopted. He then played a "fakir" or magician in a touring bill of the elder Christy's. When Christy's Minstrels♦ were established he was a charter member, and quickly became the most celebrated performer in the troupe. Skilled at playing the "bones," a good singer and comedian, he nevertheless captivated audiences mainly with his youthful charm and

vigor. He was said to be the first minstrel to employ drag routines. He left Christy's Minstrels in 1854, forming a company called Christy and Wood's Minstrels, and later organized his own George Christy's Minstrels.♦ Several of his later ensembles were unsuccessful, but he continued to be a popular performer until his early death.

Christy's Minstrels Although said to have been founded in 1842 in Buffalo, it is more likely it was organized in its traditional form a year later. Its founder, E. P. Christy,♦ was generally acknowledged to have established the basic formula of olio, minstrel ring, and burlesque that became standard in all early minstrel shows and out of which the later, larger minstrel entertainment evolved. The troupe quickly became the most famous of the pre-Civil War blackface groups. Its fame prompted other, lesser bands to use its name, forcing Christy to take out warning advertisements and initiate lawsuits. In Europe minstrel shows were sometimes called "Christy Minstrels," using the name generically. A typical 1849 show, employing ten performers, began with an act of songs such as "Watching Dinah Crow" or "The Virginia Rosebud." The second act offered a burlesque on the order of the troupe's spoof of *The Bohemian Girl*, with the opera's most celebrated aria becoming "I Thought I Lived in Hotel Halls." The final act was devoted to delineating the "peculiar characteristics" of "Southern or Plantation Negroes." E. P. Christy's ill health coupled with the departure of George Christy♦ led to the company's disbanding in 1854, but several of the members reorganized as the "Original Christy Minstrels" and toured for nearly twenty years, although they were viewed as a pale imitation of the company in its heyday.

CICERI, CHARLES (*fl.* late 18th century) Called "the first full-fledged scenic artist in America," he was born in Milan and educated in Paris, where he learned drawing. He came to San Domingo as a soldier, but there purchased his discharge and served as scene painter for the local playhouse. He returned to Europe and worked in Paris, Bordeaux, and at the London Opera House before again coming to America. He was the scene painter at Philadelphia's Southwark Theatre♦ until 1794 when a yellow fever epidemic broke out and he moved to New York. His first success was his work for the operatic spectacle, *Tammany; or, The Indian Chief.*♦ Among the works for which he provided scenery were *Hamlet,*♦ *Henry VIII, The School for Scandal,* and Dunlap's♦ *André,*♦ as well as many of the newly popular adaptations of Kotzebue. He was apparently the first scene designer in America to employ the transparent scrims which de Loutherbourg had perfected in England, and was famous as well for his artificial figure painting and his transformations, such as the one described for *Blue Beard* at the Park Theatre♦ in 1802: "On Fatima's putting the Diamond Key to the Door, the Pictures all change to scenes of Horror; the Walls of the Apartment are stained with Blood, and the Door, sinking, discovers the internal of the Sepulchre, with its ghastly inhabitants; a moment after, all resumes its former appearance." He returned permanently to Europe sometime before 1807.

Circle in the Square The company was founded in 1950 as an offshoot of the Loft Players of Woodstock, N.Y., under the direction of José Quintero♦ in association with Theodore Mann♦ and others. The postwar fascination with arena-style stages had begun, and the company was one of the first to use the new form effectively at their tiny theatre on Sheridan Square. Their opening production was *Dark of the Moon*♦ (1951), but it was their mounting of *Summer and Smoke*♦ (1952) which brought them recognition and established Geraldine Page♦ as an important actress. Their 1956 revival of *The Iceman Cometh*♦ caused critics to re-evaluate both the drama and Eugene O'Neill,♦ rekindling an interest in his works. It also gave major impetus to the career of Jason Robards, Jr.♦ A later revival of *Children of Darkness* (1959) helped propel George C. Scott♦ to stardom. When their original premises were demolished in 1960, the company moved to Bleecker Street. In 1972 they opened an uptown theatre, while continuing to present plays downtown.

Circle Repertory Company After several years of informal collaboration and exploratory discussions, the group was founded in 1969 by Tanya Berezin, Marshall W. Mason, Robert Thirkield, and Lanford Wilson♦ and was designed to promote the best in American play-writing. Among its notable productions have been Wilson's *Hot l Baltimore*♦ (1973), *The Fifth of July*♦ (1978), and *Talley's Folly*♦ (1979) as well as Jules Feiffer's♦ *Knock Knock*♦ (1976), Albert Innaurato's *Gemini*♦ (1977), *Fool for Love*♦ (1983), *As Is* (1985), *Musical Comedy Murders of 1940* (1987), and *Burn This* (1988).

Circus in America Scattered notices of professional equestrians, rope dancers, jugglers, and acts of similar ilk began to appear in American newspapers in the early years of the 18th century; however, not until John Bill Ricketts♦ came from England and in 1793 assembled a variety of such acts under one roof in Philadelphia can the American circus be said to have finally taken root. Ricketts was a celebrated rider, so his show emphasized feats of horsemanship. He later took his show to other cities, such as New York, Albany, and Boston, before making what proved a fatal return trip to England in 1799. The development of the menagerie, eventually a prominent feature of circuses, came slightly later. The earliest record of an elephant in a circus is 1812. The first traveling tent is believed to have been that employed by J. Purdy Brown in 1825 or 1826 in Wilmington, Del., although some historians credit Nathan Howe and Aaron Turner with the introduction of one a year or so earlier. In the same period Isaac Van Amburgh became our first nationally famous lion tamer, while a decade later, in the late 1840s or early 1850s, Dan Rice♦ established himself as the first pre-eminent American circus clown. During this era the rise of canals and then of railroads greatly accelerated the development and reach of the shows.

The heyday of the American circus is generally seen to have been the last three decades of the 19th century, when the shows exploded from one ring into two- and eventually three-ring entertainments. The most famous figure of the time was, of course, P. T. Barnum,♦ whose showmanship and deft publicity lifted the genre to new heights, especially after he joined with James A. Bailey to form Barnum and Bailey's Circus. Competitors included the Adam Forepaugh Circus, the Great Wallace Circus, the Lemen Brothers Circus, the Ringling Brothers Circus, and the Sells Brothers Circus. These groups merged and dissolved with dismaying frequency. At one point Barnum combined with Forepaugh to offer a four-ring circus.

At its peak in 1903, approximately 100 circuses were touring the country. Thereafter, however, economic conditions began to erode profits. By 1905 Barnum and Bailey had dropped the circus parade that long preceded the show into town and drummed up interest. After Barnum's death the Ringling Brothers bought out his interests and in 1918 merged them into the famous Ringling Brothers and Barnum and Bailey Combined Shows. Continuing financial problems and a disastrous fatal fire shortly after World War II signaled the end of "the big top," with most major surviving groups performing increasingly in huge arenas. Besides the Ringling enterprise, latter-day circuses included the Clyde Beatty Circus and the King Brothers Circus.

The circus may have played a part in inspiring the growth of arena-style theatre♦ in America. Certainly summer music tents, which began to present Broadway musicals after World War II, owe much to classic circus arrangements. Moreover, the circus served as a training ground for a number of the acrobatic comedians who once graced our musical stages, including Fred Stone♦ and Bobby Clark.♦ The circus's splashy color made it an inevitable choice of setting for numerous plays. American examples include *A Circus in Town* (1887), *A Yankee Circus on Mars* (1905), *Polly of the Circus*♦ (1907), *Everything* (1918), *Sunny*♦ (1925), *Jumbo*♦ (1935), and *Barnum* (1980).

An excellent survey of American circus history can be found in Robert C. Toll's *On with the Show* (1976).

City, The, a play in three acts by Clyde Fitch.♦ Produced by the Messrs. Shubert♦ at the Lyric Theatre. December 21, 1909. 190 performances.

George Rand, Jr. (Walter Hampden♦), seems to have his world by the tail. He has been nominated to run for governor, is engaged to marry Eleanor Vorhees (Helen Holmes), and has watched his sister, Cicely (Mary Nash♦), make an excellent marriage to his private secretary, George Frederick Hancock (Tully Marshall). Matters take an ugly turn when his father (A. H. Stuart) dies after confessing that Hancock is a secret drug addict and his illegitimate son as well. Cicely refuses to divorce Hancock, but when Rand tells him he has married his own sister, Hancock goes berserk, kills her, and attempts suicide. George prevents him from killing himself, even though Hancock has threatened to destroy Rand's career by revealing the family secrets. Rand withdraws from politics and makes a clean breast of his situation. He feared his confession to Eleanor would mean the end of their engagement, but she remains loyal.

Fitch and many of his critics considered this his best play, although just how successful he was in contrasting virtuous small-town life with corrupting city life—his expressed purpose—is debatable. The play was the last he wrote and was not mounted until after his death. The opening night was one of the most sensational in history, with near pandemonium reportedly breaking out after Hancock, learning the truth, screamed at Rand, "You're a God damn liar!" "Damn" had been employed before, but never the complete expletive.

City Center [New York] The Mecca Temple, former home of the Masonic Shriners, was opened in 1943 as an auditorium devoted to presenting opera, ballet, musicals, and straight plays at popular prices. Many of the productions were return engagements of Broadway hits which had completed their road tours, but with time the theatre began to offer its own mountings, and the practice of producing both musical and non-musical revivals there was abandoned.

Civic Repertory Theatre The company was founded by Eva Le Gallienne♦ in 1926. Her hope was to reestablish a repertory tradition in America so that actors might develop their art by playing a variety of roles in a single season, and that playgoers might be assured of a theatre devoted to presenting the classics and meritorious new plays which might not be considered commercially viable. To this end she attempted to ensure the sort of large, loyal following that would allow continuity by pricing tickets far below standard charges. The company opened at the old, out-of-the-way 14th Street Theatre on October 26, 1926, with a performance of Benavente's *Saturday Night*. Among other programs of the first season were *The Three Sisters, The Master Builder, John Gabriel Borkman,* and *La Locandiera*. Later offerings included *The Good Hope, Peter Pan,*♦ *Romeo and Juliet,*♦ *Alison's House,*♦ and, its most successful attraction, *Camille*.♦ Although Burgess Meredith,♦ Alla Nazimova,♦ and Jacob Ben-Ami♦ headed the list of distinguished performers who played in support of Miss Le Gallienne, the company was often beset by money problems. Its many and expensive mountings, low admission prices, and the onset of the Depression all combined to undermine its finances. When Actors' Equity♦ refused to allow Sunday performances, the company saw yet another source of revenue denied it and disbanded in 1933.

Civil War, see *Wars in American Drama*

CLAIRE, [FAGAN], INA (1892–1985) The svelte, blonde-haired, hazel-eyed beauty with the tipped-up nose and weak chin, who was considered the finest high comedienne of her generation, was born in Washington, D.C., and made her debut in vaudeville as a singing mimic in 1905. Her first New York appearance, in 1909, won attention with her imitation of Harry Lauder. She toured in two-a-day for several seasons, before making her musical comedy debut opposite Richard Carle♦ in *Jumping Jupiter* (1911). She played the title role in *The Quaker Girl* (1911) and then appeared in *The Honeymoon Express* (1913). After several seasons in England she returned briefly to musical comedy and vaudeville. Her performances in the 1915 and 1916 editions of the *Ziegfeld Follies,*♦ and her introduction of "Hello, Frisco" in the former were followed by her first appearance in a straight play, *Polly with a Past*♦ (1917). She won such rave notices in the title role of a girl who makes up stories about her personal history that she became one of the most sought-after comediennes. She consolidated her reputation as Jerry Lamar, the money-chasing chorus girl, in *The Gold Diggers*♦ (1919), then won further praise as Monna, the young bride determined to be her much-married playboy husband's last spouse, in *Bluebeard's Eighth Wife* (1921). Successes followed: as Lucy Warriner, who suddenly realizes she loves her ex-husband, in *The Awful Truth* (1922); Denise Sorbier, the neglected wife, in *Grounds for Divorce* (1923); the thieving heroine in *The Last of Mrs. Cheyney* (1925); and Pearl Grayston, who buys herself a title, in a revival of *Our Betters* (1928). In 1932 she toured in *Reunion in Vienna,* ♦ then played the footloose painter Marion Froude in *Biography.* ♦ Appearances in London and several American failures followed before she won applause as Leonie Frothingham, the rich woman in love with a young radical, in *End of Summer*♦ (1936). Her later plays were not major successes, although her acting and good name allowed *The Fatal Weakness* (1946) to enjoy a modest run. Her last appearance was as Lady Elizabeth Mulhammer in T. S. Eliot's♦ *The Confidential Clerk* (1954).

Writing of her last performance, John Mason Brown♦ observed, "From an audience's point of view the delight of the evening is Ina Claire as Lady Elizabeth. All the farcical joy, all the glitter of high comedy, that Mr. Eliot meant to supply in his script, she supplies in her person. She is a chic Lady Bracknell, a delectable worldling, an irresistible scatterbrain, writing comedy that is unwritten for her by the sparkle of her eyes, the laughter in her voice, and the implications of her expressions. More than a superb comedienne, Miss Claire is the Comic Spirit incarnate."

CLAPP, Henry Austin (1841–1904) Born in Dorchester, Mass., he was educated at Harvard, then taught at the Boston Latin School before becoming drama critic for the Boston *Advertiser.* He remained with the paper for more than twenty years, switching to the *Herald* two years prior to his death. Known as well as a leading Shakespearean scholar and student of dramatic history, he regularly toured the country lecturing in his field. He also wrote on theatre for many newspapers away from Boston, including such

New York dailies as the *Sun, Tribune,* and *World.* He is best remembered for his *Reminiscences of a Dramatic Critic* (1902). His style reflected the leisurely, elongated construction of his era, but was marked by genuine erudition, peppery wit, and a determined fairness.

CLARE, Joseph (1846–1917) After serving his apprenticeship at the Theatre Royal, Liverpool, he was brought to America by Lester Wallack♦ in 1871. He remained at Wallack's until the company was disbanded, and during that time earned a reputation as possibly the finest set designer in America. His settings were admired for their elegance and proper sense of period. Critics of the era rarely devoted much space to commenting on set design, but, for example, his library set for *The Man of Honor* (1873) was singled out by one reviewer as "the most exquisitely artistic thing of its kind ever presented in this City."

Clarence, a comedy in four acts by Booth Tarkington. ♦ Produced by George C. Tyler♦ at the Hudson Theatre. September 20, 1919. 300 performances.

Clarence (Alfred Lunt♦) is a timid, seemingly bumbling ex-soldier who had been wounded in the war—at target practice. He is taken into the Wheeler family, a family in desperate disarray. The harried father (John Flood) is almost at his wit's end trying to control his flighty, suspicious wife (Mary Boland♦), his wild daughter Cora (Helen Hayes♦), and his ne'er-do-well son Bobby (Glenn Hunter♦). Clarence succeeds in bringing order out of chaos and wins the hand of the daughter's governess (Elsie Mackay). Only as he is leaving does the family learn he is one of the world's greatest authorities on coleoptera—bugs.

Heywood Broun♦ wrote in the *Tribune,* "*Clarence* is the best light comedy which has been written by an American." The play, which deftly caught the optimism and excitement that was to characterize the twenties, rocketed Lunt into prominence and caused Helen Hayes to be typecast as a flapper for several seasons.

Clari, the Maid of Milan, an operetta in two acts. Libretto by John Howard Payne. ♦ Music by Henry Rowley Bishop. Produced by Stephen Price♦ and Edmund Simpson♦ at the Park Theatre. ♦ November 12, 1823. In repertory.

The Duke Vivaldi (Mr. Clarke) lures the rustic maiden Clari (Miss Johnson) to his palace with a promise of marriage, but once there insists "the splendid slavery of rank" prevents his keeping his promise. Not totally unprincipled or unfeeling, the Duke provides Clari with every possible luxury, buying her jewels, Paris gowns, and surrounding her with servants. But Clari can only lament,

"'Mid pleasures and palaces, though we may roam,

Be it ever so humble, there's no place like home." For her entertainment the Duke enlists a troupe of strolling players. Their show tells the story of another maiden enticed by a glamorous suitor. When the father in the play condemns the girl, Clari interrupts to beg his forgiveness. Later she escapes and returns home, where her own father is unforgiving. But the Duke soon appears, to announce that the king, impressed by Clari, has consented to their marriage.

The play was suggested to Payne by a Parisian ballet, *Clari; or, The Promise of Marriage.* Early advertisements in New York featured the appearance of William Pearman, ♦ the famous English singer who had portrayed Jocoso, the Duke's servant, in the original London production. Pearman's singing was praised and the New York *News* called Bishop's whole score "the most beautiful and tender we have ever heard," adding, "The scene at the old home where the flute plays the air of 'Home, Sweet Home' and Clari listens, is one of the prettiest incidents we have ever witnessed on the stage." The work was frequently revived, and "Home, Sweet Home" remains recognized.

CLARK, BARRETT H[ARPER] (1890–1953) A native of Toronto, he studied at the University of Chicago and in Paris before beginning his theatrical career as an actor and stage manager with Mrs. Fiske. ♦ After teaching at Chautauqua, he was an editor at Samuel French, Inc. ♦ from 1918 to 1936, when he was appointed executive director of the Dramatists' Play Service. For many years he was a board member of the Drama League of America as well as editor of *Drama Magazine.* Although most of his books, beginning with *The Continental Drama of Today* (1914), dealt with foreign material, he wrote one of the earliest studies of Eugene O'Neill, which was published in 1926. He also edited the multivolumed *World's Best Plays,* as well as the *America's Lost Plays* ♦ series.

CLARK, [ROBERT EDWIN] BOBBY (1888–1960) The comedian made his debut in a minor role in *Mrs. Jarley's Waxworks* in his native Springfield, Ohio, in 1902. In 1905 he teamed with Paul McCullough (1883–1936), another Springfield native, with whom

he played until McCullough's death 31 years later. They performed in minstrel shows, circuses, and vaudeville, perfecting the basic formula they would employ so successfully in musical comedy and revue. Clark, wearing painted-on glasses and wielding a sawed-off cane and a cigar, portrayed a likable but scoundrelly fellow, while the taller, heftier, mustachioed McCullough was his babyish, whimpering stooge. They first came to playgoers' attention in the 1922 and 1924 editions of the *Music Box Revue.* ♦ Thereafter they appeared in *The Ramblers* (1926), *Strike Up the Band* ♦ (1930), *Here Goes the Bride* (1931), *Walk a Little Faster* (1932), and *Thumbs Up!* (1934). After McCullough's suicide Clark appeared alone in *Ziegfeld Follies of 1936* ♦; *The Streets of Paris* (1939); *Star and Garter* (1942); *Mexican Hayride* (1944); a revival of *Sweethearts* ♦ (1947); and *As the Girls Go* (1948), his last Broadway role. In 1950 he directed *Michael Todd's Peep Show,* and in 1956 toured in *Damn Yankees.* ♦ Describing his antics in *Mexican Hayride,* Lewis Nichols wrote in the *Times,* "Bobby Clark is funny just standing still on a stage, licking ashes from his cigar and with a surprised air looking out over his audience as though he did not expect it might be there. But . . . he does not stand still. The numbers king in flight has arrayed against him the police of two countries, forcing him to such disguises as that of a flute player in a strolling band and the false-tooth merchant of tamales."

CLARK, MARGUERITE (1887–1940) A native of Cincinnati, she made her debut as a chorus girl in Baltimore in 1899 in one of Milton Aborn's ♦ touring musical companies. After understudying and playing small parts in several Broadway musicals, she won attention in *The Wild Rose* (1902). This led to her being cast opposite De Wolf Hopper ♦ in *Mr. Pickwick* (1903). She remained with Hopper to be his leading lady in a 1904 revival of *Wang* ♦; *Happyland* (1905); and *The Pied Piper* (1908). A series of short-lived assignments followed before she scored a major success as Zoie, the wife who pretends to be pregnant, in *Baby Mine* ♦ (1910). In 1912 she played opposite John Barrymore ♦ as Hilda, the hero's mistress, in *The Affairs of Anatol.* Her last important assignment was the title role in the fantasy *Prunella* (1913). At the height of her career she left the theatre to become one of its first important stars to have a film career.

CLARK, [MARGARET BROWNSON] PEGGY (b. 1915) A Baltimorean, she graduated from Smith College, then studied scenic design at Yale. Her first Broadway assignment was creating costumes for *The Girl from Wyoming* (1938). Although she later designed costumes for *Uncle Harry*♦ (1942) and *Dark of the Moon*♦ (1945), she won major recognition for her imaginative lighting design. Among the plays she lit were *Love Life* (1948), *Miss Liberty* (1949), *Gentlemen Prefer Blondes*♦ (1949), *Paint Your Wagon* (1951), *Pal Joey*♦ (1952), *The Threepenny Opera*♦ (1954), *Peter Pan*♦ (1954), *Plain and Fancy*♦ (1955), *Bye Bye Birdie*♦ (1960), and *Mary, Mary*♦ (1961), as well as many productions of the New York City Center♦ and the Los Angeles and San Francisco Light Opera Company.

CLARKE, CORSON WALTON (1814–67) Born in Elizabethtown, N.J., he made his debut in 1838 under the elder James Wallack,♦ using his middle name as a stage name. Within a short time he began to be billed with his full name. After playing several seasons with Wallack and elsewhere he moved to Barnum's American Museum♦ and there created the role of Edward Middleton in Barnum's famous production of *The Drunkard*♦ (1850). Although he later essayed many other roles, it was his performance as Middleton with which he was always identified, so much so that he was often called "Drunkard" Clarke. For many years he served as Barnum's director of amusements.

CLARKE, JOHN SLEEPER (1833–99) A native of Baltimore, the tiny, elfin-faced comedian made his "debut" in Belair, Md., in a two-man dramatic reading and minstrel show, in which his partner was his schoolmate and future brother-in-law, Edwin Booth. ♦ His first professional appearance was at the Howard Athenaeum♦ in Boston in 1851 as Frank Hardy in *Paul Pry*. He then spent several seasons at Philadelphia's Chestnut Street Theatre. ♦ In 1855 he made a brief New York debut as Diggory in *The Spectre Bridegroom*. The debut was at a second-string theatre, the Metropolitan, and caused no stir. He returned to Philadelphia to play at the Arch Street Theatre♦ and later took over its management with William Wheatley. ♦ He used this base to make regular appearances in Baltimore as well. His comic talents were recognized when he returned to New York in 1861 to play Jeremiah Beetle in *Babes in the Wood,* with the *Times* hailing him as "the best eccentric comedian now on the New York stage." His comic repertory, like Booth's tragic one, consisted largely of old favorites. Among his best parts were Dromio, Sam Scudder in *The Octoroon,* ♦ the title role in *Paul Pry,* and William Burton's♦ great role as Timothy Toodle in *The Toodles.* ♦ The

Tribune wrote of his interpretation, "His inebriety comes unconsciously out in the unsteadiness of the head, the loppiness of the neck, the thickness of the voice, the spasmodic attempt to conceal the betraying hiccup." In 1864 he became co-manager of the Winter Garden with Booth. However, after his brother-in-law John Wilkes Booth♦ assassinated Lincoln and Clarke was temporarily jailed with other members of the family, he left for England, where he spent the remainder of his career, returning occasionally for a handful of appearances.

Classic Greek Drama in America American playgoers relatively early were afforded opportunities to see many of the great Greek dramatic stories performed, albeit not in translations directly from the Greek. A version of the Medea legend was on stage in 1800, as was a production of the Oedipus myth by 1834. However, the stories were first really popularized in French versions, such as Legouvé's *Medea,* which Rachel♦ offered in the original French, Ristori♦ played in Italian, and Matilda Heron♦ in an English translation. Translations directly from the Greek had to await the rise of academic stages in the very late 19th century and the availability of the efforts of such scholars as Gilbert Murray. Not until the second decade of the 20th century did major classic revivals emerge. Margaret Anglin♦ was an important figure in the movement, offering her *Antigone* in California in 1910 and her *Electra* and *Medea* in New York in 1918. She had also played in *Hippolytus* and *Iphigenia* in other cities. John Kellerd♦ was said to have offered the first professional *Oedipus Rex* in New York in 1911. Notable modern offerings have included *Lysistrata* in 1930, the Old Vic's♦ *Oedipus Rex,* featuring Olivier,♦ in 1946, and Judith Anderson♦ in Robinson Jeffers's♦ translation of *Medea*♦ in 1947. *Medea* was revived in 1982 with Zoe Caldwell♦ in the title role and Miss Anderson as the nurse. Collegiate theatres remain important as platforms for revivals.

Claudia, a comedy in three acts by Rose Franken. ♦ Produced by John Golden♦ at the Booth Theatre. February 12, 1941. 453 performances.

David Naughton (Donald Cook♦) is a successful architect living on a colonial farm he has lovingly restored. He is more or less happily married, although he is not certain about this matter since his beautiful wife Claudia (Dorothy McGuire) has never quite grown up. She has a mother-fixation and never seems entirely sure of her sexual appeal. When she impetuously sells the farm to an opera singer and has a brief flirtation with a handsome young Englishman, David is exasperated. Then Claudia learns that her mother (Frances Starr♦) is dying. She seems suddenly to mature. "Yes, it's like a miracle," her mother remarks. "It's just as if she were the mother and I were the child." Claudia agrees to return the opera singer's check and to settle down to being a wife.

Mrs. Franken's first play since *Another Language,* ♦ nine years earlier, and her only other success, the comedy was welcomed by Richard Watts, Jr., ♦ of the *Herald Tribune* as "the best new American play of the season." The play was especially popular with women audiences.

CLAXTON, KATE (1848?–1924) Born in Somerville, N.J., she made her debut in Chicago in 1869, then played for a time opposite Charlotte Crabtree. ♦ Her first New York appearance came under Augustin Daly♦ as Jo in *Man and Wife* (1870). She scored her greatest success as the blind Louise in *The Two Orphans*♦ (1874), and was ever afterwards identified with the role, which she played frequently in ensuing years, although she gave memorable performances in several other plays, most notably as the guilty Roberte in Sardou's♦ *Ferreol* (1876). Her career was plagued by her reputation as a tragic jinx, since she was playing Louise when the Brooklyn Theatre caught fire with great loss of life in 1876 and was performing at the time of several other theatre fires. Her grandfather had been on stage at the Richmond Theatre when it burned. To overcome this stigma as well as to secure roles other than Louise, she attempted to produce plays and manage theatres, but she had little luck and returned to acting *The Two Orphans* wherever she could obtain bookings. Whatever flaws she may have possessed as an actress, according to Odell, ♦ she excelled "in sweetness, in beauty and in an innate refinement of manner." Some sources give her birth as late as 1850.

CLEMENTS, COLIN, see *Harriet*

Cleveland Play House Organized in 1915 by its first president, Charles S. Brooks, most of the original members were, curiously, painters rather than actors or other theatre people. The group began producing in 1916 under its first director, Raymond O'Neil. With the arrival in 1921 of its second director, Frederic McConnell, the group became professional. Spurred by Brooks and McConnell, the company opened a fine two-theatre complex in 1927, the larger house named for Francis E. Drury, an early fund-raiser, and the smaller hall for Brooks.

McConnell was suceeded by his associate, K. Elmo Lowe, whose conservative policies guided the Play House until his retirement in 1969. For a short while after Lowe's retirement the company seemed disoriented, but it has since found a somewhat more adventuresome if costly program under its more recent directors, notably Richard Oberlin. In late 1983 it opened its new theatre complex, including the Kenyon C. Bolton Theatre. With the appointment of Josephine Abady in 1988 the repertory has reverted to an emphasis on new plays.

CLIFTON, JOSEPHINE (1814?–47) Controversy surrounds the early years of this brawny amazon of an actress. Not only is the year of her birth uncertain, but so is her birthplace. Most historians suggest she was born in New York, although there is some reason to believe she came from Philadelphia and that her real surname may have been Miller. She made her debut at the Bowery Theatre♦ in 1831. Later the same season she appeared as Elvira in *Pizarro*♦ and as Lady Macbeth, then was seen at the Park♦ as Bianca in *Fazio.* She was the first American actress of any importance to play major roles in England, where she appeared at Drury Lane in 1835. Returning to America she played opposite the elder J. W. Wallack♦ in several new plays before embarking on her most celebrated role, the title part in the original 1837 production of *Bianca Visconti.* ♦ That American critics held reservations about her was evident in the surprise manifested when she gave a performance that was "all the author could desire . . . all that it was prophecied she would not be." Much of her career was spent in Philadelphia, where she often appeared opposite Edwin Forrest.♦ Long after her death it was revealed that their relationship was more than professional, and her name figured prominently in the Forrests' notorious divorce case.

Climax, The, a play in three acts by Edward Locke. ♦ Produced by Joseph Weber♦ at Weber's Theatre. April 12, 1909. 240 performances.

Adelina von Hagen (Leona Watson) is studying to become an opera singer, but her fiancé, Dr. John Raymond (William Lewers), fears a stage career will corrupt her, so he hypnotizes her into believing she cannot sing and, to ensure the spell holds, gives her a medicine to use daily for her throat. One day when she forgets to spray on the medicine her voice comes back and she realizes what Raymond has done. She goes on to continue her lessons and Raymond understands that her dedication and art truly cannot be corrupted.

This *Trilby*-like, low-budget play remained popular for years and was revived with some regularity into the 1930s.

Climbers, The, a play in four acts by Clyde Fitch. ♦ Produced by Amelia Bingham♦ at the Bijou Theatre. January 15, 1901. 163 performances.

Although their greed and pushiness played no small part in killing George Hunter, his wife and younger daughters return from his funeral with only bitterness toward him, for they have discovered he died bankrupt. Only Blanche Sterling (Miss Bingham), Hunter's oldest daughter, is genuinely rueful. Paying their formal respects are several women and a social butterfly of a man who, like Mrs. Hunter, have been determined social climbers. Their private comments are brutal, one noting, "Mrs. Hunter went to the most expensive decorator in town and told him, no matter what it cost, to go ahead and do his *worst!*" Even their actions are thoughtless, with the sharp-tongued Miss Godesby (Clara Bloodgood♦) dickering with Mrs. Hunter for gowns she will no longer need. Blanche's problems are exacerbated when she reads her father's papers and learns that her husband (Frank Worthing) indulged in irregular business dealings which could send him to prison. Guilt-ridden and recognizing that his wife has a loyal, loving friend in Edward Warden (Robert Edeson♦), Sterling commits suicide.

Quinn♦ has observed, "*The Climbers* is a masterly portrayal of human strength and human weakness. The strong characters are strong just in those qualities of courage, decision and unselfishness which kindle admiration, and the weak ones are tainted by a failing which, directed into a proper channel, might become legitimate ambition . . . their motives always are comprehensible."

CLINCH, C[HARLES] P[OWELL] (1797–1880) The son of a New York businessman, he was an associate of the Knickerbocker writers and served briefly as a drama critic. His first play was *The Spy, A Tale of Neutral Ground*♦ (1822), an adaptation of James Fenimore Cooper's novel. The play opened less than ten weeks after the novel was published and immediately rivaled it in popularity, playing successfully all along the Eastern seaboard. Three months later the Park Theatre♦ mounted his second play, a farce, *The Expelled Collegian.* In 1824 the same theatre offered his tragedy, *The Avenger's Vow.* His last play, another farce, *The First of May in New York* (1830), was produced at the Bowery. ♦ Thereafter he abandoned play-writing, devoting the rest of his long life to business and politics.

CLINE, MAGGIE (1857–1934) Born in Haverhill, Mass., the deep-voiced singer-comedienne made several appearances in musical comedy and revue, but was best known in the 1890s as the "Irish Queen" of vaudeville. She introduced "Nothing Too Good for the Irish," "Down Went McGinty," and "McNulty Carved the Duck." However, she was most often identified with "Throw 'em Down, McCloskey," which John W. Kelly rewrote to her specifications. Her staging of it was "a show in itself. At the words 'Throw 'em down, McCloskey!' everybody backstage seized the first object at hand—a chair, a broom, an iron rod, or something heavier—and threw it on the floor with all his might. The result was bedlam."

Clipper, The Known formally as the *New York Clipper,* it was founded in 1853 as a sporting and theatrical journal. Before it was absorbed by *Variety*♦ in 1924 it had long since minimized sporting and most general theatrical news and had become a trade sheet whose main concern was vaudeville. By the time of its demise it called itself "The Oldest American Theatrical Journal."

Clorindy; or, *The Origin of the Cake Walk.* A musical afterpiece presented by E. E. Rice♦ as part of a summer bill on the roof of the Casino Theatre♦ on July 5, 1898, it had book and lyrics by the poet Paul Laurence Dunbar♦ and music by Ernest Hogan. Its premiere marked the first occasion on which a show written and performed by blacks was presented at a major white house. Its most famous song was "Darktown Is Out Tonight."

Clothes, a play in four acts by Avery Hopwood♦ and Channing Pollock.♦ Produced by William A. Brady♦ and Wagenhals♦ and Kemper♦ at the Manhattan Theatre. September 11, 1906. 113 performances.

Olivia Sherwood (Grace George♦) likes more expensive clothes than she can afford, so she sets out to marry Richard Burbank (Robert T. Haines) for his money. Before long she has fallen in love with him and thereby winds up with the best of all worlds.

Hopwood's first play to be produced, it was reworked without his knowledge by Pollock, but he was open-minded enough to recognize the constructive additions the more experienced writer had made.

CLURMAN, HAROLD [EDGAR] (1901–80) Born in New York, he began his career at the Greenwich Village Playhouse,♦ then worked for the Theatre

Guild,♦ acting in small parts and serving as a play-reader. In 1931 he was one of the founders of the Group Theatre,♦ for which he directed *Awake and Sing!*♦ (1935) and *Golden Boy*♦ (1937), among others. After the company was dissolved his directorial assignments included *The Member of the Wedding*♦ (1950), *The Time of the Cuckoo*♦ (1952), *Bus Stop*♦ (1955), *Waltz of the Toreadors* (1957), *A Shot in the Dark* (1961), and *Incident at Vichy* (1964). He was co-producer of *All My Sons*♦ (1947). From 1949 to 1953 he served as drama critic for the *New Republic* and then for many years in the same capacity with the *Nation*. His publications include *The Fervent Years* (1945), a history of the Group Theatre; *Lies Like Truth: Theatre Essays and Reviews* (1958); *On Directing* (1973); and a loosely structured autobiography, *All People Are Famous* (1974).

COBB, Lee J. [né Leo Jacoby] (1911–76) The New York-born actor began his career in 1929 at the Pasadena Playhouse♦ and did not make his first Broadway appearance until 1935, when he assumed a minor role in *Crime and Punishment*. That same year he joined the Group Theatre,♦ where his best-remembered roles were Mr. Carp in *Golden Boy*♦ (1937) and the bankrupt Lammanawitz in *The Gentle People*♦ (1939). After playing important roles in short-lived failures such as *Thunder Rock* (1939), *The Fifth Column* (1940), and *Clash by Night* (1941), he replaced Alexander Knox as the lead in the comedy *Jason* (1942). Five years in Hollywood followed before he returned to create his most famous role, Willy Loman in *Death of a Salesman*♦ (1949). Brooks Atkinson♦ wrote in the *Times,* "Mr. Cobb's tragic portrait of the defeated salesman is acting of the first rank. Although it is familiar and folksy in the details, it has something of the grand manner in the big size and deep tone." His last appearances were in a revival of *Golden Boy* (1952), in *The Emperor's Clothes* (1953), and as King Lear (1968). He was described by Cecil Smith♦ as "a massive man . . . The face is big, each feature oversize—the large, soft, intelligent eyes; the big nose, jutting chin, wide cheekbones."

COBB, Sylvanus, Jr. (1823–87) Reputed to be the first writer to mass-produce popular romances, many of his works serialized in the New York *Ledger* and elsewhere were quickly dramatized by other authors. As plays his stories proved extremely successful at the Bowery♦ and other working-class theatres. These adaptations included *The Mystic Bride* (1856), *The Gunmaker of Moscow* (1856),

Orion, the Gold-Beater (1856), *Karmel, the Scout* (1857), *The Golden Eagle* (1857), *Alric* (1858), *The Oath of Vengeance* (1859), *The Veteran Buccaneer* (1859), *The Hunter Spy of Virginia* (1859), and *The Gipsy Daughter* (1860).

COBURN, Charles [Douville] (1877–1961) Born in Macon, Ga., he began his career as a program seller at a Savannah theatre and by the age of seventeen was the playhouse's manager. He later performed in stock in Chicago before making his New York debut in 1901 in *Up York State*. After heading a road company of *The Christian*♦ (1904), he and his first wife, Ivah Wills Coburn, formed the Coburn Shakesperian Players in 1906 and toured for several seasons playing virtually the entire Shakespearean canon. His stocky build and slightly pompous style made him an especially notable Falstaff. In 1916 he produced and took a principal role in the Chinese drama *The Yellow Jacket,*♦ a play he successfully revived on occasion. His best-known role, however, was probably the bragging Old Bill in *The Better 'Ole* (1918). None of his later appearances was quite as popular, although he won praise as David Hungerstolz, the day-dreaming button-maker, in *The Bronx Express* (1922); as Sir Percy, the English lord, in a road company of *So This Is London* (1923); and as Samuel Sweetland, the widower, in *The Farmer's Wife* (1924). In 1925 he played James Telfer in an all-star revival of *Trelawny of the Wells*. He accepted major assignments in several revivals mounted by The Players♦ and in 1934 founded the Mohawk Drama Festival & Institute. He retired from the stage after his wife's death in 1937 and enjoyed a long career in films, but returned to tour as Falstaff in *The Merry Wives of Windsor* (1946). For several summers shortly before his death he played Grandpa Vanderhof in *You Can't Take It with You*♦ on the straw-hat circuit.

COBURN, D. L., see *Gin Game,* The

Cocktail Party, The T. S. Eliot's♦ play, written in an almost conversational blank verse, and dealing with religious faith in the comfortable, modern world, was first produced in New York on January 21, 1950. Many critics could not make head or tail of it, Brooks Atkinson♦ dismissing it as "verbose and elusive." It quickly became the most talked-about and controversial play in many seasons and this, plus a superb cast headed by Alec Guinness,♦ Cathleen Nesbitt,♦ Irene Worth,♦ and Robert Flemyng, gave it a year-long run. It was revived with only small success by the APA♦ in 1968.

CODY, William Frederick (1846–1917) Better known as "Buffalo Bill," the Iowan served as a pony-express rider and as a Civil War and Indian scout. A play called *Buffalo Bill,* recounting his exploits, appeared in 1871. To capitalize on his renown he himself began to act in dramas purporting to recount his adventures, such as *The Scouts of the Prairie, The Knight of the Plains,* and *Buffalo Bill at Bay.* He toured in these for nearly a decade before founding his *Wild West Show* in 1883. Played in the open air, these entertainments allowed him to re-create vividly the old Indian skirmishes and show off his shooting and riding skills. His entrance, at the head of a large troupe, saw him clad in fringed and beaded buckskin, with a Winchester in his hand and a broad Stetson on his head. His flowing white moustache and goatee were instantly recognizable. The *Wild West Show* took on a major attraction when the great sharpshooter Annie Oakley♦ joined the company in 1885. The show prospered for many years as it toured the entire country, but eventually competition, the need to outspend that competition, and dwindling returns from a public tired of his style of entertainment forced him to merge with his major rival, Pawnee Bill's Historic Far West and Great Far East Show, in 1909. But the combined show continued to run up debts and was closed by bankruptcy in 1915.

COE, Richard L[ivingstone] (b. 1916) A native New Yorker, he became an assistant drama critic on the Washington *Post* in 1936 and its regular critic in 1946, a position he retained until his retirement in 1981. One of the leading non-New York critics, he was a warm, knowledgeable advocate of all good theatre, and his views were regularly solicited by Broadway producers, even when they did not try out their shows in Washington.

COGHLAN, Charles [Francis] (1842?–99) The brother of Rose Coghlan,♦ he was brought from England by Augustin Daly♦ as an addition to his company "where it had sometimes been found weak—in a leading man of distinction and personal charm." He made his debut in *Money* (1876). Although he impressed critics with his Orlando and Charles Surface during the season, he seemed unable to remain with any ensemble for long. By fall 1877 he was at Palmer's♦ Union Square Theatre,♦ where he scored major successes as the callous Monjoye in *The Man of Success* and as the doomed soldier Jean Renaud in *A Celebrated Case* (1878). Yet the following fall he had moved to Wallack's,♦ playing Lovelace in *Clarissa Harlowe* and Charles Surface to his sister's Lady Teazle. Thereafter he became Lillie Langtry's♦ leading man in *Enemies* (1886). He toured in the title role of *Jim, the Penman*♦ (1887), then returned to play Antony and Macbeth opposite Mrs. Langtry in 1889. At the same time he wrote two plays for his sister, *Jocelyn* (1889) and *Lady Barter* (1891). He was Lord Illingworth in Oscar Wilde's♦ *A Woman of No Importance* (1894). After a few lean seasons he won applause as Mr. Clarence, a character based on Edmund Kean, in *The Royal Box* (1897). Shortly before his mysterious death he appeared as a Sidney Carton-like figure in his own play about the French Revolution, *Citizen Pierre.*

William Winter♦ wrote of him, "He had a figure of rare symmetry, a handsome face . . . a voice of wide compass and sympathetic quality, and a natural demeanor of instrinsic superiority . . . In all Coghlan's acting there was a pleasing propriety of art. The thought preceded the speech. The gesture came before the word. All that was said and done seemed to be said and done for the first time."

COGHLAN, Rose (1851–1932) The sister of Charles Coghlan, ♦ the "wide-eyed, velvet-voiced, caressing, fascinating, divinely-smiling" actress first came to America in 1871 to play in burlesque with Lydia Thompson♦ and her British blondes. During the 1872–73 season she appeared with Wallack's♦ company in supporting roles, then returned to England. She came back to America and Wallack's in 1877 and, with two brief interruptions, remained there as a leading lady until the company disbanded in 1888. She played such classic parts as Lady Gay Spanker, Lady Teazle, and Rosalind, as well as appearing in such plays as Boucicault's♦ *Marriage,* Sardou's♦ *Diplomacy, ♦ Clarissa Harlowe,* Sardou's *A Scrap of Paper, The Silver King,* and *Lady Clare.* In 1893 she produced the first American mounting of Oscar Wilde's♦ *A Woman of No Importance,* playing Mrs. Arbuthnot. Thereafter her star began to fade, and she turned successfully to vaudeville. In 1908 she toured as Mrs. Warren in a controversial production of Shaw's♦ *Mrs. Warren's Profession,* then played opposite John Drew♦ and Mary Boland♦ in Somerset Maugham's♦ *Jack Straw.* During the 1909–10 season she was a member of the repertory company at the New Theatre, ♦ offering, among others, her Mrs. Candour, Mistress Page, and Paulina. Her last major roles were the Duchess of Saurennes in Maugham's *Our Betters* (1917) and Madame Rabouin in *Deburau* (1920). Odell♦ described her as "A ripe and radiant beauty, buxom, blithe and debonair, delightful in high comedy and effective in serious characters or in the high lights of melo-drama." Yet while she won the respect of many audiences, she seems rarely to have gained their affection and, by her admission, was never popular away from New York.

COHAN, GEORGE M[ICHAEL] (1878–1942) The first enduring figure of the modern American musical comedy stage, he was the son of vaudeville performers, with whom he made his theatrical debut. His father Jerry, his mother Helen, his sister Josephine, and he became one of vaudeville's most popular turns, The Four Cohans. Although he appeared briefly in *Daniel Boone* (1888) and toured in the title role of *Peck's Bad Boy* ◆ (1890), it was his expansion of a vaudeville skit he had written for his family that marked his entrance into musical comedy ranks. *The Governor's Son* (1901) and *Running for Office* (1903), another expanded vaudeville sketch, while only modest hits earned him the reputation as a fast-paced director and as a cocky, jaunty performer. Real success came with *Little Johnny Jones* ◆ (1904): "The Yankee Doodle Boy" and "Give My Regards to Broadway" are songs with which he nightly stopped the show. Critics dismissed his songs as tinkly Tin Pan Alley ditties and his books as too slangy, chauvinistic, and trite, but he immediately found a public that long remained loyal. In 1906 he had two of his greatest hits, *Forty-five Minutes from Broadway,* ◆ whose score included "Mary's a Grand Old Name," "So Long, Mary," and its title song; and *George Washington, Jr.,* in which he starred and introduced "You're a Grand Old Flag." Later musicals, many of which he starred in, included *The Honeymooners* (1907), a rewriting of *Running for Office; The Talk of New York* (1907); *Fifty Miles from Boston* (1908), which included "Harrigan"; *The Yankee Prince* (1908); *The American Idea* (1908); *The Man Who Owns Broadway* (1909); *The Little Millionaire* (1911); *Hello, Broadway!* (1914); *The Cohan Revue of 1916; The Cohan Revue of 1918; The Voice of McConnell* (1918); *The Royal Vagabond* (1919), a comic revision of what had been other authors' serious operetta; *Little Nellie Kelly* (1922); *The Rise of Rosie O'Reilly* (1923); *The Merry Malones* (1927); and *Billie* (1928). Although *Popularity* (1906) was a failure, he wrote several other straight plays that enjoyed long runs: *Get-Rich-Quick Wallingford* ◆ (1910), *Broadway Jones* (1912), *Seven Keys to Baldpate* ◆ (1913), *The Miracle Man* (1914), *Hit-the-Trail Holliday* ◆ (1915), *The Tavern* ◆ (1920), *Madeleine and the Movies* (1922), *The Song and Dance Man* (1923), *American Born* (1925), *The Home Towners* (1926), *The Baby Cyclone* (1927),

Whispering Friends (1928), and *Gambling* (1929). As if to bring his play-writing career full circle, his last plays were failures, even though he starred in all four: *Friendship* (1931), *Pigeons and People* (1933), *Fulton of Oak Falls* (1937), and *The Return of the Vagabond* (1940), a sequel to *The Tavern.* Between 1906 and 1920 he formed a highly successful partnership with Sam Harris. ◆ They produced all of Cohan's plays of that period and many other profitable ones as well. They also built the George M. Cohan Theatre. In 1919, as both actor and producer, he attempted to mediate the Actors' Equity ◆ strike, but the union's cold response left him permanently embittered. Following the dissolution of his partnership with Harris, he produced his own plays and those of others. Until late in his career Cohan appeared solely in his own works, except as an occasional replacement. However, two of his greatest successes were in other men's plays. In 1933 he scored a singular triumph as Nat Miller in Eugene O'Neill's ◆ *Ah, Wilderness!,* ◆ then in 1937 played President Roosevelt in Rodgers ◆ and Hart's ◆ *I'd Rather Be Right.* ◆

Amy Leslie ◆ drew a picture of the young performer "with big, soulful eyes that speak music and peer cloudily out from under soft blonde hair. His face is pale and swift to mirror sentiment . . . He is a wit, and it shows in the odd little side twist to his sensitive mouth and in the glow of fun under his long lashes; it lies about his strong, thin jaw and in the set of his head upon his slightly stooped shoulders." Walter Prichard Eaton's ◆ condemnation of Cohan for "his lack of good taste and his lack of a real knowledge of the world" typified many critics' dismissal of Cohan's early plays. With time, however, they came to appreciate his excellent technique and certain sense of what audiences wanted. Ironically, critical acceptance grew as Cohan's popularity and sure touch waned. Most of his best shows were among his first, and these fine early plays, for all their simplicity, their apparent naïveté, and their unabashed flag-waving, remain his most appealing and enduring. Perhaps it is doubly ironic, given the still lively popularity of his finest songs, that two of his straight plays, *Seven Keys to Baldpate* and *The Tavern,* are the most often revived.

Biography: *George M. Cohan: The Man Who Owned Broadway,* John McCabe, New York, 1973.

COHEN, ALEXANDER H. (b. 1920) The New York-born producer began his career in 1941 with a failure, *Ghost for Sale.* Later the same year he produced a major success, *Angel Street.* ◆ Although his record of commercial successes has been disappointing, many of his box-office failures were nevertheless meritorious. Among his productions, many of which were importations of London hits, were *King Lear*♦ (1950), *At the Drop of a Hat* (1959), *An Evening with Mike Nichols and Elaine May* (1960), *Beyond the Fringe* (1962), *The Home-coming* (1967), *6 Rms Riv Vu* (1972), and *A Day in Hollywood/A Night in the Ukraine* (1980). For many years he produced the television coverage for the annual Tony Awards. ♦

COLE, [ROBERT] BOB (1869–1911) Little is known about the earliest history of this black composer and performer, one of the first to make his mark in the theatre. Working first with Billy Johnson, then later with James Weldon Johnson♦ and Rosamond Johnson,♦ he wrote and often played in such early black shows as *A Trip to Coontown* (1898), *Kings of Koondom* (1898), *The Shoofly Regiment* (1907), and *The Red Moon* (1909). Because black shows were still subject to prejudice and never ran long in his day, he often found that a more profitable outlet for his talent was interpolating songs into white shows. His most memorable hit was "Under the Bamboo Tree," which Marie Cahill♦ introduced in *Sally in Our Alley* (1902).

COLE, JACK (1914–74) A native of New Brunswick, N. J., he began his career as a dancer in the 1934 failure *Caviar*. His first choreographic assignment was *Something for the Boys* (1943). Among the other musicals for which he created the dances were *Ziegfeld Follies of 1943,* ♦ in which he also appeared; *Kismet*♦ (1953); *Jamaica* (1957); *A Funny Thing Happened on the Way to the Forum*♦ (1962); and *Man of La Mancha*♦ (1965). His art was noted for its debt to Oriental and jazz motifs.

COLEMAN, CY [né SEYMOUR KAUFMAN] (b. 1929) A New Yorker who gave concerts as a child prodigy, he later studied at New York's High School of Music and Art and at the New York College of Music. He worked as a night-club pianist before contributing his first Broadway song to *John Murray Anderson's Almanac* (1953). His heavily jazz-influenced scores have been heard in *Wildcat* (1960), out of which came "Hey, Look Me Over"; *Little Me* (1962), which included "I've Got Your Number"; *Sweet Charity*♦ (1966), which offered "Big Spender" and "If My Friends Could See Me Now"; *Seesaw* (1973); *I Love My Wife* (1977); *On the Twentieth Century* (1978); and *Barnum* (1980), as well as new music for a 1982 revival of *Little Me*. He scored again with *City*

of Angels (1989), but his delightful *Welcome to the Club,* earlier the same year, flopped.

Colleen Bawn, The; or, The Brides of Garryowen, a play by Dion Boucicault.♦ Produced by Laura Keene♦ at Laura Keene's Theatre. March 29, 1860. 38 performances.

Mrs. Cregan (Mme. Ponisi♦) and her son Hardress (H. F. Daly) are impoverished aristocrats who will lose their lands unless one of two things happens: Mrs. Cregan must marry the corrupt attorney, Corrigan (J. G. Burnett), who holds the mortgage, or Hardress must wed rich Anne Chute (Miss Keene). Anne really loves Kyrle Daly (Charles Fisher♦), Hardress's classmate. Moreover, Hardress cannot marry Anne since he is secretly wed to Eily O'Connor (Agnes Robertson♦), a poor maiden known as the Colleen Bawn. Anne discovers a letter from Eily to Hardress, which she mistakenly believes was meant for Kyrle, and disclaims any further affection. At the same time Danny Mann (Charles Wheatleigh), Hardress's hunchback servant, is prepared to kill Eily if Hardress will give him a glove as a signal. When Mrs. Cregan innocently gives Danny the glove, he takes Eily to a grotto, where he throws her off a rock. A shot rings out, and Danny falls mortally wounded. The shot was fired by Myles na Coppaleen (Boucicault), a roguish bootlegger who has long loved Eily. Danny's dying words implicate Hardress. Corrigan comes to arrest Hardress, but Myles appears with Eily, whom he has rescued. Matters are then straightened out, with Anne agreeing to wed Kyrle. "It's a shamrock itself ye have got, sir." Myles tells Hardress, "and like that flower she'll come up every year fresh and green forenent ye. When ye cease to love her may dyin' become ye, and when ye *do* die, lave yer money to the poor, your widdy to me, and we'll both forgive ye."

Adapted from Gerald Griffin's novel, *The Collegians,* the play was the first of many by Boucicault on Irish themes to win universal acclaim. When Boucicault took it to London six months after its American premiere it ran there for 278 consecutive nights. It remained one of the most popular of 19th-century melodramas. Its title means the fair-haired girl.

College Widow, The, a comedy in four acts by George Ade.♦ Produced by Henry Savage♦ at the Garden Theatre. September 20, 1904. 278 performances.

Jane Witherspoon (Dorothy Tennant) is the daughter of the president of Atwater College. She is admired for her quick, resourceful mind. Her virtues are called into action when the best football player in the region, Billy Bolton (Frederick Truesdell), threatens to play for Atwater's archrival, Bingham. Jane sees to it he plays for Atwater and wins his affection in the process.

Walter Prichard Eaton◆ called the play "a genre picture of triumphant skill, executed with exuberant yet loving humor," adding, however, "But Mr. Ade has no power of dramatic development. He cannot penetrate the surface." The play was made into the highly successful musical comedy, *Leave It to Jane,* with music by Jerome Kern,◆ book by Guy Bolton◆ and P. G. Wodehouse,◆ and lyrics by Wodehouse. Presented at the Longacre Theatre on August 28, 1917, it ran for 167 performances. Musical numbers included a title song and "The Siren's Song." The cast included Edith Hallor and Robert Pitkin in the leads, with Oscar Shaw◆ in a major supporting role. A 1958 revival of the musical ran for two years off Broadway. Its original cast featured Kathleen Murray and Art Matthews in the leads.

COLLIER, WILLIAM (1866–1944) A New Yorker with "an inscrutable face and dry voice," he made his stage debut in a juvenile company of *H.M.S. Pinafore◆* in 1879 after running away from home when his actor parents balked at his following in their footsteps. He was a substitute not only for Dick Deadeye but for Buttercup as well. His parents forced him to return to school but in 1883 allowed him to join Augustin Daly's◆ ensemble, where for the next five years he played a number of minor roles. He first called attention to himself as John Smith, an actor, in *The City Director* (1890) and as Willis Hoss, a judge, in *Hoss and Hoss* (1891), then had another major success as Benjamin Fitzhugh, who will go to any length not to tell his wife he must serve a jail sentence, in *The Man from Mexico* (1897). He scored another hit as the secretly married student, Robert Ridgway, in *On the Quiet◆* (1901), before spending a season with Weber◆ and Fields.◆ His most famous role was Brook Travers, who innocently complicates our Latin American relations, in *The Dictator◆* (1904). More fine notices followed his portrayal of Dick Crawford, the man who promises to marry a girl sight unseen, in *Caught in the Rain◆* (1906), of which he was co-author. He participated in Weber and Fields's 1912 reunion, then played the hypochondriac, Dionysius Woodbury, in *Never Say Die* (1912), another play he co-authored. After co-starring with George M. Cohan◆ in *Hello, Broadway!* (1914), he played Robert Bennett, sworn to veracity, in *Nothing But*

the Truth◆ (1916) and Washington Cross, sworn to mendacity, in *Nothing But Lies* (1918). In 1920 he played Sam Harrington, who is mistaken for a famous jockey, in *The Hottentot,* again serving as co-author. After playing in the *Music Box Revue◆* and several other musicals he retired from the stage in 1927.

COLLINGE, PATRICIA (1894–1974) The Dublin-born actress appeared briefly in London before coming to American in 1908. Highlights of a career that spanned half a century included Bettina Dean, the stage-struck heroine, in *The Show Shop◆* (1914); the title part in *Pollyanna* (1915), a role she played for three years; leading assignments in revivals of *Hedda Gabler* (1926), *The Importance of Being Ernest* (1926), *She Stoops To Conquer* (1928), and *Becky Sharp◆* (1929); the weakling Birdie in *The Little Foxes◆* (1939); and Lavinia Pennimen, the heroine's mischievous, secretive aunt, in *The Heiress◆* (1947).

COLLINS, JOHN (1811–74) The rather sad-faced Irish comedian and tenor was perceived as successor to the late Tyrone Power◆ when he made his American debut in 1846. His first appearances were in plays and parts long identified with Power, as McShane in *The Nervous Man* and as Teddy Maloney in *Teddy the Tiler.* Among his other appearances were those in such standard works as *The Irish Ambassador, The Irish Attorney,* and *Born to Good Luck.* In 1850 he played in *The Irish Fortune Hunter,* which John Brougham◆ wrote for him. He remained in this country until the mid-1850s, then returned occasionally, most notably to create the role of Carrickfergus, the hero's buddy, in the first American production of Brougham's *The Duke's Motto* (1863). His later returns were less successful.

Colonel Sellers, a play in five acts by George Densmore and Mark Twain [Samuel Clemens]. Produced [as *The Gilded Age*] at the Park Theatre. September 16, 1874. 119 performances.

Col. George Selby (Milnes Levick), although a married man, seduces Laura Hawkins (Gertrude Kellogg). When she learns that he is married she kills him. Hovering not very far in the background is the character of Colonel Sellers (John T. Raymond◆), a perennially impoverished dreamer, who is forever concocting schemes to make millions. He sees potential fortune in oddball steamboats, corn speculation, and, if corn speculation fails, cornering the hog market and feeding the hogs corn. He obtains heat from an oven lit with a single candle and feeds his guests turnips and water, assuring them the water is good.

The play has a complicated history. It was originally written by Densmore and presented as *The Gilded Age* in San Francisco in April 1874. Clemens brought suit, forced Densmore to waive his royalties, then rewrote the play. When it was presented as *The Gilded Age* in New York, its melodramatic main plot was generally dismissed and only Raymond's Sellers praised. His performance was so memorable that the play was rewritten still further by Clemens and Charles Dudley Warner. Colonel Sellers was brought to the fore and the melodramatic frame minimized. The play thereafter was presented as *Colonel Sellers*. Raymond performed Sellers well over a thousand times. Mark Twain and William Dean Howells◆ later wrote a sequel, *Colonel Sellers as a Scientist,* which Raymond refused to play, considering the lead had been turned into a caricature and the play was itself untheatrical. His judgment was confirmed when the play was finally produced as *The American Claimant; or, Mulberry Sellers Ten Years Later* (1887) and failed.

COLT, ALVIN (b. 1915) The noted designer was born in Louisville, Ky., and attended Yale School of Drama,◆ where he studied with Donald Oenslager.◆ He has created costumes, and sometimes sets, for such shows as *On the Town*◆ (1944), *Guys and Dolls*◆ (1950), *The Golden Apple*◆ (1954), *Fanny*◆ (1954), *The Lark* (1955), *Pipe Dream* (1955), for which he won a Tony Award,◆ *Wildcat* (1960), and *Sugar* (1972).

COLTON, JOHN B. (1886–1946) Son of an English diplomat who was serving in Yokohama, Japan, at the time of his birth, he came to America where he found work as drama critic of the Minneapolis *Tribune.* His first play to reach New York was *Drifting* (1922), written with D. H. Andrews. It dealt with a woman who is ready to become a prostitute, a variation of a theme that would appear in most of his plays. His first hit was *Rain*◆ (1922), based on a Somerset Maugham◆ story and written with Clemence Randolph. Its story recounted the attempts of a not totally pure minister to reform a prostitute. *The Shanghai Gesture*◆ (1926) told of the revenge of a wronged brothel owner. His last plays were failures: *Saint Wench* (1933), recounting an unfaithful financée's religious salvation, and *Nine Pine Street* (1933), written with Carleton Miles, retelling the Lizzie Borden story.

COLVILLE, SAMUEL (1825–86) After coming from his native Ireland, he began his American career as manager of a playhouse in Sacramento, Calif. From there he moved for several years to Australia, returning to manage a playhouse in Cincinnati. Shortly after settling in New York he presented Boucicault's◆ *Flying Scud* (1867), bringing over George Belmore to re-create the role Belmore had first played in London. The next year, with George Wood, he opened Wood's Museum, and scored an immense success with his importation of Lydia Thompson◆ and her British blondes in their musical burlesques. Their popularity prompted him to make the musical theatre his main interest and he became one of the pioneering producers in the field. His Colville's Folly Company traveled the country presenting farce-comedies, those primitive precursors of musical comedy. Similarly the Henderson and Colville Opera Company and, more importantly, the Colville Opera Company crossed the country offering early operettas. He also ran the Colville Burlesque Opera Company which presented travesties of popular operettas and plays. He is credited with giving important starts to Julia Mathews and Alice Oates,◆ two prominent musical performers of the time.

COMDEN, BETTY (b. 1915), and ADOLPH GREEN (b. 1915) The New Yorkers began their professional careers performing in night clubs with Judy Holliday.◆ As co-librettists and/or co-lyricists their partnership was ultimately to become the longest-lived in Broadway history, beginning with *On the Town*◆ (1944). Their subject was almost always their native New York, whose idioms and attitudes they mirrored accurately and affectionately. Other musicals which bore their stamp were *Billion Dollar Baby* (1945), *Two on the Aisle* (1951), *Wonderful Town*◆ (1953), *Peter Pan*◆ (1954), *Bells Are Ringing* (1956), *Say, Darling* (1958), *Do Re Mi* (1960), *Subways Are for Sleeping* (1961), *Fade Out—Fade In* (1964), *Hallelujah, Baby!* (1967), *Applause* (1970), *On the Twentieth Century* (1978), *A Doll's Life* (1982), and *Singin' in the Rain* (1985). Both have also been excellent performers, appearing together in *On the Town* and in a special revue, *A Party with Betty Comden and Adolph Green* (1958).

Come Back, Little Sheba, a drama in two acts by William Inge.◆ Produced by the Theatre Guild◆ at the Booth Theatre. February 15, 1950. 190 performances.

Doc (Sidney Blackmer◆) is an alcoholic—temporarily on the wagon—who has never finished medical school. His wife, Lola (Shirley Booth◆), is a slatternly housewife, forever dreaming of their cute puppy, Little Sheba, who long ago ran away. Doc is concerned about their boarder, Marie (Joan Lorring), a young college girl. He resents her beaux, not quite aware that he is jealous of them. When he realizes the girl will soon marry, he goes on a binge. Home from the hospital, he and Lola settle back into their humdrum existence.

Inge's first play opened to sharply divided notices. The main strength of the evening came from the performances of the two principals, who won virtually every possible award for their acting. The play itself hinted at the layers of repressed sexuality that would become the major preoccupation of Inge's later works.

Come Blow Your Horn, a comedy in three acts by Neil Simon. ◆ Produced at the Brooks Atkinson Theatre. February 22, 1961. 677 performances.

Buddy Baker (Warren Berlinger) appears suddenly at the apartment of his brother Alan (Hal March), having run away from their parents' home on his twenty-first birthday. Like his older brother, Buddy wants the fun and freedom his domineering Jewish parents deny him. Both young men still work for their father (Lou Jacobi), who shows up hot on his son's trail. He is, in his own sarcastic way, understanding: "You work very hard two days a week and you need a five-day weekend. That's normal." The rest of the play is essentially a comic family feud, with the father firing his sons, but ultimately taking them back and accepting Alan's choice of a bride and Buddy's desire to live away from home.

While complaining that the comedy was repetitive, Louis Kronenberger◆ nevertheless felt, "It did squat head and shoulders above its all too recumbent rivals. It managed to keep going, it had some fresh and funny lines, it had some diverting scenes and characters." Simon's first produced play, it began a series of successes that marked him as the most knowing light comedy writer of his generation.

Come Out of the Kitchen, a comedy by A. E. Thomas. ◆ Produced by Henry Miller◆ at the Cohan Theatre. October 23, 1916. 224 performances.

The Daingerfields are an aristocratic Virginia family who have fallen on hard times and so must rent their plantation to a rich Yankee, Burton Crane (Bruce McRae◆). Crane's ideas of elegance include a staff of white servants. When he insists that as part of the arrangement the Daingerfields must become that staff, they are horrified. The younger brother,

Charles (Robert Ames◆), is particularly indignant. But his practical sister, Olivia (Ruth Chatterton◆), recognizes they have no choice and wins over the family. They adopt new names and oblige their demanding renter. Since Olivia is as beautiful and charming as she is practical she eventually wins over Crane, too, thereby keeping the plantation in the family.

The play was based on a story by Alice Duer Miller. The producer lavished special attention on the production, which many critics and playgoers came to consider his best mounting. His biographer devotes several paragraphs to details of the production, such as the imported French chintz used to cover the walls of the plantation's drawing room. In 1924 Miss Chatterton starred in a failed musical version, *The Magnolia Lady.*

Comédie Française, LA The world's oldest ongoing acting ensemble, founded in 1680, it waited 275 years before making its initial American visit in 1955. Some critics were dismayed by the relatively safe, conservative repertory it presented, which consisted of Molière's *Le Bourgeois gentilhomme,* Marivaux's *Arlequin poli par l'amour* and his *Le Jeu de l'amour et du hasard,* Beaumarchais's *Le Barbier de Seville,* and Musset's *Un Caprice.* Yet, as Louis Kronenberger◆ noted, the works were "done with not only every last nuance of phrasing and diction, but with a ballet lightness and wit." On later visits in the 1960s and 1970s the troupe ranged more broadly, offering such classics as Corneille's *Le Cid,* Montherlant's *La Reine Morte,* and Feydeau's *La Puce à l'oreille.* These subsequent visits have also offered several more Molière plays, but none by Racine. Among the notable performers who have appeared with the company have been Louis Seigner, Jacques Charon, and Robert Hirsch.

Comic Strips in American Theatre Within a few years after their first appearance in American newspapers and swift rise to popularity, comic strips were providing material for American theatrical authors. Perhaps it is significant that almost without exception they were turned not into farces or dramas, but into musicals. The first transition to enjoy major success was Victor Herbert's◆ musicalization of Winsor McKay's *Little Nemo* (1908). Its success was followed quickly by *The Newlyweds and Their Baby* (1909), based on the cartoons of George McManus. In the 1910s and 1920s *Mutt and Jeff* provided the basis for a series of slapdash musicals which toured the country with tremendous returns but rarely ventured into larger, more sophisticated cities. Titles included *Mutt and Jeff, Mutt and Jeff on the Farm,* and *Mutt and Jeff in Mexico.* During the 1914–15 season no fewer than five companies of this last edition were on tour. Another strip to prompt a series of musicals was McManus's *Bringing Up Father.* Again basically a road attraction, all through the 1920s such variations as *Bringing Up Father in Florida* and *Bringing Up Father in Ireland* traveled from small town to smaller town. For several decades thereafter the vogue faded, only to be revived with the success of *Li'l Abner* (1956), based on Al Capp's strip. *Superman* was turned into the failed *It's a Bird It's a Plane It's SUPERMAN* (1966), but two of the most popular musicals of the era were *You're a Good Man, Charlie Brown*♦ (1967), taken from Charles W. Schulz's *Peanuts,* and *Annie*♦ (1977), derived from Harold Gray's *Little Orphan Annie.* *Doonesbury* (1983), based on Gary Trudeau's celebrated cartoon, could not find an audience. While the best-known characters from the respective strips were generally retained, in virtually all instances fresh stories were created for the librettos. Many of these musicals, as might be expected, had a special appeal to young audiences.

The pervasive popularity of comic strips meant they provided subject matter for other shows. Fictitious cartoonists were the central figures in at least two shows: *King of Hearts* (1954), which dealt with an egomaniacal cartoonist who hires a "ghost" artist, and the delightful but failed *Rumple* (1957), a musical in which cartoon characters came to life to help their creator overcome a mental block. In 1981 the hero of *Woman of the Year* was also a cartoonist, and the musical made imaginative use of animated figures.

Command Decision, a play in three acts by William Wister Haines. Produced by Kermit Bloomgarden♦ at the Fulton Theatre. October 1, 1947. 409 performances.

There are some who view Brig. Gen. K. C. Dennis (Paul Kelly♦) as "A man so drunk with power he thinks he can cover anything he does with other people's blood." Dennis has been sending his bombers far beyond the range of fighter support, and even some of his officers have balked at what they consider his suicide missions. Nor will Dennis bomb installations he has been ordered to attack if he thinks other targets more important. But Dennis is no coward. He himself tests an untried enemy plane to learn its potential. When he is finally transferred to the Pacific, he reveals to his successor that their predecessor was driven to suicide by the job, and that he himself often contemplated it.

Although first published as a novel, the work had originally been written as a play. Many producers rejected it, feeling it followed too closely the war's end to have popular appeal. But the taut, compelling drama, superbly acted, won over both critics and playgoers. Haines (1908–89) was born in Des Moines, Iowa, and spent his career as a novelist and screen writer. This was his only play to reach Broadway.

Common Clay, a play in four acts by Cleves Kinkead. Produced by A. H. Woods♦ at the Republic Theatre. August 26, 1915. 316 performances.

Ellen Neal (Jane Cowl♦) is housemaid to the Fullerton family and is seduced by the Fullerton son, Hugh (Orme Caldara♦). When Hugh quickly abandons her, she sues for support of their child. At the trial she and Judge Samuel Filson (John Mason♦) make a horrifying discovery—she is the judge's illegitimate daughter. She runs away to New York, where she becomes a famous opera singer. There, Hugh Fullerton, having seen the light, comes to reclaim her and their child.

In 1914 John Craig of Boston's Castle Square Theatre offered a $500 prize for the best play submitted by a Harvard student. Kinkead (1882–1955), who had come from Louisville to study with Professor Baker♦ at his 47 Workshop,♦ submitted the script which won first prize. It was his only success. Although immensely popular, it was perceived even in its own time as contrived, if effective theatre.

Company, a musical in two acts. Book by George Furth. Music and lyrics by Stephen Sondheim.♦ Produced by Harold Prince♦ and others at the Alvin Theatre. April 26, 1970. 706 performances.

An essentially plotless musical, it centered on the birthdays of a young bachelor, Robert (Dean Jones). His married friends appear to help celebrate, at the same time revealing the flaws in their marriages and their social worlds. In the end, Robert is not certain that either bachelorhood or marriage is an answer, but he cries out, "Somebody crowd me with love" and assist him to survive "being alive."

Principal songs: Another Hundred People · The Ladies Who Lunch · The Little Things You Do Together · Side by Side by Side · Someone Is Waiting

A brilliantly innovative musical, capped by Sondheim's witty, observant lyrics and Prince's fluid staging, as well as Michael Bennett's♦ excellent dances and Elaine Stritch's♦ show-stopping delivery of "The Ladies Who Lunch," it was characterized by

Clive Barnes♦ of the *Times* as "a very New York show," filled with the sort of "masochistic fun" that especially delighted its generation of New Yorkers.

COMSTOCK, F. RAY (1880–1949) He began his career as an usher in his native Buffalo, then moved to New York where he became assistant treasurer at the Criterion Theatre. His first Broadway production was *Fascinating Flora* (1907). Shortly thereafter he mounted *Bandana Land* (1908), one of the earliest black musicals. He became manager of the Princess Theatre♦ when it was built to house experimental dramas, and when these failed he initiated a policy of intimate musical comedies that soon became known as the Princess Theatre musicals: *Nobody Home♦* (1915); *Very Good Eddie♦* (1915); *Oh, Boy!♦* (1917); *Leave It to Jane♦* (1917), not actually presented at the Princess; and *Oh, Lady! Lady!!♦* (1918). Among his successful straight plays were *Adam and Eva♦* (1919) and *Polly Preferred* (1923). He also imported a number of major foreign attractions, often in association with Morris Gest,♦ including *Chu Chin Chow* (1917), *Aphrodite* (1919), *Mecca* (1920), *Chauve-Souris* (1922), and *The Miracle* (1924), as well as the Moscow Art Theatre♦ and Eleanora Duse.♦

CONKLIN, [MARGARET ELEANOR] PEGGY (b. 1912) A native of Dobbs Ferry, N. Y., she began her career as a chorus girl in 1928 but soon revealed skills as a comedienne and serious actress. Her important assignments included Prudence Kirkland, who loves a Hessian soldier, in *The Pursuit of Happiness♦* (1933); Gabby Maple, who wins the affection of the forlorn hero, in *The Petrified Forest♦* (1935); Ellen Murray, who has liberal ideas about love, in *Yes, My Darling Daughter♦* (1937); Mrs. North, half of a husband and wife detective team, in *Mr. and Mrs. North* (1941); and Flo Owens, whose family is transformed by the arrival of a vagrant, in *Picnic♦* (1953).

Connecticut Yankee, A, a musical comedy in two acts. Book by Herbert Fields.♦ Lyrics by Lorenz Hart.♦ Music by Richard Rodgers.♦ Produced by Lew Fields♦ and others at the Vanderbilt Theatre. November 3, 1927. 418 performances.

At a party on the eve of his wedding, Martin (William Gaxton♦) flirts with Alice Carter (Constance Carpenter), which so infuriates his bride-to-be, Fay Morgan (Nana Bryant), that she knocks him unconscious with a blow from a champagne bottle. He dreams he is in King Arthur's court, where he falls in love with Alisande La Carteloise, who looks just like Alice, but where his wooing and his attempts to modernize the medieval world are thwarted by Merlin (William Norris) and the villainous Morgan Le Fay, the fire-spitting image of Fay Morgan. When he awakes he decides to marry Alice.

Principal songs: I Feel at Home with You · My Heart Stood Still · On a Desert Island with Thee · Thou Swell

A light-hearted musicalization of Mark Twain's story, and praised by Brooks Atkinson♦ in the *Times* as "a novel amusement in the best of taste," it was successfully revived in 1943, at which time Hart contributed his last Broadway lyric to a riotously black-humored song, "To Keep My Love Alive."

Connection, The, a play in two acts by Jack Gelber. Produced by Living Theatre Productions, Inc.,♦ at the Living Theatre. July 15, 1959. 722 performances.

Leach (Warren Finnerty) and his fellow drug addicts sit in his "pad" awaiting the return of Cowboy (Carl Lee) with a fresh supply of narcotics. Cowboy comes in with the innocent Sister Salvation (Barbara Winchester), who has helped him elude the police in the naïve belief that she can redeem the addicts. She cannot.

Presented as a play within a play, with the principal figures stepping slightly out of character to address the playwright, and the playwright addressing the audience, it was hailed by Kenneth Tynan♦ in *The New Yorker* as "The most exciting new play that off-Broadway has produced since the war." It foreshadowed many of the social problems and Broadway treatment of them that would follow in the 1960s. Gelber (b. 1932) was born in Chicago and attended the University of Illinois. Although nearly a dozen of his plays have been produced in New York, this has been his only success.

CONNELLY, MARC[US COOK] (1890–1981) Born in McKeesport, Penn., he began writing plays for amateur productions while working as a newspaperman in nearby Pittsburgh. In 1916 he wrote the libretto and lyrics for *The Amber Princess,* but by the time the musical reached New York others had rewritten the book and only one of his lyrics survived. After updating the libretto of *Erminie♦* for a 1921 revival, he joined forces with George S. Kaufman.♦ Together they wrote *Dulcy♦* (1921), in which a not very bright wife bumbles into saving her husband's career; *To the Ladies♦* (1922), in which a bright wife saves her bumbling husband's career; *Merton of the Movies♦* (1922), a spoof of Hollywood and a naïve grocery clerk who becomes a star; the libretto for a send-up of business, *Helen of Troy, New York* (1923); *The Deep Tangled Wildwood* (1923), mocking small town sophistication; *Beggar on Horseback♦* (1924), an expressionist satire on modern materialism; and the libretto for *Be Yourself* (1924), a musical in which a Hatfield-McCoy feud was reduced to a collegiate rivalry. They also contributed sketches to *The 49ers* (1922). After the two separated, Connelly wrote a fantasy about a man who visits himself back when he was a boy, *The Wisdom Tooth♦* (1926). With Herman J. Mankiewicz he next wrote a comedy about a pretentious carnival barker, *The Wild Man of Borneo* (1927). The play was a quick failure, but was followed by his greatest success, which he wrote alone but which was based on Roark Bradford's *Ol' Man Adam an' His Chillun.* This was *The Green Pastures♦* (1930), a recounting of the Biblical story through black eyes which won the Pulitzer Prize. ♦ His last successful play was *The Farmer Takes a Wife* (1934). Written with Frank B. Elser and based on Walter B. Edmonds's novel, *Rome Haul,* it depicted the romance of an openhearted farm boy and the daughter of riverboat people. He directed many plays, most notably *Having Wonderful Time♦* (1937), and made occasional appearances as an actor, when his bald head and avuncular face and voice prompted his casting in folksy parts.

Autobiography: *Voices Offstage,* New York, 1968.

CONNOLLY, [ROBERT] BOBBY (1895–1944) After dancing in *Hitchy-Koo, 1920* and serving as assistant choreographer for several shows, he devised the dances for *Kitty's Kisses* (1926). Among later successes for which he created the choreography were *Honeymoon Lane* (1926); *The Desert Song♦* (1926); *Good News!♦* (1927), in which he put "The Varsity Drag" on stage; *Funny Face♦* (1927); *The New Moon♦* (1928); *Follow Thru♦* (1929); *Flying High♦* (1930); *Ziegfeld Follies of 1931 ♦*; and *Take a Chance* (1932). His last Broadway assignment was *Ziegfeld Follies of 1934,* for which he also served as director. Although he was replaced as director while the revue tried out, he was generally admired for his taut, fast-paced, if not essentially original, routines.

CONOR, HARRY (1856–1931) The stocky little comedian was popular in musicals for many years, but is largely recalled for a single early success as the hypochondriacal Welland Strong in *A Trip to Chinatown♦* (1891), in which he introduced "The Bowery." He occasionally appeared in non-musicals such as *The Blue Mouse♦* (1908).

Conquerors, The, a play in four acts by Paul Potter. ♦ Produced by Charles Frohman♦ at the Empire Theatre. ♦ January 4, 1898. 128 performances.

German invaders have billeted several loutish officers in a French chateau. The officers brutally smash family heirlooms, invite ladies of dubious repute to a dinner, and generally behave scandalously. Later, when the men are drunk, one of them, Eric von Rodeck (William Faversham♦), attempts to seduce Yvonne de Grandpré (Viola Allen♦), who is not a demimonde but a noblewoman whose family owns the chateau. She handles herself so skillfully that she shames him and causes him to repent his behavior, whereupon she swoons. Von Rodeck leaves, and a second officer appears, also bent on seducing Yvonne. Learning of his intention, von Rodeck returns and kills him. When Yvonne regains consciousness she believes the second man was killed defending her honor. Von Rodeck eventually manages to convince her of the truth and to win her affection.

The most famous scene in the show occurred when Yvonne throws the contents of a glass of wine in von Rodeck's face. When Weber♦ and Fields♦ mounted a travesty of the show, their heroine threw a pie in the officer's face. Weber and Fields's biographer believes this was the first employment of the long popular slapstick device.

CONRAD, ROBERT T[AYLOR] (1810–58) The son of a famous early American publisher, he was himself a publisher and journalist as well as a lawyer, jurist, and mayor of his native Philadelphia. Like several other distinguished contemporary Philadelphians, he was also successful as a gentleman playwright. His tragedy *Conrad of Naples,* sometimes called *Conrad, King of Naples,* was mounted at Philadelphia's Arch Street Theatre♦ in 1832 with James E. Murdoch♦ in the title role. Three years later he wrote a tragedy, *The Noble Yeoman,* centering on the 1450 Kentish rebellion, for A. A. Addams. ♦ Addams was too drunk to play it on opening night, so a substitute went on. When he finally performed it in 1836 it was poorly received. Conrad revised it and offered it to Edwin Forrest,♦ who first played it as *Aylmere* in 1841, but who afterward changed the title to *Jack Cade.* ♦ It was soon one of Forrest's most celebrated roles. Conrad is also believed to be the author of a romantic tragedy, *The Heretic,* which was not produced until several years after his death.

Contests and Prizes for American Plays The earliest American theatrical companies, consisting as they did largely of English actors, were satisfied with a repertory of popular English plays. With time, however, especially after independence, larger audiences, many native-born, and companies increasingly made up of native performers sought to diversify bills and looked to American-made plays, preferably on American themes, both for patriotic and practical reasons. Yet the stigmas attached to the theatre and the poor remuneration often discouraged native playwrights. It remained for two of our great early actors, Edwin Forrest♦ and James H. Hackett,♦ to actively encourage potential American dramatists. In the New York *Critic* of November 28, 1828, Forrest offered a $500 prize for "the best tragedy, in five acts, of which the hero, or principal character, shall be an aboriginal of this country." The winner was John Augustus Stone♦ for his *Metamora; or, The Last of the Wampanoags.* ♦ The play proved to be one of Forrest's sturdiest vehicles and as a result he held eight succeeding contests, four of which were won by Robert Montgomery Bird,♦ whose plays included *The Gladiator*♦ and *The Broker of Bogota.* ♦ Hackett began offering prizes in 1831 and, while he had less luck with some of the winners, did find a popular vehicle in James K. Paulding's♦ *The Lion of the West.* ♦ The relative success of these contests and the publicity they brought the performers prompted many other performers to offer awards. G. H. Hill♦ was among the most active prize-givers, although he appears to have had only modest success with the winners. Josephine Clifton♦ was far more fortunate, finding Nathaniel Parker Willis's♦ *Bianca Visconti*♦ as the best entry in her 1837 contest. Awarding prizes for plays continued with some regularity until the Civil War, although most prize plays proved disappointments when staged. Barnum,♦ for example, offered annual prizes several years running, but winners such as Louisa Reeder's *Mary Norton; or, The Shirt Sewers* (1855) and H. J. Conway's *New York Patriots* (1856) had only short runs. Nevertheless, many producers and performers apparently still believed in the efficacy of advertising "prize play." In the 1890s newspapers adopted the policy, the *Herald* in one instance offering $1000 for the best new drama by an American on an American theme. These contests may well have been designed to stimulate circulation, but they occurred at the time of a great swell of patriotism that many later historians were to brand as jingoism. At the same time A. M. Palmer♦ and other producers were inaugurating policies of trial matinees for new plays. This practice, which persisted through the 1920s, proved a far more satisfactory mechanism for determining a play's potential. Despite this, contests for plays were

held intermittently and some have proved fruitful. When Richard Herndon♦ offered a $500 prize and promise of production in 1922, the winner was Philip Barry.♦ His play, originally called *The Jilts,* but produced as *You and I,* ♦ launched his distinguished career. Avery Hopwood♦ willed money to the University of Michigan for a prize to encourage young playwrights. The award in 1936 went to Arthur Miller.♦ The Theatre Guild♦ also offered prizes for a time.

These prizes should not be confused with such awards as the Pulitzer Prize♦ and the New York Drama Critics Circle Awards,♦ which are offered to plays already produced and not basically to encourage new playwrights or native drama.

Contrast, The, a comedy in five acts by Royall Tyler.♦ Produced by the American Company♦ at the John Street Theatre.♦ April 16, 1787. In repertory.

Mr. Van Rough (Owen Morris♦) would have his daughter, Maria (Mrs. Harper), marry the effete anglophile, Dimple (Lewis Hallam, Jr.♦), although Dimple openly flirts with Letitia (Mrs. Kenna) and Charlotte (Mrs. Morris♦). Charlotte's brother, Colonel Manly (John Henry♦), who had nobly aquitted himself during the Revolution, loves Maria but is reluctant to press what might be an unacceptable suit. When Dimple's gambling losses cost him his fortune, he is prepared to ditch Maria and marry either Letitia or Charlotte, both of whom he believes are much wealthier. Van Rough recognizes that he is well rid of the man and consents to Maria's wedding Manly. A subplot recounts how Dimple's arrogant servant, Jessamy (Mr. Harper), goads Manly's hickish servant, Jonathan (Thomas Wignell♦), into courting the maid, Jenny (Miss Tuke), but Jenny rejects them both.

The first comedy written by an American to be presented by a professional American troupe, it was modeled consciously after *The School for Scandal* and written by Tyler in three weeks. It is remembered largely for introducing Jonathan, the classic stage Yankee. Jonathan proudly denies he is a servant, even though he might polish Manly's boots: "I am a true blue son of liberty, for all that. Father said I should come as Colonel Manly's waiter to see the world, and all that; but no man shall master me: my father has as good a farm as the colonel."

CONWAY, FREDERICK B[ARTLETT] (1819–74) The son of a famous English actor, he came from his native England in 1850, making his New York debut as Charles Surface. The following night he offered a much admired Claude Melnotte in *The Lady of Lyons.* ♦ Two years later he married the sister of Mrs. D. P. Bowers, ♦ the Connecticut-born Sarah Crocker (1834–75), who had made her acting debut in Baltimore in 1849 and who as Mrs. F. B. Conway thereafter acted regularly with her husband. Although they appeared in many popular contemporary works, the couple was best liked in classic roles. Conway's major parts included Iago, Macbeth, Sir Harcourt Courtly, Sir Peter Teazle, and Malvolio. His wife's roles included Emilia, Lady Macbeth, Lady Gay Spanker, Lady Teazle, and Viola. Conway briefly managed the Metropolitan Theatre in New York. Mrs. Conway proved a better and more durable manager, assuming leadership of Brooklyn's Park Theatre in 1864. Under her aegis it was Brooklyn's principal playhouse and remained so until she left it to assume management of the new Brooklyn Theatre, which she ran until her death. T. Allston Brown, ♦ after noting briefly that Conway was "a good 'all 'round' actor" and "the best John Mildmay in 'Still Waters Run Deep' ever seen on the American stage," wrote of Mrs. Conway, "She was gifted with an intellect of strong analytic power, sufficient to fit out half a dozen leading ladies. She had a fine, expressive face, a voice full and melodious, a carriage graceful and womanly." Their daughters, Minnie and Lillian, were also popular performers.

CONWAY, William A[ugustus] (1789–1828) A handsome but thin-skinned actor, he came to America after his Hamlet was faulted by London critics. He made his American debut in the very same part in 1824. His reception was such as to convince him to remain in America, and he followed Hamlet with equally well-received interpretations of Coriolanus, Romeo, Petruchio, and Jaffier in *Venice Preserved.* This last part was played opposite the Pierre of Thomas Abthorpe Cooper, ♦ with whom he then acted Othello. For the next several seasons he continued to win laurels as he traveled the Eastern seaboard, at the same time adding such roles as the title part in *The Stranger* ♦ and Macbeth. But for all the critical praise he never proved more than moderately popular. As a result he increasingly had to resort to joint engagements with other prominent actors, including a series of appearances with Macready♦ in 1826–27. T. Allston Brown♦ observed, "Conway was six feet four inches high, well proportioned, and possessed great muscular power, and a masterly command of his countenance, which seemed to have been formed to express the passions of his soul and to delineate the characters of

Shakespeare." He left the stage to devote himself to religion, but later committed suicide by jumping from a ship in Charleston harbor.

COOK, Barbara [Nell] (b. 1927) A native of Atlanta, the doll-faced blonde with an exceptionally beautiful soprano voice made her Broadway debut as the leading lady in *Flahooley* (1951), then toured as Ado Annie in a revival of *Oklahoma!* ♦ (1953). She scored a major success in *Plain and Fancy* ♦ (1955). Another important assignment followed when she played Cunegonde in *Candide* ♦ (1956), and introduced "Glitter and Be Gay." After a brief appearance as Julie Jordan in a 1957 revival of *Carousel,* ♦ she won a Tony Award♦ for her performance in *The Music Man* ♦ (1957), in which she sang "Till There Was You" and "Goodnight, My Someone." She next starred in a 1961 revival of *The King and I,* ♦ before appearing in *The Gay Life* (1961) and introducing "Magic Moment." Her last notable success was as Amalia Balash in *She Loves Me* ♦ (1963). Later appearances were in *Something More!* (1964); as a replacement in the role of Ellen Gordon in the straight play *Any Wednesday* ♦ (1965); as Magnolia in a 1966 revival of *Show Boat* ♦; as Dolly Talbo in *The Grass Harp* (1971); and as Kleopatra in the Vivian Beaumont Theatre production of *Enemies* (1972). In later years, when increasing weight and age eliminated her from leading musical roles, she enjoyed a successful career in nightclubs. She presented a one-woman show on Broadway in 1987, but by then she required miking and amplification to project.

COOK, Donald (1901–61) The slightly foppish nasal-voiced high comedian was born in Portland, Ore., and played in vaudeville before turning to the legitimate stage. Among his memorable roles were Jim Hutton, the unfaithful young husband, in *Paris Bound* ♦ (1927); Tony Kenyon, the neglectful husband, in *Skylark* (1939); David Naughton, whose wife must grow up, in *Claudia* ♦ (1941); Elyot Chase, opposite Tallulah Bankhead♦ in a 1948 revival of *Private Lives* ♦; David Slater, the heroine's libertine father, in *The Moon Is Blue* ♦ (1951); and Larry Larkin, the egomaniacal cartoonist, in *King of Hearts* (1954). He was co-starring opposite Julie Harris♦ in the tryout of *A Shot in the Dark* at the time of his death.

COOK, George Cram (1873–1924) The founder and guiding light of the Provincetown Players, ♦ he was a versatile theatrical figure who not only ran the company but wrote a number of the plays it mounted, and directed and appeared in many others. Among his plays, some of which were written in collaboration with his wife, Susan Glaspell,♦ were *Suppressed Desires* (1915), a satire on the then scarcely voguish psychoanalysis; *Change Your Style* (1915), a comic discussion of modern versus traditional painting; *The Athenian Women* (1918), a serious treatment of the same anti-war theme Aristophanes had handled humorously in *Lysistrata;* and *The Spring* (1921), dealing with reincarnation. Among the plays he directed was the first staging of Eugene O'Neill's♦ *The Emperor Jones♦* (1920), while his roles included Yank in the original production of *Bound East for Cardiff♦* (1916). Bitter at the recognition given O'Neill and what he perceived as neglect of his own work, he left the company to spend his last years in Greece.

Biography: *Jig Cook and the Provincetown Players,* Robert Károly Sarlós, Amherst, 1982.

COOK, JOE [né JOSEPH LOPEZ] (1890–1959) The wide-mouthed, rubeish-looking comedian was born in Evansville, Ind., and played in traveling medicine shows before making his stage debut in vaudeville in 1907 as part of a juggling act that included his brothers. He soon became popular as a single in which he juggled, brought on ludicrous Rube Goldberg-style inventions, and interspersed this with his zany humor. Typically he played a landlord confronting an imaginary tenant with a demand for rent of a cottage. When, after a series of illogical arguments, he could not make the tenant pay, he walked off with the prop cottage. His most famous bit was "The Four Hawaiians," in which he started out to imitate four different islanders, digressed to tell how he became a rich man, then exited announcing he is too rich to bother with imitating four Hawaiians. His first Broadway musical was *Hitchy-Koo, 1919.* Thereafter he made important appearances in the *Earl Carroll Vanities♦* in 1923, 1924, and 1925; *Rain or Shine* (1928); *Fine and Dandy* (1930); *Hold Your Horses* (1933); *Off to Buffalo!* (1939); and *It Happens on Ice* (1940).

COOK, MADGE CARR, see *Mrs. Wiggs of the Cabbage Patch*

COOK, WILL MARION (1869–1944) Born in Washington, D.C., he studied at Oberlin College and then in Europe with Dvorak and Joachim. Although he hoped to find a place for black musical artists in serious music and, indeed, all through his life organized or worked with black choirs and orchestras, he turned to Tin Pan Alley and the Broadway theatre as a source of income. In 1898 he composed the score for the first black musical to play a white theatre, *The Origin of the Cake Walk; or, Clorindy.* ♦ His song from that score, "Darktown Is Out Tonight," was one of the reigning hits of the era. After interpolating fleetingly successful songs in several musicals, he wrote the scores for *In Dahomey♦* (1903), a musical far more successful in London than in New York; *The Southerners* (1904), the first musical to offer a racially mixed cast; *Abyssinia* (1906); and *Bandana Land* (1908). He generally orchestrated and conducted his own scores. In 1910 he provided Fanny Brice♦ with the lyric for her first *Ziegfeld Follies♦* hit, "Lovie Joe."

COOKE, GEORGE FREDERICK (1756–1812) The first great foreign actor to visit America, he was by the time of his visit a dying, emotionally troubled man. Although one of the great London actors of his era, he long had been known for his eccentricity, undependability, and frequent drunkenness. It required all of Dunlap's♦ diplomatic skills to elude his creditors and finally obtain a proper passport for him. He had a deeply lined face with a huge conspicuous nose and large, dark, soulful eyes, but was often said to lack grace. His debut, which is generally seen as having inaugurated the "star system" in America, came at the Park Theatre♦ on November 11, 1810, as Richard III. This was considered his best role. Dunlap recalled, "The high key in which he pitched his voice, and its sharp and rather grating tones, caused a sensation of disappointment in some." Nevertheless, the *Columbian* noted, "Mr. Cooke's style of acting is vivid, original, and impressive." Among the other roles he offered were Macbeth, Shylock, and Sir Giles Overreach. Unfortunately, his drinking marred many of his performances, and he soon dissipated the ardor with which he was first welcomed. Under Dunlap he toured the major theatrical centers of America until his health gave out. He died in New York City. Edmund Kean♦ later erected a monument to him in St. Paul's churchyard.

Biography: *The Life of George Frederick Cooke,* William Dunlap. London, 1813.

COOPER, THOMAS ABTHORPE (1776–1849) The son of an English surgeon, he had become a prominent young actor on the London stage when Thomas Wignell♦ persuaded him to come to America in 1796. He made his debut that year in Baltimore as Macbeth, then later played the same role in Philadelphia, which was his first American home. In 1797 he made his New York debut as Pierre in *Venice*

Preserved. The next season he offered his Hamlet, a performance the *Commercial Advertiser* praised as "transcendantly excellent." King John, Romeo, and Bland in Dunlap's♦ *André*♦ were other roles he essayed in the same engagement. When he fought with Wignell over assignments and salary he moved to New York, where he continued to enlarge his repertory both of classic works and contemporary pieces. He won special applause in the title part of *The Stranger*♦ and in several plays by the newly popular Kotzebue.♦ After Dunlap went bankrupt he assumed the management of the Park Theatre.♦ Although Ireland♦ noted, "With a handsome face and noble person, a fine mellow voice, unusual dignity of manner and grace of action, and in his declamation most forcible and eloquent, as a trage-dian he was without rival," many critics felt he was not totally professional, given as he was to waving and winking at friends in the audience and often failing properly to learn a part and requiring prompting. With time his popularity began to fade. In 1827 the *Albion* noted, "His style is, as it ever was, harsh, and his gestures stiff and ungraceful; but there is in his expression and movement an earnest-ness and passion, which are not surpassed by any of his contemporaries . . . The time is speedily ap-proaching when this eminent individual must re-tire." A disastrous visit to London was followed by his return to New York, where he appeared at the Bowery Theatre♦ playing Othello to Edwin Forrest's♦ Iago. He later managed the failing Chatham Theatre and continued to act to ever smaller audiences and increasing suggestions that he was too old to continue. In his last New York appearance in 1835, at the age of sixty-one, he played Antony in *Julius Caesar.*♦ He continued to tour, giving his final performance in Albany in 1838, then spent his last years as Inspector of the New York Custom House, a post to which he was appointed by President Polk at the urging of his daughter's father-in-law, President Tyler. Whatever his origins and failings, his acceptance of American citizenship has led to his generally being called the first great American tragedian.

Biography: *A Memoir of the Professional Life of Thomas Abthorpe Cooper,* Joseph N. Ireland, Bos-ton, 1888.

Copperhead, The, a play in four acts by Augustus Thomas.♦ Produced by John D. Williams♦ at the Shubert Theatre. February 18, 1918. 120 perfor-mances.

Milt Shanks (Lionel Barrymore♦) is a reasonably prosperous farmer in southern Illinois at the time of the Civil War. His neighbors are certain that he is a Confederate sympathizer, possibly even a rebel spy. They cannot prove their suspicions, but circumstan-tial evidence is strong enough to turn even his wife and son against him. All through this Shanks remains silent. Not until decades later, when his behavior in the war is turned against his beloved granddaughter, does he reveal that the secret work he did was for the Northern cause. He has a letter to prove it—from a grateful Abraham Lincoln.

Based on a story by Frederick Landis, the play is generally considered Thomas's last important work. Coming as it did during World War I, it was sometimes read as a plea for tolerance of pacifists and even apparent German sympathizers. A large measure of its success was attributable to Barry-more. Many critics and playgoers felt his Shanks was Barrymore's finest performance. In the original production the parts of Shanks's wife and grand-daughter were played by the same actress, a popular device at the time to suggest continuing family characteristics.

COQUELIN, Benoît Constant (1841–1909) Like his compatriot Sarah Bernhardt♦ before him, the great French actor had just broken a long history with the Comédie-Française♦ when he made his American debut in 1888. For his first appearance he offered what was then considered his finest role, Mascarille, in *Les Precieuses Ridicules.* He later became the original Cyrano de Bergerac, an interpre-tation he offered on his third and last American tour in 1900. One critic concluded, "Coquelin is a rare artist, and his portrayal of Cyrano is his rarest, finest and greatest work." On the tour, in which he played opposite Bernhardt, he also essayed Scarpia in *La Tosca,* Flambeau in *L'Aiglon,* Duval in *La Dame aux Camélias,* and the First Gravedigger to Miss Bernhardt's Hamlet. A large man with a resonant voice and an expressive face, he was the author of numerous books on the theatre.

Coquette, a play in three acts by George Abbott♦ and Ann Preston Bridgers. Produced by Jed Harris♦ at Maxine Elliot's Theatre. November 8, 1927. 366 performances.

Norma Besant (Helen Hayes♦), the quintessen-tial giddy, flirtatious flapper, loves Michael Jeffrey (Eliot Cabot♦), a handsome, insolent, and at heart shiftless young man. When Norma's father, Dr. Besant (Charles Waldron♦), refuses to consider Michael's request to marry Norma and angrily orders him out of the house, Michael blurts out that he and Norma have slept together, so Dr. Besant's objections no longer matter. The doctor shoots Michael. Rather than face the physical examination that would almost certainly be demanded at her father's trial, Norma commits suicide.

"A fragile and exquisite tragedy, a truly rare and touching evening in the theatre," was John Anderson's assessment in the *Evening Post*. The original idea for the play came from Miss Bridgers, an actress who had worked with Abbott in several plays. Their earliest drafts, called either *Norma* or *Norma's Affairs,* treated the story as a comedy with a happy ending. Harris demanded the revised treatment and suggested the final title. Ironically, the play was forced to close when Miss Hayes revealed she was pregnant with her "act of God" baby.

CORBETT, JAMES J. (1866–1933) The San Franciscan who won the world heavyweight championship by knocking out John L. Sullivan used his fame to become a stage and vaudeville celebrity for a time. His vehicles included the leads in such works as *Gentleman Jack* (1892) and *Cashel Byron's Profession* (1906), as well as playing the wrestler in *As You Like It*♦ (1899).

CORBIN, JOHN (1870–1959) The Chicagoan was educated at Harvard and Oxford (England), then between 1896 and 1917 served stints as drama critic for *Harper's Weekly,* the New York *Sun,* and the New York *Times.* His views at the time were generally conservative and unexceptional, but he startled many admirers in 1933 when he wrote an article in *Scribner's Magazine* in which he blamed the lowering of standards in the theatre on the influx of Jews.

Cordelia's Aspirations, a play with music in three acts. Book and lyrics by Edward Harrigan.♦ Music by David Braham.♦ Produced by Harrigan and Hart♦ at the Theatre Comique. November 5, 1883. 176 performances.

When Cordelia Mulligan's jealous brother and sisters arrive in America they are quick to plant seeds of ambition and discontent in her fertile mind. Before long Cordelia (Annie Yeamans♦) has forced her husband Dan (Harrigan) to leave their happy old home and to move uptown, where Dan's easy, comfortable life gives way to Cordelia's starchy pretensions. Cordelia's brother Planxty (H. A. Fisher) overreaches himself when he attempts to trick his sister into signing away her property. Driven to distraction, Cordelia attempts suicide by gulping down a bottle of "Roach Poison" kept by her

black maid, Rebecca Allup (Tony Hart). The poison is simply Rebecca's secret cache of booze. The Mulligans are soon heading back to their old neighborhood.

Principal songs: Dad's Dinner Pail · Mulligan Guard's March

The work is generally acknowledged as the best in Harrigan's series of plays dealing with the Mulligan family, Irish immigrants who have settled in the rough and tumble Irish ghettos of New York.

CORMACK, BARTLETT, see *Racket, The*

CORNELL, KATHARINE (1893–1974) The daughter of a onetime theatre manager, she was born in Berlin, where her father had gone to study medicine, and made her stage debut with the Washington Square Players♦ in 1916. She afterwards continued her apprenticeship in her hometown of Buffalo and in Detroit with Jessie Bonstelle's♦ stock company. Following a successful sojourn in London, she called attention to herself as the determined flapper, Eileen Baxter-Jones, in *Nice People*♦ (1921). Further accolades came when she portrayed Sydney Fairfield, the daughter who stands by her mentally disturbed father, in *A Bill of Divorcement* (1921); as the lively Mary Fitton in *Will Shakespeare* (1923); and as the shy, homely Laura Pennington, who learns beauty is in the eye of the beholder, in *The Enchanted Cottage* (1923). Her performance as Candida in 1924 consolidated her reputation, and was followed by two of her most sensational roles, first as the carnal, doomed Iris March in *The Green Hat* (1925) and next as Leslie Crosbie, who kills her lover, in *The Letter* (1927). In 1928 she played Ellen Olenska in a dramatization of *The Age of Innocence,* then appeared as another woman ready to murder her lover, Madeline Carey in *Dishonored Lady* (1930). With her husband, Guthrie McClintic,♦ whom she had married in 1921, she embarked on a career as actress-manager, and scored her greatest triumph in her very first offering when she played Elizabeth Barrett, who is courted and won by the poet Robert Browning, in *The Barretts of Wimpole Street*♦ (1931). "By the crescendo of her playing," Brooks Atkinson♦ observed, "by the wild sensitivity that lurks behind her ardent gestures and her piercing stares across the footlights she charges the drama with a meaning beyond the facts it records. Her acting is quite remarkable for the carefulness of its design as for the fire of her presentation." In 1933 she played the displaced Elsa Brandt in *Alien Corn,*♦ then barnstormed as Juliet to Basil Rathbone's Romeo, as Candida, and as Elizabeth

Barrett in 1934, acting in 77 cities in seven months. After appearing as St. Joan in Shaw's◆ play, she depicted Oparre, the tragic princess, in *Wingless Victory*◆ (1936). Her performance as Linda Esterbrook, who convinces her playwright husband to stick to what he writes best, in *No Time for Comedy*◆ (1939) gave her a major success. She followed this with her Jennifer Dubedat in a 1941 revival of *The Doctor's Dilemma* and her Masha in a 1942 revival of *The Three Sisters,* which were both well received. She then spent much of the war years playing Candida and Elizabeth Barrett for soldiers. After the war she appeared in a modernized version of *Antigone* (1946) and as Shakespeare's Cleopatra (1947). Among her better later parts were Constance Middleton in a revival of *The Constant Wife* (1951); Mary Prescott, a U.N. delegate, in *The Prescott Proposals* (1953); and the Countess in Christopher Fry's◆ verse play, *The Dark Is Light Enough* (1955). Her last appearances were as Mrs. Patrick Campbell◆ in *Dear Liar* (1960). Although she seemed tall and regal on stage, she was not quite five feet seven inches, with dark hair, a dark complexion and broad features that were called Oriental and even negroid. With Lynn Fontanne◆ and Helen Hayes,◆ she was one of the great actresses of her era, and even though she hated performing, she was far more willing than either of her rivals to extend her range and attempt classics from the entire history of the theatre.

Biography: *Leading Lady: The World and Theatre of Katharine Cornell,* Tad Mosel◆ with Gertrude Macy, Boston, 1978.

Corsican Brothers, The A French melodrama in which a brother is prompted to avenge the death of his twin by that twin's ghost, it was first played in America in 1852 and held the stage for over half a century in various adaptations, including those by Boucicault◆ and Charles Fechter.◆ Among the more famous interpreters of Fabian and Louis de Franchi were Edward Eddy,◆ J. A. J. Neafie,◆ Charles Kean,◆ Fechter, F. C. Bangs, and Robert Mantell.◆

CORT, John (1860?–1929) The son of a Newark, N.J., minister, he entered the theatre over his father's objections. He began as half of a vaudeville comedy team, Cort and Murphy. Before long, however, he abandoned performing to build his first theatre. He was so successful at the start that he soon had a major chain of vaudeville houses. When he lost his theatres through overexpansion he started again, this time building legitimate playhouses. As head of the Northwest Theatrical Circuit he dominated the theatre in his area. Later he expanded eastward, and eventually there were Cort Theatres in New York, Boston, and Chicago, as well as in San Francisco and throughout the West. He once claimed that over the years he had owned between 200 and 300 playhouses. For several years he served as president of the National Theatre Owners' Association. He was also active as a producer, especially of musicals. Among his hits were Victor Herbert's◆ *The Princess Pat* (1915), *Flo-Flo* (1917), *Listen Lester* (1918), and *Shuffle Along*◆ (1921).

COSTA, David (d.1873) After beginning his dancing career in the early 1840s in his native Italy, he turned to choreography about 1853 and soon was in demand in Rome, Florence, Naples, and other major cities. He came to America in 1866 and his ballets that year for *The Black Crook*◆ were credited with a large measure of the musical's phenomenal success. For the next several seasons he was indisputably the leading Broadway choreographer, his dances seen in such musicals as *The White Fawn* (1868), *Humpty Dumpty*◆ (1868), *Hiccory Diccory Dock* (1869), and *The Twelve Temptations*◆ (1870). He also served as dance director for the Globe Theatre, an early vaudeville house. His work was totally in the classical romantic tradition, employing huge corps of dancers and using startling scenic effects to heighten its theatricality.

COTTEN, Joseph [Cheshire] (b. 1905) The gravelly voiced actor was born in Petersburg, Va., and had been on Broadway since 1930 before calling attention to himself as a member of the Mercury Theatre. ◆ He later scored a major success as Dexter Haven, who gets his ex-wife to remarry him, in *The Philadelphia Story*◆ (1939), then spent many years in films. Subsequently he played Linus Larrabee, Jr., the misanthropic rich man who marries his chauffeur's daughter, in *Sabrina Fair*◆ (1953); Victor Fabian, the temperamental conductor, in *Once More, with Feeling* (1958); and Julian Armstrong, who must prevent a business take-over, in *Calculated Risk* (1962).

COTTRELLY, Mathilde [née Mathilde Meyer] (1851–1933) Born in Hamburg, where her father was an opera conductor and several other family members were performers, she made her stage debut at the age of eight. At sixteen she was singing important roles in contemporary light operas. She also appeared in straight plays and performed in circuses with her husband. In 1875, several years after her husband's death, she came to America. Within a few seasons she was a popular player in German-language productions at the Irving Place Theatre as well as in similar theatres around the country. Shortly thereafter she joined McCaull's Comic Opera Company, becoming not only its leading comedienne but one of its leading directors and costume designers. Her business acumen was such that McCaull♦ made her his silent partner and generally allowed her to determine the company's budget and handle its finances. In the mid-1890s she abandoned musicals and embarked on a career as a character actress. Her first major role in this field was Mme. Vinard, the heroine's friend, in *Trilby*♦ (1895). Because of her accent she was often assigned Jewish parts and played in many of the comedies of the *Potash and Perlmutter*♦ series, making her final appearance in *Potash and Perlmutter, Detectives* (1926). Her most famous characterization was probably Mrs. Isaac Cohen, who can talk of little but her operation, in *Abie's Irish Rose*♦ (1922).

COULDOCK, C[HARLES] W[ALTER] (1815–98) One of the leading character actors of the 19th century, he was born in London and decided on a stage career after watching Macready♦ perform. His professional debut occurred in 1836. Thirteen years later he came to America, where playgoers first saw him in the title role of *The Stranger*♦ opposite Charlotte Cushman's♦ Mrs. Haller. He next spent four seasons at Philadelphia's Walnut Street Theatre,♦ then embarked on a long tour as Luke Fielding, an old farmer driven insane by his daughter's shameful ways, in Boucicault's♦ early play, *The Willow Copse*. He continued to return to this role as late as 1885. In 1858 he joined Laura Keene's♦ company and later successfully essayed such roles as Iago and Hamlet. However, his most celebrated part was that of Dunstan Kirke, who unjustly banishes his daughter, in *Hazel Kirke*♦ (1880). Clara Morris♦ described the heavy-set, curly-haired actor as looking like "the beau-ideal wealthy farmer" and noted, "The strong point of his acting was in the expression of intense emotion—particularly grief or frenzied rage. He was utterly lacking in dignity, courtliness, or subtlety. He was best as a rustic."

Counsellor-at-Law, a play in three acts by Elmer Rice.♦ Produced by Rice at the Plymouth Theatre. November 6, 1931. 397 performances.
George Simon (Paul Muni♦) is an aggressive Lower East Side Jew, who has clawed his way just about as far as a Jew could go in the legal profession of his day. With a probable eye to inching a few steps

further, he marries a prominent, if cold, socialite. His career is jeopardized when a bigoted society lawyer discovers that years before Simon had falsified evidence in a case. At the same time his wife runs off to Europe with her lover. Simon would jump from a window, but with the help of his sympathetic secretary, Regina (Anna Kostant), he unearths incriminating material about the society lawyer, presses him into silence, and concludes he can lead a happy life with the loyal Regina.
Although some critics felt there was a superfluity of characters, and that many of them verged on caricature, Robert Coleman spoke for the majority when he wrote of the play in the *Daily News,* "It has an inspired fire, a dramatic, compelling surge, a human realism and sufficient comedy relief." The work was successfully revived in 1942.

COUNT JOANNES [né GEORGE JONES] (1810–79) One of the more memorable and pathetic eccentrics of 19th-century American theatre, he is generally believed to have been born in London and brought to Boston while still a child, although he sometimes told interviewers that he was born at sea or was the son of a Boston policeman. He made his debut at Boston's Federal Street Theatre♦ in 1828, then moved to the Bowery,♦ at the time in its heyday, where he won acclaim as Richard III, Hamlet, and other tragic figures. In later years he played opposite such leading figures as Forrest♦ and Edwin Booth,♦ usually to solid acclaim. However, his eccentricities were noticeable almost from the start. Even early on he assumed all applause was for him and so took bows meant for his associates. In 1833 he announced that he had become Count of Sertorii of the Holy Roman Empire of the First Commander of the Imperial Order of Golden Knight and Count Palatine. Thereafter he was never seen in public without his full regalia. His absurdities led to widespread publicity. In turn this led many playgoers to come to the theatre with the intention of scoffing, only to be impressed by his real skills. With time, however, his eccentricities became more flagrant and audiences rowdier, forcing him to call the police to keep order. T. Allston Brown♦ described him as "of medium height, fine figure with an animated countenance, high forehead, expressive dark eyes, resolute chin, and fine, white, even teeth; he wore a heavy moustache, with a fresh and ruddy complexion."

Count of Monte Cristo, The In this dramatization of Dumas's 1845 novel, a wrongly imprisoned Frenchman learns of a vast buried treasure, escapes from prison, finds the treasure, and comes to Paris to be revenged on those who imprisoned him. J. Wallack♦ was the first American to play the hero, Edmund Dantès, in 1848. Edward Eddy♦ was a popular Dantès of the 1860s. Charles Fechter♦ made his own version about 1870, and for many years was considered the best interpreter of the Dantès role. However, in 1883 James O'Neill,♦ who had played in earlier versions, appeared in the Fechter redaction to great acclaim. Two years later he purchased the rights to it, made revisions, and thereafter was generally acknowledged as the greatest of all American Dantès.

Country Girl, The, a play in two acts by Clifford Odets.♦ Produced by Dwight Deere Wiman♦ at the Lyceum Theatre.♦ November 10, 1950. 235 performances.

Over the objections of his author and producer, Bernie Dodd (Steven Hill), a young director, hires Frank Elgin (Paul Kelly♦) to star in a new play. Elgin had long since destroyed a promising career by drinking. He blames his problems on his wife, Georgie (Uta Hagen♦), whom he insists became a suicidal alcoholic after the death of their daughter. When Elgin goads Georgie into seeking a raise and long-term contract for him from Dodd, the director concludes she is also a meddler and orders her to stay away. But Elgin turns up on opening night too drunk to act, and Dodd learns from Georgie that it is Elgin who is the real would-be suicide. Elgin sobers up in time to make a hit at the New York premiere. Although Georgie has grown to admire and even love Dodd, she realizes she must stay with her weakling husband.

Praised by Howard Barnes of the *Herald Tribune* as "a fiercely affectionate anecdote about backstage doings," it has been revived several times, not always with success.

County Chairman, The, a comedy in four acts by George Ade.♦ Produced by Henry W. Savage♦ at Wallack's Theatre. November 24, 1903. 222 performances.

Jim Hackler (Maclyn Arbuckle♦), the county chairman, is determined to defeat the shady Judge Rigby (Charles Fisher) in his bid for the prosecuting attorney's office. To that end he nominates his young partner, Tillford Wheeler (Earle Brown), to run against the judge. This creates a dilemma for Tillford, who loves Rigby's daughter, Lucy (Miriam Nesbitt). Hackler has a story that could destroy Rigby if given to the local paper, but the tearful pleas of Lucy and her mother prompt him to tear it up. Tillford wins anyway.

Of Ade's first straight play, Quinn♦ has written, "As is usual with Ade, the minor characters establish the atmosphere of the town and provide rather obvious comedy. The plot is of no real significance. What carried the play was the character study of Jim Hackler, who represents the politician that dominates his town by his personality . . . and has the saving grace of decency which marks him out from the herd."

Typical of Ade's minor figures was the jingoistic Jefferson Briscoe (Edward Chapman). He has firm and belligerent opinions on the Bering Sea controversy, but when asked where the Bering Sea is, replies, "Don't make no difference where it is. The question is, air we, the greatest and most powerful nation of earth, goin' to set back and be bully-ragged an' hornswoggled by some Jim Crow island that looks, by ginger, like a freckle on the ocean!"

County Fair, The, a play in four acts by Charles Barnard. Produced at Proctor's 23rd Street Theatre. March 5, 1889. 105 performances.

Abigail Prue (Neil Burgess♦) is in danger of losing her New England farm because she has not enough money to make payments on the mortgage. But she has a horse named Cold Molasses, and when she runs him in a race at the county fair he wins the $3000 she needs to buy back the mortgage. This makes everyone happy since Abigail is a nice old lady who has smoothed many a path to the altar for neighboring youngsters.

A clean, homey comedy, featuring the era's leading female impersonator, it returned the following two seasons for even longer runs, and remained in Burgess's repertory for over a decade. Barnard (1838?–1920), best known for his long association with *Scribner's Monthly,* was the author of a number of plays, including his collaboration with Henry C. de Mille,♦ *The Main Line* (1886).

Courage, a comedy in three acts by Tom Barry. Produced at the Ritz Theatre. October 8, 1928. 280 performances.

The widowed Mary Colebrook (Janet Beecher♦) brings her seven children east from Iowa in the hopes that the rich Massachusetts Colebrooks will help support and educate them. However, Caroline Colebrook (Helen Strickland) resents the fact that one of the children, Bill (Junior Durkin), is illegitimate and succeeds in alienating the other youngsters from their mother and brother. When Bill comes into an unexpected inheritance, Mary and he head back west, where Mary will wed Bill's father.

For all the unpleasant situations in the play, its

treatment was essentially sentimental when not comic. It typifies the sort of theatre that could skim the surface of ugliness and still find a large market before the development of sound films, radio soap operas, and television. Although two other of his plays reached Broadway, this was the only success for Barry (1885–1931), a minor dramatist and screen writer who was born in Kansas City, Mo.

COURTENAY, WILLIAM [LEONARD] (1875–1933) Born in Worcester, Mass., he made his stage debut with a traveling company that was playing Portland, Me., in 1891. He continued to tour until 1896, when he joined Richard Mansfield's♦ company, where he remained for three seasons. After further seasons under the aegis of first Daniel,♦ then Charles Frohman,♦ he became leading man to Virginia Harned,♦ whom he later married, and toured with her in *Iris, Camille,*♦ and *The Light That Lies in a Woman's Eyes.* He scored his first major success as Walter Corbin, in whose bachelor apartment are found *Mrs. Leffingwell's Boots*♦ (1905). Another tour followed with Miss Harned before he played opposite Clara Bloodgood♦ in *The Truth,* then scored another success as the Duke of Charmerace in *Arséne Lupin* (1909). In 1912 he enjoyed a run as Stephen Baird, the innocent recipient of counterfeit wealth, in *Ready Money,* and the following year created one of his most memorable roles, Bishop Armstrong, who loves an opera singer, in *Romance.* ♦ He began another long run as Stephen Denby, the distressed heroine's lover, in *Under Cover*♦ (1914), then turned to a wartime spy melodrama, *Under Fire* (1915). *Pals First* (1917), in which a tramp impersonates a millionaire, gave him another meaty role. In 1919 he played Matt Peasley, the first mate in love with his captain's daughter, in *Cappy Ricks.* A series of less successful plays followed until he enjoyed one final run as the vamped husband, Tom Burton, in David Belasco's♦ controversial production of *The Harem* (1924). His last appearance was as Governor Hazleton in the gangster melodrama *The Inside Story* (1932).

Courtenay was essentially a matinee idol, but one of the handsomest and most durable. Oliver Morosco♦ felt "he had all the requisites of a star. His voice was perfectly modulated and his poise admirable. He knew how to reach a climax, how to put over comedy, and his intonations and transitions of speech were perfect. He was about six feet tall, slight and very handsome." Women who came to gape cared little if critics such as Walter Prichard Eaton♦ considered him "sing-song and artificial," capable only of "playing himself."

COWARD, NOËL [PEIRCE] (1899–1973) The English actor, playwright, and composer first appeared before American audiences in his own play, *The Vortex* (1925). He was a small, excessively suave man with a studiously clipped enunciation. He returned to America in his revue, *This Year of Grace* (1928), recalled for "A Room with a View." Subsequently he performed in *Private Lives*♦ (1931), a comedy which contained the song "Someday I'll Find You"; *Design for Living* (1933); *Tonight at 8:30* (1936); and *Nude with Violin* (1957). Among his other plays, in which he did not appear in this country, were *Hay Fever* (1925); *Bitter Sweet* (1929), remembered for "I'll See You Again"; *Blithe Spirit* (1941); *Present Laughter* (1946); and *Sail Away* (1961). At his peak, he represented to many Americans the ultimate in urbane Englishmen.

Biography: *Remembered Laughter: The Life of Noël Coward,* Cole Lesley, New York, 1976.

COWELL, JOE [né JOSEPH HAWKINS WITCHETT] (1792–1863) Born in Torquay, England, he hastily decided on a theatrical career after fleeing the Royal Navy rather than face a court-martial for striking an officer. He made his acting debut in 1812 and had become a favorite at Drury Lane by the time he first appeared in America at the Park Theatre♦ in 1821. A small, round-faced, balding man, with large, circular eyes and a long, quizzical mouth, he excelled at comedy but was also adept at scene-painting and playhouse-managing. He spent several seasons at Philadelphia's Walnut Street Theatre♦ and was later one of the first actors to gain widespread recognition by touring even the smaller theatrical centers. Throughout his career his most called-for role was the one in which he had made his American debut, Crack in *The Turnpike Gate.* Kate Bateman♦ was his granddaughter.

Autobiography: *Thirty Years Passed Among the Players,* New York, 1844.

COWL, JANE (1884–1950) Born in Boston, she studied at Columbia, then began her career under the aegis of David Belasco,♦ appearing first in his 1903 production of *Sweet Kitty Bellairs,*♦ and then in *The Music Master,*♦ *The Rose of the Rancho,*♦ *A Grand Army Man,*♦ *The Easiest Way,*♦ and *Is Matrimony a Failure?* She left Belasco to play leading roles in a failure, *The Upstart* (1910), and a success, *The Gamblers* (1910), before catapulting to stardom as Mary Turner, the wronged, vengeful woman, in *Within the Law*♦ (1912). She scored another success as a wronged woman, Ellen Neal, in *Common Clay*♦ (1915), then turned to sentimental romance as Jeannine, the French girl in love with an English aviator, in *Lilac Time* (1917), which she co-authored. She was also a collaborator on her next play, *Information Please* (1918), a comedy that failed. She won applause as a devoted actress in *The Crowded Hour* (1918), and followed this with a hugely successful tear-jerker, *Smilin' Through* (1919), which she co-authored, she and her collaborator working under a single pen name, and in which she played both a modern young lover and the girl's ill-fated grandmother when she was a girl. She earned additional laurels with her highly praised Juliet in 1923, after which she appeared as Melisande and Shakespeare's Cleopatra. Stark Young♦ observed in the *New Republic,* "Miss Cowl's Juliet is beautiful, first of all, to see. She is a child, a tragic girl, a woman convincing to the eye as few Juliets ever have had the good fortune to be. She has quiet too and naturalness and a right simplicity of method. Her readings are often . . . quite traditional . . . but well studied and made into her very own." Her next success came as Larita, the mismarried heroine of Noel Coward's♦ *Easy Virtue* (1925). In 1927 she portrayed Amytis, the noble beauty who dissuades Hannibal from sacking her beloved city, in *The Road to Rome.*♦ Years later John Mason Brown♦ recalled her in this part as "lilting, lovely, and not a little coy, her hands fluttering around her mouth like doves around a cote." Her next role was a puppet come to life in *The Jealous Moon* (1928). Following a brief run as Francesca in *Paolo and Francesca* (1929), she played the title role of the glamorous actress in *Jenny* (1929). The failure of her Viola in 1930 signaled a series of disappointments before she again scored as Katherine Markham, the dedicated writer, in *Old Acquaintance* (1940). Her last appearance was in a 1947 revival of *The First Mrs. Fraser.* To the end she remained a slim, dark-haired, dark-eyed beauty—her eyes "so black, so limpid, it was a wonder they didn't dissolve and run down her cheeks."

COWLES, EUGENE [CHASE] (1860–1948) The Canadian-born basso was raised in Vermont and studied singing while working as a bank clerk in St. Paul. He then joined the Boston Ideal Opera Company,♦ remaining as their leading basso for several seasons. During his tenure he played Will Scarlet in the original *Robin Hood*♦ (1891), introducing "Brown October Ale." After leaving the group he appeared in *The Fortune Teller*♦ (1898), in which he sang "Gypsy Love Song." He later appeared in numerous Gilbert♦ and Sullivan♦ revivals.

CRABTREE, CHARLOTTE [MIGNON] (1847–1924) The petite, red-headed, dark-eyed beauty, best known simply as Lotta, was one of the most successful and beloved of all American entertainers. Although born in New York, she was taken to California at the age of six. There she was befriended by the celebrated Lola Montez,♦ who taught her to sing and dance. She was soon plying her art in mining camps and small-town variety houses. Her first San Francisco appearance is believed to have been in 1858 in *The Loan of a Lover.* Her rise was relatively rapid and with each year she added new works to her repertory, playlets that allowed her to exhibit the singing and dancing at which she excelled. She made her New York debut in 1864 in two of these playlets, *The Mysterious Chamber* and *Jenny Lind.* The critic for the *Herald* described her as "a very extended and most versatile talent. She plays the banjo with great spirit, and dances a breakdown in such style as to cause the star of the champion in that line to pale. Added to which Miss Lotta possesses a quick and ready repartee, which she launches at her audience with infinite grace." She returned to New York in 1867, appearing in two plays with which she was long identified, *The Pet of the Petticoats* and *Family Jars.* In the same year she first essayed the dual title parts in *Little Nell and The Marchioness,* ♦ John Brougham's dramatization of *The Old Curiosity Shop.* Among her other famous vehicles, in which she toured incessantly, were *Hearts Ease, or, What's Money Without; Musette, or, Little Bright Eyes; The Firefly, or, The Friend of the Flag;* and *Zip, or, Point Lynde Light.* ♦ All of these had basically melodramatic parts into which she interpolated her happy musical numbers. Retaining her youthful looks and vigor, she continued performing in these plays until her retirement in 1891. When she died, she left a $4,000,000 estate.

Biography: *The Triumphs and Trials of Lotta Crabtree,* David Dempsey with Raymond P. Baldwin, New York, 1968.

Cradle Snatchers, a comedy in three acts by Russell Medcraft and Norma Mitchell. Produced by Sam H. Harris♦ (by arrangement with Hassard Short♦) at the Music Box Theatre. September 7, 1925. 485 performances.

Having caught her own husband lunching with an attractive flapper, Kitty Ladd (Margaret Dale) has no trouble convincing her friends Susan Martin (Mary Boland♦) and Ethel Drake (Edna May Oliver) that their husbands' sporting weekends are not what they're made out to be. They invite three attractive college boys to a party of their own.

Champagne flows freely and before long all six are tipsy and not a little disorderly. Of course, the husbands walk in at this very moment. An uproar ensues, but in the end the boys go off to seek younger women and the married couples are pleasantly, if not irrevocably, chastened.

The comedy was hailed by Walter Winchell♦ in the *Graphic* as "unquestionably the funniest play in town." Many critics gave their brightest adjectives to the performance of Humphrey Bogart as one of the college boys. Russell Graham Medcraft (1897?–1962) was an actor, director and playwright. This was his only major play. However, his partner, Miss Mitchell (d. 1967), an actress and playwright, enjoyed a second hit when she collaborated with her husband, Wilbur Daniel Steele, on *Post Road* (1934), a comedy melodrama about a kidnapping.

Cradle Snatchers was made into the successful musical *Let's Face It!*, with book by Herbert♦ and Dorothy Fields,♦ music and lyrics by Cole Porter.♦ The musical opened at the Imperial Theatre on October 29, 1941, and ran for 547 performances. Its cast included Danny Kaye,♦ Eve Arden, Mary Jane Watson, and Nanette Fabray.♦ Porter's songs were not among his best, but did include the humorous "Farming."

Cradle Will Rock, The, a musical drama in ten scenes by Marc Blitzstein.♦ Presented as a Mercury Theatre♦ production at the Windsor Theatre. January 3, 1938. 108 performances.

Steeltown is run by the rich, greedy Mr. Mister (Will Geer). He dominates not merely the town's industry but its press, its church, and its social organization. Larry Foreman (Howard da Silva) organizes the workers into a union and fights for the cause of the little man.

This view of the world through red-colored glasses has a curious history. Dropped as a WPA project in Washington, its June 16, 1937, New York premiere was stopped by an injunction. Led by John Houseman♦ and Orson Welles,♦ the cast and audience trekked twenty blocks to another, vacant theatre where the players, to circumvent the injunction, performed from seats in the theatre. Because the musicians' union refused to cooperate, Blitzstein played the score from an on-stage piano. After a series of special matinees, the musical was allowed to begin a regular run at the tiny Windsor. In the climate of the time its radical position won some support, but a 1947 revival was dismissed as an "angry, theatrical prank" and quickly folded. Later revivals, off-Broadway, have sometimes received better press, yet have failed to find a large audience.

Craig's Wife, a drama in three acts by George Kelly.♦ Produced at the Morosco Theatre. October 12, 1925. 360 performances. PP.

Harriet Craig (Chrystal Herne♦) is a woman obsessed by her home and her possessions. She will not even allow her husband to smoke in the house, lest he stain or mar something. Luckily Walter Craig (Charles Trowbridge) is blind to her faults. His maiden aunt, Miss Austen (Anne Sutherland), is anything but blind and she warns Harriet her obsession will cost her all her friends and her family as well: "other people will not go on being made miserable indefinitely for the sake of your ridiculous idolatry of house furnishings." Matters are brought to a head not by a piece of furniture but by the suicide of a neighbor. Walter would call the police to offer help, since he visited the man's home shortly before the suicide. Harriet, however, will not permit her name to be brought in, even indirectly. In a fury Walter breaks one of Harriet's favorite knicknacks, then sits down to enjoy a cigarette. Both Walter and his aunt leave, taking the housekeeper with them.

Alexander Woollcott♦ wrote in the *World*, "*Craig's Wife* is a thorough, unsmiling, patiently detailed and profoundly interesting dramatic portrait of a woman whom every playgoer will recognize with something of a start and yet whose prototype has never before appeared in any book or play that has passed my way." Its only major revival, in 1947, was unsuccessful.

CRANE, WILLIAM H[ENRY] (1845–1928) A native of Leicester, Mass., he made his debut in 1863 as the Notary in *The Daughter of the Regiment* in Harriet Holman's touring company, with which he remained for eight seasons. He then played low comedian roles with the Alice Oates Light Opera. In 1874 he created the role of Le Blanc, the Notary, in the original production of *Evangeline.*♦ Three years later he was first teamed with Stuart Robson,♦ beginning a celebrated partnership that would survive until 1889. Their initial success was as the quarreling neighbors in *Our Boarding House*♦ (1877), with Crane in the role of Colonel M. T. Elevator, the Corn Exchange operator. In their subsequent engagements Crane appeared as Dromio of Ephesus in *The Comedy of Errors* (1878, revived 1885); as Bachelor Jowler in *Our Bachelors* (1878); as Dullstone Flat in *Sharps and Flats* (1880); as Sir Toby Belch in *Twelfth Night*♦ (1881); as John Pownceby in *My Mother-in-Law* (1884); and as Nicholas Van Alstyne, the rich father, in their biggest success, *The Henrietta*♦ (1887). After the team split Crane continued to act until 1917. Among his most notable later roles were the manipulative, but sympathetic Senator Hannibal Rivers in *The Senator*♦ (1890); W. Farragut Gurney, the seemingly innocent American abroad, in *For Money* (1892); and the likable horse-trader, the title role of *David Harum*♦ (1900). In *Famous Actors of the Day* Lewis C. Strang♦ concluded, "Although Mr. Crane's versatility and his talent for impersonation are limited, his comedy powers . . . are exceptionally authoritative. His humor, especially, is broad, unctuous, and perfectly understandable . . . there is neither bite nor sting to the fun that he invokes. His command of pathos is not so sure, and he is not always successful in scenes that require sustained emotion."

Autobiography: *Footprints and Echoes,* New York, 1927.

CRAVEN, Frank (1875–1945) Born in Boston, he was the son of actors and made his first stage appearance with them as a child in *The Silver King* in 1887. On completing his schooling he returned to learn his trade in stock. Although he made his New York debut in *Artie* in 1908, he did not create a stir until he appeared as Jimmy Gilley, the heroine's brazenly parasitic brother-in-law, in *Bought and Paid For*♦ (1911). He followed this by playing Albert Bennett, the newlywed beset by relatives, in his own play *Too Many Cooks*♦ (1914). Lesser successes came as Charlie Brown in the spy melodrama *Under Fire* (1915), and as Jimmie Shannon, who must marry within 24 hours to inherit a fortune, in *Seven Chances* (1916), before he enjoyed a long run as Robert Street, who is forced into an airplane race although he knows nothing about flying, in the musical *Going Up* (1917). His own fine comedy, *The First Year*♦ (1920), afforded him the chance to play another young husband, Thomas Tucker. His *Spite Corner* (1922) told of young lovers temporarily parted by an old family feud. For several years thereafter he seemingly had little luck, but he then enjoyed a modest run as the golf-addicted writer, Vernon Chase, in his own play *The Nineteenth Hole* (1927). A bigger hit was his *That's Gratitude* (1930), in which he played Robert Grant, a good samaritan who doesn't know when to stop. He next won applause as Kirk, the reporter who helps solve a crime, in *Riddle Me This* (1932), which he directed. In the same season he also directed the comedy hit, *Whistling in the Dark*. Virtually his last major assignment was one of his finest, the Stage Manager in *Our Town*♦ (1938). Brooks Atkinson wrote of his performance, "Frank Craven plays with great sincerity and understanding, keeping the sublime well

inside his homespun style." His final appearance was as the former President in *Mrs. January and Mr. X* (1944).

CRAWFORD, Cheryl (1902–86) Born in Akron, Ohio, she started her theatrical career by staging plays while a student at Smith College. She later worked for the Theatre Guild♦ before helping to found the Group Theatre♦ in 1931, where she directed *The House of Connelly* (1931) and several other plays. Her first successful independent production after leaving the Group Theatre was a 1942 revival of *Porgy and Bess.*♦ Among her later productions were *One Touch of Venus*♦ (1943), *The Tempest*♦ (1944), *Brigadoon*♦ (1947), *The Rose Tattoo*♦ (1951), *Paint Your Wagon* (1951), *Oh, Men! Oh, Women!*♦ (1953), and *Sweet Bird of Youth*♦ (1959). While working as an independent producer she was also a founder of the short-lived American Repertory Theatre,♦ a founder of the Actors Studio,♦ and Joint-General Director of the ANTA♦ play series.

Autobiography: *One Naked Individual,* Indianapolis, 1977.

CREWS, Laura Hope (1880–1942) She began her career as a child actress in her native San Francisco, where she played for many years in stock before coming to New York in 1901 to perform in stock there. She started to attract notice when she appeared as Rosie Leadbetter in *Merely Mary Ann* (1903) and as Evelyn Kenyon, the hero's sweetheart, in *Brown of Harvard* (1906). For the next several seasons she was a prominent member of Henry Miller's♦ company. In 1913 she played Beatrice in *Much Ado About Nothing,*♦ then portrayed Louise Marshall, the daydreaming wife, in Belasco's♦ production of Molnar's♦ *The Phantom Rival* (1914). Walter Prichard Eaton said of her performance, "She has, to a degree possessed by almost no other player of her age on our stage, the technical command of her trade . . . [she] plays Louise, the wife, with a skill, a variety, a force and a charm that delight the soul. Dignified and womanly under the torture of her husband's jealousy, she wins absolute conviction for the character." Although she regularly earned such praise and remained a sought-after performer, she never quite became a star of the first rank. Among her later roles were Mistress Page in a 1916 Boston revival of *The Merry Wives of Windsor;* Mrs. Deane in *Peter Ibbetson* (1917); Olivia Marden, who may have entered a bigamous marriage inadvertently, in *Mr. Pim Passes By* (1921); Dora Faber in a comedy about mate-exchanging,

The Changelings (1923); Judith Bliss in *Hay Fever* (1925); the possessive mother, Mrs. Phelps, in *The Silver Cord*♦ (1926); Amalia in *Right You Are If You Think You Are* (1927); and the flighty Aunt Min in *Her Master's Voice*♦ (1933). Her last Broadway appearance was in *Save Me the Waltz* in 1938, although in 1941 she headed a road company of *Arsenic and Old Lace.* ♦

Crimes of the Heart, a play in three acts by Beth Henley. Produced at the John Golden Theatre. November 4, 1981. 535 performances. PP.

The story depicts a day in the life of three unhappy Mississippi sisters. Babe (Mia Dillon) is out on bail after shooting her husband because she "didn't like his looks." Meg (Mary Beth Hurt) is a failed singer who has spent more time in psychiatric wards than in performing. Lenny (Lizbeth Mackay) is unloved and frustrated. The sisters are not alone in their troubles; their family history is dismal. They are visited by Babe's lawyer, Barnette Lloyd (Peter MacNicol). He cannot offer much real encouragement, but the girls are sure their strong family loyalty will see them through.

Another in the sort of Chekovian-style plays that have long been popular and which Max Beerbohm once classified as "adramatic," it nevertheless was written with great warmth and wit. It was presented off-Broadway the spring preceding its opening, following mountings by several major regional theatres. Frank Rich♦ wrote in the *Times,* "Be grateful that we have a new writer from hurricane country who gives her characters room to spin and spin and spin."

Miss Henley (b. 1952) was born in Jackson, Miss., and attended Southern Methodist University and the University of Illinois. Her other plays, including *The Miss Firecracker Contest* (1984) and *Abundance* (1990), have been less successful.

Criminal Code, The, a melodrama in a prologue and three acts by Martin Flavin.♦ Produced by William Harris, Jr.,♦ at the National Theatre. October 2, 1929. 174 performances.

Robert Graham (Russell Hardie), an amiable brokerage clerk, is sent to prison by the state's attorney, Martin Brady (Arthur Byron♦), for a murder which Graham insists was self-defense. " 'An eye for an eye,' That's the basis and foundation of our criminal code," Brady tells the young man, although the attorney is not without sympathy for the man's plight. Six years pass. Graham has remained a model prisoner, although his spirit is broken. Brady's daughter, Mary (Anita

Kerry), works at the prison. She has taken a liking to Graham and prevailed on her father to seek his parole. But when another prisoner is killed, Graham, accepting the fact that there is a code among criminals, too, refuses to testify. Mary, her father, and the prison officials beg and cajole, but Graham will not budge. Moved, they proceed with the parole, which is granted. But one cruel prison officer, Gleason (Leo Curley), beats Graham, who kills him in reprisal. There is nothing now that anyone can do for Graham. "It's just the way things break sometimes," a stunned Brady tells his daughter.

Quite possibly the best of all American prison dramas, it was hailed by Burns Mantle♦ as "a thoughtful study, not only of our methods of prison conduct and corrective punishments, but also of the normal reactions, of both prisoners and keepers, to the law, to the system, and to their respective codes."

CRISTOFER, MICHAEL, see *Shadow Box, The*

CROMWELL, JOHN (1887–1979) A native of Toledo, Ohio, he enjoyed a career as actor, director, and producer that spanned nearly three-quarters of a century. After making his debut in 1907 with the R. C. Herz stock company in Cleveland, he toured for three years before coming to New York in 1910 to appear in *Baby Mine.* ♦ He next spent several seasons as director and actor with William A. Brady,♦ then embarked on his own. Among the many plays he directed were *The Man Who Came Back*♦ (1916), *At 9:45* (1919), *The Law Breaker* (1922), *The Silver Cord*♦ (1926), and *Yankee Point* (1942). His productions included *Oh, Mama!* (1925) and *Lucky Sam McCarver*♦ (1925). He appeared as Sam McCarver; as Babe Callahan in the Chicago company of *Ned McCobb's Daughter*♦ (1926); as Captain McQuigg in *The Racket*♦ (1927); as John Gray in *Point of No Return*♦ (1951), for which he received a Tony Award♦; Linus Larrabee in *Sabrina Fair*♦ (1953); and Oscar Nelson in *Mary, Mary*♦ (1961). In his later years he directed at the Cleveland Play House♦ and acted at both the Tyrone Guthrie Theatre♦ in Minneapolis and the Long Wharf♦ in New Haven. He was also active as a director of films.

CRONYN, HUME (b. 1911) A small man with a long face and prominent mouth and teeth, he was born in London, Ontario. After performing in Canada and in stock in Washington, D.C., he took additional training at the American Academy of Dramatic

Arts♦ and elsewhere, then joined the Barter Theatre♦ as performer and director. Early Broadway appearances were in *Hipper's Holiday* (1934), *Boy Meets Girl*♦ (1936), *Room Service*♦ (1937), *High Tor*♦ (1937), and *The Three Sisters* (1939). In 1950 he directed *Hilda Crane,* which starred his wife, Jessica Tandy,♦ and thereafter appeared with her as Michael, the husband, in the two-character study, *The Fourposter* (1951), and as Dr. Brightlee, the devil, in *Madam, Will You Walk* (1953). He created the role of Jimmy Luton, the fussy art teacher, in *Big Fish, Little Fish*♦ (1961) before spending a season with his wife at the Tyrone Guthrie Theatre♦ in Minneapolis. There he played leading roles in *The Miser, The Three Sisters,* and *Death of a Salesman.*♦ He received a Tony Award♦ for his Polonius in 1964. Following another season at the Guthrie, in which he played the title role in *Richard III*♦ and other leads in classic plays, he and his wife returned to play the loveless couple in *A Delicate Balance*♦ (1966). He appeared with her again in a double bill of Noel Coward♦ one-act plays, *Noel Coward in Two Keys* (1974). In 1977 he scored as Weller Martin, a cantankerous patient at a home for the aged, playing opposite his wife, in *The Gin Game.*♦ He played opposite her again as Hector, a crotchety backwoodsman, in *Foxfire* (1982), which he also helped to dramatize, and as Gen. Sir Edmund Milne, who is aghast at his wife's liberalism, in *The Petition* (1986).

CROSMAN, HENRIETTA [FOSTER] (1861–1944) A native of Wheeling, W. Va., she made her first appearance on the stage in 1883 as Lily in *The White Slave.*♦ She was an attractive, if slightly pouty-faced actress, who rose rapidly in ever more important roles as she moved from one major management to another. By the turn of the century she had performed for Augustin Daly,♦ both Daniel♦ and Charles Frohman,♦ and A. M. Palmer.♦ However, it was not until she approached middle age that she achieved stardom in the role of Nell Gwynne in *Mistress Nell*♦ (1900). Her performance was generally acknowledged as one of the sensations of the season. In 1902 she enjoyed praise and a long run as Rosalind in *As You Like It.*♦ The next year she was acclaimed as the wily Irish heroine of *Sweet Kitty Bellairs.*♦ Thereafter she toured successfully in such plays as *All-of-a-Sudden Peggy, The Christian Pilgrim, Anti-Matrimony,* and *The Real Thing,* although their New York stands were short. For many years she alternated between vaudeville and the legitimate theatre. In her last active years she played prominent roles in several all-star revivals, including

Mrs. Candour in *The School for Scandal;* The Countess de Linière in *The Two Orphans*♦; Mrs. Telfer in *Trelawny of the Wells;* Mistress Ford in *The Merry Wives of Windsor;* and Lady Bountiful in *The Beaux Stratagem.* Her final New York appearance was in *Thunder in the Air* (1929), although she continued to act until shortly before her death. In *Sixty Years of Theatre,* J. Rankin Towse♦ suggested, "Henrietta Crosman is an actress who is entitled to more general critical and popular appreciation than she has obtained. She is an exceedingly bright and capable performer, of considerable range and much technical expertness. Spontaneous vivacity is one of the potent charms in her various embodiments. Her Nell Gwynn . . . will long be remembered for its variety, its animation, its delightful deviltry, and its general fascination."

CROTHERS, RACHEL (1878–1958) Born in Bloomington, Ill., she had dabbled at play-writing before she entered the State Normal School of Illinois. She studied acting at the Stanhope-Wheatcroft School, then played professionally for several seasons. Although she directed all her own works, she abandoned acting when her first play, *Nora* (1903), was produced. It failed, as did her second play, *The Point of View* (1904), but she realized a major success with her next play, *The Three of Us*♦ (1906), a story of a spunky sister who protects her brothers' interests in a Nevada mine. Several subsequent plays had short runs before she enjoyed a modest success with *A Man's World* (1910), a story of a woman who learns that a man she admires is the father of her adopted child. *Young Wisdom* (1914) examined the virtues and flaws of trial marriages. In *Old Lady 31* (1916), adapted from a novel by Louise Forsslund, an elderly sea captain masquerades as a woman in order to join his wife in a home for ladies. *A Little Journey*♦ (1918) described how a train wreck educates a selfish society belle, while *39 East* (1919) recounted the comic misadventures of a group of boarders. *He and She*♦ (1920) focused on a self-sacrificing wife. She had another major success with *Nice People*♦ (1921), which followed the destinies of three determined flappers. The rebellion of another flapper was the subject of *Mary the Third*♦ (1923). In 1924 she took the side of a mother determined to expose her son's parasitic bohemian friends in *Expressing Willie.*♦ She continued her line of hits with *A Lady's Virtue* (1925), in which a bored wife forces her husband into infidelity, but came a cropper with *Venus* (1927), a fantastic comedy in which a scientific discovery makes men more feminine and women more masculine. One of her best comedies was *Let Us Be Gay*♦ (1929), the story of a lady's attempt to rescue a young girl from the advances of her ex-husband. *As Husbands Go*♦ (1931) offered two women considering divorce or remarriage. *When Ladies Meet*♦ (1932) presented a classic triangle of husband, wife, and mistress. Her last play was *Susan and God*♦ (1937), describing the problems that ensue when a rich matron discovers religion. During World War I she founded the Stage Women's War Relief.♦ She was a consummate craftsman, who, as Howard Taubman noted, "used the stage to articulate the case for woman's freedom. When the battle was won, she did not shrink from poking fun at the liberated woman's pretensions. Her work had sanity and humor, often sophistication and maturity. Although she did not dig deeply . . . she was always timely and bright."

CROUSE, RUSSEL (1893–1966) A native of Findlay, Ohio, he was seventeen when he embarked on a career as journalist, first in Cincinnati and then in New York. In the late 1920s he tried a brief fling as an actor, then served as press agent for the Theatre Guild.♦ He collaborated on the librettos of two musicals, *The Gang's All Here* (1931) and *Hold Your Horses* (1933), prior to first teaming with his most famous partner, Howard Lindsay.♦ Their initial effort came when they were called in to rewrite the libretto of *Anything Goes*♦ (1934), after its story of a shipwreck was made unusable by the sinking of the *Morro Castle*. Subsequently he wrote with Lindsay *Red, Hot and Blue!* (1936); *Hooray for What!* (1937); *Life with Father*♦ (1939), which went on to establish a contemporary long-run record; *Strip for Action* (1942); *State of the Union*♦ (1945), which won a Pulitzer Prize♦; *Life with Mother* (1948); *Call Me Madam*♦ (1950); *Remains To Be Seen* (1951); *The Prescott Proposals* (1953); *The Great Sebastians* (1956); *Happy Hunting* (1956); *Tall Story* (1959); *The Sound of Music*♦ (1959); and *Mr. President* (1962). With Lindsay he also presented *Arsenic and Old Lace*♦ (1941), *The Hasty Heart* (1945), and *Detective Story*♦ (1949), as well as several of their own plays. He served as president of the Authors' League of America, and on the boards of several theatrical organizations.

CROWLEY, MART, see *Boys in the Band, The*

Crucible, The, a play in a prologue and two acts by Arthur Miller.♦ Produced by Kermit Bloomgarden♦ at the Martin Beck Theatre. January 22, 1953. 197 performances.

Abigail Williams (Madeleine Sherwood), the pro-miscuous niece of the Reverend Samuel Parris (Fred Stewart), is employed by John Proctor (Arthur Kennedy♦) until Proctor's wife, Elizabeth (Beatrice Straight), fires her. In revenge she accuses Elizabeth of being a witch. In the highly charged climate of 1692 Salem, her charges are given ample credence. Proctor comes to his wife's defense, but in the process admits to adultery with Abigail. Hoping to save his own life, he signs a confession, but soon recants and is sentenced to death by Deputy-Governor Danforth (Walter Hampden♦).

Appearing at the height of the McCarthy era, the play was perceived as a thinly veiled indictment of McCarthy and his followers. *Time* felt the work demonstrated "more fieriness of purpose than vision . . . The material seems not there for the sake of the play, but the play for the sake of the material." Revivals after the McCarthy era had passed, most notably in London in 1965, suggest that the drama, for all its preachiness, may have more universal and permanent validity than any other of Miller's works.

CULLUM, JOHN (b. 1930) The Knoxville native studied at the University of Tennessee. Among his early assignments were understudying Richard Burton♦ in *Camelot*♦ and impersonating Laertes in Burton's 1964 presentation of *Hamlet.*♦ He replaced the principal players in serveral musicals before finding acclaim as the leading man of *Shenandoah*♦ (1975). He won a Tony Award♦ as the flamboyant producer in the musical *On the Twentieth Century*♦ (1978), then spent the 1979–80 season as replacement to the lead in *Deathtrap.*♦ Subsequently he was Victor in the 1983 Burton-Taylor revival of *Private Lives,*♦ Gus, the tennis buff, in *Doubles* (1985), and a 50-year-old Tom Sawyer in *The Boys in Autumn* (1986). In 1990 he headed a revival of *Shenandoah.*

CUMBERLAND, JOHN (b. 1880) The Canadian-born actor began his career in 1900 playing opposite Sol Smith Russell.♦ He was a short, balding man with a round face and puzzled mien whose brief heyday came when he played the central male roles in a number of slam-bang sex farces: *Twin Beds*♦ (1914), *Fair and Warmer*♦ (1915), *Parlor, Bedroom and Bath*♦ (1917), *Up in Mabel's Room*♦ (1919), and *Ladies' Night*♦ (1920). His career faltered when the vogue for this sort of farce waned.

CURRAN, HOMER F. (1885–1952) Called at his death the "dean of West Coast theatrical producers," he was born in Springfield, Mo., and attended

Stanford University, where he developed an interest in theatre. He later purchased the Cort Theatre in San Francisco, but sold it after he built the Curran Theatre in 1922. When the Depression discouraged New York producers from taking their plays to California, Curran, in association with Fred Butler and Edward Belasco, brother of David Belasco,♦ regularly bought the rights and mounted the plays for Western tours. He also revived a number of older works in order to keep playhouses lit. As a result he is generally credited with retaining interest in live theatre on the West Coast. In 1939 he founded the San Francisco Light Opera Company, later combining it with Edwin Lester's♦ Los Angeles Light Opera Company. He collaborated on the writing of *Song of Norway*♦ (1944) and *Magdalena* (1948), which his and Lester's joint company produced. He also brought to New York his highly successful 1946 revival of *Lady Windermere's Fan.*

CUSHING, CATHERINE CHISHOLM (d. 1952) The Ohio-born playwright scored a modest success with her first comedy, *The Real Thing* (1911). After writing an acceptable vehicle for May Irwin,♦ *Widow by Proxy* (1913), in which the heroine pretends to be a widow to help a friend win a legacy, she enjoyed a smash hit with *Kitty Mackay*♦ (1913), the story of a Scottish girl who falls in love with her half-brother. The major virtue of her next play, *Jerry* (1914), was the performance of Billie Burke♦ as the girl determined to marry a much older man. Her adaptation of Eleanor Porter's novel, *Pollyanna* (1916), told the story of an incurably cheerful, helpful waif. Her later straight plays were unsuccessful, most of them not even reaching New York. However, she had better luck as a librettist and lyricist. In 1918 *Glorianna,* a musical version of *Widow by Proxy,* proved popular on the road, if not in New York. *Lassie* (1920), a musicalization of *Kitty Mackay,* won critical praise, but failed. *Marjolaine* (1922) was more to the public's liking, and was followed in 1923 by her biggest hit, *Topsy and Eva.* ♦ This musical version of *Uncle Tom's Cabin* was written as a vehicle for the Duncan Sisters♦ and was one of the most profitable musicals of the decade.

CUSHMAN, CHARLOTTE [SAUNDERS] (1816–76) A relatively tall, burly, homely woman, she is generally acknowledged as the first great tragedienne of the American stage. Born in Boston and descended from several old, distinguished New England families, she is said to have suffered hardships as a child after her father's business failed. One consequence is that she is believed to have been self-educated.

She had intended to become an opera singer, but when her singing voice gave out she turned to acting, making her debut in New York in 1835 as Lady Macbeth, a role afterwards considered among her finest, although she continued to sing operatic roles later that season in New Orleans. She caused a stir in 1837 when she essayed Romeo, thus displaying early on a penchant for men's roles that persisted almost until the end of her career. That same year she first performed the role much of her public most admired her for, Meg Merrilies in the popular dramatization of *Guy Mannering.* While some critics carped at her departure from Scott, her public and fellow artists accepted her version unquestioningly. Mary Anderson♦ recalled, "When, in the moonlight of the scene, she dashed from her tent on to the stage, covered with the gray, shadowy garments of the gypsy sibyl, her appearance was ghost-like and startling in the extreme. In her mad rushes on and off stage she was like a cyclone. During her prophecy . . . she stood like one great withered tree, her arms stretched out, her white locks flying, her eyes blazing under their shaggy brows. She was not like a creature of this world, but like some mad majestic wanderer from the spirit-land. When Dick Hatterick's fatal bullet entered her body, and she came staggering down the stage, her terrible shriek, so wild and piercing, so full of agony and yet of the triumph she had given her life to gain, told the whole story of her love and her revenge." In the fall of 1837 she became a member of the Park Theatre♦ company, where her roles included Goneril, Emilia, and Volumnia to Edwin Forrest's♦ Coriolanus. She first played another of her famous roles, Nancy Sykes in *Oliver Twist,* in 1839. "The horror of her death scene was unmatched," Odell♦ recorded years later. In 1841 she was the first American Lady Gay Spanker. After briefly managing Philadelphia's Walnut Street Theatre,♦ she performed with Macready♦ in 1844. He saw in her a fine but imperfect actress, so advised her to improve her art in London, where she spent the next several years. When she returned to America in 1852 she had added one more of her celebrated interpretations, Katherine in Shakespeare's *Henry VIII.* The *Tribune* felt her London experience had improved her noticeably, writing, "She is less hard, less metallic in her passions . . . more tender, more delicate." During the season she added another of her controversial portrayals of men, Claude Melnotte in *The Lady of Lyons.* ♦ She continued to play actively until 1857, when she announced her "farewell" tour. She was to have several of these during her career, bringing her a share of unnecessary ridicule. In fact she did leave to return to England, but began performing again in America in 1860. Her repertory was extensive, including Beatrice, Rosalind, Bianca, and Pauline (in *The Lady of Lyons*) as well as important roles in contemporary plays. Of course, she continued to play men's parts as well, eventually adding Hamlet and Cardinal Wolsey to her list. Her last New York appearance was as Lady Macbeth in 1874. During her final years age and ill-health plagued her, so she often abandoned traditional acting in favor of readings. Her last performance—a reading—was in Easton, Pennsylvania, in 1875.

Although there was little dissent about the greatness of her acting, especially in serious and tragic roles, some controversy exists about her personality. Most published recollections are highly favorable, recalling her consideration and charity, but several associates remember her peculiarly masculine hardness and her occasional slugging of performers who annoyed her.

In 1907 a club was established in Philadelphia as a hostel for traveling actresses and gathering place for theatrical aficionados. Named in her honor, it houses a collection of her personal memorabilia.

Biography: *Bright Particular Star,* Joseph Leach, New Haven, 1970.

Cyrano de Bergerac This tale of a huge-nosed, comic-tragic poseur who is so homely he must woo by proxy remains one of the great French romantic plays of the late 19th century. Rostand's♦ work was first presented by Richard Mansfield♦ in New York in 1898 and by Augustin Daly♦ in Philadelphia with a cast headed by Charles J. Richmond,♦ Ada Rehan,♦ and Mrs. Gilbert.♦ Daly's mounting drew disappointing notices and was withdrawn before reaching New York, but Mansfield enjoyed a major triumph. Within a month of its opening Weber♦ and Fields♦ presented their famous spoof, *Cyranose de Bric-a-Brac,* while in 1899 Victor Herbert's♦ failed musical version was produced with Francis Wilson♦ as star. Walter Hampden♦ revived the play in 1923 and returned to it at intervals. In 1946 José Ferrer♦ led a successful revival. A second musical version, called simply *Cyrano,* failed in 1973. The Royal Shakespeare Company's♦ revival, with Derek Jacobi, earned rave notices in 1984.

D

DA COSTA, MORTON, [né TECOSKY] (1914–89) As a
teen-ager he acted in plays in Philadelphia, but it
was only while attending Temple University that he
seriously determined to become professional. He
served as president of the Templers and later taught
at Temple's School of the Theatre. He worked with
Clare Tree Major's♦ Children's Theatre, and in
1937 co-founded the Civic Repertory Theatre in
Dayton, Ohio. From 1938 to 1945 he was also an
actor and director at the Port Players Summer
Theatre in Port Washington, Wis. He made his New
York debut as an actor, playing the Broadcast
Official in *The Skin of Our Teeth*♦ (1942). Among
his other roles were Osric in Maurice Evans's♦
Hamlet♦ (1945) and Henry Straker in *Man and
Superman*♦ (1949). His first New York directorial
assignments were at the New York City Center,♦
where he staged *The Alchemist* (1948), *She Stoops
To Conquer* (1949), *Captain Brassbound's Conversion* (1950), *Dream Girl*♦ (1951), and *The Wild
Duck* (1951). Regular Broadway credits included
Plain and Fancy♦ (1955); *No Time for Sergeants*♦
(1955); *Auntie Mame*♦ (1956); *The Music Man*♦
(1957); *Saratoga* (1959), for which he also wrote the
book; *The Wall* (1960); *Maggie Flynn* (1968), for
which, again, he was co-librettist; a revival of *The
Women*♦ (1973); and *A Musical Jubilee* (1975).
Although he was one of the finest directors of his
era, no singular characteristic of style differentiates
him from his leading competitors.

Daddies, a comedy in four acts by John L. Hobble.
Produced by David Belasco♦ at the Belasco Theatre. September 5, 1918. 340 performances.

Several confirmed bachelors, who insist "marriage
was made for women" and who dread the thought of
raising children, nevertheless are talked into adopting war orphans. Their experiences vary, with one of
them finding himself saddled with triplets, and
several, on coming to care for the tots, agreeing to
wed the mothers when they are found. But one
bachelor, the writer Robert Aubrey (Bruce
McRae♦), is disconcerted to discover that his
orphan is not a tot but a seventeen-year-old beauty,
Ruth Atkins (Jeanne Eagels♦). She not only persuades him to turn his writing skills toward helping
the orphans' cause but wins his love in the process.

During the war Belasco produced a number of
successful comedies such as this, a departure from
his more serious earlier productions. But his sense
of production values remained steadfast. George
Abbott,♦ who, in only his second Broadway acting
experience, was cast as the bachelor with the
triplets, recalled that in the first act soda siphons
sometimes drowned out actors' laugh lines. When
the actors complained to Belasco he replied. "I'd
rather lose three laughs than lose the atmosphere
created by that sound."

Daddy Long-Legs, a comedy in four acts by Jean
Webster. Produced by Henry Miller♦ at the Gaiety
Theatre. September 28, 1914. 264 perfomances.

The selfish superintendent of the John Grier
Home for Orphans has refused to allow Judy Abbott
(Ruth Chatterton♦) to be adopted, telling prospects
the girl is incorrigibly selfish, because she really
wants to keep her on as a drudge and to help raise
the younger children. One day in front of all the
trustees, Judy rebels, arguing, "I might have had a
home too—like other children—and you stole it
away from me . . . I can make my own way in the
world. Just give me a chance." One fortyish trustee,
Jervis Pendleton (Charles Waldron♦), is so impressed that he quietly insists the girl be sent to
college at his expense. At first Judy does not know
who her benefactor is. She has seen him only briefly,
when the lights of his limousine cast his elongated
shadow on the ground, so she calls him Daddy Long-
Legs. In time they meet, with Judy still unaware of
his role in her life, and fall in love. The romance
grows, and only after Judy at first rejects his
proposal of marriage does Jervis reveal his full
identity.

The warmly written comedy was one of the major
hits of its day and made Ruth Chatterton a star.
Miller, sensing that the play would be important in
her career, decided not to play the role of Pendleton
lest he steal the limelight. Miss Webster [Mrs. Glen
Ford McKinney] (1876–1916) was born in Fredonia,
New York, and was known primarily as a novelist.
She adapted this, her only successful play, from one
of her own books.

DAILEY, PETER F. (1868–1908) The hefty but nimble *farceur,* famous for his humorous ad-libs, made his debut as a child dancer at the Globe Theatre in his native New York in 1876. Following a brief stint with a circus he became one of "The American Four," a popular vaudeville act for many years. In 1884 he joined the Howard Athenaeum♦ company in Boston and remained there for three seasons. He earned New York's praise in 1891, virtually stealing J. J. McNally's♦ *A Straight Tip* from its star, James T. Powers,♦ with his performance as Jack Postand Poole, a race track habitué. So pleased was McNally that he wrote two starring vehicles for Dailey: *A Country Sport* (1893), in which Dailey played Harry Hardy, whose uncle leaves him a fortune provided he prove "a thoroughbred sport"; and *The Night Clerk* (1895), in which he played the overextended, not-altogether-honest clerk, Owen More. He joined Weber♦ and Fields♦ in 1897, and was a favorite in their celebrated burlesques. Dailey left that troupe to star in *Hodge, Podge, and Co.* (1900), playing the victim of a series of mistaken identities, Rudolf Roastemsum. After two short-lived failures, *A Little Bit of Everything* (1904) and *In Newport* (1904), he scored a major success as Benton Scoops, whose excursion-boat party is highjacked to South America, in *The Press Agent* (1905). His last appearances were for his old associates, first in Fields's revue *About Town* (1906), then in Weber's *The Merry Widow Burlesque* (1908).

Weber and Fields's biographer, Felix Isman, eulogized Dailey as "Inimitable Peter! Born comedian, the quickest-witted man that ever used grease paint; splendid voice; an acrobat and agile dancer despite his two hundred and fifty pounds; no performance ever the same; needing neither lines nor business, but only to be given the stage."

Daisy Mayme, a comedy in three acts by George Kelly.♦ Produced at the Playhouse. October 25, 1926. 112 performances.

Cliff Mettinger (Carlton Brickert) is a 43-year-old real estate broker and a bachelor who has long been the principal support of his married sisters. When one of his sisters dies, he takes her daughter May (Madge Evans) to Atlantic City to recover from her bereavement. Mettinger's surviving sisters, Olly Kipax (Josephine Hull♦) and Laura Fenner (Alma Kruger), come to his house to put things in order for his return. They come somewhat grudgingly, for there is little genuine love in the family. To their dismay, Mettinger returns not only with May, but with Daisy Mayme Plunkett (Jessie Busley), an outgoing, slightly uncouth spinster. A horrified

Laura is certain she knows Daisy Mayme's type—the sort of woman who "has no more home . . . than a tomcat" and who will "hang around fashionable hotels, with their ear to the ground." The sisters set aside their animosities in an attempt to cool their brother's ardor for his newfound friend. Although she shrewdly fights back, they succeed in convincing Daisy Mayme that Cliff wants her solely as a companion for May. But Cliff proves he is fond of Daisy Mayme for herself. She agrees to marry him, purring, "I'll sit here in the lady's chair. I've always wanted to *be* a lady."

"When Daisy finally carries the fray," Brooks Atkinson♦ noted, "the audience is accordingly unable to rejoice over the triumph of virtue. For Mr. Kelly has carefully indicted every character in the play." So unrelentingly observant a comedy commanded at best a modest audience, and only the healthy theatrical economics of the 1920s allowed the play to become a commercial success. It remains, however, a valid, if biting, portrait of aspects of American society.

DALE, ALAN [né ALFRED J. COHEN] (1861–1928) Born in Birmingham, England, he first became a New York drama critic on the *Evening World* in 1887. Later he moved to the *Journal* and then to the *American,* where his often vitriolic notices helped sell papers and so won the backing of William Randolph Hearst. They did, however, alienate producers and theatre owners who often tried to ban him from theatres. Whereas the *Dramatic Mirror*♦ once noted, "When he takes pen in hand the playhouses throughout the land tremble upon their foundations and the faces of actors burn white with fear," *Who's Who in the Theatre*♦ observed, "His criticisms probably carried more weight than any others in New York." His precise position on the theatre was unclear. He could praise one great artist by noting, "Our emotional actresses weep from their temples and foreheads. Afraid to ruin their make-up. Nazimova shed tears from her eyes, mopped them with a handkerchief, and at the end of her grief, she actually had a red nose." He was Jerome Kern's♦ earliest and for many years only advocate. But he could also dismiss a lesser Shaw♦ play, *John Bull's Other Island,* as "A thick glutinous and imponderable four-act tract," even though his own plays proved pompous absurdities. He also wrote several books on theatre.

DALE, JIM [né JAMES SMITH] (b. 1935) The lithe, lanky actor, who at one time studied ballet, was born in England, where he made his debut in 1951. Stints at the National Theatre♦ and the Young Vic followed before he first appeared in America in the Young Vic mountings of *The Taming of the Shrew*♦ and *Scapino* in 1974. His acting in the latter won him wide recognition. In 1979 he played in *Privates on Parade* at the Long Wharf,♦ returning to the comedy a decade later off-Broadway. He is best recalled for the title role in the musical *Barnum* (1980). Subsequently he appeared as Bri in a 1985 revival of *Joe Egg* and replaced the original star in 1987 in *Me and My Girl.* ♦

Dallas Theater Center "DTC," as it is popularly called, was founded in 1959 under the leadership of Robert D. Stecker, Sr., and Beatrice Handel to offer the best in professional theatre for Dallas. Plays are presented in the only public playhouses designed by Frank Lloyd Wright, the 516-seat Kalita Humphreys Theatre and the 56-seat Down Center Stage. The company also uses the Arts District Theatre, which allows for easy rearranging of seating and stage plans. Repertory consists of both classics and new works and has included the premieres of Preston Jones's *A Texas Trilogy*. The company continues a regular children's program. For a time the DTC offered graduate school studies in conjunction with Trinity University in San Antonio, but that has been discontinued. Adrian Hall♦ served as director from 1983 to 1989.

DALRYMPLE, Jean (b. 1910) Although she became best known for her work with the New York City Center♦, Miss Dalrymple, who was born in Morristown, N.J., began her professional career writing vaudeville sketches. For a time she worked with John Golden,♦ then established her own office as publicist and manager in 1937. In the late 1940s she produced several shows on Broadway, most notably a revival of *Burlesque*♦ (1946) and *Red Gloves* (1948). She had been associated with the City Center since its inception, but not until she was named to its board of directors did she start to mount productions there. Her first, all in 1953, were a series of plays with José Ferrer,♦ *Cyrano de Bergerac,* ♦ *The Shrike,* ♦ *Richard III,* ♦ and *Charley's Aunt.* ♦ Later dramatic productions at the house, all in 1956, ranged from *King Lear*♦ to *Mister Roberts.* ♦ From 1957 to 1968 she was general director of the City Center Light Opera Company,♦ mounting 47 revivals of thirty different musicals, the most frequently staged of which were *Brigadoon*♦ and *South Pacific.* ♦ She has also written several books on theatre and the autobiographical *September*

Child (New York, 1963) and *From the Last Row* (Clifton, N.J., 1975).

DALY, [Peter Christopher] Arnold (1875–1927) The Brooklyn-born actor began his theatrical career as an office boy for Charles Frohman. ♦ His first acting assignment was a small role opposite Fanny Rice in *The Jolly Squire* (1892). After touring for several seasons he made his New York debut as Chambers in *Pudd'nhead Wilson* (1895). Among his important early roles were the rejected Jack Negly in *Barbara Frietchie*♦ (1899); the drunken, brutal husband in *Hearts Aflame* (1902); and the hero's Irish servant in *Major André* (1903). Daly's Irish parents, and, more especially, his uncles and aunts remaining in Ireland, were close friends of George Bernard Shaw♦ and Shaw's family, so Daly had followed closely Shaw's new career as dramatist. While he was playing in *Major André,* Daly and Winchell Smith♦ pooled their resources of $350 to mount a special matinee of *Candida,* ♦ with Daly as Marchbanks. The *Herald* complained that "there is too much of a muchness in *Candida*—of talk, for instance" and that "Daly walked up and down the stage like a caged lion." Nevertheless, an audience was found, the play moved to a theatre for a regular run, and Daly became Shaw's strongest advocate in America. In 1904 he organized, with Liebler and Company,♦ an ensemble devoted to presenting Shaw, in several instances giving the first New York or American mountings of the plays. The repertory included *You Never Can Tell, Candida, The Man of Destiny, How He Lied to Her Husband, John Bull's Other Island,* and *Mrs. Warren's Profession*. The performance of the last play led to his arrest for presenting an immoral work, but he was acquitted in court. Constant harassment from authorities continued, however, and this, coupled with the continuing disdain from moralistic critics, led him to abandon his hope for "a theatre of ideas." His last years were spent largely in standard commercial vehicles, most notably creating the role of The Vagabond in George M. Cohan's♦ *The Tavern*♦ (1920).

A somewhat stocky man with a large round head, Daly was considered a good, if occasionally erratic and temperamental, actor. He possessed "an Irish voice of lilting cadence and great variety of tone."

Biography: *Arnold Daly,* Berthold H. Goldsmith, New York, 1927.

DALY, [John] Augustin (1838–99) Although he became the most respected producer and director of his day as well as a playwright of no mean repute,

Daly's origins were scarcely theatrical. His father, who died while Daly was still a child, was a sea captain and his mother a soldier's daughter. His first exposure to the theatre was in Norfolk, Va., where his mother had moved from Daly's earlier North Carolina home, following her husband's death. After seeing James E. Murdoch♦ play in *Rookwood,* he began to organize amateur theatricals. The family's move to New York placed him closer to the theatrical mainstream. He took work at the *Sunday Courier,* soon becoming its drama critic. In 1862 he turned to play-writing, dramatizing S. H. von Mosenthal's *Deborah* as *Leah, The Forsaken.*♦ First produced at the Boston Museum♦ and brought to New York in January 1863, the play was an immediate hit. Several subsequent efforts were less successful, but in 1867 he wrote a largely original work, *Under the Gaslight,*♦ which enjoyed widespread acclaim. Its sensational effects of an approaching railroad train and a man tied to the tracks in its path were widely copied. Two years later he leased the Fifth Avenue Theatre.♦ His intention was to assemble the finest company and offer seasons mixing the best new works with revivals of the classics—although one of Daly's few faults was his insistence on rewriting even the most famous plays. "The old playwrights must have turned in their graves at his ruthlessness," Otis Skinner♦ observed. In a remarkable departure from accepted practice he broke with the tradition of having each performer play only those roles in his or her "line"— for example, leading man or first old woman. He expected his artists to be able to switch from comic roles to serious ones and from heroes to villains. He annoyed some players by assigning them minor roles after they had played major ones. However, his plans succeeded famously, and within a short time his company was the only serious rival to Wallack's.♦ His tiny playhouse became known as the "parlor home of comedy." One of his few disappointments was the reaction to most of the new American plays he offered. "American press writers," he noted, "are proud of everything American except other American writers." When the Fifth Avenue burned in 1873, he quickly restored another old theatre, continuing until he temporarily retired in 1877. Among the plays he offered during this first period were *London Assurance,*♦ *Twelfth Night,*♦ *As You Like It,*♦ *Frou-Frou,*♦ *Fernande, Saratoga,*♦ *Divorce,*♦ *Article 47, The Fast Family, The School for Scandal, The Big Bonanza,*♦ *Our Boys,* and *Pique.*♦ His company included Mrs. Gilbert,♦ James Lewis,♦ William Davidge,♦ Charles Fisher,♦ and several young ladies whose careers he

promoted—Agnes Ethel,♦ Fanny Morant,♦ Fanny Davenport,♦ and Clara Morris.♦ During this time Daly attempted to operate other New York theatres, including the Grand Opera House, where he presented opéra bouffe and some musical spectacles. These proved burdensome and unpopular, and were soon dropped.

In 1879 Daly restored yet another old playhouse, renaming it after himself, and initiated what Odell♦ called "one of the most distinguished theatres in the history of the American stage." Many of his former actors returned to his fold, including Lewis, Davidge, Fisher, and the rising John Drew.♦ Mrs. Gilbert also returned. Although none of his leading young actresses was re-engaged, Daly enlisted the woman who would become probably his finest and most beloved performer, Ada Rehan.♦ One curious decision, soon abandoned, was to include operettas and musical comedies in the repertory. Late in his career, however, Daly imported several London musicals, but did not use his regular company for them. The list of major hits this company did offer included *Needles and Pins,*♦ *Boys and Girls, 7-20-8,*♦ *The Country Girl, Red Letter Nights, She Would and She Would Not, A Night Off, The Magistrate, The Taming of the Shrew,*♦ *Dandy Dick, The Railroad of Love,*♦ *A Midsummer Night's Dream,*♦ *The Lottery of Love,*♦ *The Last Word,*♦ and Tennyson's *The Foresters.* Daly had sent out road companies of his earlier hit plays, but this second company he took as an ensemble not only across country, but on one visit to Germany, three visits to France, and numerous visits to England.

As playwright, Daly claimed credit for approximately 100 plays, although virtually all his works were adapted from foreign pieces. Most of Daly's sources were German or French, though he was not above rewriting Shakespeare and the 18th-century English playwrights. Indeed, his modern editor, Catherine Sturtevant, suggests that so few of his plays are without known sources that it is not unreasonable to suppose we are merely ignorant of the models for his so-called original plays. One of these, *Under the Gaslight,* appears to have been inspired by Wallack's *Rosedale,*♦ while its famous railroad scene may have been derived from an English play, *The Engineer.* No source has been found for what many consider his finest work, *Horizon*♦ (1871), a story set in the Wild West and recounting the adventures of a girl adopted by a villainous type after her father's murder. *Divorce* (1871) and *Pique* (1875), two additional outstanding successes, are exceedingly free adaptations of novels. Modern research has revealed that many of the plays he took credit for were written largely by his brother Joseph.

William Winter♦ summed up Daly by noting, "He made the Theatre important, and he kept it worthy of the sympathy and support of the most refined taste and the best intellect of his time."

Biography: *The Life of Augustin Daly,* Joseph Francis Daly, New York, 1917.

DALY, CHARLES PATRICK (1816–99) The distinguished New York jurist, a devoted lover of theatre, often gave legal counsel free or at cost to needy actors and producers. He collected a notable theatrical library and was the author of *First Theatre in America: When Was the Drama First Introduced in America?* (1896), a pioneering work.

DALY, DAN (1858–1904) The lanky performer began as a circus and variety acrobat "who seems to be boneless one moment and in the next stands on his head with his feet in the air, and in that position plays the castanets with a grace of manner that would do credit to Carmencita." However, he soon discovered his true métier was pure comedy. Harry B. Smith♦ recalled that his "method and manner were unlike those of any one else; a 'knight of the rueful countenance,' drawling his lines in a guttural bass voice. If he ever laughed or smiled it must have been in seclusion." His first legitimate appearance in *The City Directory* (1891) was followed by increasingly important roles in *A Society Fad* (1892), *The Golden Wedding* (1893), *About Town* (1894), *The Twentieth Century Girl* (1895), *The Merry World* (1895), *The Merry Countess* (1895), *The Lady Slavey* (1896), *The Whirl of the Town* (1897), *The Belle of New York♦* (1897), *The Rounders* (1899), *The Cadet Girl* (1900), *The Girl from Up There* (1901), *The New Yorkers* (1901), and *John Henry* (1903).

Damn Yankees, a musical comedy in two acts. Book by George Abbott♦ and Douglass Wallop. Lyrics and music by Richard Alder♦ and Jerry Ross.♦ Produced by Frederick Brisson,♦ Robert E. Griffith,♦ Harold S. Prince,♦ and others at the 46th Street Theatre. May 5, 1955. 1,019 performances.

For years the New York Yankees have won the pennant, while the forlorn Washington Senators remain in the cellar. A Senators' fan, middle-aged Joe Boyd (Robert Shafer), blurts out that he would sell his soul to have his team in first place. Obligingly, the Devil in the person of Mr. Applegate (Ray Walston) appears and transforms the aging Joe into young Joe Hardy (Stephen Douglass). As "Shoeless Joe from Hannibal, Mo." he sparks the

team into surging ahead, giving it the "Heart" it needs to aim for the top. But something inside the new Joe yearns for the wife he left behind. To overcome the loneliness, Applegate changes a hag into the beautiful Lola (Gwen Verdon♦), who cuddles up to Joe and assures him, "Whatever Lola Wants" Lola gets. This time she is wrong. Joe cannot forget his wife. He reneges on his agreement and returns home to watch the Senators embark on another losing streak.

Other principal songs: Near to You · Two Lost Souls

Although the 1905 baseball musical, *The Umpire,* had enjoyed a long run in Chicago, this was the first successful New York musical dealing with the national pastime. The work was based on Wallop's popular novel *The Year the Yankees Lost the Pennant.*

DANA, LEORA [SHEPHERD] (1923–83) A native New Yorker, she made her Broadway debut as Irma, the starry-eyed waitress, in *The Madwoman of Chaillot* (1948). Her performance earned her the Clarence Derwent Award. She then played the loving Maman in *The Happy Time♦* (1950) and Nancy Gray, the hero's ambitious wife, in *Point of No Return* (1951). Unfortunately she was one of many fine talents for whom a shrinking theatre no longer afforded proper opportunities. Virtually her only other memorable assignment was Alice Russell, wife of the high-principled presidential candidate, in *The Best Man♦* (1960).

Dancin', a choreographic revue in three acts. Produced by the Shubert♦ Organization and others at the Broadhurst Theatre. March 27, 1978. 1,774 performances.

A series of dances conceived and directed by Bob Fosse♦ to music by such diverse composers as Johann Sebastian Bach, George M. Cohan,♦ Neil Diamond, and John Philip Sousa,♦ the show enjoyed an exceptionally long run not only because of the excellence of its numbers but because it became a prime attraction for foreigners, who found it offered no language problems.

Dancing Mothers, a play in four acts by Edgar Selwyn♦ and Edmund Goulding. Produced by Selwyn at the Booth Theatre. August 11, 1924. 311 performances.

Ethel Westcourt (Mary Young) is not sympathetic when a friend is expelled from their club for unseemly behavior, but she is concerned when priggish young Kenneth Cobb (Michael Dawn), a suitor to her daughter Kittens (Helen Hayes♦), informs her that Kittens spends time in the rooms of Gerald Naughton (John Halliday♦), a notorious man-about-town. The ultimate shock for Ethel comes when she learns her husband, Hugh (Henry Stephenson), is actively philandering. Her reaction is to teach her free-thinking friend, daughter, and husband a lesson by outdoing them in socially unacceptable wildness. "Times have changed," she announces, "I have become a woman of today. I have become a dancing mother." She even competes with Kittens for Naughton's attentions. Throwing over her straitlaced ways gives her so much pleasure that she throws over her family, too. She heads for Europe, leaving her husband and daughter to console each other.

Although the play received largely lukewarm notices, it caught the public's fancy, capturing for its audiences an apparently accurate, if over-dramatic, view of the new flapper morality. Many commentators felt that the startling ending was the key to the play's success.

DANIELS, Frank [Albert] (1860–1935) Although born in Dayton, Ohio, the genial, bantam, imp-faced Daniels grew up in Boston, where he attended business school before being apprenticed to a wood engraver. While learning his trade he also studied singing at the New England Conservatory of Music. He made his professional stage debut as the Sheriff in *The Chimes of Normandy* in 1879, then served a second apprenticeship with several light opera companies. Daniels first won major recognition in New York as Old Sport, the drug store clerk whose only ambition is to shake the hand of heavyweight boxing champion John L. Sullivan, in Charles Hoyt's♦ *A Rag Baby* (1884). He then capered in *Little Puck* (1888) as the father transformed into his schoolboy son. Further applause came when he played Shrimps, the loyal if comic lighthouse man, in *Princess Bonnie* (1895) and the title role in Victor Herbert's♦ *The Wizard of the Nile* (1895). His success in the latter musical was so pronounced that Herbert immediately wrote two more vehicles especially for him, *The Idol's Eye* (1897) and *The Ameer* (1899). *Miss Simplicity* (1902), *The Office Boy* (1903), and *Sergeant Bruce* (1905) all depended on his antics for their popularity. In 1907 Herbert created a fourth vehicle for Daniels, *The Tattooed Man,* inspired by a song of the same name which the comedian had sung in *The Idol's Eye.* Daniels later appeared in *The Belle of Brittany* (1909) and a touring company of *The Pink Lady♦* (1911). He retired after performing in Weber♦ and Field's♦ last

double bill, *Roly Poly* and *Without the Law* (1912). A broad comedian, Daniels was famous for his vividly expressive eyebrows, which were often put to best use in his equally celebrated curtain speeches. Describing one of these a critic noted, "He rambled about in a mock effort at forensic eloquence that brought tears to the eyes of a good many people out front."

Danites, The; or, The Heart of the Sierras, a play in five acts by Joaquin Miller. Produced at the Broadway Theatre. August 22, 1877. 30 performances.

When a band of Danites, members of a Mormon secret society, attempt to murder the Williams family, two youngsters escape. One is Nancy Williams (Kitty Blanchard), who, fearing the Mormons will continue to pursue her, disguises herself as a boy and takes the name Billy Piper. She seeks refuge in a mining camp. There a comely young scoolteacher, Huldah Brown (Lillie Eldridge), falls in love with the supposed young man. Huldah is courted by Alexander "Sandy" McGee (McKee Rankin♦), and when Billy refuses to return her affection she agrees to marry Sandy. Learning Billy's true identity, Huldah takes her into her confidence and carelessly invites her into the privacy of her rooms. Sandy misconstrues these actions and becomes ragingly jealous. Several Danites appear at the camp, having searched out Nancy, and try to incite the mob into lynching the presumed boy. Luckily, Sandy discovers that Billy is a girl, dissuades the mob, and turns its ire against the Mormons.

The work was first contrived in London with the help of an unidentified English actor and was based on Miller's stories, *The First Woman in the Forks* and *The Last Man in the Camp.* At the time it was called *The First Families of the Sierras.* The play was revised by a Philadelphia actor, Alexander Fitzgerald, as a vehicle for Rankin and his wife Kitty Blanchard. It has also been known as *The Danites in the Sierras.*

Although it was not the first play about Western life, the success of *The Danites* initiated a vogue for such plays. It remains of interest as well because of its cruel depiction of Mormons. For half a century the Mormon was portrayed either as the blackest of villains or as a somewhat unsavory comic. So long as this view had popular currency, the play remained well received. It was regularly revived, and Rankin himself played in it for many years.

Miller (1841?–1913), whose real first name was Cincinnatus, was well known as a writer of Western stories. *The Danites* was his first play and the only to achieve prolonged success. Miller's other plays included *Forty-nine* (1881), telling of a pioneer who retains his hope when all seems lost; *Tally Ho!,* in which a man is prepared to sacrifice himself when his wife is accused of murder; and *An Oregon Idyll,* centering on the misfortunes of a part-Indian hero. The last two were not given major mountings.

Dark at the Top of the Stairs, The, a play in three acts by William Inge.♦ Produced by Saint Subber and Elia Kazan♦ at the Music Box. December 5, 1957. 468 performances.

The Floods are a lower-middle-class family living in a small Oklahoma town in the 1920s. Rubin Flood (Pat Hingle♦) is a harness salesman, at a time when automobiles are killing the demand for harnesses. His wife, Cora (Teresa Wright), is the daughter of a schoolteacher and has married somewhat below her station. Their children are Reenie (Judith Robinson), a teenager, and Sonny (Charles Saari), a ten-year-old. The Floods' humdrum life is shaken by three events: Cora's sister, Lottie (Eileen Heckart♦), comes for dinner and confesses she is frigid; Reenie's date at a dance, a young Jewish boy, commits suicide after he is humiliated by an anti-Semite; and Rubin announces the harness company is going out of business. The incidents contrive to bring about a certain understanding and compassion, and with them the small hope of a somewhat happier life.

Although Louis Kronenberger♦ felt "Inge's most definite quality—his feeling for human loneliness—became too insistent," most critics and playgoers applauded the semi-autobiographical play, which was a revision of a 1947 work, *Farther Off from Heaven.*

Dark of the Moon, a legend with music in two acts by Howard Richardson and William Berney. Music by Walter Hendl. Produced by the Messrs. Shubert♦ at the 46th Street Theatre. March 14, 1945. 318 performances.

John (Richard Hart) is a witch boy, the son of a buzzard father and a witch mother. He lives with the witches of the Smoky Mountains until he notices beautiful Barbara Allen (Carol Stone) in the valley below, and falls in love with her. So that he can marry Barbara, John cajoles the Conjur Woman (Georgia Simmons) into making him human. Their pact guarantees that he will stay a human if Barbara remains true for a year. When Barbara has his child, however, it proves to be a witch child, so the midwives burn it. Barbara's relatives persuade her to sleep with a local man, thereby destroying the spell.

Barbara dies, and John becomes a witch boy once more.

Freely adapted from the famous old ballad, the play was a surprise success despite numerous critical complaints about the writing and, more especially, the production. Subsequent revivals have shown it to be a superior, durable fantasy.

Howard Dixon Richardson (1917–84) was born in Spartanburg, S.C., and later studied at the University of North Carolina, at Iowa, and elsewhere. He has been an actor and director as well as a playwright. Although none of his other works was commercially successful, they included such critically praised dramas as *Design for a Stained Glass Window* (1950) and *Protective Custody* (1956). All these plays were written with Berney (1921–61), who was born in Birmingham, Ala. and studied at the University of Alabama and at Iowa. Berney was also a published poet.

DARLING, EDWARD V. (1890–1951) Born in Waterbury, Conn., he was still in his teens when he went to work for Edward Albee.♦ He soon rose to be Albee's confidential secretary. Later Albee made him the booker of talent for all Keith theatres, including the Palace Theatre♦ when that house was in its heyday. Unlike either Keith♦ or Albee, he had a reputation for kindness and fairness and was much admired by the great stars as well as the lowest level performers who dealt with him.

Darling of the Gods, The, a play in five acts by David Belasco♦ and John Luther Long.♦ Produced by Belasco at the Belasco Theatre. December 3, 1902. 182 performances.

Prince Saigon of Tosan (Charles Walcot) has invited the outlawed Prince Kara (Robert T. Haines) to a banquet because Kara saved Saigon's daughter, Princess Yo-San (Blanche Bates♦), from death and respected her innocence. Yo-San is betrothed to the effete Tonda-Tanji (Albert Bruning), but she does not love him and hopes to discourage him by insisting that before their wedding he must kill a dangerous outlaw. Her wish falls in with the plans of the sinister war minister, Zakkuri (George Arliss♦), who is determined to kill Kara. He has planted assassins around Saigon's house, but Kara eludes them. When he and Yo-San meet again, Yo-San falls in love with him and hides him from Zakkuri's men. For 40 days she lives secretly with the outlaw. Kara eventually decides he must join his band; he leaves and is captured by Zakkuri's men. Zakkuri refuses to kill Kara at once, hoping Kara will lead him to more outlaws. Kara declines. Yo-San visits Zakkuri to plead for Kara's life. The cynical Zakkuri, knowing Yo-San has lost her reputation after concealing a man in her apartments, attempts to turn her into his courtesan. She rebuffs him, but he does succeed in having her reveal the whereabouts of Kara's band. Zakkuri releases Kara, who joins his men, but they are immediately attacked, and Kara is mortally wounded. Yo-San appears to confess her love. They agree they will meet a thousand years hence in the First White Heaven. After Kara dies, Yo-San commits suicide. A thousand years pass. The lovers do meet, and arm in arm prepare to ascend to the next celestial level.

Following the success of their *Madame Butterfly*, ◆ Belasco suggested to Long that they write a full-length drama with a Japanese setting and gave him an older work, *Il Carabiniere,* to use as an outline. Even in its day the play was judged contrived and its dialogue ("How is your honorable health? Do you happily eat well?") preposterous. Fine acting and sumptuous settings were its main attraction for many, although here, too, not all critics were totally pleased. One wrote that the "stage scenes, however gorgeous, never rise to the altitude of high art, but they give a very real delight to the vast multitudes who considerately forbear to wear out the steps of the Metropolitan Museum with their sole leather." Nevertheless, the same critic noted the ten settings were "a triumph of richly artistic light and movement and color."

D'ARVILLE, CAMILLE (1863–1932) The Dutch-born singing actress made her American debut as Lillian Russell's◆ co-star in *The Queen's Mate* (1888), and for a short while was considered Miss Russell's leading rival in comic opera. Her biggest hit was *Madeleine; or, The Magic Kiss* (1895). She was also popular in vaudeville.

DAVENPORT, [BENJAMIN] BUTLER (1871–1958) A versatile but mildly eccentric figure, the New York-born Davenport began his career playing walk-ons and serving as understudy in Augustin Daly's◆ company. He later played small parts opposite Richard Mansfield, ◆ John Drew, ◆ Duse, ◆ and Bernhardt◆ and worked with David Belasco. ◆ In 1910 the Messrs. Shubert◆ produced his play, *Keeping Up Appearances,* centering on a family dominated by a cruel father. The play failed, and Davenport decided to strike out on his own. He opened several little theatres at which he produced, directed, and starred in his own plays. To encourage patronage he charged no admission, merely passing

the hat after each performance. Bearing titles such as *The Importance of Coming and Going, The Depths of Purity,* and *The Comforts of Ignorance,* they attracted small audiences. Only his 1916 revival of *Keeping Up Appearances* enjoyed an appreciable run, and that one was apparently somewhat forced. His Davenport Free Theatre continued to offer his own plays and those of others in intermittent seasons as late as 1943–44.

DAVENPORT, E[DWARD] L[OOMIS] (1815–77) The son of a Boston innkeeper, Davenport made his debut in Providence, R.I., in 1837, billed simply as Mr. E. Dee and playing opposite Junius Brutus Booth◆ in *A New Way To Pay Old Debts.* He then toured for several seasons before making his first New York appearance as Frederick Fitzallen in *He's Not A-Miss,* in a company led by Mrs. Henry Hunt (the future Mrs. John Drew◆). He continued to tour until he left for England in 1848. Returning in 1854, he demonstrated the range of his repertory by first playing Othello to F. B. Conway's◆ Iago, followed by Hamlet, Claude Melnotte, Sir Giles Overreach, and William (in *Black-Eyed Susan*). The next year he created the part of Lanciotto in Boker's◆ *Francesca da Rimini.* ◆ His performances regularly won critical acclaim, but for some reason he was never able to earn the affection of play-goers. His fellow actors, however, admired his talents, and at one time or another he was welcomed into all the major ensembles of his day—Burton's, ◆ Wallack's, ◆ and Daly's. ◆ Much of the time he toured in a company headed by himself and his wife, the former Fanny [Elizabeth] Vining (1829–91). In 1875 he played Brutus to Lawrence Barrett's◆ Cassius in a celebrated mounting of *Julius Caesar,* ◆ and a year later was Edgar to Barrett's Lear. This marked his final New York appearance. His farewell was as Dan'l Druce in Washington in 1877. Attempting to explain Davenport's lack of popularity with the public, Odell◆ suggested, "Perhaps his versatility, his finish, his lack of sensational clap-trap, militated against him with a people that admired the physical vigour of Forrest and the electrical effects of the elder Booth." Whatever his failings, he fathered a large theatrical family. Four of his children attained some distinction in the theatre, most notably Fanny Davenport.◆ His younger daughter, May (1856–1927), was an important member of the companies at the Chestnut Street Theatre◆ in Philadelphia, Daly's, ◆ and the Boston Museum. ◆ His son Edgar L[ongfellow] (1862–1918) played at both the Chestnut and the Walnut Street◆ in Philadelphia, toured as leading man with Kate Claxton◆ and McKee

Rankin,♦ and was long a major actor at the Boston Museum. A younger son, Harry [George Bryant] (1866–1949), first gained fame as Sir Joseph Porter in the celebrated 1879 children's company of *H.M.S. Pinafore*♦ and later became a popular leading man in both straight plays and musical comedies, creating the leading man's role of Harry Brown in *The Belle of New York*♦ (1897). He was one of the earliest important performers to leave the stage for a career in silent films, though he continued to return to theatre as late as 1935.

Biography: *Edward Loomis Davenport,* Edwin Francis, New York, 1901.

DAVENPORT, FANNY [LILY GYPSY] (1850–98) To many observers the position of this celebrated actress was precisely the opposite of that of her father, E. L. Davenport.♦ She was adored by her public but accorded a grudging respect by fellow professionals. Born in London, during her American parents' English visit, she made her stage debut shortly after their return when she played one of the children in a Boston mounting of *Metamora.*♦ In 1862 she played New York for the first time, performing Charles II to her father's Ruy Gomez in *Faint Heart Never Won Fair Lady.* Augustin Daly♦ found great promise in some of her early work and enlisted her as a member of his first major ensemble. "What Daly saw in her," his brother recalled, "besides her dazzling beauty, splendid presence, and blooming health were confidence and self-possession." Among her most popular roles at Daly's were Lady Gay Spanker, Maria in *Twelfth Night,*♦ Lu Ten Eyck in *Divorce,*♦ Lady Teazle, and Eugenia in *The Big Bonanza.*♦ She also won applause for masking her beauty as the haggish Ruth Tredgett in *Charity,* and, most of all, for her portrayal of Mabel Renfrew, the mother of the kidnapped child, in *Pique.*♦ She toured successfully in the last role, and it apparently played a large part in her decision to assume dramatic roles instead of comic ones. Her success also prompted her to leave Daly and strike out on her own. Four major plays occupied the remainder of her career. In *Fedora* (1883) she played the heroine whose determination to avenge her fiancé's death ultimately destroys her. The role had been created by Bernhardt♦ in Paris, as were all Miss Davenport's subsequent parts, including her next major role, the tragic heroine of *La Tosca* (1888). Yet another Sardou♦ drama, *Cleopatra* (1890), gave her a third successive hit. Her last important new role was the vengeful duchess in Sardou's *Gismonda* (1894). Miss Davenport had produced all four Sardou dramas, thus

markedly increasing her profits. The not entirely flattering assessment of her associates was recorded by Otis Skinner♦ in his autobiography: "Miss Davenport was a handsome woman, her business sense keen and her industry untiring. To these qualities rather than her acting, she owed the late success in which she accumulated a fortune in her productions."

David Harum, a play in three acts by R. and M. W. Hitchcock (and Edward E. Rose,♦ uncredited). Produced by Charles Frohman♦ at the Garrick Theatre. October 1, 1900. 148 performances.

In the small New England town of Homeville, David Harum (William H. Crane♦) is known as a shrewd banker, an even shrewder horse-trader, and kindly philosopher. He gives the all-too-lordly Deacon Perkins (Homer Granville) a costly lesson in horses, pays a long-standing "debt" to patient Widow Cullum (Eloise Frances Clark), and sees to it that his young assistant, John Lenox (George S. Probert), wins the hand of comely Mary Blake (Katherine Florence).

Crane toured in this successful dramatization of Edward Noyes Westcott's best-seller for four seasons, while secondary companies criss-crossed the country for over a decade.

DAVIDGE, WILLIAM [PLEATER] (1814–88) Long popular as a principal comedian, the English-born actor made his professional debut in 1836. His first American appearance was at the Broadway Theatre in 1850, when he played Sir Peter Teazle. He remained at the Broadway for several seasons, then moved to the Bowery♦ and the Winter Garden. He also supported the Conways♦ in Brooklyn. Later he acted with Daly's♦ first ensemble throughout its entire existence, and afterward for Palmer♦ at the Madison Square.♦ "Rare old Bill," as he was popularly known, was awarded a special testimonial on the occasion of his fiftieth year on the stage and continued acting almost until the time of his death. Generally regarded as an actor of the old formal school, his assignments ranged from classic roles such as Bottom and Sir Toby Belch to important comic parts in newer, ephemeral works.

Autobiography: *Footlight Flashes,* New York, 1866.

DAVIS, J. FRANK, see *Ladder, The*

DAVIS, JESSIE BARTLETT (1861–1905) Born on a farm near Morris, Ill., the contralto studied voice in Chicago, where she made her debut in 1879 in

H. M. S. Pinafore.♦ She then spent several years with various opera companies before joining the Boston Ideal Opera Company.♦ An early member, she was one of the few who remained with this troupe for virtually its entire history. Her most famous role was the trouser part of Alan-a-Dale in *Robin Hood*♦ (1891), in which she introduced "Oh, Promise Me."♦ She later was briefly popular in vaudeville, and also appeared in several other Broadway musicals.

DAVIS, OWEN (1874–1956) After graduating from Harvard, the Portland, Maine-born Davis tried his hand unsuccessfully at blank-verse tragedy. To support his family he began churning out cheap melodramas for popular touring companies. Finishing them at the rate of one every second or third week, he wrote over 200, with titles such as *Edna, the Pretty Typewriter; Nellie, the Beautiful Cloak Model; Driven from Home;* and *Convict 999.* In his autobiography Davis called them "practically motion pictures," observing, "one of the first tricks I learned was that my plays must be written for an audience who, owing to huge, uncarpeted, noisy theaters, couldn't always hear the words and who, a large percentage of them having only recently landed in America, couldn't have understood them in any case. I therefore wrote for the eye rather than the ear." When dialogue was necessary he filled it with "noble sentiments so dear to audiences of that class." He was first represented on Broadway as author of the Hippodrome♦ musical spectacle *The Battle of Port Arthur* (1908). His first regular play to reach New York was *Making Good* (1912), a quick failure, but he scored commercial successes with *The Family Cupboard* (1913), in which a jilted mistress seduces her former lover's son; *Sinners*♦ (1915), recounting a fallen girl's attempt to keep her history from her crippled mother; *Forever After*♦ (1918), telling of a poor boy who wins a rich girl only after he becomes a hero in the war; and *Opportunity* (1920), depicting a young man's overreaching ambitions. To many playgoers' surprise, Davis then wrote two highly praised dramas: *The Detour*♦ (1921), in which a mother's high hopes are dashed, and *Icebound*♦ (1923)—which told of a greedy family disinherited by their mother—which won a Pulitzer Prize.♦ Although several of his other plays, such as *The Nervous Wreck*♦ (1923) and *Mr. and Mrs. North* (1941), were commercially profitable, they did not fulfill the promise he briefly displayed. Many of his later works, including the two just mentioned, were dramatizations of other writers' stories.

Autobiography: *I'd Like To Do It Again,* New York, 1931, and *My First Fifty Years in the Theatre,* Boston, 1950.

DAVIS, OSSIE, see *Purlie Victorious*

DAVIS, RICHARD HARDING (1864–1916) Although best known as a war correspondent and short-story writer, Davis, a native of Philadelphia, wrote several successful plays, while his stories provided other men with material for dramatization. In 1895 Robert Hilliard♦ adapted "Her First Appearance" for the stage and played it for several seasons as *The Littlest Girl.* Later Augustus Thomas♦ made a play of *Soldiers of Fortune* (1902). Davis himself met small success with *The Taming of Helen* (1903) or with his adaptation of *Ranson's Folly* (1904), but followed those failures with two popular comedies, *The Dictator*♦ (1904), in which an American playboy suddenly finds himself at the head of a volatile Latin American banana republic, and *The Galloper* (1906), in which the hero poses as a famed war correspondent. Both these comedies were later made into musicals. He was the brother of the noted critic Charles Belmont Davis (1866?–1926).

Biography: *Richard Harding Davis: His Day,* Fairfax Downey, New York, 1933.

DAVIS, SAMMY, JR. (1925–90) The versatile song-and-dance man was born in New York and studied with Bill Robinson.♦ He was a popular night-club and vaudeville performer before starring in two Broadway musicals: *Mr. Wonderful* (1956), in which he introduced "Too Close for Comfort," and *Golden Boy* (1964).

Autobiography: *Yes I Can,* with Jane and Burt Boyar, New York, 1965.

Davy Crockett; or, Be Sure You're Right, Then Go Ahead, a play in five acts by Frank Murdoch.♦ Produced at Wood's Museum. June 2, 1873. 12 performances.

Davy Crockett (Frank Mayo♦) returns to his forest home carrying a buck he has shot and bearing the news that his childhood sweetheart, Little Nell, has come back from a long stay abroad. Little Nell now calls herself by her proper name, Eleanor Vaughn (Rosa Rand), and she brings with her her guardian, Major Hector Royston (T. W. Keene), and her fiancé, Neil Crampton (Harry Stewart). The travelers are headed for the estate of Neil's uncle, Oscar Crampton (J. J. Wallace). Davy is quick to sense something is wrong. He decides to run ahead of the party and offer them the shelter of his hunting hut, since it has started to snow. The decision proves wise, for Neil has been hurt and his blood has attracted wolves. Davy singlehandedly keeps the wolves at bay, while Eleanor reads him Scott's poem of Lochinvar. When the party finally reaches old Crampton's estate, the uncle is revealed as a villain who is blackmailing Royston with forged papers and forcing his nephew to marry. Davy, like young Lochinvar, arrives to rescue his sweetheart. He takes her home and marries her, then destroys the uncle's papers.

Although the play is usually set down among the major works dealing with frontier life, it is actually little more than a drawing room melodrama unfolding in the wilderness. Despite Crockett's first appearance with a deer over his shoulder, his later fending off of wolves, and dialogue such as, "Yes, this is my crib. This is where I come and bank when I'm out on a long stretch arter [*sic*] game," the play could have been set elsewhere with little change. Still, the contrast of the rough and the polished, the openhearted and the venal, was underscored by the setting.

The play was first produced in Rochester, N.Y., in 1872 and was received coolly. However, Mayo had faith in the piece and kept rewriting it. Even its initial New York reception was reserved. But the public took to it, so Mayo was able to play it for the rest of his life. Indeed, he played it as late as two days before his death in 1896. This last point is especially telling, since Mayo was in his late fifties and Crockett supposedly twenty-five. By the same token, Eleanor, always played by mature women, was supposedly sixteen. Loyalty to favorite performers and the relatively dim stage lighting of the period were thus added to a willing suspension of disbelief in permitting the practice to flourish here and elsewhere.

DAWN [Tout], Hazel (1891–1988) One of those performers remembered largely for the playing of a single role, the "dewy-eyed blonde" was born in Ogden City, Utah, studied violin and singing in Europe, and made her theatrical debut in London. Her first American assignment was her most memorable, Claudine, the demimondaine, who was also known as *The Pink Lady*♦ (1911). In this popular musical she introduced "My Beautiful Lady," both singing it and playing it on the violin. Three more musicals followed: *The Little Cafe* (1913), *The Debutante* (1914), and *The Century Girl* (1916). Generally forgotten is the fact that she was also an excellent *farceuse*. In 1919 she created the role of Mabel Essington in *Up in Mabel's Room*,♦ and two years later played Gertie Darling in *Getting Gertie's*

Garter.♦ Both plays dealt with a former lover's attempts to retrieve embarrassing evidence. She scored again as Gloria Graham, the temperamental actress, in *The Demi-Virgin* (1921). After touring in the *Ziegfeld Follies of 1923,*♦ she appeared in three more revues: *Nifties of 1923, Keep Kool* (1924), and *Great Temptations* (1926). Her last appearance was in *Wonder Boy* (1931).

Dawn of a Tomorrow, The, a play in three acts by Frances Hodgson Burnett.♦ Produced by Liebler and Co.♦ at the Lyceum Theatre.♦ January 25, 1909. 152 performances.

When Sir Oliver Holt (Fuller Mellish) concludes he is terminally ill, he takes a pistol and wanders the streets of London to get up enough nerve to kill himself. He meets a poor young girl, Glad (Eleanor Robson♦), whose enthusiastic belief that good works can overcome despair and pain lifts his spirits. Glad's ruffian boyfriend, Dandy (Henry Stanford♦), is accused of a crime he did not commit. He promises Glad that if he is exonerated he will behave thereafter. But the only man who can provide Dandy with a real alibi is Holt's ne'er-do-well son (Aubrey Boucicault♦). Prodded by Glad, the young man tells the police the real story. The four walk away confident that their futures are bright.

The play was inspired by the growing popularity of Mary Baker Eddy's Christian Science movement.

DAY, Edith (1896–1971) The beautiful, round-faced, dark-haired singing actress, who was born in Minneapolis, made her stage debut in 1915. By 1917 she was the leading lady of *Going Up*. She scored a huge success in the title role of *Irene*♦ (1919), in which she introduced "Alice Blue Gown," then enjoyed further acclaim in *Orange Blossoms* (1922), in which she sang "A Kiss in the Dark," and in *Wildflower* (1923), in which she sang "Bambalina." For many years thereafter she was one of London's leading musical stars.

DAY, Edmund, see *Round Up, The*

Days Without End, a modern miracle play in four acts by Eugene O'Neill.♦ Produced by the Theatre Guild♦ at the Henry Miller Theatre. January 8, 1934. 57 performances.

John Loving is two men simultaneously: John (Earle Larimore♦), his generous, idealistic half, and Loving (Stanley Ridges), his baser self. Embittered at life, he has abandoned religion and made a god of love. But he has not been faithful even to his new deity. He decides to write a book about his experiences. He tells the story to his priest (Robert Loraine♦) and his wife Elsa (Selena Royle). The shock of hearing her husband's history makes Elsa deathly ill. Mortified, John prostrates himself before the cross and re-embraces Catholicism. John's reaffirmation kills Loving and saves his wife.

Although highly praised by the Catholic press, most other American critics treated the play harshly, seeing it largely as a failed literary exercise rather than a vital drama. Curiously, the play was accorded a better reception the following year when it opened in London.

The play's American failure may have played some part in the withdrawal of O'Neill, heretofore prolific, from the stage. He did not return to Broadway until twelve years later with *The Iceman Cometh,* ♦ though, of course, he continued to write.

DAZEY, C[HARLES] T[URNER] (1855–1938) The Lima, Illinois-born playwright attended the College of Arts in Lexington, Ky., and Harvard University. Most of his plays were period melodramas designed for popular-priced touring companies, although nearly a dozen of his works reached New York, from *Elsa* (1882) to *The Stranger* (1911). His fame rests solely on one play, *In Old Kentucky*♦ (1893), in which a mountain girl wins a young patrician by racing a horse to victory, and in which Dazey incorporated his observations of the Kentucky life he knew while at school. According to Quinn♦ the play was performed in New York or on the road for 27 consecutive seasons.

Dazian's Theatrical Emporium Founded in 1842 by a Bavarian immigrant, Wolf Dazian, as a supplier of fancy and dry goods, it quickly became the leading supplier of materials and, most importantly, costumes to the theatrical trade. In short order the house was costumer to P. T. Barnum♦ and other leading producers. It provided the celebrated costumes for *The Black Crook.* ♦ After Wolf's death his son, Henry, took charge, but he abandoned the practice of providing finished costumes in 1919, prefering to sell bulk goods to other costume houses.

Dead End, a drama in three acts by Sidney Kingsley.♦ Produced by Norman Bel Geddes♦ at the Belasco Theatre. October 28, 1935. 684 performances.

On a New York street, dead-ending at the river, a crippled, failed young architect, Gimpty (Theodore Newton), sits sketching and observing the occupants of the new luxury apartments on one side of the street and of the tenements on the other. Among

those he observes are Tommy (Billy Halop), who exercises a precarious hold on his gang of youthful ruffians. Tommy's well-meaning, loving sister, Drina (Elspeth Eric), desperately tries to keep him on the straight and narrow, but Tommy leads his gang in stealing the watch of a rich boy who lives in the swank apartment house, and when the boy's father attempts to recover the watch, Tommy stabs him. At the same time Babyface Martin (Joseph Downing), once a gang member on the same street and now a major racketeer and murderer, returns on a secret visit to his mother (Marjorie Main), only to find she will have nothing to do with him. He is killed by the police, while Tommy is hauled off to jail. Gimpty is left to comfort Drina and to continue his sketching.

One highlight of the evening was Bel Geddes's magnificent setting depicting the new high-rise and the tenements. In between, construction equipment cluttered the set. The front of the stage was a pier, and the orchestra pit represented the river, into which characters occasionally jumped. Reviewers took note of the fact that the play was housed at the Belasco, where in earlier years Belasco♦ himself had offered his own famous realistic settings.

The play was hailed as a compassionate, forthright study of New York low-life, although most critics were offended at what, for the time, was its shocking language. A successful 1937 film version featured Humphrey Bogart and initiated the brief popularity of the Dead End Kids.

DEAN, JULIA (1830–68) Born in Pleasant Valley, N.Y., the daughter and granddaughter of performers, she made her professional debut in Louisville, in 1845 as Lady Ellen in *Lady of the Lake.* Her first New York appearance was at the Bowery in 1846 as Julia in *The Hunchback.* ♦ The *Herald* hailed her as "a child of nature," while Laurence Hutton♦ later recalled, "we have never seen her equal. Her light, graceful figure and beautiful face won her the sympathy and interest in the first act that her genius and fire enabled her to maintain until the fall of the curtain." She had deep blue eyes and golden hair. She followed her success with equally acclaimed performances in *The Lady of Lyons*♦*; The Stranger*♦*; Pizarro*♦*;* and *Romeo and Juliet.* ♦ For several seasons she continued to tour and expand her repertory. She briefly performed as Julia Dean Hayne after her marriage to the son of Daniel Webster's senatorial opponent, and played an exceptionally profitable California engagement. She then apparently retired from the stage, until she divorced Hayne for non-support. When she returned to New York in 1867, critics felt her acting had coarsened, a view they frequently took of performers who had spent considerable time in the West. She nonetheless found a loyal public, but her career was cut short when she died in childbirth after her second marriage. Perhaps because of her early sudden death, she was long remembered with a special fondness.

DEAN, JULIA (1880–1952) A beautiful blonde with warm, vivid eyes, Miss Dean was born in St. Paul, Minn., but raised in Salt Lake City, where she made her first stage appearances with a local stock company. After playing briefly with Joseph Jefferson,♦ James O'Neill,♦ and in vaudeville, she made her New York debut in *The Altar of Friendship* (1902). Small roles followed in *Merely Mary Ann* (1903) and *The Serio-Comic Governess* (1904) before she won attention as Anna Gray, who destroys evidence that might incriminate her lover, in *The Little Gray Lady* (1906). The play was a failure, and she was reduced to accepting a supporting role in *A Marriage of Reason* (1907). She next scored as the carefree Polly Hope in *The Round Up*♦ (1907), then toured as Emma Brooks in *Paid in Full*♦ (1908). Her performance as Christiane, the young girl desperate for love, in *The Lily* (1909) earned her further recognition, and she played the part for two seasons. More acclaim followed when she portrayed Virginia Blaine, the poor telephone operator who marries a cruel, selfish rich man, in *Bought and Paid For*♦ (1911), and for her acting as Mrs. Harding, who murders her vicious husband and is protected by her friends, in *The Law of the Land*♦ (1914). Several failures followed, including her last New York appearance, opposite George Arliss,♦ in *Poldekin* (1920). Miss Dean was praised as an actress of "absolute naturalness and much varied emotional expressiveness."

DE ANGELIS, [THOMAS] JEFFERSON (1859–1933) The San Francisco-born comedian made his debut shortly before his eleventh birthday at a Baltimore vaudeville house. In the early 1880s he toured the world at the head of his own dramatic company but soon recognized that his forte was acrobatic clowning. From 1887 to 1889 he was a principal comedian with John McCaull♦ and then served in the same capacity from 1891 to 1895 at the Casino Theatre.♦ He co-starred in the first major American revue, *The Passing Show* (1894), and with many of the leading prima donnas of his day, including Lillian Russell,♦ in shows such as *The Tzigane* (1895), *Fleur-de-Lis* (1895), *The Wedding Day* (1897), *The Jolly Musketeer* (1899), and *Fantana* (1905). Of his performance in this last musical the *Times* noted,

"his familiar sallies into broad humor met with much approval. He appears first as a valet, then disguises himself as a Japanese ambassador . . . in a wild chase around the stage after the tassle of his hat which has the habit of flying in his face at every possible opportunity." He continued to play in musicals but gradually varied his assignments with roles in straight comedies. One of his most memorable portrayals was that of Oscar Wolfe, the Broadway producer, in *The Royal Family*♦ (1927). His last appearance was in *Apron Strings* (1930).

Autobiography: *A Vagabond Trouper* (with Alvin E. Harlow), New York, 1931.

Dear Ruth, a comedy in two acts by Norman Krasna.♦ Produced at the Henry Miller Theatre. December 13, 1944. 683 performances.

Miriam Wilkins (Lenore Lonergan) is almost sweet sixteen and determined to do her share for the war effort. One way she is sure she can help is to write a lonely American soldier overseas. And she does. In fact, she writes him 60 letters. Only she isn't totally honest with him, for she signs all her letters with the name of her sister, Ruth (Virginia Gilmore), and sends him Ruth's picture. Home on leave, the soldier, Lt. William Seawright (John Dall), appears at the Wilkins home without warning, on the very day that Ruth has accepted a proposal of marriage from Albert Kummer (Bartlett Robinson). Although Bill has only two days to spare, it is time enough for Ruth to fall in love with him and ditch Albert. Ruth's father (Howard Smith), a judge, performs a hasty wedding ceremony, and the newlyweds rush off to a quick honeymoon. They are no sooner gone than the doorbell rings. It is a young sailor looking for Ruth. Miriam has obviously been doing more than her share.

Welcomed by Howard Barnes of the *Herald Tribune* as "slight but eminently satisfying," the play typified the vogue for preposterous but joyous comedies that went out several years later when television flooded the market with situation comedies.

Dearest Enemy, a musical comedy in three acts. Book by Herbert Fields.♦ Lyrics by Lorenz Hart.♦ Music by Richard Rodgers.♦ Produced at the Knickerbocker Theatre. September 18, 1925. 286 performances.

When General Howe (Harold Crane) stops at the home of Mrs. Robert Murray (Flavia Arcaro) for some rest and refreshment, the good lady contrives to delay him and his associates until the American troops of General Putnam (Percy Woodley) have time to escape and join Washington (H. E. Eldridge) at Harlem Heights. The delay allows Mrs. Murray's niece, Betsy Burke (Helen Ford♦), to fall in love with British Captain Sir John Copeland (Charles Purcell♦). The romance seems to fall apart when Copeland believes Betsy has signaled the Americans, but after the war he reconsiders and returns to consummate the courtship.

Principal songs: Bye and Bye · Here in My Arms

Hailed by Arthur Hornblow♦ in *Theatre♦* as "something very akin to a genuine comic opera," the musical was Rodgers and Hart's first book show following their success with the *Garrick Gaieties*. It united the pair with Herbert Fields, thus creating a new team that for several seasons gave promise of rivaling the great Princess Theatre♦ trio—Bolton♦–Wodehouse♦–Kern.♦

Death of a Salesman, a play in two acts by Arthur Miller.♦ Produced by Kermit Bloomgarden♦ and Walter Fried at the Morosco Theatre. February 10, 1949. 742 performances. PP, NYDCCA.

Willy Loman (Lee J. Cobb♦) is a salesman who has seen better days, or at least lets himself believe he was once more appreciated by his employers. His life has been devoted to his work, his wife Linda (Mildred Dunnock♦), and his sons, Happy (Cameron Mitchell) and Biff (Arthur Kennedy♦). His boys are the apple of his eye, so he cannot see that they will probably never amount to much and that Biff has never gotten over his disgust at finding his father in a hotel room with a woman. At sixty-three Willy loses his job and rejects the suggestion of rich Uncle Ben (Thomas Chalmers) that he try a new life in Alaska. Willy kills himself in an automobile crash, hoping his $20,000 insurance policy will resolve financial problems and give his boys another chance. At his funeral a neighbor characterizes Willy as "a man way out there in the blue, riding on a smile and a shoeshine. And when they start not smiling back—that's an earthquake." The long-suffering Linda can only sob, "We're free and clear. We're free."

John Mason Brown♦ noted the "play is the most poignant statement of man as he must face himself to have come out of our theatre," but added, "Mr. Miller's play is a tragedy modern and personal, not classic and heroic. Its central figure is a little man sentenced to discover his smallness rather than a big man undone by his greatness." A 1984 revival starred Dustin Hoffman.♦

Death of General Montgomery, The, a blank-verse tragedy written by H. H. Brackenridge♦ in 1777 as an exercise for his students at the Somerset Academy in Maryland. It described Montgomery's ill-fated attack on Quebec, but all the real action took place offstage and was merely recounted. Nevertheless it was perceived as a serious attempt at historical reporting and is credited with bolstering patriotic sentiments at a low point in the Revolution.

Deathtrap, a play in two acts by Ira Levin.♦ Produced by Alfred de Liagre, Jr.,♦ and Roger L. Stevens♦ at the Music Box. February 26, 1978. 1,809 performances.

Sidney Bruhl (John Wood♦), a mystery writer suffering a dry spell, tells his wife, Myra (Marian Seldes), that he intends to steal the story a young writer, Clifford Anderson (Victor Garber), has sent him and then kill the young man. To his wife's horror he apparently carries out his plan, burying the young man in their garden. When Clifford later seemingly returns from the dead, it proves too much for Myra, and she dies of a heart attack. That was Sidney's intention from the start, for Sidney has homosexual leanings and would set up a new life with Clifford. The murder was a hoax. But in a falling out Sidney mortally wounds the young man, who has just enough life in him before he dies to kill Sidney.

John Beaufort of the *Christian Science Monitor* wrote, "Mr. Levin has a fiendishly clever way of mixing chills and laughter, clues and climaxes . . . He can twist a plot until it almost cries out for mercy." If many playgoers felt the evening was sometimes more claptrap than deathtrap, the play's small cast and low budget allowed it to become the longest-running mystery in New York history. On the road the play was somewhat less successful.

DE BAR, Ben[edict] (1812?–77) A pioneering actor-manager, he was born in London to parents of French background and settled in New Orleans in 1834. A year later he made his acting debut at that city's St. Charles Theatre as Sir Benjamin Backbite in *The School for Scandal*. At the time he was slim and handsome enough (with attractive blue eyes and a round, boyish face) to assume roles such as Mazeppa, albeit from the start he excelled as a comedian. Two years later he joined J. W. Wallack's♦ company at the National in New York. Although he subsequently played several seasons in New York, he preferred what was then known as "the Western circuit"—the cities along or near the Mississippi. In 1853 he bought out Noah Ludlow♦ and Sol Smith's♦ New Orleans interests and in 1855 bought out John Bates in St. Louis. Thereafter he commuted by riverboat between the two cities, running playhouses and acting. He also arranged regional tours for companies based in those cities. In his later years he grew quite corpulent, so Falstaff became his most celebrated role.

Déclassée, a drama in three acts by Zoë Akins.♦ Produced at the Empire Theatre. ♦ October 6, 1919. 257 performances.

When Sir Bruce Haden (Harry Plimmer) catches one of his wife's guests, Edward Thayer (Vernon Steel), cheating at cards, Lady Helen (Ethel Barrymore♦), the wife, comes to her guest's defense. She is not one to avoid a fight since she is the last of the "Mad Varvicks," who for 500 years have been dying for causes in which they believe. Indeed, she has married a bit below her station, since Sir Bruce is a new knight, a butcher lately elevated by the king. But after Lady Helen catches Thayer cheating again, she threatens to expose him, although he counters by vowing to reveal letters she has written to him. Undeterred, she exposes him and thus ruins her own reputation. She moves to New York, where she befriends a rich Jew, Rudolf Solomon (Claude King), and where she lives by selling her jewelry. Solomon proposes and Helen accepts, though she confesses that she still loves Thayer. Thayer suddenly reappears, so Solomon offers to release Helen from her promise. Misunderstanding Solomon's change of heart, Helen rushes out into the night, where she is struck down by a taxi. Only as she is dying and sees Thayer does she understand Solomon's action.

Although critics were impressed with the sensitivity and acuity with which the Missouri-born Akins depicted English high society, it was generally agreed that the strength of the evening came from Barrymore's acting. Dorothy Parker,♦ so often venomously critical, wrote that she had never seen "any other performance so perfect."

Deep Are the Roots, a play in three acts by Arnaud d'Usseau♦ and James Gow.♦ Produced by Kermit Bloomgarden♦ and George Heller at the Fulton Theatre. September 26, 1945. 477 performances.

Brett Charles (Gordon Heath) grew up in the home of Senator Langdon (Charles Waldron♦), where his mother was a servant. Though Brett was black he was allowed to play with the Senator's daughters, Genevra (Barbara Bel Geddes♦) and Alice (Carol Goodner). Now Brett has returned home from the war with several decorations and with ideas about his place in life that disturb the conservative Southern Senator. When Brett enters

the public library through the front door, the town begins to gossip and turn against him, and when he is accused of stealing a watch he is arrested. But Brett has the support of Genevra and Alice. Genevra, in fact, is fond enough of him and optimistic enough about the future to suggest that Brett marry her. Brett, a realist, rejects her suggestion, but he is grateful for the girls' support. "We're on the same side," he tells Alice, whose father's sentiments remain unyielding.

An effectively written propaganda play, its suggestion of miscegenation offended some conservative playgoers, but its essentially reasonable stand on racial tolerance found a welcome in the liberal climate of the period. It typified the hopeful outlook for the future expressed frequently in early postwar dramas.

DEETER, JASPER, see *Hedgerow Theatre*

Deformed, The; or, Woman's Trial, a play in five acts by Robert Penn Smith. ♦ Produced at the Chestnut Street Theatre,♦ Philadelphia. February 4, 1830. 4 performances.

> Nature has lavish'd with unsparing hand,
> The choicest gifts upon her meanest works;
> But, in her boundless prodigality,
> Not one has fallen here. I—I alone,
> Move through this world of vast variety,
> A species in myself—disown'd by all.

Indeed, Adorni (Mr. Maywood) is so deformed he cannot understand why his wife Eugenia (Mrs. Rowbotham) loves him. He prevails on his friend Claudio (Mr. Forbes) to test her fidelity, then turns on Claudio and has him condemned to death. At the last minute he recognizes how blindly jealous he has been, so prepares to take Claudio's place at the execution. But the Duke of Florence (Mr. Wemyss♦) pardons Adorni.

The *United States Gazette* began its notice by welcoming a serious new drama into a season given over to musical spectacles and frivolous comedies, a perennial critical cry. It continued, "The character of the Deformed is entirely new, and we believe unique in the whole range of the drama . . . There are so many bold traits in this character, such as entitle Mr. Smith to a distinguished rank as a dramatic observer."

The play is an early example of the intermittent fascination that American playwrights have had for freaks and disabled people, a fascination still evident in plays such as *The Elephant Man,* ♦ *The Miracle Worker,* ♦ and *Children of a Lesser God.* ♦

The sympathetic portrait of Adorni won favor for the drama, as did a subplot of a good girl debased by a worthless man, which Smith derived from Dekker's *The Honest Whore* and Dunlap's♦ *The Italian Father*. The play was revived as late as 1839.

DE GRESAC, FRED, see *Gresac, Fred de*

DE KOVEN, [HENRY LOUIS] REGINALD (1859–1920) The composer of *Robin Hood*♦ (1891), the first enduring American operetta, De Koven was for a very brief time the most respected and promising melodist of the American theatre. Born in Middletown, Conn., he was thirteen when his clergyman father moved the family to England. He was educated at Oxford, then pursued his musical studies in Germany and France, where he was a pupil of Leo Delibes. His initial score was for Harry B. Smith's♦ libretto for *The Begum* (1887). The work was written in conscious imitation of Gilbert♦ and Sullivan,♦ and failed. So did their second effort, *Don Quixote* (1889). *Robin Hood* won instant acclaim, and its great songs, "Oh, Promise Me"♦ and "Brown October Ale," earned De Koven national fame and fortune. His later scores included *The Knickerbockers* (1892), *The Algerian* (1893), *The Fencing Master* (1893), *Rob Roy* (1894), *The Tzigane* (1895), *The Mandarin* (1896), *The Highwayman* (1897), *The Three Dragoons* (1899), *Papa's Wife* (1899), *Foxy Quiller* (1900), *The Little Duchess* (1901), *Maid Marian* (1902), *The Jersey Lily* (1903), *The Red Feather* (1903), *Happyland* (1905), *The Student King* (1906), *The Girls of Holland* (1907), *The Golden Butterfly* (1908), *The Beauty Spot* (1909), *The Wedding Trip* (1911), and *Her Little Highness* (1913). Although several of these later shows were commercial successes, the arrival on the scene of Victor Herbert♦ and other fresh talents, coupled with De Koven's archly conservative musical composition and the perception that his later scores were derivative and repetitive, forced critics and playgoers to reassess their earlier evaluation. It appears doubtful that any of his works, except possibly *Robin Hood,* will survive.

Biography: *A Musician and His Wife,* Anna De Koven, New York, 1926.

Delicate Balance, A, a play in three acts by Edward Albee.♦ Produced at the Martin Beck Theatre. September 22, 1966. 132 performances. PP.

Sitting in their comfortable library after dinner, Agnes (Jessica Tandy♦) confides to her husband that she sometimes worries about losing her mind. But her husband, Tobias (Hume Cronyn♦), assures

her he knows no saner woman. In short order the couple are visited by Agnes's younger sister (Rosemary Murphy), a bitter, malicious alcoholic; by Tobias's best friend (Henderson Forsythe) and the friend's wife (Carmen Mathews), both of whom are frightened by something they cannot identify; and by the couple's much married daughter (Marian Seldes). The visits force Agnes and Tobias to reevaluate all their relationships and to recognize that they must maintain a delicate balance between sanity and madness.

A curiously elusive play filled with stilted dialogue ("I apologize that my nature is such to bring out in you the full force of your brutality"), it was often more satisfying as an intellectual exercise than as a dramatic theatre piece.

DE LIAGRE, ALFRED, JR. (1904–87) A Yale graduate, the Passaic, N.J.-born De Liagre entered the theatre in 1930, working at the Woodstock Playhouse and serving as stage manager for a New York revival of *Twelfth Night.*♦ With Richard Aldrich♦ he produced *Three Cornered Moon* (1933), which he also directed. Together they produced several other plays, the most successful of which was *Petticoat Fever* (1935). In 1937 he began producing on his own. His best-known productions, many of which he directed, have included *Yes, My Darling Daughter*♦ (1937), *Mr. and Mrs. North* (1941), *The Voice of the Turtle*♦ (1943), *The Madwoman of Chaillot* (1948), *Second Threshold* (1951), *The Deep Blue Sea* (1952), the Phoenix Theatre♦ production of *The Golden Apple*♦ (1954), *Janus*♦ (1955), *J.B.*♦ (1958), and *Photo Finish* (1963). With Roger Stevens♦ he produced *Deathtrap*♦ (1978).

DE MILLE, AGNES [GEORGE] (b. 1905) The New York-born daughter of William C. de Mille,♦ she was graduated with honors from the University of California, and then studied dancing in London with Theodore Koslov, Marie Rambert, Anthony Tudor, and others. In 1928 she appeared as a dancer in the *Grand Street Follies* and a year later created the choreography for a much discussed revival of *The Black Crook*♦ in Hoboken. The next several seasons were spent dancing and choreographing in London before she returned to New York to develop the dances for *Hooray for What!* (1937) and *Swingin' the Dream* (1939). Major success and popular renown came to her with her ballets for *Oklahoma!*♦ (1943). Her dances for the show changed the nature of choreography in Broadway musicals. Heretofore there had been little ballet, and when ballet had been employed it had been usually ornamental and classical, except for a few notable examples by George Balanchine♦ and in some progressive revues. More than any other choreographer Miss de Mille popularized modern ballet styles in the musical theatre and made ballets dramatic, often allowing them to develop the story. The major ballet in *Oklahoma!* had been a "dream ballet," in which the heroine dreamed of the consequences of her behavior, and for several seasons thereafter "dream ballets" were a fad in musicals. Miss de Mille's subsequent choreography was seen in *One Touch of Venus♦* (1943), *Bloomer Girl♦* (1944), *Carousel♦* (1945), *Brigadoon♦* (1947), *Allegro♦* (1947), *Gentlemen Prefer Blondes♦* (1949), *Paint Your Wagon* (1951), *The Girl in Pink Tights* (1954), *Goldilocks* (1958), *Juno* (1959), *Kwamina* (1961), *110 in the Shade* (1963), and *Come Summer* (1969). Her work for traditional ballet ensembles included the celebrated *Fall River Legend* (1948). She also served as director for *Allegro; Out of This World* (1950); and *Come Summer.* She has written several books about both her life and her art, including *Dance to the Piper* (1952), *And Promenade Home* (1957), and *Speak to Me; Dance with Me* (1973).

DE MILLE, Henry C[hurchill] (1855?–93) De Mille came to New York from his North Carolina home with the intention of studying for the clergy, but his exposure to the theatre changed his plans. After graduating from Columbia, he joined the faculty of the Columbia College Grammar School, where he helped write school plays. His work came to the attention of the Frohmans♦ at the Madison Square Theatre♦ and he was hired as a play reader. At the same time he wrote his first play to be produced professionally, *John Delmer's Daughters; or, Duty,* a story of overreaching social climbers. With David Belasco♦ directing, it was produced in 1883 but failed. His next work, a collaboration with Charles Barnard,♦ was a railroad melodrama called *The Main Line; or, Rawson's Y* which told of the romance of a beleaguered girl who serves as a telegraph operator at a small train station. Produced by Daniel Frohman♦ in 1886, it was an immediate hit and was played around the country for many years. The four plays that followed were written with Belasco and were all huge successes: *The Wife♦* (1887) recounted how a kind, loving husband wins back his straying spouse; *Lord Chumley* (1888), a comedy centering on an eccentric Englishman; *The Charity Ball♦* (1889), in which a clergyman forces his selfish brother to wed the girl the brother has ruined; and *Men and Women♦* (1890), a story built around a bank scandal. After Belasco's departure to work on his own productions, de Mille adapted

Ludwig Fulda's *Das verlorene Paradies* as *The Lost Paradise♦* (1891). This early serious look at labor-management problems was hailed by the *Times* as "an uncommonly good play." At the time of his death, de Mille was working on a drama entitled *The Promised Land.* His modern editor, Robert Hamilton Ball, has noted, "The factor which determined the nature of these plays was the stock company. For that purpose they were admirably suited. They gave great and enduring pleasure to a large number of people. Moreover, Henry De Mille would have gone much farther, had he not died before he was forty years old." De Mille was the father of William C.♦ and Cecil B. de Mille, and the grandfather of Agnes.♦ His wife, Beatrice, was a well-known playwrights' agent.

DE MILLE, William C[hurchill] (1878–1955) The son of Henry C.♦ and father of Agnes,♦ he was born in Washington, N.C., and studied at Columbia U., then at the American Academy of Dramatic Arts.♦ He enjoyed a modest success with his first produced play, *Strongheart* (1905), in which an Indian chief relinquishes the white woman he loves for the sake of his tribe. Less successful was the comedy he wrote with his brother, Cecil B., *The Genius* (1906), centering on an amiable charlatan. In collaboration with Margaret Turnbull he next wrote a well-received comedy, *Classmates* (1907), in which two West Point cadets fight over the same girl, but its popularity was overshadowed by the tremendous success of his own play, *The Warrens of Virginia♦* (1907), one of many Civil War dramas recounting the romantic difficulties of a Southern girl and a Northern soldier. *The Royal Mounted* (1908), which told of the dilemma of a Mountie who must arrest the brother of his fiancée, was his second joint effort with his brother and was no more successful than the first. His biggest success came with *The Woman♦* (1911), in which corrupt politicians attempt to destroy an honest insurgent by linking him to a woman with whom he once registered at a hotel. A final collaboration with his brother, *After Five* (1913), also failed. The play described the comic suicide attempts of a young guardian after he loses his ward's money. Shortly thereafter he followed his brother west, where he spent the rest of his career in films.

DENHAM, Reginald (1894–1983) The English-born author, actor, and director first came to American playgoers' attention with his direction of *Rope's End* (1929) and *Josef Suss* (1930). He settled in America in 1940 and thereafter directed such plays as *Ladies in Retirement* (1940), which he wrote, and in which an old actress is murdered by her housekeeper; *Guest in the House* (1942); *The Two Mrs. Carrolls*♦ (1943); *Dial M for Murder* (1952); *Sherlock Holmes*♦ (1953); *The Bad Seed* (1954); and *Hostile Witness* (1966). His forte seemed to be plays with an element of mystery to increase dramatic suspense. With his wife, Mary Orr, he wrote several plays as well as a book of reminiscences, *Footlights and Feathers* (1966).

DENKER, Henry, see *Far Country, A*

D'ENNERY, Adolphe-Philippe (1811–99) Alone or with collaborators this French dramatist was one of the most successful authors of melodrama, many of which were huge hits when adapted for the American stage. By far the most notable of these triumphs were *The Two Orphans*♦ (1874) and *A Celebrated Case* (1878). Other works included: *Cartouche, the Highwayman of Paris* (1864); *Michael Strogoff* (1880); and *The Creole* (1881).

DENNIS, [Sandra Dale] Sandy (b. 1937) Born in Hastings, Neb., she first called attention to herself as Sandra, the compassionate social worker, in *A Thousand Clowns*♦ (1962), then played Ellen Gordon, the kooky mistress, in *Any Wednesday*♦ (1964). In 1974 she appeared in *Absurd Person Singular*. Between these major Broadway assignments she assumed many leading roles at major regional theatres, in touring productions, and in films.

DEROSA, Eugene An architect who alone or as part of the firm of Derosa and Pereira designed such Broadway theatres as the Apollo, Coliseum, Colony (now the Broadway), Gallo, Klaw, Times Square, and Vanderbilt.

DERWENT, Clarence (1884–1959) The English-born actor made his first New York appearance as Stephen Undershaft in *Major Barbara* in 1915 and for the next 31 years played important supporting roles in a wide variety of works, including *The Letter of the Law* (1920), *Love for Love* (1925), *The Woman of Bronze* (1927), *The Three Musketeers*♦ (1928), *Serena Blandish* (1929), *Topaze* (1930), *The Late Christopher Bean* (1932), *Kind Lady* (1940), *The Doctor's Dilemma* (1941), *The Pirate*♦ (1942), and *Rebecca* (1945). His last appearance was as the President in *The Madwoman of Chaillot* (1948). He served two terms as president of Actors' Equity♦ and for many years was president of ANTA.♦ In

1945 he established the annual Clarence Derwent Awards to be given for the best performances in supporting roles in both London and New York.

Autobiography: *The Derwent Story,* New York, 1953.

Desert Song, The, an operetta in two acts. Book by Otto Harbach,♦ Oscar Hammerstein II,♦ and Frank Mandel.♦ Lyrics by Harbach and Hammerstein. Music by Sigmund Romberg.♦ Produced by Laurence Schwab♦ and Mandel at the Casino Theatre.♦ November 30, 1926. 465 performances.

In the mountains of Morocco the French are fighting the rebellious Riffs who are led by a mysterious figure known as The Red Shadow. Pierre Birabeau (Robert Halliday♦), the son of the French commander, loves one of the beautiful women at the encampment, Margot Bonvalet (Vivienne Segal♦), but she has little time for the shy, seemingly backward young man. Matters come to a head when The Red Shadow kidnaps Margot. The French bribe a Riff dancing girl into betraying the leader, but he escapes, leaving behind only a red cloak. All that the French discover is Pierre wandering aimlessly in the desert. The French and the Riffs reach an accommodation. Margot, however, is forlorn, since she has fallen in love with her romantic captor. She looks on Pierre with new eyes when he reveals he was the leader.

Principal songs: The Desert Song · One Alone · The Riff Song · Romance

Suggested by the real life exploits of a contemporary Berber chieftain named Abd-el-Krim, the exotic backgrounds and Romberg's lush score made this one of the biggest and best-loved hits of the era, albeit Richard Watts, Jr.,♦ observed in the *Herald Tribune,* "The lyrics gave indication that W. S. Gilbert had lived and died in vain."

Desire Under the Elms, a drama in three parts by Eugene O'Neill.♦ Produced at the Greenwich Village Theatre. November 11, 1924. 208 performances.

Ephraim Cabot (Walter Huston♦), unsparing and miserly, works the New England farm he inherited from his second wife with the help of his three sons. The youngest, Eben (Charles Ellis), blames his father for his mother's death, insisting he killed her with overwork. Eben's older half-brothers, Simeon (Allen Nagle) and Peter (Perry Ivins), long for a better life in California—"at t'other side of the world." The 75-year-old Ephraim appears with his third wife, an ambitious young widow, Abbie Putnam (Mary Morris), so the older boys sell their shares to Eben and head for the gold fields. Abbie seduces Eben, and when their child is born, Ephraim, believing the child his, makes the baby his heir. Eben denounces Abbie, but she has come to love him. To prove her love, she kills the baby. Eben calls the police, but recognizing that he, in turn, has come to love Abbie, claims he assisted in the killing. Ephraim prepares to tend the farm alone as the young couple are taken away.

Stark Young♦ saw the work's similarity to *Beyond the Horizon*♦ but judged it "better written throughout; it has as much tragic gloom and irony, but a more mature conception and a more imaginative austerity." When the play was moved uptown it was not particularly successful until the police attempted to close it. The notoriety helped the play achieve an acceptable run.

DESLYS, GABY [Gabrielle Claire] (1884–1920) The tiny French dancer was a star in Paris and London before making her American debut in 1911. She appeared here in *Vera Violetta* (1911), *The Honeymoon Express* (1913), and *Stop! Look! Listen!* (1915). Despite some language problems, she was so popular that a once well-known dance, "The Gaby Glide," was written in her honor.

DE SYLVA, [GEORGE GARD] B. G. (1895–1950) Known popularly as "Buddy," he was born in New York and raised in Los Angeles. While attending the University of Southern California, he performed with a small ukulele combo and wrote some of their songs. One of these songs, " 'N' Everything," caught the ear of Al Jolson,♦ who used it in *Sinbad* (1918). Afterward De Sylva collaborated on several other songs that became Jolson standards: "Avalon," "April Showers," and "California, Here I Come." In 1919 he wrote the lyrics to George Gershwin's♦ score for *La, La Lucille,* and in 1922 and 1924 the words to Gershwin's melodies for *George White's Scandals,*♦ including the hit songs "I'll Build a Stairway to Paradise" and "Somebody Loves Me." He also created the lyrics for Jerome Kern's♦ "Look For the Silver Lining" and Victor Herbert's♦ "A Kiss in the Dark." He wrote several other less successful shows with Gershwin and served as lyricist for *Big Boy* (1925), whose songs included "If You Knew Susie," as well as lyricist and co-librettist for *Queen High* (1926), whose hit song was "Cross Your Heart." In 1925 he joined with Lew Brown♦ and Ray Henderson,♦ and for the next five years the team of De Sylva, Brown, and Henderson was the most successful in the musical theatre, their shows deemed the quintessential musical comedies and revues of the

era. Henderson fashioned the melodies; Brown and De Sylva, the lyrics; while De Sylva often collaborated on the librettos. Their songs were characterized by jazz-inspired rhythms and simple, upbeat lyrics. The shows, all hits, and the songs included: *George White's Scandals of 1925; George White's Scandals of 1926* ("Birth of the Blues," "Black Bottom," "Lucky Day"); *Good News!*♦ (1927) (title song, "Lucky in Love," "The Best Things in Life Are Free," "Just Imagine," and "Varsity Drag"); *Manhattan Mary* (1927); *George White's Scandals of 1928; Hold Everything*♦ (1928) ("You're the Cream in My Coffee"); *Follow Thru*♦ (1929) ("Button Up Your Overcoat"); and *Flying High*♦ (1930). After the team split, De Sylva produced and wrote the lyrics for *Take a Chance* (1932), whose songs included "Eadie Was a Lady," "Rise 'n' Shine," and "You're an Old Smoothie." In 1939 he was producer and co-librettist for *Du Barry Was a Lady,*♦ while the following year he was co-producer of *Louisiana Purchase*♦ and producer and co-librettist of *Panama Hattie.*♦

Detective Story, a melodrama in three acts by Sidney Kingsley.♦ Produced by Howard Lindsay♦ and Russel Crouse♦ at the Hudson Theatre. March 23, 1949. 581 performances.

Detective McLeod (Ralph Bellamy♦) of the 21st Precinct, New York, is a fanatically committed policeman whose ideas of justice and law are in some ways as warped as those of the hoodlums with whom he deals. He seems to hold that suspects are guilty until proven innocent, and even when they are acquitted in the courts insists "There's a higher court," and, by implication, that he is it. He is not above brutally treating suspects such as Dr. Kurt Schneider (Harry Worth), a suspected abortionist. But when he learns that his wife, Mary (Meg Mundy), once had an abortion and that Schneider performed it, his world collapses. He walks into a suspect's gun, and the man shoots him dead.

Although the main story was well written and its principal figures perceptively drawn, much of the evening's strength came in its vignettes of minor figures: burglars, shoplifters, shady lawyers, and policemen. Burns Mantle,♦ who had been a police reporter early in his career, observed that the "melodrama possesses so much naturalism and realism, and performs so easily, that a careless onlooker might use a film term and call it a documentary."

Detour, The, a domestic drama in three acts by Owen Davis.♦ Produced by the Messrs. Shubert♦

at the Astor Theatre. August 23, 1921. 48 performances.

Helen Hardy (Effie Shannon◆), wife of a Long Island truck farmer, Stephen Hardy (Augustin Duncan◆), has secretly saved her egg money over the years to give her daughter Kate (Angela McCahill) a proper education and better life. When Stephen learns of this, he is furious, but Helen threatens to leave and accompany her daughter. Kate, however, proves to have no real talent and prefers to settle down with the neighboring garage-owner. Mrs. Hardy can only continue hoarding so that her grandchild can have that better life.

Davis called the play "the first attempt on my part to write of life simply and honestly." Alexander Woollcott◆ concurred, hailing the work "a thoughtful human play, one that has more than its normal share of wisdom and kindly humor and knowledge of folks." Despite a generally laudatory press, the play was not successful.

Devil and Daniel Webster, The, a musical folk play in one act. Text by Stephen Vincent Benét. Music by Douglas Moore. Produced at the Martin Beck Theatre. May 18, 1939. 6 performances.

Jabez Stone (John Gurney), a New Hampshire farmer who has sold his soul to the devil in return for a decade of prosperity, is confronted on his wedding day by Mr. Scratch (George Rasely) demanding payment. Jabez prevails on his neighbor Daniel Webster (Lansing Hatfield) to defend him before a jury of the devil's selection. Webster's eloquence carries the moment, and Jabez is acquitted.

Despite its brief New York run, the work, which was based on Benét's own short story, remains a favorite of small dramatic and musical groups.

Devil's Disciple, The Shaw's◆ only important work set in America and dealing with events during the Revolutionary War, the play was his second to receive a professional mounting, when Mansfield◆ offered it in 1897 with himself as Dick Dudgeon. William Winter◆ called his performance "picturesque, sympathetic, and effective." The production ran for seven weeks, a run far exceeded when the Theatre Guild◆ revived it in 1923. With Basil Sydney◆ as Dick and Roland Young◆ in the brilliant cameo part of General Burgoyne, the production was hailed by the *Times* as "one of the few great comedy hits of the season" and ran six months. A superb 1950 revival starred Maurice Evans◆ as Dick but was stolen by Dennis King◆ as the General. Brooks Atkinson◆ called his performance "humorously insufferable," adding, "The

sardonicism rolls off his lips with wonderful grace and condescension." The comedy was revived in 1988 at the Circle in the Square. ◆

DE WALDEN, T. B., see *Kit, the Arkansas Traveller*

DEWHURST, Colleen (b. 1926) Born in Montreal, she studied at the American Academy of Dramatic Arts◆ and with Harold Clurman◆ before making her debut as a neighbor in a 1952 revival of *Desire Under the Elms*. ◆ Although she has kept busy she has rarely found the great roles her major talents suggest she deserves. Much of her early work was off-Broadway, including her highly praised performance of the ostentatiously ladylike Laetitia in *Children of Darkness* (1958) at the Circle in the Square.◆ On Broadway she has received Tony Awards◆ for her Mary Follet, the devout wife, in *All the Way Home*◆ (1960) and as Josie in a 1973 revival of *A Moon for the Misbegotten*. ◆ In 1988 she appeared in revivals of *Ah, Wilderness!*◆ and *Long Day's Journey into Night*. ◆ Two years later she toured in A. R. Gurney's◆ *Love Letters*.

DE WOLFE, Elsie , see *Other Girl, The*

DIAMOND, John (1823–57) The New Yorker made his debut in 1838, when he was known as Master Diamond or Master Jack Diamond, and, though white, quickly gained a reputation as a pre-eminent dancer of black jigs and songs. He was famous for issuing challenges to other performers to outdance him, but only the black performer, William Henry Lane,◆ who was known as Juba or Master Juba, was said to have genuinely outclassed him. As he grew older his vogue waned, and he died in poverty. Minstrel troupes held a huge benefit to pay burial costs.

Diamond Lil, a play in three acts by Mae West.◆ Produced at the Royale Theatre. April 9, 1928. 171 performances.

Lil (Miss West) is the mistress of Gus Jordon (J. Merrill Holmes), who runs a Bowery saloon and dance joint known as Suicide Hall and who trafficks in white slavery on the side. Gus is not especially loyal to Lil, but then when Gus is not around Lil is delighted to entertain any number of men friends. She even falls for Captain Cummings (Curtis Cooksey), a Salvation Army evangelist. When Cummings breaks up the white slave trade and discloses that he is really a police officer, Lil is not too shocked. She has grown tired of Gus and, well, just might even reform.

Although more straitlaced critics assailed the show as "lurid," more liberal reviewers took a line not unlike that of Charles Brackett in *The New Yorker,* who wrote, "Pure trash, or rather impure trash though it is, I wouldn't miss *Diamond Lil* if I were you." A nearly year-long run in London during the 1947–48 season prompted a New York revival in 1949. By then the play was perceived as harmless hokum, but with Miss West again as star it ran 181 performances and might have run longer had she not broken her ankle.

Diary of Anne Frank, The, a play in two acts by Frances Goodrich and Albert Hackett. Produced by Kermit Bloomgarden♦ at the Cort Theatre. October 5, 1955. 717 performances. PP, NYDCCA.

Shortly after the war Otto Frank (Joseph Schildkraut♦) returns with his former stenographer, Miep Gies (Gloria Jones), to the attic where Mr. Kraler (Clinton Sundberg) had hidden from the Gestapo Frank, his family, and other Jews. There Frank discovers the diary kept by his thirteen-year-old daughter Anne (Susan Strasberg). His thoughts fly back to the months they spent there, often in silence lest they give away their whereabouts—to happy moments such as a Chanukah celebration and to bitter ones such as catching a fellow Jew stealing their food. The announcement of Allied landings brings hope of a quick release, but shortly before the liberation their hiding place is betrayed. Anne and the others are sent to the gas chambers. Only Mr. Frank manages to escape. Now he reads the last line in the diary. "In spite of everything," Anne writes, "I still believe people are really good at heart." "She puts me to shame," the still bitter Frank acknowledges.

The play was based on the real Anne Frank's diary (published in English as *Anne Frank: The Diary of a Young Girl),* which had become a world-wide bestseller after the war. Richard Watts, Jr.,♦ of the New York *Post* noted, "By wisely shunning any trace of theatricality or emotional excess, the playwrights have made the only-too-true story deeply moving in its unadorned veracity." It was successfully produced in almost every major theatre center.

New Yorker Hackett (b. 1900) and his wife, Miss Goodrich (1891–1984), a native of Belleville, N.J., began their careers as performers. Their first two plays were moderately successful comedies: *Up Pops the Devil* (1930), in which a pair of free-thinking Greenwich Village bohemians create problems when they attempt to legalize their relationship; and *Bridal Wise* (1932), in which a youngster reconciles his divorced parents. After a long, successful career

as film writers they returned to Broadway with *The Great Big Doorstep* (1942), a failure.

Dictator, The, a farce in three acts by Richard Harding Davis.♦ Produced by Charles Frohman♦ at the Criterion Theatre. April 4, 1904. 64 performances.

Believing he has fatally struck a cab driver in a fight over a fare, Brooks Travers (William Collier♦) and his valet (Edward Abeles♦) take the first boat for Porto Banyos, where revolutions are weekly events. The latest revolution was engineered by none other than the American Consul (George Nash) with the aid of General Santos Campos (Robert McWade, Jr.). But the Consul's reign as dictator is short, for the General organizes another coup and makes himself dictator. Fearing for his life, the Consul assigns Travers both his position and a battle-ax widow (Louise Allen) who has been pursuing him. Travers must choose between returning to America and going to jail, or fighting not only the General but the harridan señora. He elects to fight. To give his men backbone, he ups their pay from 28 cents a day to thirty, then announces the next revolution will take place at 11 o'clock. But the general proves a determined opponent until Travers gets his cocktail-swilling telegraph operator (John Barrymore♦) to send a message asking that Admiral Dewey come to his aid with the *Olympia.* The result is that the opposition capitulates. At the same time, however, Travers learns that the cab driver was not seriously hurt. He decides to take the next ship back, preferring obnoxious taxi men to Latin instability.

One critic wrote of Davis, "We always knew he had a real play somewhere concealed upon his person, and now, having given over the attempt to dramatize his stories, he has delivered himself of it. 'The Dictator' is his best play, and in fact his first real play." The piece toured successfully for several seasons and was frequently revived by little theatre groups. A musical version was presented in 1920 as *The Girl from Home.*

DIETZ, HOWARD (1896–1983) One of Broadway's most urbane lyricists and librettists, the New York-born Dietz was a classmate of Oscar Hammerstein II♦ and Lorenz Hart♦ at Columbia. While in college his witty verses began to appear in newspapers, notably in Franklin P. Adams's famous "Conning Tower." Broadway first heard his rhymes when he wrote a lyric for "Alibi Baby" in *Poppy* (1923). He soon came to the attention of Jerome Kern,♦ who asked him to create the lyrics for *Dear Sir*

(1924). During this time he also began a successful career as publicist for the MGM film company. In 1927 he wrote lyrics and sketches for *Merry-Go-Round*. He then joined with composer Arthur Schwartz to create songs for the leading revues of the day: *The Little Show*♦ (1929), which included "I Guess I'll Have To Change My Plan"; *The Second Little Show* (1930); *Three's a Crowd* (1930), offering "Something To Remember You By"; *The Band Wagon*♦ (1931), from which came "Dancing in the Dark," "I Love Louisa," and "New Sun in the Sky"; and *Flying Colors* (1932), whose score included "A Shine on Your Shoes" and "Louisiana Hayride." Dietz wrote sketches for many of these revues and served as director for the last. He was lyricist, librettist, and director for *Revenge with Music* (1934), then wrote the lyrics and dialogue for *At Home Abroad* (1935) and *Between the Devil* (1937). In 1944 he collaborated with Vernon Duke on songs for *Jackpot* and *Sadie Thompson,* writing the libretto for the latter. Later he rejoined Schwartz for the revue *Inside USA* (1948) as well as *The Gay Life* (1961) and *Jennie* (1963).

Autobiography: *Dancing in the Dark,* New York, 1974.

DIGGES, DUDLEY (1879–1947) The Dublin-born actor had distinguished himself with the Irish National Players before embarking for America in 1904. Among his early appearances were roles in *The Rising of the Moon* (1908), opposite Mrs. Fiske♦; *The Spitfire* (1910); and *The Squaw Man*♦ (1911). After playing opposite George Arliss♦ in *Disraeli* (1911), he served as Arliss's stage manager for seven years. In 1919 he joined the newly formed Theatre Guild♦ and quickly established himself as one of its finest character actors. He remained with the Guild for eleven years, giving nearly 3000 performances under its aegis. The avuncular, gravel-voiced actor's notable assignments included the cowardly, selfish Henry Clegg in *Jane Clegg* (1920); Boss Mangan in *Heartbreak House* (1920); the villainous Sparrow in *Liliom*♦ (1921); the foredoomed Mr. Zero in *The Adding Machine*♦ (1923); Rev. Thompson, the heavenly examiner, in *Outward Bound* (1924); the helpful Critic in *The Guardsman* (1924); Feodor in *The Brothers Karamazov* (1927); the wise Chu-Yin in *Marco Millions*♦ (1928); Andrew Undershaft in *Major Barbara* (1928); and the atheistic Ramsey Fife in *Dynamo*♦ (1929). He also directed a number of Guild productions, among them: *Candida*♦ (1925); *Pygmalion*♦ (1927); *Love Is Like That* (1927); and *The Doctor's Dilemma* (1927). He scored as Gramps, who defies

death's messenger, in *On Borrowed Time*♦ (1938), then appeared as the rich Uncle Stanley in *George Washington Slept Here*♦ (1942) and as Mr. Burgess in *Candida* (1942). His last appearance was as Harry Hope, owner of the seedy bar, in *The Iceman Cometh*♦ (1946). Of this performance Brooks Atkinson♦ commented, "To anyone who loves acting, Dudley Digges' performance as the tottering and irascible saloon proprietor is worth particular cherishing. Although the old man is half dead, Mr. Digges' command of the actor's art is brilliantly alive; it overflows with comic and philosophic expression."

DILLINGHAM, CHARLES [BANCROFT] (1868–1934) Born in Hartford, Conn., the son of an Episcopalian clergyman, Dillingham rejected college in favor of becoming a journalist and served on newspapers in Hartford, Washington, and Chicago before moving to the New York *Evening Sun*. A stint as that paper's drama critic convinced him his future lay in the theatre. In 1896 he wrote and produced a play called *Ten P.M.* Although the play was a failure, it brought him to the attention of Charles Frohman,♦ who hired him as a press agent and production assistant. In 1898 he became Julia Marlowe's♦ manager and began to produce actively. In the next 30 years he produced over 200 plays. Straight plays he mounted included *Man and Superman*♦ (1905), *A Bill of Divorcement* (1921), *Bulldog Drummond* (1921), and *The Last of Mrs. Cheyney* (1925). However, he was most celebrated for his musical productions, which in lavishness and taste were considered second only to Florenz Ziegfeld's.♦ Among his many successes were *Mlle. Modiste*♦ (1905), *The Red Mill*♦ (1906), *Chin-Chin*♦ (1914), *Watch Your Step*♦ (1914), *Jack o'Lantern* (1917), *Apple Blossoms*♦ (1919), *Tip Top* (1920), *Good Morning, Dearie* (1921), *Stepping Stones* (1923), *Sunny*♦ (1925), and *Criss Cross* (1926). In 1910 he built the Globe (now Lunt-Fontanne) Theatre, and from 1915 to 1922 ran the mammoth Hippodrome.♦ Dillingham was famous for his gentlemanly conduct and his dapper appearance—his derby became a trademark. So respected was he that when he went bankrupt in the Depression his friends regularly took up collections to support him and even mounted a show, giving him credit as producer.

Dinner at Eight, a play in three acts by George S. Kaufman♦ and Edna Ferber.♦ Produced by Sam H. Harris♦ at the Music Box. October 22, 1932. 232 performances.

The guests invited to the dinner party of Millicent

Jordan (Ann Andrews) have all seemed to reach turning points in their lives. Larry Renault (Conway Tearle), a broke, alcoholic, fading matinee idol, loses his last chance for a comeback, so commits suicide. His young mistress, Paula Jordan (Marguerite Churchill), is the daughter of Oliver Jordan (Malcolm Duncan), who is seriously ill and whose shaky shipping interests are in danger of being taken over by the greedy upstart Dan Packard (Paul Harvey). Packard's sluttish wife Kitty (Judith Wood), a former hatcheck girl, is in love with Dr. Wayne Talbot (Austin Fairman), but Talbot has tired of her and prefers to return to his wife Lucy (Olive Wyndham). The long-retired star, Carlotta Vance (Constance Collier), once Jordan's mistress, has sold her stock in his company, unaware that his interests are beleaguered. Even Millicent's servants are touchy and quick to blow up. Then the cook announces that part of the dinner has been spoiled. Nevertheless, tired of waiting for Renault and unaware of his suicide, the guests and their hostess head for the dining room to make the best of it.

Praised by the *Herald Tribune* as "one of the best of the shrewdly literate Broadway dramas," the play broke theatre records in its early weeks. But its large cast, expensive production, and effects of the Depression, then at its nadir, prevented the play from spanning the summer. The 1933 MGM film version featured an all-star cast. A 1966 Broadway revival again with an all-star cast somehow missed capturing the original's glitter and failed.

Diplomacy A drama by Victorien Sardou,♦ it was first offered in America by Lester Wallack♦ in an adaptation by Saville and Bolton Rowe in 1878. Its story centers on Dora, a poor girl who is married to Julian Beauclere after he had spurned the Countess Zicka. The countess steals an important document and implicates Dora in the theft. The play, which proved one of Wallack's greatest successes, featured H. J. Montague♦ as Julian, Maude Granger♦ as Dora, and Rose Coghlan♦ as the Countess. It remained a favorite for fifty years, its last important revival coming in an all-star production in 1928 with a cast that included Margaret Anglin,♦ Jacob Ben-Ami,♦ Charles Coburn,♦ William Faversham,♦ Helen Gahagan,♦ Rollo Peters,♦ and Tyrone Power. ♦

DITHMAR, EDWARD A[UGUSTUS] (1854–1917) The son of a newspaper composing-room foreman, he was born in New York and began his own newspaper career as a reporter for the *Evening Post* in 1871. Six years later he moved to the *Times,* where he

remained for the rest of his life. He became the paper's principal drama critic in 1884 and held the post until 1901. His approach was what he himself called "Impressionistic," judging a play by his immediate reaction to it and not by academic canons of correctness or by primarily puritanical moralistic considerations. He also wrote such works as *Memories of Daly's Theatre* (1897) and *John Drew* (1900).

DITRICHSTEIN, LEO [JAMES] (1865–1928) Son of a count and grandson of a famous Austrian novelist, the heavy-set, gruffly handsome, round-faced actor apprenticed in Berlin before coming to America in 1890. His first appearances were in German plays at the Amberg Theatre. After learning sufficient English he toured in *Mr. Wilkinson's Widows* before making his New York debut under Charles Frohman's♦ aegis in *The Other Man* (1893). He first caught Broadway's eye as Zou Zou in *Trilby* (1895), then enhanced his reputation as the comic Otto Whisky in *A Stag Party* (1895) and the mad scientist Achille Rabon in *Under the Polar Star* (1896). In 1898 he was George Tesman in a special matinee of *Hedda Gabler,* its first New York performance. Later notable performances included the explosive Colonel Larivette in *Before and After* (1905), which he adapted from the French; the cynical Bernard in *The Lily* (1909); Gabor Arany, the philandering pianist, in his adaptation of *The Concert* (1910); Jacques Dupont in his adaptation of *The Temperamental Journey* (1913); Sascha Taticheff, whose wife sees him in daydreams as her imagined lover, in his adaptation of Molnar's♦ *The Phantom Rival* (1914); the modern-day Don Giovanni, Jean Paurel in *The Great Lover♦* (1915); the title role in *The King* (1917); and Napoleon's adversary, Armand, in *The Purple Mask* (1920). His last appearance was in *The Business Widow* (1923). Even in cameo parts, such as Bernard in *The Lily,* Ditrichstein won critical respect. One reviewer observed, "In a brief role confined to the first act [he], with perfect art, also delivered a little gem of characterization—the figure of a middle-aged cynic, a role expressed with complete naturalness and splendid touches of acrid humor." Alone or with collaborators, he wrote or adapted many plays, often appearing in them or directing them. He retired while still at the height of his fame and returned to Europe.

Divorce, a play in five acts by Augustin Daly.♦ Produced by Daly at the Fifth Avenue Theatre.♦ September 5, 1871. 200 performances.

The day of the marriage of convenience of her daughter, Lu Ten Eyck (Fanny Davenport♦), to the much older De Wolf De Witt (William Davidge♦), Mrs. Ten Eyck (Fanny Morant♦) learns that Alfred Adrianse (D. H. Harkins) has returned from a long trip abroad. Alfred had left New York when Mrs. Ten Eyck cut short his courtship of her other daughter, Fanny (Clara Morris♦), insisting Fanny was too young. Now that Fanny is older, Mrs. Ten Eyck's objections fade, so Alfred and Fanny are married along with Lu and De Wolf. Both marriages, however, quickly fall apart, Alfred becomes unjustly suspicious of Fanny, especially of her actually innocent relations with Captain Lynde (Louis James♦), while Lu finds her aged mate dismayingly complacent—"He says I may do what I like. I may buy all New York up, and begger him—says all he can do is to submit to my whims. Did you ever hear such outrageous language?" Her bemused lawyer, Jitt (James Lewis♦), can only look at her in amazement and despair. Fanny and Alfred's problems are more serious, and Fanny leaves, taking their young son with her. Alfred kidnaps the boy, and Fanny follows them to Florida to reclaim the child. Alfred and Lu are brought to their senses in time for a happy ending.

Daly took his characters and incidents from Anthony Trollope's novel, *He Knew He Was Right,* but rearranged matters with a free hand, moving the setting to America, adding a subplot, and contriving reconciliations at the close. The *Herald* commented, "The subject . . . is a real live one, and certainly its treatment evinces rare delicacy and skill and a thorough knowledge of society of the present day . . . The play is a very long one . . . but there is not a weak or uninteresting scene in it." The play was the reigning hit of the day, at one point playing simultaneously in New York, Boston, Philadelphia, Buffalo, and St. Louis. Its New York run was said to have been a record for a comedy at the time. It was also the first play performed in Chicago after the fire. Later critics looked less kindly on the play, but it was revived successfully in Philadelphia as late as 1892.

Divorçons This play by Victorien Sardou♦ deals with a foolish young wife, Cyprienne, who feels she must divorce her husband, des Prunelles, and marry a handsome ne'er-do-well. Her husband's kindness and generosity bring her to her senses. The work was first offered in an English version in 1882 with an undistinguished cast, but quickly became a major success and was revived regularly as late as World War I.

DIX, Beulah Marie (1876–1970) Born in Kingston, Mass., and educated at Radcliffe, she wrote numerous plays in the early years of the 20th century. Her two most successful were those she wrote with Evelyn Greenleaf Sutherland♦: *A Rose o' Plymouth Town* (1902), dealing with Priscilla Alden, and *The Road to Yesterday♦* (1906), telling of a woman who dreams of imaginary past adventures.

DIXEY, Henry E. (1859–1943) After making his debut at the age of ten at the Howard Atheneum♦ in his native Boston playing Peanuts in *Under the Gaslight,* ♦ he trained with the pantomimist James S. Maffitt, then made his first New York "appearance" as one-half of the heifer in E. E. Rice's♦ *Evangeline♦* in 1874. Subsequently he appeared in numerous other musicals before creating the role for which he was afterward famous, the statue brought to life as *Adonis♦* (1884). His comic cavortings, which included a celebrated spoof of Henry Irving, a bit in drag, and another bit as a madcap barber, helped the musical become the first show in Broadway history to run more than 500 performances. He played the part for several seasons and later returned to tour with it occasionally. Unlike most comedians, he was an exceptionally handsome man, who later sought roles that allowed him to display his figure in tight-fitting period costumes. Unfortunately, the rest of his career was anticlimatic. Two major musicals written especially for him, *The Seven Ages* (1889) and *Rip* (1890), both failed. Thereafter he alternated between musicals and straight plays, usually comedies, but never again savored the acclaim he had won in *Adonis.* One of his better later roles was the absurdly troublesome Peter Swallow opposite Mrs. Fiske♦ in *Mrs. Bumpstead-Leigh♦* (1911).

"Dixie" A song written in November 1859 by Dan Emmett♦ and whose correct title was "I Wish I Was in Dixie's Land." Whether the song was introduced immediately thereafter at Bryant's Minstrels♦ or on February 6, 1860, when Bryant first performed his production of "Dixie's Land," has been argued by minstrel scholars. In any case, the song's real popularity came not from Bryant's but from Mrs. John Wood, ♦ who interpolated it into one of her burlesques while she was touring the South, first singing it to much acclaim in New Orleans. Picked up by the local citizenry, it quickly spread throughout the area and became virtually the anthem of the Confederacy.

DIXON, George Washington (1808?–61) One of the earliest blackface entertainers, he was briefly popular in the late 1820s and early 1830s, and claimed to have written and introduced the once well-known "Old Zip Coon." He later abandoned the stage to edit a notoriously scurrilous newspaper and died in poverty in New Orleans.

Do I Hear a Waltz?, see *Time of the Cuckoo, The*

Dock Street Theatre (Charleston, S.C.). An announcement in the *South Carolina Gazette* for January 24, 1736, read: "On Thursday, February 12, will be opened the New Theatre in Dock Street in which will be perform'd 'The Recruiting Officer'." The paper took no note of the fact that the street recently had been officially renamed Queen Street, while its readers apparently cared little that the playhouse's name was simply the New Theatre. The house became known as the Dock Street Theatre for the two years it was in operation. It closed in 1738 and burned in the great Charleston fire of 1740. Two more playhouses were built on or near its site, one in 1754 and a second in 1766. The modern theatre of the name was an outgrowth of the little theatre movement. ◆

DOCKSTADER, Lew [né George Alfred Clapp] (1856–1924) Dockstader became a professional minstrel about 1873, after having performed in amateur blackface ensembles for several years in his native Hartford, Conn. He played with a number of groups, including his celebrated travesty of *Camille* ◆ with Wood's Minstrels, before joining with Charles Dockstader to form the Dockstader Brothers' Minstrels in 1876, at which time he changed his name. In 1886 he opened his own theatre in New York, later giving it up to tour in vaudeville. By this time traditional blackface minstrelsy was all but dead, and had, in any case, evolved from its original small troupes into mammoth companies that offered spectacle as much as old-fashioned minstrelsy. In 1898 he combined with George Primrose, ◆ a more conservative old minstrel, to form a company that presented a show that was an amalgam of minstrelsy and vaudeville, not much different from a blackface revue. One important innovation that kept his troupe popular was his injection of topical satire, with Dockstader, a huge man usually dressed in oversized clothing and shoes, impersonating not plantation blacks but celebrated figures of the day. His spoof of President Cleveland, another large man, was especially applauded. After Primrose's withdrawal, Dockstader continued to tour with his own company. From 1913 to 1923 he frequently performed in vaudeville and in 1922 appeared in an unsuccessful Broadway revue *Some Party.*

Doctor of Alcantara, The, an opéra bouffe in two acts. Libretto by Benjamin Edward Woolf. ◆ Music by Julius Eichberg. Produced at the French Theatre. September 25, 1866. 12 performances.

Two young lovers, Carlos and Isabella, are ordered by their fathers, Doctor Paracelsus and Senor Balthazar, to marry mates they have never seen. No one realizes that the mates the parents have selected are none other than the lovers themselves. Carlos's adventures in the difficult courtship include hiding in a basket, which is thrown in the river with Carlos inside, and being mistaken for dead after drinking a sleeping potion.

The comic opera had its first performances in Boston, where its authors were based, in 1862. For several years it was regularly included in the repertory of numerous traveling opera companies and was presented in most major cities. Of negligible value, it represents the style and drift of operetta in America before the coming of Offenbach ◆ and Gilbert ◆ and Sullivan. ◆

DODGE, D. Frank One of the busiest turn-of-the-century set designers, he specialized in colorful settings for musicals as exemplified by his work for De Koven's ◆ *Rob Roy* (1894); the Lillian Russell ◆ vehicle, *An American Beauty* (1896); and the long-running importation *A Chinese Honeymoon* (1902). His work for non-musicals ranged from spectacular settings for *Ben Hur* ◆ (1899) to realism in *Salvation Nell* ◆ (1908) and *Mrs. Bumpstead-Leigh* ◆ (1911).

Dodsworth, a play in three acts by Sidney Howard. ◆ Produced by Max Gordon ◆ at the Shubert Theatre. February 24, 1934. 317 performances.

A rich, retired automobile manufacturer, Samuel Dodsworth (Walter Huston ◆), decides to take his wife Fran (Fay Bainter ◆) on a grand tour of Europe. To his chagrin, however, Fran is more interested in indiscreet affairs with other men than in Europe's treasures. On the eastward sailing Dodsworth has met Edith Cortright (Nan Sunderland), a woman Fran's age but more mature. When the time comes to sail back, Dodsworth decides to remain in Europe with Edith. Fran, alone on the ship, can only exclaim dazedly, "He's gone ashore. He's gone ashore."

This dramatization of Sinclair Lewis's novel was one of the most successful transfers from book to stage of the era, helped immensely by Huston's and

Miss Bainter's luminous performances and Gordon's skillful production. Burns Mantle♦ noted, "It combined the homeliness of subject and the vigorous honesty of the best plays of the year."

Dog Dramas In the 1840s Barkham Cony and Edwin Blanchard introduced plays at the Bowery Theatre♦ in which trained dogs took a significant part in the action—holding villains at bay, rescuing the heroine, or uncovering evidence that exonerates the hero. With titles such as *The Planter and His Dogs* and *The Dogs of the Wreck* the plays soon became popular features at the theatre. When Cony and Blanchard separated at the end of the decade, Cony, with his young son Eugene and their dog Yankee, continued to appear at the Bowery in a number of specially written vehicles, among them *The Cross of Death; or, The Dog Witness* and *The Butcher's Dog of Ghent*. At the same time Blanchard, with his dogs Hector and Bruin, moved to the National Theatre, where they starred in *The Watch Dogs, The Fisherman and His Dogs,* and similar pieces. All through the 1850s and 1860s dog dramas continued to be popular, especially in the less elite playhouses. Cony soon disappeared from the scene, but Blanchard found a new rival in Fanny Herring,♦ who with her dogs Lafayette and Thunder performed in *The Rag Woman and Her Dogs* and other such plays. By the early 1870s the vogue for the genre had largely exhausted itself, while trained dogs found new opportunities on the rapidly multiplying vaudeville stages.

DOLLY, JENNIE [née JANSZIEKA DEUTSCH] (1892–1941) and ROSIE [née ROSZIKA DEUTSCH] (1892–1970) These small, dark-complexioned, almond-eyed beauties were the most successful sister act of their day, their four-week run at the Palace♦ being the longest such stand for any sister act at that theatre. Born in Hungary, but raised on New York's Lower East Side, they were headliners in vaudeville before they were chosen to sing and dance in the *Ziegfeld Follies of 1911.♦* Other major appearances included *A Winsome Widow* (1912), the national tour of *Oh, Look!* (1918), and *Greenwich Village Follies of 1924.♦* Rosie appeared alone in *The Whirl of New York* (1914), after Jennie temporarily broke up the act to team with her husband Harry Fox. Stark Young♦ wrote of them: "The smartest part of the bill was the Dolly sisters, who bring on the stage a real chic and make you wish they would lend some of what they have by way of point and style to our Broadway stage in its more serious aspects."

DONAHUE, JACK (1892–1930) A native of Charlestown, Mass., the supple, eccentric dancer had begun making a name for himself in vaudeville before his Broadway debut in 1919 in *Angel Face*. His best known appearances came when he played opposite Marilyn Miller,♦ in *Sunny♦* (1925) and in *Rosalie* (1928) and starred in *Sons o' Guns* (1929), for which he was co-librettist.

DONALDSON, WALTER, see *Whoopee*

Donaldson Awards Established in 1944 in honor of the founder of *Billboard,♦* W. H. Donaldson (1864–1925), they were offered in numerous categories, including best new play, best new musical, best performances, best debuts, and best costumes and set designs. They were discontinued in 1955 when it was recognized that they were redundant and overshadowed by more prestigious honors.

DONNELLY, DOROTHY [AGNES] (1880–1928) Daughter of the manager and lessee of New York's Grand Opera House, she made her acting debut in the stock company run by her brother, Henry V. Donnelly, at the Murray Hill Theatre. She came to critics' and playgoers' attention in 1903 when she played the title roles in Yeats's *Kathleen ni Houlihan* and Shaw's♦ *Candida♦* in their first American performances. In the next year she was the first American to play The Lady in Shaw's *The Man of Destiny*. Her most celebrated performance was in the title role of *Madame X* (1910), in which she played the part of a woman who had years before deserted her husband and young child, and now finds that the husband is the judge and the son her defense attorney when she is tried for murdering her blackmailing lover. She continued to act for another decade. In 1916 she was co-librettist for *Flora Bella* and two years later for *Fancy Free*. The success of her book and lyrics for Sigmund Romberg's♦ adaptations of Schubert's melodies in *Blossom Time♦* (1921) prompted her to abandon performing. Further success came with her libretto for *Poppy* (1923), but her biggest hit was *The Student Prince♦* (1924), for which she wrote the lyrics to such popular Romberg songs as "Deep in My Heart, Dear," "The Drinking Song," "Golden Days," and "Serenade." *Hello, Lola* (1926), a failure, was followed by her third profitable collaboration with Romberg, *My Maryland* (1927). Among her lyrics were those for "Mother," "Silver Moon," "Won't You Marry Me?" and "Your Land and My Land." Shortly before her death she joined Romberg again to write *My Princess* (1927), their only unsuccessful work.

Don't Bother Me, I Can't Cope, a musical revue in two acts by Micki Grant. Produced at the Playhouse. April 19, 1972. 1,065 performances.

An intimate revue featuring songs relating to black experience. Miss Grant is a Chicago native who studied at several important universities. She has written background and incidental music for a number of shows and has performed in her own material and that of others. This show has been her most memorable achievement.

DOOLEY, [RACHEL RICE] RAY (1891–1984) Daughter of a circus clown who gave her her earliest training, she was born in Scotland but grew up in Philadelphia. While still a child she made her debut at that city's Keith's Theatre with Tim McMahan's "Watermelon Girls." Soon afterward she created a similar act called "Ray Dooley's Minstrels," which eventually played the Palace. ♦ Her Broadway debut was in *Words and Music* (1917), followed by appearances in the 1919, 1920, and 1921 *Ziegfeld Follies,* ♦ *The Bunch and Judy* (1922), *Nifties of 1923, Ziegfeld Follies of 1925, No Foolin'* (1926), *Sidewalks of New York* (1927), *Earl Carroll Vanities of 1928,* ♦ and *Thumbs Up!* (1934). She specialized in playing young spoiled brats, often named Gertie. Typical of her antics was a skit in *No Foolin'* in which she taunted a train conductor, refusing to give him her ticket and leading him a merry chase over seats and passengers alike. She was married to Eddie Dowling. ♦

DORO, MARIE [KATHRYN] [née STUART] (1882–1956) Born in Duncannon, Pa., the lithe, delicately beautiful actress made her acting debut in St. Paul in 1901 and first appeared in New York in *The Billionaire* (1903). She next played in *The Girl from Kay's* (1903), before essaying Lady Millicent in James Barrie's *Little Mary* (1904). Shortly thereafter she toured with William Gillette ♦ in *The Admirable Crichton.* Her first starring part was in the title role of the waif in *Friquet* (1905), but the play was a quick failure. Following a London visit and American tour as Gillette's leading lady, she returned to New York with him to play the doctor's assistant in love with her boss, the title part in Gillette's *Clarice* (1906). She scored a major success as Carlotta, the ingenuous girl in love with the bookish young man, in *The Morals of Marcus* (1907). One critic noted, "she has a persuasive little personality, with eerie beauty as an asset. And she is charming in comedy

and genuinely touching in emotion." Most of her later successes were in London, but she did delight her American public as Oliver Twist (1912) and in the title role of *Patience* (1912). Her last appearance was as the wronged wife whose revenge is to dabble in prostitution in *Lilies of the Field* (1921).

DOUGHERTY, HUGHEY (1844–1918) The Philadelphia-born minstrel made his debut in his hometown in 1858 with Sanford's Minstrels. ♦ During his long career he worked with many troupes and came to be considered the greatest "stump speech" artist in minstrelsy. Despite his widespread travels and fame, he spent most of his career in Philadelphia, where he popularized the expression "Stick a pin in dar, Brudder Bones."

Doughgirls, The, a comedy in three acts by Joseph Fields. ♦ Produced by Max Gordon ♦ at the Lyceum Theatre. ♦ December 30, 1942. 671 performances.

Just as Edna (Virginia Field) is about to be evicted from her hotel suite in overcrowded wartime Washington she discovers the woman who is taking the rooms is her old friend Vivian (Arleen Whelan), so she forces Vivian to let her remain. Before long another old friend, Nan (Doris Nolan), joins the group. All three women have been living with men to whom they are not married. The quarters are further crowded when a Russian sniper, Natalia Chodorov (Arlene Francis), is imposed on them. Natalia, who has shot 397 Nazis, is a vigorous, forceful woman who, for exercise, takes short hikes—to Baltimore and back. All sorts of complications ensue. A wife of one of the lovers suddenly appears; a marriage is put off when divorce papers turn out to be a report from the Wordsworth Chemical Laboratory; an admiral, a general, and even a group of Marines briefly make their home in the suite. In the end, of course, the difficulties are resolved—in no small part by the aid of Natalia.

Although some cries were raised that the comedy was immoral, most playgoers and critics agreed with Lewis Nichols of the *Times,* who hailed this "mad salute to wartime Washington" as "very funny indeed."

Douglas John Home's only successful tragedy tells of Lady Randolph, who, after the death of her husband and disappearance of her son, has married Lord Randolph. When he goes off to war he is rescued from certain death by the brave Young Norval, who has been raised by a shepherd, Old Norval. The young man, of course, turns out to be Lady Randolph's long-lost son and assumes his rightful name of Douglas. But Lord Randolph's mind is poisoned against Douglas by the crafty Glenalvon. Douglas is murdered; Lady Randolph throws herself from a cliff; and Lord Randolph, recognizing the wrong he has abetted, goes off, hoping to die in battle. The play apparently was first produced in America in 1758, two years after its London premiere, although the original cast has not survived. It was revived shortly afterwards in Philadelphia with the young Hallam♦ as Young Norval, David Douglass♦ as Lord Randolph, and Mrs. Douglass (the elder Hallam's widow) as Lady Randolph. The play remained popular for about one hundred years, and the role of Young Norval became a popular debutant role for such performers as John Howard Payne.♦

DOUGLAS, MELVYN [né MELVYN EDOUARD HESSELBERG] (1901–81) The suave leading man who developed into a fine character actor was born in Macon, Georgia, and made his stage debut in Chicago. He next spent several seasons with Jessie Bonstelle♦ before briefly operating his own company in Madison, Wis. He first appeared in New York as Ace Wilfong, the gambler whose conventional ideas of morality lead him into murdering his free-thinking wife's escort, in *A Free Soul* (1928). Several more praised performances in failures followed, including his role of "The Unknown Gentleman," a suitor mistaken for a gigolo, in *Tonight or Never* (1930). His acting in plays landed him a Hollywood contract. He returned to Broadway in 1934 to play Sheridan Warren, the philandering husband, in *No More Ladies* and to win acclaim for his direction of O'Casey's♦ *Within the Gates*. When his next appearances were all in failures, he returned to Hollywood until he re-emerged after World War II as co-producer of the ex-soldier revue, *Call Me Mister* (1946). In 1949 he played Tommy Thurston, the newspaperman determined to expose the absurdity of government bureaucracy, in *Two Blind Mice,* then portrayed Wally Williams, the callous night-club owner, in *The Bird Cage* (1950). He scored a small success as Steve Whitney, the middle-aged bachelor who learns he is a father, in *Glad Tidings* (1951), which he also directed, then enjoyed a bigger hit as Howard Carol, the staid banker whose tomboyish daughter makes the football team, in a frivolous farce, *Time Out for Ginger* (1952). He played this part for three seasons, before replacing Paul Muni♦ in 1956 as the Clarence Darrow-like Henry Drummond in a modern retelling of the Scopes evolution trial, *Inherit the Wind.* ♦ Following several failures, he won a Tony Award♦ for his portrayal of

William Russell, the idealistic presidential candidate, in *The Best Man* ♦ (1960). His last Broadway appearance was as a retired chicken farmer encroached on by suburbanites, the title role in *Spofford* (1967).

DOUGLASS, DAVID (d. 1786) In 1754 John Moody, who had returned to London from Jamaica, where he had given theatrical performances, organized a new company to play the West Indian island. Shortly before Moody was set to sail, however, he accepted an important position offered by David Garrick, and so entrusted his band to Douglass, whose earlier career is unknown. By coincidence, a company led by Lewis Hallam, Sr.,♦ was also playing in the island. The troupes were merged, Hallam died, and Douglass married Mrs. Hallam.♦ The company came to New York in 1758, where it built a new playhouse, and soon was traveling up and down the coast, playing not only in New York but in Philadelphia, Annapolis, Newport, and elsewhere. Douglass was not a distinguished actor. By consensus the best member of the troupe was Lewis Hallam, Jr.♦ But Douglass was a tactful politician and forceful businessman. His diplomacy was required because wherever he went he encountered puritanical opposition to the theatre, opposition he was usually successful in overcoming, at least for a time. His business acumen helped him to arrange the construction of proper playhouses in the cities where his company played. Among the theatres for whose erection he was largely responsible were the Southwark♦ in Philadelphia, the John Street♦ in New York and the third New or Dock Street Theatre♦ in Charleston. His company adopted the name The American Company♦ as early as 1763. Under his aegis colonists were offered a large repertory of classics and new London successes, as well as the first professional mounting of a play by an American author, *The Prince of Parthia*♦ (1767). He also brought to America such popular performers as Miss Cheer♦ and John Henry.♦ With the onset of the Revolution he returned to Jamaica, where he became a government official and died leaving an estate of £25,000.

DOWLING, EDDIE [né JOSEPH NELSON GOUCHER] (1894–1976) Born in Woonsocket, R.I., he made his stage debut in nearby Providence in 1909 in *Quo Vadis?*. After spending some time in England, he returned to America to join the *Ziegfeld Follies of 1918,* ♦ then on tour. His first New York appearance was as a policeman in Victor Herbert's♦ *The Velvet Lady* (1919), after which he performed as a song and dance man in the 1919 and 1920 editions of the *Ziegfeld Follies*. Following another tour in a second Herbert musical, *The Girl in the Spotlight* (1921), he was starred in a musical of which he was co-author, *Sally, Irene and Mary* (1922). He played in this show for three seasons, then co-authored another starring vehicle for himself, *Honeymoon Lane* (1926). The show was also a success, although one reviewer could say no more about Dowling than he was "a popular, likeable, if a bit unctuous, performer." He co-authored and starred in a third musical, this time with his wife, Ray Dooley,♦ but *Sidewalks of New York* (1927) was a modest hit at best. For several seasons he and his wife toured in vaudeville. A final musical appearance (except to replace a star in later years) was in *Thumbs Up!* (1934), which he also produced. Thereafter his career took an unusual turn for a performer until then identified with the most frivolous musicals. He was acclaimed for his work in a number of distinguished straight plays, although his triumphs were interspersed with several dismaying dry spells. In 1938 he produced and appeared in Philip Barry's♦ curious religious fantasy, *Here Come the Clowns*. The next year he toured briefly as the Stage Manager in *Our Town,*♦ then directed and played in *The Time of Your Life.*♦ Another major success was Tennessee Williams's *The Glass Menagerie*♦ (1945), which he directed and co-produced, and in which he created the role of Tom Wingfield, the brother-narrator. In 1946 he directed *The Iceman Cometh.*♦ John Mason Brown♦ wrote of his direction, "His groupings are fluid; his modulations of pace admirable; and his eye for the pictorial unflagging. He never fails to heighten and interpret the meannesses of life, so that they cease to be photography and emerge as art." He won further praise when he directed and acted in a bill of one-act plays, the best of which was *Hope Is the Thing with Feathers* (1948). Except for his stint as James Barton's♦ replacement in *Paint Your Wagon* (1952), all his subsequent endeavors were short-lived.

D'Oyly Carte Opera Company Founded after the success of Richard D'Oyly Carte's London production of *Trial by Jury,* the troupe enjoyed its greatest West End successes with its Gilbert♦ and Sullivan♦ productions, although early in its career it also mounted works by other men. It survived just over one hundred years, in its later decades doing only Gilbert and Sullivan. Its founder and some members of the company first appeared in America in 1879 to offer *H.M.S. Pinafore*♦ and the world premiere of *The Pirates of Penzance.*♦ However, American performers were also enlisted in these casts, and American musicians were employed. This remained the practice for all its original Gilbert and Sullivan mountings in this country. The company as a whole did not appear in America until 1934, after Winthrop Ames♦ revived what had been a flagging interest in the Savoyard comic operas. Between then and its dissolution the ensemble made numerous American visits. At first the tours were immensely successful and popular, and offered such great performers as Martyn Green, Derek Oldham, and Darrell Fancourt. However, in its last seasons its members seemed relatively talentless, its productions trapped in tradition, and it relied heavily on only the most popular works. As a result its final tours were not commercial successes. An attempt has been made to revive the company under a bequest from Bridget D'Oyly Carte, but the new ensemble has met with small success and its future is doubtful.

DRAKE, ALFRED [né ALFREDO CAPURRO] (b. 1914) Someone identified only as a "Broadway old-timer" is reputed to have said, "Nobody looks at a woman like Alfred Drake. It turns out he looks at *everything* like that. It's a good look." Whatever the reason for his particular magnetism, the darkly handsome Drake was the finest leading man of the 1940s and 1950s, combining a superb baritone voice with exceptional acting and comic skills. He studied singing in his native New York, then made his debut in the chorus of several 1935 Gilbert♦ and Sullivan♦ revivals. The next year he was in the chorus of *White Horse Inn,* after which he played increasingly important roles in *Babes in Arms*♦ (1937), *The Two Bouquets* (1938), *One for the Money* (1939), *The Straw Hat Revue* (1939), and *Two for the Show* (1940). In the last show he introduced "How High the Moon." Widespread recognition followed when he created the role of Curly, the hero of *Oklahoma!*♦ (1943), where he introduced "Oh, What a Beautiful Morning," "Oklahoma," "People Will Say We're in Love," and "The Surrey with the Fringe on Top." He won praise for his performances in *Sing Out, Sweet Land* (1944), *The Beggar's Holiday* (1946), *The Cradle Will Rock*♦ (1947), and as Alexander Soren, the Orson Welles-like hero of the comedy *Joy to the World* (1948), before starring as the shrew-taming Fred Graham in *Kiss Me, Kate*♦ (1948). After a brief appearance as the egotistical David Petri in *The Gambler* (1952), he scored again as the wily Hajj in *Kismet*♦ (1953), then played Othello and Benedick for the American Shakespeare Festival.♦ He later garnered excellent notices in three failures, *Kean* (1961), *Lorenzo* (1963), and *Gigi* (1973). Drake helped adapt several Italian plays, including *The Gambler,* and directed a number of shows.

DRAKE [BRYANT], SAMUEL (1768–1854) Born in Barnstable, England, it is believed he was a strolling player before coming with his family to America in 1810. He made his debut that year at Boston's Federal Theatre, ◆ remaining there until he was appointed manager for John Bernard ◆ at the latter's theatre in Albany in 1813. When his wife died in 1814, he packed up his family and embarked on a pilgrimage along the Ohio, Allegheny, and Mississippi rivers. In many of the cities along the way his was the first professional company ever to offer theatrical performances. Young Noah Ludlow, ◆ who was a member of his troupe for a time, has painted a vivid picture of their vicissitudes in *Dramatic Life as I Found It.* Ludlow also noted that "Drake was quite successful the first ten or twelve years." Thereafter, however, his age and increasing competition made touring less profitable for him. He had made prudent investments and retired to a farm in Kentucky. Among his most notable roles were Lear, Julius Caesar, and Shylock. Although he elected to spend a good part of his career in backwaters, his contemporaries were virtually unanimous in suggesting that he was a fine enough actor to have become a major star had he chosen to remain in the important theatrical centers.

Drama Criticism in America All too little is known about early American drama critics. Newspapers of the 18th and even early 19th century were published as much for the convenience of classified advertisers as they were for the dissemination of other news, so that there was room for few theatrical reviews, and these were often written to please advertisers. Most criticism was unsigned or at best given a fictitious byline. Eola Willis, in her history of the 18th-century Charleston stage, records what she claims was "the first dramatic criticism given of an American performance," but the unsigned excerpt she quotes from the Charleston *Gazette* of May 28, 1737, simply acknowledges that a performance of *The Recruiting Officer* had taken place and was well attended, and passes no judgment on either the play or the mounting. It was typical of many later notices.

Not until the early years of the 19th century did a few such critics as Stephen Cullen Carpenter of the Charleston *Courier,* J. W. S. Hows ◆ of the New York *Albion,* or, more importantly, Washington Irving ◆ begin to make names for themselves with

what today would be perceived as proper criticism. Yet even here, they and others frequently published initially under pseudonyms—although cognoscenti undoubtedly were aware of the real authorship— and their work was often first given major recognition when republished in contemporary theatrical magazines or in book form. Indeed, much of the more interesting criticism of the period came not in newspapers but in the usually short-lived theatrical journals that sprang up in larger theatrical centers. As a rule newspapers remained largely uninterested or blatantly partisan in favor of (or against) certain theatres or performers.

By general consensus, not until after the Civil War and the emergence of William Winter ◆ did American theatrical criticism come of age. His lead was followed by the appearance of such noted writers as T. Allston Brown, ◆ Henry Austin Clapp, ◆ E. A. Dithmar, ◆ William Dean Howells, ◆ James Huneker, ◆ Laurence Hutton, ◆ J. R. Towse, ◆ and A. C. Wheeler. ◆ Many, though not all, of these early critics were archly conservative, relating dramatic merit to moral standards and observance of traditional forms. The arrival on the scene of Ibsen ◆ and realism ◆ sharply divided critics into essentially an older, unyielding school and a newer, more open one. The controversy probably played a significant role in rushing American dramatic criticism into final maturity by broadening the scope of interest and knowledge required of critics, sharpening their reasoning and writing faculties, and attracting new readers. At about the same time the flowering of American newspapers and the concurrent rivalries caused papers to seek better critics, thereby improving standards everywhere. Only Clapp, among the critics just named, was not based in New York, but the simultaneous proliferation of both theatres and newspapers led to the rise of any number of fine critics away from New York. As a rule, these men rarely achieved national celebrity, but they were known and respected in the trade. Cincinnati's Montgomery Phister ◆ is a typical example.

The list of great 20th-century drama critics is long. Among them might be cited Brooks Atkinson, ◆ Robert Benchley, ◆ John Mason Brown, ◆ Claudia Cassidy, ◆ Percy Hammond, ◆ Walter Kerr, ◆ George Jean Nathan, ◆ Dorothy Parker, ◆ Henry Taylor Parker, ◆ Ashton Stevens, ◆ Alexander Woollcott, ◆ and Stark Young. ◆ Many of these critics departed from the Brahmin-like aloofness and impersonal approach of their predecessors, giving their writings a fresh vigor and a feistiness. However, not all newspapers maintained a totally impartial approach, and as late as the 1920s there were papers that refused to review plays if not advertised, and, in the same spirit, some papers bent over backwards to be kind to advertisers.

In recent years several problems have arisen. The marked shrinkage of theatrical production, especially on Broadway and in major road houses, has given critics fewer chances to hone their art. Moreover, in many cities newspaper competition has disappeared and the surviving paper has often viewed what is left of local theatre with indifference, even to occasionally appointing men or women with no real theatrical background as critics. The result has been a drastic falling off of the quality of dramatic criticism in several major cities, a falling off sometimes marked not only by ineptitude and ignorance, but coupled with a monopolistic arrogance as well. Of course, some newspapers and national magazines have retained high standards. Television has attempted to take up some of the slack, but the brevity of the reviews and television's insistence on the attractive appearance of its reviewers do not bode well for the future.

Although a few critics have been accorded biographies or other studies, the whole field of American dramatic criticism remains ripe for scholarship.

Drama Desk Founded in 1949 and chartered as a non-profit corporation in 1974, this association of writers on the theatre holds monthly luncheons in New York at which prominent theatre people are invited to talk and to discuss modern problems with the members.

Dramatic Mirror Founded in 1879 as the *New York Mirror,* but soon changed to the *New York Dramatic Mirror,* the theatrical trade paper was popularly known by its shorter name. Under the editorship of Harrison Grey Fiske♦ it was for many years the leading American theatrical trade journal, offering not only a wealth of important professional information but gossipy items for non-professionals as well. Fiske often turned the paper into a crusading sheet, as in his successful attempt to establish the Actors' Fund♦ and in his far less successful effort to fight the Trust's♦ monopolistic practices. Fiske retired in 1911. Under less imaginative editors the paper's popularity declined, and by the time it suspended publication in 1922 *Variety*♦ had long since supplanted it.

Dramatic Review for 1868, The, a burlesque afterpiece in one act by John Brougham.♦ Produced by Brougham at Brougham's Fifth Avenue Theatre.♦ January 25, 1869. 28 performances.

This afterpiece opened with an allegory featuring Manhatta and Brooklyna, "the oldest of Manhatta's family, and a remarkably forward young lady . . . holding but ferry little intercourse with her Ma, and that she means to abridge." Other characters in the opening were New Jersia, North Rivero (a fluent individual), East Rivero, and Public Opinion. Succeeding skits travestied *opéra bouffe* as "Bouffe à la Mode," G. L. Fox♦ and *Humpty Dumpty* as "The Fox's Nest," as well as new theatres and straight plays. A number of songs included one making fun of the velocipede craze.

The work is significant only as a curiosity, a precursor to the revues which first took hold of New York in 1894 with *The Passing Show.* ♦

Dramatists Guild, Inc., THE The most successful and enduring of organizations designed to protect the rights of dramatists, it was not the first. In 1878 Steele MacKaye♦ and Clay M. Greene♦ had established the American Dramatic Authors' Society "to secure protection for their work," but the group was short-lived and was followed in 1891 by the American Dramatists Club, which was later known as the Society of American Dramatists and Composers,♦ and which was headed by Bronson Howard. ♦ This group quickly enlisted 33 leading playwrights, but made little headway and remained for a time largely a social organization. In 1911 the Authors League of America was founded and included playwrights among its members. A subcommittee was formed in 1914 to work "towards the standardization of a dramatic contract," although initial attempts proved fruitless. Following the successful 1919 strike of Actors' Equity,♦ Channing Pollock♦ suggested the League form "an autonomous committee" to work exclusively for dramatists' rights. Out of this came the Dramatists Guild. Matters were brought to a head in 1925 when it was discovered that Fox Films had contracts with seven important producers which granted Fox uncontested film rights in return for backing plays. In March 1926 the committee met with producers, and on April 27 the first contract was signed. The Guild became an independent corporation in 1946 and has continued to serve as guardian of dramatists' welfare, guaranteeing, among other matters, minimum royalties and competitive bidding for film and other rights. According to George Middleton,♦ Howard's old group remained for many years as a separate affiliate of the Guild, known as the American Dramatists.

Dramatists Play Service, Inc. Disgruntled with the contracts offered playwrights for amateur rights, in 1936 Sidney Howard, ♦ then president of the Dramatists Guild, ♦ encouraged the establishment of this new group. Many leading authors of the period, including Howard Lindsay, ♦ George S. Kaufman, ♦ and others, quickly joined in support. Today the company is the principal rival to Samuel French, Inc. ♦ Although it does offer the work of some leading English dramatists, its emphasis has been on American writers, for many of whom it is now the exclusive agent for amateur rights. It also encourages young American authors. The Dramatists Guild remains a major partner in the company.

Dramatists' Theatre, Inc. Founded in 1923 to present the works of its members and other playwrights, the group may be seen as an unsuccessful predecessor to the Playwrights' Company. ♦ Founding members were Edward Childs Carpenter, ♦ Owen Davis, ♦ James Forbes, ♦ Cosmo Hamilton, ♦ and Arthur Richman, ♦ but their first offering, *The Goose Hangs High* ♦ (1924), was by an outsider, Lewis Beach. Subsequent productions included *Cock o' the Roost* (1924), *Young Blood* (1925), and *Scotch Mist* (1926)—the last two by Forbes—but when none of these presentations was as well received as the first, the organization was disbanded.

DRAPER, RUTH (1884–1956) The most famous of all American monologuists, she made her debut as a maid in *A Lady's Name* (1916), but shortly thereafter decided that her gifts for mimicry were best disclosed when she was alone on a bare stage, with little more than a scarf and a hat for props. She began to write her own monologues, offering them professionally first in London in 1920, and in New York the following year. Some of her monologues dealt with a single character, others with a succession of people. She frequently departed from her own script, improvising as the moment suggested. Her characters ranged from the most lordly to the most beggarly, and on some occasions, as in her depiction of a French wife saying goodbye to her husband who is leaving to join the Free French in the war, were done entirely in a foreign language. But her unique gift of expression made every line intelligible. For many years she began her bills with "Opening a Bazaar," in which she portrayed an English country lady. Brooks Atkinson ♦ noted, "Miss Draper does poke fun at her beflustered manners and her tea party grimaces. But the essence of the bazaar lady is thoroughly admirable. She is genuinely interested in the people of the village. She is kindly and thoughtful." She won applause throughout the world and was offering her show in New York, in her early seventies, when she died in her sleep after a performance.

Biography: *The Art of Ruth Draper,* Morton D. Zabel, New York, 1960.

Dream Girl, a comedy in two acts by Elmer Rice. ♦ Produced by the Playwrights' Company ♦ at the Coronet Theatre. December 14, 1945. 348 performances.

Georgina Allerton (Betty Field), who writes unpublishable novels and runs a small bookshop, wakes up to confront the likelihood of another awful day. To escape from her mundane existence, she daydreams. The moment she flicks on the radio as she dresses and hears the voice of a broadcasting psychiatrist, she imagines she is on the air with him, pouring out her problems. All through the day, a word here, a gesture there send her into fantasyland. Her life changes only when she meets a young man, Clark Redfield (Wendell Corey), who reviews books he doesn't read and hopes to be a sportswriter. They fall in love and will probably marry, "as long," Clark insists, "as you run your dreams, instead of letting them run you." She promises to try, because this newfound reality seems "some wonderful dream."

One of Elmer Rice's few ventures into light comedy, its principal part required the heroine to be on stage all but two minutes of the performance. Betty Field was Mrs. Rice. June Havoc and Richard Widmark led the road company. A musical version, *Skyscraper* (1965), starred Julie Harris. ♦

Dreamgirls, a musical in two acts. Book and lyrics by Tom Eyen. Music by Henry Krieger. Produced by Michael Bennett, ♦ the Shubert Organization, ♦ and others at the Imperial Theatre. December 20, 1981. 1,522 performances.

The Dreams are a black singing group who have emerged from the ghetto to scale the heights of success in the 1960s. However, just as they appear to reach the pinnacle their manager, Curtis Taylor, Jr. (Ben Harney), decides to dump one of the trio, Effie (Jennifer Holliday). Although he is her lover as well as her manager, Curtis has decided that Effie lacks the class to push the group to the top and keep it there. Besides, he has a new girl. Effie goes on to achieve a personal success alone.

Principal song: And I Am Telling You I Am Not Going

The real talent behind this show's success was

Bennett, who served not only as co-producer, but as director and choreographer. He worked with a solid, although by now traditional book about sordid backstage manipulations and a score that effectively re-created the black musical styles of the 1960s. Added strengths were the superb performances of Miss Holliday and a physical production which Elliot Norton♦ of the Boston *Herald-American* described as "a vivid moving pageant of lights in perpendicular towers and horizontal bridges, lights visible and invisible, that move about the stage to frame the actors and keep the action moving."

DRESSER, LOUISE (1882–1965) The blue-eyed, blonde singer was best known as a vaudevillian and identified with one song, "My Gal Sal." Her real surname was Kerlin, and she was the daughter of a railroad engineer who had once stopped some rowdies from badgering a fat newsboy on the train. That newsboy became the celebrated composer Paul Dresser, and it was Dresser who, in grateful memory of her father, gave the singer her stage name and wrote "My Gal Sal" for her. She also played in many Broadway shows, including *About Town* (1906), *The Girl Behind the Counter* (1907), *A Matinee Idol* (1910), *Broadway to Paris* (1912), *Potash and Perlmutter♦ (1913), and Rock-a-Bye Baby* (1918).

DRESSLER, MARIE [née LEILA MARIE KOERBER] (1869–1934) Famous as a hefty, bulldog-faced comic harridan, she was born in Coburg, Canada, and made her debut as Cigarette, the camp follower, in *Under Two Flags,* but soon switched to musicals. Her first New York appearance was in *The Robber of the Rhine* (1892). Later appearances included *Princess Nicotine* (1893), *Giroflé-Girofla* (1894), *Madeleine* (1895), *A Stage Party* (1895), *The Lady Slavey* (1896), *Hotel Topsy-Turvy* (1898), *The Man in the Moon* (1899), *Miss Prinnt* (1900), *The King's Carnival* (1901), *The Hall of Fame* (1902), *King Highball* (1902), *Higgledy Piggledy* (1904), *Twiddle Twaddle* (1906), and *The Boy and the Girl* (1909). In 1910 she created her most famous Broadway role, Tillie, the drudge who dreams of richer worlds, in *Tillie's Nightmare* and introduced "Heaven Will Protect the Working Girl." After *Roly Poly* (1912), she played largely in revues: *Marie Dressler's All-Star Gambols* (1913), *The Century Girl* (1916), *The Passing Show of 1921,♦* on tour in *Cinderella on Broadway* (1921), and in a book show that many critics felt to be a revue, *The Dancing Girl* (1923). She was long popular in vaudeville but received more universal recognition in films.

Autobiographies: *The Life Story of an Ugly*

Duckling, New York, 1924; and *My Own Story,* Boston, 1934.

DREW, JOHN (1827–62) He came as a ten-year-old with his parents from his native Dublin to New York, where his father assumed the post of treasurer at Niblo's Garden. ♦ Taking the theatre for granted and finding little interest in it, John elected to go to sea. However, after several years he changed his mind and in 1845 made an unsuccessful debut at the failing Richmond Hill Theatre. Discouraged, he sailed for Ireland, where he tried his hand at running a dry-goods store. He was soon back in America, first playing a season in Rochester, N.Y., then touring. He scored his first New York success as Dr. O'Toole in *The Irish Tutor* at the Bowery Theatre. ♦ Thereafter most of his best received roles were his Irish characters. In 1850 he joined the company at the Albany Museum, where he met and married Louisa Lane. Two years later he and Mrs. John Drew♦ joined the ensemble at Philadelphia's Chestnut Street Theatre,♦ and in 1853 they became co-managers of the Arch Street Theatre♦ with William Wheatley. ♦ An attempt by Drew to run the National Theatre in Washington quickly failed, so he returned to touring, both in America and in Ireland and England. When Mrs. Drew took over sole management of the Arch Street in 1861, he appeared under her aegis, playing not only his famous Irish parts but Meddle in *London Assurance,♦* William in *Black-Eyed Susan,* and Sir Lucius O'Trigger in *The Rivals,* as well as Sir Andrew Aguecheek and Dromio. He died as a result of injuries sustained in a fall.

DREW, JOHN (1853–1927) Like his namesake father his familiarity with theatre made him decide to look elsewhere for work, but a brief stint as a clock salesman for a department store in his native Philadelphia proved so boring that he reluctantly agreed to go on stage. He made his first appearance at his mother's Arch Street Theatre♦ in 1873 and continued to act there for two seasons, until Augustin Daly♦ spotted him and invited him to New York. His New York debut was as Bob Ruggles, the seemingly impecunious suitor, in *The Big Bonanza♦* (1875). He remained with Daly for many years, earning particular renown as a high comedian after the producer formed his second company in 1879. Among his great successes with the ensemble was his Petruchio. Of his performance one critic wrote, "His acting was consistently vigorous, and his speech, as usual, flawless." But it was as a polished gentleman—a roué, a blasé prince, or an avuncular guardian—in the era's drawing room comedies that he was best known. When he moved from Daly to Charles Frohman,♦ the striking-looking actor, with the large, heavy-lidded eyes and a drooping black moustache, continued in similar parts, mostly in works now long-forgotten. In 1908 he played the title role in Somerset Maugham's♦ *Jack Straw,* prompting the *Times* to exclaim, "John Drew at fifty, reveling like a boy, full of the spirit of juvenile lightheartedness, is an agreeable sight to see . . . He has the absolute assurance of a man who only needs to disclose his real self to walk away with all the honors." Among his last appearances were Maugham's *The Circle* (1921), *The School for Scandal* (1923), and *Trelawny of the Wells* (1925 and 1927). He was the uncle of Lionel,♦ Ethel,♦ and John Barrymore.♦

Autobiography: *My Years on the Stage,* New York, 1922.

DREW, Mrs. John [née Louisa Lane] (1820–97) Born in Lambeth Parish, London, she was the daughter of performers who traced their theatrical heritage to Elizabethan times. After her father's death she was brought to America by her mother, and made her American debut in 1827 playing the Duke of York to Junius Brutus Booth's♦ Richard III at Philadelphia's Walnut Street Theatre.♦ Shortly thereafter she played Albert to Edwin Forrest's♦ William Tell in Baltimore, then won critical acclaim in her New York debut at the Bowery Theatre♦ as Little Pickle in *The Spoiled Child.* She continued to act for the next seventy years, her most celebrated role being Mrs. Malaprop in *The Rivals,* in which she often toured with Joseph Jefferson♦ as Bob Acres. T. Allston Brown♦ called her "the most wonderfully versatile actress on the American stage." But her principal claim to fame was her stint as manager of Philadelphia's Arch Street Theatre,♦ which she ran with an iron hand from 1861 to 1892 and which, under her rule, was generally considered to offer the finest company and finest productions outside of New York. She presented a repertory of classics interspersed with many of the most popular new plays of her era. A small, somewhat wispy woman, with large eyes, which she passed on to her Barrymore heirs, her appearance belied her inner strengths. She was married at least three times, always to actors—to Henry Hunt, whom she divorced, to George Moosop, and to John Drew.♦ Under her stern tutelage her son John Drew♦ and her daughter Georgiana Drew Barrymore♦ began their own careers, and she was responsible for much of the upbringing of Georgiana's children—Lionel,♦ Ethel,♦ and John Barrymore.♦

Autobiography: *Autobiographical Sketch of Mrs. John Drew,* New York, 1899.

Driving Miss Daisy, a play (performed without intermission) by Alfred Uhry. Produced at the Playwrights Horizons Theatre. April 15, 1987. 1,195 performances. PP.

Daisy Werthan (Dana Ivey) is an aging Jewish matron in post-World-War-II Atlanta. Because she cannot safely drive herself any longer, her son (Ray Gill) hires Hoke (Morgan Freeman), a black man, to drive her around and to look after her as unobtrusively as possible. At first the relationship is prickly, but with time the pair develops a rewarding friendship.

A small, warm but fundamentally unimportant play, its winning of the Pulitzer Prize attested again to the paucity of serious and meritorious writing either on Broadway or off. Wisely, this production remained off-Broadway for its entire run. A film version earned Jessica Tandy♦ an Oscar.

Uhry (b. 1936), a native Atlantan and graduate of Brown University, had worked on numerous musicals, but only *The Robber Bridegroom* (1975) enjoyed any measure of success. He has also written for television. This was his first straight play.

Drunkard; The or, The Fallen Saved, a play in five acts by W. H. Smith. See production details below.

The villainous Lawyer Cribbs has long held a grudge against the Middleton family, even though he has served as their attorney. When young Edward Middleton's father dies, Cribbs attempts to persuade Edward to dispossess a poor mother and daughter who are Middleton's tenants. Instead, Edward falls in love with the daughter, Mary, and marries her. But Edward has a weakness—drink. Cribbs insidiously encourages Edward's weakness, until Edward, ashamed and seemingly impoverished, flees to the degradation of New York's Five Points. Cribbs follows him there and attempts to turn him into a forger, but Edward's better nature prevails. Edward's foster-brother William and a rich philanthropist Arden Rencelaw seek him out, rehabilitate him, and reunite him with his wife and young daughter. Cribbs is forced to reveal that he has hidden Edward's grandfather's will and that Edward is really still a wealthy man.

The play was first presented, as part of a temperance crusade, in Boston on February 25, 1844. Within a year it had been played there a hundred times, including performances at the

Tremont Temple and at the Boston Museum.♦ It was offered by a temperance group in New York in 1844 but failed to cause a stir. However, in 1850 it was revived by several New York theatres, most notably at Barnum's American Museum,♦ where its run of one hundred consecutive performances, beginning July 8, set a long-run record for the time. C. W. Clarke,♦ who played Edward at Barnum's, was ever afterward identified with the role and was known popularly as "Drunkard Clarke." A revival in 1933 in a small Los Angeles theatre was played for laughs but ran twenty years, chalking up an American record of 7,510 performances. Only the musical *The Fantasticks*♦ has run longer in this country.

W[illiam] H[enry] [Sedley] Smith (1806–72), the son of a British army officer, was born in Wales and came to America to perform at the Walnut Street Theatre♦ in Philadelphia in 1827, making his debut as the sponging Jeremy Diddler in *Raising the Wind*. He also played in New York and Boston before joining the Boston Museum in 1843 as actor and stage manager. He remained there until 1860. In later years he managed San Francisco's California Theatre♦ for Barrett♦ and McCullough.♦

Du Barry, a play in five acts by David Belasco.♦ Produced by Belasco at the Criterion Theatre. December 25, 1901. 165 performances.

Jeanette Vaubernier (Mrs. Leslie Carter♦) is a sweet Parisian milliner, who promises to meet a young soldier, Cosse-Brissac (Hamilton Revelle), but instead is lured into a gambling house by Comte Du Barry (Campbell Gollan). There she becomes the plaything of French society and is married to Du Barry's brother to give her a certain respectability. She continues to love Cosse-Brissac, although their meetings bring them little but pain. In the end, like her royal associates, she is caught up in the revolution and sent to the guillotine.

Although William Winter♦ bemoaned the fact that the play contained "a plenitude of needless talk," his dissent was in the minority. Shortly after the play opened, a sensational, headline-grabbing lawsuit disclosed that Belasco had taken most of the play from *La Du Barry,* a work by a French poet-dramatist Jean Richepin.

Du Barry Was a Lady, a musical comedy in two acts. Book by B. G. De Sylva♦ and Herbert Fields.♦ Lyrics and music by Cole Porter.♦ Produced by De Sylva at the 46th Street Theatre. December 6, 1939. 408 performances.

Louis Blore (Bert Lahr♦) is a night-club washroom attendant. He loves the club's star, May Daley

(Ethel Merman♦), who has eyes only for a reporter, Alex Barton (Ronald Graham). Louis attempts to give Alex a mickey, but accidentally drinks it himself. Unconscious, he dreams that he is Louis XV and that May is Madame Du Barry. When he awakes he realizes the futility of his quest, so resumes scrubbing basins.

Principal songs: Do I Love You? · Friendship

Although the show's weak score typifies the slump many Broadway composers suffered about this time, the brashness and brassiness of the musical and its superb stars turned the offering into a hit.

DU BOIS, Raoul Pène (1914?–85) A New York-born designer, famous for his colorful, often gaudy costumes and sets, his work was first seen on Broadway when he created costumes for the *Ziegfeld Follies of 1934.*♦ He later designed costumes for such shows as *Jumbo*♦ (1935), *Ziegfeld Follies of 1936, Hooray for What!* (1937), *Leave It to Me!*♦ (1938), *Carmen Jones*♦ (1943), *The Music Man*♦ (1957), and *Gypsy*♦ (1959). He created both costumes and sets for, among others, *Du Barry Was a Lady*♦ (1939), *Panama Hattie*♦ (1940), *Call Me Madam*♦ (1950), *Wonderful Town*♦ (1953), *No, No, Nanette*♦ (1971), and *Irene*♦ (1973).

DUFF, James C. (1854–1928) A theatrical producer, best known for first bringing *H.M.S. Pinafore*♦ to New York, he offered the American or New York premieres of many other Gilbert♦ and Sullivan,♦ Strauss,♦ and Von Suppe operettas as well as French opéra bouffe♦. His J. C. Duff Opera Company was an important touring ensemble in the 1880s and 1890s, bringing comic opera to many large and small theatrical centers. Harry B. Smith♦ called him the "most able and artistic producer of operetta" in this early period. He remained active, although on a reduced scale, all through his life, his last production being a revival of *The Beggar's Opera* a few months before his death. He was the son of John A. Duff (1820–89), who was born in Ireland but came to America as a young man. After successfully operating restaurants in Albany and New York he took over the Olympic Theatre in 1866 and later operated the Broadway and Standard theatres. He was the father-in-law of Augustin Daly,♦ with whom he worked closely for many years.

DUFF, John (1787–1831) The Dublin-born actor left a successful stage career in his homeland to try his luck in America. He made his debut in Boston in 1810. Philadelphia first saw him and his "stupendous" range when he acted Macbeth and the Three Singles (Pertinax Single, Peregrine Single, and Percival Single) in *Three and the Deuce* for his first appearance there in 1812. Two years later he made his New York debut playing Octavian and the Three Singles. Among his most famous parts were the title roles in the tragedy *Richard III*♦ and the melodrama *The Stranger,* ♦ and Jeremy Diddler, the impecunious sponger, in the farce *Raising the Wind.* He frequently performed with his wife, Mrs. Duff,♦ and made a profitable trip to England with her shortly before his death.

DUFF, JOHN A., see *Duff, James*

DUFF, MRS. JOHN [née MARY ANN or MARIANNA DYKE] (1794–1857) She made her debut in her native Dublin as a dancer, but soon showed ability as an actress. After rejecting a proposal of marriage from the poet Thomas Moore (who later married her sister) in favor of one from fellow performer John Duff,♦ she came to America with him. She made her American debut in Boston in 1810 as Juliet, remaining there for two years before following her husband to Philadelphia, where she initially appeared in 1812 and where she remained five years. Her first New York performance was in 1823, when she played Hermione in *The Distressed Mother* opposite the Orestes of Junius Brutus Booth.♦ She soon came to eclipse her husband in esteem and popularity and is generally looked back upon as one of the first great artists of our stage. Among her major roles were Ophelia, Jane Shore, Belvidera, Portia, and Lady Macbeth. According to William Winter,♦ who never saw her, "Mrs. Duff seems to have been lovely more than beautiful; strong in affectionate, melting charms of womanhood rather than in resolute, commanding, brilliant intellect . . . She had dark, brilliant eyes, and she had a voice that ranged from the clarion call of frantic passion to the softest accents of maternal love." The elder Booth, writing from closer experience, called her simply "the greatest actress in the world." She continued to act after her husband's death, made a brief, unfortunate second marriage during a period of mental instability, then retired shortly after her third marriage to a New Orleans lawyer.

Biography: *Mrs. Duff,* Joseph N. Ireland, Boston, 1882.

DUFF, MARY (1811?–52) The daughter of John♦ and Mrs. Duff,♦ she made her debut as Ernestine in *The Somnambulist* in 1831 at Philadelphia's Arch Street Theatre.♦ Her first New York appearance

followed shortly thereafter, but she performed largely at the Arch Street Theatre until she married A. A. Addams♦ in 1835. Joseph N. Ireland♦ recalled, "On her first appearance she was radiant in youthful loveliness. Her person was eminently beautiful and above the medium height, her voice was of extensive compass and beautiful in every tone, and her spirits so exuberant, that even in her novitiate her best friends feared that 'overacting' would be the rock on which her bark would split—an apprehension all too truthfully fulfilled." The marriage was short-lived, as was her second to Joseph Gilbert. Meanwhile she began to tour the Eastern seaboard, but also played extended engagements in the Western states, whose baleful influences New York critics blamed for her increasingly broad style. Among her more popular roles were Kate Hardcastle, Lady Teazle, and Lady Macbeth, along with such now forgotten parts as Donna Hypolita in *The Phantom Bride* and Genevra in *The Dragon Knight.* After her marriage to J. G. Porter she sometimes performed as Mrs. Porter, but playbills usually included the reminder that she had been Mary Duff. She died while still at the height of her popularity.

Duffy [James] **and Sweeney** [Fred] "Mr. Duffy and Mr. Sweeney" was a celebrated vaudeville "nut" act. Typically, the team would begin with Sweeney telling a pointless story and Duffy falling asleep. Sweeney would then wake Duffy; Duffy would start to bow by way of apology; and a bowing match would ensue which would quickly deteriorate into a slapping match. The act was considered one of the funniest on stage, but was booked only reluctantly, for the pair had earned a reputation for irresponsible pranks, and Duffy was a notorious drunkard. Once in Memphis, playing to a particularly lifeless audience, Duffy took a somewhat forced bow, then announced to the surprised watchers, "And now, ladies and gentlemen, my partner will go through the aisles with a baseball bat and beat the bejesus out of you." Often one or the other would not appear at all, prompting Albee♦ to tell his manager, "When you get them together, cancel them." According to vaudeville historian Douglas Gilbert, their antics made them "the most talked-of two-act in the profession," and their notoriety sometimes helped get them bookings. Duffy was found dead on a New York street, while Sweeney ended his days in straitened circumstances.

DUKE, VERNON [né VLADIMIR DUKELSKY] (1903–69) A Russian-born composer, classically trained, he wrote scores for London musicals before coming to

New York in the early thirties. His first American score, for *Walk a Little Faster* (1932), included "April in Paris." In 1934 he interpolated "Autumn in New York" in *Thumbs Up!*, as well as creating melodies for the *Ziegfeld Follies.* ♦ Out of his music for the *Ziegfeld Follies of 1936* came "I Can't Get Started." His best score is generally acknowledged to be that for his first American book show, *Cabin in the Sky* ♦ (1940), which offered "Taking a Chance on Love" and the title song. Eddie Cantor ♦ introduced "We're Having a Baby" in Duke's score for *Banjo Eyes* (1941), but thereafter all Duke's efforts failed to please playgoers: *The Lady Comes Across* (1942), *Jackpot* (1944), *Sadie Thompson* (1944), *Two's Company* (1952), and *The Littlest Revue* (1956).

Autobiography: *Passport to Paris,* Boston, 1955.

Dulcy, a comedy in three acts by George S. Kaufman ♦ and Marc Connelly. ♦ Produced by George C. Tyler ♦ and H. H. Frazee ♦ at the Frazee Theatre. August 13, 1921. 246 performances.

Dulcinea Smith (Lynn Fontanne ♦) is an ambitious but feather-brained young lady given to spouting bromides and getting her husband, Gordon (John Westley), into jams whenever she attempts to help him out. Since Gordon is about to merge his business with that of C. Rogers Forbes (Wallis Clark), Dulcy invites the Forbeses and their daughter Angela (Norma Lee) for a weekend. She also invites the scenario writer Vincent Leach (Howard Lindsay ♦), who is in love with Angela; her brother, Bill (Gregory Kelly ♦); and a rich young man she has met at a party, Schuyler Van Dyck (Gilbert Douglas). She manages to irritate Mr. Forbes by encouraging Angela and Vincent to elope and by having Schuyler offer to support Gordon in a venture in opposition to Mr. Forbes. But Blair Patterson (George Allison) arrives, announcing that Schuyler is actually simply a harmless madman who thinks he is rich. Luckily for Dulcy, Forbes sees Patterson, who is an attorney for the real Van Dycks, and offers Gordon an even better deal than he did at first. And then it is discovered that Angela eloped not with Vincent, but with Bill. Though things have turned out well, Dulcy promises never again to meddle. After all, "A burnt child dreads the fire. Once bitten—"

Heywood Broun ♦ wrote in the *Tribune,* "*Dulcy* is an ingenious trick play and the patter which introduces the legerdemain is even better than the stunts." The play not only established the reputations of Kaufman and Connelly but made a star of Lynn Fontanne.

Dummy, The, a comedy in four acts by Harvey J. O'Higgins and Harriet Ford. ♦ Produced at the Hudson Theatre. April 13, 1914. 200 performances.

Young Barney Cook (Ernest Truex ♦) may still be in knickers, but he has earned a reputation as a brilliant boy detective. So when little Beryl Meredith (Joyce Fair) is kidnapped, he poses as a dim-witted youngster to catch the kidnappers and free the child.

Based on O'Higgins's popular Detective Barney stories, the play successfully blended elements of the then voguish "crook play" with comedy. Joyce Fair was later better known as Clare Boothe ♦ [Luce].

Dumont's Minstrels Founded by Frank Dumont, who had served with John L. Carncross, ♦ the group took over Philadelphia's Eleventh Street Opera in 1895 and continued there until the playhouse was demolished in 1911. Since the theatre had been employed uninterruptedly for blackface entertainments from 1855, when Sanford's Minstrels took over its stage, it earned distinction as the most enduring minstrel theatre in American history. With his old theatre gone, Dumont took over the old Dime Museum in Arch Street and converted it to Dumont's Theatre. He remained there with his troupe until his death in 1913. Dumont's Minstrels were essentially a traditional company, looked upon by many critics as a threadbare vestige of the past but by others as a valid holdover. Among its most celebrated members were Harry Shunk, Johnny Murphy, and, best of all, Hughey Dougherty, ♦ generally acknowledged as the finest stump speaker of his day. Dougherty eventually published a popular book of his stump speeches and jokes. After Dumont's death, the troupe continued under other management until 1928, giving Philadelphia the distinction of offering the longest tradition of permanent minstrelsy as well as the last major professional ensemble.

DUNBAR, PAUL LAURENCE (1872–1906) Most famous as a black poet and novelist, he was also an important figure in the development of black musical theatre. In 1898 he wrote the libretto and lyrics for the first major black musical to play a first-class white house, *Clorindy;* ♦ *or, the Origin of the Cake Walk;* although the entertainment was not a full-length show and the house was the Casino's ♦ summer roof garden. But Dunbar also served as lyricist for the first full-length black musical to play a standard Broadway theatre, *In Dahomey* ♦ (1903). He wrote lyrics for several songs that were interpolated into other musicals.

DUNCAN, Augustin (1873–1954) After making his debut in 1893 in his native San Francisco, he toured for seven years before first appearing in New York in 1900 as Jamy opposite the Henry V of Richard Mansfield. ◆ He continued to play opposite such celebrated figures as William Gillette ◆ and Charles Coburn ◆ in increasingly important roles both in New York and London. In 1919 he was a charter member of the Theatre Guild, ◆ and his performance in the title role of *John Ferguson* as well as his direction of the play helped give the new company its first success. Shortly thereafter he severed his connections with the Guild over artistic differences. Among the shows he both directed and acted in were *The Cradle Song* (1921), in which he took the minor role of The Poet; *The Detour* ◆ (1921), in which he portrayed the unsympathetic father, Stephen Hardy; Eugene O'Neill's ◆ *The First Man* (1922), in which he played Curtis Jason, the anthropologist who must reach an understanding with the son he did not want; *Hell-Bent fer Heaven* ◆ (1924), in which he played the small part of the old father, David Hunt; and *Juno and the Paycock* (1926), in which he was Captain Jack Boyle. He also directed plays in which he did not appear, such as *Kempy* ◆ (1922). In the late 1920s his eyesight began to fail and by the early 1930s he was blind. Nevertheless he continued to perform, playing John of Gaunt and the Ghost in Maurice Evans's ◆ productions of *Richard II* ◆ (1937) and *Hamlet* ◆ (1938), and making his last appearance as the Father in *Lute Song* (1946). He was the brother of the famed dancer Isadora Duncan.

DUNCAN, Rosetta (1900–1959) and Vivian (1902–86) A sister singing and dancing act, the girls were Los Angeles natives who were given their start in vaudeville by Gus Edwards. ◆ They played two-a-day for many years and appeared in several Broadway shows, but are best remembered for one vehicle, *Topsy and Eva* ◆ (1924), which they helped write and in which they performed for four years. They revived it as late as 1942.

DUNCAN, [Robert] Todd (b. 1903) The black singer was born in Danville, Ky. His Broadway appearances have been rare but always memorable. He was the original Porgy in *Porgy and Bess* ◆ (1935) in which he introduced "Bess, You Is My Woman Now" and "I Got Plenty O' Nuttin'," and later played in *Cabin in the Sky* ◆ (1940) and *Lost in the Stars* ◆ (1949), in which he sang the title song.

DUNHAM, Katherine (b. 1910) The Chicago-born dancer and choreographer appeared in *Cabin in the Sky* ◆ (1940) and in *Carib Song* (1945); but is best remembered by playgoers for dance-revues she created and starred in, and which featured black dancing from around the world: *Tropical Revue* (1943), *Bal Negre* (1946), and a titleless 1950 offering.

DUNLAP, William (1766–1839) The earliest enduring figure of the American theatre, he was born in Perth Amboy, N.J., and although he apparently had little formal education, he read Shakespeare while still a youth. His attraction to the theatre was consolidated during the Revolutionary War when he watched British soldiers perform in New York, where his parents had moved. Nevertheless, he decided to become a professional painter and sailed for London in 1784 to study with Benjamin West. However, London theatres proved an irresistible lure. Watching the latest plays and classics performed by Mrs. Siddons, Charles Kemble, and the other leading performers of the day established standards which he strove to maintain throughout his career. He returned to America in 1787, where, inspired by Royall Tyler's *The Contrast,* ◆ he wrote a play, *The Modest Soldier; or, Love in New York,* for the American Company. ◆ The play was rejected, but a second play, *The Father; or, American Shandyism* ◆ (1789), a comedy examining love among the rich and their servants, was accepted and produced successfully. He continued to write for the company and in 1796 was made one of its partners, along with John Hodgkinson ◆ and Lewis Hallam. ◆ When Hallam withdrew from the partnership in 1797, Dunlap and Hodgkinson continued, and together opened the Park Theatre ◆ in 1798. Two of his most successful plays appeared in 1798: *André,* ◆ recounting the last days of the Revolutionary spy; and *The Stranger,* ◆ in which the mysterious central figure turns out to be a nobleman, who is reconciled with his erring wife. This latter work was a translation from the German of August Friedrich Ferdinand von Kotzebue, ◆ then the rage of Continental theatres and called "the German Shakespeare." The translation initiated Kotzebue's American vogue, and Dunlap translated at least ten more of his plays, though none proved as enduring as *The Stranger.* At the same time, Hodgkinson resigned, so Dunlap continued to run the Park alone as well as provide plays for it. He also leased the Haymarket in Boston and worked closely with the Chestnut Street Theatre ◆ in Philadelphia. Under his aegis the Park presented a repertory of modern and traditional works and offered English performers opportunities of appearing in America. He was forced to relinquish his management in 1805, when he declared bankruptcy, but a year later returned to serve as assistant to the new manager, Thomas Abthorpe Cooper. ◆ In 1812 he accompanied George Frederick Cooke on his American tour, then retired. But he continued to write plays—some sixty or seventy in all, mostly adaptations from the French or German—and in 1832 published his monumental *History of the American Theatre*. He also attempted to publish his plays, but only one volume was issued before his death.

During his theatrical career Dunlap endeavored, with only limited success, to overcome the snobbish preference for things British. Although he welcomed the best artists and works from overseas, he actively encouraged American actors and playwrights. He was also aware of the conflict in the theatre between commercialism and art, and tried, without result, to get the government to subsidize playhouses. A highly puritanical man, he frequently eliminated what he deemed offensive passages in works he translated, and he fought futilely against the accepted practice of allowing a special section in theatres set aside for ladies of questionable virtue.

Quinn◆ concluded a long chapter devoted to Dunlap by noting, "[he] had the soul of an artist and the intrepidity of the pioneer, and his place in our dramatic literature will remain secure."

Autobiography: *Diary of William Dunlap*, New York, 1930.

DUNNING, PHILIP , see *Broadway*

DUNNOCK, MILDRED [DOROTHY] (b. 1900) Born in Baltimore, the actress made her debut in *Life Begins* (1932) and later appeared in such plays as *The Corn Is Green* (1940) and *Another Part of the Forest* (1946). For years one of the most respected supporting actresses in American theatre despite her mousy looks and plaintive voice, she is best remembered for three roles: Linda Loman, the long-suffering, loving wife, in *Death of a Salesman*◆ (1949); the weak, boozy Mrs. Constable in *In the Summer House*◆ (1953); and Big Mama, the vacuous, subjugated wife, in *Cat on a Hot Tin Roof*◆ (1955).

DUPREE, MINNIE (1875?–1947) Born in La Crosse, Wis., the gamin-faced actress made her debut in 1887 in a touring company of the *The Unknown*. The following year she appeared in New York in *Held by the Enemy*, playing the small part of Susan McCreery. Her talents were immediately recog-

nized, and for the next dozen years she was awarded important supporting roles in an unending series of plays. Her first leading role was Mary Andrews, the hapless heroine caught between two murderous rivals, in *Women and Wine* (1900). She next played the piquant Clara in *The Climbers*◆ (1901); was starred for the first time as the capricious but good-hearted Rose in *A Rose o' Plymouth-town* (1902); and then played the waitress who loves but loses her student prince in *Heidelberg* (1902). A major success came as Helen Stanton, the daughter loyal to her long-lost father, in *The Music Master*◆ (1904), and was followed by a second one as both Elspeth and Lady Elizabeth Tyrrell in *The Road to Yesterday*◆ (1906), a play in which the heroine dreams she lives in the England of 300 years before. After portraying the unhappily married Kate Grayson in *The Real Thing* (1911), she spent several years touring vaudeville in short plays. Most of her later appearances were in failures, the notable exceptions being Matilda, the patient wife of a topering husband, in *The Old Soak*◆ (1922); Mrs. Burns, the sullen stepmother, in *The Shame Woman*◆ (1923); and Mrs. Midget, one of the newly dead, in a touring company of *Outward Bound* (1924). In 1941 she was a replacement in the role of Martha Brewster in *Arsenic and Old Lace*. ◆ Her final appearance was as the grandmother in *Land's End* (1946).

DUPREZ, CHARLES H. (1830–1902) Acknowledged as one of the most astute impresarios of the minstrel era, he was born in Paris and came to this country as a young man. He settled in New Orleans, where he began his stage career in 1852. In a short while he established several minstrel troupes, the most famous and long-lived being Duprez and Benedict's Minstrels. He and Lew Benedict founded the company in 1865 and, after Benedict's retirement, he ran it alone until his own retirement in 1885. Besides handling both financial and artistic matters with great acumen, he was considered among the shrewdest advertisers in the trade. In one clever promotional stunt he published a book known as "Rules for Visiting a Place of Amusement," a tongue-in-cheek discussion of theatrical etiquette, which offered such advice as "As soon as you have been seated eat peanuts, whistle and stamp your feet so everybody will know you're an old theatre-goer."

DURANG, JOHN (1768–1822) Dancer, acrobat, puppeteer, and actor, he was born in Lancaster, Pa., but grew up in York, where he attended the German school attached to Christ Lutheran Church, and in Philadelphia. It was in this latter city that he was first exposed to theatricals, and he made his debut there at the Southwark Theatre♦ in 1785 as a dancer, having been hired by Lewis Hallam, Jr.♦ Although Philadelphia remained his base, he performed up and down the Northeastern coast and made an extended tour of Canada. He worked under all the great managers of his day, including William Dunlap,♦ John Bill Ricketts,♦ Thomas Wignell,♦ and Alexander Reinagle.♦ He appeared in numerous pantomimes, often taking the role of Scaramouche, entertained between acts, and sometimes accepted small dramatic parts—a necessity in an era of quick-changing repertory. For a time he was so popular that he was often the only performer mentioned in the cramped newspaper advertisements of his day. From 1806 to 1810 he headed a small troupe which brought theatre to Pennsylvania's "Dutch" country. In his later years he wrote and illustrated a memoir, which was not published until a century and a half after his death. Durang had five children, all of whom spent some time on the stage. Charles (1796–1870) was an actor, dancer and choreographer of some celebrity in Philadelphia and New York, but is best remembered as the author of *The Philadelphia Stage from the Year 1749 to the Year 1855,* much of it derived from his father's papers, and published serially by the Philadelphia *Sunday Dispatch* between 1854 and 1860. Ferdinand (1798–1831), like his father and brother, was both a dancer and an actor. He made his debut in Philadelphia, but spent most of his short professional life at the Chatham Garden Theatre and Bowery Theatre♦ in New York. Reliable accounts credit him with suggesting to Francis Scott Key that the old drinking song "To Anacreon in Heaven" would fit the lyric Key had written as "The Star-Spangled Banner." Augustus (1800–1818?) was briefly something of a child prodigy, making his debut in Philadelphia as Tom Thumb at the age of six, but he abandoned the stage to become a sea captain and was lost at sea. Charlotte (1803–24) danced briefly in Philadelphia, while Juliet (1805–49) toured for many years under her married name, Mrs. Godey, playing leading roles in provincial companies. Durang's sister, Catherine, was a popular singer.

Autobiography: *The Memoir of John Durang,* Pittsburgh, 1966.

DURANTE, [JAMES FRANCIS] JIMMY (1893–1980) Famed for his prominent nose which he called his "schnozzola," his raspy voice, his fractured English, and his stiff-kneed strut, the comedian began his career in 1910 as a honky-tonk pianist at Diamond Tony's Saloon on Coney Island. Sometime between 1919 and 1923 he formed a trio with Lou Clayton and Eddie Jackson. Their "nut" act won instant popularity, and they were invited to play Loew's State in 1926. A year later they played the Palace.♦ From the start Durante was the center of attraction, so when the team appeared in *Show Girl* (1929) and *The New Yorkers* (1930) he was assigned important roles while his partners played bit parts. The act was disbanded in 1931, although it was frequently reunited for special appearances. Durante then appeared in *Strike Me Pink* (1933), *Jumbo♦* (1935), *Red, Hot and Blue!* (1936), *Stars in Your Eyes* (1939), and *Keep Off the Grass* (1940). At a time when much humor was increasingly biting, his humor remained sunny and he himself the butt of his sharpest digs—"There are a million good lookin' guys, but I'm a novelty." In a typical rough and tumble antic, he sang "Wood" in *The New Yorkers* while cluttering the stage with every conceivable wooden object. Another favorite routine was his wild dismantling of a piano. In later years he was popular in nightclubs and on radio and television.

DUSE, ELEONORA (1858–1924) The greatest Italian actress of her age, she made her American debut in 1893 as Marguerite Gautier in *La Dame aux Camélias.* This tour was followed by several more over the next eleven years; then, after a 19-year hiatus, she made a farewell tour in 1923, during which she died in Pittsburgh. She was a small, darkish, lithe, woman, with sad eyes, who was credited by many with furthering the movement toward realistic acting. She is said to have eschewed the heavy makeup common at the time and, despite occasional marked moments of fidgetiness, to have usually seemed to underplay and to have been most eloquent in repose. Among her notable vehicles were *Magda, Ghosts, Rosmersholm, The Lady from the Sea,* and three by her lover D'Annunzio: *La Gioconda, Francesca da Rimini,* and *La Citta Morta.* Although many American critics sensed a falling away from her earlier excellence during her last tour, Alexander Woollcott♦ insisted, without any irony, that she retained "a kind of physical eloquence, a beauty in motion" equaled only by Charlie Chaplin.

Biography: *Eleonora Duse,* Arthur Symons, London, 1926.

D'USSEAU, ARNAUD, see *Deep Are the Roots* and *Tomorrow the World*

Dynamo, a play in three acts by Eugene O'Neill.◆ Produced by the Theatre Guild◆ at the Martin Beck Theatre. February 11, 1929. 50 performances.

The Reverend Light (George Gaul), a devout but somewhat arrogant Christian, and Ramsay Fife (Dudley Digges◆), an atheist, are unfriendly neighbors. When the minister's son, Reuben (Glenn Anders◆), falls in love with Fife's daughter, the teasing Ada (Claudette Colbert), father and son have a falling out. Reuben denounces religion and goes in search of truth. He returns years later, having made science his god, but when he is seduced by Ada he kills her and then electrocutes himself by throwing himself on the dynamo.

Although Brooks Atkinson◆ observed, "Writing on the most essential theme of modern life, Mr. O'Neill has strength and breadth, and a lashing poetry," the play, which O'Neill planned as the first of a trilogy, was a failure. For some critics Lee Simonson's◆ brilliant second-act setting, showing the interior of a hydro-electric plant was the most memorable feature of the evening.

E

EAGELS, JEANNE (1894–1929) For a brief time one of the most exciting and promising actresses of the American theatre, the slender, intense blonde beauty had her career cut down at its height by her erratic personal behavior and a reputed drug addiction. Born in Kansas City, Mo., she made her debut at the age of seven as Puck in *A Midsummer Night's Dream.* ◆ She first appeared in New York in 1911 when she took a small part in the musical *Jumping Jupiter.* Minor roles followed in *The Mind-the-Paint Girl* (1912); on tour in *The Crinoline Girl* (1914); and *Outcast* (1916). She first garnered critical attention after George Arliss◆ hired her to play opposite him in *Paganini, The Professor's Love Story, Disraeli,* and *Hamilton.* In his autobiography, Arliss echoed the praises of contemporary critics, extolling her as an "amazingly clever" performer "with unerring judgment and artistry." She next scored as Ruth Atkins, a war orphan adopted by a confirmed bachelor, in *Daddies* ◆ (1918), and as Mary Furlong, a store mannequin brought to life by a love-sick artist, in *A Young Man's Fancy* (1919). In the wake of several failures she was selected at the urging of Maxine Elliott◆ to portray the role with which she was identified thereafter, Sadie Thompson, a prostitute who seduces a proselytizing minister, in *Rain* ◆ (1922). The *Times*'s John Corbin◆ described her as acting "with an emotional power as fiery and unbridled in effect as it is artistically restrained. Among her sailor cronies she rollicks and drinks whisky with more than the swagger of the Bowery. Her conduct toward the gentle folk of the hotel party is a marvelous mingling of social awe and human arrogance. Her demeanor toward Davidson is subtly felt and inerrantly expressed in all the gamut of its tragic moods." She played the part for over four years before essaying the role of Simone, a rich lady who falls in love with a man she had hired to masquerade as her paramour, in *Her Cardboard Lover* (1927).

Biography: *The Rain Girl,* Edward Doherty, Philadelphia, 1930.

EAMES, CLARE (1896–1930) Born in Hartford, Conn., and raised in Cleveland, the petite, aristocratic actress, who was a niece of soprano Emma Eames, studied in Paris and at the American Academy of Dramatic Arts◆ before making her debut in 1918 in a triple bill that included Eugene O'Neill's◆ *Ile.* She won critical attention when she played the title role in John Drinkwater's *Mary Stuart* (1921). Woollcott◆ observed, "Miss Eames brings much to the part—the keen wit, the entire comprehension, the royal quality. It is only as Mary, the arch fascinator, that she is a little lacking." Although other critics also lamented the absence of a certain fire or glamour, she kept busy for the remainder of her short career before her early death. Among her notable roles were Miss Tiffany in *Fashion;* Lady Macbeth opposite James K. Hackett◆; and Hedda Gabler, in a series of 1924 revivals. She also played important parts in two plays by her husband, Sidney Howard◆: Carlotta Ashe, the amoral socialite who marries the upstart hero of *Lucky Sam McCarver* ◆ (1925), and Carrie Callahan, the title role of the girl who turns on her criminal husband and brother-in-law, in *Ned McCobb's Daughter* ◆ (1926).

Earl Carroll Vanities A series of revues produced by Carroll◆ annually from 1923 through 1932 (except for 1927 and 1929) and again in 1940, they were celebrated and sometimes attacked for their emphasis on nude girls and salacious humor. Joe Cook, ◆ W. C. Fields,◆ and Sophie Tucker◆ were among the many stars who appeared in the shows, which left behind few memorable melodies.

Earl of Pawtucket, The, a comedy in three acts by Augustus Thomas. ◆ Produced by Kirke La Shelle◆ at the Madison Square Theatre. ◆ February 5, 1903. 191 performances.

To escape a summons from the House of Lords and to see how well he can survive without his title, Lord Cardington (Lawrence D'Orsay) sails to America and adopts the name of an old American friend, Putnam, who lives in England. Once landed, he falls in love with Harriet Fordyce, unaware that she was once Mrs. Putnam. The Lord's mysterious disappearance leads to the belief that the real Putnam, with whom he was last seen publicly, may have murdered him. So the fake Putnam finds himself pursued by the police as well as by lawyers seeking alimony payments due from his namesake.

Written as a vehicle for D'Orsay, the play was rejected by Charles Frohman♦ on the grounds that the actor could not sustain so large a role. He was proved wrong, and the comedy became a huge success.

EARLE, VIRGINIA (1875–1937) The statuesque singing actress from Cincinnati began her career playing Nanki-Poo in an all-children company of *The Mikado♦* in 1888. A prominent prima donna from 1894 on, she had her biggest hit in *Sergeant Kitty* (1903). She played for a time in vaudeville before retiring.

Easiest Way, The, a play in four acts by Eugene Walter.♦ Produced by David Belasco♦ at the Belasco-Stuyvesant Theatre. January 19, 1909. 157 performances.

Laura Murdock (Frances Starr♦) is a mediocre actress who has been unable to make a living by acting, so has allowed herself to be kept in style by Willard Brockton (Joseph Kilgour). While appearing in Denver, however, she meets and falls in love with a young newspaper man, John Madison (Edward H. Robins). John's romantic view of women clashes with both Brockton's cynical one and Laura's situation. When Brockton learns of Laura's feelings, he makes her write to John and test him by revealing the truth. Laura reluctantly writes the letter, but after Brockton leaves, she burns it. Eventually, John earns a small fortune and prepares to marry Laura, until he learns of her past life and deserts her. Laura is left to take "the easiest way" out by remaining a kept woman. She tells her maid to get her best dress ready. "I'm going to Rector's to make a hit," she announces, "and to hell with the rest."

Burns Mantle♦ appraised the play as "the first bold denial of the happy ending in modern [American] drama, the first deliberate attempt to prove that a play could be emotionally appealing because of its essential truth and the validity of its performance." Certainly the ending, its famous curtain line, and Miss Starr's performance were the talk of the season. Belasco is reported originally to have wanted to rewrite the ending, allowing John and Laura to wed, but Walter obstinately refused. He felt that other contemporary plays, such as *Leah Kleschna,♦* had been irreparably damaged artistically by contrived happy endings.

East Is West, a comedy in three acts and a prologue by Samuel Shipman♦ and John B. Hymer. Produced by William Harris, Jr.♦ at the Astor Theatre. December 25, 1918. 680 performances.

Although she was given a proper Chinese upbringing, Ming Toy (Fay Bainter♦) is something of a hoyden. Brought to San Francisco's Chinatown, she falls in love with a handsome young American, Billy Benson (Forrest Winant). Two obstacles stand in the way of their marrying. First, both laws and sentiment argue against an interracial marriage. Also, a cynical Chinese man-about-town, Charlie Yang (George Nash), has purchased Ming Toy, and by Chinese custom is thereby entitled to her. Matters turn out satisfactorily when it is learned that Ming Toy was adopted while still a baby and is Spanish by birth.

Although the play itself was dismissed by most critics as absurd hokum, the gorgeous settings of Livingston Platt♦ and Miss Bainter's droll performance turned it into one of the greatest hits of its era.

East Lynne, a play in five acts by Clifton W. Tayleure.♦ Produced at the Winter Garden Theatre. March 23, 1863. Approximately 20 performances.

Lady Isabel Mount Severn (Lucille Western♦) marries her childhood sweetheart, Archibald Carlyle (A. H. Davenport), but after several years of happiness she is led by Sir Francis Levison (Lawrence Barrett♦) to believe that Archibald is unfaithful. She elopes with Sir Francis, who later refuses to keep his promise of marriage. Carlyle remarries. Years pass. Ill and dying, Isabel returns to Carlyle's home, East Lynne, to see her children and to beg her husband's forgiveness. She comes disguised as a Madam Vine. Archibald, who quickly recognizes her, does forgive her as she dies.

Miss Western paid Tayleure $100 to adapt Mrs. Henry Wood's popular Victorian novel of the same name. It served her as a vehicle for many years and was also popular with other actresses. It became such a favorite of touring and stock companies that "Next week, *East Lynne*" was soon a well-known, if slighting, expression to indicate the seemingly inevitable nature of their repertories. From the start, however, the play was never as well received by critics as it was by the public, the *Albion* dismissing its first presentation as "sickly nonsense."

EATON, CHARLES HENRY (1813–43) The son of a prosperous Boston merchant, he made his debut in his hometown in 1833 in the title role of *The Stranger.♦* Although he remained primarily a Boston actor, he toured all the leading theatrical centers winning praise for his interpretations of Richard III, Hamlet, William Tell, and other popular figures. A fatal fall in Pittsburgh cut short a career of growing acclaim and promise.

EATON, MARY (1902–48) A native of Norfolk, Va., the petite blond dancer began performing professionally while still a child and made her New York debut as Tyltyl in *The Blue Bird* (1915). She was spotted by Ziegfeld,♦ who groomed her as a successor to Marilyn Miller,♦ and she appeared for him in the 1920, 1921, and 1923 editions of the *Ziegfeld Follies*♦ and as Eddie Cantor's♦ leading lady in *Kid Boots* (1923). However, her biggest and last success came only after she left the producer to star in *The Five O'Clock Girl* (1927), in which she introduced "Thinking of You."

EATON, WALTER PRICHARD (1878–1957) Born in Malden, Mass., he graduated from Harvard and accepted a position as assistant drama critic on the *Tribune* before becoming principal drama critic for the *Sun* and *American Magazine.* He wrote numerous books on theatre, including *The American Stage of To-Day* (1908), *At the New Theatre and Others* (1910), *Plays and Players* (1916), *The Actor's Heritage* (1924), and *The Theatre Guild—The First Ten Years* (1929). In 1933 he accepted the post of Associate Professor of Playwriting at Yale. Although he consistently argued for a progressive, serious drama, Eaton's views were fundamentally conservative and he welcomed much that now would be unpalatable. His sharp observations and pleasant style make his criticisms eminently readable.

Eaves-Brooks The principal costume maker for modern plays, the company was formed in 1981 by a merger of the two leading manufacturers. Brooks was the older of the two, having been founded in 1861, that of Charles Eaves in 1864. At the turn of the century the Geoly family took over Eaves and now heads the merged company.

EBB, FRED (b. 1932) The New York-born lyricist and librettist was educated at Columbia and first contributed lyrics to Broadway in the revue *From A to Z* (1960). Beginning in 1965 he teamed with John Kander♦ and wrote lyrics to Kander's scores for *Flora, the Red Menace* (1965); *Cabaret*♦ (1966); *The Happy Time*♦ (1968); *Zorba* (1968); *70, Girls, 70* (1971), for which he also collaborated on the book; *Liza* (1974); *Chicago*♦ (1975), again serving as co-librettist; *Woman of the Year* (1981); and *The Rink* (1984). His lyrics have rarely displayed any excep-

tional characteristics other than admirably suiting the mood and period of text and music.

ECKART, WILLIAM [JOSEPH] (b. 1920) and JEAN [née LEVY] (b. 1921) A successful husband and wife team, he was born in New Iberia, La., and studied architecture at Tulane and stage design at Yale; she was born in Chicago and also studied stage design at Yale. Beginning with *Glad Tidings* (1951), they created sets for such productions as *Oh, Men! Oh, Women!* (1953); *The Golden Apple*♦ (1954) for which they won a Donaldson Award♦; *Damn Yankees*♦ (1955); *Li'l Abner* (1956); *Take Her, She's Mine* (1961); and *Mame*♦ (1966). They often designed lighting for their sets and occasionally, the costumes. In later years they moved to Texas, thereafter designing primarily for regional playhouses across the country. Their work is excellent but hard to characterize.

Economics of the American Theatre The American theatre has moved from humble beginnings through decades of great strength and huge financial returns only to lapse, in the last decades of the 20th century, into a curious situation. Now rewards for occasional success are enormous but on balance production and consequent employment have dwindled and most theatrical enterprises are economically precarious. The earliest years left behind little solid statistical evidence but it may be safely assumed that the lots of performers and other professionals were uncertain and hard. Not until late in the 18th century had American cities grown populous enough and Americans themselves sufficiently prosperous to allow larger centers to support permanent ensembles. Even so, the record is unclear about how well the average professional lived. A few early luminaries were apparently able to save comfortable sums for retirement, and John Henry,♦ sometimes called America's first matinee idol, led a flamboyant, expensive life, even maintaining a private coach. He realized a then significant $10,000 when he sold his interest in the American Company,♦ but seemingly never saved much and was in relatively poor financial condition when he drowned. Nor were theatrical impresarios or playwrights in better shape, as witnessed by the problems of Dunlap♦ and others. Costs of production, however, must have been comparatively small, since individual sets and costumes were rarely provided. Actors were expected to supply their own costumes, and most theatres kept a handful of basic sets—a domestic interior, a castle, a woods, a garden—which saw service in whatever play was being performed. Some of the figures relating to New York's Park Theatre♦ are enlightening. Opened in 1798, it had been projected to cost just over $42,000, a considerable sum at the time, but actually cost an exceptional $130,000. (Not until after the Civil War would most playhouses begin to cost that much and even years afterward many, especially away from major cities, were constructed for considerably less.) Top seats were 75¢, soon raised to $1, and the cheapest tickets were either 12½¢ or 25¢. Because of the house's large capacity a performance could gross over $1200. Ironically, this figure remained about the standard for capacity houses for over a century, since the higher ticket prices that came into being at the time of the Civil War were coupled with the development of more intimate theatres. The cost to the Park's management of the entire ensemble's salaries came to a mere $480 per week, with Hodgkinson♦ receiving top reimbursement at $20 per week, plus $5 per week for wardrobe and $30 for his managerial concerns. When all other expenses were included (among them $150 for orchestra, $109 for lighting, and $68 for printing), the weekly nut was $1200. In theory, the theatre could have been extremely profitable, especially since it was the city's only playhouse for many years, but extant records reveal many nights and longer stretches of dismal business.

The coming of stars in the early 1800s proved both a source of additional revenue and a drain on those revenues as most stars' contracts called for them to receive a sizable portion of the gross. Yet even the Kembles♦ rarely filled the Park, and on nights when they did not perform grosses averaged only $150. With the coming of competition, both in New York and elsewhere, theatres encountered new problems, often having to lower prices to attract trade. For a time during the lean years of the early 1840s, 75¢ was generally the top ticket price. At the same time, actors' salaries began to creep up, albeit slowly. For example, the Bowery♦ paid J. R. Scott♦ $40 a week in 1845, although most salaries at the house ranged between $4 and $15. While most theatres continued to provide the same basic sets, some productions were given special mountings and with them we begin to obtain a notion of these theatrical costs. Thus, when Edwin Forrest♦ mounted a totally new *Macbeth*♦ in 1852, his outlay for scenery and costumes was $8000. Until the panic of 1857, the 1850s were comparatively prosperous times for theatres, and tickets again went to a $1 top. A few exceptional attractions demanded more, but Rachel♦ is believed to have encountered stiff opposition when she charged a $3 top and a $1 minimum. (Three decades later her compatriot,

Sarah Bernhardt,♦ dared ask only a $2 top.) At the same time actors' salaries again rose. For the 1857–58 season at Wallack's, Lester Wallack♦ received a weekly $100 as both actor and director. W. R. Blake♦ was listed as earning $80, and the emerging Mrs. Hoey♦ $55. It should be noted that contracts for all leading performers allowed them one or more benefit nights, at which they were entitled to a substantial share of the gross. Lesser players at the house were paid about $25 and shared no benefits. The leading scene designer received a salary on a par with lesser actors.

By 1861, with the coming of wartime prosperity, salaries had risen still further. Mrs. Hoey, for example, was now listed at $100 per week. Prosperity and rising costs allowed Edwin Booth♦ and his brothers to charge a then record $5 top when they appeared together in their 1864 special production of *Julius Caesar*♦; and two years later, in 1866, Wallack led the way to a standard $1.50 top, a figure which was to prevail at first-class houses for the rest of the century, although some lowered it briefly during the 1873 panic. While most straight plays continued to be mounted for a few thousand dollars, with the coming of elaborate musicals new record figures followed one another rapidly. *The Black Crook*♦ (1866) is said to have cost $50,000, and subsequent spectacles advertised yet larger, if somewhat suspect, figures. In 1869 the *Times* listed the previous year's grosses for leading Broadway houses. In all of 1868 Niblo's Garden,♦ the home of spectacle, was reported taking in $359,879; the Olympic Theatre, where G. L. Fox♦ was the reigning star, had garnered $349,921; while the elite Wallack's, given over to non-musical attractions, grossed $263,319. (In the 1980s, large musicals often grossed as much in a single week.)

The typical comic opera of the 1890s is believed to have cost between $10,000 and $25,000 to produce. Moreover, the basically healthy economic climate of the time allowed most shows to recoup their costs after four weeks at capacity business. De Wolf Hopper♦ claimed that many of the era's musicals ran at a loss in smaller New York theatres, so that they could claim long Broadway stands and retrieve their investments at larger touring houses. His statement cannot be corroborated precisely, but as late as the 1920s many shows that failed in New York went on tour and closed with a profit. At the end of 1911, Adolph Klauber♦ reported in the *Times* that in the first half of the 1911–12 season, from August 8 to December 31, sixty-four plays of all variety had opened on Broadway and thirty of them had already recouped their costs. However, the road began to change noticeably in the early years of the 20th century when films arrived to lure less affluent and less educated playgoers away from live theatre. Cheap touring companies such as the ten-twent'-thirt'♦ groups, which presented lurid melodramas, treacly comedy, and old operettas at prices between 10¢ and 30¢, quickly disappeared.

Real changes started to affect theatrical economics about the time of World War I. Wartime inflation was coupled with the rise of unions,♦ most notably Actors' Equity.♦ The justice of union demands for rehearsal pay, overtime pay, better working conditions, and higher salaries cannot be gainsaid, but nonetheless played a major role in the marked escalation of costs and therefore of ticket prices. Top prices, which had remained a $1.50 or at best $2 since the Civil War, rose during World War I to $3.50. By 1919, while straight plays, unless unusually elaborate, could still be mounted for under $10,000, musical production costs had soared. The *Ziegfeld Follies*♦ of the era cost about $200,000 apiece, admittedly an exceptional figure. *Irene*♦ (1919), a more typical example, cost $40,000. The prosperity of the 1920s and increasing union demands continued the upward spiral all during the decade. By 1927 *Good News,*♦ again typical, cost $75,000 and charged a $6 top. Some musicals went as high as $8. Nonetheless, both *Irene* and *Good News,* along with many other successes of the era, returned their investments in four weeks.

The economic pinch began to be felt during the Depression when the theatre found itself competing with radio's and Hollywood's glittering rewards and confronting union militancy. Although ticket prices plummeted ($3 and $4 became standard tops again), the costs of productions did not necessarily fall proportionally. Shows began to take longer and longer to pay off. These discouraging developments led to fewer mountings, and in the late 1930s the number of major productions dropped below 100 for the first time in the century and never again passed the mark.

World War II brought a measure of prosperity, and the theatre seemed reasonably healthy for the next decade, albeit the number of plays continued to fall and the percentage of shows to repay their investment decreased. For example, *Variety*♦ reported that for the 1955–56 season only about a dozen of some fifty commercial productions showed a profit. A one-set, small-cast comedy such as *Fallen Angels* could run nearly 300 performances and a musical such as *Mr. Wonderful* run almost a year without closing in the black.

The rampant inflation that was precipitated by the Vietnam War and the international oil cartel threw theatrical economics into turmoil. By the early 1980s simple straight plays cost hundreds of thousands of dollars to mount and musicals were budgeted at a million or more. *Cats* (1982) was reputed to have cost five million. Top ticket prices skyrocketed to $55, actually not excessive in view of inflation and the rise of other prices, but dissuading to many casual theatregoers kept at home by "free" television. Producers, too, had to be dissuaded since a $55 top for a musical costing five million could not possibly promise the prompt payoff that a $6 top could for a $75,000 production. No small part of the problem derived from the absurdity of union demands. Union bonds alone, which had to be figured into initial costs, were in the hundreds of thousands of dollars. Nor were union demands conducive to reasonable weekly running costs. Actors' Equity, for example, negotiated contracts in which a performer's minimum salary per week was $850 (1990) at the same time that the Bureau of Labor Statistics reported the average American's weekly salary at $399. Ever more questionable were such practices as the musicians' union frequently requiring producers to pay musicians who were not used. Many smaller theatres, especially on the road, became uneconomical, and producers, who now demanded huge guarantees from playhouses instead of simply a percentage of the gross, sought out grotesquely large old film-houses and convention halls as auditoriums for their attractions. At the end of the 1980–81 season, *Variety* recorded that only three of the forty-odd productions were commercial successes, although one or two others were expected to prove profitable eventually. The picture has not improved appreciably in subsequent seasons.

EDDINGER, Wallace (1881–1929) The Albany, N.Y.-born performer made his debut as a child actor in 1888, and continued to play children's roles for the next five years, notably as Cedric in *Little Lord Fauntleroy.* He then abandoned the stage to finish his education, returning in 1902 as a replacement in *Soldiers of Fortune.* He quickly made playgoers note his polished skills both as a comic and a serious actor, as well as the boyish, down-home attractiveness he was never to lose. Prominent supporting roles followed in *The Optimist* (1906), *Caught in the Rain*♦ (1907), and *Classmates* (1907). His versatility was further demonstrated when he assumed the leads in *The Third Degree*♦ (1909) and *The Aviator* (1910), playing Howard Jeffries, a weakling wrongly accused of a crime, in the former, and Robert Street, the author of a book on flying who is forced into an air race although he had never really been inside an airplane, in the latter. He scored again as Travers Gladwin, the young art collector who borrows a policeman's uniform in an inept attempt to prevent his paintings from being stolen in *Officer 666*◆ (1912), and as William Magee, the novelist tricked into a scary time at an empty summer hotel, in *Seven Keys to Baldpate*◆ (1913). He next enjoyed a long run as Budd Woodbridge, a young man desperately trying to cure his jealousy, in *The Boomerang*◆ (1915). Another hit was *Wedding Bells* (1919), where as Reginald Carter he is lured away from his second wedding by his first wife. In *Captain Applejack* (1921) he was Ambrose Applejack, an English squire who dreams he is a pirate. His last successes were *The Haunted House* (1924), in which he played The Novelist who lives out all his plots, and *And So to Bed* (1927), in which as Samuel Pepys he makes an innocent visit to a lady's house, only to have his actions misconstrued by both his wife and the king.

EDDY, EDWARD (1822–75) Long the leading star at the popular-priced Bowery Theatre,◆ the manly, handsome, stentorian-voiced actor was born in Troy, N.Y., and first appeared in public at a New York recital in 1839. He then toured for several seasons before making his New York acting debut in 1846 playing Othello at the New Greenwich Theatre. In the same season he offered his Claude Melnotte (*The Lady of Lyons*◆), Clifford (*The Hunchback*◆), and the title part in *The Stranger,*◆ all of which were to be favorite interpretations in his later Bowery years. His debut there was in 1851, when he played Richelieu. During the same season he first played Edmond Dantes in *The Count of Monte Cristo,* another of his most demanded roles. His Richard III was also highly popular. He remained at the Bowery for a dozen years, although he occasionally performed elsewhere and made several unsuccessful attempts at management. His emotive, scene-chewing style of acting led to his being called "robustious Eddy." Throughout these years he continued to essay a wide range of parts, even participating in the dog dramas◆ that were briefly the rage, but, whether he wore out his welcome or playgoers became more sophisticated, he eventually lost popularity. In the late 1860s and early 1870s he drifted among a number of lesser theatres before leaving to set up a theatrical troupe in the West Indies, where he died in poverty.

EDESON, ROBERT (1868–1931) The sternly handsome actor, himself the son of an actor, was born in New Orleans and made his stage debut in Brooklyn in 1887, playing two small parts, Earle Sparks and Captain Windsor, in *Fascination.* After several other minor assignments, both on the road and in New York, he accepted a position with the Boston Museum◆ where he remained until he was spotted by Charles Frohman,◆ who cast him as Harry Winters, one of three look-alikes whose resemblance causes confusion, in *Incog* (1892). He remained with Frohman for several seasons, his most notable assignment being Rev. Gavin Dishart opposite Maude Adams◆ in *The Little Minister* (1897). In 1901 he was applauded for his portrayal of the faithful Edward Warden in *The Climbers.*◆ His performance earned him the starring role of Clay, the mining engineer who thwarts a revolution in Latin America, in *Soldiers of Fortune* (1902). Another success came as Soangataha, the Indian who gives up his white sweetheart for the sake of his tribe, in *Strongheart* (1905). Two years later he played Duncan Irving, the cruel, cynical cadet who loses his girl to his rival, in *Classmates.* Thereafter he moved from play to play with little success, often accepting supporting roles. At the same time he became one of the earliest important theatrical figures to move into films. His last Broadway appearance was as The Vagrant in Owen Davis's◆ adaptation of Capek's *The World We Live In* (*The Insect Comedy*) (1922).

Edgewood Folks, a pastoral comedy-drama in four acts by J. E. Brown. Produced at the Park Theatre. August 23, 1880. 32 performances.

As far as most residents of the small New England town are concerned, Tom Dilloway (Sol Smith Russell◆) is an overgrown boy, given to spending his time singing and clowning with children. But when the shady Ferguson (J. W. Lanergan) appears and attempts to overthrow a will which would benefit sweet Faith Hardewick (Carrie McHenry), Tom puts his histrionics to good use. He disguises himself as a toping young German, as a tramp, as a possible confederate for Ferguson, and even as a deacon's spinster sister to thwart the villain. He succeeds, thus winning his amazed neighbors' approval.

Described by one anonymous critic as "flimsy and uninteresting; full of anomalies that would be objectionable if the movement of the characters concerned anybody seriously," the play helped establish its young star, although both the work and Russell were always more popular in smaller towns and cities than in larger ones. It remained in his repertory for many years.

EDOUIN, [William Frederick] Willie [né Boyer] (1846–1908) Although he spent little more than a decade on American stages, he became an especially popular comedian and was one of the progenitors of American musical comedy. The son of an English dance instructor, he and his five brothers and sisters made their debuts in children's shows in London and Brighton. He then performed in pantomime and spent some time in Australia before coming to America in 1869, where he first appeared under Barrett♦ and McCullough♦ at San Francisco's California Theatre. ♦ He won quick celebrity there with his travesties of popular plays and local figures. His initial New York appearance was in 1870 playing Narcissus Fitzfrizzle in *The Dancing Barber,* a skit in an olio that was on the bill along with a burlesque about Lydia Thompson♦ and her British blondes. Later in the year he joined Dan Bryant♦ to perform Murphy in *Handy Andy.* In 1871 he was enlisted in Miss Thompson's troupe as its principle male comedian. He remained with her, apart from one short return to London, for six years, appearing in *Blue Beard, Lurline, Robin Hood, Mephisto and the Fourscore,* and *Robinson Crusoe.* His make-up, clowning, and acrobatics as Friday in the last named earned him special praise, as did his double role of Corporal Zoug Zoug and Wishee-Washee, the Heathen Chinee, in *Blue Beard.* At this time, a genre called farce-comedy,♦ elementary, prototypical musical comedies, began to take hold. Edouin performed briefly in 1877 with an early farce-comedy troupe, Colville's♦ Folly Company, then switched to an even more famous band, Rice's♦ Surprise Party. He performed with Rice's ensemble for two years in such pieces as *Babes in the Woods, The Lost Children,* and *Horrors.* In 1880 he organized his own troupe, Willie Edouin's Sparks, collaborating on one of the most successful of farce-comedies, *Dreams,* and taking several of the principal roles in it as well. He left for England in 1884, returning only occasionally, most memorably to play Tweedlepunch in *Florodora*♦ (1900).

EDWARDES, George , see *English Musical Comedy in America*

EDWARDS, Gus [né Simon] (1879–1945) Born in Germany, he was brought to America while still a child and soon was employing his boy soprano voice to help support his family. In his late teens he organized the first of many similar vaudeville acts consisting entirely of promising youngsters. The first act was called either "The Newsboy Quintet" or "The Newsboy Quartet," depending on how many performers he had at the moment. His eye for young talent was so impressive that he was nicknamed "The Star Maker." Among the many future stars to whom he gave starts in his acts were Eddie Cantor,♦ George Jessel,♦ Georgie Price, Walter Winchell,♦ and the Duncan Sisters. ♦ While assembling acts he also began to write songs. Still popular are his "In My Merry Oldsmobile," "By the Light of the Silvery Moon," and "School Days." On Broadway his scores or songs were heard in *When We Were Forty-one* (1905), *Hip! Hip! Hooray!* (1907), *School Days* (1908), *The Merry-Go-Round* (1908), and the [*Ziegfeld*] *Follies of 1910.* ♦

EDWARDS, Julian (1855–1910) The English-born composer studied in Edinburgh and London before accepting a post as conductor of the Carl Rosa Opera Company. James C. Duff♦ brought him to New York and produced his first show to reach Broadway, *Jupiter* (1892). Between that premiere and his death 18 years later he wrote the scores for 17 musicals to play New York. Among the best received or more interesting were *King René's Daughter* (1893); *Madeleine* (1895); *The Goddess of Truth* (1896); *The Wedding Day* (1897); *The Jolly Musketeer* (1898); *Princess Chic* (1900); *Dolly Varden* (1902); *When Johnny Comes Marching Home*♦ (1902), his best work; *Love's Lottery* (1904); and *The Girl and the Wizard* (1909). Although none of his music remains popular, he was highly respected in his own time and his work was sufficiently admired to lure such stars as Digby Bell,♦ Carmen D'Arville,♦ Lillian Russell,♦ Jefferson De Angelis,♦ Della Fox,♦ Christie MacDonald,♦ Lulu Glaser,♦ and Ernestine Schumann-Heink.

Effect of Gamma Rays on Man-in-the-Moon Marigolds, The, a play in two acts by Paul Zindel. Produced at the Mercer-O'Casey Theatre. April 7, 1970. 819 performances. PP.

Beatrice (Sada Thompson) is a slatternly, widowed housewife who takes her hatred of the world out on her two children, Ruth (Amy Levitt) and Matilda or Tillie (Pamela Payton-Wright). She badgers them and often keeps them out of school to help with housework, which never gets properly done anyway. The extroverted Ruth is an epileptic and has little love or respect for her mother. The younger Tillie escapes her nightmarish daily life by making scientific experiments in school, studying the effects of cobalt-60 on marigolds. Only her laboratory work sustains her.

The play was originally written for television, and

was later staged at Houston's Alley Theatre♦ and the Cleveland Play House♦ before being presented off-Broadway. Jerry Talmer of the New York *Post* wrote, "I don't know of a better play of its genre since *The Glass Menagerie*. It is stronger and funnier and tougher than I can report." In 1971 the play became only the second off-Broadway production to receive the Pulitzer Prize,♦ having won the New York Drama Critics Circle Award♦ earlier. However, some critics considered it too derivative, the sort of mood-memory play that was flooding the theatre, and a road company headed by Dorothy Loudon failed.

Zindel (b. 1936), a native of Staten Island, has been a high school science teacher and a novelist. His other plays include *And Miss Reardon Drinks a Little* (1971) and *The Secret Affair of Mildred Wild* (1972). Neither these nor later works have found a large audience.

Eighth of January, The, a play in three acts by Robert Penn Smith.♦ Produced at the Chestnut Street Theatre,♦ Philadelphia. January 8, 1829. In repertory.

The War of 1812 has divided the Bull family. John Bull (William Warren♦), its aging patriarch, remains loyal to England, although he refuses to take an active part in the battle. His son Charles (Mr. Southwell) thinks differently. He is a loyal American and willing to lay down his life for his country and for General Jackson (Mr. Rowbotham). Jackson fights the battle of New Orleans on January 8, unaware a peace treaty has been signed. A lovable Cockney, Billy Bowbell (the first Joseph Jefferson♦), wanders in and out of the play.

One of the few plays written about the war, it was inferior as drama to the best play about the conflict, *The Triumph at Plattsburg.*♦ Indeed, the *United States Gazette* complained of its "peculiarly undramatic nature." Actually, however, it was hastily written to celebrate Jackson's 1828 election. For all its faults, the *Gazette* welcomed it as "uncommonly interesting," especially in that it "displays effectually more variety of humor than the generality of pieces in which national peculiarities are harped upon."

El Capitan, a comic opera in three acts. Book by Charles Klein.♦ Lyrics by Tom Frost and John Philip Sousa.♦ Music by Sousa. Produced at the Broadway Theatre. April 20, 1896. 112 performances.

Don Medigua (De Wolf Hopper♦), the viceroy of Peru, captures the rebel El Capitan, executes him, and assumes his place in disguise. The rebels capture Medigua's servant, Pozzo (Charles Klein), mistaking him for his master, and news of the viceroy's apparent capture prompts his wife (Alice Hosmer) and daughter (Bertha Waltzinger) to go in search of him. Meanwhile, as El Capitan, Medigua flirts with Estrelda (Edna Wallace Hopper), a former viceroy's daughter. When the Spanish army arrives, Medigua leads the rebels in circles until they are too tired to fight. The revolution is put down, but Medigua has some explaining to do to his wife about his flirtation.

Principal songs: El Capitan's Song · Sweetheart, I'm Waiting · A Typical Tune of Zanzibar

Sousa's great score and Hopper's superb clowning were in large measure responsible for the success of the original production. "El Capitan's Song," later known as "El Capitan March," was the most famous melody to come from a Sousa operetta. In his autobiography Sousa insisted that Klein's libretto was the finest ever written for a comic opera. While that assessment is open to dispute, the book proved durable enough when the work was revived in the 1970s by the Goodspeed Opera House.♦

ELDRIDGE, FLORENCE [née FLORENCE MCKECHNIE] (1901–88) The Brooklyn-born actress made her professional debut in the chorus of a 1918 musical but first won major attention when she portrayed Annabelle West, the terrified heroine, in *The Cat and the Canary*♦ (1922), and the Step-daughter in *Six Characters in Search of an Author* (1922). In 1927 she married Fredric March♦ and subsequently played opposite him in many shows, most notably *The Skin of our Teeth*♦ (1942), *Years Ago*♦ (1946), and *Long Day's Journey into Night*♦ (1956).

ELIOT, T[HOMAS] S[TEARNS] (1888–1965) The expatriate American poet, who spent most of his creative career in England as a British subject, is remembered by American playgoers largely for three plays: *Murder in the Cathedral*♦ (1936), *The Cocktail Party*♦ (1950), and *The Confidential Clerk* (1954). None of the three was received in America with unequivocal acclaim. The merits of the poet's unique dramatic blank verse were open to serious question, the writing seen as verbose and elusive, and the plotting perceived as frequently too shaky. Nevertheless, all three works found reasonably large audiences and have been revived occasionally. That many audiences, especially earlier ones, were attracted by the controversy and notoriety surrounding some of his famous poems and by the esteem in which he was held cannot be gainsaid. But it should be noted that despite the plays' pretensions and flaws, in competent productions they were capable of holding an audience's attention at the most elemental level—as good theatre. Indirectly Eliot may have been far more important to modern theatre in several ways. In his position as an arbiter of taste he was instrumental in promoting a reconsideration of long neglected Jacobean playwrights. His *Sweeney Agonistes: Fragments of an Aristophanic Melodrama* is recognized as a precursor of the now popular style and approach of such later writers as Samuel Beckett,♦ Harold Pinter,♦ and Sam Shepard,♦ a style branded by Professor Arthur Holmberg of Harvard as "taut, nervous, jangling" and an approach that communicated "the anguish of the marrow, the fever of the bone." Lastly, his tremendous prestige made him a leading voice in the rebellion, however unsuccessful, against the reigning school of Ibsenite realism. His *Old Possum's Book of Practical Cats* provided the lyrics for the 1982 musical *Cats.* ♦

Elitch's Gardens Theatre (Denver) America's oldest summer playhouse, in continuous operation since May 1, 1890, it was founded by John Elitch, a former actor, and his wife Mary. The Elitches had come to Denver in 1882 and purchased a 16-acre plot where they eventually built a wooden, octagonal theatre. Elitch died before the theatre opened, so Mrs. Elitch assumed its management. The house was used at first for vaudeville, but in 1897 a stock company was organized. In the 1950s a modern stagehouse was added. For many years regular plays touring summer circuits were booked, but this was discontinued after 1987. Vaudeville and concert attractions are now the mainstay. However, there are some tentative plans to reintroduce a few Broadway shows. The theatre was equally famous for the gardens which surrounded it, including a large greenhouse where Colorado carnations were grown. The gardens were later enlarged to 32 acres. Among its early attractions was a cart, pulled by an ostrich, in which rides were offered. In 1932 Caroline Lawrence Dier wrote its history in *The Lady of the Gardens.*

Elizabeth the Queen, a drama in three acts by Maxwell Anderson.♦ Produced by the Theatre Guild♦ at the Guild Theatre. November 3, 1930. 147 performances.

The aging Queen Elizabeth (Lynn Fontanne♦) has fallen in love with her young, handsome courtier Robert Devereaux (Alfred Lunt♦), the Earl of Essex. While he is away on an Irish campaign Sir Walter Raleigh (Percy Waram) and Lord Cecil (Arthur Hughes) conspire to make the Queen doubt

not merely his love, but his loyalty as well. To test Essex, the Queen orders him to disband his army. He does, after which Elizabeth has him arrested and sentenced to death. She calls him to her, hoping he will plead for mercy and forgiveness, thereby allowing their romance to resume. But the proud, stubborn Essex refuses and is sent to his death. Alone, Elizabeth laments that she is old and only Essex's love could have given her a breath of youth.

Brooks Atkinson♦ hailed the blank-verse tragedy as "magnificent drama. It is a searching portrayal of character, freely imaginative in its use of history, clearly thought out and conveyed in dialogue of notable beauty." The play was revived successfully in 1961 and 1966 with Eva Le Gallienne♦ and Judith Anderson♦ in the title role.

Elizabethan and Jacobean Plays [Other Than Shakespeare] in America Although some non-Shakespearean Tudor and Stuart plays were performed by the earliest professional ensembles, these productions were few and far between, a situation which persisted all through the 19th century. There was, however, one notable exception, Massinger's *A New Way To Pay Old Debts.* The play seems to have first been staged during the 1794–95 season in Philadelphia, and soon became one of the leading vehicles for early American tragedians. The meaty role of the villainous Sir Giles Overreach afforded J. B. Booth♦ and Edwin Booth,♦ as well as many other less distinguished actors, a chance for a tour de force. The play held the stage with marked regularity as late as 1886, when the younger Booth offered his last revival of the work.

The rise of academic playhouses in the late 19th and early 20th century may have whetted interest in many of these long neglected plays, and the 20th century did see some notable revivals, although they were highly infrequent and never fully in the theatrical mainstream. A few of the more noteworthy revivals have been the Theatre Guild's♦ 1928 staging of *Volpone;* Elisabeth Bergner's♦ 1946 mounting of *The Duchess of Malfi;* and the Phoenix Theatre's♦ 1950 production of *The White Devil.*

ELLIOTT, Maxine [née Jessie Dermot] (1868–1940) The daughter of a New England sea captain, she had no specific affection for the stage but took up acting solely as a means of support and quit when she had made her fortune, although much of her wealth actually derived from gifts and from following the financial suggestions of her well-placed admirers. From the beginning of her career it was recognized that her dramatic abilities were limited. However, her beauty and charm, coupled for a time with a careful selection of vehicles, made her a favorite for some twenty years. Her biographer-niece pictured her as having "brilliant black hair, ivory skin, enormous eyes . . . described as 'mid-night eyes,' and features of even proportion." After assuming her stage name at the suggestion of Dion Boucicault,♦ she made her debut in New York in 1890 in *The Middleman,* then toured with its star, E. S. Willard,♦ in a repertory of plays for two years. Several short-lived failures and a season opposite Rose Coghlan♦ followed before she briefly joined the company of Augustin Daly.♦ Although Daly immediately assigned her important roles, his policy of frequently changing plays and of making the star of one play a bit player in the next displeased the ambitious actress. She left and suffered a few more quick failures before teaming with Nat Goodwin,♦ whom shortly she married. Among the plays in which she co-starred with Goodwin were *An American Citizen* (1897), where she played Beatrice Carew, who is uncertain whether her husband, who married her to help her secure her rights, really loves her; *The Rivals* (1897), in which she played Lydia Languish; Clyde Fitch's♦ *Nathan Hale* (1899), in which she portrayed Alice Adams, Hale's fiancée; Fitch's *The Cowboy and the Lady* (1899), in which she was Mrs. Weston, the elegant, good-hearted wife of the villain, who marries the hero after her first husband's murder; *When We Were Twenty-one* (1900), in which as Phyllis Erleson she wins her clubman lover away from a more flashy rival; and *The Merchant of Venice*♦ (1900), with her as Portia. After divorcing Goodwin she scored a success as Georgiana, who is torn between a heartless suitor able to destroy her family fortunes, and a sweetheart fighting overseas in the Spanish-American War, in Fitch's *Her Own Way*♦ (1903). Her last success was Fitch's *Her Great Match* (1905), in which as an American girl, Jo Sheldon, she declines a morganatic marriage to a prince. In 1908 she opened her own theatre in New York, but her play for the occasion, like all her later plays, was a failure. She announced her retirement in 1911, although she made several brief subsequent appearances, the last as Cordelia, the woman who returns home twenty years after deserting her family, in *Trimmed in Scarlet* (1920). Of her work in this last play Alexander Woollcott♦ repeated what had been often said, "Besides her lustrous beauty, she has dignity, a pleasing and thoroughly mastered voice, taste, humor and intelligence." She passed her remaining years in France and England.

Biography: *My Aunt Maxine,* Diana Forbes-Robertson, New York, 1964.

ELLISTON, Grace [née Rutter] (1881–1950) The beautiful leading lady was born in Memphis, Tenn., and made her New York debut in a series of Frank Daniels♦ musicals. Although she later appeared opposite George Arliss,♦ Richard Bennett,♦ Henry Miller,♦ and other prominent leading men, her most famous role was Shirley Rossmore, the fighting heroine of *The Lion and the Mouse*♦ (1905).

ELLSLER, Effie (1855?–1942) Born in Cleveland, where her parents were popular actors and her father ran the leading playhouse, she made her debut while still a child and for many years played supporting and ingenue roles, acting with Edwin Booth,♦ Lawrence Barrett,♦ John McCullough,♦ and other celebrities during their Cleveland visits. She came to New York in 1880, making a sensation in her very first part, the title role of *Hazel Kirke,*♦ a girl who is thrown out of her home by her father after she announces she will not marry a groom of his choosing and who then is led to believe that the man she does marry has deceived her. She won ecstatic notices for her forceful yet natural portrayal of the part, which she played for three years. Thereafter, however, her choices of starring parts were ill-advised. She appeared in numerous unsuccessful plays of a sort that today would be dismissed as claptrap melodrama: *Courage* (1883), *Storm Beaten* (1883), *Woman Against Woman* (1886), *The Keepsake* (1888), and *Judge Not* (1888). For most of the 1890s she toured in road companies, and in 1900 headed the tour of *Barbara Frietchie.*♦ Three years later she was Jessica to Maxine Elliott's♦ Portia in *The Merchant of Venice.*♦ Minor roles in a number of plays followed before she scored one last hit as Cornelia Van Gorder, who rents a summer home and finds herself in the middle of a murder, in *The Bat*♦ (1920).

ELSSLER, Fanny (1810–84) One of the almost legendary figures of early classic ballet, rivaled in Europe only by Marie Taglioni, she had won the approbation of Paris, Vienna, and London before making her American debut at the Park Theatre♦ in May 1840. For her first appearance she danced in *La Cracovienne* and *La Tarentule*. The *Spirit of the Times*♦ praised the "faultless taste of every attitude, the charming simplicity and grace of her gestures and motions, the rapidity and strength of her execution, and the perfect ease with which she produced the most astounding effects." For the next

26 months, before she left in July 1842, she made a triumphant national tour in her repertory, giving ballet a popularity and cachet it had never before enjoyed in this country. Because there were no such things as modern concert halls she played almost entirely on legitimate stages. She was, according to Odell,♦ "the most sensational performer up to that time seen on the American stage."

ELTINGE, JULIAN (né WILLIAM JULIAN DALTON] (1883–1941) The most celebrated of American female impersonators, ♦ he was born in Newtonville, Mass., and made his debut in Boston at the age of ten, playing a little girl. His appearance was so well received that he continued to develop his art and made his New York debut in 1904 in E. E. Rice's♦ production of *Mr. Wix of Wickham*. The musical was a failure, but he quickly began to make a name for himself in vaudeville. Unlike most earlier female impersonators, who had emphasized the comic, often grotesquely exaggerated, side of their trade, Eltinge portrayed beautiful young women, carefully and tastefully imitating their make-up, dress, and mannerisms. His comedy came from the situations his women found themselves in and only incidentally from the fact that he was a man in drag. In 1908 and 1909 he toured with the Cohan and Harris Minstrels, then in 1911 returned to Broadway to portray Hal Blake, who is forced to disguise himself as a Mrs. Monte to pursue his courtship of his sweetheart, in *The Fascinating Widow*. Producer Al Woods♦ made so much money from this production that when he built a new theatre a year later he named it in Eltinge's honor. Eltinge appeared in two more musicals, *The Crinoline Girl* (1914) and *Cousin Lucy* (1915), and continued to star in vaudeville throughout the 1920s. Thereafter his vogue faded, and his few attempts to revive it were poorly received.

EMENS, HOMER [FARNHAM] (1862–1930) One of the distinguished set painters of his era, he was born in Volney, N.Y., and started his career as an apprentice to Philip Goatcher♦ at the Madison Square Theatre.♦ He spent several years at the Chestnut Street Theatre♦ in Philadelphia, before returning to New York. In keeping with the practice of his day he frequently designed only one or two of the several settings used in a play, generally creating the outdoor scenes which were considered his forte. His setting for the fourth act of *Gismonda* (1894), showing a star-lit vista just before dawn, was called by one critic "probably the most beautiful ever put on stage" for its "simplicity, grandeur, hint of splendid architecture, [and] poetic reflection."

Among the other plays for which he did some or all of the scenery were *Blue Jeans*♦ (1890), *Mavourneen*♦ (1891), *Alabama*♦ (1891), *Babes in Toyland*♦ (1903), *Twelfth Night*♦ (1904), *Mlle. Modiste*♦ (1905), *The Red Mill*♦ (1906), and *Kismet*♦ (1911). He retired in 1922.

EMERSON, BILLY [né WILLIAM EMERSON REDMOND] (1846–1902) Born in Ireland, but brought to America while still a babe in arms, he made his debut with Joe Sweeney's Minstrels in 1857 and moved from band to band before arriving in San Francisco in 1870, where his personal success helped Thomas Maguire,♦ the famed San Francisco impresario, to survive a spell of bad business. With Maguire's backing, Emerson immediately formed a company that remained the city's leading minstrel ensemble for a decade. In the 1880s he toured with several important troupes, then returned for a time to San Francisco. He continued performing until his death. At once a superb singer and comedian, he was also a composer of numerous songs that were popular in their day, including "Big Sun Flower," "Love Among the Roses," and "The Yaller Gal That Looked at Me."

EMERSON, JOHN (1874–1956) After preparing for the ministry at Oberlin, Heidelberg, and the University of Chicago, he decided to enter the theatre and made his acting debut in 1904 in *Tit for Tat*. He continued to act for several seasons, including a tour with Mrs. Fiske, before turning his hand to directing. He successively served the Shuberts,♦ Charles Frohman,♦ and Al Woods,♦ staging such diverse pieces as Clyde Fitch's♦ *The City*♦ (1909) and the Julian Eltinge♦ musical, *The Crinoline Girl* (1914). He served as president of Actors' Equity,♦ during its 1919 strike. In the 1920s he wrote several plays with his wife, Anita Loos,♦ including *The Whole Town's Talking* (1923), in which a small-town braggart finds he must make good his boasts of having loved a movie star; and a 1926 dramatization of Miss Loos's *Gentlemen Prefer Blondes*. ♦ He was a native of Sandusky, Ohio.

EMERY, GILBERT, see *Hero, The*

EMERY, MISS [also known as MRS. BURROUGHS] (d. 1832) A fine tragedienne whose ghastly death gave her greater notice than any of her performances, she had become a favorite at the Surrey Theatre in her native London before Wemyss♦ brought her to America. She made her American debut in 1827 at Philadelphia's Chestnut Street

Theatre♦ as Belvidera (*Venice Preserved*) and also won acclaim there and in New York for her Portia, Bianca (*Fazio*), and other popular heroines of the era. For reasons now lost she was suddenly denied parts and finally sank to prostitution in the notorious Five Points slum, where she was discovered dying after a bloody brawl. T. Allston Brown♦ adds the unusual note that she was "the largest woman ever seen on the American stage."

EMMET, J[OSEPH] K[LEIN] (1841–91) Born in St. Louis, he was apprenticed after his father's early death to a sign painter who also painted sets for local playhouses. Working on these gave him a taste for the stage and before long he was performing his own song and dance act. He made his debut in St. Louis in 1866. A stint in minstrelsy, including an engagement with Dan Bryant,♦ was followed by several seasons in variety, where he perfected a "Dutch" act, wearing a green blouse and cap and wooden shoes, and singing in broken English. In 1870 the wide-eyed actor with curly black hair first appeared as Fritz, the young man seeking his long-lost sister, in *Fritz, Our Cousin German.* ♦ The play, in which he sang a number of songs and for which he eventually wrote the famous "Emmet's Lullaby," made him a star and provided him with a vehicle for the rest of his life. Between engagements in this work he appeared in a number of similar pieces such as *Carl, the Fiddler* (1871), *Max, the Merry Swiss Boy* (1873), and *Fritz in Ireland* (1879). His skill with such instruments as the guitar, the violin, and the harmonica, and his fine Irish tenor voice and supple dancing combined with his winning personality to assure him steady occupation in what were essentially the flimsiest of plays. He died, apparently of paresis, while still at the height of his popularity.

EMMETT, DAN[IEL DECATUR] (1815–1904) One of four men who in 1843 founded the Virginia Minstrels,♦ generally acknowledged to be the first traditional blackface minstrel troupe, he lived long enough to watch the small minstrel bands grow into mammoth companies and ultimately fade away in the wake of vaudeville and silent films. He was apparently a performer of no special merit and with time played smaller and smaller roles in companies such as Dan Bryant's.♦ His real claim to fame came as a composer of such minstrel standards as "Old Dan Tucker," "Early in the Morning," "The Blue Tail Fly," and, most of all, "Dixie."♦ As a result of the celebrity his songs brought him he was able to tour in the 1880s, appearing as part of a nostalgic minstrel quintet in Leavitt's♦ Gigantean Minstrels.

Emperor Jones, The, a play in eight scenes by Eugene O'Neill.♦ Produced by the Provincetown Players♦ at the Neighborhood Playhouse. November 1, 1920. 204 performances.

A former Pullman porter, Brutus Jones (Charles S. Gilpin♦), escapes from a prison he has been sent to as the result of a fight in a crap game and flees to a West Indies island. There he establishes himself as emperor, running an abusive, corrupt dictatorial regime. A white Cockney trader, Smithers (Jasper Deeter♦), warns him that the incessant drum beating signifies an imminent revolt, but Jones is cocky and assures Smithers only a silver bullet can kill him. The revolt forces him to hide in the forest. There the troops of Lem (Charles Ellis), a native chief, find him and kill him with a silver bullet that Lem has had specially made. Looking at the body, Smithers remarks, "Where's yer 'igh an' mighty airs now, yer bloomin' Majesty? Silver bullets! Gawd blimey, but yer died in the 'eight of style, any'ow."

Based loosely on an incident in Haitian history, the play was originally called *The Silver Bullet*. George Jean Nathan♦ thought the play a compelling drama "touched by a visionary ecstasy." It was also seen as an early attempt by O'Neill at expressionism, albeit framed in two realistic scenes. Jones was perceived to represent modern man, and the jungle a modern, destructive civilization. Stylized settings and a persistent beating of drums in the background accentuated the theme. The play has been revived on several occasions, was a standard in the repertory of the Hedgerow Theatre,♦ and remains popular with little theatre and college groups.

Empire Theatre For many years the oldest and most prestigious playhouse in New York, it was built by Al Hayman♦ and Charles Frohman♦ and stood directly across Broadway from the Metropolitan Opera House, one door away from 40th Street. The architect was J. B. McElfatrick,♦ and while his design was undistinguished it was nonetheless attractive. A long lobby, in later seasons hung with portraits of noted stars, led to a rococo auditorium decorated in rich reds and gold. The theatre opened in 1893 with *The Girl I Left Behind Me,*♦ and for the next 22 years, until Frohman's death, served as his flagship. The producer was insistent that the theatre's first attraction be an American play on an American theme, but his penchant for English and French successes meant that its early bills were primarily importations. Thus, the house witnessed the American premieres of numerous works by Pinero,♦ Jones,♦ Barrie,♦ and Maugham.♦ *Peter Pan*♦ (1905) opened there, as did *Captain Brass-*

bound's Conversion (1907). The house was also the home of Frohman's most celebrated stars, such as Maude Adams,♦ Ethel Barrymore,♦ and John Drew.♦ After Frohman's death the theatre continued to offer the greatest stars, often in fine plays. Miss Barrymore performed *Déclassée*♦ (1919) there; Katharine Cornell♦ appeared in several plays, including her most famous vehicle, *The Barretts of Wimpole Street*♦ (1930). Judith Anderson,♦ Ruth Chatterton,♦ Jane Cowl,♦ Julie Harris,♦ Doris Keane,♦ Helen Menken,♦ Lunt♦ and Fontanne,♦ and Ethel Waters♦ were all stellar attractions, as was *Hamlet* (1936) with John Gielgud♦ and *Life with Father*♦ (1939). For all its fame the theatre was threatened with loss of its license in 1926 when it housed a controversial play about lesbianism, *The Captive*. Authorities closed the play but never otherwise penalized the theatre. Its last play was *The Time of the Cuckoo*♦ (1952), starring Shirley Booth.♦ The building was demolished in 1953.

End of Summer, a comedy in three acts by S. N. Behrman.♦ Produced by the Theatre Guild♦ at the Guild Theatre. February 17, 1936. 152 performances.

Leonie Frothingham (Ina Claire♦) is a rich woman of old stock, as her mother, Mrs. Wyler (Mildred Natwick♦), is only too happy to point out. However, Leonie's concern is not her mother, but her daughter Paula (Doris Dudley), who is courted by two men. The older of the suitors is Dr. Kenneth Rice (Osgood Perkins♦), who is obviously something of a fortune hunter but promises to maintain Paula in her comfortable world. The other suitor is Will Dexter (Shepperd Strudwick), a young radical who promises only revolution and a new social order. When Paula decides in Will's favor, Leonie acquiesces, accepting the likelihood that the brilliant summer of her own life is about to fade. She even agrees to back a radical magazine which Will's friend, Dennis McCarthy (Van Heflin), hopes to publish.

Although Brooks Atkinson♦ suggested that Behrman's play was "one of those tolerant, witty, gently probing essays in modern thinking," he concluded, "you scarcely know which side he is taking." Yet the play, perhaps more clearly than any other Behrman comedy, suggested that the playwright was all in favor of a more open, even-handed society, provided it subscribed to some of the elegances and graces of the old order.

Enemy, The, a play in four acts by Channing Pollock.♦ Produced by Crosby Gaige♦ at the Times Square Theatre. October 20, 1925. 203 performances.

Pauli Arndt (Fay Bainter♦) has become almost a mother to her widowed father, Dr. Arndt (Russ Whytal), just as she seems to be to her poetic fiancé, Carl Behrend (Walter Abel). The men in her life are both pacifists, Carl even writing a play, *The Enemy,* which proclaims "Hate is the enemy of mankind." The Arndts have a welcome boarder, an English student, Bruce Gordon (Lyonel Watts). But matters change when World War I breaks out. Carl, who has married Pauli, enthusiastically joins the army and brands Bruce a traitor. Carl's father, profiteering from the war, similarly condemns Dr. Arndt's pacifist teachings. The war and its effects horrify Pauli. Carl is killed in battle. After the war Bruce returns, tells Pauli he has arranged for a London production of Carl's play, and asks her to marry him. Watching children playing soldier in the street, Pauli is uncertain how to respond. "God give us Love!," Bruce exclaims. "God give us Peace!," Pauli answers.

Praised highly by critics and editorial writers during its tryout, the play was coolly received in New York, where it was viewed merely as a well-meant jeremiad. Nevertheless, in an age of arch conservatism, preoccupied with financial success and good times, it found a substantial audience.

ENGEL, LEHMAN (1910–82) The Mississippi-born composer, conductor, author, and teacher studied at the University of Cincinnati, the Juilliard School of Music, and with Roger Sessions before writing incidental music for a 1934 production of *Within the Gates*. He later composed background music for several other shows as well as creating the score for *A Hero is Born* (1937). He was better known, however, as a conductor. Beginning with *The Cradle Will Rock*♦ (1937), he conducted the orchestras for such musicals as *Call Me Mister* (1946), *Wonderful Town*♦ (1953), *Fanny*♦ (1954), *Li'l Abner* (1956), *Jamaica* (1957), *Take Me Along*♦ (1959), *Do Re Mi* (1960), and *I Can Get It for You Wholesale* (1962). His lively response to performers on stage and his singing along as he conducted made him a happy part of the entertainment for those who could see him. But he was also a serious student of musical theatre, teaching both at the American Musical and Dramatic Theatre Academy and at New York University. Among his books are *Musical Shows: Planning and Producing* (1957), *The American*

Musical Theatre (1967), *Words with Music* (1972), and an autobiography, *This Bright Day* (1974).

ENGLANDER, LUDWIG (1859–1914) Born in Vienna, where he received his earliest musical training, he moved briefly to Paris and there worked for a time with Offenbach.♦ On coming to America he took a post as conductor for the Thalia Theatre, a playhouse catering to German immigrants. His first musical score, *Der Prinz Gemahl* (The Prince Consort), was presented there and failed. After a time he moved to the Casino Theatre,♦ at first solely as its musical director, but in short order provided a score for its production of *The Passing Show*♦ (1894), the first American revue. Following the opening he left the house to write independently. During the next 14 years he wrote the music for nearly 30 shows to reach Broadway. Among his works were *The Casino Girl* (1900), *The Strollers* (1901), *The Wild Rose* (1902), *Sally in Our Alley* (1902), *The Office Boy* (1903), *The Rich Mr. Hoggenheimer* (1906), and *Miss Innocence* (1908). After a long hiatus he wrote one final show shortly before his death, *Madam Moselle* (1914). He regularly made his own orchestrations and frequently conducted his own and other men's scores. For all his prolificacy he produced no songs of lasting fame. His lack of melodic inspiration was recognized even in his own day—critics described his work as "tinkly"—and many of his musicals had interpolations which proved far more popular and enduring than his contributions.

English Musicals [Other Than Gilbert and Sullivan] in America It is not generally recognized that, while American musicals have won world-wide fame for their daring and excellence, English musicals have time and again been the real pioneers. American lyric works have simply moved forward from the impetus provided by West End examples. The importance of Gilbert♦ and Sullivan♦ is detailed in the entry on them. While many of their contemporaries such as Cellier and Solomon enjoyed some popularity with American audiences, and *Erminie*'s♦ success was exceptional, it was the Savoyard comic operas which served as exemplars to American writers of the period and which opened all American stages to song and dance entertainments. When the vogue for comic opera faded, the Gaiety Theatre musical comedies that George Edwardes had instituted in London came across the Atlantic, beginning in 1894 with *A Gaiety Girl,* to speed the development of the new genre. Of course, America had also been evolving its own musical comedy

tradition. Harrigan♦ and Hart♦ and farce-comedy,♦ especially those advanced farce-comedies of Hoyt♦ as exemplified by *A Trip to Chinatown,*♦ suggested America could create its own musical comedy tradition. But the sophistication and elegance of the Gaiety musicals set new standards and propelled the advance, albeit it was not a Gaiety musical but *Florodora*♦ (1900) which proved the most popular importation. In the 1920s the popularity of *Charlot's Revue*♦ similarly promoted the cause of the intimate revue and signaled the end of the gargantuan extravaganza of the Ziegfeld♦ school. A handful of later English musicals were noteworthy successes, such as *Bitter Sweet,*♦ *The Boy Friend, Oliver,*♦ *Stop the World—I Want To Get Off.* However, these were looked upon as almost *sui generis* and had little real influence on the development of American musicals. Since then such Andrew Lloyd Webber♦ musicals as *Evita,*♦ *Cats,*♦ and *The Phantom of the Opera*♦ have enjoyed remarkable successes, but their influence on mainstream American lyric theatre remains to be seen. It seems unlikely that the long Broadway run of *Me and My Girl*♦ will prove meaningful.

English Restoration and Eighteenth-Century Drama and Comedy in America Although the earliest Restoration (1660–1700) plays were about eighty years old when professional theatre emerged in America, and while the last of these works were approaching the half-century mark, they remained among the most popular and frequently revived pieces on the London stage, so constituted a substantial part of the repertory of the first actors to play in America. Dryden, Otway, Congreve, Vanbrugh, and Farquhar appeared regularly in the lists of playwrights offered by Murray♦ and Kean, ♦ by Upton,♦ and by the elder Hallam.♦ At the same time such later authors as Cibber, Garrick, Rowe, and Lillo began to make numerous appearances. The Elizabethan♦ and Jacobean♦ plays that completed the repertory are discussed in a separate entry.

From the start Otway's *Venice Preserved* and Farquhar's *The Beaux' Stratagem,* possibly along with his *The Recruiting Officer,* were the most popular of the Restoration works. Indeed, throughout the first half of the 19th century *Venice Preserved* remained far and away the most revived work from this era. The roles of Jaffier and Pierre were favored parts of such early American tragedians as Forrest♦ and the two great Booths.♦

Congreve's *Love for Love* came early to American stages, and while revivals were not numerous, the play did return at intervals, always respected and admired. Curiously, the first professional American staging of his equally great *The Way of the World* seems not to have taken place until 1924!

Rowe's *The Tragedy of Jane Shore* and eventually Gay's *The Beggar's Opera* were the most often produced of the earlier 18th-century pieces. Later, Home's *Douglas*♦ became for a long time one of the most familiar of all the period's plays. During the last years of the century, by which time professional theatre was permanently established in America, five then new plays won huge audiences. Mrs. Cowley's *The Belle's Stratagem* retained its popularity throughout the 19th century, especially at great houses known for their ensemble playing of comedy, such as Wallack's,♦ Mrs. Drew's♦ in Philadelphia, and the Boston Museum.♦ Sheridan's♦ *Pizarro*♦ was a standard vehicle for many early 19th-century tragedians. Of course, the three greatest comedies of this period, all of which continue to hold the boards, were Goldsmith's *She Stoops To Conquer* and Sheridan's *The School for Scandal* and *The Rivals*. Of these three *The School for Scandal* was the most regularly seen.

In the 20th century, mountings of the 18th-century and, on the rarest of occasions, of Restoration plays became very infrequent and were largely special events. The Players♦ offered several highly acclaimed all-star revivals in the 1920s and, to cite one later example, Cyril Ritchard♦ headed a superb revival of *The Relapse* in 1950. Visiting English ensembles have generally provided the best presentations, such as John Gielgud's♦ *Love for Love* in 1947. To a small extent regional and collegiate theatres have helped fill the void.

ENNERY, A.-P., see *D'Ennery, Adolphe-Philippe*

Enter Madame, a comedy in three acts by Gilda Varesi and Dolly Byrne. Produced by Brock Pemberton♦ at the Garrick Theatre. August 16, 1920. 350 performances.

Gerald Fitzgerald (Norman Trevor) has been married for more than 20 years to the great prima donna Lisa Della Robbia (Miss Varesi), but has tired of following her all over the world in the wake of her sycophantic entourage. When one newspaper calls him Gerald Della Robbia and another nominates him as "President of the Only Her Husband's Club," he decides enough is enough. He has met a sedate widow, Flora Preston (Jane Meredith), and fallen in love with her. Lisa agrees to a divorce, although she still loves Gerald. After the divorce comes through, Lisa invites Gerald and Flora to dinner. Turning on

the charm, she persuades him to leave Flora and marry her again.

Heywood Broun♦ noted, "here is an excellent light comedy . . . The story is slight, but it is briskly told." The play was revived for a successful road tour in 1930 with Helen Menken♦ as the prima donna. Miss Varesi, a popular actress, was the daughter of the celebrated opera star, Elena Varesi, and acknowledged that much of the play derived from memories of her own childhood with her mother.

EPHRON, Phoebe and Henry, see *Three's a Family.*

Equity Library Theatre Founded in 1943 by Sam Jaffe, representing Actors' Equity,♦ and George Freedley,♦ at the time curator of the New York Public Library Theatre Collection, ELT, as it is often referred to, was designed to provide a showcase for young actors, directors, and technicians and to create an audience from among those who could not afford commercial theatre. A non-profit organization, it originally presented its plays at libraries and charged no admission, but asked instead for a contribution to help sustain it. Since 1949 it has operated its own theatre, first at the Lenox Hill Playhouse, and later at other auditoriums. Actors whose careers were helped by early appearances with the organization include James Earl Jones,♦ Richard Kiley,♦ and Jason Robards, Jr.♦ Financial problems forced its closing during the 1989–90 season.

Equity Players An acting and producing ensemble formed in 1922 by members of Actors' Equity♦ for the presentation of superior new plays and classical revivals. Although most of its mountings won critical praise they proved unappealing to a majority of playgoers. One notable exception was a 1922 production of Jesse Lynch Williams's♦ *Why Not?*. After some reorganization the name was changed to the Actors' Theatre. Under this banner during the 1924–25 season it offered distinguished revivals of *Candida*♦ and *The Wild Duck,* the former directed by Dudley Digges,♦ the latter by Digges and Clare Eames.♦ In 1927 the group was absorbed by Kenneth MacGowan's♦ company in Greenwich Village.

Equus Peter Shaffer's♦ 1973 London success, centering on a psychiatrist and his young male patient who is obsessed with horses, was produced by Kermit Bloomgarden♦ and others at the Plymouth Theatre on October 24, 1974. It compiled 1,209 performances. Anthony Hopkins was the original doctor, and Peter Firth, the boy. Several other notable actors, including Anthony Perkins♦ and Richard Burton,♦ later assumed the role of the doctor.

ERLANGER, A[BRAHAM] L[INCOLN] (1860–1930) As a young boy in his native Cleveland, he sold opera glasses at John Ellsler's Academy of Music. When Ellsler went bankrupt after building the Euclid Avenue Opera House, Mark Hanna bought the theatre and appointed Erlanger treasurer. Hanna and Erlanger became friends and the young man accepted Hanna's cynical business philosophy. At the same time he developed an interest in Napoleon, beginning a collection of Napoleonic memorabilia and busts which would later clutter his office and which his enemies would point to with glee. The blocky, balding, bull-faced man began to direct and produce contemporary melodramas and shortly thereafter entered into partnership with a lawyer, Marc Klaw.♦ The pair came East and bought out the Taylor Theatrical Exchange, changing its name to the Klaw and Erlanger Exchange. Among the celebrated performers they represented were John Ellsler's daugher Effie,♦ Joseph Jefferson,♦ and Fanny Davenport.♦ Theatrical bookings of the day were loosely organized and often chaotic. In 1895 the pair met quietly with Charles Frohman,♦ Al Hayman,♦ William Harris,♦ Fred Nixon-Nirdlinger,♦ and Fred Zimmerman♦ to attempt to bring some order to the system, and in the following year the group established what became known as the Theatrical Syndicate or Trust,♦ with Erlanger in effective control. Within a short time the Syndicate controlled several hundred theatres across the country, almost always the principal houses in each city. Whatever the group's original intention, and that has been subject to argument ever since, the Syndicate's power quickly led to gross abuse, with performers and producers who refused to meet its often unreasonable demands denied suitable theatres. Such distinguished players as Mrs. Fiske♦ and Sarah Bernhardt♦ were reduced to performing in tents and lesser theatres, but won huge audiences and widespread admiration for their defiance. In 1907 the Syndicate seemingly attempted to take over vaudeville as well, but in a short while sold out to Keith♦ for well over a million dollars, suggesting to many that the move was merely a gigantic blackmail attempt against Keith. The Messrs. Shubert♦ succeeded in breaking Erlanger's stranglehold, and films further diminished his empire.

Although most theatre figures looked on him as a vicious, callous, arrogant man, Erlanger had a number of loyal admirers, such as George M. Cohan♦ and, until he fought with them late in their careers, Florenz Ziegfeld♦ and Charles Dillingham.♦ He bankrolled most of their productions, including the first *Follies.*♦ Ziegfeld claimed that when they went to Europe together Erlanger was only interested in seeing places of cultural importance, and Cohan often told of his wit. His detractors, however, insisted his artistic inclinations were small and his wit unintentional, such as the time he changed the title of a show from *Little Miss Springtime* to *Miss Springtime,* insisting nothing little could play his flagship, the New Amsterdam Theatre.♦

Beginning with *The Great Metropolis* (1889), he produced hundreds of plays in New York and silently underwrote many others. Although he took public credit, usually as co-producer, for such plays as *Rebecca of Sunnybrook Farm*♦ (1910), *Kismet*♦ (1911), *Pollyanna* (1916), *The Famous Mrs. Fair*♦ (1919), and *To the Ladies*♦ (1922), he was better known as producer or co-producer of such musicals as *Forty-five Minutes from Broadway*♦ (1906), *The Pink Lady*♦ (1911), *The Count of Luxembourg* (1912), *Two Little Girls in Blue* (1921), and *Honeymoon Lane* (1926).

Erminie An English musical with libretto by Harry Paulton and music by Edward Jacobowski, it opened at the Casino Theatre♦ in 1886, less than a year after its English premiere, and enjoyed the longest run of any musical during that playhouse's early heyday, 571 performances. Only one contemporary American musical, *Adonis,*♦ had run longer on Broadway. *Erminie*'s musical audiences especially admired the clowning of Francis Wilson♦ as the comic vagabond, Cadeaux, and one song, "Lullaby (Dear Mother, in Dreams I See Her)." Though the work was long held in affection and esteem and was successfully revived as late as 1921, it had little real importance in the development of the American musical theatre.

ERROL, LEON (1881–1951) The balding, sour-faced comic, famous for his rubber-legged drunk scenes, was born in Australia and originally planned a medical career. To earn money for tuition he played in vaudeville, where he was so successful that he abandoned his medical ambitions. He performed in Shakespearean repertory, with a circus, and in comic opera before coming to San Francisco. The 1906 earthquake prompted him to work his way East, where Ziegfeld♦ eventually discovered him and enrolled him in the *Ziegfeld Follies of 1911.*♦ He scored a huge success, and Ziegfeld next cast him in *A Winsome Widow* (1912), and in the 1912, 1913, 1914, and 1915 editions of the *Follies,* and in *The Century Girl* (1916). After appearing in the 1917 and 1918 editions of *Hitchy-Koo,* he returned to the Ziegfeld fold to play Connie, the impoverished nobleman who befriends the heroine-waif in *Sally*♦ (1920). Later appearances were in *Louie the 14th* (1925), *Yours Truly* (1927), and *Fioretta* (1929). Describing his antics in this last musical one critic wrote, "For these many years Mr. Errol has never stood quietly on his feet. In 'Fioretta' he slides down pairs of stairs, handicapped by a metal breast-plate and a basket of fruit, falls into a canal, bends, sags, and teeters all evening." He was also skilled behind the scenes, occasionally writing his own sketches and serving as director or co-director for the 1914 and 1915 *Follies, The Century Girl, Words and Music* (1917), and *The Blue Kitten* (1922). In later years he was famous for his film shorts in which he often portrayed a henpecked husband.

Esmeralda, a play in four acts by Francis Hodgson Burnett♦ and William Gillette.♦ Produced at the Madison Square Theatre.♦ October 29, 1881. 350 performances.

Esmeralda Rogers (Annie Russell♦), a winsome North Carolina farm girl, falls in love with her rugged, good-natured neighbor, Dave Hardy (Eben Plympton♦), but her ambitious mother, Lydia Ann (Kate Denin Wilson), objects. As always, her acquiescent father, Elbert (Leslie Allen), accepts his wife's ultimatums. When some gold is found on what the Rogerses believe is their property, the newly rich Lydia Ann rushes Esmeralda off to Paris, where she hopes to marry her daughter to the Marquis de Montessin (Davenport Bebus). The facetious but kindly Mr. Estabrook (Thomas Whiffen), sensing Esmeralda's unhappiness, manages to delay the wedding until it is learned that the gold is really on Dave Hardy's land. Mrs. Rogers looks on Hardy with new eyes, returns home, and allows Esmeralda to marry Dave. The young couple settle into wedded bliss.

Called a "sweet, harmless play" by Odell,♦ the dramatization of Mrs. Burnett's novelette was criticized by some contemporary critics, who suggested that the play really ended in the second act, when Esmeralda marries Hardy. The rest of the story described their early married life. Audiences had no time for such quibbles, so the play enjoyed one of the longest runs of its era and afforded both Russell and other actresses a popular vehicle for the next twenty years.

Ethan Frome, a play in a prologue, three acts and an epilogue by Owen Davis♦ and Donald Davis. Produced by Max Gordon♦ at the National Theatre. January 21, 1936. 120 performances.

When Mattie Silver (Ruth Gordon♦) comes to live with her cousin, Zenobia Frome (Pauline Lord♦), and Zenobia's husband, Ethan (Raymond Massey♦), Ethan and Mattie fall in love. Zenobia orders Mattie from the house. On the way to the station, Ethan and Mattie attempt suicide, but are instead crippled for life, leaving the slatternly, bitter Zenobia to care for them.

This dramatization of Edith Wharton's short novel was enhanced by Jo Mielziner's♦ superb settings and Guthrie McClintic's♦ brilliant staging, but most of all by the luminous performances of its three stars.

ETHEL, AGNES (1853–1903) Briefly one of the most popular and promising of American actresses, she trained with Matilda Heron♦ and made her debut in New York in 1868, playing Miss Heron's most famous role, Camille. Her performance caught the attention of Augustin Daly,♦ who enlisted her as a member of his first Fifth Avenue Theatre♦ ensemble. She portrayed Rosie Farquhere in the opening attraction, *Play* (1869). "What the audience saw," Daly's biographer wrote, "was a slender figure, candid eyes, flowing auburn hair, an oval face, and regular features always lit up by an expression of childish appeal. These and a low voice of penetrating quality dwelt in the public memory . . . Her gifts were not varied or marked, but she filled the eye and ear so completely that no one asked for more." She scored her biggest success at Daly's as Gilberte, the spoiled child bride whose irresponsible behavior finally destroys her, in *Frou-Frou*♦ (1870). Her success led her to refuse several roles not to her liking, most notably the role of Ann Sylvester in *Man and Wife* (1870), in which Clara Morris♦ went on to make a hit. Daly thereafter rarely cast her, but lent her to his father-in-law, James C. Duff,♦ to play Med, the gun-toting "Wild Flower of the Plains," in *Horizon*♦ (1871), which furthered her popularity. She then moved to the rival Union Square Theatre,♦ winning applause in the title role of *Agnes* (1872), a work reputedly written especially for her by Victorien Sardou.♦ However, her rejection of subsequent parts led to her dismissal and she retired when she married in 1873.

ETTING, RUTH (1907–78) Born in David City, Nevada, the blonde torch singer, whose personal life often mirrored the sad songs she sang, was best known as a night-club performer, but appeared in several Broadway shows. She introduced "Shaking the Blues Away" in *Ziegfeld Follies of 1927,* ◆ "Love Me or Leave Me" in *Whoopee* ◆ (1928), "Get Happy" in *9:15 Revue* (1930), and "Ten Cents a Dance" in *Simple Simon* (1930). She also revived "Shine On Harvest Moon" in *Ziegfeld Follies of 1931.*

Eugene O'Neill Memorial Theater Center Founded in 1963 by George C. White, the center is housed in Waterford, Conn., in an old home that had been slated for demolition until White and his associates intervened. White felt the American theatre at the time was in dire need of revitalization, so established his "forum of ideas," whose principal aim was "to provide channels for communication between artists of the highest caliber." To this end, regular summer seminars were instituted which have served to encourage new playwrights, technicians, and critics. The National Playwrights Conference, ◆ National Critics Institute, ◆ National Theatre Institute (for college students), National Musical Theatre Conference, and the National Theatre of the Deaf ◆ have all been developed under its aegis. The Center also operates the O'Neill Library and Museum at Monte Cristo Cottage, the former home of James O'Neill ◆ and Eugene O'Neill ◆ at nearby New London.

Evangeline; or, The Belle of Acadia, a musical burlesque in three acts. Book and lyrics by J. Cheever Goodwin. ◆ Music by E. E. Rice. ◆ Produced at Niblo's Garden. ◆ July 27, 1874. 16 performances.

When her people are expelled by the British from their Acadian village, Evangeline (Ione Burke) and her lover, Gabriel (Connie Thompson), are separated. Evangeline wanders the world, from the wilds of Africa to the wilder West, before she is reunited with her fiancé.

Freely adapted from Longfellow's poem, the burlesque included such characters as a dancing heifer, an amorous whale, and the Lone Fisherman, who is forever looking for the sea with his telescope but who never utters a word. The burlesque began the careers of both Goodwin and Rice, later giving an important leg up to such later famous performers as Henry E. Dixey ◆ and Francis Wilson ◆ (both of whom played half of the heifer) and W. H. Crane. ◆ Originally a Boston production, this most popular and enduring of American musical burlesques was played incessantly for the remainder of the century, although it produced no songs of note.

EVANS, CHARLES E[VAN] (1856–1945) After running away from his Rochester, N.Y., home to try his luck in vaudeville, he joined James Niles to create the successful team of Niles and Evans. Later the men banded with Fred C. Bryant and William F. Hoey ◆ to form another popular act, "Meteors." When the team dispersed, Evans and Hoey asked the famous minstrel Frank Dumont ◆ to write a sketch for them. The result was "The Book Agent," which the pair performed for several seasons before requesting Charles Hoyt ◆ to expand it into a full-length play. Hoyt's version, *A Parlor Match* ◆ (1884), gave them a vehicle for the next ten years. Although Hoey dominated the show with his portrayal of a seedy tramp, the short, slight, dapper Evans won rounds of laughs with his uncontrollable feet. The partnership dissolved in 1894, and Evans took over the old Park Theatre, refurbished it, and renamed it the Herald Square. He remained as manager for several seasons, then resumed his acting career. He won applause as the happily married husband pursued by his old flame in George Arliss's ◆ *There and Back* (1903) and later toured vaudeville in a one-act version, "It's Up to You, William." His last appearance was as a replacement in the role of Judge Townsend in *Lightnin'* in 1919.

EVANS, [WILLIAM] GEORGE (1870–1915) Born in Wales, the bantam-sized minstrel joined Balser's Musical Minstrels in 1891, later moving to Haverly's Minstrels, Cleveland's Minstrels, and to Primrose and West's company. Sometime early in this period he first sang his "I'll Be True to Honey Boy" and was ever afterwards known as "Honey Boy" Evans. With the decline of minstrelsy he appeared briefly in several musicals and composed the music for "In the Good Old Summertime," which Blanche Ring ◆ introduced in *The Defender* (1902). In 1904 he toured briefly as a jockey in a musical of his own composition, named after his 1902 song success. When George M. Cohan ◆ and Sam Harris ◆ attempted to revive the vogue for minstrel shows in 1908 with the Cohan and Harris Minstrels, he was one of the company's stars. In later years he played vaudeville with a blackface monologue. Although Evans arrived on the scene long after minstrelsy's heyday, he is recalled as one of the finest of blackface artists, a fine singer, and capital comic.

EVANS, MAURICE (1901–89) The English-born actor came to America in 1935, after establishing himself on the London stage, including a stint with the Old Vic. ◆ His first appearance was as Romeo to Katharine Cornell's ◆ Juliet, followed by the Dauphin to her Saint Joan. He then played Napoleon in *St. Helena* (1936). Major recognition came when he mounted his interpretation of *Richard II* (1937). Brooks Atkinson♦ called his a "glowing performance," one of "infinite subtlety and burning emotion," although some dissenters suggested his clear diction was marred by a singsong delivery and his interpretations were more intellectual than deeply felt. Additional accolades appeared in the wake of his full-length *Hamlet*♦ (1938) and his portrayal of Sir John Falstaff in *Henry IV, Part 1*♦ (1939). By this time recognized as the finest and most loyal proponent of Shakespeare on the New York stage, he continued his series of highly praised performances with his cockney Malvolio opposite Helen Hayes's♦ Viola in 1940 and his Macbeth to Judith Anderson's♦ Lady Macbeth the following year. During World War II he entertained troops with a cut-down version of *Hamlet,* which he later successfully mounted on Broadway in 1945. He next scored as John Tanner in *Man and Superman*♦ (1947), then played in a double bill of *The Browning Version* and *Harlequinade* (1949), before returning to Shaw to play Dick Dudgeon in *The Devil's Disciple*♦ (1950). In 1952 he began a long run as Tony Wendice, who bungles his attempt at a perfect crime, in *Dial M for Murder.* After appearances as King Magnus in Shaw's♦ *The Apple Cart* (1956) and Captain Shotover in *Heartbreak House* (1957), his luck at picking hits ran out when he essayed the crusading Rev. Brock in the musical *Tenderloin* (1960). In 1962 he toured with Helen Hayes in *Shakespeare Revisited: A Program for Two Players.* Besides being the producer of most of his own productions, he was co-producer of two Broadway hits: *The Teahouse of the August Moon*♦ (1953) and *No Time for Sergeants*♦ (1955). In later years he appeared on television and in occasional films.

　Autobiography: *All This—and Evans Too!,* Columbia, S.C., 1987.

Eve of St. Mark, The, a drama in two acts by Maxwell Anderson.♦ Produced by the Playwrights' Company♦ at the Cort Theatre. October 7, 1942. 305 performances.

　Shortly before America enters World War II, Private Quizz West (William Prince) returns home on leave to his family's farm in upstate New York, and announces to his mother, Nell (Aline McMahon), and father, Deck (Matt Crowley), that he has fallen in love with a neighbor girl, Janet Feller (Mary Rolfe). Back at camp he remains loyal when his buddies take him to a local honky-tonk, while Janet, too, is faithful at home. After the war comes,

Quizz is sent to the Philippines. The lovers correspond, but Quizz comes to her even more vividly in her dreams. Before long news arrives that Quizz has been killed. Janet and Quizz's family accept his death stoically. When his younger brothers enlist Deck tells them, "Make a new world, boys."

　Hailed by Howard Barnes of the *Herald Tribune* as "a war drama of emotional tension, humor and poetic splendor," the play was a far cry from Anderson's less romantic, less sentimental *What Price Glory?,* ♦ the most celebrated American play about World War I. It was one of the few plays dealing with World War II which succeeded at the time.

EVELYN [MORRIS], JUDITH (1913–67) The darkish, somewhat stern looking actress was born in Seneca, S.D., and made her acting debut when she was fifteen. She is recalled primarily for two notable performances: as Mrs. Manningham, whose husband is trying to drive her insane, in *Angel Street*♦ (1941), and Ann Downs, the vicious wife, in *The Shrike*♦ (1952).

Evita A musical about Eva Peron, wife of the Argentine dictator with Patti LuPone in the title role, it was written by two Englishmen, Andrew Lloyd Webber♦ and Tim Rice, and staged by Harold Prince.♦ The show opened in New York in September 1979 and at the time of its close was the longest run foreign musical in Broadway history.

EWELL, TOM [né S. YEWELL TOMPKINS] (b. 1909) A native of Owensboro, Ky., the quizzical-faced comedian enjoyed a stage career that spanned nearly fifty years but is best known as Richard Sherman, the summer bachelor who falls in love with his upstairs neighbor, in *The Seven Year Itch*♦ (1952).

EWEN, DAVID (1907–85) Brought to the United States from his native Austria at the age of three, he studied briefly at the City College of New York and at Columbia. In 1943 he wrote *The Story of George Gershwin,* a biography of the composer designed for young readers. He later published similar biographies of Irving Berlin,♦ Jerome Kern,♦ Cole Porter,♦ and Richard Rodgers,♦ as well as a general history of our musical theatre. For adults he has written biographies of Gershwin,♦ Kern, and Rodgers, and a survey of composers in the American theatre. His best-known work is *The Complete Book of the American Musical Theatre* (1950), which was drastically revised and updated as *The New Complete Book of the American Musical Theater* in 1970.

Although some later scholars have criticized his work as frequently careless, his books remain readable and useful, and his importance as a pioneer in books on modern American musicals and their composers cannot be gainsaid.

Excess Baggage, a comedy in three acts by John McGowan.♦ Produced at the Ritz Theatre. December 26, 1927. 216 performances.

Eddie Kane (Eric Dressler) and Elsa McCoy (Miriam Hopkins) are a small-time vaudeville act. Eddie juggles while the attractive Elsa merely stands by to assist. She is, she claims, only excess baggage. Hoping for a more important career, Elsa tries out for a film and is soon a star. Eddie quits performing and lives off Elsa until shame drives him back to the stage. His single act seems about to fail, but Elsa, sitting in the audience, runs to join him.

The play appeared to many critics a more superficial, comic version of *Burlesque,*♦ which had opened earlier in the same season. The play itself was one of eleven openings on the busiest night in Broadway history and the only one to enjoy a huge commercial success, although *Behold the Bridegroom,*♦ another opening that night, received far more critical acclaim and attention and had a respectable run.

Experience, a play in ten scenes by George V. Hobart.♦ Produced at the Booth Theatre. October 27, 1914. 255 performances.

Youth (William Elliott, who was also the producer), goaded by an insidious but faint-hearted Ambition, leaves his happy garden and sets out on the Road of Life. His journeys take him to the Street of Vacillation, the Primrose Path, the Corridors of Chance, and the Street of Disillusion. His fortunes fail, and he moves from one frustrating, unhappy adventure to the next. When he is about to take up with Crime (Frank McCormack), the voices of his past call to him and he stumbles home. There, with the help of Love (Miriam Collins), he finds a better life.

Originally presented as a one-act play at The Lambs,♦ it was enlarged by the author and became one of the few out-and-out morality plays to find commercial success.

Experimental Theatre, The Conceived in 1940 and incorporated under the aegis of ANTA♦ as a nonprofit organization in New York in 1941, with Antoinette Perry♦ as president, it began to offer plays in early 1947 at the Princess Theatre.♦ During the 1947–48 season it moved to Maxine Elliott's

Theatre, where it presented well-received productions of *Galileo* (1947), *Skipper Next to God* (1948), *Hope Is the Thing with Feathers* (1948), and *Ballet Ballads* (1948). Several notable actors, including Charles Laughton♦ and John Garfield,♦ appeared in these productions, performing for token salaries, and several of the plays moved on to extended runs. The group was assailed early on for its emphasis on foreign playwrights, so changed its program. But even a change of program and praiseworthy productions could not cut the mounting deficits that eventually caused abandonment of its plans.

Expressing Willie, a comedy in three acts by Rachel Crothers.♦ Produced at the 48th Street Theatre. April 16, 1924. 293 performances.

Willie Smith (Richard Sterling), scion of a toothpaste magnate, builds a luxurious Italianate mansion on Long Island and is soon surrounded by hosts of sycophantic spongers and social climbers. Notable among them is Frances Sylvester (Merle Maddern), a pushy but talentless actress who is determined to marry Willie for his money. Willie's observant mother, Mrs. Smith (Louise Closser Hale♦), sets about to save him from Frances's clutches by inviting Minnie Whitcomb (Crystal Herne♦), his music teacher and friend, to help bring Willie to his senses. Minnie's artistry and reasonableness put the pretentious actress to shame. Willie is made to recognize where his affections and money belong.

John Corbin♦ wrote in the *Times,* "The sallies of [Miss Crothers's] wit took the audience by storm . . . The varied group of her characters was so subtly and saliently limned that half a dozen actors, long loved and honored, seemed lifted above themselves as by the touch of genius." At a time of many large new fortunes and conspicuous nouveau-riches consumption the play treated lightly the same theme F. Scott Fitzgerald would approach more seriously the next year in *The Great Gatsby.* Yet the real center of interest was not Willie or his predicaments, but, as in all Miss Crothers's best plays, the relationships and interaction of her principal women.

Expressionism in American Theatre Although evident in the latter plays of Strindberg♦ and a few other late 19th-century playwrights, the movement—which found advocates in almost all the arts—was not given formal theatrical definition until shortly before World War I and then primarily in Germany. It did not affect American drama and production until after the war. Most immediately it was a reaction to neo-romanticism and impressionism but mainly it sought to move behind the façade of naturalism, and to unmask inner emotions and hidden realities. For a time Eugene O'Neill♦ was its major American exponent, employing it with great skill in such works as *The Emperor Jones*♦ (1920), *The Hairy Ape*♦ (1922), and *The Great God Brown*♦ (1926). The irresistibly pulsating drums of the first, the total indifference of the rich shoppers to the hero's rough jostling of them in the second, and the symbolic masks of the last were all audible or visible manifestations of the points the playwright was driving home in his texts. Perhaps the most famous and completely successful expressionistic play in our literature is Elmer Rice's♦ *The Adding Machine*♦ (1923), in which huge numbers whirled around the bookkeeper-hero and he was dwarfed by a gigantic adding machine. Another famous play was the work of two unlikely figures, George S. Kaufman♦ and Marc Connelly,♦ who set their *Beggar on Horseback*♦ (1924) in a fantastic dream world. Also popular were European playwrights such as Ernst Toller and Karel Capek, especially the latter's 1922 offerings: *R.U.R.* and *The World We Live In* (*The Insect Comedy*). By the late twenties the movement's vogue had waned, although its characteristics remained to be seen in the distorted dialogue, the flattened figures, and surrealistic settings and props of later post-expressionistic theatre.

Eyes of Youth, a comedy drama in three acts by Charles Guernon and Max Marcin.♦ Produced by Al Woods♦ and the Messrs. Shubert♦ at Maxine Elliott's Theatre. August 22, 1917. 414 performances.

Worried about her future, Gina Ashling (Marjorie Rambeau♦) consults a yogi who gazes into his ball and tells her he can see several paths, one of which he may not reveal. The first path makes Gina a schoolteacher, dismissed for incompetence and deserted by her caddish lover; the second turns her into a prima donna in an amoral world. Another road takes her into a disastrous marriage, a divorce court on trumped-up charges of infidelity, and finally into prostitution. In the end, Gina elects to take the one course the yogi cannot reveal.

Considered, in theatrical parlance of the time, a "trick melodrama," the play was one of the runaway successes of its day. Alma Tell♦ and her sister Olive led the principal road companies which played long engagements in many cities. Because the play was listed as a comedy drama, playgoers could assume the implied correctness of the path Gina took, all the while enjoying the sensationalism of the episodes depicted.

EYTINGE, ROSE (1835–1911) Born in Philadelphia, and raised there and in Brooklyn, the "black-eyed, black-haired Jewess," as Daniel Frohman♦ described her, made her debut in 1852 in Syracuse N.Y., as Melanie in Dion Boucicault's♦ *The Old Guard.* Ten seasons in stock followed before she became an understudy to Laura Keene♦ and made an unscheduled New York debut in 1863, playing Nellie O'Donaghue in *Bantry Bay* when Miss Keene was indisposed. Coming to Edwin Booth's♦ attention, he hired her as his leading lady for his 1864 New York stand. Thus, critics first saw her as Fiordelisa opposite his Bertuccio in *The Fool's Revenge* (*Le Roi s'amuse*). They were immediately impressed. She also played with Booth in *The Marble Heart*♦ and *Richelieu.*♦ She won more laudatory notices when she appeared with J. W. Wallack♦ and E. L. Davenport♦ in 1865 as Hortense de Piermont in Bayle Bernard's♦ *The Iron Mask* and as Mrs. Sternhold in *Still Waters Run Deep.* Later in the same year she portrayed Florence to John Sleeper Clarke's Asa Trenchard in *Our American Cousin.*♦ By the time she played Kate Peyton, the wife falsely accused of murdering her husband, in Augustin Daly's♦ *Griffith Gaunt* in 1866, the *Time*'s critic could write, "We have long considered Miss Eytinge the leading actress of the American stage." The next year she returned to Wallack's ensemble where she portrayed, among others, Nancy Sykes in *Oliver Twist,* Lady Gay Spanker, and Beatrice as well as the leading roles in many long-forgotten, but once-popular contemporary plays. She left the group temporarily to perform in Daly's *Under the Gas Light*♦ (1867), creating the role of Laura Courtlandt, who saves a benefactor from death under the wheels of a speeding train. After several seasons abroad she returned to play Gabrielle, the French wife who saves her German husband from being executed as a spy during the Franco-Prussian War, in *The Geneva Cross* (1873), and then was Armande, the unsatisfied wife, in *Led Astray.*♦ In 1874 she accepted the small but crucial role of Marianne, the outcast who takes the place of one of the heroines in exile, in *The Two Orphans.*♦ To many her greatest performance came in the title part of *Rose Michel*♦ (1875), as the woman who, in order to protect her daughter's future, allows an innocent young man to pay for her husband's crime. According to the *Herald,* her performance "attained to the exalted pitch of perfect truth, in delineation of horror and agony, and it swept to this apex with the spontaneity of perfect ease." Unfortunately, the hyper-temperamental actress's battles with management and with talkers in her audience, notorious since early in her career, seem to have become uncontrollable. Engagements with Mrs. Drew♦ in Philadelphia and at the California Theatre♦ in San Francisco were both abruptly terminated. In the latter instance she stopped a performance when a drunkard made some comments and, according to a local paper, she told her audience that "she acted by inspiration, she was not a mechanician, and they must pardon her if, under the circumstances, her sensibilities being so deeply affected, she refused to conclude the performance." Thereafter she toured for many years with her own company, mostly in her old successes, and appeared in New York only on occasion. Her last appearance was in the short role of the hero's mother in *In the Bishop's Carriage* (1907).

Autobiography: *The Memories of Rose Eytinge,* New York, 1905.

F

FABRAY, NANETTE [née RUBY BERNADETTE NANETTE THERESA FABARES] (b. 1922) The bubbly, snub-nosed redhead made her debut at the age of three in vaudeville in Los Angeles, not far from her native San Diego, and afterward toured as Baby Nanette. Later she won scholarships to the Max Reinhardt School of the Theatre and appeared in its productions of *The Miracle, Six Characters in Search of an Author,* and *Servant with Two Masters.* Broadway first saw her in *Meet the People* (1940), then in *Let's Face It!*♦ (1941), *By Jupiter*♦ (1943), *My Dear Public* (1943), and *Jackpot* (1944). After replacing Celeste Holm♦ as the lead in *Bloomer Girl*♦ (1945), she was awarded the role of Sara Longstreet in *High Button Shoes* (1947), introducing "Papa, Won't You Dance with Me?" and "I Still Get Jealous." She next played Sara Cooper, whose marriage covers the entire range of American history, in *Love Life* (1948), in which she sang "Here I'll Stay" and "Green-up Time." In 1950 she was Jo Kirkland, the American girl who loves a Hessian soldier, in *Arms and the Girl,* and the following year played Jeanette, the orphan on a tour of Paris, in *Make a Wish.* Her last important appearance in a musical was as Nell Henderson, the First Lady, in *Mr. President* (1962). In 1973 she played Roberta Bartlett, the wife in a shaky marriage, in the comedy *No Hard Feelings.*

FAGAN, BARNEY (1850–1937) Although he is best remembered for a single song, "My Gal's a High-Born Lady," Fagan was admired in his heyday not only as a prolific songwriter but as a fine minstrel. He was the organizer of a number of blackface bands, including Fagan and Fenton's Minstrels and Sweatnam, Rice and Fagan's Minstrels. With the decline of minstrelsy he appeared in vaudeville occasionally, and on Broadway in *A Higher Roller* (1891).

Fair and Warmer, a farce in three acts by Avery Hopwood.♦ Produced by Selwyn and Co.♦ at the Eltinge Theatre. November 6, 1915. 377 performances.

Billy Bartlett (John Cumberland♦) is content to be a stay-at-home, although his wife Laura (Janet Beecher♦) would prefer a steady diet of fun on the town. By contrast Billy's friend, Jack Wheeler (Ralph Morgan♦), is forever making excuses to get away from his homebody wife Blanche (Madge Kennedy♦). So when Laura also makes excuses and joins Jack for a night out, Billy and Blanche decide to spend a quiet evening together. They sit around and chat and drink—and before long get drunk and innocently cozy. The gadabout spouses return in time to misconstrue everything. Tempers flare, followed by explanations and a return to normal.

Comparing the play with similar contemporary farces, the *Times* concluded it was "twice as well written and about four and half times as amusing." The public agreed, so the play became one of the longer running hits of its day.

FAIRBANKS, DOUGLAS [né ULMAN] (1883–1939) The handsome, flamboyant actor, whose acrobatic antics were as celebrated off-stage as on, was born in Denver and made his stage debut in Richmond, Va., in 1900 as Florio in *The Duke's Jester.* His New York debut occurred two years later in the small part of Glen Masters in *Her Lord and Master.* After a season on tour in *Mrs. Jack,* and several short New York engagements, he played his first leading role as Benny Tucker, the bellboy out to make a million in *A Case of Frenzied Finance* (1905). The play closed after one week. He was reduced to playing his "now familiar, breezy, attractive" young men in several supporting roles. Major success came as "Bud" Haines, a Senator's secretary who gets his boss out of a politically embarrassing situation, in *A Gentleman from Mississippi*♦ (1908). He toured with the play for several seasons before portraying the impoverished Philosopher Jack, who hopes for a large reward after finding a bracelet, in *The Lights o' London* (1911), and then Robert Pitt, an amateur crook, in *A Gentleman of Leisure* (1911). For a time he turned his attention to vaudeville, appearing in a skit called "A Regular Businessman," then replaced Wallace Eddinger♦ as Travers Gladwin in *Officer 666.*♦ His next important success came as the swashbuckling Anthony Hamilton Hawthorne, who sweeps a foreign princess off her feet, in *Hawthorne of the U.S.A.* (1912). He scored again as Bertie, the wonder boy of Wall Street, in *The New Henrietta* (1913). His last role was Jerome Belden, a rich young man who becomes an actor to please his sweetheart, in *The Show Shop*♦ (1914). The rest of his career was spent in films, where he was long a leading romantic, swashbuckling figure.

Faith Healer, The, a play in three acts by William Vaughn Moody. ♦ Produced by Henry Miller♦ at the Savoy Theatre. January 19, 1910. 13 performances.

Ulrich Michaelis (Miller), a faith healer in the Middle West, comes to the farm of the skeptical Matthew Beeler (Harold Russell) and makes Beeler's wife, Mary (Mable Bert), walk for the first time in many years. Mary urges Ulrich to go out in the world and heal others, but Ulrich is reluctant to leave the area since he loves Rhoda Williams (Jessie Bonstelle♦), Mary's niece. Ulrich's ministrations are opposed by the Reverend John Culpepper (Edward See), who suspects the occult, and by the local physician, Dr. Littlefield (Theodore Friebus). When Rhoda admits to Ulrich that Littlefield has been her lover, Ulrich's self-confidence wanes, and with it his faith-healing abilities. On Easter morning he determines to fight back and to love Rhoda despite her history. As his gifts return he tells Rhoda, "You needed what the whole world needs— healing, healing, and as I rose to meet that need, the power that I had lost poured back into my soul."

Miller, who had so successfully produced and starred in *The Great Divide,* ♦ mounted the play out of a sense of obligation to the dying Moody, knowing it would almost certainly fail. Contemporary critics dismissed the work as closet drama, but Quinn♦ praised the play, noting, "To have let the play run on to tragedy would have been not a more logical but a more obvious treatment," and concluding it was "the most significant of Moody's dramas because the theme is the largest and the treatment most secure . . . it had a deeper imaginative quality than *The Great Divide.*"

FALK, BENJAMIN J[OSEPH] (1853–1925) Born in New York, he began his photographic career shortly after graduating from City College. His studio was located on the site of the future Flatiron Building, a site then in the heart of the theatrical district. Until his time theatrical photographs consisted almost entirely of formally posed portraits of stars and other prominent figures. At midnight, May 1, 1883, after a performance of Daniel Frohman's♦ production of *A Russian Honeymoon,* he and Frohman assembled the play's cast on the stage of the Madison Square Theatre♦ and had them pose for a photograph of the closing tableau of Act II. This was the first full-stage scene ever photographed. Later in

his career he took similar pictures of scenes from other plays, but unlike several photographers who followed in his pioneering efforts, he never devoted himself primarily to theatrical photography.

Fall Guy, The, a comedy in three acts by James Gleason♦ and George Abbott. ♦ Produced by the Messrs. Shubert♦ [and others] at the Eltinge Theatre. March 10, 1925. 177 performances.

Gullible little Johnnie Quinlan (Ernest Truex♦) finds himself out of a job and with a wife and a sponging brother-in-law and sister to support, so when "Nifty" Frank Herman (Hartley Power) offers him good money simply to deliver a suitcase filled with "valuables," Johnnie accepts, although he suspects the valise contains bootleg whiskey. After all, he asks, "How can you be sure about this here Eighteenth Amendment, huh? Some guy says there must be something wrong with a law that so many people want to break." Johnnie's attempt to hide the suitcase leads to complications, especially when his sister's suitor, Charles Newton (Henry Mortimer), arrives. Newton is apparently a member of a rival gang. He is convinced the suitcase holds not whiskey, but drugs. When Herman shows up, Johnnie tricks him into admitting that he is the leader of his ring, whereupon Newton reveals that he is a federal agent. Herman is arrested, and Newton, impressed by the way Johnnie handled Herman, offers him a job.

One of two hits which Gleason co-authored in the same season—the other was *Is Zat So?*♦—this roustabout picture of lower-middle-class life and its attitudes toward prohibition was enhanced by Truex's memorable clowning.

FALL, LEO (1873–1925) Known in Europe as a composer of Viennese operetta,♦ he was best known in America for the success of his early work, *The Dollar Princess*♦ (1909). Among his other works performed here were *The Siren* (1911), *The Doll Girl* (1913), *The Rose of Stamboul* (1922), and *Madame Pompadour* (1924).

Fall of British Tyranny, The; or, American Liberty Triumphant, a political satire ("tragi-comedy") by John (or, in some sources, Joseph) Leacock. Published in 1776. No record of production is known.

Lord North and Governor Hutchinson, called Lord Catspaw and Judas in the play, conspire to convince the English cabinet that the American rebels can be readily defeated. They are opposed by Camden, Wilkes, Burke, and Pitt, called Lord Justice, Lord Patriot, Bold Irishman, and Lord

Wisdom respectively. The battle of Lexington and the war in Virginia are depicted, after which Generals Gage, Howe, and Burgoyne, called here Lord Boston, Elbow Room, and Mr. Caper, blame each other for the early debacles. A final scene shows Washington and his men at camp.

Probably both the earliest American chronicle play and the first to portray Washington on stage, this sprawling prose piece was designed to stimulate patriotism among the colonists. Leacock (1729–1802) was a goldsmith and silversmith, and later a farmer. A well-known Philadelphian, he was a member, possibly a founder, of the Patriotic Society of the Sons of St. Tammany and was also an acceptable poet.

Famous Mrs. Fair, The, a play in four acts by James Forbes.♦ Produced by A. L. Erlanger♦ at Henry Miller's Theatre. December 22, 1919. 343 performances.

Nancy Fair (Blanche Bates♦), having served as an ambulance driver in World War I and earned a Croix de Guerre for her bravery, returns after the armistice to find a lucrative contract for a lecture series awaiting her. Being an ardent feminist, Nancy would accept the offer, but she gradually realizes that in her absence her family had drifted away from her and from her standards of behavior. Mr. Fair (Henry Miller♦) has been paying very close attention to a neighboring widow; Nancy's daughter, Sylvia (Margalo Gillmore♦), has become rebellious and has taken up with an ambitious, loose-moraled young man; and her son, Alan (Jack Devereaux), seems all at sea and loves a stenographer. Matters come to a head when Sylvia elopes. She is brought back, and Mrs. Fair is brought to her senses. She will devote her time to her family and forget her feminist inclinations.

Hailed by Burns Mantle♦ as "the most timely of the post-bellum dramas and easily the most entertaining," the play opened to largely ecstatic notices. One of the few dissenters was Dorothy Parker,♦ who lamented in *Vanity Fair,* "it is almost impossible to discern just what all the raving is about." Although now something of a period piece, it remains interesting for its rueful observations on feminism, the incipient flapper rage, and upper-middle-class social mores of its day.

Fanchon, the Cricket, a play in five acts. Produced at Laura Keene's Theatre. June 9, 1862. 24 performances.

Fanchon (Maggie Mitchell♦) is a sharp-tongued, wild, and somewhat mysterious young country girl whose mother long ago deserted her and who has been raised by her grandmother, Old Fadet (Mrs. A. Hind), a reputed witch. Villagers avoid the girl, not only because she, too, may be a witch, but because they believe she is poor. The relatively well-to-do bourgeois Barbeauds, are no exceptions. Even when she helps the Barbeaud son Landry (J. W. Collier) locate his missing twin brother, Didier (A. H. Davenport), Landry is reluctant to seem grateful. But with time Landry discovers and brings to light Fanchon's basic commonsense and goodness. He proposes to her only to discover she will not marry him because his parents, especially the haughty, strict Father Barbeaud (J. H. Stoddart♦), are dead set against her. "I will not marry a man who did not honor his father and mother," she tells Landry. However, she has come to love Landry, so she sets about winning over his stern parent and soon succeeds. Landry then learns that while his bride-to-be may have magic powers, she will be a rich lady when Old Fadet dies.

The play was one of several dramatizations of George Sand's *La Petite Fadette.* Miss Mitchell, who served as her own producer, apparently used the version of Charlotte Birch-Pfeiffer, which she altered to suit her special talents. Her "Shadow Dance" and the scene in which she wins over the older Barbeaud were among the most famous theatrical moments of the era. She continued to return to this play for over twenty seasons. Odell♦ has written, "As Jefferson's Rip Van Winkle, Kate Claxton's Louise in The Two Orphans, and Mrs. G. C. Howard's Topsy, Maggie Mitchell's Fanchon the Cricket was for years and years a household word in America." Some advertisements and programs listed the play as *Fanchon; or, The Cricket.*

Fanny, a musical play in two acts. Book by S. N. Behrman♦ and Joshua Logan.♦ Music and lyrics by Harold Rome.♦ Produced by David Merrick♦ and Logan at the Majestic Theatre. November 4, 1954. 888 performances.

César (Ezio Pinza♦), owner of a small Marseilles café, hopes his son, Marius (William Tabbert), will marry their young neighbor, Fanny (Florence Henderson), and take over the business. Instead, Marius runs off to sea, leaving Fanny pregnant but unwed. Frightened, Fanny marries a benevolent old sailmaker, Panisse (Walter Slezak♦). Years pass, and Marius returns, hoping to marry Fanny. César, however, not wanting his friend Panisse to be hurt, chases Marius away. On his deathbed, Panisse urges Fanny to marry Marius after all, so that Fanny and Marius's young son can have a proper home.

Principal songs: Fanny · Love Is a Very Light Thing

Based on Marcel Pagnol's film trilogy, *Marius, Fanny,* and *César,* this over-written, over-produced musical was a major hit in a season of superior musicals, thanks largely to Rome's fine score and the performances of Pinza and Slezak.

Fantasticks, The, a musical in two acts. Book and lyrics by Tom Jones. Music by Harvey Schmidt. Produced by Lore Noto at the Sullivan St. Playhouse. May 3, 1960. Still running at press time.

The parents of The Boy called Matt (Kenneth Nelson) and The Girl called Luisa (Rita Gardner) build a wall between their homes, not because of any real animosity but on the assumption that the best way to kindle a romance is to appear to oppose it. They even hire El Gallo (Jerry Orbach♦) to stage a mock rape so The Boy can rescue The Girl and seem a hero. The youngsters discover their parents' ploy, fall out, and go their separate ways. Eventually, however, they return to each other, disillusioned but mature.

Principal songs: Try To Remember · Soon It's Gonna Rain

The musicalization of Edmond Rostand's *Les Romanesques* opened to indifferent notices at the 150-seat theatre and seemed in danger of closing, but a small band of loyalists helped publicize it, and it went on to win the Vernon Rice Award for the best off-Broadway show of the season. When "Try To Remember" became popular, the musical's success was assured. It has become the longest running show in New York theatre history (although comparison with shows playing much larger regular theatres is unfair) and has been popular with little theatres, college playhouses, and dinner theatres.

Composer Harvey Lester Schmidt (b. 1929) and lyricist and librettist Tom Jones (b. 1928) were Texans who began their collaboration while students at the University of Texas. Some of their earliest work was heard in the 1957 version of the *Shoestring Revue.*♦ Subsequently they wrote *110 in the Shade* (1963), *I Do! I Do!* (1966), *Celebration* (1969), and songs for *Colette* (1970). Schmidt is also an accomplished painter.

Far Country, A, a play in three acts by Henry Denker. Produced by Roger L. Stevens♦ and others at the Music Box Theatre. April 4, 1961. 271 performances.

As Sigmund Freud (Steven Hill) prepares to leave Nazi-occupied Vienna in 1938, his thoughts wander back to 1893 and a case that helped him establish his medical theories. The case concerned a young girl, Elizabeth von Ritter (Kim Stanley♦), who is so crippled she can walk only with the aid of crutches. Every other doctor in Vienna has failed to cure her, so her brother-in-law has brought her to Freud in a last, desperate effort. Freud's attempts to hypnotize the girl lead nowhere. Instead he tries letting her talk, hoping something from her past will give him a clue. His difficulties with Elizabeth are compounded by the anti-Semitism of his colleagues, who mistrust his odd methods. In the end, Elizabeth is made to realize that she longed for her sister's death in order to marry her brother-in-law. The knowledge allows her to walk again.

Louis Kronenberger♦ wrote, "Thanks to a sturdy union of play and production, *A Far Country* proved engrossing. If historically it was Freud's play, dramatically it was Elizabeth's story," and many playgoers felt Miss Stanley's bravura performance was largely responsible for the play's run.

Denker (b. 1912) is a New Yorker who studied at New York University. His other plays to reach Broadway were less successful. The most notable was *Time Limit!* (1956), written with Ralph Berkey and describing the trial of a soldier who is accused of collaboration with the enemy during the Korean War.

Farce-comedy, the name given to a genre of prototypical musical comedies. The first is generally acknowledged to have been *Patchwork* (1875), a piece by Nate Salsbury (1846–1902), with which he toured with some small success for several years. However, it was the popularity of Salsbury's sequel, *The Brook*♦ (1879), which established the vogue for the type and led to a rash of imitators. These pieces could hardly be said to have a plot. Rather, they placed four or five performers in a situation—in the case of *The Brook,* a picnic—and let them offer songs, dances, and other turns all tied together with the simplest dialogue. The tremendous and sudden rage for farce-comedy inevitably led writers and producers to expand them, enlarging the once tiny casts, complicating the originally elementary story lines. Some early successes of the type include *Our Goblins* (1880), *Dreams; or, Fun in a Photographic Gallery* (1880), and *Greenroom Fun* (1882). The names of early farce-comedy troupes were entertainments in themselves, running to Salsbury's Troubadors, Rice's Surprise Party, and Edouin's Sparks. Within a decade these plays had ineluctably evolved into full-fledged musical comedy. The term persisted well into the 1890s, when many of Charles Hoyt's♦ plays were offered as farce-comedies.

FARNUM, Dustin (1874–1929) The brother of William Farnum,♦ the popular matinee idol was born in Hampton Beach, N.H., and took part in amateur theatricals in Maine before turning professional in 1897. Although he appeared briefly in New York in *A War Correspondent* (1898), *A Romance of Athlone* (1899), and *Marcelle* (1900), his first years were occupied largely with touring and playing in stock. He won major recognition as Lieutenant Denton, who resigns his commission to fight false accusations of theft and murder, in *Arizona*♦ (1901). He played the role for several seasons and then scored an even greater success in 1904, playing the rugged but chivalrous cowboy who woos and wins the heroine, the title role in *The Virginian.*♦ Once again his success gave him several seasons' work. His personal popularity was largely responsible for the appeal of *The Ranger* (1907), in which, as Captain Esmond, he fought off thieving miners and murderous Mexicans to win a mine-owner's daughter. For something of a change of pace, he next played Dr. Prince, a reformed train robber turned minister whose kindness earns him the hand of a girl pursued by a hot-headed rival, in *The Rector's Garden* (1908). His next role was Eugene Kirby, a gambler whose actions are misunderstood by the girl he loves, in *Cameo Kirby* (1909). Following his portrayal of Jim Carston in a revival of *The Squaw Man*♦ (1910), one final major success was as Lt. Colonel Morrison, the Yankee who risks court-martial by writing passes for a Southern tot he has befriended and for her father, in *The Littlest Rebel* (1911). One unidentified critic wrote of him, "There is no more ingratiating and charming personality on our stage . . . and in roles of the romantic hero type there is no other man who acts half as well." After appearing in a 1913 revival of *Arizona,* he devoted the rest of his career to films, frequently in cowboy roles.

FARNUM, William (1876–1953) Although never quite as popular on stage as his older brother Dustin,♦ he too became a celebrated matinee idol. He was born in Boston and made his debut in 1890 in Richmond, Va., as Lucius in *Julius Caesar.*♦ A decade of touring, with occasional New York engagements, passed before he won attention when he replaced Edward Morgan in the title role of *Ben Hur*♦ in 1900. He toured in the play for several seasons. He won further applause as Prince Mohammed, who is ready to fight the world for his beloved princess, in *The Prince of India* (1906). In 1909 he played Capt. Severi, who commits suicide when he cannot persuade his fiancée, who has taken the veil,

believing him dead, to marry him, in *The White Sister,* and then assumed the title role in a revival of *Ingomar.*♦ He next co-starred with his brother, portraying Capt. Cary, the Southern officer who is the father of *The Littlest Rebel* (1911), and Colonel Bonham to his brother's Denton in a revival of *Arizona*♦ (1913). Although he, too, then turned to films, he made occasional New York appearances, most notably as Banquo in a 1928 revival of *Macbeth.* ♦ His last appearance was as Inspector Bill Regan, who believes his daughter has committed the crime he is investigating, in *Headquarters* (1929).

Farren Riots A benefit for the English comedian, George F. Farren, who had served for several seasons as a performer and stage manager at the Bowery Theatre,♦ was announced for July 9, 1834. Edwin Forrest,♦ who was about to sail for Europe, was slated to perform *Metamora*♦ at the benefit. In his diary for the next day Philip Hone recorded what happened initially.

Our city last evening was the scene of disgraceful riots. The first was at the Bowery Theatre. An actor by the name of Farren, whose benefit it was, had made himself obnoxious by some ill-natured reflections upon the country, which called down the vengeance of the mob, who seemed determined to deserve the bad name which he had given them. An hour after the performance commenced, the mob broke open the doors, took possession of every part of the house, committed every species of outrage, hissed and pelted poor Hamblin [Thomas S. Hamblin,♦ manager of the Bowery], not regarding the talisman which he relied upon, the American flag, which he waved over his head. This they disregarded, because the hand which held it was that of an Englishman, and they would listen to nobody but "American Forrest."

Later the mob moved on to sack the house of an abolitionist. The riots presaged the more destructive Astor Place Riots,♦ although no one has suggested that Forrest had a hand in the Farren affair as he did in the later one.

Fashion; or, Life in New York, a comedy in five acts by Anna Cora Mowatt.♦ Produced at the Park Theatre.♦ March 24, 1845. 20 performances.

The upstart Mrs. Tiffany (Mrs. Barry) is determined to make her way in the world. To this end she hires a large staff and teaches herself French, dropping "jenny-says-quois" and "ee-lights" everywhere she goes. She rejects all her daughter's suitors, insisting instead that Serphina (Miss K. Horn) marry the Count di Jolimaitre (Mr. Crisp). A thorn in her side is brusque but honest Adam Trueman (Mr. Chippendale), a fine specimen of

Yankee integrity. Trueman is an old friend of Mr. Tiffany (Thomas Barry♦), a not entirely honest businessman, who is being blackmailed by one of his daughter's suitors, Snobson (Mr. Fisher). Trueman's long-lost grand-daughter helps expose the Count as merely an old French chef whose real name is Gustave Treadmill. With this brought out into the open, Trueman is able to persuade Tiffany to send his wife and daughter to the country to learn simple values and to rid him of Snobson.

Edgar Allan Poe,♦ then a drama critic with the *Broadway Journal,* observed, "Compared with the generality of modern dramas, it is a good play—compared with most American dramas it is a *very* good one." The play's run was an American record for its day, and it has been revived regularly ever since. One notable revival, produced by Kenneth MacGowan,♦ Robert Edmond Jones,♦ and Eugene O'Neill♦ at the Provincetown Playhouse in 1924, chalked up 235 performances.

Father, The; or, American Shandyism, a comedy in five acts by William Dunlap.♦ Produced at the John Street Theatre.♦ September 7, 1789. In repertory.

Mr. Racket (Lewis Hallam, Jr.♦) is a carefree young merchant whose fun-loving ways have not always included Mrs. Racket (Mrs. Owen Morris♦). As a result, Mrs. Racket has been flirting with Ranter [in some versions, Rusport] (Mr. Biddle), who is masquerading as a British officer, though he is really the servant of Captain Haller (Mr. Harper). Ranter is not actually interested in Mrs. Racket. His aim is to marry Mrs. Racket's sister, Caroline (Mrs. Henry), for her money. Ranter's plans are frustrated by the arrival of Haller and his long-lost father, Colonel Duncan [in some versions, Colonel Campbell] (John Henry♦). Interwoven throughout the action was a charlatan-doctor, Tattle [in some versions, Quiescent] (Thomas Wignell♦).

While the *Gazette of the United States* recorded that "sentiment, wit and *comique* humor are happily blended" and that "This *Comedy* bids fair to be a favorite entertainment," Dunlap himself concluded, "Its merits have never entitled it to a revival." Some modern scholars, such as Quinn,♦ have questioned Dunlap's harsh assessment, but the fact remains that the play has rarely been performed even by collegiate theatres, although it was played occasionally in the early 19th century under the title of *The Father of an Only Child.* The "Shandyism" of the subtitle refers to Sterne's popular novel *Tristram Shandy.*

FAVERSHAM, WILLIAM (1868–1940) Born and trained in London, the actor made his New York debut as Dick in *Pen and Ink* in 1887. The play was a quick failure, so he found himself stranded in America, but his boyish, curly-haired good looks and his patent dramatic abilities had caught Daniel Frohman's♦ attention. He quickly won acceptance in Frohman's productions and later played opposite Mrs. Fiske.♦ In 1893 he signed with Charles Frohman,♦ and for the next eight years assumed a variety of parts for the producer, including Algernon in the first American production of *The Importance of Being Earnest* (1895), and Romeo to Maude Adams's♦ Juliet, as well as leading roles in *Under the Red Robe,♦ The Conquerors,♦ Phroso,* and *Lord and Lady Algy.* He was first starred above the title as the dissolute yet noble Don Caesar de Bazan in *A Royal Rival* (1901). A major success was as Capt. James Wynngate, the exiled Englishman who loves and loses an American Indian girl, in *The Squaw Man♦* (1905), a play written especially for him. He won further acclaim in the title role of the tragedy *Herod* (1909), which he produced and directed, and as the demi-god who becomes a human prince in *The Faun* (1911), which again he produced and staged. Two high points in his career followed when he staged *Julius Caesar♦* (1912) and *Othello♦* (1914), playing Marc Antony and Iago. Walter Prichard Eaton♦ wrote of the latter, "Where his 'Othello' differs from tradition is chiefly in Mr. Faversham's own interpretation of Iago, and the consequent hue that gives to the entire play. It is a novel, refreshing, stimulating impersonation, and it gives the drama a new vitality, a new holding power . . . The keynote of his Iago is humor." He scored another hit when he played the Bishop of Chelsea in Shaw's♦ *Getting Married* (1916), which he produced and directed. Thereafter his career faltered, and much of it was spent in revivals of earlier successes. His final Broadway appearances were as Georges, the exiled king who falls in love with an American widow, in *Her Friend, the King* (1929) and in some 1931 Shakespearean revivals. The public last saw him when he toured as Jeeter Lester in *Tobacco Road♦* in 1934.

FAWCETT, GEORGE (1860–1939) The Virginia-born actor, who made his professional debut in 1886, was best known for the company he headed from 1900 to 1905 in conjunction with his wife, Percy Haswell (1871–1945), at Albaugh's Lyceum Theatre in Baltimore. The ensemble was nationally respected for its fine productions of a wide variety of classic and modern plays, but the day for such quality stock troupes had passed and Fawcett was unable to sustain it. He remained a highly admired character actor on Broadway until the early 1930s and appeared in numerous films.

FAY, [FRANCIS ANTHONY] FRANK (1897–1961) The "handsome, saturnine and brilliantly redheaded" monologuist was born in San Francisco and made his stage debut as the child in *Quo Vadis?* in 1901. His early career ran a theatrical gamut, from playing a teddy bear in the original *Babes in Toyland*♦ (1903) to walking on as one of the crowd in Sir Henry Irving's♦ *The Merchant of Venice*♦ (1903). As a young adult he formed the vaudeville team of Dyer and Fay, with Johnny Dyer, but the act was short-lived, and by 1918 critics and playgoers were taking note of him as a lone storyteller. His soft-spoken, daffy yarns told of such quirky people as the little boy who would not get off the wagon and the family who saved scraps of string. During this same period, from 1918 to 1933, he also appeared in a number of Broadway musicals, generally failures. Then his career languished for about a decade until he scored his greatest and most memorable success when he returned to Broadway to play Elwood P. Dowd, the boozer whose best friend is an invisible rabbit, in *Harvey*♦ (1944).

Autobiography: *How To Be Poor,* New York, 1935.

FECHTER, CHARLES [ALBERT] (1824–79) Born in London, the son of a French father of German lineage and a Flemish mother of Italian lineage, the short, hulky, bull-necked actor was acclaimed for many years in romantic melodrama, in both Paris and London, before coming to America in 1869. After a brief tour, he opened at Niblo's Garden♦ in 1870, offering his Ruy Blas, Lagardere in *The Duke's Motto,* and Hamlet. He immediately became the center of controversy. Laurence Hutton♦ wrote, "The acting of no man, native or foreign, in the whole history of the American stage has been the subject of so much or of such varied criticism as his. There was no medium whatever concerning him in public opinion. Those who were his admirers were wildly enthusiastic in his praise; those who did not like him did not like him at all." William Winter♦ detested his Hamlet, noting, "His speaking of it was much marred by a sing-song cadence, and his delivery of English blank verse, accordingly, was abominable." Conversely, Henry Austin Clapp♦ praised his interpretation for its "outward and visible charm, its vitality, directness, and fervid sincerity." In later engagements he appeared as Claude Melnotte in *The Lady of Lyons,*♦ as Monte Cristo, and as Obenreizer in *No Thoroughfare.*

Winter was more complacent about his interpretations of these roles, observing, "With his romantic ideals in melodrama, and with his effective methods of expressing them, his audience was always pleased." His Monte Cristo was performed from a dramatization he himself had prepared in collaboration with Arthur LeClercq, and which James O'Neill♦ was later to employ with even greater success. Fechter continued to perform for several seasons, making his last appearances in 1877. By that time his waning health, coupled with a reputation for arrogance that verged on madness, had lost him his audiences. He died in poverty on his farm in Quakertown, Penn.

Biography: *Charles Albert Fechter,* J. R. Osgood, Boston, 1882.

FEDER, ABE (b. 1909) A native of Milwaukee, he studied at the Carnegie Institute of Technology before providing the lighting for *Trick for Trick* in 1932. Since then he has designed the lighting for dozens of plays and musicals, including the original *My Fair Lady*♦ (1956). He has created the basic lighting arrangements for many new theatres, including Washington's Kennedy Center,♦ and has taught workshops in several universities.

Federal Street Theatre [sometimes called the Boston Theatre] The first auditorium built in Boston specifically for theatrical presentations, it was erected from designs by the famous architect Charles Bulfinch and opened in 1794. A handsome brick structure with an arcaded front, it seated approximately 1000 people and was said by John Bernard♦ to display "a taste and completeness that was worthy of London." The theatre burned to the four walls in 1798, but was promptly rebuilt. Although it was sometimes plagued by mismanagement, it retained a virtual monopoly on Boston theatricals for nearly 30 years and continued to house drama after the arrival of competition. In the early 1870s it was converted into a business establishment, but was totally destroyed by another fire shortly thereafter.

Federal Theatre Project Established under the Works Progress Administration (WPA) in 1935 by an act of Congress, it was designed to offer work to theatrical professionals idled by the Depression. A second aim, according to President Roosevelt's assistant, Harry Hopkins, was to provide "free, adult, uncensored theatre." Hallie Flanagan,♦ director of the Vassar Experimental Theatre, was named national director. For a time it succeeded in both its aims. At its height it employed 10,000 people, most of whom had been on relief rolls. In New York alone in 1936, some 5,385 professionals were at work, and during its just over three years of life no fewer than 12 million people attended performances in the city. Numerous companies sprang up across the country, officially directed from Washington, but in reality semi-autonomous, and these also provided hard-pressed playgoers with a wide variety of inexpensive and often very good theatre. Productions ranged from imaginative revivals of old classics through new plays, children's plays, plays in foreign languages, marionette shows, and evenings of dance. Elmer Rice♦ was placed in charge of the New York branch. One of his most noteworthy, albeit controversial innovations was the Living Newspaper—plays which were essentially theatrical documentaries. The very first offering was to be *Ethiopia,* which dealt with Mussolini's attack on that country and employed excerpts from his speeches and Roosevelt's response. The State Department, fearful of offending the dictator, ignored Hopkins's promise and attempted to censor the play, which prompted Rice's resignation. The play never opened. The most successful of the Living Newspapers was Arthur Arent's *One Third of a Nation* (1938), which took its title from Roosevelt's claim that one-third of the country was ill-housed, ill-clad, and ill-nourished. Orson Welles♦ and John Houseman♦ also encountered censorship problems from bureaucrats and subservient or frightened unions when they attempted to mount the virulently left-wing musical *The Cradle Will Rock*♦ (1938), but they successfully defied their opposition. Numerous black theatre projects flourished in Harlem and elsewhere, as did specifically Catholic and Jewish mountings. One particularly successful offering was a black, jazzed version of Gilbert♦ and Sullivan♦ offered as *The Swing Mikado.* However, because many of the productions were perceived as and indeed, often were, blatantly left-wing propaganda pieces, opposition to the project grew, especially among conservatives. In 1939, after heated debate, Congress abolished the project. A detailed, highly readable account of the Federal Theatre can be found in Miss Flanagan's *Arena* (1940).

Feiffer, JULES, see *Knock Knock* and *Little Murders*

Female Impersonation Female impersonation has never been as popular on American stages as in England and elsewhere. One reason may be that the English tradition of pantomimes, which featured comic crones and other women played by men, never gained a lasting foothold in this country.

Nevertheless, notable examples do exist. Probably the two most famous impersonators of the 19th century were Francis Leon,♦ who worked largely in the minstrel tradition and who spoofed famous figures as well as characters from contemporary plays, and Neil Burgess,♦ who specialized in dear old spinster or widow ladies. Tony Hart,♦ of Harrigan♦ and Hart, was famous for his character of Mrs. Welcome (Rebecca) Allup, the sassy black serving wench, although he just as often appeared in regular men's parts. The greatest 20th-century impersonator was Julian Eltinge,♦ who brought the art to a refinement unequaled before or since. A major rival was Bert Savoy,♦ who was far more outrageous and grotesque in his characterizations. In recent times T. C. Jones offered superb satires of famous ladies, but his promising career was cut short by his early death.

Female Patriotism; or, The Death of Joan d'Arc, a blank-verse tragedy in five acts by John Daly Burk.♦ Produced at the Park Theatre.♦ April 13, 1798. In repertory.

The young maiden is so determined to lift France from tyranny that she is willing to sacrifice her home, her love, and her life. Many Frenchmen see her as a divine manifestation, but she disabuses them:

> I am no more of heaven than yourselves;
> Nor inspiration do I feel, beyond
> The stretch and compass of the human mind,
> Develop'd by its own innate exertions.

Rather, she comes as an advocate of reason and republicanism. Condemned to death and abandoned by the king and her former friends, she writes to her beloved Chastel predicting not only the French Revolution but an alliance of England and France in the cause of democracy.

Although the play was a failure, according to Dunlap♦ because of a slipshod performance, scholars generally consider this Burk's best play. Certainly it is lacking in the bombast and obvious spectacle of his more successful *Bunker-Hill; or, The Death of General Warren* (1797).

Fences, a play in two acts by August Wilson.♦ Produced at the 46th St. Theatre. March 26, 1987. 526 performances. PP, NYDCCA.

Troy (James Earl Jones♦) is an ignorant black man, stuck in a low-grade job. He is bitter because even his supposed athletic abilities have not allowed him to rise in a white world. He is building a fence around his house—not only to keep the white world at a distance, but also to keep away Death, with whom he insists he has wrestled and won. He is unhappy because his young son, Cory (Courtney B. Vance), has given up an after-school job to play football. Cory eventually joins the Marines. Troy finishes his fence. But the fence doesn't keep out Death in the end.

Jones's powerful performance made the play interesting theatre.

FENNELL, JAMES (1766–1816) The son of an employee in the British naval offices, he was slated for the law but over family objections elected to become an actor. Exceedingly tall for his day—he stood over six feet—he made his debut in Edinburgh, using the name Mr. Cambray to spare his family embarrassment. Later he acted at Covent Garden, but was not well received, so he toured the provinces until coming to America at Wignell's◆ behest in 1794. Because of a yellow fever epidemic in Philadelphia, he made his debut, apparently as Othello, in Annapolis. Although he acted for Wignell in Philadelphia, a dispute about a Baltimore engagement led him to sever temporarily his Philadelphia connections. His New York debut was as Zanga in *The Revenge* in 1797. When he played Jaffier in *Venice Preserved* at the Park Theatre◆ in 1799, the *Commercial Advertiser* remarked, "Few things can excel the performance of the excellent Fennell. The power of expression by countenance and gesture he possesses in an eminent degree." At the same time, when not appearing in plays, he gave numerous evenings of recitation, a policy he had initiated after his fight with Wignell. Whether it was this independence, the fecklessness he displayed in his autobiography, or the pressure of his outside business interests—which were ultimately to bankrupt him—he slowly fell from popularity and was forced to accept occasional small assignments. He made several comebacks, with varying success. But on his last performances as Othello (always considered his best role), Richard III, and Macbeth he was criticized for his ungainly stance, his rigid expression, and unexciting voice.

Autobiography: *An Apology for the Life of James Fennell,* Philadelphia, 1814.

FERBER, EDNA (1887–1968) Born in Kalamazoo, Mich., the celebrated novelist was also a noted playwright, although most of her better plays were collaborations. In 1915, working with George V. Hobart,◆ she gave Ethel Barrymore◆ one of the actress's favorite roles as the traveling saleswoman who rises high in the business world, in *Our Mrs.*

Chesney. Following an unsuccessful solo effort, *The Eldest,* and a collaboration with Newman Levy, *$1200 a Year,* both in 1920, she joined with George S. Kaufman◆ to write the plays for which she is best remembered: *Minick* (1924), in which an old man attempts to live with his son and daughter-in-law; *The Royal Family*◆ (1927), a comedy about a famous theatrical family; *Dinner at Eight*◆ (1932), in which the guests at a gala dinner party all prove to be tragically interrelated; and *Stage Door*◆ (1936), centering on young actresses in a theatrical rooming-house. Less well received were two other collaborations with Kaufman: *The Land Is Bright* (1941), depicting three generations of a wealthy family; and *Bravo!* (1948), which told of the efforts of refugee actors to find a place in America. Two of her novels were made into musicals, *Show Boat*◆ (1927) and *Saratoga* (1959), the latter from *Saratoga Trunk.*

Biography: *Ferber,* Julie Goldsmith Gilbert, New York, 1978.

FERGUSON, ELSIE (1885–1961) An exquisite beauty, the New York-born actress made her debut in the chorus of *The Belle of New York*◆ (1901), and graduated to small parts in both musicals and straight plays before calling prominent attention to herself as Jen Galbraith, a young girl who inadvertently delivers orders for her brother's arrest, in *Pierre of the Plains* (1908), and as Jenny, the tenement waif whose distress drives her father to attempt murder, in *The Battle* (1908). She became a star as Anna Victoria, who is willing to relinquish her throne so that her husband may rule, in *Such a Little Queen* (1909). Successful assignments followed in a revival of *Caste* (1910); a long tour in *A Matter of Money;* the title role in *Dolly Madison,* also called *The First Lady of the Land* (1911); and in a revival of *Rosedale*◆ (1913). She next portrayed Inez de Pierrefond, a woman of the world whose behavior shocks a small Iowa town, in *The Strange Woman* (1913). In *Outcast* (1914) she played Miriam, a girl of the streets whose warmth wins over a good man. She received additional applause as the alien who falls in love with the Prime Minister she is sent to spy on, the title role of *Margaret Schiller* (1916), then later the same season played Portia to Sir Herbert Tree's◆ Shylock. Turning to light comedy, she pleased audiences as the unfettered patrician suffragette who rescues her father from ruin, the title role of *Shirley Kaye* (1916). For the next several seasons she devoted herself to films, interrupting her cinema career in 1920 to play Carlotta Peel, who saves a former lover fallen on hard times, in *Sacred and Profane Love,* and the following year to play Madam Leland, a legendary old grand dame whose hidden past is revealed after her death, in *The Varying Shore*. Critics had long extolled her gorgeous looks and charm, but had felt her acting abilities were limited, so when several later shows in which she played the leading role— *The Moonflower* (1924), *The Grand Duchess and the Waiter* (1925), *The House of Women* (1927), and *Scarlet Pages* (1929)—all failed, she retired from the stage, returning only for a last appearance in 1943 as Crystal Grainger, the mysterious woman who tries to make an unhappy family understand itself, in *Outrageous Fortune*.

FERRER, JOSÉ [VICENTE] (b. 1912) Born in Puerto Rico, but educated in New York and at Princeton, the rather well built, heavy-featured, rich-voiced actor made his professional debut in 1934 in a series of melodramas performed on a show boat cruising Long Island Sound. Broadway first saw him as a policeman in *A Slight Case of Murder* (1935). He won critical attention in the role of The Lippincott, a gadfly, in *Spring Dance* (1936), then later the same season essayed his first important part, Dan Crawford, a meddling cadet, in *Brother Rat*. ♦ Important supporting assignments followed as Billy Gashade, Jesse James's loyal associate, in *Missouri Legend* (1938); as the white St. Julien in the black *Mamba's Daughters* (1939); and as Victor d'Alcala, the poet who dies for his beliefs in the Spanish Civil War, in *Key Largo*♦ (1939). Major success came when he appeared as Lord Fancourt Babberley in a revival of *Charley's Aunt*♦ (1940) and subsequently starred in two more highly praised revivals, playing Iago to Paul Robeson's♦ Othello in 1943 and the title role in *Cyrano de Bergerac*♦ (1946). "His Cyrano," Brooks Atkinson♦ noted, "has sardonic wit, a strutting style, a bombastic manner of speech and withal a shyness and modesty." In 1948 Ferrer was appointed general director of the New York City Theatre Company at the City Center,♦ producing and appearing in *Volpone; Angel Street;* a bill of Chekhov♦ one-act plays; *The Alchemist; S.S. Glencairn*♦; and *The Insect Comedy*. Later that year he scored a hit as Oliver Erwenter, who brings a bit of joy to a home for old folks, in *The Silver Whistle*. He next played the frantic producer, Oscar Jaffe, in a revival of *Twentieth Century*♦ (1950). Another important success was as Jim Downs, a mental patient trapped by a demanding wife, in *The Shrike*♦ (1952), a play he also produced and directed. In 1953 he revived the work at the City Center, also playing in revivals of *Charley's Aunt* and *Richard III*. ♦ In 1963 he appeared for the first

time in a musical, portraying the Prince Regent in *The Girl Who Came to Supper*. Thereafter, he appeared largely as replacements for original stars or in productions outside New York. He has also directed and occasionally produced plays, including *Strange Fruit* (1945); *Stalag 17*♦ (1951); *The Four-poster* (1951); *The Chase* (1952); *My Three Angels* (1953); *Oh, Captain!* (1958), for which he was also co-librettist; and *The Andersonville Trial* (1959).

FEUER, CY (b. 1911) and **MARTIN,** ERNEST [né MARKOWITZ] (b. 1919) The pair were, for a time, the most successful producers of musicals on Broadway. Beginning with *Where's Charley?*♦ (1948), they presented *Guys and Dolls*♦ (1950); *Can-Can*♦ (1953); *The Boy Friend* (1954); *Silk Stockings* (1955); *Whoop-up* (1958), for which they were co-librettists; *How to Succeed in Business Without Really Trying*♦ (1961); *Little Me* (1962); *Skyscraper* (1965); *Walking Happy* (1966); and a straight play, *The Goodby People* (1968). Feuer also directed *Little Me, Skyscraper,* and *Walking Happy*. Since 1975 they have been co-managers of the Los Angeles and San Francisco Light Opera Association. Feuer was born in New York, Martin in Pittsburgh.

FEUILLET, OCTAVE (1821–90) A French novelist and playwright, his theatre pieces, which ran to sentimental romances and highly charged melodramas, were frequently adapted to American tastes. Not only were his plays translated but his novels dramatized as well. Four works enjoyed relatively long careers on American stages: *Led Astray*♦ (1873); *The Sphinx* (1874); *The Romance of a Poor Young Man* (1874); and the play that gave Richard Mansfield♦ his earliest fame, *A Parisian Romance* (1883).

Fiddler on the Roof, a musical in two acts. Book by Joseph Stein. ♦ Lyrics by Sheldon Harnick. ♦ Music by Jerry Bock. ♦ Produced by Harold Prince♦ at the Imperial Theatre. September 22, 1964. 3,242 performances.

Tevye (Zero Mostel♦) is a pious dairyman living in the impoverished Jewish shtetl of Anatevka. He and his wife, Golde (Maria Karnilova), hire a matchmaker, Yente (Beatrice Arthur), to find husbands for their five daughters. The daughters, however, have minds of their own. One even runs off with a Christian soldier, so is disowned by the family. A pogrom and threats of increasing anti-Semitism finally force Tevye and his neighbors to leave Anatevka and seek homes in other countries.

Principal songs: If I Were a Rich Man · Matchmaker · Sunrise, Sunset · To Life

Based on Sholom Aleichem's *Tevye's Daughters,* this warm, melodic, if somewhat soap-opera-ish operetta, established a long-run record that held for a decade. It is revived regularly.

FIELD, JOSEPH M. (1810–56) Born to English parents in Dublin, and distantly related to the Elizabethan playwright Nathaniel Field, he was brought to America at the age of two and made his acting debut at Boston's Tremont Theatre in 1827. By 1830 he had performed in all the major American theatre centers, and had written a popular afterpiece, *Down South; or, A Militia Training.* Although he excelled at comedy roles such as Jeremy Diddler in *Raising the Wind,* Sir Benjamin Backbite in *The School for Scandal,* and Flutter in *The Belle's Stratagem,* he was not unsuccessful in essaying Sir Giles Overreach, Romeo, Othello, Jaffier, Claude Melnotte, and other tragic and melodramatic parts. In 1835 Noah Ludlow♦ brought him West, where he began to figure as an important playwright and performer, especially in St. Louis. Indeed, Ludlow's editor speaks of Field as "the first Western playwright who in any sense could wear that label, and a Western actor who almost made the grade into the rarefied air of stardom." During this period he also played New York, Philadelphia, Mobile, and New Orleans, temporarily abandoning the stage in 1841 to become the New Orleans *Picayune*'s foreign correspondent. He returned to America in 1842 to become William Mitchell's♦ right-hand man at the Olympic. While continuing to act and write in later years, he also managed a theatre in Mobile and Field's Varieties Theatre in St. Louis. Among his many plays are *Victoria; or, The Lion and the Kiss* (1839), in which James Gordon Bennett♦ pays a visit to the young English queen to determine her policy; *Tourists in America* (1840), a spoof of English visitors who return home to write nasty articles about our country; *Oregon, or, The Disputed Territory* (1846), a drama about the Northwest boundary dispute; and *Family Ties; or, The Will of Uncle Josh* (1846), written with J. S. Robb, and which won a prize Dan Marble♦ offered for the best new Yankee play.

FIELDS, BENNY, see *Seeley, Blossom*

FIELDS, DOROTHY (1905–74) Daughter of Lew Fields♦ and sister of Herbert Fields♦ and Joseph Fields,♦ she was born in Allenhurst, N.J., and became in her own right a lyricist whose work was distinguished by a sophistication coupled with a down-to-earth humor that frequently gave refreshing slants to clichés. Her lyrics were heard in *Blackbirds of 1928,* ♦ where she put words to Jimmy McHugh's♦ "I Can't Give You Anything But Love" and "Diga Diga Doo"; *Hello, Daddy* (1928); *International Revue* (1930), teaming again with McHugh for "Exactly Like You" and "On the Sunny Side of the Street"; *Stars in Your Eyes* (1939); *Up in Central Park*♦ (1945); *Arms and the Girl* (1950); *A Tree Grows in Brooklyn*♦ (1951); *By the Beautiful Sea* (1954); *Redhead* (1959); *Sweet Charity*♦ (1966), collaborating with Cy Coleman♦ to write "Big Spender" and "If My Friends Could See Me Now"; and *Seesaw* (1973). With her brother, Herbert, she also wrote the librettos for *Let's Face It!*♦ (1941), *Something for the Boys* (1943), *Mexican Hayride* (1944), *Up in Central Park* (1945), *Annie Get You Gun*♦ (1946), *By the Beautiful Sea* (1954), and *Redhead* (1959).

FIELDS, HERBERT (1897–1958) Son of Lew Fields♦ and brother of Dorothy Fields♦ and Joseph Fields,♦ he was born in New York and educated at Columbia before turning his hand to librettos. His earliest work, done with Richard Rodgers♦ and Lorenz Hart,♦ was considered to be among the most advanced and sophisticated of its day. His works included *Dearest Enemy*♦ (1925), *The Girl Friend* (1926), *Peggy-Ann*♦ (1926), *Hit the Deck!*♦ (1927), *A Connecticut Yankee*♦ (1927), *Present Arms* (1928), *Chee-Chee* (1928), *Hello, Daddy* (1928), *Fifty Million Frenchmen*♦ (1929), *The New Yorkers* (1930), *America's Sweetheart* (1931), *Pardon My English* (1933), *Du Barry Was a Lady*♦ (1939), and *Panama Hattie*♦ (1940). From 1941 on all his works were collaborations with his sister: *Let's Face It!*♦ (1941), *Something for the Boys* (1943), *Mexican Hayride* (1944), *Up in Central Park*♦ (1945), *Annie Get Your Gun*♦ (1946), *Arms and the Girl* (1950), *By the Beautiful Sea* (1954), and *Redhead* (1959).

FIELDS, JOSEPH [ALBERT] (1895–1966) Son of Lew Fields♦ and brother of Dorothy Fields♦ and Herbert Fields,♦ he was born in New York and attended New York University with the intention of becoming a lawyer. While in the navy during World War I, he wrote sketches for shows and appeared in them, and then decided to make the theatre his career. He contributed sketches to some revues and afterward spent some time in Hollywood before collaborating with Jerome Chodorov♦ on a spoof of film life, *Schoolhouse on the Lot* (1938). The team next wrote two major hits, *My Sister Eileen*♦ (1940), dealing with the adventures of two young girls in New York;

and *Junior Miss*♦ (1941), centering on an overly imaginative teenager. He also succeeded with a solo venture, *The Doughgirls*♦ (1942), a comedy about women in crowded, wartime Washington. He then collaborated again with Chodorov on a story of a French actor opposing the Nazis, *The French Touch* (1945), but the play was a failure. He worked with Anita Loos on the libretto for *Gentlemen Prefer Blondes*♦ (1949), then returned to Chodorov to write a libretto for *Wonderful Town*♦ (1953), a musical version of *My Sister Eileen*; a libretto for *The Girl in Pink Tights* (1954); and a comedy about a married couple who dismay their children when they reveal their premarital life, *Anniversary Waltz*♦ (1954). With Chodorov he also adapted Eudora Welty's *The Ponder Heart* (1956) for the stage, and the following year collaborated with Peter De Vries on a dramatization of De Vries's *The Tunnel of Love*. His last work was his collaboration with Oscar Hammerstein II♦ on the libretto of *Flower Drum Song* (1958). Fields also occasionally served as a director.

FIELDS, LEW [né LEWIS MAURICE SHANFIELD] (1867–1941) One of the most successful and popular of American theatrical figures, he was born to immigrant parents on New York's Lower East Side, just a few blocks from his childhood friend and longtime partner Joe Weber. ♦ As a boy he worked as a soda jerk, but in his spare time was part of an amateur vaudeville act, The Standard Four. To get into the group he was forced to oust Weber, who later rejoined the act. When their partners dropped out, Weber and Fields moved on to their first paying job, doing a skit nine times a day at the Chatham Square Museum in 1877. The Museum folded shortly thereafter, so they moved to the Globe Museum, changing acts every second week. It was here they first began devising the "Dutch" routines that made them famous. The routine, in a German or Yiddish accent, frequently consisted of Fields suggesting some course of action to Weber, of Weber's bungling the matter, and of a wild-eyed Fields then pummeling or choking Weber. Within a few years they were touring the country in vaudeville houses and even circuses, and by 1887 they had a complete company. Their "Dutch" act emphasized the fact that they were modern comedians, for dialect comics had come to replace the grotesque comedians who had been the rage. But Weber and Fields always had a respect for tradition, so their act was performed in the grotesque costumes and make-up just then beginning to lose favor. Fields, the taller, slimmer of the pair, wore an undersized derby

hat, oversized checkered suit, and a hayseed beard. Weber dressed in similar fashion, but exaggerated his shorter, stockier build with excessive padding. Sometime during this period they reputedly developed one of the most famous of all American jokes, with Weber delivering the punch line, "Dat vas no lady. Dat vas my wife." In 1896 they took over the tiny Broadway Music Hall, renaming it Weber and Fields' Music Hall, and began a series of double bills that quickly became among Broadway's most popular tickets. The bills consisted of a shorter than ordinary musical comedy, with the stars playing characters such as Herman Dillpickle and Meyer Schmartzgeezer, and a burlesque of a popular play. The burlesques were changed at intervals. The musicals had such names as *Hurly Burly* (1898); *Helter Skelter* (1899); *Fiddle-Dee-Dee* (1900); *Hoity Toity* (1901); *Twirly Whirly* (1902); and *Whoop-Dee-Doo* (1903). The burlesques made a mockery of both the story of the play, often of its scenery and costumes, and almost always of its title. For example, in 1896 *The Geisha* became *The Geezer,* while in 1898 *Cyrano de Bergerac*♦ was distorted into *Cyranose de Bric-a-brac.* The satires proved so popular that managements supposedly offered Weber and Fields bribes to spoof their plays, and the entertainments as a whole were in such demand that the partners were able to auction off opening night seats at outlandish prices. The popularity of the entertainments was enhanced by the striking productions squeezed onto the small stage, the gorgeous chorus line—the most famous before Ziegfeld's♦— and a host of great supporting performers, including Lillian Russell,♦ Fay Templeton,♦ Bessie Clayton, Sam Bernard,♦ Peter Dailey,♦ David Warfield,♦ and De Wolf Hopper. ♦ So costly were the productions that they made little money during their New York stands and depended upon road tours for profit. By 1903, however, Weber and Fields had a falling out, Weber supposedly claiming Fields had better parts. When the team broke up in 1904, Fields began a highly successful career as a producer, often starring in his own productions. His first offerings were *It Happened in Nordland* (1904) and *About Town* (1906), in both of which he was starred. In 1907 he produced and starred in *The Girl Behind the Counter,* playing a soda jerk in its most famous scene. This hit was followed by twelve musicals in four years; many of them distinguished by their elaborate production, exceptional for Broadway at the time. *The Midnight Sons* (1909), for instance, opened with the audience seemingly watching a show from the back of a stage, with footlights shining at them and another audience watching both the show and them; *The Summer Widowers* (1910) sent miniature planes through the audience and also revealed an entire apartment house with its several floors of apartments seen at the same time. In 1912 Weber and Fields were temporarily reconciled and appeared together in *Hokey Pokey* and *Roly Poly*. The reunion, joyously welcomed, was short-lived. Thereafter Fields's career slowly waned, catching fire again only in the late 1920s when he successfully produced a series of musicals written by his son Herbert Fields,♦ Richard Rodgers,♦ and Lorenz Hart♦: *The Girl Friend* (1926), *Peggy-Ann♦* (1926), *A Connecticut Yankee♦* (1927), and *Present Arms* (1928). He also co-produced *Hit the Deck!♦* (1927) with Vincent Youmans. ♦ His last Broadway production was *The Vanderbilt Revue* (1930).

Although Fields was hardly an innovator and in interviews disclosed his commercial philosophy as pragmatic, at his peaks he gave the public what it wanted and expected, but with a special panache and style.

Biography: *Weber and Fields,* Felix Isman, New York, 1924.

FIELDS, W. C. [né William Claude Dukenfield] (1879–1946) Born in Philadelphia, the great comic began his career in 1897 as a tramp juggler, an act he continued to develop and perform world-wide until 1914. For a time in 1905 he incorporated the routine into McIntyre♦ and Heath's *The Ham Tree*. He played briefly in *Watch Your Step♦* (1914), before being signed by Ziegfeld, ♦ for whom he appeared in six editions of the *Follies♦* between 1915 and 1921, missing only the 1919 production. It was during these seasons that he largely abandoned his juggling to perfect the misanthropic character he is remembered for. A portly man with grayish blond hair, a bulbous nose, vulpine eyes, and a voice described as reedy or croaky, he clowned dead-pan, with a bored, slightly haughty air. His characters were amoral, and contemptuous of suckers, children, animals, teetotalers (he was a notorious drinker), and sentimentalists. In one skit he decided to rob a man, but, finding the victim was larger than he and armed, walked away pontificating that robbery isn't honest. Playing a dentist, he discovered a bird flying out of his patient's beard, so he donned a hunting cap and shot the bird. He left Ziegfeld to appear in *George White's Scandals of 1922, ♦* then starred as Eustace McGargle in *Poppy* (1923). After playing in *The Comic Supplement* (1925), which folded on the road, he joined the 1925 *Follies*. His final Broadway appearances were in the *Earl Carroll Vanities of 1928♦* and as Q. Q. Quayle in *Ballyhoo* (1930).

Between shows he continued to be a popular attraction in vaudeville. In the 1930s he made several immensely popular films and later appeared regularly on radio.

Biography: *W. C. Fields, His Follies and Fortunes* Robert Lewis Taylor, Garden City, 1949.

FIERSTEIN, Harvey, see *Torch Song Trilogy*

Fifth Avenue Theatre The name was given to two different playhouses, neither of which was on Fifth Avenue and both of which were for a time connected with Augustin Daly. ♦ The first was built on 24th Street in 1862 as an adjunct to the once-famous Fifth Avenue Hotel and stood at the rear of the hostelry. Conceived as a stock exchange, it was not turned to theatrical uses until 1865, when it was occupied by George Christy's♦ Minstrels. In 1867 it began booking other sorts of light entertainment but closed soon after when a playgoer was murdered in a brawl. James Fisk then bought the house, redecorated it, and leased it to John Brougham, ♦ who attempted unsuccessfully to run it. His stay lasted only a few weeks, so Daly took it over later in 1869 and housed his first great company there until the building was destroyed by fire in 1873. *Frou-Frou, ♦ Saratoga, ♦ Horizon, ♦* and *Divorce♦* were among Daly's notable hits there. It lay in ruins for several years until shortly before Steele MacKaye♦ obtained control. Since by that time Daly had opened his new Fifth Avenue Theatre, MacKaye called his auditorium the Madison Square Theatre. ♦

Meanwhile, Daly had immediately set about remodeling Gilsey's Apollo Hall on 28th Street, just west of Broadway. The New Fifth Avenue Theatre's beginnings were inauspicious, for while Daly had retained most of his ensemble intact he could not at first find plays to please critics and playgoers. Moreover, the 1873 financial panic was hurting all theatrical trade. Daly was close to bankruptcy when his 1875 production of *The Big Bonanza♦* saved the day. After Daly went into temporary retirement in 1878 the theatre came under the management of others. The world premiere of *The Pirates of Penzance♦* was offered there in 1879. Mary Anderson♦ and Modjeska♦ both made their New York debuts on its stage. The house underwent several name changes, burned in 1891, was rebuilt and served as a vaudeville, film, and cheap burlesque theatre before being torn down in 1938.

Fifth Column, The, a drama in two acts by Ernest Hemingway and Benjamin Glazer. Produced by the

Theatre Guild♦ at the Alvin Theatre. March 6, 1940. 87 performances.

Philip Rawlings (Franchot Tone♦), a newspaperman, works with the Loyalist counter-espionage forces during the Spanish Civil War along with his even more rabidly anti-Nazi friend Max (Lee J. Cobb♦). During a bombardment, Rawlings despairs of victory, gets drunk, and attacks a woman in a neighboring hotel room. Later, sober and remorseful, he takes the girl to Paris and marries her. But the situation in Spain is deteriorating, so when Max urges Rawlings to return to help, he does.

Hemingway wrote the play while under fire in Spain, but had trouble getting it produced. He finally allowed Glazer to write revisions which made the play acceptable to the Guild. Many critics felt the love interest was extraneous and diverted the story from its hard look at the war. A brilliant performance by Tone and a supporting performance by Lenore Ulric♦ as a Spanish trollop, along with Lee Strasberg's♦ direction and Howard Bay's♦ superb settings, were unstintingly hailed. Nevertheless, the play found only a small audience, and but for the Guild's advance subscription sales might have had an even shorter run.

Fifth of July, The, a play in two acts by Lanford Wilson.♦ Produced by the Circle Repertory Company♦ at the Circle Theatre. April 27, 1978. 158 performances.

Kenneth Talley, Jr. (William Hurt), who lost both of his legs in Vietnam, lives with his male lover Jed (Jeff Daniels). He has been a schoolteacher, but has decided to give up teaching. Some friends and relatives are visiting with the boys on a July 4th weekend. The friends are an odd lot, into drugs and hoping to do something in country and rock music. The relatives include an aunt who carries around her husband's ashes and a sister who comes with her illegitimate daughter. That daughter's father, it seems, is one of the visitors, a married man. The group reminisces bitterly and fights, but in the end appears no more the wiser or happier for the soul-searching.

One of a series of plays which Wilson wrote about the Talley family and which included *Talley's Folly,*♦ it was described by Otis L. Guernsey, Jr.,♦ as "a not-very-tightly structured study of human spirit in the aftermath of stress." Revived on Broadway in 1980, it ran for 511 performances.

Fifth Season, The, a comedy in two acts by Sylvia Regan. Produced at the Cort Theatre. January 23, 1953. 645 performances.

Max Pincus (Menasha Skulnik♦) and Johnny Goodwin (Richard Whorf♦) run a faltering garment company. The company is in trouble to some extent because of the traditional ups and downs of the industry, but also because Johnny spends too much time away—philandering. So most of the company's woes fall on the already woeful Max. Luckily, Max is lovable and good enough to help matters to a happy ending.

This slim, cliché-ridden comedy succeeded handsomely on the strength of the tiny, doleful Skulnik's clowning.

Sylvia Regan [née Hoffenberg] (b. 1908), New York-born, has been an actress and a press agent as well as a playwright. Although several of her plays reached Broadway, this has been her only success.

Fifty Million Frenchmen, a musical comedy in two acts. Book by Herbert Fields.♦ Lyrics and music by Cole Porter.♦ Produced by E. Ray Goetz♦ at the Lyric Theatre. November 27, 1929. 257 performances.

Rich Peter Forbes (William Gaxton♦) bets a friend $25,000 that he can win Looloo Carroll (Genevieve Tobin♦) without disclosing how wealthy he is. He takes a job as a guide and wins Looloo away from the titled Russian whom her snobbish parents hope she will marry.

Principal songs: Find Me a Primitive Man · You Do Something to Me · You've Got That Thing

This show's sets were so lavish that they had to be cut down before they would fit into the theatre, but the musical's biggest problem was the onset of the Depression, which shortened what might have been a longer run.

Fighting Hope, The, a play in three acts by William J. Hurlbut.♦ Produced by David Belasco♦ at the Stuyvesant Theatre. September 22, 1908. 231 performances.

When Robert Granger (Howell Hansel) is sent to prison for stealing huge sums from his employer, his wife Anna (Blanche Bates♦) assumes an alias and goes to work for his old boss, Burton Temple (Charles Richman♦), convinced that Temple is the real thief and that she can find the evidence to exonerate her husband. What she does find is proof of her husband's guilt, and this proof she promptly destroys. Temple catches her but, since he has begun to fall in love with her, is forgiving. Granger appears, announcing that he has been paroled. He discerns the affection that Temple has developed for Anna and questions her motives in going to work for him. It is then quickly discovered that he has not been paroled, but rather that he has escaped and hidden a small fortune with which to go off and live with another woman. The police close in, killing Granger as he flees. Temple and Anna are free to pursue their budding romance.

Although the merits of the melodrama sharply divided the critics, Belasco's fine mounting and Miss Bates's popularity gave the work a long run.

Finian's Rainbow, a musical fantasy in two acts. Book by E. Y. Harburg♦ and Fred Saidy. Lyrics by Harburg. Music by Burton Lane. ♦ Produced at the 46th Street Theatre. January 10, 1947. 725 performances.

Finian McLonergan (Albert Sharpe) and his daughter Sharon (Ella Logan♦) come to America from Glocca Morra lugging a crock of gold, which Finian hopes to plant at Fort Knox and watch grow. They are pursued by a mischievous leprechaun, Og (David Wayne♦). Stopping at Rainbow Valley, Missitucky, Sharon falls in love with Will Mahoney (Donald Richards). The McLonergans also encounter the racist, xenophobic Senator Billboard Rawkins, who whines, "My whole family's hated immigrants ever since we *came* to this country." Through the magic power of the crock Rawkins is turned black and made to see the penalties of his attitudes. But Sharon reveals that her father lives in a fantasy world and, even without her, must continue his wanderings. Although Glocca Morra is only a figment of her father's imagination, it is a lovely place nonetheless, and she lets him go on alone hoping "we meet in Glocca Morra some fine day."

Principal songs: How Are Things In Glocca Morra? · If This Isn't Love · Look to the Rainbow · Old Devil Moon

This show, which twitted reactionaries, was so sunny, so witty, and so melodic, that it delighted almost everyone. Billboard Rawkins, for example, spoofed Mississippi's notorious Senator Bilbo and Congressman Rankin. Because much of the humor was topical, revivals have proved unsuccessful.

Finishing Touches, a comedy in three acts by Jean Kerr. ♦ Produced by Robert Whitehead♦ and Roger L. Stevens♦ at the Plymouth Theatre. February 8, 1973. 164 performances.

Jeff Cooper (Robert Lansing) is a college professor, and his wife, Katy (Barbara Bel Geddes♦), the loyal, somewhat caustic mother of their three sons. Jeff, however, has a roving eye, and when he announces that he has fallen in love with one of his graduate students, he unwittingly drives Katy into considering the offer of an affair with a neighbor,

Fred Whitten (Gene Rupert). However, the Coopers are brought back to their senses and their good old-fashioned moral precepts when their son Stevie (James Woods) comes home from college with his mistress, Felicia Andrayson (Pamela Bellwood). After Felicia leaves, confessing she really does not love Stevie, middle-class morality reigns supreme.

Although Richard Watts♦ of the New York *Post* wrote, "It is funny, it is wise, and it is believable in characterizations and story," some critics and playgoers felt the comedy reflected attitudes of the 1950s rather than of the more freewheeling 1970s. Nevertheless, Jean Kerr's unfailing humor carried the day.

FINKLEHOFFE, Fred, see *Brother Rat*

FINN, Henry James (1785–1840) Born in Cape Breton, he was brought to New Jersey while still a child. He enrolled at Princeton, intent on law as a career, but abandoned his plans in favor of the theatre. He became an assistant prop boy at the Park Theatre♦ and may have been the Mr. Finn who played minor roles there in 1804. After his father's death he went to London and performed at the Haymarket. He returned to New York to play Shylock in 1818, then spent several seasons in Charleston. Back again in New York in 1820, he offered his Hamlet, The Stranger, and Othello. His interpretations, however, were compared unfavorably with those of other major actors, so he began to gravitate toward comic roles. At the same time, he began his association with Thomas Kilmer as a manager in Boston. By 1824 he was accepted as a fine comedian in parts such as Sir Andrew Aguecheek, Paul Pry, Sir Peter Teazle, and Bob Logic. The New York *Mirror* noted, "Mr. Finn's style of playing is broadly ludicrous. His delineations are sketched with a strong and masterly hand, and are generally correct, though sometimes rough likenesses." He scored a major success as Sergeant Welcome Sobersides, who saves a half-breed Indian girl from a villain, in his own play *Montgomery; or, The Falls of Montmorency* (1825). He may also have been the author of *The Indian Wife* (1830), which made Sobersides a major character. Later, he wrote a farce about President Jackson's battle with the United States Bank, *Removing the Deposits* (1835). Finn died in a ship fire, while traveling between New York and Boston.

Fiorello!, a musical in two acts. Book by Jerome Weidman and George Abbott. ♦ Lyrics by Sheldon Harnick. ♦ Music by Jerry Bock. ♦ Produced by Robert Griffith♦ and Harold Prince♦ at the

Broadhurst Theatre. November 23, 1959. 795 performances. PP, NYDCCA.

When Fiorello La Guardia (Tom Bosley♦) is told by his loyal secretary, Marie (Patricia Wilson), and her friend Dora (Pat Stanley) that a labor organizer, Thea (Ellen Hanley), has been arrested on trumped-up charges, he rushes to Thea's defense and berates the corrupt policeman, Floyd (Mark Dawson), who arrested her. Later, he runs for mayor with the grudging approval of the Republican ward leader, Ben Marino (Howard da Silva). Meanwhile Floyd rises in Tammany ranks and befriends Dora, who drifts away from her old crowd. La Guardia marries Thea, who dies during his second campaign and then fires Marie so he can propose to her. But his romances never stop his battles against injustice.

Principal songs: Little Tin Box · Politics and Poker · Till Tomorrow

Characterized by Walter Kerr♦ of the *Herald Tribune* as "a song-and-dance jamboree with a curious streak of honest journalism and a strong strain of rugged sobriety about it," the original production was made especially memorable by Bosley's affectionate portrayal of the mayor.

Firebrand, The, a comedy in three acts by Edwin Justus Mayer.♦ Produced by Laurence Schwab,♦ Horace Liveright, and Frank Mandel♦ at the Morosco Theatre. October 15, 1924. 287 performances.

Benvenuto Cellini (Joseph Schildkraut♦) has purchased his beautiful model, Angela (Florence Mason), from her haggish mother for forty ducats. His plans to romance her, however, are frustrated by the arrival in his workshop of the flighty Duke of Florence (Frank Morgan♦), who is instantly captivated by Angela and takes her to his palace. Cellini is in no position to argue since the sight of Angela has prompted the Duke to pardon Cellini for a murder he has committed. Moreover, Cellini has been having an affair with the Duchess (Nana Bryant). Later, Cellini attempts to steal Angela away from the Duke. Once again his plans are thwarted, so he must content himself with continuing to see the Duchess.

Based loosely on an incident in Cellini's autobiography, the play was perceived as "racy" entertainment at a time when such plays were felt to demonstrate a new freedom and maturity on the stage. A musical version, *The Firebrand of Florence,* with songs by Ira Gershwin♦ and Kurt Weill,♦ failed in 1945.

Firefly, The, an operetta ["comedy opera"] in three acts. Book and lyrics by Otto Harbach. ♦ Music by Rudolf Friml. ♦ Produced by Arthur Hammerstein♦ at the Lyric Theatre. December 2, 1912. 120 performances.

To flee from her drunken guardian, a young street urchin, Nina Corelli (Emma Trentini♦), disguises herself as a boy and boards a yacht headed for Bermuda. On board are Jack Travers (Craig Campbell) and his bitchy fiancée, Geraldine Van Dare (Audrey Maple). Nina falls in love with Jack but cannot disclose her real identity. However, when she is mistaken for a sought pickpocket she is forced to reveal that she is a girl. A kindly musician, who has heard her sing, sends her to Europe to be educated. She returns as a celebrated prima donna and marries Jack.

Principal songs; Giannina Mia · Love is Like a Firefly · Sympathy

The operetta was originally to have had a score by Victor Herbert,♦ but after a series of rows with Miss Trentini, Herbert asked to be released from his contract. The score was Friml's first and won him immediate recognition.

Fires in American Theatres Until the early 20th century, when stringent laws and safer building materials were developed, the threat of fire was omnipresent in American theatres. The first major fire recorded in an American playhouse occurred at the Federal Street Theatre♦ in Boston in 1798. Between then and 1903 over one hundred serious fires destroyed and heavily damaged theatres, although most occurred when no performance was on and lives were not lost. No fewer than five New York theatres—Barnum's,♦ "444" Broadway, the Academy of Music, the New Bowery, and the Winter Garden—burned in the period from July 1865 to March 1867. Walter Leman♦ noted that in these years fires were so frequent that theatrical people felt the average life of an auditorium was only 15 years. The three worst catastrophes were the burning of the Richmond (Va.) Theatre, during the playing of an afterpiece, *Raymond and Agnes; or; The Bleeding Nun,* on December 26, 1811, when 71 people perished; the destruction of the Brooklyn Theatre during a performance of *The Two Orphans*♦ on December 5, 1876, with the loss of 197 lives; and the fire at the newly opened, supposedly fireproof Iroquois Theatre in Chicago during a performance of the musical *Mr. Bluebeard* on December 30, 1903, which claimed over 600 lives.

First Year, The, a comedy in three acts by Frank Craven. ♦ Produced by John Golden♦ at the Little Theatre. October 20, 1920. 725 performances.

Grace Livingston (Roberta Arnold) of Rochester, Ill., has been proposed to by young, ambitious Dick Loring (Lyster Chambers). She has also been courted by shy Tommy Tucker (Craven), who is not nearly as handsome as Dick and will probably spend all his life as a Rochester realtor. Grace's Uncle Myron (Tim Murphy) finally goads Tommy into proposing, and Grace accepts. But their married life is not all bliss. Tommy thinks their problems are merely the dark before the dawn, but Grace suggests they've "had a long arctic night." Just as a dinner party starts to fall to pieces, Tommy blames Loring, who has returned on a visit, for breaking up a big deal he had in the works. In a snit, Grace runs home to mother. There Grace learns that Tommy's deal has, in fact, gone through and he is rich. But Tommy appears just after Loring again arrives and is talking to Grace. A melee ensues, with Grace, attempting to stop Dick from hurting Tommy, inadvertently knocking out her husband with a vase meant for Dick's head. Tommy misconstrues her behavior. It takes all of Uncle Myron's persuasive abilities, plus the announcement that Grace is pregnant, to reunite the couple.

Welcomed by Burns Mantle, ♦ who called it "one of those true, homely little comedies which are a blend of character, keenly observed, and the human comedy situation, overlaid with a suggestion of farce," the play was the biggest hit of the 1920–21 season. At the time of its closing it was the third longest-run show in Broadway history.

FISHER, CHARLES (1816–91) The English-born actor had already made a name for himself at London's Princess Theatre when William Burton♦ enlisted him for his American company. He made his debut as Ferment in *The School of Reform* in 1852, then won acclaim the following year as Triplet, the humble art fancier, in *Masks and Faces.* He remained with Burton for several seasons before moving to Laura Keene's♦ company. In 1855 he created the role of Pepe, the treacherous jester, in *Francesca da Rimini.* ♦ He joined Wallack's♦ ensemble in 1861 and for many years was one of Wallack's principal supporting players, assuming such roles as Joseph Surface and important parts in newer plays, including Matthew Leigh in *Rosedale*♦ (1863). During one summer hiatus he created the role of the villainous Colonel Crafton in *Fritz, Our Cousin German.* ♦ In 1872 he became a member of Augustin Daly's♦ troupe, where he remained for the rest of his life. As at Wallack's, he played important roles in many of the new plays Daly mounted as well as interpreting such classic roles as Falstaff and Sir Peter Teazle. Daly's biographer characterized his style as "more French then English," suggesting his forte for light, elegant impersonations, and although he never became a star he remained one of the most respected American performers for nearly forty years.

FISHER, CLARA [later known as CLARA FISHER MAEDER or MRS. JAMES G. MAEDER] (1811–98) Born in London, where her father was a well-known librarian and auctioneer, she was a child prodigy who began to perform at the age of six. She played such standard child prodigy favorites as Little Pickle and Richard III and at sixteen made her American debut at the Park Theatre♦ in 1827. The *Albion* wrote of her performance that night as Albina Mandeville in *The Will,* "Miss Fisher succeeded most admirably . . . In her hoydenish airs, there was nothing vulgar; in her passion, nothing indelicate; in her gentility, nothing affected." During the following seasons she was immensely popular, displaying a remarkable range of talents that allowed her to perform with equal applause such diverse roles as Ophelia, Lady Teazle, and Clari (in the operetta of the same name). In 1834 she married James G. Maeder, a well-known conductor and musical coach. She retired from the stage shortly after the birth of their son Frederick. ♦ When she attempted a comeback in the 1880s she met with only small success. According to Ireland, ♦ "Her person, below middle height, and just reaching but not exceeding a delicate plumpness, was exquisitely formed . . . her expression arch and intelligent . . . her fine hair closely cut on the back of the head, while on her brow she wore the then fashionable rolls, or puffs, a style that was immediately adopted by all fashionable ladies under twenty-five."

Autobiography: *Autobiography of Clara Fisher Maeder,* New York, 1897.

FISKE, HARRISON GREY (1861–1942) The New York-born son of a wealthy hotel owner, he early on developed an interest in theatre. While still in his teens, he became drama critic for the Jersey City *Argus* but quit after he discovered the paper was in debt to his father and had hired him as a courtesy. He matriculated at New York University, only to leave when his father bought him a one-third interest in the *Dramatic Mirror*♦ in 1880 and he was made editor. He himself bought the remaining two-thirds several years later. In 1890 he married Minnie

Maddern, who had already developed a reputation as a promising actress and who thereupon changed her professional name to Mrs. Fiske. ♦ As editor, Fiske had been a crusader from the start. His 1880 editorials were instrumental in establishing the Actors' Fund of America. ♦ When stories about the practices of the newly formed Theatrical Syndicate or Trust ♦ began to gain currency, Fiske printed them without editorial comment. But after the members of the Trust threatened to destroy his paper if he mentioned it again, he initiated a mammoth crusade against the monopoly. The result was that his wife was barred from playing in Trust houses. He was forced to lease theatres and produce plays to keep his wife on the boards. He also wrote several plays, including *Hester Crewe* (1893), *The District Attorney* (1895), *Marie Deloche* (1896), and *The Privateer* (1897). He withdrew from the *Dramatic Mirror* in 1911 but continued to produce plays, both for Mrs. Fiske and others. Ironically, one of his biggest hits was *Kismet* ♦ (1911), produced in association with his old adversaries from the Trust, Frohman, ♦ Klaw, ♦ and Erlanger. ♦

FISKE, MINNIE MADDERN [née MARY or MARIE AUGUSTA DAVEY] (1865–1932) Born in New Orleans, she was the daughter of Thomas Davey, manager of the St. Charles Theatre in that city, and of Lizzie Maddern, an actress. Her maternal grandfather, Richard Maddern, had emigrated from England with his family, organized them into the Maddern Family Concert Company, and toured for many years. "Little Minnie Maddern" was first carried on stage at the age of three by her mother. She made her New York debut on May 30, 1870, in *A Sheep in Wolf's Clothing.* Just over a month later she created the role of Little Fritz in the premiere of J. K. Emmet's ♦ long-popular vehicle, *Fritz, Our Cousin German.* ♦ In 1871 she played opposite Laura Keene ♦ as Willie Leigh in *Hunted Down,* and later created the part of Little Alice in the premiere of another play destined for years of popularity, Frank Chanfrau's ♦ vehicle, *Kit, The Arkansas Traveller.* ♦ Although her role was relatively small, the *Herald* singled her out for praise, hailing her as "a wonder" and suggesting her talents surpassed "that [of] some of the mature artists who surround her." For much of 1872 she assumed the role of Little Eva in *Uncle Tom's Cabin.* ♦ Nearly a decade of touring ensued in which she played, among other parts, Prince Arthur in John McCullough's ♦ production of *King John.* By 1882, when she returned to New York as Chip in *Fogg's Ferry,* she was being universally applauded as an ingenue. She followed

with the part of Mercy in young Charles Frohman's ♦ production of *Caprice* (1884). Daniel Frohman ♦ awarded her stardom when she played Stella in Steele MacKaye's ♦ adaptation of Sardou's ♦ *In Spite of All* (1885). In 1888 she portrayed Mrs. Coney in James Albert's *Featherbrain.* In 1890, several years after a brief, unsuccessful marriage to Legrand White, she married Harrison Grey Fiske ♦ and announced her retirement. For the moment she satisfied her theatrical yearnings by writing plays. Her *Countess Roudine,* written with Paul Kester, ♦ was mounted by Modjeska. ♦ *The Rose, The Eyes of the Heart, A Light from St. Agnes,* and *Fontenelle* (written with her husband) met with varying degrees of success. By 1893 the lure of the footlights proved irresistible, and she returned to the stage in *Hester Crewe,* a play by her husband. A new-style drama, heavily influenced by Ibsen, the play was a quick failure, so Mrs. Fiske switched to Ibsen himself. Special performances as Nora in *A Doll's House* (1894) earned her recognition as a serious actress. Her *Tess of the D'Urbervilles* (1897) was one of her biggest triumphs, but it coincided with the Fiskes' problems with the Trust, ♦ an organization they were determined to buck. The Trust denied her access to theatres and even bribed amenable critics to write scathing reviews. Like Sarah Bernhardt, ♦ the Fiskes were forced to play undesirable houses and even in tents. Neither the Fiskes nor their followers were discouraged, and in 1899 Langdon Mitchell's ♦ *Becky Sharp* ♦ proved another vastly popular play. Several less successful shows followed. In 1903, at the Manhattan Theatre, which the Fiskes bought and renovated in order to have a New York playhouse, she won accolades as Hedda Gabler. A year later C. M. S. McLellan's ♦ *Leah Kleschna* ♦ gave her one of her finest roles. More triumphs came in its wake: as Mrs. Karslake in Langdon Mitchell's *The New York Idea* ♦ (1906); as Rebecca West in *Rosmersholm* (1907); Edward Sheldon's ♦ *Salvation Nell* ♦ (1908); as Lona Hessel in *Pillars of Society* (1910); and the title role of *Mrs. Bumpstead-Leigh* ♦ (1911). Unfortunately, the costs of maintaining the Manhattan were too much for the Fiskes, and they lost the house. For a number of years Mrs. Fiske appeared in a series of relatively weak plays, which only her acting and her loyal admirers kept afloat. During World War I she was a member of an all-star cast for *Out There.* Not until the end of her career, when she appeared in several superb revivals, did she again know the acclaim that had been hers earlier. Her Mrs. Malaprop in *The Rivals* (1925) gave place to Mrs. Alving in *Ghosts* (1927) and Mistress Page in *The Merry Wives of Windsor*

(1928). Her last New York appearance was as Mrs. Tyler in *It's a Grand Life* (1930). Ill health and age forced her to withdraw from a pre-Broadway tour of *Against the Wind*.

Short and red-headed, Mrs. Fiske was one of the greatest American actresses. Ward Morehouse♦ has written, "Mrs. Fiske never had beauty, but she had magnetism. She had with all of her nervous, jerky manner, subtlety and finesse, and she was as much at ease in light-handed drawing-room comedy as she was in the problem plays of Ibsen." Many critics saw her style as heavily influenced by Duse's♦ underplaying. Mrs. Fiske herself called it "natural, true acting." She once created a furor by delivering an important speech to George Arliss♦ with her back to the audience, and elsewhere awed playgoers by holding their attention for ten minutes without moving and without speaking as she cradled her drunken lover's head in her lap in *Salvation Nell*. Yet she was also sometimes too subservient to the demands of less thoughtful playgoers. She forced C. M. S. McLellan to write an extra act for *Leah Kleschna*, giving the play a contrived happy ending instead of his original, ambiguous one. Much of the criticism leveled at her during her career is suspect, possibly written by critics susceptible to the Trust's bribes. In a curious way, Franklin P. Adams's droll verse best sums up most playgoers' reactions:

> Somewords she runstogetherso,
>   Some others are distinctly stated.
> Somecometoofast and s o m e   t o o s l o w
>   And some are syncopated,
> And yet no voice—I am sincere—
>   Exists that I prefer to hear.

FITCH, [WILLIAM] CLYDE (1865–1909) Considered the finest American playwright at the turn of the century, he was born in Elmira, N.Y., the son of a Union army officer and a Maryland belle. (He would later pay a sort of tribute to their courtship in his 1899 success, *Barbara Frietchie.* ♦) His "sissy" manners made him a loner at school, but the same effeminacy won him major women's roles in the dramatic club at Amherst College. After graduation, he went to New York where, at his parents' behest, he sought a career as an architect and interior decorator. While applying for work, he wrote a number of stories and short plays, one of which, *Betty's Finish* (1890), was afterwards successfully performed at the Boston Museum.♦ He also made a number of important theatrical friends, including the critic for the New York *Times,* Edward A. Dithmar. ♦ It was Dithmar, along with William Winter,♦ who suggested to Richard Mansfield♦ that

Fitch provide the actor with a dramatization of the life of Beau Brumell. *Beau Brumell* ♦ (1890) was an immediate hit and launched his career. During the next nineteen years he wrote nearly sixty plays, thirty-three of them original, and the remainder translations of foreign plays or adaptations of novels. Among his more important works were *Nathan Hale* (1898), which interwove historic incidents with a love story; *The Moth and the Flame* (1898), depicting the power of a clever, but dissipated man over an innocent young girl; *The Cowboy and the Lady* (1899), centering on a man falsely accused of murdering the villanous husband of the woman he loves; *Barbara Frietchie,* turning the famous story into a tragic romance; *The Climbers* ♦ (1901), examining the viciousness of people striving for social position; *Captain Jinks of the Horse Marines* ♦ (1901), focusing on the romance of an American girl who has become an opera singer; *The Girl with the Green Eyes* ♦ (1902), in which a woman's unreasoning jealousy drives her to attempt suicide; *The Truth* (1907), portraying the disastrous consequences of a woman's pathological lies; and *The City* ♦ (1909), showing the corrupting influences of a big city on a country-bred family.

The range and variety of Fitch's plays are startling, as is his prolificacy. One anonymous poem in the New York *World* read in part:

> He shoves his pen until he makes it sizz.
> Biff!
> Act I, —Act II, —Act III, as if
> The things were a cigarette to whiff.
> Slambang,
> The word goes out to the Broadway gang:
> Hooray!
> Clyde Fitch has written another play!

Yet his works were rarely perceived as hastily written, and what unevenness was evident was no greater than that of less productive authors. Indeed, Quinn♦ made a point of insisting that "thirty-three original plays in twenty years is not an extraordinary total," continuing, "while his adaptations took comparatively little effort, his original work was slowly developed in his mind and he came to its creation on paper with plan and even dialogue fully conceived." Quite probably his most glaring fault by modern standards was his contrived happy endings. Thus, the jealous woman in *The Girl with the Green Eyes* is thwarted in her suicide attempt and the lying girl in *The Truth* is ultimately brought to her senses. These conclusions were not the result of haste on Fitch's part, but of his need to please contemporary audiences and thereby provide him with the income required for his notoriously luxurious way of life. Quinn has pointed to Fitch's three salient virtues as "the ability to visualize any place or period in terms of its social values, the power to incarnate virtues and vices in characters who are essentially dramatic, and the gift of writing clever dialogue." Walter Prichard Eaton♦ added to this list Fitch's dramatized observations of small details such as the thumping of steam-pipes in one play and the sound of an object falling down an airshaft in another. He concluded, "If we took Fitch's worlds and correctly illustrated them, they would give to future generations a better idea of American life from 1890 to 1910 than newspapers or historical records." Certainly Fitch's best plays, whatever their flaws, remain gripping reading and are probably exceptionally playable even today.

Biography: *Clyde Fitch and His Letters,* Montrose J. Moses and Virginia Gerson, Boston, 1924.

Fit-Up A name given in the 18th and 19th centuries to small bands of actors, often composed largely of members of a single family, who traveled with plays to backwater villages. They customarily performed in makeshift theatres, using barns, store porches, or any other available site. A number of celebrated American performers, such as John Durang♦ and G. L. Fox,♦ were at one time members of such companies.

Five Star Final, a melodrama in three acts by Louis Weitzenkorn. Produced by A. H. Woods♦ at the Cort Theatre. December 30, 1930. 175 performances.

Caring only about circulation, the callous newspaper owner, Bernard Hinchcliffe (Berton Churchill), orders Randall (Arthur Byron♦), his editor, to revive the sordid, long-buried story of Nancy Vorhees (Merle Maddern), who had been acquitted of the charge of shooting her lover. Nancy is now married to Michael Townsend (Malcolm Duncan) and is preparing for the wedding of her daughter Jenny (Frances Fuller). When a reporter visits her, she gives him a picture of Jenny, thinking it is for the marriage notices. Learning the truth, Nancy begs Randall to kill the story, but he insists it is still news. The story is published on Jenny's wedding day, and Nancy and Michael commit suicide. Jenny comes to the paper to kill Randall, but learning that Randall has quit in revulsion, walks away.

Richard Lockridge of the *Sun* observed that the play displayed such "scathing contempt for tabloid journalism and its supporters that in the end only a few charred bones remain to mark the place." The Theatre Guild had produced a similar play the night before, Claire and Paul Sifton's *Midnight,* which some critics thought had more literary value. But the dramatic effectiveness of Weitzenkorn's play succeeded, while *Midnight* failed.

Weitzenkorn (1893–1943) was born in Wilkes-Barre, Penn., and later studied at Columbia. He was primarily a newspaperman, but wrote several plays, of which this alone was successful.

FLANAGAN, HALLIE [née FERGUSON] (1890–1969) Born in Redfield, S.D., she studied at Grinnell College, then spent time as an assistant to Professor George Pierce Baker♦ at his 47 Workshop♦ before returning briefly to teach at the Grinnell Experimental Theatre. In 1925 she was appointed professor of drama and director of experimental theatre at Vassar. She took a leave of absence between 1935 and 1939 to serve as the head of the Federal Theatre Project. ♦ Afterwards she returned to Vassar, retiring in 1952. Besides writing numerous articles for leading magazines and journals, she was the author of *Shifting Scenes of the Modern European Theatre* (1928), *Arena, the Story of the Federal Theatre* (1940), and *Dynamo, the Story of the Vassar Theatre* (1943).

Flash of Lightning, A, a play in five acts by Augustin Daly. ♦ Produced at the Broadway Theatre. June 10, 1868. 52 performances.

Garry Fallon (J. H. Jack) is a greedy, ambitious man who rules his family with an iron hand. He has made his wife totally subservient and devoted all his attentions to advancing his haughty daughter, Rose (Kitty Blanchard), neglecting his other daughter, Bessie (Blanche Grey). Shortly after Rose's beau Chauncey (McKee Rankin♦) has presented her with some gold jewelry, Bessie's former suitor Jack Ryver (J. K. Mortimer) visits Bessie and steals the jewelry. The family blames Bessie, who runs away. She takes refuge on a steamboat, which catches fire. Luckily, Chauncey and Ryver have followed her and rescue her at the last minute. Ryver also manages to make the family believe that the electricity from a flash of lightning moved the jewelry, which he has quietly replaced.

Daly derived the basic plot from Sardou's♦ *Le Perle noire,* adding the burning ship to provide the requisite thrill required by contemporary "sensation drama." Coming on top of his successes with *Leah, the Forsaken♦* and *Under the Gaslight,* ♦ the play not only consolidated Daly's reputation but helped give him the wherewithal to consider founding a permanent company.

FLAVIN, Martin [Archer] (1883–1967) Born in San Francisco, he was raised in Chicago, where he attended the University of Chicago and spent several years as a businessman before seriously turning his hand to play-writing. Two of his one-act dramas were produced on Broadway in 1921. His first full-length play to reach New York was *Children of the Moon* (1923), in which a family's history of insanity claims a daughter and her lover. The play was much admired, but had only a modest run. Less successful were *Lady of the Rose* (1925), a Pirandellish story of a playwright's search for a perfect heroine; and *Service for Two* (1926), in which a groom's old flame demonstrates his vacuity to his bride. In the first half of the 1929–30 season three of Flavin's plays reached New York. All three won substantial critical endorsement, although only two had relatively successful runs. Best received was *The Criminal Code,* ♦ a stark study of a model prisoner debased and destroyed by prison life. *Broken Dishes* described a family's rebellion against a domineering mother, while *Cross Roads,* a quick failure, told of the trouble a young medical student encounters in choosing between his career and marriage. Several other plays were mounted by community theatres in the early 1930s, but not until 1935 did any reach New York. *Achilles Had a Heel* recounted the trials of a black war hero reduced to being a zoo-keeper; *Tapestry in Gray* described how a nurse destroys the friendship and lives of two men who had been buddies since medical school. Apparently discouraged by the poor public reception of his plays, Flavin turned to writing novels and was successful.

FLEXNER, Anne Crawford, see *Mrs. Wiggs of the Cabbage Patch*

FLORENCE, W[illiam] J[ames or Jermyn] [né Bernard Conlin] (1831–91) Born in Albany, N.Y., where he early showed dramatic ability and became an important member of the local Murdoch Dramatic Association, he made his professional debut in Richmond, Va., in 1849, playing Tobias in *The Stranger.* ♦ He then moved from one stock company to another during the season before first appearing in New York in 1850 as Hallagan in John Brougham's ♦ *Home.* His Irish good looks and charm coupled with his "frank, ingenuous" acting style kept him playing preponderantly Irish parts for the next dozen years, often in conjunction with his wife, the former Malvina Pray (1831–1906). They also appeared successfully in a number of burlesques. He broke away from this relatively narrow pattern on his return in 1860 from some seasons in London, first re-creating the late William Burton's ♦ great roles of Toodle and Cap'n Cuttle, even using Burton's own costumes. Critics were uncertain whether his performances were fine acting or fine mimicry. He scored a more important success when he became the first American Bob Brierly, the maligned parolee, which is the title part in *The Ticket-of-Leave Man* ♦ (1863). In 1867 he produced the first American presentation of *Caste,* ♦ taking for himself the part of George D'Alroy, who rescues his wife from poverty and snobbery. Both the production and Florence's performance were highly praised, but his reputation was severely tarnished, since Lester Wallack ♦ had bought the rights to the work and had announced his own production. Wallack sued to stop Florence's mounting, only to have Florence win on a technicality, Florence claiming he had memorized the entire play while watching London performances. He next turned from hero to tricky villain when he played Obenreizer in the American premiere of *No Thoroughfare* (1868). One final long run was as the garrulous Hon. Bardwell Slote in a spoof of Washington political corruption, *The Mighty Dollar* ♦ (1875). His last years were spent largely reviving his repertory, but he won praise in 1890 as Sir Lucius O'Trigger and Zekiel Homespun in Joseph Jefferson's ♦ mountings of *The Rivals* and *The Heir-at-Law.* William Winter ♦ recalled, "The secret of his success lay in his profound feeling, guided by good taste and perfect self-control. He was an actor of humanity, and he diffused an irresistible charm of truth and gentleness."

Florodora An 1899 English musical comedy with book by Owen Hall, lyrics by E. Byrd Jones and Paul Rubens, and music by Leslie Stuart, it told the story of an attempt to cheat a beautiful young heiress out of her rights to a famous perfume. Its New York premiere, with a somewhat revised book by Frank Pixley, ♦ opened at the Casino Theatre ♦ on November 12, 1900, and ran for 505 performances. The run was one of the longest of its era in the American theatre and was even more unusual in that it surpassed the London run, an unheard-of phenomenon until then, when English stands were as a rule far lengthier than American runs. No small part of the show's popularity stemmed from the fame of its sextette (actually a double sextette of six men and six women) who sang "Tell Me Pretty Maiden," the first major song hit from a Broadway show not sung by the principals. Legend has it that the six original women of the sextette—Daisy Greene, Marjorie Relyea, Vaughn Texsmith, Margaret Walker, Agnes Wayburn, and Marie L. Wilson—all married millionaires. The musical was revived on frequent occasions, including a very successful production during the 1919–20 season.

Flying High, a musical comedy in two acts. Book by Jack McGowan,♦ B. G. De Sylva,♦ and Lew Brown.♦ Lyrics by De Sylva and Brown. Music by Ray Henderson.♦ Produced by George White♦ at the Apollo Theatre. March 3, 1930. 347 performances.

While the flashy aviator, Tod Addison (Oscar Shaw♦), pursues a courtship of Eileen Cassidy (Grace Brinkley) that began when he parachuted onto her apartment balcony, his dithering mechanic, "Rusty" Krause (Bert Lahr♦), attempts to escape the advances of hefty, lovelorn Pansy Sparks (Kate Smith). Her dogged pursuit prompts "Rusty" to steal Tod's plane. Only when he is airborne does he remember that he has no idea of how to land the plane. Without meaning to, he breaks records for sustained flight.

Principal songs: Red Hot Chicago · Thank Your Father

This final De Sylva, Brown, and Henderson musical was a success largely because of Lahr's comic antics.

Folger Shakespeare Memorial Library (Washington, D.C.) The library was founded in 1930 and opened in 1932, with monies and a collection of Shakespeariana bequeathed it by Henry Clay Folger (1857–1930). While a student at Amherst, Folger, who finally was chairman of the board of Standard Oil of New York, was inspired by Ralph Waldo Emerson to begin his life-long acquisitions. The collection includes 79 first folios, and is equaled only by collections in the British Museum and the Bodleian Library at Oxford. The Library has been administered by Amherst under the direction of Dr. Joseph Quincy Adams, Louis B. Wright, and other respected scholars. In 1970, its director at that time, O. B. Hardison, Jr., joined with Richmond Crinkley to found the Folger Theatre Group, and to mount numerous Shakespearean revivals as well as modern plays in the Elizabethan-style theatre housed within the Library. In 1985 the theatre end became a separate entity, incorporated as the Shakespeare Theatre at the Folger. Michael Kahn took over as director in 1986. The repertory no longer includes new plays.

Folksbiene (People's Stage) Called by the Yiddish theatre historian, Nahma Sandrow, "one of the most illustrious of Yiddish amateur groups," it has certainly been the most durable. It was formed in 1915 by a merger of several older companies, including the Progressive Dramatic Club and the Hebrew Dramatic League. From the start it was closely allied with left-wing and labor organizations, and still operates under the auspices of the Arbeter Ring (Workmen's Club). No season since its founding has gone by without its offering at least one presentation, and usually more. It performs generally serious plays, mostly by Yiddish writers, but has often turned to Eugene O'Neill,♦ Upton Sinclair, and important European playwrights as well. The group frequently hires distinguished professional directors and because its actors are amateurs performs only on weekends.

Follies, a musical [performed without intermission]. Book by James Goldman. Lyrics and music by Stephen Sondheim.♦ Produced by Hal Prince♦ and others at the Winter Garden Theatre. April 4, 1971. 522 performances.

With the Weismann Theatre under demolition, many of the aging performers who had played in the various editions of Weismann's *Follies* gather for a last, bittersweet reunion. As they talk about what has happened to them since their earlier successes and as they recall those bygone days, "memory figures" of their younger selves help jolt the recollections. The reunion over they leave, and one of them concludes that "life is empty; there is no hope."

Principal songs: I'm Still Here · Losing My Mind · Too Many Mornings

The musical was probably suggested by the demolition of the great Ziegfeld Theatre.♦

Follow the Girls, a musical comedy in two acts. Book by Guy Bolton,♦ Eddie Davis, and Fred Thompson.♦ Music and lyrics by Dan Shapiro, Milton Pascal, and Phil Charig. Produced at the Century Theatre. April 8, 1944. 882 performances.

When Bubbles La Marr (Gertrude Niesen), a burlesque queen, takes over a servicemen's canteen as her contribution to the war effort, her 4-F suitor, Goofy Gale (Jackie Gleason), is forced to disguise himself as a Wave to gain entrance.

Principal song: I Wanna Get Married

This loosely structured "girlie" show, whose thin plot served for little more than to frame its many vaudeville turns and skimpily clad chorus girls, was of a type often called "glorified burlesque." No small part of its attraction was its appeal to servicemen in town on leave. The show was Bolton's last successful effort as a collaborator on musical comedy books, although it was a marked comedown in quality from his work of two or three decades earlier.

Follow Thru, a musical comedy in two acts. Book by Laurence Schwab♦ and B. G. De Sylva.♦ Lyrics by De Sylva and Lew Brown.♦ Music by Ray Henderson.♦ Produced by Schwab and Frank Mandel♦ at the 46th Street Theatre. January 9, 1929. 403 performances.

Lora Moore (Irene Delroy) and Ruth Van Horn (Madeline Cameron) are rivals both for their country club's golf championship and for handsome Jerry Downs (John Barker). At the same time brash Angie Howard (Zelma O'Neal♦) attempts to catch Jack Martin (Jack Haley♦). Angie has no rivals, but the shy, oddball Jack proves remarkably elusive. In the end, however, Lora and Angie win their men, and Lora also gets her loving cup.

Principal songs: Button Up Your Overcoat · My Lucky Star · You Wouldn't Fool Me, Would You?

Called in its programs "a musical slice of country club life"—a small indication of its punning humor—the show expressed the zesty, sometimes frenetic hedonism of the 1920s in melody and comedy. Gilbert Gabriel wrote in the *Sun* that it seemed "dedicated to the task of making youth flame and love shout out, with crisp, crazy, lusty, ankle-loosing, hip-seizing songs, and lyrics that give this whole razzing, jazzing society circus its cue to get gay."

FONDA, Henry [Jaynes] (1905–82) The lanky, slightly twangy-voiced actor was born in Grand Island, Neb., and raised in Omaha, where he first appeared on stage in 1925 as Ricky in *You and I*♦ with the Omaha Community Playhouse. After performing with various stock groups for several years, he made his Broadway debut as a walk-on in *The Game of Love and Death* (1929). Shortly thereafter he joined the University Players♦ and remained with them until 1932. He next appeared on Broadway in *I Love You Wednesday* (1932), *Forsaking All Others* (1933), and *New Faces*♦ (1934), before winning acclaim as Dan Harrow, the canal man determined to return to the land, in *The Farmer Takes a Wife* (1934). Apart from a brief run in *Blow Ye Winds* (1937), he devoted himself to films until he returned to play the title role of the officer forever sticking up for his crew in *Mister Roberts*♦ (1948). John Mason Brown♦ wrote of his performance, "He is to the full the unheroic hero; the shy, modest, everyday young man whose decencies and hidden strength have somehow made a leader of him. His is a quiet performance . . . Its power is its understate-

ment, its reticence, its utter and communicated honesty." His work won him a Tony Award.♦ Thereafter he became one of the few major stars to shuttle regularly between Hollywood and Broadway. In 1951 he portrayed Charles Gray, the businessman seeking to recover his self-respect, in *Point of No Return*. He earned further encomiums as Lt. Greenwald, the reluctant prosecuting attorney, in *The Caine Mutiny Court-Martial* (1954), and as Jerry Ryan, the staid Irish lawyer in love with a kooky Jewish girl, in *Two for the Seesaw*♦ (1958). Later New York appearances were less successful: John, who finds an evening of love in a New England inn, in *Silent Night, Lonely Night* (1959); Parker Ballantine, a critic who must review his wife's play, in *Critic's Choice* (1960); and Charles Wertenbaker, who is dying of cancer, in *A Gift of Time* (1962). He finally enjoyed another long run as Jim Bolton, the conservative executive who finds himself saddled with a free-thinking daughter, in *Generation*♦ (1965). He toured in several productions before returning to New York in 1974 in a one-man show, *Clarence Darrow*. His last appearance was as Justice Daniel Snow, who is taken aback to learn a woman has been appointed to the Supreme Court, in *First Monday in October* (1978).

Autobiography: *Fonda: My Story,* with Howard Teichman, New York, 1981.

FONTANNE, Lynn [née Lillie Louise Fontanne] (1887–1983) One of the great ladies of the American stage, the willowy, dark-haired, sharp-eyed actress with the throaty contralto voice and regal bearing was born in England, where she studied with Ellen Terry♦ before making her debut in 1905 in *Cinderella*. She came to America in 1910, appearing in *Mr. Preedy and the Countess*, but shortly returned home and did not settle here permanently until 1916. Thereupon she appeared in a rapid succession of plays, including *A Young Man's Fancy* (1916), in which she met her future husband, Alfred Lunt.♦ Among her early assignments was the role of Anna in the original production of *Anna Christie*, ♦ which was then called *Chris Christopherson* (1920). This production was withdrawn and Miss Fontanne was replaced. However, she enjoyed a major hit as Dulcinea, the pushy, cliché-ridden wife, in *Dulcy*♦ (1921). Her first important joint appearance with her husband was as The Actress in *The Guardsman* (1924), after which she appeared, often with him, in such Theatre Guild♦ productions as *Arms and the Man* (1925); *The Goat Song* (1926); *Pygmalion*♦ (1926); and *The Brothers Karamazov* (1927). In 1927 she also created the role of Mrs. Frayne, understanding mistress to Lunt's Clark Story, in *The Second Man,* ♦ and later that year was Jennifer Dubedat to Lunt's Louis Dubedat in *The Doctor's Dilemma*. She next created the role of Nina Leeds, whose insatiable possessiveness wrecks the lives of the men closest to her, in *Stange Interlude* ♦ (1928). Lunt was not in this play, but the couple permanently reunited when she played another of his mistresses, Ilsa, in *Caprice* (1928). A short run followed in *Meteor* (1929) as Ann Carr, wife to Lunt's greedy financier. The 1930s saw the Lunts in some of their most memorable roles, in plays often written with them in mind. She was Elizabeth to his Essex in *Elizabeth the Queen* ♦ (1930); and Elena, a former prince's mistress who must decide what to do when the prince returns for another fling, in *Reunion in Vienna* ♦ (1931). The couple then cavorted with Noel Coward in his *Design for Living* (1933), with Miss Fontanne as Gilda, who finds her two wild former beaux still courting her after her marriage. Following a brief failure in *Point Valiant* (1935), she undertook Katherine to Lunt's Petruchio, then played Irene, an old show girl traveling as a rich man's mistress, in *Idiot's Delight* ♦ (1936). A year later, in *Amphitryon 38* (1937), she was Alkmena, a mortal loved by a god. In 1938 she was Ilena in *The Seagull*. For the following seasons the couple toured in a repertory of their successes. They did not return in a new piece until they appeared in *There Shall Be No Night* ♦ (1940), with Miss Fontanne as Miranda Valkonen, the American wife of a Finnish scientist during the Russo-Finnish War. She next played the romantic, naive Manuela, who is wooed away from a dull husband by a strolling player in *The Pirate* ♦ (1942). The Lunts spent the war years in England, entertaining British audiences first with *There Shall Be No Night* and then with a written-to-order comedy, *Love in Idleness,* which they brought to New York in 1946 as *O Mistress Mine*. Miss Fontanne portrayed Olivia Brown, a woman living with a man who cannot divorce his wife because of his position. The play signaled a decline in the quality of the pieces the couple had to work with, so in the late 1940s and early 1950s it was largely their acting that was responsible for the success of three weak shows. In *I Know My Love* (1949), the long history of a marriage, Miss Fontanne was Emily Chandler, the wife; in *Quadrille* (1954), the Marchioness of Heronden, who elopes with a railroad magnate after her husband has fled with the magnate's wife; and in *The Great Sebastians* (1956), Essie Sebastian, a member of a mind-reading act caught behind the Iron Curtain. They found a powerful vehicle for their farewell

performances, *The Visit* (1958), with Miss Fontanne playing Claire Zachanassian, a rich woman who returns to the town of her girlhood to wreak vengeance on a faithless lover. The play was mounted at the old Globe Theatre, renamed in their honor the Lunt-Fontanne.

Always the more restrained, controlled performer of the team, Miss Fontanne was early on characterized by Brooks Atkinson ♦ as an actress with "glamour, poise and subtlety." Theresa Helburn, ♦ who worked with her for years, called her "a brilliant and beautiful tiger," and suggested that both she and Lunt always retained something of the characters they first made famous. In Miss Fontanne's case that meant she ever afterward displayed a touch of Dulcy's inherent cruelty in all her roles.

Biography: *The Fabulous Lunts,* Jared Brown, New York, 1986.

Fool, The, a melodrama in four acts by Channing Pollock. ♦ Produced at the Times Square Theatre. October 23, 1922. 360 performances.

Parishioners at New York's Church of the Nativity are disturbed by their new assistant rector, Daniel Gilchrist (James Kirkwood), who has condemned the fancy Christmas decorations. He has also read contributors to the church a lecture on the rich man entering heaven, and spoken of "ill gotten gains." As if that were not enough, he has welcomed poor worshippers into the upper-class church and even given his own overcoat to an impoverished Jew who was shivering in the cold. The rector, Rev. Wadham (Arthur Eliot), has warned Gilchrist that he courts trouble. "What would happen if anybody really tried to live like Christ?" Gilchrist asks. Wadham replies it cannot be done. Gilchrist is dismissed. He takes his private ministry to striking workers, and when he is slapped for his pains, he turns the other cheek. He next opens a mission. Even here he is beaten by hoodlums. Although he helps a crippled woman (Sara Sothern) walk again and saves a marriage, he continues to be assailed as a "nut." Only the woman whose paralysis he cured retains faith in him. Her name is Mary.

Pollock was turned down by virtually every important producer, until he got Arch Selwyn ♦ to back the play. When it opened to generally unfavorable notices, Selwyn was ready to close it, but Pollock, who owned 25 percent of the work, would not let him. Pollock began a primitive publicity campaign, writing letters, making speeches, and printing advertisements with favorable remarks from the few notables, such as Nicholas Murray Butler, Charles Dana Gibson, and David Belasco, ♦

who had liked the play. The publicity turned business around. According to Pollock, "Before the end of the season, seven companies were touring . . . reaching audiences of not less than 85,000 people each week, or close to five million theatregoers in a single season."

Fool for Love, a play (performed without intermission) by Sam Shepard. ♦ Produced by the Circle Repertory Company♦ at the Circle Theatre. May 26, 1983. 1000 performances.

May (Kathy Whitton Baker) and Eddie (Ed Harris), both low-lifes, are half-brother and half-sister. They long have had a love-hate relationship. At a cheap motel, with their hopelessly besotted or senile father (Will Marchetti) sharing their room, they once again rage through their gamut of emotions, until Eddie finally walks out.

Although the play dealt with ill-educated, sometimes inarticulate people, it made for good theatre. Its small cast helped earn it a long run, and it remains popular in regional theatres.

Fool There Was, A, a play in three acts by Porter Emerson Browne. ♦ Produced at the Liberty Theatre. March 24, 1909. 93 performances.

There are two kinds of love, says The Woman (Katherine Kaelred), one like white roses, wan and bloodless, and the other like red roses, warm and vital. When The Husband (Robert Hilliard♦) sails on an important diplomatic mission, he sees The Woman, throws his wife's pale bouquet overboard, and before long is in The Woman's clutches. She destroys his career and his marriage, and drives him to drink. Realizing the damage The Woman has wrought, he attempts to strangle her. The struggle proves too much, and he falls dead. The Woman laughingly scatters red rose petals over his body.

This unrelenting, if obvious, melodrama was even more popular on the road and was eventually made into a famous silent film.

FORBES, JAMES (1871–1938) Born in Canada, he moved to America to seek a career, first trying his hand as an actor, a press agent, and a drama critic for the Pittsburgh *Dispatch* and later for the New York *World.* He found play-writing most congenial, so began by writing vaudeville sketches. It was one of these, written for Rose Stahl, ♦ that he turned into his first produced full-length play, *The Chorus Lady*♦ (1906). Telling of a chorus girl willing to sacrifice her own reputation to save her sister's, it was a smash hit. Equally popular was *The Traveling Salesman*♦ (1908), in which the hero falls in love

with a telegraph operator and prevents her land being sold from under her. In *The Commuters* (1910), a suburban wife decides to emulate her gallivanting husband. He suffered his first failure with *A Rich Man's Son* (1912), which he produced, a comedy about a young man's courtship of his father's secretary, then scored another hit with *The Show Shop*♦ (1914), in which a rich young man is forced to underwrite a play to retain his actress-sweetheart's love. When styles of play-writing began to change with the coming of World War I, Forbes attempted to change with them. His best play was *The Famous Mrs. Fair*♦ (1919), in which a militant feminist learns the price of neglecting her family. Thereafter, however, his gift for effective theatre eluded him. *Endless Chain* (1922), the story of a pushy young wife; *Young Blood* (1925), a father-son conflict; *Precious* (1929), showing the problems of a hasty marriage; and *Matrimony PFD* (1936), a French comedy adapted in collaboration with Grace George, ♦ were all failures. Forbes was one of the founders of the Dramatists' Theatre. ♦ Admired in his own day for his pungent dialogue, he was also respected as a director. He staged all of his own plays along with several by other playwrights.

FORBES-ROBERTSON, JOHNSTON (1853–1937) The handsome, if ascetic, slightly craggy-featured English actor made his American debut in 1885, playing Orlando opposite Mary Anderson. ♦ On his numerous subsequent visits he offered many of his most admired Shakespearean interpretations, including Shylock and Hamlet. Comparing his Dane with that of another English artist, Sir Henry Irving, ♦ Walter Tallmadge Arndt observed in *Current Literature,* "Irving's is artistic artificiality, while Mr. Robertson's is artistic naturalness." However, for most American playgoers his greatest role was The Passer-by, a divine figure who comes in human form to visit a Bloomsbury lodging house, in *The Passing of the Third Floor Back* (1909). Adolph Klauber♦ wrote of his performance in this play, "There is something so illusive in the appeal of Mr. Forbes-Robertson's acting as almost to baffle complete description. It has been termed an aloofness or a certain spiritual-like quality . . . His reading alone is balm for ears tired of the raw and raucous utterance of most players . . . In gesture and action he is simple and sparing, but every movement tells of a purpose and a thought behind it." After formally retiring from the London stage in 1913 he spent three seasons touring America. He was married to the sister of Maxine Elliott. ♦

Autobiography: *A Player Under Three Reigns,* Boston, 1925.

Forbidden Broadway A very small-scale revue that spoofed Broadway shows and Broadway stars, it was first presented at Palsson's, a supper club, on January 15, 1982. Although much of the music was borrowed from shows being kidded, the satirical text was entirely by Gerard Alessandrini. Since its opening the entertainment, which is regularly updated, has moved to several different venues, but, with minor hiatuses, continues to play year in year out. At this writing (1991) it is on stage at an off-Broadway playhouse.

FORD, HARRIET (1863–1949) A native of Seymour, Conn., she studied acting at the American Academy of Dramatic Arts♦ and performed for several seasons before turning to play-writing. Nearly two dozen of her works, almost all either adaptations of novels or collaborations, were given major productions, among them, *A Gentleman of France*♦ (1901), *The Fourth Estate* (1909), *A Little Brother of the Rich* (1909), *The Argyle Case* (1912), and *The Dummy*♦ (1914).

FORD, HELEN [ISABEL] [née BARNETT] (1897?–1982) The petite, vivacious singer, who was one of the more popular musical comedy queens of the 1920s, was born in Troy, N.Y., and made her debut there as a child performer. Although she had played New York earlier, she first came to critics' attention as Toinette Fontaine, the French nurse who wins the doughboy hero, in *Always You* (1920). Later that year she was Natalie Blythe, the girl who wins an artist beau in *The Sweetheart Shop.* After assuming a less important role in *For Goodness Sake* (1922), she had one of her biggest hits as Mary Thompson, who sets up her own business while waiting for her playboy fiancé to settle down, in *The Gingham Girl* (1922). *Helen of Troy, N.Y.* (1923), which seemed named after her but was not, was stolen from her by young Queenie Smith.♦ After another failure, *No Other Girl* (1924), she began a long relationship with Richard Rodgers,♦ Lorenz Hart,♦ and Herbert Fields,♦ playing Betsy Burke, the American girl in love with a redcoat, in their *Dearest Enemy*♦ (1925); the title role of a girl who daydreams of a better life in *Peggy-Ann*♦ (1926); and the title role of the Chinese wife who saves her husband from becoming a eunuch, in *Chee-Chee* (1928). In *Dearest Enemy* she introduced "Here in My Arms" and "Bye and Bye"; in *Peggy-Ann,* "A Tree in the Park." Between engagements she toured in vaudeville. She later played Adele in a 1933 version of *Fledermaus,* called *Champagne Sec.* Her last appearance in a major musical was in *Great Lady* (1938), although she performed in several straight plays before retiring.

FORD, HUGH (1868–1952) After beginning his career as an actor, he served several seasons in stock, both as a player and a director, before coming to the attention of George C. Tyler.♦ For many years thereafter he was the leading director for Tyler and for the company with which Tyler was long connected, Liebler and Co.♦ Tyler came to consider him "the greatest director alive," and Owen Davis♦ recalled that he "had probably the longest unbroken string of successes of any contemporary director." While these may have been exaggerations, his list of credits included *Salomy Jane*♦ (1907), *The Man from Home*♦ (1908), *The Melting Pot* (1909), *The Dawn of a Tomorrow*♦ (1909), *Alias Jimmy Valentine*♦ (1910), *The Deep Purple* (1911), *The Garden of Allah*♦ (1911), *Potash and Perlmutter*♦ (1913), *The Yellow Ticket* (1914), and *Merton of the Movies*♦ (1922). He was also famous as a director of silent films.

FORD, JOHN T[HOMPSON] (1829–94) Descended from an old Maryland family, he was born in Baltimore, which remained his base throughout his career as a builder and manager of theatres. As a young man he worked in a family tobacco factory, but left the company in 1850 to become business manager and press agent for a concert ensemble. In 1854 he assumed management of Baltimore's famed Holliday Street Theatre,♦ which he ran for the next 25 years. He quickly took over the running of numerous other theatres in the South and eventually built many playhouses, including Ford's Theatre♦ in Washington, where Lincoln was assassinated and which remains an active legitimate theatre today; Ford's Theatre in Baltimore, which remained the city's principal playhouse until the 1960s; and the Academy of Music in Philadelphia, which is still the main concert hall there. He was generally acknowledged as one of the most honest and important theatrical figures of his day.

FORD [WEAVER], PAUL (1901–76) An actor with a drolly grim long face, he was born in Baltimore and made his debut in summer stock in 1920 as Sir Lucius O'Trigger. His first Broadway appearance was as Sgt. Carey in *Decision* (1944). Although he was a fine dramatic actor, he is remembered largely for his comic portraits, notably the befuddled Colonel Purdy in *Teahouse of the August Moon*♦

(1953); a variety of characters in *A Thurber Carnival* (1960); and Harry Lambert, the middle-aged husband who suddenly finds he is to become a father, in *Never Too Late*♦ (1962).

Ford's Theatre (Washington, D.C.) In 1861 John T. Ford♦ converted the empty First Baptist Church into a playhouse. It was operating profitably when it burned down a year later. Ford then built a new, brick theatre holding 1700, which he opened in August 1863 as Ford's New Theatre. Once again the theatre flourished until President Lincoln♦ was shot there on April 14, 1865, while watching a performance of *Our American Cousin.* ♦ The War Department prevented Ford from reopening the auditorium and purchased it from Ford and his brothers. The building was gutted and converted into an office building and storage facility, but its jinx continued. Part of the building collapsed in the 1890s, killing 22 government employees. Between 1965 and early 1968 the building was restored to its original appearance but with a seating capacity of only 741. In January 1968 it reopened as a playhouse.

Forest Rose, The; or, American Farmers, a play in two acts by Samuel Woodworth.♦ Music by John Davies. Produced at the Chatham Garden Theatre. October 7, 1825. In repertory.

Although William (Arthur Keene), a decent country lad, loves Harriet (Mrs. Burke), Harriet and her friend Lydia (Mrs. Henry Wallack), two New Jersey farm girls or "forest roses," long to escape their bucolic life for the excitement of the city. Lydia's prospects for escape seem better than Harriet's, since she is loved by the rich Blandford (Mr. Howard). However, the romance must be kept secret in order not to offend Blandford's snobbish father. Blandford's English-born friend Bellamy (Edward N. Thayer) courts Harriet, whom he promises Blandford he will love for a whole month. Later he persuades a seemingly naïve Yankee shopkeeper-turned-farmer, Jonathan Ploughboy (Alexander Simpson), to help him kidnap Harriet. But Jonathan is not as gullible as he appears. A servant girl is substituted. Harriet marries William, and Lydia weds Blandford.

Principal songs: Here in Scenes of Sweet Seclusion · When Bashful Lubin Sought My Hand · The Morn Awakes · The Heart Sustained by Hope Alone · Is There a Light?

Often called a "pastoral opera," the play was one of the first, and for many years the most popular, American rural drama. Woodworth apparently based his Jonathan Ploughboy on the Jonathan in

Royall Tyler's♦ *The Contrast,* ♦ but it was Ploughboy who kindled the real vogue for such Yankee characters. Virtually all the great 19th-century Yankee specialists and other fine comedians— G. H. Hill,♦ Dan Marble,♦ Henry Placide,♦ and Joshua Silsbee♦—frequently played the part.

Forever After, a play in three acts by Owen Davis. ♦ Produced by William A. Brady♦ at the Central Theatre. September 9, 1918. 312 performances.

A grievously wounded soldier, Ted (Conrad Nagel), recounts the tale of his unfulfilled romance to his buddy. Before the war he had loved a rich girl, Jennie (Alice Brady♦), but Jennie's ambitious, snobbish mother had forced her to break off the affair. Now Ted is taken to a field hospital where Jennie serves as a Red Cross nurse. Their tearful reunion and her obvious love give him the strength to survive.

Davis recalled this mawkishly romantic play as "one of the best money-makers I have ever had," at the same time recognizing that along with such other works as *Sinners*♦ and *At 9:45* it marked a major turning point in his career, representing "one step up" from the cheap melodramas of his earlier years.

FORREST, EDWIN (1806–72) Generally acknowledged as the first grand tragedian of the American stage, Forrest was born in Philadelphia to the impoverished, runaway son of a Scottish squire and the daughter of middle-class German immigrants. His theatrical debut came about by accident in 1817 when the manager of the Southwark Theatre,♦ noting his attractiveness, asked him to substitute for an ailing actress in the small role of Rosina, a captive odalisque, in *Rudolph; or, The Robber of Calabria*. The experience thrilled him and though he had little formal education he studied elocution and organized a Thespian Club. His real debut was as Norval in *Douglas*♦ at the Walnut Street Theatre♦ in 1820. He spent the next several seasons touring what was called the Western circuit—western Pennsylvania, Ohio, and Kentucky—then played in New Orleans. During this time he first performed many of the roles for which he would become famous, including Damon in *Damon and Pythias,* Jaffier in *Venice Preserved,* Tell in *William Tell,* and the Indian chief in *She Would Be a Soldier.* ♦ His New York debut was as Othello in July 1826 at the Park Theatre,♦ and he repeated his performance at the Bowery Theatre♦ the following November. Both playhouses were to figure importantly in his career. His welcome was promising. What critics and playgoers saw was a dark-haired, sardonically handsome man of noticeably muscular build—he always favored roles which allowed him to display his arms and legs—who stood five feet ten inches tall and had a deep, stentorian voice, which he sometimes employed with a crude vigor. Implicit in his appearance and acting were the seeds of class differences that would beset his career. From the start Forrest's appeal was to the mass of playgoers, the more genteel members of the audience often balking at what they perceived as his sometimes vulgar display of physique and his unlettered readings. In 1828 he offered prizes for new American plays, preferably on American themes. First prize went to John Augustus Stone♦ for *Metamora,* ♦ which was soon one of Forrest's most popular vehicles. Other winners included Richard Penn Smith's♦ *Caius Marcus*♦; three plays by Robert Montgomery Bird♦: *The Gladiator*♦, *Oralloossa,* ♦ and *The Broker of Bogota*♦*;* and Robert T. Conrad's *Jack Cade.* ♦ Of these only *Metamora* and *Oralloossa* could be said to have had American themes, while only *The Gladiator* (with Forrest as Spartacus) and *Jack Cade* endured alongside *Metamora* in Forrest's repertory. But the well-intentioned contest also added to the actor's increasingly questionable personal reputation, for he was accused of not paying money owed to several of the playwrights. On the other hand he used some of his income at this time to pay his late father's debts. As his career progressed, he made several trips to Europe. He also added a number of major roles to his repertory, including the title parts of *King Lear,* ♦ *Hamlet,* ♦ *Macbeth,* ♦ and *Virginius.* He had attempted several of these roles early in his career, but they did not become accepted standards for some seasons. His career may be said to have peaked in the late 1840s, after which two incidents further tarnished his reputation. In 1849 his rivalry with the English actor William Macready♦ came to a head in the bloody Astor Place Riots,♦ in which Forrest almost certainly had a hand. In 1851 he and his wife were divorced after each had noisily—and probably accurately—accused the other of infidelity. In Forrest's case, his affair with Josephine Clifton♦ had become common knowledge. Thereafter, his popularity began to wane, although he still retained a large and vocal following, especially in the upper reaches of theatres. But increasing age, a sameness in repertory—although this was a policy of most 19th-century tragedians—as well as new faces and newer styles of performing also militated against the actor. Loss of favor embittered Forrest, but he continued to play until shortly before his death.

William Winter♦ called Forrest a "vast animal, bewildered by a grain of genius," who was personally an "utterly selfish" man. But while he was reluctant to "canonize" Forrest, Winter concluded, "As an actor Forrest, at his best, was remarkable for iron repose, perfect precision of method, immense physical force, capacity for leonine banter, fiery ferocity and occasional felicity of elocution."

Biography: *Edwin Forrest—First Star of the American Stage,* Richard Moody, New York, 1960.

FORREST, George, see *Wright, Robert*

FORREST, Sam (1870–1944) Born in Richmond, Va., he made his debut as an actor but soon turned to directing. His first Broadway assignment as a director was Booth Tarkington's♦ *Springtime* (1909). He caught the attention of George M. Cohan♦ and Sam Harris, ♦ for whom he co-directed his first major hit, *Get-Rich-Quick Wallingford*♦ (1910). Over the next thirty years he staged approximately one hundred plays, mainly for Cohan and Harris. Among his notable successes were *Officer 666*♦ (1912), *Seven Keys to Baldpate*♦ (1913), *On Trial*♦ (1914), *The Great Lover*♦ (1915), *A Tailor Made Man*♦ (1917), *Three Faces East*♦ (1918), *Six-Cylinder Love*♦ (1921), *The Hero*♦ (1921), *Icebound*♦ (1923), *Cradle Snatchers*♦ (1925), and *Baby Cyclone* (1927). His final assignment was Cohan's *The Return of the Vagabond* (1940).

Fortune Hunter, The, a comedy in four acts by Winchell Smith.♦ Produced by George M. Cohan♦ and Sam Harris♦ at the Gaiety Theatre. September 4, 1909. 345 performances.

Spoiled as a youth by a rich father who eventually died penniless, Nat Duncan (John Barrymore ♦) is at a loss to provide himself with champagne and lobster. His friend Henry Kellogg (Hale Hamilton) suggests the best way is to marry a rich girl and that the best place to find that rich girl is a small town which the more ambitious young men have left for more lucrative territory. The two friends bet on the outcome. Nat selects a small town and picks as his objective the banker's daughter, Josie Lockwood (Edna Bruna). Taking a job as a drug store clerk, Nat finds himself falling in love instead with the druggist's daughter, Betty Graham (Mary Ryan). He decides Betty means more to him than champagne and lobster.

This fresh, wholesome comedy gave a major boost to Barrymore's career. A musical version, *The City Chap* (1925), failed.

Fortune Teller, The, a comic opera in three acts. Book and lyrics by Harry B. Smith. ♦ Music by

Victor Herbert.♦ Produced at Wallack's Theatre. September 26, 1898. 40 performances.

Irma (Alice Nielsen♦), an heiress studying ballet in Budapest, is in love with a handsome hussar, Ladislas (Frank Rushworth), but is being pressed to marry Count Berezowski (Joseph Herbert♦). She is able to discourage the Count by having Musette (also Miss Nielsen), the fiery gypsy fortune teller who so remarkably resembles her, take her place for a while. This creates problems for Musette and her gypsy lover Sandor (Eugene Cowles♦). But matters are eventually resolved happily.

Principal songs: Always Do as People Say You Should · Gypsy Love Song · Only in the Play · Romany Life

Written as a vehicle for Miss Nielsen, the musical had a short Broadway run mainly because it had been booked for an entire season on the road before it opened. The score was Herbert's finest up to that time and established him as the leading American composer of operetta. Revivals were frequent until the early 1930s.

Forty-five Minutes from Broadway, a play with music in three acts by George M. Cohan.♦ Produced by Klaw♦ and Erlanger♦ at the New Amsterdam Theatre.♦ January 1, 1906. 90 performances.

When Tom Bennett (Donald Brian♦) learns he is the sole heir of his uncle, who died in New Rochelle apparently without leaving a will, he announces he will marry the actress Flora Dora Dean (Lois Ewell). The townsfolk had hoped the uncle would leave his money to his loyal maid Mary (Fay Templeton♦). Dan Cronin (James H. Manning) had courted Mary in hope of getting his hands on the money. Tom's wise-guy secretary, Kid Burns (Victor Moore♦), falls in love with Mary and finds the will, which in fact leaves the estate to her. But Mary fears Kid might also be a fortune hunter. Realizing this, Kid tears up the will, and Mary agrees to marry him. Cronin is exposed as a crook and Miss Dean and her mother as little more than accomplices. Tom is left with the money but no sweetheart.

Principal songs: Forty-five Minutes from Broadway · Mary's a Grand Old Name · So Long, Mary

Not truly a musical comedy—there were no songs in the second act—the play remains one of Cohan's best, and is still revived on occasion. The show helped establish Moore as a star comic.

42nd Street, a musical comedy in two acts. Book by Michael Stewart♦ and Mark Bramble. Lyrics by Al Dubin and others. Music by Harry Warren. Pro-

duced by David Merrick♦ at the Winter Garden Theatre.♦ August 25, 1980. 3,486 performances.

Julian March (Jerry Orbach♦), the harassed, sardonic director of a new musical, is having no end of trouble with his impossibly difficult leading lady, Dorothy Brock (Tammy Grimes♦). When Dorothy breaks her ankle he pushes young, aspiring Peggy Sawyer (Wanda Richert) into the lead. She becomes a star overnight.

Principal songs: About a Quarter to Nine · 42nd Street · Lullaby of Broadway · Shuffle Off to Buffalo · You're Getting To Be a Habit with Me

In recent years the old trend of adapting shows into films has been turned about and many films have become the source of musicals or even straight plays. This show took the famous 1933 musical film and simply plunked it on the stage, telling the same basic story and adding Warren songs from other films. To a public satiated with socially significant musicals, its harmless story, melodic songs, and colorful sets and costumes proved a tonic, although its biggest attraction was unquestionably the huge, happy tap routines devised by Gower Champion,♦ who died the day of the opening.

47 Workshop An outgrowth of Professor George Pierce Baker's♦ course at Harvard in play-writing—the course was listed as English 47—it offered his students a chance to produce their plays, although without academic credit. The course had been started in 1905 and the workshop in 1913. Among the many aspiring playwrights who profited from the workshop were George Abbott,♦ Philip Barry,♦ S. N. Behrman,♦ Sidney Howard,♦ and Eugene O'Neill.♦ Other later important theatrical figures also enrolled, including critic John Mason Brown,♦ executive Theresa Helburn,♦ and designer Donald Oenslager.♦ The course and the workshop are generally acknowledged to have been among the most significant academic contributions to the creative commercial stage.

FOSSE, [ROBERT LOUIS] BOB (1927–87) Born in Chicago, he began dancing professionally at the age of fourteen and later appeared in the choruses of several Broadway musicals before choreographing *The Pajama Game*♦ (1954). He was immediately recognized as a fresh, imaginative talent, whose style leaned heavily on clever, angular groupings and showed a marked debt to ghetto street dancing. He later did the dances for *Damn Yankees*♦ (1955); *Bells Are Ringing* (1956), in collaboration with Jerome Robbins♦; *New Girl in Town* (1957); *Redhead* (1959), which he also directed; *How To*

Succeed in Business Without Really Trying♦ (1961); *Little Me* (1962), also serving as director for this and all subsequent shows; *Sweet Charity*♦ (1966); *Pippin*♦ (1972); *Liza* (1974); *Chicago*♦ (1977), for which he was co-librettist as well; *Dancin'*♦ (1978); and *Big Deal* (1986). He received numerous Tony Awards♦ for his work. In 1963 he played the title role in a City Center♦ revival of *Pal Joey.*♦

Biography: *All His Jazz: The Life and Death of Bob Fosse,* Martin Gottfried, New York, 1990.

FOSTER, STEPHEN COLLINS (1826–64) The most popular of 19th-century American songwriters, he composed many "Ethiopian" songs which were either introduced or readily adopted by the minstrel troupes of his day. He told E. P. Christy,♦ who first sang and even took credit for "Old Folks at Home" ("Swanee River"), that he hoped "to establish my name as the best Ethiopian songwriter." Among his many melodies associated with minstrelsy are "De Camptown Races," "Old Black Joe," "Massa's in the Cold, Cold Ground," and "My Old Kentucky Home."

Four Mortons, THE   A popular act in the early days of vaudeville, the turn consisted of Sam and Kitty Morton and their children Paul and Clara. The act centered on family arguments which were resolved in song and dance. Both the humor and the music were distinctly Irish.

Four Saints in Three Acts, an opera in four acts. Libretto by Gertrude Stein.♦ Music by Virgil Thomson. Produced at the 44th Street Theatre. February 20, 1934. 48 performances.

Despite her title, Miss Stein's libretto took four acts to tell a generally unfathomable story about no fewer than sixteen saints, including a female St. Theresa and her male alter ego. Critics had kind words for Thomson's fine score and for the all-black cast that performed in costumes and sets that made heavy use of cellophane. The work was revived unsuccessfully on Broadway in 1952. Two of Miss Stein's most famous lines, "Pigeons on the grass alas" and "When this you see remember me," are from the libretto. Virgil Garnett Thomson (1896–1989), a native of Kansas City, Mo., studied at Harvard and with Nadia Boulanger. He is a distinguished American composer whose other theatrical contributions include a second work with Miss Stein, *The Mother of Us All* (1947), as well as incidental music for such productions as Leslie Howard's♦ *Hamlet* (1936), *Ondine* (1954), and several mountings by the American Shakespeare Festival.♦

FOX, DELLA [MAY] (1871–1913) Born in St. Louis, the round-faced, snub-nosed tiny blonde beauty made her acting debut in the chorus of one of the numerous all-children-cast versions of *H.M.S. Pinafore*♦ in 1879. She spent many seasons with the Bennett and Moulton Opera Company, one of the era's most famous traveling light-opera troupes, before being cast as the soubrette, Blanche, opposite De Wolf Hopper♦ in *Castles in the Air* (1890), then enjoyed her greatest success in the trouser role of the Siamese prince, Mataya, again opposite Hopper, in *Wang*♦ (1891). After a final appearance as Hopper's leading lady in *Panjandrum* (1893), she received star billing in the musicals *The Little Trooper* (1894) and *Fleur-de-Lis* (1895). In 1897 she co-starred with Lillian Russell♦ and Jefferson De Angelis♦ in *The Wedding Day.* She was appearing in *The Little Host* (1899) when illness forced her to retire temporarily. On her return she played mostly vaudeville engagements, although she also performed in *The Rogers Brothers in Central Park* (1900); *The West Point Cadet* (1904); and, shortly before her death, in one straight play revival, *Rosedale*♦ (1913). Many critics professed to be baffled by her popularity, seeing her as possessing little real talent and attributing her popularity simply to "magnetism." Nevertheless, for about a decade she remained one of the principal attractions of our musical theatre.

FOX, FREDERICK (b. 1910) Born in New York, and educated at Yale and the National Academy of Design, he spent an apprenticeship at the Ivoryton, Conn., summer theatre before creating the Broadway sets for *Farewell Summer* (1937). Between then and the mid-1960s he created the sets, and occasionally the lighting, for nearly one hundred shows, including *Johnny Belinda*♦ (1940), *Junior Miss*♦ (1941), *The Doughgirls*♦ (1942), *The Two Mrs. Carrolls*♦ (1943), *Anna Lucasta*♦ (1944), *Dear Ruth*♦ (1944), *Make Mine Manhattan* (1948), *Light Up the Sky*♦ (1948), and *The Seven Year Itch*♦ (1952).

FOX, G[EORGE WASHINGTON] L[AFAYETTE] (1825–77) The greatest American exponent of classical pantomime and often called the first "star" of the American musical theatre, he was born in Boston into a family of "actors of a mediocre kind such as used to delight rural New England audiences but rarely appeared before city theatre-goers." He did play Boston, however, at the age of seven, appearing in *The Hunter of the Alps,* but did not make his New York debut until 1850, when he joined the

271

company of the National Theatre, using the name Lafayette Fox. He remained there for several seasons, playing a large variety of roles, and is generally credited with persuading the company to mount *Uncle Tom's Cabin,* ♦ the theatre's greatest success. He later moved to the Bowery Theatre, ♦ where as manager he regularly inserted pantomimes into the bill. His greatest success came, after he moved to the Olympic Theatre, as Clown and in the title role in *Humpty Dumpty* ♦ (1868), which he wrote, possibly in collaboration with his brother Charles, and which established a long-run record for the day. This was followed by another pantomime, *Hiccory Diccory Dock* (1869), He also scored heavily in a burlesque of *Hamlet* ♦ (1870), at a time when both Edwin Booth ♦ and Charles Fechter ♦ were offering their more serious versions. A burlesque of *Macbeth* ♦ (1870) was less successful, but Fox enjoyed another long run in the pantomime *Wee Willie Winkie* (1870). Afterwards, he continued to play for several seasons in various versions of *Humpty Dumpty* until increasingly erratic behavior—he once ran into the auditorium and attacked members of the audience without provocation—forced his removal from the stage. He died a short time later, apparently of paresis.

Fox was a small, lean man with sharp darting eyes and pointed features that reflected his name. At the height of his popularity he was the highest-paid entertainer in America, with a yearly income that exceeded $20,000.

FOY, EDDIE [né EDWIN FITZGERALD] (1856–1928) Described by Stanley Green ♦ as a "Puckish comic with pointed nose and wide V-shaped mouth, noted for his slurred way of speaking and his acrobatic dancing," he began his career in vaudeville in 1869 and later toured Western mining towns with a minstrel troupe. He also occasionally appeared in comedies and melodramas before settling in Chicago, where he clowned in such musicals as *The Crystal Slipper* (1888), *Bluebeard, Jr.* (1890), *Sinbad the Sailor* (1891), *Ali Baba* (1892), and *Little Robinson Crusoe* (1893). In 1894 he toured in *Off the Earth,* then played in *Hotel Topsy Turvey* (1898) and a reworking of *Ali Baba,* called *An Arabian Girl and Forty Thieves* (1899). He next scored as a principal comedian in *The Strollers* (1901) and *The Wild Rose* (1902). By 1903 he was a popular star when he appeared as Sister Anne in *Mr. Bluebeard.* One of his high points in the show was his routine with a stubborn bustle that determined to go its own way. But the humor turned to tragedy when he was performing the show at Chicago's Iroquois Theatre

at the matinee at which the worst fire in American theatre history occurred. More starring roles followed in *Piff! Paff!! Pouf!!!* (1904), *The Earl and the Girl* (1905), *The Orchid* (1907), *Mr. Hamlet of Broadway* (1908), *Up and Down Broadway* (1910), and *Over the River* (1912). Between engagements he regularly played in vaudeville, and in 1910 first brought his children into the act. Eddie Foy and the Seven Little Foys rapidly became one of the most popular two-a-day turns, so after 1912 Foy abandoned musical comedy. The group appeared in such skits as "Fun in the Foy Family" and "Slumwhere in New York." A typical bit would have one little daughter ask him to bring home a doll, and when he inquired what sort of doll, she would respond, "Mama says you know all about dolls." After World War I, as the children grew older, the act was disbanded, and Foy toured alone.

Autobiography: *Clowning Through Life,* with Alvin F. Harlow, New York, 1928.

FOY, EDDIE, JR. [né EDWIN FITZGERALD, JR.] (1905?–83) The son of the famous older comedian was born in New Rochelle, N.Y., and while still a child made his debut in his father's famous vaudeville act, Eddie Foy and the Seven Little Foys. Among his early Broadway appearances were *Show Girl* (1929), *Ripples* (1930), *Smiles* (1930), *The Cat and the Fiddle* ♦ (1931), and *At Home Abroad* (1935). However, he is best recalled for his starring roles in a 1945 revival of *The Red Mill* ♦ and in *The Pajama Game* ♦ (1954), as well as for playing the comic lead in the tour of *High Button Shoes.* His last New York appearance was in *Donnybrook* (1961).

Francesca da Rimini, a tragedy in five acts by George H. Boker. ♦ Produced at the Broadway Theatre. September 26, 1855. 8 performances.

In hope of putting an end to the long feud between Guelfs and Ghibellines, Lanciotto (E. L. Davenport ♦) of Rimini is engaged to Francesca (Elizabeth Ponisi ♦) of Ravenna. Lanciotto is a spindly hunchback whose brother Paolo (Mr. Lanergan) has often had to defend him from cruel jibes. The brothers love each other, so Lanciotto asks Paolo to go to Ravenna to bring back the bride. Paolo and Francesca fall in love, but at first both attempt to constrain themselves. The sight of Lanciotto, however, drives Francesca into the handsome Paolo's arms. When the vicious jester, Pepe (Charles Fisher ♦), reports the rendezvous to Lanciotto, Lanciotto kills him. In a jealous fury he rushes to find Paolo and Francesca in an embrace. He kills them, too, then stabs himself.

Derived from an incident in Dante, the drama was only moderately successful at first. Fine revivals by Lawrence Barrett♦ in 1882 and Otis Skinner♦ in 1901 led to a further appreciation of its merits. Boker's modern biographer, Professor Sculley Bradley, has written in *Literary History of the United States,* "In *Francesca da Rimini* . . . Boker found his masterpiece. Of seven plays on this theme in four languages, his is the only one to conceive the pathos of the deformed husband, Lanciotto, without sacrificing the enduring appeal of the young lovers, Paolo and Francesca, and to recognize that callous society, not fate, was the agent of the tragedy. . . . With this play, romantic tragedy in America achieved the dignity of art."

FRANKEN, Rose, see *Another Language; Claudia*

Franklin, Benjamin Within eight years of his death the great American philosopher-stateman was being depicted in the popular allegorical spectacles of the late 18th century. That depiction, like those of his celebrated contemporaries, tended to be largely hagiographic. Thus, in *Americana* (1798) he was shown as "Fulmenifer" who, "with an electrical rod in his hand," helps bring the light of understanding to his new nation. Franklin remained a relatively popular stage character throughout the 19th century, albeit rarely in plays of any importance. He was the hero of several, including John Brougham's♦ 1846 stage biography, *Benjamin Franklin.* Brougham, who portrayed the lead in all but the first scene, took Franklin from his boyhood through his days at Louis XVI's court, and drew him as a rather canny, lovable personage. That was the approach employed by 20th-century writers, most notably in such musicals as *Ben Franklin in Paris* (1964) and *1776*♦ (1969).

FRANKLIN, Irene (1876–1941) Born in St. Louis, Mo., where her parents were members of a local stock company, she began her career at the age of six, assuming children's roles in such plays as *Shore Acres,*♦ *Editha's Burglar,* and *The Fire Patrol.* At the age of fifteen she toured Australia in a vaudeville act, taking it to London in 1894 and bringing it home the following year. By now she was a busty, red-headed young woman who specialized in imitating resentful little girls and a mixed bag of older ladies—such characters as a flirtatious schoolmarm, a hotel maid seduced and deserted by a traveling salesman, or a lippy waitress at Childs Restaurant. Her imitations were interspersed with appropriate songs, usually accompanied by one of her pianist-husbands. The *Dramatic Mirror*♦ said of her act,

"She injects so much humor, she touches such a vibrant note of pathos that she is quite irresistible. Her 'kid' songs are unforgettable, and her slangy dissertation of a chorus girl invading the Great White Way was a little masterpiece of characterization." Most popular among her songs were "I'm Nobody's Baby Now" and "Red Head." She also appeared in musical comedy, most notably as Lulu in Jerome Kern's♦ *Sweet Adeline*♦ (1929).

FRAZEE, H[arry] H[erbert] (1880–1929) Beginning his career in his hometown of Peoria, Ill., at the age of sixteen as a theatre usher, he quickly rose to be treasurer of the theatre. He soon became an advance man for traveling shows. In 1902 he produced his first play, *Uncle Josh Perkins,* which toured successfully but never reached New York. His later productions included *Madame Sherry*♦ (1910); *Ready Money* (1912); *A Pair of Sixes*♦ (1914); *A Full House* (1915); *Nothing But the Truth*♦ (1916); *Dulcy*♦ (1921), produced in conjunction with George C. Tyler♦; and *No, No, Nanette*♦ (1925), his biggest success. He was also a major figure in the sports world and it was he, as owner of the Boston Red Sox, who sold Babe Ruth to the Yankees.

FREEDLEY, George [Reynolds] (1904–67) Born in Richmond, Va., he attended Yale, where he enrolled in Professor George P. Baker's♦ Workshop, then began his career as an actor and technical director with the Theatre Guild.♦ In 1931 he joined the New York Public Library and shortly thereafter established its theatre collection, becoming its first curator in 1938. He also served as secretary to the New York Drama Critics Circle,♦ and, for a time, as drama critic of the *Morning Telegraph.* He lectured and wrote books and articles on the theatre, including many entries for *The Oxford Companion to the Theatre.*

FREEDLEY, Vinton (1891–1969) Born in Philadelphia, and educated at Harvard and the University of Pennsylvania, he began his theatrical career as an actor, appearing in such diverse entertainments as the musical comedy *For Goodness' Sake* (1922) and the expressionist drama *The World We Live In* (1922). In 1923 he joined forces with Alex A. Aarons,♦ and for the next ten years the team produced some of Broadway's most interesting musicals, including *Lady, Be Good!*♦ (1924), *Tip-Toes*♦ (1925), *Oh, Kay!*♦ (1926), *Funny Face*♦ (1927), *Hold Everything!*♦ (1928), and *Girl Crazy*♦ (1930). The men also built the Alvin Theatre, deriving its name from the first syllables of theirs. With the coming of the Depression they lost the theatre and dissolved their partnership. Freedley continued to produce alone, his more successful or memorable offerings being *Anything Goes*♦ (1934), *Red, Hot and Blue!* (1936), *Leave It to Me!*♦ (1938), *Cabin in the Sky*♦ (1940), and *Let's Face It!*♦ (1941). His last production was *Great To Be Alive* (1950). At various times he also served as president of the Actors' Fund of America,♦ the American National Theatre and Academy,♦ and the Episcopal Actors' Guild, as well as holding important positions with the American Theatre Wing♦ and the Council of Living Theatre.

FREEMAN, Max (d. 1912) Beginning his theatrical career in his native Germany, he made his American debut at New York's German-language Germania Theatre in 1873. After spending some time at the California Theatre♦ in San Francisco, he toured with the Emily Melville♦ Light Opera Company. He first appeared in New York in an English-speaking role in *Divorçons*♦ (1882), playing the small part of Joseph. By that time his English was sufficiently fluent to allow him to adapt plays and direct, all the while continuing to act. To always complimentary receptions he performed a variety of roles in plays, from the melodrama *Siberia*♦ (1883) and the comedy *The Rajah*♦ (1883) to later comedies such as *Over Night* (1911). Similarly, his adaptations ranged from opéra bouffe, *Orpheus and Eurydice* (1893), to melodrama, *Claudius Nero* (1890). For many years he was Rudolph Aronson's♦ director at the Casino Theatre,♦ staging, among many others, the 1890 revival for Lillian Russell♦ of *The Grand Duchess*♦ and Reginald De Koven's♦ *The Fencing Master* (1892). After leaving the Casino he continued to direct until shortly before his death, working primarily with musicals.

French Opéra Bouffe, see *Opéra Bouffe in America*

FRENCH, Samuel, see *Samuel French, Inc.*

Fresh, the American, a play in four acts by A. C. Gunter.♦ Produced at the Park Theatre. February 7, 1881. 63 performances.

Ferdinand Nervy Fresh (J. T. Raymond♦) is a brash, somewhat uncouth, but likable Yankee. His attempts to corner the market on Wall Street and other grandiose schemes have failed, but he has always found simple, practical ways of extricating himself from the mess his failures create and of rationalizing the failures. His wanderlust takes him to Egypt, where he falls in love with a harem beauty, Erema Almi (Laura Don). Despite the machinations of the Egyptians he manages to marry the girl, remove her from the harem, and escape the dire revenge the Egyptians plan for the couple.

Written by Gunter at Raymond's request, this loosely contrived farce provided the actor with a major hit for two years. He returned to it occasionally later in his career. Next to Colonel Sellers, it was considered his best role. Harry B. Smith♦ recalled a different origin for the play, stating that it was first mounted at McVicker's Theatre in Chicago as a serious piece, but that the audience laughed so much at its patent absurdities that Miss Don, McVicker's♦ leading lady, persuaded the producer to play it as comedy.

Friars, The Originally organized in 1904 as the Press Agents' Association, or the National Association of Press Agents, by Charles Emerson Cook, Channing Pollock,♦ John W. Rumsey, and several other men, it rapidly became a popular theatrical club, so changed its name and constitution in 1907. Although the name has no real connection with the theatre, the club has been consistent in its nomenclature, calling its clubhouse a monastery and its chief officer an abbot. Its clubhouses were first situated in the heart of the theatre district, but the last of these was disposed of during the Depression. A new clubhouse was established in 1948, away from the main theatre area, and in 1956 the club moved to its present building on East 55th Street. The organization has regularly mounted celebrated shows known as Frolics, giving the proceeds to charity. George M. Cohan♦ served as abbot for nearly twenty years, while later abbots have included George Jessel,♦ Milton Berle, Joe E. Lewis, who served for eighteen years, Ed Sullivan, and Frank Sinatra. As the record of leadership indicates, the club has drifted away from primarily legitimate theatre membership. A Los Angeles Friars was organized with permission of the New York club.

FRIEDMAN, Bruce Jay, see *Scuba Duba*

Friendly Enemies, a comedy drama in three acts by Samuel Shipman♦ and Aaron Hoffman.♦ Produced by A. H. Woods♦ at the Hudson Theatre. July 22, 1918. 440 performances.

Henry Block (Sam Bernard♦) and Karl Pfeifer (Louis Mann♦) are German-born Americans who have been life-long friends. When World War I breaks out in Europe, however, their friendship is sorely tested, for Block is totally American in his outlook, while Pfeifer retains strong loyalties toward the fatherland. To Pfeifer's horror, his son William (Richard Barbee) leaves college and enlists in the American army. Pfeifer's wife, Marie (Mathilde Cottrelly♦), is caught in the verbal crossfire. When William is lost in a troop-ship sinking, Block proves a loyal and compassionate friend. The animosities are put aside, and the men agree to work toward peace in the world.

At a time of raging hatred, this plea for tolerance of divergent views in war became the biggest hit of its season. John Corbin wrote in the *Times*, "As dramatic literature the play may, perhaps, not win any high rank. . . . But it has the rarer virtues of broaching a new, vital, and timely subject . . . in a spirit that is wholesome and invigorating. Among the many plays touching upon our part in the war it stands quite alone."

FRIGANZA, TRIXIE [née DELIA O'CALLAHAN] (1870–1955) Born in Grenola, Kansas, the large bouncy performer made her stage debut in 1889 in *The Pearl of Pekin*. Thereafter she appeared in numerous musicals including *The Orchid* (1907), *The Passing Show of 1912,♦* and *Canary Cottage* (1917), but won her greatest celebrity as a vaudeville comedienne. Hers was a jolly, clean act in which she had fun kidding her own figure—describing herself as "a perfect forty-six." She added to her girth by coming on stage wearing several costumes, one under the other, and in effect doing a chaste striptease as she discarded each outer garment in turn. She was often billed as "Broadway's Favorite Champagne Girl."

FRIML, [CHARLES] RUDOLF (1879–1972) Born in Bohemia into a poor but musical family, he displayed remarkable abilities so early that his neighbors took up a collection to send him to the Prague Conservatory. While there he eventually won a scholarship and studied with Antonin Dvořák. After graduating he began to compose, but in order to support himself accepted a position as violinist Jan Kubelik's accompanist. He made two trips to America with Kubelik, on the second journey electing to remain permanently. Here he continued to give concerts and write light compositions. His chance came when Victor Herbert♦ refused to create a second score for Emma Trentini♦ after fighting with her over *Naughty Marietta.♦* Friml's score for the Trentini vehicle, *The Firefly♦* (1912), included "Giannina Mia," "Love Is Like a Firefly," and "Sympathy." The operetta's success established Friml immediately in the front rank of composers,

and he followed it with *High Jinks* (1913), which included "Something Seems Tingle-Ingleing"; and *Katinka♦* (1915), which offered "Allah's Holiday." Several subsequent operettas were less successful, so Friml tried his hand at musical comedies. Some of these enjoyed profitable runs, but left behind nothing memorable. In 1924 he returned to operetta and wrote his greatest success, *Rose-Marie.♦* This proved to be the most popular operetta of the 1920s, and its vogue was world-wide. From its great score came the title song as well as "The Mounties" and "Indian Love Call." Another fine operetta, *The Vagabond King♦* (1925), produced "Song of the Vagabonds," "Only a Rose," "Someday," and numerous other standards. His final hit was *The Three Musketeers♦* (1928), whose score included "March of the Musketeers," "Ma Belle," and "Your Eyes." Friml's principal competitor during the 1920s was Sigmund Romberg.♦ Although Friml's music was generally perceived to have more melodic originality and fervor, it was Romberg who proved more pliable when musical tastes changed in the 1930s. Friml wrote only two short-lived operettas at the time, *Luana* (1930), and *Music Hath Charms* (1934), then retired.

FRINGS, KETTI, see *Look Homeward, Angel*

FRISCO, JOE [né LOUIS WILSON JOSEPH] (1890?–1958) The diminutive, stuttering comedian, brandishing his derby hat, cane, and trick cigar, was long a headliner at the Palace Theatre.♦ Born in Milan, Ill., and reared in Dubuque, Iowa, he began his career entertaining in Chicago cabarets. There he developed his comic "Frisco Dance," a soft-shoe routine performed to "Darktown Strutters' Ball." His humor was off-beat. At a time when many comedians had fun with lighters that failed to work, he would pull a lighter from his pocket, have it light instantly, and throw it away saying it was too good to be true. He was also praised for his travesty of Helen Morgan♦ singing atop a piano. His rare appearances in Broadway musicals included the *Ziegfeld Follies of 1918♦* and the *Earl Carroll Vanities of 1928.♦*

Fritz, Our Cousin German, a play in four acts by Charles Gayler.♦ Produced at Wallack's Theatre. July 11, 1870. 63 performances.

Fritz (J. K. Emmet♦) arrives in America to seek both his long-lost sister and money his father left with the girl. On shipboard he has fallen in love with another immigrant, Katarina (Georgia Langley). His courtship of Katarina is cut short temporarily when the villainous Colonel Crafton (Charles

Fisher♦) kidnaps her. Fritz rescues her, and later finds his sister has been adopted by Crafton. Fritz's singing of an old family lullaby brings about recognition and reunion. Fritz and Katarina marry, and before long they have a child. But they have not heard the last of Crafton. He now kidnaps Little Fritz (Minnie Maddern, later Mrs. Fiske♦), so Fritz must once more come to the rescue. This time he kills Crafton.

Principal songs: Emmet's Lullaby (added some years later) · Oh, Schneider, How You Vas? · Valking Dat Broadway Down

Written expressly for Emmet's manifold talents, it provided a vehicle for him for the rest of his life. Sequels telling basically the same story included *Carl, the Fiddler* (1871) and *Max, the Merry Swiss Boy* (1873), but these were less successful, as were attempts by his son and others to assume the role of Fritz after Emmet's death.

FROHMAN, CHARLES (1860–1915) The youngest of three brothers who made names for themselves in the theatrical arena, he was born in Sandusky, Ohio. His father was an itinerant peddlar. At the age of twelve he came to New York and took work first with the *Tribune* and later with the *Daily Graphic.* But having long loved theatre, he took an evening job as well, selling tickets at Hooley's Theatre in Brooklyn. By 1877 he was serving as advance agent for traveling shows, including Haverly's Minstrels.♦ Steele MacKaye♦ invited Charles and his brothers Daniel♦ and Gustave to help manage the Madison Square Theatre,♦ and in sending out complete duplicate road companies of the theatre's hits they are credited with inaugurating a policy that was to change the nature of provincial theatre. In 1888 he was an agent for Bronson Howard,♦ whose play *Shenandoah*♦ had been mounted with only small success at the Boston Museum. ♦ Frohman, nevertheless, saw possibilities in it, and with money supplied by Al Hayman♦ and W. R. Hooley, remounted and produced it the following year in New York. The show was an immediate success and launched Frohman's career as a producer. At the same time, William Gillette♦ signed with Frohman to allow Frohman to produce his plays. In 1890 Frohman took over Proctor's Theatre and organized a stock company there, which later moved to the Empire Theatre,♦ which he built with Hayman in 1893. Two years later Frohman met secretly with Hayman, Abe Erlanger,♦ Mark Klaw,♦ and several other men to organize what became known as the Theatrical Syndicate or Trust.♦ Ostensibly the group's aim was to bring order out of chaos in cross-country bookings, but it soon controlled all the important theatres in the country and demanded exhorbitant fees from producers and performers. Failure to meet its demands often meant a show could not play in a major city. Frohman's precise role in the organization has remained a matter of dispute. His supporters have claimed that he was the idealist in the group, looking the other way at its shady practices because he felt more benefits than harm came from its methods. Others have seen him as playing Spenlow to Erlanger's Jorkins. Most likely the truth lies somewhere in between. But the certainty of comfortable bookings allowed him to work with ease, develop a roster of great stars, and present a steady stream of popular plays. Among the many stars who played for years under his auspices were John Drew,♦ Ethel Barrymore,♦ Maude Adams,♦ and Billie Burke.♦ Drew had already earned a distinguished reputation, but the women were relative unknowns when they signed with him, and his careful nurturing made all of them stellar attractions. Their celebrity was important to Frohman, since he recognized that a star could attract audiences even when his or her vehicle was weak, while a fine play without a star often had to struggle for business. Detractors have suggested that, as a result of this thinking, Frohman cared little about the value of his plays, ignoring promising American playwrights and preferring to buy up wholesale the rights to tested European works. Moreover, they add, his policy destroyed the interest in classics that his predecessors such as the Wallacks♦ and Augustin Daly♦ had carefully nurtured. While all this remains correct, especially his preoccupation with modern plays, it remains equally important to note that not all the plays Frohman offered were merely effective but ephemeral theatre pieces. He was responsible for the American premieres of many works by such significant and durable playwrights as Oscar Wilde,♦ Sir James Barrie,♦ Arthur Wing Pinero,♦ Somerset Maugham,♦ and Georges Feydeau. Among plays given their American premieres by Frohman were *The Importance of Being Earnest* (1895), *The Girl from Maxim's* (1899), *Peter Pan*♦ (1905), *Alice Sit-by-the-Fire* (1905), and *What Every Woman Knows* (1908). Nor did he totally neglect the best American talent, producing several of Clyde Fitch's♦ plays, including *Barbara Frietchie*♦ (1899). Moreover, he promoted an international respect for rising American playwrights by presenting their works abroad even when he had not produced the original New York mountings. Frohman was at the height of his career when he died in the sinking of the *Lusitania*. He has been described as a "little, round, slant-eyed Buddha."

Biography: *Charles Frohman: Manager and Man,* Isaac F. Marcosson and Daniel Frohman, New York, 1916.

FROHMAN, DANIEL (1851–1940) Like his younger brother Charles, ♦ he was born in Sandusky, Ohio, and came to New York, where he served in various capacities on several newspapers, including the *Tribune,* the *Standard,* and the *Daily Graphic,* before becoming an advance man for the Georgia Minstrels from 1874 to 1879. With Charles and his other brother Gustave, he then helped manage Steele MacKaye's♦ Madison Square Theatre, ♦ also assisting in sending out road companies of the theatre's hits. In 1885 he took over the old Lyceum Theatre♦ and opened it with *In Spite of All,* MacKaye's version of Victorien Sardou's♦ *Andrea.* Employing an excellent stock company that he developed there he quickly mounted such successes as *The Highest Bidder* (1887), *The Wife*♦ (1887), *Lord Chumley* (1888), and *The Charity Ball*♦ (1889). The performances of E. H. Sothern♦ in two of these helped start that actor on his career as a major figure. An important later success was *The Prisoner of Zenda*♦ (1895). He also produced several plays by Henry Arthur Jones♦ and Arthur Wing Pinero, ♦ offering the American premieres of such plays as *The Case of Rebellious Susan* (1894) and *Trelawny of the Wells* (1898). For a time in 1899, after Daly's death, he managed Daly's Theatre. He relinquished Daly's shortly after the Lyceum was demolished in 1902, and he built a new Lyceum a year later. With time he gradually abandoned producing, but remained active in theatrical affairs. From 1904 until his death he served as president of the Actors' Fund of America. ♦ He found time as well to write several books, including two volumes of reminiscences, *Memories of a Manager* (1911) and *Daniel Frohman Presents* (1935), and a collection of essays on theatrical history, *Encore* (1937). Unlike his squat, clean-shaven brother Charles, he was a wiry, balding man with a closely cropped beard and moustache.

Front Page, The, a play in three acts by Ben Hecht♦ and Charles MacArthur. ♦ Produced by Jed Harris♦ at the Times Square Theatre. August 14, 1928. 276 performances.

To his fellow newsmen hanging around the press room of Chicago's Criminal Court Building awaiting a murderer's execution, Hildy Johnson (Lee Tracy♦) announces that he is quitting the *Herald Examiner,*

getting married, and heading for New York. His plans are temporarily stymied when the murderer, Earl Williams (George Leach), escapes, and Hildy phones in a scoop to his paper. Williams suddenly appears in the press room, and Hildy and a prostitute, Molly Malloy (Dorothy Stickney), hide him in a folding desk. Hildy's dapper, devilish editor Walter Burns (Osgood Perkins♦) appears, prepared to take over. Amid the mayhem that ensues it is discovered that the governor has pardoned Williams. Telling Hildy of his gratitude for the scoop, Burns presents him with a watch, apologizing for the fact that the watch has his own name engraved in it. Hildy and his fiancée head off to catch the train. But Burns really has had no intention of allowing Hildy to go. He sends a wire to the chief of police in La Porte, Ind., telling him to arrest Hildy—"The son of a bitch stole my watch!"

Alison Smith of the *World* rejoiced, " 'The Front Page,' with its rowdy virility, its swift percussion of incident, its streaks of Gargantuan derision, is as breath-taking an event as ever dropped . . . on Broadway." The play, while not the first to be set in a press room, remains an exemplar of its kind and has enjoyed numerous revivals, the most notable American one in 1969, with Bert Convy as Hildy and Robert Ryan as Walter Burns. A 1986 revival at Lincoln Center♦ received mixed notices. It has been made into at least three films.

Frou-Frou Meilhac and Halévy's♦ French play was adapted for American audiences by Augustin Daly♦ and first presented by him in 1870. The story tells of an irresponsible young wife who invites her staid sister to live with her and her family so that she herself can flit about the town. She loses everyone's affection and returns home to repent and to die. Agnes Ethel♦ was the original heroine Gilberte. The play was revived regularly until the early years of the 20th century and was one of Bernhardt's♦ most popular vehicles on her American tour.

FRY, CHRISTOPHER [né HARRIS] (b. 1907) The English dramatist's attempt to restore blank-verse drama to the stage caused a flurry of interest in the 1950s. However, what success his works did have in this country could be largely attributed to the allure of the stars who appeared in his plays: *The Lady's Not for Burning* (1950), with John Gielgud♦ and Pamela Brown; *A Sleep of Prisoners* (1951), performed in a small church without stars; *Venus Observed* (1952), with Rex Harrison♦ and Lilli Palmer; and *The Dark Is Light Enough* (1955), with Katharine Cornell♦ and Tyrone Power. ♦ He has also provided excellent translations of two French plays: *Ring Round the Moon* (1950) and *Tiger at the Gates* (1955).

FRYER, ROBERT (b. 1920) A native of Washington, D.C., who studied at Western Reserve University, he has produced, alone or with others, such shows as *A Tree Grows in Brooklyn*♦ (1951), *Wonderful Town*♦ (1953), *Auntie Mame*♦ (1956), *Sweet Charity*♦ (1966), *Mame*♦ (1966), *Chicago*♦ (1975), *California Suite* (1976), *Sweeney Todd*♦ (1979), *Noises Off* (1983), and *Benefactors* (1985).

FULLER, LOIE (1863–1928) Born in Fullersburg, Ill., she demonstrated her precociousness by giving temperance lectures while still a small child. From the lecture stage to the legitimate stage was a simple move, which she made still in her teens, playing in a variety of touring companies. Her New York debut was in *Humbug* (1886), and she thereafter acted with Nat Goodwin♦ in *Little Jack Sheppard* (1886), *Turned Up* (1886), *The Skating Rink* (1887), and *The Gentlemanly Savage* (1887). Her performances won her commendatory notices, especially in the trouser title role of Sheppard. She next played Aladdin in *Arabian Nights* (1887) and Ustane in a musical dramatization of Rider Haggard's *She* (1887). She then went to England, where she was reportedly hired as Nellie Farren's understudy. While there she claimed a friend gave her a beautiful white Indian silk skirt, and this prompted her to devise the skirt or serpentine dance that made her famous, although there is reason to believe she had danced similar dances before. She performed with the voluminous drapery twirling and shedding prismatic hues in the calcium light. She first offered the dance in America in *Quack, M.D.* (1891) and later in *Uncle Celestin* (1892) and in *A Trip to Chinatown*♦ (1892). Although she appeared briefly in several other Broadway entertainments she spent most of her remaining career in dance recitals. She eventually produced two books, *Fifteen Years of My Life* (1908) and *Fifteen Years of a Dancer's Life* (1913).

Funny Face, a musical comedy in two acts. Book by Fred Thompson♦ and Paul Gerard Smith. Lyrics by Ira Gershwin.♦ Music by George Gershwin.♦ Produced by Alex A. Aarons♦ and Vinton Freedley♦ at the Alvin Theatre. November 22, 1927. 250 performances.

When Jimmie Reeves (Fred Astaire♦), her strait-laced guardian, refuses to allow Frankie (Adele Astaire♦) to have her jewels, Frankie arranges with her friend Peter Thurston (Allen Kearns♦) to steal them. Two comic burglars, Herbert (Victor Moore♦) and Dugsie (William Kent), are also after the jewels. The burglars, however, have a falling out, although Herbert is unable to shoot Dugsie since he has forgotten to get a shooting license. So everything ends happily, with Frankie keeping both her jewels and her man.

Principal songs: The Babbitt and the Bromide · Funny Face · He Loves and She Loves · 'S Wonderful

Originally, the show was produced as *Smarty* with a libretto by Thompson and Robert Benchley.♦ Benchley bowed out when the show was drastically rewritten and renamed. Applauded by Brooks Atkinson♦ as "uncommonly rollicking entertainment," the musical was blessed with a rare melange of melody, comedy, and superb dancing. It was in this show that Astaire first danced in evening clothes and a top hat.

Funny Girl, a musical comedy in two acts. Book by Isobel Lennart. Lyrics by Bob Merrill. Music by Jule Styne. ♦ Produced at the Winter Garden Theatre. ♦ March 26, 1964. 1,348 performances.

Sitting in her *Follies* dressing room, Fanny Brice (Barbra Streisand) reminisces about her career. Her thoughts wander back to the days when she was a gawky, stage-struck young girl, to her first failure at Keeney's Music Hall, and her eventual success there. That success brings two men into her life, the great Broadway producer Florenz Ziegfeld, who sets about making her a star, and an attractive gambler, Nicky Arnstein (Sydney Chaplin), whom she marries. Her career flourishes, although her marriage is destroyed by Arnstein's gambling and prison sentence.

Principal songs: Don't Rain on My Parade · People

Despite some glaring faults—a skimpy production, a no more than competent score, and a grotesquely glamorized interpretation of Arnstein—the show was made into an electric entertainment by its young star, Miss Streisand. Ted Kalem of *Time* welcomed her as "the theatre's new girl for all seasons" and described her as "an anthology of the awkward graces, all knees and elbows, or else a boneless wonder, a seal doing a balancing act." Miss Streisand [née Barbara Streisand] (b. 1942) was a New Yorker who had garnered attention earlier in an off-Broadway revue, *Another Evening with Harry Stoones* (1961), and as the comic secretary, Miss Marmelstein, in *I Can Get It for You Wholesale* (1962). *Funny Girl* was her last Broadway appearance before she went on to become a major film and recording star.

Funny Thing Happened on the Way to the Forum, A, a musical comedy in two acts. Book by Burt Shevelove and Larry Gelbart. Music and lyrics by Stephen Sondheim.♦ Produced by Harold Prince♦ at the Alvin Theatre. May 8, 1962. 967 performances.

Pseudolus (Zero Mostel♦), a Roman slave, attempts to earn freedom by procuring the sexy, but brainless, courtesan Philia (Preshy Marker) for his master, Hero (Brian Davies). Hero's own father, Senex (David Burns♦), also has his eye on the girl, but the dashing Miles Gloriosus (Ronald Holgate) apparently has first claim, as he has purchased her from Lycus (John Carradine). Pseudolus spreads the word that Philia has contracted the plague and died. A mock funeral degenerates into a wild chase. Miles learns that Philia is his sister, so he gives her to Hero. Pseudolus is set free.

Principal songs: Comedy Tonight · Free · Lovely

Based very loosely on material in Plautus, the musical was described by Howard Taubman of the *Times* as "noisy, coarse, blue and obvious like the putty on a burlesque comedian." Other fine clowns in the cast included Jack Gilford as the hysterical Hysterium and Raymond Walburn as the doddering Erronius. The show was the first for which Sondheim composed both lyrics and music, demonstrating from the start that, whatever his gift for melody, it was as a lyricist that he excelled.

FURNESS, Horace Howard (1833–1912) Born in Philadelphia, the son of a Unitarian minister, he attended Harvard and was admitted to the bar, but devoted most of his life to the study of Shakespeare and the preparation of variorum editions of his works. Beginning with *Romeo and Juliet*♦ he edited fifteen plays, while his wife, Helen Kate Furness, compiled *A Concordance to the Poems of Shakespeare.* After his death, his son, Horace, Jr., and other scholars attended to editions of the remaining plays.

FURNISS, Grace Livingston, see *Man on the Box, The,* and *Pride of Jennico, The*

FURST, William [Wallace] (1852–1917) Born in Baltimore, Furst was for many years conductor of the orchestra and composer of background music at the Tivoli Theatre♦ in San Francisco. New York first heard his incidental music in a dramatization of Rider Haggard's *She* (1887). He moved permanently to New York in 1893, to become conductor for the orchestra at the new Empire Theatre.♦ For the remainder of his career he was busy conducting theatre orchestras and creating background material for such successes as *The Conquerors*♦ (1898); *The Christian*♦ (1898); *A Royal Family* (1900); and a 1916 revival of *The Yellow Jacket.*♦ If theatre orchestras were then commonplace for even straight plays, so, unfortunately, was the writing of comic operas by conductors for star-centered musicals. Furst composed the scores for Thomas Seabrook's♦ *The Isle of Champagne* (1892); Lillian Russell's♦ *Princess Nicotine* (1893); Della Fox's♦ *The Little Trooper* (1894); and Miss Fox's and Joseph De Angelis's♦ *Fleur-de-Lis* (1895). This practice led the *Dramatic Mirror*♦ to complain, "It is time that orchestral leaders of the [Gustave] Kerker and Furst order should cease to figure as operatic composers." The situation was not remedied until Victor Herbert♦ and his later great successors appeared on the scene, by which time there was also increasingly little demand for incidental music. A dedicated amateur horticulturist, Furst died as the result of a fall sustained from tripping over a flower pot.

FYLES, Franklin (1847?–1911) Born in Troy, N.Y., where he began his career as a newspaperman, he served as drama critic for the New York *Sun* for twenty-five years. In 1893 he tried his hand at playwriting, working first in collaboration with David Belasco.♦ The successful result was *The Girl I Left Behind Me,*♦ in which an army officer accused of cowardice rides through hostile Indians to save a fort and reclaim his doubting sweetheart. His subsequent plays, generally not so well received but often popular, were *The Governor of Kentucky* (1896), in which corrupt politicians attempt to prevent an honest governor from being nominated senator; *Cumberland '61* (1897), in which an old family feud threatens lovers during the Civil War; *A Ward of France* (1897), written with Eugene Presbrey♦ and recounting the adventures of a noblewoman exiled to Louisiana after the French Revolution, who falls in love with her persecutor's son; and *Kit Carson* (1901), telling of Carson's escapes from rustlers and Indians. He was also the author of *The Theatre and Its People* (1900).

G

GAHAGAN, HELEN [MARY] (1900–80) Although best known for her later political career, Miss Gahagan was a highly respected actress in the 1920s and early 1930s. Born in Boonton, N.J., and educated at Barnard College, she made her initial New York appearances in *Shoot!* (1922) and *Manhattan* (1922). Her first important assignment was as Anne Caldwell, whose choice between two lovers will determine the outcome of an old family feud, in *Dreams for Sale* (1922). She next played Paula, the avaricious secretary who finally marries her kind, but impoverished former employer, in *Fashions for Men* (1922) and Jean Trowbridge, a flapper determined to retain her independence, in *Chains* (1923). In 1924 she assumed the title role in a revival of *Leah Kleschna.* ◆ After several failures, she scored as Laura Simmons, the schoolmaster's wife loved by a young student, in *Young Woodley* (1925), then played Rose and Countess Zicka in revivals of *Trelawny of the Wells* (1927) and *Diplomacy* ◆ (1928). She returned from a tour of Europe, where she sang in opera, to play The Prima Donna, who finds real love with a supposed gigolo, in *Tonight or Never* (1930). Her leading man was Melvyn Douglas, ◆ whom she married. Apart from touring in the role of the spiteful Elizabeth to Helen Hayes's ◆ Mary in *Mary of Scotland* ◆ in 1934, the remainder of her theatre career was undistinguished. Her last appearance was at the City Center ◆ as Lucy Chase Wayne in a 1952 revival of *First Lady,* but this was long after she had become famous for her espousal of liberal causes and her career as Congresswoman had been destroyed by Richard M. Nixon.

Gaiety Theatre, see *English Musicals*

GAIGE, CROSBY [né ROSCOE CONKLING GAIGE] (1882–1949) Born in Skunk Hollow, N.Y., and educated at Columbia, he served a brief stint on the New York *Times* before joining the famous theatrical agent Elisabeth Marbury. ◆ Soon thereafter he became a partner with Edgar Selwyn ◆ and Arch Selwyn, ◆ producing with them such celebrated hits as *Within the Law* ◆ (1912) and *Why Marry?* ◆ (1917). After severing his connections with the firm, he produced on his own, among others, *The Butter and Egg Man* ◆ (1925), *The Enemy* ◆ (1925), *The*

Shannons of Broadway (1927), *Little Accident* ◆ (1928), and *Accent on Youth* ◆ (1934). He occasionally directed plays and also served as vice-president of the Managers Protective Association. ◆ Respected as a gourmet, he wrote several books on cooking as well as an autobiography *Footlights and Highlights* (New York, 1948).

GALE, ZONA (1874–1938) Born in Portage, Wisc., and educated at the University of Wisconsin, she became best known as a novelist, although she was also the author of several respected dramas. Her one-act play *The Neighbors* (1917) was produced by the Washington Square Players. ◆ She won a Pulitzer Prize ◆ for her dramatization of her novel *Miss Lulu Bett* ◆ (1920), the story of a drudge who prefers marrying a bigamist to remaining a spinster. Less successful was her dramatization of her novel *Birth* as *Mr. Pitt* (1924), the chronical of a likable ne'er-do-well. Several other original plays and adaptations were presented by amateur groups, but never reached Broadway.

Biography: *Still Small Voice,* August W. Delreth, New York, 1940.

GALLAGHER [EDWARD] (1873?–1929) **and SHEAN** [AL] (1868–1949) One of the greatest and most popular of vaudeville teams, their career together was surprisingly short. The American-born Gallagher was relatively tall, slim, bespectacled, and sported a mini-moustache, while the German-born Shean, whose real surname was Schonberg, was stockier and clean-shaven. Gallagher was a superb straight-man, who had spent much of his early career in partnership with Joe Barrett, generally performing comic military sketches. Shean began his career in vaudeville in 1890 as a member of the Manhattan Comedy Four. This group disbanded in 1900, after which Shean teamed with Charles L. Warren for several seasons. Gallagher and Shean joined ranks in 1910, appearing in vaudeville and in the 1912 Broadway musical *The Rose Maid,* before splitting for reasons never divulged. Both then played single turns in vaudeville, while Shean also appeared in such Broadway musicals as *The Princess Pat* (1915) and *Flo-Flo* (1917). They were reunited in 1920 through the good offices of Minnie Marx,

Shean's sister and mother of the Marx Brothers. ◆ Because their new act initially was called "Mr. Gallagher and Mr. Shean in Egypt," Gallagher thereafter wore a straw hat and Shean a fez. Sometime during the next year they first sang the song that helped make them famous, "Mister Gallagher and Mr. Shean," with its celebrated tagline, "Positively, Mr. Gallagher—Absolutely, Mr. Shean." The team at first claimed authorship of the song, but later became entangled in litigation over it. While Gallagher then claimed Ernest Ball assisted in the composition, the real author was apparently Bryan Foy, son of Eddie Foy. ◆ The song was reprised when the pair appeared in the *Ziegfeld Follies of 1922.* ◆ They later continued in vaudeville and performed in the *Greenwich Village Follies of 1924.* ◆ In 1925 the team split for a second time. Gallagher briefly developed another vaudeville act before suffering a nervous breakdown and dying shortly thereafter. Shean continued in vaudeville, Broadway shows, and films for many years.

Galley Slave, The, a play with five acts by Bartley Campbell. ◆ Produced at Haverly's Theatre. December 1, 1879. 101 performances.

Cicely Blaine (Maude Granger◆), an American girl in Europe, loves Sidney Norcott (Frank Evans), but is led to believe he has been unfaithful by the treacherous Baron Le Bois (J. J. Sullivan), who himself has wed and deserted a girl named Francesca (Emily Rigl◆). When Sidney is caught visiting Cicely he pretends to be a thief rather than compromise her position, and so is sent to prison. There he meets Francesca. Cicely has learned his whereabouts and goes to talk with him. The Baron follows her, but is confronted by Francesca. With the truth exposed, Cicely and Sidney are free to wed.

Originally presented at Philadelphia's Chestnut Street Theatre◆ with a different cast except for Miss Rigl, the play remained popular for a quarter of a century, although there is some reason to question whether it could have compiled 101 performances in a two-and-a-half-month New York run, as its advertisements and some historians have claimed. Theda Bara later made it into one of her earliest films, around 1910.

GALSWORTHY, JOHN (1867–1933). The English novelist and dramatist was much admired for his serious examination of the inequities of contemporary life. *The Silver Box* (1907), his study of the double standard employed by English courts in treating rich and poor subjects, although highly praised, failed despite the fine acting of its star, Ethel Barrymore. ◆ Nor did *Strife* (1909), a play about labor troubles, fare any better when mounted by the New Theatre. ◆ However, his grim picture of prison life in *Justice* (1916) appeared at the same time that a young Eugene O'Neill◆ and other American playwrights were beginning to move drama away from 19th-century artificiality and overwrought plots and was instantly recognized by more venturesome playgoers and critics as another important breakaway from fading traditions. The work's popularity was enhanced by the brilliant performance of John Barrymore, ◆ whose stardom was then assured. Among his subsequent successes were *The Skin Game* (1920), *Loyalties* (1922), and *Escape* (1927). While most of his dramas could be seen as extensions of the older problem plays, he dealt with larger social issues rather than difficulties raised by narrow and artificial conventions of social propriety, and he treated his figures with a singular honesty.

Game of Love, The, a play in five acts by John Brougham. ◆ Produced by J. W. Wallack◆ at Wallack's Theatre. September 12, 1855. 23 performances.

After Alice Devereux (Mrs. Hoey◆) is jilted by her betrothed, she decides to marry the first man who comes her way. That man proves to be the well-educated but poor Paul Weldon (Lester Wallack◆). Because Alice is wealthy, Paul readily agrees, only to find that the marriage contract makes him little more than a servant. It takes all of Councillor Foxglove's (Henry Placide◆) thoughtful diplomacy to make Alice and Paul realize they love each other and settle into a happy marriage.

Although one of Brougham's modern editors, Eugene R. Page, suggests that the story was derived from an incident in Dickens's *Bleak House,* the connection is not obvious. Nor are any special aesthetic merits or historical significance apparent. But the play exemplifies the ephemeral material which Wallack so skillfully mounted along with revivals of great classics and which helped establish his playhouse and ensemble as the greatest of its day.

GANNON, MARY (1829–68) Born in New York, she made her debut as a child actress and dancer but shortly evolved into a brilliant comedienne whose career was cut short by her early death. The date and place of her debut remain a matter of argument. T. Allston Brown◆ places it at the Richmond Hill Theatre in 1832 in *The Daughter of the Regiment;* Ireland,◆ in some of Cony's dog dramas◆ at the

Bowery Theatre♦ in 1835; and Odell,♦ later that same year at the Franklin Theatre opposite Mrs. Duff♦ in *The Wonder.* By 1840 she was assuming all seven roles in *The Actress of All Works,* a popular tour-de-force, and offering her imitation of Fanny Elssler,♦ which prompted the *Spirit of the Times*♦ to call the youngster "the genius of the dance." She spent successful seasons at the Bowery and at William Mitchell's♦ Olympic. "She was in those days," Brown recalled, "a beauty, fresh and plump, with a foot that Titania might have envied, eyes that sparkled . . . a sweet ever ready laugh, and a vivacious nature." She never lost her vivacity, but her plumpness increased until before long she had a marked double chin. In 1855 she joined Wallack's♦ company, where she remained until her death. Among her many roles at Wallack's were Betty in *The Clandestine Marriage;* Jenny in *The Provoked Husband;* Atalanta Cruiser in Boucicault's♦ *How She Loves Him;* and Mary Netley in *Ours.* Her comedy was generally viewed as not merely lively but imbued with a peculiarly pleasing archness. Describing her as "literally perfection," Ireland, writing shortly before her death, added, "Entirely original in style, with a truthfulness to nature almost unparalleled, and a fund of quiet humor apparently inexhaustible, she has in some characters never been approached in merit, is in none surpassed, and is now universally acknowledged to be the best general comic actress in the city."

Garden of Allah, The, a play in four acts by Robert Hichens and Mary Anderson.♦ Produced by Liebler and Co.♦ at the Century Theatre. October 21, 1911. 241 performances.

At first the beautiful Domini (Mary Mannering♦) sees little to admire in the boorish stranger, Boris Androvsky (Lewis Waller), who seems far more out of place than even she in the warm, romantic, and exotic desert lands. But with time she falls in love and marries him. Only then does she discover he is a runaway monk. He eventually returns to his monastery and she is left to raise their child alone.

Miss Anderson was lured out of retirement by George Tyler♦ to assist the English author Hichens (1864–1950) in dramatizing his novel. This tale of Christian love set against the lush backgrounds of Islam was considered one of the most elaborate and gorgeous spectacles ever mounted on Broadway and was one of the few major successes at the huge Century (formerly New♦) Theatre. It was a type of play and production Hollywood was soon to usurp.

GARDNER, HERB, see *I'm Not Rappaport*

GARFIELD, JOHN [né JULES GARFINKEL] (1913–52) The handsome if pug-faced actor was born in New York, where he was an amateur boxer and then later studied at the Heckscher Foundation and Maria Ouspenskaya drama schools. He made his debut in 1930 playing small parts with the Civic Repertory Theatre,♦ but called attention to himself only after he joined the Group Theatre.♦ Among his notable roles there was Ralph Berger, the ambitious but embittered son, in *Awake and Sing!*♦ (1935). He left the company after not being cast for the title role in *Golden Boy*♦ (1937). He showed a gift for comedy as Chick Kessler, the young, amorous law student earning his tuition by working at a summer camp, in *Having Wonderful Time*♦ (1937). After playing the Overland Kid, an almost legendary hobo who rides a mythical train, in *Heavenly Express* (1940), he spent several years in films before returning to portray Captain Joris Kuiper, the Dutch sea captain attempting to rescue Jewish refugees, in *Skipper Next to God* (1948). He next played Charlie Castle, a Hollywood star who must sign a long-term contract or have his sordid past revealed, in *The Big Knife* (1949). In 1951 he assumed the title role in a revival of *Peer Gynt,* and the following year gave his last performance, somewhat ironically, as Joe Bonaparte, the title role of the man who chooses a prizefighting career over being a violinist, in a revival of *Golden Boy.* Garfield was a likable, realistic actor, best in parts requiring a streak of toughness.

Biography: *Body and Soul: The Story of John Garfield,* Larry Swindell, New York, 1975.

Garrick Gaieties, The A series of revues produced by the Theatre Guild♦ in 1925, 1926, and 1930. The 1925 edition was originally mounted only for two Sunday performances on May 15 in an effort to raise funds for tapestries for the new Guild Theatre. However, it was so well received that it was soon brought back for a regular run. Richard Rodgers♦ and Lorenz Hart♦ wrote the songs for the first two editions, including "Manhattan" (1925) and "Mountain Greenery" (1926), as well as a short jazz opera, "The Joy Spreader" (1925), and a spoof of operetta, "The Rose of Arizona" (1926).

GASSNER, JOHN [WALDHORN] (1903–67) Born in Hungary, he was brought to America while still a youngster and was educated at Columbia. He served as a drama critic, professor, and adviser to several important theatrical organizations, but was best known to the public for his numerous anthologies of plays and such books as *The Theatre in Our Times*

(1954), *Form and Idea in Modern Theatre* (1956), and *Theatre at the Crossroads* (1960).

GATES, WILLIAM F. (d. 1843) One of the many theatrical meteors who briefly shone brightly and then burned out, his early history is unknown. He was generally assumed to have been American-born, and Noah Ludlow,♦ with whom he worked for a time, recalled being told that he began his career with a circus. In any case, his New York debut occurred in 1828 at the Chatham Theatre as Orson in *Valentine and Orson,* but it was during his thirteen seasons at the Bowery,♦ commencing in 1830 and ending just before his death, that he won his real fame. Although he sometimes essayed serious roles, his forte was low comedy. He excelled as Trinculo and the First Gravedigger, but was best known for his acting in contemporary, long-discarded comedies such as Joshua Jenkin in *The Cannibals,* Timothy Shrewdboy in *Blue Laws,* and Peter Spyk in *Loan of a Lover.* He had a round, wide-eyed, youthful face, with an impish quality appropriate to his sort of roles, and a broad, unpolished style. Something of both the nature of his acting and the class distinctions that prevailed at the time can be read from Ireland's♦ remark, "He could not justly be ranked with Hilson, Barnes, Burton or Placide, but the audiences to which he generally played would have been unwilling to acknowledge his inferiority." T. Allston Brown♦ stated simply that "he became, as low comedian, the greatest favorite ever seen."

Gates and Morange A firm of set designers and builders founded in 1894 by Frank and Richard Gates and Edward A. Morange. Their first contract was painting a curtain with one of the landscapes popular on drops of that era. Soon thereafter their sets for a touring musical *Off the Earth* (1895) and the Broadway musical *Kismet* (1895) won them widespread praise and numerous subsequent assignments. The firm remained active for 40 years. Among their most noteworthy settings were the orchard scene in *Leah Kleschna*♦ (1904) and the London Bridge set for a 1912 production of *Oliver Twist.* Their designs for *Pomander Walk* (1910) are said to have inspired a New York City development of the same name and similar appearance.

GAUNT, PERCY (1852–96) The Philadelphia-born composer was best known as musical director for Charles Hoyt,♦ whom he joined in 1883. He composed the scores for several of Hoyt's farce-comedies, most notably for *A Trip to Chinatown*♦ (1891), which included "The Bowery," "Push Dem

Clouds Away" (played at his funeral by an organ-grinder), and "Reuben and Cynthia," this last adapted from an older song. Many felt his early death deprived the musical theatre of a promising melodist.

GAXTON, WILLIAM [né ARTURO ANTONIO GAXIOLA] (1893–1963) The distinguished looking comedian, whose pushy, frenetic style somewhat belied his appearance, was born in San Francisco and educated at military school and the University of California. He entered vaudeville at the age of fifteen and was soon doing a popular single turn, "A Regular Business Man." His debut in Broadway musicals was in the *Music Box Revue*♦ (1922). He rose to leading man status as Martin in *A Connecticut Yankee,*♦ in which he introduced "My Heart Stood Still," and as Peter Forbes, the rich man who bets he can win a girl without revealing his wealth, in *Fifty Million Frenchmen*♦ (1930), in which he sang "You Do Something to Me." After returning to vaudeville in the successful sketch, "Kisses," he scored his biggest hit when he first teamed with Victor Moore♦ to play President Wintergreen in *Of Thee I Sing*♦ (1931), in which he sang "Of Thee I Sing, Baby" and "Who Cares?" His manly, brash style proved a superb counterpart to Moore's wispy timidity, so they were paired again in a sequel, *Let 'Em Eat Cake* (1933). Another hit was *Anything Goes*♦ (1934), in which he played Billy Crocker to Moore's Reverend Moon and introduced "All Through the Night" and "You're the Top." After appearing without Moore in *White Horse Inn* (1936), he rejoined him for his remaining roles in *Leave It to Me!*♦ (1938), *Louisiana Purchase*♦ (1940), *Hollywood Pinafore* (1945), and *Nellie Bly* (1946).

Gay Divorce, a musical comedy in two acts. Book by Dwight Taylor. Music and lyrics by Cole Porter.♦ Produced by Dwight Deere Wiman♦ and Tom Weatherly at the Ethel Barrymore Theatre. November 29, 1932. 248 performances.

To give her husband grounds for divorce, Mimi Pratt (Claire Luce) arranges to be caught with a paid co-respondent, Tonetti (Erik Rhodes). But a young man named Guy (Fred Astaire♦), who has fallen in love with Mimi, manages to get himself confused with the co-respondent and uses the confusion to pursue his courtship.

Principal songs: After You · Mister and Missus Fitch · Night and Day

In Astaire's only Broadway appearance without his sister, both he and the show were greeted with a certain indifference at first. However, the popularity of "Night and Day" and Astaire's superb performance, his last on Broadway, turned the musical into a hit. Hollywood codes forced the film version to be called *The Gay Divorcée.*

GAYLER, CHARLES (1820–92) One of the most prolific dramatists of the second half of the 19th century, as well as a sometime actor and novelist, he is said to have written well over 100 plays, covering a range from minstrel skits through farce, comedy, spectacle, melodrama, and tragedy. Many of his plays were written to order for some of the most popular and respected performers of the era, and though a number of his works held the stage for years, none is probably performable today. Among his more notable vehicles were *Taking the Chances* (1856), written for J. M. McVicker♦; *The Love of a Prince* (1857), written for Laura Keene♦; *There's Many a Slip 'Twixt the Cup and the Lip* (1859), written for Mr. and Mrs. W. J. Florence♦; *The Magic Marriage* (1861), written for J. W. Wallack's♦ company; *The Connie Soogah; or, The Jolly Peddler* (1863), written for Mr. and Mrs. Barney Williams♦; and *Atonement; or, The Child Stealer* (1866), written for Lucille Western.♦ His most durable success was another vehicle, J. K. Emmet's♦ *Fritz, Our Cousin German*♦ (1870). *The Son of the Night,* adapted from the French, was originally performed by E. L. Davenport♦ and Lawrence Barrett,♦ and enjoyed revivals for several decades. Writing swiftly, he had *Bull Run; or, the Sacking of Fairfax Courthouse* (1861) on stage less than a month after the battle, and *Hatteras Inlet; or, Our Naval Victories* (1861) ready three months after the incidents described in the play. Some of his other earlier plays included *Olympiana; or, a Night with Mitchell* (1857), a nostalgic look back at William Mitchell♦ in his heyday; and *Our Female American Cousin* (1859) and *Our American Cousin at Home; or, Lord Dundreary Abroad* (1861), both sequels to Tom Taylor's♦ *Our American Cousin.*♦ By the 1880s the New York-born writer's style was no longer in vogue, although plays such as *Jacqueline, Lord Tatters: The Bohemian,* and *Lights and Shadows* found audiences at lesser houses and on the road.

GAZZARA, [BIAGIO ANTHONY] BEN (b. 1930) The small, darkly handsome actor was born in New York and studied at City College, Erwin Piscator's Dramatic Workshop, and the Actors Studio♦ before making his debut in summer stock in 1952. He won immediate recognition when he portrayed the vicious Jocko de Paris in *End as a Man* (1953), then portrayed the guilt-ridden Brick in *Cat on a Hot Tin Roof*♦ (1955). He next scored as the drug-addicted Johnny Pope in *A Hatful of Rain*♦ (1955). His later successes were in two Eugene O'Neill♦ revivals, as Edmund Darrell in *Strange Interlude*♦ (1963) and as "Erie" Smith in *Hughie* (1974).

GAZZO, MICHAEL V., see *Hatful of Rain, A*

GEAR, LUELLA [GARDNER VAN NORT] (1899–1980) The New Yorker made her debut in the 1917 musical *Love o' Mike* and over the next decade used her often acid, knowing style of comedy to win increasingly important roles in such comedies and musicals as *The Gold Diggers*♦ (1919), *Poppy* (1923), and *Queen High*♦ (1926). She enjoyed major assignments in *Gay Divorce*♦ (1932), *Life Begins at 8:40* (1934), and *On Your Toes*♦ (1936). In later years her best role was Julia McKinlock, the bitter worldling, in *Sabrina Fair*♦ (1953).

GELBER, JACK, see *Connection, The*

Gemini, a play in two acts by Albert Innaurato. Produced by the Circle Repertory Company♦ at the Circle Theatre. March 13, 1977. 1,778 performances.

The Geminiani family is not quite typical of South Philadelphia's many Italian families, for their son Fran (Robert Picardo) has gone to Harvard. On his 21st birthday he is visited by two friends from his college days, Randy (Reed Birney) and Judith (Carol Potter), who are brother and sister. Both love Fran, and Fran, being uncertain of his own sexual proclivities, loves them. Among the other visitors who come to the party are the Geminiani's Jewish neighbors, Bunny Weinberger (Jessica James) and her fat son Herschel (Jonathan Hadary).

Although the play trafficked in such contemporary concerns as homosexuality and neuroses, it took a fresh and funny slant and placed its action in a setting, South Philadelphia, usually ignored by New York-centered playwrights. The play was quickly transferred to Broadway.

Innaurato (b. 1948) is a Philadelphia-born playwright who first called attention to himself with his one-act play, *The Transfiguration of Benno Blimpie* (1977), the study of an unloved man who becomes a compulsive eater. Later plays include *Ulysses in Traction* (1977), *Coming of Age in Soho* (1985), and *Gus and Al* (1989).

GENÉE, ADELINE (1878–1970) The famous Danish ballerina won wide acclaim when she starred in the American musical *The Soul Kiss* (1908), for which

Ziegfield♦ advertised her as "the world's greatest dancer." She capitalized on her success by appearing in two more musicals, *The Silver Star* (1909) and *The Bachelor Belles* (1910).

General Theatrical Fund An organization founded in Philadelphia in 1829 to help incapacitated or indigent actors. Its founding coincided with the loss of theatrical primacy by Philadelphia to New York, so that within a few years the fund was in difficulty. Edwin Forrest♦ had been one of its founders and chief contributors, and in his loyalty to his home town he stubbornly refused to allow the organization to merge with the newer and stronger New York-based American Dramatic Fund Association. ♦ The merger was finally effected in 1856.

GENET, JEAN (1910–86). The French dramatist, who spent many years in institutions and prisons, has written numerous plays which serve as vehicles for his hatred of society. He is best known to American audiences for *The Balcony* (1960) and *The Blacks* (1961). The latter had 1,408 performances off-Broadway,♦ a record there for a serious non-musical. Although never mounted on Broadway and scarcely in the mainstream of popular modern drama, Genet's works continue to find audiences in colleges and more experimental regional theatres.

GENNARO, PETER (b. 1924) Born in Metairie, La., he made his debut as dancer with the San Carlo Opera Company and later danced in the chorus of numerous Broadway musicals before creating the choreography for *Seventh Heaven* (1955). Later choreographic assignments included *West Side Story*♦ (1957), on which he worked with Jerome Robbins♦; *Fiorello!*♦ (1959); *The Unsinkable Molly Brown* (1960); *Mr. President* (1962); *Bajour* (1964); *Jimmy* (1969); *Irene*♦ (1973); *Annie*♦ (1977); and *Carmelina* (1979). He also served for many years as choreographer at the Radio City Music Hall.

Gentle People, The, a play in three acts by Irwin Shaw.♦ Produced by the Group Theatre♦ at the Belasco Theatre. January 5, 1939. 141 performances.

Jonah Goodman (Sam Jaffe) and Philip Anagnos (Roman Bohnen) are gentle souls who would like nothing better than to fish off a pier near their home. Their simple, idyllic life is threatened by a racketeer, Harold Goff (Franchot Tone♦), who demands protection money. Goff would also have Jonah's daughter Stella (Sylvia Sydney), and, when he learns the men have saved money to buy a small fishing boat, he would have that, too. So the men take Goff out in the boat, kill him, and throw him overboard, but not before retrieving the money and additional sums from his wallet.

Shaw called his work a "Brooklyn fable," adding, "justice triumphs and the meek prove victorious over arrogant and violent men. The author does not pretend this is the case in real life." Seen by some as an anti-fascist allegory, it was dismissed by Brooks Atkinson♦ as "pleasant, discursive writing" which had "the disadvantage of seeming a little uneventful."

Gentleman from Mississippi, A, a play in four acts by Harrison Rhodes and Thomas A. Wise.♦ Produced by William A. Brady♦ and Joseph R. Grismer♦ at the Bijou Theatre. September 29, 1908. 407 performances.

William H. Langdon (Wise) is a new Senator from Mississippi. He is a quiet, honest gentleman and proud of his state. When the brash young reporter "Bud" Haines (Douglas Fairbanks♦) announces he is from New York, Langdon replies he knows it as "the Vicksburg of the North." The men strike up a friendship, and Haines is appointed Langdon's private secretary. Some corrupt Senators hope to push through a bill establishing a naval base in Mississippi and have secretly been buying up land. They have even involved the Senator's daughter Hope (Lola May). But Langdon and Haines thwart the plan, and Haines wins Hope.

Described by one critic as "full of bright lines, tender sentiment, and genuine local color," this straightforward, wholesome if simplistic play was one of the major hits of its day.

Gentleman of France, A, a play in seven scenes by Harriet Ford.♦ Produced by Liebler and Co.♦ at Wallack's Theatre. December 30, 1901. 120 performances.

Gaston de Marsac (Kyrle Bellew♦) loves Mlle. de la Vire (Eleanor Robson♦), but he will not have her if the villainous M. de Bruhl (John Blair) succeeds in his machinations. Not until de Marsac kills de Bruhl and several of his cohorts (with Mlle. de la Vire assisting by conking another over the head) can he safely claim her.

This swashbuckler was taken from Stanley Weyman's novel. Although *Harper's Weekly* joined others in complaining that the somewhat effeminate Bellew was miscast, it concluded the play was "better worth seeing than most dramatizations of historical novels that have been recently produced."

Gentlemen Prefer Blondes, a comedy in three acts by Anita Loos♦ and John Emerson. ♦ Produced by Edgar Selwyn♦ at the Times Square Theatre. September 28, 1926. 199 performances.

Lorelei Lee (June Walker♦), a gold-digging little girl from Little Rock, has all her expenses paid by a rich button manufacturer, Gus Eisman (Arthur S. Ross). He even sends Lorelei and her friend Dorothy (Edna Hibbard) to Europe, where Lorelei wangles a tiara from an English knight and dates dashing young Henry Spofford (Frank Morgan♦). When she learns that Spofford may be richer than Eisman, she would dump Eisman. By that time, however, Dorothy has claimed Spofford.

Based on Miss Loos's famous novel, the story was also used in a musical of the same name, with a book by Miss Loos and Joseph Fields,♦ lyrics by Leo Robin, and music by Jule Styne.♦ The show was produced by Herman Levin♦ and Oliver Smith♦ at the Ziegfeld Theatre♦ on December 8, 1949, and ran for 740 performances. The main roles were taken by Carol Channing♦ (Lorelei), Yvonne Adair (Dorothy), Jack McCauley (Gus), and Eric Brotherson (Spofford).

Principal songs: Bye Bye Baby · Diamonds Are a Girl's Best Friend · A Little Girl from Little Rock

The musical has been successfully revived both in its original version and in a revised version called *Lorelei*. In both the straight play and the musical versions, the eternal gold-digger, noticeably caricatured, was set against the background of the hedonistic 1920s.

GEORGE, GRACE (1879–1961) The fair-haired, blue-eyed beauty was born in New York and educated at a convent. She later studied at the American Academy of Dramatic Arts♦ before making her debut as a schoolgirl in *The New Boy* (1894). Her first important role was Juliette, the innkeeper's daughter whose marriage plans are constantly frustrated by a rival, in *The Turtle* (1898). She quickly mastered a style which her husband, William A. Brady, ♦ would later describe as "the fast-building, vivacious, chin up and tongue-sparkling sort of thing, with wit and tears mingled." She demonstrated these skills in over 50 subsequent plays. Among her notable roles were Peg Woffington in *Pretty Peggy* (1903); Louise in an all-star revival of *The Two Orphans♦* (1904); Lady Kitty, a flighty woman who always does the wrong thing at the wrong time, in *The Marriage of William Ashe* (1905); Olivia Sherwood, whose attempts to keep up appearances backfire, in *Clothes♦* (1906); Cyprienne in a revival of *Divorçons♦* (1907);

Marion Stanton, who wins back her fickle husband, in *A Woman's Way♦* (1909); Lady Teazle in *The School for Scandal* (1909); Kitty Constable, who gives her philandering husband his comeuppance, in *Sauce for the Goose* (1911); Lady Cicely in *Captain Brassbound's Conversion* (1916); Anne De Rhonde, the rich society woman who is unaware the shanty dweller she likes is her sister, in *The Merry Wives of Gotham* (1924); Janet Fraser, who is courted by her former husband, in *The First Mrs. Fraser* (1929); Mary Herries, a gentle spinster whose home is taken over by a vicious man hoping to gain her fortune, in *Kind Lady* (1935); and Mother Hildebrand, the mistress of a school, who gently prevents her bishop from firing a faculty member, in *The Velvet Glove* (1949). Her last appearance was as Mrs. Culver opposite Katharine Cornell♦ in a revival of *The Constant Wife* (1951). She also adapted several plays, some of which she acted in.

George Spelvin, see *Spelvin, George*

George Washington Slept Here, a comedy in three acts by George S. Kaufman♦ and Moss Hart. ♦ Produced by Sam H. Harris♦ at the Lyceum Theatre. ♦ October 18, 1940. 173 performances.

When Newton Fuller (Ernest Truex♦) shows his wife Annabelle (Jean Dixon) a decrepit country home in which George Washington reputedly slept, Annabelle can only remark, "Martha wasn't a very good housekeeper." But when Newton surprises his wife with the news that he has bought the place, she becomes angry enough to "spit from here to Mount Vernon." The Fullers' problems have only begun. The old well, for example, has long since run dry. Even after the house is virtually in order—they are still drilling for water—their family's problems have hardly ended. Their daughter Madge (Peggy French) is going around with a married man, an actor in a local summer stock company. And of course, there are hosts of visitors, including rich Uncle Stanley (Dudley Digges♦), a bore from way back whose deadening conversations suddenly seem all the more excruciating when he announces he is broke. Worse, the Fullers learn it was not Washington who slept there, but Benedict Arnold. However, when the property is about to be foreclosed, Uncle Stanley slyly comes to the rescue.

The last of the Kaufman-Hart collaborations, it was awaited with such exalted expectations that disappointment was almost inevitable. Malcolm Goldstein, Kaufman's biographer, condemned the comedy: "The play proceeds with intermittent merriment, but without a display of true wit. The characterization is slight and the twists of plot improbable, excessive, and dull." Nevertheless, the play has enjoyed occasional successful summer stock revivals.

George White's Scandals, a series of revues produced by White♦ from 1919 through 1926, and then in 1928, 1929, 1931, 1935, and 1939. Although given to elaborate show numbers much like the *Ziegfeld Follies,* ♦ these revues were less ornate and cumbersome. Their comedy tended to be far more topical, and because White had been a dancer, the productions were fast-paced and featured better dancing and music than similar revues. Most of the scores were written either by George Gershwin♦ or by De Sylva,♦ Brown,♦ and Henderson.♦ Memorable songs from these shows included "I'll Build a Stairway to Paradise" (1922); "Somebody Loves Me" (1924); "Black Bottom," "Birth of the Blues" and "Lucky Day" (1926); and "Life Is Just a Bowl of Cherries" (1931).

GERMON, EFFIE (1843?–1914) The daughter of performers and great-granddaughter of the first Joseph Jefferson,♦she was born in Augusta, Ga., and raised in Baltimore. After making her debut with a Philadelphia stock company in 1857, she joined Laura Keene's♦ New York ensemble in 1858, appearing first as Kate Rocket in *Old Heads and Young Hearts,* and a short time later creating the role of Augusta in the first American performance of *Our American Cousin*♦ (1858). In 1865 she played Ophelia to Edwin Booth's♦ Hamlet, then spent several seasons with John Brougham.♦ She joined Wallack's♦ company in 1868, essaying as her first assignment Naomi Tighe, the East Indian heiress, in Robertson's♦ *School.* Her "rollicking" performances quickly won the doll-faced actress the position formerly held in the troupe by the late Mary Gannon,♦ and she remained with the company for 17 years. After the company disbanded she continued to play important roles such as Audrey to Helena Modjeska's♦ Rosalind in 1886 and the comic servant in *Little Lord Fauntleroy* (1888). Much of her later career was spent touring, notably as Aunt Polly in *David Harum.* ♦

Gerry Society Formally known as the New York Society for the Prevention of Cruelty to Children, it was founded by Elbridge T. Gerry, Henry Bergh, John D. Wright, and others in 1875. Gerry, a banker, lawyer, and grandson of a signer of the Declaration of Independence, was by far the most prominent of the figures, so that the writings of many late 19th-

century theatrical figures simply called the group by his name. For the most part the group successfully attacked abuses by inconsiderate producers and selfish stage mothers, but occasionally went too far in its zeal. One memorable instance occurred when Francis Wilson,♦ charmed by two black waifs he saw dancing in the streets, gave them a number in his latest musical. The Gerry Society went to court to forbid the children's performing, thus depriving the needy youngsters of paychecks and a chance to improve their talents and audiences of a harmless entertainment. Gerry himself wrote, "I am a friend of the stage, but I am a better friend of the children." Although most of the abuses disappeared with the coming of child labor laws and the rise of unions, theatrical producers must still get the Society's approval for children to perform, and the group still monitors the treatment of child actors as well as seeing that they have proper schooling.

GERSHWIN, GEORGE [né JACOB GERSHVIN] (1898–1937) One of the greatest and most original of Broadway composers, he was born in Brooklyn to a poor, immigrant family. His father was an unsuccessful businessman. Young George's love of music came early on and was helped by his friendship with his classmate, violinist Max Rosen. When the Gershwins purchased a piano for his older brother Ira,♦ it was George, then twelve, who monopolized it. At fourteen he began lessons with a key figure in his musical life, Charles Hambitzer, a composer and pianist of broad, advanced musical tastes. From Hambitzer, Gershwin received a thorough classical training. But he was also aware of the native musical upheaval around him. At the wedding of an aunt he heard the orchestra play some songs which struck him as far superior to anything he yet knew. These songs turned out to be the interpolations Jerome Kern♦ added to *The Girl from Utah*♦ (1914). Kern became Gershwin's exemplar. Gershwin's name achieved recognition after Al Jolson♦ sang "Swanee" in *Sinbad* in 1919. That same year he composed his first score, for *La La Lucille.* From 1920 to 1924 he created scores for *George White's Scandals,* ♦ including such hit songs as "I'll Build a Stairway to Paradise" (1922) and "Somebody Loves Me" (1924). During these seasons he also wrote two less successful shows, *Our Nell* (1922) and *Sweet Little Devil* (1924). From late 1924 on he worked almost exclusively with Ira. Their first hit was *Lady, Be Good!*♦ (1924) a show that marked a turning point in American musical comedy. Its jazz-based melodies, harmonies, and rhythms set a new standard and allowed musical comedy to be clearly distinguished from operetta, which retained allegiances to European mannerisms. Gershwin's melodic lines tended to be angular and aggressive, as exemplified by the show's "Fascinating Rhythm" and title song, but could on occasion be soft, sentimental, almost wailing, as in "So Am I," suggesting that his Jewish background as well as black sources influenced his composition. A succession of hits and near misses followed: *Tell Me More!* (1925); *Tip-Toes*♦ (1925), which offered "Looking for a Boy," "Sweet and Low Down," "That Certain Feeling" and "When Do We Dance?"; *Song of the Flame* (1925), an operetta written in collaboration with Herbert Stothart,♦ which produced Gershwin's rousing title song; *Oh, Kay!*♦ (1926), which offered "Clap Yo' Hands," "Do, Do, Do" "Maybe," and "Someone To Watch Over Me"; *Funny Face*♦ (1927), from which came "The Babbitt and the Bromide," "He Loves and She Loves," " 'S Wonderful," and the title song; *Rosalie* (1928), written in collaboration with Sigmund Romberg♦ and offering "How Long Has This Been Going On?"; *Treasure Girl* (1928), which contained "I've Got a Crush on You"; *Show Girl* (1929), offering "Liza," for which Gus Kahn wrote the lyric; *Strike Up the Band*♦ (1930), which gave us "Soon" and the title song; *Girl Crazy*♦ (1930), which included "Bidin' My Time," "But Not for Me," "Could You Use Me?," "Embraceable You," and "I Got Rhythm"; *Of Thee I Sing*♦ (1931), the first musical to win a Pulitzer Prize,♦ which presented "Of Thee I Sing, Baby," "Love Is Sweeping the Country," "Wintergreen for President," and "Who Cares?"; *Pardon My English* (1933); and *Let 'Em Eat Cake* (1933), which included "Mine." From early in his career Gershwin had been interested in more serious composition, writing numerous concert pieces that remain popular today. Even his political musicals can be seen as a step away from traditional material. In 1935 he attempted a folk opera, *Porgy and Bess.*♦ The initial reception was mixed and public response lukewarm, but the musical's popularity has grown with time and may well prove his most durable work. Out of it came "Bess, You Is My Woman Now," "I Got Plenty o' Nuttin'," "It Ain't Necessarily So," and "Summertime," for many of which the librettist, Dubose Heyward, served as Ira's co-lyricist.

Biography: *The Gershwin Years.* Edward Jablonski and Lawrence D. Stewart, Garden City, N.Y., 1958.

GERSHWIN, IRA [né ISRAEL GERSHVIN] (1896–1983) Born in New York, and the older brother of George Gershwin,♦ he was a bookish, introspective youth.

When he first decided to write lyrics professionally he did it under a pseudonym derived from the first names of another brother and a sister, Arthur Francis. It was as Francis that he created lyrics for Vincent Youmans's♦ *Two Little Girls in Blue* (1921), writing the words for such songs as "Dolly" and "Oh Me, Oh My." During the twenties he occasionally wrote with composers other than his brother, most successfully when he provided words for "Sunny Disposish" in *Americana* (1926). That title suggests the nature of his writing, which was usually cheery, colloquial, and marked by a unique, slangy shorthand. His work with his brother is listed in the entry for George immediately above. He wrote lyrics for *Life Begins at 8:40* (1934) and the 1936 edition of the *Ziegfeld Follies,*♦ producing the hit "I Can't Get Started with You" with Vernon Duke.♦ After his brother's death he wrote *Lady in the Dark*♦ (1941) with Kurt Weill,♦ creating such songs as "[The Saga of] Jenny," "My Ship," "This Is New," and "Tschaikowsky." His last two shows were failures: *The Firebrand of Florence* (1945), written with Weill; and *Park Avenue* (1946), written with Arthur Schwartz.♦

GEST, MORRIS (1881–1942) Although born in Russia, he came to America as a child and was educated in the Boston public schools. He made his debut as a producer there in 1903, but soon moved to New York, where in 1905 he went into partnership with F. Ray Comstock.♦ Many of their successes were large spectacles such as *The Wanderer* (1917) or light comedies such as *Polly Preferred* (1923), but they were best known as importers of such attractions as the English musical *Chu Chin Chow* (1917); the Russian revue, *Chauve Souris* (1922); the Moscow Art Theatre♦ (1923); and Eleonora Duse♦ (1923), most of which Gest is believed to have negotiated. In 1924 they offered Max Reinhardt's♦ production of *The Miracle.* After the partnership dissolved in the late 1920s, Gest continued to produce until shortly before his death, but his later record was undistinguished. He was married to David Belasco's♦ daughter and is said, along with his father-in-law and Jed Harris,♦ to have inspired the character of the producer in *Twentieth Century*♦ (1932).

Get-Rich-Quick Wallingford, a comedy in four acts by George M. Cohan.♦ Produced by Cohan and Sam H. Harris♦ at the Gaiety Theatre. September 19, 1910. 424 performances.

J. Rufus Wallingford (Hale Hamilton) and his crony, Horace "Blackie" Daws (Edward Ellis), are consummate con-men. They move from town to town setting up promising businesses, selling stock in the companies by telling the local "boobs" that "There's millions in it!," then disappearing before the bubble bursts. A favorite Wallingford trick is to walk into a hotel when he first arrives, and, as he signs the register, beg the clerk not to sell his autograph. But when he comes to Battlesburg to set up a plant for the manufacture of covered carpet tacks that will match any carpet, his plans go awry. The company succeeds, and Battlesburg prospers. Wallingford looks to become richer than he ever dreamed and even wins the hand of Fannie Jasper (Frances Ring), who believed in him.

Based on George Randolph Chester's short stories in the *Saturday Evening Post,* the play was Cohan's first successful work without music. His fast-paced co-direction (with Sam Forrest♦) glossed over myriad improbabilities, while the colorful minor figures that filled the play led the Boston *Evening Transcript* to note that his characters were "Americans, keenly observed, shrewdly put to speaking [for] themselves in their own idiom."

Getting Gertie's Garter, a farce in three acts by Wilson Collison and Avery Hopwood.♦ Produced by A. H. Woods♦ at the Republic Theatre. August 1, 1921. 120 performances.

When Gertie (Hazel Dawn♦) was dating Ken Waldrick (Donald MacDonald), Ken gave her a diamond-studded garter with his picture in it. But that was a year ago. Now Gertie is married to Teddy Darling, while Ken has married a girl named Pattie, so it seems time to return the garter before the spouses learn of it. Quietly returning the garter, however, proves easier said than done. It turns out to involve all sorts of misunderstandings, including a curious romp in a haystack.

Because many of the figures involved with the show had been involved with the earlier *Up in Mabel's Room,* ♦ comparisons were obvious and not altogether flattering. Percy Hammond♦ of the *Herald Tribune* judged it "duller," adding, "There is no more interest in a garter as a naughty thing than there is in a virgin's wimple." The public disagreed. Not only were the original production and its road companies highly profitable, but for many years the play remained popular with stock companies and on summer circuits.

Getting Out, a play in two acts by Marsha W. Norman.♦ Produced by the Phoenix Theatre♦ at the Marymount Manhattan Theatre. October 19, 1978. 22 performances.

Arlene Holsclaw (Susan Kingsley) when released from prison is determined to lead a decent life, but remains haunted by her old, more vicious self, Arlie (Pamela Reed). Settling into the dingy room that she expects to call home, Arlene is visited by her mother (Madeleine Thornton-Sherwood), who dredges up old memories; by Carl (Lee Burmester), a pimp who was her lover and who would have her return to prostitution; and by Bennie (Barry Corbin), her former jailer, who tries to seduce her. With the help of an understanding neighbor, Ruby (Joan Pape), she begins to realize that she can handle herself properly and even live with the vestiges of Arlie that still cry within her.

A sordid, foul-mouthed, yet compassionate and moving play, the work was first mounted in 1977 by the Actors' Theater of Louisville,♦ and later won the American Theatre Critics Association♦ award as the season's outstanding play. After its original New York engagement it reopened May 15, 1979, at the Theatre de Lys and ran an additional 237 performances.

GEVA, TAMARA [née TAMARA or SHEVERSHEIEVA GEVERGEVA] (b. 1907) The Russian-born ballerina, who was once the wife of George Balanchine,♦ made her American debut in *Chauve Souris* in 1927 and subsequently appeared in such musicals as *Three's a Crowd* (1930) and *Flying Colors* (1932), as well as several straight plays. However, she is best remembered as one of the original stars of *On Your Toes♦* (1936), in which she introduced "Slaughter on Tenth Avenue"♦ with Ray Bolger.♦

GIBBS, [OLIVER] WOLCOTT (1902–58) A descendant of Oliver Wolcott, signer of the Declaration of Independence, and a cousin of the novelist Alice Duer Miller, Gibbs was born in New York and attended the Hill School, but not college. He held such odd jobs as architect's apprentice and railroad conductor before joining *The New Yorker,* where he became drama critic when Robert Benchley retired in 1939. He held the post until his death. He could be acerbic, as when he wrote of Saroyan's♦ *My Heart's in the Highlands,* ♦ "This collision between the most completely undisciplined talent in American letters and the actors of the Group Theatre bored me utterly to distraction and I would advise you to stay away from it unless you are especially fond of being badgered in the name of experimental drama." But he could also be warm and open, as when he confessed to a "feeling of rising excitement" while watching *Abe Lincoln in Illinois,* ♦ concluding, "I suppose it was just the surprise and gratitude and somehow sorrow of seeing a very great man exactly as he must have been." He was one of those rare critics who successfully worked both sides of the footlights, writing *Season in the Sun*♦ (1950), a well-received comedy about a writer attempting to work on a novel while his summer cottage becomes a meeting place for all sorts of hangers-on.

GIBSON, WILLIAM (b. 1914) A native of New York, he studied at City College and saw his earliest dramas produced at regional theatres. His first play to reach Broadway was *Two for the Seesaw*♦ (1958), which depicted the romance of a prim Midwestern lawyer and a bohemian New York girl. *The Miracle Worker*♦ (1959) recounted the early history of Helen Keller and her tutor, Annie Sullivan. He later collaborated on the book of the musical *Golden Boy*♦ (1964) and then rewrote *A Cry of Players* (1968), an earlier play dealing with Shakespeare's decision to become a playwright. His *Golda* (1977) dealt with the Israeli political leader. He returned to the Keller-Sullivan relationship for a play that looked at their later years, *Monday after the Miracle* (1982). A number of his other plays have been produced by regional stages.

Gideon, a play in two acts by Paddy Chayefsky.♦ Produced at the Plymouth Theatre. November 9, 1961. 236 performances.

God comes to earth as an Angel (Fredric March♦) and exhorts the young farmer, Gideon (Douglas Campbell), to lead his people against the Midianites. At first Gideon is disbelieving, but when the Angel performs miracles and even gives Gideon the very plan that wins the battle, Gideon accepts that the Angel is indeed Yahweh or Jehovah. But later Gideon refuses God's order to slay the elders of Succoth. Gideon's head has been swelled by praise and so he comes to attribute his success not to God but to "historico-economic, socio-psychological forces." The Angel can only rue that for all Man's belief in God, Man believes first and foremost in himself.

Hailed by Howard Taubman of the *Times* as "A graceful conceit tinged with innocent wonder and wise laughter," the play demonstrated Chayefsky's increasing preoccupation with mystical and metaphysical concerns.

GIELGUD, [ARTHUR] JOHN (b. 1904) A grand-nephew of Ellen Terry,♦ the slightly arch, musical-voiced actor first appeared in New York in 1928 as the Grand Duke Alexander in *The Patriot*. However, he did not win major American recognition until his 1936 Hamlet. The consensus was that his interpreta-

tion was intelligent and exquisitely recited but lacking in a certain passionate power. In 1947 he scored major successes when he starred in his revivals of *The Importance of Being Earnest* and *Love for Love*. Later that same year he played Jason to Judith Anderson's♦ Medea, which he directed, and also appeared as Raskolnikoff in *Crime and Punishment*. He returned to America in 1950 to play Thomas Mendip in *The Lady's Not for Burning*. He read selections from Shakespeare in *Ages of Man* (1958); directed and played Benedick in *Much Ado About Nothing*♦ (1959); directed *Five Finger Exercise* (1959); staged *Big Fish, Little Fish* (1961); played Joseph Surface in *The School for Scandal* (1963); portrayed the beleaguered Brother Julian in *Tiny Alice*♦ (1964); directed and starred in a revival of Chekhov's *Ivanov* (1966); acted the part of Harry, the mild-mannered mental patient, in *Home* (1970); and directed *Private Lives*♦ and *The Constant Wife* (1975).

GILBERT, MRS. [GEORGE HENRY], [neé ANN HARTLEY] (1821–1904) No beauty—she had an angular, pinched face and heavy-lidded protruding eyes—she was for many decades one of the most skillful and beloved American comediennes. She was born in England and trained as a dancer in London at the ballet school of Her Majesty's Theatre. In 1846 she married Gilbert, an actor and dancer, and together they toured England and Ireland before coming to America, where they first settled in Milwaukee. Work next took them to Chicago, Cleveland, Cincinnati, Louisville, and finally New York. During these seasons Mrs. Gilbert developed her acting skills, dancing less and less. She performed opposite many of the era's stars, including J. M. Wallack,♦ William Burton,♦ John Brougham,♦ and Edwin Booth,♦ playing Lady Macbeth to Booth's Macbeth and Osric to his Hamlet. She made her New York debut in 1864 as Baroness Freitenhorsen in *Finesse* with Mrs. John Wood's company. Soon afterwards Mr. Gilbert was hurt in a fall and died in 1866. Mrs. Gilbert first earned major plaudits as the Marquise de St. Maur, whose son marries below his station, in the American premiere of Robertson's♦ *Caste* (1867). Two years later she joined Augustin Daly's♦ company and, with very short breaks, remained with it through its 30-year history. She acted comic old women in approximately 150 different plays for Daly, ranging from Shakespeare and Sheridan through such important new plays as *Saratoga*♦ (1870) and *Pique*♦ (1875) to many long-discarded contemporary pieces. During the last years of Daly's heyday she was, with Ada Rehan,♦ John Drew,♦

and James Lewis,♦ the core of his great comic productions. After Daly's death she worked for Charles Frohman.♦ Her last appearance was as "Granny" Thompson, who must reconcile herself to her widowed son-in-law's remarrying, in *Granny* (1904). One critic said of her at this time, "The older and broader school never had anything richer and truer in its sphere, and the new school of naturalism cannot show anything of finer and firmer veracity." She died while touring in this play.

Autobiography: *The Stage Reminiscences of Mrs. Gilbert*, New York, 1904.

GILBERT, JOHN [né GIBBS] (1810–89) One of the finest actors of his day, most distinguished in comic parts such as Sir Anthony Absolute and Sir Peter Teazle, he was born in Boston, where his next-door neighbor and childhood friend was Charlotte Cushman.♦ His widowed mother put him to work at age fifteen in a dry-goods store, but he soon realized his true calling and made his debut at the Tremont Theatre in 1828 as Jaffier in *Venice Preserved*. Shortly thereafter he left to work in Mississippi River towns, remaining in that part of the country until 1834. He made his New York debut in 1839 as Sir Edmund Mortimer in *The Iron Chest*. Although he continued for several years to play in tragedy and melodrama, he turned increasingly to comic parts. His somewhat portly build and round, sober-miened face led him to prefer roles as older men. In 1847 he enjoyed a season in London, then spent some time in Paris. He returned to New York to play at the Park Theatre♦ until it burned down, then served unsuccessfully as manager of the Chestnut Street Theatre♦ in Philadelphia. In 1862 he joined Wallack's♦ company, making his first appearance there as Sir Peter. He remained with Wallack until the company disbanded in 1888, serving not only as a principal comedian but as stage manager as well. He also assumed serious roles such as Miles McKenna in *Rosedale*♦ (1863). He died while touring with Joseph Jefferson♦ in *The Rivals*.

Gilbert was an archly conservative actor of the old school. He fought with Jefferson over the changes that the actor made in *The Rivals*, branding them as "sacrilege," and generally protested every innovation and change of fashion. He was considered a cold, haughty person, but respected as a conscientious and skilled artist. He prided himself as well on his learning and had amassed a fine library before his death.

GILBERT [WILLIAM SCHWENCK] (1836–1911) **and SULLIVAN** [ARTHUR SEYMOUR] (1842–1900) The masters of English comic opera were first represented in America in 1875 by a failed production of their *Trial by Jury*. However, their *H.M.S. Pinafore*♦ became one of the biggest successes in the history of the American theatre after its premiere during the 1878–79 season. So many companies were hurriedly put on the stage that contemporaries spoke of "a *Pinafore* craze." More importantly (as detailed in the entry for the show), it opened all American stages to musical entertainments and served as a model for American musicals that shortly followed. All of their subsequent offerings received immediate American productions, the most successful being *The Pirates of Penzance*♦ (1879); *Patience* (1881), whose success was helped by the concurrent arrival in America of a figure satirized in it, Oscar Wilde♦; and *The Mikado* (1885), whose debunking of the Orientalia then so fashionable was aped by numerous contemporary American musicals. By the turn of the century the vogue for these Savoyard gems had waned noticeably. The period saw the rise of amateur groups dedicated to producing the works and also several mammoth all-star revivals. Winthrop Ames's♦ highly praised revivals in the 1920s once again whetted interest, as did visits of the D'Oyly Carte♦ in the 1930s. With the decline of that company several unsuccessful attempts were made after World War II to form an American ensemble devoted to producing the works. Tyrone Guthrie also staged successful revivals. Sensing that the tradition of pure D'Oyly Carte no longer appealed to most Americans, Joseph Papp♦ brought out a defiantly unconventional *The Pirates of Penzance* in 1981, a production that enjoyed far and away the longest run ever accorded a Gilbert and Sullivan work in America.

Gilded Age, The, see *Colonel Sellers*

GILDER, ROSAMUND (1891?–1986) The daughter of writer and editor Richard Watson Gilder, she was born in Marion, Mass., and was for many years the drama critic and editor of *Theatre Arts Monthly*. Besides serving as secretary of the National Theatre Conference,♦ director of the Playwrights' Bureau of the Federal Theatre Project,♦ and a secretary of the American National Theatre and Academy,♦ she wrote numerous books on the theatre, including: *Enter the Actress* (1931); *A Theatre Library* (1932); *Theatre Collections in Libraries and Museums* (1936), written with George Freedley,♦ and *John Gielgud's Hamlet* (1937).

GILFERT, CHARLES (1787–1829) Born in Germany, he was brought to America while still a youngster and was soon a violinist at the Park Theatre. ♦ He advanced quickly, often composing incidental music and occasionally giving concerts. When the Theatrical Commonwealth ♦ was organized in 1813 to fight the virtual monopoly the Park held over talent, he was appointed its musical director. The venture was short-lived, and he did not emerge again as a significant theatrical figure until the opening of the Bowery Theatre, ♦ of which he was the first manager and lessee. Whatever his musical talents, his managerial abilities were much less. His stint was plagued by competition, lack of attendance because of the theatre's location, the fire that destroyed the first and apparently uninsured Bowery, and by a poor selection of plays and artists. He went bankrupt in 1829, suffered a nervous breakdown, and died shortly thereafter.

GILLETTE, WILLIAM (1855–1937) The lean, haughtily handsome actor and writer with vivid blue eyes and an aquiline nose was born in Hartford, Conn., the son of a United States senator. He studied at Yale, Harvard, and the Massachusetts Fine Arts Institute and made his acting debut at New Orleans in *Across the Continent* ♦ in 1875. This was an amateur production, and he did not make his professional debut until later the same year, when he played Guzman in *Faint Heart Ne'er Won Fair Lady* in Boston. He then joined the Boston Museum, ♦ where he performed numerous supporting roles. His first New York appearance was as the Prosecuting Attorney in *The Gilded Age* ♦ in 1877. In 1881 he appeared in the title role of his own play, *The Professor,* ♦ which dealt with an unworldly pedant. He then toured in *Young Mrs. Winthrop* ♦ and played briefly in his own verson of von Moser's *Der Bibliothekar,* called *Digby's Secretary* (1884). Three major successes followed when he wrote *Held by the Enemy* ♦ (1886), a Civil War drama in which he eventually assumed the role of the comic newspaper correspondent, Thomas Beene [or Bean]; *Too Much Johnson* ♦ (1894), in which he played Augustus Billings, a man whose incessant lying causes comic complications; and *Secret Service* ♦ (1896), another Civil War drama in which he played the Northern spy who operated under the alias Captain Thorne. His greatest success came in the title role of *Sherlock Holmes* ♦ (1899), which he adapted from Conan Doyle's famous stories. One critic wrote that the actor, famous for his "scarce gesture and staccato sentence," "looks the part and carries it in his accustomed nonchalant and pictorially effective

way." He scored again in the title role of Barrie's ♦ *The Admirable Crichton* (1903). Most of his later career was spent reviving his earlier successes, but he enjoyed popularity as Henry Wilton, the millionaire who pretends to be ruined in order to enjoy a night out at a prizefight, in *A Successful Calamity* (1917); and as Mr. Dearth, who dreams of what might have been, in Barrie's fantasy *Dear Brutus* (1918). Of this last performance John Corbin ♦ wrote in the *Times* that Gillette "has never been more humanly gracious and delicately real," while Helen Hayes, ♦ who was in the play, recalled his "silken quality," his "felicitous combination of grain and polish" and added, "I was never again to see such timing as this man had."

Among the many other plays which Gillette wrote were such adaptations as *Esmeralda* ♦ (1881), written with F. H. Burnett ♦; *She* (1887); *All the Comforts of Home* (1890); *Mr. Wilkinson's Widows* ♦ (1891), and *Settled Out of Court* (1892).

Biography: *Sherlock Holmes and Much More,* Doris E. Cook, Hartford, 1970.

GILLMORE, MARGALO (1897–1986) A member of an old acting family, she was born in London, but while still a child was brought to America. She studied at the American Academy of Dramatic Arts, ♦ then made her professional debut in *The Scrap of Paper* (1917). Several more roles followed before she was cast as Sylvia Fair, the rebellious daughter, in *The Famous Mrs. Fair* ♦ (1919). She followed this by playing Eileen Carmody, the tubercular patient who believes two men have jilted her, in Eugene O'Neill's ♦ *The Straw* (1921). Her first appearance with the Theatre Guild, ♦ with which she was long associated, was as Consuelo, the little bareback rider whom the hero poisons to save her from a cruel marriage, in *He Who Gets Slapped* (1922). Although she never became a star, she was much admired for her beauty and fine talent. Among her later roles were Ann, one of the newly dead, in *Outward Bound* (1924); Venice Pollen, who marries the man the heroine loves, in *The Green Hat* (1925); Hester, whose engagement is destroyed by her fiancé's possessive mother, in *The Silver Cord* ♦ (1926); Monica Gray, who loses the man she really loves, in *The Second Man* ♦ (1927); Kukachin, who loves but loses Marco Polo, in *Marco Millions* ♦ (1928); Helen Pettigrew, who dies before she can marry the man who loves her, in *Berkeley Square* ♦ (1929); Mary Philipse, George Washington's first love, in *Valley Forge* ♦ (1934); Mary Haines, who wins back her husband from a bitchy rival, in *The Women* ♦ (1936); Amanda Smith, who would turn a light-hearted writer into a serious dramatist, in *No Time for Comedy*♦ (1939); and Mrs. Darling in the musical version of *Peter Pan*♦ (1954).

Autobiography: *Four Flights Up,* Boston, 1964.

GILPIN, CHARLES S[IDNEY] (1878–1930) The black actor was born in Richmond, Va., and spent some time apprenticing as a printer's devil before taking to the stage in 1903. He toured for many years with black companies and in 1916 became director of the Lafayette Theatre♦ in Harlem, the first black stock company in the city. His fine performance on Broadway as William Curtis, the black clergyman, in *Abraham Lincoln* (1919), prompted Eugene O'Neill♦ to cast him as Brutus Jones in *The Emperor Jones.*♦ (1920) Although Gilpin's performance was praised, problems soon emerged. An arrogance born of sudden fame, coupled with an increasing drinking problem, made him difficult to work with. He was not signed for the London production, his role going to Paul Robeson,♦ whom many considered even better in the part. Gilpin rarely worked after *The Emperor Jones.* He appeared in a 1926 revival and in 1928 was cast for a part in *The Front Page,*♦ but when he appeared at rehearsal too drunk to act, he was dismissed and the role eliminated. He never again performed professionally. Moss Hart,♦ who acted Smithers in the 1926 revival, wrote of Gilpin, "He had an inner violence and a maniacal power that engulfed the audience." Hart concluded, "Gilpin was the greatest actor of his race."

GILROY, FRANK D., see *Subject Was Roses, The*

GILSON, LOTTIE [née LYDA DEAGON] (1869?–1912) Billed as "The Little Magnet," she was one of the most popular entertainers in the last years of Tony Pastor's♦ heyday. Today her figure would be considered plump, but it was pleasing to her generation, and, while playgoers generally agreed she was hardly beautiful, she had a winning personality that allowed her to put over both tear-jerkers and songs that were considered risqué. Her most celebrated song was "The Sunshine of Paradise Alley." She is reputed to have been the first blatant song-plugger, for a fee introducing even the dreariest material. She is also credited with being the first vaudeville performer to plant in the audience a stooge who would sing along with her.

Gin Game, The a play in two acts by D. L. Coburn. Produced by the Shubert Organization♦ at the John Golden Theatre. October 6, 1977. 517 performances. PP.

At a home for the aged, cantankerous, somewhat unstable Weller Martin (Hume Cronyn♦) invites Fonsia Dorsey (Jessica Tandy♦) to play gin rummy with him. As the couple play, they reveal their personal histories. But Fonsia's persistent winning provokes Weller's ire, and when he explodes in a profane rage, the games are apparently over.

This play may well come to exemplify the sorry or peculiar state of American play-writing of its day. Soaring costs made two-character plays a commonplace, and this was the first to win a Pulitzer Prize. ♦ Almost by necessity these plays had minimal plots and action, consisting instead simply of dialogue. Yet when this play toured, it was often performed in large auditoriums, and the Cronyns, supposedly fine, thoroughly trained actors, frequently resorted to amplification. Thus the production offered neither real drama nor genuine intimacy; not even totally live theatre.

D. L. Coburn was born in Baltimore in 1938, then spent time in the navy and in business before writing this, his first play.

GINGOLD, HERMIONE [FERDINANDA] (1897?–1987) The frowsy-miened comedienne who combined a certain hauteur with a streak of raffishness was born in London and was long a favorite on West End stages before making her American debut in *John Murray Anderson's Almanac* (1953). She later starred in several Broadway and West Coast productions and occasionally replaced other stars in shows, most notably in *Oh, Dad, Poor Dad.*♦ However, her most memorable Broadway role was the grande dame, Mme. Armfeldt, in *A Little Night Music*♦ (1973).

GIRARDOT, ETIENNE (1856–1939) One of many actors remembered for a single role, the London-born actor captivated Broadway when he made his New York debut as Lord Fancourt Babberley, who helps his college roommate by dressing as an old lady and pretending he is *Charley's Aunt*♦ (1893). He later played in several revivals of the farce. Although he continued to appear regularly for the next forty years, often in important supporting roles, he never again equaled his early success. Among his other roles was Valentine, opposite Mrs. Fiske♦ in *Leah Kleschna*♦ (1904). His last assignment was as Matthew Clark, the religious zealot, in the original *Twentieth Century*♦ (1932).

GIRAUDOUX, [Hippolyte] Jean (1882–1944) Thanks to a number of fine productions, Giraudoux has been the most successful of more serious modern French playwrights in the American theatre. Although several of his plays failed, he met varying measures of popularity with four works: *Amphitryon 38* (1937), *The Madwoman of Chaillot* (1948), *Ondine* (1954); and *Tiger at the Gates* (1955). His best works were felicitously witty mixtures of fantasy and realism.

Girl and the Judge, *The,* a play in four acts by Clyde Fitch.◆ Produced by Charles Frohman◆ at the Lyceum Theatre.◆ December 4, 1901. 125 performances.

When Judge Chartris (Orrin Johnson) grants the Stantons a separation he allows their daughter Winifred (Annie Russell◆) to choose which parent she will live with. She elects to live with her mother, for she knows the real reasons for the separation, a reason she withheld from the judge. Mrs. Stanton (Mrs. McKee Rankin) is a kleptomaniac, and Winifred hopes to cure her. The judge has fallen in love with Winifred and proposes. His mother, old Mrs. Chartris (Mrs. Gilbert◆), comes to visit, and Mrs. Stanton promptly steals the lady's jewels. Winifred forces her mother to confess. Mrs. Stanton's husband returns and agrees to accompany her to a special home.

Fitch took the story from a real incident told to him by an Ohio judge. The play was the last to be seen at the old Lyceum.

Girl Crazy, a musical comedy in two acts. Book by Guy Bolton◆ and Jack McGowan.◆ Lyrics by Ira Gershwin.◆ Music by George Gershwin.◆ Produced by Alex A. Aarons◆ and Vinton Freedley◆ at the Alvin Theatre. October 14, 1930. 272 performances.

Fleeing night-clubs, gambling casinos, and women, Danny Churchill (Allen Kearns◆) hires a New York taxi driven by Gieber Goldfarb (Willie Howard◆) to take him to Custerville, Arizona. There Danny hopes to rest on a dude ranch. Before long, however, he has transformed the ranch into a club with gambling rooms and bevies of girls. One of the girls is Molly Gray (Ginger Rogers), whom Danny woos and wins, another is Kate Fothergill (Ethel Merman◆), daughter of a local saloonkeeper.

Principal songs: Bidin' My Time · Boy! What Love Has Done to Me! · But Not for Me · Embraceable You · I Got Rhythm · Sam and Delilah

This was the last traditional musical comedy by the Gershwins before they attempted their political satires. The show was Miss Merman's debut, and her singing of "I Got Rhythm" and "Sam and Delilah" helped propel her to stardom.

Girl from Utah, *The* A 1913 English musical with book by James T. Tanner, lyrics by Percy Greenbank, Adrian Ross, and Paul A. Rubens, and music by Rubens and Sidney Jones, it told of an American girl who is pursued to England by a Mormon, but who is saved from a bigamous marriage by a handsome musical comedy star. Charles Frohman◆ presented the American version at the Knickerbocker Theatre on August 24, 1914, with Julia Sanderson,◆ Joseph Cawthorn,◆ and Donald Brian◆ in the leading roles. What made this production so important in American musical theatre history were its Jerome Kern◆ interpolations, which included "The Land of Let's Pretend," "Same Sort of Girl," "Why Don't They Dance the Polka?," as well as "You Never Can Tell" and which made Kern a composer of major significance. But it was another Kern song which was the hit of the show: "They Didn't Believe Me."◆ This song singlehandedly established the ascendancy of the modern 4/4 ballad over the older waltz and set the pattern for musical comedy love songs for the next half-century or more.

Girl I Left Behind Me, *The,* an "American Drama" in four acts by David Belasco◆ and Franklin Fyles.◆ Produced by Charles Frohman◆ at the Empire Theatre.◆ January 25, 1893. 208 performances.

When American soldiers disrupt a Blackfoot Indian religious ceremony, the Indians, led by Jack Ladru or Scar Brow (Theodore Roberts), plan their revenge. Their hope is to cut off communication between Fort Assinaboine and Post Kennion, both in Blackfoot territory in Montana, then attack the post. The post is named after General Kennion (Frank Mordaunt), whose daughter Kate (Sydney Armstrong) loves one of its officers, Lt. Edgar Hawkesworth (William Morris◆). But his rival for Kate's hand, Lt. Morton Parlow (Nelson Wheatcroft), spreads stories of Hawkesworth's cowardice, which circumstances lend credence to. Only when Hawkesworth rides through the hostile Indian forces to call for relief are matters set right. Seeing Kate and Hawkesworth embrace, the General comments, "This looks like—union forever."

According to Belasco, Frohman commissioned the play in order to open the Empire Theatre with an American work on a native theme. The drama's modern editors, Glenn Hughes and George Savage, remarked, "The keynote of the play was suspense, and it was suspense *par excellence* that Belasco's maturing art achieved in its production." The play was revived regularly for a decade after its premiere.

Girl of the Golden West, The, a play in four acts by David Belasco.♦ Produced by Belasco at the Belasco Theatre. November 14, 1905. 224 performances.

The Girl (Blanche Bates♦), whose name is really Minnie Falconer, may be the owner of the Polka Saloon in a California mining camp called Cloudy Mountain, but she is also the town's respected schoolmarm, and she is courted by the gentlemanly but dangerous sheriff, Jack Rance (Frank Keenan). While the town seeks a bandit named Ramerrez, The Girl falls in love with a handsome young man named Dick Johnson (Robert Hilliard♦), who she soon discovers is none other than the hunted bandit. When Johnson is shot by Rance, The Girl hides him in her loft, but his whereabouts are revealed to Rance by blood dripping from the ceiling. The Girl agrees to play a game of poker with Rance, Johnson's fate to be determined by the winner. She cheats to win, pulling a pair of aces from her petticoat after distracting the sheriff. However, the miners would still hang Johnson. Only The Girl's pleas spare him. Reluctantly she agrees to leave her beloved golden hills, and she and Johnson ride off to find a new life.

Responding to criticism about the mechanics of his plot, especially the dripping blood, Belasco wrote, "I know the period of Forty-nine as I know my alphabet, and there are things in my *The Girl of the Golden West* truer than many of the incidents in Bret Harte." However, Belasco's biographer, Craig Timberlake, has suggested the many debts the dramatist owed Harte, among them a heroine who ran a Polka Saloon. Typical of Belasco's striking theatrical effects was his opening, in which a vertically moving panorama took audiences from The Girl's cabin high in the hills down a path to the front of the saloon. The rest of the stage was then lit to reveal the first act set. The play was made into an opera by Puccini in 1910.

Girl with the Green Eyes, The, a play in four acts by Clyde Fitch.♦ Produced by Charles Frohman♦ at the Savoy Theatre. December 25, 1902. 108 performances.

A streak of pathological jealousy besets the Tillmans. Geoffrey Tillman (John W. Albaugh, Jr.), having married a housemaid while drunk, enters into a bigamous marriage with Ruth Chester (Lucille Flaven) lest a rival wed her. Geoffrey tells his brother-in-law, John Austin (Robert Drouet), of his first marriage but John learns the horrifying truth when Ruth reveals she, too, has married him. Ruth breaks down while telling John the news, and John's wife Jinny (Clara Bloodgood♦), who is also Geoffrey's sister, enters in time to misconstrue the scene. Her jealousy is boundless, and destroys Jinny and John's marriage, John refusing to betray the dark secret he has learned. Jinny is driven to attempt suicide, but John arrives to rescue her.

What to many critics was a play moving compellingly toward tragedy was marred by the contrived happy ending which Fitch felt obligated to attach in order to assure popular acceptance. Some other critics felt the play was weakened by an absence of any genuine motive for John Austin's persistent silence.

GISH, DOROTHY, see *Gish, Lillian*

GISH, LILLIAN (b. 1899?) Born in Springfield, Ohio, she made her debut at a small theatre in Rising Sun, Ohio, in 1902, in the melodrama *In Convict Stripes*. She continued in children's roles for many years, once acting with Sarah Bernhardt, ♦ and later under David Belasco.♦ She left the stage to become one of the first important silent film stars and did not return to Broadway until 1930, when she appeared as Helena in *Uncle Vanya*. Two years later she played Marguerite Gautier in *Camille.*♦ Among her subsequent assignments were Ophelia to John Gielgud's Hamlet (1936) and Martha Minch, who is returned to the days of her youth and given a chance to rearrange her life, in *The Star Wagon*♦ (1937). She served as replacement of the leads in such important plays as *The Old Maid*♦ and *Life With Father*♦ and also gave highly praised performances in a number of failures. Her sister, Dorothy (1898–1968), had a similar career of early stage parts and later success in films before returning to New York in 1928 as Fay Hilary, who tries some mate-swapping, in *Young Love*. Later appearances included Aaronetta Gibbs, the unhappy spinster sister, in *Morning's at Seven*♦ (1939) and Fanny Dixwell Holmes, the Chief Justice's wife, in *The Magnificent Yankee* (1946). Like Lillian, she was one of many actresses to serve a stint as Vinnie, the mother in *Life with Father*.

Autobiography [Lillian]: *Dorothy and Lillian Gish*, New York, 1973.

Gladiator, *The,* a tragedy in five acts by Robert Montgomery Bird.♦ Produced at the Park Theatre.♦ September 26, 1831. In repertory.

To free his wife, Senona (Mrs. Sharpe) and young son (Julia Turnbull), the captive Thracian, Spartacus (Edwin Forrest♦), agrees to fight in a Roman gladiatorial contest. But when his opponent turns out to be his brother, Phasarius (Thomas Barry♦), and the Romans insist they fight to the death, the brothers decide to rebel. Spartacus cries:

> Death to the Roman fiends, that make their mirth
> Out of the groans of bleeding misery!
> Ho, slaves, arise! It is your hour to kill!
> Kill, and spare not—For wrath and liberty!—
> Freedom for bondmen—freedom and revenge!

But Phasarius' impetuosity, aggravated by his obsession with the praetor's niece Julia (Mrs. Wallack), undermines their plans. With his brother, wife, and son all dead, Spartacus fights on until he, too, is slain.

One of Forrest's most successful roles—he played it more than 1000 times—the actor never fully paid Bird for the work, but at the same time refused to allow Bird or his heirs to publish it. After Forrest's death, it was revived by John McCullough and others until the end of the century.

Glance at New York, A, a "local drama" in two acts by Benjamin A. Baker.♦ Produced by William Mitchell♦ at the Olympic Theatre. February 15, 1848. Approx. 75 performances.

When George Parsells (G. Clark), a "green-horn" from the country, comes to New York to visit his cousin Harry Gordon (G. J. Arnold), they embark on a tour of the city, often encountering the most unsavory con-men, but they also disguise themselves as women to enter a "ladies' bowling saloon." Helping them out of their scrapes, and once or twice unwittingly getting them into trouble, is a handsome, rugged fireman, Mose (Frank Chanfrau♦), one of the "B'hoys."

One of the earliest, and certainly the most successful, of American plays using the tour-of-the-city theme taken from Pierce Egan's *Tom and Jerry; or, Life in London,* the play was performed in city after city, with the title and setting changed to reflect local pride and points of interest. It made frequent use of contemporary slang, until then a rarity in plays. The show boosted the career of Frank Chanfrau, who played in numerous other sequels written around the character of Mose, and also performed in local versions in such cities as Philadelphia, New Orleans, Cincinnati, Chicago, Montreal, and Louisville as late as 1857.

GLASER, Lulu (1874–1958) Born in Allegheny City, Penn., she came to Broadway with no previous professional experience and was placed in the chorus of *The Lion Tamer* (1891), where she was assigned to understudy the prima donna. In one of those rare instances when a popular theatrical motif becomes reality, she was catapulted to stardom when the leading lady was taken ill. The show's principal male comedian, Francis Wilson,♦ wrote, "She was graceful in form and action and had wonderfully luminous eyes," though he diplomatically neglected to mention that critics were divided about her singing ability. For the next twenty years she was a reigning favorite, appearing in revivals of *The Merry Monarch* (1892) and *Erminie*♦ (1893); and in *The Devil's Deputy* (1894); *The Chieftain* (1895); *Half a King* (1896); *The Little Corporal* (1898); *Cyrano de Bergerac* (1899), the Victor Herbert♦ operetta; *Sweet Anne Page* (1900); *The Prima Donna* (1901); *Dolly Varden* (1902), her greatest success; *The Madcap Princess* (1904); *Miss Dolly Dollars* (1905); *Lola from Berlin* (1907); *The Merry Widow Burlesque* (1908); *Mlle. Mischief* (1908); and *The Girl and the Kaiser* (1910). She performed in several straight plays and was long popular in vaudeville.

GLASPELL, Susan (1882–1948) Born in Davenport, Iowa, the playwright and novelist studied at Drake University and the University of Chicago. With her husband, George Cram Cook,♦ she was a founder and director of the Provincetown Players.♦ Alone or with Cook, she wrote several one-act plays for the troupe, including *Suppressed Desires* (1914), a spoof of the then new psychoanalysis; *Trifles* (1916), showing the provocations that lead a farm wife to kill her husband; *Close the Book* (1917), which depicts the consequences of a respectable young girl's believing her parents were gypsies; *A Woman's Honor* (1918), in which women will lie to win the love of a handsome murderer but he prefers to die for having defended a woman's honor; and *Tickless Time* (1918), in which a couple replace their clocks with a sun-dial to protest mechanization. Her full-length works include *Bernice* (1919), in which a woman is fully understood only after her death; *The Inheritors* (1921), depicting the generation gap between liberals and conservatives; *The Verge* (1921), portraying a woman's mental breakdown; and *Alison's House*♦ (1930), in which the secrets of a long-dead spinster-poet are revealed and which won the Pulitzer Prize.♦ With her second husband, Norman Matson, she wrote *The Comic Artist,* in which a cartoonist learns that real life is as violent as his cartoons. The work was successfully presented in

Europe in the late 1920s, but failed when brought to America in 1933. Shortly after the commercial failure of this play she abandoned the theatre. Her plays often reflected the most advanced intellectual thinking of her time and recorded her frequently telling observations, although many of them seemed more like literary exercises than theatrically knowing and effective dramas.

Glass Menagerie, The, a drama in two acts by Tennessee Williams.♦ Produced by Eddie Dowling♦ and Louis J. Singer at the Playhouse. March 31, 1945. 561 performances. NYDCCA.

Looking back, Tom Wingfield (Dowling) recalls his life in a shoddy St. Louis tenement with his mother Amanda (Laurette Taylor♦), who lives in dreams of a probably imaginary past, and his crippled sister Laura (Julie Haydon♦), who seems to live only for a collection of glass animals. At Amanda's insistence, Tom invites a friend from the warehouse where he works. That friend, Jim (Anthony Ross), went to high school with Laura, who has long been quietly in love with his memory. The evening proves a disaster. Jim persuades Laura to dance with him, only to break her favorite glass unicorn as they move about. Then Jim mentions he is engaged to be married. After Jim has gone, Amanda scolds Tom, who runs off to join the merchant marine.

Called "a memory play" by Williams, and "a mood-memory play" by some later writers, it was hailed by Ward Morehouse♦ of the *Sun* as "fragile and poignant . . . a vivid, eerie and curiously enchanting play." Its success placed Williams in the front ranks of contemporary dramatists. Miss Taylor's performance was considered one of the memorable acting gems of the time. Pauline Lord♦ headed the road company. A 1983 revival with Jessica Tandy♦ failed.

GLASS, Montague [Marsden] (1877–1934) The English-born playwright and short story writer was brought to America while very young and began his career by contributing to various magazines. All his successful plays were collaborations, and many of them were based on his stories about a pair of comic Jewish business partners: *Potash and Perlmutter*♦ (1913), written with Charles Klein♦; *Abe and Mawruss* (1915), written with Roi Cooper Megrue♦; *Business Before Pleasure*♦ (1917), written with Jules Eckert Goodman♦; *His Honor Abe Potash* (1919), with Goodman; *Partners Again* (1922), with Goodman; and *Potash and Perlmutter, Detectives* (1926),

with Goodman. Although several of his other plays received favorable notices, they had short runs.

GLEASON, [Herbert John] Jackie (1916–87) The burly, aggressive Brooklyn-born comedian is best known to Americans for his popular television series. He first appeared on Broadway in *Keep Off the Grass* (1940), but is recalled primarily for his clowning in *Follow the Girls*♦ (1944), *Along Fifth Avenue* (1949), and *Take Me Along*♦ (1959).

GLEASON, James (1886–1959) Born in New York into an old family of troupers, he was carried on stage at the age of two, then performed around the country with numerous touring and stock companies. He returned to New York in 1914 to appear in *Pretty Mrs. Smith*. He soon graduated to such important roles as Nathaniel Alden, who returns to his hometown pretending to be a millionaire, in *Like a King* (1921), and James Leland, the disillusioned playwright, in *The Deep Tangled Wildwood* (1923), before scoring a major success as "Hap" Hurley, the tough-talking fight manager, in *Is Zat So?*♦ (1925), which he wrote with Richard Taber. Later that same season he collaborated with George Abbott♦ to write another hit, *The Fall Guy*♦ (1925), centering on a young, befuddled married man tricked into helping a dope ring. With his wife, Lucille Webster, he wrote *The Shannons of Broadway* (1927), a successful comedy about two troupers determined to give up the theatre. He also produced several plays. With the coming of sound films, he moved to Hollywood, where he was long typecast in tough guy roles.

Glengarry Glen Ross, a play in two acts by David Mamet.♦ Produced at the Golden Theatre. March 25, 1984. 378 performances. PP.

In three separate scenes at a Chinese restaurant: Shelly Levene (Robert Prosky), a failing real-estate salesman, pleads with his boss, John Williamson (J. T. Walsh), for a better list of prospects; Dave Moss (James Tolkan) tries to inveigle George Aaronow (Mike Nussbaum) into robbing the real-estate office to obtain the same lists; and the high-flying Richard Roma (Joe Mantegna) hustles James Lingk (Lane Smith), an unsuspecting prospect. However, when the office is burglarized it turns out that Levene, not Aaronow, is the culprit. Moss quits, Aaronow reluctantly continues in a job he hates, and the foul-mouthed Roma continues to bull his way from sale to sale.

This "drama-cum-comedy," as Bernard Weiner of the San Francisco *Chronicle* branded it, was an unflinching, powerful play doing for the cynical, hard-nosed real-estate world of the 1980s what *The Front Page* did for the newspaper world of the 1920s.

GLENVILLE, PETER (b. 1913) London-born, he has been active in England as an actor, producer, and director, but is known in America primarily for his staging. Among the many shows to carry his stamp have been *The Browning Version* (1949), *The Innocents* (1950), *Separate Tables* (1956), his own translation of *Hotel Paradiso* (1957), *Take Me Along*♦ (1959), *Becket* (1960), and *A Patriot for Me* (1969).

GOATCHER, PHILIP W. (1852–1931) The son of a London scene painter, he served his apprenticeship under his father, then worked in Australia before coming to America in 1875. After several seasons at the Park Theatre he became the principal set designer at Wallack's.♦ Among his many notable achievements were the settings for the W. H. Crane♦-Stuart Robson♦ *Comedy of Errors* (1878), such Wallack productions as *The Silver King* (1883) and *Hoodman Blind* (1885), the musical *The Lady or the Tiger?* (1888), and Daly's♦ 1889 revival of *As You Like It.*♦ Of his work for *Hoodman Blind,* the *Times* noted, "The views of English rural scenery by Mr. Philip Goatcher are full of mellow beauty: A moonlit grove, with a rustic stile and winding pathway, is notable for excellent perspective; the Thames Embankment scene, showing the Egyptian Column, the semicircle of lights, and the 'dark, flowing' river called forth a storm of cheers when displayed. Mr. Goatcher was summoned to the front three times during the evening." After losing a divorce case in 1890, he returned to England, then moved to Australia, where he remained an important scene painter until just before World War I.

GODFREY, THOMAS (1736–1763) Born in Philadelphia, his father, the elder Thomas Godfrey, was the inventor of a sea quadrant. He was thirteen when his father died and he was apprenticed to a watchmaker, but William Smith, provost of the College of Philadelphia, saw potential in the boy, released him from his indentures, and began his education. Smith had encouraged dramatic performances at the school and young Godfrey quickly found theatricals to his liking. He wrote his first and only play, *The Prince of Parthia,*♦ while still in his early twenties. At the same time Smith helped him obtain a commission in the Pennsylvania militia. He served in the expedition against Fort Duquesne and later was promoted to lieutenant. Shortly thereafter he moved to North Carolina, where he died of a sudden fever. His play was not mounted until after his death, when

it became the first American work to be given a professional performance. Godfrey was also a poet of some repute.

Godspell, a musical in two acts. Book by John-Michael Tebelak. Music and lyrics by Stephen Schwartz.♦ Produced at the Cherry Lane Theatre. May 17, 1971. 2,124 performances.

John the Baptist interrupts a meeting of the great men of history, from Socrates to Buckminster Fuller, to announce the coming of Jesus. This Jesus (Stephen Nathan) sports a red nose, a heart painted on his forehead, and a Superman shirt. His history, following the Gospel according to St. Matthew, is then told by means of circus and commedia dell' arte tricks, a parody of TV quiz shows, cartoon voices, and similar devices.

Principal song: Day by Day

Although no one found the treatment of the gospel sacrilegious, many critics objected to a persistent tone of cuteness. For the most part, playgoers apparently disagreed, so not only did it enjoy a long run off-Broadway but it was revived on Broadway at the Broadhurst Theatre in 1976 and ran an additional 527 performances.

GOETZ, E. RAY (1886–1954) Born in Buffalo, N. Y., he began to write lyrics and sometimes melodies for Broadway shows in 1910, when he set words to A. Baldwin Sloan's♦ score for *The Prince of Bohemia.* He remained active until better songwriters emerged about the time of World War I. Thereafter he confined himself largely to producing, mounting several musicals for his wife, Irene Bordoni—*As You Were* (1920); *The French Doll* (1922); and *Paris* (1928), as well as several of Cole Porter's earliest musicals—*Paris; Fifty Million Frenchmen*♦ (1929); and *The New Yorkers* (1930).

GOETZ, RUTH and AUGUSTUS, see *Heiress, The*

Gold Diggers, The, a comedy in three acts by Avery Hopwood.♦ Produced by David Belasco♦ at the Lyceum Theatre.♦ September 30, 1919. 720 performances.

When rich, proper Stephen Lee (Bruce McRae♦) learns that his nephew, Wally Saunders (Austen Harrison), would marry a chorus girl, Violet Dayne (Beverly West), he is duly alarmed. He decides to talk to Jerry Lamar (Ina Claire♦), a worldly-wise show girl he has known and who, he learns, has taken Violet under her wing. Jerry assures Stephen that Violet is an exception to the rule that all chorus girls are out to marry rich men solely for their money, a rule exemplified by Mable Monroe (Jobyna Howland), Trixie Andrews (Lilyan Tashman), Eleanor Montgomery (Luella Gear♦), and Gypsy Montrose (Gladys Feldman). But while she is reassuring Stephen she is also plying him with whiskey. When he is drunk he proposes, and she accepts. Because she is in love with him, she soon confesses her trickery, but since Stephen loves her in return, he is forgiving.

Although Arthur Hornblow♦ of *Theatre*♦ magazine typified the many negative critical reactions when he dismissed the play as a "trivial hodge-podge of chorus girl slang, bedroom suggestiveness and false sentiment," the play was the second longest-running show in Broadway history when it closed, and it gave popular currency to the expression "gold digger." In the original production one celebrated bit part was Cissie Gray, the oldtime Broadway beauty reduced to peddling soap. The role was played by the musical comedy queen of decades earlier, Pauline Hall.♦ The play later was the basis of several successful Hollywood musicals.

Golden Apple, The, a musical in two acts. Libretto by John Latouche.♦ Music by Jerome Moross. Produced by the Phoenix Theatre♦ at the Phoenix Theatre. March 11, 1954. 173 performances. NYDCCA

Angel's Roost, Washington, is a small turn-of-the-century American village where little that is exciting seems to happen. Matters change at an annual fair when a traveling salesman, Paris (Jonathan Lucas), arrives in a balloon and so beguiles Helen (Kaye Ballard), the wife of Sheriff Menelaus (Dean Michener), that she elopes with him to Rhododendron. Ulysses (Stephen Douglass) and his neighbors pursue the pair, while Rhododendron's mayor, Hector (Jack Whiting♦), throws road blocks in the pursuers' path. After Ulysses outclasses Paris in a boxing match, the Angel's Roost soldiers begin their detour-laden journey home, where Ulysses finds Penelope (Priscilla Gillette) waiting for him.

Principal songs: Doomed, Doomed, Doomed · Lazy Afternoon

This brilliant re-creation of *The Iliad* and *The Odyssey* in terms of 1900 America garnered general critical approbation and won the New York Drama Critics Circle Award♦ as the best musical of the season, but failed to find a large public. While there was virtually no dialogue, Latouche's adroit, witty lyrics and Moross's charming music were at once contemporary yet period in flavor. Thus, in the song "Scylla and Charybdis" the returning soldiers were beguiled by two shady financial manipulators to a melody and words reminiscent of Gallagher♦ and Shean.♦ The show has enjoyed several revivals.

Golden Boy, a drama in three acts by Clifford Odets.♦ Produced by the Group Theatre♦ at the Belasco Theatre. November 4, 1937. 250 performances.

Although Joe Bonaparte (Luther Adler♦) knows his father (Morris Carnovsky♦) wants him to become a violinist, Joe feels the best way out of the slums is with his fists, as a professional fighter. He enjoys some early victories, and, when he breaks his hand, doubts about his choice seem resolved. "Hallelujah!! It's the beginning of the world!" he exclaims. But that world quickly turns sour when his girl, Laura (Frances Farmer), seems to desert him and when he kills a man in the ring. Laura returns to console Joe, and the two drive off. They are killed in a car crash.

One of Odets's least political early plays, "its pungent, flashy story" was marred, according to Brooks Atkinson♦ of the *Times,* by "an unwillingness to be simple in style." For all its faults it proved popular and has been revived frequently, most notably in 1952 with John Garfield.♦ It was also the basis for a 1964 black musical of the same name, starring Sammy Davis, Jr.♦

GOLDEN, JOHN (1874–1955) Born in New York, his first theatrical job was as a super at Niblo's Garden.♦ He later entered New York University, intending to study law, but while there produced a college play and abandoned the notion of becoming a lawyer. He served briefly as actor-manager for a touring company, then turned his hand to lyric writing. His major successes as a lyricist included "Goodbye Girls, I'm Through" (from the 1914 musical *Chin-Chin*♦) and "Poor Butterfly" (from *The Big Show,* a 1916 Hippodrome♦ extravaganza). Royalties from these songs allowed him to produce his first play, *Turn to the Right*♦ (1916). Among his many later productions were *Lightnin'*♦ (1918); *Three Wise Fools*♦ (1918); *The First Year*♦ (1920); *Seventh Heaven*♦ (1922); *The Wisdom Tooth*♦ (1926); *Let Us Be Gay*♦ (1929); *That's Gratitude* (1930); *As Husbands Go*♦ (1931); *Susan and God*♦ (1937); *Skylark* (1939); and *Claudia*♦ (1941). Some measure of his acute judgment of contemporary public taste can be gauged by the fact that, at the time of *Seventh Heaven*'s closing, Golden was on record as the producer of three of the five longest-running shows in Broadway history, with *Lightnin'* in first place, *The First Year* in fourth place, and *Seventh Heaven* in fifth. For the most part his plays avoided material that might offend many playgoers. He wrote in his autobiography, "I think *Mrs. Warren's Profession* is a great play, but personally I prefer *Turn to the Right*. Given equal literary value, I should infinitely prefer a wholesome play. Where there is a wide discrepancy in literary merit, I confess I still lean towards wholesomeness." In 1926 he built the John Golden Theatre but lost it in the Depression. He later purchased the more centrally located Masque Theatre and renamed it for himself.

Autobiography: *Stage-Struck John Golden,* with Viola Brothers Shore, New York, 1930.

GOLDFADEN, Avrom (1840–1908) Often called the "Father of Yiddish Theatre," he is generally acknowledged to have been the first to put it on a professional basis and to have written its earliest plays, which remained part of the repertory as long as Yiddish theatre flourished. He was born in Russia and spent most of his life in Europe. His first trip to America was in 1887, but his reception was cool since many performers, with whom he had worked in Europe, considered him too arrogant and his plays dated. When he first appeared at a New York theatre for rehearsal, the cast walked out, so he was forced to find other actors and produce his play himself. It failed, and after several attempts to produce Yiddish drama in other American cities he returned home. One story of this trip tells of Boris Thomashefsky♦ being so shocked by the playwright's threadbare shoes that he bought him a new pair. He returned to New York in 1902, living largely off doles contributed by Thomashefsky and Jacob Adler.♦ His last play, *Ben-Ami* (Son of My People), was produced in New York shortly before his death. Among his plays long popular with Yiddish-speaking audiences in America were *Koldunye* (The Witch); *Bar Kochba* (The Last Days of Jerusalem); and his masterpiece, *Shulamis.*

GOLDMAN, James, see *Lion in Winter, The*

GOLDSMITH, Clifford, see *What a Life*

Good Gracious Annabelle, a play in three acts by Clare Kummer.♦ Produced by Arthur Hopkins♦ at the Republic Theatre. October 31, 1916. 111 performances.

A group of nice young things have gathered at the posh St. Swithen Hotel. They are nice, but they are all broke. So when one of their group, a pert lady named Annabelle Leigh (Lola Fisher), suggests they sign on as servants at the Wimbledon mansion on Long Island, they agree. Annabelle was married to a strange mining man when she was sixteen. She ran away, but he has continued to support her, although she regularly lives beyond her means. The new servants find the mansion has been rented in Wimbledon's absence by a handsome, rich miner, John Rawson (Walter Hampden♦). When Wimbledon returns unexpectedly, he and Rawson prove to be rivals, at first only in business but soon for Annabelle. Rawson wins, turning out to be not merely a decent man but Annabelle's old husband as well.

Miss Kummer had originally approached Hopkins, hoping to have her script turned into a musical, but Hopkins liked the piece as written. Alexander Woollcott♦ described the farce as belonging to "the leisure class," adding, "It is idle with a lorgnette and orange pekoe idleness. At times it is a little vague within, but it is always vogue without." The play might have run longer but for the depression that hit Broadway immediately before our entry into World War I. Ironically, when the show was finally turned into a musical, with Ziegfeld♦ as producer, it failed. The musical version was called simply *Annie Dear* (1924).

Good News!, a musical comedy in two acts. Book by Laurence Schwab♦ and B. G. De Sylva.♦ Lyrics by De Sylva and Lew Brown.♦ Music by Ray Henderson.♦ Produced by Schwab and Frank Mandel♦ at the 46th Street Theatre. September 6, 1927. 557 performances.

Tom Marlowe (John Price Jones), the star of football-mad Tait College's team, may not be able to play if he fails his astronomy exam. Connie Lane (Mary Lawlor) agrees to tutor Tom, since she loves him even if she suspects he really loves another girl. Tom passes, Tait wins, and Connie gets Tom.

Principal songs: The Best Things in Life Are Free · Good News · Just Imagine · Lucky in Love · Varsity Drag

This melodic, roistering musical has often been called the quintessential musical of the 1920s. Walter Winchell♦ welcomed the show as "flip, fast, furious, free and flamingly festive." A botched 1974 revival lasted only two weeks in New York.

Goodbye Again, a comedy in three acts by Allan Scott and George Haight. Produced at the Masque Theatre. December 28, 1932. 212 performances.

Years before Kenneth Bixby (Osgood Perkins♦) had become a famous author, he had a brief affair with a fatuous, wispy young lady named Julia (Katherine Squire). Now that he is successful and lecturing around the country, Julia suddenly appears at his hotel room, anxious to rekindle the old flame. By this time, however, Julia is Mrs. Wilson, and Mr. Wilson (Leslie Adams) soon appears on the scene to further complicate Kenneth's life. Luckily Kenneth's loyal, loving secretary, Anne Rogers (Sally Bates), is also on the scene, and she finally helps Kenneth explain away everything. Kenneth begins to look at Anne in a new light.

Writing in *Judge*, George Jean Nathan♦ praised the work as "A humorously observant fable . . . told with a saucy eye to authentic character."

Goodbye, My Fancy, a comedy in three acts by Fay Kanin. Produced at the Morosco Theatre. November 17, 1948. 446 performances.

Agatha Reid (Madeleine Carroll), a famous liberal author and Congresswoman, returns to her alma mater to accept an honorary degree. She had been expelled years before, covering up for her fiancé. Now that ex-fiancé James Merrill (Conrad Nagel) is the president of the college. He is also a widower and a stuffy, confirmed arch-conservative. Nevertheless he falls in love with Agatha again. But Agatha is repelled by his politics, so after threatening to reveal the truth about her expulsion if he doesn't allow his daughter to pursue her own liberal ways, she heads off with a charming magazine photographer.

An amusing if slightly preachy play, its success was enhanced by the popularity of the former film star, Miss Carroll. Mrs. Kanin was an actress and screen writer, as well as the sister-in-law of Garson Kanin. ♦

GOODMAN, JULES ECKERT (1876–1962) Born in Gervais, Ore., and educated at Harvard and Columbia, he spent some time as a journalist, including a stint on the *Dramatic Mirror,*♦ before turning his hand to play-writing. Most of his plays were adaptations or collaborations, but he enjoyed a few small successes with original, solo efforts. His first long run was with *Mother* (1910), in which the mother stands by her erring sons even if it means family ruin. Subsequent successes included *The Silent Voice* (1914), based on a story by Gouverneur Morris recounting how a snooper unwittingly discovers his wife's infidelity; *Treasure Island*♦ (1915), based on Stevenson's novel; and *The Man Who Came Back*♦ (1916), based on John Fleming Wilson's novel telling the tale of a prodigal son. Several of his most popular works were collaborations with Montague Glass♦ on the Potash and Perlmutter series: *Business Before Pleasure*♦ (1917); *His Honor Abe Potash* (1919); *Partners Again* (1922); and *Potash and Perlmutter, Detectives* (1926). Two other moderately popular plays were *Chains* (1923), in which a

rebellious flapper rejects parental demands that she marry her lover; and *Many Mansions* (1937), written with his son Eckert, in which a progressive theology student battles religious orthodoxy.

GOODMAN, PHILIP (1885–1940) The self-educated, Philadelphia-born entrepreneur used some of his profits from his garment district enterprises briefly to become a successful producer. His lightweight hits were *The Old Soak*♦ (1922), *Poppy* (1923), *The Ramblers* (1926), and *The Five O'Clock Girl* (1927). Curiously, his few attempts at trying something a little out of the ordinary all failed: Jerome Kern's♦ *Dear Sir* (1924), Marc Connelly's♦ *The Wild Man of Borneo* (1927), and Vincent Youmans's♦ *Rainbow* (1928). He also wrote a book of childhood reminiscences, *Franklin Street* (1942).

Goodman Theater Center of the Art Institute of Chicago Founded in 1925 with a memorial gift from the family of Kenneth Sawyer Goodman, who had been active in little theatre movements and had written some plays before being killed in World War I, the theatre was designed by Howard Van Doren Shaw and built alongside the Art Institute on Lake Shore Drive, where city ordinances relating to height forced it to be placed underground. It seats 683 playgoers. The theatre opened in 1925 with the first American performance of Galsworthy's♦ *The Forest,* and its resident company continued to mount original plays and classics until it was forced to disband temporarily in 1930 because of the Depression. It served as a drama school before it was reactivated in 1969. Since then it has continued to mount a responsible repertory in both the original auditorium and its smaller, more experimental Stage 2. The school was dissociated from the organization in 1978 and was moved to DePaul University.

Goodspeed Opera House (East Haddam, Conn.) Built in 1876 by William H. Goodspeed to contain a local playhouse and offices for his mercantile endeavors, the Victorian Gothic wooden structure closed as a theatre in 1920. In 1959, shortly before it was slated to be demolished, conservationists organized the Goodspeed Opera House Foundation to restore and reactivate the auditorium. It reopened in 1963. Since then it has presented three musicals each season, usually two revivals and one original. Great imagination and taste have been shown in the selection of offerings. Among the new musicals first tried out at the theatre have been *Man of La Mancha*♦; *Shenandoah*♦; *Something's Afoot;* and *Annie.* ♦ Similarly, an all too rare sense of responsibility, daring, and theatrical history have been manifest in the choice of revivals, which have ranged as far back as Sousa's♦ *El Capitan.*♦ Unfortunately, the mountings themselves have been bedeviled by a faithlessness that has prompted substantial revisions of text and interpolation of songs not written for the shows in question and by a tastelessness exemplified by stagings that lean toward a snickering style called "camp." These failings have not, however, displeased audiences and critics who seek light entertainment and are unruffled by purist considerations. In the 1980s a second theatre, named for Norma Terris, a musical star of the 20s and early 30s, was opened in hopes of promoting new works. Unfortunately, the project could not gain widespread support.

GOODWIN, J. Cheever (1850–1912) The first American to enjoy a long, successful career as a librettist, Goodwin was born in Boston, and graduated from Harvard. He spent a short time in support of E. A. Sothern♦ before joining forces with E. E. Rice♦ to write *Evangeline*♦ (1874), the musical burlesque which was to remain a favorite for the rest of the century. He continued to act and also translated French opéra bouffe♦ until *H.M.S. Pinafore*♦ (1879) began the modern rage for musicals, allowing him to work virtually full time at creating books and lyrics for musical shows. Among his more popular efforts were *The Merry Monarch* (1890); *Wang*♦ (1891); *Dr. Syntax* (1894); *Fleur-De-Lis* (1895); *Lost, Strayed or Stolen* (1896); and *An Arabian Girl and Forty Thieves* (1899). Noting that Goodwin had sold his rights in the hugely profitable *Wang* for a mere fifty dollars a week, De Wolf Hopper♦ in his autobiography said that the librettist never fully realized his abilities because of a lack of business acumen and a certain personal irresponsibility. "Had he possessed a rudder," Hopper observed, "Goodwin might have become the American Gilbert. Gilbert himself never excelled Goodwin's 'The Man with an Elephant on His Hands' song in 'Wang.' " Toward the end of his career he worked solely as a lyricist. He also wrote several straight plays and was active in politics.

GOODWIN, Nat[haniel Carl] (1857–1919) The comedian, who was as famous in his own day for his off-stage roistering as for his performances, was born in Boston and educated at the Little Blue Academy in Farmington, Maine. His acting in school productions came to the attention of several famous performers, and though he wanted to become an actor he spent some time as a clerk in a dry-goods store. Later Stuart Robson♦ gave him his

professional start when he persuaded John B. Stetson♦ to cast him as a shoeblack at Boston's Howard Atheneum♦ in *Law in New York* (1874). After appearing as a mimic at Tony Pastor's,♦ he played for several seasons in E. E. Rice's♦ musicals and then organized his own farce-comedy troupe, the Froliques. He performed in many written-to-order pieces such as *The Skating Rink* (1885); *Little Jack Sheppard* (1886), *Turned Up* (1886), and *Lend Me Five Shillings* (1887). He scored a major hit as Chauncey Short, the rich young man who proves to his fiancée that he can make a fortune on his own, in *A Gilded Fool* (1892). A year later he essayed a more serious role, Jim Rayburn, the sheriff who persuades his fiancée not to elope with a train robber, in *In Mizzoura.*♦ Augustus Thomas,♦ who wrote the play, recalled; "In person he [was] under the average height, and, then, was slight, graceful, and with a face capable of conveying the subtlest shades of feeling. The forehead was ample; the eyes were large and blue, clear and steady. The nose was mildly Roman; the hair was the colour of new hay. His voice was rich and modulated." Among his subsequent later successes were the title role in *Nathan Hale* (1899) and as Richard Carewe, who would reform the ways of an impish youngster, in *When We Were Twenty-one* (1900), both opposite his wife, Maxine Elliott.♦ His final success came shortly before his death, when he portrayed Uncle Everett, who talks glibly on divorce, but is a monogamist at heart, in *Why Marry?*♦ (1917). In his early career Goodwin espoused the broad, grotesque low comedy so popular at the time, but as styles changed so did he. In his later roles he was praised for his warmth and polished restraint. Although he longed throughout his career to play Shakespeare, his attempts at Bottom, the First Gravedigger, and Shylock were failures.

Autobiography: *Nat Goodwin's Book*, Boston, 1914.

Goose Hangs High, The, a play in three acts by Lewis Beach. Produced by the Dramatists' Theatre, Inc.♦ at the Bijou Theatre. January 29, 1924. 186 performances.

Bernard Ingals (Norman Trevor) and his wife have scraped and sacrificed so that their three children could have a better life. Bernard, in fact, gave up dreams of being a horticulturist, taking a political desk job instead. The children—Hugh (John Marston), Bradley (Eric Dressler), and Lois (Miriam Doyle)—seem indifferent to their parents' sacrifices, living expensively while chattering on about the benefits of socialism. Suddenly Ingals loses his job, and the children are forced to go to work. To everyone's surprise, they do so with gusto and skill. They even persuade their snobbish grandmother (Mrs. Thomas Whiffen♦) to set their father up in the horticultural business.

Although many critics questioned the facile happy ending, the play suggested that there was another, deeper, and more responsible side to the era's high-living flappers.

Beach was born in Saginaw, Mich. and educated at Harvard. His one-act play *The Clod* (1916) was produced by the Washington Square Players.♦ Later full-length works included *A Square Peg* (1923) and *Merry Andrew* (1929).

GORDIN, Jacob [Michailovitch] (1853–1909) Born in Russia, the son of a well-to-do merchant, he was given a good education, but soon came into conflict with growing Russian anti-Semitism. He emigrated to America in 1891 to help found a socialistic farming commune. When it failed he began to write plays to support his large family. His first play, *Siberia* (1891), was a success. His most famous plays were *The Jewish King Lear* (1892); *Mirele Efros* (1898), telling a similar story but with a woman as the tragic protagonist; a version of the Faust legend, *God, Man and Devil* (1900); and *The Kreutzer Sonata* (1902), depicting a woman's tragic downfall. In all he wrote at least 35 plays, and possibly many more, since he often employed pen names. Gordin eschewed the particularly Jewish stories, especially the sentimental and comic ones, that had been the mainstay of Yiddish theatres. He wanted to depict Jewish life in terms of larger and more universal themes. He also rebelled against the freewheeling ways of contemporary Yiddish actors, insisting they follow his dialogue precisely and wear clothes proper to the time and characters of his plays. His seriousness of purpose is generally said to have initiated the Golden Age of Yiddish-American theatre.

GORDON, Leon, see *White Cargo*

GORDON, Max [né Mechel Salpeter] (1892–1978) The New York-born producer started his career as a press agent for Hyde♦ and Behman,♦ later becoming a vaudeville agent. For a time he was associated with Sam H. Harris,♦ before embarking on his own. In the 1930s and during much of the 1940s he was one of Broadway's most successful producers. His offerings included: *Three's a Crowd* (1930), *The Band Wagon♦* (1931), *The Cat and the Fiddle♦* (1931), *Flying Colors* (1932), *Design for Living*

(1933), *Her Master's Voice♦* (1933), *Roberta♦* (1933), *Dodsworth♦* (1934), *The Great Waltz* (1934), *The Farmer Takes a Wife* (1934), *Jubilee♦* (1935), *Ethan Frome♦* (1936), *The Women♦* (1936), *My Sister Eileen♦* (1940), *Junior Miss♦* (1941), *The Doughgirls♦* (1942), *The Late George Apley♦* (1944), *Born Yesterday♦* (1945), and *The Solid Gold Cadillac♦* (1953). A small, professorial looking man, Gordon was known for his mercurial behavior, once perching himself on a window ledge and threatening to jump if money was not forthcoming for a new production. Nevertheless, George S. Kaufman♦ characterized him as "the comparable Max Gordon."

Autobiography: *Max Gordon Presents,* with Lewis Funke, New York, 1963.

GORDON [Jones], Ruth (1896–1985) Born in Wollaston, Mass., she determined to become an actress after watching Hazel Dawn♦ in *The Pink Lady.* ♦ To this end she studied at the American Academy of Dramatic Arts♦ before making her stage debut as Nibs opposite Maude Adams♦ in a 1915 revival of *Peter Pan.* ♦ One of her first important assignments was as Lola Pratt in *Seventeen♦* (1918), after which she played Cora Wheeler in the road company of *Clarence♦* (1920). Subsequent important roles included Bobby, who finds marriage disappointing, in *Saturday's Children♦* (1927); the title part of the guileless girl who loses her chance to marry a rich man, in *Serena Blandish* (1929); Mattie Silver, whose joint suicide attempt with the hero leaves them both crippled, in *Ethan Frome♦* (1936); Mrs. Pinchwife in a revival of *The Country Wife* (1936); Nora in *A Doll's House* (1937); Natasha in *The Three Sisters* (1942); Paula Wharton, a writer who helps her husband through officer's candidate school, in her own comedy, *Over 21♦* (1944); and Dolly Levi, the pushy lady who arranges marriages, including her own, in *The Matchmaker♦* (1955). Brooks Atkinson,♦ writing of the tiny, gravel-voiced actress's performance in *The Matchmaker* suggested she gave "her most extravagant performance—sweeping wide, growling, leering, cutting through her scenes with sharp gestures." She also wrote a successful, semi-autobiographical play about a stage-struck young girl, *Years Ago♦* (1946). One of the last old-school performers to demand footlights whenever she appeared, she was married to the promising young actor Gregory Kelly♦ and, after his death, to Garson Kanin. ♦

Autobiography: *Myself Among Others,* New York, 1971.

GORDONE, Charles, see *No Place To Be Somebody*

GOW, James, see *Deep Are the Roots* and *Tomorrow the World*

GRAIN, F., P., and P. Jr. (fl. first half of the nineteenth century) A family of set designers, they first appeared on the New York scene about 1823, when they were advertised as having gained fame in Charleston, Savannah, and Richmond. Among their early work in New York were settings for Barriere's◆ production of *The Lady of the Lake* (1826) and *The Battle of Algiers* (1829). Later they were important designers for the Bowery◆ and Niblo's Garden.◆ They also created sets for the Floating Theatre in 1845, shortly before their names disappeared from advertisements. However, the mere fact that their names appeared in numerous advertisements attested to their fame, and one critic called them "among the best artists in the country."

Grand Army Man, A, a play in four acts by David Belasco,◆ Pauline Phelps, and Marion Short. Produced by Belasco at the Stuyvesant Theatre. October 16, 1907. 149 performances.

Wes Bigelow (David Warfield◆), a Civil War veteran, has adopted and raised Robert (William Elliot), the son of a comrade killed in the war. Unfortunately, Robert gets into bad company, lends one worthless friend funds he has been given in trust, and is sent to jail when that friend squanders the money. Matters are eventually set right, and Robert returns to marry Hallie (Antoinette Perry◆), the daughter of the judge who imprisoned him.

Although this was the least successful of the Belasco-Warfield vehicles, it nonetheless enjoyed a reasonable success thanks to the theatrical brilliance of the two men.

Grand Duchess, The [*La Grande Duchesse de Gérolstein*] This Offenbach operetta was first presented in America in 1867 with Lucille Tostée in the title role. It tells of a duchess who hopes to win the love of a common soldier by promoting him, but finds he remains loyal to his simple sweetheart. Its great aria, "Voici le sabre de mon père," became one of the most ragingly popular melodies of its day. The show began the decades-long vogue for French opéra bouffe◆ in this country and was regularly revived. One of the most successful of American duchesses was Lillian Russell.◆ When it was first performed in English a short time after its American premiere, which had been in French, some playgo-

ers and critics took offense at what they deemed its salaciousness, but today the work seems harmless enough. Contemporary revivals usually are mounted as part of opera companies' repertories.

GRANGER, Maude [neé Anna Brainerd Follen] (1851?–1928) Something of a curiosity, Miss Granger began her career as a celebrated beauty and ended it as a fine character actress. In between she was occasionally a star, but her stardom was precarious and intermittent. Odell◆ wrote, "Miss Granger was in her youth one of the most beautiful and most photographed of actresses. Every college man, every sentimental girl, every collector had numerous pictures of her." She made her New York debut in 1873 in *Without a Heart,* and quickly rose to such important assignments as Clare Dart, whose earlier romance presents problems for her marriage, in *The Mighty Dollar*◆ (1875), and Olivia Schuyler, the millionairess who marries her rescuer from a shipwreck and later stands by him when he is falsely accused of murder, in *Fifth Avenue* (1877). In 1877 she also was leading lady to John McCullough◆ in revivals of *Virginius, The Gladiator,*◆ *Richelieu,*◆ and *Othello.*◆ She was judged a good enough actress to appear with Lester Wallack's◆ company as Dora, falsely accused of theft, in *Diplomacy*◆ (1878), and then was chosen by Augustin Daly◆ to play the humiliated, doomed Gervaise in *L'Assommoir* (1879). After this she appeared in two successive Bartley Campbell◆ plays, as Mary Brandon, who makes a disastrous marriage, in *My Partner*◆ (1879), and as Cicely Blaine, who nearly makes a disastrous marriage and must help clear her lover of false charges stemming from his attempt to save her reputation, in *The Galley Slave*◆ (1879). She next portrayed Antonia, the adventuress, in *Two Nights in Rome* (1880). Apparently her early promise was not being fully realized, for by this time her acting ability was coming under question, one critic suggesting, "a few gestures, postures, facial expressions, and verbal tones—these are her effects and these she repeats to a tiresome extent." After playing in a series of revivals of popular contemporary plays opposite James O'Neill,◆ her star quickly began to fade. For some years she played either important roles in lesser touring companies or supporting roles in major productions. With time, however, she appears to have carefully honed her limited abilities, and she won plaudits for her final appearances as Mrs. Livingston, the heroine's mother, in *The First Year*◆ (1920) and as the selfish, domineering Grandma Spenser in *Pigs* (1924).

GRAU, Maurice (1849–1907) Although best known for his successful tenure as head of the Metropolitan Opera, he was also important in the growth of popular musical theatre in America. He was born in Brünn, Austria, and brought to this country at the age of five. After studying at Columbia and embarking on a law practice, he abandoned his legal career to help his uncle, Jacob Grau, then manager of the French Theatre in New York. His first venture on his own was to bring to America the great French star of opéra bouffe,♦ Marie Aimée. The success of her performances helped consolidate the vogue for opéra bouffe in particular and musical theatre in general. He later persuaded Jacques Offenbach♦ to make an American tour, and sponsored the great Italian actor, Salvini.♦ At various times he was occupied with the management of several New York legitimate theatres.

Grease, a musical with book, lyrics, and music by Jim Jacobs and Warren Casey. Produced at the Eden Theatre. February 14, 1972. 3,388 performances.

Innocent little Sandy Dumbrowski (Carole Demas) transfers from Immaculata to Rydell High, where she promptly wins the affection of Danny Zuko (Barry Bostwick), a member of the "Burger Palace Boys," a tough-talking, but harmless gang of youngsters who are known as greasers because of their slicked-down hair. When Danny refuses to conform to her canons of behavior, she dons tight jeans, a bouffant hair-do, and stoops to conquer. At the same time she gives her rival, Betty Rizzo (Adrienne Barbeau), her comeuppance.

Principal songs: Greased Lightin' · Look at Me, I'm Sandra Dee

After expressing the bewilderment of so many that this totally undistinguished musical, whose songs reverted to the early rock and roll styles of the 1950s, could become (for a time) the longest running show in Broadway history, musical theatre historian Stanley Green♦ attempted to explain its success by concluding, "But obviously the musical hit a nerve. Though the air was primarily one of parody, *Grease* let us see with unerring authenticity and total lack of sentimentality the way kids actually looked and acted and felt during those . . . days that we look back on as somehow being both placid and plastic."

Great Divide, The, a play in three acts by William Vaughn Moody.♦ Produced by Henry Miller♦ at the Princess Theatre. October 3, 1906. 238 performances.

Although of old New England stock, Ruth Jordan (Margaret Anglin♦) has come to Arizona to get away from the stifling, effete East and to help her brother's Western venture. She rejects a proposal of marriage from a New England doctor who seems too bloodless to her. Left alone in the Jordan cabin, she finds herself confronting three rough-hewn men, who would apparently attack her. She pleads to the most decent looking, Stephen Ghent (Miller), to help her. He buys off the others, but then demands that Ruth come and live with him as his wife. She does. Although Ghent proves both an honorable man and a successful entrepreneur, drawing strength and goodness from his wife, Ruth cannot bring herself to love him. She remains haunted by her puritanical upbringing. She returns to New England, only to have Ghent follow her. There he reveals he has helped save her brother's enterprise. At first Ruth remains reluctant to return, but at last she sees she must. She tells Ghent, "You found me, a woman in whose ears rang night and day the cry of an angry Heaven to both of us—'Cleanse yourselves!' And I did it the only way I knew—the only way my fathers knew—by wretchedness, by self-torture, by trying blindly to pierce your careless heart with pain." And she begs him to teach her how to live.

Basing his play on an actual incident which did not end happily, Moody was inspired to develop the story as a classic battle between the tight puritanical mind and the free spirit of the West. The play was first performed at Miss Anglin's urgings in Chicago as *The Sabine Woman,* then slightly rewritten. Walter Prichard Eaton♦ noted, shortly after the New York premiere, "No other American play has ever gone so deep, has ever seized hold of so powerful an idea; and no other American play has ever wrought an idea into a dramatic story with such dignity and grace of language, such poetry of image and emotion."

Great God Brown, The, a play in prologue, four acts and epilogue by Eugene O'Neill.♦ Produced by Kenneth MacGowan,♦ Robert Edmond Jones,♦ and O'Neill at the Greenwich Village Theatre. January 23, 1926. 271 performances.

William A. Brown (William Harrigan) and Dion Anthony (Robert Keith) are the sons of business partners and will themselves soon take over the business. Both men love Margaret (Eleanor Wesselhoeft), but she chooses Dion, although it is not the real Dion she elects, not the tortured, sensitive, and artistic Dion, but rather the Dion of the mocking, cynical mask. Indeed, when Dion briefly removes his mask in a moment of ecstatic passion, Margaret is revolted. Dion retires from the business partnership, fails in his attempt to become a painter, returns as Brown's employee, but soon withers and dies. Taking Dion's mask, Brown also takes his place as Margaret's husband, until the deception is revealed. By that time the real, inner Brown has languished. When Brown is accused of murdering his true self, only the prostitute, Cybel (Anne Shoemaker), who wears no mask, comforts him. Years after both men's deaths Margaret looks back and swears eternal love to Dion, or at least to Dion's mask.

"From passages of winged poetry he shifts quickly to mordant irony," Brooks Atkinson♦ noted of O'Neill's writing, continuing, "from the abstract he passes to the concrete without missing a beat." Although many playgoers were baffled by the work, in which the actors often spoke from behind masks, enough were intrigued to give the production a surprising commercial success. The play is reputed to have been O'Neill's own favorite among his works. A 1959 revival was unsuccessful.

Great Lover, The, a play in three acts by Leo Ditrichstein♦ and Frederic and Fanny Hatton.♦ Produced by Cohan♦ and Harris♦ at the Longacre Theatre. November 10, 1915. 245 performances.

Jean Paurel (Ditrichstein) is the world's greatest bass-baritone, the highest paid, most glamorous star of New York's Gotham Opera Company. His most famous part is Don Giovanni, a role he is notorious for playing off-stage as well as on. But at the height of his career his great voice fails, and he must stand in the wings listening to a new star challenge his supremacy. As his career fades away so do the women who were once only too willing to be his conquests. He sits alone in despair when the phone rings. The caller is a lady for whom he never could find time, but with whom he now eagerly agrees to meet.

Written entirely as a vehicle for one star, the play created a furor because the settings were designed to look precisely like rooms at the Metropolitan Opera House and the hero's name was so similar to that of the Met's great Don, Victor Maurel. Walter Prichard Eaton,♦ despite some reservations, granted it "was about as sure fire as anything can be in the theatre."

Great White Hope, The, a play in three acts by Howard Sackler. Produced by Herman Levin♦ at the Alvin Theatre. October 3, 1968. 556 performances. PP, NYDCCA.

To the dismay of racists, Jack Jefferson (James Earl Jones♦), a black prizefighter, rises to the top of his profession and becomes the heavyweight champion.

But even some people who would not consider themselves racists bristle at Jefferson's arrogant, impolitic behavior. He flaunts his wealth and, worse, flaunts his white girl friend Ellie (Jane Alexander). The pressures finally drive Ellie to suicide. To the joy of many, Jack is toppled by a white fighter, but not before he has first pounded his opponent to a pulp.

Based on the career of Jack Johnson, this gripping, magnificently mounted blank-verse drama was initially presented at Washington's Arena Theatre.♦

Sackler (1929–82) was born in New York and educated at Brooklyn College, served as a record director, screen writer, and poet, as well as author of several plays mounted in regional theatres, before he was represented on Broadway by this play.

GREEN, ABEL (1900–73) Born in New York and educated at New York University, he began his career as a cub reporter for *Variety*♦ in 1919. He remained with the publication for the rest of his life, first organizing its European news service and establishing its Paris office, briefly directing its Hollywood office, and then becoming editor in 1933. He continued the policy of Sime Silverman♦ of attempting full, impartial coverage of all forms of entertainment. Among his books are *Inside Stuff on Popular Songs* (1927); *Show Biz, From Vaude to Video* (1951); and *The Spice of Variety* (1952).

GREEN, ADOLPH, see *Comden, Betty*

Green Book, The A periodical first published in 1909 as *The Green Book Album* it called itself "The Magazine of the Passing Show." In 1912 the title was changed to *The Green Book Magazine*. The publication featured "novelized" versions of current plays as well as biographical, critical, and other essays, but rarely attempted first-night coverage. It regularly offered pages of superb, rare photographs, all too often neglected by modern theatrical historians. Publication ceased in 1921.

GREEN, CAROLYN, see *Janus*

Green Pastures, The, a fable play in eighteen scenes by Marc Connelly.♦ Produced at the Mansfield Theatre. February 26, 1930. 640 performances. PP.

In a small black church in the South, Mr. Deshee (Charles H. Moore) sets out to teach his children the Bible. He begins with a pre-Creation fish fry which is interrupted when the angel Gabriel (Wesley Hill) arrives and announces, "Gangway! Gangway for de Lawd God Jehovah!" The Lawd God (Richard B. Harrison♦) enters, dressed in a Prince Albert coat, black trousers, and Congress gaiters. The story then proceeds through the legends of Adam and Eve, Cain and Abel, Noah, Moses, and other Old Testament figures and continues up to the crucifixion of Jesus.

Based on Roark Bradford's stories, the play was praised by Heywood Broun♦ in the *Telegram* as "more stirring than anything I have seen in the theatre," and by Robert Littell in the *World* as "simply and briefly one of the finest things that the theatre of our generation has seen . . . it will move you to tears and make you gasp with the simple beauty of the Old Testament pageantry." Theatre historian William Torbert Leonard has called Gabriel's announcement "one of the greatest entrance cues ever written for the stage." A revival in 1954 failed.

GREEN, PAUL [ELIOT] (1894–1981) Born in Lillington, N.C., and educated at the University of North Carolina and at Cornell, he wrote numerous one-act plays before one of them, *The No 'Count Boy* (1925), made New York aware of his skills. The following year his first full-length play, *In Abraham's Bosom,* ♦ won the Pulitzer Prize. It told of a Negro who would better the lot of his fellow blacks only to be rejected by them and lynched by whites. His next play, *The Field God* (1927), described the problems of a poor white farmer and his crippled wife. *The House of Connelly* (1931) centered on the weak son of a declining old Southern family and his rejuvenation after he marries a poor girl. It was the first play produced by the Group Theatre.♦ *Roll, Sweet Chariot* (1934) told of a small town's opposition to a new road which would destroy its isolation, while *Johnny Johnson*♦ (1936) recounted the disintegration of a pacifist. His later work for the traditional theatre consisted of dramatizing Richard Wright's novel *Native Son*♦ (1941) and providing a new version of *Peer Gynt* for a 1951 revival. Much of Green's early work was looked on as folk plays, stories of the most downtrodden people, often written with explicit or implicit left-wing attitudes. In 1937 he wrote the first of his outdoor historical pageants, *The Lost Colony,* which has been presented on Roanoke Island, N.C., regularly ever since, except for the years of World War II. Similar pageants followed, including *The Common Glory* (for Williamsburg, Va.) and *Faith of Our Fathers* (for Washington, D.C.). Green also taught drama at the University of North Carolina and elsewhere.

Biography: *Paul Green,* Vincent B. Kenny, New York, 1971.

GREEN, STANLEY (1923–90) Born in New York and educated at Union College and the University of Nebraska, Green became a leading modern authority of our musical theatre. His works included *The World of Musical Comedy* (1960, and later revised editions); *The Rodgers and Hammerstein Story* (1963); *Ring Bells! Sing Songs!* (1971), a detailed examination of the musical theatre of the 1930s; *Starring Fred Astaire* (1973); *Encyclopedia of the Musical Theatre* (1976); *The Great Clowns of Broadway* (1984), and *Broadway Musicals* (1985). These books were characterized by an accuracy all too rare in popular show-business histories, sound judgment, and an especially felicitous writing style.

GREENE, CLAY M[EREDITH] (1850–1933) Born in San Francisco and educated at Santa Clara College and the University of California, Greene had established himself as a successful San Francisco stock broker and businessman before turning his attention to play-writing and occasional acting. His first success was *M'liss*♦ (1878), a dramatization of Bret Harte's story of a determined waif. Altogether he wrote about 80 plays including *Sharps and Flats* (1880), written with Slason Thompson and telling how a San Francisco stock broker goads a parson-turned-hotelkeeper into speculating; *Chispa* (1882), also written with Thompson and depicting California backwoods life; *The New South* (1892), written with Joseph R. Grismer♦ and telling of a Northerner framed for murder by still resentful Southerners; and *Under the Polar Star* (1896), in which a woman joins an Arctic expedition to uncover her guardian's murderer. At the same time he wrote librettos for such musicals as *Bluebeard, Jr.* (1890); *The Maid of Plymouth* (1894); *The Little Trooper* (1894); and *In Gay Paree* (1899). He also mounted his own version of the *Passion Play* in California. For twelve successive years he was president of The Lambs,♦ using his own money to tide the club over troubled times, and holding an annual ritual known as the Lambs' Wash at his Long Island estate. When his own financial problems forced him to sell his estate, he returned to San Francisco, where he remained active in local theatricals until his death. He typifies the many creative theatrical figures, long popular and successful, who have left nothing enduring behind.

Greenwich Village Follies, The This was a series of revues originally presented in a small Greenwich Village theatre, but later moved to larger playhouses uptown. Editions were offered from 1919 through 1925, and again in 1928. The brainchild of John Murray Anderson, ♦ they were considered the principal rival to the *Ziegfeld Follies*♦ in elegance and taste, and Ziegfeld early on tried to prevent them from using the word "Follies" in the title. The shows were also admired for their fine comedy, including excellent female impersonators, and their imaginative ballets. Famous songs from these productions included Ted Lewis's♦ "When My Baby Smiles at Me" (1919); "Three O'Clock in the Morning" (1921); and Cole Porter's♦ "I'm in Love Again" (1924).

GREENWOOD, [FRANCES] CHARLOTTE (1893–1978) The tall, thin comedienne, with blonde hair and large blue eyes, was most celebrated for her long-legged, flat-footed kicking. Born in Philadelphia, where her mother ran a theatrical boarding house, she made her debut as an eccentric dancer in *The White Cat* (1905). After appearances in vaudeville and several more Broadway musicals, including two editions of *The Passing Show,*♦ she won critical acclaim for her performance as Letitia Proudfoot, a supporting role in *Pretty Mrs. Smith* (1914). The show was a failure, but its producer, Oliver Morosco,♦ ordered a musical written to order for her around the character of Letty. For nearly a decade she toured in such "Letty" shows as *Long, Lanky Letty* (1915), *So Long, Letty* (1916), *Linger Longer, Letty* (1919), *Let 'Er Go, Letty* (1921), and *Letty Pepper* (1922). These shows attempted no consistent characterization, but simply attached the name "Letty" to any suitable comic heroine. Only three of them played New York, where they were quickly dismissed as too unsophisticated. But in other cities and smaller towns, Miss Greenwood built a special following that long remembered her with affection. Afterwards she appeared in several revues: *Music Box Revue*♦ (1922), *The Ritz Revue* (1924), and *Rufus LeMaire's Affairs* (1927). In the 1930s, when not in films, she appeared in several California and London productions, including a final "Letty" show, *Leaning on Letty* (1935). She toured for two years as Mama in the road company of *I Remember Mama* (1947 to 1949), then made a final appearance in New York when she portrayed Juno in the musical *Out of This World* (1950).

Autobiography: *Never Too Tall,* New York, 1947.

GREET, [PHILIP] BEN (1857–1936) The noted English actor, director, and producer spent twelve seasons in America, from 1902 to 1914. Although he mounted a few original plays, he was best known for his Shakespearean revivals and for his production of *Everyman.* His troupe toured the country and served as a training ground for many young actors.

GRESAC, FRED[ERIQUE ROSINE] DE (1867?–1943) The French wife of the famed opera singer Victor Maurel, she was a successful playwright and librettist. Among her better known librettos were *The Enchantress* (1911) and *Sweethearts*♦ (1913), both written with Harry B. Smith♦; as well as *The Purple Road* (1913), with William Cary Duncan; *Flo-Flo* (1917); and *Orange Blossoms* (1922), which was based on her play *La Passerelle.*

GRESHAM, HERBERT (1852–1921) The lean, handsome English-born actor made his New York debut in 1883 as Gabriel Gadforth in *The Frolics of a Day.* He won excellent notices the following year when he created the role of the comically villainous Marquis de Baccarat in *Adonis,* ♦ and remained with the musical for several seasons. In 1891 he joined Augustin Daly's♦ famous company. With that ensemble he created the roles of Little John in the American premiere of Tennyson's *The Foresters* (1892) and Sir John Garnett in *The Great Ruby* (1899). In between he appeared as Flutter in *The Belle's Stratagem,* Meddle in *London Assurance,*♦ and Dandy Dinmont in *Meg Merrilies,* as well as in such Shakespearean parts as Malvolio, Speed, Touchstone, Stephano, and Gratiano. On occasion he left the group to act for Daly in some of the English musicals the producer was importing. After Daly's death he became a director for Klaw and Erlanger, and their associates, staging such diverse offerings as *The Rogers Brothers in Paris* (1904); *The Ham Tree* (1905); *The Prince of India* (1906); the 1907 and 1908 editions of *The* [*Ziegfeld*] *Follies*♦; *The Round-Up*♦ (1907); and *The Trail of the Lonesome Pine* (1912).

GREVILLE [first name and dates unknown] He is said to have been a student at Princeton who abandoned his studies to join David Douglass's♦ company at the John Street Theatre♦ in 1767. This would make him probably the first native American to become a professional, since all known earlier performers appear to have been English-born. He played only minor roles, such as Marcellus in *Hamlet* and Escalus in *Romeo and Juliet,* and after a single season seems to have retired or moved elsewhere, where no record has been found. According to Dunlap,♦ John Martin♦ was the first American-born actor to make a career on the stage, performing in the 1790s in Philadelphia and New York.

GREY, JOEL [né KATZ] (b. 1932) The pint-sized son of comedian Mickey Katz was born in Cleveland and made his professional debut with his father while still a youngster. Although he headed road companies or served as Broadway replacements for leads, he did not gain major attention until he appeared as the Master of Ceremonies in the musical *Cabaret*◆ (1966). He next assumed the title part of *George M!* (1968). Thereafter he starred in several musicals but his earlier success eluded him until he headed a 1987 revival of *Cabaret*.

GRIFFITH, Robert E. (1907–61) Born in Methuen, Mass., he co-produced a series of musical hits with Harold Prince◆: *The Pajama Game*◆ (1954), *Damn Yankees*◆ (1955), *New Girl in Town* (1957), *West Side Story*◆ (1957), and *Fiorello!*◆ (1959). His last two productions with Prince, *Tenderloin* (1960) and a straight play *Call on Kurpin* (1961), were failures.

GRIMES, Tammy (b. 1934) The petite blonde, with a voice that has been compared to a buzz-saw, was born in Lynn, Mass., and studied at the Neighborhood Playhouse◆ School of Theatre before making her professional debut by replacing Kim Stanley◆ as Cherie in *Bus Stop*◆ (1955). She later appeared in *The Littlest Revue* (1956) and several lesser failures before starring in the title role of *The Unsinkable Molly Brown* (1960). Long runs also followed as Cyrenne, the prostitute who helps an effeminate man find his masculinity, in *Rattle of a Simple Man* (1963); Elvira, the blithe spirit who returns from the dead, in *High Spirits* (1964); and Amanda Prynne in a 1969 revival of *Private Lives*.◆ In 1980 she was co-starred in *42nd Street*.◆

GRISMER, Joseph R[hode] (1849–1922) Born in Albany, N.Y., he made his debut as an actor about 1870, later rising to leading man at the Grand Opera House in Cincinnati and at several major theatres in San Francisco. He managed to make many roles believable, although his stubby appearance was decidedly against him. As he reached middle age, however, he gradually abandoned acting in favor of writing, directing, and producing. His first effort in this line was *The New South* (1892), a drama about regional hatred continuing after the Civil War, which he wrote in collaboration with Clay M. Greene.◆ Later plays, all adaptations or collaborations, included *A Gay Deceiver* (1898) and *The Manicure* (1899). His greatest success came when he rewrote a play by Lottie Blair Parker called *Annie Laurie*, changing its title to *Way Down East*◆ and producing it with William A. Brady◆ in 1898. Brady later recalled Grismer as "the finest play-doctor who ever made a spavined manuscript jump through hoops." They enjoyed another success after Grismer rewrote

As Ye Sow (1905), as well as with their productions of *The Man of the Hour*◆ (1906) and *A Gentleman from Mississippi*◆ (1908). He continued as Brady's reconstructor, director, and associate producer, sometimes uncredited, for many years.

GRIZZARD, George (b. 1928) The boyish looking actor, who specialized in wimpy or seemingly wimpy characters, was born in Roanoke Rapids, N.C. As a teen he acted in summer stock, then joined the Arena Stage◆ in 1952. He played important roles on Broadway in *The Desperate Hours* (1955), *The Happiest Millionaire* (1956), and *Big Fish, Little Fish* (1962), but really called attention to himself as Nick, the puzzled young professor, in *Who's Afraid of Virginia Woolf?*◆ (1962). He portrayed a variety of leading characters in two evenings of one-acters, *You Know I Can't Hear You When the Water's Running*◆ (1967) and *California Suite* (1976). Between Broadway appearances he works with major off-Broadway and regional companies. In the late 1980s he starred in several A.R. Gurney◆ plays, including a tour of *The Perfect Party* and an off-Broadway mounting of *Another Antigone*.

GROODY, Louise (1897–1961) One of the brightest musical comedy stars of the 1920s, the vivacious, dimpled performer was born in Waco, Texas, and began her career in cabarets. She first appeared on Broadway as a dancer in *Around the Map* (1915). After playing important supporting roles in *Toot-Toot!* (1918), *Fiddlers Three* (1918), and *The Night Boat* (1920), she was awarded the part of Rose-Marie, the heroine who must ditch a gangster beau to marry into society, in *Good Morning, Dearie* (1921). Following a less profitable run in an importation, *One Kiss* (1923), she scored her biggest success as Nanette, who finds love after running away from her guardians, in *No, No, Nanette*◆ (1925). She introduced the show's great hits, "I Want To Be Happy" and "Tea for Two." Her last major appearance was as Loulou, who chases the sailor she loves around the world, in *Hit the Deck!*◆ (1927), in which she sang "Sometimes I'm Happy." She later played in vaudeville and in several non-musical failures.

GROS, Ernest M. Born in Paris, he came to America originally to paint the huge, realistic panoramas that were in fashion in the 1880s and 1890s. His mastery of realism quickly made him one of the most sought after set designers, especially by advocates of this style such as David Belasco.◆ Among the dozens of Broadway shows displaying his work were *El Capitan*♦ (1896), *Sherlock Holmes*♦ (1899), *Ben Hur*♦ (1899), *The Darling of the Gods*♦ (1902), *The Music Master*♦ (1904), *Adrea*♦ (1905), *Peter Pan*♦ (1905), *The Girl of the Golden West*♦ (1905), *Salvation Nell*♦ (1908), *The Easiest Way*♦ (1909), *The Bird of Paradise*♦ (1912), *The Gold Diggers*♦ (1919), and *Kiki* (1921). One of his most memorable scenes was a rocky pass in North Africa in which the heroine rides through a sand storm in *Under Two Flags*♦ (1901). The ride, not unlike one in *Mazeppa,* took the heroine and her horse virtually up into the flies.

GROSSMITH, LAWRENCE (1877–1944) The English actor, member of a once famous theatrical family, often played America, taking major roles in such musicals as *About Town* (1906), *Nobody Home*♦ (1915), *Flora Bella* (1916), *Love o' Mike* (1917), and *The Cat and the Fiddle*♦ (1931), as well as in such plays as *Too Many Husbands* (1919) and *Call It a Day* (1936).

Group, The, a play in two acts by Mercy Otis Warren.♦ Printed in 1775.

A group of men who, for a variety of reasons and with varied shades of enthusiasm, have embraced the loyalist cause, gather to discuss the growing movement toward rebellion in the colonies. They implore Sylla (read General Gage) to take action, but Sylla is torn between his sense of duty and a compassion for the plight of the colonials.

> And shall I rashly draw my guilty sword,
> And dip its hungry hilt in the rich blood
> Of the best subjects that a Brunswick boasts,
> And for no cause, but that they nobly scorn
> To wear the fetters of his venal slaves!

Described by Quinn♦ as more conversation than play, the text was widely circulated among anti-British factions. No record of performance survives, although the title page states "As lately acted." The principal characters, with the figures they are believed to represent in parentheses, were Lord Chief Justice Hazelrod (Peter Oliver), Judge Meagre (Foster Hutchinson), Brigadier Hateall (Timothy Ruggles), Sir Sparrow Spendall (William Pepperell), and Dupe (Thomas Flucker).

Group Theatre, THE After about a year of discussions, the Group Theatre was founded in 1931 by Harold Clurman,♦ Cheryl Crawford,♦ and Lee Strasberg.♦ An early announcement described the company as "an organization of actors and directors formed with the ultimate aim of creating a perma-nent acting company to maintain regular New York seasons." All three founders had been associated in one capacity or another with the Theatre Guild♦ and their breakaway was to a large extent a protest over the Guild's essentially apolitical policies. The founders, especially Strasberg and Clurman, were committed leftists and felt the theatre should provide a stage for more sharply oriented political plays. In retrospect, the rupture was seen to mark the beginning of the Guild's decline. The group's first effort was *The House of Connelly* (1931). Among its notable productions were *Men in White*♦ (1933); *Awake and Sing!*♦ (1935), *Waiting for Lefty*♦ (1935), *Johnny Johnson*♦ (1936), *Golden Boy*♦ (1937), *Rocket to the Moon*♦ (1938), *The Gentle People*♦ (1939), and *My Heart's in the Highlands*♦ (1939). The company ceased production in 1940 and disbanded. Although most of the playwrights whose works were mounted had already established their reputations, the Group Theatre was the first to present Clifford Odets♦ and Marc Blitzstein♦ to playgoers. The many theatrical figures whose careers were boosted by the company included Luther Adler,♦ Stella Adler,♦ John Garfield,♦ Elia Kazan,♦ and Franchot Tone,♦ who provided much of the financial backing in the early seasons. A detailed history of the company was written by Clurman in *The Fervent Years* (1945).

GROVER, LEONARD, see *Our Boarding House*

GUARE, JOHN, (b. 1938) Nephew of a Hollywood casting director, he was born in New York and studied at the Yale School of Drama.♦ He won an Obie Award♦ for his one-act play, *Museeka* (1968), in which a young musician rebels at slick, canned music. A major success was *The House of Blue Leaves*♦ (1971). Subsequent full-length plays have included *Rich and Famous* (1976); *Marco Polo Sings a Solo* (1977); *Landscape of the Body* (1977); *Bosoms or Neglect* (1979), done unsuccessfully on Broadway; and *Lydie Breeze* (1982). Not until *Six Degrees of Separation* (1990), dealing with a black imposter who gulls white socialites, did he enjoy another major hit.

GUERNSEY, OTIS L[OVE], JR. (b. 1918) Born in New York and educated at Yale, he has served as a drama critic for the *Herald Tribune* and *Show,* and as a lecturer on theatre. He also edits the *Dramatists Guild Quarterly.* However, he is best known as the editor of the *Best Plays*♦ series. He has been its editor since the 1964–65 volume, making his stint the longest save for the first editor, Burns Mantle.♦

GUINNESS, Alec (b. 1914) The versatile, often sly-seeming English actor who first came to the attention of Americans in droll British film comedies has only made two major New York appearances. His first was as The Unidentified Guest in T.S. Eliot's◆ *The Cocktail Party*◆ (1950); the second, in the title role of *Dylan* (1964). However, Canadians and those Americans traveling north could have seen him as Richard III and as the King in *All's Well That Ends Well* at the 1963 Stratford Shakespearean Festival.

GUNTER, A[rchibald] C[lavering] (1847–1907) The English-born author was raised in California and studied at the University of California. While working as a chemical and civil engineer he wrote his first play, *Found a True Vein* (1872), dealing with life in a mining camp. Its success prompted him to come East, where he scored a success with a crude but powerful drama, *Two Nights in Rome* (1880), the story of a Corsican adventuress who nearly destroys her husband, an artist and baronet, before he leaves her for a better woman. His later plays included *Fresh, the American*◆ (1881), which told of a brash Yankee who courts an Egyptian odalisque; *A Dime Novel* (1883), which told the adventures of a young man susceptible to the trashy stories he reads; Richard Mansfield's◆ popular vehicle, *Prince Karl*◆ (1886), in which a poor, improvident prince fights to win the hand of a girl he believes to be wealthy; and two successful adaptations of novels, *Mr. Barnes of New York* (1888) and *Mr. Potter of Texas* (1891). In all about two dozen of his plays were produced. They were generally perceived as lacking in real merit, but theatrically effective. He also wrote thirty-nine novels.

GURNEY, A[lbert] R[amsdell] Jr. (b. 1930) A native of Buffalo, N.Y., he studied at Williams College and at Yale, and for years has supplemented his writing income by teaching at a college level. His plays reveal him as the logical heir to Philip Barry◆ and S. N. Behrman,◆ time and again presenting an amused look at rich WASP American society, where mothers doggedly try to squelch their daughters' intellectual aspirations and where shallowness and lovelessness are kept from chaos by a studied observance of polite form. Among his more noted plays have been *Scenes from American Life* (1971), a hop, skip, and jump through society from the 1930s to the revolution; *The Dining Room* (1982), generations as seen from the fourth wall of a dining room; *The Middle Ages* (1982), in which a step-sister and brother find their own world after the death of their socialite father; and *The Perfect Party* (1986), in

which a college professor's attempt at hosting and winning celebrity goes askew. All these were mounted off-Broadway and at regional theatres. His first play to reach Broadway was *Sweet Sue* (1987), in which a mother, and her alter ego, contemplate a romance with her son's college roommate and his alter ego. His 1988 *The Cocktail Hour* told of a playwright who returns home to confront his past. In *Love Letters* (1989) two characters read from their years-long correspondence.

GUTHRIE, Tyrone (1900–1971) The distinguished English director, long associated with the Old Vic, first came to America to direct *Call It a Day* (1936), later returning to stage a 1946 revival of *He Who Gets Slapped.* Thereafter he moved back and forth between continents, offering New York his stagings of *The Matchmaker*◆ (1955); Marlowe's *Tamburlaine the Great* (1956); *Candide*◆ (1956); *The Makropoulos Secret* (1957); *The Tenth Man*◆ (1959); *Gideon*◆ (1961); and a revival of *Dinner at Eight*◆ (1966). He was largely responsible for the creation of the Shakespearean Festival Theatre in Stratford, Ontario, in 1953 and the Guthrie Theatre and Guthrie Theatre Foundation◆ in Minneapolis in 1963. Guthrie was at his best in bringing to life Elizabethan, especially Shakespearean, plays, but he displayed his fine sense of pacing, tension, and understanding in productions of many modern works. He also wrote a number of books, including *Theatre Prospect* (1932), *A New Theatre* (1964), and *In Various Directions* (1965).

Autobiography: *A Life in the Theatre*, New York, 1959.

Guthrie Theatre, The and The Guthrie Theatre Foundation, (Minneapolis, Minnesota) Established by Oliver Rea, Peter Zeisler, and Guthrie◆ with the idea of forming a permanent repertory company away from New York, it was placed in Minneapolis after the Walker Art Center offered the men a $400,000 grant and land on which to build a playhouse. Guthrie and his designer, Tanya Moiseiwitsch, worked out details for an auditorium seating 1,437 people in a 200-degree arc around an asymmetrical thrust stage. The theatre opened in 1963 with a performance of *Hamlet.*◆ Among Guthrie's personal successes there were his mountings of *The Three Sisters, Henry V, Volpone,* and *Richard III.*◆ After Guthrie's death the season was expanded, the company went on occasional tours, and a smaller theatre opened for the presentation of experimental plays.

Guys and Dolls, a musical comedy in two acts. Book by Jo Swerling and Abe Burrows. ♦ Music and lyrics by Frank Loesser. ♦ Produced by Feuer ♦ and Martin ♦ at the 46th Street Theatre. November 24, 1950. 1200 performances.

Nathan Detroit (Sam Levene ♦), who runs the oldest established permanent floating crap game in New York, is hard up for money, a special problem since the biggest plunger of all, Sky Masterson (Robert Alda ♦), is in town, ready to play. When Sky boasts that he can have any woman he wants, Nathan sees his chance. He wagers that Sky cannot win any woman Nathan points to. Sky takes the bet. At that moment, Sister Sarah (Isabel Bigley) of the Salvation Army comes marching by, and Nathan points to her. When Sky wins big at dice he forces the losers to attend a Salvation Army rally in order to help his pursuit of Sarah. He eventually lures her to Havana, but in the end she converts him to her ways. Meanwhile Nathan agrees to wed Adelaide (Vivian Blaine ♦), a night club singer with whom he has had a fourteen-year courtship.

Principal songs: Adelaide's Lament · A Bushel and a Peck · If I Were a Bell · I'll Know · I've Never Been in Love Before · More I Cannot Wish You · Sit Down, You're Rockin' the Boat

Based on Damon Runyon's ♦ short stories, especially "The Idyll of Miss Sarah Brown," and billed as "a musical fable of Broadway," the entertainment created its own special, raffish world, with people sporting such colorful monikers as Nicely-Nicely Johnson and Harry the Horse. The work won every prize offered to a musical in its season. Only its music at first seemed weak, and that has grown in popular affection. Howard Barnes of the *Herald Tribune* noted that "The work uses music and dancing as embellishments to the libretto, rather than making the latter a loose clothesline for assorted capers," while John Chapman in selecting his *Best Plays* thought its cohesiveness and brilliance made it better than any straight play of the season. The show has enjoyed regular revivals, including a highly praised mounting by Great Britain's National Theatre ♦ in 1982.

Gypsy, a drama in three acts by Maxwell Anderson. ♦ Produced by Richard Herndon ♦ at the Klaw Theatre. January 14, 1929. 64 performances.

David Hastings (Lester Vail), a failed violinist who conducts an orchestra in a film house, is deeply in love with his wife Ellen (Claiborne Foster), whom he calls "Gypsy." She insists she is in love with him but also confesses to a restlessness and malaise which she blames on her hated mother, a woman whom she recalls as having many lovers. Yet Gypsy has also had lovers, and while they have been attractive, the affairs have been unsatisfactory. When she becomes pregnant with David's child, she has an abortion. She does not, she claims, want a new generation to grow up as unhappily as she and her mother have. Her own discontent growing, she leaves David and takes a small shabby room, where she commits suicide.

Burns Mantle ♦ labeled the play "an honestly written drama inspired by changing social standards and values, a play of purpose, the artistic integrity of which cannot be questioned whatever the reaction may be to its characters and its story." While the critical response was largely favorable, the play could not find a public, even when Anderson revised it to include a happy ending. It remains one of his best, most neglected works.

Gypsy, a musical in two acts. Book by Arthur Laurents. ♦ Lyrics by Stephen Sondheim. ♦ Music by Jule Styne. ♦ Produced by David Merrick ♦ and Leland Hayward ♦ at the Broadway Theatre. May 21, 1959. 702 performances.

Rose (Ethel Merman ♦), a typical pushy stage-mother, is determined to make a star of her daughter, "Baby June." To this end she even leaves her phlegmatic husband and takes up with Herbie (Jack Klugman), a man who sells candy to vaudeville houses. But as June (Lane Bradbury) grows up she develops a mind of her own and runs away, so Rose centers her drive on her other daughter, Louise (Sandra Church). In time Louise becomes the great burlesque queen, Gypsy Rose Lee, but Rose is left uncertain whether all the ambition and sacrifice were worth the effort.

Principal songs: Everything's Coming Up Roses · Rose's Turn · Small World · Together · You'll Never Get Away from Me

Based on Gypsy Rose Lee's ♦ autobiography, the musical inspired Styne's finest score and Miss Merman's finest performance. The show was successfully revived in 1973 with Angela Lansbury ♦ as Rose and in 1989 with Tyne Daly.

H

HACKETT, Albert, see *Diary of Anne Frank, The*

HACKETT, J[ames] H[enry] (1800–1871) Born in New York, he studied briefly at Columbia, but left to read law. After his first marriage in 1819 he went into business. He had long been interested in amateur theatricals, so when his mercantile ventures failed in late 1825, he decided to perform professionally. His debut at the Park Theater♦ in March 1826 as Justice Woodcock in *Love in a Village* caused few ripples. Not until he essayed Dromio of Ephesus the following fall did he win widespread fame. That his initial success was in such a role is significant, for Hackett's career was to have two distinct aspects. Cognoscenti were to consider him probably the finest Shakespearean comedian of his day; ordinary playgoers, to admire him for his Yankee characterizations. In 1828, on his return from the first of several London visits, he scored in the earliest of these Yankee roles when he rewrote an old English comedy *Who Wants a Guinea?,* calling it *Jonathan in England* and creating the role of Solomon Swop. Two years later he offered his Rip Van Winkle and his Colonel Nimrod Wildfire, an unlettered Kentuckian elected to Congress, in *The Lion of the West.*♦ This latter character proved so popular that in 1833 Hackett appeared in a specially written play about him, *The Kentuckian.* That same year he gave his first American performances as Falstaff, which traditional critics looked upon as his finest achievement. William Winter♦ wrote, "He interpreted a mind that was merry, but one in which merriment was strongly tinctured with scorn. It cared nothing about virtue, except that some persons trade on that attribute; and it knew nothing about sweetness, except that it is a property of sugar and a good thing in sack." Later in his career Hackett attempted Lear and Hamlet, but these were unsuccessful, so most of his long theatrical life was passed playing roles he popularized early on.

He also spent time in managing theatres, including the Bowery,♦ the Chatham, the National, and the Astor Place Opera House—this last at the time of the Astor Place Riots.♦ Considered something of a Shakespearean scholar as well, he was instrumental in New York's erecting a statue of Shakespeare in Central Park. His first wife, Catherine Leesugg (1797–1848), was a popular singer and actress.

HACKETT, James K[eteltas] (1869–1926) The Canadian-born son of J. H. Hackett,♦ like his father he studied law before electing to become an actor. He made his debut early in 1892, and later the same year joined Augustin Daly's♦ ensemble, where his assignments ranged from Master Wilford in *The Hunchback*♦ to Jacques in *As You Like It.*♦ From 1895 to 1899 he worked with Daniel Frohman♦ at the Lyceum,♦ playing in a series of romantic comedies and dramas. His most famous role there was the one with which he was afterwards always identified, Rudolf in *The Prisoner of Zenda.*♦ Hackett did not create the role; E. H. Sothern♦ did. But Sothern went on to greater achievements, while Hackett, a tall, slim, dark-haired, handsome man, was a relatively wooden actor whose career was largely confined to similar, if less memorable roles. Typical of his later characterizations were Basil Jennico, whose swashbuckling valor wins the hand of a princess disguised as a serving maid, in *The Pride of Jennico*♦ (1900), and Jack Frobisher, who exposes the hypocrisies of English high society, in *The Walls of Jericho* (1905). Late in his career he attempted a number of Shakespearean revivals, which met with only modest success. His last Broadway appearance was in 1924 as Macbeth. For a short time, he also ran the theatre originally built as the Lew Fields', renaming it for himself during his tenure.

HAGAN, James S., see *One Sunday Afternoon*

HAGEN, Uta (b. 1919) Born in Germany but educated in America, she studied at England's Royal Academy of Dramatic Arts before making her Broadway debut as Nina in *The Seagull* (1938). After winning praise for her Desdemona opposite Paul Robeson's♦ Othello in 1943, her career faltered for several seasons until she replaced Jessica Tandy♦ as Blanche Du Bois in *A Streetcar Named Desire*♦ in 1948. She next played Georgie, the loyal, misunderstood wife of an alcoholic actor, in *The Country Girl*♦ (1950), then won excellent notices in the title role of Shaw's *Saint Joan*♦ (1951). Her performance, which displayed the high intelligence she brought to all her work, was admired for its common sense, down-to-earth qualities. In 1962 she created the role of Martha, the unhappily married woman, in *Who's Afraid of Virginia Woolf?*. ◆ In the 1980s she starred in several Shavian revivals off-Broadway. For many years she taught acting at a school run by her second husband, Herbert Berghof. ◆

HAGGIN, [James] Ben Ali [Jr.] (1882?–1951) Playgoers recalled Haggin for the sumptuous tableaux or "living pictures," often revealing draped beauties, that he created for the *Ziegfeld Follies*◆ and for Ziegfeld's◆ cabaret shows, the *Midnight Frolics*. Revue historian Robert Baral has said of Haggin's tableaux, "He incorporated drama and historical sweep, making groupings look like old masters." But writers of his obituaries generally ignored this. To them he was the New York-born son of the famous horseman, James B. A. Haggin (who had once displayed his equestrian abilities in the 1888 show *A Run of Luck*), and grandson of James B. Haggin, who had been the owner of the Anaconda copper mine. Young Haggin studied art in Munich and returned home to become a celebrated society portrait painter. He also staged numerous lavish pageants and balls. In 1912 he successfully tried his skill at performing when he played the old father in *Lucy Moore; or, The Prune Hater's Daughter,* which Everett Shinn and other members of the Ash Can School of painters produced privately. Apart from similar amateur affairs and occasionally designing tableaux for vaudeville, his professional career was almost entirely associated with Ziegfeld. After Ziegfeld's death he directed *Field of Ermine* (1935), a failure.

HAINES, William Wister, see *Command Decision*

Hair, a musical in two acts. Book and lyrics by Gerome Ragni and James Rado. Music by Galt MacDermott. Produced by Joseph Papp◆ at the New York Shakespeare Festival Public Theatre. October 29, 1967. 1,836 performances, including Broadway run.

Claude (Walker Daniels) is a somewhat bewildered, long-haired, hippie rebel. Although he was born and raised in Brooklyn, he gives his birthplace as Manchester, England. He shares his apartment with his friend Berger (Ragni) and Berger's girl Sheila (Jill O'Hara). His own girl, Jeannie (Sally Eaton), is pregnant with another man's child. Around their lives swirl problems of racial inequal-

ity, drugs, homosexuality, and poverty, but most of all the Viet Nam War. For a time Claude considers burning his draft card, but finally enters the army, is sent to Viet Nam, and killed. His friends mourn his senseless death.

Principal songs: Aquarius · Frank Mills · Good Morning, Starshine

Filled with anti-establishment protest, profanity, and seediness, the musical nevertheless caught the spirit of the decade and was one of the earliest to adapt rock music successfully for the popular theatre. After a short run off-Broadway,◆ it was revised, recast, and restaged, including a much publicized nude scene, and moved to Broadway, where publicity and the vogue of its best songs assured it a long run.

Hairy Ape, The, a play in eight scenes by Eugene O'Neill. ◆ Produced by the Provincetown Players◆ at the Provincetown Theatre (N.Y.). March 9, 1922. 120 performances.

Richard "Yank" Smith (Louis Wolheim◆) is an ape-like coal stoker on a luxury liner. Mildred Douglas (Mary Blair), do-gooder daughter of the line's president, visits the boiler room and faints at the sight of the brutish man. Her behavior causes Yank to question his worth and his place in society. He leaves the ship to stroll up Fifth Avenue, where his boorish behavior lands him in jail. Cell mates urge him to join the "Wobblies," but the union refuses him. Confused and upset, he heads for a zoo. After asking a gorilla, "Where do I fit in?" he attempts to release the animal. But the beast, like everyone else, misunderstands him, and kills him.

One of O'Neill's most popular early plays, it was welcomed by Woollcott◆ as "a bitter, brutal, wildly fantastic play of nightmare hue and nightmare distortion." It has enjoyed occasional revivals.

HAJOS, Mitzi [Magdalena] (b. 1891) Born in Budapest, where she began to perform professionally while still a young child, she came to America in 1909 and played cabarets and vaudeville before appearing in the 1911 *La Belle Paree*. After performing in *Her Little Highness* (1913), the petite singer and dancer became a star when she assumed the title role in the operetta *Sari* (1914). Soon afterwards she changed her billing simply to Mitzi, and starred in *Pom-Pom* (1916), *Head Over Heels* (1918), *Lady Billy* (1920), *The Magic Ring* (1923), and *Naughty Riquette* (1926). In later years she accepted supporting roles in numerous straight plays.

HALE, GEORGE (1902–56) A choreographer, who began his career as a tap dancer, he performed in *The Rise of Rosie O'Reilly* (1923) and other musicals, before creating the dances for *Heads Up!* (1929), *Strike Up the Band*♦ (1930), *Girl Crazy*♦ (1930), *The New Yorkers* (1930), *Earl Carroll Vanities of 1931*♦, *Of Thee I Sing*♦ (1931), *Pardon My English* (1933), and *Red, Hot and Blue!* (1936). His work was generally considered lively but unexceptional. He later co-produced some musicals, including *Hold On to Your Hats* (1940).

HALE, LOUISE CLOSSER (1872–1933) Born in Chicago, she studied at the American Academy of Dramatic Arts♦ before making her debut in Detroit in 1894 in *In Old Kentucky.*♦ After touring with W. H. Crane♦ and in *Arizona,*♦ she made her first New York appearance as Prossy in Arnold Daly's♦ production of *Candida*♦ (1903). Later important appearances included the Fairy Berylune in Maeterlinck's *The Blue Bird* (1910); Mrs. Atkins in *Beyond the Horizon*♦ (1920); the cantankerous Mrs. Bett in *Miss Lulu Bett*♦ (1920); Ase in *Peer Gynt* (1923); and the understanding mother, Mrs. Smith, in *Expressing Willie*♦ (1924). Mrs. Hale also wrote several novels dealing with theatre life.

HALÉVY, LUDOVIC (1834–1908) and MEILHAC, and HENRI (1831–97) The French collaborators first gained fame in America for their librettos to such Offenbach works as *La Grande Duchesse de Gérolstein*♦ (1867), *La Belle Hélène* (1868), and *La Vie Parisienne* (1868), all of which helped initiate the rage for opéra bouffe♦ in this country and all of which were first performed here with their original French texts. Augustin Daly's♦ adaptation and production of their play *Frou-Frou*♦ (1870) launched it on a career that ran well into the 20th century. Their other non-musical plays, however, were generally less successful here.

HALEY, [JOHN] JACK (1902–79) Born in Boston, the wide-eyed, eager comedian made his professional debut in vaudeville in the early 1920s, when he teamed with Charlie Crafts as Crafts and Haley. He later teamed briefly with Helen Eby Rock. His first Broadway appearances were in two revues, *Round the Town* (1924) and *Gay Paree* (1925 and 1926 editions). He scored heavily as Jack Martin, the shy chain-store heir, in *Follow Thru*♦ (1929), introducing "Button Up Your Overcoat," then was starred as Steve Potter, a rich man's son mixed up in radical politics, in *Free for All* (1931). The musical was a failure, but he fared better as the shady Duke Stanley in *Take A Chance* (1932), in which he sang "You're an Old Smoothie." After a long sojourn in Hollywood he appeared in *Higher and Higher* (1940) and *Show Time* (1942), then returned for one final appearance, playing opposite Bea Lillie♦ in the revue *Inside U.S.A.* (1949).

HALL, ADELAIDE [LOUISE] (b. 1895) The short, hefty black singer, who was celebrated for her sizzling renditions of popular songs, was born in Brooklyn and first appeared before a New York audience in the chorus of *Shuffle Along*♦ (1921). She performed in night clubs, in vaudeville, including star turns at the Palace,♦ and in several other black Broadway musicals, but was best known for her appearance in *Blackbirds of 1928,*♦ in which she introduced "Diga Diga Doo," "I Can't Give You Anything But Love," and "I Must Have That Man." Her last important assignment was as Grandma Obeah in the musical *Jamaica* (1957).

HALL, ADRIAN (b. 1928) A native of Van, Texas, he studied at Texas State Teachers' College, the Pasadena Playhouse,♦ and with Lee Strasberg.♦ After staging plays off-Broadway and at regional threatres he helped found the Trinity Square Repertory Company♦ in Providence. In 1983 he assumed double duty by also taking over the directorship of the Dallas Theatre Center. His choice of plays and his mountings have often been controversial. In 1989 he left Trinity to concentrate on Dallas, but later the same year left Dallas. He now works independently with various major regional troupes.

HALL, BETTINA (b. 1906) A native of North Easton, Mass., she won major notices when she appeared in a series of Gilbert♦ and Sullivan♦ revivals beginning in 1926. Later she played leading roles in *The Cat and the Fiddle*♦ (1931), in which she introduced "She Didn't Say 'Yes,'" and *Anything Goes*♦ (1934). Her older sister, Natalie (b. 1904), who was born in Providence, R.I., was also a prominent musical comedy performer, introducing the title song in *Through the Years* (1932) and "The Song Is You" in *Music in the Air*♦ (1932).

HALL, PAULINE [née PAULINE FREDERICKA SCHMIDGALL] (1860–1919) One of the most popular turn-of-the-century prima donnas, she began her career as a dancer in her native Cincinnati in 1875. Shortly thereafter she joined the Alice Oates Opera Company, leaving it to spend time touring in straight plays with Mary Anderson.♦ By 1880 she was working for E. E. Rice,♦ who cast her in several of his musical productions, giving her, among others, the trouser role of the hero Gabriel in a revival that year of *Evangeline*. ♦ Her shapely figure allowed her to take men's parts, as she did most notably in the title role of *Ixion* (1885). However, her greatest success came when she played the title role in the first American production of *Erminie*♦ (1886). In 1892 she portrayed the hero, Earl Trevelyan, in a comic opera written especially for her, *Puritania*. In all, she played in over two dozen Broadway operettas. Her last appearance came just before her death, when she created the role of the impoverished old prima donna in *The Gold Diggers*♦ (1919).

HALL, THURSTON (1882–1958) The rather heavyset, mannishly handsome actor was born in Boston and made his professional debut in 1901. New York first saw him as Bob, the courting editor, in *Mrs. Wiggs of the Cabbage Patch*♦ (1904). After some years touring he returned to New York to take the romantic leads in such musicals as *The Only Girl* (1914) and *Have a Heart* (1917). When he turned to character parts in non-musicals he scored notable successes as Sam McGinnis, who wins over his snobbish wife, in *Civilian Clothes* (1919), and Robert Lyle, father of a spoiled daughter, in *Behold the Bridegroom*♦ (1927). His last years were spent as a featured performer in films.

HALLAM, LEWIS (1714–56) His father, Adam, and brother, William, were both actors at London's Covent Garden. William later became a manager, and though he failed, he was left with enough theatrical properties and supporters to organize a company of actors for the American colonies. To this end, he appointed Lewis as head of the troupe, and together they assembled players and repertory. With William remaining in London, Lewis and the company set sail in May 1752 on the *Charming Sally,* bound for Yorktown, Va. Lewis is said to have rehearsed the company daily during the crossing. Arriving in Virginia, he quickly obtained the Governor's permission to act and set about refurbishing the primitive auditorium he found. On September 15, the company offered its first bill, consisting of *The Merchant of Venice*♦ and *The Anatomist*. The following summer Hallam moved the troupe to New York, where he had to battle formidable antitheatrical sentiment as well as rebuild another inadequate playhouse. Puritanical opposition plus the limited audiences to be attracted in what were still relatively small cities forced Hallam to keep on the move. So after his New York stand he traveled with his players to Philadelphia and then to Charleston. In all of these cities he attempted to offer as broad and extended a repertory as possible, ranging from Shakespeare through the Restoration and contemporary dramatists. Some time in late 1754 or early 1755, he took the company to Jamaica, in the West Indies, where he died.

HALLAM, LEWIS, JR. (1740–1808) He came to America with his parents in 1752 and gave his first performance in Williamsburg as Portia's servant when the Hallam company offered *The Merchant of Venice*♦ for its American debut. He continued to act small parts with the troupe until it left for Jamaica. In 1758 he returned with a new company organized by his mother and step-father, David Douglass, ♦ the ensemble that shortly was known as the American Company. ♦ By this time his art had matured and he was the company's leading man. He was thin, of medium height, and not unattractive despite a noticeable cast in one eye. To him fell the honor of being the earliest known American Hamlet and of playing Arsaces, the hero of the first professionally produced American play, *The Prince of Parthia*♦ (1767). He essayed Romeo to his mother's Juliet, and ranged from Young Norval to central figures in contemporary comedies. After spending the Revolutionary War years in the West Indies, he returned in 1784 to reopen the Southwark Theatre♦ in Philadelphia and the John Street Theatre♦ in New York. With John Henry♦ he revitalized the American Company, working with John Hodgkinson♦ and William Dunlap♦ after Henry's withdrawal. He also performed occasionally in Baltimore and Annapolis. Although he was approaching fifty, he continued to play the same leading parts he had assumed twenty years before. Some protests were heard, but older actors' tackling younger roles was not uncommon, and not only was Hallam as good a performer as was active at the time, but he frequently staged imaginative, responsible, and applauded productions. For example, he restored *Hamlet*'s Grave Diggers' scene, which traditionally had been shortened or eliminated, and attempted some semblance of correct costuming. He appears, however, to have grown increasingly dour. Moreover, his second wife, the former Miss Tuke, antagonized his associates. With the opening of the Park Theatre♦ he withdrew from management but continued to act almost until his death. Seemingly improvident, he is said to have died in poverty. Looking back, John Durang♦ recalled him as "a sterling actor, but an inactive manager. His stile of acting was of the old school. He was celebrated in all the gentlemanly dashing profligateness of young men, in epilogues, correct in Harlequin, and performed them with ease and spirit to a great age."

HALLAM, MRS. LEWIS (d. 1773) Already established as an actress of some small importance in London, she came with her husband to America in 1752. Ireland◆ described her as "a woman of great beauty and elegance, still in the prime of life and enabled to play the youthful heroines of tragedy and comedy with due effect. Far superior to any actress who had preceded her, she retained for many years all the kind feelings of the public, who regarded her with an admiration reaching almost to idolatry." Her most popular roles included Desdemona, Juliet, Cordelia, Portia, Jane Shore, and the leading ladies of some contemporary comedies. After Hallam's death, she married David Douglass. ◆ She retired in 1769. Although Odell◆ points to a Mrs. David Douglass performing in 1774, most historians agree she died in 1773.

HALLIDAY, JOHN (1880–1947) Although born in Brooklyn, he was raised in England where he studied to become an engineer. He returned to America in order to work for Western mining interests, but soon decided to join Nat Goodwin,◆ who was touring the region. His first New York appearance was as the Earl of Brancaster in *The Whip* (1912). He quickly rose to become a leading man. Among his subsequent parts were Leonard Hunt, the troubled sculptor, in *The Woman of Bronze* (1920); George Conway, whose despair over not telling his friend the truth about that friend's future wife drives him to suicide, in *East of Suez* (1922); Gerald Naughton, the caddish man-about-town, in *Dancing Mothers*◆ (1924); Chartrand the Great, a magician who finds himself involved in a murder, in *The Spider* (1927); Maurice, who strangles his fiancée's guardian, in *Jealousy* (1928); and Prince Mikail, the nobleman reduced to being a servant, in *Tovarich* (1936).

HALLIDAY, ROBERT (b. 1893) The Scottish-born baritone came to America in 1913 and appeared in vaudeville before touring with several Broadway musicals. His New York debut was in the chorus of *The Rose Girl* (1921), after which he was assigned increasingly important roles, in *Dew Drop Inn* (1923); *Paradise Alley* (1924); *Topsy and Eva*◆ (1924); *Holka Polka* (1925); and *Tip-Toes*◆ (1925). He rose to leading man when he took the part of "The Red Shadow" in *The Desert Song*◆ (1926), introducing the title song, "The Riff Song," and "One Alone." Two years later he was Robert Misson in a second Sigmund

Romberg◆ operetta, *The New Moon,*◆ singing "Stouthearted Men" and "Wanting You." Subsequent musicals in which he appeared were *Princess Charming* (1930); *Music Hath Charms* (1934); *White Horse Inn* (1936); and *Three Wishes for Jamie* (1952). He was married to Evelyn Herbert. ◆

HAMBLIN, THOMAS S[OWERBY] (1800–1853) Born in London, he had performed in the English provinces, at Sadler's Wells and at Drury Lane, and had risen to some prominence as an actor, before coming to America in 1825. He made his debut at the Park Theatre◆ as Hamlet, immediately becoming embroiled in controversy. Some critics suggested his interpretation surpassed Thomas Abthorpe Cooper's,◆ while others thought he was vastly overrated. He continued to act for several years, although increasingly troubled by asthma. In 1830 he found a more congenial theatrical niche when he took over the Bowery Theatre,◆ which he ran, with only minor interruptions, for the next twenty years. These seasons are looked on as the heyday of the house. At first Hamblin made it the principal rival to the Park, albeit the great performers who appeared there, such as J. H. Hackett◆ and Edwin Forrest,◆ relied on a broader based, less elite following than the stars of the older theater. As competition increased with the opening of several fine new playhouses, Hamblin gradually moved the theatre toward melodrama, and in his last years it became New York's main home for blood-and-thunder pieces. He was a tough-fibered man, undaunted by three fires which destroyed the theatre during his tenure, and even ignored critics' complaints and falling attendance whenever he persisted in returning to the stage. In 1848 he assumed management of his former opposition, the Park, only to have this house, too, destroyed by fire later the same year. For all his vicissitudes, he is said to have retired with a sizable fortune.

Hamlet Shakespeare's most famous play was first offered to Americans in Garrick's version at a theatre in Philadelphia's Society Hill in 1759 with the younger Hallam◆ in the title role and remains the most frequently produced of all Shakespeare's works. At one time or another every great American classical tragedian assumed the role. In his *Curiosities of the American Stage,* Laurence Hutton◆ devoted an extended chapter to comparing all the major interpreters up to his time. Besides Hallam, his list includes such notables as John Hodgkinson,◆ Thomas Abthorpe Cooper,◆ James Fennell,◆ John Howard Payne,◆ George Frederick Cooke,◆ Edmund Kean,♦ Junius Brutus Booth,♦ James William Wallack,♦ John Jay Adams,♦ William Macready,♦ Charles Kemble,♦ Edwin Forrest,♦ Charles Kean,♦ Edward Eddy,♦ George Vandenhoff,♦ Edward L. Davenport,♦ Lawrence Barrett,♦ James Murdoch,♦ Charles Fechter,♦ Daniel Bandmann,♦ and Tommaso Salvini.♦ He attempted brief descriptions and comparisons of their performances. Noting that Forrest and Edwin Booth♦ offered interpretations in 1860, he concluded that "the contrast between the powerful robustious figure, deep chest tones, and somewhat ponderous action of the elder actor, and the lithe, poetic, romantic, melancholy rendition of the younger was very marked," and added, "In many minds Booth *is* Hamlet, and Hamlet is Booth." All these 19th-century artists performed in mountings that today would be perceived as top-heavy with scenery and slow-moving. In 1912 a relatively minor star, John E. Kellerd,♦ established a then long-run record of 102 performances. Noted contemporary Hamlets have included John Barrymore,♦ Leslie Howard,♦ John Gielgud,♦ and Richard Burton.♦ As a rule these actors played in versions that included substantial cuts in text and limited, more suggestive scenery, and allowed the strength and depth of their interpretations to carry the evening. Only Maurice Evans♦ offered anything approaching a totally uncut version, but his often sing-song delivery was seen by some critics as standing in the way of a completely satisfying study.

HAMLISCH, MARVIN (b. 1944) A New Yorker who won a scholarship to Juilliard when he was only seven and who studied music at Queens College, he became a well-known composer of screen background music before writing the scores for two exceptionally long-run Broadway musicals: *A Chorus Line*♦ (1975), recalled for "One" and "What I Did for Love," and *They're Playing Our Song*♦ (1979). His *Smile* (1986) failed.

HAMMERSTEIN, ARTHUR (1872–1955) The son of the first Oscar Hammerstein,♦ he began his theatrical career as his father's assistant, and became a producer when his father, leaving the theatre to resume his work as an opera impresario, handed over the flourishing *Naughty Marietta*♦ to him. Among his own noteworthy mountings were *The Firefly*♦ (1912); *High Jinks* (1913); *Katinka*♦ (1915); *Wildflower* (1923); *Rose-Marie*♦ (1924); *Song of the Flame* (1925); and *Sweet Adeline*♦ (1929). In 1927 he built the Hammerstein Theatre, which he lost shortly thereafter in the Depression.

HAMMERSTEIN, OSCAR (1847–1919) Born in Berlin, he ran away from home in 1863 and emigrated to America. Unable to employ his musical training, he accepted work with a cigar manufacturer. His alert, inventive mind quickly saw ways to mechanize many of the laborious operations, and his patents soon made him wealthy. He then wrote several one-act musicals for New York's Germania Theatre, and his success prompted him to become manager of the Stadt Theatre. In 1889 he built his first theatre, the Harlem Opera House, but soon lost it because of his reckless management. Much of his history would be a sad repetition of this building and then losing of playhouses, including the Columbus Theatre, the Manhattan, the Olympia, and the Republic. For a time his most successful venture was the Victoria, which briefly served as New York's leading vaudeville theatre. The house opened in 1899 as a legitimate theatre, switching to two-a-day in 1904. Attractions were booked by his son William, who found a special success with such freak acts as The Cherry Sisters.♦ Oscar also wrote a number of musicals, which he produced, including *Santa Maria* (1896), *In Greater New York* (1897), and *War Bubbles* (1898). However, his most successful Broadway production was Victor Herbert's *Naughty Marietta*♦ (1910). But for his obsession with opera, which caused several of his Broadway enterprises to fail, he might have been a more important figure in popular musical theatre.

Biography: *Oscar Hammerstein I,* Vincent Sheean, New York, 1956.

HAMMERSTEIN, OSCAR II (1895–1960) Generally acknowledged as the most successful lyricist of his generation, he was the grandson of the first Oscar Hammerstein♦ and the nephew of Arthur Hammerstein.♦ He was educated at Columbia, where he wrote lyrics for collegiate musicals. His collaborator was young Richard Rodgers.♦ He began his professional career as stage-manager for his uncle's production of *Sometime* (1918). The following year he attempted a serious drama, which quickly failed. In 1920 he wrote the book and lyrics for *Always You,* and in that same year came under the tutelage of Otto Harbach.♦ Together they wrote the book and lyrics for such shows as *Wildflower* (1923); *Rose-Marie*♦ (1924); *Sunny*♦ (1925); *Song of the Flame* (1925); and *The Desert Song*♦ (1926). Many critics consider his masterpiece to be *Show Boat*♦ (1927), which he wrote with composer Jerome Kern♦ and which included his lyrics to "Can't Help Lovin' Dat Man," "Make Believe," "Ol' Man River," and "Why Do I Love You?" The show was the first successful modern musical play with an American theme and employing American idioms. Another success was a more traditional operetta, *The New Moon*♦ (1928), for which he created the book and lyrics to Sigmund Romberg's♦ melodies for "Lover, Come Back to Me," "One Kiss," "Softly, As in a Morning Sunrise," "Stouthearted Men," and "Wanting You." He returned to Kern to create *Sweet Adeline*♦ (1929), whose major songs included "Don't Ever Leave Me" and "Why Was I Born"; and *Music in the Air*♦ (1932), which offered "I've Told Every Little Star" and "The Song Is You." Apart from this last show, the 1930s were barren years for Hammerstein, although one failure written with Kern, *Very Warm for May* (1939), produced the classic "All The Things You Are." His greatest and best-known success came when he rejoined Richard Rodgers in 1943. Between then and 1959 they wrote nine shows, five of which were among the most towering triumphs of the American musical theatre. *Oklahoma!*♦ (1943) offered the title song, "Oh, What a Beautiful Mornin'," "People Will Say We're in Love," and "The Surrey with the Fringe on Top." *Carousel*♦ (1945) included "If I Loved You," "June Is Bustin' Out All Over," "Soliloquy," and "You'll Never Walk Alone." Both of these shows followed in the pioneering path of *Show Boat* by using the American past to tell American stories (although *Carousel* was based on the European *Liliom*♦) in American terms. As much as possible in musical theatre, these plays attempted to integrate songs and story and even went so far as to attempt the integration of dance. Rodgers and Hammerstein began to drift away from Americana with *South Pacific*♦ (1949), whose great songs included "Bali Ha'i," "I'm Gonna Wash That Man Right Outa My Hair," "Some Enchanted Evening," "There Is Nothin' Like a Dame," "A Wonderful Guy," and "Younger Than Springtime." Although its story told of Americans in the Pacific during World War II, the romantic settings and an alien hero indicated Hammerstein was exploring new fields. Certainly there was little American, except a ballet telling of *Uncle Tom's Cabin,* in their next major success, *The King and I*♦ (1951), which produced "Getting To Know You," "Hello, Young Lovers," and "I Whistle a Happy Tune." Their last major success was *The Sound of Music*♦ (1959), set in Austria and perceived by some critics as a return to traditional operetta, and which presented "Climb Every Mountain," "Do-Re-Mi," "My Favorite Things," and the title song. Hammerstein's other collaborations with Rodgers were *Allegro*♦ (1947), *Me and Juliet* (1953), *Pipe Dream* (1955), and *Flower Drum Song*

(1958). At the time he resumed his collaboration with Rodgers, he also wrote on his own a modern version of *Carmen,* told in terms of contemporary black America and called *Carmen Jones*♦ (1943). With Rodgers he also entered into a successful career as producer, not only mounting all their shows from *South Pacific* on, but such other hits as *I Remember Mama*♦ (1944), *Annie Get Your Gun*♦ (1946), *Happy Birthday*♦ (1946), and *John Loves Mary*♦ (1947). In his early career Hammerstein directed such works as *Show Boat, The New Moon,* and *Music in the Air.*

Although critics sometimes complained about his excessive sentimentality and preachiness, Hammerstein's best lyrics displayed a colloquial freshness and a recourse to genuinely poetic imagery rare in popular musical theatre. As a librettist he was respected for his sharp dialogue and superb ability to trim a cumbersome script.

Biography: *Getting To Know Him,* Hugh Fordin, New York, 1977.

HAMMOND, Percy (1873–1936) Born in Cadiz, Ohio, where he fell in love with the theatre at the age of thirteen after witnessing a tent show, he began his newspaper career with small Ohio papers. Soon afterwards he joined the Chicago *Evening Post,* quickly becoming its drama critic. In 1908 he moved to the Chicago *Tribune,* then in 1921 became critic for the New York *Tribune* (later *Herald Tribune*), a position he held until his death. His criticism was sharp, and his style a curious, identifiable mixture of hominess and latinate phrases. He opened one notice, "Well, as Grandfather would say, draw up your chair and let's talk about the *Follies of 1917.*" Later, reviewing Alexander Woollcott's♦ acting debut, he wrote, "Observation of his billowy amplitudes suggests that the world might be a safer globe on which to live were the abdomens of its inhabitants more convex and less concave." Probably his most famous bon mot, often attributed to others, was his succinct review of a vaudeville act: "They've played it so often that they can play it in their sleep, which yesterday they did." On another occasion, when Florenz Ziegfeld♦ sent him an early morning telegram scolding him for panning a Ziegfeld show and demanding the producer's telegram be printed in rebuttal, Hammond, who had been one of the few critics to speak favorably of much of the show, obliged by not only printing the telegram but also the more damning reviews of his fellow critics. His best writings were anthologized in *But— Is It Art?* and *This Atom in the Audience.* After his death Franklin P. Adams and other writers published *Percy Hammond, A Symposium in Tribute* (1936).

HAMPDEN [DOUGHERTY], WALTER (1879–1955) Although born in Brooklyn and educated at the Brooklyn Polytechnic Institute and at Harvard, he served his theatrical apprenticeship with F. R. Benson's company in England, learning a wide range of Shakespearean parts. His American debut came in 1907 when Henry Miller◆ hired him to play opposite Alla Nazimova◆ as Comte Silvio in *The Comtesse Coquette,* Halvard Solness in *The Master Builder,* and Dr. Rank in *A Doll's House.* Success then followed in more commercial ventures, notably as Manson, the reincarnation of Jesus, in *The Servant in the House*◆ (1908); as George Rand, Jr., whose hopes of a governorship are destroyed, in *The City*◆ (1909); and as John Rawson, the miner-suitor, in *Good Gracious Annabelle*◆ (1916). In the 1920s Hampden starred in a number of Shakespearean revivals, offering his Marc Antony, Hamlet, Romeo, Macbeth, Shylock, and Othello, but had even greater success with two 19th-century classics, *Cyrano de Bergerac*◆ and *Richelieu.*◆ He continued to revive some of these for many years, in between engagements in lesser contemporary plays. He was an important member of the American Repertory Theatre◆ in the mid-1940s, playing Cardinal Wolsey in *Henry VIII* and Charles Venable in *What Every Woman Knows.* His last Broadway appearance was as Deputy-Governor Danforth, the cruel, bigoted judge, in *The Crucible*◆ (1953).

A tall, slim, handsome man, he was an advocate of the older, romantic school of acting and fortunate that in his prime years an audience still existed for his style of play and performance. He served for many years as president of The Players.◆

Hanlon-Lees, THE [originally known as The Six Hanlons] A troupe of acrobats and jugglers, it originally comprised George, William, Edward, Thomas, Alfred, and Frederick, the six sons of Thomas Hanlon, who managed the Theatre Royal in Manchester, England. They changed the name of the troupe primarily to honor their teacher, "Professor" John Lees, but also because injury and eventually death affected their numbers. Their American debut occurred in 1858 at Niblo's Garden when they appeared as part of a circus entertainment imported from Astley's Amphitheatre in London. Although they regularly toured the world, they eventually settled in America. Among their most successful shows were *La Voyage en Suisse* (1881) and *Fantasma* (1883). By this time they were only five,

one brother having died from injuries sustained in a fall. In the former show a brother lit a cigarette as he somersaulted from the top of a stagecoach; another fell through the floor of a fast moving train and slid in and out among the wheels. Later in the same show the five turned an elegant dinner into a storm of spinning plates and cutlery. According to Brander Matthews,◆ when they learned of the Continental success of Léotard, the originator of the flying trapeze, one of the brothers was hastily dispatched to Europe to learn Léotard's tricks.

HANSBERRY, LORRAINE, see *Raisin in the Sun, A*

HAPGOOD, NORMAN (1868–1937) Although best known as editor of *Collier's* when it was a leading muckraking magazine, and later of *Harper's Weekly* and *Hearst's International,* the Chicago-born, Harvard-educated author was also a distinguished drama critic and writer on theatre. He served as critic for the New York *Commercial Advertiser* and the *Bookman,* while his works included *The Stage in America* (1901); *Why Janet Should Read Shakespeare* (1929); and his autobiography, *The Changing Years* (1930).

Happy Birthday, a comedy in two acts by Anita Loos.◆ Produced by Richard Rodgers◆ and Oscar Hammerstein II◆ at the Broadhurst Theatre. October 31, 1946. 564 performances.

Addie Bemis (Helen Hayes◆), a mousy librarian, has fallen so in love with a young bank clerk, Paul (Louis Jean Heydt), that she follows him to the Jersey Mecca Cocktail Bar and there has her first drinks—some Scotch and a few Pink Ladies, which she has been told is a "tart's" drink. The alcohol sends her spinning, but also liberates her from her inhibitions. These gone, she wins Paul away from a jezebel, Myrtle (Jacqueline Page).

Written as a vehicle for Miss Hayes, it was her brilliant performance which lured playgoers.

Happy Time, The, a comedy in three acts by Samuel Taylor. ◆ Produced by Richard Rodgers◆ and Oscar Hammerstein II◆ at the Plymouth Theatre. January 24, 1950. 614 performances.

Bibi (Johnny Stewart) is the adolescent son of a Scottish Maman (Leora Dana◆) and a French-Canadian Papa (Claude Dauphin). Maman worries that Bibi will be corrupted by Papa's heavy-drinking brothers. But as Bibi embarks on his first puppy-love affair, all seems secure.

Based on Robert Fontaine's novel, this affectionate comedy was made into a musical in 1968.

HARBACH, OTTO [né HAUERBACH] (1873–1963) Born in Salt Lake City to Danish immigrant parents, he taught English and public speaking after graduating from Knox College. He came to New York in 1901 to work toward a doctorate at Columbia but failing eyesight forced him to abandon his studies and take odd jobs, mostly in journalism. He met Karl Hoschna♦ in 1902 and together they wrote an operetta, *The Daughter of the Desert,* which was never produced. In 1908 he wrote lyrics to Hoschna's melodies for *Three Twins,* a huge success whose hit song was "Cuddle Up a Little Closer, Lovey Mine." Thereafter he collaborated with Hoschna on five more musicals. Most notable was *Madame Sherry*♦ (1910), for which he created both book and lyrics. Its "Every Little Movement" remains familiar. Following Hoschna's death he worked with Rudolf Friml on *The Firefly*♦ (1912), among whose songs were "Giannina Mia" and "Sympathy"; *High Jinks* (1913), which offered "Something Seems Tingle-Ingleing"; and *Katinka*♦ (1915), which included "Allah's Holiday." With Louis Hirsch♦ he wrote *Going Up* (1917), whose hit song was "The Tickle Toe," and *Mary* (1920), remembered for "The Love Nest." In 1923 he joined forces with his protégé Oscar Hammerstein II,♦ Vincent Youmans,♦ and Herbert Stothart♦ to write *Wildflower,* then in 1924 worked with Hammerstein, Stothart, and Friml to create the biggest musical success of the 1920s, the operetta *Rose-Marie,*♦ His next effort was the greatest musical comedy hit of the era, *No, No, Nanette*♦ (1925), although the lyrics for that show's most popular songs were by Irving Caesar.♦ In that same year he worked with Jerome Kern♦ and Hammerstein on *Sunny,*♦ and with Hammerstein, Stothart, and George Gershwin♦ on *Song of the Flame.* With Hammerstein and Sigmund Romberg♦ he created *The Desert Song*♦ (1926). His last successful collaborations were with Kern: *The Cat and the Fiddle*♦ (1931), from which came "The Night Was Made for Love" and "She Didn't Say 'Yes' "; and *Roberta*♦ (1933), which offered "Smoke Gets in Your Eyes," "The Touch of Your Hands," and "Yesterdays." In all, he helped write over thirty musicals. His work was sometimes assailed as heavy-handed and humorless, but at best was fresh and even poetic. Shortly before his death his son William spent many hours taping his recollections. Although they have never been published, they have proven a valuable source for researchers.

HARBURG, E[DGAR] Y. [né ISIDORE HOCHBERG] (1898–1981) Popular lyricist and sometime librettist, familiarly known as "Yip," he was born in New York and educated at City College. He turned to lyric-writing after his appliance business failed in the Depression. His efforts were first offered to Broadway in *Earl Carroll's Sketch Book* (1929), with music by Jay Gorney. With Gorney he wrote his first big hit, "Brother, Can You Spare a Dime?" Included in the 1932 edition of *Americana,* it soon became a Depression theme song. That same year *Walk a Little Faster* produced "April in Paris," with music by Vernon Duke.♦ Collaborating with Ira Gershwin,♦ he wrote the lyric for Harold Arlen's♦ "Let's Take a Walk Around the Block" in *Life Begins at 8:40* (1934), then wrote "Down with Love" with Arlen for *Hooray for What!* (1937). Again with Arlen he wrote one of his biggest hits, *Bloomer Girl*♦ (1944), which included his plea for racial equality, "The Eagle and Me," as well as "Evelina" and "Right as the Rain." In 1947 he served as lyricist and co-librettist for *Finian's Rainbow,*♦ among whose songs were "How Are Things in Glocca Morra?," "If This Isn't Love," and "Old Devil Moon." Later shows were *Flahooley* (1951); *Jamaica* (1957); *The Happiest Girl in the World* (1961); and *Darling of the Day* (1968). Probably the most politically committed of major Broadway lyricists and certainly the most patently leftist, his lively, impish wit usually made his most controversial rhymes palatable.

HARDS, IRA (1872–1938) Born in Geneva, Ill., he made his New York debut as an actor in 1893 under the aegis of Charles Frohman,♦ for whom he continued to work for ten years. However, he was best known as a director. Among his more successful efforts were *The Thirteenth Chair*♦ (1916); *Pals First* (1917); *The Unknown Purple*♦ (1918); *Intimate Strangers* (1921); *Twelve Miles Out* (1925); *Dracula* (1927); *Jarnegan* (1928); and *The Bishop Misbehaves* (1935).

HARKRIDER, JOHN The Texas-born artist began his career in films, playing opposite such silent favorites as Mary Pickford and Theda Bara. He later turned to costume designing and created costumes for virtually all of Ziegfeld's♦ final productions, including *Rio Rita*♦ (1927), *Ziegfeld Follies of 1927,*♦ *Show Boat*♦ (1927), *Rosalie* (1928); *The Three Musketeers*♦ (1928), *Whoopee*♦ (1928), *Show Girl* (1929), *Simple Simon* (1930), *Smiles* (1930), and the 1931 edition of the *Follies.* Since the heyday of the *Follies* had passed, his costumes were less extravagantly imaginative than those in the earlier Ziegfeld shows, but nonetheless retained the rich, sumptuous beauty that had become the producer's trademark.

He also designed the costumes for *Music in the Air*♦ (1932), which Ziegfeld had hoped to produce before his death, and much later for *Let's Face It!*♦ (1941). However, most of his later years were spent either as a designer for films or in various personal entrepreneurial endeavors.

HARNED [HICKES], VIRGINIA (1868–1946) Born in Boston but raised in England, she returned to America to make her stage debut in *Our Boarding House.*♦ The precise date is a matter of dispute. After touring for several seasons she made her first Broadway appearance in 1890 in *A Long Lane*. Later that same year she was enlisted by Daniel Frohman♦ for his Lyceum Theatre♦ company, playing opposite E. H. Sothern,♦ whom she eventually married. She scored a popular success as Drusilla Ives, a libertine Duke's doomed mistress, in *The Dancing Girl* (1891), then consolidated her reputation when she played Fanny Haddon, who wins the young man too proud to marry for money, in *Captain Lettarblair* (1892). Perhaps her most memorable assignment came when she created the title role of *Trilby* (1895), playing the young woman who comes under the influence of the nefarious Svengali. Another well-received role was Julie de Varion, who loves the Huguenot leader (played by Sothern) in *An Enemy to the King* (1896). In 1902 she portrayed the part of the improvident, doomed heroine in Pinero's *Iris,* then switched to comedy to play the lady who wins her man away from a rival by staging a Shakespearean rehearsal in *The Light That Lies in a Woman's Eyes* (1903). Her repertory included several classic parts, including Ophelia, which she played to Sothern's Hamlet, as well as Pauline in *The Lady of Lyons,*♦ and Camille. She continued to perform in both new plays and revivals until her retirement in 1918. One writer described her as a mature actress with "sex, vitality, dignity and beauty."

HARNICK, SHELDON [MAYER] (b. 1924) Born in Chicago, he was graduated from Northwestern University, where he wrote songs for college shows. He continued his musical studies elsewhere before creating songs which were interpolated into such revues as *New Faces of 1952*♦; *Two's Company* (1952); *John Murray Anderson's Almanac* (1953); and *Shoestring Revue*♦ (1955). Joining with Jerry Bock, he wrote the lyrics to Bock's music for *The Body Beautiful* (1958); the Pulitzer Prize♦-winning *Fiorello!*♦ (1959), whose songs included "Little Tin Box" and "Till Tomorrow"; *Tenderloin* (1960); *She Loves Me*♦ (1963), which offered "Dear Friend,"

"Ice Cream," and the title song; *Fiddler on the Roof*♦ (1964), from whose score came "If I Were a Rich Man," "Matchmaker, Matchmaker," and "Sunrise, Sunset"; *The Apple Tree* (1966); and *The Rothschilds* (1970). After the team split, Harnick wrote lyrics for Richard Rodgers's♦ music to *Rex* (1976). At their best Harnick's lyrics caught the flavor of periods and places in which his musicals were set, without ever becoming truly imitative of older styles. They also offered a compassionate, yet often witty, understanding of human longings.

Harriet, a play in three acts by Florence Ryerson and Colin Clements. Produced by Gilbert Miller♦ at the Henry Miller Theatre. March 3, 1943. 377 performances.

When Harriet Beecher (Helen Hayes♦) marries Professor Calvin Stowe (Rhys Williams), she is not fully aware that she has done so partly to escape her overbearing family. Her writing, too, begins as a way of removing herself from family pontifications. At first, the Beechers are not altogether pleased. But then Harriet's novel, *Uncle Tom's Cabin,* makes her famous and wealthy. Soon what started as an escape becomes a crusade, and she even supports her son when he goes off to the war that President Lincoln has suggested she helped precipitate.

Robert Sherwood♦ had been working on a play about Mrs. Stowe for Miss Hayes, but Miller persuaded his somewhat reluctant star to accept this already finished work instead. The play was leisurely and loose-jointed, but sustained in the theatre by Miss Hayes's artistry.

Florence Ryerson [Willard] (1892–1965), who was born in Glendale, Calif., and Colin Clements (1895–1948) a native of Omaha, were a husband and wife team, both having studied with Professor George Pierce Baker♦ at his 47 Workshop.♦ Their only other success was *Strange Bedfellows* (1948), a comedy focusing on the suffragette movement.

HARRIGAN, EDWARD (1844–1911) Born in New York, where he originally apprenticed in the ship-building trade, he ran away from home and sailed to San Francisco. Although he had appeared briefly as a youngster with Campbell's Minstrels, he made his real debut in the burgeoning West Coast variety theatres, such as the Bella Union.♦ In short order he teamed first with Alexander O'Brien and then with Sam Rickey, creating for the later act a sketch called "The Little Fraud." This was a success, but Rickey's drinking problems caused the act to disband. While looking for a new partner, Harrigan met Tony Hart♦ in Chicago. The fatherly or avuncular-looking Harrigan, with his dry wit, and the almost femininely beautiful Hart, with his more rambunctious style, proved perfect foils. They quickly became one of vaudeville's most popular attractions. Harrigan wrote the sketches, as well as the lyrics for their songs, which Harrigan's father-in-law, David Braham,♦ set to music. Soon Harrigan began writing extended playlets, and these proved so popular that he eventually started expanding some. The pair took over the Theatre Comique, where their shows were presented. At first the entertainments consisted of an olio followed by one of the playlets, but in time the latter continued to be so popular that Harrigan turned them into full-length musicals. One of the earliest was *The Mulligan Guards,* a spoof of contemporary paramilitary groups and dealing with the adventures of Dan Mulligan, his wife, and son. Harrigan used the Mulligan family in many of his best works, including *The Mulligan Guards' Ball*♦ (1879); *The Mulligan Guards' Surprise* (1880); *The Mulligans' Silver Wedding* (1880); and *Cordelia's Aspirations*♦ (1883). This last, centering on Cordelia Mulligan's comically overreaching ambitions, is considered by many to be Harrigan's finest work. Harrigan played Dan, while Hart played either his son or the Mulligans' raucous black maid Rebecca. Harrigan peopled his plays largely with immigrant classes and treated not only the Irish but also the blacks, Italians, Germans, and Jews. Among his other successes at this time were *The Major* (1881); *Squatter Sovereignty* (1882); and *McSorley's Inflation* (1882). Harrigan and Hart separated as a result of ill-feeling stemming from the burning of their theatre. Thereafter Harrigan's skills began to wane, although he enjoyed one final important success with *Reilly and the Four Hundred*♦ (1890), with which he opened the new theatre he had built and named after himself. His last new work was *The Woolen Stocking* (1893). In later years he leased the theatre and acted intermittently in a few plays by other men.

Harrigan's songs were among the most popular of his era. Hits such as "The Mulligan Guard March," "The Babies on Our Block," and "Maggie Murphy's Home" had widespread and long-lasting vogues. While they are largely forgotten today by modern playgoers and singers, they have, oddly, been absorbed into active folk traditions and have been collected in the United States and Canada by folklorists.

His works presented working-class life in relatively realistic, if comic, terms. The characters he created were richly developed and three-dimensional, and their virtues and flaws depicted consistently from one work to the next. At first Harrigan's works appealed only to regular theatregoers and were especially popular with newsboys and similar gallery gods of the time. Eventually, however, they attracted the notice and respect of leading critics and of writers such as William Dean Howells,♦ whose praise gave the pieces a new cachet. Harrigan has been called both the Dickens and the Hogarth of 19th-century American theatre.

Biography: *Ned Harrigan: From Corlear's Hook to Herald Square,* Richard Moody, Chicago, 1980.

HARRIS, ELMER, see *Johnny Belinda*

HARRIS, HENRY B. (1866–1912) The "pudgy, friendly, aggressive" son of William Harris, Sr.,♦ who was one of the founders of the Theatrical Syndicate or Trust,♦ and brother of William, Jr.,♦ he was born in St. Louis and raised in Boston. After assisting his father's theatrical enterprises he embarked on his own producing career with *Soldiers of Fortune* (1901). Subsequent productions included *Strongheart* (1905), *The Lion and the Mouse*♦ (1905), *The Chorus Lady*♦ (1906), *The Struggle Everlasting* (1907), *The Traveling Salesman*♦ (1908), and *The Third Degree*♦ (1909). In 1911 he built the Folies Bergere dinner theatre in conjunction with Jesse Lasky, a house which they converted into the Fulton Theatre shortly before Harris died in the sinking of the *Titanic*.

HARRIS, JED [né JACOB HOROWITZ] (1900–1979) The abrasive but brilliant producer and director, who once described himself as "an adventurer with a passion for the theatre and an indifference to show business," was born in Vienna. Brought to America while still very young, he was educated at Yale. After a brief stint in journalism, including time with the New York *Clipper,* ♦ he produced *Weak Sisters* in 1925. The play was a failure, but his next production, *Love 'Em and Leave 'Em* (1926), enjoyed a small success. Apart from one *succès d'estime, Spread Eagle* (1927), he then produced a series of hits that were not merely fine theatre but eminently "show business": *Broadway*♦ (1926), *Coquette*♦ (1927), *The Royal Family*♦ (1927), and *The Front Page*♦ (1928). Although he quickly earned a reputation as the "wonder boy" of Broadway, his eccentric behavior antagonized many. Once he called several of his associates to his apartment to discuss revisions for a play. When they arrived they found him lounging, totally naked, and he remained so throughout the discussions. As one of the men was leaving (some accounts say it was George S. Kaufman,♦

others, Charles MacArthur♦) he said to Harris, "Jed, your fly is open." Later, aware that Kaufman had developed an intense dislike for him, he told young Moss Hart,♦ then looking for a partner, to tell Kaufman that he, Harris, had recommended him. This nearly prevented Kaufman and Hart's celebrated association. He gained national notoriety when he sued Helen Hayes,♦ who was leaving *Coquette* to have a baby. He argued that an actress should not be pregnant when accepting a role or become pregnant while playing a part. Miss Hayes countered that a baby was an "act of God." The brouhaha resulted in "act of God" clauses being inserted in subsequent contracts to protect actresses. In the 1930s he began directing his productions, including interesting revivals of *Uncle Vanya* and *The Inspector General* and a mounting of the controversial *The Green Bay Tree* (1933). For the most part, however, his earlier success eluded him until he produced and directed *Our Town♦* (1938). Thereafter only his productions of a slight comedy, *Dark Eyes* (1943), and the drama *The Heiress♦* (1947) were commercial successes, although some of his mountings, such as the thriller *The Traitor* (1949), received good notices. In 1953 he directed *The Crucible.♦*

Autobiography: *A Dance on the High Wire*, New York, 1979.

HARRIS, [JULIA ANN] JULIE (b. 1925) Born in Grosse Point, Mich., and educated at the Yale School of Drama,♦ the somewhat elfin actress made her Broadway debut in *It's a Gift* (1945). That appearance was the first in a series of failures before she won high praise and the Donaldson Award♦ for her performance as Frankie Addams, the lonely tomboy, in *The Member of the Wedding♦* (1950). Further laurels came when she starred as the drifting, amoral Sally Bowles in *I Am a Camera♦* (1951). Brooks Atkinson♦ wrote of her performance, "She plays with a virtuosity and an honesty that are altogether stunning, and . . . has the quicksilver and the genius we all long to discover on the stage." She next essayed the title role of the girl who abandons her stodgy husband for the stage in *Mademoiselle Colombe* (1954). In 1955 she was a gamin Joan of Arc in *The Lark*. Thereafter she was unable to find superior plays. Nevertheless she enjoyed lengthy runs as Georgina, who lives for her dreams, in *Skyscraper* (1965), a musical version of *Dream Girl♦; * Ann Stanley, a middle-aged divorcée who flirts with a younger man, in *Forty Carats* (1968); and Lydia Crutwell, the dying wife who fears her husband no longer cares, in *In Praise of Love*

(1974). She had a lengthy tour in *The Belle of Amherst* (1976), a one-woman show based on the life and poetry of Emily Dickinson. Following the failure of *Break a Leg* (1979), a play about Viennese theatre-life, she assumed the lead in the West Coast company of *On Golden Pond♦* in 1980. In 1988 she toured in *Driving Miss Daisy.♦*

HARRIS, ROSEMARY [ANN] (b. 1930) The beautiful English-born actress, who has artfully combined elegance and warmth, made her American debut in *The Climate of Eden* (1952) and returned to New York as a member of the Old Vic♦ to play Shakespeare's Cressida in 1956. Among her subsequent American appearances were several important roles with the Association of Producing Artists,♦ including Alice in *You Can't Take It with You♦* and Lady Teazle. Afterwards she starred as Eleanor of Aquitaine in *The Lion in Winter♦* (1966), as Julie Cavendish in a 1975 revival of *The Royal Family,♦* as Hesione Hushabye in a 1983 revival of *Heartbreak House,* as Barbara Jackson, the worried wife, in *Pack of Lies* (1985), and later the same year as Judith Bliss in a revival of *Hay Fever*. She has also appeared in leading roles with numerous important American regional theatres.

HARRIS, SAM H[ENRY] (1872–1941) Born on New York's Lower East Side, Harris had been a newsboy, cough drop salesman, and steam laundry operator before becoming manager of Terry McGovern, a prizefighter. Between bouts McGovern had been appearing in a touring burlesque show, *The Gay Morning Glories*. Harris purchased an interest in the affair, and found himself in show business. He next formed the company of Sullivan, Harris and Woods,♦ with P. H. "Paddy" Sullivan and A. H. Woods,♦ sending popular melodramas such as *The Bowery After Dark* on tour. In 1904 he met George M. Cohan♦. The two became friends and organized a new company, Cohan and Harris. Among their many productions were *Little Johnny Jones♦* (1904); *The Talk of New York* (1907); *The Fortune Hunter♦* (1909); *The Man Who Owns Broadway* (1909); *Get-Rich-Quick Wallingford♦* (1910); *Seven Keys to Baldpate♦* (1913); *The House of Glass♦* (1915); *Hit-the-Trail Holliday♦* (1915); *The Great Lover♦* (1915); *A Tailor-Made Man♦* (1917); *Going Up* (1917); *Three Faces East♦* (1918); and *The Royal Vagabond* (1919). When the partnership was dissolved in 1920, Harris embarked on a career as solo producer. His productions included the *Music Box Revues♦* for the Music Box Theatre, which he built with Irving Berlin,♦ as well as *The Hero♦*

(1921); *Six-Cylinder Love*♦ (1921); *Rain*♦ (1922); *Icebound*♦ (1923); *The Nervous Wreck*♦ (1924); *The Jazz Singer*♦ (1925); *Cradle Snatchers*♦ (1925); *The Cocoanuts* (1925); *Chicago*♦ (1926); *Animal Crackers* (1928); *June Moon*♦ (1929); *Once in a Lifetime*♦ (1930); *Of Thee I Sing*♦ (1931); *Face the Music* (1932); *Dinner at Eight*♦ (1932); *As Thousands Cheer*♦ (1933); *Let'Em Eat Cake* (1933); *Merrily We Roll Along*♦ (1934); *Jubilee*♦ (1935); *Room Service*♦ (1935); *Stage Door*♦ (1936); *You Can't Take It with You*♦ (1936); *I'd Rather Be Right*♦ (1937); *Of Mice and Men*♦ (1937); *The Man Who Came to Dinner*♦ (1939); *George Washington Slept Here*♦ (1940); and *Lady in the Dark*♦ (1941). Besides the Music Box, he also managed the Harris Theatres in New York and Chicago. Obviously a shrewd judge of plays, Harris was equally admired for his integrity and courtesy.

HARRIS, WILLIAM, SR. (1844–1916) Born in Prussia and brought to America at the age of six, he was removed from school after only three months and put to work at his father's clothing store. He later took employment as a cigar stripper before becoming a minstrel in 1867. After several seasons he moved from minstrelsy to vaudeville, then in the 1880s took over the management of Boston's Howard Atheneum. ♦ His success was so marked that he soon began acquiring other playhouses. In 1895 he joined Klaw,♦ Erlanger,♦ Charles Frohman,♦ and others in forming the Theatrical Syndicate or Trust.♦ At the time of his death he controlled no fewer than six New York theatres and at least as many in other cities. He also worked closely with Klaw, Erlanger, and Frohman in producing plays. His sons, Henry B.♦ and William, Jr.,♦ were both well-known producers.

HARRIS, WILLIAM, JR. (1884–1946) Son of William Harris,♦ one of the founders of the Theatrical Syndicate or Trust,♦ and brother of Henry B. Harris,♦ he was born in Boston but raised in New York, where he studied at Columbia. After working briefly under his father, he tried his hand unsuccessfully as a lyricist and librettist. He soon found more congenial work by following in his father's and brother's footsteps as a producer. Usually alone, but occasionally in collaboration with others, he produced such hits as *The Yellow Jacket*♦ (1912); *Twin Beds*♦ (1914); *The Thirteenth Chair*♦ (1916); *East Is West*♦ (1918); *Abraham Lincoln* (1919); *The Bad Man* (1920); *In Love with Love* (1923); *Outward Bound* (1924); *The Criminal Code*♦ (1929); and *The Greeks Had a Word for It* (1930). Late in his career he often directed his own productions. Described as

"tall, lank and frequently caustic," he retired in 1939.

HARRISON, BERTRAM (1877–1955) Although he began his career as an actor, eventually playing important supporting roles with Henry Miller,♦ he found even greater success when he turned to directing. He staged a wide range of plays, but seemed to have best luck with fast-paced farces. Among his hits were *Little Women* (1912); *Parlor, Bedroom and Bath*♦ (1917); *Up in Mabel's Room*♦ (1919); *Ladies' Night*♦ (1920); *Getting Gertie's Garter*♦ (1921); *The Demi-Virgin* (1921); *Partners Again* (1922); *Lawful Larceny* (1922); *The Kiss in the Taxi* (1925); and *Swing Your Lady!* (1936).

HARRISON, [REGINALD CAREY] REX (1908–90) The slim, suave, slightly reptilian, English-born actor made his first American appearance as Tubbs Barrow, the heroine's witty friend, in *Sweet Aloes* (1936). The play was a failure, and Harrison did not return to the New York stage until after he had become a celebrated film star. He then starred as Henry VIII in *Anne of the Thousand Days*♦ (1948). He next played Shepherd Henderson, the publisher ensnared by a designing witch, in *Bell, Book and Candle*♦ (1950). In 1952 he portrayed Hereward, the philandering Duke who yearns for a quieter life, in *Venus Observed.* Following that he played The Man, the comically evil spirit who bedevils the officers' amours, in *The Love of Four Colonels* (1953). His greatest success came when he created the role of Henry Higgins, the professor who attempts to make a lady of a street urchin, in *My Fair Lady*♦ (1956). Walter Kerr wrote of his performance, "Mr. Harrison's slouch was a rhythmic slouch. His voice was a showman's voice—twangy, biting, confident beyond questioning . . . But most of all Mr. Harrison was still an actor, believing every cranky, snappish, exhilarating syllable of the Alan Jay Lerner lyric he was rattling off, and a fourteen-carat character simply crashed its way onto the stage." Among the lyrics he helped make famous were "I've Grown Accustomed to Her Face" and "The Rain in Spain." Harrison played the role for several years and revived it afterwards. He later appeared as The General, who would reorder the world along his own old-fashioned lines, in *The Fighting Cock* (1959); in the title role of *Emperor Henry IV* (1973); as Sebastian Crutwell, the seemingly indifferent husband of a dying wife, in *In Praise of Love* (1974); Hawkins, the aging man who briefly rekindles an old love, in *The Kingfisher* (1979); Captain Shotover in a 1983 revival of

Heartbreak House; as Lord Gresham in a 1985 revival of *Aren't We All?;* and as Lord Porteous in a 1989 revival of *The Circle.*

Autobiography: *Rex,* New York, 1974.

HARRISON, RICHARD B[ERRY] (1864–1935) One of many actors remembered for a single role, it was his interpretation of De Lawd in *The Green Pastures*◆ (1930) which made that play so mesmerizing. He played the part nearly 2000 times before his death. Marc Connelly◆ recalled him thus: "Topping his six-foot height was a head of leonine gray hair. Below it, we saw a face that had managed to weather sixty-five years of struggle and disheartenment . . . He spoke with a voice like a cello's." Harrison was the son of slaves who had escaped to Canada via the underground railroad. Moving later to Detroit, he studied elocution and then offered Shakespearean and other recitals on the L. E. Behymer and Chautauqua circuits. *The Green Pastures* marked his only professional appearance in a play.

Harry Burnham, a play in four acts by James Pilgrim. ◆ Produced at the National Theatre. March 10, 1851. 18 performances.

Harry Burnham (Harry Watkins◆) rouses his fellow Yale students against the British. He joins the Revolutionary army, is wounded and captured, but escapes. At the Battle of Trenton he replaces the British flag with an American one, and is hailed as a hero.

Typical of the melodramatic patriotic spectacles that appeared in the wake of the Mexican-American war, the story was dramatized from a novel then being serialized in a newspaper and featured George Washington as an important character. According to Watkins's biographers, Otis Skinner◆ and Skinner's wife, Maud, the version played represented Watkin's revision of Pilgrim's adaptation. Certainly, Watkins claimed as much in his diary, but his claims are often suspect. The Skinners refer to the producer as H. O. Pardy, but Odell◆ lists him as A. H. Purdy. Both men were active in New York theatricals at the time.

HART, LORENZ [MILTON] (1895–1943) Born in New York, he was educated at Columbia, where he wrote lyrics for college shows to music by the man who would be his life-long partner, Richard Rodgers. ◆ He left college to accept a job as translator for the Messrs. Shubert,◆ but continued collaborating with Rodgers. Broadway first heard his lyrics when Lew Fields interpolated "Any Old Place with You" in *A Lonely Romeo* (1919). The song's impudent rhym-

ing of "go to hell for ya" with "Philadelphia" and "corner ya" with "California" caught critics' ears, but nothing came of it. Even their songs for *Poor Little Ritz Girl* (1920) seemingly led nowhere. Not until they created the songs for the 1925 and 1926 editions of the *Garrick Gaieties*◆ did they begin to find a niche. Hits from these revues were "Manhattan" and "Mountain Greenery." Subsequent successes included *Dearest Enemy*◆ (1925), which offered "Bye and Bye" and "Here in My Arms"; *The Girl Friend* (1926), whose score contained "The Blue Room" and the title song; *Peggy-Ann*◆ (1926); *A Connecticut Yankee*◆ (1927), from which came "My Heart Stood Still" and "Thou Swell"; *Present Arms* (1928), whose hit was "You Took Advantage of Me"; *Spring Is Here* (1929), which produced "With a Song in My Heart"; and *Simple Simon* (1930), remembered for "Ten Cents a Dance." After a stint in Hollywood, they returned to New York to create a series of even more memorable shows: *Jumbo*◆ (1935), which included "The Most Beautiful Girl in the World" and "My Romance"; *On Your Toes*◆ (1936), which gave us "There's a Small Hotel"; *Babes in Arms*◆ (1937), whose hit-filled score contained the title song, "I Wish I Were in Love Again," "Johnny One Note," "The Lady Is a Tramp," "My Funny Valentine," and "Where or When"; *I'd Rather Be Right*◆ (1937); *I Married an Angel*◆ (1938), which produced the title song and "Spring Is Here"; *The Boys from Syracuse*◆ (1938), which offered "Falling in Love with Love" and "This Can't Be Love"; *Too Many Girls* (1939), whose score provided "I Didn't Know What Time It Was"; *Higher and Higher* (1940); *Pal Joey*◆ (1940), whose hit was "Bewitched"; and *By Jupiter*◆ (1942), from which came "Everything I've Got." Hart also collaborated on the books for *On Your Toes; Babes in Arms;* and *I Married an Angel.*

Hart was a master at polysyllabic and internal rhymes and at innovative lyric forms. His work was pervaded with his essentially misanthropic view of the world. Although personal problems, especially alcoholism, beset his later years, his gifts never waned. His lyric for "To Keep My Love Alive," which was added to the 1943 revival of *A Connecticut Yankee,* just before his death, was the equal in wit and style to anything he had written earlier.

Biography: *Rodgers and Hart,* Samuel Marx and Jan Clayton, New York, 1976.

HART, Moss (1904–61) Born in New York, he received his earliest theatrical training as assistant to producer Augustus Pitou. ◆ His first plays, *The Beloved Bandit,* also called *The Hold Up Man*

(1923), and *Jonica* (1930), the latter written with Dorothy Heyward, were failures. Success came when he collaborated with George S. Kaufman♦ on *Once in a Lifetime*♦ (1930), a spoof of Hollywood. Turning to musicals he wrote the libretto for *Face the Music* (1932), sketches for *As Thousands Cheer*♦ (1933), and adapted *The Great Waltz* (1934). With Kaufman he next wrote *Merrily We Roll Along*♦ (1934), which examined the career of a disillusioned playwright. In 1935 he wrote the libretto for *Jubilee,*♦ then reunited with Kaufman on seven successive plays: the Pulitzer Prize♦-winning *You Can't Take It with You*♦ (1936), a comic look at a zany family; the book for *I'd Rather Be Right*♦ (1937), a fantasy in which President Roosevelt was a central figure; *Sing Out the News* (1938), a revue; *The Fabulous Invalid* (1938), a nostalgic glimpse of American theatre; *The American Way* (1939), a patriotic spectacle revolving around an immigrant family; *The Man Who Came to Dinner*♦ (1939), focusing on an Alexander Woollcott-like figure; and *George Washington Slept Here*♦ (1940), in which a city family attempts to restore a dilapidated country house. *Lady in the Dark*♦ (1941), for which he wrote the libretto, sought to psychoanalyze a woman editor, while *Winged Victory* (1943) was a wartime play about the air force. *Christopher Blake* (1946), in which a youngster is forced to choose between divorcing parents was a mixture of realism and fantasy and was a failure, but his next work, *Light Up the Sky*♦ (1948), which told in comic terms of a play's tryout, was a popular success. His last work was *The Climate of Eden* (1952), adapted from Edgar Mittelholzer's novel, *Shadows Move Among Them,* and telling of a missionary and his daughters confronted by a mentally unstable man. Because so many of Hart's earlier works were collaborations it is difficult to assess his precise contribution to them, but his solo efforts revealed a gift for superior, literate dialogue, and probing characterization, this last quality probably reflecting his interest in human psychology following his own much-publicized psychoanalysis. Besides directing many of his own shows, he also staged such hits as *Junior Miss*♦ (1941), *Dear Ruth*♦ (1944), *My Fair Lady*♦ (1956), and *Camelot*♦ (1960). On occasion he served as producer as well.

Autobiography: *Act One,* New York, 1959.

HART, TONY [né ANTHONY J. CANNON] (1855–91) However brief his heyday, Hart was one of the finest and most popular performers of his era. He is remembered today entirely for his association with Edward Harrigan♦ in the team of Harrigan and Hart. His early life was unhappy. Born into a poor Irish family in Worcester, Mass., he apparently was the shortest member of the household and thus the butt of much unpleasant humor. His response was often so abusive that he was sent to reform school. He soon ran away, coming to New York, where he sang and danced for pennies in saloons. Some time with a circus company was followed by stints with several minstrel troupes. While appearing with one in Chicago he came to Harrigan's attention at the very moment Harrigan was seeking a new partner. Hart was sixteen at the time. Although small, he was exceptionally handsome and had a fine tenor voice. By contrast Harrigan was relatively tall, fatherly looking, and had a light baritone voice. The men recognized that their appearances and abilities were complementary. They quickly ranked high among variety bills, performing in skits written by Harrigan. When Harrigan began writing longer plays, Hart was always given major roles. In the series of plays dealing with the Mulligan family Hart played either the Mulligan son, Tommy, or else the Mulligans' rambunctious black maid, Rebecca. This later was his most famous role. The pair broke up following mutually recriminatory accusations after their theatre burned. Hart's subsequent roles included Isaac Roost, the desperate editor who resorts to numerous disguises to save his failing paper, in *A Toy Pistol* (1886) and Upton O. Dodge, the befuddled assistant moonshiner, opposite Lillian Russell♦ in *The Maid and the Moonshiner* (1886). His behavior, however, was becoming increasingly erratic and he was committed to a home, where he died of paresis.

HART, WILLIAM S. (1870–1946) Although most famous as an early film cowboy, this rugged actor had an interesting stage career. A native of Newburgh, N.Y., he made his debut in Daniel Bandmann's♦ company in 1889. He then played leads opposite such distinguished actresses as Modjeska♦ and Julia Arthur,♦ offering his Armand Duval, Benedick, Macbeth, Ingomar, Romeo, and Orlando. He was the original Messala in *Ben Hur*♦ (1899), and between 1907 and 1910 headed a touring company of *The Virginian.* ♦

HARTE, BRET, see *M'liss* and *Ah Sin*

Harvard Dramatic Club Founded in 1908 to encourage play-writing among undergraduates and alumni, it produced only their plays until 1917. Its offerings included the premiere of Percy Mackaye's♦ *The Scarecrow*♦ in 1909. After World War I it abandoned its original policy, but for many years offered the American premieres of interesting foreign plays. In recent years it has combined with the Radcliffe dramatic club and operates much like any other college theatrical organization, albeit it works closely with the American Repertory Theatre at the Loeb Center.

Harvey, a comedy in three acts by Mary Chase.♦ Produced by Brock Pemberton♦ at the 48th Street Theatre. November 1, 1944. 1,775 performances. PP.

Flibbertigibbet Veta Louise Simmons (Josephine Hull♦) and her haughty, homely spinster daughter, Myrtle Mae (Jane Van Duser), are exasperated with Veta's boozy brother, Elwood P. Dowd (Frank Fay♦), who has befriended Harvey. Harvey, you see, is not only an extraordinarily large rabbit—over six feet tall—but he is also invisible. Matters come to a head after Elwood introduces Harvey to Mrs. Chauvenet (Frederica Going), a social leader. The dowager quickly makes her excuses, leaving a furious Myrtle Mae to insist Uncle Elwood be sent to a "booby hatch," Chumley's Rest. There, however, it is Myrtle Mae who is mistaken for the prospective patient. The confusion is soon settled and Elwood admitted. But a taxi driver who has driven Veta to the mental home describes how nice the patients are when he brings them there, and how when they are "cured," "They crab, crab, crab. They yell at me to watch the lights, watch the brakes, watch the intersection. They scream at me to hurry." Veta realizes that she prefers Elwood as the harmless, benign man he has always been. So Elwood is allowed to leave Chumley's, taking Harvey with him.

Originally called *The Pooka,* a Celtic term describing a fairy spirit in animal form, Pemberton produced the play against the advice of his fellow professionals and after all his initial choices for Elwood turned him down. His casting of Fay, a reformed alcoholic who had fallen on hard times, was a desperate inspiration. John Chapman♦ of the *Daily News* called the comedy, "the most delightful, droll, endearing, funny and touching piece of stage whimsey I ever saw." It has been revived regularly.

HARWOOD, JOHN EDMUND (1771–1809) Although Harwood was indisputably among the ranking comedians of his time, there is some question whether he was American-born or English-born. Some sources contend he initially read for the law. Certainly his entire stage career was spent in America, where he made his professional debut in 1794 at Philadelphia's

Southwark Theatre♦ under Wignell's♦ auspices as Gradus in the comic afterpiece *Who's the Dupe?* Later in the same season he played such roles as Sir Fretful Plagiary in *The Critic* and Stephano in *The Tempest.* ♦ He also played for Wignell in Annapolis and New York, before temporarily retiring from the stage. This withdrawal was urged upon him by his in-laws, the Baches, who were Benjamin Franklin's daughter and son-in-law. They deemed the theatre an unworthy profession and helped set him up as a bookseller, but he shortly failed and returned to acting. Dunlap♦ engaged him for the Park Theatre♦ in 1803, where he enjoyed a huge success as Dennis Brulgruddery in *John Bull; or, An Englishman's Fireside.* Growing increasingly corpulent, he soon established himself as the finest Falstaff America had yet seen. While much of his early reputation was established in low comedy roles, in his last years he was often acclaimed for his high comedy parts. He died at the height of his popularity.

HASTINGS, THOMAS, see *Carrère and Hastings*

Hasty Pudding Club, THE Founded as a social club in 1795 by a group of Harvard undergraduates, it calls itself "the third oldest theatrical organization in the world," outranked only by the Comédie Française♦ and the Oberammergau Passion Players. The claim is exaggerated since the club did not enter the theatrical arena for many years. Early in its history the organization began staging mock trials, at what it called its "High Court of Equity." By 1835 these trials were theatricalized by costuming participants. Musical numbers were introduced in 1850. The first more or less original Hasty Pudding show was written in 1884 by Lemuel Hayward. It was a collegiate burlesque of a then popular commercial burlesque, *Bombastes Furioso.* Although the club mounted several shows a year, it was generally its spring production on which it lavished special attention and which often toured. Since the time of World War I a separate committee, the Hasty Pudding Theatricals, has overseen the productions. Among performers and writers were such later famous figures as Oliver Wendell Holmes, Franklin Roosevelt, William Randolph Hearst, Henry Cabot Lodge, Owen Wister, Robert Sherwood,♦ and Alan Jay Lerner. ♦ After Harvard became co-educational, women were allowed to be active behind the scenes. However, the casts of Hasty Pudding musicals, including "female" leads and chorus "girls," remain steadfastly male.

Hatful of Rain, A, a drama in three acts by Michael V. Gazzo. Produced at the Lyceum Theatre.♦ November 9, 1955. 398 performances.

Johnny Pope (Ben Gazzara♦), who had picked up a drug habit in the hospital and had overcome it, suffers a relapse. He hides his problem from his wife, Celia (Shelley Winters), and his father, John, Sr. (Frank Silvera). His wife suspects his sometimes peculiar behavior means there is another woman; his father is also alienated by his actions. Only his brother Polo (Anthony Franciosa) understands him and supplies the money he needs. Johnny finally confesses to his wife, and they agree to work through the hell of withdrawal.

One of the earliest plays after World War II to deal openly with a growing problem, it was faulted by many critics for failing to explore many aspects of the personal relationships it brought up—such as the interaction of father and son—but was nevertheless seen as a powerful piece of theatre.

Gazzo was born in Hillside, N.J., in 1923, and studied at the Dramatic Workshop. Although this was his only successful play, he also directed and acted.

HATTON, FANNY LOCKE (1870?–1939) and FREDERIC H. (1879–1946) A husband and wife team who worked together on the drama desks of several Chicago newspapers before turning to play-writing, they found success with their first produced play, *Years of Discretion* (1912), a story of a New England widow who has a fling in New York. Subsequent hits included *The Great Lover*♦ (1915), written with Leo Ditrichstein♦ and centering on the romantic life of an aging opera star; *Upstairs and Down*♦ (1916), in which the worlds of the rich and their servants are shown to be equally clawing; and *Lombardi, Ltd.*♦ (1917), recounting a successful dress designer's unfortunate wooing of a young gold digger. One critic described this last work as "just another of those Hatton plays, in which familiar characters bounce along through an even more familiar stage love story, to the accompaniment of a patter of racy and spicy lines attuned to the mood of the all too familiar Broadway audience." While the Hattons were regularly represented on Broadway until the early 1930s, all of their later efforts failed. Their last plays were not originals, but adaptations. Hatton was born in Peru, Ill., and studied chemistry at the University of Wisconsin and at Princeton. Mrs. Hatton was a Chicago native.

HATTON, MRS., see *Tammany*

HAVERLY, JOHN H. (1838–1901) Born somewhere in eastern Pennsylvania he was removed from school at an early age and apprenticed to a shoemaker, whom he found excessively demanding and violent. He ran away, reaching Pittsburgh, where he took employment as a railway newsboy. He soon found the attractions of Pittsburgh's theatres irresistible and quickly rose from usher to treasurer. At the same time he tried his luck at performing, but proved to have little talent. He left Pittsburgh to become advance man for Sand's Minstrels. Later he moved to the Wagner Minstrels, which he eventually took over. He soon developed the largest company in the country, turning the once intimate minstrel show into a gigantic spectacle. Haverly's Mastodon—Forty, Count 'Em, Forty—Minstrels was for a time the pre-eminent touring ensemble in the country. He also began leasing theatres, beginning with the old Adelphi in Chicago. Often he renamed the theatres after himself. Long before the advent of the Theatrical Syndicate or Trust,♦ he envisaged a chain of playhouses spanning the continent. At his height in the 1880s he is said to have headed six theatres and had fourteen touring troupes. But Haverly placed too much faith in the continuing vogue for blackface entertainments, and when vaudeville surpassed minstrel shows in public favor he proved surprisingly and damagingly inflexible. He moved on to other commercial ventures, none of which was successful. At the time of his death he was managing a small mine.

Having Wonderful Time, a comedy in three acts by Arthur Kober. Produced by Marc Connelly♦ and others at the Lyceum Theatre.♦ February 20, 1937. 372 performances.

Having quarreled with an older man whom she had been dating, Teddy Stern (Katherine Locke), a Bronx stenographer, comes to Camp Kare-Free in the Berkshires for a vacation. She is quickly courted by a young lawyer, Chick Kessler (John Garfield,♦ still billed as Jules Garfield), who is working as a waiter to meet expenses. Chick's eagerness puts off Teddy, but when she is next courted by an unscrupulous Lothario, Pinkie Aaronson (Sheldon Leonard), she comes to appreciate Chick's sincerity.

This comic view of Jewish camp life was turned into an even more successful musical, *Wish You Were Here,* with a book by Kober and Joshua Logan♦ and music by Harold Rome.♦ The show opened at the Imperial Theatre on June 25, 1952, and ran for 598 performances. Patricia Marand was Teddy; Jack Cassidy, Chick; and Paul Valentine,

Pinky. Principal songs were "Wish You Were Here"; and "Where Did the Night Go?."

Kober (1900–1975) was born in Austria. These were his only successful plays.

HAYDON, JULIE [née DONELLA LIGHTFOOT DONALD-SON] (b. 1910) The shyly beautiful daughter of a publisher and editor and his musician wife, she was born in Oak Park, Ill., but raised in California. Her stage debut was as a maid in a 1929 West Coast revival of *Mrs. Bumpstead-Leigh.* ♦ She first appeared in New York in *Bright Star* (1935), and is best remembered for three later performances: Brigid, the maid caught in the feud between a canon and a schoolmaster, in *Shadow and Substance* (1938); Kitty Duval, the streetwalker who dreams of a better world, in *The Time of Your Life* ♦ (1939); and Laura, the crippled girl who lives for her collection of figurines, in *The Glass Menagerie* ♦ (1945). In 1955 she married George Jean Nathan, ♦ the critic, who was many years her elder, and after his death toured in a program of readings from his work.

HAYES [BROWN], HELEN (b. 1900) The daughter of a small-time actress and a traveling salesman, she was born in Washington, D.C., and made her stage debut there at the age of five with a local stock company. She soon came to the attention of Lew Fields, ♦ who cast her as Little Mimi in *Old Dutch* (1909), her Broadway debut. After appearing in several more of his musicals she moved on to such teen-age roles as Pollyanna in the show of the same name in 1917, as Margaret Schofield in *Penrod* (1918), and as Margaret in *Dear Brutus* (1918). In the early 1920s she won recognition and seemed for a short while type-cast as a flapper, including the parts of Cora Wheeler in *Clarence* ♦ (1919); Elsie Beebe in *To the Ladies* ♦ (1922); and Catherine Westcourt in *Dancing Mothers* ♦ (1924). In 1925 she played Cleopatra in *Caesar and Cleopatra* ♦ and the following year appeared for the first time in what became her favorite part, Maggie Wylie in *What Every Woman Knows.* This role of a seemingly mousy, unassertive woman who bends everyone to her will succinctly caught the dichotomy that characterized much of her later acting, a curious and unique combination of apparent softness, even cuteness, with a hard, iron resolve. Because she was a tiny woman with a round, friendly face her inner strengths were not always instantly obvious. A major success was her playing of Norma Besant, the doomed flapper, in *Coquette* ♦ (1927). The role brought her some unsought national notoriety when she left the cast to have her "act of God" baby. In

1933 she was Mary Stuart in *Mary of Scotland.* ♦ After its tour she then essayed what is probably her most famous part, the title role in *Victoria Regina* (1935). She portrayed the Queen from her young, innocent years into aged widowhood. Robert Garland of the *World-Telegram* hailed her performance as one of "consummate skill and comprehension." She took the play on extended tour. Following a brief stint as Viola in a 1940 revival of *Twelfth Night,* ♦ she played Madeleine Guest, an American actress determined to rescue her lover from the Nazis, in *Candle in the Wind* (1941). She returned to history to enact Harriet Beecher Stowe in *Harriet* ♦ (1943), then moved on to a light comedy, playing Addie Bemis, the librarian who goes on a toot, in *Happy Birthday* ♦ (1946), her longest New York run. Subsequent performances, all highly praised but less successful commercially, included Lucy Andree Ransdell (read Madame Ranevskaya) in *The Wisteria Trees* (1950), a modern version of *The Cherry Orchard* set in 19th-century Louisiana; Mrs. Howard V. Larue II, whose son is spirited away by a wicked witch, in *Mrs. McThing* (1952); the Duchess of Pont-au-Bronc, who hires a milliner to impersonate her nephew's dead sweetheart, in *Time Remembered* (1957); and Nora Melody, the loyal wife of a drunken innkeeper, in *A Touch of the Poet* ♦ (1958). For the rest of her career, playing in both America and Europe, she appeared largely in revivals. The most notable of these was *The Show Off* ♦ (1967), in which she portrayed the sweetly calculating Mrs. Fisher. She retired from the stage after playing the flustered Veta Louise Simmons in a 1970 revival of *Harvey.* ♦ However, in her heyday she ranked with Katharine Cornell ♦ and Lynn Fontanne ♦ as one of the theatre's great ladies. She was married to Charles MacArthur. ♦

Autobiography: *My Life in Three Acts,* New York, 1990.

HAYMAN, AL (1847–1917) Born in Wheeling, W.V., he apparently began his theatrical career as manager of a touring company of *The Black Crook* ♦ in 1871. The tour covered not only the Southern states but Mexico and Central America as well. In Panama he met Harry Keller, ♦ the magician, and agreed to manage his South American tour. Shortly thereafter Hayman was engaged by M. B. Leavitt ♦ to run Leavitt's Australian interests. In 1882 Leavitt transfered him to San Francisco, where he was placed in charge of the Bush Street Theatre. While there he met Charles Frohman, ♦ who was helping with the tours of Lyceum Theatre ♦ productions from New York. The two became friends, and

Hayman resigned his position with Leavitt to work with Frohman. Hayman seemingly had been prudent with his finances, for it was largely with his money that Frohman was able to buy the rights to *Shenandoah,* ♦ the play that launched his career as producer. Similarly it was Hayman's financial manipulation which allowed the men to build the Empire Theatre♦ in 1893. With Klaw, ♦ Erlanger, ♦ and others they then formed the Theatrical Syndicate or Trust, ♦ ostensibly to bring order out of chaotic booking practices but in reality to exert monopolistic powers over the theatre of their day. He served from 1901 to 1904 as president of the Actors' Fund♦ and was the largest personal contributor in the drive to erect a home for retired actors, which was opened during his tenure. Hayman's decision to leave artistic matters to Frohman and to allow Frohman lone public credit for productions mounted largely with Hayman's money meant that to playgoers he was little more than a shadowy figure. His fiscal acumen, however, was such that he left an estate of $1,692,815, while his more visible partner, Frohman, left behind a mere $451.

HAYMAN, Alf[red] (1865–1921) The younger brother of Al Hayman, ♦ with whom he is sometimes confused, he was born in Wheeling, W.V., and tried his hand as a salesman before his brother induced him to become treasurer of the Baldwin Theatre♦ in San Francisco. By the mid-1890s he was right-hand man to Charles Frohman, ♦ and after Frohman's death he continued as head of Frohman's production company. Under the Frohman name he produced such shows as *Dear Brutus* (1918); *Déclassée*♦ (1919); and *Mary Rose* (1920).

HAYWARD, Leland (1902–71) Born in Nebraska City, Neb., and educated at Princeton, he spent some years working in films before becoming a talent agent. In 1944 he produced *A Bell for Adano*♦ and for the next two decades was one of New York's most successful producers. Among his other hits, produced alone or in collaboration, were *State of the Union*♦ (1945); *Mister Roberts*♦ (1948); *Anne of the Thousand Days*♦ (1948); *South Pacific*♦ (1949); *Call Me Madam*♦ (1950); *Point of No Return* (1951); *Wish You Were Here*♦ (1952); *Gypsy*♦ (1959); and *The Sound of Music*♦ (1959). He was married to Margaret Sullavan. ♦

Hazel Kirke, a play in four acts by Steele MacKaye. ♦ Produced by MacKaye at the Madison Square Theatre. ♦ February 4, 1880. 486 performances.
Hazel Kirke (Effie Ellsler♦) is disowned by her father, Dunstan Kirke (C. W. Couldock♦), when she marries Arthur Carrington (Eben Plympton♦) instead of the man of his choice. Carrington's mother, Emily Carrington (Mrs. Cecil Rush), is equally unhappy about the marriage, since Carrington is also Lord Travers and his mother feels he has married below his station. She leads Hazel to believe the marriage is illegal. Hazel rushes off and attempts suicide by drowning, but becomes frightened and screams for help. Her father, who has gone blind by this time, hears her but can do nothing. Fortunately, Arthur appears and rescues her.

The play was originally produced as *The Iron Hand* and failed. It was rewritten and served as an early attraction at MacKaye's new theatre. Although it received a divided press, it was an immediate hit and enjoyed the longest run up to its day of any non-musical play. It could be seen as a typical late 19th-century melodrama, but it was distinguished from them, as Quinn♦ has noted, by "the quiet natural dialogue and the absence of the usual stage villain." It was also among the very first plays to send out road companies, five of them touring while the original production remained in New York.

HAZELTON, George, see *Mistress Nell* and *The Yellow Jacket*

HAZZARD, John E., see *Turn to the Right!*

He and She, a play in three acts by Rachel Crothers. ♦ Produced at the Little Theatre. February 12, 1920. 28 performances.
Ann Herford (Miss Crothers) and her husband, Tom (Cyril Keightley), are architects whose seventeen years of happy marriage seem threatened when each submits a separate entry to a contest for a frieze design. Ann wins the $100,000 prize, but soon comes to recognize that she has won it at the cost of probably losing her husband and of neglecting her daughter Millicent (Faire Binney). She declines the prize, prepares to spend time with Millicent in Europe, and knows that she has lost neither the money nor Tom, since he was second and will now be the winner.

The play had an interesting history. Originally produced as *The Herfords* (1911), it failed, and Miss Crothers blamed the failure on miscasting. However, she was not able to find another producer until she persuaded the Messrs. Shubert♦ to produce it with her. Even then she was unable to find an actress to play Ann, so took the part herself. The play was hailed by almost every major critic, who looked on it as a fine study of the plight of the modern, emancipated woman. Yet the play did not find an audience, although (or because) an equally fine play on the same theme, *The Famous Mrs. Fair,* ◆ had succeeded earlier in the season.

Heart of Maryland, The, a drama in four acts by David Belasco. ◆ Produced by Belasco at the Herald Square Theatre. October 22, 1895. 229 performances.

The Civil War has split apart Maryland families. Colonel Alan Kendrick (Maurice Barrymore◆) fights for the North, while his father, General Hugh Kendrick (Frank Mordaunt), is a Confederate. Similarly, Alan's sweetheart, Maryland Calvert (Mrs. Leslie Carter◆), remains loyal to the South and so has broken their engagement, while her brother, Lloyd (Edward J. Morgan), spies for the Federal troops. When Alan sneaks through the lines to see Maryland he is captured by Colonel Fulton Thorpe (John E. Kellerd◆), a former Northern officer whom Alan once court-martialed and who now fights with the Confederate troops. Seeking revenge, Thorpe arranges to have Alan shot as a spy. Maryland comes to plead for Alan's life, only to have Thorpe attempt to seduce her. She takes a bayonet that Thorpe uses as a candlestick and stabs him with it, giving Alan time to escape. The wounded Thorpe orders the local church bell rung to announce a prisoner's escape, but Maryland climbs into the belfry and, shouting "The bell shall not ring!," grabs the clapper and swings with it to prevent the bell from sounding. Later Alan returns with Federal troops and besieges Thorpe. He also intercepts letters from General Robert E. Lee in which Lee reveals he has learned that Thorpe is an untrustworthy double agent. Thorpe is imprisoned, and Alan and Maryland are reunited.

Written as a vehicle for Mrs. Carter and suggested by the poem "Curfew Shall Not Ring Tonight!," it was this play which firmly established Belasco's reputation as author, producer, and director. Many critics felt the story was unduly complicated and cliché-ridden, but the fine production and, most of all, the famous scene with Maryland swinging on the clapper made the play a huge success. It toured for three consecutive seasons and was occasionally revived.

HECHT, BEN (1894–1964) Born in New York and raised in Wisconsin, Hecht made unsuccessful attempts at becoming an acrobat and a violinist before finding a niche as a flamboyant Chicago newspaperman. Besides his newspaper writing, novels, and other literary works he wrote numerous plays. The most memorable were two acerbic comedies written in collaboration with Charles MacArthur◆: *The Front Page*◆ (1928), in which Chicago newsmen cover an execution; and *Twentieth Century*◆ (1932), in which a fading producer makes a desperate attempt at a comeback. Among his other plays were *The Egotist* (1922); *The Stork* (1925), an adaptation of a Hungarian play; *The Great Magoo* (1932), written with Gene Fowler; the libretto for *Jumbo*◆ (1935), with MacArthur; *To Quito and Back* (1937); *Ladies and Gentlemen* (1939), with MacArthur; *Swan Song* (1946), with MacArthur; *A Flag Is Born* (1946); and the libretto of *Hazel Flagg* (1953).

Autobiography: *A Child of the Century,* New York, 1954.

HECKART, [ANNA] EILEEN (b. 1919) A native of Columbus, Ohio, she made her New York debut in 1943 and soon rose to important supporting roles in such plays as *Picnic*◆ (1953), *The Bad Seed* (1954), *A View from the Bridge*◆ (1955), and *The Dark at the Top of the Stairs*◆ (1957). She achieved stardom in a failed comedy, *Everbody Loves Opal* (1961), then went on to play a variety of roles in *You Know I Can't Hear You When the Water's Running*◆ (1967) and Mrs. Baker, the possessive mother, in *Butterflies Are Free*◆ (1969). She continues to appear off-Broadway and in regional theatre, but her luck on Broadway has soured.

Hedgerow Theatre Founded in 1923 by Jasper Deeter (1893–1972), the theatre was housed in a converted mill in Moylan, near Philadelphia. The company, which usually consisted of about thirty actors, performed in traditional repertory style, giving different plays nightly during a season that generally ran from early spring until late fall. In winter months they would offer occasional performances and sometimes would tour. The repertory eventually consisted of over 200 plays, with Chekhov,◆ Ibsen,◆ Shaw,◆ and O'Neill◆ special favorites. Along with the classics the troupe revived many rarities and gave the world premieres of such plays as *Rancour* (1928), *The Cherokee Night* (1932), *Winesburg, Ohio* (1934), and *In the Summer House*◆ (1951). A school was established by the troupe, offering a three-year course in all aspects of theatre. The school continues, although the repertory policy was abandoned in 1956. Shows are now mounted for brief runs. The theatre burned in 1985 but has been restored.

HEGGEN, THOMAS, see *Mister Roberts*

HEGGIE, O. P. (1879–1936) An Australian-born character actor, he spent many years on his native and London stages before coming to America in 1907 with Ellen Terry♦ to appear as Alexander Oldworthy in *Nance Oldfield* and as Osman in *Captain Brassbound's Conversion.* He later returned to settle in New York and to become the first American Androcles in *Androcles and the Lion* (1915). Subsequent memorable roles included Robert Cokeson, the solicitors' clerk, in *Justice* (1916); Oliver Blayds, the famous poet whose best work was really not his own, in *The Truth About Blayds* (1922); and Old Man Minick, who prefers a home for the aged to his daughter-in-law's, in *Minick* (1924). He also appeared in numerous revivals of classics ranging from Shylock in *The Merchant of Venice*♦ to Diggory in *She Stoops To Conquer.* His last Broadway assignment was as William Owen, who kills his son's degenerate benefactor, in *The Green Bay Tree* (1933). Although never a star of the first magnitude, Heggie was almost always praised for his singularly warm, knowing interpretations.

Heidi Chronicles, The, a play in two acts by Wendy Wasserstein. Produced by the Shubert♦ Organization and others at the Plymouth Theatre. March 9, 1989. 621 performances. PP, NYDCCA.

Heidi Holland (Joan Allen) lectures on women's matters, but she herself is not the happiest of women. In fact, she's unfulfilled and very unhappy. The would-be politician (Peter Friedman) she loves goes off to marry someone else. She befriends a homosexual doctor (Boyd Gaines), although he obviously will not marry her. Finally, she adopts a baby. Yet the doctor is probably right when he warns she will continue "Looking back at your life and regretting your choices."

A reasonably entertaining, if unexceptional work, it nonetheless walked away with the season's major awards despite the opening of such superior plays as A.R. Gurney's♦ *The Cocktail Hour* and, most especially, *Other People's Money.*♦

Wasserstein (b. 1950) was born in Brooklyn. She attended Mount Holyoke College and Yale Drama School.♦ An earlier play, *Isn't It Romantic,* which treated the lives of young women in New York, was originally done off-Broadway in 1981, then, in 1983, began a nearly two-year run in a revised version.

HEIN, Silvio (1879–1928) Although the New York-born composer came from a musical family, sources disagree about his own musical training. Some say he studied in Vienna and Trieste, others that he was self-taught. Certainly his melodic gifts were limited

and the fact that he was asked to compose scores for approximately two dozen musicals is generally attributed to his prolifacy and gentle disposition. He seems to have pleased associates as often as he displeased reviewers. One critic noted, "All the one-finger composers of musical comedies, since the halcyon days of [George] Lederer, have ground for action for petit larceny against Silvio Hein." Like most composers of his day he began by interpolating songs in other men's scores. Between 1905, when he wrote the score for *Moonshine,* and 1922, when he composed much of the music for *Some Party,* he created the melodies for such shows as *Marrying Mary* (1906); *The Boys and Betty* (1908); *The Yankee Girl* (1910); *When Dreams Come True* (1913); *Flo-Flo* (1917); and *Look Who's Here* (1920).

Heiress, The, a play in two acts by Ruth and Augustus Goetz. Produced at the Biltmore Theatre. September 29, 1947. 410 performances.

Dominated by her unloving father, Dr. Austin Sloper (Basil Rathbone♦), Catherine Sloper (Wendy Hiller) is receptive to the courtship of Morris Townsend (Peter Cookson). But Townsend is a fortune-hunter, so when he learns Catherine will be disinherited if they wed, he jilts her. After Dr. Sloper's death, Catherine gets her revenge by allowing Townsend to seek her hand again and then spurning him.

Based on Henry James's *Washington Square,* the play was rejected by several important producers who insisted on a happy ending. The Goetzes finally acquiesced, but the production failed out of town. Recast and revived with the ending the authors had initially written, it succeeded. Robert Coleman of the *Daily Mirror* called it "a bitter, relentless, absorbing character study."

Ruth (b. 1912), the daughter of producer Philip Goodman,♦ and her husband Augustus Goetz (1901–57) were also the authors of *One Man Show* (1945), telling of a father-daughter relationship; *The Immoralist* (1954), based on André Gide's novel; and *The Hidden River* (1957), based on Storm Jameson's novel of the postwar search for a French traitor.

HEISTER, George (b. 1822?) Probably the most important set designer in New York in the 1850s, he seems to have been a native New Yorker. His name first appears in credits in 1840 when he designed sets for *Gamblers of the Mississippi* at the Franklin and later that year became a scenic artist at the Bowery. ♦ When the new Broadway Theatre opened in 1847 he was its principal designer and it was during the next decade at this house that he did his best-known work. Among the productions he helped create there were such elaborate mountings as *Faustus* (1851), *The Vision of the Sun* (1851), *The Cataract of the Ganges*♦ (1853), and *A Midsummer Night's Dream*♦ (1854). In one of his effects in *The Vision of the Sun*, after a character is thrown into a lake, "The waters become agitated and rise, and in their progress to the whole height of the Stage, they assume various tints, till a most Brilliant Palace rises out of the Water!" Not without humor, he wrote the *Herald* in regard to complaints about his work, offering to take lessons in perspective from its critic. During the 1860s he designed sets for Philadelphia theatres. Although his celebrity waned in later years he remained busy, designing, among other offerings, Augustin Daly's♦ *Le Roi Carotte* (1872) and that producer's *A Midsummer Night's Dream* (1873); the panoramas from an 1877 revival of *Antony and Cleopatra*♦ at Niblo's Garden♦; the Kiralfys'♦ touring production of *Around the World in Eighty Days*♦ (1878); and Wallack's♦ mounting of *Wolfert's Roost* (1879).

HELBURN, THERESA (1887–1959) Born in New York, she became interested in professional theatre while studying at Bryn Mawr. After continuing her studies at Radcliffe, the Sorbonne, and with Professor George Pierce Baker,♦ she tried her hand briefly at acting and also served as drama critic for *The Nation.* She then joined the Theatre Guild♦ and soon became its executive director, a post she held for the rest of her career. Her associate, Lawrence Langner,♦ described her as "a wild-looking . . . woman with a high forehead," but added, "She possessed the faculty of conscientiously carrying out the decisions of the Board, yet at the same time holding to her own opinions . . . her nerves were like whipcord and her power like steel."

Autobiography: *A Wayward Quest,* Boston, 1960.

HELD, ANNA (1873–1918) The tiny, slightly plump, coquettish entertainer, with reddish-brown hair and large, expressive brown eyes was born in Paris of Polish-French parentage. Her early years were impoverished, and when her father died young her mother took her to London. There she began to appear in the chorus of some musicals. After her mother's death she continued to learn her trade throughout Europe. In 1895 Florenz Ziegfeld,♦ who later married her, saw her perform and brought her to America. Playgoers first saw her in an 1896 revival of *A Parlor Match.* ♦ The "veiled naughtiness

of her songs" coupled with her sly, teasing delivery won her instant fame. She appeared in *La Poupee* (1897); *Papa's Wife* (1899); *The Little Duchess* (1901); *Mam'selle Napoleon* (1903); *Higgledy Piggledy* (1904); *The Parisian Model* (1906); and *Miss Innocence* (1908). After her separation from Ziegfeld she devoted most of her time to vaudeville, but she returned to musical comedy for a final time in *Follow Me* (1916). Among the songs associated with her were "Won't You Come and Play with Me?," "I Just Can't Make My Eyes Behave," and "It's Delightful To Be Married."

Held by the Enemy, a play in five acts by William Gillette. ♦ Produced at the Madison Square Theatre.♦ August 16, 1886. 70 performances.

When Federal troops capture a Confederate city, Brigade Surgeon Fielding (Melbourne McDowell) falls in love with a Southern belle, Rachel [in some texts and programs, Eunice] McCreery (Kathryn Kidder), although she is engaged to Lieutenant Gordon Hayne (John E. Kellerd♦). Hayne comes through the lines to spy for the Confederacy and is captured. Fielding serves as the judge in his court-martial. Hayne escapes and is shot. He plays dead to allow Rachel and her family to carry him to safety. When Fielding recognizes the ploy, Rachel agrees to marry him if he will allow Hayne to escape. Later Hayne returns and forces Fielding to release Rachel from her promise.

Although the play now seems merely an effective melodrama, it was long looked upon as the first meritorious drama about the Civil War. It held the stage for nearly a decade.

Hell-Bent fer Heaven, a play in three acts by Hatcher Hughes. ♦ Produced by Marc Klaw♦ at the Klaw Theatre. January 4, 1924. 122 performances. PP.

The courtship of Sid Hunt (George Abbott♦) and Jude Lowry (Margaret Borough) promises to end their mountain families' long feud. But Rufe Prior (John F. Hamilton), who has refused to fight in the recent World War and who has beome a religious fanatic, rekindles the hatred so that he can win Jude away from Sid. He nearly succeeds in destroying both the courtship and family reconciliation, until he is exposed and cravenly flees.

A controversial play from the start, condemned by some for its excessive melodramatics and by others for what they deemed was its irreverence, it won the Pulitzer Prize♦ and immediately became embroiled in further controversy. The play jury had actually selected George Kelly's♦ *The Show-Off,* ♦

but was overruled by a higher committee. One jurist resigned and another issued a letter of protest.

HELLMAN, LILLIAN (1905–84) The New Orleans-born playwright studied at New York University and Columbia, then took employment as a manuscript reader for Herman Shumlin♦ and book reviewer before her first play was produced. That play was *The Children's Hour*♦ (1934), a story of two school teachers falsely accused of lesbianism, and its success established her as a major new voice in the theatre. A drama about the effects of a labor strike on a Midwestern family, *Days To Come* (1936), was a quick failure, but her third play, *The Little Foxes*♦ (1939), was a huge hit and is generally acknowledged to be her finest work. It depicted the vicious in-fighting among members of a rapacious Southern family. With the coming of World War II, Miss Hellman turned to current affairs, writing two popular dramas, *Watch on the Rhine*♦ (1941), examining the problems of an exiled German resistance leader in America, and *The Searching Wind* (1944), centering on a fence-straddling career diplomat who is brought to his senses when his son is crippled in the war. She returned to the family which figured in *The Little Foxes* to show its earlier history in *Another Part of the Forest* (1946). In 1949 she adapted Emmanuel Robles's French drama, *Montserrat,* in which hostages give their lives to protect Simón Bolívar. *The Autumn Garden* (1951) told how idlers at a summer resort are forced to face the reality of their failures. She was next represented by her translation of Jean Anouilh's version of the Joan of Arc story, *The Lark* (1955), and then by her libretto for *Candide*♦ (1956). Her last success was *Toys in the Attic*♦ (1960), in which a weak young man is destroyed by his doting spinster sisters. *My Mother, My Father and Me* (1963), based on Burt Blechman's novel, *How Much?,* and recounting the problems of a greedy, amoral Jewish family, was a short-lived failure. Miss Hellman's best writing has been characterized by a superb sense of theatre, taut construction, and acute personal observation of human behavior, often coupled with an attempt to probe major moral and political issues.

Biography: *Lillian Hellman,* William Wright, New York, 1986.

Hello, Dolly!, a musical in two acts. Book by Michael Stewart.♦ Lyrics and music by Jerry Herman.♦ Produced by David Merrick♦ at the St. James Theatre. January 16, 1964. 2,844 performances.

Dolly Levi (Carol Channing♦) will jump in wherever there is a quick buck to be made. As she puts it, "I meddle." Her meddling becomes self-serving when she sets about to find a mate for Horace Vandergelder (David Burns♦). She suggests two possible candidates, Irene Molloy (Eileen Brennan), a milliner, and Ernestina Money (Mary Jo Catlett), a rich woman. But because Horace is "half-a-millionaire . . . that means he's got at least sixty thousand cash," she really sets out to grab him for herself. A night on the town, where they meet Vandergelder's assistants, Barnaby (Jerry Dodge) and Cornelius (Charles Nelson Reilly), who are supposedly at home minding the store, leads to both complications and marriage.

Principal songs: Hello, Dolly! · It Only Takes a Moment · Put On Your Sunday Clothes

Based on *The Matchmaker,* ♦ the musical almost certainly would have enjoyed a reasonable run on the strength of Miss Channing's clowning and Gower Champion's♦ stylish staging alone. The show's success was immeasurably enhanced by the popularity of its title song. For a brief time it was the longest running musical in Broadway history.

Hellzapoppin, a revue in two acts. Sketches mostly by Ole Olsen♦ and Chic Johnson. ♦ Lyrics mostly by Charles Tobias. Music mostly by Sammy Fain. Produced by Olsen and Johnson at the 46th Street Theatre. September 22, 1938. 1,404 performances.

This was a zany revue in which men carried ladders through rows of seated playgoers, a woman stopped the show on occasion to look for her missing spouse, a man peddled a plant that grew larger with each appearance, a magician offered tricks that would not work, and dozens of pistol shots rang out from all corners of the theatre.

The show opened to divided, if largely favorable reviews, but owed much of its success to persistent plugging by Walter Winchell, ♦ at the time probably the most influential Broadway columnist.

HENDERSON, DAVID (1853–1908) Born in Scotland, where he was orphaned at the age of twelve, he apprenticed himself in the newspaper trade and when he was satisfied that he had mastered his work came to America at the age of eighteen. He served on papers from New York to California before settling in Chicago. There he continued in the newspaper field but also began to take an active role in that city's theatricals. He built the Chicago Opera House and in 1887 began to produce a series of musicals that enjoyed long runs and toured the country. These musicals included *The Arabian Nights; The Crystal Slipper; Bluebeard, Jr.; Sinbad the Sailor;* and *Ali Baba.* He also worked closely with John McCaull,♦ mounting many Midwestern versions of McCaull's comic opera productions. He ran several theatres in Chicago as well as houses in Denver, Kansas City, Pittsburgh, and New York. He was often credited with re-establishing Chicago as a major theatre center after the great fire and of initiating its heyday as a producing center second only to New York, a heyday that lasted until World War I.

HENDERSON, RAY[MOND] [né BROST] (1896–1970) Born and raised in Chicago, he studied at the Chicago Conservatory of Music, then played piano in local dance bands, before moving to New York, where he served as song-plugger and arranger. In 1922 his publisher introduced him to lyricist Lew Brown,♦ and together they wrote "Georgette," a hit song in the *Greenwich Village Follies of 1922.*♦ When the pair was joined by lyricist B. G. De Sylva♦ they wrote the songs for some of the biggest musical successes of the 1920s: *George White's Scandals of 1925*♦; *George White's Scandals of 1926,* which included "The Birth of the Blues," "Black Bottom," and "Lucky Day"; *Good News!*♦ (1927), whose score offered "The Best Things in Life Are Free," the title song, "Just Imagine," "Lucky in Love," and "Varsity Drag"; *Manhattan Mary* (1927); *George White's Scandals of 1928; Hold Everything!*♦ (1928), from which came "You're the Cream in My Coffee"; *Follow Thru*♦ (1929), remembered for "Button Up Your Overcoat"; and *Flying High*♦ (1930). After the team split, Henderson continued to write melodies for Broadway shows, although none of his later songs proved popular, except those he wrote with Brown for *George White's Scandals of 1931,* including "Life Is Just a Bowl of Cherries" and "The Thrill Is Gone." His work was last heard in the *Ziegfeld Follies of 1943.*♦ On occasion Henderson also served as co-librettist and producer. Although his melodies were simple and hardly innovative, probably no other contemporary composer captured so well the upbeat qualities and raffish harmonies of the era. One historian has described the work of De Sylva, Brown, and Henderson as possessing a "distinctive vernacular touch—lowdown in rhythm, piquant in love."

HENLEY, BETH, see *Crimes of the Heart.*

Henrietta, The, a play in four acts by Bronson Howard.♦ Produced at the Union Square Theatre.♦ September 26, 1887. 158 performances.
   Gruff but kindly Nicholas Van Alstyne (W. H. Crane♦) has made a fortune in a bullish stock market, but his unscrupulous son Nicholas Jr.

(Charles Kent) attempts to make his own fortune by creating a bear market and destroying his father. He even steals some of his father's securities to serve his own ends. Young Nicholas's faithlessness extends to his loving wife, Rose (Sibyl Johnstone), but his philandering is kept from her by Nicholas's younger brother Bertie, "the Lamb" (Stuart Robson♦), who burns incriminating evidence. Just as Nicholas manages to create a panic, his father learns of his treachery and confronts him. Young Nicholas dies of a heart attack, while Bertie gives his father all his savings to help revitalize the market and save the family wealth. The loyal Rose at first refuses to believe any charges against her husband, but is finally made to see the truth. She marries a man who has long loved her.
   One of the most memorable entertainments of its era, its initial run was cut short when the Union Square Theatre burned. But the play continued to be revived regularly until the early 1900s, and an updated version was offered in 1913 as *The New Henrietta.* The sub-plot of Rose's and Nicholas's affairs was derived from Thackeray's *Vanity Fair.*

Henry IV Shakespeare's historical drama was first performed in New York with Douglass♦ as Falstaff, though only Part I was traditionally played until about 1820, and even then Part II was mounted only intermittently. James H. Hackett♦ was by far the most famous American interpreter of Falstaff. Curiously, after Hackett's retirement the plays virtually disappeared from the boards. Almost no major revivals were mounted in the last decades of the 19th century or the early years of the 20th century. One reason may have been suggested by a review in the *Spirit of the Times*♦ of one of Hackett's last appearances, in which Falstaff was called "this most difficult" of all Shakespearean parts. The only interesting mounting of this period came in 1896 when Julia Marlowe♦ assumed the role of Prince Hal. The major Falstaff after Hackett's day was Ben De Bar,♦ but he rarely played in New York, preferring to tour. In more modern times Maurice Evans♦ played Falstaff in a 1939 revival, and the Old Vic♦ presented a brilliant mounting in 1946 with Ralph Richardson♦ as Falstaff, and Olivier♦ as Hotspur and Justice Shallow. Of course, collegiate and festival stages have presented the play with some regularity.

HENRY, JOHN (1738–94) Sometimes called the first matinee idol in America, although matinees were not given in his day, he was born in Ireland and had appeared both in Dublin and at London's Drury

Lane before sailing to America. He made his debut under Douglass♦ at the John Street Theatre♦ in 1767 as Aimwell in *The Beaux' Stratagem*. Although a handsome and apparently accomplished actor, he seems to have been somewhat weak in his personal determination, so for a long while he was assigned relatively minor roles. After the Revolution he joined the younger Hallam♦ in the management of the American Company.♦ He is thought to have been responsible for the production of William Dunlap's first play and was also the first professional performer to play Sir Peter Teazle in America, which he played with his "incurable Irish brogue." In 1792 he encouraged John Hodgkinson♦ to come to America, but Hodgkinson quickly turned against him, not only assuming his roles but forcing him to sell his interest in the American Company for $10,000. His attempts to regain his stature failed and he drowned while sailing to New England, where he may have hoped to start another company.

His personal life was flamboyant and led to much unfavorable gossip. His flamboyance was signaled by the fact that he was the only actor of his time to maintain a private coach. Aware of the jealousy it might arouse he had painted on it two crutches and the motto "This or These." He let it be known that he suffered from gout, although this seems highly unlikely, and the carriage was therefore a necessity. The scandal grew largely out of his romances with the Storer sisters. He married the eldest, who died in a fire at sea. After her death he had an affair with her younger sister, who bore him a child. He later married the youngest of the sisters. She went insane at the time of his death.

HEPBURN, KATHARINE [HOUGHTON] (b. 1907) A lithe, horsy beauty with a haughty voice, she enjoyed a long, distinguished career as much by dint of glamour and dedication as by any exceptional acting abilities. She was born in Hartford, Conn., and educated at Bryn Mawr. Her acting debut was in 1928 with the Edwin Knopf Stock Company in Baltimore in *The Czarina*. Under the stage name of Katherine Burns she made her New York debut that same year as one of the hostesses in *Night Hostess*. Recognition came when she portrayed Antiope, the determined Amazon, in *The Warrior's Husband* (1932), but a certain ignominy followed when she attempted the part of Stella Surrege, who loves one man but marries another, in *The Lake* (1933). It was of this performance that Dorothy Parker♦ complained Miss Hepburn's gamut of emotions ranged from "A to B." Although she subsequently toured in the title role of *Jane Eyre* in 1937, she did not return

to Broadway until after she had become a celebrated film star. Her vehicle was *The Philadelphia Story*♦ (1939), written expressly for her by Philip Barry.♦ In it she played Tracy Lord, a rich woman brought to her senses in time to avoid a probably disastrous marriage. The play was a tremendous success, but another Barry play, *Without Love* (1942), in which she was Jamie Coe Rowan, whose marriage of convenience blossoms into real romance, failed. She did not again play Broadway until she essayed Shakespeare's♦ Rosalind in 1950. Moving from Shakespeare to Shaw♦ she was The Lady in *The Millionairess* (1952). In 1957 and 1960 she appeared at the American Shakespeare Festival♦ as Portia, Beatrice, Viola, and Cleopatra. Three later appearances were in lightweight vehicles which ran largely on the strength of her attraction: the musical *Coco* (1969), in which she played the famous designer Chanel; *A Matter of Gravity* (1976), in which as Mrs. Basil she was an aging lady confronting changing mores; and *West Side Waltz* (1981), in which she was Margaret Mary Elderdice, an old curmudgeon battling loneliness.

Biography: *Kate: The Life of Katharine Hepburn*, Charles Higham, New York, 1976.

Her Master's Voice, a comedy in two acts by Clare Kummer.♦ Produced by Max Gordon♦ at the Plymouth Theatre. October 23, 1933. 224 performances.

Ned Farrar (Roland Young♦), a would-be singer and ineffectual businessman, has just lost another job. This creates problems for him with his affectionate but rattled wife Queena (Frances Fuller) and his battle-axe mother-in-law Mrs. Martin (Elizabeth Patterson). However, they are nothing like the problems that arrive with Queena's regal Aunt Min (Laura Hope Crews♦), who has disapproved of Queena's marriage from afar and never met Ned, and who now mistakes him for a servant. When Aunt Min seemingly breaks up the marriage, Ned accepts her offer to indeed be her new servant. She calls him George, and after he sneaks into her bed, believing Queena is there, she likes him even more. Of course, nothing happens that night. Eventually Ned becomes a radio crooner. Mrs. Martin runs off with Ned's sponsor; Aunt Min is made to understand the situation; and Ned and Queena go home together.

Based on Mrs. Kummer's earlier vaudeville sketch, "The Choir Boy," the play was written for her son-in-law, Young. Burns Mantle♦ saw the comedy as "written with many graceful twists of dialogue and many revealing bits of character observation." A 1964 off-Broadway revival was unsuccessful.

Her Own Way, a play in four acts by Clyde Fitch.♦ Produced by Charles Dillingham♦ at the Garrick Theatre. September 28, 1903. 107 performances.

Believing that Georgiana Carley (Maxine Elliott♦) prefers Sam Coast (Arthur Byron♦) to him, Richard Coleman (Charles Cherry) quietly sails for the Philippines. Actually, Georgiana does not love Sam, who hopes to destroy her family's fortune in order to force her to marry him. When he nearly succeeds at the same time that Richard is reported to have died, Georgiana's future looks bleak. But Richard returns in time to rectify everything.

Written expressly for Miss Elliott, who rejected all of the author's suggested titles, leaving him to call it what he did out of exasperation, it was judged by many critics to be his finest comedy up to that time as well as Miss Elliott's best performance.

HERBERT, EVELYN [née HOSTETTER] (b. 1898) Although she was generally acknowledged as the finest singer in Broadway musicals of her era, her theatre career was brief and remembered for two parts. Born in Philadelphia, she was taken to New York while still in her teens to study with Caruso, who prevailed on the Chicago Opera to hire her. She sang important roles there and in New York before developing voice problems. Retrained, she took a job in a touring company of *Honeydew,* then made her Broadway debut in *Stepping Stones* (1923). She soon graduated to leading roles in *The Love Song* (1925): *Princess Flavia* (1925), and in the revue, *The Merry World* (1926). In 1926 she also created the role of Barbara Frietchie in *My Maryland,* ♦ playing the part through most of its record-breaking 40-week Philadelphia tryout and then in New York. Among the songs she introduced in the operetta were "Mother," "Silver Moon," and "Your Land and My Land." Another success followed when she portrayed Marianne in *The New Moon♦* (1928), introducing "Lover, Come Back to Me," "One Kiss," and "Wanting You." Thereafter the vogue for full-throated operettas waned, so her final appearances were in two short-run musicals, *Princess Charming* (1930) and *Melody* (1933), as well as in a 1934 revival of *Bitter Sweet.* She was married to Robert Halliday.♦

HERBERT, F[REDERICK] HUGH (1898?–1958) Born in Vienna, but raised in England, he studied at London's Royal School of Mines with the intention of becoming an engineer. However, wounded in World War I, he elected to take a position in the advertising office of a London department store. He came to America to write for films. His first stage play satirized Hollywood morals, telling how an actress subdues her philandering husband by having an affair with a gas station attendant. Called *Quiet Please* (1940), it was written in collaboration with Hans Kraly and ran two weeks. By contrast his first solo effort became a smash hit. *Kiss and Tell♦* (1943) dealt with the complications that arise when a young teenager pretends she is going to have a baby. *For Keeps* (1944), centering on a neglected daughter of divorced parents and her comic antics, disappeared quickly, but *For Love or Money* (1947), a comedy about a young girl's pursuit of an older man, enjoyed a long run. In 1950 Herbert collaborated on the book for the musical *Out of This World,* then had the lengthiest stay of his career with *The Moon Is Blue♦* (1951), in which a wholesome girl is caught between a young architect she has met at the Empire State Building and a suave libertine. A subsequent comedy, *A Girl Can Tell* (1953), relating the quandary of a lady with six suitors, failed, as did his adaptation of an Italian play, *The Best House in Naples* (1956).

HERBERT, JOSEPH (1867–1923) Born in Liverpool, he came to America while still a young man and embarked on a career as an actor. He made his first appearances with John McCaull's♦ comic opera company. When Augustin Daly♦ began importing English musicals, Herbert appeared in many of them and quietly helped revise them for American audiences. At the same time he wrote the successful burlesque *Thrilby* (1895). He later moved to Weber♦ and Fields,♦ writing some of their celebrated burlesques, notably *The Geezer* (1896), and occasionally performing in them. For the rest of his career he continued both to write and act, and sometimes direct. Alone or with partners, he wrote such musicals as the American version of *A Waltz Dream* (1908); *The Honeymoon Express* (1913); *The Beauty Shop* (1914); and *Honeydew* (1920). He appeared in such shows as *The Fortune Teller♦* (1898); *It Happened in Nordland* (1904); and *Deburau* (1920).

HERBERT, VICTOR (1859–1924) The first great American composer of operetta, he was born in Dublin. (His grandfather was Samuel Lover, a well-known novelist and musician.) He studied music in Germany and afterwards played cello in several major German orchestras. While there he met and married the prima donna Therese Foerster, and it was her signing to sing with the Metropolitan Opera that brought Herbert to New York. His first position was as a cellist with the Met. Shortly thereafter he accepted the post of director of the 22nd New York National Guard Band, succeeding the leading band-master Patrick Gilmore. In 1893 he composed an operetta for Lillian Russell, ♦ *La Vivandière,* but the work was never produced. A year later, however, the Bostonians♦ mounted his *Prince Ananias.* Although the musical was a failure, the company kept it in its repertory for several seasons. In 1895 *The Wizard of the Nile* gave Herbert his first success. From its score came "Star Light, Star Bright." *The Gold Bug* (1896), *The Serenade* (1897)—with its hit song, "I Love You, I Adore You"—and *The Idol's Eye* (1897) followed. His first great, enduring achievement was *The Fortune Teller*♦ (1898), whose score included "Gypsy Love Song" and "Romany Life." Subsequent offerings were *Cyrano de Bergerac* (1899), *The Singing Girl* (1899), *The Ameer* (1899), and *The Viceroy* (1900). He then briefly abandoned the stage to become conductor of the Pittsburgh Symphony, returning in 1903 with one of his best-loved scores, *Babes in Toyland.* ♦ Its still familiar melodies included "March of the Toys" and "Toyland." His 1904 success *It Happened in Nordland* produced "Absinthe Frappé." Many critics considered *Mlle. Modiste*♦ (1905), with its popular "I Want What I Want When I Want It" and "Kiss Me Again," the best American operetta written up to its day. In the following year he turned to what he perceived as musical comedy to write another enduring success, *The Red Mill.* ♦ Among its many memorable melodies were "Every Day Is Ladies' Day with Me," "The Isle of Our Dreams," "Moonbeams," and "The Streets of New York." His next major success was *Naughty Marietta*♦ (1910), generally acknowledged to be his masterpiece. Besides the classic "Ah, Sweet Mystery of Life," its brilliant score offered "I'm Falling in Love with Someone," "Italian Street Song," " 'Neath the Southern Moon," and "Tramp, Tramp, Tramp." "The Land of My Own Romance" was part of his 1911 *The Enchantress.* In 1913 *Sweethearts*♦ offered a fine group of songs, almost the equal of *Naughty Marietta's,* including "The Angelus," "Every Lover Must Meet His Fate," "Pretty as a Picture," and the title song. *The Only Girl* (1914) left behind "When You're Away" and *The Princess Pat* (1915) contained "Love Is the Best of All" and "Neapolitan Love Song," but Herbert was to write just one more great score, for *Eileen* (1917). Luxuriating in his Irish heritage, he created such gems as its title song, "The Irish Have a Great Day To-night," and "Thine

Alone." In 1919 *The Velvet Lady* included "Life and Love" and *Angel Face,* "I Might Be Your Once-in-a-While." "A Kiss in the Dark" came from *Orange Blossom* (1922), while the posthumously produced *The Dream Girl* (1924) contained "My Dream Girl." Several of his failures also left behind notable melodies, such as "Twilight in Barakeesh" and "Rose of the World" from *Algeria* (1908). Conversely, a long-run success such as *The Lady of Slipper* (1912) contained nothing of merit. In all he composed scores for over forty musicals.

His other scores, aside from those already named, were for *Babette* (1903), *Miss Dolly Dollars* (1905), *Wonderland* (1905), *Dream City* and *The Magic Knight* (1906 double bill), *The Tattooed Man* (1907), *Little Nemo* (1908), *The Prima Donna* (1908), *Old Dutch* (1909), *When Sweet Sixteen* (1911), *The Duchess* (1911), *The Madcap Duchess* (1913), *The Débutante* (1914), *The Century Girl* (1916), *Miss 1917,* *Her Regiment* (1917), *My Golden Girl* (1920), and *The Girl in the Spotlight* (1920).

Although Herbert in his lifetime made distinctions between what he considered his musical comedies and his operettas, his richly lyrical music today is perceived as almost wholly operetta-ish. He sometimes claimed that he was writing in an American idiom, and his contemporaries often agreed with him, but, again, today his influences are seen largely as French and Middle European. He moved from thumping marches to lilting waltzes to sentimental ballads with grace and ease. Whatever his sources he raised the artistic level of American theatrical music and for many years did so virtually alone.

Herbert was also one of the organizers of ASCAP,♦ which he was moved to found after hearing his music played in restaurants without his receiving any remuneration.

Biography: *Victor Herbert: A Life in Music,* Edward Waters, New York, 1955.

HERMAN, [GERALD] JERRY (b. 1932) Born in New York and raised in Jersey City, he had no formal musical education although his mother taught piano and voice. At Miami University, where he majored in drama, he wrote a musical revue that was later reproduced off-Broadway. Several more off-Broadway revues followed before he wrote his first musical for Broadway, *Milk and Honey* (1961). Because the show dealt with Americans visiting Israel, Herman's fine score ranged from traditional Jewish harmonies to modern American idioms. His second score was for his biggest success, *Hello, Dolly!*♦ (1964), a success aided no end by the tremendous popularity of the title song. A similar title song helped *Mame*

(1966) enjoy a long run. Unfortunately, his three early hits were followed by three failures, *Dear World* (1969), *Mack and Mabel* (1974), and *The Grand Tour* (1979). In 1983 he retrieved his fortunes with *La Cage aux Folles*. ◆ A retrospective revue of his songs was offered as *Jerry's Girls* (1985). Herman's best songs are light, lively, and quickly hummable, but lack the innovative twists and richness of better composers. However, his lyrics have all too often been underrated.

HERNDON, RICHARD G[ILBERT] (1873?–1958) Herndon was born in Paris and educated at private schools. In 1914 he produced his first play, but it failed to reach New York, so he began importing celebrated foreign performers and companies including Théâtre du Vieux Colombier and Théâtre Parisien, as well as several famous ballet troupes. With his profits from these tours he returned to more traditional, commercial theatre. From there on his career was a curious mixture of commonplace and daring. He took over two of Broadway's most intimate playhouses, the Belmont and the Klaw. In 1922 he produced Elliot Nugent's◆ first play, *Kempy*. The next year, working with Professor George Pierce Baker◆ of Harvard, he offered a prize for a new play. The result was that Philip Barry◆ was given his first New York hearing with *You and I*. Among his other successes were *Hurricane* (1923); *The Patsy* (1925); *Americana,* a revue which gave starts to Helen Morgan◆ and Charles Butterworth◆; *Sinner* (1927); and *The Unexpected Husband* (1931). His more noteworthy failures included Maxwell Anderson's◆ *Gypsy*◆ (1929).

HERNE, [KATHERINE] CHRYSTAL (1883–1950) The daughter of James A. Herne,◆ she was born in Dorchester, Mass., and made her earliest appearances in plays of her father, beginning in 1899. As a mature actress, she was best as regal, if sometimes haughty or cold, women. Among her more memorable roles were Mrs. Clayton, the forgiving wife who nonetheless demands there be no double standards, in *As a Man Thinks* (1911); Lady Grayston in the original American production of Maugham's◆ *Our Betters* (1917); Minnie Whitcomb, the music teacher who teaches the hero some sense, in *Expressing Willie*◆ (1924), and the houseproud Mrs. Craig in *Craig's Wife*◆ (1925).

HERNE, JAMES A. [né AHEARN] (1839–1901) The son of a poor Irish immigrant who had adopted the rigorous philosophy of the Dutch Reformed Church, he was taken out of school in his native Cohoes,

N.Y., at the age of thirteen and put to work in a brush factory. Although his father forbade his attending theatricals, when he was fourteen he saw Edwin Forrest◆ perform. That decided him on a career. However, it was not until he was twenty that he joined a traveling troupe performing the dog dramas◆ then popular. His first role was the Seneschal in *The Dog of Montagris* in West Troy, N.Y. He next played a season in nearby Troy, before moving on to act for John T. Ford◆ in Washington and Baltimore. An engagement followed at Philadelphia's Walnut Street Theatre.◆ From there he moved to Montreal and then to New York. Many of these moves were prompted by his romances with Lucille Western◆ and her sister, Helen, to whom he was married briefly. After more touring and a season's stint as manager of New York's Grand Opera House, he left for California, where he managed several theatres and, more importantly, met David Belasco◆ and married Katharine Corcoran. He had already begun to adapt novels for the stage, but it was with Belasco that he wrote his first important play. The idea came from Belasco, who never informed Herne that the story was actually derived from another contemporary play, *The Mariner's Compass*. The collaborators originally called their work *Chums*, but at Herne's suggestion the title was changed to *Hearts of Oak* (1880). The story told of an old sailor who raises two orphans, one a girl, the other a boy. The old man falls in love with the girl and would marry her, but loses her to the boy. The play was unusual for its day, offering neither a clear hero or a clear villain. After quarreling with Belasco, Herne wrote an unsuccessful patriotic drama, *The Minute Men of 1774–75* (1886). The movement toward naturalistic writing which Herne had manifested in *Hearts of Oak* was seen more clearly in his next play, *Drifting Apart* (1888), in which a nightmare convinces an alcoholic sailor to give up drinking. Although the play failed financially, it brought him to the attention of such important literary figures as Hamlin Garland and William Dean Howells. ◆ Along with his actress wife, both men encouraged him as he worked on his next play, *Margaret Fleming*◆ (1891). The study of a cultivated woman's reaction to the consequences of her husband's philandering, it was the first important American play to demonstrate a significant debt to Ibsen. ◆ That connection was held against it by many contemporary playgoers. Even Mrs. Herne's fine acting of the title role could not ensure its acceptance. However, Herne's next play, *Shore Acres*◆ (1893), in which a lovable ne'er-do-well finally discovers the strength to best his malicious brother, enjoyed widespread success with the author in the leading role. *The Reverend Griffith Davenport♦* (1899), a study of a Southern family divided by the Civil War, was based on Helen H. Gardener's novel *An Unofficial Patriot.* Herne's last play was *Sag Harbor♦* (1900), which contrasts the love of two brothers for the same woman. The author himself assumed the role of an aging guardian angel, Captain Dan Marble.

Herne was more of an enlightened, progressive writer than a great one. Even if his plays had revealed greater literary or artistic merits, it seems doubtful that they would have been more successful, for he paid the price for being in the avant garde—forced runs, small profits, and often downright commercial failure. As a result, even when his reputation as a playwright was established, to make ends meet he was often required to act in or direct other men's works. For example, he took the part of Sampson, the black murderer, in Joseph R. Grismer♦ and Clay Greene's♦ *The New South* (1893). The role was a departure for him, for with his bulky figure and round, kindly face he was generally cast in homier roles. Similarly, shortly before his death he revised and directed Israel Zangwill's *Children of the Ghetto* (1899) for American audiences. However, his principal celebrity comes from his effectively introducing Ibsen's theories into American drama. His daughter was Chrystal Herne.♦

Biography: *James A. Herne—The American Ibsen,* John Perry, Chicago, 1978.

Hero, The, a play in three acts by Gilbert Emery. Produced by Sam H. Harris♦ at the Belmont Theatre. September 5, 1921. 80 performances.

Andrew Lane (Richard Bennett♦), an insurance salesman, has struggled during the war years to support his wife, his son, his widowed mother, and a Belgian refugee the Lanes had taken in. On the other hand, Andrew's brother, Oswald (Robert Ames♦), has been fighting overseas and comes home a wounded, much-decorated hero. Before the war, Oswald had been something of a blackguard, so the family hopes his experiences have changed him. They have not. He is no sooner home than he seduces the refugee and steals church funds. But as he is running off he stops to rescue some boys from a fire and is burned to death. Andrew can only conclude that Oswald was a hero after all.

Originally presented the preceding season for four special matinees, it was given a regular booking on the strength of its excellent notices. The notices were once again enthusiastic, but playgoers appar-

ently found the drama discomfiting. It remains one of the best plays to come out of World War I.

The New York-born, Amherst-educated Emery [né Gilbert Emery Bensley Pottle] (1875–1945), was an actor, playwright, and short-story writer. His longest-run success was *Tarnish* (1923), in which a girl is taught to be tolerant of others' failings. *Love in a Mist* (1926), a social comedy written with Amelie Rives♦ and centering on a lady who cannot say "no," was his only other work to achieve a modest run.

HERON, Matilda [Agnes] (1830–77) Born in Ireland and brought to America while still quite young, she studied with Peter Richings♦ before making her professional debut at Philadelphia's Walnut Street Theatre♦ in 1851 as Bianca in *Fazio.* Her intelligent reading and fine acting won her instant plaudits, although she was not an especially attractive woman. Even by the standards of the time her figure was "ample," while her facial features were heavy. Nevertheless she followed her Bianca with equally praised interpretations of Juliet, Lady Macbeth, Ophelia, Parthenia (in *Ingomar♦*), Pauline (in *The Lady of Lyons♦*), and Julia (in *The Hunchback♦*). Her New York debut was at the Bowery Theatre♦ in 1852 as Lady Macbeth. The following year she went to California, where she scored a considerable success. During a trip to Paris in 1855 she saw a performance of *La Dame aux Camélias* and made her own English version of it, which she first offered in 1857. Other adaptations had been on American stages since 1853, but it was her performance that was considered definitive by American critics and playgoers for as long as she lived. The *Tribune* wrote: "She exuded the electricity of genius . . . there was about her a halo of individuality—a brilliancy of vitality—which convinced everyone present able to distinguish gauds from glories, that the palpitating actuality of perceptive genius was before them." Shortly thereafter she offered her version of Legouve's *Medea* and was also admired for her Nancy in *Oliver Twist.* She continued to perform these and other roles until illness forced her premature retirement. Her many loyal students, including Agnes Ethel,♦ gave numerous benefits for her, but because of medical expenses she died in poverty. Her daughter, Hélène Stoepel, known professionally as Bijou Heron (1862–1937), who married Henry Miller,♦ was also a popular actress.

HERRING, Fanny (1832–1906) The daughter of popular performers, the tiny, dark-haired, hoydenish actress was born in London and came to America four years later. T. Allston Brown♦ lists her debut as taking place at the Bowery Theatre♦ in 1842, but most sources place it in 1847. As a teenager she moved from theatre to theatre and it was not until she returned to the Bowery Theatre in the late 1850s that she found her niche. There she soon became the darling of the gallery gods, offering them everything from her Ophelia and Juliet to leading roles in such now forgotten pieces as *The Female Detective* and *The Dumb Girl of Genoa*. However, her forte was trouser roles, and she won the loudest cheers for characterizations on the order of Mose in *A Glance at New York*♦ and the title parts of *Jack Sheppard* and *Sinbad the Sailor*. By the early 1870s her popularity at the Bowery began to wane, so she often took herself to important vaudeville houses. She continued to perform, still frequently playing youthful street urchins, well into the 1890s, when she was billed at once comically and pathetically as "The Bernhardt of the West Side."

HERRMANN, ALEXANDER (1844–1896) Billed as "Herrmann, the Great," he was the son of one magician and the nephew of the even more famous "Professor" Carl Herrmann (1821–1887), who made several American visits beginning in 1861. Whether the Alexandre (*sic*) who accompanied "Professor" Herrmann in that year was the older man's nephew or brother is a matter of dispute. Certainly by 1874 Alexander was appearing with his wife, Adelaide, in entertainments that included catching a bullet with his teeth and seemingly allowing himself to be cremated. Despite the intense drama inherent in such stunts, Herrmann was a casual performer, who delighted in debunking his own and others' deceptions. While he occasionally appeared on vaudeville stages, he usually offered whole evenings of magic at legitimate playhouses. He provided jugglers and other acts between his stunts. He several times attempted to run his own theatres, most notably when he converted the old San Francisco Minstrels theatre at 29th and Broadway into Herrmann's Theatre.

HERTS, HENRY B[EAUMONT] (1871–1933) A native New Yorker, he was graduated from Columbia in 1893, then spent seven years in Europe studying architecture at Paris's Beaux Arts, and the universities of Rome and Heidelberg. Between 1900 and the outbreak of World War I he designed over thirty theatres and is credited with perfecting the principles of cantilevered arch construction that eliminated the need for pillars to support balconies.

Among his New York playhouses were the Booth, the Fulton (later Helen Hayes), the Gaiety, the Liberty, the Lyceum,♦ the New Amsterdam,♦ and the Shubert, as well as the Brooklyn Academy of Music.

HEWITT, JAMES, see *Tammany*

HEWLETT, JAMES (fl. early 19th century) Possibly the first professional black actor in America, he seems to have been a performer of modest merit, although his opportunities were few and his career was beset by prejudice, particularly at the hands of vociferous white hooligans. In 1821 he attempted *Richard III*♦ with an all-black cast and himself in the principal role. The *National Advocate* reviewed the performance, which seems to have been unintentionally comic, with Richard shouting "Gib me noder horse," and dying with "the rolling eye, white teeth gnashing, clenched fists and phrenzied looks." He later may have played either Othello or Iago with the same company. Both productions were interspersed with lighthearted songs and dances. In 1823 he assumed the title role in *The Drama of King Shotaway*, based on a West Indies insurrection and conceivably the first black play in American history. Thereafter he seems to have confined his appearances to recitals devoted largely to imitations of famous white actors. An 1826 advertisement called him "the most astonishing phenomena of the age: a young man, who, notwithstanding the thousand obstacles which the circumstance of complexion must have thrown in his way of improvement, has, by the mere dint of natural genius and self-strengthened assiduity, risen to a successful competition with some of the first actors of the day." He was later billed as "Shakespeare's proud Representative." After a farewell benefit in 1831 he disappears from the records.

HEYWARD, [EDWIN] DUBOSE (1885–1940) South Carolina novelist and poet, he worked as an insurance agent before publishing his first poems and short stories in the early 1920s. He is important to the theatre because with his wife, the former Dorothy Hartzell Kuhns (1890–1961), he dramatized two of his novels of black life: *Porgy*♦ (1927), which told of the love of a crippled peddler for a weak-willed beauty; and *Mamba's Daughters* (1939), a melodrama about three generations of blacks in which the principal story concerns the killing by one daughter of her own daughter's seducer and of her subsequent suicide. In 1931 he wrote an unsuccessful original drama, *Brass Ankle*

(1931), in which a Southern woman who learns she has Negro blood arranges her own death. Heyward also collaborated on the musical version of *Porgy, Porgy and Bess*♦ (1935).

Biography: *Dubose Heyward, the Man Who Wrote Porgy,* Frank Durham, Columbia, S.C., 1954.

HIELGE [sometimes spelled HEILGE], GEORGE Called "a native artist" when he painted both scenery and murals for the Franklin Theatre in 1837, he soon moved to Philadelphia and became a major scene painter for that city's Walnut Street Theatre♦ and Arch Street Theatres. ♦ It was apparently at the Arch that he met William E. Burton,♦ who was managing it at the time. The two men developed a mutual respect and he became Burton's set designer for the rest of that great actor-manager's career. Among the many productions for which he designed the sets were Burton's famous revivals of *The Merry Wives of Windsor* (1853) and *A Midsummer Night's Dream*♦ (1854). After Burton's retirement Hielge served as P. T. Barnum's♦ chief set designer. He disappears from the records about 1865. During his career he was also famous for panoramas and landscape paintings.

HIGGINS, DAVID K. (1858?–1936) Chicago-born actor and playwright, he wrote numerous melodramas and rustic comedies at the turn of the century. Most of these plays had only short New York runs, frequently in secondary houses, but toured in smaller towns for many years. His best work was probably *At Piney Ridge* (1897), whose principal love story turns on the revelation that a vengeful slave had once switched two babies. Among his other plays were *Our Rich Cousin* (1886), written with his brother Milton; *The Plunger* (1890); *The Vendetta* (1891); *Kidnapped* (1892); *The Turn of the Tide* (1896); *A Union Soldier* (1898); *Up York State* (1901); and *His Last Dollar* (1904). Higgins often performed in his own plays, and after the market for his writings was destroyed by the rise of silent films he continued to act in other men's works.

High Tor, a fantasy in three acts by Maxwell Anderson. ♦ Produced by Guthrie McClintic♦ at the Martin Beck Theatre. January 9, 1937. 171 performances. NYDCCA.

Van Van Dorn (Burgess Meredith♦) is disgusted with civilization. Having fought with his sweetheart Judith (Mab Maynard), he flees to a hill that he owns, overlooking the Hudson. There, with an Indian (Harry Irvine), he spends an eventful night. The pair encounter bank robbers, land-developers determined to buy Van Dorn's hill, and the ghosts of old sailors. Come morning, the ghosts vanish, the robbers are apprehended, and a profitable deal is consummated with the developers. Van Dorn is even reconciled with Judith. Although he may appear to have sold out to the forces of progress, he has not totally capitulated, for the Indian assures him, "Nothing is made by men, but makes, in the end, good ruins."

This blank-verse fantasy was one of Anderson's best, if lightest, plays.

HILL, ARTHUR [EDWARD SPENCE] (b. 1922) A low-keyed, solid Canadian actor, he had appeared in several London productions before making his Broadway debut in *The Matchmaker*♦ (1955). He is best recalled for three roles: Ben Gant, the hero's frail brother, in *Look Homeward, Angel*♦ (1957); Jay Follet, the doomed father, in *All the Way Home*♦ (1960); and George, the husband in an unhappy marriage, in *Who's Afraid of Virginia Woolf?*♦ (1962). He was also Simon Harford, the weakling son and husband, in *More Stately Mansions* (1967).

HILL, G[EORGE] H[ANDEL] (1809–49) Best known as "Yankee" Hill, he was born in Boston, the son and brother of celebrated musicians. His early career was given over to acting in minor roles and to offering recitals based on New England character sketches. With the rise in popularity of similar figures in American comedy Hill quickly found stardom as the best Yankee interpreter of his day. Among his famous roles were Jonathan Ploughboy, Major Enoch Wheeler, Nathan Tucker, Jedediah Homebred, Hiram Dodge, and Solomon Swop. *The Knickerbocker Magazine* for May, 1838 noted, "In the exhibition of the quiet, dry humor peculiar to *the* Yankee, par excellence, he stands unrivalled. His acting is nature itself." An elongated, naïvely cheerful face enhanced his attraction. His personal behavior appears to have been quirky, and he retired from the stage on several occasions for various reasons, only to soon return. He was also plagued by poor health. Despite his many retirements he continued to act until his death, although in his last years his pre-eminence was challenged by several fine newcomers.

Autobiography: *Scenes from the Life of an Actor,* New York, 1853 (reissued New York, 1969).

HILLIARD, ROBERT C. (1857–1927) Considered "the handsomest, as well as one of the best leading men" of his era, he was born in New York and educated at colleges in his hometown and in Canada. He made his stage debut in Brooklyn in 1886 in *False Shame,* and later that year first appeared on Broadway in *A Daughter of Ireland.* He then succeeded Maurice Barrymore♦ as leading man to Lillie Langtry.♦ In 1891 he played Johann Tonnessen in *The Pillars of Society,* one of the earliest American productions of Ibsen's play. Although he was a star for many years, most of the plays in which he acted were popular but ephemeral works. His best-known roles were Dick Johnson, the bandit who finds salvation in love, in *The Girl of the Golden West*♦ (1905); John Schuyler, or The Man, whose life is destroyed by a femme fatale, in *A Fool There Was*♦ (1909); and Asche Kayton, the cool-headed detective, in *The Argyle Case* (1912). William J. Burns, the famous American detective, was part author of the play, and the character of Kayton was modeled after him and his experiences. Between plays Hilliard was equally popular on the vaudeville stage, where he appeared in numerous playlets.

HILSON, Thomas [né Hill] (1784–1834) Born in England into a family careful of its respectability, he dutifully changed his name when he embarked on a theatrical career so as not to embarrass his parents. He made his American debut in 1811 at the Park Theatre♦ playing Walter in *The Children of the Wood.* His success was immediate, and he soon earned a reputation in comedy parts such as Falstaff, Figaro, Sir Peter Teazle, Touchstone, and Tony Lumpkin. But his range was remarkable, and he seems to have been equally skilled in playing the passionate figures of the romantic plays of the time. He was also an accomplished tragedian. He offered a fine Richard III, while Thomas Abthorpe Cooper♦ considered him the best contemporary Iago. His popularity extended to all the American theatre centers of his day. Mrs. Hilson, the former Ellen Augusta Johnson (1801–37), was a well-thought-of actress.

HINGLE, [Martin] Pat[terson] (b. 1924) A native of Denver, Colo., he made his debut in *End as a Man*♦ (1953), and after playing Cooper, the hero's brother, in *Cat on a Hot Tin Roof*♦ (1955), scored major successes as Rubin Flood, the troubled harness salesman, in *The Dark at the Top of the Stairs*♦ (1957), and as the Job-like title figure in *J.B.*♦ (1958). Subsequently he played Macbeth and Hector at the American Shakespeare Festival,♦ then appeared as Sam in a 1963 revival of *Strange*

Interlude.♦ His only other long run has been as Victor Franz, the failed brother, in *The Price* (1968).

Hippodrome Theatre The largest theatre of its day, it had a seating capacity of 5200 and room for nearly 800 standees. Its stage was 110 feet deep and over 200 feet long. The theatre, which stood on Sixth Avenue between 43rd and 44th Streets, and which was the only major legitimate theatre ever built that far east of Broadway, opened in 1905 with the musical spectacle *A Society Circus* and for the next seventeen years offered similar spectacles annually, generally giving two performances a day. In its heyday the theatre was the most successful in New York, and its productions often chalked up the longest runs of their seasons. Besides choruses that reputedly numbered over 500 the theatre was famous for its horses, which dove into the huge tank in front of the stage. The productions all featured exceedingly lavish scenery. Between the runs of the major spectacles the house offered vaudeville, and when growing competition from even more spectacular films and an increasing sophistication put an end to the spectacle's attraction, the house was used solely for vaudeville. It later converted to films, but shortly before it was demolished in 1939 it returned to the legitimate fold to house *Jumbo*♦ (1935).

HIRSCH, Louis A[chille] (1881–1924) Born in New York, next door to where Jerome Kern♦ was to grow up, he began his career as a staff composer for the Shuberts,♦ writing with Kern some of the score for *The Golden Widow* (1909), a musical which folded during its tryout. That same year he interpolated songs into *The Girl and the Wizard.* His first full score was heard in *He Came from Milwaukee* (1910). After writing melodies for Winter Garden♦ revues, he spent some time in London. He returned in 1915 to write much of the music for that season's *Ziegfeld Follies,*♦ including the hit song, "Hello, Frisco." In all he wrote the principal scores for eighteen Broadway musicals, best remembered of which are *Going Up* (1917), from which came "The Tickle Toe," and *Mary* (1920), the hit song of which was "The Love Nest." Many of his contemporaries felt that his early death deprived the American musical of a composer who had not yet reached his inventive zenith.

HIRSCHFELD, Al[bert] (b. 1903) The St. Louis-born artist began working for the New York *Times* as a caricaturist specializing in theatrical figures in 1925 and has illustrated a number of books with similarly witty, observant line drawings. Since 1945 he has hidden his daughter's name, Nina, in many of his cartoons, indicating the number of Ninas alongside his signature.

Hit the Deck!, a musical comedy in two acts. Book by Herbert Fields. ♦ Lyrics by Leo Robin and Clifford Grey. Music by Vincent Youmans. ♦ Produced by Youmans and Lew Fields ♦ at the Belasco Theatre. April 25, 1927. 352 performances.

Loulou (Louise Groody ♦) runs a coffee house on the docks at Newport, but is prepared to throw it all up to follow a sailor, "Bilge" Smith (Charles King), around the world. She finally persuades him to marry her, only to have him change his mind when he learns she is an heiress. He changes his mind again after she agrees to assign her inheritance to their children.

Principal songs: Hallelujah · Sometimes I'm Happy.

Based on Hubert Osborne's 1922 play, *Shore Leave,* the musical had the longest Broadway run of any original Vincent Youmans show. It was welcomed by Percy Hammond ♦ of the *Herald Tribune* as "a clean, pretty, bright and happy show."

Hit-the-Trail Holliday, a farce in four acts by George M. Cohan. ♦ Produced by Cohan and Harris ♦ at the Astor Theatre. September 13, 1915. 336 performances.

Billy Holliday (Fred Niblo), a celebrated New York barman, comes to a small New England town to help open a new hotel. But when he has a falling out with the local liquor magnate, he turns prohibitionist. He campaigns so vigorously that he puts the local bars and breweries out of business, and he wins the hand of Edith Holden (Katherine La Salle), the minister's daughter.

Many saw this play, based on a plot suggested to Cohan by George Middleton ♦ and Guy Bolton, ♦ as a spoof of Billy Sunday, the leading evangelist of the day, and no doubt Cohan intended them to. But in his autobiography, Middleton suggested he had patterned the original story after a bookmaker named Peter De Lacey, whose business was shut down after racing track interests forced his patrons to bet at the tracks and who then successfully crusaded against the immorality of the tracks, closing them down. Niblo was Cohan's brother-in-law.

HITCHCOCK, RAYMOND (1865–1929) Described by Stanley Green ♦ as "a lanky, raspy-voiced comic with sharp features and straw-colored hair that he brushed across his forehead," he was born in Auburn, N.Y., and came to the theatre after some unhappy years in other trades, including time as a shoe-store clerk. From 1890 on he began to call attention to himself in musicals such as *The Brigands* and *The Golden Wedding.* His performance in *King Dodo* (1901) made him a star, and he subsequently played principal roles in *The Yankee Consul* (1904), *Easy Dawson* (1905), *The Galloper* (1906), *The Student King* (1906), *The Yankee Tourist* (1907), *The Man Who Owns Broadway* (1909), *The Red Widow* (1911), and *The Beauty Shop* (1914). Beginning in 1917 he produced and starred in a series of revues called *Hitchy-Koo.* In 1921 he appeared in the *Ziegfeld Follies.* ♦ When another revue, *Raymond Hitchcock's Pinwheel,* failed in 1922, he took to the road as Clem Hawley in *The Old Soak.* ♦ Thereafter, his fortunes began to wane. His last Broadway appearance was as Boniface in *The Beaux' Stratagem* (1928). At his best, Hitchcock had a casual, homespun humor not unlike that of the later Will Rogers. ♦

H.M.S. Pinafore; or, The Lass That Loved A Sailor A landmark Gilbert ♦ and Sullivan ♦ comic opera, it tells of a young lady who is pursued by the head of the English navy but who loves an ordinary tar. Her loyalty is rewarded when it is discovered that the sailor is really entitled to be a captain. Among its memorable songs were "I'm Called Little Buttercup," "Never Mind the Why and Wherefore," "We Sail the Ocean Blue," and "When I Was a Lad." The American premiere in Boston took place on November 25, 1878, and the first New York performance on January 15, 1879. Within weeks what was called "the *Pinafore* craze" swept the nation. In New York alone three companies performed at the same time, when New York had only a dozen first-class theatres. By season's end twelve theatres had offered a version on one occasion or another. The reason was twofold. First and most obvious was the excellence of the work—its literate, witty libretto and captivating melodies. Secondly, it was such a clean show that ministers who had heretofore railed against the theatre encouraged their flocks to attend performances of the piece. The real beginnings of the popular American musical theatre can be traced to this work's unprecedented success. Prior to its appearance only the smallest handful of what could be called musicals were presented each season. Immediately thereafter and for almost the next hundred years Broadway never again saw fewer than fifteen or twenty musicals a year. The earliest great American musicals were openly modeled on this and other Gilbert and Sullivan works. It is, of course, still revived regularly.

HOBART, [PHILPOTT] GEORGE V[ERE] (1867–1926) One of the most prolific librettists, lyricists, vaudeville sketch writers, and playwrights of his day, he was born at Cape Breton, Nova Scotia, and spent time as a journalist in New York prior to writing for the stage. Alone or with collaborators he wrote such musicals as *Broadway to Tokio* (1900), *The Wild Rose* (1902), *The Boys and Betty* (1908), and *Buddies* (1919), and sketches for the *Ziegfeld Follies,* ♦ *Hitchy-Koo,* and the *Greenwich Village Follies.* ♦ His most successful plays were *Wildfire* (1908), written with George Broadhurst ♦ and in which Lillian Russell ♦ played the somewhat unwilling owner of a racing stable; *Experience* ♦ (1914), a morality play in which Youth deserts Mother and Love and is reduced to trafficking with Crime, Delusion, and Poverty; and *Our Mrs. McChesney* (1915), which he wrote with Edna Ferber ♦ and in which Ethel Barrymore ♦ portrayed a traveling saleswoman. He directed many of his own works. While clearly a knowing theatrical craftsman, he left nothing of importance behind.

HODGE, WILLIAM T[HOMAS] (1874–1932) Born in Albion, N.Y., he is said to have formed his own amateur repertory company while still a boy. He was in his teens when he turned professional, but did not make his New York debut until 1898 in *The Heart of Chicago.* He won recognition as Freeman Whitemarsh, the smug, gabby bumpkin, in James A. Herne's ♦ *Sag Harbor* ♦ (1900). Another major assignment was Mr. Stubbins, the husband disillusioned to learn his wife did not bake her own pies, in *Mrs. Wiggs of the Cabbage Patch* ♦ (1904). In 1907 he first played Daniel Vorhees, the shrewd but kindly American who saves his ward from foreign entanglements in *The Man from Home.* ♦ His performance made him a star and kept him occupied for five years. Thereafter he made a career of appearing in similar roles in similar plays, all of them written by himself: Jim Whitman in *The Road to Happiness* (1915); John Otis in *Fixing Sisters* (1916); Dr. Pendergrass in *A Cure for Curables* (1918); John Weatherbee in *The Guest of Honor* (1920); George Oliver in *Beware of Dogs* (1921); Tom Griswold in *For All of Us* (1923); Joe Kirby in *The Judge's Husband* (1926); and Eugene Thomas in *Straight Through the Door* (1928). His plays usually enjoyed only modest runs in New York, where they were perceived as superannuated hokum, but continued to have long, profitable road tours. Hodge was a rather attractive man with a slightly gaunt face and sharp features.

HODGKINSON, JOHN [né MEADOWCROFT] (1767–1805) Son of a farmer turned publican, he left home after his father's death and enlisted in a troupe playing in Bristol and Bath. At the same time he adopted his stage name. In 1791 he wrote to Lewis Hallam, Jr., ♦ and John Henry ♦ requesting a position in their company. Henry responded favorably, so Hodgkinson made his American debut at Philadelphia's Southwark Theatre ♦ in 1792 as Belcour in *The West Indian.* Dunlap ♦ described him as "five feet ten inches in height, but even at the period we speak of, at the age of twenty-six, he was too fleshy to appear tall, and in a few years became corpulent . . . His face was round, his nose broad and not prominent, his eyes gray, and of unequal sizes, but with large pupils and dark eyelashes." Among his early roles, both in Philadelphia and in New York, were Macheath, Macbeth, Marc Antony, Bob Acres, and Jaffier. He later distinguished himself in the title role of *André* ♦ and as Rolla in Dunlap's version of *Pizarro.* ♦ His looks and fine acting won him rapid public approval. But behind the scenes he was apparently a ruthless, ambitious, and quarrelsome man, squeezing first Henry then Hallam out of their positions. However, he was a skilled manager, and his partnership with Hallam at the John Street Theatre ♦ resulted in several excellent seasons. He was prepared to open the Park Theatre ♦ with Dunlap, but after numerous arguments with members of the company he agreed to leave. He played in other cities, and continued to act in New York, although the rising star of Thomas Abthorpe Cooper ♦ tarnished his celebrity and at one point he was reduced to playing Banquo to Cooper's Macbeth. He died in a yellow fever epidemic. For all his flaws, he was probably the finest actor American audiences had seen up to his time.

HOEY, MRS. JOHN [née JOSEPHINE SHAW] (1824?–1896) A slightly mousey, but still attractive actress with a style that many critics insisted was too stilted and artificial, she was nevertheless a reigning favorite for several seasons under the Wallacks. ♦ Born in Liverpool, she came to America with her musician father and made her debut at the Museum in Baltimore in 1839. She acted for several years first under her maiden name, then as Mrs. W. H. Russell. Under the latter name she appeared briefly with W. E. Burton ♦ in New York. On her second marriage, to a rich shipping magnate, she retired from the stage, but James Wallack, Sr., persuaded her to return in 1854. That not only Wallack, but a large segment of the public, disagreed with the critics who rejected her can be read in T. Allston Brown's◆ recollections: "Her peculiar forte lay in rendering that class of characters in which the manners of the modern lady of fashion were required. Yet, as the arch and wayward Beatrice, or the intense and melodramatic Pauline, she also gained the highest praise. Whoever has been fortunate enough to see her in the enchanting character of Rosalind has beheld a portrayal which for delicacy, sensibility, and grace, never, perhaps, had its equal." Her gift for playing ladies of fashion was enhanced by her reputation as an extravagantly rich and beautiful dresser. In 1865 she quarreled with Wallack and retired permanently.

HOEY, WILLIAM F. (1855–97) Alone or with partners he was for many years a popular vaudeville performer. However, his greatest fame came when he joined with his brother-in-law, Charles E. Evans,◆ in a new team. In 1885 they first appeared in a play they helped Charles H. Hoyt◆ write, *A Parlor Match.*◆ Hoey played a bibulous, bearded tramp, "Old Hoss," and was regularly afterwards known as "Old Hoss" Hoey. He continued in the part with only intermittent interruptions almost until his death. Among his other legitimate appearances were *The Flams* (1894) and *The Globe Trotter* (1895).

HOFFMAN, AARON (1880–1924) St. Louis-born playwright, who began creating vaudeville skits and monologues while still a student at the University of Chicago, he became fully professional when he wrote such turn-of-the-century touring shows as *Bankers and Brokers* and the libretto for *The Belle of Avenue A.* He came to New York's attention when he collaborated on the libretto of *The Rogers Brothers in Panama* (1907). His best-known plays were *Friendly Enemies*◆ (1918), written with Samuel Shipman◆ and telling of two German-Americans with divergent loyalties in World War I; *Nothing But Lies* (1918), in which an advertising man complicates his life when he feels he cannot tell the truth; *Welcome Stranger*◆ (1920), in which a likable Jew overcomes small-town anti-Semitism; and *Give and Take* (1923), dealing with a father and son who have different ideas on how to run a business.

HOFFMAN, DUSTIN (b. 1937) A native of Los Angeles, he studied acting at the Pasadena Playhouse◆ and with Lee Strasberg,◆ among others. He won fine notices off-Broadway in the mid-1960s and on Broadway in *Jimmy Shine* (1968) before beginning a long, highly successful film career. He returned to Broadway to star in a 1984 revival of *Death of a Salesman*◆ and a 1989 revival of *The Merchant of Venice.* ◆

HOFFMAN, GERTRUDE [née KITTY HAYES] (1898?–1955) Her early years are shrouded in obscurity. In different interviews she gave her birthplace as several different cities, but most often as San Francisco, where she claimed she made her debut as a child performer. She was apparently at least in her teens when she caused a stir in New York performing opposite Anna Held◆ in *A Parisian Model* (1906), so even the birthdate customarily given for her is suspect. She rapidly rose in popularity as a flamboyant dancer and choreographer, most famous for routines that were considered highly suggestive at the time. In 1912 she was starred in (*From*) *Broadway to Paris* and later appeared in numerous other revues. She also toured vaudeville with her own miniature revue, and provided the dances and girls for several Broadway shows. Highly eccentric, she spent her last years as a clairvoyant in Washington, D.C.

Hogan's Goat, a play in two acts by William Alfred. Produced by the American Place Theatre at St. Clement's Church. November 11, 1965. 607 performances.

Matt Stanton (Ralph Waite) determines to take on the incumbent, Edward Quinn (Tom Ahearne), in a contest for the mayorality of Brooklyn in 1890. Stanton is consumed by ambition and subordinates everything to his attempt to rise to power. He finally alienates his wife, Kathleen (Faye Dunaway), who is killed in a fall down the stairs when she goes to leave him. Her death destroys his overreaching hopes.

In selecting entries for the *Best Plays*◆ series, editor Otis L. Guernsey, Jr.◆ called this blank-verse drama "the very best play of 1965–66," adding, "its examination of a human being's drive to emerge from the ruck in defiance of all rules and risks is extremely pertinent to our modern population-swelling, status-seeking, amoral society."

Alfred was born in Brooklyn in 1922 and studied at Harvard, where he now teaches English. He co-authored the book and lyrics for *Cry for Us All* (1970), a musical version of *Hogan's Goat,* and also wrote *The Curse of an Aching Heart* (1981)—both failures.

347

HOLBROOK, [Harold Rowe, Jr.], Hal (b. 1925) A native of Cleveland, he made his professional debut in 1942. Although he later assumed leading roles in such important Broadway offerings as the 1964 revival of *Marco Millions*♦; *After the Fall*♦ (1964), in which he alternated with Jason Robards, Jr.♦; and *I Never Sang for My Father* (1968), he is recalled primarily for his one-man show, *Mark Twain Tonight!*, which he first performed in 1955 and afterwards toured with for many seasons. In 1990 he played King Lear off-Broadway.

Hold Everything!, a musical comedy in two acts. Book by B. G. De Sylva♦ and John McGowan.♦ Lyrics by De Sylva and Lew Brown. ♦ Music by Ray Henderson. ♦ Produced by Alex A. Aarons♦ and Vinton Freedley♦ at the Broadhurst Theatre. October 10, 1928. 413 performances.

"Sonny Jim" (Jack Whiting♦) is a welterweight contender. When he agrees to fight in a charity bout his trainer suggests he pull his punches rather than risk problems, but his sweetheart, Sue Burke (Ona Munson), tells him to fight as if it meant the title. "Sonny Jim" is also pursued by the flashy Norine Lloyd (Betty Compton). He is uncertain whether to follow his trainer's or his sweetheart's advice until his opponent slaps Sue. Then he quickly wins both the bout and Sue.

Principal songs: Don't Hold Everything · To Know You Is To Love You · Too Good To Be True · You're the Cream in My Coffee

Prizefights had become big in this sports-mad era, enjoying what for the time were record-breaking gates. Earlier in the same season several straight plays had centered on boxing, so this show was bringing to the musical stage a popular subject. For many critics and playgoers, the highlight of the evening was the clowning of Bert Lahr♦ as a punchdrunk fighter, Gink Schiner. His antics in this show made him a star.

Holiday, a play in three acts by Philip Barry.♦ Produced by Arthur Hopkins♦ at the Plymouth Theatre. November 26, 1928. 230 performances.

Having made a small fortune while still a young man, Johnny Case (Ben Smith) decides to use his wealth to live a carefree, easy life. As he tells his prospective sister-in-law, Linda Seton (Hope Williams), "I just want to save part of my life for myself. There's a catch, though. It's got to be part of the young part." He can work again later, if need be. This philosophy sits well with Linda, but not with Johnny's fiancée, Julia Seton (Dorothy Tree), nor with her father. So when Johnny goes off to put his ideas into action, it is Linda, not Julia, who follows him.

While critics saw this play as everything from an intellectual defense of 1920s' hedonism to an Edith Whartonish satire on society, Barry's modern editor, Brendan Gill, viewed it as "an embodiment of Barry's continued preoccupation with the relations between outsiders and insiders," noting that at the time of its premiere Barry was a newly rich young man, watching with fascination from outside the curious games of society insiders.

HOLLAND, George (1791–1870) The son of a London tradesman, he himself spent several years in trade before electing to make a career of acting. He was already an experienced comedian when he came to America in 1827 and won over Bowery Theatre♦ playgoers as Jerry in *A Day After the Fair.* The role required him to assume seven disguises, including that of a drunken cobbler, a madman, and a French songstress. He soon migrated south, where he became a regional favorite, especially in New Orleans. Returning to New York in the 1840s he acted in the burlesques of William Mitchell, ♦ but left again for New Orleans in 1849. Sol Smith♦ recalled that during this engagement "he enjoyed a popularity never perhaps equalled by any other actor in that city." By 1853 he was again in New York, a member of W. E. Burton's♦ celebrated company. Two years later he joined what was to prove an even greater and longer-lived ensemble, James Wallack's.♦ Except for a brief stint with Christy's Minstrels♦ in 1857 he remained a principal comedian with Wallack until 1869, when he briefly joined Augustin Daly.♦ T. Allston Brown♦ observed, "He was unlike any other actor I ever saw. His appreciation of a part had nothing to do with the opportunity it might afford of developing a passion or an eccentricity of mind, but simply the amount of practical fun he could extract from it. An opportunity of tumbling over a chair, upsetting a table or burning his nose with a candle, was worth to him more than all the finest sentences of wit and sentiment. In the overstrained, unnatural and exaggerated style of farce . . . George Holland was in many respects unequalled." Yet it was not his art but an incident after his death for which he is best remembered. His son and the actor Joseph Jefferson♦ went to arrange his burial, only to be told by the Reverend Lorenzo Sabine that his church did not welcome actors, but that there was "a little church around the corner where they do that sort of thing." Holland's funeral thus gave a special cachet to New York's Church of the Transfiguration in American theatrical history.

Biography: *Holland Memorial: Sketch of the Life of George Holland, the Veteran Comedian, with Dramatic Reminiscences,* William B. Maclay, New York, 1871.

HOLLAND, John Joseph (1776?–1820) The English-born architect, painter, and set designer was reputedly a pupil of Marinelli in London before being brought to America by Wignell♦ to serve at Philadelphia's Chestnut Street Theatre.♦ He later moved to New York, where he was largely responsible for the 1807 redesigning of the Park Theatre,♦ at which he served for several seasons as principal scenic artist. In 1813 he left to become one of the leaders of the rebellious, short-lived Theatrical Commonwealth.♦ His skills were such, however, that when that company collapsed he was welcomed back to the Park. The Gothic settings he created for the Park's 1809 mounting of *De Montfort* are sometimes said to be the first American attempt at historical accuracy in scenery. Dunlap♦ suggested he was a slow, deliberate worker who insisted "an Artist was not bound to work by the hour like a mechanick," whereas Ireland♦ recalled, "He was an artist of great taste, and as a scenic and decorative painter, surpassed all who had been known before him in this country."

HOLLIDAY, Judy [née Judith Tuvim] (1922–65) A New York-born, baby-voiced blonde, she began her theatrical career as a telephone operator with the Mercury Theatre.♦ She spent time with a night-club act, "The Revuers," which also included Betty Comden♦ and Adolph Green,♦ before appearing in films and then making her Broadway debut as Alice in *Kiss Them for Me* (1945). She is remembered primarily for two roles: Billy Dawn, the dumb mistress of a crass junk dealer, in *Born Yesterday*♦ (1946), and Ella Peterson, who finds love while running a telephone answering service, in the musical *Bells Are Ringing* (1956). Her last appearance was as Sally Hopwinder, a Peace Corps volunteer, in the musical *Hot Spot* (1963).

Biography: *Judy Holliday,* Will Holtzman, New York, 1982.

Holliday Street Theatre (Baltimore) Opened on September 25, 1794, by Thomas Wignell♦ and Alexander Reinagle,♦ it was a wooden structure and stood on Holliday Street near Peale's Museum and directly across from the site of Baltimore's future city hall. Although it was officially the New Theatre, it soon became known as the Holliday. Later managers included William Warren♦ and William B. Wood.♦ After playing there John Howard Payne♦ noted, "the attraction was the acting, not the scenery, of which the less said the better, nor the comfort experienced by the audience, since the seats were long, uncushioned benches without backs." In 1813 it was replaced by a brick structure called the Baltimore Theatre, but again called the Holliday by Baltimoreans. "The Star Spangled Banner" received its first public performance there on October 19, 1819. The playhouse burned in 1873. It was rebuilt with a similar facade by John T. Ford♦ and finally officially called the Holliday Street Theatre. Management was later assumed by John W. Albaugh.♦ Long known as Baltimore's "Old Drury," it remained an important playhouse until shortly before its demolition in 1917.

HOLM, Celeste (b. 1919) The versatile, bright-eyed blonde, a native New Yorker, made her professional debut in 1936 and later that year understudied Ophelia in Leslie Howard's♦ *Hamlet.*♦ However, her greatest fame came when she created the role of the irrepressible Ado Annie in *Oklahoma!*♦ (1943), in which she sang "I Cain't Say No." She next starred in *Bloomer Girl*♦ (1944), but thereafter never seemed to be able to find major roles worthy of her. She did briefly replace Gertrude Lawrence♦ in *The King and I*♦ and later led a touring company of *Mame.*♦ She also spent several years touring in *Theatre in Concert.*

HOLM, Hanya [née Johanna Eckert] (b. 1893) German-born choreographer who worked with Max Reinhardt♦ before emigrating to America, she performed alone or with an ensemble prior to choreographing *The Eccentricities of Davy Crockett* in the Broadway production of *Ballet Ballads* (1948). Later assignments included *Kiss Me, Kate*♦ (1948), *Out of This World* (1950), *The Golden Apple*♦ (1954), *My Fair Lady*♦ (1956), and *Camelot*♦ (1960). Her work was eclectic, ranging from the lively, witty routines for *Kiss Me, Kate* and *The Golden Apple* to the elegant dances of *My Fair Lady.*

Biography: *Hanya Holm: The Biography of an Artist,* Walter Sorrell, Middletown, Conn., 1969.

HOLM, John Cecil, see *Three Men on a Horse*

HOLMAN, Libby [née Elizabeth Holtzman] (1906–71) One of the most celebrated torch singers of the 1920s and early 1930s, the dark-haired beauty was born in Cincinnati and studied at the university there. She made her professional debut, simply as an actress, in a 1924 touring company of *The Fool,*♦ then first appeared on Broadway in the *Garrick Gaieties*♦ (1925). Assignments in several other revues and as the sultry Lotta in Vincent Youmans's♦ *Rainbow* (1928) followed before she scored heavily in the revue *The Little Show*♦ (1929), in which she sang "Moanin' Low." She introduced "Body and Soul" and "Something to Remember You By" in *Three's a Crowd* (1930), and "You and the Night and the Music" in *Revenge with Music* (1934). Later appearances were in *You Never Know* (1938) and in a one-woman show *Blues, Ballads and Sin Songs* (1954). Besides occasional performances in straight plays in summer stock, she frequently sang in cabarets.

HOLTZ, Lou (1898–1980) Yiddish-dialect comedian, famed for his zany version of "O Sole Mio" with which he often ended his vaudeville act, he was born in San Francisco and made his vaudeville debut in Newark, N.J., in 1914. A year later he made his Broadway debut in *A World of Pleasure.* Thereafter he moved back and forth between two-a-day and the legitimate stage. Musicals in which he appeared included the 1919, 1920, and 1921 editions of *George White's Scandals*♦*; The Dancing Girl* (1923); *Tell Me More* (1925); *Manhattan Mary* (1927); *You Said It* (1931), which he also produced; *Calling All Stars* (1934); *Priorities of 1942;* and *Star Time* (1944). Holtz's popularity was mainly in cities with large Jewish communities. His humor, which was highly ethnic, was sometimes assailed for exceeding the boundaries of good taste.

HOOKER, [WILLIAM] BRIAN (1880–1946) A professor of English at both Yale and Columbia, his translation of *Cyrano de Bergerac*♦ was used by both Walter Hampden♦ and José Ferrer.♦ Hampden also used his version of *Ruy Blas* (1933). Hooker served as well as lyricist and librettist for several musicals, the best remembered of which is *The Vagabond King*♦ (1925).

HOOLEY, RICHARD M. (1822–93) One of the earliest minstrels, he made his debut with E. P. Christy's♦ company in 1845. Later he formed his own troupe, with which he toured Europe as well as all major American cities. In 1862 he opened Hooley's Opera House in Brooklyn, initially as a minstrel auditorium, but with time found management so congenial that he abandoned minstrelsy to run theatres as far west as Chicago.

HOPE, [LESLIE TOWNES] BOB (b. 1903) Born in England, but raised in Cleveland, he made his professional debut in vaudeville. His Broadway debut was in the chorus of *The Ramblers* (1926), and he subsequently appeared in *Sidewalks of New York* (1927), *Ups-a-Daisy* (1928), *Smiles* (1930), and *Ballyhoo of 1932.* By 1932 he had become a headliner at the Palace Theatre,♦ where Max Gordon♦ caught his act, which consisted largely of brash one-liners, and cast him for the part of Huck Haines in *Roberta*♦ (1933). He played similar wise-cracking roles in *Say When* (1934), *The Ziegfeld Follies of 1936,*♦ and *Red, Hot and Blue!* (1936), then abandoned the theatre for films and radio, where he became one of the most successful comedians of the time, especially during his extended tours of army camps in World War II.

HOPKINS, ARTHUR [MELANCTHON] (1878–1950) One of the most distinguished of Broadway producers, he was born in Cleveland, and spent time as a newspaper reporter before turning to the theatre. As a newsman, he was the first to uncover background material on Leon Czolgocz, President McKinley's assassin. He left the newspaper field to become a vaudeville press agent, and later worked with Irene and Vernon Castle. ♦ His first production *Steve* (1912) was a failure, but *The Poor Little Rich Girl* (1913) gave him his initial success. Later hits included *On Trial*♦ (1914), produced in association with George M. Cohan♦ and Sam Harris♦; *Good Gracious Annabelle*♦ (1916); *A Successful Calamity* (1917); *The Jest* (1919); *Anna Christie*♦ (1921); *The Hairy Ape*♦ (1922); *The Old Soak*♦ (1922); *What Price Glory?*♦ (1924): *Burlesque*♦ (1927), which he co-authored; *Paris Bound*♦ (1927); *Machinal*♦ (1928); *Holiday*♦ (1928); *The Petrified Forest*♦ (1935), produced in association with Gilbert Miller♦ and Leslie Howard♦; and *The Magnificent Yankee* (1946). He was also responsible for bringing John Barrymore♦ to the stage in *Richard III*♦ (1920) and *Hamlet*♦ (1922), as well as for Ethel Barrymore's♦ Juliet in 1922 and Lionel Barrymore's♦ Macbeth in 1921. As a rule, Hopkins directed all his own productions. His play *Conquest* (1933), which retold the Hamlet story in terms of modern-day, commercial New England, was highly praised, but failed. In conjunction with the Shuberts, ♦ he built the Plymouth Theatre in New York. He also wrote two books: *How's Your Second Act?* (1931) and an autobiography, *To a Lonely Boy* (1937). In the latter he expressed a philosophy of producing: "It would seem to me that the final test of producers or producing groups is the amount of new talent they have brought into the theater. It was the joy of old producers like Belasco and Tyler to develop new talent. That was the high adventure of the theater. To the extent that I have succeeded in doing this I can assure you that therein lies the chief joy of producing." John Mason Brown♦ remembered him as "that amazing, moon-faced little cherub . . . looking like a small town banker and thinking like an artist."

HOPPER, DE WOLF [WILLIAM D'WOLF HOPPER] (1858–1935) Descendant of a family that traced its ancestry back to colonial America, he was born in New York and raised in expectation of following in his father's footsteps as a lawyer. A few months of studying law changed his mind, and after his father's death he used his inheritance to form his own theatrical company. The company failed, so while playing minor roles he studied voice with the idea of singing in opera. However, when John McCaull♦ cast him as a singing comedian in *Désirée* in 1884, his success was so pronounced that he realized immediately he had found his life's work. Among his major early musicals were *The Black Hussar* (1885), *The Beggar Student* (1885), *The Begum* (1887), *The Lady or the Tiger* (1888), and *Castles in the Air* (1890), his first starring vehicle. A major success was his performance as the conniving regent, the title role of *Wang*♦ (1891), in which he stopped the show with a comic "topical" song, "Ask the Man in the Moon." *Panjandrum* (1893) and *Dr. Syntax* (1894) were somewhat less popular, but in 1896 he first played the role with which he is most identified, the wily viceroy of Peru, Don Medigua, who under the guise of his arch enemy thwarts a rebellion, in John Philip Sousa's♦ *El Capitan,*♦ introducing "El Capitan's Song." In subsequent seasons he appeared in *The Charlatan* (1898); *Fiddle-Dee-Dee* (1900); *Hoity Toity* (1901); *Mr. Pickwick* (1903); *Happyland* (1905); *The Pied Piper* (1908); *A Matinee Idol* (1910); a series of Gilbert♦ and Sullivan revivals; *Lieber Augustin* (1913); *Hop o' My Thumb* (1913); more Gilbert and Sullivan revivals; *The Passing Show of 1917*♦; *Everything* (1918); as Bill in the main road company of *The Better 'Ole* (1919); a revival of *Erminie*♦ (1921); *Snapshots of 1921;* and *Some Party* (1922). He also played Falstaff, as well as David in *The Rivals.* By this time his popularity had waned with Broadway audiences, but he found a welcome touring in revivals of *El Capitan, The Chocolate Soldier,* and a road company of *The Student Prince*♦ (1927). After clowning in the musical *White Lilacs* (1928), he performed in two short-lived straight plays and toured briefly in

others. An exceedingly tall, thin man with a deep basso voice, he made famous the poem "Casey at the Bat"♦ early in his career and thereafter recited it either in his shows or as part of his curtain calls. He was notorious for having been married six times.

Autobiography: *Once a Clown, Always a Clown,* with Wesley Winan Stout, Boston, 1927.

HOPPER, EDNA WALLACE (1864?–1959) The exceptionally tiny—said to be well under five feet—singer and comedienne was born in San Francisco and made her New York debut in 1891. She was a rising member of Charles Frohman's♦ stock company when she married De Wolf Hopper♦ and turned to the musical stage. She played major roles in such shows as *El Capitan*♦ (1896) and *Florodora*♦ (1900). In later years she remained popular in vaudeville, where she traded on her deceptively youthful appearance.

HOPWOOD, [JAMES] AVERY (1882–1928) One of the most successful playwrights of his day, he was born in Cleveland, and educated at the University of Michigan. Like many other contemporary playwrights he spent time as a newspaperman before seeing his first play produced. That play was *Clothes*♦ (1906), the story of comic complications besetting a poor girl when she attempts to dress like a rich one. Inspired by Hopwood's reading of Carlyle's *Sartor Resartus*, it was rewritten by the more experienced Channing Pollock♦ before it opened. But Hopwood profited from studying Pollock's revisions. He never laid claim to serious artistic pretensions, wanting only to be a successful, respected commercial craftsman. In the future he worked alone or with collaborators and frequently wrote to order. More often than not his plays were looked upon as risqué, although only once did the police suggest he had overstepped the line of decency. His most successful works were *Seven Days*♦ (1909), written with Mary Roberts Rinehart♦ and telling of an odd assortment of characters trapped together by a quarantine; *Nobody's Widow*♦ (1910), depicting a lady's attempt to deny her husband; *Fair and Warmer*♦ (1915), describing the marital misunderstandings of two couples; *The Gold Diggers*♦ (1919), centering on grasping chorus girls; *The Girl in the Limousine* (1919), written with Wilson Collison and in which a motorist's troubles begin when he stops to aid a seemingly stranded girl. *Ladies' Night* ♦ (1920), a story of an innocent young man who finds himself in a Turkish bath on the wrong evening, written with Charlton Andrews; *Spanish Love* (1920), written with Mary Roberts

Rinehart and narrating the love of two young men for the same girl; *The Bat*♦ (1920), a whodunit, also with Mrs. Rinehart; *Getting Gertie's Garter*♦ (1921), written with Collison and telling of the attempt by a married man to retrieve a present given an old sweetheart; *The Demi-Virgin* (1921), relating the on-again off-again romance of a tempestuous Hollywood pair; *Why Men Leave Home* (1922), recounting the adventures of some summer bachelors; *Little Miss Bluebeard* (1923), describing the confusions of two newlyweds; *The Best People* (1924), written with David Gray and telling of a rich brother and sister who fall in love with a chorus girl and chauffeur respectively; *The Harem* (1924), an adaptation of a Hungarian play in which a wife poses as an odalisque to test her husband; and *Naughty Cinderella* (1925), in which a French secretary's flirtations lead to problems.

Brooks Atkinson♦ wrote, "The mechanical formula for play-writing that made the value of American drama negligible was perfect for Hopwood, and he developed it with the skill and polish of an ingenious workman." A tall, thin man with blue eyes and blond hair, he was known for his exceedingly grave expression. That demeanor apparently masked serious private problems, for Hopwood eventually became a heavy drinker and may have committed suicide by drowning himself in the Mediterranean. He left his alma mater a large bequest to be made the basis of an annual award for play-writing.

Biography: *Avery Hopwood: His Life and Plays*, Jack F. Sharrar, Jefferson, N.C., 1989.

Horizon, a play in five acts by Augustin Daly.♦ Produced by John A. Duff♦ at the Olympic Theatre. March 21, 1871. 65 performances.

Alleyn Van Dorp (Hart Conway), a recent West Point graduate, is dispatched to the Far West on his first commission. He employs his spare time seeking the lost daughter and husband of his foster-mother. He soon learns Med (Agnes Ethel♦), whom the Indians call "the White Flower of the Plains," and her drunkard father Wolf (J. B. Studley♦) are the very persons he seeks. After Wolf is murdered, a notorious criminal, John Loder (J. K. Mortimer), who is known as "Panther Loder" or "the White Panther," takes Med under his protection. He loves her and treats her well, but she is kidnapped by the Indian chief, Wannamucka (Charles Wheatleigh). Van Dorp rescues her, and Loder kills Wannamucka. For all his cruelty and dishonesty, Loder cares enough about Med to recognize she will fare better with Van Dorp, so he relinquishes her to the soldier.

Critics praised the play for its reasonably accurate picture of the contemporary West and for its willingness to see virtue in villains and faults in heroes and heroines. One of Daly's great rivals, A. M. Palmer,♦ later said not only was it Daly's best play but the finest American play he had ever seen. Despite critical and professional admiration for the work, its public acceptance was minimal.

HORN, [Evan] Eph (1823–77) Born in Philadelphia, he began his career as part of a hypnotist act, but while still in his teens became a minstrel. His success was instant and he quickly became a favorite not only across the country, but in England as well. He worked at one time or another with most of the great troupers of his day, including E. P. Christy♦ and Dan Bryant. ♦ He was not an especially good-looking man, with a high forehead, huge nose, prominent chin, and walrus moustache, but in blackface his comic and dramatic skills made audiences indifferent to his appearance. Among his most famous routines were his imitation of various locomotives and his stump speech on "Woman's Rights." His act "The Stage Struck Darkey" was apparently especially effective, T. Allston Brown♦ recalling, "For depth of feeling and pathos, [it] has not been exceeded on any stage."

HORNBLOW, Arthur (1865–1942) The English-born writer and editor studied literature and painting in Paris before moving to America in 1889. He became a member of the staff of the *Dramatic Mirror,* ♦ supplementing his salary by serving as a play reader for A. M. Palmer. ♦ From 1901 to 1926 he was the editor and principal dramatic critic for *Theatre Magazine.* ♦ During this period he novelized several successful Broadway plays as well as writing several plays of his own. He also wrote his two-volume *A History of the Theatre in America, from Its Beginnings to the Present Time* (1919).

HORNE, Lena (b. 1917) The Brooklyn-born singer, better known for her work in films and night clubs, first appeared on Broadway in a 1939 black drama. However, her major theatrical successes were *Jamaica* (1957) and her one-woman show, *Lena Horne: The Lady and Her Music* (1981). A light-skinned black, she is distinguished by her exquisitely lacquered beauty and her extraordinarily precise enunciation, although, like many of her contemporaries, she apparently requires a microphone to project in even the smallest Broadway house.

Horseshoe Robinson, a play in three acts by Clifton W. Tayleure.♦ Produced at the Holliday Street Theatre♦ (Baltimore). May 5, 1856.

The roughhewn woodsman and Indian fighter, Galbraith "Horseshoe" Robinson (William Ellis), is helping his friend Major Arthur Butler (George C. Boniface♦) sneak through redcoat lines during the Revolution. Not only does Butler want to reach friendly forces, but he wants to stop for a visit at the Lindsay home. Although Mr. Lindsay (J. H. Jack) is a loyalist, his daughter Mildred (Mrs. I. B. Phillips) is a rebel supporter who has secretly married Butler. At one point Butler and Robinson are surrounded. Robinson escapes and uses all his wiles to enlist further aid to free Butler, now under sentence of death. His ruses include making himself and one associate appear to outnumber the British force.

Based on John P. Kennedy's historical romance, *Horseshoe Robinson: A Tale of the Tory Ascendency,* it was originally adapted (probably by Charles Dance) as a vehicle for the elder Hackett♦ in 1836. Hackett played the role for several seasons. Whether Tayleure made his own version or simply revamped Dance's is unknown, for Tayleure's alone survives. It is a lively piece, filled with colorful characters. In one form or another, the play remained popular, especially at lower-class houses, well beyond the Civil War.

HORTON, EDWARD EVERETT (1886–1970) The effeminate Brooklyn-born comedian had a long, but minor stage career before becoming a popular supporting player in films. With his newfound fame he toured off and on for many years as Henry Dewlip, the aging playboy who is almost reformed, in *Springtime for Henry.*

HOSCHNA, KARL (1877–1911) Born in Kushchwarda, Bohemia, he graduated with honors from the Vienna Conservatory and accepted a post as oboist in the Austrian army band. He came to America in 1896 and found work with Victor Herbert. ♦ According to rumor, he developed a fear that oboe playing would affect his mind, so he left Herbert to work as a copyist at a music publisher. While there he composed three operettas which were produced but folded before reaching New York. His luck changed when he wrote the score for *Three Twins* (1908), from which came the hit songs "Cuddle Up a Little Closer, Lovey Mine" and "The Yama Yama Man." *Bright Eyes* and *Madame Sherry*♦ opened in 1910, the latter his biggest hit and the source of the still recognized "Every Little Movement." In the follow-ing year *Jumping Jupiter, Dr. Deluxe, The Girl of My Dreams,* and *The Fascinating Widow* all reached Broadway, while his *The Wall Street Girl* (1912) was mounted posthumously. Hoschna was a fine melodist, his work characterized by great charm. His death at thirty-four left unanswered how he would have developed.

Hot Corn: Life Scenes in New York Illustrated Solon Robinson's collection of loosely interconnected stories depicting the drink-doomed habitués of Five Points, a notorious Manhattan slum, was first published in mid-1853 in the New York *Tribune,* then a year later was expanded into a hardcover bestseller. Dramatizations, according to Odell,♦ soon "swept the stages with a blast second only to that of Uncle Tom's Cabin." New York saw no fewer than three popular versions during the 1853–54 season. The first to appear was *Little Katy; or, The Hot Corn Girl,* which opened at the National Theatre on December 5. This version was by C. W. Taylor♦ and featured Cordelia Howard♦ as Katy. The next afternoon, December 6, another version, *Hot Corn; or, Little Katy,* was presented at Barnum's American Museum.♦ The Bowery Theatre♦ offered its adaptation, *The Hot Corn Girl,* on April 3. The versions varied greatly, often changing characters' names and, apparently, sometimes adding original materials. If programs are any indication, that of the Bowery seems to have been most faithful to the original. Its characters included the Reverend Mr. Pease, a Protestant missionary whose House of Industry shelters and attempts to reform the mostly Catholic drunkards; Wild Maggie and her father, Jim Reagan, two shining examples of the minister's reform efforts; Athalia Lovetree, a daughter of a drunken farmer, who comes to New York to accept work as a seamstress and marries a rich merchant's son, only to have his drinking wreck her life; Madalina, a small girl whose death spares her the life of prostitution her ragpicker mother would force her into; and, most of all, Little Katy, a tot selling peanuts in winter and hot corn in summer, who dies after her drunken mother beats her for falling asleep and allowing a thief to steal her nightly quota of corn.

Hotel Universe, a play [performed without intermission] by Philip Barry.♦ Produced by the Theatre Guild♦ at the Martin Beck Theatre. April 14, 1930. 81 performances.

Ann Field (Katherine Alexander) has invited a variety of guests to her Riviera estate. They include Ann's old beau, Pat Farley (Glenn Anders♦); Lily

Malone (Ruth Gordon♦), an actress; Tom Ames (Franchot Tone♦), a publisher, and his wife Hope (Phyllis Povah); Norman Rose (Earl Larimore♦), a rich Jew; and Alice Kendall (Ruthelma Stevens), who is in love with Rose. Also present is Ann's strange old father, Stephen (Morris Carnovsky♦), a scientist and a mystic as well. The guests have all found their promising beginnings somehow thwarted. Moreover, they have been unnerved by odd stories about the house and by the suicide of a young friend. Stephen's probing questions and incisive remarks force them to examine their past and exorcise the demons that have bedeviled them. They leave filled with new hope, and unaware Stephen has quietly died while sitting in his chair.

Although the play baffled most critics and was rejected by playgoers, it remains one of Barry's more interesting excursions away from his high comedy forte, yet is filled with his typically witty lines and trenchant observations.

Hot l Baltimore, The, a play in three acts by Lanford Wilson.♦ Produced by Kermit Bloomgarden♦ and Roger Ailes at the Circle in the Square.♦ March 22, 1973. 1,166 performances. NYDCCA.

The Hotel Baltimore, once fashionable, but now home to prostitutes, petty thieves, drifters, and indigents, has become seedy. The "e" in "hotel" in its sign has gone out, but no one has bothered to replace it since the building is about to be torn down. Little happens in the hotel. People reminisce about their past, the prostitutes come and go with their trade, one tenant robs another, and a young man, who turns out to be an escapee from a work farm, comes seeking his grandfather, who may or may not have lived there.

Originally produced off-off-Broadway by the Circle Repertory Company,♦ this was a compassionate but somewhat unfocused play. In the original production Judd Hirsch played Bill, the night clerk.

HOUDINI, Harry [né Erik Weisz] (1874?–1926) Born in Budapest, he was brought to America as a child and raised in Appleton, Wis., where his father was a rabbi. As a youngster he was apprenticed to a locksmith, mastering skills that would later make him famous. He seems to have purposely shrouded his theatrical beginnings in some mystery, but most often claimed to have first performed in medicine shows. With a friend, Jacob Hyman, he formed an acrobatic and magic act in 1891. They called their act "The Brothers Houdini," in honor of the famous French illusionist Robert Houdin. The team lasted only a short while when Houdini embarked on his

own. He quickly became a major vaudeville celebrity, although some of his most publicized feats took place of necessity outside of theatres. His forte was escape from seemingly indefiable locks and shackles, and he even allowed himself to be chained and thrown into a river to demonstrate his ability. He also escaped from supposedly impregnable jail cells in which he was imprisoned as a stunt. A consummate showman, he was often billed as "The King of Handcuffs." He garnered additional publicity exposing fraudulent séances.

Biography: *Houdini: The Untold Story,* Milbourne Christopher, New York, 1969.

HOUGH, Will M. (1882–1962) With Frank R. Adams,♦ his fellow student at the University of Chicago, he collaborated on the book and lyrics for a Chicago musical, *His Highness the Bey* (1904). The composer was Joe Howard.♦ Over the next several seasons the trio offered Chicago some of its most successful musical comedies, including *The Isle of Bong Bong* (1905); *The Umpire♦* (1905); *The Girl Question* (1906); *The Time, the Place and the Girl♦* (1906), which established a Chicago long-run record for its day; *The Land of Nod* (1907); *Honeymoon Trail* (1908); *A Stubborn Cinderella* (1908); *The Prince of Tonight* (1909); *The Golden Girl* (1909); *The Flirting Princess* (1909); *The Goddess of Liberty* (1909); and *Miss Nobody from Starland* (1910). Although several of these shows toured successfully after their Chicago runs, none was popular in New York. Hough's and Adams's writing had a down-to-earth directness, and a slanginess not unlike George M. Cohan's,♦ but was far less brash and chauvinistic. After splitting with Howard, Hough and Adams wrote *The Heartbreakers* (1911) with Harold Orlob. With collaborators other than Adams, Hough later wrote *The Girl at the Gate* (1912), a major Chicago success, and *Pitter Patter* (1920).

House of Blue Leaves, The, a play in two acts by John Guare.♦ Produced at the Truck and Warehouse Theatre. February 10, 1971. 337 performances. NYDCCA.

News of the Pope's impending visit seems to unhinge the zany Shaughnessy family. The father, Artie (Harold Gould), is a zookeeper who dreams of becoming a show business celebrity and writes lyrics such as "Where is the devil in Evelyn?" The mother, Bananas (Katherine Helmond), is flakier still, sometimes confusing Brillo pads and hamburgers. Their son, Ronnie (William Atherton), has gone AWOL in hopes of blowing up the Pope. Even Artie's mistress, Bunny (Anne Meara), is kooky. Her idea of real life is what she reads in *Modern Screen*. Ronnie's plans backfire, and he is blown up by his own bomb. Bunny runs off with a Hollywood producer whom Artie had hoped would help him. Artie's reaction to all this is to compose another inane ditty.

The play was a superb black comedy. It was revived to great acclaim in 1986.

House of Flowers, a musical in two acts. Book by Truman Capote. Lyrics by Capote and Harold Arlen. ◆ Music by Arlen. Produced at the Alvin Theatre. December 30, 1954. 165 performances.

During a trade war between two brothel keepers, Madame Tango (Juanita Hall) and Madame Fleur (Pearl Bailey ◆), the latter sells one of her girls, Ottilie (Diahann Carroll), to a rich man. But Ottilie prefers young, handsome Royal (Rawn Spearman) and, despite Madame Fleur's machinations, she gets her way.

Principal songs: House of Flowers · A Sleeping Bee · Two Ladies in de Shade of de Banana Tree

The show had a superb Arlen score and an exceptionally beautiful production featuring Oliver Messel's pastel settings and costumes, but it could not overcome indifferent notices and unusually strong competition. Although it became one of those failures that develops a cult following, an off-Broadway revival in 1968 quickly failed. Capote (1924–84; né Truman Streckfus Persons), a New Orleans native better known as a novelist, also wrote the play *The Grass Harp* (1952). Several of his other works were adapted for the stage by other writers, albeit unsuccessfully.

House of Glass, The, a play in four acts by Max Marcin. ◆ Produced by Cohan ◆ and Harris ◆ at the Chandler Theatre. September 1, 1915. 245 performances.

Margaret Case (Mary Ryan) is sent to prison for a crime she did not commit. After she is paroled she hides her prison record from the man she eventually marries, Harvey Lake (Frederick Burt). However, Lake believes one of his employees is stealing, and when he calls in a detective to get the evidence, he learns the truth about his wife from him. A kindly state governor helps reconcile the couple.

Because of similarities in the early part of its story, many critics compared the play with *Within the Law* ◆ and found the new work somewhat inferior, but still agreed it was gripping theatre. Cohan is said to have helped Marcin whip the play into shape. A sign of the healthy theatrical economics of the time was the fact that while this was Marcin's first play,

the very next show to open on Broadway (the next night) was another Marcin play.

HOUSEMAN, JOHN [né JACQUES HAUSSMANN] (1902–88) The Rumanian-born, English-educated actor, director, and producer first came to playgoers' attention when he directed *Four Saints in Three Acts* ◆ (1934). He consolidated his reputation that same year by directing a revival of *The Lady from the Sea* and *Valley Forge,* ◆ and then producing Archibald MacLeish's ◆ *Panic* (1935). The following year he staged Leslie Howard's ◆ *Hamlet.* ◆ He then joined the Federal Theatre Project. ◆ Perhaps his most notable achievement was the founding of the Mercury Theatre ◆ in 1937 with Orson Welles. ◆ Designed largely to offer "plays of the past—preferably those which seem to have emotion or factual bearing on contemporary life," the company in its all too short existence mounted several notable productions. The most remarkable may have been its modern-dress version of *Julius Caesar.* ◆ After the troupe disbanded, Houseman directed *The Devil and Daniel Webster* ◆ (1939) and Philip Barry's ◆ *Liberty Jones* (1941). He also co-produced *Native Son* ◆ (1941). He did not work again in the theatre until after World War II. On his return he directed *Lute Song* (1946), Louis Calhern's ◆ *King Lear* ◆ (1950), and the Phoenix Theatre's ◆ *Coriolanus* (1954). From 1956 to 1959 he was artistic director for the American Shakespeare Festival, ◆ then held a similar position until 1964 with the Theatre Group of the University of California. He next headed the drama division of Juilliard. From 1972 he staged several productions of the Acting Company, ◆ which he headed.

Autobiographies: *Run-Through,* New York, 1972; *Front and Center,* New York, 1979; and *Final Dress,* New York, 1983.

How To Succeed in Business Without Really Trying, a musical comedy in two acts. Book by Abe Burrows, ◆ Jack Weinstock, and Willie Gilbert. Lyrics and music by Frank Loesser. ◆ Produced by Feuer ◆ and Martin, ◆ in association with Frank [Loesser] Productions, at the 46th Street Theatre. October 14, 1961. 1,417 performances. PP.

Although J. Pierpont Finch (Robert Morse ◆) is only a windowwasher, he is determined that nothing will stop his rise to the top of the business world. Nothing does. Reading from his "How To" book, he proceeds to step over every obstacle (read fellow employees) at World Wide Wickets, including the boss's ambitious nephew, Bud Frump (Charles Nelson Reilly), until all that stands in the way is the boss himself, J. B. Biggley (Rudy Vallee). Finch manages to blame a television fiasco which he engineered on Biggley, and has Biggley kicked upstairs. As Finch is about to assume office, Frump is seen washing the windows and reading from the same "How To" book that helped Finch.

Based on Shepherd Mead's novel of the same name, the musical was praised by Walter Kerr♦ in the *Herald Tribune* as "a sassy, gay and exhilarating evening." It was Loesser's last show. The musical was marked by its cleverly iconoclastic placement of songs. Thus, "Grand Old Ivy," a seemingly traditional college fight song, was used to spoof sentimental alumni susceptibility, while the principal song of the show, the hit "love song" "I Believe in You," was sung by the egomaniacal hero as he admired himself in a men's room mirror.

HOWARD, Bronson [Crocker] (1842–1908) Often called "the dean of the American drama," he is generally considered the first American playwright to earn a living entirely by play-writing. He came from old American stock, and his father, a successful merchant, served as mayor of Detroit, where Howard was born. Forced to leave Yale because of eye problems, he accepted a post as drama critic with the Detroit *Free Press*. While in that position he wrote *Fantine* (1864), a play based on incidents in Hugo's *Les Miserables*. Shortly after its Detroit production, he moved to New York, accepting positions with the *Tribune* and then the *Post*. In 1870 Augustin Daly♦ produced his *Saratoga,*♦ recounting the comic adventures of a gay blade whose lady friends all descend on him at once. A huge success, it was later played profitably in England and Germany. Howard, however, was uncertain whether its popularity was a fluke, so continued for several more years in the newspaper field. At the same time he wrote *Diamonds* (1872), a comedy of manners which included a controversial shooting scene patterned after Stokes's killing of Fisk; *Moorcroft* (1874), based on a short story by John Hay and telling of a man who sells his half-brother into slavery and of the loving woman who buys him only to find he does not share her feelings; and *The Banker's Daughter*♦ (1878), a rewriting of his 1873 play *Lillian's Last Love* and depicting how a woman grows to love the older man she married for his money. This play remained popular for many years, and confirmed Howard in his eventual decision to abandon newspaper work. Several lesser plays followed before he wrote *Young Mrs. Winthrop*♦ (1882), in which a wife's preoccupation with social position and her husband's overriding concern with

business threaten their marriage. *One of Our Girls* (1885) contrasted the openhandedness of an American heiress with French social proprieties. His next success was *The Henrietta*♦ (1887), a comedy-drama of family intrigue on Wall Street. Two years later, *Shenandoah,*♦ a story of lovers separated by the Civil War, proved to be his last popular work, although several others were mounted before his death.

Quinn♦ has written, "It is just because Howard so well illustrated, in the broadening of his own grasp of dramatic material and the refinement of his own skill, the development of American playwriting during the period of his creative achievement from 1870 to 1906, that his work becomes of such significance." Howard had little time for social significance in the theatre and apparently even less for artistic pretensions. He insisted that the divorce of drama and literature "should be made absolute and final," adding, "I have felt this so strongly, at times, as to warmly deny that I was a 'literary man,' insisting on being a 'dramatist.' " However, he fought to have American themes made more welcome on stage and to secure the position of the American playwright. To the latter end, in 1891 he organized the American Dramatists Club,♦ which evolved into the Society of American Dramatists and Composers.♦ Although he left no personal autobiography and no full-fledged biography of him has been written, his *The Autobiography of a Play* (1914) gives a detailed, fascinating history of *The Banker's Daughter* and provides numerous insights into his character.

HOWARD, Cordelia (1848–1941) A niece of G. L. Fox,♦ the tiny, dark-haired charmer was only four and a half years old when she first played Little Eva in *Uncle Tom's Cabin,*♦ a role she performed or regularly returned to for several years. One writer noted, "The name of Little Cordelia has become synonymous with that of Little Eva." She withdrew from the stage while still in her teens.

HOWARD, Eugene , see *Howard, Willie*

HOWARD, [Joseph E.] Joe (1867–1961) Best remembered as the composer of a song he did not write, Howard was a performer and entertainer for over three-quarters of a century. Born in New York, he claimed to have run away from home as a youngster to begin singing for pennies on sidewalks outside saloons and theatres. He soon was performing in two-a-day as a boy soprano. By the turn of the century he had won fame as composer of "Goodbye,

My Lady Love" and "Hello, My Baby." He was also celebrated for his performance of "The Handicap March," in which he impersonated horses, jockeys, bookies, and bettors at a race. About the same time he established Chicago as his base and began composing scores for Chicago musicals, most of which toured successfully and a few of which reached New York, where they were not welcomed. His songs were heard in *His Highness the Bey* (1904); *The Isle of Bong Bong* (1905); *The Umpire*◆ (1905); *The District Leader* (1906); *The Girl Question* (1906); *The Time, The Place and the Girl*◆ (1906), which established a Chicago long-run record for its time; *The Land of Nod* (1907); *Honeymoon Trail* (1908); *A Stubborn Cinderella* (1908); *The Flower of the Ranch* (1908); *The Prince of Tonight* (1909); *The Golden Girl* (1909); *The Flirting Princess* (1909); *The Goddess of Liberty* (1910); and *Miss Nobody from Starland* (1910). The song hit of *The Prince of Tonight* was the song with which he was most identified, "I Wonder Who's Kissing Her Now," but a lawsuit decades later revealed he had bought the melody from Harold Orlob. It was this doubt about the source of his melodies that prompted music publisher Edward B. Marks to brand him "the opportunist of song," but whatever its origin, the music for which he took credit had a distinctive homey warmth and, early on, displayed a flare for the then new ragtime. He was still performing when he died at the age of ninety-four.

HOWARD [STAINER], LESLIE (1893–1943) The suave, slender, handsome English-born actor first appeared before New York audiences as Sir Calverton Shipley, who accompanies his friend, the Prince of Wales, on an American tour, in *Just Suppose* (1920). Thereafter he played in New York more than in England. Best recalled among his many roles were Henry, the suicide who may be given another chance at life, in the fantasy *Outward Bound* (1924); Napier Harpenden, who loyally loves but loses the doomed heroine, in *The Green Hat* (1925); André Sallicel, the hired lover, in *Her Cardboard Lover* (1927); Matt Denant, who fails in his efforts to flee the prison where he has been sent for manslaughter, in *Escape* (1927); Peter Standish, who transcends the centuries, in *Berkeley Square*◆ (1929); Joseph, the prince's valet who impersonates his master, in *Candle Light* (1929); Tom Collier, the publisher who chooses his mistress over his wife, in *The Animal Kingdom*◆ (1932); and Alan Squier, the disillusioned idealist who seeks his own death, in *The Petrified Forest*◆ (1935). His last Broadway appearance was in 1936 as Hamlet. He also enjoyed

a successful career in films before his death in a plane downed during World War II. John Mason Brown◆ recalled, "Howard was a player supreme as a water-colorist but without strength for oils. Of a negative he made a positive; of diffidence, an act of caring. No one could write of him . . . without falling back on the word 'charm,' which he had in such easy abundance that he could turn nighttime theatregoers into matinee audiences. Immaculate, quizzical and stylish, he had in Savile Row terms something of Chaplin's pathos."

Biography: *A Quite Remarkable Father*, Leslie Ruth Howard, New York, 1959.

HOWARD, SIDNEY [COE] (1891–1939) Born to pioneer stock in Oakland, Calif., he studied at the University of California and with Professor George Pierce Baker◆ in his 47 Workshop◆ at Harvard. He then worked on magazines and newspapers while awaiting production of his plays. The first to reach New York was *Swords* (1921). This romantic verse drama set in Renaissance Italy was a failure, as were several subsequent offerings. His first success was *They Knew What They Wanted*◆ (1924), recounting a December-May romance in the Napa Valley. It won a Pulitzer Prize.◆ *Lucky Sam McCarver*◆ (1925) centered on a callous, greedy bootlegger, while *Ned McCobb's Daughter*◆ (1926) examined the efforts of a tough-fibered lady to deal with her worthless family. An even better play was *The Silver Cord*◆ (1926), a study of a destructively possessive mother. A series of failures followed before Howard found success with *The Late Christopher Bean* (1932), recounting the effects of an artist's posthumous fame on his family. *Alien Corn*◆ (1933), examining the plight of a sensitive artist in a deadening college community, was enhanced immeasurably by the performance of Katharine Cornell. ◆ His 1934 dramatization of Sinclair Lewis's *Dodsworth*, ◆ focusing on a retired businessman and his disillusionment with his wife, enjoyed a long run. In 1938 he joined in founding the Playwrights' Company. ◆ For the rest of his career his new plays met with divided notices and poor box office response. Ironically, after he died in an accident on his farm, two of his works found better receptions. The first was an adaptation of an old Chinese classic which he wrote with Will Irwin and which was produced as *Lute Song* (1946); the second was a play that had originally closed during its 1939 tryout but was superbly revived in 1953 by the Phoenix Theatre,◆ *Madam, Will You Walk,* a Faustian fantasy in which the devil falls in love with his intended victim.

Theatre historian Glenn Hughes had observed, "Howard's work was always vigorous and biting, but frequently repellent. At times, too, it lacked form and compactness. He was a headstrong writer, and his enthusiasms were apt to carry him beyond the bounds of dramatic propriety." But his best work also showed a compassionate, tolerant understanding of human foibles and a zest for life.

HOWARD, WILLIE [né WILHELM LEVKOWITZ] (1886?–1949) Born in Germany, he grew up on New York's Lower East Side and made his debut in vaudeville in 1897 as a boy soprano. He later appeared with Anna Held♦ in *The Little Duchess* (1901). In 1903 the tiny, tousle-haired, impish-faced Willie joined his taller, heavy-set, dapper brother EUGENE [né ISIDORE] (1880–1965), who had made his debut in the chorus of *The Belle of New York* (1897), in a vaudeville act called "The Messenger Boy and the Thespian." At about the same time Willie began his well-liked imitations of other popular performers. The brothers remained in vaudeville for ten years. Two of their most famous turns were "French Taught in a Hurry," in which Willie played a language teacher whose French was more Yiddish and broken English than Gallic, and a spoof of the quartet from *Rigoletto,* in which Willie was a singer who could not keep his eyes off the prima donna's huge bust. In a later sketch, "Tomorrow Comes the Revolution," Willie played a Communist agitator promising everyone strawberries and cream. When one listener insisted he hated strawberries and cream, Willie replied that when the revolution comes the listener would eat strawberries and cream whether he liked it or not. In 1912 they joined the first *Passing Show,* ♦ remaining with later editions and in other Shubert♦ revues until 1922. They then returned to vaudeville until appearing in *George White's Scandals of 1926*♦ and several later editions. They also appeared in *Ballyhoo of 1932,* the *Ziegfeld Follies of 1934,* ♦ and *The Show Is On* (1937). Willie played without Eugene in *Sky High* (1925) and *Girl Crazy*♦ (1930), and, after Eugene's retirement in 1940, in *Crazy with the Heat* (1941), *My Dear Public* (1943), and a 1948 revival of *Sally.* ♦

Howard Athenaeum (Boston) Built in 1843 as a church by the Millerite sect, its congregation abandoned it following disappointment with the minister's promise that the end of the world would occur in 1844. It was converted to a theatre in 1846. For several decades thereafter it vied with the Boston Museum♦ as that city's leading playhouse, but while the Museum relied largely on its great stock company, the Howard became the home of leading touring actors. Edwin Booth,♦ Charlotte Cushman,♦ and other stellar performers played there regularly. In the early 1870s, faced with increasing competition, the theatre became a vaudeville house and in 1920 turned to bump-and-grind burlesque. The city refused to renew its license in 1953, so the auditorium was dark for many years. In 1960 the Howard National Theatre and Museum Committee was formed to raise $1,500,000 to refurbish "Boston's most celebrated theatre" and restore it to the legitimate fold. However, before the committee could realize its ambition the building burned to the ground in 1961.

HOWE, TINA (b. 1937) The daughter of the celebrated radio newsman, Quincy Howe, she was born in New York. She earned a B.A. at Sarah Lawrence and later studied at several teachers colleges. She received her first professional mounting in 1970. To date her work has been confined to off-Broadway and regional theatres, where she has established a reputation as something of a playwright's playwright. Her best plays have been warm, intelligent, and fundamentally decent-minded. Most memorable have been *The Art of Dining* (1979), describing events which take place in a restaurant; *Painting Churches* (1983), in which a daughter must help her aging parents move out of their home; and *Coastal Disturbances* (1987), examining late summer romances at the beach.

HOWELL, ALFRED (1809–62) An Englishman who came to America as an actor and spent most of his career in Boston, he gained widespread fame as a costumer at a time when most actors had to provide their own clothes and when the idea of a costume designer was virtually unheard of.

HOWELLS, WILLIAM DEAN (1837–1920) Although this distinguished man of letters was best known as a novelist, editor, essayist, and critic, he also figured prominently in the development of the American theatre. He states in his autobiography that he could scarcely remember a time when the stage was not among his passionate interests, and he attempted his first play, *Samson* (1874), only two years after the publication of his earliest novel. The play was basically a translation of D'Aste's *Sansone* and was written for the actor Charles Pope. It held the stage intermittently for twenty-five years. Lawrence Barrett♦ was responsible for the presentation of Howells's two best-known dramas, *A Counterfeit Presentment* (1877) and *Yorick's Love* (1878). The first recounted the awkward romance of an artist and a woman, when the artist so strikingly resembles the woman's first fiancé—a man who turned out to be a criminal. The latter work was a free adaptation in blank verse of Tamayo y Baus's Spanish play, *Un Drama Nuevo*, and gives Shakespeare's jester an imaginary, tragic romance. One of his more interesting efforts was his collaboration with Mark Twain♦ on *Colonel Sellers as a Scientist*. It was a failure when it was offered in 1887 as *The American Claimant*. In all, Howells wrote about three dozen plays, many of them one-acters. Most center on Back Bay Boston characters. Their dialogue is infinitely superior to most stage dialogue of the time, and their scenes would appear to make for good theatre. Yet many of them were never produced, and those that were often had small success. They were collected in 1960 and published by New York University Press with Walter J. Meserve as editor, who provided an excellent introduction. Howells's generous nature prevented his becoming embittered by his relative failure in the theatre, and his writings in the *Atlantic Monthly* and elsewhere played a large share in popularizing the plays of Edward Harrigan♦ and James A. Herne.♦

Biography: *William Dean Howells: A Critical Study,* Delmar G. Cooke, New York, 1922.

HOWS, JOHN W. S. (1797–1871) Born in London, he came to America where he taught at Columbia and was the editor or author of numerous books on theatre, including *The Shakesperian Reader, The Modern Standard Drama,* and *Golden Leaves from the British and American Dramatic Poets.* However, playgoers may have known him best for his long stint as drama critic for the *Albion.*

HOWSON, FRANK A[LFRED] (1841–1926) When he was a year old, the London-born Howson was taken to Australia, where his parents were said to have introduced opera. He came to America with his family's Howson Opera Company in 1866. After his father's death he moved to New York, becoming conductor of the orchestra at the Academy of Music and then musical director for Daniel Frohman♦ at the Madison Square♦ and the Lyceum.♦ He later was musical director for Charles Frohman.♦ In this capacity he was responsible for writing incidental music for the producers' plays, and was soon recognized as the best in the field. His music for such plays as *The Prisoner of Zenda*♦ (1895), *If I Were King*♦ (1901), and E. H. Sothern's♦ 1900 mounting of *Hamlet*♦ were often singled out for special praise.

HOYT, CHARLES H[ALE] (1860–1900) The only child of a railway mail clerk who also served one term as a state legislator, Hoyt was born in Concord, N.H. His mother died when he was eight years old, so the youngster was alone for long stretches while his father was away. This created in the youth a certain fecklessness he was never to lose. In his early years he briefly attended Boston Latin School, tried studying law, and served on a Western cattle ranch before accepting work with the Boston *Post*. Within a few months he was awarded a humorous column called "All Sorts," and in its paragraphs can be found the prototypes of many of his later characters. He made friends with the theatre magnate, William Harris,♦ and when Harris suddenly found himself with an empty week at the Howard Atheneum♦ in 1881 Hoyt quickly threw together a farce, *Gifford's Luck*. The play was a hit but a second effort, *Cazalia* (1882), failed. Both plays have been lost. About the same time Willie Edouin♦ was having trouble with his farce-comedy *Dreams* and prevailed on Hoyt to revise the play. Hoyt's revisions turned the piece into a success, so the following year Edouin persuaded Hoyt to write a new play. The result was *A Bunch of Keys* (1883), centering on an ineptly run hotel. The play was an immediate success and was regularly performed as late at 1900. *A Rag Baby* (1884) managed to find fun in a mother's attempt to recover her child, whom her estranged husband has kidnapped, while a rambunctious tramp's effect on a sedate household was the principal source of mirth in an even bigger hit, *A Parlor Match*♦ (1884). Both *A Tin Soldier* (1885) and *The Maid and the Moonshiner* (1886) were disappointments, the latter so much so that the superstitious Hoyt resolved never again to use the definite article in a title. *A Hole in the Ground* (1887) had fun at the expense of railroads. Curiously, given his own superstitious nature, *A Brass Monkey* (1888), was a satire on superstition. *A Midnight Bell* (1889) was a comic melodrama in which a deacon confronts a crooked banker. The play was the first in which Hoyt, however gingerly, touched on larger issues, a trend he continued with his satire on political corruption, *A Texas Steer* (1890), describing how a Texas rancher brazenly buys his way into Congress. He reverted to pure farce for his greatest success, *A Trip to Chinatown*♦ (1891), in which youngsters, their chaperone, and their guardian become comically entangled. Social comment grew more marked in *A Temperance Town* (1893), ridiculing prohibition; and *A Milk White Flag* (1894), satirizing paramilitary groups. *A Runaway Colt* (1895) was written by Hoyt as a vehicle for the Chicago baseball celebrity,

"Captain" Andrian Anson, and naturally centered on the game, telling of professional gamblers attempting to bribe players. Frontier journalism provided the subject for *A Black Sheep* (1896), while *A Contented Woman* (1897) took a jaundiced look at the suffragette movement. The pretensions of the monied set were spoofed in *A Stranger in New York* (1897); and a supposedly prim New Jersey deacon allowed a fling in *A Day and a Night in New York* (1898). By this time Hoyt was displaying symptoms of mental instability. When his next play, *A Dog in a Manger* (1899), opened in Washington to a severe drubbing and immediately closed, the failure apparently proved too much. His mind snapped and he was committed to an insane asylum. He was soon released, but died a few months later.

With Hoyt, farce-comedy reached its peak. Indeed, even more than the works of Edward Harrigan,♦ with whom he was often compared and whom his contemporaries suggested he had succeeded, most of his plays can be seen as primitive musical comedies. Their loosely structured plots allowed the insertion of numerous songs, usually with what one critic termed a "that reminds me of a song" lead-in. However, where Harrigan was interested mainly in what today would be viewed as New York ethnic types, Hoyt built his plays around more established, acclimated American figures. Both men wrote essentially sunny, wholesome works, of questionable literary merit, especially in Hoyt's case, but eminently theatrical.

Biography: *The Life and Work of Charles H. Hoyt,* Douglas L. Hunt, Nashville, Tenn., 1945.

HOYT, HENRY E. (1834–1906) The early history of this New Hampshire-born scene designer is uncertain. However, in the 1880s and 1890s he was probably the most respected member of his profession. In keeping with the practice of the day, he frequently created only one or two of the settings for a particular production, but his reputation was such that he sometimes was asked to devise all the scenes of important mountings. His work regularly graced the Casino Theatre♦ musicals when that playhouse was new and in its prime. He also executed major assignments for Augustin Daly.♦ His 1888 designs for Daly's *A Midsummer Night's Dream*♦ were described as "severely Greek in pillars and vistas for the palace of Theseus, and soft and dreamy for the wood of perplexity." These designs included a moving panorama for the final return from the woods to Athens. Hoyt also conceived Daly's decor for *As You Like It*♦ (1889), *The Foresters* (1891), and *Twelfth Night*♦ (1893). Among his other designs

were those for Fanny Davenport's♦ 1890 production of *Cleopatra;* Lillian Russell's♦ 1891 vehicle, *Apollo;* and the first American mounting—done in a legitimate theatre, not an opera house—of *Cavalleria Rusticana* in 1891.

HUBBELL, RAYMOND (1879–1954) A prolific composer, who left behind only one enduring song, Hubbell was born in Urbana, Ohio, and grew up in Chicago. There he studied music and led a dance orchestra before taking a position as staff composer with Charles K. Harris's company. His songs were soon being sung in vaudeville and interpolated into Chicago musicals. His first full score was offered to Chicago as *Chow Chow* and later brought to New York as *The Runaways* (1903). One of his biggest successes was *Fantana* (1905). Thereafter he composed the music for many of Lew Fields's♦ musical productions; for the 1911, 1912, 1913, 1914, and 1917 editions of the *Ziegfeld Follies*♦; and for six of the extravaganzas at the Hippodrome.♦ It was for the 1916 Hippodrome production, *The Big Show,* that he composed his best remembered song, "Poor Butterfly." By 1922 the appearance of numerous superior talents and changes in style had lessened the demand for his services. In the late twenties he wrote only two shows, the last being *Three Cheers* (1928). In all he composed the scores for over thirty musicals, most of them highly successful in their day.

HUDSON, LEO (1839–73) Born in England to American performers who were playing an engagement there, she grew up to become a celebrated equestrienne and actress. A "handsome, dashing" woman, she excelled at trouser roles. In 1863 she became the Bowery Theatre's♦ first Mazeppa, the role for which she was best known and which she played for many years. She died as a result of injuries sustained when a horse threw her during a performance. Only Adah Isaacs Menken♦ was more famous in the part.

HUFFMAN, J[ESSE] C. (1869–1935) The son of a Civil War general, he was born in Bowling Green, Ohio, and began to act professionally at sixteen. He abandoned acting to become director of a Pittsburgh stock company. Richard Mansfield♦ brought him to New York. In 1911 he became general dramatic director for the Shuberts.♦ He directed many straight hit plays, such as *Whispering Wires* (1922), but was best known for his work in such musicals as the various editions of *Passing Show,*♦ *Sinbad* (1918), *Blossom Time*♦ (1921), *The Student Prince*♦ (1924), *Countess Maritza* (1926), and *My Maryland*

(1927). He is credited with staging more than 200 Broadway shows. Some sources spell his first name Jessie.

HUGHES, HATCHER (1883–1945) Born in Polkville, N. C., he was educated at the University of North Carolina and at Columbia, where he later taught drama for many years. In 1921 his play, *Wake Up, Jonathan,* written with Elmer Rice, ♦ reached Broadway. It told of stratagems employed by a clever wife to bring about a reconciliation with her husband. The play had originally been written as a vehicle for David Warfield, ♦ but was later revised for Mrs. Fiske. ♦ His next play, *Hell-Bent fer Heaven* ♦ (1923), centering on a hypocritical religious fanatic, won a Pulitzer Prize. ♦ *Ruint* (1925) was a comedy in which backwoods folk force a philandering city man to marry their daughter. Another comedy, *Honeymoon* (1927), told of newlyweds who learn their marriage is not legal. For Mrs. Fiske he then wrote *It's a Grand Life* (1930), a study of a woman whose self-satisfaction allows her to ignore problems around her. His last play was *The Lord Blesses the Bishop* (1934), in which the husband of a busy career woman invites another lady to have his child.

HUGHES, LANGSTON, see *Mulatto*

HULL, HENRY (1890–1977) Like his brother Shelley Hull, ♦ this handsome leading man was born in Louisville, Ky. He made his name largely in weakling roles such as the degenerate Henry Potter in *The Man Who Came Back* ♦ (1916); Paul Jones, the seemingly diffident suitor, in *The Cat and the Canary* ♦ (1922); George Randall, the white barber vamped by the black prostitute, in *Lulu Belle* ♦ (1926); and the black sheep Baron von Gaigern in *Grand Hotel* (1930). He also won success as Richard Winslow, the shy hero of *The Youngest* (1924). In later years he served as the replacement to the original lead in *Springtime for Henry,* then created the part of Jeeter Lester, the shiftless sharecropper, in *Tobacco Road* ♦ (1933). Thereafter he rarely enjoyed success and eventually accepted supporting roles.

HULL, JOSEPHINE [née MARY JOSEPHINE SHERWOOD] (1886–1957) Born in Newtonville, Mass., and educated at Radcliffe, she studied for the stage with the popular 19th-century actress, Kate Reingolds. Her earliest experience was with stock troupes, Boston's Castle Square Theatre Company among them, and in a few Broadway failures. She retired when she married Shelley Hull ♦ in 1910 and did not return to the stage until after his death. In the 1920s she began to attract notice in plays such as *Neighbors* (1923), *Fata Morgana* (1924), *Craig's Wife* ♦ (1925), and *Daisy Mayme* ♦ (1926), but did not win widespread acclaim until she portrayed Penelope Sycamore, the daffy unproduced playwright, in *You Can't Take It with You* ♦ (1936). She consolidated her reputation as a comic character actress when she created the role of Abby Brewster, one of the murderous sisters, in *Arsenic and Old Lace* ♦ (1941). Her next assignment was Veta Louise Simmons, whose brother has befriended an invisible rabbit, in *Harvey* ♦ (1944). One final success was *The Solid Gold Cadillac* ♦ (1953), in which she played Mrs. Laura Partridge, the stockholder whose questions play havoc with a corporate giant. A tiny, heavy-set woman with huge brown eyes (and, early on, brown hair), she excelled at dithering, but lovable old ladies.

Biography: *Dear Josephine,* William G. B. Carson, Norman, Okla., 1963.

HULL, SHELLEY (1883–1919) Born in Louisville, Ky., where his father was drama critic of the *Courier-Journal,* he first came to New York's attention playing the small part of Captain de Crespigny in *The Crossing* (1906). For several seasons he moved from play to play, unable to find a suitable success, until he was cast as leading man to Billie Burke ♦ in *The Mind-the-Paint Girl* (1912). He continued to play opposite her in *The Amazons* (1913), *The Land of Promise* (1913), and *Jerry* (1914). She remembered him as "a graceful actor, lithe and handsome, one of the first to play with the light and natural touch. He was whimsical, sometimes faun-like, much like a young, blond Faversham." He scored a major hit as Anthony Quintard, the impoverished poet whose charms win him an heiress, in *The Cinderella Man* (1916). Another highly praised impersonation was his Ernest, the young scientist who would wed his laboratory assistant, in *Why Marry?* ♦ (1917). In 1918 he was Petruchio to Laurette Taylor's ♦ Kate. That same year he gave his last performances in the duel roles of Arthur Ford and Captain Hartzmann, cousins who find themselves on opposite sides in the war, in *Under Orders.* Many critics considered this his finest moment, but his early death cut short his promising career.

HUMMEL, ABRAHAM HENRY (1850–1926) The son of a Jewish peddler, he was born in Boston and raised in New York. At age thirteen he became office boy to the famed lawyer William F. Howe. He so impressed Howe that the lawyer had the young man admitted to the bar six years later. As Howe and Hummel they became "the cleverist, most picturesque, most sought-after, most highly remunerated criminal lawyers in the country." Hummel was a small man with a large, bald head who always dressed in black. He was also a bon vivant, counting many celebrated performers and other theatrical figures among his friends. These friendships led to his handling major, often highly publicized cases for Maurice Barrymore,♦ Edwin Booth,♦ Abe Erlanger,♦ Henry Irving,♦ Lillie Langtry,♦ and Lester Wallack♦ and becoming the most renowned theatrical attorney of his era. Unfortunately, his ethics were not the highest, and he was disbarred in 1905.

HUMPHREYS, DAVID, see *Yankey in England, The*

HUMPHREYS, JOSEPH [né MURPHY] (1861–1904) Born in Boston, he served as a clerk in a dry-goods store and then worked for several circuses before becoming a character actor and director for the Kiralfy brothers.♦ In 1889 Charles Frohman♦ placed him in charge of casting all Frohman productions, except for their stars, and also made him his house director. He staged many of Frohman's early successes such as *The Masqueraders* (1894), *Under the Red Robe*♦ (1896), *The Little Minister* (1897), *The Liars* (1898), and *Quality Street* (1901). His briskness and firmness antagonized many performers, but Frohman admired his work and kept him at his post until his death.

Humpty Dumpty, a musical pantomime in seventeen scenes. Produced at the Olympic Theatre. March 10, 1868. 483 performances.

The musical recounted the adventures of Humpty Dumpty (George L. Fox♦), Goody Two Shoes (Emily Rigl♦), Dan Tucker (G. K. Fox), and One Two Button My Shoe (F. Lacy) as they traipse about not only the sights of New York such as City Hall, a famous candy store, and the Olympic Theatre itself, but in such marvelous places as the Farm of Plenty, an Enchanted Garden, and the Retreat of the Silver Sprites. Their cavortings at an end, they are transformed, in classic pantomime fashion, into Clown, Columbine, Pantaloon, and Harlequin.

The longest running musical up to its day, it marked the apogee both of Fox's career and of traditional pantomime in America. Its authorship was by various hands, including A. Oakey Hall, once mayor of New York, and Fox himself. Music was attributed to one A. Reiff, Jr. In the pattern of the time the musical was regularly revised to prompt return visits.

Hunchback, The Sheridan Knowles's♦ romantic drama was written for Fanny Kemble♦ and first acted by her in 1832 in London. The story centers on a country girl, Julia, who comes to London where her eyes are seemingly blinded by the allures of high society. She would throw over her faithful, good-natured lover and marry a much richer man. Luckily she sees the error of her ways, repents, and is happily reunited with the right man. The first New York performance, also in 1832, offered Mrs. Sharpe as Julia. The drama remained extremely popular for the rest of the century. In 1870 the *Times* referred to it as "the play that has stirred the hearts of lovers more than, with one exception, any other in the modern repertory" and called Julia "the most difficult serious part written for a heroine in the last fifty years." Among the great interpreters of the role on American stages were Miss Kemble, Charlotte Cushman,♦ Clara Morris,♦ Mary Anderson,♦ Julia Marlow,♦ and Viola Allen.♦ Opinions on the play changed with the coming of the new century, and in 1902 the same *Times* dismissed the work by branding it "as absurd and false a play as ever took the manner of Shakespeare in vain."

110 in the Shade, see *Rainmaker, The*

HUNEKER, JAMES GIBBONS (1859?–1921) Born in Philadelphia of Irish-Hungarian parentage, he studied law briefly, then moved to Paris to prepare for a career as a concert pianist. That career never materialized, and he became a music critic instead. He did not become a drama critic until 1902 when, at the age of forty-two, he replaced Franklin Fyles♦ on the New York *Sun.* He immediately took up the cudgels for Ibsen♦ and Shaw,♦ two playwrights who were confusing and infuriating the more traditional reviewers. He wrote of Ibsen, "In his bones he is a moralist, in practice an artist." Although he later was to have reservations about Shaw, he wrote the introduction to a 1906 edition of Shaw's collected criticisms and called him "jester to the cosmos and the most serious man on the planet." He also warred against the prudery that infused so much contemporary dramatic criticism. In 1912 he left the *Sun* to write for the New York *Times,* but eventually returned to the former. Brooks Atkinson♦ called him "the best critic Broadway ever had." Among his books, which ranged broadly and knowingly among all the arts, was *Iconoclasts: A Book of Dramatists.*

HUNTER, GLENN (1893?–1945) Born in Highland Mills, N. Y., the boyish-looking actor made his first professional appearances with the Washington

Square Players♦ in 1916. After replacing the original performers as Willie Baxter in *Seventeen* (1918) and as Robert Williams in *Penrod* (1918), he scored as the infatuated Bobby Wheeler in *Clarence*♦ (1919). His biggest success came as Merton Gill, the grocery clerk who almost accidently becomes a film star, in *Merton of the Movies*♦ (1922), but he won equal praise when he portrayed the title role of the sensitive schoolboy in love with his headmaster's wife, in *Young Woodley*♦ (1925). Although he continued to perform regularly thereafter, none of his subsequent work was in successful plays. Best received of his later roles was his robustly boorish Tony Lumpkin in an all-star 1929 revival of *She Stoops To Conquer,* a limited engagement.

HUNTER, RICHARD (dates unknown) Sometime between May 1699 and May 1702 a Richard Hunter petitioned the acting governor of New York, John Nanfan, that "having been at great charge and expense in providing persons and necessary's in order to the acting of Play's in this Citty," he be allowed to stage performances. Whether Hunter was an actor or merely a producer, and whether he actually staged any performances is unknown. If he did, he antedated Anthony Aston.♦

HUNTER, ROBERT, see *Androboros*

HURLBUT, WILLIAM (1883–?) Born in Belvidere, Ill., he studied art in St. Louis and Chicago with the intention of becoming a painter, but soon decided to try his hand at play-writing. His first play to reach New York was a major success. *The Fighting Hope*♦ (1908) told of a wife who, believing her husband innocent, destroys incriminating evidence, only to learn her husband was actually guilty. Although nearly thirty of his plays eventually played New York, the best received invariably dealt with women confronting crises. *The Strange Woman* (1913) described the problems of a worldly lady in a small farm community. *Lilies of the Field* (1921) recounted the descent of a wronged wife into prostitution. *Bride of the Lamb* (1926) was a study of an unhappy wife's breakdown.

HUROK, SOL (1888–1974) Russian-born impresario, best known for his work in the fields of music and ballet, he frequently brought over major foreign theatrical companies to America, including the Habimah Players in 1926, the Moscow Art Players♦ in 1935, and, after World War II, Compagnie Madeleine Renaud–Jean Louis Barrault♦; Théâtre Nationale Populaire; Comédie Française♦; the

D'Oyly Carte Opera Company♦; the Bristol Old Vic; and many others. He also occasionally arranged tours for such American artists as Margaret Webster♦ and Eva Le Gallienne.♦

Autobiography: *Impresario,* with Ruth Goode, New York, 1946.

Hurtig and Seamon In the 1880s Jules Hurtig (1867–1928), who had begun his career as a candy-seller in a Cincinnati theatre and had risen to an important position with Barnum and Bailey, met a young juggler, Harry J. Seamon. They organized a vaudeville booking agency and sent out a show called "The Bowery Burlesquers." Their success prompted them to lease the old Eden Musee. Before long they had put together one of the nation's largest vaudeville organizations, running theatres and managing touring attractions. They occasionally ventured into the legitimate with entries such as the early black musical *In Dahomey*♦ (1903). With the decline of two-a-day, their empire collapsed.

HUSTON, WALTER [né HOUGHSTON] (1884–1950) The gruff-voiced, Canadian-born actor made his debut in Toronto in 1902. He first appeared in New York in *In Convict Stripes* (1905). From 1909 to 1924 he toured in vaudeville with his second wife, Bayonne Whipple, in an act that never quite reached the top. He then returned to Broadway, making a pronounced impression as Ephraim Cabot, the unyielding old farmer, in *Desire Under the Elms*♦ (1924). The following year he played Ponce de Leon in a less important Eugene O'Neill♦ drama, *The Fountain* (1925). In 1926 he was the sadistic black ruler, Flint, in *Kongo,* then moved on to Nifty Miller, the glib pitchman, in *The Barker* (1927). He won praise for his performance as Elmer Kane, the brainless baseball pitcher, in Ring Lardner's *Elmer the Great* (1928), although the play failed. After another failure a year later he spent time in films before returning to New York in 1934 to play the title role of the unhappy retired businessman in *Dodsworth.*♦ In 1937 he offered his Othello, then turned to the musical theatre to portray Pieter Stuyvesant in *Knickerbocker Holiday*♦ (1938), introducing "September Song." The remainder of his stage career offered nothing noteworthy. His final appearance was as Sam Stover, an old farmer in love with a young girl, in *Apple of His Eye* (1946).

HUTTON, JOSEPH (1787–1828) Born in Philadelphia, where he served as a schoolmaster for several years, he turned to the stage to become both an actor and a playwright. He seems to have been a restless person, spending much of his career traveling up and down the coast. His plays ranged widely: a broad comedy, *The School for Prodigals* (1808); a Gothic melodrama, *The Orphan of Prague* (1808); a musical afterpiece, *The Wounded Hussar; or, The Rightful Heir* (1809); and a social satire, *Fashionable Follies,* written about 1810 and revised later. In after years he is said to have abandoned the stage to take up farming and possibly newspaper work in the South, but much of his history is uncertain.

HUTTON, Laurence (1843–1904) Born in New York and educated at Princeton, he served as drama critic for the New York *Evening Mail* in the 1870s, then became literary editor of *Harper's Magazine.* He held the post until 1898, frequently contributing reviews and essays on the theatre. He was one of the first to revive interest in books on American theatrical history and to have his criticisms collected in hardcover editions. Among his books, which have been described as "chatty, impressionistic," were *Curiosities of the American Stage* (1891) and the five-volume *American Actor Series* (1881–82). He was an organizer of the Authors' Club and of the International Copyright League.

HWANG, David Henry, see *M. Butterfly*

HYDE [Richard] (1856–1912) **and BEHMAN** [Louis C.] (1855–1902). The pair, who had been schoolmates in their native Brooklyn, opened their first theatre in Philadelphia during the 1876 Centennial. Like almost all their later theatres, the playhouse was devoted primarily to what would now be considered vaudeville. During the same year they took over a second theatre, this time in Baltimore, and in 1877 returned to Brooklyn to establish a base, and where, by the end of the century they dominated the vaudeville scene, as well as running two-a-day houses in numerous other locations. They established the Hyde and Behman Amusement Company in 1899. The company not only controlled all their theatres and managed many important acts but sent whole bills touring. Behman was considered the real force behind the enterprise. Having something of a sense of history he attempted to put into manuscript form the dialogue used in his theatres. Unfortunately these invaluable records were destroyed in a fire. Among the organization's clients were "The Four Cohans," and he produced, without his partner, *The Governor's Son* (1901), a musical comedy which was based on a skit "The Four Cohans" employed and which launched the Broadway career of George M. Cohan. ◆ The organization faltered after Behman's death as much because of the monopolistic practices of such larger magnates as Keith◆ and Albee◆ as because of Hyde's lesser acumen.

I

I Am a Camera, a play in three acts by John van Druten.♦ Produced at the Empire Theatre.♦ November 28, 1951. 262 performances. NYDCCA.

Sitting in his room in Fräulein Schneider's flat in Berlin, the young writer, Christopher Isherwood (William Prince) records his impressions of the city. It is a city disturbed by ominous Nazi rioting. Isherwood is also disturbed but tries not to be, noting, "I am a camera, with its shutter open, quite passive." Some of his carefully nurtured passivity disappears when he is introduced to Sally Bowles (Julie Harris♦), an attractive, flamboyant singer at a local night club. They strike up an immediate friendship. Neither Sally's insistence that Isherwood never ask about her past, nor her becoming pregnant by another man seriously affects their relationship. What does come between them is the growing political turmoil. Isherwood elects to leave Berlin, but Sally, as apolitical as she is amoral, chooses to remain.

Based on Isherwood's autobiographical *Berlin Stories,* the play was perceived by many critics as a loosely strung together but theatrically effective series of scenes. To most playgoers its main attraction was Miss Harris's incandescent performance. The play served as the basis for the 1966 musical, *Cabaret.♦*

I Married an Angel, a musical comedy in two acts. Book by Richard Rodgers♦ and Lorenz Hart.♦ Lyrics by Hart. Music by Rodgers. Produced by Dwight Deere Wiman♦ at the Shubert Theatre. May 11, 1938. 338 performances.

Willie Palaffi (Dennis King♦), a banker and ladies' man, breaks off his engagement to Anna (Audrie Christie) and swears he will marry only an angel. A real angel (Vera Zorina) promptly flies into his life. He marries her, but her angelic honesty causes no end of problems for him until his sister, Countess Palaffi (Vivienne Segal♦), teaches the angel the ways of a cynical world. The Countess also bribes cab drivers to delay Willie's creditors until a way is found to save her brother's bank.

Principal songs: I Married an Angel · Spring Is Here

Basing it on a Hungarian play, Rodgers and Hart had originally worked on it with Moss Hart♦ as a musical film. The film was scrapped, so the work was rewritten for the stage. In the *Journal-American,* John Anderson characterized it as "a winged wonder-work from the musical heavens of Rodgers and Hart."

I Remember Mama, a comedy in two acts by John van Druten.♦ Produced by Rodgers♦ and Hammerstein♦ at the Music Box Theatre. October 19, 1944. 714 performances.

Katrin (Joan Tetzel), a writer, reads from her memoirs of growing up in turn-of-the-century San Francisco. She recalls Mama (Mady Christians♦) forever putting away pennies in a home "bank-account" for a rainy day. She also remembers cantankerous Uncle Chris (Oscar Homolka), who promises to leave his money to the family, and her mother's defending Aunt Trina (Adrienne Gessner) when other aunts objected to Trina's marriage. And then there was the time when Mama was not allowed to visit a daughter after the daughter's operation, so Mama disguised herself as a hospital scrubwoman to get in. Uncle Chris finally dies, and the family discovers that through the years he had given his money away to help crippled children. Moreover, Mama is forced to confess that there is no bank account. She had lied because "It is not good for little ones to be afraid." So, though Mama urges Katrin to write about all the other members of the family, Katrin concludes, "First and foremost, I remember Mama."

Based on Kathryn Forbes's *Mama's Bank Account,* the play appeared during the height of World War II and was welcomed by Burns Mantle♦ as "a pleasantly undisturbing evening in the theatre." A musical version with a score by Rodgers, starring Liv Ullmann as Mama, failed in 1979.

IBSEN, Henrik [Johan] (1828–1906) Probably no foreign dramas caused debate so prolonged and impassioned as did the emergence of Ibsen's Norwegian plays in the American theatre. What was the first American production of Ibsen is uncertain, but Scandinavian performers did offer the world premiere of *Ghosts* to Chicago and other Midwestern cities in 1882, and that same year the play later known as *A Doll's House* was offered in English as

The Child Bride, albeit given a happy ending. The same play, with a similar happy ending, was presented by Modjeska♦ as *Thora* in 1883. However, it fell to an 1889 production of *A Doll's House,* faithfully translated and given its correct name, to spread Ibsen's fame and precipitate the controversy. To the leading anti-Ibsenite, William Winter,♦ Ibsenism was seen as "rank, deadly pessimism . . . a disease, injurious alike to the Stage and to the Public,—in as far as it affects them at all,—and therefore an evil to be deprecated." Aligned against Winter and his allies were such other leading figures as Walter Prichard Eaton,♦ William Dean Howells,♦ and James Huneker.♦ The cause was taken up by such distinguished performers as Mrs. Fiske,♦ Alla Nazimova,♦ and Richard Mansfield.♦ Their appearances in Ibsen plays gained the writer such widespread acceptance that by 1908 Eaton could write, "Ibsen is one of the most popular playwrights in America today." Mrs. Fiske had done *A Doll's House* (1894), *Hedda Gabler* (1903), and *Rosmersholm* (1907). Late in her career she would star in *Ghosts* (1927). Nazimova did *Hedda Gabler* (1906), *A Doll's House* and *The Master Builder* (1907), and *Little Eyolf* (1910). In 1906 Mansfield offered *Peer Gynt.* Blanche Bates♦ and Nance O'Neill♦ offered their Heddas about the same time and Ethel Barrymore♦ her Nora. For a while interest in and enthusiasm for Ibsen dwindled, but Duse's♦ performance in *The Lady from the Sea* sparked a revival, as did the Theatre Guild's♦ production of *Peer Gynt* with Joseph Schildkraut.♦ Eva Le Gallienne♦ and Walter Hampden♦ both became advocates and appeared in several major revivals. Miss Le Gallienne was the more doggedly loyal of the two. Beginning in 1925, when she portrayed Hilda Wangel in *The Master Builder,* she appeared in or staged numerous mountings, including several of *Hedda Gabler* (1928, 1934, 1948), *John Gabriel Borkman* (1926, 1946), and *Rosmersholm* (1935). She also played Mrs. Alving in *Ghosts* (1948). Hampden's most notable offering was *An Enemy of the People* (1928, 1937). A somewhat lesser performer, Blanche Yurka, headed revivals of *The Wild Duck* (1925, 1928), *Hedda Gabler,* and *The Lady from the Sea* (1929).

In the 1930s and 1940s a reaction set in, prompted by the perception that the problems Ibsen dealt with were no longer those of immediate concern to contemporary American society. Probably the most interesting production of this period was Thornton Wilder's♦ adaptation of *A Doll's House* (1937), which Jed Harris♦ presented with Ruth Gordon♦ and Paul Lukas.

Ibsen's appeal waxed again in the 1950s, which saw Arthur Miller's♦ version of *An Enemy of the People* (1950); Lee Strasberg's♦ staging of *Peer Gynt* (1951); and the Phoenix Theatre's♦ productions of *The Master Builder* (1955) and *Peer Gynt* (1960). In the 1960s David Ross offered a much admired cycle of Ibsen plays off-Broadway.♦

Of recent years there have been few major mountings. Liv Ullmann appeared in *Ghosts* (1982), while a musical attempting to show Nora's life after she walked out was called *A Doll's Life* (1982). Both shows were failures.

The influence of Ibsen's sociological realism was immediately felt in American play-writing. James A. Herne♦ was the first to openly acknowledge his debt, but his work was overshadowed in later decades by the plays of such writers as Eugene O'Neill♦ and Arthur Miller, both of whom looked to Ibsen as an exemplar.

Icebound, a play in three acts by Owen Davis.♦ Produced by Sam H. Harris♦ at the Sam H. Harris Theatre. February 10, 1923. 170 performances. PP.

At the old Jordan homestead near Veazie, Maine, the Jordan clan greedily and impatiently await Mother Jordan's death. They wait, as she has told Judge Bradford (Willard Robertson), "like carrion crows around a sick cow in a pasture, watchin' till the last twitch of life is out of me before they pounce." When she dies, her family is furious to learn that she has left her entire estate to a distant cousin, Jane Crosby (Phyllis Povah). Only Jane, with the help of a loyal hired hand, Hannah (Edna May Oliver), faithfully tended Mother Jordan during her last days. The sole exception to the family chagrin is the black sheep son, Ben (Robert Ames♦). With time Jane reforms Ben, falls in love with him, and agrees to marry him. Hannah sends them on their way happy that marriage will further assure Ben's reformation.

In *Theatre,*♦ Arthur Hornblow♦ wrote, "The breath of life sweeps through this pack of New England jackals and exposes them roundly, honestly and effectively." The play marked a conscious move away from claptrap melodrama for Davis.

Iceman Cometh, The, a play in four acts by Eugene O'Neill.♦ Produced by the Theatre Guild♦ at the Martin Beck Theatre. October 9, 1946. 136 performances.

At Harry Hope's seedy bar, a group of down-and-out, besotted regulars live on their booze and their dreams. Besides Harry (Dudley Digges♦), a former Tammany wardheeler, the regulars include a Harvard-trained lawyer, Willie Oban (E. G. Marshall); a Boer War general, Piet Wetjoen (Frank Tweddell); an old newspaper man, James Cameron (Russell Collins); a onetime anarchist, Larry Slade (Carl Benton Reid); and a young, frightened drifter, a newcomer, Dan Paritt (Paul Crabtree). Into their midst comes a hardware salesman, Theodore Hickman (James Barton♦), more familiarly known as "Hickey." Hickey tells the barflies he is out for a toot, since his wife is "with the iceman," and he would make the drinkers rid themselves of "the damned guilt that makes you lie to yourselves you're something you're not, and the remorse that nags at you and makes you hide behind lousy pipe dreams about tomorrow." One probable effect of Hickey's insistence is to goad Slade into convincing Paritt to commit suicide. But all Hickey's talk goes for naught when he confesses that he has murdered his wife and that the "iceman" is Death. After the police take away Hickey, the men return to their whiskey and their illusions, without which they cannot live.

This four-hour-long play, based on O'Neill's 1917 short story, *Tomorrow,* and marking his return to the theatre after an absence of twelve years, was welcomed by most critics, albeit with reservations. Howard Barnes of the *Herald Tribune* wrote the work was "mystical and mystifying . . . the stuff of a great and moving tragedy gleams through scene after scene of the drama, but it has not been properly refined." A superior 1956 revival at the Circle in the Square♦ won the work renewed respect and made José Quintero,♦ who staged it, and Jason Robards, Jr.,♦ who played Hickey, names to be reckoned with. A highly praised 1985 revival, again with Robards, failed.

I'd Rather Be Right, a musical comedy in two acts. Book by George S. Kaufman♦ and Moss Hart.♦ Lyrics by Lorenz Hart.♦ Music by Richard Rodgers.♦ Produced by Sam H. Harris♦ at the Alvin Theatre. November 2, 1937. 290 performances.

Peggy Jones (Joy Hodges) and Phil Barker (Austin Marshall) would like to marry but cannot until Phil receives a raise in pay contingent on President Roosevelt's balancing the budget. Falling asleep in Central Park, Phil dreams that he and Peggy meet Roosevelt (George M. Cohan♦). The President summons his Cabinet and even goes to battle with the Supreme Court to help the youngsters. Seemingly stymied, Roosevelt suggests the couple marry anyway, and when Phil awakes from his dream that is precisely what he and Peggy decide to do.

Principal songs: Have You Met Miss Jones? · Off the Record

Apparently the first important American play to employ a living President as the leading figure, the show was Cohan's only appearance in a musical which he did not write himself, and was also his last song and dance role. Of the writers, only Moss Hart was in top form. Nevertheless, Cohan's ingratiating performance (despite his much publicized hatred of Roosevelt) and generally satisfactory writing turned this affectionate satire of the New Deal into a hit.

Idiot's Delight, a comedy in three acts by Robert E. Sherwood. ♦ Produced by the Theatre Guild♦ at the Shubert Theatre. March 24, 1936. 299 performances. PP.

The Hotel Monte Gabrielle had been an Austrian sanitorium until the area was ceded to Italy after World War I. Now, with another war looming, a handful of guests, caught by border closings, sit languidly in the hotel's cocktail lounge. They are unsure just when the war will begin and how sides will be drawn. As one guest remarks, "The map of Europe supplies us with a wide choice of opponents. I suppose, in due time, our government will announce its selection—and we shall know just whom we are to shoot at." Into their midst comes a mediocre American song-and-dance man, Harry Van (Alfred Lunt♦) and his bevy of girls, returning from a Balkan tour. Among the guests, Harry spots a supposed Russian countess, Irene (Lynn Fontanne♦), who is traveling with a rich munitions manufacturer, and recognizes her as a former trouper with whom he once had a brief fling in Omaha. As the war clouds darken they gingerly resume their old affair. The other guests leave, but Harry stays behind to convince Irene to flee with him and create a new mind-reading act. They share a bottle of champagne and sing "Onward, Christian Soldiers" as bombs begin to fall.

Brooks Atkinson♦ observed, of this strongly pacifist and ardently anti-fascist comedy "Mr. Sherwood has spoken passionately about a grave subject and settled down to writing a gusty show." A musical version, *Dance a Little Closer* (1983), was unsuccessful.

If I Were King, a play in four acts by Justin Huntly McCarthy. Produced by Daniel Frohman♦ at the Garden Theatre. October 14, 1901. 56 performances.

To the humble Tavern of the Fir Cone, where the vagabond poet François Villon (E. H. Sothern♦) recites poetry and sneers at his weak king, come none other than a disguised Louis IX (George W. Wilson) and Lady Katherine de Vaucelles (Cecilia Loftus♦). At once impressed and irked, the King discloses himself and gives Villon a week in which to make good his boasts, after which he will die. Villon, in fact, defeats the Burgundians. Louis would still hang Villon, but the suicide of the loyal camp follower, Huguette (Suzanne Sheldon), and Katherine's announcement that she will marry the poet, dissuade the King.

This most famous play by the renowned Irish politician and writer was performed in America before it was offered to London. The play consolidated Sothern's stardom and was revived regularly until World War I. In 1925 it became the source of the operetta *The Vagabond King*. ♦

ILLINGTON, MARGARET [née MAUDE ELLEN LIGHT] (1881–1934) This "lovely, stately, talented actress," as her first husband, Daniel Frohman,♦ described her, was born in Bloomington, Ill. She studied at Illinois Wesleyan and then at a Chicago dramatic school. Her first professional appearance was made under Frohman, in *The Pride of Jennico*♦ (1900). In 1903 she scored a major success as Yuki, the young Japanese girl who abandons her American husband and enters a monastery to appease her family, in *A Japanese Nightingale*. The following year she played Henrietta in an all-star revival of *The Two Orphans*. ♦ One of her most memorable assignments was as the wife falsely accused of having an affair with a young man in whose rooms her quilted silk slippers have been found, in *Mrs. Leffingwell's Boots*♦ (1905). She next headed a road company of *The Lion and the Mouse*,♦ playing Shirley Rossmore, who saves her father from impeachment. After appearing in the same part in London, she returned to New York to act opposite John Drew♦ as Nina Jesson, the unhappy second wife, in *His House in Order* (1906). For many admirers, her finest achievement was her portrayal of Marie Louise Voysin, who allows an admirer to take the blame for a crime she has committed, in *The Thief* (1907). As often happens she found it hard to find an equally effective successor to this play. She did not have another major success until she played Maggie Shultz, a poor girl willing to steal to support the baby her husband says they cannot afford, in *Kindling* (1911). This was her last significant new role, although she later took leading parts in several road companies. She retired in 1919 after appearing in the quick failure *A Good Bad Woman*.

I'm Not Rappaport a play in two acts by Herb Gardner. Produced at the Booth Theatre. November 19, 1985. 890 performances.

Two very old men, Nat (Judd Hirsch), a Jew who constantly makes up stories about his imaginary pasts, and Midge (Cleavon Little), a black who has little time for Nat's lies but nowhere else to go, regularly occupy adjacent benches in Central Park. Callous or interfering people or even vicious muggers sometimes interrupt their conversations, which seemed destined to go on until one of the men dies.

A slight, ingratiating play, it exemplified a vogue for light pieces pitting a somewhat eccentric Jew against a more down-to-earth black, as did the later *Driving Miss Daisy*. ♦

Gardner (b. 1934) is a Brooklyn native who has worked primarily in television. His only other big Broadway success has been *A Thousand Clowns* (1962), which told of turmoil in the life of an unhappy TV writer, although *Thieves* (1974), which used a woman's debate about getting both an abortion and a divorce as a frame for pictures of New York life, ran nine months.

Impossible Years, The, a comedy in two acts by Bob Fisher and Arthur Marx. Produced at the Playhouse. October 13, 1965. 670 performances.

Dr. Jack Kingsley (Alan King) is a famous psychiatrist who sets about writing an all-knowing book on how to raise teenagers. What he does not reckon with are his own teen-aged daughters, the slightly kooky, free-wheeling Linda (Jane Eliot) and the precocious, impertinent Abbey (Neva Small). They run in and out of the Kingsley household with an odd assortment of friends and associates. Mrs. Kingsley (Janet Ward) tries to keep order and prevent Jack from losing his mind. But when Linda announces she left her virginity on a beach, Mrs. Kingsley becomes so rattled that she bids "three no-virgins" at her weekly bridge game. Clearly, the book that the doctor will eventually write will be quite different from the one he originally envisaged.

A slick but well-written comedy, it far outran most of the season's superior offerings. Many critics credited night-club comedian King for much of the comedy's success. Fisher and Marx, the son of Groucho Marx,♦ are film and television writers.

In Abraham's Bosom, a play in seven scenes by Paul Green. ♦ Produced by the Provincetown Players♦ at the Provincetown Theatre. December 30, 1926. 277 performances. PP.

Near the Turpentine Woods of eastern North Carolina, Abraham McCranie (Jules Bledsoe♦) has grown up, the troubled son of white Colonel McCranie (L. Rufus Hill) and a black woman. He is determined to "rise him up wid eddication" and to become the black man's savior, "to lead 'em up out'n ignorance." But his all-white half-brother, the Colonel's vicious son Lonnie (H. Ben Smtih), is just as determined to thwart him, to close the school he would open for blacks, and to keep him in his place. Only Goldie McAllister (Rose McClendon♦) offers him love. As the years pass Lonnie's tormenting becomes too much for him and in a rage Abraham kills him. He in turn is shot dead by other local white men.

Hailed by the *Herald Tribune* as "so well-written and so well-played that even near-Southerners who applaud *Dixie* the loudest may be urged to sympathy," the play nevertheless struggled to find an audience. It had already closed when the announcement that it had won the Pulitzer Prize♦ prompted a quick reopening.

In Dahomey, a musical comedy in three acts. Book by J. A. Shipp. Lyrics by Paul Laurence Dunbar.♦ Music by Will Marion Cook.♦ Produced by Hurtig♦ and Seamon♦ at the New York Theatre. February 18, 1903. 53 performances.

When Rareback Pinkerton (George Walker) is sent to Florida by the black Get-the-Coin Syndicate to bamboozle a rich old man, he discovers that his bumptious companion, Shylock Homestead (Bert Williams♦), is an even richer man. So he proceeds to bamboozle Shylock and uses the money to live a sporting life both in Florida and Africa until Shylock suddenly sees through him.

While *The Origin of the Cake Walk; or, Clorindy*♦ (1898) was the first all-black-written, black-performed show to play before major white audiences, it was a relatively short afterpiece and was performed on a summer roof garden. *In Dahomey* thus became the first black musical to play a regular New York legitimate theatre. Despite generally favorable reviews and many raves for Williams, large segments of traditional white playgoers refused to attend. In London, where prejudices against black performers were not so widespread, the musical ran seven months.

In Mizzoura, a play in four acts by Augustus Thomas.♦ Produced by Nat Goodwin♦ at the Fifth Avenue Theatre.♦ September 4, 1893. 64 performances.

Sheriff Jim Radburn (Goodwin) of Bowling Green, Mo., is a kindly, middle-aged man who never shoots to kill and will even stop to make a cast for a wounded dog. Having something of a private income, he has paid for the education of young Kate Vernon (Mabel Amber), his neighbors' daughter, whom he has grown to love. But Kate returns from school with new-found airs. She his little time for Jim, instead falling for a dashing young man, Robert Travers (Emmett Corrigan). However, Travers turns out to be a train robber, and when he shoots a man, Radburn gives him a pony with which to escape rather than see Kate's feelings hurt. The village would turn against the sheriff, until they recognize the good-heartedness behind his action. Even Kate begins to love Radburn, but he has come to realize they must go their separate ways. When Mrs. Vernon (Jean Clara Walters) suggests that Kate is "comin' to her senses" and that Radburn need only talk to her to win her hand, he replies laconically, "Some other time."

Written as a vehicle for Goodwin, this comedy of rural manners remained popular for many years. Its compassion, acute observation, and theatrical effectiveness make it one of Thomas's best plays, all too neglected.

In Old Kentucky, a play in four acts by Charles T. Dazey.♦ Produced at the Academy of Music. October 23, 1893. 160 performances.

Madge Brierly (Bettina Gerard) is a girl who longs to escape from the ages-old feuding and fanaticism of her fellow Kentucky mountain folk. When she meets handsome, young, and rich Frank Layson (William Courtleigh), she sees her chance. She is skilled with horses, and Layson had entered his prize runner in the Ashland Oaks Derby. Overcoming treachery and the opposition of his snobbish friends, who would cut any woman in jockey's clothes, she wins both the race and Layson.

One of the most popular of all late-19th-century melodramas, the play remained a favorite for several decades. Quinn♦ records that "The play was performed for twenty-seven consecutive seasons in New York or on the road."

In the Palace of the King, a play in six scenes by Lorimer Stoddard. Produced by Liebler and Co.♦ at the Republic Theatre. December 31, 1900. 138 performances.

To be near her beloved hero, Don John (Robert T. Haines), the spunky Dona Maria Dolores (Viola Allen♦) disguises herself as a blind woman at the court of Philip II (Eben Plympton♦). She witnesses an attempted murder for which Don John is framed by her treacherous rival and wins his acquittal by defending him before the king.

One of the many dramatizations of floridly romantic novels that were popular at the time, this was based on F. Marion Crawford's best-seller. Stoddard was an actor and dramatist, probably best remembered for his adaptation of *Tess of the D'Urbervilles* (1897) for Mrs. Fiske. ◆

In the Summer House, a play in two acts by Jane Bowles. Produced by Oliver Smith◆ and the Playwrights' Company◆ at the Playhouse. December 29, 1953. 55 performances.

Gertrude Eastman-Cuevas (Judith Anderson◆) is a viciously domineering mother who would keep her daughter, Molly (Elizabeth Ross), firmly under her thumb. By contrast, the boozy, weak Mrs. Constable (Mildred Dunnock◆) has long since been deserted by her family. When Molly finally finds the strength to leave her harridan mother, Gertrude finds herself helpless, while Mrs. Constable continues to take solace in her drink.

Originally presented at the Hedgerow Theatre, ◆ the play was written with great insight and style, but remained too demanding and dramatically ineffectual to recruit large audiences. A high point was Gertrude's ten-minute monologue, which opened the play.

Jane Auer Bowles (1917–73), the wife of composer and author Paul Bowles, was best known for her novels and short stories. This was her first, and only important, play.

In the Zone, a play in one act by Eugene O'Neill. ◆ Produced by the Washington Square Players◆ at the Comedy Theatre. October 31, 1917.

Seeing Smitty (Frederick Roland) furtively remove a little black box from his suitcase, his mates on the *S.S. Glencairn* conclude he may be a spy. They bind and gag him, then rummage through his belongings until they find the box. Its contents prove to be letters from an old sweetheart who left him because of his drinking.

The only one of the four plays which eventually comprised *S.S. Glencairn* not to be produced by the Provincetown Players,◆ it was mounted by the group out of which came the Theatre Guild,◆ O'Neill's principal producer in his heyday.

INCLEDON, CHARLES (1757–1826) The great English tenor, known as "The Wandering Melodist," was sixty years old when he first faced American audiences in 1817 at the Park Theatre◆ as Hawthorn in *Love in a Village.* Although his excellent reputation had preceded him, he proved a major disappointment. He was seen to have grown fat and slovenly, to be an exceptionally poor actor even for a singer, and to refuse stubbornly to play several of his most requested roles. He returned to England after only a year.

Indian Princess, The; or, La Belle Sauvage, an "operatic melo-drama" in three acts by James Nelson Barker. ◆ Music by John Bray. Produced at the Chestnut Street Theatre, ◆ Philadelphia. April 6, 1808. In repertory.

The English land to establish a settlement at Jamestown. Some of the men sing of their sweethearts back home, but one lovesick traveler attacks the wife of another settler. Captain Smith (Mr. Rutherford) leads an expedition into the hinterlands, where he is captured by the Indians. Lieutenant Rolfe (William Wood◆) and his comrades set out to find their leader. They come to the Indian encampment. There Pocahontas (Mrs. Wilmot) falls in love with Rolfe, to the fury of the Indian Prince Miami (Mr. Mills). When the Englishmen return to their settlement, Miami plans an attack. But Pocahontas alerts the settlers.

Originally conceived simply as a blank-verse drama by Barker, the music helped make the piece a huge success. The love scene in Act III between Pocahontas and Rolfe was especially well done. When the play was offered in New York two months after its Philadelphia premiere, the *Evening Post* called it, "in point of dramatic composition, one of the most chaste and elegant plays ever written in the United States." It was the first American play to be done in London, where it was performed at the Drury Lane in 1820 under the title *Pocahontas; or, The Indian Princess.*

Indians in American Drama The immediacy of white-Indian wars and the proximity of many settled Indians to our 18th-century cities made native Americans figures of interest to several early American dramatists. The first play to center on American Indians, however, was written not in English but in French. *Le Père-Indien* was the work of LeBlanc de Villeneuve, a French officer stationed in New Orleans, and was given an amateur mounting there in 1753. Although it had no influence on later plays, its story of an Indian father who sacrifices his life for the sake of his son foreshadowed numerous pictures of noble, tragic primitives that would long characterize American plays of Indian life. Villeneuve is also believed to have written a second tragedy, *Poucha-Houmma.*

In 1766 the maverick Major Robert Rogers published his semi-historical if romanticized tragedy of *Ponteach,* ♦ but no record of performance survives. One reason for its failure to find a stage may have been an implicit contempt or at least condescension on the part of most whites toward Indians. This could explain why the earliest Indian plays to reach the stage and sometimes find success, although they, too, generally depicted the Indian as wronged and doomed, were couched in musical terms. *Tammany* ♦ (1794), *The Indian Princess* ♦ (1808), and *Harlequin Panattatah; or, The Genii of the Algonquins* (1809) are examples. *The Indian Princess* is probably the first play to deal with Pocahontas, who for decades remained a favorite of dramatists, including George Washington Parke Custis, Robert Dale Owen, and John Brougham. ♦ Custis, indeed, wrote several Indian plays besides *Pocahontas* (1830), among them *The Indian Prophecy* (1827) and the apparently unacted *The Pawnee Chief.* Quinn ♦ credits Custis with "the honor of introducing the vogue" for Indian dramas.

But the immediate inspiration for the deluge of Indian stories that flooded our stages in the 1830s and 1840s certainly can be ascribed to John Augustus Stone's ♦ *Metamora* ♦ (1828), which was turned into one of the raging successes of contemporary theatre by Edwin Forrest. ♦ Perhaps because by this time most theatrical centers were far removed from Indian territory, such plays could generally offer a romanticized view of these imposed-upon natives, often fighting to the death to protect what they saw as their heritage. The lengthy list of now forgotten works would include *Sassacus, or, The Indian Wife; Onylda, or, The Pequot Maid; Ontiata, or, The Indian Heroine; Osceola; Tuscalomba; Carabasset; Narramattah; Wacousta; Wissahickon;* and many others.

Apart from *Metamora,* the most popular Indian play of the first part of the 19th century was undoubtedly Brougham's burlesque, *Pocahontas; or, The Gentle Savage* ♦ (1855). Taking a lighthearted look at both Indians and settlers it served as a sort of bridge between the basically humanistic, romanticized pictures that preceded it and the more indifferent, even negative depictions that arose after the Civil War and which reflected the callous, cynical treatment of Indians in the push for Western lands. Indians in the late 19th century almost never served as heroes or heroines as they had before. They were generally minor figures or, more often, a band of drink-crazed marauders doing the villain's bidding. *Across the Continent* ♦ (1871) is a typical example. The Wild West shows offered by Buffalo Bill ♦ and others also fostered period perceptions.

The pendulum swung back at the beginning of the 20th century with such plays as *Strongheart* (1905) and *The Squaw Man* ♦ (1905), although the latter might be seen as simply a variation of the tragic alien or exotic heroine so popular for many years in diverse works such as *Leah, the Forsaken* ♦ and *Madame Butterfly.* ♦ However, a further rise in the popularity of Indian themes in the theatre may have been discouraged by the growth at the time of silent films which offered a greater range and freedom of action when recounting tales of the Wild West. Thereafter Indians rarely appeared in American drama. At best they were consigned minor roles, often comic. The wise Sitting Bull in *Annie Get Your Gun* ♦ (1946) exemplifies this treatment.

A notable exception was Arthur Kopit's ♦ *Indians* (1969), which attempted to make modern audiences share the guilt for their forefathers' behavior toward Indians. The play failed.

INGE, WILLIAM (1913–1973) A playwright who wrote knowingly of lonely, sexually obsessed but otherwise normal Midwesterners, he was born in Independence, Kansas, and educated at the University of Kansas. He was employed as a schoolteacher and as an actor before accepting the post of drama critic for the St. Louis *Star-Times* in 1943. He left the paper when his first play, *Farther Off from Heaven* (1947), was presented by Margo Jones ♦ at her Dallas theatre. The play never reached New York. However, his second play, *Come Back, Little Sheba* ♦ (1950), recounting the unhappy marriage of an alcoholic and his frowsy, day-dreaming wife, was an immediate success on Broadway. *Picnic* ♦ (1953), in which a handsome, swaggering vagrant brings into the open the sexual frustrations of some small-town Kansas women, won both the Pulitzer Prize ♦ and the New York Drama Critics Circle Award. ♦ Two more successes followed. In *Bus Stop* ♦ (1955) Inge depicted the romance of a cheap singer and a lovesick cowboy who are stranded by a storm, while *The Dark at the Top of the Stairs* ♦ (1957) dealt with an unhappy Oklahoma family. This semi-autobiographical play was a rewriting of *Farther Off from Heaven.* Thereafter Inge's plays were failures, the critics sensing a certain limited sameness of outlook and subject as well as a falling away of theatricality. *A Loss of Roses* (1959) described the futile romance of a show girl and a young man who has been smothered with mother love. *Glory in the Flower* (1959), a one-act play, brought together oddly assorted travelers at a roadhouse. *Natural Affection* (1963) examined a triangle consisting of a successful department store buyer, her lover, and her son. The young couple in *Where's Daddy?* (1966) struggled with the idea of giving up their child for adoption. During this time several of his other plays folded on the road. His final drama, *The Last Pad* (1970), dealt with three men on death row and was done off-Broadway. ◆ His death was a suicide.

Biography: *William Inge,* Robert B. Shuman, New York, 1965.

Ingomar This romantic drama adapted by Maria Lovell from a German play by Friedrich Halm premiered in 1851 simultaneously at the Broadway and the Bowery. ◆ The story tells of a sweet, comely maiden, Parthenia, who wins over Ingomar, the leader of the invading Allemanni barbarians—a beauty and the beast legend set in classic times. The play was famous for its celebrated couplet, "Two souls with but a single thought,/Two hearts that beat as one," which closed the second act. Mme. Ponisi◆ and F. B. Conway◆ were the leads in the Broadway's production, Amelia Parker and Edward Eddy◆ at the Bowery. The play was revived regularly as late as 1909. Among its famous interpreters were Mary Anderson◆ and Julia Marlowe.◆ Salvini◆ was a controversial Ingomar.

Inherit the Wind, a play in three acts by Jerome Lawrence◆ and Robert E. Lee◆ Produced by Herman Shumlin,◆ in association with Margo Jones,◆ at the National Theatre. April 21, 1955. 806 performances.

When Bertram Cates (Karl Light) is brought to trial for violating his state's law against teaching Darwinian evolution, the great liberal, flamboyant lawyer, Henry Drummond (Paul Muni◆), leads his defense. Heading the prosecution is the equally flamboyant orator and politician, Matthew Harrison Brady (Ed Begley). The appearance of these men brings the press en masse, led by the famed curmudgeon from Baltimore, E. K. Hornbeck (Tony Randall). The trial quickly becomes a circus, in which Drummond devastates Brady. But when the trial is over, with Cates found guilty and given a token fine, and with Brady dead, Drummond surprises Hornbeck by coming to the defense of Brady and the Bible. "You never pushed a noun against a verb except to blow something up," he says, insisting every man has the right to be wrong and that Brady's fault was that "he was looking for God too high up and far away."

Closely following the events of the 1925 Scopes "Monkey" Trial in Tennessee, the authors made little attempt to hide the fact that Drummond was Clarence Darrow; Brady, William Jennings Bryan; and Hornbeck, H. L. Mencken. Writing in the *Daily News,* John Chapman◆ hailed the play as "one of the most exciting dramas of the last decade."

INNAURATO, ALBERT, see *Gemini*

IONESCO, EUGÈNE (b. 1912) The French-Roumanian playwright, an exponent of the Theatre of the Absurd, has been a favorite of off-Broadway◆ companies, and collegiate and regional theatres since the early 1950s. Among his better-known works are *The Lesson* (1956), *The Chairs* (1958), and *The Bald Soprano* (1958). His only major commercial success on Broadway was *Rhinoceros* (1961), although the remarkable performance of Zero Mostel◆ was as much responsible for its success as were the excellences of the play. This absurdist allegory in which a man is turned into a rhinoceros was seen by some as an attack of fascism and by others as a satire on excessive individuality.

IRELAND, JOSEPH N[ORTON] (1817–98) One of the major early historians of the American theatre, he entered his father's business after graduating from high school in his native New York. He left the company in 1855 and retired to Bridgeport, Conn. where he devoted the rest of his long life to studying and writing about the stage. His major work was *Records of the New York Stage from 1750–1860* (2 vols., 1866–67). Although the work may be faulted for some factual errors, most of which Odell◆ later corrected in his own *Annals,* ◆ Ireland was an excellent historian who filled the book with numerous useful biographical sketches and other background information. He also wrote two biographies: *Mrs. Duff* (1882) and *A Memoir of the Professional Life of Thomas Abthorpe Cooper* (1888).

Irene, a musical comedy in two acts. Book by James Montgomery. ◆ Lyrics by Joe McCarthy. ◆ Music by Harry Tierney.◆ Produced at the Vanderbilt Theatre. November 18, 1919. 670 performances.

Irene O'Dare (Edith Day◆), "a little bit of salt and sweetness," is a poor shopgirl who is sent on an errand to the Marshalls' Long Island estate. There Donald Marshall (Walter Regan) falls in love with her, and helps her land a job at a couturier's shop run by a man known as Madam Lucy (Bobby Watson). At first both families oppose the match. Mrs. O'Dare (Dorothy Walters) is suspicious of the rich, and Donald's family feels he would be marrying beneath him. But when Irene sings and dances while she models at a party held by the

J. P. Bowdens, she wins everyone's heart—and a wedding ring from Donald.

Pricipal songs: Alice Blue Gown · Irene · The Last Part of Every Party

This charming, intimate musical is generally credited with initiating the vogue for Cinderella librettos, a vogue which dominated Broadway until 1924. From the time of its closing, until *Pins and Needles* ◆ surpassed it in 1939, *Irene* remained the longest-running musical in Broadway history. A 1973 revival, which took many liberties with the original text and score, and which starred Debbie Reynolds, also enjoyed a long run.

Irish in American Theatre and Drama Early Irish immigrants, speaking English as they did, found a relatively easy acceptance in colonial society, especially since there were not too many of them and they represented a better educated class than their countrymen who began to leave their homeland during the potato famine of the 1840s. English plays about Irishmen, while not all that numerous, generally treated their figures without prejudice, and such plays as *The Irish Widow* (1773) and *The True-born Irishman* (1787) retained a certain popularity for many decades. The maverick playwright, John Daly Burke, ◆ an Irish immigrant, was one of the first noteworthy contributors to the American drama, although his feisty, often violent plays apparently were not major successes, and, in any case, scarcely touched on Irish material. It was the vogue of the great Irish comedian, the first Tyrone Power, ◆ who made his American debut in 1833, that may be said to have started the real rage for Irish themes on American stages and which initiated the century-long ascendancy of the Irish in our theatre. As a rule Power impersonated Irish gentlemen of "debonair manners and some sense of the impetuosity for which his countrymen were remarkable." When Power was drowned in the sinking of the *President* in 1841 his place was taken by such diverse actors as John Broughham ◆ (who soon moved on to other types of plays) and John Collins. ◆ Their appearances coincided with the beginnings of mass Irish immigration to America, with the Irish settling primarily in the great cities which were also the theatrical centers of the time. An explosion of pieces followed with Irishmen as central figures and with Ireland itself often the scene. In the 1850s dozens of such plays held the stage for longer and shorter times. Their titles ranged from *The Irish Ambassador,* which had first been seen in this country in 1828 and in which Power later made his debut, through *The Irish Fortune Hunter* and *The Irish Know*

Nothing to *The Irish Yankee,* as well as *Ireland and America* and *Ireland as It Is.* The character of the sophisticated Irish gentlemen, popularized by Power, gave way, in the face of increasing gallery patronage by the less educated Irish immigrants, to the working-class Irishmen, raucous, bibulous, and sly, if not very bright. The increasing immigration also brought on increasing anti-Catholic and specifically anti-Irish prejudices, making many of the Irish-centered plays unfashionable for certain groups and confining the works to cheaper playhouses. But the cream of the Irish artists and Irish plays still found widespread audiences.

By the post-Civil War period the Irish had infiltrated and influenced the American theatre beyond all proportion to their numbers in society. Three figures represent the broad-ranging development of Irish talent. Two were American-born, the other Irish-born, but he spent much of his career in the United States. For many Augustin Daly ◆ represented the pinnacle of theatrical excellence and achievement in his era. A playwright, director, and producer, he established in New York two of the great acting ensembles in the history of the American theatre. Though much of his early success came from his writing or adapting dramas, his ensembles were distinguished for their great comic playing and with them he offered many of the best comedy successes of the era as well as some of the most memorable comedic Shakespearean revivals of his day. He was, for example, the first American producer to mount *The Taming of the Shrew* ◆ in a version closely approximating Shakespeare's original. He made stars of such distinguished Irish performers as John Drew ◆ and Ada Rehan. ◆

If Daly exemplified the Irish in the elite theatre of the later 19th century, the Dublin-born Dion Boucicault ◆ was the leading figure in what might be called the middle-brow stage of the period. An actor, playwright, director, and sometime producer, he had established a London reputation and written *London Assurance,* ◆ the only enduring comedy of the early 19th century, before coming to America. However great his popularity as an actor, he is remembered now largely for his plays, which ranged from sensation-filled melodramas with American settings, such as *The Octoroon,* ◆ to his more rustic, but still sensation-crammed plays of Irish life, such as *The Shaughraun.* ◆ He wrote comedy, too, but those of his later years were inferior to *London Assurance* and quickly faded from the scene.

Catering initially to working-class audiences, the plays of Edward Harrigan ◆ lovingly if amusingly depicted the lives and struggles of immigrants in

New York. His characters were mostly Irish, and his Mulligan family became one of the most beloved and enduring families in American dramatic literature. But he drew blacks, Jews, Italians, and other ghetto denizens with equal warmth and validity. As sometimes happens with artists of Harrigan's ilk, his work eventually attracted the attention and admiration of a Brahmin figure such as William Dean Howells♦ and ultimately drew audiences from all classes.

Harrigan was a product of the early vaudeville stages, and as such he rubbed elbows with a long list of great Irish entertainers both in variety and in minstrelsy. Besides his partner, Tony Hart,♦ there were such noted figures as Dan Bryant,♦ Hughey Dougherty,♦ and Dan Emmett,♦ to name a few. Harrigan's plays also served as a bridge between the comedies of his day, which often were interspersed with songs, and the later American musical theatre. In this latter field the Irish were also pre-eminent at the time. Victor Herbert♦ was unquestionably the first truly great composer of American operetta, while George M. Cohan♦ could be called the father of American musical comedy. His exuberant, patriotic, brash shows have been seen by some as the essence of the working-class Irish contribution to the contemporary stage. The romantic plays with music that featured Chauncey Olcott♦ appeared during roughly these same years and appealed hugely to working-class Irish audiences.

The awesome roster of other notable Irish-Americans of the 19th-century stage ranged from Lawrence Barrett♦ to Annie Yeamans♦ and included not only actors but writers, producers, directors, and designers, among them the Drews,♦ Barney Fagan,♦ James A. Herne.♦ John McCullough,♦ J. B. McElfatrick,♦ John J. McNally,♦ James H. McVicker,♦ and James O'Neill.♦

In the years just before World War I the Irish hegemony, at least in the musical theatre and in the business end of the theatre, was challenged and largely routed by Jews. But at the same time, or shortly thereafter in the teens and 1920s, several Irish-American playwrights emerged who may, in the long run, be seen as the most significant Irish contributors yet to the American stage. By far the most important was the man generally acknowledged as the greatest of American playwrights, Eugene O'Neill.♦ There was nothing specifically Irish about O'Neill's tragic vision of life, and few of his characters can be deemed to represent any sort of stage Irishman. However, his Catholicism, or his reaction to it, did condition several of his later works. The high comedies of Philip Barry♦ are only

marginally more Irish, touching as they occasionally do on Irish who have made it to the top of the social ladder. For the most part, however, his society figures could have come from any ethnic background. Yet, like O'Neill, Barry had another side, a mystic streak closer to traditional Catholic mysticism than O'Neill's religious explorations were to basic Catholic questioning. Coincidentally both playwrights were less successful commercially, and probably artistically, when their religious concerns obtained the upper hand. The third major Irish playwright, George Kelly,♦ from the start mixed a comic view of life with a certain "black Irish" bitterness. A few of his characters, especially in his early *The Show Off,*♦ could be branded Irish, but as a rule he, too, wrote in general American terms. His later plays failed when his bitterness got the better of his humor. A number of lesser Irish playwrights, such as James Gleason,♦ dealt with more readily identifiable Irish types, but even their plays attested to the fundamental assimilation of the Irish into American society. One curious phenomenon in the early 1920s was in the musical theatre, where during the so-called Cinderella Era musical comedy after musical comedy told essentially the same story—a poor Irish girl, often a secretary, winning the hand of a rich man, usually the boss's son. That the men generally had Waspish names further attested to the acceptance of a certain easy mingling. The long-run *Abie's Irish Rose*♦ trafficked in the stalest steretypes.

Playwrights aside, the Irish, while no longer looming as large as they had in the preceding century, still contributed substantially to every aspect of the American theatre. Random examples would include Fred Allen,♦ William Brady,♦ Marc Connelly,♦ Homer Curran,♦ Frank Fay,♦ Eddie Foy,♦ Helen Gahagan,♦ Frank Gilroy,♦ Terrence McNally,♦ Laurette Taylor,♦ and Harry Tierney.♦ Gilroy may be perceived as the last important playwright to use identifiably Irish material.

Only in recent years does Irish-American interest in and involvement with the American theatre seem to have slackened. A rash of religious plays (see Religious Drama in America♦) centering on Catholicism have had no special Irish-Catholic tinge to them.

IRVING, HENRY [né JOHN HENRY BRODRIBB] (1838–1905) The renowned English actor-manager, who was long the subject of both adulation and savage criticism, was credited with making acting a respectable profession in his homeland and with ridding English playgoers of Puritan obsessions. He was the first actor to be knighted. He made six visits to America between 1883 and 1903, most in the company of Ellen Terry. ♦ For his American debut he selected one of his most celebrated roles, the guilt-ridden Mathias in *The Bells.* Among his other American offerings were his Shylock, Hamlet, Macbeth, Doricort (*The Belle's Stratagem*), Dubosc (*The Lyons Mail*), Benedick, and Richelieu. Neither good-looking nor well-built, and with a peculiar style of delivery, he divided American critics much as he did English reviewers. Henry Austin Clapp, ♦ in his *Reminiscences of a Dramatic Critic,* spent pages attempting to analyze Irving's style, noting, among other things, "He has not learned how to sit, stand or move . . . and even worse than this, he does not know how to speak his own language"; yet he concluded, "The principal source of Mr. Irving's professional power and success lies in the character and quality of his intellect." Odell♦ drew a similar conclusion, observing more succinctly, "There was a soul of drama in his rather hampered body." Despite critical complaints, his tours were among the most financially profitable of his era, and he was often able to charge twice the going rate for tickets.

Biography: *Henry Irving, the Actor and His World,* Laurence Irving, London, 1951.

IRVING, JULES, see *Actor's Workshop*

IRVING, WASHINGTON (1783–1859) If this great early American writer is best remembered for his biographies, histories, and romantic short stories, he was also an important, if largely indirect, figure in the American theatre of his day. Among his first published pieces were "The Letters of Jonathan Oldstyle, Gent.," which were serialized in 1802–03 in the New York *Morning Chronicle* and also published separately, and which offered his personal views of contemporary plays and performers. Further observations on the theatre, usually satirical and not nearly as important, appeared in *Salmagundi,* which he wrote in 1807–08 with his brother, William, and J. K. Paulding. ♦ Both in America and in Europe, where he spent some time, he made many important theatrical friends, including John Howard Payne. ♦ With Payne he collaborated on half a dozen plays, the most important of which were *Charles the Second; or, The Merry Monarch*♦ (1824) and *Richelieu, A Domestic Tragedy* (1826). Only *Charles the Second* enjoyed widespread popularity. The failure to find mountings for the remaining plays discouraged Irving. He wrote Payne, "I am sorry to say I cannot afford to write any more for the theatre . . . The experiment has satisfied me that I

should never at any time be compensated for my trouble." In the long run, it was other men's adaptations of his stories, especially *Rip Van Winkle,* ♦ which made him an enduring figure in our theatre.

IRWIN, MAY [née ADA MAY CAMPBELL] (1862–1938) In 1899, when she was at the height of her fame, Lewis C. Strang, ♦ a popular writer on theatrical themes, observed, "May Irwin is a personality rather than an artist, an entertainer more than an actress. Her career has vacillated between the variety stage and the legitimate, until at last she has become identified with that hybrid species of the theatrical amusement called farce comedy. Miss Irwin is a famous fun-maker; of jolly rotund figure, and with a face that reflects the gaiety of nations, she is the personification of humor and careless mirth, a female Falstaff." The Canadian-born blue-eyed blonde made her professional debut with her sister, Flora, at a Buffalo vaudeville house in 1875. By the early 1880s she was a popular attraction at Tony Pastor's, ♦ appearing both in his olios and his versions of Gilbert♦ and Sullivan♦ favorites. She left Pastor in 1883 to assume important supporting roles in Augustin Daly's♦ great ensemble. Four years later she returned to vaudeville, then began appearing in those prototypical musicals that were called farce-comedies♦ at the time. Stardom came in 1895 when she appeared in *The Widow Jones* and introduced "The Bully Song." Her singing of this song placed her in the forefront of what then were termed "coon shouters." Subsequent hits, all of a similar nature, included *Courted into Court* (1896), *The Swell Miss Fitzwell* (1897), *Kate Kip, Buyer* (1898), *Sister Mary* (1899), *Madge Smith, Attorney* (1900), and *Mrs. Black is Back* (1904). Thereafter she alternated between vaudeville and musical plays, although her vogue had begun to wane. Her last Broadway assignment was in *The 49ers* (1922). She retired after making an appearance in a 1925 "Old Timers' Week" at the Palace. ♦

Is Zat So?, a comedy in three acts by James Gleason♦ and Richard Taber. Produced at the 39th Street Theatre. January 5, 1925. 634 performances.

Chick Cowan (Robert Armstrong), a boxer, and Hap Hurley (Gleason), his manager, are down on their luck when they meet rich young Clinton Blackburn (Sidney Riggs). Clinton is determined to prove his brother-in-law, Robert Parker (John C. King), is a crook and to sock it to him in more ways than one. To this end, he takes on Chick and Hap as his sparring partner and trainer, and introduces them into his household as butler and footman. When Chick is accidentally knocked out in a fight, his somewhat befuddled mind becomes clear, and it is he who provides the evidence Clinton needs to unmask Parker.

This "rough and ready comedy" competed successfully with another Gleason farce of the same season, *The Fall Guy,* ♦ and far outran it, though most critics thought *The Fall Guy* the better work.

ISAACS, EDITH J[ULIET] R[ICH] (1878–1956) Born in Milwaukee and educated at Downer College, she served as drama critic for *Ainslee's Magazine* in 1913. In 1918 she became editor of *Theatre Arts* ♦ magazine and retained that post until 1946. Under her aegis the magazine was the leading intellectual theatrical periodical of the era. She also edited *Theatre: Essays on the Arts of the Theatre* (1927) and *Plays of American Life and Fantasy* (1929), and wrote *The Negro in the American Theatre* (1947).

ISHERWOOD, HENRY (1803–1885) The son of famous New York confectioners, he was hired by the Park Theatre ♦ in 1817 as a super and apprentice scene-painter. Although he continued to act until the mid-1850s, it was his work as a scene-painter for which he was most admired. By the mid-1840s he was designing important sets for productions at Niblo's Garden ♦ and elsewhere. In 1857 he was signed by James Wallack ♦ to be the principal scene-painter for his great company. His salary was $25 a week, actually not a bad salary when Lester Wallack, ♦ then the company's leading man, received $100. Isherwood remained with the Wallacks until his retirement in 1875. He designed everything from Shakespeare to contemporary comedies. One of his last assignments was to create the sets of Wallack's tremendously successful production of *The Shaughraun* ♦ (1874).

It Pays To Advertise, a farce in three acts by Roi Cooper Megrue ♦ and Walter Hackett. Produced by Cohan ♦ and Harris ♦ at the Cohan Theatre. September 8, 1914. 399 performances.

Cyrus Martin (John W. Cope) so dominates the soap business that one of his associates remarks, "If

he were to go busted, the whole country would go dirty." But Martin is dismayed at the refusal of his playboy son Rodney (Grant Mitchell ♦) to settle down to work. So is Rodney's fiancée, Mary Grayson (Ruth Shepley). Irked by their disapproval, Rodney joins with Ambrose Peale (Will Deming) to found a rival soap company. He invents a soap that costs three cents a bar to make and, with proper advertising, they plan to sell for a dollar a bar. They call their soap "#13" and launch a huge publicity campaign announcing "Number Thirteen Soap Is Unlucky for Dirt." The demand for the new soap overwhelms the men, for they have exhausted their funds in advertising and have no money left to manufacture the product. Father Martin buys them out. But Rodney has caught the fever, and as soon as he marries Mary, promises to settle down to business.

The *Times*'s unidentified critic praised the work for having "something more than the gayety of the average farce" and for humor rich in "genuineness and substance."

It's a Wise Child, a comedy in three acts by Laurence E. Johnson. Produced by David Belasco ♦ at the Belasco Theatre. August 6, 1929. 378 performances.

Although she is engaged to G. A. Appleby (Harlan Briggs), a prosperous middle-aged banker, Joyce Stanton (Mildred McCoy) meets and falls in love with a younger man, Roger Baldwin (Humphrey Bogart). To break her engagement, she announces darkly that she is pregnant, an idea which she gets on learning the condition of one of the Stantons' serving girls. But her plan backfires when she loses both Appleby and Baldwin. However, the family's young attorney, James Stevens (Minor Watson), is so taken with Joyce that he proposes marriage.

"It's a wise child in the theatre who can write so comic a play," Brooks Atkinson ♦ noted in his review. Its popularity allowed the comedy to override the onset of the Depression.

Johnson (1872–1933) was a minor playwright who wrote half a dozen plays which were produced on Broadway between 1925 and 1933. This was his only success.

J

J.B., a play in two acts by Archibald MacLeish. Produced by Alfred de Liagre, Jr.,♦ at the ANTA Theatre. December 11, 1958. 364 performances. PP.

J.B. (Pat Hingle♦) is a successful businessman who seems to have everything in life. Walking through the great traveling circus that is the world he comes to the attention of Mr. Zuss (Raymond Massey♦), a downtrodden balloon seller, and Nickles (Christopher Plummer♦), a sardonic popcorn vendor. After Nickles puts on the Satanmask and Zuss the Godmask, they confront J.B. One by one his blessings are taken away—his wealth lost, his children killed, his body diseased, his wife deserting him. But J.B. refuses to condemn God, so his wounds are healed. He concludes,

> We *are*—and that is all our answer.
> We are, and what we are can suffer . . .
> But . . . what suffers, loves.

The American poet MacLeish (1892–1982) a native of Glencoe, Ill., who studied at Yale and at Harvard Law School, had written several other verse dramas, such as *Panic* (1935) and *The Music Crept by Me upon the Waters* (1953), but *J.B.* was his only commercial success. Louis Kronenberger♦ noted, "Judged as a theatre piece, *J.B.*—at least in the first half—had a striking theatricality . . . Judged as philosophic drama, though an effort of a sort and size unusual in today's American theatre, *J.B.* was not altogether satisfying." For all its flaws, this play, suggested by the Book of Job, was a noteworthy success.

Jack Cade, a play in four acts by Robert T. Conrad.♦ Produced by F. C. Wemyss♦ at the Walnut Street Theatre,♦ Philadelphia. December 9, 1835. In repertory.

The villainous Lord Say (Mr. Connor), who typifies the arbitrary power of the nobles, cruelly oppresses his people. He has long since killed Jack Cade's father and exiled Jack (Mr. Ingersoll), who now returns to take his revenge. He succeeds in capturing London, forcing the king to flee. Confronting Say, Cade stabs him fatally, but Say has enough strength left in him before he dies to dig his poisoned dagger into Cade. As Cade is dying, his wife Mariamne appears, crazed by an attack on her by Lord Clifford (Mr. Porter), whom she has murdered in self-defense. She dies moments before her husband, whose last words are, "The bondman is avenged, my country free!"

Conrad originally wrote this verse drama as a vehicle for A. A. Addams♦ under the title *Aylmere,* but Addams was too drunk to appear on opening night. Conrad based his story on the Kentish rebellion of 1450. However, he emphasized the social rather than the political aspects of the revolt. The play was only a modest success until Edwin Forrest♦ assumed the leading role in 1841. Thereafter it remained in Forrest's repertory until his death. Afterwards John McCullough assumed the part on several occasions, and it was revived with some regularity as late as 1887.

JACKSON, ANNE (b. 1926) Born in Allegheny, Penn., she made her professional debut in 1944 but called attention to herself when she played Mildred, the peevish wife, in *Oh, Men! Oh, Women!*♦ (1953) and The Daughter, who opposes her father's remarriage, in *Middle of the Night*♦ (1956). Many of her subsequent appearances have been with her husband, Eli Wallach,♦ in such plays as *Rhinoceros* (1961), *The Typists* and *The Tiger* (double bill, 1963), *Luv*♦ (1964), a 1973 revival of *The Waltz of the Toreadors, Twice Around the Park* (1982), a 1988 revival of *Cafe Crown,* and a 1990 tour of *Love Letters.*

JACKSON, ETHEL (1877–1957) Although the New Yorker appeared on stage off and on from 1897 to 1939, she is recalled almost entirely as the original Sonia for the first American production of *The Merry Widow*♦ (1907), in which she introduced "The Merry Widow Waltz" and "Vilja."

JACKSON, JOE [né JIRANEK] (1880?–1942) In his teens a bicycle racing champion in his native Austria, he first took to performing publicly in a straight, daredevil act. He turned to comedy after witnessing an audience's reaction to his behavior when his handlebars came loose during a turn-of-the-century appearance in London. Coming to America he developed the tramp cyclist act that kept him in the vaudeville spotlight for the next forty years. He would wander on stage downtrodden and lugubrious, forlornly trying to fix a cuff that would not stay put. Soon he would discover a bicycle, which he would begin to ride with "lyric rapture" until piece by piece it fell apart. He died immediately after taking his curtain calls at an appearance in New York.

JACOBS, Bernard, see *Shubert, Lee, Sam S., and J.J.*

JAMES, Henry [Jr.] (1843–1916) This famous expatriate novelist was also a passionate playgoer and harbored serious ambitions for a place in the theatre. He dramatized his own novel, *Daisy Miller* (1883), as well as writing such plays as *Guy Domville* (1895) and *The High Bid* (1908), but none was commercially viable. He also wrote numerous essays on the theatre. These essays were collected after his death and published as *The Scenic Art* (1949). His plays were edited and published in 1948. Ironically, several of his novels provided the bases for popular plays long after his death. The most notable were *Berkeley Square*♦ (1929), suggested by his unfinished *A Sense of the Past; The Heiress*♦ (1947), derived from *Washington Square;* and *The Innocents* (1950), whose source was *The Turn of the Screw.*

JAMES, Louis (1842–1910) A much respected actor who never quite attained the highest order of public acceptance, he was born in Tremont, Ill., and made his debut with a Louisville stock company in 1863. He left to join Mrs. John Drew♦ at Philadelphia's Arch Street Theatre,♦ then in 1872 became a member of Augustin Daly's♦ great ensemble. Five years later he began a series of engagements with Lawrence Barrett. ♦ In 1886 he branched out on his own, producing and starring in a series of Shakespearean revivals, beginning with *Othello*♦ (1886); *Hamlet*♦ (1888); and *Much Ado About Nothing*♦ (1888); and continuing through *Henry VIII* and *The Comedy of Errors* during the 1907–08 season. The productions were generally admired by critics, but found more welcome on the road than in New York.

JANAUSCHEK, [Francesca Romana Magdalena] Fanny (1830–1904) The tempestuous Czech actress had become a reigning favorite on European stages before she made her American debut in 1867. Her opening play was *Medea,* which she performed in German with a company she had brought with her from the Continent. The selection invited comparison with Ristori,♦ who had only recently triumphed

in the part, and comparisons were not totally favorable to the newcomer. Nevertheless, she soon developed a loyal following. In 1870 she decided to learn English well enough to act in English-language productions. Thereafter, most of her career was spent in America. Among her best roles were Lady Macbeth and the title parts in *Deborah* and *Mary Stuart.* Otis Skinner,♦ who played opposite her when he was a young man, recalled her as "a short, rather stockily built woman . . . Her eyes were of hazel-gray, large and weary-lidded, but when they suddenly opened, it was the unmasking of a battery." In 1900 she suffered a stroke, which left her paralyzed. She died nearly blind and impoverished and was to be buried in an indigent's grave until her fellow actors took up a collection for a proper funeral.

Janie, a comedy in three acts by Josephine Bentham and Herschel Williams. Produced by Brock Pemberton♦ at the Henry Miller Theatre. September 10, 1942. 642 performances.

When 17-year-old Janie Colburn (Gwen Anderson) meets Pvt. Dick Lawrence (Herbert Evers), the son of her mother's old friend, she instantly forgets her high school beau, Scooper Nolan (Frank Amy). And when her parents and their friends go out for the night, Janie has Dick invite all his army buddies to a hastily got-up party at the Colburn house. The older Colburns return to find the house overrun. Of course, Dick must go off to war, so Janie realizes she will have to make up with Scooper.

Almost every critic compared this play unfavorably with the earlier *Junior Miss.* ♦ Both comedies exemplified the recourse playwrights had to youngsters and old folks as principals when so many draft-age men, and women, had joined the war effort. Although business was slow at first, good word-of-mouth and wartime prosperity turned the play into a hit. Williams (b. 1909) was a native of Savannah, Ga., and studied at Tulane and Yale. Most of his career was spent in radio. This was his only successful play.

JANIS, Elsie [née Bierbower] (1889–1956) Best known as the "Sweetheart of the A.E.F.," for her entertaining of troops during World War I, the slim, hoydenish performer was born in Columbus, Ohio, and made her debut in her hometown as a boy in *The Charity Ball*♦ in 1897. She quickly rose to popularity in vaudeville as "Little Elsie." She turned to Broadway in 1906 in *The Vanderbilt Cup,* later appearing in *The Hoyden* (1907); *The Fair Co-ed* (1909); *The Slim Princess* (1910), in which she introduced "Fo' de Lawd's Sake, Play a Waltz"; and *The Lady of the Slipper* (1912). But two-a-day remained her main stamping grounds, where her singing and imitations won the loudest applause. The *Dramatic Mirror*♦ wrote of her, "You caught a splendid semblance of the divine fire—enough to truly thrill you," while Sime Silverman♦ called her "the most natural person in vaudeville." She continued to perform throughout the twenties, but retired after the death of her infamous stage mother in 1932.

Autobiography: *So Far, So Good!*, New York, 1932.

JANSEN, MARIE [née JOHNSON] (1857–1914) The Boston-born singing comedienne joined Colonel McCaull's♦ company in 1883, then appeared in principal roles at the Casino. ♦ However, she is best recalled as leading lady to Francis Wilson♦ in such shows as *The Oolah* (1889) and *The Merry Monarch* (1890).

Janus, a comedy in three acts by Carolyn Green. Produced by Alfred de Liagre, Jr.,♦ at the Plymouth Theatre. November 24, 1955. 251 performances.

Every summer Jessica (Margaret Sullavan♦) and Denny (Claude Dauphin) go off to an apartment in Washington Square, where they write novels under the pen name Janus. Jessica and Denny are married, but not to each other. Even their spouses don't know where they go and what they do. But this particular summer their idyll is interrupted successively by their aggressive agent (Mary Finney), Jessica's husband (Robert Preston♦), and the tax man (Richard Emhardt). It is some time before they can return to their writing.

A delightful escapist comedy of what even in 1955 was becoming an old school, it did good business to no small extent because of its fine performers. Miss Green was born in New York and educated at Vassar. This was her only successful play.

JARRETT, HENRY C. (1828–1903) Jarrett began his career as an actor in amateur theatricals in his native Baltimore. In 1851 he purchased the Baltimore Museum and four years later assumed the management of Washington's National Theatre♦. The following year he endeavored to recruit John E. Owens,♦ Joseph Jefferson,♦ and other major performers in a company to offer Londoners some idea of American drama and American acting at its best, but the project fell through, reputedly because every performer wanted all the important roles for himself. In 1861 he added the new Brooklyn Academy of Music to his roster of theatres and in 1864 the Boston Theatre. When he brought the "Parisienne Ballet Troupe" to New York for an engagement, the burning of Manhattan's Academy of Music, where they were to appear, led to the ballerinas being added to a melodrama about to be mounted at Niblo's Garden. ♦ The result was *The Black Crook*♦ (1866), a milestone in the history of the American musical theatre. At the same time Jarrett took over management of Niblo's. In 1874 he joined A. M. Palmer♦ to take over Booth's Theatre, and to produce plays, including a highly successful revival of *Uncle Tom's Cabin.* ♦ He retired to England in the mid-1880s.

Jazz Singer, The, a comedy-drama in three acts by Samson Raphaelson. ♦ Produced by Al Lewis, Max Gordon♦ and Sam H. Harris♦ at the Fulton Theatre. September 14, 1925. 303 performances.

Jackie Rabinowitz (George Jessel♦) fights with his cantor father (Howard Lang), who objects to his obsession with jazz music and his neglect of his religion. Running away from home he takes the name of Jack Robin and quickly rises as a popular singer. His big break comes when he lands a major role in a new Broadway revue. But on the eve of its premiere, he learns his father is dying. He rushes to his father, who persuades him to return to the synagogue and follow in the older man's footsteps.

Although this tear-jerker was one of the major hits of its season—called by one paper "a shrewd and well-planned excursion into the theatre"—it is best remembered as the source of Al Jolson's♦ famous early "talkie" of the same name. From the start critics felt the story was based on Jolson's career, but Raphaelson is said always to have denied this.

JEFFERS, [JOHN] ROBINSON (1887–1962) The famed American poet, a native of Pittsburgh, was best known to playgoers for his modern translation of *Medea,* ♦ which Judith Anderson♦ performed to great acclaim in 1947. She later appeared in his *The Tower Beyond Tragedy*♦ (1950), which he dramatized from his own poem on the Electra legend. In 1954 Washington's Arena Stage♦ mounted his version of the Phaedra story, *The Cretan Woman*.

Biography: *The Stone Mason of Far House*, Melba Bennett, Los Angeles, 1966.

JEFFERSON, JOSEPH (1774–1832) Although best remembered as the grandfather of the famous Joseph Jefferson, ♦ he was one of the most accomplished and beloved comedians of his own day. He was born in Plymouth, England, and given his earliest tutelage by his father, Thomas Jefferson, a minor actor at Drury Lane. Hodgkinson♦ brought him to America in 1795, and he made his American debut with Hodgkinson's company when it was appearing in Boston, playing La Gloire in *The Surrender of Calais.* His New York debut was at the John Street Theatre♦ as Squire Richard in *The Provoked Husband* in February 1796. He was a small, slender man, with a Grecian nose and blue eyes "full of laughter." After an argument with Hodgkinson, he left for Philadelphia in 1803. There, with his brother-in-law, the first William Warren,♦ he became the mainstay of the Chestnut Street Theatre.♦ His best roles were in then popular, if now forgotten, light comedies, such as Farmer Ashfield in *Speed the Plough,* Jeremy Diddler in *Raising the Wind,* and Jacob Gawky in *The Chapter of Accidents.* He left Philadelphia during the theatrical depression of 1830, attempting to find work in the hinterlands. But by then his age had begun to tell on him, and he was unsuccessful. His son Joseph, Jr. (1804–1842) was an actor and scene-painter of only modest repute.

JEFFERSON, JOSEPH (1829–1905) Beyond question the most popular and respected American comedian of the 19th century, he was the scion of an old theatrical family. His father was attempting, unsuccessfully, to manage a theatre in Philadelphia when the future actor was born there. The youngster did not wait long before making his debut at the age of four, performing alongside of and mimicking the celebrated singer of "Jim Crow," T. D. Rice.♦ He had little schooling, and after his father's death when he was thirteen, he toured with his actress mother in theatrical backwaters. Within a few years he was playing important roles in support of the great actors of the day, including Marrall to the Sir Giles Overreach of Junius Brutus Booth.♦ In 1853 he became stage manager of the Baltimore Museum, and a year later was hired by John T. Ford♦ to manage a theatre in Richmond, Va. There he played with Edwin Forrest♦ and other noted performers. The turning point in his career came after his return in 1857 from a visit to London, when he was hired by Laura Keene♦ as a member of her company. Under her aegis he scored notable successes as Dr. Pangloss in *The Heir-at-Law* and as Asa Trenchard in *Our American Cousin.*♦ Moving to the Winter Garden, he consolidated his reputation when he played Caleb Plummer in *Dot,* Dion Boucicault's♦ dramatization of *The Cricket on the Hearth,* and Salem Scudder in

Boucicault's *The Octoroon.*♦ In 1859 he produced his own version of *Rip Van Winkle,* but it was unsuccessful. During a second trip to London he prevailed on Boucicault to give him a revised version. This he played with great success in London in 1865, and a year later in New York. The performance brought him fame and fortune, and for many years he played little else. Not all critics were pleased at first, but within a year his performance had been so refined and honed that even the *Times,* which had been among the dissenters, wrote, "In *Rip Van Winkle* he evinces all his abilities and sounds the gamut of all quiet and natural emotions. He is no doubt the best comedian America has yet produced, and probably unsurpassed in England, that *nidus* of comedians. His face and body were formed to inspire mirth, and this lends additional force to his rendering of pathetic parts. In *Rip,* for instance, the smile excited by his scarecrow figure actually forces more quickly the tear we bestow on his misery." A year later the paper added of his performance, "In many important respects it more nearly approaches positive perfection than any single piece of acting now before the public." In 1880 he produced his version of *The Rivals,* playing Bob Acres to the Mrs. Malaprop of Mrs. John Drew.♦ While some critics condemned his rewriting of Sheridan, his performance was universally hailed and added one final great portrait to his theatrical canon. In 1893 he succeeded his friend, Edwin Booth,♦ as president of the Players.♦ He made his last appearance, as Caleb Plummer, in 1904, ending a stage career of 71 years.

Jefferson was a man of slightly over average height, with a noticeably smallish head and long brown hair. Even as a relatively young man his quizzical face was wizened. He had a prominent nose and chin, and described himself as presenting "a classical contour, neither Greek nor Roman, but of the pure Nut-cracker type." His beguiling *Autobiography of Joseph Jefferson* (1890) is filled with superb pictures of the theatre of his day and remains one of the landmarks in American theatrical writing.

Jefferson, Thomas Although Jefferson was personified early on as Monticello in the anti-Sedition Act satire, *The Essex Junto* (1802), the later perception of the man as a towering intellectual rather than a dramatic activist may have long denied him a place as a major character in American drama. Even in modern theatre he has not been written about that often nor has he been well served. Two major exceptions might be Sidney Kingsley's♦ *The Patriots*♦ (1943) and the musical *1776*♦ (1969).

JENKINS, GEORGE (b. 1911) Born in Baltimore and educated at the University of Pennsylvania, he worked under Jo Mielziner♦ from 1937 to 1941. In 1943 he designed the sets and lighting for *Early to Bed,* and for the next twenty years was in steady demand. Among his credits are *Mexican Hayride* (1944), *I Remember Mama*♦ (1944), *Dark of the Moon*♦ (1945), *Lost in the Stars*♦ (1949), *Bell, Book and Candle*♦ (1950), *Two for the Seesaw*♦ (1958), *The Miracle Worker*♦ (1959), *A Thousand Clowns* (1962), *Generation* (1965), and *Sly Fox* (1976).

JEROME, WILLIAM, see *Schwartz, Jean*

JESSEL, GEORGE [ALBERT] (1898–1981) Born into a poor Jewish family in the Bronx, he took to the stage in 1907 to help support his sick father. He formed an act called The Imperial Trio, the other youngsters being Jack Wiener, who became a Hollywood agent, and Walter Winchell.♦ Later Winchell and Jessel joined Gus Edwards's♦ famous schoolchildren act, performing alongside Georgie Price and Eddie Cantor.♦ By 1920 he was producing his own miniature revues for vaudeville. About the same time he first did his most celebrated turn, his monologue which pretended to be a phone call to his demanding mother. In it he swore he knew nothing about the money missing from the cupboard, he hadn't eaten a piece of the cake she had baked for a charity affair, and no, that was not his cigar butt, since he didn't smoke. He appeared on Broadway in the *Shubert Gaieties of 1919, The Passing Show of 1923,*♦ *Sweet and Low* (1930), and *High Kickers* (1941). He co-produced the latter as well as several other shows. On occasion Jessel also appeared in straight plays, most notably as Jackie Rabinowitz, who must choose between the stage and the synagogue, in *The Jazz Singer*♦ (1925). His last years were spent as a Hollywood producer and as a celebrated after-dinner speaker.

Autobiography: *So Help Me,* New York, 1943.

Jessie Brown; or, The Relief of Lucknow, a drama in three acts by Dion Boucicault.♦ Produced at Wallack's Theatre. February 22, 1858. 42 performances.

Led by the treacherous Nena Sahib (Boucicault), the Sepoy Rebellion has succeeded in trapping a garrison of European troops at Lucknow. As the days move on the situation seems more and more hopeless. The women and children, even the soldiers, though they are reluctant to admit it, have begun to despair. It would appear that surrender is their only recourse. As fear grows, a young Scottish girl, Jessie Brown (Agnes Robertson♦), slowly raises her head and listens. She tells her neighbors she can hear the Campbell's pibroch. At first they are disbelieving, but in time the sound of the bagpipes grows louder, and before long kilted Highlanders have broken through to rescue the besieged.

So fresh was the memory of these events that, according to popular theatre legend, no actor would assume the role of Nena Sahib for fear of being hissed off stage. Boucicault was forced to play the role himself. Pronounced a "capital drama" by William Winter,♦ the play held the boards for over twenty years.

JESSOP, GEORGE H. (d.1915) Born in Ireland, the younger son of an Irish family of Cromwellian stock, who were at one time Oliver Goldsmith's landlords, he was educated at Trinity College and used his small inheritance to come to America in 1873. His first play, *A Gentleman from Nevada* (1880), dealt with an uncouth American who becomes the guest of a cultured English countess. Critics accused him of plagiarism and bad writing, but the play was popular with the public. His next work, *Sam'l of Posen*♦ (1881), centered on a Jewish peddler. For several years afterwards he collaborated with William Gill on a series of similar comedies with melodramatic overtones: *In Paradise* (1883); *Facts; or, His Little Hatchet* [later called *Our Governor*] (1883); *Stolen Money* (1884); *Mam'zelle* (1884); and *A Bottle of Ink* (1885). In 1889 he offered the first of three long-popular romantic Irish comedies, *Myles Aroon.* The same year New York saw *A Gold Mine,* which he had written two years earlier with Brander Matthews♦ as a vehicle for John T. Raymond,♦ and which Nat Goodwin♦ played after Raymond's death. It was, like his first play, a melodramatic comedy about an American, a miner, opposing more sophisticated Englishmen. He turned to pure melodrama for *The Great Metropolis* (1889), which he wrote with Ben Teal,♦ then reunited with Matthews to write *On Probation* (1889), a well-received comedy in which William H. Crane♦ portrayed a flirtatious man placed "on probation" by his annoyed fiancée. His 1891 play *The Power of the Press,* written with Augustus Pitou,♦ told of a young man seduced into committing a crime by an older cohort who covets the younger man's wife. Two more romantic Irish plays followed: *Mavourneen*♦ (1891) and *The Irish Artist* (1894).

JEWETT, HENRY (1861–1930) The Australian-born actor came to America in 1891 and shortly was leading man to Julia Marlowe,♦ Fanny Davenport,♦ and other noted actresses. He also played second leads opposite Richard Mansfield.♦ At the turn of the century he moved to Boston where he established the Henry Jewett Players (also known as the Repertory Theatre), a company that soon gained national recognition for the excellence of its repertory and acting. One observer described him as "a robust and powerful fellow, with the chest and muscles of an athlete" and noted "sincerity was the chief characteristic of his work."

Jews in American Theatre and Drama Jewish immigration to America began in the mid-17th century, and small enclaves developed in Rhode Island, New Amsterdam, and several other more tolerant settlements. Because their numbers and influence were so small there appears to have been little overt or organized anti-Semitism. Moreover, they appear to have served largely as tradesmen and to have taken no part in the beginnings of American theatre. Thus scarcely any significance can be attached to the fact that *The Merchant of Venice*♦ was one of the first professionally mounted plays in America—the initial American offering by the elder Hallam's♦ company. That the villain was a Jew seems not to have mattered more to 1752 or later audiences than that Iago was Italian or Macbeth a Scot. Some suggestion that there existed a widespread willingness to view Jews sympathetically can be assumed from the success which attended the American premiere of Richard Cumberland's *The Jew* (1795), less than a year after its English premiere. In his humane portrayal of Sheva, Cumberland publicly acknowledged that he was attempting to discard derogatory stereotypes and present Jews "according to the new doctrine of human perfectibility . . . and the universal sentiment of tolerance associated with the era of the French Revolution." On the other hand, Lessing's great German play, *Nathan the Wise,* which was an even stronger plea for tolerance, remained unknown to American playgoers for decades, despite the long popularity of German plays. And the earliest known depiction of a Jew in American drama in Susanna Haswell Rowson's *Slaves of [in?] Algiers* (1794) had the villain describe himself "as a forger and a crook, as one who cheated the Gentiles because Moses so commanded."

In the early 19th century the older sterotype was perpetuated in such foreign works as the comic *The Jew and the Doctor* (1808), which held American stages for decades. One curious piece was Henry E.

Milner's once famous *The Jew of Lubeck* (1819), in which a disgraced aristocrat disguises himself as a Jew. At the same time actors such as Edmund Kean♦ attempted more compassionate portrayals of such sterotypical figures as Shylock and Marlowe's Barabas. Yet while Jewish men continued to be presented as sly, callous, mercenary, and pushy, a new figure began to appear. This was the tragically beset, but rather beautiful and noble Jewish woman. Rebecca in Scott's novel *Ivanhoe* and Rachel in the Scribe♦-Halevy opera, *La Juive,* gave widespread currency to the figure. *The Hebrew* (1823) was a successful dramatization of the former, while *The Jewess* (1835), taken from the latter and frequently mounted without the music, remained a favorite for many years. Sol Smith's♦ and Noah Ludlow's♦ version tacked on a happy ending to ensure its acceptance with less sophisticated audiences.

The most important Jewish playwrights of the era studiously avoided plays with Jewish themes or even Jewish characters, perhaps out of fear of rejection but more likely because they felt no need for advocacy. Best known was Mordecai Manuel Noah,♦ whose plays ranged from romantic melodrama to contemporary comedy such as *She Would Be a Soldier*♦ (1819). The Charlestonian Isaac Harby (1788–1828), who gained attention as an editor and drama critic as well as dramatist, wrote the well-received romantic revenge melodramas *The Gordian Knot* (1807) and *Alberti* (1819) before his early death, while Jonas B. Phillips (d.1862) created numerous claptrap melodramas during a busy career as director, but left behind only one superior play in the *Coriolanus*-like *Camillus* (1833).

The idea of the tragic Jewish beauty may have played a small part in public approval in this country of the great French actress Rachel.♦ Indeed, it is interesting that many of the earliest reigning Jewish stars were to be women, such as Rose Eytinge♦ and Sarah Bernhardt,♦ all of whom excelled at tragic parts, although these two women came sometime later. In the pre-Civil War period under discussion, however, characters such as the venal Solomon Isaac of *London Assurance*♦ (1841), the sleazy Melter Moss in *The Ticket-of-Leave Man*♦ (1863), as well as Fagin in numerous versions of *Oliver Twist* continued to typify the stage Jew. Augustin Daly's♦ earliest success came when he took another play dealing with the figure of the noble Jewess, S. H. von Mosenthal's *Deborah,* and transformed it into *Leah, the Forsaken*♦ (1863).

Following the Civil War both American society and its attitude toward Jews changed perceptibly. The number of Jews arriving in America increased sharply with the turmoil that upset Europe in the late 1840s. Many of these new arrivals soon began to make their mark importantly in business and elsewhere. But at the same time the new rich created by the War represented a moneyed upper stratum that often lacked the culture and tolerant philosophy of an older order. Moreover, it found itself confronting not only a rising Jewish presence but a growing number of Catholics, who were also perceived as an alien and possibly disruptive force. Religious and other groups suffered a pigeonholing previously unknown.

For the most part, during the last half of the century the stage picture of the Jew changed little, although many intellectuals attempted minor rebellions. One of the most interesting was the leading character of *Sam'l of Posen*♦ (1861), a character written to order for the Jewish actor M. B. Curtis by the Irish-American George H. Jessop.♦ Curtis was determined to offer a picture of an affectionate, kindly Jew with whom audiences could immediately sympathize. Ironically, while Curtis succeeded and had his biggest hit, he himself was long a controversial figure, often brought into court for his unethical behavior. Whether this notoriety reflected a certain bigotry or simply a response to genuinely unsocial behavior cannot be determined with certainty. Curtis aside, few Jewish actors of the era attained so much as secondary rank. Numerous memoirs of the era recall encountering a "Hebrew" performer here and there, although the writer rarely can remember the player's name. But even if the legitimate theatre was seemingly closed to Jews, except the infrequent leading lady, the vaudeville stage began offering outlets. On the other side of the footlights, Jews were becoming increasingly important as theatregoers. Looking back in her memoirs, Clara Morris♦ recalled "Hebrew citizens [as] enthusiastic and most generous patrons of the theatre," adding, "better judges of matters theatrical it would be hard to find."

Behind the scenes a similar state of affairs began to emerge. The late 19th century saw no American-Jewish playwrights of any significance, but American playgoers welcomed plays by European Jews. Among the most popular were Adolphe-Philippe D'Ennery♦ and Arthur Wing Pinero.♦ Pinero treated his occasional Jewish figures with circumspection and tact, but D'Ennery refused to create Jewish personages, noting, "If I had put a Jew on stage, naturally I would have been obliged to make him a usurer or a crook or a traitor, or some sort of nasty type . . . So what did I do? I completely eliminated the Jew. You won't find a single one in my plays." At the same time, the business side of the theatre started to attract a growing number of Jews. Jonas Philip's brother, H. B. Phillips, for example, was the manager of Ford's Theatre♦ until it was closed by the assassination of Lincoln. Jews soon entered the producing field both directly or as backers, but more importantly they increasingly took over the ownership and running of theatres. The Frohmans,♦ playwright David Belasco,♦ and Oscar Hammerstein♦ are prominent examples. The extent to which they rapidly took over virtual control of the American theatre became public with the formation in 1895 of the Theatrical Syndicate or Trust.♦ This group, which sought to monopolize major bookings, consisted almost entirely of Jews, headed by A. L. Erlanger.♦ Their success exacerbated some anti-Semitic tensions, largely because it gave to many a specific complaint and target, but their monopoly was broken after little more than a decade by other Jews, the Shubert♦ brothers. To this day the business end of the American theatre remains largely Jewish-dominated.

Early in the 20th century Jewish creative talent and Jewish performers came ever more into the forefront. Nowhere was this more evident than in the musical theatre, where one has only to think of such composers as Jerome Kern,♦ Irving Berlin,♦ Sigmund Romberg,♦ George Gershwin,♦ Richard Rodgers,♦ Arthur Schwartz,♦ and Harold Arlen.♦ Joe Weber,♦ Lew Fields♦ and his children, especially Herbert♦ and Dorothy,♦ Ira Gershwin,♦ and Lorenz Hart♦ were but a few of the other talented Jews to play important creative roles. Lew Fields was also a comedian of first rank. Fields, his partner Weber, and others such as Sam Bernard♦ gained fame initially as "Dutch" comedians, a term employed to suggest they used a German or, usually, Yiddish dialect. If many other early Jewish stars flourished as comedians or comic singers—Al Jolson,♦ Eddie Cantor,♦ and Fanny Brice♦ are notable examples—some Jewish performers distinguished themselves in more serious endeavors. Many of these came out of the Yiddish theatre, which had sprung up in the 1880s with the onrush of Russian-Jewish immigrants and which served as a platform for such famous players as Jacob Adler,♦ Bertha Kalish,♦ and Maurice Schwartz.♦

The treatment of Jews on stage began to change noticeably in the 1920s. Two totally different plays were pivotal to the change. One was a superficial, somewhat outlandish American comedy, *Welcome Stranger*♦ (1920), which was one of the earliest American theatre pieces to deal directly with native anti-Jewish sentiment. The other was John Galsworthy's ♦ perceptive and understanding examination of English anti-Semitism, *Loyalties* (1922), which nonetheless owed much of its success to the fact that it was perceived first and foremost as a rattling good thriller. The series that began with *Potash and Perlmutter* ♦ (1913), and the long-running *Abie's Irish Rose* ♦ (1922), although they trafficked almost entirely in comic stereotypes, helped move Jews into a social mainstream. Nevertheless, for many years Jews were depicted in American plays as people a bit apart socially, albeit not unlike others by nature.

Many of these plays were written by Jewish writers such as Aaron Hoffman ♦ and Montague Glass. ♦ Both writers and their plays were aiming for success in the broadest theatrical terms. Jewish writers of more serious purport, such as Elmer Rice ♦ and S. N. Behrman, ♦ also began to appear during this time as did such a uniquely talented figure as George S. Kaufman. ♦ But the real explosion of Jewish writing talent on Broadway occurred with the Depression. Historian Ellen Schiff has called Clifford Odets's ♦ *Awake and Sing!* ♦ (1933) "the earliest quintessentially Jewish play outside the Yiddish theatre," and it certainly signaled a movement away from the more universal or at least largely non-sectarian interests of even Rice, Behrman, or Kaufman toward interest in a specifically Jewish experience. The theatre of protest and rebellion that sprang up so violently in the 1930s seemed a particularly fertile field for Jewish playwrights, and has remained so long after the initial reasons for protest have receded into history. Thus, Arthur Miller, ♦ one of the two major American dramatists to emerge in the 1940s, wrote almost totally in this tradition, deriving much of his inspiration from Jewish life and Jewish concerns even when he couched in non-Jewish terms his stories such as *Death of a Salesman* ♦ (1949), which could be seen to examine the futility and emptiness of much lower-middle-class Jewish commercial life, or *The Crucible* ♦ (1953), which responds to the perennial Jewish story of unjust persecution. In a sense Miller might be said to be the ultimate Jewish-American playwright, in whose works Jewish problems are American problems while American dilemmas encompass Jewish dilemmas. A writer such as Paddy Chayefsky, ♦ on the other hand, remained more redolently Jewish and injected a distinctly Talmudic mysticism into some of his stories. In recent seasons the voguish thrust of plays with preminent Jewish characters, has been to show them interacting with blacks, as in *I'm Not Rappaport* ♦ (1985) and *Driving Miss Daisy* ♦ (1987).

Other important Jewish names, to cite but a few,

include Leonard Bernstein, ♦ Betty Comden ♦ and Adolph Green, ♦ Joseph Papp, ♦ Jerome Robbins, ♦ Stephen Sondheim, ♦ Neil Simon, ♦ and Jule Styne, ♦ as well as such performers as John Garfield ♦ and Eli Wallach. ♦

Not everyone has seen the large—disproportionately large in relation to their percentage of the population—contributions of American Jews to American theatre as beneficial. Writing in May 1933 in *Scribner's Magazine,* John Corbin, ♦ who had served as drama critic for the *Times* off and on from 1902 to 1933, complained of the "acrid intelligence of our new Jewry," insisting, "For years now Jewish playwrights have repeatedly attempted the thing Edmund Burke declared impossible, the indictment of the American people entire." The result, according to Corbin, was that "Americans of elder stock have suffered an eclipse of what is best in their drama heritage." What Corbin was attempting to state, in his own petulant, soured way, was nothing new. Years before Walter Prichard Eaton ♦ had gone to a library to borrow some Ibsen ♦ plays, and finding them all out inquired who had borrowed them. "The Jews," the librarian informed him. In short, regardless of how one editorializes, the Jews, so often excluded from mainstream establishments and thus able to observe those establishments with the fresh, if sometimes bitter eyes of the outsider, have long advocated change of one sort or another. Given the opportunity they have helped expand the horizons of the American stage, often thereby giving it both new depth and new breadth. This same advocacy of progress may at times have driven them to promote objectionable excesses in the name of intellectual freedom, but it has also resulted in such great forces for good as the early Theatre Guild, ♦ in its heyday the most exciting and responsible producer in American history. Only the Irish, among American minorities, can claim an influence on the American theatre equal to the Jewish loyalty and influence.

Jim, the Penman Sir Charles Young's drama, about an attractive forger who is eventually unmasked by a wife he had deceived, was presented by A. M. Palmer ♦ at the Madison Square Theatre ♦ on November 1, 1886, within months of its London premiere, and became what Odell ♦ called "one of the greatest triumphs in the history of the New York stage." Frederic Robinson was the first American Jim Ralston, but Charles Coghlan ♦ was among the later actors who scored successes in the part. The play was revived regularly for thirty years.

JOB, THOMAS, see *Uncle Harry*

Joe Turner's Come and Gone, a play in two acts by August Wilson. ◆ Produced at the Ethel Barrymore Theatre. March 27, 1988. 105 performances. NYDCCA.

At a turn-of-the-century black boarding house in Pittsburgh, a rather spooky Herald Loomis (Delroy Lindo) appears, claiming that he has escaped from Joe Turner's forced labor and is seeking his wife (Angela Bassett). He finds her, recognizes that she has become a religious fanatic, stabs himself, and walks out, leaving his wife to raise their child alone.

A note in the program claimed Turner was a historic figure.

John Loves Mary, a comedy in three acts by Norman Krasna. ◆ Produced by Richard Rodgers◆ and Oscar Hammerstein II, ◆ in association with Joshua Logan, ◆ at the Booth Theatre. February 4, 1947. 423 performances.

When John (William Prince) returns from the war he does so with an English bride. She is not his sweetheart, but the fiancée of a buddy who saved his life in the war. Since the girl is English, marrying her was the only way to get her into the country promptly. John's real love is Mary (Nina Foch), and when he returns her parents insist they marry at once. Obviously, John cannot until he divorces his English bride. Rather than simply tell the true story, John piles lie on lie. Each lie further complicates matters. Mary's father is a Senator, so the lies have far-reaching but ultimately harmless effects.

Several critics suggested that the play was a return to the seemingly moribund tradition of "farce-comedy," while Ward Morehouse◆ of the *Sun* concluded it was a play "definitely of the manufactured variety, and one for which there would be no second and third acts if the simple truth has been told in the first."

John Street Theatre The first permanent playhouse in New York, it was erected at the behest of David Douglass◆ and opened in December 1767. It remained the town's principal and, usually, only theatre for thirty-one years, when it was demolished after the erection of the Park Theatre. ◆ Dunlap◆ says that it was modeled after Philadelphia's Southwark Theatre◆ and that "It was principally of wood; an unsightly object, painted red." He adds that the stage was as large as that of London's Haymarket Theatre. The house was opened with *The Beaux Stratagem* and was naturally given over primarily to plays imported from England. Nevertheless, it was here that two historically important American plays had their premieres: Royall Tyler's◆ *The Contrast* ◆ (1787) and Dunlap's *The Father; or, American Shandyism*◆ (1789). During the Revolutionary War the playhouse was known as the Theatre Royal, but reverted to its original name after the end of hostilities. It then housed the American Company◆ first under Lewis Hallam◆ and John Henry, ◆ and later under John Hodgkinson. ◆

Johnny Belinda, a drama in three acts by Elmer Harris. Produced at the Belasco Theatre. September 18, 1940. 321 performances.

Belinda McDonald (Helen Craig) is a deaf mute held in contempt by her harsh father and her insensitive neighbors. When Dr. Jack Davidson (Horace McNally) arrives in her Prince Edward Island village he takes an instant liking to her, so sets about to teach her sign language. He slowly falls in love with her, even though she is pregnant with the child of a village ruffian, Locky McCormick (Willard Parker). After the child is born, McCormick attempts to take it from her. She kills him. Davidson defends her at the trial. She is acquitted and then agrees to marry the doctor.

Most critics found the play overwrought and even offensive, John Mason Brown◆ of the *Post* branding it "barely passable" and Richard Watts, Jr., ◆ in the *Herald Tribune* dismissing it as "just trash." Yet the play quickly found a loyal public. It was later made into a film which earned Jane Wyman an Academy Award for her performance.

Elmer Blaney Harris (1878–1966) was a Chicago-born playwright whose first produced play was *Sham* (1909). Apart from *Johnny Belinda,* his major successes were his collaboration with Oliver Morosco◆ on the libretto for *So Long Letty* (1916) and his comedy, *Young Sinners* (1929), in which a playboy suddenly finds himself a fervent moralist.

Johnny Johnson, a play with music in three acts by Paul Green. ◆ Music by Kurt Weill. ◆ Produced by the Group Theatre◆ at the 44th Street Theatre. November 19, 1936. 68 performances.

While Johnny Johnson (Russell Collins) is a quiet, dedicated pacifist, he eventually finds himself fighting in World War I, where he is wounded. As an act of protest, he sprays the Allied High Command with laughing gas. The act lands him in a mental institution. There he and his fellow inmates pretend they are great statesmen and establish a League of World Republics. When he is released, he returns home to peddle non-martial toys in his war-happy village.

Principal songs: Johnny's Song · Song of the Guns

Called by Stanley Green♦ a "daring fusion of music and satiric fantasy," the show mirrored the widespread pacifist feelings of the 1930s. Weill's first American musical, it was a failure, but enjoys frequent revivals away from Broadway and remained a regular attraction in Iron Curtain countries.

JOHNSON, ALBERT [RICHARD] (1910–67) The set designer credited with perfecting the use of revolving stages, which he employed to stunning effect in *The Band Wagon*♦ (1931), was born in La Crosse, Wis., and began his theatrical career painting scenery for the Farmingdale Opera House on Long Island. After studying briefly with Norman Bel Geddes,♦ he was hired at the age of nineteen to create the sets of *The Criminal Code*♦ (1929). His designs were praised for their realism, but he insisted he had not gone near a jail and that he would not work "from real life." The requirements of the play and its audience were what counted for him. His designs were also seen in *Three's a Crowd* (1930); *Face the Music* (1932); *As Thousands Cheer*♦ (1933); *Let 'Em Eat Cake* (1933); *Ziegfeld Follies of 1934*♦; *Life Begins at 8:40* (1934); *The Great Waltz* (1934); *Jumbo*♦ (1935); *Leave It to Me!*♦ (1938); *The Skin of Our Teeth*♦ (1942); and the 1956 revival of *Show Boat*. ♦

JOHNSON, JAMES WELDON, see *Johnson, J. Rosamond*

JOHNSON, J[OHN] ROSAMOND (1873–1954) and JAMES WELDON (1871–1938) The brothers, born in Jacksonville, Fla., were among the pioneers in black musicals. They were educated at Atlanta University and at Columbia. At the turn of the century, working with Bob Cole,♦ they began interpolating what were then called "coon songs" into Broadway musicals. Best remembered of their lyrics was that for "Under the Bamboo Tree," although they were not given proper credit on the published sheet music. Attempting to get away from this sterotype, they later wrote several highly thought of, if commercially disappointing, musicals, including *The Shoo-Fly Regiment* (1907) and *The Red Moon* (1909). Music publisher Edward B. Marks later recalled, "The Johnson brothers were emphatically new Negro. Their father was a minister—and they combined a clerical dignity, university culture, and an enormous amount of talent . . . They wrote songs sometimes romantic, sometimes whimsical, but they eschewed the squalor and squabbles, the razors, wenches and chickens of the first ragtime." Perceptions are relative, however, and today the difference between their work and that of other black writers of the time is seen as one of degree, not kind. Sensing this, perhaps, James left the theatre to pursue a career as a diplomat, poet, and essayist. J. Rosamond remained in the theatre and continued to provide music for black shows into the 1930s. Because these shows rarely had long runs, he was also forced to serve as musical director for his own and other shows and to act in black musicals. Among those in which he performed were *Porgy and Bess*♦ (1935), *Mamba's Daughters* (1939), and *Cabin in the Sky*♦ (1940).

JOHNSON, LAURENCE E., see *It's a Wise Child*

JOLSON, AL [né ASA YOELSON] (1886–1950) Born in Srednike in what is now Lithuania, he was brought to America when still a youngster. His family settled in Washington, D.C., where his father was a cantor. In the 1897–98 season he ran away from home to join Rich and Hoppe's Big Company of Fun Makers. He next worked in a circus and then as a super in the Washington tryout of *Children of the Ghetto* (1899), until his father forced him to return home. Within a few months he was back on stage, in vaudeville. For the next eleven years he moved back and forth between two-a-day, burlesque, and minstrelsy. He signed with the Shuberts♦ in 1911 and appeared in *La Belle Paree* when it opened the Shuberts' new flagship, the Winter Garden,♦ two months later. He performed in blackface, with an exuberance and warmth that quickly made him the most popular box-office attraction in New York. As one critic was later to write, "He sang with his old-time knee-slapping, breast-beating, eye-rolling ardor, sang with a faith that moved mountains and audiences." Major assignments followed in *Vera Violetta* (1911), *The Whirl of Society* (1912), *The Honeymoon Express* (1913), *Dancing Around* (1914), *Robinson Crusoe, Jr.* (1916), *Sinbad* (1918), *Bombo* (1921), and *Big Boy* (1925). Among the many songs he introduced in these shows, and with which he was afterwards identified, were "April Showers," "Avalon," "California, Here I Come," "My Mammy," "Rockabye Your Baby with a Dixie Melody," and "Toot, Toot, Tootsie! Goo'bye." In many of his early vehicles he reputedly often dismissed the cast and spent much of the evening singing to audiences from directly in front of the footlights or on ramps leading out into the house. His most famous pose was down on one knee, arms outstretched. By 1925 his popularity had begun to slip slightly, so following appearances in *Artists and Models* (1926), to whose cast he was added after the opening, and a tour in *A Night in Spain* (1927), he went to Hollywood, where he starred in the first "talkie," *The Jazz Singer,* and for a few years was a major film star. He returned to Broadway only twice, in *The Wonder Bar* (1931) and *Hold On to Your Hats* (1940), which he co-produced. In neither show did he play the blackface clown that made him famous.

Biography: *Jolson: The Legend Comes to Life,* Herbert G. Goldman, New York, 1988.

JONES, GEORGE, see *Count Joannes*

JONES, HENRY ARTHUR (1851–1929) Along with Pinero♦ and Shaw♦ a leading English dramatist of his day, he was an advocate of the tautly constructed problem play. He made his reputation in America as in England with his collaboration with Henry Herman, *The Silver King* (1883). On his own he later wrote such notable successes as *The Middleman* (1890), *The Dancing Girl* (1891), *The Bauble Shop* (1894), *The Masqueraders* (1894), *The Case of Rebellious Susan* (1894), *The Rogue's Comedy* (1896), *The Liars* (1898), and *Mrs. Dane's Defense* (1900). Although his gift for comic aphorisms was inferior to Wilde's♦ and his characters rarely as fascinating as Pinero's, his best works remain interesting period pieces.

JONES, JAMES EARL (b. 1931) The Mississippi-born black actor studied at the University of Michigan and with Lee Strasberg♦ before making his Broadway debut in *Sunrise at Campobello♦* (1958). He began to call himself to playgoers' attention when he essayed a number of roles for the New York Shakespeare Festival,♦ including Caliban, Mac-Duff, and Othello. His performance as Jack Jefferson, the despised black boxer, in *The Great White Hope♦* (1968), won him a Tony Award.♦ However, important roles for black actors continued to be hard to come by, so for many seasons he performed off-Broadway,♦ usually with the same New York Shakespeare Festival. In 1973 he played Hickey in a Circle in the Square♦ revival of *The Iceman Cometh,♦* and the following year was Lenny in a Broadway revival of *Of Mice and Men.♦* He won further laurels in 1982 when he played Othello on Broadway to Christopher Plummer's♦ Iago, then served as a replacement in *Master Harold and the Boys.* In 1987 he played Troy, who would keep the white world and Death at a distance in *Fences.♦* He has a deep, rich bass voice and strong physical presence.

JONES, JOSEPH STEVENS (1809–1877) The "indefatigable Dr. Jones"—playwright, actor, theatre manager, and surgeon—was one of the most prolific of American dramatists. Estimates of his output range from a low of 60 plays to a high of more than 150. He was born in Boston, and after making his acting debut in 1827 in Providence as Crack in *The Turnpike Gate,* returned to Boston. For the next ten years he acted regularly at one or another Boston playhouse. His first successful play, *The Liberty Tree; or, Boston Boys in '76,* was premiered in 1832, with the author in the part of "Yankee" Bill Ball. The next year his *The Green Mountain Boy* gave G. H. Hill♦ one of his most famous roles, Jedediah Homebred, the servant whose outrageous sayings disconcert his stuffy betters. In 1839 Jones assumed management of the Tremont Theatre and at the same time wrote one of his two most popular plays, *The People's Lawyer♦* (later better known as *Solon Shingle*). It describes the trial of a sincere but poor man falsely accused of theft. These plays were all on American themes and depicted recognizable American characters. But Jones also wrote many romantic melodramas "of a wild and strenuous type," such as *The Usurper; or, Americans in Tripoli* (1835?); *The Surgeon of Paris; or, The Massacre of the Huguenots* (1838); and *The Carpenter of Rouen; or, The Massacre of St. Bartholomew* (1840). Jones's letters suggest he was bitter about the chances of making a proper living in the theatre. When the Tremont was forced to close in 1843, he withdrew from the profession, returning only on occasion. His withdrawal was assisted by Harvard's making him a Doctor of Medicine that same year. Thereafter he practiced medicine and lectured on anatomy and physiology. On one of his rare returns in 1852 he wrote *The Silver Spoon,♦* the second of his two best-known plays. The play centered on the Honorable Jefferson S. Batkins, a rural delegate. It gave William Warren♦ one of his greatest roles and was played regularly as late as World War I. His last play was *Paul Revere and the Sons of Liberty* (1875).

JONES, MARGO (1913–1955) Born in the town of Livingston, Texas, she attended Texas State College for Women at a time when it had no drama department, and so majored in psychology. After graduation she worked at the Pasadena Playhouse♦ and other community theatres, until she was hired to be assistant director of the Federal Theatre Project♦ in Houston. The project was a failure, but she remained in Houston, producing plays for that city's recreation department. It was during this time that she first employed the arena-style stage so long identified with her. During the war she taught at the University of Texas. In 1944 she applied to the Rockefeller Foundation for a grant to open an arena theatre for professional repertory in Dallas. While waiting for that plan to come to fruition she helped direct *The Glass Menagerie*♦ (1945) and then directed Ingrid Bergman in *Joan of Lorraine*♦ (1946). Her Dallas auditorium opened in 1947 as Theatre '47, a name that was updated yearly. Among the plays first presented at her house were William Inge's♦ *Farther Off from Heaven* (later rewritten as *The Dark at the Top of the Stairs*♦); *Summer and Smoke*♦; and *Inherit the Wind.*♦ Even more important than the new talents she encouraged was her theatre's influence in spreading the vogue for arena-style staging. Her theatre closed in 1959, four years after her all too early death. In 1961 Jerome Lawrence♦ and Robert E. Lee♦ established the Margo Jones Award, given each year "to the producing manager of an American or Canadian theatre whose policy of presenting new dramatic works continues most faithfully in the tradition of Margo Jones."

JONES, Robert Edmond (1887–1954) One of the most influential figures in 20th-century American theatre, the New Hampshire-born designer, producer, director, and lecturer was educated at Harvard. He began designing sets in 1911, but it was his work for *The Man Who Married a Dumb Wife* (1915) that is said to have "sounded the note that began the American revolution in stage scenery." Jones rebelled against the various forms of realism that dominated set design at the time—the meticulously painted flats in general use or the careful reconstructions of Belasco.♦ "The artist," he was later to write, "should omit details, the prose of nature, and give only the spirit and the splendor." Not all his sets were so strikingly poetic, but after his death John Mason Brown♦ was to remember "The Renaissance glories of his backgrounds for *The Jest;* the ominous outline of the Tower of London which dominated his *Richard III;* the great arch at the top of the long flight of steps in John Barrymore's *Hamlet;* the brooding austerity of his New England farm house in *Desire Under the Elms;* the background of mirrors, as bright as Congreve's wit, in *Love for Love;* the lovely Sunday-school innocence of his cut-outs for *The Green Pastures;* the way in which he connected the portico of the Mannons' Greek Revival home in *Mourning Becomes Electra* with the house of Agamemnon; the subtle suggestions of decadence in his living room for *The Green Bay Tree;* the bold bursts of Chinese Red in *Lute Song;* or the George Bellows-like depths and shadows of his barroom for *The Iceman Cometh.*" In 1925 he joined forces with Kenneth MacGowan♦ and Eugene O'Neill♦ to produce Eugene O'Neill's♦ and other fine plays at the Greenwich Village Playhouse. Among the productions he directed were Gilbert♦ and Sullivan's♦ *Patience* (1924); and O'Neill's *The Fountain* (1925) and *The Great God Brown*♦ (1926). Most critics felt his direction was less innovative than his design work. With MacGowan he wrote *Continental Stagecraft* (1922).

Biography: *The Theatre of Robert Edmond Jones,* Ralph Rendelton (ed.), Middletown, Conn., 1959.

JONES, Tom, see *Fantasticks, The*

Juba, see *Lane, William Henry*

Jubilee, a musical comedy in two acts. Book by Moss Hart.♦ Lyrics and music by Cole Porter.♦ Produced by Sam H. Harris♦ and Max Gordon♦ at the Imperial Theatre. October 12, 1935. 169 performances.

As the anniversary of the coronation approaches, The King (Melville Cooper) and The Queen (Mary Boland♦) admit they have become jaded with their luxurious but constrained life. Prince James (Charles Walter) and Princess Diana (Margaret Adams) agree. When a royal nephew leads an insurrection the royal family rushes into seclusion and emerges incognito. The Queen flirts with a movie star, the Princess has a brief romance with a writer, and the Prince takes a celebrated dancer out for a night on the town. The King is happy to remain home, playing his beloved parlor games. Inevitably they are recognized, so when the insurrection dies aborning the royal family returns to its comfortable, restricted world.

Principal songs: Begin the Beguine · Just One of Those Things

The musical, suggested by the Silver Jubilee of the English royal family, was written while Hart and Porter were on a world cruise together. As they so often did on first hearing, many critics insisted Porter's score was not up to snuff. Time proved them wrong.

JUDAH, Mrs. [née Marietta Starfield] (1812?–83) Hailed as "San Francisco's Favorite Actress" and eventually as the "Grand Old Woman of the Western Stage," she was born in New York State and was married at an early age to actor Emmanuel Judah. They traveled together throughout the South until Judah was drowned in a shipwreck while sailing between Florida and Cuba in 1839. She made her New York debut a year later. In 1851 she remarried but contined to perform as Mrs. Judah. Shortly after this marriage she moved to San Francisco at the behest of Thomas Maguire.♦ The small, stocky, square-faced, and stern-visaged actress remained an important artist there for a quarter century. She was praised for a wide range of interpretations from shrews in contemporary comedies to Lady Macbeth, but her most famous role was the Nurse in *Romeo and Juliet,* which she first performed in 1855 and beside which, according to reliable critics, many a celebrated Juliet paled. Although she retired in 1878, she continued to play at benefits and similar special occasions until just before her death.

JUDAH, Samuel B[enjamin] H[elbert] (1804–76) Shortly after graduating from college in his native New York he wrote a melodrama, *The Mountain Torrent* (1820), in which a girl marries a man she does not love to save her father from financial ruin. Two years later he wrote a revenge melodrama, *The Rose of Arragon.* After the premiere of his last play, a historical comedy, *A Tale of Lexington* (1922), he devoted the rest of his life to practicing law. Although most scholars condemn Judah's writing as absurdly stilted and his dramatic scenes as minimal, the plays were not unpopular in their day.

Jujamcyn Theatres Founded in 1956 by Virginia and James Binger, and named for their children Judy, James, and Cynthia, the organization became a major force on Broadway in the last quarter of the 20th century. It operates the Eugene O'Neill, the Martin Beck, the St. James, the Virginia, and the Walter Kerr (formerly, Ritz). It actively encourages productions and has selected so intelligently that its record of housing hits is outstanding. Rocco Landesman, the company's president, is credited with much of this success.

JULIA, Raul (b. 1940) Born in San Juan and educated at the University of Puerto Rico, his first New York appearance was in an off-Broadway mounting of *La Vida Es Sueño.* He has played major roles, ranging from Shakespeare through Shaw and Coward, with such groups as the New York Shakespeare Festival♦ and the Circle in the Square.♦ However, he is probably best known to Broadway audiences as the leading man in two musicals: *Two Gentlemen of Verona* (1971) and *Nine*♦ (1982).

Julius Caesar By far the most popular of Shakespeare's Roman histories, the work is believed to

have been first performed in America in Charleston, S.C., in 1774. Most of the great 19th-century tragedians appeared in it. Thomas Abthorpe Cooper♦ long held a virtual monopoly on the role of Antony, although late in his career he was forced to portray Cassius while ceding the role of Antony to Edwin Forrest,♦ who did not make a particular success of it. For decades the drama was a standby at the Bowery Theatre.♦ The work also holds the dubious distinction of being the last play in which John Wilkes Booth♦ appeared in New York, when he acted Antony in 1864 to Edwin Booth's♦ Brutus and Junius Brutus Booth, Jr.'s Cassius. The most memorable modern production was Orson Welles's♦ modern-dress version for the Mercury Theatre,♦ staged in 1937 with anti-fascist slanting. It remains popular with collegiate and festival theatres.

Jumbo, a musical comedy in two acts. Book by Ben Hecht♦ and Charles MacArthur.♦ Lyrics by Lorenz Hart.♦ Music by Richard Rodgers.♦ Produced by Billy Rose♦ at the Hippodrome.♦ November 16, 1935. 233 performances.
Two feuding circus magnates, Matthew Mulligan (W. J. McCarthy) and John A. Considine (Arthur Sinclair), are dismayed to learn that their children, Matt, Jr. (Donald Novis) and Mickey Considine (Gloria Grafton), have fallen in love. Considine's problems are compounded by his drinking and his imminent bankruptcy. The money difficulties are solved when his unorthodox press agent, Claudius B. Bowers (Jimmy Durante♦), burns down Considine's house, allowing him to collect his insurance. And when the youngsters bring about a reconciliation between the two older men, Considine promises to put the bottle on the shelf.
Principal songs: Little Girl Blue · The Most Beautiful Girl in the World · My Romance
The show marked Rodgers and Hart's return from a four-year stay in Hollywood. It was also the last legitimate production to play the famed Hippodrome, which Rose reconstructed to make it resemble a circus arena. Gilbert Gabriel of the *American* found the entertainment "chockful of so many thrills, musical, scenic, gymnastic and humanitarian, it deserves an endowment as an institution."

June Moon, a comedy in three acts by Ring Lardner♦ and George S. Kaufman.♦ Produced by Sam H. Harris♦ at the Broadhurst Theatre. October 9, 1929. 273 performances.
Fred M. Stevens (Norman Foster) gives up his job as a shipping clerk in Schenectady to try his luck as a Tin Pan Alley lyricist. He hits it big when Paul Sears

(Frank Otto), who has been living off the meagre royalties of his song hit "Paprika," puts music to Fred's lyric for "June Moon." Success goes to Fred's head, and he abandons his old sweetheart, Edna Baker (Linda Watkins), in favor of the beautiful, but vicious and rapacious Eileen (Lee Patrick), Paul's sister-in-law. Eileen succeeds in persuading her sister, Lucille (Jean Dixon), to leave Paul and have an affair. She also sets about to live beyond Fred's means. Just as Fred is about to leave for Europe with Eileen—he has tickets as Mr. Frederick M. Stevens and wife—his eyes are opened up by the caustic pianist, Maxie (Harry Rosenthal). Fred asks Maxie if the steamship line would mind his changing wives. Maxie assures him there will be no problem, "If you don't do it in midstream."

Robert Littell of the *World* called the comedy "a lively show that gave *Tin Pan Alley* . . . a rich and merciless kidding." The work was based on Lardner's short story "Some Like 'Em Cold." Lardner later described the writing of the play in his "Second-Act Curtain."

Junior Miss, a comedy in three acts by Jerome Chodorov♦ and Joseph Fields.♦ Produced by Max Gordon♦ at the Lyceum Theatre. ♦ November 18, 1941. 710 performances.

Thirteen-year-old Judy Graves (Patricia Peardon) has seen too many movies and believed them all. Being an over-imaginative child she convinces herself that her father (Phillip Ober) is having an affair with his boss's daughter, Ellen (Francesca Bruning), and that her Uncle Willis (Alexander Kirkland) is a reformed criminal. To set matters right, she and her friend, Fuffy Adams (Lenore Lonergan), determine to mate Willis with Ellen. None of this sits well with Ellen's father, J. B. Curtis (Matt Briggs). With every move, Judy and Fuffy seem to make matters worse. Things return to normal only when Judy finds herself about to have her first date. She is now a young lady, a junior miss, with her own problems to work on.

Greeted by Brooks Atkinson♦ as "a harum-scarum antic and a darlin' play," *Junior Miss* was one of the first shows, at a time when the draft was taking many men and when women were beginning to look toward the forthcoming war effort, to use younger talents as principals and older performers in support. The comedy was based on short stories by Sally Benson, which had appeared in *The New Yorker*.

K

KALISH [also transliterated KALISCH or KALICH], BERTHA (1874–1939) Born in Galicia, when it was part of the Austro-Hungarian empire, she studied at the Lemberg Conservatory and appeared in Yiddish productions before moving to Rumania to become a leading lady in the Bucharest National Theatre. Anti-Semitic prejudices prompted her to sail for America. Her first New York appearances were in operetta at the Thalia Theatre, but she soon began to demonstrate her skill as a tragedienne and comedienne, appearing in Yiddish versions of *A Doll's House, Fedora, Madame Sans-Gêne,* and other contemporary plays. Her performance as the Jewess whose marriage to a Russian nobleman leads to tragedy in Jacob Gordin's◆ *The Kreutzer Sonata* (1902) brought many major New York critics to the Lower East Side to witness and praise her abilities. This was her greatest role, and after she perfected her English she played it on Broadway in 1906. Among her other English-speaking assignments were *Fedora* (1905), *Monna Vanna* (1905), *Sappho and Phaon* (1907), *Marta of the Lowlands* (1908), *The Unbroken Road* (1909), and *The Witch* (1910). After she played in *The Riddle: Woman* (1918), failing eyesight forced her to act less frequently, though she did make occasional appearances as late as 1924, when she revived *The Kreutzer Sonata,* in 1926, when she portrayed the title role in *Magda,* and finally in 1935, when she revived *Sappho*. She was described as "a woman of classic beauty with a magnificent voice."

KALMAN, EMMERICH (1882–1953) The Hungarian-born composer of Viennese operetta◆ found Americans cool to his first imported work, *The Gay Hussars* (1909). However, his lovely collection of waltzes for *Sari* (1914) turned the tide. His fine score helped *Miss Springtime* (1916) chalk up a run, but his work for *Her Soldier Boy* (1916) needed interpolations. *The Riviera Girl* (1917), which used many of his songs from *Czardasfürstin,* was also subjected to interpolations. Although his *Die Bajadere* was a failure as *The Yankee Princess* (1922), despite its superb melodies, he scored two major successes with *Countess Maritza* (1926), his most famous work, and *The Circus Princess* (1927). Later in 1927 he composed much of the music for an American musical, *Golden Dawn,* which was only a moderate success. While a refugee during World War II he wrote the lovely melodies for *Marinka* (1945), but when the show opened disdain for operetta was at a peak and it quickly closed. Yet despite his failures and while Lehar's◆ *The Merry Widow*◆ was a far bigger hit than any of his works, on the whole he was probably the most successful of all 20th-century Viennese composers on American stages.

KALMAR, BERT (1884–1947) While best known as a lyricist and librettist, he began his career as a child magician in tent shows and later appeared in vaudeville. In 1923 he teamed with Harry Ruby◆ to create the songs for *Helen of Troy, New York*. Among his subsequent hits, all written with Ruby, were *The Ramblers* (1926), which included "All Alone Monday"; *The Five O'Clock Girl* (1927), remembered for "Thinking of You"; *Good Boy* (1928), whose score contained "I Wanna Be Loved by You"; and the Marx Brothers◆ vehicle *Animal Crackers* (1928), from which came "Hooray for Captain Spalding." After a brief Hollywood career in the 1930s, he was last represented on Broadway by *High Kickers* (1941).

KANDER, JOHN [HAROLD] (b. 1927) Born in Kansas City, Mo., he studied at Oberlin College and Columbia prior to spending nine years in journeyman work at summer theatres and as an orchestrator. His first score was heard in *A Family Affair* (1962). That same year he was introduced to Fred Ebb.◆ Their debut as a team was with *Flora, the Red Menace* (1965). A year later they enjoyed their first hit, *Cabaret*◆ (1966). Subsequent musicals were *The Happy Time*◆ (1968), *Zorba* (1968), *70, Girls, 70* (1971), *Chicago*◆ (1975), *The Act* (1977), *Woman of the Year* (1981), and *The Rink* (1984). Stanley Green◆ has written, "If, like their creators, [their] songs have escaped individual acclaim, they have nevertheless performed the demanding function of heightening the emotion and strengthening the texture of the varied dramatic works for which they were created."

KANE, HELEN [née SCHROEDER] (1904–66) Celebrated as the "Boop-Boop-a-Doop" Girl, the petite, moon-faced, baby-voiced singer, who was born in New York, was one of the meteoric stars of the late 1920s. She appeared on Broadway in *A Night in Spain* (1927) and *Good Boy* (1928), introducing "I Wanna Be Loved by You" in the latter. For a brief time she was a headliner in vaudeville and appeared in early talkies. Her last Broadway role was in *Shady Lady* (1933).

KANIN, GARSON (b. 1912) The Rochester-born playwright and director began his career as an actor, playing a small part in *Little Ol' Boy* (1933). For several years he served as assistant director to George Abbott,♦ before accepting directorial chores for *Hitch Your Wagon* (1937). After serving in World War II he achieved success both as director and playwright with his *Born Yesterday*♦ (1946), in which a crass junk-dealer's attempt to educate his mistress backfires. That same year he directed *Years Ago,*♦ a play by his wife, Ruth Gordon.♦ He later wrote and directed three interesting, but unsuccessful plays: *The Smile of the World* (1949) in which the wife of a stodgy Supreme Court justice falls in love with his clerk; *The Rat Race* (1949) depicting the romance of a jazz musician and a dance-hall hostess; and *The Live Wire* (1950) centering on a group of actors. Subsequent directorial assignments included *The Diary of Anne Frank*♦ (1955); *A Hole in the Head*♦ (1957); the musical *Do Re Mi* (1960), for which he wrote the libretto; and *Funny Girl*♦ (1964). He was also active in television and films, sometimes working in collaboration with his wife.

KAPP, JACK (1901–49) The Chicago-born record company executive was president of Decca Records from 1934 until his death. It was in this capacity that he produced the original cast recording of *Oklahoma!*♦ in 1943. The album was so successful that it sparked a parade of similar recordings of other shows. Oddly, the English had been producing original cast recordings since the turn of the century, but Americans had not. One quirky result was that the only large-scale cast recordings of American shows before 1943 were recordings made with their London casts.

Katinka, an operetta in three acts. Book and lyrics by Otto Harbach.♦ Music by Rudolf Friml.♦ Produced by Arthur Hammerstein♦ at the 44th Street Theatre. December 23, 1915. 220 performances.

Katinka (May Naudain) loves Ivan Dimitri (Samuel Ash), so when she is forced to marry Boris Strogoff (Count Lorrie Grimaldi) she runs away and

hides in a harem. Matters are resolved when it is learned that Boris is already married to another woman.

Principal songs: Allah's Holiday · Rackety Coo · 'Tis the End

Although this operetta competed for attention with the far more American and contemporary *Very Good Eddie*♦ and *Stop! Look! Listen!,* which opened the same week, it held its own for public esteem.

KAUFMAN, GEORGE S[IMON] (1889–1961) The great comic playwright and director was born in Pittsburgh and served on the staffs of newspapers in Washington, D.C., and New York before joining with Marc Connelly♦ to write his first successful play, *Dulcy*♦ (1921), which centered on a brainless, meddling young wife who inadvertently helps her husband in a business matter. The collaboration continued for three more years and resulted in seven additional offerings. Most notable were *To the Ladies*♦ (1922), which, in something of an about-face, dealt with an intelligent wife who saves her husband from making a fool of himself; *Merton of the Movies*♦ (1922), based on a story by Harry Leon Wilson♦ and recounting the adventures of a film-struck grocery clerk in Hollywood; and *Beggar on Horseback*♦ (1924), an expressionistic fantasy which satirized modern business. In 1924 he also collaborated with Edna Ferber♦ for the first time. The play was *Minick,* in which an old man must choose between living with his child or in an old-age home. His next play was his only successful solo effort, *The Butter and Egg Man*♦ (1925), a story of an innocent whose eyes are opened when he backs a Broadway show. His other popular works in the late 1920s were librettos for two Marx Brothers♦ vehicles, *The Cocoanuts* (1925) and *Animal Crackers* (1928), the latter written with Morrie Ryskind; *The Royal Family*♦ (1927), written with Miss Ferber and dealing with a theatrical family not unlike the Barrymores; and *June Moon*♦ (1929), a collaboration with Ring Lardner♦, which offered a jaundiced view of Tin Pan Alley. Although he first worked with Moss Hart♦ on *Once in a Lifetime*♦ (1930), one of the period's best travesties of Hollywood, most of his memorable work in the early 1930s was in musicals. With Ryskind he revised his political satire, *Strike Up the Band*♦ (1930). He had originally written the libretto alone for the musical's unsuccessful 1927 tryout. In 1932 he, Ryskind, and Ira Gershwin♦ were awarded a Pulitzer Prize♦ for an even more brilliant political spoof, *Of Thee I Sing*♦ (1931). He also contributed the sketches to the 1931 revue, *The Band Wagon.* ♦ *Dinner at Eight* ♦ (1932), written with Ferber and describing an elegant, if disastrous soirée, was his major straight play of the time. After the failure of *Let 'Em Eat Cake* (1933), a third, more bitter political satire, he rejoined Hart to write *Merrily We Roll Along* ♦ (1934), which examined the guilt feelings of a popular playwright. His 1936 collaboration with Ferber, *Stage Door,* ♦ depicted the heartaches and triumphs of some aspiring actresses. That same year he began a series of plays with Hart, the best being *You Can't Take It with You* ♦ (1936), a story of a zanily unconventional family, which won him another Pulitzer Prize; the libretto of *I'd Rather Be Right* ♦ (1937), a send-up of the New Deal; *The Man Who Came to Dinner* ♦ (1939), which spotlighted a family who have an Alexander Woollcott-like curmudgeon imposed on them; and *George Washington Slept Here* ♦ (1940), in which a city family decides to renovate an old farm. Thereafter he enjoyed fewer successes. In 1944 he helped John P. Marquand dramatize Marquand's novel, *The Late George Apley.* ♦ *The Solid Gold Cadillac* ♦ (1953), written with Howard Teichmann, told of a little old lady's confrontation with big business. With his second wife, Leueen McGrath, he wrote the libretto for *Silk Stockings* (1955), a musical version of the film *Ninotchka.* Kaufman was also a much-sought-after director. Besides staging many of his own plays, he directed such hits as *The Front Page* ♦ (1928), *My Sister Eileen* ♦ (1940), and *Guys and Dolls* ♦ (1950).

To the public, Kaufman was a master of the barbed riposte, but his professional associates also admired his ability as a play doctor and his impeccable sense of timing.

Biography: *George S. Kaufman: His Life, His Theater,* Malcolm Goldstein, New York, 1979.

KAUSER, ALICE (1872–1945) Born in Budapest, where her father was the American consul, she received most of her schooling on the Continent. Her mother was a celebrated opera singer, Berta Gester, who introduced her to many theatrical figures. These connections served her handsomely when she became a play broker in the late 1890s. She helped get several Sardou ♦ plays produced here and was one of the first to take up cudgels for Ibsen. ♦ She also fought to achieve recognition for such early American clients as Edward Sheldon ♦ and Langdon Mitchell, ♦ proving instrumental in the production of such plays as *Salvation Nell* ♦ and *The New York Idea.* ♦ Among her other clients were Channing Pollock ♦ and Edward Childs Carpenter. ♦

KAY, HERSHY (1919–81) Although better known as a composer of light concert pieces and of the music for such modern ballets as *Stars and Stripes,* the Philadelphia native was also an important orchestrator of Broadway musicals. He was a classmate of Leonard Bernstein ♦ at the Curtis Institute of Music, and his first major Broadway assignment was Bernstein's *On the Town* ♦ (1944). His notably breezy arrangements were later heard in such shows as *The Golden Apple* ♦ (1954), *Candide* ♦ (1956), *Milk and Honey* (1961), *A Chorus Line* ♦ (1975), *On the Twentieth Century* (1977), and *Evita* (1980).

KAYE, DANNY [né DAVID DANIEL KOMINSKY] (1913–87) The slim, supple, Brooklyn-born comedian worked in vaudeville and at summer camps before making his Broadway debut in *The Straw Hat Revue* (1939). He called attention to himself as the effeminate Russell Paxton in *Lady in the Dark* ♦ (1941), in which he sang the tongue-twisting "Tschaikowsky." After appearing in *Let's Face It!* ♦ (1941) he left for Hollywood and, except for appearances in vaudeville at the Palace ♦ and at the Ziegfeld, ♦ did not return to New York until he starred in the musical *Two by Two* (1970), in which he clowned as the Biblical Noah.

Biography: *The Danny Kaye Story,* Kurt Singer, New York, 1958.

KAZAN, ELIA (b. 1909) Born in Istanbul, but raised in America, he attended Williams College and did graduate work at Yale before joining the Group Theatre ♦ as an apprentice. He appeared with the company as an actor in such plays as *Men in White* ♦ (1933), *Waiting for Lefty* ♦ (1935), *Johnny Johnson* ♦ (1936), *Golden Boy* ♦ (1937), and *The Gentle People* ♦ (1939). His first major directorial assignment was *Casey Jones* (1938), but it was his freshly imaginative staging of *The Skin of Our Teeth* ♦ (1942) that gave his career its major boost. Among his subsequent successes were *Harriet* ♦ (1943); *One Touch of Venus* ♦ (1943); *Deep Are the Roots* ♦ (1945); *All My Sons* ♦ (1947), which he co-produced; *A Streetcar Named Desire* ♦ (1947); *Death of a Salesman* ♦ (1949); *Tea and Sympathy* ♦ (1953); *Cat on a Hot Tin Roof* ♦ (1955); *The Dark at the Top of the Stairs* (1957), which he also co-produced; *J.B.* ♦ (1958); *Sweet Bird of Youth* ♦ (1959); and *After the Fall* ♦ (1964). He staged this last play when he assumed the co-directorship (with Robert Whitehead ♦) of the Repertory Theatre of Lincoln Center. ♦ But his tenure was not a success, and after he withdrew he retired from the theatre in general. He was also a founding member of the Actors

Studio.♦ As his list of credits suggests, he was the most important American director of the late 1940s and the 1950s, bringing a vitality and poetic intensity to virtually all his efforts. John Mason Brown♦ observed of his work on *Streetcar,* "Mr. Kazan's direction is brilliantly creative. His imagination is at all times equal to Mr. Williams'. He succeeds in combining stylization with realism. He is able to capture to the full the inner no less than the outer action of the text. He knows when to jab a climax, when to rely on mood, when to focus the attention pitilessly on the principals, or when to establish . . . the tenement atmosphere."

KEAN, CHARLES [JOHN] (1811–68) The son of Edmund Kean,♦ he had only begun his career as an actor when he made his American debut at the Park Theatre♦ in 1830 as Richard III. He continued by offering many of the same parts associated with his father, including Shylock, Othello, Hamlet, and Sir Giles Overreach. Most critics judged him an immature but promising artist, although the seeds for his later success were firmly planted. He returned in 1837 and, with his wife Ellen Tree,♦ in 1845 and 1864. Their repertory consisted of many of the standard classic favorites interspersed with such once popular contemporary works as *The Hunchback*♦ and *The Iron Chest.* James E. Murdoch♦ recalled, "Charles Kean was an imitator of his father's style of acting. But to the method which made the elder Kean famous the son added a grace and finish that gave repose and beauty to what would otherwise have been a mere copy . . . Of all our tragedians of the analytic and passionate order, approaching the mechanical in execution, Charles Kean may be said to have been the most finished, and yet the most earnest." In her autobiography, *Life on the Stage,* Clara Morris♦ has left a vivid, endearing picture of him on his last American visit.

Biography: *The Life and Theatrical Times of Charles Kean,* John W. Cole, London, 1859.

KEAN, EDMUND (1787?–1833) The first great English actor to visit America while still at the height of his powers, he made his debut at the Anthony Street Theatre in 1820 as Richard III, the most popular Shakespearean role of his era. The *Evening Post* remarked, "We saw the most complete actor . . . that ever appeared on our boards," continuing, "Mr. Kean appears to be beneath the middle size . . . his features are good and his eye particularly expressive and commanding; his voice, in which he is most deficient, is, however, in its lower tones, sonorous, and he has the power of throwing it out so as to be

heard at the extremity of the house." He followed his Richard with Othello, Shylock, Brutus (in Payne's♦ tragedy), Hamlet, Sir Giles Overreach, King Lear, and Macbeth. He performed for a percentage of the gross and for many nights received £125, far and away the highest figure yet paid to a performer in America. However, his tour ran into problems when he refused to appear before an uncrowded house in Boston later in the season. The brouhaha that ensued prompted him to leave the country. After he returned in 1825 less temperate journals revived the controversy, and when he attempted to appear again as Richard at the Park Theatre♦ a riot broke out. He soon mollified playgoers, and acted around the country for the rest of the season and part of the next, but never again revisited America.

Biography: *Edmund Kean: The Story of an Actor,* W. J. Macqueen-Pope, Edinburgh, 1960.

KEAN, THOMAS (fl. mid-18th century) Little is known about this early actor-manager. In 1749, with his partner Walter Murray, ♦ he staged some Shakespearean and Restoration revivals as well as contemporary plays in Philadelphia, and a year later appeared in a similar repertory with what may have been the same troupe in New York. Among the plays were *The Beggar's Opera, Richard III,* ♦ *Cato,* and *Love for Love.* Kean's New York stay was marred by conflicts with authorities and apparently by religious opposition, by atrocious weather, and by accusations that he oversold his houses. Although this overselling may have been either accidental or a reflection of a certain lack of ethics, it also suggests that a definite demand for theatricals existed at the time. After New York, he headed a company of players in Virginia, then disappears from the record.

KEANE, DORIS (1881–1945) One of many performers remembered for a single role, this piquant beauty was born in Michigan and educated largely in Europe. She apparently also spent some time at the American Academy of Dramatic Arts♦ and with the school associated with the Empire Theatre. ♦ Her first professional assignment was a small role in *Whitewashing Julia* (1903), although reviews for that play suggest she had caught some critics' eyes in earlier student productions. She rose rapidly to leading roles such as Joan Thornton, the neglected wife, in Clyde Fitch's♦ *The Happy Marriage* (1909); Bess Marks, who remains loyal to her wrongly imprisoned husband, in a 1911 revival of *The Lights o'London;* and Mimi, the vulgar music-hall performer, in the *The Affairs of Anatol* (1912). In 1913 she first appeared as Margherita Cavallini, the great opera star who forsakes her young clergyman lover rather than ruin his career, in Edward Sheldon's◆ *Romance.* ◆ Walter Prichard Eaton wrote of her in this part, "Miss Keane . . . has dark, magnetic eyes, a curious mouth that is extremely mobile and can suggest either impish glee or profound sorrow very easily . . . and a general attractiveness of face and figure which arrests our attention. Having arrested our attention, we soon realize other features of her personality, notably her humor, not without its capacity for a sarcastic edge, her sensitiveness to impressions, her alert mind. We sense her as rather an unusual person." She played Cavallini uninterruptedly in America and Europe for the next five years and returned to the role in regular revivals until the late 1920s. Although she afterward appeared as the heroine in several other plays, among them a 1919 revival of *Romeo and Juliet*◆ and Eugene O'Neill's◆ failed *Welded* (1924), her only other success was as Catherine the Great in *Czarina* (1922), a European play especially revised for her by Sheldon.

KEARNS, ALLEN (1893–1956) A native of Ontario, he began his career as a chorus boy in musicals and with a vaudeville act. By the 1920s he was in demand as a leading man. He appeared in such musicals as *Mercenary Mary* (1925); *Tip-Toes*◆ (1925), in which he sang "That Certain Feeling"; *Funny Face*◆ (1927), in which he introduced " 'S Wonderful"; *Here's Howe* (1928); and *Girl Crazy*◆ (1930), in which he performed "Embraceable You."

KEENE, LAURA (1826?–73) The early history of this London-born actress-manager is obscure. Even her birth year has been given as anywhere from 1820 to 1836, although her daughters insisted their mother was forty-seven at her death. Her real surname is given as Foss, Moss, or Lee. Similarly, the year and place of her professional debut are uncertain, though it is known she did at one time act with Madame Vestris. She came to America in 1852 and first appeared before New York audiences as Albina Mandeville in J. W. Wallack's◆ mounting of *The Will.* In the year she remained at Wallack's she became a popular favorite, but she left without warning to assume management of a Baltimore theatre. When this failed she toured California and Australia before returning to New York in 1855 to open her own playhouse. Her return coincided with the retirement of William Burton, ◆ so her ensemble quickly became Wallack's only serious rival. Although she staged some highly praised Shakespear-

ean mountings, her company was best known for its contemporary works. Among her successes were *Camille,* ◆ *Jane Eyre, The Heir-at-Law* (a somewhat older piece), and *Our American Cousin.* ◆ It was in these productions that Joseph Jefferson◆ and E. A. Sothern◆ rose to prominence. Her mounting of *Our American Cousin* established a long-run record at "a first class house," although *Uncle Tom's Cabin*◆ and *The Drunkard*◆ had run longer at more popular theatres. The onset of the Civil War presented financial problems for her, which she met initially by offering elaborate musical spectacles. When these finally palled, she abandoned her theatre and took to the road. She was playing *Our American Cousin* at Ford's Theatre◆ in Washington when Lincoln was assassinated there. While she had no part in the assassination, her career never recovered from her association with the incident.

Although a somewhat puffy-faced, heavy-featured woman, she was, Jefferson noted, "esteemed a great beauty in her youth; even afterwards her rich and luxuriant auburn hair, clear complexion and deep chestnut eyes, full of expression, were greatly praised; but to me it was her style and carriage that commanded admiration, and it was this quality that won her audience. She had, too, the rare power of varying her manner, assuming the rustic walk of a milkmaid or the dignified grace of a queen."

Biography: *The Life of Laura Keene,* John Creahan, Philadelphia, 1897.

KEENE, THOMAS WALLACE [né EAGELSON or EAGLESON] (1840–98) An actor long more popular in small towns than in New York or other major theatre centers, he spent his early career in such playhouses as the Bowery, ◆ when it was turning to melodrama, and Wood's, under Edward Eddy. ◆ There he learned the emotive, scene-chewing style of acting he was never fully to abandon. Although he played in support of such great actors as J. H. Hackett◆ and Edwin Booth, ◆ he seems to have profited little from them. His Richard III was much admired in the backwaters, but his repertory consisted largely of tried and true melodramas such as *Across the Continent*◆; *Drink (L'Assommoir); The French Spy;* and *Ten Nights in a Barroom.* ◆ He was said to be a huge, florid man.

KEISTER, GEORGE An architect whose New York houses include the Astor, Belasco, Earl Carroll, George M. Cohan's, and Selwyn theatres.

KEITH, B[ENJAMIN] F[RANKLIN] (1846–1914) Born in Hillsboro, N.H., he left his family farm to join a circus. He worked for a time under P. T. Barnum♦ and later with Forepaugh's and Batcheller and Doris's circuses. By the early 1880s he had moved into the realm of theatre management. In 1885 he took over the Gaiety Musée in Boston. He claimed that a dream convinced him of the value of continuous vaudeville, which he initiated at the theatre. His policy's success was immediate, and he soon owned a series of theatres east of the Mississippi. At the turn of the century he enlarged his chain by merging with F. F. Proctor,♦ at the same time forming the United Booking Office♦ to control the hiring and firing of performers. At its height his organization controlled well over a hundred theatres. There is some dispute as to whether he or his associate E. F. Albee♦ was the driving force behind the company's expansion and tactics, but it is generally agreed that Keith was responsible for the rigid moral code which all performers in his theatres were required to adhere to.

KELCEY, HERBERT [né LAMB] (1856–1917) The eldest son of a well-to-do English country family, he was intended for the army, but elected to become an actor instead. He changed his name to avoid hurting his family. After two years on English stages he came to America, where he made his debut with Wallack's♦ company in 1882. Two years later he moved to the Madison Square Theatre♦ company, but soon returned to Wallack's. In 1887 he became the leading man in Daniel Frohman's♦ Lyceum Theatre♦ ensemble, remaining there nine seasons. He left in 1896 to replace Maurice Barrymore♦ as Alan Kendrick in *The Heart of Maryland.*♦ The round-faced, heavy-lidded, but handsome actor became a star with his appearance as Edward Fletcher, the dissipated, balefully influential man-of-the-world, in Clyde Fitch's♦ *The Moth and the Flame* (1898). Important assignments followed as des Grieux in *Manon Lescaut* (1901) and as Richard Milbank, the compassionate financeer, in *The Daughters of Men* (1906). In 1907 he played William De Burgh Cockane in Shaw's♦ *Widowers' Houses.* Whether because of age or because he failed to enlist the support of sufficient New York playgoers, much of his remaining career was spent performing major roles in touring companies of Broadway successes. These plays included *The Bridge, The Walls of Jericho,* and *The Thief.* His last New York appearance was as Dr. Chilton in *Pollyanna* (1916).

KELLAR, HARRY (1842–1922) The Pennslyvania-born magician began to make his name in the mid-1880s with his incomparable sleight-of-hand. Doug-

las Gilbert, the vaudeville historian, has written, "Few could approach him in deftness of touch; remarkable, for he was an awkward, powerfully built man with such enormous hands his apparatus had to be specially made for him." In time he developed many larger tricks featuring levitation and disappearing rooms. Apparently his education was meager, for one of the most blistering reviews he received was from the acerbic Alan Dale, who criticized not his performance, but his grammar and pronunciation. His response was to take a correspondence course in English, and his diction soon improved.

KELLERD, JOHN E. (1863–1929) The English actor first came to America in 1883 to appear at the Boston Museum.♦ Subsequently he played important roles in such New York productions as *Held by the Enemy*♦ (1886), *Shenandoah*♦ (1889), and *The Heart of Maryland*♦ (1895). He pioneered in presenting classical Greek drama professionally. However, his place in American theatrical history came when he performed Hamlet in New York for 102 consecutive showings in 1912, thus surpassing Edwin Booth's♦ old record.

KELLERMANN, ANNETTE (1887?–1975) Born in Australia, she learned to swim as therapy for a childhood attack of polio. She was in her teens when she won attention by swimming long distances in the rivers of Europe. Her feats led her into British music-halls and in 1907 to America, where her vaudeville act rapidly made her a star. E. F. Albee♦ placed mirrors around the stage so audiences could see her performance better. In 1914 she appeared in the Hippodrome♦ extravaganza *Neptune's Daughter* and returned to the theatre to play in *A Daughter of the Gods* (1916). Shortly afterwards she organized "Annette Kellermann's Big Show," a 40-minute turn in which she sang, danced, and did acrobatics, but no swimming. The act was only moderately successful, since theatregoers thought of her primarily as a swimmer. Within a few years her vogue had waned, so she retired.

KELLEY, EDGAR STILLMAN (1857–1944) The distinguished American composer was born in Sparta, Wisc., and educated at the Chicago Conservatory of Music. Much of his work for the theatre was incidental music, notably his material for an 1885 San Francisco revival of *Macbeth*♦ and for William Young's♦ dramatization of *Ben Hur*♦ (1899). For a time in the late 1880s and early 1890s he conducted comic opera, and in 1892 wrote the score for one,

Puritania; or, The Earl and the Maid of Salem. He has been described as "a composer of refinement and taste," whose music demonstrated a marked Teutonic bent.

KELLY, ANTHONY PAUL, see *Three Faces East*

KELLY, EMMETT [LEO] (1898–1979) Born in Sedan, Kansas, he began his professional career as a cartoonist in 1920, creating the character of "Weary Willie." A year later he joined the circus, first as an acrobat, but from 1931 until his death performing as a sad-faced cabbage-chewing clown whom he named after his cartoon character. He spent fourteen seasons with Ringling Bros. and Barnum and Bailey Circus, and was the most famous circus clown of his generation.

KELLY, GEORGE [EDWARD] (1887–1974) The Philadelphia-born playwright was the brother of Walter C. Kelly,♦ the vaudevillian, and John B. Kelly, the Olympic sculler, as well as the uncle of Princess Grace of Monaco. He entered the theatre when he was twenty-one, playing juvenile roles, then drifted into vaudeville about 1916. There he performed in his own sketches. He wrote his first full-length play, *Mrs. Ritter Appears,* in 1917, but it failed to reach Broadway. His first successful work was *The Torch-Bearers*♦ (1922), a satire on the little theatre movement. His next comedy, *The Show-Off*♦ (1924), centered on a young braggart and barely missed winning a Pulitzer Prize,♦ but he did win the award a year later for *Craig's Wife*♦ (1925), a study of a blindly possessive woman. *Daisy Mayme*♦ (1926) recounted the romance of a shrewish spinster and a put-upon middle-aged bachelor. In 1927 he wrote sketches for the revue *A la Carte,* along with a powerful study of the degeneration of a rich, spoiled woman, *Behold the Bridegroom.*♦ Many critics felt the play baffling and sensed a certain falling away in Kelly's heretofore sure theatricality. Certainly his next two plays demonstrated little of his earlier skill. *Maggie the Magnificent* (1929) depicted the conflict between a vulgar mother and her sensitive daughter. In *Philip Goes Forth* (1931), a talentless playwright renounces his aspirations and enters his father's business. Apparently embittered by these two failures, Kelly did not return to the theatre until he offered *Reflected Glory* (1936), in which an actress must choose between career and family. This, too, failed, and the playwright had only two more plays produced, both in the mid-1940s and both failures. *The Deep Mrs. Sykes* (1945) was a darkly probing study of a woman who refuses to believe that her unkind intuitions about her husband are wrong, while *The Fatal Weakness* (1946) focused on an absurdly romantic woman whose behavior loses her her husband. At his best Kelly was a superb technician, trenchant observer, and satirist of human folly. But a certain coldness and misanthropy eventually made his later plays unpalatable to most critics and theatregoers.

KELLY, GREGORY (1891?–1927) The boyish-looking actor from New York, whose promising career was cut short by his early death, performed in stock with his wife, Ruth Gordon,♦ then won rave notices as Willie Baxter, the puppy-love-lorn hero, in *Seventeen*♦ (1918), and as Peter Jones, the yokel looking to strike it rich on Broadway, in *The Butter and Egg Man*♦ (1925).

KELLY, PAUL (1899–1956) Born in Brooklyn, the lean, sternly handsome actor made his debut in 1907 in *A Grand Army Man.*♦ He spent time in stock before returning to Broadway as George Cooper in *Seventeen* (1918) and Robert Williams in *Penrod* (1918). He won praise for his performance as John Allen, the jazz-age husband destroyed by his hedonism, in *Up the Ladder* (1922), then enjoyed a long run as Barry McGill, who must help solve a bizarre murder, in *Whispering Wires* (1922). His next assignment was as Harry, the rejected lover, in *Chains* (1923). None of his subsequent roles in the 1920s and early 1930s were in successful plays, so he left for Hollywood in 1933. He is best remembered for two roles he played after he returned from films: Brigadier General K. C. Dennis, who agonizes over his orders which send his men on dangerous missions, in *Command Decision*♦ (1947), and Frank Elgin, the alcoholic actor trying for a comeback, in *The Country Girl*♦ (1950).

KELLY, WALTER C. (1873–1939) Famed as "The Virginia Judge," an act he performed in vaudeville, on the legitimate stage and in films for over thirty years, the pudgy comedian was born in Mineville, N.Y., and was the older brother of playwright George Kelly.♦ He planned on becoming a naval engineer, but while working as a shipyard machinist he visited the courtroom of the celebrated Judge Dudley Brown and saw in Brown possibilities for a rich character. He began acting in his courtroon sketches in 1899. However, it was not until Marie Dressler♦ included him in one of her entertainments that he achieved recognition. He performed in a baggy black alpaca coat, standing behind a pedestal and flourishing his gavel. Whether he was recounting the pleas of a poor black, a Southern gentleman, or an Irish laborer, his accents were perfect. Indeed George Ade♦ called him "storyteller to the world, prince of raconteurs, Phi Beta Kappa student of dialect . . . a humorist of the first order."

Autobiography: *Of Me I Sing,* New York, 1953.

KEMBLE, CHARLES (1775–1854) A member of a distinguished English acting family and father of Fanny Kemble,♦ he paid only one two-year visit to America and that relatively late in his career. He made his debut in 1832 at the Park Theatre♦ as Hamlet. He was warmly greeted, but was even more eagerly applauded for such later roles as Charles Surface and Benedick. Indeed, Wemyss♦ afterward looked back on him as "the best representative of high comedy belonging to the British stage." He was a rather boyishly handsome, curly-headed man, whose career in England had been overshadowed by those of his brother, John Philip, and sister, Mrs. Siddons, and whose American appearances were often distracted by adulation accorded his beautiful daughter. However, his polished performances established him as a model of an English gentleman and set an example for future American players.

Biography: *Charles Kemble, Man of the Theatre,* Jane Williamson, Lincoln (Nebraska), 1970.

KEMBLE, [FRANCES ANNE] FANNY (1809–93) This great beauty was the heir to a distinguished English acting tradition. Her father was Charles Kemble,♦ her uncle, John Philip Kemble, and her aunt, Mrs. Siddons. She came to America with her father in 1832, making her debut at the Park Theatre♦ as Bianca in *Fazio.* She continued by demonstrating her skill as Juliet, Portia, Belvidera, and as other classic heroines of the period's standard repertory. One of her most famous roles was Julia in *The Hunchback,*♦ a part she had created in England. She retired from the stage in 1834 following her marriage to Pierce Butler, later U.S. Senator from South Carolina. Out of this marriage came her diary of Southern life. After her divorce some years later she largely confined herself to offering formal readings, before returning permanently to England in 1868. Perhaps because she acted here so briefly and retired at the height of her powers, she was remembered with a special affection. T. Allston Brown♦ recalled, "She was full of the true, heavenly fire, with every other requisite of physical and intellectual endowment, but her representations were mere dash sketches, though with here and there a touch of the most masterly and overwhelming power." Less critical, Anna Cora Mowatt♦

wrote of watching her perform, "I thought I had never beheld any creature so perfectly bewitching. The tones of her voice were richest music, and her dark, flashing eyes seemed to penetrate my very soul."

Biography: *Fanny Kemble,* J. H. Furnas, New York, 1982.

KEMPER, COLLIN, see *Wagenhals, Lincoln*

Kempy, a comedy in three acts by J. C. and Elliott Nugent. ♦ Produced by Richard G. Herndon♦ at the Belmont Theatre. May 15, 1922. 212 performances.

James Kemp (Elliott Nugent), who is known as "Kempy," is a plumber who dreams of becoming an architect. He is also somewhat naïve and pliable. Coming to the house of his fiancée, Ruth Bence (Ruth Nugent), to fix a leaky pipe, he is confronted by Ruth's sister Katherine (Lotus Robb), who has just had a nasty fight with her boyfriend, "Duke" Merrill (Grant Mitchell♦), and decides to get even by bamboozling Kempy into marrying her. But that night she makes him sleep alone on the living room couch. The next morning more sober thoughts win the day, so Duke, who is a lawyer, arranges to pair everyone happily.

Written with an uncredited assist from Howard Lindsay,♦ the play was the comedy sleeper of the season and helped establish Elliott, whose family had heretofore been largely associated with vaudeville, as an important figure in the legitimate theatre.

KENDAL, MR. [né WILLIAM HUNTER GRIMSTON] (1843–1917) and MRS. [née MARGARET (MADGE) ROBERTSON] (1848–1935) One of the finest English acting teams, they made their American debut in 1889 under Daniel Frohman's♦ aegis in Sardou's♦ *A Scrap of Paper.* The *Dramatic Mirror*♦ noted of Mrs. Kendal, "Her art is as fine as old point lace, and yet it is laid upon a temperament so genuinely sympathetic and so pliant and transitional that there is no sign of effort, no direct exhibition of method in anything she does"; while the *Times* called her husband's performance "deliberate, careful, good-humored, and unquestionably effective." Their repertory consisted entirely of contemporary plays. They made several highly successful visits to America over the next several seasons, although they ultimately antagonized more prudish players and critics, led by William Winter,♦ when they gave the first American mounting of the then shocking Pinero♦ play, *The Second Mrs. Tanqueray,* in 1893.

Their final American appearances came during the 1899–1900 season.

Biography: *The Kendals,* T. Edgar Pemberton, New York, 1900.

KENNEDY, [JOHN] ARTHUR (1914–90) A native of Worcester, Mass., the light-haired, slightly boyish-looking actor, who always conveyed an impression of intense dedication, made his debut in Maurice Evans's♦ 1937 revival of *King Richard II.* He won major recognition as Chris Keller, who holds his father responsible for his brother's death, in *All My Sons*♦ (1947). His later roles included Biff, the troubled son of the failing commercial traveler, in *Death of a Salesman*♦ (1949); John Proctor, who is caught up in the Salem witchhunts, in *The Crucible*♦ (1953); Col. William Edwards, the judge advocate in the trial of an officer who deserted, in *Time Limit!* (1956); Patrick Flannigan, the hot-tempered father who is determined his daughter will not marry a man he dislikes, in *The Loud Red Patrick* (1956); Thomas Becket in a touring company of *Becket* (1961); and Walter Franz, the selfish but successful brother, in *The Price* (1968).

Kennedy Center for the Performing Arts (Washington, D.C.) In 1958 President Eisenhower signed P.L. 85-874, which provided land and authorized a private fund campaign to establish the National Cultural Center in Washington. Shortly thereafter Edward Durell Stone was selected to be the architect. Following the assassination of President Kennedy and just before the ground-breaking, President Johnson changed the center's name to the John F. Kennedy Center for the Performing Arts, making it the only Washington monument to the late President. The Center, housed in a single, imposing building, contains three major auditoriums: the 2,318-seat Opera House, the 1,142-seat Eisenhower Theatre, and a 2,750-seat Concert Hall. There are also three small houses, including the 512-seat Terrace Theatre and a 120-seat Theater Lab. The Opera House has been home to some large touring musicals, while the Terrace and Theater Lab have offered experimental productions. However, the principal legitimate activity has been in the Eisenhower. Under the chairmanship of Roger L. Stevens,♦ the theatre has offered a series of distinguished new plays and revivals, several of which, such as the 1983 production of *You Can't Take It with You,*♦ have gone on to Broadway. Stevens retired in 1988. Ralph Davidson followed Stevens and was in turn succeeded by James D.

Wolfensohn in 1990. There appear to be no major policy changes.

KENNEDY, CHARLES RANN (1871–1950) Grandson of the famous classical scholar of the same name, the English-born actor and playwright made his first American appearance as the Doctor and Messenger in a 1903 revival of *Everyman.* While the fact that his American debut was in a medieval morality play may have been mere coincidence, it remains significant that most of his plays had markedly religious bents. He is best remembered for *The Servant in the House*♦ (1908), in which Christ returns to earth in the guise of a servant to assist a disturbed family. Among his other works were *The Winterfeast* (1908); *The Terrible Meek* (1912); and *The Army with Banners* (1918). In later years he produced and played in an annual festival of Greek plays at Millbrook, N.Y.

KENNEDY, MADGE (1892–1987) The Chicago-born comedienne became a professional in 1910. Among her notable roles were Blanche Hawkins, who is pursued by a drunken tenor, in *Twin Beds*♦ (1914); Blanche Wheeler, the determinedly stay-at-home wife, in *Fair and Warmer*♦ (1915); the title role in the musical *Poppy* (1925), and Mary Hutton, who learns to live with infidelity, in *Paris Bound*♦ (1927).

Kentuckian, The, see *Lion of the West, The*

KERKER, GUSTAVE [ADOLPH] (1857–1923) Born in Germany, where he began studying cello at the age of seven, he continued his musical studies when his family moved to Louisville, in 1867. He started his professional career playing in pit orchestras at the city's theatres, and soon rose to the post of conductor. His 1879 operetta, *Cadets,* toured the South, coming to the attention of E. E. Rice,♦ who offered the composer-conductor a chance to work with him. Shortly after moving to New York he became the principal conductor at the Casino Theatre.♦ Although he interpolated his songs into other men's scores, notably in Lecocq's *The Pearl of Pekin,* his first complete score was not heard in New York until the production of *Castles in the Air* (1890). Over the next two decades he provided the music for more than twenty shows. His best known work was *The Belle of New York*♦ (1897), which was an international success. Among his other musicals were *An American Beauty* (1896), which starred Lillian Russell♦; *The Girl from Up There* (1901); *Winsome Winnie* (1903); *The Tourists* (1906); and *Fascinating Flora* (1907). His work was musicianly and highly popular in its day, but none of it has proved memorable.

KERN, JEROME [DAVID] (1885–1945) Born in New York, he moved at the age of ten to Newark. His father was a German-born immigrant who became a moderately successful merchandiser; his American-born mother, of Bohemian descent, had once contemplated a career as a professional pianist. She gave her son his first piano lessons. While still in high school Kern composed music for a class show as well as for a production by the Newark Yacht Club. His success prompted him to quit high school after his junior year and enroll instead at the New York College of Music, where his teachers included Paolo Gallico, Alexander Lambert, and Austin Pierce. He also claimed to have studied briefly with private tutors in Germany. Kern employed what was then the accepted method of breaking into Broadway—interpolating songs into other men's scores. Playgoers first heard Kern melodies when Lew Fields♦ accepted "Wine, Wine! (Champagne Song)" and "To the End of the World Together" for insertion into a 1903 importation, *An English Daisy.* The songs caused little stir. However, a year later, when E. E. Rice♦ allowed Kern to write half the score for another importation, *Mr. Wix of Wickham,* recognition began to come Kern's way. His first big hit, "How'd You Like To Spoon with Me?," followed in the 1905 importation, *The Earl and the Girl.* For the next decade the young composer shuttled back and forth between New York and London. His trips to England were eye-openers for him, making him a life-long Anglophile and leaving him with an abiding love for Gaiety musical comedy. On one trip he fell in love with an English girl, Eva Leale, and in 1910 married her. Among the shows in which Kern inserted melodies during these years were *The Doll Girl, The Dairymaids, Fascinating Flora, Fluffy Ruffles,* and *The Girl from Montmartre.*

The years of apprenticeship and of shuttling back and forth allowed Kern to develop a unique musical idiom, a distinct amalgam of his German and Bohemian heritage, turn-of-the-century English musical theatre styles, and identifiable American mannerisms. An especially important influence was "the dancing craze," a rage for ballroom dancing that exploded across America shortly before World War I. This new pastime gave only secondary consideration to the traditional waltz, and emphasized instead new dances such as the tango and the fox trot. It was in answer to this demand for new dance songs that Kern finally found his first real style and achieved lasting recognition. In 1914 Charles Frohman♦ brought the London hit *The Girl from*

Utah♦ to New York. He had Kern provide the American interpolations. Kern's songs, such as "Same Sort of Girl," "You Never Can Tell," "Why Don't They Dance the Polka?" and "The Land of Let's Pretend," were among his most beguiling. But it was another of his songs for the show, "They Didn't Believe Me,"♦ that changed the course of American musical comedy writing. This great, enduring composition established the ballad as the most basic style of popular song in place of the heretofore reigning waltz. Within a year Kern had joined forces with Guy Bolton,♦ and, after a failure, *Ninety in the Shade,* in which Kern nevertheless consolidated his new style of dance-based writing, the pair began to write intimate musical comedies for the tiny Princess Theatre.♦ The first, *Nobody Home♦* (1915), a drastically rewritten version of an English musical, was a modest hit; the second, *Very Good Eddie♦* (1915), a huge success, remembered for "Babes in the Wood." When P. G. Wodehouse♦ joined the team, adding his incomparable lyrics, the shows hit full stride, with *Oh, Boy!♦* (1917), from which came "Till the Clouds Roll By" and *Oh, Lady! Lady!!♦* (1918). Two other shows the trio wrote with the Princess in mind were presented elsewhere, *Have a Heart!* (1917) and *Leave It to Jane♦* (1917). These musical comedies, with their sensible books about believable people, their literate and witty lyrics and their enchanting melodies—songs which were well integrated into the story—became exemplars of their kind. In the next decade most of Kern's scores were far more blatantly commercial enterprises. As vehicles for Marilyn Miller♦ he wrote *Sally♦* (1920), which offered "Look for the Silver Lining," "Whip-poor-will," and "Wild Rose," and *Sunny♦* (1925), whose hits were its title song and "Who?"; for Fred Stone♦ he wrote *Stepping Stones* (1923) and *Criss Cross* (1926). In 1924 Kern broke away from his dance-based style to attempt a more ambitious musical line in *Dear Sir,* a failure. But three years later he found the answers he was looking for when he collaborated with Oscar Hammerstein II♦ on the first successful, totally American operetta, *Show Boat.♦* Its masterful score included "Bill," "Can't Help Lovin' Dat Man," "Make Believe," "Ol' Man River," and "Why Do I Love You?" The success of the pair's next work, *Sweet Adeline♦* (1929), recalled for "Don't Ever Leave Me" and "Why Was I Born?," was dampened by the onset of the Depression. In the early 1930s Kern attempted still another style of operetta writing, interweaving Middle-European and American mannerisms. *The Cat and the Fiddle♦* (1931), written with Otto Harbach,♦ and *Music in the Air♦* (1932), written with Hammerstein, both enjoyed long runs. The former is remembered for "The Night Was Made for Love," "She Didn't Say 'Yes'," and "Try To Forget"; the latter for "I've Told Ev'ry Little Star" and "The Song Is You." A dreadful Harbach libretto nearly scuttled *Roberta*♦ (1933), but Kern's luminous score saved the day. The score included "Smoke Gets in Your Eyes," "The Touch of Your Hand," "Yesterdays," and "You're Devastating." For the rest of the decade Kern worked in Hollywood, returning only in 1939 for the unsuccessful *Very Warm for May*, which left behind "All the Things You Are." He was preparing to write the score for the musical that became *Annie Get Your Gun*♦ when he died in 1945.

Kern's remarkable melodic gifts and his crucial pioneering—popularizing the ballad, modernizing musical comedy, and creating the modern American operetta or musical play—have won him general recognition as the father of the American musical theatre as we know it today. Harold Arlen,♦ George Gershwin,♦ Cole Porter,♦ Richard Rodgers,♦ Arthur Schwartz,♦ and Vincent Youmans♦ all at one time or another acknowledged that he had served as their idol and model. For all his experimentation, however, Kern could be a difficult, obstinate associate. He almost never would write a melody to a lyric, and once he did create a melody he refused to change a note of it. As a result, even when his lyricist was a master such as Wodehouse or Hammerstein, there were occasional clashes of words and music. Witness, for example, the verse to "Make Believe."

Kern's full scores, other than those already mentioned, were *The Red Petticoat* (1912); *Oh, I Say!* (1913); *Miss Information* (1915); *Love o' Mike* (1917); *Toot-Toot!* (1918); *Head Over Heels* (1918); *Rock-a-Bye Baby* (1919); *Zip Goes a Million* (1919), closed on tryout; *She's a Good Fellow* (1919); *The Night Boat* (1920); *Hitchy-Koo, 1920*; *Good Morning Dearie* (1921); *Sitting Pretty* (1924); *The City Chap* (1925); *Lucky* (1927); and *Gentleman Unafraid* (1938), done in St. Louis but never brought to New York.

Biography: *Jerome Kern: His Life and Music*, Gerald Bordman, New York, 1980.

KERR, [BRIDGET] JEAN [née COLLINS] (b. 1923) The popular playwright was born in Scranton, Penn., and educated at Marywood College and Catholic University. Her first play to reach New York was *Jenny Kissed Me* (1948), in which a crotchety priest tries to make a swan of an ugly duckling. With her husband, Walter Kerr,♦ she wrote sketches for *Touch and Go*

(1949). Her next play, written with Eleanor Brooke, was *King of Hearts* (1954), a comedy about an egocentric cartoonist. In 1958 she collaborated with her husband on the book for *Goldilocks*. Her biggest hit was *Mary, Mary*♦ (1961), centering on an outspoken young lady whose caustic wit almost destroys her marriage. *Poor Richard* (1964) told of a comic love triangle consisting of a poet, his publisher, and the publisher's secretary. *Finishing Touches*♦ (1973) depicted the problems of a middle-aged college professor and his family. *Lunch Hour* (1980) was a comedy about mate-swapping. Her work is marked by a biting wit and shrewd personal observation.

KERR, WALTER [FRANCIS] (b. 1913) The distinguished drama critic and playwright was born in Evanston, Ill., and educated at De Pauw and Northwestern universities. From 1938 to 1945 he taught speech and drama at Catholic University in Washington. At the same time he co-authored his first Broadway show, the musical *Count Me In* (1942) Two years later he wrote and directed *Sing Out, Sweet Land!* With his wife, Jean Kerr,♦ he wrote the sketches for the revue *Touch and Go* (1949), which he also directed. In 1950 he became drama critic for *Commonweal* and the next year for the *Herald Tribune*. It was during his tenure on this paper that he staged his wife's comedy, *King of Hearts* (1954), and with her wrote the book for the musical *Goldilocks* (1958), which he directed. With the demise of the *Herald Tribune* in 1966 he became drama critic for the *Times*. He held the post only briefly, confining himself to Sunday critiques beginning in 1967. Among his books are *How Not To Write a Play* (1955); *Criticism and Censorship* (1957); *Pieces at Eight* (1957); *The Decline of Pleasure* (1962); and *Theatre in Spite of Itself* (1963). His writings earned him a Pulitzer Prize. ♦

KESSELRING, JOSEPH, see *Arsenic and Old Lace*

KESSLER, DAVID (1859?–1920) Yiddish actor and manager, he was born in Russia but spent most of his career on New York's Lower East Side. A tall, broad man, with a markedly peasant neck, he seemed to have the highest artistic principles and instinct even though he apparently had little or no formal education. While he performed in highly praised productions of such works as Sudermann's *Heimat* [*Magda*] and Jacob Gordin's♦ *God, Man and Devil*, he was forced by his public to appear mostly in plays which he considered trash. He ran several theatres and it was his move to a new playhouse on Second

Avenue which is often credited with moving the American-Yiddish theatre's center there from the Bowery. When he appeared on Broadway in *The Spell* (1907) one critic, citing his "emotional gymnastics and physical contortions," branded him an actor of "the old German school."

KESTER, PAUL (1870–1933) Born in Delaware, Ohio, he was a cousin of William Dean Howells♦ and was only twenty-two when he collaborated with Mrs. Fiske♦ on a vehicle for her. Their play, *Countess Roudine* (1892), was a romantic piece about nihilism in Russia and was unsuccessful. His later plays were of a similarly romantic, often highly sentimental nature and were usually written with specific stars in mind. Among his successes were *Sweet Nell of Drury Lane* (1901), *When Knighthood Was in Flower*♦ (1901), and *Dorothy Vernon of Haddon Hall* (1903), the last two dramatizations of novels. When styles of dramaturgy changed at the time of World War I, Kester attempted to change with them. However, he had only one later success, *The Woman of Bronze* (1920), the story of a sculptor who cannot at first realize that his true source of inspiration is his loyal wife. Noting that he "flourished in an era of different proportions," George Middleton♦ recalled, "He could and did write only for stars—good or limited. He deliberately restricted his skill to their exploitation. He was a stage tailor: he skillfully cut his cloth to the figure which was to wear it. He took the blame for technical deficiencies he was aware of, rather than ask the star to do what he knew was beyond her power."

Key Largo, a drama in a prologue and two acts by Maxwell Anderson. ♦ Produced by the Playwrights' Company♦ at the Ethel Barrymore Theatre. November 27, 1939. 105 performances.

Concluding his side has lost the Spanish Civil War, King McCloud (Paul Muni♦) urges his men to join him in deserting. They refuse, and die fighting. Back in America, King is beset by guilt. He attempts to expiate his feelings by visiting the families of his fallen comrades. Among these families are the D'Alcalas, who run a small hotel in Key Largo. The D'Alcalas are being menaced by gangsters. At first King would wave away the problem, but concluding his life is now worthless he kills one gangster and is himself killed. His death spares two innocents' being framed for the killings the gangster has committed.

Although the play was dismissed by many critics as a well-intentioned tract, poorly developed, it reflected the deep concern of many theatrical figures over the events and implications of the war.

Kick In, a play in four acts by Willard Mack. ♦ Produced by A. H. Woods♦ at the Longacre Theatre. October 15, 1914. 188 performances.

Chick Hewes (John Barrymore♦) is an ex-convict who is determined to go straight. However, when a former cellmate is shot during a robbery, Chick and his wife, Molly (Jane Grey), offer to hide him. The cellmate dies, but not before a valuable necklace he has stolen disappears. Although Chick and Molly dump the body in the river, they are still arrested in the case. When Molly's drug-addicted brother, Charles Cary (Forrest Winant), learns his pregnant sister may go to prison, he confesses that he took the necklace. By rights, Chick and Molly should still be held for harboring a criminal, but a compassionate police commissioner decides to give them another chance.

The play was hailed by one critic as "engrossing from beginning to end." Chick was one of Barrymore's best interpretations and led directly to his being cast in more serious, artful works.

KIDD, MICHAEL [né MILTON GREENWALD] (b. 1919) Born in New York, he left City College, where he was studying chemical engineering, to become a pupil at a ballet school. He performed with the Eugene Loring Dance Players and the Ballet Theatre before choreographing *Finian's Rainbow*♦ (1947). His choreography was later seen in such musicals as *Love Life* (1948), *Guys and Dolls*♦ (1950), and *Can-Can*♦ (1953). In 1956 he co-produced, directed, and staged the dances for *Li'l Abner.* In all he choreographed, and sometimes directed, a score of musicals. His work was often characterized by a raffish liveliness.

KIDDER, EDWARD E. (1846–1927) Born in Charleston, Mass., but raised in New York, he was an actor's manager—working with Charlotte Crabtree,♦ John T. Raymond,♦ and others—before turning playwright. Between 1883, when he wrote *Three of a Kind* for Nate Salsbury and Nellie McHenry, and 1905, when he created *Easy Dawson* for Raymond Hitchcock,♦ he was the author of some twenty or thirty Broadway and touring plays, most of them vehicles for important stars. His biggest success was *A Poor Relation* (1889), written for Sol Smith Russell♦ and centering on a likable, inventive hobo.

KILEY, RICHARD [PAUL] (b. 1922) A native Chicagoan, he played in summer stock before assuming the role of Stanley Kowalski in a road company of *A Streetcar Named Desire*♦ in 1950. New Yorkers first saw him as Joey Percival in a 1953 revival of Shaw's *Misalliance*. He switched to musicals later that year, appearing as the Caliph in *Kismet*♦ and introducing "Stranger in Paradise," then further displayed his versatility as Major Harry Cargill, the suspected P.O.W. turncoat, in the drama *Time Limit!* (1956). Continuing to move into the lyric theatre he portrayed the leading men in *Redhead* (1959), *No Strings*♦ (1962), and *I Had a Ball* (1964). His other major straight play during those years was *Advise and Consent* (1960), in which he took the part of Brig Anderson, a young Senator who commits suicide after he is blackmailed about his homosexual past. His most memorable assignment came with the dual roles of Cervantes and Don Quixote in *Man of La Mancha*♦ (1965), in which he introduced "The Impossible Dream." He won a Tony Award♦ and other honors for this performance. Thereafter he was unable to find roles in other outstanding successes, but appeared regularly in revivals of *La Mancha*. In 1987 he portrayed Joe Keller in a revival of *All My Sons.*♦

KILNER, THOMAS (1777–1862) An English actor who made his American debut at the Park Theatre♦ in 1818, his fame rests on his career as manager of Boston's Federal Street Theatre,♦ where he not only provided fine productions but distinguished himself in such "old men" roles as Sir Anthony Absolute and Polonius. He retired in the early 1830s.

King and I, The, a musical play in two acts. Book and lyrics by Oscar Hammerstein II.♦ Music by Richard Rodgers. ♦ Produced by Rodgers and Hammerstein at the St. James Theatre. March 29, 1951. 1,246 performances.

When English Anna Leonowens (Gertrude Lawrence♦) arrives in Siam to tutor the children of The King (Yul Brynner), she hides her fears by acknowledging "I Whistle a Happy Tune." She finds The King is a despot, so she is especially sympathetic to the furtive youngsters who would marry without his permission. Indeed, greeting them with "Hello, Young Lovers," she recalls that she, too, was once in love. To the younger tots she expresses her joy in "Getting To Know You." The lovers, who confess "We Kiss in a Shadow," are caught and sentenced to death, but The King's head wife, Lady Thiang (Dorothy Sarnoff), begs Anna to be patient and assures her that for all his cruelty The King can often do "Something Wonderful." Slowly, Anna and The King come to understand each other and at one point Anna even asks The King, "Shall We Dance?"

As a result of this mutual understanding, Anna perseveres, and when The King is on his deathbed he confesses he has begun to see the wisdom of her more civilized ways.

Based on Margaret Landon's novel, *Anna and the King of Siam,* it portrayed, as Richard Watts, Jr.,♦ wrote in his *Post* review, "an East of frank and unashamed romance seen through the eyes of . . . theatrical artists of rare taste and power." Although for many Miss Lawrence's luminous performance was a high point of the show, after her death during the run Brynner's acting was thrown in the spotlight and he usually headed its many major revivals.

Brynner (1920?–1985) gave varying birthplaces and birth dates. Several obituaries gave his birthplace as Sakhalin Island and his real name as Taidje Khano. He had made Broadway appearances, including a 1941 revival of *Twelfth Night* and *Lute Song* (1946) before this role catapulted him into the limelight. His subsequent career was largely in films, including the movie version of *The King and I,* except when he toured in several revivals of the musical, ultimately performing his part over four thousand times. He also starred in a failed musical, *Home Sweet Homer* (1976).

KING, DENNIS [né PRATT] (1897–1971) While best remembered as the leading man of many 1920s operettas, the handsome, English-born King was a versatile performer who enjoyed a long and varied career. His earliest professional assignment was as a call-boy with the Birmingham Repertory Theatre. He rose rapidly in the company to stage manager and finally actor. He came to America in 1921 to play the Marquis de Trois Fleurs in *Clair de Lune,* but first called prominent attention to himself when he essayed Mercutio to Jane Cowl's♦ Juliet in 1923. He became a star the following year when he took the role of Jim Kenyon in *Rose-Marie,* ♦ introducing the title song and "Indian Love Call." This was followed by two more popular Rudolf Friml♦ operettas, *The Vagabond King*♦ (1925) in which as François Villon he sang "Only a Rose" and "Song of the Vagabonds"; and *The Three Musketeers*♦ (1928), in which he played D'Artagnan and introduced "My Sword" and "March of the Musketeers." In 1931 he played the title role in a revival of *Peter Ibbetson,* then appeared as Ravenal in a 1932 revival of *Show Boat.*♦ Turning to farce, he scored as Dascom Dinsmore, the isolated, sex-hungry telegraph operator, in *Petticoat Fever* (1934). He won praise for his Dr. Rank in a 1937 revival of *A Doll's House* before reverting to musical comedy in *I Married an Angel*♦ (1938). In the 1940s he headed road companies or succeeded the Broadway leads in such diverse works as *Blithe Spirit, Medea,*♦ *Pygmalion,*♦ and *Edward, My Son.* The same decade saw him play Colonel Vershinin in a 1942 revival of *The Three Sisters,* and Alexander Hazen, the fence-straddling diplomat, in *The Searching Wind* (1944). Among his major roles in the 1950s were General Burgoyne in a 1950 revival of *The Devil's Disciple;* Captain Vere in *Billy Budd* (1951); Bruno Mahler in a 1951 revival of *Music in the Air*♦*;* and the boozy Judge Sullivan in *Lunatics and Lovers* (1954). His last success was as Sam Elderly, a writer's playboy alter ego, in *Photo Finish* (1963), and his last appearance was as the homosexual Baron von Epp in *A Patriot for Me* (1969). King served for many years as president of The Players. ♦

King Lear Shakespeare's tragedy was first mounted in New York in 1754 and soon became a popular vehicle for all the great American tragedians. Junius Brutus Booth,♦ himself a little mad, was a noteworthy interpreter as was Edwin Forrest. ♦ It was also a favorite role of Edwin Booth,♦ though critics divided on the merits of his performance, which, especially in early years, seemed to have been copied from his father's. Modern revivals, including those featuring Louis Calhern,♦ Orson Welles,♦ and Paul Scofield,♦ have found surprisingly little favor at the box office.

KING, WALTER WOOLF [né WOOLF] (1899–1984) A popular leading man in operetta in the 1920s, he was born in San Francisco and began his career in vaudeville. His notable appearances included *The Lady in Ermine* (1922), in which he introduced "When Hearts Are Young"; *The Dream Girl* (1924), in which he sang "My Dream Girl"; and *Countess Maritza* (1926), in which he sang "Play Gypsies—Dance Gypsies."

KINGSLEY, SIDNEY [né KIRSCHNER] (b. 1906) The Philadelphia-born playwright, director, and producer studied at Cornell, where he wrote one-act plays for the University's drama club. After graduation he acted for a short time. His first play to reach Broadway, *Men in White*♦ (1933), explored the dilemma of a young intern torn between a wealthy marriage and dedication to his profession. Produced by the Group Theatre,♦ it won a Pulitzer Prize.♦ He was a slow, careful writer, and did not have another play ready until two years later. But *Dead End*♦ (1935), a searing yet compassionate study of youth gangs, gave him another success. He directed the play, as he did all his subsequent offerings. His

next two works were failures. *Ten Million Ghosts* (1936) was an anti-war tract, focusing on the conflict between a young poet and a munitions salesman. *The World We Make* (1939), based on Millen Brand's novel *The Outward Room,* described the attempts of a mental patient to lead a normal life. Kingsley produced both of these failures, losing much of his own money in the process. *The Patriots*♦ (1943), centering on the conflict between Jefferson and Hamilton, was given a better reception and won the New York Drama Critics Circle Award,♦ but he did not have another major success until *Detective Story*♦ (1949), which recounted the events leading to the death of an over-zealous policeman. He won a second award from the New York Drama Critics Circle for his adaptation of Arthur Koestler's novel *Darkness at Noon* (1951), a grim picture of life in Communist Russia. In a notable change of pace he enjoyed a final success with something approaching farce, *Lunatics and Lovers* (1954), which depicted the complications that ensue when a shady Broadway roustabout attempts to obtain cheap legal advice. His last play, which he produced as well as directed, was *Night Life* (1962), set in a café where an assortment of figures attempt to untangle their lives. Kingsley's best works were hard-hitting dramas with a moral and social point of view. He also served as president of the Dramatists Guild. ♦

KINKEAD, CLEVES, see *Common Clay*

KIRALFY, BOLOSSY (1848?–1932) and IMRE (1849?–1919) were Hungarian-born dancers and acrobats who, with their sister Haniola, made their American debut in George L. Fox's♦ production of *Hiccory Diccory Dock* (1869). They performed in numerous spectacles at Niblo's Garden♦ before turning producers there with *The Deluge* (1874), said to have been the first production to employ a primitive form of electricity for its lighting. Some historians suggest it was their later production of *Enchantment* (1879) which can actually claim this distinction. Certainly for about fifteen years they were New York's principal purveyors of spectacle, including *Azurine* (1877), *Excelsior* (1883), *Sieba and the Seven Ravens* (1884), and *The Water Queen* (1889). During that time they sent out lavish touring companies of two popular extravaganzas, *The Black Crook*♦ and *Around the World,*♦ both of which made seasonal visits to New York. In later years they assisted with the staging of Barnum and Bailey's circus and in mounting spectacles in arenas and elsewhere. Their last years were spent in England.

Autobiography, *Bolossy Kiralfy, Creator of Great*

Musical Spectacles, Barbara M. Barker, ed., Ann Arbor, Mich. 1988.

KIRBY, J. HUDSON (1810–48) The idol of the cheap theatres of his day, he was born in London and came to America apparently in 1837, making his debut at Philadelphia's Walnut Street Theatre.♦ He first appeared in New York at Wallack's National Theatre in 1838, when he played Antonio to J. M. Wallack's♦ Shylock. Since Wallack was a shrewd and demanding judge of talent, this suggests that the young actor might have made a career in better roles. Instead he chose to star in the tawdry, overwrought melodramas of the time. His most notable success came from 1840 to 1845 when he was the leading man at the Chatham Theatre. T. Allston Brown♦ describes the ruggedly handsome actor as "of medium height, of slight build, with complexion and hair rather dark. His chief charm was his voice, which was melodious, strong, ringing and clear as a bell." Brown continued, "Even on noisy nights, such as Christmas, New Year's, and the Fourth of July, when audiences used to talk, shout, and scream so that the actors went through their parts in dumb show, Kirby's voice would ring out above the din. His greatest successes were in melodramas such as 'Six Degrees of Crime'—the old-fashioned 'blood and thunder' style, on which the curtain did not drop until one o'clock in the morning." Kirby's scene-chewing technique gave rise to the expression "Wake me up when Kirby dies." He returned to England in 1845, becoming a star in similar pieces at London's Surrey Theatre, but was preparing to come back to America at the time of his death.

KIRKLAND, JACK, see *Tobacco Road*

Kismet, a play in three acts by Edward Knoblauch.♦ Produced by Charles Frohman♦ and Klaw♦ and Erlanger♦ at the Knickerbocker Theatre. December 25, 1911. 184 performances.

The wily Baghdad beggar and poet Hajj (Otis Skinner♦) is arrested on a minor infraction by the Wazir Mansur (Hamilton Revelle), who agrees to release him if he will kill the Caliph Abdullah (Fred Eric). Hajj's attempt fails, and he is thrown in jail alongside his old enemy Sheik Jawan (Sheridan Block). He kills Jawan and escapes in the Sheik's clothing. Learning his daughter Marsinah (Rita Jolivet) has become a concubine in the Wazir's harem, he drowns the Wazir and frees Marsinah. The Caliph, who has disguised himself as a gardener to court Marsinah, now marries her. By law he must banish Hajj, which he does, but he looks the other way when Hajj simply returns to his old haunts to beg and write poetry again.

Initially rejected by all the major Broadway producers, it was presented in New York only after its successful London premiere. Walter Prichard Eaton♦ wrote that "the touch of genius in Mr. Knoblauch's achievement [was] to dare to write a play in ten scenes, to dare to make it primitive as a folk tale, bloody and passionate and humorous and farther from the present than when old Omar sang before his tent of the modern unrest and doubt, a tale from the childhood of the race." The role of Hajj was generally considered Skinner's most popular. In 1953 a musical version, with book and lyrics by Robert Wright and George Forrest, and music based on Aleksandr Borodin themes, began a run of 583 performances at the Ziegfeld Theatre♦ with Alfred Drake♦ as Hajj and Richard Kiley♦ as the Caliph. Hit songs included "And This Is My Beloved," "Baubles, Bangles and Beads," and "Stranger in Paradise." It has been revived several times. A 1978 revival with a black cast was called *Timbuktu.*

Kiss and Tell, a comedy in three acts by F. Hugh Herbert.♦ Produced by George Abbott♦ at the Biltmore Theatre. March 17, 1943. 957 performances.

The Archers and the Pringles have been feuding, especially since they caught their teenage daughters, Corliss Archer (Joan Caulfield) and Mildred Pringle (Judith Parrish), selling kisses for charity. So when Lt. Lenny Archer (Richard Widmark) elopes with Mildred, he swears Corliss to secrecy. Mildred, it turns out, is soon pregnant, but it is only Corliss Mrs. Pringle sees leaving the obstetrician's office. Since she is sworn not to reveal the truth, Corliss says she is pregnant. That means she will have to marry her dim-witted boyfriend, Dexter Franklin (Robert White), whose limited vocabulary consists largely of "Holy Cow." Matters are properly resolved after Lenny becomes a war hero and reveals his marriage.

Welcomed by John Anderson of the *Journal-American* as "a fresh, funny and completely beguiling comedy," it was another of the many successful plays of the war which relied heavily on young performers.

Kiss Me, Kate, a musical comedy in two acts. Book by Sam and Bella Spewack.♦ Music and lyrics by Cole Porter.♦ Produced by Saint Subber and Lemuel Ayers♦ at the New Century Theatre. December 30, 1948. 1,077 performances.

While cast members of a revival of *The Taming of the Shrew* celebrate "Another Op'nin', Another Show," the show's stars, Fred Graham (Alfred Drake♦) and Lilli Vanessi (Patricia Morison), celebrate the first anniversary of their divorce. They take time from their bickering to recall they had once sung "Wunderbar" in a long-forgotten operetta. Lilli receives a bouquet from Fred, leading her to believe he still loves her, and she confesses she is still "So In Love" with him, but when she learns the flowers are meant for someone else she determines to be revenged. Fred's problems are compounded when another member of the company, Bill Calhoun (Harold Lang), signs Fred's name to a gambling debt. Opening night is peppered by warfare between Fred and Lilli, and by demands by two comic hoods for payment of the debt. Fred convinces the hoods that they must force Lilli to perform. Bill's promiscuous girl, Lois (Lisa Kirk), helps him try to reform by promising she will be "Always True to You in My Fashion," and the hoods eventually leave when the debt proves no longer valid on a technicality. They decide it might be more profitable to "Brush Up Your Shakespeare." In the course of the evening, Fred and Lilli recognize they still do love each other.

Called by Brooks Atkinson♦ "a blissfully enjoyable musical show," the work is generally acknowledged as Porter's masterpiece. Not only did he employ Shakespearean lines and whole passages with wit and taste, but his songs actually seemed to come out of and be a part of the libretto, both in the *Shrew* scenes and in the backstage story, a rare thing for the cavalier composer. A worldwide success, it has been revived often.

Kiss the Boys Goodbye, a comedy in three acts by Clare Boothe. ♦ Produced by Brock Pemberton♦ at the Henry Miller Theatre. September 28, 1938. 286 performances.

Into Hollywood's frantic search for an actress to play Velvet O'Toole in the filming of a novel about the Civil War, *Kiss the Boys Goodbye,* comes Georgia belle Cindy Lou Bethany (Helen Claire). Whether she is the "half Hepburn, half Bette Davis, half Myrna Loy" that one figure says is required is moot. To a collection of show-wise characters assembed in Westport, Conn., she is merely a bore. Furious at the other guests' behavior toward her, she punches one and shoots at another. In the end she decides she prefers marriage to a career.

Despite critical reservations that the comedy was mechanical and contrived, the play was a huge success and quickly sent out a road company. Although most critics and playgoers saw it as a spoof of Hollywood's search for an actress to play Scarlett O'Hara, Miss Boothe muddied the waters by insisting in her preface to the published version that it was really an attack on fascism and Southern fascism in particular.

Kit, the Arkansas Traveller, a play in five acts by T. B. De Walden and Edward Spencer. Produced at Niblo's Garden. ♦ May 8, 1871. 40 performances.

Young Kit Redding (Frank Chanfrau♦), an Arkansas farmer, and his wife Mary (Rose Evans) live happily with their young daughter Alice (Minnie Maddern [Fiske♦]) until Mary's former suitor, the crooked gambler Manuel Bond (George C. Boniface♦), abducts both mother and child. Years pass. Kit has become a wealthy, but disconsolate merchant, who continually searches for his wife and child when he is not in his cups. He finally encounters Manuel, who now calls himself Hastings, and a grown Alice (played by Miss Evans) on a Mississippi River steamboat. Mary has died. He is able to convince Alice that she is his daughter. At the same time, Hastings sets fire to the boat, hoping in the confusion to rob it. The passengers are shipwrecked on a small island, where Kit kills Hastings and reclaims Alice.

The play had toured the country for over a year before coming to New York. It was well received, the *Times* noting it offered "Realistic pictures of every-day life in the West—reasonably realistic, be it understood—[and] exciting situations" as well as "representative types from distant places." It became Chanfrau's principal vehicle for the rest of his life. After his death it continued to be played well into the 1890s.

De Walden [né Thomas Blades] (1811–73) was a London-born actor, playwright, and manager, who made his American debut in 1844. He was Chanfrau's business manager for many years. His last play, written for Edward Eddy,♦ was *The Life and Death of Natty Bumpo.*

KITTREDGE, GEORGE LYMAN (1860–1941) The distinguished American scholar taught Shakespeare and early English literature at Harvard. His writings, such as his 1916 *Shakespere* and his monographs, were often referred to by producers and actors planning Shakespearean revivals.

Kitty Mackay, a comedy in three acts by Catherine Chisholm Cushing. ♦ Produced at the Comedy Theatre. January 7, 1914. 278 performances.

Kitty McNab (Molly McIntyre), a foundling, has been lovingly raised in Scottish backwaters by Sandy

McNab (Ernest Stallard) and his wife. For all his goodness, Sandy's dark religious upbringing convinces him he will be sent to a heaven filled with goats. This so bothers Kitty that she sets about rewriting the Bible, commenting, "It's no fair making Christianity like walking a tight-rope." Suddenly, the family who abandoned her calls to bring her back to London. There, as Kitty Mackay, she falls in love with Lt. David Graham (Eugene O'Brien). But when the lovers learn she is Graham's half-sister, the marriage is called off and Kitty returns to Scotland. Graham follows her with the news that as a baby she was switched for his real half-sister, who had died. Since they are not blood relatives, they can wed.

This sentimental comedy was highly praised by critics for its warm-heartedness and humor and was one of the major hits of its day. A musical version, *Lassie* (1920), failed.

KIVIETTE [née YETTA KIVIAT] Said to have been born on Staten Island, she attended the Women's School of Applied Design and worked closely for a time with Charles Le Maire. ◆ Her costume designs began to attract attention in the late 1920s when she worked on such musicals as *Here's Howe!* (1928), but her heyday was the 1930s. Her clothes were seen in, among others, *Girl Crazy*◆ (1930), *Three's a Crowd* (1930), *The Band Wagon*◆ (1931), *The Cat and the Fiddle*◆ (1931), *Face the Music* (1932), *Take a Chance* (1932), *Walk a Little Faster* (1932), *Let 'Em Eat Cake* (1933), *Roberta*◆ (1933), *Ziegfeld Follies of 1934,*◆ *Life Begins at 8:40* (1934), and *Between the Devil* (1937). Thereafter she worked less frequently on Broadway, one of her last important assignments being a non-musical, *Light Up the Sky*◆ (1948). The fashion show in *Roberta* may have represented the high point in her career, the streamlined simplicity and elegance of its gowns exemplifying her best work.

KLAUBER, ADOLPH (1879–1933) Born in Louisville and educated at the University of Virginia, he began his career on the staffs of the *Commercial Advertiser* and the *Tribune.* In 1906 he was appointed drama critic of the New York *Times,* a post he held until 1918. He left the paper when he became a producer and scored a modest hit with his first solo offering, *Nighty-Night* (1919). In 1920 he was the uncredited co-producer of the two Eugene O'Neill◆ plays, *The Emperor Jones*◆ and *Diff'rent.* His 1922 production of *The Charlatan* was well received, but had only a mediocre run. With the Selwyns◆ and his wife, Jane Cowl,◆ he produced many of her starring vehicles,

such as *Lilac Time* (1917), *Smilin' Through* (1919), *Pelleas and Melisande* (1923), and *Antony and Cleopatra* (1924), although he remained a silent partner in these enterprises.

KLAW, MARC (1858–1936) Although he was born in Paducah, Ky., his widowed mother moved the family to Louisville when he was five, and it was there that he received his degree in law and began to practice. In 1881 he was employed by Gustave and Daniel Frohman◆ to act against pirated productions of *Hazel Kirke.* ◆ His work was so successful that he soon came to the attention of Abe Erlanger. ◆ In 1888 the pair bought out the Taylor Theatrical Exchange, renaming it the Klaw and Erlanger Exchange. By 1895 they were the second largest agency in the country, representing such notables as Joseph Jefferson◆ and Fanny Davenport,◆ and controlled most of the principal Southern theatres. That same year they met secretly with Charles Frohman,◆ Al Hyman,◆ William Harris, Sr.,◆ and others to organize what became known as the Theatrical Syndicate or Trust.◆ Their avowed aim was to bring order into chaotic booking practices. They succeeded, but at the same time developed a stranglehold of the American theatre that often was viciously manipulative and was widely resented. The organization's monopoly was not broken until the arrival of the Shuberts◆ a decade later and remained a powerful force until it was quietly dissolved in 1916. During those years Klaw and Erlanger also produced numerous shows, including many George Arliss◆ vehicles and Otis Skinner's◆ *Kismet*◆ (1911), as well as such musicals as *Forty-five Minutes from Broadway*◆ (1906) and *The Pink Lady*◆ (1911). Unlike his crass partner, Klaw was gentlemanly in appearance and demeanor. Their personal differences apparently led to an irrevocable rupture in 1919. A year later Klaw formed his own production company and in 1921 built the Klaw Theatre. Most notable among his solo ventures was *Hell-Bent fer Heaven*◆ (1924). He retired in 1927.

KLEIN, CHARLES (1867–1915) Coming to America at the age of fifteen from his native London, he began his career as an actor in juvenile roles. His first play to be produced was *A Mile a Minute* (1891), a comedy which he wrote with Charles Coote. Success came to him when he wrote the libretto for *El Capitan*◆ (1896). Over the next 19 years he wrote several dozen plays—comedies, melodramas, and musical librettos. The most notable were *Heartsease* (1897), written with Joseph Clark, in which a young composer avenges the theft of his opera; *The Auctioneer*♦ (1901), depicting the struggles of a Jewish entrepreneur; *The Music Master*♦ (1904), a story of a musician's search for his lost daughter; *The Lion and the Mouse*♦ (1905), which centered on the confrontation between a young lady muckraker and the millionaire who destroyed her father's career; and *The Third Degree*♦ (1909), in which a weak young man is goaded into falsely confessing a murder. Although his best works are now perceived as too sentimental or as contrived melodrama, they were widely praised and highly popular in their time. Klein also served as Charles Frohman's♦ playreader, and he died with the producer when the *Lusitania* was sunk. His brother Manuel (1876–1919) resided in America between 1903 and 1913, during much of that time serving as conductor at the Hippodrome♦ and composing scores for extravaganzas mounted during his tenure. His most popular song was "Moon Dear" from *A Society Circus* (1906).

KLEIN, MANUEL, see *Klein, Charles*

KLINE, KEVIN (b. 1947) The lanky actor was born in St. Louis and studied at Indiana University and at Julliard. Much of his earliest work was done in a variety of roles with the New York Shakespeare Festival♦ and the Acting Company.♦ He won priase as Paul, the writer attracted to an unsettled girl, in *Loose Ends*♦ (1979). In recent years he has undertaken such roles as Richard III, Hamlet and Benedick at the New York Shakespeare Festival. But larger numbers of playgoers probably recall him best from his two Tony Award♦ winning performances in the musicals *On the Twentieth Century*♦ (1978) and *The Pirates of Penzance*♦, the latter a freewheeling 1980 revival.

KLOTZ, FLORENCE The work of this New York-born costume designer has been seen in such shows as *Take Her, She's Mine* (1961), *Never Too Late*♦ (1962), *The Owl and the Pussycat*♦ (1964), *Follies*♦ (1971), *A Little Night Music*♦ (1973), *Pacific Overtures*♦ (1976), *On the Twentieth Century*♦ (1978), the 1981 revival of *The Little Foxes*♦, and *Jerry's Girls* (1985).

Knickerbocker Holiday, a musical comedy in two acts. Book and lyrics by Maxwell Anderson.♦ Music by Kurt Weill.♦ Produced by the Playwrights Company♦ at the Ethel Barrymore Theatre. October 19, 1938. 168 performances.

As he writes his history of New York, Washington Irving (Ray Middleton) seems to wander back into the 17th century just as New Amsterdam is awaiting the arrival of Pieter Stuyvesant (Walter Huston♦). The town council seeks to divert the new governor from its corruption and ineptitude by staging a hanging, and they select a rebellious young man, Brom Brock (Richard Kollmar♦), who brashly has asked for the hand in marriage of Tina Tienhoven (Jeanne Madden), daughter of one councillor. Stuyvesant pardons Brock, but refuses to allow him to marry Tina. Stuyvesant himself decides to marry her. This prompts Brom to rouse the citizens against the governor, who senses the way the political winds are blowing and backs down. His decision is aided by Irving's warning him he must think of his place in history.

Principal song: September Song

Many critics considered Anderson's libretto preachy and cumbersome. However, Huston's memorable performance, especially his singing of "September Song," gave the show a modest popularity.

KNOBLAUCH [later anglicized to KNOBLOCK], Edward (1874–1945) Although born in New York and educated at Harvard, he spent most of his professional career in England, where he became a British subject in 1916. He began his career as an actor but soon switched to play-writing. He is best remembered for his *Kismet*♦ (1911), the story of a resourceful beggar who outwits the law in Baghdad. Among his other popular plays were *The Faun* (1911) and *Marie-Odile* (1915). Like many other theatrical figures with German names, he anglicized the spelling from World War I on.

Autobiography: *Round the Room,* London, 1939.

Knock Knock, a comedy in three acts by Jules Feiffer.♦ Produced at the Biltmore Theatre. February 24, 1976. 192 performances.

Two cantankerous middle-aged recluses, Cohn (Daniel Seltzer) and Abe (Neil Flanagan), who share a cabin in the woods, seem doomed to spend the rest of their days in petty quarrels. Suddenly their touchy existence is interrupted by the arrival of Joan of Arc (Nancy Snyder)—and her famous voices. Joan settles in with the men, cooking for them and helping them to try to understand each other better. When she leaves, apparently headed for heaven, it is debatable whether or not she has succeeded.

Critic Otis L. Guernsey, Jr.,♦ found this "mixture of old and new jokes, acrobatic language, an exploding kitchen, constantly lurking violence, etc."

at once "hilarious" and "perplexing." It was Feiffer's biggest Broadway success.

KNOWLES, [JAMES] SHERIDAN (1784–1862) The Irish actor-playwright performed with only passing success in America during the 1834–35 season. His relative failure, however, in no way diminished the opinion of many of his contemporaries that he was the greatest dramatist of his day. Such plays as *William Tell* (1825) and *The Wife* were in the American repertory for many years, but it was another pair of dramas that capped his reputation. *Virginius* (1820) and *The Hunchback*◆ (1832) both held the stage for the rest of the century and served as vehicles for many of the greatest American actors and actresses, from Junius Brutus Booth◆ and Edwin Forrest◆ through Mary Anderson◆ and Ada Rehan.◆

KOBER, ARTHUR, see *Having Wonderful Time*

KOLLMAR, RICHARD (1910–71) A native of Ridgewood, N.J., who studied at Yale with Professor George Pierce Baker,◆ he played prominent roles in such musicals as *Knickerbocker Holiday*◆ (1938) and *Too Many Girls* (1939) before turning producer. Alone or with others, he then offered *By Jupiter*◆ (1942), for which he was associate producer, *Early to Bed* (1943), *Are You with It?* (1945), and *Plain and Fancy*◆ (1955).

KOPIT, ARTHUR [LEE] (b. 1937) A native New Yorker, his first plays were produced at Harvard, where he was a student. In fact, the work that called most playgoers' attention to him, *Oh Dad, Poor Dad, Mamma's Hung You in the Closet and I'm Feelin' So Sad*◆ (1962), was acted at Harvard and in London before being presented off-Broadway. Focusing on a devouring woman who keeps her husband's corpse in the closet and who dominates her son, it was later moved to Broadway. He was subsequently represented on Broadway by *Indians* (1969), which blamed white Americans for the wanton annihilation of the redmen, and *Wings* (1979), a study of a woman recovering from a stroke. Both had first been performed at important regional theatres. Kopit wrote numerous other plays which were mounted successfully both at regional playhouses and off-Broadway, but which were not considered commercial prospects for Broadway. In 1982 he turned to the musical stage to create the book for the successful musical comedy *Nine.*◆

Korean War, see *Wars in American Drama*

Koster and Bial's For a brief time New York's most prestigious vaudeville house, it was established in 1879 by John Koster and Rudolf Bial as a concert hall in a building that had formerly been occupied by Dan Bryant's◆ Ministrels on 23rd Street. Within two years the concert program had been abandoned and a policy of changing variety bills introduced. Unlike Tony Pastor,◆ Koster and Bial placed a strong emphasis on importing foreign talent. In 1893 they moved to 34th Street, again renovating an existing theatre. The management was the first to introduce primitive films as part of a bill in 1896. Koster died in 1894, but the house continued its policy until 1901, when it was demolished to make way for Macy's Department Store.

KOTZEBUE, AUGUST FRIEDRICH FERDINAND VON (1761–1819) The playwright who was hailed briefly by some of his contemporaries as the German Shakespeare burst upon the American scene in Dunlap's◆ translation of his *Menschenhass und Reue,* here called *The Stranger.* ◆ The play's tremendous success not only saved Dunlap's faltering fortunes at the new Park Theatre◆ but also initiated the vogue of theatrical romanticism. The play retained its popularity for decades, as did his *Die Spanier in Peru,* which was played in America both in Dunlap's and Richard Brinsley Sheridan's◆ versions as *Pizarro.*◆ Between the first production of *The Stranger* and Dunlap's retirement in 1805 well over a dozen of Kotzebue's plays were premiered in New York and elsewhere, their increasing sensationalism precipitating the deluge of melodrama, much as *The Stranger* helped open the gates to romanticism. Among Dunlap's translations were *Lover's Vows* from *Das Kind der Liebe; False Shame* from *Falsche Scham; The Wild Goose Chase* from *Der Wildfang; The Force of Calumny* from *Die Verläumder;* and *The Virgin of the Sun* from *Die Sonnenjungfrau.* Except for *The Stranger* and *Pizarro,* few of the plays held the stage for long.

KRAMM, JOSEPH, see *Shrike, The*

KRAPP, HERBERT J. (1887–1973) The most productive of all American theatre architects, he was born in New York and studied at the Cooper Union Institute. At the height of his career he was the principal designer of playhouses for the Shuberts◆ as well as for other theatre owners. In New York alone he drew up the plans for the Alvin, the Ambassador, the Bijou, the Biltmore, the Central, the Century, the Ethel Barrymore, the Forrest (now the Eugene O'Neill), the 49th Street Theatre, the

46th Street Theatre, Hammerstein's, the Imperial, the Majestic, the Mansfield (now the Brooks Atkinson), the Masque (now the Golden), the Morosco, the Plymouth, the Ritz, the Royale, and the Waldorf.

KRASNA, NORMAN (1909–84) Born in Corona, N.Y., he studied at Columbia and at St. John's Law School before becoming a dramatic critic for the *World* and then the *Evening Graphic*. His first play, *Louder, Please* (1931), told of a press agent who fabricates a story of a shipwreck to ensure his client publicity. *Small Miracle* (1934) recounted the melodramatic events which ensue in a theatre lobby while a play is in progress. After many years as a film writer he returned to Broadway with *The Man with Blond Hair* (1941), a tale of an escaped German prisoner of war trapped in a Jewish tenement. His first success was *Dear Ruth*♦ (1944), a comedy about a teenager who writes letters to a lonely soldier but signs them with her sister's name. Thereafter all Krasna's best work was of a similar order. *John Loves Mary*♦ (1947) dealt with a returning soldier who complicates his life by marrying his buddy's English sweetheart in order to bring her to America. *Time for Elizabeth* (1948), a failure, written with Groucho Marx,♦ centered on a man's attempt to retire. *Kind Sir* (1953) depicted the romance of an actress and a banker. *Who Was That Lady I Saw You With?* (1958) described the problems that follow when two men pretend they are FBI agents. His last success was a lightweight sex comedy, *Sunday in New York* (1961), which told how a 22-year-old virgin finds real romance. Only two of his later plays reached New York, and both were failures: *Love in E Flat* (1967) was another sex comedy, this time about untrusting lovers who spy on each other, while *We Interrupt This Program* (1975) was a melodrama in which a gang holds playgoers hostage in order to secure the release of a gang member from prison.

KREMER, THEODORE (1871?–1923) Born in Cologne, he performed in both Europe and Australia before arriving in San Francisco in 1896. Almost immediately he began churning out melodramas for popular priced theatres. Among his titles were *The Slaves of the Orient, The Great Automobile Mystery, Secret Service Sam,* and *Fallen by the Wayside.* However, he is probably best recalled for writing one of the most successful of the many dramatizations of the story *Bertha, the Sewing Machine Girl.*♦

KRONENBERGER, LOUIS (1904–80) Born in Cincinnati and educated at the University there, he served as drama critic for *Time* (1936–61), for *PM* (1940–48), and briefly for *Town and Country*. At the same time he taught drama at numerous universities, including Columbia and Harvard, but most importantly at Brandeis, where he remained for many years. For Broadway he adapted Anouilh's♦ *Mademoiselle Colombe* (1954). He was also the author of many books, and from 1952 to 1961 edited the *Best Plays*♦ series. His writing featured a rapier wit and a unique sense of stylistic balance, which reflected his admiration of the elegances of the 18th century.

Autobiography: *No Whippings, No Gold Watches,* New York, 1970.

KRUGER, OTTO (1885–1974) One of Broadway's most popular leading men in the 1920s, he was born in Toledo and educated at the University of Michigan and Columbia. He first appeared before the public in 1900 in a Toledo production of *Quo Vadis?* Over a decade in stock and touring companies followed before he made his New York debut as Jack Bowling in *The Natural Law* (1915). Among his best remembered roles were Adam Smith, who reforms a spoiled family, in *Adam and Eva*♦ (1919); Stephen Murray, the tubercular patient who falls in love with a fellow patient, in *Eugene O'Neill's*♦ *Straw* (1921); Lee Randall, the reformed crook, in a 1921 revival of *Alias Jimmy Valentine*♦; Leonard Beebe, the conceited but incompetent salesman, in *To the Ladies*♦ (1922); the title role in *Will Shakespeare* (1923); Henry Williams, the hypochondriac who inadvertently becomes a hero, in *The Nervous Wreck*♦ (1923); and Anthony Cavendish, the John Barrymore-like actor, in *The Royal Family*♦ (1927). In the early 1930s he led several important road companies and was a replacement for important leading men on Broadway. After many years in films, he returned to Broadway in the 1940s without ever finding a successful play.

KRUTCH, JOSEPH WOOD (1893–1970) Born in Knoxville, he earned his bachelor's degree at the University of Tennessee and advanced degrees at Columbia, where he taught for many years. From 1924 to 1952 he was also drama critic for *The Nation*. Among his many works on theatre are *The American Drama Since 1918* (1939), and *'Modernism' in Modern Drama* (1953). He served as president of the New York Drama Critics Circle for the 1940–41 season. Krutch's interest was not so much in the presentation and immediacy of plays as in their value as enduring literature.

KUMMER, CLARE [RODMAN] [née BEECHER] (1873?–1958) She began her career as a song writer, but enjoyed a huge success with her first produced play, *Good Gracious Annabelle*♦ (1916), in which some moneyless society youngsters hire themselves out as servants. Her second play, *A Successful Calamity* (1917), was also a hit. Written as a vehicle for her cousin, William Gillette,♦ it told of a millionaire who feigns bankruptcy in order to enjoy a night away from his family. Although over a dozen more of her plays were produced on Broadway, her only other important successes were two vehicles written for her son-in-law, Roland Young♦: *Rollo's Wild Oat*♦ (1920), in which a talentless, stage-struck youngster mounts his own version of *Hamlet;* and *Her Master's Voice*♦ (1933), centering on a luckless husband who dreams of becoming a famous singer.

L

La Cage aux Folles, a musical comedy in two acts, based on a French play of the same name. Book by Harvey Fierstein.♦ Lyrics and music by Jerry Herman.♦ Produced at the Palace Theatre.♦ August 21, 1983. 1,761 performances.

Georges (Gene Barry), a night-club operator, and Albin (George Hearn), a female impersonator, long have been lovers, although Georges once had a heterosexual affair which left him with a son (John Weiner). Now that son wants to marry. His prospective father-in-law (Jay Garner), a crusader against homosexuals, presents problems when the two families meet, and Albin, in drag, is introduced as mama.

Principal Songs: I Am What I Am · Look Over There · Song on the Sand.

Despite a potentially difficult and offensive theme, the musical's essential lightheartedness and melodiousness, coupled with a gaudy production, made it a success.

La Mama Experimental Theatre Club Founded in Greenwich Village in 1962 by Ellen Stewart, a native of Alexandria, La., who had previously served as an elevator operator and clothing designer, initially it was a combination boutique and theatre, but soon became a leading off-off-Broadway center, presenting numerous avant-garde plays and companies. It is popularly known as Café La Mama.

LACKAYE, WILTON (1862–1932) Born in Loudon County, Va., and educated at Georgetown University, he was barely out of college when he made his debut as Lucentio opposite Lawrence Barrett♦ in an 1883 revival of *Francesca da Rimini.*♦ Afterwards he played important roles in support of Fanny Davenport♦ and other stars. Among his most significant early assignments were Gouroc, the nobleman turned villainous revolutionary, in *Paul Kauvar*♦ (1887), and Robert, the thieving twin brother of the hero, in *Allan Dare* (1887). He followed this with appearances in similar dramas and in contemporary comedies such as *Featherbrain* (1889), *Shenandoah*♦ (1889), *Money Mad* (1890), *The Power of the Press* (1891), and *Aristocracy* (1892). His most famous role was the villainous Svengali in *Trilby*♦ (1895). In 1898 he was Sir Lucius

O'Trigger in Joseph Jefferson's♦ revival of *The Rivals,* then played leading roles in, among others, *The Children of the Ghetto* (1899), *Don Caesar's Return* (1901), *Colorado* (1901), *A Modern Magdalen* (1902), and *The Frisky Mrs. Johnson* (1903). In 1904 he produced and starred in a much praised version of *The Pillars of Society.* He continued to appear both in new plays and revivals, especially of *Trilby,* until shortly before his death. Lackaye had a pleasant, round face, with large eyes, and for many years sported a prominent handle-bar moustache.

Ladder, The, a play in three acts by J. Frank Davis. Produced by Brock Pemberton♦ at the Mansfield Theatre. October 22, 1926. 794 performances.

Margaret Newell (Antoinette Perry♦) has proposals from two men, the charming, but vacillating Roger Crane (Vernon Steele) and the ruthless Stephen Pennock (Hugh Buckler), who has ruined Roger in business. Thinking back, Margaret realizes that the men's proposals are nothing new. In the 14th century, when Stephen was the Earl of Orleton, he murdered Roger to win her. Under other names Stephen did similar dastardly acts in the 17th and 19th centuries. So Margaret throws her lot with Roger again, come what may.

Ridiculed by most critics, the play nevertheless was the fourth longest running show in Broadway history when it closed. It was able to run so long because a millionaire oil man, Edgar B. Davis, who believed in reincarnation as much as the author, underwrote the play for its entire stand and even admitted the public free when playgoers would not buy tickets. The play never made a profit and Davis is reputed to have spent between a half million and a million dollars on it.

J. F. Davis (1870–1941) was born in New Bedford, Mass., and spent many years in newspaper work. This was his only play to reach Broadway.

Ladies' Night [often called *Ladies' Night in a Turkish Bath*], a farce in three acts by Avery Hopwood♦ and Charlton Andrews. Produced by A. H. Woods♦ at the Eltinge Theatre. August 9, 1920. 375 performances.

Because Jimmy Walters (John Cumberland♦) is so shy and prudish his friends decide to take him to an artists' ball, a sort of pseudo-pagan ritual where he will see lots of bare flesh. Unfortunately, the police raid the party, so Jimmy flees through a window into the building next door. That building houses a Turkish bath, and it so happens it is a special night catering only to ladies. It takes Jimmy two acts to calm down and explain his actions.

A brainless but funny farce, it was one of the major hits of its day and was long popular in summer stock. It was revived off-Broadway in 1961.

Lady, Be Good!, a musical comedy in two acts. Book by Guy Bolton♦ and Fred Thompson.♦ Lyrics by Ira Gershwin.♦ Music by George Gershwin.♦ Produced by Alex A. Aarons♦ and Vinton Freedley♦ at the Liberty Theatre. December 1, 1924. 330 performances.

After Dick Trevor (Fred Astaire♦) rebuffs Josephine Vanderwater (Jayne Auburn), she evicts him and his sister Susie (Adele Astaire♦) from an apartment she owns. By coincidence both the Trevors and Josephine have the same lawyer, "Watty" Watkins (Walter Catlett♦), so he sets about righting matters. Since Watkins himself is in a jam, his fee to the moneyless Trevors is to demand that Susie pose as a Mexican. In the end, Susie marries Jack Robinson (Alan Edwards), and Dick ditches Josephine permanently for Shirley Vernon (Kathlene Martyn).

Principal songs: Fascinating Rhythm · Oh, Lady Be Good! · So Am I

This was one of the most important of American musicals, for its Gershwin score established the ascendancy of native, jazz-based lyricism in American musical comedy and helped promote a clear distinction between musical comedy and operetta. The first collaboration of George and Ira to reach Broadway—their *A Dangerous Maid* (1921) had folded out of town—it gave them instant fame as a team. It also consolidated the growing reputation of the Astaires.

Lady in the Dark, a musical comedy in two acts. Book by Moss Hart.♦ Lyrics by Ira Gershwin.♦ Music by Kurt Weill.♦ Produced by Sam H. Harris♦ at the Alvin Theatre. January 23, 1941. 467 performances.

Although Liza Elliott (Gertrude Lawrence♦) is a successful fashion magazine editor, privately she is an unhappy woman. She tells her analyst that while her dreams are filled with familiar figures, they act in unfamiliar ways. Most prominent in her dreams are Kendall Nesbitt (Bert Lytell), her lover and the man who has helped her to the top of her profes-

sion; Charley Johnson (MacDonald Carey), her crusty advertising manager; Russell Paxton (Danny Kaye♦), the magazine's effeminate photographer; and Randy Curtis (Victor Mature), a handsome but stupid movie star. By recounting her dreams, Liza comes to realize that her father's disdain for her when she was a child has warped her relations with men.

Principal songs: My Ship · [The Saga of] Jenny · Tschaikowsky

John Anderson wrote in the *Journal-American,* "It is a play that requires nearly three hours and four revolving stages to reach a given, and I must say rather obvious point, a play partly psychoanalysis, part ballet, and part drama. Whatever else it is, though, it is a triumph of stagecraft, a beautiful and imaginative production . . . but wearisomely long and a little prententious." While most critics held fewer reservations, the play, whether because of the lavishness required or because none of its songs became exceptionally popular, has received no major revival. The employment of songs in the show was interesting. Only one song, "My Ship," used in snatches as a motif until near the end of the evening, was sung during the frame sections—the visits to the doctor. All the other songs were presented during the essentially surrealistic dream sequences, including Danny Kaye's show-stopping rendition of the tongue-twisting "Tschaikowsky" and Miss Lawrence's witty delivery of "[The Saga of] Jenny."

Lady of Lyons, The This romantic drama by Bulwer-Lytton♦ centers on Pauline Deschapelles, who is tricked by her rejected suitor, the Marquis Beauséant, into marrying Claude Melnotte, her gardener's son. Beauséant had persuaded Melnotte to pose as a foreign prince, but when, after the marriage, Melnotte takes Pauline to the home of his widowed mother she learns the truth. The remorseful Melnotte joins the army and the marriage is annulled. Beauséant induces Pauline to marry him to save her father from bankruptcy. However, Melnotte returns from the wars as a hero and Pauline realizes that she truly loves him. The original American cast at New York's Park Theatre♦ in 1838 included Mrs. Richardson as Pauline, Edwin Forrest♦ as Melnotte, and Peter Richings♦ as Beauséant. No less than Charlotte Cushman♦ was the Widow Melnotte. The work remained one of the most popular of all plays for the rest of the century. The list of important performers in this play would include virtually every major serious actor and actress of the period. Among the many Paulines were Fanny Morant,♦ Fanny Janauschek,♦ Emma

Waller,♦ Fanny Davenport,♦ Mary Anderson,♦ Adelaide Neilson,♦ and Mrs. Langtry.♦ Notable Melnottes included Edwin Booth,♦ Charles Fechter,♦ H. J. Montague,♦ Charles Coghlan,♦ and Eben Plympton.♦

Lafayette Theatre Along with the Apollo, a vaudeville house, the Lafayette was the most famous theatre in Harlem. Built in 1912, at a time when New York's major black district was moving from San Juan Hill to the area, it gained widespread celebrity when it offered the hugely successful *Darktown Follies* (1913). The emphasis on musicals was abandoned when Anita Bush moved her stock company to the theatre in 1915. The company soon became known as the Lafayette Players and helped black performers such as Charles Gilpin♦ gain recognition. Its repertory ranged from Shakespeare to new plays of contemporary black life. The Players disbanded in 1932. Later in the 1930s it became the Harlem center for the Federal Theatre♦ under whose aegis it offered highly praised mountings of such works as *Run, Little Chillun!, Stevedore, Macbeth,*♦ and *The Swing Mikado.* Thereafter the house fell on hard times and for a while was used as a church. It burned in 1968, soon after an attempt had been made to restore it to live theatre. The theatre was sometimes called "The House Beautiful," and a large tree, reputedly an elm, which stood in front of it, was considered a talisman by struggling black performers, who felt that touching it would bring them luck and so named it the "Tree of Hope."

LAHR, BERT [né IRVING LAHRHEIM] (1895–1967) The rubber-faced, caterwauling comedian—famous for his "gnong-gnong" and "Some fun, eh kid?"—began his career in vaudeville and burlesque. His first Broadway assignment was in *Delmar's Revels* (1927), but it was his clowning as the punch-drunk Gink Schiner in *Hold Everything!*♦ (1928) that made him a star. Appearances followed in *Flying High* (1930), *Hot-Cha!* (1932), *George White's Music Hall Varieties* (1932), *Life Begins at 8:40* (1934), *George White's Scandals of 1935,*♦ *The Show Is On* (1936), *Du Barry Was a Lady*♦ (1939), and *Seven Lively Arts* (1944). In 1946 he was praised for his performance as Skid in a revival of *Burlesque,*♦ then, after touring in *Make Mine Manhattan* (1948) and appearing in *Two on the Aisle* (1951), he won further laurels for his portrayal of Estragon in *Waiting for Godot*♦ (1956), a role he claimed he never understood. He next played Boniface in the farce *Hotel Paradiso* (1957), and toured as the General in *Romanoff and Juliet* (1959). He returned

briefly to revue in the unsuccessful *The Boys Against the Girls* (1959), after which he toured as Bottom in *A Midsummer Night's Dream*♦ (1960). His performance in a number of quick-change roles in *The Beauty Part* (1962) was one of his most memorable achievements, but the play opened in the midst of a newspaper strike and had only a short run. His last Broadway appearance was in the musical *Foxy* (1964). Describing his antics in this musical, critic Richard Gilman noted, "The eyes roll upward toward heaven or the house dick, the great moose calls shake the furniture, the miracle of lust wedded to innocence and appetite to ineptness is once more effected. 'Play me like a harp!' the temptress challenges him. [He responds with] An exquisitely fractional silence, a baring of the teeth, and an 'I can't, I got a sore pinky.' "

Biography: *Notes on a Cowardly Lion,* John Lahr, New York, 1969.

LAMB, THOMAS (1871–1942) Born in Dundee, Scotland, he came to America while still a youth and studied architecture at the Cooper Union Institute. Although he is best remembered for his Adamesque movie palaces and for designing the second Madison Square Garden, he also was the architect for numerous legitimate theatres. His New York playhouses were the Eltinge, the Harris, the Mark Hellinger, and, with Joseph Urban,♦ the Ziegfeld.♦

LAMBS, THE In 1874 a group of men, most of whom were members of the cast of *The Shaughraun,*♦ formed a supper club and named it after a similar London society. Until that time most actors had used either Union Square or public bars as meeting places. The club was incorporated in 1877 and moved to its first permanent home shortly thereafter. In short order the members became famous for their camaraderie and conviviality. Their president was known as their Shepherd, their vice president as the Boy. In 1904 the club moved into impressive new quarters on 44th Street just east of Broadway, complete with its own theatre, all designed by Stanford White. One of the group's most famous functions was the Lambs' Gambols, in which members performed for no fee and whose proceeds were offered to charity. During the club's heyday, several of these Gambols toured the country. Financial difficulties forced the club to sell its building in 1974, and the organization now operates on a more restricted scale.

LANDER, MRS. [née JEAN MARGARET DAVENPORT] (1829–1903) The daughter of English performers, she made her American debut in 1838 as a child prodigy. Her first appearance was as Young Norval, and was followed by her Shylock and Sir Peter Teazle, as well as roles in less well remembered plays. When she returned to New York in 1849, both she and her art had matured. She won applause for her interpretation of the heroines in such popular plays as *Romeo and Juliet,* ◆ *The Hunchback,* ◆ *The Lady of Lyons,* ◆ and *Ingomar.* ◆ In 1853 she was the first actress to portray Adrienne Lecouvreur and Camille in English to American audiences. She retired briefly after her marriage in 1860 to Frederick Lander, but resumed her career after he was killed in the Civil War. She then appeared in English versions of many of the plays Adelaide Ristori◆ had offered. Among her later parts were the title role in Legouvé's *Medea,* Colombe in Browning's *Colombe's Birthday,* Peg Woffington in Reade's *Masks and Faces,* and Hester Prynne in *The Scarlet Letter.* A small, attractive woman, she was, according to William Winter,◆ "remarkable for thoroughness of impersonation, complete command of the essential implements of histrionic art, a fine intellect, a lovely feminine temperament, peculiar clarity and sweetness of elocution, and the controlling faculty of taste."

LANE, BURTON [né LEVY] (b. 1912) The New York native began his professional career by writing the music for songs which were interpolated into the revues *Three's a Crowd* (1930) and *The Third Little Show*◆ (1931). He then wrote the score for *Earl Carroll's Vanities of 1931,* ◆ after which he spent a decade in Hollywood. His next score was for *Hold On to Your Hats* (1940), and included "There's a Great Day Coming, Mañana." No memorable songs emerged from his work for *Laughing Room Only* (1944), but his great score for *Finian's Rainbow*◆ (1947), written with lyricist E. Y. Harburg,◆ offered "How Are Things in Glocca Morra?," "If This Isn't Love," and "Old Devil Moon." Of his score for *On a Clear Day You Can See Forever* (1965) only the title song has remained popular, while another fine score was neglected after the failure of *Carmelina* (1979).

LANE, WILLIAM HENRY (1825?–52) A black, probably born in New York, he first attracted attention in the early 1840s with his superb jigs and other dances at a hall in the notorious Five Points district where he performed as Juba or Master Juba. Dickens saw him there in 1842 and wrote about him. He was considered for a time the major rival to Master John Diamond,◆ the young white dancer, and is said to have bested him in several challenge dances. He

performed in 1846 with White's Serenaders, a minstrel band, but in 1848 left for England, where he died.

LANGNER, LAWRENCE (1890–1962) Born in Wales, he drifted into theatrical work in London before emigrating to America. In 1914 he was one of the founders of the Washington Square Players,◆ and after that troupe disbanded he was an organizer of the Theatre Guild,◆ which he was to run with Theresa Helburn◆ for all of its greatest years, supervising over 200 productions. He also built the Westport (Conn.) Country Playhouse and was founder and president of the American Shakespeare Festival◆ in Stratford (Conn.). Alone or with his wife, Armina Marshall, he wrote several plays, the most notable of which was *The Pursuit of Happiness*◆ (1933).

Autobiography: *The Magic Curtain,* New York, 1951.

LANGTRY, LILLIE (sometimes spelled LILY) [née EMILIE CHARLOTTE LE BRETON] (1853–1929) The daughter of a minister on the island of Jersey, she married into London society and became one of the first Englishwomen from that society to embark on a stage career. Known popularly as "The Jersey Lily," she was a great beauty who was not always careful of the proprieties of the time. One of her extended affairs was with Edward, Prince of Wales. Her glamour and the hints of scandal helped make her a celebrity. Her American debut was to have been at a theatre which burned just hours before her first appearance in 1882, so she made her debut a week later at Wallack's as Hester Grazebrook in Tom Taylor's◆ old play, *An Unequal Match.* Although she attempted such classic roles as Rosalind and Lady Macbeth, she was at her best in contemporary pieces. She made a number of American visits and was best received in such plays as *Gossip* (1895) and the controversial *The Degenerates* (1900). Surprisingly, given his customarily strict moral attitudes, William Winter◆ was one of her admirers. He praised "her well proportioned, lissome figure, shapely and finely poised head, long, oval face, pure white complexion, large gray eyes—innocent, candid, and sweet in expression—abundant chestnut hair, and rich, cordial, winning voice," adding that her acting "put detraction to silence and won and held a large measure of public sympathy and critical respect."

Biography: *Because I Loved Him: The Life and Loves of Lillie Langtry,* Noel B. Gerson, New York, 1971.

LANSBURY, ANGELA [BRIGID] (b. 1925) The London-born actress came to Broadway after a long career in films. Her first New York role was Marcelle, the high-strung wife, in the farce *Hotel Paradiso* (1957). In 1960 she was Helen, the heroine's cheerfully independent mother, in *A Taste of Honey.* Her first venture into musicals came as Cora Hoover Hoople in Stephen Sondheim's♦ *Anyone Can Whistle* (1964). However, her best-remembered roles were in four subsequent musicals, playing the leading roles in *Mame*♦ (1966), in which one critic praised her "wit, poise, warmth and a very taking coolth"; *Dear World* (1969), a 1974 revival of *Gypsy,*♦ and *Sweeney Todd*♦ (1979), in which she offered an interpretation of Mrs. Lovett remarkable for its blending of cruelty and humor. She won Tony Awards♦ for all four performances.

LAPINE, JAMES (b. 1949) A native of Mansfield, Ohio, he studied design at the California Institute of the Arts and apprenticed at the Yale School of Drama. But his interest in writing and directing grew. He first called attention to his abilities with his play *Table Settings* (1980), then earned wide aclaim for his staging of the off-Broadway musical *March of the Falsettos* (1981). In 1982 his staging of *A Midsummer Night's Dream*♦ for the New York Shakespeare Festival♦ was well received. He won more applause for the book and direction of *Sunday in the Park with George*♦ (1984), then successfully revamped an older Sondheim♦ musical, *Merrily We Roll Along,* for a remounting in La Jolla, Calif. In a further collaboration with Sondheim, he staged and provided the book for *Into the Woods* (1987). His 1989 revival of *A Winter's Tale* for the New York Shakespeare Festival added to his fine record.

LARDNER, RING[GOLD WILMER] (1885–1933) The famed humorist and short-story writer was best known to playgoers as George S. Kaufman's♦ collaborator on *June Moon*♦ (1929), a spoof of Tin Pan Alley. A year earlier he had been the author of a play about baseball, *Elmer the Great.* He also contributed sketches and lyrics to several musicals, among them some editions of the *Ziegfeld Follies,*♦ *The 49ers* (1922), and *Smiles* (1930).

LARIMORE, EARLE (1899–1947) A fine actor who was never able to capitalize on his early promise, he was born in Portland, Ore., where he began acting while still a child. He made his New York debut in 1925 and was afterwards seen as George, the ruthless husband, in *Ned McCobb's Daughter*♦ (1926); Robert, the cowed son, in *The Silver Cord*♦ (1926); Alistin Lowe, a determined suitor, in *The Second Man*♦ (1927); Sam Evans, a weak man accepted by the possessive heroine, in *Strange Interlude*♦ (1928); Norman Rose, the rich Jew, in *Hotel Universe*♦ (1930); Orin Mannon, the Orestes-like son, in *Mourning Becomes Electra*♦ (1931); Richard Kurt, the radical editor, in *Biography*♦ (1932); and John, the better half of the hero's split personality, in *Days Without End*♦ (1934). Following this impressive series his career inexplicably faltered.

LARRIMORE, FRANCINE [née FANYA LEVOVKSY] (1898–1975) Niece of the great Yiddish actor, Jacob Adler,♦ the blue-eyed beauty with reddish-gold hair was born in France, but came to America while still very young. She made her debut as a child in 1910 in *A Fool There Was.*♦ Her first major success came when she headed the Chicago company of Avery Hopwood's♦ *Fair and Warmer*♦ (1916), playing Blanche Wheeler, the baby-talking, homebody of a wife who complicates the lives of all her friends. Among her later successes were her performances as Nita Leslie, the hired "other woman," in *Parlor, Bedroom and Bath*♦ (1917); Theodora Gloucester, the brazen flapper who finally finds real love, in *Nice People*♦ (1921); Roxie Hart, the publicity-seeking murderess, in *Chicago*♦ (1926); Kitty Brown, the divorcée who reclaims her ex-husband, in *Let Us Be Gay*♦ (1929); and Abbey Fane, the night-club singer who marries into society, in *Brief Moment*♦ (1931).

LA SHELLE, KIRKE (1862–1905) Born in Wyoming, Ill., he left school to work in newspapers, eventually rising to managing editor of several Chicago dailies. E. S. Willard♦ persuaded him to become his business manager. He followed this with time as a partner to George Lederer♦ and then as business manager for the Bostonians.♦ With monies he had saved he embarked on an independent producing career by co-producing the comic opera *The Wizard of the Nile* (1895). For that show's star, Frank Daniels,♦ he later mounted *The Idol's Eye* (1897); *The Ameer* (1899), for which he also served as co-librettist; and *Miss Simplicity* (1902). Among the successful straight plays he produced were *Arizona*♦ (1900); *The Earl of Pawtucket*♦ (1903); and his collaborative dramatization with Owen Wister of that author's *The Virginian*♦ (1904). Failing health forced him to retire when he was in his early forties.

Last Mile, The, a drama in three acts by John Wexley. Produced by Herman Shumlin♦ at the Sam

H. Harris Theatre. February 13, 1930. 285 performances.

The prisoners in death row at Keystone State Penitentiary help Richard Walters (James Bell) sit out his last moments. Two weeks later it is Eddie Werner's turn to die. But as a guard comes to give Eddie (George Leach) his final meal, the other prisoners, led by the hardened, ruthless John Mears (Spencer Tracy), seize the guard and kill him. A bloody mutiny has begun, which for a time appears to be succeeding. However, the odds against the prisoners ultimately prove irresistible. Realizing the futility of his uprising, Mears walks out to surrender and is gunned down.

Noting that it had been many years since a play caused so much excitement in theatrical circles, Burns Mantle♦ found it "a tragedy so tense, so stripped of theatrical artificialities, and emotionally so moving that even calloused reviewers of plays were frank to admit its disturbing and unsettling effect upon their nerves . . . [a play] that must be reckoned among the greatest theatre exhibits of the time."

The first act was derived largely from a short play called *The Law Takes Its Toll*, which had been published in the *American Mercury* in 1929 and had been written by Robert Blake, an inmate who had been executed shortly afterward. He claimed his dialogue was mostly verbatim transcriptions of actual conversations. The New York-born Wexley (1907–85) was a nephew of Maurice Schwartz♦ and was also an actor. He wrote numerous one-act plays as well as two other full-length plays that were presented in New York: *Steel* (1931), a story of labor agitation; and *They Shall Not Die* (1934), a dramatization of the Scottsboro case. Tracy (1900–1967), a native of Milwaukee, had appeared in a number of Broadway plays during the 1920s, but only achieved major attention with this performance. His distinguished film career began when he re-created this role. Except for starring in the short-lived Robert Sherwood♦ drama *The Rugged Path* (1945), the remainder of his career was in films.

Last of the Red Hot Lovers, The, a comedy in three acts by Neil Simon.♦ Produced at the Eugene O'Neill Theatre. December 28, 1969. 706 performances.

Barney Cashman (James Coco), the owner of a fish restaurant, is middle-aged, overweight, married—and anxious to have one last fling. Discovering that his mother's apartment is empty on certain days, he lures three totally different types of women there and attempts to seduce them. He bungles

every attempt. In desperation he asks up the only other woman he can think of—his wife, Thelma. But apparently even she is not too eager to accept his invitation.

One of Simon's many gag-filled yet probing comedies, it was assessed by Richard Watts, Jr.,♦ of the New York *Post* as "delightfully hilarious and witty, as well as filled with the wisdom about human nature characteristic of all his work."

Last Word, The, a comedy in four acts by Augustin Daly.♦ Produced by Daly at Daly's Theatre. October 28, 1890. 101 performances.

When Faith Rutherwell (Isabel Irving) announces she will marry Boris Bagoleff (Sidney Herbert) instead of the Baron Stuyve (Sidney Bowkett), whom her father (George Clarke) has selected for her, she is forced to leave her father's house. The Baroness Vera Boraneff (Ada Rehan♦), a beautiful and rich "Witch from the Neva," whose laugh is "a full yard of velvet sunshine," and who is also Boris's sister, takes Faith under her wing. Faith's brother, Harry (John Drew♦), a conscientious but bookish physician, comes to Vera's house to demand that Faith change her mind. But Vera not only proves to Harry that the Baron is treacherous and her brother worthwhile, she makes Harry realize that he loves her. Together they make the elder Rutherwell see things their way.

Based on Shoenthan's *Das letzte Wort,* the play was one of Daly's last major successes in modern comedy.

Late George Apley, The, a comedy in three acts and an epilogue by John P. Marquand and George S. Kaufman.♦ Produced by Max Gordon♦ at the Lyceum Theatre.♦ November 21, 1944. 385 performances.

George Apley (Leo G. Carroll♦) is a Harvard-educated Boston Brahmin who has lived a happy, if stolidly conventional life. But his contentment is jolted when his daughter Eleanor (Joan Chandler) falls in love with a Greenwich Village bohemian who is, horror of horrors, a Yale graduate. At the same time, George's son, John (David McKay), announces he will marry the daughter of a rich manufacturer from Worcester. Eleanor has the gumption to marry, but John goes off to Europe after his fiancée's father also objects to John's marriage plans. Twelve years later George is dead and John has become a stuffy Brahmin, thereby continuing the family tradition.

Although some critics found the play formless, little more than a series of amusing, loosely related incidents, Robert Garland of the *Journal-American* hailed it as "an evening of sheer delight, wise, witty and enchantingly satirical." The performance of Carroll captured Brahmin stuffiness to a T, but never lost the audience's interest or affection. The comedy was based on Marquand's Pulitzer Prize-winning novel of the same name.

LATEINER, JOSEPH (1853–1935) For many years this European-born author of Yiddish plays and operettas was one of the most prolific and popular figures in American-Jewish theatricals, although, as historian Nahma Sandrow has written, his name is now "synonymous with vulgar baked goods or uncertain freshness." He wrote over eighty plays, including *Ezra; or, The Eternal Jew, Mishke and Moshke; or, Europeans in America,* and *The Jewish Heart.*

LATHAM, FREDERICK G. (1853?–1943) The English-born producer and director had a long, successful career in London before coming to America in 1897 to work with Maurice Grau. Shortly thereafter he managed the American tours of Sarah Bernhardt♦ and Coquelin.♦ For many years he was an important director of musicals, including *Mlle. Modiste*♦ (1905), *The Red Mill*♦ (1906), *The Firefly*♦ (1912), *The Only Girl* (1914), *The Princess Pat* (1915), *Eileen* (1917), *Apple Blossoms*♦ (1919), and *The Night Boat* (1920).

LATOUCHE, JOHN [TREVILLE] (1917–56) The brilliant lyricist, and occasional librettist, whose early death deprived the musical theatre of a major talent, was born in Richmond, Va., and contributed his first lyrics to *From Vienna* (1939). He called attention to his art with his work in *Cabin in the Sky*♦ (1940). Subsequent collaborations included *Banjo Eyes* (1941), *Beggar's Holiday* (1946), and *Ballet Ballads* (1948). His finest achievement was his libretto for *The Golden Apple*♦ (1954), a recounting of the *Iliad* and the *Odyssey* in terms of turn-of-the-century America. Since there was no spoken dialogue, his lyrics in effect comprised the complete libretto. His last work was heard in *The Vamp* (1955) and in *Candide*♦ (1956).

LAUDER, HARRY [né HUGH MACLENNAN] (1870–1950) A wry, wee Scot, he was almost certainly the most popular foreign entertainer in American vaudeville, although, curiously, he never played the Palace.♦ Between 1907 and 1934 he made 25 American tours. Dressed in a kilt and all the other classic Scottish regalia, and brandishing a crooked

walking stick, he would saunter grumpily on stage, then slowly warm to his audience with his homespun stories and his songs. *Variety*♦ wrote, "It is impossible to catch and analyze the peculiarly elusive charm of this great artist. It is a thing so subtle and indefinable it has not a name, and yet it exerts a force that cannot be escaped . . . His every word and gesture gives a line or faithful touch of color to the picture he seeks to draw, and the whole is a vivid, forceful characterization." Among his best-loved songs were "I Love a Lassie," "Just a Wee Deoch-an-Doris," "She is Ma Daisy," "Stop Yer Tickling, Jock," and his most famous, "Roamin' in the Gloamin'."

Biography: *Valiant Minstrel, the Story of Harry Lauder,* Gladys Malvern, New York, 1943.

LAUGHTON, CHARLES (1899–1962) The heavyset, wry-faced English actor first appeared in America in two thrillers, *Payment Deferred* (1931) and *The Fatal Alibi* (1932). He did not return to the stage until after a long, distinguished film career. In 1947 he appeared in his own adaptation of *Galileo,* then played the Devil in *Don Juan in Hell* (1951), also directing the production. He next adapted and directed *John Brown's Body* (1953) and staged *The Caine Mutiny Court-Martial* (1954). His last appearance was as Undershaft in a 1956 revival of *Major Barbara,* which he staged.

LAURENTS, ARTHUR (b. 1918). The Brooklyn-born playwright and director was educated at Cornell. His first play, *Home of the Brave* (1945), a story of anti-Semitism in the war, was praised by many critics, but failed commercially. Although he wrote several other plays that pleased many critics, his only major success was one of the lightest of these, *The Time of the Cuckoo*♦ (1952), which centered on the bittersweet romance of an American spinster in Italy. He found more favor as a librettist, especially with *West Side Story*♦ (1957) and *Gypsy*♦ (1959). His other librettos were *Anyone Can Whistle* (1964), which he directed as well; *Do I Hear a Waltz?* (1965); and *Hallelujah, Baby!* (1967). He also directed the musicals *I Can Get It for You Wholesale* (1962) and *La Cage aux Folles*♦ (1983).

Law of the Land, *The,* a play in four acts by George Broadhurst.♦ Produced by Broadhurst at the 48th Street Theatre. September 30, 1914. 221 performances.

Mrs. Harding (Julia Dean♦) puts up with her savagely sadistic husband (Charles Lane) for the sake of her young son, Bennie (Master Macomber), but when Harding slashes at Bennie with a bullwhip, Mrs. Harding grabs a gun and shoots. The understanding family doctor is willing to declare the death accidental, Mrs. Harding's friends are prepared to tamper with the evidence to exonerate her, and her most ardent admirer, Geoffrey Morton (Milton Sills), stands ready to claim he shot Harding. For a time Mrs. Harding seems willing to let Morton take the blame, only finally to blurt out a confession. However, the kindly Inspector Cochrane (George Fawcett♦), seeing the whip marks on the young boy, writes a report that assures no jury would convict the woman.

While not as successful as Broadhurst's earlier and not dissimilar *Bought and Paid For,♦* the play was sufficiently taut and thrilling to find a wide audience.

LAWRENCE, GERTRUDE [née GERTRUD ALEXANDRA DAGMAR LAWRENCE KLASEN] (1898–1952) Although she could not dance well and sang off-key, this graceful, haughty beauty was one of the great stars of the musical stage, as well as of straight comedy. She was born in London, where she had begun to make an important name for herself in revues before coming to America with *Charlot's Revue♦* (1924). After appearing in a 1926 version of the same show, she was starred in *Oh, Kay!* (1926), in which she introduced "Someone To Watch Over Me" and "Do, Do, Do." Assignments followed in the musical *Treasure Girl* (1928); the romantic comedy *Candle-Light* (1929); and *The International Revue* (1930). She then scored a major success as Amanda Prynne, playing opposite Noel Coward,♦ with whom she was long and closely associated, in his *Private Lives♦* (1931). She returned to New York in 1936 to again play opposite Coward in his *Tonight at 8:30,* a bill of one-act plays. Successes followed as Susan Trexel, who finds religion by helping her family, in *Susan and God♦* (1937), and as Lydia Kenyon, the neglected wife, in *Skylark* (1939). She returned to musicals to play the lead in *Lady in the Dark♦* (1941), in which she sang "[The Saga of] Jenny." After the war she appeared as Eliza Doolittle in a revival of *Pygmalion♦* (1945), then toured and finally played New York in a revival of *Tonight at 8:30* (1948). Her last appearance was as the English tutoress, Anna Leonowens, in the musical *The King and I♦* (1951), in which she introduced "Getting To Know You," "Hello, Young Lovers," "I Whistle a Happy Tune," and "Shall We Dance?."

Biography: *Gertrude Lawrence,* Sheridan Morley, New York, 1981.

LAWRENCE, JEROME (b. 1915) A native of Cleveland and a graduate of Ohio State University, the playwright has collaborated on all his major works with Robert E. Lee (b. 1918), a native of Elyria, Ohio, who was educated at Ohio Wesleyan and Drake. They have written the books for such musicals as *Look, Ma, I'm Dancin'!* (1948) and *Mame* (1966), the latter taken from their popular play, *Auntie Mame♦* (1956), which in turn had been based on a best-selling novel. Their most notable drama was *Inherit the Wind♦* (1955), a retelling of the 1925 Scopes "Monkey" trial. Another work, *The Night Thoreau Spent in Jail,* was popular with amateur groups.

LAWSON, JOHN HOWARD (1894–1977) The controversial playwright was born in New York and educated at Williams College. He began writing plays while still in college, and several were produced away from New York. His first play to reach Broadway was *Roger Bloomer* (1923), an expressionistic satire centering on a young man's rebellion against bourgeois society. His extreme left-wing bent was even more pronounced in *Processional* (1925), in which a West Virginia miners' strike was seen largely in terms of good Marxists versus bad Fascists. He continued, although with less success, to write similar pieces until 1937, when the Group Theatre♦ mounted his *Marching Song,* another story of strikers against strikebreakers. Ironically, he left the theatre for more lucrative film-writing, remaining an important screenwriter until he was blacklisted in the McCarthy era. Lawson was also the author of *Theory and Technique of Playwriting* (1936).

LAYTON, JOE [né JOSEPH LICHTMAN] (b. 1931) The Brooklyn-born choreographer and director made his debut as a dancer in the chorus of *Oklahoma!♦* in 1947 and danced in several other shows before choreographing a 1959 off-Broadway revival of *On the Town.♦* He subsequently created the dances for *Once Upon a Mattress* (1959), *The Sound of Music♦* (1959), *Greenwillow* (1960), *Tenderloin* (1960), and *Sail Away* (1961). In 1962 he handled both the choreography and over-all direction of *No Strings,♦* and did similar double duty in *The Girl Who Came to Supper* (1963), *Drat! The Cat!* (1965), *Sherry!* (1967), *George M!* (1968), *Dear World* (1969), *Two by Two* (1970), *Bette Midler's Clams on the Half-Shell Revue* (1975), *An Evening with Diana Ross* (1976), *Platinum* (1978), and *Barnum* (1980). He won Tony Awards♦ for his work in *No Strings* and *George M!.*

LEACOCK, J., see *Fall of British Tyranny, The*

League of American Theatres and Producers, THE Founded in 1930 as the League of New York Theatres, its purpose was "to protect the general public, patrons of the theatre, owners of theatrical entertainments, operators of theatres and reputable theatre ticket brokers against the evils of speculation in theatre tickets." Since its founding it has significantly enlarged its scope, most notably in the field of labor relations. It now regularly negotiates with all major theatre unions as well as with the Dramatists Guild. ♦ In 1973 the name was broadened to the League of New York Theatres and Producers. The new name was adopted in 1985.

League of Historic American Theatres, THE A nonprofit association, founded in 1977 by Michael P. Price of the Goodspeed Opera House♦ and Gene Chesley, professor of theatre design at the University of California, its purpose is to promote the preservation and use of historic auditoriums. The League defines an historic theatre as one built before 1940, which 1) is an architecturally significant structure deemed worthy of preservation; 2) has played an important role in the history of the American stage; or 3) can be used as a performing-arts facility. More than forty important historic theatres are members.

League of Resident Theatres Founded in 1965 by Peter Zeisler of the Tyrone Guthrie Theatre, ♦ Thomas C. Fichandler of the Arena Stage, ♦ and Morris Kaplan, an attorney. Its purpose was to serve as a trade organization for resident professional theatres. It regularly negotiates contracts with pertinent theatrical unions. More than sixty theatres across the country are members.

Leah Kleschna, a drama in five acts by C. M. S. McLellan. ♦ Produced by Minnie Maddern Fiske♦ and Harrison Fiske♦ at the Manhattan Theatre. December 12, 1904. 131 performances.

Leah Kleschna (Mrs. Fiske) has long admired a man who saved her during a shipwreck, but she does not know the man's name. Her admiration would seem to be one of Leah's few commendable qualities, for Leah is a thief who steals at her father's behest. Her father sends her to steal jewels from the home of Paul Sylvaine (John Mason♦). Sylvaine catches her in the act, and she recognizes him as the man who saved her life. A certain rapport is instantly kindled between the two. While they are talking, however, Raoul Berton (George Arliss♦),

the dissolute brother of Sylvaine's fiancée, enters and himself steals the jewels Sylvaine had meant for his betrothed. Sylvaine's refusal to blame Leah for the theft, which is what Raoul hopes will happen, and his reluctance to implicate the real thief, alienate Sylvaine's fiancée. So in the end, it is Sylvaine and Leah who marry.

McLellan's original ending, when the play was called *Into the Great White Light,* was equivocal, leaving Leah's future open to conjecture. But the Fiskes, bowing to the era's theatrical requirements, insisted he add a fifth act in which Sylvaine marries the heroine. It was revived in 1924 as the author had first written it, but by that time styles of dramaturgy had changed and the work was perceived merely as a dated "crook play."

Leah, the Forsaken, a play in five acts by Augustin Daly. ♦ Produced by H. L. Bateman♦ at Niblo's Garden. ♦ January 19, 1863. 35 performances.

Against the laws of 17th-century Germany, Leah (Kate Bateman♦), a Jewess, loves a young Christian farmer, Rudolf (Edwin Adams♦). Their liaison is discovered by an apostate Jew, Nathan (J. W. Wallack, Jr. ♦), who betrays them to the authorities. The Jews are threatened with expulsion from the village, and Rudolf is led to believe that Leah has deserted him in return for a payment of silver. In despair, Rudolf marries a local Christian girl, Madelena (Mrs. Frank Chanfrau). Some time thereafter the Jews, who have kept their part of the bargain in dissuading Leah, are nevertheless ordered to leave. Just before their departure word arrives that the laws against the Jews have been abrogated. But by that time Madelena has had a child and Leah's heart has been broken. Rudolf learns of Nathan's treachery and of Leah's loyalty. He comes to beg forgiveness just as Leah dies.

The play, loosely adapted by Daly from S. H. von Mosenthal's German drama, *Deborah,* gave the author his first success and started him on his distinguished career. It also gave Kate Bateman the role with which she was thereafter identified.

LEAN, CECIL (1878–1935) The Canadian-born song and dance man first came into prominence when he played opposite Frank Daniels♦ in *Miss Simplicity* (1902). Settling in Chicago, he quickly became a star in that city's musical comedies, often sharing star billing with his first wife, Florence Holbrook. His important assignments included *The Isle of Bong Bong, The Yankee Regent, The Umpire,* ♦ *The Time, the Place and the Girl,* ♦ *The Honeymoon Trail,* and *The Girl at the Helm.* He continued to appear both in musical comedies and vaudeville with his second wife, Cleo Mayfield [née Cleonte Empy], throughout the teens and 1920s. Together they played in such shows as *Look Who's Here!, The Blushing Bride,* and a touring company of *No, No, Nanette.* Like many performers of the day, Lean and his wives were always more popular on the road than in New York.

Leave It to Jane, see *College Widow, The*

Leave It to Me!, a musical comedy in two acts. Book by Bella and Sam Spewack. ◆ Lyrics and music by Cole Porter. ◆ Produced by Vincent Freedley◆ at the Imperial Theatre. November 9, 1938. 291 performances.

Mrs. Goodhue (Sophie Tucker◆) has contributed so generously to Roosevelt's campaign coffers that the President makes her husband, "Stinky" (Victor Moore◆), ambassador to Russia. There his undiplomatic behavior, like kicking a Nazi and shooting a counter-revolutionary, is brushed aside. But when he proposes a plan for world peace he is declared persona non grata. His problems are often compounded by a brash newspaperman, Buckley Thomas (William Gaxton◆), who is courting a girl named Colette (Tamara).

Principal songs: Get Out of Town · Most Gentlemen Don't Like Love · My Heart Belongs to Daddy

Typical of the highly topical musical comedies of the period, the musical made a star of Mary Martin,◆ who was selected to sing "My Heart Belongs to Daddy" only after another actress was dropped. Her performance of the song included a genteel striptease. When the show went on tour the following season, the Stalin-Hitler pact had been signed, so some of the characters and topical references were eliminated or changed. The musical was based on the Spewacks' 1932 comedy, *Clear All Wires.*

LEAVITT, Michael Bennett (1843–1935) While his obituaries stressed that he was one of the founders of the Elks, they also took note of the fact that he was an important pioneer in the American theatre. Born in Posen, Poland, he was brought to this country while still a child and raised in Boston. He was in his teens when he organized a minstrel ensemble with himself and W. H. Crane◆ as endmen. Before long he had numerous large minstrel troupes touring under his aegis, such as Leavitt's Gigantean Minstrels and Mme. Rentz's Female Minstrels. As the vogue for minstrelsy waned, he conceived the idea of turning his female

minstrels into a burlesque company, featuring not the classic, satirical burlesque, but the sort of "leg show" that has since come to characterize the genre. At about the same time he formed two chains of legitimate theatres, one moving from coast to coast along the southerly railroad routes, the other along the northern tracks. In this manner he could send plays and musicals across the country and back without duplicating cities. His idea is said to have served as the inspiration for the Theatrical Syndicate or Trust◆ a few years later. Indeed, Al Hayman,◆ one of the group's founders, had been Leavitt's manager in San Francisco. Unlike the Frohmans,◆ or Klaw◆ and Erlanger,◆ or other subsequent figures, Leavitt was apparently never able to consolidate and retain his organizations. He retired in 1912 and in the same year wrote his memoirs, *Fifty Years in Theatrical Management.*

Leblang's Ticket Office In its heyday situated in the basement of Gray's Drug Store on Broadway between 42nd Street and 43rd Street, it was founded by Hungarian immigrant Joe Leblang. He started in business with a small tobacco shop at 30th Street and Sixth Avenue. At the time it was customary to give free passes to shopkeepers who displayed theatrical advertisements in their windows. Not only did Leblang sell his own passes, he collected them from other shopkeepers and sold them at cut-rate prices. He was so successful that before long theatres were sending him unsold seats several hours prior to curtain time. During the twenties he is said to have sold as many as 3,000 seats a night both to knowledgeable playgoers and less aware passers-by lured into his office by pitchmen barking the virtues of the various plays. Leblang died in 1931, but his widow and associate ran the agency until shortly after World War II, when the marked drop in the number of theatres seemed to make the operation unprofitable.

Led Astray, a drama in five acts by Dion Boucicault. ◆ Produced at the Union Square Theatre. ◆ December 6, 1873. 161 performances.

Armande (Rose Eytinge◆) marries a widower, Count Rudolphe Chandoce (C. R. Thorne, Jr. ◆), but he proves an indifferent and faithless husband, soon enmeshed in an affair with the calculating Suzanne O'Hara (Elizabeth Weathersby). Although Armande loves both the Count and his daughter, Mathilde (Kate Claxton◆), she is eventually driven into an affair of her own, with the poet George de Lesparre (McKee Rankin◆). When the Count learns of their relationship, he challenges George to a duel, but he purposely shoots to miss and then promises Armande he will be faithful thereafter.

Based loosely on Octave Feuillet's *La Tentation*, the play was described by the *Times's* critic as "told with cleverness and a thorough knowledge of dramatic effect; its personages are not so conventional as to be absolutely commonplace; and the language assigned to them is generally appropriate and often impressive." It soon became, as Odell♦ noted, "one of the most famous dramas of its decade in America."

LEDERER, GEORGE W. (1861–1938) The once-famous producer was born in Wilkes-Barre, Penn., and began his professional career as an actor in an 1873 production of *The Naiad Queen*. In his teens he began to write vaudeville sketches and also served a stint on the drama desk of the New York *Journal*. His first producing venture came in 1878, when he collaborated with Sydney Rosenfeld♦ in sending out a tour of *Florizel*. In 1893 he took over the Casino Theatre♦ with Thomas Canary, though it quickly became clear that Lederer was the dominant partner. During the decade in which he ran the theatre he produced numerous highly successful musicals, including the first important American revue, *The Passing Show*♦ (1894), and the first American musical to achieve major international success, *The Belle of New York*♦ (1897). He directed many of these productions. In after years he joined H. H. Frazee♦ to produce such hits as *Madame Sherry*♦ (1910) and *Angel Face* (1919). His last years were spent as general manager for Sam H. Harris. ♦

LEE, CANADA [né LEONARD CANEGATA] (1907–1952) The New York-born black actor made his first professional appearance in *Meek Mose* (1928), but did not gain attention until he played Blacksnake in a Civic Repertory Theatre♦ revival of *Stevedore* (1934). Much of his work for the rest of the decade was with black troupes. He came into real prominence when he played Bigger Thomas, the chauffeur hunted down for the slaying of his employer's daughter, in *Native Son*♦ (1941). He won additional laurels for his Caliban in a 1945 revival of *The Tempest*. In 1946 he played Daniel de Bosola in white-face, opposite Elisabeth Bergner,♦ in a revival of *The Duchess of Malfi*. His last appearance was as George, whose treachery defeats an uprising of his fellow blacks, in *Set My People Free* (1948).

LEE, GYPSY ROSE [née ROSE LOUISE HOVICK] (1913–70) Although she was probably the most famous of all American "strip-teasers," she was also a successful actress and author. Under the guidance of her pushy stage-mother, she began her career in a children's act in vaudeville, and after vaudeville began to fade moved into burlesque, where she quickly became one of its greatest stars, her restraint and elegance separating her from the vulgar, sexually suggestive run-of-the-mill strippers. She also played small roles in such musicals as *Hot-Cha!* (1932), *Strike Me Pink* (1933), and the *Ziegfeld Follies of 1936,*♦ and acted briefly in the comedy *I Must Love Someone* (1939). Her most important Broadway assignment was as co-star to Bobby Clark♦ in *Star and Garter* (1942). A year later she wrote a semi-autobiographical comedy about a burlesque queen with literary ambitions, *The Naked Genius* (1943). She afterward appeared in *A Curious Evening with Gypsy Rose Lee* (1961). Her 1957 autobiography, *Gypsy,* provided the basis for the musical of the same name.

LEE, ROBERT E., see *Lawrence, Jerome*

LEE, [SAMUEL] SAMMY [né LEVY] (1890–1968) One of the leading choreographers of the 1920s, Lee, a New York native, began his career as a dancer in *The Firefly*♦ (1912) and other pre-World War I musicals. His fast-paced routines enlivened such shows as *Mary Jane McKane* (1923), *Lady, Be Good!*♦ (1924), *No, No, Nanette*♦ (1925), *The Cocoanuts* (1925), *Tip-Toes*♦ (1925), *Queen High* (1926), *The Ramblers* (1926), *Oh, Kay!*♦ (1926), *Rio Rita*♦ (1927), *Ziegfeld Follies of 1927,*♦ and *Show Boat*♦ (1927).

Left Bank, The, a play in three acts by Elmer Rice. ♦ Produced by Rice at the Little Theatre. October 5, 1931. 242 performances.

For several years John Shelby (Horace Braham) and his wife, Claire (Katherine Alexander), have been living in Europe, especially France, and enjoying what John insists is "the most civilized country that there is in the world today." He adds, "No civilized man can live decently in America." But Claire has begun to miss the American way of life she grew up with. Arriving at the same Left Bank hotel at which they are housed is an American couple. Waldo Lynde (Donald MacDonald) clearly is educated, but remains totally Yankee in his interests. His wife, Susie (Merle Maddern), is more of a restless, free spirit. Before long John and Susie have gone off to tour the Midi together, so Claire elects to take her young son and return with Waldo to the States.

Brooks Atkinson♦ considered the play "the

shrewdest contribution to the literature of the American émigré in Paris" and suggested it represented "the modern American theatre at its best." Perhaps because expatriates no longer loom large in our artistic culture the play has become one of Rice's most neglected.

LEFTWICH, ALEXANDER (1884–1947) The Philadelphia native began his career as an actor at the age of fourteen in Baltimore. After spending some years in stock he worked as assistant to Jesse Lasky and Cecil B. De Mille when both men were still active on Broadway. After grooming acts for B. F. Keith,♦ he became a general director for Daniel Frohman♦ in 1915 and then for the Shuberts♦ in 1924, directing for the latter such shows as *Big Boy* (1925). He is best remembered for the musicals he staged after leaving the Shuberts, including *Hit the Deck!*♦ (1927), *A Connecticut Yankee*♦ (1927), *Rain or Shine* (1928), *Present Arms* (1928), *Spring Is Here* (1929), *Strike Up the Band*♦ (1930), and *Girl Crazy*♦ (1930). In later years he was director of the Federal Theatre Project♦ in California.

Legal Wreck, A, a play in four acts by William Gillette.♦ Produced by Gillette at the Madison Square Theatre.♦ August 14, 1888. 102 performances.

Olive Grey (Nina Boucicault) is the adopted daughter of an eccentric old New England sea captain, Edward Swift (Alfred Hudson), and is courted by both Swift's ruffian son Ed (George Fawcett♦) and suave Henry D. Leverett (Boyd Putnam). The men fight over the girl, after which a young attorney, Richard Merriam (Sidney Drew), leads each man to believe he has murdered the other. But there is some method in Merriam's cavalier humor, since he knows who Olive's real mother and sister are. He hopes to effect a match for himself by reuniting them.

This light summer entertainment was later turned into a novel by Gillette, one of the earliest examples of a practice that for many years was popular both in the theatre and in films.

LE GALLIENNE, EVA (b. 1899) Daughter of the famous novelist and poet Richard Le Gallienne, she was born in London and trained at the Royal Academy of Dramatic Arts. She acted briefly in England before making her American debut as Rose in *Mrs. Boltay's Daughters* (1915). She scored her first major success as Julie, who loves the ne'er-do-well hero, in *Liliom*♦ (1921), and consolidated her new-found fame when she played Princess Alexan-

dra, who falls in love with her tutor, in a second Molnar♦ play, *The Swan* (1923). In the 1925–26 season she mounted her own productions of *The Master Builder* and *John Gabriel Borkman,* playing Hilda Wangel and Ella Rentheim, and later the same year established her Civic Repertory Theatre♦ in an attempt to offer low-priced productions of classics. She directed and appeared in many of its productions over the next six years, playing, among others, Masha (*The Three Sisters*), Viola (*Twelfth Night*♦), Sister Joanna (*The Cradle Song*), Elsa (*Alison's House*♦), the White Queen (*Alice in Wonderland*), and the title roles of *Hedda Gabler* and *Peter Pan.*♦ In 1942 she won applause as Lettie, the spiteful sister who allows herself to be executed for her brother's crime, in *Uncle Harry.*♦ With Cheryl Crawford♦ and Margaret Webster♦ she made another attempt at forming a permanent ensemble in 1946, calling it the American Repertory Company,♦ but its life was short. Many of her subsequent appearances were in even more short-lived failures, but she scored a major success as Fanny Cavendish, the dowager of a great acting family, in a 1975 revival of *The Royal Family.*♦ Her last appearance was in *To Grandmother's House We Go* (1981). A small woman, with a tiny, tight-featured face, her acting struck many as too studiously mannered, but she brought an exceptional intelligence and dedication to all her work.

Autobiographies: *At 33,* New York, 1934; and *With a Quiet Heart,* Westport, Conn., 1953.

LEHAR, FRANZ (1870–1948) The Hungarian composer who was the most famous exponent of 20th-century operetta is best known world-wide for his masterpiece, *The Merry Widow*♦ (1907). Of his other works only two were successful in America, *Gypsy Love* (1911) and *The Count of Luxembourg* (1912), although their popularity by no means matched that of the earlier hit. Several of his operettas were produced later, only to fail, while a number of his greatest works have never been given major professional mountings in New York. As a composer Lehar moved away from the more florid, quasi-operatic style of 19th-century Viennese operetta.♦

LEIBER, FRITZ (1883–1949) After making his stage debut in 1902 with a stock company in his native Chicago, he joined the Ben Greet Players, learning the basic Shakespearean repertory with them and first appearing before New York audiences in 1905 as Macduff in their *Macbeth.*♦ He later spent many seasons as a principal supporting player to Robert

Mantell,♦ often alternating with Mantell in the roles of Othello and Iago. He then organized his own Shakespearean company. John Corbin,♦ the critic of the *Times,* said of his Hamlet, "His lean, trim figure and poetic masque are well suited to the role. In enunciation he at times lacks purity, and his voice has no great variety or range, but his reading is for the most part cultivated and intelligent." From 1929 to 1932 he directed and appeared with the Chicago Civic Shakespeare Company, then toured with a reorganized Shakespeare ensemble in the mid-thirties. He said to have played over a hundred different Shakespearean parts.

LEIGH, MITCH, see *Man of La Mancha*

LEIGHTON, MARGARET (1922–76) The slender English actress first came to America with the Old Vic♦ in 1946, but did not receive major attention until she essayed two disparate roles in Terence Rattigan's♦ double bill, *Separate Tables♦* (1956). After playing Beatrice to John Gielgud's♦ Benedick in 1959, she won a Tony Award♦ for her portrayal of Hannah Jelkes, the gentle spinster, in Tennessee Williams's♦ *The Night of the Iguana* (1961). Subsequently she was seen as Pamela Pew-Pickett, the starchy Englishwoman who has an affair with a rough-hewn Italian, in *Tchin-Tchin* (1962); in two roles in Williams's double bill, *Slapstick Tragedy* (1966); and as Regina in a 1967 revival of *The Little Foxes.♦*

LEMAIRE, CHARLES (1897–1985) Born in Chicago, but raised in Salt Lake City, he served in World War I and tried his luck as a song and dance man before turning to costume design. Although he had no formal design training, his talent was quickly recognized by Florenz Ziegfeld,♦ who allowed him to create some dresses for the 1919 editions of the *Midnight Frolics* and the *Follies.♦* Between then and his work for the 1939 edition of *George White's Scandals♦* he designed costumes for numerous extravaganzas of Ziegfeld, White,♦ and Earl Carroll♦ as well as for such shows as *Wildflower* (1923), *Poppy* (1923), *Rose-Marie♦* (1924), *The Cocoanuts* (1925), *The New Moon♦* (1928), *Strike Up the Band♦* (1930), *Flying High* (1930), *Fine and Dandy* (1930), *Of Thee I Sing♦* (1931), and *Take a Chance* (1932). Among the most memorable of his imaginative, colorful conceptions were the costumes simulating totem poles worn by the forty chorus girls in *Rose-Marie* for the "Totem Tom Tom" number.

LEMAN, WALTER M. (b. 1810) An actor and playwright who was born in Boston and spent most of his career there, in Philadelphia and in San Francisco playing important supporting roles, he is remembered solely for his autobiographical *Memories of an Old Actor* (1886). Although the work is largely a catalogue of the names of figures with whom he worked, it does offer some unusual and telling glimpses into the theatre of his day.

LENIHAN, WINIFRED (1898–1964) A New Yorker, she studied at the American Academy of Dramatic Arts♦ before making her debut in 1918. Although she portrayed Anne, the would-be eloper, in *The Dover Road* (1921), Anne Hathaway in *Will Shakespeare* (1923), and the resourceful Mary Todd in *White Wings♦* (1926), she is recalled mostly as Joan in the original American production of *Saint Joan♦* (1923).

LENYA, LOTTE [née KAROLINE BLAMAUER] (1900–1981) Best known as the wife of composer Kurt Weill♦ and as Jenny in the 1954 revival of his *Threepenny Opera,* she was born in Vienna and was a popular cabaret and musical star in Berlin before the advent of the Nazis forced her to flee Germany. She had, during her Berlin career, appeared in several of her husband's works, including creating the role of Jenny in 1928. Her first American appearance was in *The Eternal Road* (1937). She later played in *Candle in the Wind* (1941) and in Weill's *The Firebrand of Florence* (1945). The year before the revival of *Threepenny Opera,* she won applause for her portrayal of Xantippe in Maxwell Anderson's♦ *Barefoot in Athens* (1951). She later appeared in *Brecht on Brecht* (1962), and in *Cabaret♦* (1966). Her "steel-file voice" made her the definitive interpreter of her husband's songs.

LEON, [PATRICK] FRANCIS [né GLASSER] (b. 1840) The greatest female impersonator in minstrelsy, he was born in New York and educated at Fordham University. In his youth he had been noted as a boy soprano. He joined a minstrel company when he was fourteen years old and in 1864 formed Kelly and Leon's Minstrels with Edwin Kelly. The troupe quickly became famous for its "Africanized opéra bouffe," spoofs of such contemporary comic operas as *The Grand Duchess♦* or *La Belle Hélène* as "The Grand Dutch S" and "La Belle L.N.," with Leon in the prima donna parts. The *Clipper♦* observed that his clowning was never offensive, "He does it with such dignity, modesty, and refinement that it is truly art." He wore only the finest, most expensive costumes and excellent imitation jewelry. He was also an accomplished dancer in ballet as well as in the clogs and other standard routines of the time. Kelly and Leon disbanded their company in 1869, but continued to perform together in other minstrel troupes and in vaudeville. They played successfully in Australia in late 1879 and the early 1880s, after which Kelly remained there while Leon returned home. Leon continued to be a star attraction, often billed as "The 'Only' Leon," in minstrel groups, vaudeville, and in the loosely contrived musical comedies of the day well into the 1890s.

LEONARD, EDDIE [né LEMUEL GORDON TOONEY] (1875–1941) One of the last of the great, traditional minstrels, he was born in Richmond, Va., into a poor Irish family and put to work while still a youngster at a steel rolling mill. He was entertaining his co-workers during a break by singing and dancing when an agent for Lew Dockstader◆ happened to pass by. He was immediately signed and continued with Dockstader for most of the 1890s before moving on to other minstrel ensembles. With the passing of minstrelsy he took his blackface act into vaudeville, remaining a headliner at the Palace◆ until it abandoned two-a-day. He also appeared on Broadway in *The Southerners* (1904) and *Roly-Boly Eyes* (1919), the latter named after a song he wrote and popularized. An even more famous song of his was "Ida, Sweet as Apple Cider."

Autobiography: *What a Life, I'm Telling You,* New York, 1934.

Leonor de Guzman, a tragedy in five acts by George H. Boker.◆ Produced at the Walnut Street Theatre,◆ Philadelphia. October 3, 1853. 6 performances.

When Leonor (Julia Dean◆), who has been the real power behind the Spanish throne, learns that King Alfonso XII has been killed in battle she determines to retain her influence. But the courtiers quickly desert her and flock to the new king, Don Pedro (Mr. Perry), and his mother, Queen Maria (Mrs. Duffield). Both are strongly influenced by Don Juan Albuquerque (Mr. Adams), who, as prime minister, is determined to assure a peaceful transfer of the royal reins. But Leonor's persistent machinations finally prompt Maria to stab her to death.

Quinn◆ has observed that "The most marked advance in *Leonor de Guzman* lies in the character drawing." He calls attention to how well Boker evokes sympathy for Leonor while at the same time painting a three-dimensional portrait of an even

more interesting figure, Maria. The Queen's all-consuming jealousy bridles at Don Albuquerque's hatred of Leonor, since Maria perceives that his hatred somehow dilutes hers. The blank-verse drama was less successful when it was later presented in New York than it was at its Philadelphia premiere.

LERNER, ALAN JAY (1918–86) Born into a wealthy New York family, he was educated at selective private schools and at Harvard, where he collaborated on two Hasty Pudding◆ musicals. He worked as a radio script writer before joining composer Frederick Loewe◆ to write *What's Up* (1943), a quick failure. Their second show, *The Day Before Spring* (1945), was an imaginative, if heavy-handed musical comedy that also failed commercially. Turning to romantic fantasy they scored a huge hit with *Brigadoon◆* (1947), whose major songs included "Almost Like Being in Love," "Come to Me, Bend to Me," and "The Heather on the Hill." *Paint Your Wagon* (1951), set in gold rush days, is remembered for "I Talk to the Trees." Their greatest success was a musical version of Shaw's◆ *Pygmalion,◆* called *My Fair Lady◆* (1956). Among its many fine songs were "Get Me to the Church on Time," "I Could Have Danced All Night," "I've Grown Accustomed to Her Face," and "On the Street Where You Live." The final Lerner and Loewe collaboration was *Camelot* (1960), whose hit song was "If Ever I Would Leave You." However, a theatricalization of the screen musical *Gigi* was offered to Broadway in 1973. During this same period Lerner wrote another innovative, but failed musical, *Love Life* (1948), with music by Kurt Weill.◆ After Loewe's retirement, he wrote two musicals with Burton Lane,◆ *On a Clear Day You Can See Forever* (1965), and *Carmelina* (1979), as well as one with André Previn, *Coco* (1969), one with Leonard Bernstein,◆ *1600 Pennsylvania Avenue* (1976), and one with Charles Strouse,◆ *Dance a Little Closer* (1983). While Lerner's librettos offered excellent dialogue they often betrayed an inability at proper construction and a lack of theatrical tension. On the other hand, as a writer of elegantly literate and witty lyrics he had no peer among his contemporaries.

Autobiography: *The Street Where I Live,* New York, 1978.

LESLIE, AMY (1860–1939) Born in West Burlington, Iowa, she made a small reputation for herself as a prima donna in operetta during the 1880s and early 1890s, performing under the name Lillie West. She retired from the stage to become drama critic for the

Chicago *Daily News,* a position she held for 40 years. She was the first woman to have such a prestigious assignment. Her criticisms leaned over backward to be kind to even the most woe-begone entertainments and as a result she was sometimes accused of "puffing," writing favorable notices to help at the box office. She nonetheless won the respect of her fellow reviewers and of the theatrical profession as well. Although the tradition of women drama critics has continued in Chicago, none followed in her considerate footsteps.

LESLIE, ELSIE [née LYDE] (1881–1966) Daughter of a prosperous New Yorker, she made her debut in 1885 and two years later became the darling of playgoers when she played Editha, the tot who can more than hold her own as she encounters *Editha's Burglar.* Successes followed in the title roles of *Little Lord Fauntleroy* (1888) and *The Prince and the Pauper* (1890), after which she temporarily retired. When she returned eight years later she was not able to capture her early appeal.

LESLIE, LEW [né LEWIS LESSINSKY] (1886–1963) Born in Orangeburg, N.Y., he began his career as a performer in vaudeville and later became manager of the famous New York night-club Café de Paris. While there he recognized the growing popularity of black entertainers and so produced the *Plantation Revue* (1922) for Broadway. With one exception, all his subsequent productions were black musicals: *Dixie to Broadway* (1924), *Rhapsody in Black* (1931), and a series of *Blackbirds*♦ revues, with editions in 1928, 1930, 1933, and 1939. His lone production to feature white performers was his *International Revue* (1930).

Les Misérables A musical in two acts. Book by Alain Boublil and Claude-Michel Schönberg (from an original French text by Boublil and Jean-Marc Natel), music by Schönberg and English lyrics by Herbert Kretzmer. This musical version of Hugo's novel was originally released as a recording, then given a Paris production. The English producer, Cameron Mackintosh,♦ ordered a revised and expanded script, which he mounted first in London and then in New York at the Broadway Theatre on March 12, 1987. The work is basically undistinguished, but the overblown, overamplified production was also grotesquely overpraised and so became a tremendous success. It long since has supplanted *La Plume de Ma Tante* as the longest running Continental musical in Broadway history and continues to play to good business at press time.

LESTER, EDWIN (1895–1990) Probably the last important West Coast theatrical producer, he was born in Providence, R.I., and settled in California after serving in World War I. He spent many years as an executive for a music company before becoming an artists' representative in the early 1930s. In 1935 he organized the Los Angeles Light Opera Festival. Two years later with Homer Curran♦ he founded the more permanent San Francisco Light Opera Association, then in 1938 established the companion Los Angeles Light Opera Association. He headed both groups until his retirement in 1976. Under his aegis the companies mounted yearly series of splendid revivals of past musicals, interspersed with new productions. Among these original mountings were *Song of Norway*♦ (1944), *Magdalena* (1948), *Kismet*♦ (1953), and *Peter Pan*♦ (1954). During his last years, rising costs forced him to resort increasingly to booking traveling companies of Broadway successes.

Let Us Be Gay, a comedy in a prologue and three acts by Rachel Crothers. ♦ Produced by John Golden♦ at the Little Theatre. ♦ February 21, 1929. 363 performances.

When Kitty Brown (Francine Larrimore♦) and her husband, Bob (Warren William), quarrel, Bob stalks out of the house vowing never to return. Three years pass. Old Mrs. Boucicault (Charlotte Granville) is worried about her young granddaughter, Deirdre Lessing (Rita Vale), who has seemed too receptive to the advances of a divorced man. So Mrs. Boucicault invites Kitty to a weekend house party, hoping to distract the suitor. Of course the divorced man is Bob, and by the time the guests are ready to leave, he and Kitty have kissed and made up.

One of the most successful of Rachel Crothers's frothy but observant high comedies, the play remained a favorite in summer stock and little theatres for many years.

Let's Face It!, see *Cradle Snatchers*

LEVENE, SAM[UEL] [né LEVINE] (1905–80) The sour-faced comedian who spoke with the pronounced accent of his native New York studied at the American Academy of Dramatic Arts♦ before making his professional debut in *Wall Street* (1927). Major recognition came eight years later when he played Patsy, the racing addict, in *Three Men on a Horse*♦ (1935). Successes followed as Gordon Miller, the shoestring producer desperately trying to keep his troupe together, in *Room Service*♦ (1937), and as Officer Finkelstein, the Jewish policeman who must solve the murder of a Nazi diplomat, in *Margin for Error*♦ (1939). Not until he played Sidney Black, the aggressive, foul-mouthed producer, in *Light Up the the Sky*♦ (1948) did he enjoy another long run. Immediately thereafter he assumed the role for which he is best remembered, Nathan Detroit in the musical *Guys and Dolls*♦ (1950). He subsequently portrayed stereotypical New York Jewish types in such plays as *Fair Game* (1957), *Make a Million* (1958), and *Paris Is Out!* (1970), all of which owed what runs they achieved to his clowning. More interesting interpretations were his Boss Mangan in a 1959 revival of *Heartbreak House,* and Oscar Wolfe, the great producer, in a 1975 revival of *The Royal Family.* ♦ His last appearance was as Samuel Horowitz in a quick failure, *Horowitz and Mrs. Washington* (1980).

LEVIN, HERMAN (1907–90) The Philadelphia-born lawyer-turned-producer was first represented on Broadway in 1946 by the musical revue *Call Me Mister* and the Sartre drama *No Exit.* In 1949 he produced the successful musical version of *Gentlemen Prefer Blondes.* ♦ His greatest success came when he presented *My Fair Lady*♦ (1956). *The Great White Hope*♦ (1968) was his only subsequent hit.

LEVIN, IRA (b. 1929) A New Yorker who studied at New York University, he scored a huge hit with his first work to reach Broadway, his adaptation of the novel *No Time for Sergeants*♦ (1955), which centered on a hillbilly soldier. Although he has written for Broadway with some regularity his only other successes have been *Critic's Choice* (1960), a comedy about a critic who must review his wife's play, and *Deathtrap*♦ (1978), in which a writer seemingly would murder another author to steal his work. Levin has also enjoyed success as a novelist.

LEWIS, ADA (1875–1925) Discovered performing in her native San Francisco by Edward Harrigan,♦ she virtually stole the show when he brought her East to play a rough girl of the streets in his *Reilly and the 400*♦ (1890). For the next decade or so she played similar characters, then aged into the imperious grande dame. Her numerous appearances included *The Widow Jones* (1905), *Fascinating Flora* (1907), *Very Good Eddie*♦ (1915), *The Night Boat* (1920), and *Good Morning, Dearie* (1921).

LEWIS, FREDERICK G. (1873–1946) A native of Oswego, N.Y., he made his debut in Savannah as Armand Duval in 1891 and for six years played in stock. After becoming a leading man in touring productions sent out by the Lyceum Theatre,♦ he began to make a niche as a Shakespearean specialist. He was Henrietta Crosman's♦ Orlando in 1903, long the second male lead in the Julia Marlowe♦– E. H. Sothern♦ company, and at the age of fifty played Horatio to John Barrymore's♦ Hamlet.

LEWIS, HENRY, see *Lewis, Mrs. Henry*

LEWIS, MRS. HENRY [née BERTHA (?) HARVEY] (d. 1855) The London-born actress was reputed to have been a great favorite in her native city before coming with her husband to New York in 1835. Although she was said to have been an attractive, graceful woman and a skilled dancer, her principal fame derived from interpretation of men's parts such as Richard III and Othello. She spent all of her American career traveling with her specialties from city to city, never establishing the firm base that many more ordinary performers were able to achieve. Her husband, from whom she was divorced in 1849, began his career in pantomine and later won respect as a director and delineator of old men. He spent much of his career in Pittsburgh, retiring in the late 1860s and dying at the age of ninety in 1892.

LEWIS, JAMES (1838–96) The slim, short comedian with blue pop-eyes and reddish-blond hair was born in Troy, N.Y., and began his theatrical apprenticeship touring the western part of the state while still in his early teens. He came to New York in 1866, quickly making a name for himself in Mrs. John Wood's♦ burlesques at the Olympic Theatre and in similar pieces at Lina Edwin's Theatre. When Augustin Daly♦ began assembling his soon famous ensemble in 1869, Lewis was one of his first choices. Within a brief time he became the company's leading farceur and remained with the group until his early death. Along with John Drew,♦ Mrs. Gilbert,♦ and Ada Rehan♦ he was considered a mainstay of the organization. Most of his assignments were in now forgotten comedies; but he was also applauded for such roles as Captain Lynde in *Divorce*♦ (1873); Bob Sackett in *Saratoga*♦ (1874); Tony Lumpkin in *She Stoops To Conquer* (1874); Professor Cawallader in *The Big Bonanza*♦ (1875); Sammy Dymple in *Pique*♦ (1875); Sir Benjamin Backbite in *The School for Scandal* (1876); Bottom in *A Midsummer Night's Dream*♦ (1888); Touchstone in *As You Like It*♦ (1891); and Sir Toby Belch in *Twelfth Night*♦ (1893). William Winter♦ recalled, "Lewis was an artist. He caused effects in acting not by grimace, posturing and extravagance, but by getting inside of characters and permitting his droll humor to permeate them and show itself through amusing peculiarities of demeanor and felicities of comic expression, visual and vocal. For each of the many parts that he played he provided a distinct identity and an appropriate, characteristic 'make-up,' and each part that he thus presented was a coherent, consistent, authentic type of credible human nature—the pervasive quality of all being genial, comic eccentricity."

LEWIS, ROBERT (b. 1909) The New Yorker studied at City College and at Juilliard before turning to acting. In 1938 he directed the road company of *Golden Boy*♦ and thereafter was known primarily for his staging. Among his later efforts were Saroyan's♦ *My Heart's in the Highlands*♦ (1939), *Brigadoon*♦ (1947), *The Happy Time*♦ (1950), *An Enemy of the People* (1950), *The Teahouse of the August Moon*♦ (1953), *Witness for the Prosecution* (1954), *Jamaica* (1957), and *On a Clear Day You Can See Forever* (1965). He has also taught at leading schools and directed for major regional playhouses.

Autobiography: *Slings and Arrows,* New York, 1984.

LEWIS, TED [né THEODORE LEOPOLD FRIEDMAN] (1891–1971) Born in Circleville, Ohio, where he made his professional debut singing in a nickel-odeon, he learned to play clarinet in school. Coming to New York he established the Ted Lewis Nut Band, playing what at the time was called "jazz." By 1919 he was a headliner in vaudeville and in night clubs. He also performed on Broadway in such revues as *Ziegfeld's Midnight Frolics* in 1919; several editions of *Greenwich Village Follies*♦; and *Artists and Models of 1927.* ♦ He would appear with his battered top hat and his clarinet and ask with a mocking sentimentality, "Is ev'rybody happy?" Performing in his cheerily forlorn style he made famous such songs as "When My Baby Smiles at Me" and "Me and My Shadow." In the latter his leisurely strutting was often mimicked by a black youngster.

Liberty Theatres Huge, temporary wooden auditoriums, erected during World War I, largely to entertain troops at military camps. Touring companies of Broadway shows or hastily assembled vaudeville bills would perform in them for soldiers who had paid to see the entertainments with coupons from Smileage Books, which sold for nominal amounts and which were usually bought by the public and then donated to the troops.

Lie of the Mind, a play in three acts by Sam Shepard.♦ Produced at the Promenade Theatre. December 5, 1985. 185 performances. NYDCCA

Jake (Harvey Keitel) believes he has beaten his wife to death and so runs away. He beat her because she was an amateur actress who, he felt, was becoming the slut she had portrayed on stage. Actually, his wife, Beth (Amanda Plummer), is not dead but she has suffered brain damage. When she is returned to her family, Jake's brother, Frankie (Aidan Quinn), visits them, hoping to bring about a reconciliation or at least an understanding. Jake returns home to his flighty mother (Geraldine Page♦). But his mother eventually goes off with her daughter. In the end Jake and Beth are left to work out for themselves their probably bleak futures.

Although the play took four hours to perform, it was always gripping, especially in the fine production accorded it. However, viewed from a distance it could be seen as a modern-day *Tobacco Road,*♦ crossed with strong influences of *The Glass Menagerie*♦ school of drama.

LIEBERSON, GODDARD (1911–1977) Born in England but raised in America, where he studied at the University of Washington and the Eastman School of Music, he became president of Columbia Records. In this capacity he produced numerous original cast recordings of Broadway musicals, following in the pioneering footsteps of Decca's Jack Kapp.♦ But he moved one important step further, re-creating, often with Lehman Engel,♦ virtually complete versions of the scores of Broadway shows that predated the era of contemporary recordings. His re-creation of *Pal Joey*♦ is generally credited with prompting the highly successful 1952 revival of that musical.

LIEBLER, THEODORE (1852–1941) Born in New York, shortly after his father was forced to flee Germany for partaking in an insurrection, he began his working life as a commercial artist. Before long he had a modestly successful lithograph firm in Park Place. When his establishment was destroyed by fire, George Tyler♦ persuaded him to join forces to produce *The Royal Box* (1897). The play was a success, inaugurating the long career of Liebler and Company. Among its memorable productions were *The Christian*♦ (1898), *The Children of the Ghetto* (1899), *Sag Harbor*♦ (1900), *In the Palace of the King*♦ (1900), *A Gentleman of France*♦ (1901),

Raffles♦ (1903), *Mrs. Wiggs of the Cabbage Patch*♦ (1904), *The Squaw Man*♦ (1905), *Salomy Jane*♦ (1907), *The Man from Home*♦ (1908), *Alias Jimmy Valentine*♦ (1910), *Pomander Walk* (1910), *Disraeli* (1911), and *The Garden of Allah*♦ (1911). Liebler was also responsible for bringing to America such celebrated foreign artists as Mrs. Patrick Campbell,♦ Duse,♦ and Rejane.♦ His importation of the Irish Players of the Abbey Theatre♦ in 1911 precipitated a riot when many Irishmen objected to the sentiments in their production of *The Playboy of the Western World*. After a series of expensive failures during World War I the company was dissolved and Liebler retired.

Life with Father, a comedy in three acts by Howard Lindsay♦ and Russel Crouse.♦ Produced by Oscar Serlin at the Empire Theatre.♦ November 8, 1939. 3,224 performances.

Clarence Day (Lindsay) is certain he dominates his Madison Avenue brownstone and his family, which includes four young sons and his wife, Vinnie (Dorothy Stickney). He constantly berates Vinnie about her housekeeping, and his blustering tantrums have cost the Days many a maid. But when the Rev. Dr. Lloyd (Richard Sterling) pays a visit, Day reveals he has never been baptized. Although her husband argues, "They can't keep me out of heaven on a technicality," Vinnie is determined that the oversight must be rectified. Clarence, however, is adamant, until in a weak moment, when he believes Vinnie may be dying, he agrees. Vinnie holds him to his promise, so he goes off to church bellowing, "I'm going to be baptized, damn it!"

The comedy, based on Clarence Day, Jr.'s *New Yorker* recollections, remains the longest running non-musical play in Broadway history. Arriving as war broke out in Europe and while America was still feeling the effects of the Depression, its affectionate portrait of 19th-century home life evoked a past of simple values. A sequel, *Life with Mother* (1948), had only a modest run despite generally warm notices.

Light Up the Sky, a comedy in three acts by Moss Hart.♦ Produced at the Royale Theatre. November 18, 1948. 216 performances.

Just before the opening of a new play in Boston, the leading figures involved in the show assemble in the Ritz-Carlton suite of the leading lady, Irene Livingston (Virginia Field). The others include the coarse-mouthed producer, Sidney Black (Sam Levene♦), his brassy wife Frances (Audrie Christie), the swishy, lugubrious director, Carleton Fitzgerald

(Glenn Anders♦), and the young playwright, Peter Sloan (Barry Nelson♦). They are gushily sweet and loving to each other until they return from the first performance, which they believe to be a flop. Then a screaming, name-calling session ensues. When the reviews prove encouraging the sweetness and camaraderie return.

The show was originally written by Hart as a more philosophic comedy, but after a Boston tryout that mirrored the fictitious events in the play, it was rewritten as a slam-bang farce. Insiders recognized that the vain, effusive Irene was a send-up of Gertrude Lawrence♦; the Blacks, of Billy Rose♦ and his wife Eleanor Holm; and Fitzgerald, of Guthrie McClintic.♦ The play was Hart's only successful solo venture, aside from the wartime *Winged Victory*♦ (1943), but appearing in a season of exceptional competition it never enjoyed the run it deserved.

Lightnin', a play in a prologue and three acts by Winchell Smith♦ and Frank Bacon.♦ Produced by Smith and John Golden♦ at the Gaiety Theatre. August 26, 1918. 1,291 performances.

When "Lightnin'" Bill Jones (Bacon) meets young John Marvin (Ralph Morgan♦) in Marvin's cabin near Tahoe, the two men take an instant liking to one another, although Marvin quickly realizes that Jones is a chronic boozer and teller of tall tales. Marvin is in trouble with some shady speculators who work for the railways, and Jones promises to lie in court to help Marvin. Jones and his wife (Jessie Pringle) own a hotel which straddles the California and Nevada line. A line has been painted across the Calivada's lobby for the benefit of guests coming to procure a divorce or avoid arrest. The same speculators that have caused trouble for Marvin convince Mrs. Jones to sell the hotel, but Jones refuses to co-sign the agreement. Mrs. Jones, finally fed up with Jones's drinking and prevaricating, files for divorce. However, Jones manages to expose the speculators as crooks and win back his wife. At the same time Marvin and Jones's stepdaughter, Millie (Beatrice Nichols), fall in love.

Arthur Hornblow♦ wrote in *Theatre Magazine,*♦ "The authors have put into their play something—a character, in fact, that seems to be drawn from life. Mr. Bacon's impersonation of the central figure is Jeffersonian in its simplicity and understanding." Because many thought Bacon's performance was necessary to the success of the play, no road company was sent out at first. When the play closed on Broadway it was the longest running show in American history, a record broken seven years later by *Abie's Irish Rose.* ♦ Bacon died, however, during the post-Broadway tour, and other actors were able to keep it on the road through 1925. A 1938 revival with Fred Stone♦ failed.

Liliom Ferenc Molnar's play, with fantastic overtones, which told of the star-crossed romance of a carnival barker and a serving girl, was first produced in America by the Theatre Guild♦ at the Garrick Theatre on April 20, 1921, and ran for 300 performances. Joseph Schildkraut♦ and Eva Le Gallienne♦ were the principals. It has been revived on several occasions and was the source of the 1945 musical *Carousel.* ♦

Liliputians, THE A group of German or Austro-Hungarian-born midgets, who, for about a decade beginning in 1890, were tremendously popular entertainers in musical vehicles written especially for them, such as *The Pupil in Magic* (1890), *Candy* (1892), and *A Trip to Mars* (1893). They performed both in German and in English. The leading figures in the troupe were Selma Gomer, Adolf Zink, and Fritz Ebert.

LILLIE, BEATRICE [GLADYS] (1894–1989) Born in Toronto, she became a popular London comedienne before making her New York debut in *Charlot's Revue*♦ (1924). Her uproarious clowning as she led a totally disorganized brigade and sang "March with Me" made her an overnight star. She consolidated her reputation in the *Charlot Revue of 1926; Oh, Please!* (1926), in which she introduced Vincent Youmans's♦ "I Know That You Know"; and *She's My Baby* (1928). In *The Third Little Show*♦ (1931) she helped popularize "Mad Dogs and Englishmen." After appearing in *Walk a Little Faster* (1932), she scored a major success in *At Home Abroad* (1935), in which she sang "Get Yourself a Geisha" and created havoc with her tongue-twisting order for "a dozen double damask dinner napkins." She next appeared in *The Show Is On* (1936) and *Set to Music* (1939). During World War II she returned to America in the revue *Seven Lively Arts* (1944), then cavorted in *Inside U.S.A.* (1948). She repeated many of her favorite routines in *An Evening with Beatrice Lillie* (1952), then found herself in a disastrous failure, *The Ziegfeld Follies of 1957.* ♦ In 1958 she succeeded Rosalind Russell♦ in *Auntie Mame.* ♦ One of her finest performances was her last, as Madame Arcati, the medium, in a musical version of *Blithe Spirit* called *High Spirits* (1964). Howard Taubman of the *Times* wrote of her performance, "Overflowing with coziness, she begins to move like a ballerina. Her hands

flutter as she takes mincing little steps, then they wave broadly as the afflatus of Terpsichore possesses her . . . And when the audience roars for more and won't let the show go on, she flutters through a devastating mockery of curtsies and fond gestures of farewell." A tiny, slender woman, who wore her hair in a mannishly short bob, she was generally recognized as the greatest comedienne of her era. No small part of her genius came from her retaining her lady-like decorum even in the coarsest, most vulgar bits.

Biography: *Beatrice Lillie: The Funniest Woman in the World,* Bruce Laffey, New York, 1990.

Lincoln, Abraham Although Lincoln appeared, often mute, in patriotic Civil War spectacles and later was assigned roles of varying importance in a handful of plays, such as James A. Herne's♦ *The Reverend Griffith Davenport*♦ (1899), it was not until the 20th century that he figured in the central role of two major dramas of some durability. Oddly, the first was the work of an Englishman, John Drinkwater's *Abraham Lincoln* (1919). Of course, the most famous and successful play about the murdered President was Robert Sherwood's♦ *Abe Lincoln in Illinois*♦ (1938), which focused on his early years and which starred Raymond Massey. ♦ Less successful works in which he figured included *If Booth Had Missed* (1932) and *Prologue to Glory* (1938). In 1959 excerpts from the Lincoln-Douglas debates provided the basis for *The Rivalry.*

Lincoln Center, see Repertory Theatre of Lincoln Center

LINDSAY, ADAM (fl. late 18th century) Few details of personal history exist for this man whom theatrical historian George O. Seilhamer called "with [Thomas] Wall, the first manager under the Stars and Stripes" and of whom Eola Willis in her *The Charleston Stage of the XVIII Century* wrote, "To Wall and Lindsay must be accorded the honor of reviving drama in America after the Revolution." With Wall♦ he built the first theatre in Baltimore in 1781, all the while apparently running a tavern there as well. He seems to have been an actor of modest talent, and never assumed major roles. After two seasons he retired from both managing and performing, and disappeared from the records.

LINDSAY, HOWARD [né Herman Nelke] (1889–1968) Born in Waterford, N.Y., and educated at Harvard, he began his theatrical career as an actor, touring in *Polly of the Circus*♦ in 1909 and later appearing in support of McKee Rankin♦ and Margaret Anglin. ♦

He continued to act and occasionally direct all through the 1920s, but found a more successful métier when he dramatized *She Loves Me Not*♦ (1933), an Edward Hope novel, then joined Russel Crouse♦ to rewrite the book for *Anything Goes*♦ (1934) after the original story of a shipwreck had to be jettisoned because of the sinking of the *Morro Castle*. The team then wrote the books for *Red, Hot and Blue!* (1936) and *Hooray for What!* (1937). In 1939 they wrote *Life with Father,*♦ a nostalgic, comic look at a 19th-century household. The play remains the longest running non-musical in New York history. Their next play was *Strip for Action* (1942), a comedy about a burlesque troupe's visit to an army base. It was followed by their political satire, *State of the Union*♦ (1945), which won a Pulitzer Prize.♦ *Life with Mother* (1948), a sequel to their earlier success, was well received by critics, but failed at the box office. In 1950 they wrote the book for *Call Me Madam.*♦ *Remains To Be Seen* (1951) was a mediocre comedy-mystery, while their next two plays were at best competent vehicles for great stars. In *The Prescott Proposals* (1953) Katharine Cornell♦ played an idealistic United Nations delegate caught in a potential scandal; Alfred Lunt♦ and Lynn Fontanne♦ cavorted as a mind-reading act trapped behind the Iron Curtain in *The Great Sebastians* (1956). Neither their book for *Happy Hunting* (1956) nor their comedy about a high school basketball star asked to take a bribe, *Tall Story* (1959), was liked by most critics. Nor did critics enjoy their book for *The Sound of Music*♦ (1959), although the musical was a major success. Their last collaboration was their book for *Mr. President* (1962). As producers the team's offerings included *Arsenic and Old Lace*♦ (1941) and *Detective Story*♦ (1949). Although their works may have had minimal merit as dramatic literature, they were excellent, show-wise writers whose best plays were consummately theatrical.

LINGARD, W[ILLIAM] H[ORACE] [né THOMAS] (1839–1927) The English-born comedian had established a reputation in London music halls before emigrating to America in 1868. He specialized in short, satirical character sketches and songs and was quickly recognized as the best in his line. Odell♦ recalled, "His versatility was remarkable, he exactly hit off some of the foibles of the day, and his protean changes were extraordinary." His comic flair was immensely enhanced by his youthful, drolly pixyish face. Although he frequently acted in regular plays and musicals, often with his wife, Alice Dunning Lingard, his skits and songs were in such demand that he was forced to offer them between acts when they could not be incorporated into the plays themselves. He also tried his hand successfully at managing theatres and producing plays.

Lion and the Mouse, The, a play in four acts by Charles Klein.♦ Produced by Henry B. Harris♦ at the Lyceum Theatre.♦ November 20, 1905. 586 performances.

Under the alias of Sarah Green, Shirley Rossmore (Grace Elliston♦) has written a muck-raking book exposing the methods of the multimillionaire John Burkett Ryder (Edmund Breese♦), who is known as "Ready-money" Ryder. Her writing the book was partly in revenge for Ryder's destroying the career of her father Judge Rossmore (Walter Allen), whose decisions had gone against Ryder's monopolies. But she is also determined to clear her father's name, and to this end allows Ryder's son, Jefferson (Richard Bennett♦), to court her. Neither father nor son realize she is the Sarah Green who wrote the exposé. The older Ryder asks her to write a book answering Green's charges. Shirley agrees, but insists on having access to all Ryder's papers. When she comes across the papers that clear her father, she confronts the Ryders and discloses her identity.

The greatest hit of its season (its opening followed closely those of *Peter Pan*♦ and *The Girl of the Golden West,*♦ neither of which ran nearly as long), it was seen as a powerful, skillful if contrived, and not very subtly veiled portrait of Ida Tarbell and John D. Rockefeller.

Lion in Winter, The, a play in two acts by James Goldman. Produced at the Ambassador Theatre. March 3, 1966. 92 performances.

Henry II (Robert Preston♦) allows Queen Eleanor (Rosemary Harris♦), whom he has long imprisoned, to join the family's Christmas festivities. The King is determined to select an heir. He favors their youngest son, John (Bruce Scott), but Eleanor favors the eldest, who has long been her pet, Richard (James Rado). The argument that ensues is conditioned as much by the couple's ambivalent love-hate relationship as by genuine political considerations. It is made more complex when all three sons unite against their father. In the end Henry has little choice but to forgive the children—and to send Eleanor back into imprisonment.

A largely fictitious, often wittily anachronistic treatment of historical figures, the play received generally excellent notices but failed to find a public. However, it remains popular with amateur groups.

The Chicago-born Goldman (b. 1927) was also the author of *Blood, Sweat and Stanley Poole* (1961) as well as the books for the musicals *A Family Affair* (1962) and *Follies*♦ (1971).

Lion of the West, The; or, A Trip to Washington, a play in four acts by James Kirke Paulding.♦ Produced at the Park Theatre.♦ April 25, 1831. In repertory.

Cecilia Bramble (Mrs. Sharpe) is a giddy young girl who dreams of marrying a titled Frenchman and living in Paris. She is the daughter of testy old Governor Bramble (Mr. Blakely) and the cousin of the unlettered but sage new Kentucky Congressman, Col. Nimrod Wildfire (J. H. Hackett♦). Her dream seems to come true when she is courted by one Count de Grillon (Peter Richings♦), who persuades her to elope. The elopement is thwarted by another suitor, the upright American Mr. Roebuck (Mr. Woodhull). A third suitor, Mr. Higgins (Mr. Collett), appears on the scene to complicate matters. The complications include mistaken identities and a noisy but harmless series of gunshots, after which Wildfire exposes the Count as a swindler and Higgins as a coward. Cecilia refuses to marry Roebuck until she can prove she deserves him.

The play was presented by Hackett after it won a prize of $300 which he had offered for "an original comedy whereof an American should be the leading character." William Cullen Bryant and Fitz-Greene Halleck were among the contest's judges. Many contemporaries saw in Wildfire a good-natured spoofing of Davy Crockett, but Paulding and Hackett strenuously denied this. However, the play was not totally successful, so was immediately withdrawn for revisions, which Paulding allowed John Augustus Stone♦ to write. Stone retained only the basic plot and the character of the Congressman. In his three-act redaction, Cecilia becomes Fredonia, the daughter of a long-lost British officer, and is raised by the benevolent Peter Bonnybrown. She is courted by a fortune hunter who calls himself Lord Luminary and by the fake Count Rousillon, but, with Wildfire's help, wins a proposal from Trueman Casual.

During his 1833 trip to London, Hackett had William Bayle Bernard♦ provide him with yet a third similar vehicle about Wildfire, which was in two acts and was called *The Kentuckian: or, A Trip to New York,* although it was sometimes offered as *A Kentuckian's Trip to New York in 1815.* The play centered on a dinner given by Mr. and Mrs. Freeman. The guests include Mr. Freeman's nephew, Wildfire; the Freemans' daughter Caroline; Mrs. Wollope, a haughty Englishwoman who hopes to make a fortune teaching Americans good manners and who promises, once her plans for quick

riches come to naught, to write a scathing travelogue on her American trip; and Caroline's two suitors, Percival, a rich, decent English merchant, and Jenkins, an English fortune hunter who is posing as a Lord and who is actually Mrs. Wollope's brother. Mrs. Wollope was a putdown of Mrs. Trollope, so the character's name was changed in England to Mrs. Luminary. In later years, until his retirement, Hackett used this play and, apparently on some occasions, Stone's, to keep Wildfire before an adoring public. Typical of Wildfire's Americanisms was his calling lawyers catfish, " 'cause you see they're all head, and they're head all mouth." Hackett played the part in "buckskin clothes, deerskin shoes, and a coon-skin hat." Laurence Hutton♦ noted, "He had many contemporary imitators, who copied his dress, his speech and his gait."

LITHGOW, JOHN [ARTHUR] (b. 1945) Born in Rochester, N.Y., he studied at Harvard and at the London Academy of Music and Dramatic Art. He previously had made his acting debut in 1953 as Mustardseed in the Antioch Shakespeare Festival's mounting of *A Midsummer Night's Dream.*♦ His Broadway debut as Kenny Kendal, one of the athletes, in *The Changing Room* (1973) earned him a Tony Award.♦ In the checkered career that followed he has performed to acclaim in several Broadway failures, off-Broadway, and in regional theatres. He appeared as Mat Burke in the 1977 revival of *Anna Christie*♦ and as Walter Burns in the 1986 production of *The Front Page,*♦ but is probably best remembered as René Gallimard, the troubled diplomat, in *M. Butterfly*♦ (1988).

LITT, JACOB (1860–1905) While still a youngster he began his theatrical career by selling programs at the Grand Opera House in his native Milwaukee. Within a few years he was treasurer of the house. Shortly thereafter he acquired two theatres of his own in Milwaukee and began mounting popular melodramas, which he sent on tour throughout the Midwest. With profits from these shows he was able to buy additional theatres in Minneapolis and St. Paul as well as Milwaukee. He found his greatest moneymaker in the melodrama *In Old Kentucky*♦ (1899), which major New York managements had rejected. By the time a nervous disorder forced his early retirement he had theatres as far east as New York and was sending out not only companies of his own plays but handling Midwestern operations for Charles Frohman♦ and other Broadway producers. Despite his short career, his estate amounted to well over a million dollars.

Little Accident, a comedy in three acts by Floyd Dell and Thomas Mitchell.♦ Produced by Crosby Gaige♦ at the Morosco Theatre. October 9, 1928. 304 performances.

On the eve of his wedding to Madge Ferris (Elvia Enders) Norman Overback (Mitchell) discovers that he is the father of Isabel Drury's child. When Isabel (Katherine Alexander) tells Norman she is putting the baby up for adoption, Norman kidnaps it. Madge is willing to marry Norman anyway. So is his landlady's daughter. But Norman decides he really likes Isabel, who was his sweetheart at college.

Based on Dell's novel, *The Unmarried Father,* the slight but amusing comedy was a major hit of its season.

Little Church Around the Corner, THE The Protestant-Episcopal Church of the Transfiguration at 1 East 29th Street in New York. At George Holland's♦ death in 1870, Joseph Jefferson♦ and Holland's son went to arrange the funeral service at a nearby Episcopal church. Refused on the grounds that Holland was an actor, they were informed, "There is a little church around the corner where they do that sort of thing." As a result, the Church of the Transfiguration acquired its nickname and has ever since served popularly for theatrical weddings and funerals. It was featured prominently in the musical *Sally.* ♦

Little Foxes, The, a drama in three acts by Lillian Hellman.♦ Produced by Herman Shumlin♦ at the National Theatre. February 15, 1939. 410 performances.

The Hubbards are a rapacious, hate-filled family who dominate a small Southern town at the turn of the century. Oscar (Carl Benton Reid) has married Birdie Bagtry (Patricia Collinge♦) for her family's money, and now that they again need cash, Oscar and his older brother Ben (Charles Dingle) reluctantly offer their crafty sister Regina (Tallulah Bankhead♦) one-third interest in a new cotton mill they plan in return for a $75,000 loan. When Regina's husband, Horace Giddens (Frank Conroy), refuses to lend the money, Oscar goads his weakling son, Leo (Dan Duryea), into stealing Horace's bonds. Since the bonds were willed to Regina, Horace says nothing. An argument ensues between Regina and Horace. The quarrel induces Horace's heart attack, but Regina refuses to get his medicine and lets him die. She then demands not one-third but a three-quarters interest in the business for her silence.

Comparing the work with her earlier success, *The*

Children's Hour, ♦ Richard Watts, Jr.,♦ of the *Herald Tribune* commented, "Miss Hellman's new play is a grim, bitter and merciless study, a drama more honest, more pointed and more brilliant." It has been revived regularly, most notably in 1967 by the Repertory Theatre of Lincoln Center♦ and in 1981 with Elizabeth Taylor. It provided the basis for Marc Blitzstein's♦ 1949 opera *Regina.* The opera featured, among others, Jane Pickens as Regina, Brenda Lewis as Birdie, and William Warfield as Cal. Although the work was a commercial failure, it has since found a place in the repertory of several opera companies.

Little Johnny Jones, a musical play in three acts by George M. Cohan.♦ Produced by Sam H. Harris♦ at the Liberty Theatre. November 7, 1904. 52 performances.

Johnny Jones (Cohan) comes to England to ride in the Derby. Anthony Anstey (Jerry Cohan) offers him a bribe to throw the race, but Johnny refuses. Johnny loses anyway, and when he does the vindictive Anstey spreads rumors that he lost intentionally. Johnny returns to America in disgrace, but a friendly detective obtains evidence to clear him. Anstey then kidnaps Johnny's sweetheart, Goldie Gates (Ethel Levey), and Johnny must scour San Francisco's Chinatown to recover her.

Principal songs: Give My Regards to Broadway · Life's a Funny Proposition After All · The Yankee Doodle Boy (I'm a Yankee Doodle Dandy)

Although the play was assailed by most critics as too slangy, contrived, and chauvinistic, the public adored it. Within a few months after its original run, Cohan twice brought it back for return engagements. A largely rewritten, poorly mounted 1982 revival failed.

Little Journey, A, a play in three acts by Rachel Crothers.♦ Produced by the Messrs. Shubert♦ at the Little Theatre. December 26, 1918. 252 performances.

When Julie Rutherford (Estelle Winwood♦), a New York society belle, loses both her fortune and her fiancé in quick succession, she decides to head west to live with her brother. She is nearly kicked off the train when it is discovered she has lost her ticket, but a handsome young rancher, Jim West (Cyril Keightley), lends her the money to remain aboard. He quickly grows fond of her, but she remains enamored of her old frivolous way of life, without which she sees no reason to live. The train is involved in a horrendous wreck, in which the widowed young mother of a baby is killed. Her own close brush with death, her motherly instincts at seeing the orphaned baby, and Jim's obvious manly virtues all contrive to offer Julie new hope and a new life.

Not typical of Miss Crothers's best work, usually dealing with the interaction of women, this rather ordinary, if theatrical love story was made memorable by her subtle drawing of an essentially rootless young lady.

Little Katy, see *Hot Corn*

Little Mary Sunshine, a musical comedy in two acts by Rick Besoyan. Produced at the Orpheum Theatre. November 18, 1959. 1,143 performances.

Little Mary Sunshine (Eileen Brennan) runs a lodge in the Rockies, but is in danger of being evicted. The Colorado Rangers, led by Captain Jim (William James), all love her and on their way to hunt the villainous Yellow Feather stop to help her. Eventually they capture the Indian and save Mary from eviction.

Principal songs: Colorado Love Call · Little Mary Sunshine

Although *Little Mary Sunshine,* unlike the English spoof of 1920s' musicals, *The Boy Friend,* which ridiculed a particular type of musical comedy, aimed its barbs all over the theatrical arena of the same era, it did so with deadly and hilarious accuracy. The basic object of satire was operettas such as *Rose-Marie*♦ and *Rio Rita,* ♦ which told similar stories. Of course, "Colorado Love Call" was a send-up of *Rose-Marie*'s "Indian Love Call." But other songs ranged farther afield. For example, "Look For a Sky of Blue" recalled Kern's♦ "Look For the Silver Lining" from the musical comedy *Sally.* ♦ The show remains popular with amateur groups.

Little Murders, a play in two acts by Jules Feiffer. Produced by Alexander H. Cohan♦ at the Broadhurst Theatre. April 25, 1967. 7 performances.

The Newquists are a rather kooky family trying to make the best of the bad deal life has dealt them. The father, Carol (Heywood Hale Broun), would like to have a less feminine name; the mother, Marjorie (Ruth White), would like to have a different family; the son, Kenny (David Steinberg), would like to be of a different sex. Only the sweet but spunky daughter, Patsy (Barbara Cook♦), seems vaguely content, although she is in love with a thin-skinned liberal, Alfred Chamberlain (Elliott Gould), who thinks the best way to deal with muggers is to let them beat you. The jangle and blare around them grows increasingly hectic and menacing until Patsy is killed by someone shooting through the window. At that point, the Newquists decide to shoot back.

Although the play failed initially, it was produced with great success in England by the Royal Shakespeare Company♦ and this led to an off-Broadway revival at the Circle in the Square. ♦ The revival opened January 5, 1969, and ran 400 performances with a cast that included Vincent Gardenia as Carol, Elizabeth Wilson as Marjorie, Jon Korkes as Kenny, Linda Lavin as Patsy, and Fred Willard as Alfred. Jules [Ralph] Feiffer (b. 1929) is a New Yorker best known as a cartoonist.

Little Nell and the Marchioness, a play in four acts by John Brougham. ♦ Produced at Wallack's Theatre. August 14, 1867. 28 performances.

Nell (Lotta Crabtree♦) and her Grandfather Trent (T. J. Hind) are forced from the Old Curiosity Shop by the rapacious Quilp (E. Coleman). They wander the country roads of England until the old man finds work at a small church. Eventually the grandfather's long-lost rich brother returns to help him retrieve his shop, but by that time the wear and tear has been too much for Little Nell, who dies and is lifted bodily to heaven. In a second, interwoven story Dick Swiveller (J. C. Williamson) falls in love with the poor servant girl of Quilp's unscrupulous lawyer, Simon Brass (W. J. Leonard). He names her "The Marchioness" (Lotta Crabtree) and after she nurses him through an illness marries her.

Based on Dickens's *The Old Curiosity Shop,* the play was written as a vehicle for Lotta. It became the most popular piece in her repertory, and she played it as long as she performed. Neither her Nell nor her Marchioness was totally faithful to the original, but served as excuses for her banjo playing, her clog dances, and other turns. For example, the fair at Highgate, which Nell visits, prompted a miniature minstrel show with Lotta performing a jig and a breakdown. The show's short original run is in no way indicative of its popularity, since it was a limited engagement. T. Allston Brown♦ noted, "Rarely in the history of New York theatricals has a summer engagement proved so profitable." Receipts averaged a then exceptional $1,100 per night, the run was extended one week, and Lotta herself realized $10,000 from the stand. The J. C. Williamson, who played Swiveller, later became the leading Australian theatre magnate.

Little Night Music, A, a musical in two acts. Book by Hugh Wheeler. ♦ Lyrics and music by Stephen Sondheim. ♦ Produced by Harold Prince♦ and others at the Shubert Theatre. February 25, 1973. 600 performances.

Having fallen in love with his former mistress Désirée (Glynis Johns), Fredrik Egerman (Len Cariou♦) would dissolve his marriage to his child bride (Victoria Mallory). Count Carl-Magnus (Laurence Guittard), Désirée's lover, attempts to cool the romance. However, after a dinner given by Désirée's mother, Mrs. Armfeldt (Hermione Gingold♦), Fredrik's son, Henrik (Mark Lambert), runs off with his young mother-in-law, the Count returns to his wife, and Fredrik and Désirée are free to pursue their romance.

Principal songs: Liaisons · Send in the Clowns

Based on the Swedish film, *Smiles of a Summer Night,* the musical's score was written entirely in three-quarter time or variations thereof. Though the show displayed much of Sondheim's misanthropy, it was mellower than most of his later works.

Little Shop of Horrors, a musical in two acts. Book and lyrics by Howard Ashman. Music by Alan Menken. Produced by David Geffen, Cameron Mackintosh,♦ and the Shubert♦ organization at the Orpheum Theatre. July 27, 1982. 2,209 performances.

Seymour (Lee Wilkof) brings a small plant into Mushnik's florist shop, where he works, and names it Audrey II, after the girl (Ellen Greene) he loves. The plant begins to grow and grow, preferably feeding on bits of Seymour's rival for Audrey's affections and eventually on Mushnik, Audrey, and Seymour himself. It seems the plant has hopes to take over the world.

Based on a film of the same name, this delightful, small spoof enjoyed world-wide success. Audrey II was a huge puppet manipulated by a puppeteer; its voice came from an actor off stage.

Little Show, The, a series of intimate revues presented on Broadway in 1929, 1930, and 1931. The first edition featured songs by Arthur Schwartz♦ and Howard Dietz♦ and sketches by Dietz and George S. Kaufman. ♦ It starred Fred Allen,♦ Clifton Webb,♦ and Libby Holman.♦ Among its songs were "I Guess I'll Have To Change My Plan" (Webb) and "Moanin' Low" (Holman's famous torch song), the latter with music by Ralph Rainger. The final edition starred Beatrice Lillie♦ and Ernest Truex♦ and offered Noel Coward's "Mad Dogs and Englishmen," and "When Yuba Plays the Rhumba on the Tuba" and "There Are Fairies at the Bottom of My Garden."

Little Theatre in America If regionally oriented amateur production is considered the essence of Little Theatre, then the first American example might be said to have been the performance by one Colonel Ornate's troops of the prosletyzing *Los Moros y los Christianos* before an audience of probably bewildered Indians in 1598 in what afterwards became New Mexico. As theatre later spread across the colonies in succeeding centuries scattered amateur entertainments no doubt were offered occasionally. The controversial playing of *The Bear and the Cub* ♦ is possibly another instance, as would be performances by General Burgoyne's troops during the Revolutionary War. Amateur groups sprang up across the country all through the 19th century from the Lobero Theatre in Santa Barbara, California, to the Comedy Club in New York City, the latter group, founded in 1885, still active today. But a concerted effort to develop such theatres did not occur until early in the 20th century when such important figures as Percy MacKaye♦ began trumpeting the merits of "a theatre wholly divorced from commercialism." MacKaye's plea, in his 1909 *The Playhouse and the Play,* came precisely at the moment when silents films began to make noticeable inroads, luring away many less educated, less affluent playgoers from cheap melodrama and farce, and forcing the closing or conversion of many marginal live theatres. Although MacKaye attempted to promote the term Civic Theatre the somewhat more descriptive term Little Theatre quickly took hold and spread. Indeed the rapidity of the spread was remarkable. Chicago was the cradle of several important little theatres, including that at the Hull House in 1900 and the later group founded by Maurice Browne,♦ who is sometimes called the father of the Little Theatre movement in America. Kenneth MacGowan♦ was also an avid supporter of such playhouses. Historian Joseph Wesley Ziegler noted, "In the number of theatres created and the number of amateur talents working in them, the Little Theatre movement was the farthest-reaching homegrown theatre in American history. It was also the most self-consciously noble; it is no accident that even now we speak of the phenomenon in capital letters." The heyday of the movement was in the 1920s, when prosperity, a general renaissance in dramatic writing and an awareness of that renaissance sharpened interest everywhere. As a rule the troupes presented recognized Broadway successes and occasionally the more accessible or at least undemanding of the classics. A few attempted original drama, though virtually nothing of importance emerged from these theatres. Contrary to

MacKaye's hopes, they were at heart only a little less conservative, if that, than Broadway. Many of the more successful groups were able to finance the erection of attractive, well equipped playhouses, usually seating only a few hundred patrons. In their informative study of the movement, *Curtains Going Up* (1938), Albert McCleery and Carl Glick were able to list more than 500 community groups that had functioned or were still flourishing in the then forty-eight states. (The book also provides excellent photographs of the often beautiful playhouses and the fine physical productions.) With the coming of sound films, followed immediately by the Depression and eventually World War II, interest in the movement waned. While a number of durable amateur groups continue to prosper in various localities, the sheen and the excitement that once surrounded the Little Theatre movement have long since been transferred to the fine professional regional theatres that have developed since the war. The nature of amateur collegiate theatre unusually depends on the quality of the institution and the vision and industry of its theatrical director.

Little Tycoon, The, a comic opera in two acts by Williard Spenser.♦ Produced at the Standard Theatre. March 29, 1886. 104 performances.

General Knickerbocker (R. E. Graham) is returning home from Europe with his daughter Violet (Carrie M. Dietrich) and Lord Dolphin (E. H. Van Veghten), the monosyllabic nobleman he has decided his daughter must marry. But Violet loves Alvin (W. S. Rising), so, after they arrive at the Knickerbocker estate, Alvin comes disguised as "His Royal Highness Sham, The Great Tycoon of Japan" and with his flattery gulls the social-climbing general into allowing him to wed Violet.

Principal songs: The Cats on Our Back Fence · Love Comes Like a Summer Sigh

After a long run in Philadelphia, the musical played New York as part of its road tour. Although New York critics dismissed it as typifying the Philadelphia School of Comic Opera,♦ its original engagement was extended by popular demand and continued until the hot weather. It toured or was revived regularly for about a decade.

Living Models Living pictures or tableaux vivants had been popular in American theatre from very early on. Patriotic spectacles in particular were wont to have such finales, often with the personification of Liberty at the center of a carefully posed ensemble. It also became the custom to have the first curtain call taken in a dramatically held pose.

These extravagant tableaux remained popular through the era of Ziegfeldian♦ revues. However, during the 1847–48 season a special variety of tableau was the rage—carefully posed reproductions of famous statues and paintings. Excuses were found to place them in all types of entertainment. As so often happens, the vogue faded when excesses, especially posing of virtually nude female figures, led to moral protests and finally to police action.

Living Newspaper, see *Federal Theatre Project*

Living Theatre Company, THE Established as a repertory ensemble in 1947 by Julian Beck and his wife Judith Malina, it first performed at the Cherry Lane Theatre and after 1951 at its own theatre on lower Sixth Avenue. From the start its repertory leaned heavily on plays that had little chance of commercial success. The choices, and often the mountings, were daring, frequently leftish in bent, and increasingly controversial. Among the writers whose plays were produced were Gertrude Stein,♦ T. S. Eliot,♦ Pirandello,♦ and Cocteau. The company's most famous production was not a revival but an original play, Jack Gelber's *The Connection*♦ (1959), one of the earliest attempts to look candidly at the growth of drug addiction. In 1961 and 1962 the troupe made two well-received visits to Europe, but growing concern with what was perceived as its increasingly confrontational, iconoclastic nature embroiled the company in legal and critical battles and may have speeded the onset of the financial difficulties that forced the theatre to close in 1963. The Becks later attempted to run the company in Europe. A 1984 return was not made welcome.

LOCKE, EDWARD (1869–1945) Born in England, he came to America while still in his early teens and soon became an actor both in the theatre and in vaudeville. After writing some vaudeville sketches, he turned to full-length plays. Several were done by cheaper touring companies before he reached Broadway with *The Climax*♦ (1909), which told of a beautiful young opera singer who comes under the mesmerizing influence of an evil, lustful doctor. It was a huge success, and although Locke subsequently was the author or co-author of numerous other plays, none proved nearly as popular. Among his other works were *The Case of Becky* (1912), in which a girl with a dual personality is cured by hypnosis; and *The Dancer* (1919), written with Max Marcin♦ and Louis K. Anspacher,♦ recounting the romance of a showgirl and a socialite which is opposed by the young man's snobbish parents.

LOCKE, GEORGE E. (1817–1880) Known popularly as "Yankee" Locke for his impersonation of native types, he was born in Epsom, N.H. and made his theatrical debut in Boston. He played there and in Providence, R.I., for many seasons before he found his special métier and began to make a name for himself across the country. The names of the characters he played suggest their nature and the nature of the vehicles written around them— Jedediah Homebred, Zedediah Short, Solomon Swop, and Moderation Easterbrook. He was one of the many performers who played the major cities only briefly, finding warmer welcomes on the stages of smaller cities and towns.

LOESSER, FRANK [HENRY] (1910–69) Although Loesser was born into a musical New York family, his father, a piano teacher, disapproved of popular music, so young Loesser was largely self-taught. His earliest professional work was writing lyrics and sketches for vaudeville and radio, and Broadway first heard of him solely as a lyricist when he set words to some Irving Actman melodies for *The Illustrators' Show* (1936). By the time he returned to the theatre in 1948 as both composer and lyricist for *Where's Charley?,* ♦ he had long since established himself as a songwriter in films and what was left of Tin Pan Alley. His melodic and wide-ranging, if essentially nostalgic score for the show included the march, "The New Ashmoleon Marching Society and Student Conservatory Band"; the popular ballad, "My Darling, My Darling"; and the enduring soft-shoe, "Once in Love with Amy." His songs for the great musical comedy *Guys and Dolls* ♦ (1950) unerringly caught the piece's raffish colorings. Among its hits were "Adelaide's Lament," "A Bushel and a Peck," "If I Were a Bell," and "More I Cannot Wish You." He blended opera, musical play, musical comedy, and vaudeville in his next work, *The Most Happy Fella* ♦ (1956), a lyric version of *They Knew What They Wanted,* ♦ for which Loesser provided the book as well as the songs. The show's popular successes were its more immediately show-wise numbers such as "Big D" and "Standing on the Corner." *Greenwillow* (1960), for which he provided the songs and collaborated on the book, was an interesting, fundamentally bucolic work that failed commercially, but he shared a Pulitzer Prize ♦ for his final work, his songs for the satirical *How To Succeed in Business Without Really Trying* ♦ (1961), best remembered for "I Believe in You." Loesser's music was probably the wittiest of any contemporary composer and regularly caught the flavor and rhythms of colloquial speech. His lyrics, too, were singularly fresh. In a trade notoriously jealous of its fame and success, Loesser was known for his generosity to other songwriters and gave important boosts to the Broadway careers of Richard Adler, ♦ Jerry Ross, ♦ and Meredith Willson. ♦

LOEWE, FREDERICK (1901–88) Born in Germany, the son of a popular leading man in operetta, he studied with such notable figures as Ferruccio Busoni and Eugène d'Albert. He came to America in 1924, but for a decade found he could not make a living with his music, so took numerous odd, unrelated jobs. In 1935 Dennis King ♦ introduced his song "Love Tiptoes Through My Heart" in the farce *Petticoat Fever.* A year later he had a single song interpolated into *The Illustrators' Show.* His first complete score was heard in New York in *Great Lady* (1938), a quick failure, although St. Louis had earlier heard another score in *Salute to Spring* (1937). In 1942 he was introduced to lyricist-librettist Alan Jay Lerner, ♦ with whom he was to write all his subsequent musicals. Their first effort, *Life of the Party* (1942), got no further than Detroit, while their next collaboration, *What's Up* (1943), closed almost as soon as it reached New York. In 1945 they wrote an interesting, off-beat musical, *The Day Before Spring,* but it failed to attract playgoers. So it remained for the fantasy *Brigadoon* ♦ (1947) to establish their reputations. Among the memorable songs from the show were "Almost Like Being in Love," "Come to Me, Bend to Me," and "The Heather on the Hill." Their next work, *Paint Your Wagon* (1951), re-created the rough-and-tumble gold rush days, and left behind "I Talk to the Trees." Their greatest success was *My Fair Lady* ♦ (1956), a musical version of Shaw's ♦ *Pygmalion.* ♦ Among its enduring songs were "Get Me to the Church on Time," "I Could Have Danced All Night," "I've Grown Accustomed to Her Face," and "On the Street Where You Live." The last Loewe score heard on Broadway was *Camelot* ♦ (1960) and included "If Ever I Would Leave You." However, in 1973 a theatrical version of their film, *Gigi,* was offered to Broadway. Loewe was a traditionalist whose music followed long-established patterns, but it was marked by his uncommon gift for fresh melody and his ability to capture the essence of a far-off time or place.

LOFTUS, [MARIE] CECILIA (1876–1943) One of the most versatile of performers, who moved successfully back and forth between vaudeville and musical comedy on the one hand and romantic drama and Shakespeare on the other, she was born in Glasgow the daughter of popular music hall entertainers. The attractive, dark-haired woman, often known as

Cissie, first called attention to herself as a mimic, and it was in this capacity that she made her American debut at Koster♦ and Bial's♦ in 1895. She later returned to America to appear in the operetta *The Mascot* (1900), then joined Helena Modjeska's♦ ensemble to appear as Viola in *Twelfth Night♦* and Hero in *Much Ado About Nothing. ♦* She next played briefly under Daniel Frohman's♦ aegis, before joining E. H. Sothern♦ as his leading lady. Her most famous roles for Sothern were Lady Sacheverell in *Richard Lovelace* (1901) and Katherine in *If I Were King♦* (1901), the latter written with her in mind by her husband, Justin Huntly McCarthy. She continued to alternate between London and New York, and between vaudeville and the legitimate theatre for many years. During the 1913–14 season she toured America playing Juliet and Desdemona opposite William Faversham.♦ She remained a headliner at the Palace♦ throughout the 1920s, winning applause for her imitations of the Barrymores and other popular performers. One of her last assignments was the small role of Mrs. Riley in *Merrily We Roll Along♦* (1934). Her final appearance was in *Little Dark Horse* (1941), in which she played a tyrannical grandmother.

LOGAN, CORNELIUS A[MBROSIUS] (1806–1853) Little is known for certain of this briefly popular playwright and comedian's early history. He is generally said to have been born in Baltimore and to have made his acting debut in Philadelphia in 1825. Noah Ludlow♦ adds that he had been a painter by trade and at one time had considered entering the priesthood. He also notes that Logan eventually manifested ambitions as a tragedian, but that his "unchangeable comic" face denied him success. Much of his acting career was spent in the Midwest (called the West in his day), where he specialized in Yankee roles. He was the author of several comedies in which such Yankee characters were pivotal figures. *Yankee Land; or, The Foundling of the Apple Orchard* (1834) centered on one Lot Sap Sago, who turns out to be the long-lost son of an English lord. *The Wag of Maine* (1835) is apparently lost. *The Vermont Wool Dealer* (1840), which focused on a hoodwinked guardian named Deuteronomy Dutiful, provided Danforth Marble♦ with a lucrative vehicle for many years. Logan's last known work, *Chloroform; or, New York a Hundred Years Hence* (1849), told how Aminadab Slocum, buried as dead after he was chloroformed while having a tooth pulled, is resuscitated a century later and confronts his descendants. Logan himself played Aminadab when William Burton♦ mounted the

work. Logan was the father of three talented daughters, Eliza,♦ Celia, and Olive. ♦

LOGAN, ELIZA (1830–1872) The eldest daughter of Cornelius A. Logan,♦ she was given a careful education by her father in the hope that she would not follow in his wandering footsteps. However, he supported her final decision to become an actress. She made her debut as Young Norval in Philadelphia's Walnut Street Theatre♦ when she was only eleven. Her New York debut took place in 1850 as Pauline in *The Lady of Lyons. ♦* Most of her career was spent performing as a major star in the South or in what was then called the West (now the Midwest). She is said to have possessed an attractive, expressive face, a fine figure, and a sweet, adaptable voice. The critic for the New York *Herald* described her acting as "impulsive, electric and at times singularly impressive from the power she throws into a few brief words." She retired in 1859 when she married George Wood, who operated theatres in St. Louis and Cincinnati.

LOGAN, ELLA (1913–69) The Scottish singer who never quite lost her brogue came to America in 1932 and sang with dance bands and in cabarets before appearing in *Calling All Stars* (1934), *George White's Scandals of 1939–40, ♦* in which she introduced "Are You Havin' Any Fun?," *Sons o' Fun* (1941), and *Show Time* (1942). Her last appearance was her best known, when she introduced "How Are Things in Glocca Morra?" in *Finian's Rainbow♦* (1947).

LOGAN, JOSHUA [LOCKWOOD] (1908–88) Born in Texarkana, Texas, he studied at Princeton and with Stanislavsky♦ in Moscow. In 1928 he was a founder of the University Players,♦ with whom he remained until 1933. On Broadway his first solo directorial assignment was *To See Ourselves* (1935), but it was his staging of *On Borrowed Time♦* (1938) which called attention to his talent and inaugurated a string of successes. His work was subsequently seen in *I Married an Angel♦* (1938); *Knickerbocker Holiday♦* (1938); *Stars in Your Eyes* (1939); *Morning's at Seven♦* (1939); *Two for the Show* (1940); *Higher and Higher* (1940), for which he was also co-author of the book; a 1940 revival of *Charley's Aunt♦; By Jupiter♦* (1942); *This Is the Army♦* (1942); *Annie Get Your Gun♦* (1946); *Happy Birthday♦* (1946); *John Loves Mary♦* (1947), for which he was also co-producer; *Mister Roberts♦* (1948), which he helped adapt from Thomas Heggen's novel besides directing; and *South Pacific♦* (1949), for which he served as co-librettist and co-producer as well as director.

Following the failure of his modern rewriting of *The Cherry Orchard* as *The Wisteria Trees* (1950), which he directed and co-produced, he was director, co-producer, and co-librettist of *Wish You Were Here* (1952), and co-producer and director of *Picnic*♦ (1953). He served as both producer and director of *Kind Sir* (1953). He next directed and helped write and produce *Fanny*♦ (1954). After producing and directing *Middle of the Night*♦ (1956), he staged *Blue Denim* (1958) and *The World of Susie Wong*♦ (1958). Although he was afterward associated with numerous worthwhile plays, none was commercially successful. At his best his direction was distinguished by a deep insight into character and a remarkable fluidity, the latter especially evident in his staging of often cumbersome musicals. He was sometimes criticized in his later years, however, for too heavy a touch.

LOGAN [Sykes], Olive (1839?–1909) The versatile, persistent, but never totally successful youngest daughter of Cornelius A. Logan,♦ she made her debut as a child actress playing opposite her father in the South and Midwest. After his death she spent several seasons in important roles at Philadelphia's Arch Street Theatre,♦ when it was under the management of William Wheatley♦ and the first John Drew.♦ She left her position to study in Europe, where she published her first novel and travel book. Returning to America she assumed the title role in her own play, *Eveleen* (1864). The play failed, so she toured the South and Midwest until she returned to New York to act the part of Laura Roslyn opposite Frank Chanfrau♦ in *Sam* (1866) and also offered her interpretation of Lady Gay Spanker. That same year she briefly joined a troupe of French actors who were appearing in New York and acted with them in *500 Francs de Récompense*. Thereafter she performed only on occasion, preferring to lecture on women's rights and other topics of interest to her, and to write. Her plays included *Surf* (1870); *A Business Woman* (1873); *La Cigale* (1878), which she adapted from the French for Charlotte Crabtree♦; and *Newport; or, The Swimmer, the Singer, and the Cypher* (1879). Among her books was *The Mimic World* (1871).

Lombardi, Ltd., a comedy in three acts by Frederic and Fanny Hatton. ♦ Produced by Oliver Morosco♦ at the Morosco Theatre. September 24, 1917. 296 performances.

Tito Lombardi (Leo Carrillo) is a skilled dressmaker whose simple honesty and quiet morals seem out of place in the often harsh, cynical world of fashion. Apart from his work his one love is a chorus girl named Phyllis Manning (Sue MacMannamy). Unfortunately she is a scheming gold-digger who returns his affections only so long as it serves her purposes. When she runs out on him and his business seems on the verge of bankruptcy, he looks with new eyes on his self-sacrificing, long-suffering assistant, Norah Blake (Janet Dunbar).

Although many critics found the play trite and contrived, the Hattons' professional know-how, their varied pictures of theatrical showgirls, Carrillo's warm performance, and a number of scenes with scantily clad mannequins made the play exceedingly popular both in New York and on the road. Morosco called the show "as completely gratifying as anything I ever did in show business."

London Assurance The only enduring British comedy of the first half of the 19th century, this earliest Dion Boucicault♦ success tells of a lordly Belgravia fop, Sir Harcourt Courtly, whose suit of a Gloucestershire heiress is thwarted by none other than his own son. Romping in and out of the amorous adventures is a determined horsewoman, Lady Gay Spanker. The American premiere occurred at the Park Theatre♦ in 1841 with a cast that included Henry Placide♦ as Harcourt Courtly and Charlotte Cushman♦ as Lady Gay Spanker. The premiere was a landmark in the annals of the American theatre. First of all, it followed the innovation employed in its original London production by Mme. Vestris♦ of using a box set, so that audiences appeared to be watching the action from the fourth wall of a real house. Equally important was the comedy's stand of three uninterrupted weeks, the first "long run" in our history. The play was regularly revived by J. W. ♦ and Lester Wallack♦ in productions in which John Gilbert♦ invariably played Harcourt Courtly and in which such actresses as Fanny Davenport♦ and Rose Coghlan♦ portrayed Lady Gay Spanker. Laura Keene's horsewoman was also admired, as was Ada Rehan's♦ in Augustin Daly's♦ 1896 revival. Thereafter the play was brought back with increasing infrequency and with little success. Even a superb Royal Shakespeare Company♦ production, imported in 1974, attracted few American playgoers.

LONERGAN, Lester (1869?–1931) The Irish-born director came to America as a young man and acted in Western stock companies before graduating to important supporting roles opposite such notables as John Barrymore,♦ John Drew,♦ and Helena Modjeska.♦ In his later years he largely abandoned acting and was responsible for staging such successes as *Abraham Lincoln* (1919), *The Bad Man* (1920), *The Road to Rome*♦ (1927), and *The Command To Love* (1927).

Long Day's Journey into Night, a play in four acts by Eugene O'Neill.♦ Produced by Leigh Connell, Theodore Mann,♦ and José Quintero♦ at the Helen Hayes Theatre. November 7, 1956. 390 performances. PP, NYDCCA.

On an uncomfortably hot day in their New England summer home, the Tyrones confront their pasts and each other. James Tyrone (Fredric March♦) is an aging actor, famous but miserly. He has continued to perform in the same trashy melodrama rather than risk failure in more adventuresome plays. To save pennies he had called in a quack doctor when his wife gave birth to their third son, Edmund (Bradford Dillman). As a result of the quack's treatment, Mary Tyrone (Florence Eldridge♦) has been a drug addict ever since. Their eldest son, James, Jr. (Jason Robards, Jr.♦), is a rakish, boozing ne'er-do-well, who is jealous of his younger brother. As the day turns into night the destructively probing conversations continue, until the rattled, drugged Mary appears in her wedding gown, reliving a happier, unreclaimable time.

Louis Kronenberger♦ wrote, "This relentless chronicle of O'Neill's riven and tormented family, mingling the fierce thrust of unblushing theatre with the harsh, unsoftened truth, may very possibly come to seem O'Neill's most substantial legacy to the American stage." Written as a sort of autobiographical catharsis, its production violated O'Neill's stipulation that it not be performed until 25 years after his death. A mediocre revival in 1986, with Jack Lemmon in the lead, failed, but so did a much praised production two years later with Robards now portraying the elder James.

LONG, JOHN LUTHER (1861–1927) Born in either Philadelphia or Hanover, Penn., he was a successful Philadelphia attorney who had published short stories. Belasco's♦ popular dramatization of his *Madame Butterfly*♦ (1900) prompted him to try his own hand at play-writing, so he collaborated with Belasco on another tragic Oriental romance, *The Darling of the Gods*♦ (1902). They followed this with the story of a tricked and doomed 5th-century princess, *Adrea*♦ (1904). His next work, written with Edward Childs Carpenter,♦ was *The Dragon Fly* (1905), which told of a young Spanish woman caught by the divided loyalties of the Mexican-American War. That these exotically set themes

were Long's became more clearly evident when on his own he wrote *Dolce* (1906) for Mrs. Fiske.♦ It told the story of a countess who finds that her childhood sweetheart still retains affectionate memories of their platonic affair. *Kassa* (1909), written for Mrs. Leslie Carter,♦ focused on a girl who runs away from a convent only to be betrayed by the man she thought loved her. After a lapse of 13 years, his last produced play, *Crowns* (1922), was mounted in New York, but the time for his style of romantic drama had passed. The play recounted the tragic love story of a prince and princess, who are visited by Jesus in the hope that they will bring peace to their feuding countries, but who die in their thwarted effort to carry out Christ's will. In a sense Long was an early-20th-century throwback to the 18th- and 19th-century Philadelphia tradition of gentleman-lawyer-writer.

LONG, SUMNER ARTHUR, see *Never Too Late*

Long Voyage Home, The, a play in one act by Eugene O'Neill.♦ Produced by the Provincetown Players♦ at the Playwright's Theatre. November 2, 1917.

Having been paid off that afternoon, several crew members of the *S. S. Glencairn* have come to Fat Joe's sleazy bar on the London waterfront. One of them, Olson (Ira Remsen), tells of his joy to be finished with the sea and of his plans to go home to Sweden. But his joy is short-lived, for he is given a mickey and shanghaied aboard the *Amindra,* bound for Cape Horn. The *Amindra,* he notes before he passes out, is the "worst ship dat sail to sea."

The only one of the four plays which ultimately comprised *S. S. Glencairn*♦ not set on the ship, it is considered by many critics to be the finest of the group.

Long Wharf Theatre (New Haven, Conn.) Founded in 1965 by Harlan Kleiman and Jon Jory, it is situated in a former warehouse near the waterfront. A three-quarter thrust stage was erected into an auditorium that originally seated about 440 people, but that was slightly enlarged soon after the opening. Arvin Brown has been the artistic director since 1967. The repertory consists of new plays and revivals. Among the original works presented there that later moved to Broadway were *The Changing Room* (1973), *Streamers*♦ (1976), and *The Shadow Box*♦ (1977). *Quartermaine's Terms* (1983) became an off-Broadway hit. In 1977 a 199-seat "Stage II" was added, offering works in progress, and regular repertory as well.

Look Back in Anger This play by John Osborne♦ served in 1957 as America's introduction to the new post-war school of British playwrights known as "the angry young men." The drama focuses on the raging discontent of a poor young Englishman and on his tortured relations with his wife and his best friend. The play was first produced in New York by David Merrick♦ at the Lyceum Theatre♦ on October 1, 1957, and ran for 407 performances. Kenneth Haigh, Mary Ure, and Alan Bates were the original leads. Many critics pointed out that America long had had drama of strident social protest, so that the new English school did not seem so really new. However, it soon became evident that these English playwrights did bring about a subtle change in protest plays in that the expression of the anger and not its actual causes frequently became central to the play. While a similar evolution might have occurred on its own in American drama in the undisciplined 1960s, the success of the British school hastened the appearance of plays that trafficked more in self-pity and self-flagellation than in self-improvement, and which at best mirrored the hopelessness of many weaker people to change their lot.

Look Homeward, Angel, a play in three acts by Ketti Frings. Produced by Kermit Bloomgarden♦ and Theatre 200, Inc., at the Ethel Barrymore Theatre. November 28, 1957. 564 performances. PP, NYDCCA.

Eugene Gant (Anthony Perkins♦) is a moonstruck, sensitive boy, who lives in the boardinghouse run by his domineering mother Eliza (Jo Van Fleet). His father, W. O. Gant (Hugh Griffith), is a blustering, frequently drunk, would-be tyrant and a dreamer. His brother Ben is too frail to live in the real world he longs for. Eugene's own world seems shattered when Ben dies and when his affection for the Gants' boarder, Laura James (Frances Hyland), is not returned. As he goes off to college he can only hope to pick up the pieces and make something of himself.

This fine adaptation of Thomas Wolfe's autobiographical novel of the same name was by an author [née Catherine or Katherine Hartley (1910?–81)] who was born in Columbus, Ohio, and gained major attention with her novel *Hold Back the Dawn*. Better known as a screen-writer, her other Broadway efforts were failures.

LOOS, ANITA (1893–1981) Born in Sisson, Calif., she was an actress before turning to writing. Her earliest hits were written with her husband, John Emerson.♦ *The Whole Town's Talking* (1932) cen-tered on a young man who boasts about an affair with a film star, while *Gentlemen Prefer Blondes*♦ (1926), based on her popular novel, focused on a gold-digger. The couple also wrote several less successful plays. In later years she enjoyed success with *Happy Birthday*♦ (1946), in which a shy librarian goes on a toot; her collaboration with Joseph Fields♦ on the book for a 1949 musicalization of *Gentlemen Prefer Blondes;* and her dramatization of Colette's novel *Gigi* (1951).

Autobiography: *A Girl Like I,* New York, 1966.

Loose Ends, a play in eight scenes by Michael Weller.♦ Produced at the Circle in the Square.♦ June 6, 1979. 284 performances.

Paul (Kevin Kline), a writer, teacher, and former Peace Corps volunteer, and Susan (Roxanne Hart), an attractive drifter and photographer, meet on a beach in Bali but soon go their separate ways. Paul later arranges to meet Susan again in Boston, and before long they are living together. After a few years they marry, but Paul's desire to have a child does not sit well with Susan. When she becomes pregnant she has an abortion, so they again split up. They meet several years later, and while they recognize they will always be friends they also understand that their relationship is at an end.

An episodic, but intelligent and sympathetic character study, the play was awarded the American Theatre Critics Association♦ Award after its 1979 premiere at Washington's Arena Stage.♦

LORAINE, ROBERT (1876–1935) The handsome English actor-manager, whose huge repertory ranged from the heroes of Shakespearean drama and 18th-century comedy through swash-buckling melodrama and modern drawing-room comedy, first played for American audiences in 1901 as the gallant Ralph Percy in *To Have and To Hold*. From then until shortly before his death he made numerous return visits. By far his best known part, at least for American theatregoers, was John Tanner, which he played in the American premiere of Shaw's♦ *Man and Superman*♦ (1905). He portrayed Tanner for six months in New York, then toured the country in the part for two seasons. During World War I he was an aviator and earned a DSO.

LORD, PAULINE (1890–1950) Born in Hanford, Calif., she made her debut in San Francisco stock in 1903 and afterwards toured with Nat Goodwin♦ and played in stock in Milwaukee and in Springfield (Mass.) before winning recognition in New York as Ruth Lennox, a young girl whose innocence is corrupted, in *The Talker* (1912). Her next major success came as Sadie, a girl of the streets, in *The Deluge* (1917). The part of another prostitute, the title role of *Anna Christie*♦ (1921), is generally considered her most memorable achievement, but she followed that with what many critics rated an equally artful portrayal, Amy, the young waitress who is courted by an aging Italian winemaker, in *They Knew What They Wanted*♦ (1924). Later in the 1920s she appeared in *Trelawny of the Wells* (1925 and 1927); *Sandalwood* (1926); *Mariners* (1927); *Salvation* (1927); and replaced Lynn Fontanne♦ as Nina Leeds in *Strange Interlude*♦ (1928). Her most notable parts in the 1930s were Abby, the neglected painter's loyal cook, in *The Late Christopher Bean* (1932); and Zenobia, the embittered, unkempt wife, in *Ethan Frome*♦ (1936). In 1946 she headed the touring company of *The Glass Menagerie,*♦ playing Amanda Wingfield. She was an actress with a singularly identifiable style of performing, which Ward Morehouse♦ described as "so jerky, so halting, so gasping, so volatile, and so brilliant." Brooks Atkinson♦ found her "elusive, tremulous, infinitely gifted."

LORRAINE, LILLIAN [née EULALLEAN DE JACQUES] (1892–1955) A San Franciscan who began performing professionally at the age of four, she grew to be an exquisite beauty and the reputed mistress of Florenz Ziegfeld.♦ She appeared in over a dozen Broadway musicals between 1906 and 1922, including the 1909, 1910, 1911, 1912, and 1918 editions of the *Ziegfeld Follies.*♦ Songs she introduced included "My Pony Boy" in *Miss Innocence* (1908), "By the Light of the Silvery Moon" in the 1909 *Follies,* and "Row, Row, Row" in the 1912 edition. Some sources give her real name as Mary Ann Brennan, but others suggest this was her mother's maiden name.

Los Angeles (California) For many years the city played second fiddle to its northern rival San Francisco, although it was a good legitimate theatre town with men such as Oliver Morosco♦ running theatres and producing plays there. By the late Depression only the Biltmore remained as a regular touring house. However, some other playhouses, often much smaller, enjoyed long runs with locally produced plays. Among these were a record run of *The Drunkard*♦ and a revue, *Blackouts.* Only in recent years has the city not only surpassed San Francisco but become virtually the second most important theatre town in America. The erection of a huge cultural center, at least one new legitimate theatre, and the conversion of some old film houses

all hastened the growth. While the Los Angeles and San Francisco Light Opera Company is now based in the city, this once active producing organization today does little but book in large musicals. However, the other organizations, such as the Mark Taper Forum,♦ associated with the cultural center have occasionally mounted new works or important revivals which have later toured successfully.

Lost in the Stars, a musical in two acts. Book and lyrics by Maxwell Anderson.♦ Music by Kurt Weill.♦ Produced by the Playwrights' Company♦ at the Music Box Theatre. October 30, 1949. 273 performances.

Stephen Kumalo (Todd Duncan♦), a black preacher in the South African hinterlands, goes to Johannesburg to seek his straying son Absalom (Julian Mayfield). But Absalom has killed a white man and is sentenced to death. All Stephen can do is comfort Absalom's girl, Irina (Inez Matthews), and reach a compassionate understanding with the murdered man's father, James Jarvis (Leslie Banks).

Principal songs: Lost in the Stars · Stay Well · Thousands of Miles.

A musical version of Alan Paton's acclaimed novel, *Cry, the Beloved Country,* it was revived unsuccessfully in 1972.

Lost Paradise, The, a play in three acts by Henry C. de Mille.♦ Produced by Charles Frohman♦ at Proctor's 23rd Street Theatre. November 16, 1891. 138 performances.

Andrew Knowlton (Frank Mordaunt) is a rich Boston manufacturer who has turned over the day-to-day operation of his huge factory to his trusted, good-hearted manager, Reuben Warner (William Morris♦), so that he may devote his time to his daughter, Margaret (Sydney Armstrong). He wants her to marry Ralph Standish (Orrin Johnson), and to further the chance takes the snobbish young man in as a partner. They treat the workers so cruelly that the employees strike. Warner sides with the workers and, to Knowlton's dismay, so does Margaret. She breaks off her engagement to Standish and agrees to marry Warner, who, it turns out, was the inventor of the device which has allowed Knowlton to become successful.

Based on Ludwig Fulda's *Das verlorene Paradies,* the play was told entirely in American terms and appealed to the sympathy of playgoers aware of the frequent callous and selfish abuse of workers in this country.

LOTITO, Louis A[NTHONY] (1900–1980) An orphan who became an usher at the Hippodrome♦ in his native New York to help support his family, he soon caught the eye of Charles Dillingham♦ and later of Vincent Youmans,♦ for both of whom he worked as treasurer and office manager. He next worked for Martin Beck,♦ and after Beck's death was asked by Mrs. Beck to run the Martin Beck Theatre. The playhouse had been a white elephant, but under his aegis became one of the most profitable in New York. As a result, in 1943 he was elected president of City Investment Corp. and ran its Morosco, Fulton, Coronet, Bijou, and 46th Street theatres as well as the Beck. His record of successes in booking was unique, but he also led the way in refurbishing worn-out playhouses. Noted for his honesty and loyalty in a profession in which both are all too rare, he was elected to serve as president of the Actors' Fund of America. ♦

Lotos Club, THE Founded in 1870 in response to a New York mayor's plea for a suitable place to entertain foreign visitors, the club soon broadened its aim "to let in such businessmen as were lovers of literature and art." It has been called "The Godfather of the Arts." Since 1947 it has been housed in a onetime Vanderbilt residence. Many famous theatrical personalities have either been members or have been honored by the organization.

LOTTA, see *Crabtree, Charlotte*

Lottery Man, The, a comedy in three acts by Rida Johnson Young.♦ Produced by the Messrs. Shubert♦ at the Bijou Theatre. December 6, 1909. 200 performances.

Jack Wright (Cyril Scott) is a handsome, charming newspaperman who is deeply in debt. To obtain the money he needs to pay back his loans he decides to raffle himself off. Women flock to buy chances on the likable bachelor, but in the midst of the hubbub Jack falls in love with Helen Heyer (Janet Beecher♦). He and his friends buy up as many chances as possible in Helen's name to give her the best opportunity to win. Helen learns of the schemes and is furious. Of course, all ends happily.

Lottery of Love, The, a comedy in three acts by Augustin Daly.♦ Produced by Daly at Daly's Theatre. October 9, 1888. 105 performances.

Mrs. Zenobia Sherramy (Mrs. G. H. Gilbert♦) a "strong-minded, woman's rights, female suffrage platform apostle," who was jailed in her youth for parading in bloomers, makes life so miserable for her new son-in-law, Adolphus Doubledot (John Drew♦), and his bride, Diana (Sara Chalmers), that on the very afternoon of the wedding they agree upon a divorce. Two years later Adolphus has married Josephine (Ada Rehan♦), daughter of the widower Benjamin Buttercorn (James Lewis♦). He is horrified when Buttercorn suddenly appears with his own new bride, none other than Diana, with Mrs. Sherramy in tow. But the harridan again makes life so miserable that Adolphus and Buttercorn conspire to foist Diana on the doting Tom Dangerous (Frederick Bond), who agrees to take daughter and mama to Brazil with him.

Based on Bisson and Mars's *Les Surprises du divorce,* which by coincidence Coquelin♦ was performing across the street during the play's run, the work was called by one of Daly's biographers "the best of Daly's adaptations from the French." At Daly's and elsewhere it held the stage for the rest of the century.

Louisiana Purchase, a musical comedy in two acts. Book by Morrie Ryskind.♦ Lyrics and music by Irving Berlin.♦ Produced by B. G. De Sylva♦ at the Imperial Theatre. May 28, 1940. 444 performances.

When Senator Loganberry (Victor Moore♦) is sent to investigate the corrupt Louisiana Purchase Company, the firm's lawyer, Jim Taylor (William Gaxton♦), attempts to compromise him with the vampish Marina Van Linden (Vera Zorina) and with the coquettish Madame Bordelaise (Irene Bordoni♦). But the good Senator proves incorruptible.

Principal songs: It's a Lovely Day Tomorrow · You're Lonely and I'm Lonely

Another of the many musicals of the era that reflected the day's headlines, this show was based on a story by De Sylva that was a thinly veiled satire on the Huey Long machine.

Love in '76, a "comedietta" in two acts by Oliver Bunce.♦ Produced by Laura Keene♦ at Laura Keene's Theatre. February 28, 1857. 10 performances.

Although her father is a Tory loyalist, Rose Elsworth (Miss Keene) loves Captain Walter Armstrong (M. V. Lingham) of the American army. When Armstrong is trapped in her home by British troops, she attempts to claim he is someone else. The ruse fails, so she is forced to try another ploy. She feigns affection for British Captain Arbald (Mr. Benson) and secures the promise of the British Major Cleveland (J. G. Burnett), who has his own eyes on her, that he will protect "the captain who is her husband." Suspecting another deception, however, Cleveland arranges to marry Armstrong to Rose's maid Bridget (Miss Howell). Rose, in disguise, changes places with Bridget at the ceremony and is married to Captain Armstrong. She then confronts Cleveland with his promise and threatens to question his word of honor publicly if he reneges.

While Quinn♦ has called the comedy "the best of the Revolutionary plays," its wartime setting was hardly essential to the story. Despite its short initial run, it remained popular until the end of the century.

Lovers' Lane, a play in four acts by Clyde Fitch.♦ Produced by William A. Brady♦ at the Manhattan Theatre. February 6, 1901. 127 performances.

The Reverend Thomas Singleton (Ernest Hastings) has alienated many of the small minds in his backwater flock. After all, he has not only fed the undeserving poor and taken in an unruly orphan the local orphanage could not handle, but he allows a divorced woman to sing in his choir and sees nothing wrong with billiards and cards. The conservative Deacon Steele (Julian Barton) speaks for these petty churchgoers when he announces, "a hell that was good enough for our grandfathers is good enough for us." But the liberal minister is unswayed.

Brady was reluctant to produce this play, since it depended for much of its appeal on the secondary characters whom Fitch drew so cuttingly, but after a tryout in Trenton (N.J.), he wired the author, "Great success. All the little Fitchisms going like hell."

LOWELL [ROBB], HELEN (1866–1937) The New Yorker was a popular actress for fifty years, although her moments of stardom were few and her best roles were secondary parts. She made her debut in 1884 as Iolanthe in one of the many all-children casts common at the time. She is especially recalled as the snubbed, pessimistic Miss Hazy in *Mrs. Wiggs of the Cabbage Patch*♦ (1904) and Mrs. Fisher, the mother of *The Show-Off*♦ (1924).

LUCE, CLARE B., see *Boothe, Clare*

Lucky Sam McCarver, a play in three acts by Sidney Howard.♦ Produced by William A. Brady, Jr.♦ and Dwight Deere Wiman♦ (in association with John Cromwell♦) at the Playhouse. October 21, 1925. 29 performances.

Sam McCarver (Cromwell) has risen from a drinks and towel hustler at a Hoboken Turkish bath to owner of one of New York's most fashionable night clubs, but he is ambitious to climb even

further. To help his rise, he courts the cold, amoral socialite, Carlotta Ashe (Clare Eames♦). After he skillfully covers up a shooting during a party Miss Ashe holds at his club, she agrees to marry him. His luck continues when he moves to Wall Street, although Carlotta runs off to Venice with some of her less savory friends. Eventually Carlotta returns to New York. She is ill when Sam visits her and he agrees to take her back if she will mend her ways. She refuses and dies of a heart attack. Sam is left to continue making money alone.

After the play was greeted by a largely unfavorable press and resoundingly rejected by playgoers, Howard wrote a bitter preface to the published text, calling the work "an attempt at dramatic biography" and noting, "Those who misunderstood 'Lucky Sam McCarver' found nothing in it to enjoy—neither plot, idea, hero, nor heroine. Well, I can only strike a defiant note in pleading guilty to the omission of those elements. There is no plot in biography." The play nevertheless remains a probing character study of timeless greed and degeneracy set against the more specific corruptions and hedonistic excesses of its day.

LUDERS, GUSTAV (1865–1913) A thoroughly trained musician, he emigrated from his native Bremen in 1888, settling first in Milwaukee and then in Chicago. He was a theatre conductor there when he wrote his first score for *Little Robinson Crusoe* (1899). Thereafter he wrote most of his shows with either Frank Pixley♦ or George Ade.♦ His most notable musicals were *The Burgomaster* (1900); *King Dodo* (1902); *The Prince of Pilsen*♦ (1903), his best and most popular work; *The Sho-Gun* (1904); *Woodland* (1904); *The Grand Mogul* (1907); *The Fair Co-ed* (1909); and *The Old Town* (1910). Although popular in their era, none of his songs is remembered today. Luders's range as a melodist was restricted, and he appeared not to grow artistically. Nevertheless, at his best his was a small, clear, and enchantingly sweet musical voice.

LUDLOW, NOAH M[ILLER] (1795–1886) One of the great pioneers of the American theatre, he was born in New York, but moved to Albany after his father's death. He made his debut as an actor there in 1813. Two years later he was engaged by Samuel Drake♦ to perform at theatres in Lexington, Frankfort, and Louisville, which Drake managed. Following a falling out with Drake in 1817 he organized his own troupe, the American Theatrical Commonwealth Company, with which he toured regions of the South and Midwest (then the West). Many of these areas had never seen proper live theatre before. In New Orleans he offered the first extended seasons of plays in English. He continued to tour for over a decade. At the invitation of Thomas Abthorpe Cooper♦ he came to New York in 1828 to manage the Chatham Theatre, but the venture was unsuccessful, so Ludlow returned to touring the regions he knew best. In 1835 he joined with Sol Smith♦ to form a reorganized, reinvigorated American Theatrical Commonwealth Company, which soon was managing theatres in all the major cities along the Mississippi River and in some inland towns as well. Joseph Jefferson,♦ who worked briefly with them, recalled the company was notorious for its "economy of organization." The company was dissolved when Ludlow elected to retire after a farewell entertainment at the New Orleans St. Charles Theatre in April 1853. Ludlow was considered a competent actor, especially in comic roles, but his claim to fame rests on two other achievements. The first was his acumen and courage as a theatrical producer and theatre manager in regions largely ignored by most professional luminaries. The second was his superb autobiography, *Dramatic Life as I Found It* (1880), written when he himself was in his eighties and filled with historically important and fascinating pictures of America and its playhouses.

Lulu Belle, a play in four acts by Edward Sheldon♦ and Charles MacArthur.♦ Produced by David Belasco♦ at the Belasco Theatre. February 9, 1926. 461 performances.

Lulu Belle (played in blackface by Lenore Ulric♦) is a flamboyant black prostitute who pounds the pavements both of San Juan Hill and Harlem. She succeeds in luring a white barber, George Randall (Henry Hull♦), away from his wife and family, only to desert him for Butch Cooper (John Harrington), a prizefighter. She leaves him, too, when the Vicompte de Villars (Jean Del Val) promises to set her up in luxury. But the passions she evokes overwhelm all the figures in her life. Butch winds up with a knife in his ribs, and the probably demented Randall follows her to Paris and strangles her in her posh apartment.

Brooks Atkinson♦ concluded, " 'Lulu Belle' is splendid showmanship; but it retains few of the elements of drama." Although black groups protested against the lurid picture the play painted of black life, Belasco's reputation and skill turned the melodrama into one of the era's biggest, most colorful successes.

LUNT, Alfred [David] (1892–1980) Considered by many the greatest actor of his generation, he was born in Milwaukee and educated at Carroll College. He abandoned his early ambition to become an architect and made his theatrical debut with the Castle Square Theatre stock company in Boston in 1912. He later toured with Lillie Langtry♦ and Margaret Anglin.♦ Broadway first saw him in *Romance and Arabella* (1917), but it was his performance as the shy, bumbling young man, the title role of *Clarence♦* (1919), that brought him important recognition. In 1922 he married Lynn Fontanne♦ and rarely thereafter performed without her. One of his few important assignments alone was as Mr. Prior, the boozy, newly dead young man, in *Outward Bound* (1924). Their first great triumph together was in *The Guardsman* (1924), in which he played the suspicious, jealous Actor. Miss Fontanne did not appear with him when he played Babe Callahan, the flashy bootlegger, in *Ned McCobb's Daughter♦* (1926), but she was the mistress to his Clark Story, the egocentric novelist, in *The Second Man♦* (1927), and was Jennifer Dubedat to his Louis Dubedat in *The Doctor's Dilemma* (1927). Without his wife, he created the role of Marco Polo in *Marco Millions♦* (1928). From the 1930s on, the couple were never apart. Lunt's important roles included the Earl of Essex in *Elizabeth the Queen♦* (1930); Rudolf, the former crown prince reduced to driving a taxi, in *Reunion in Vienna♦* (1931); Otto, one-third of an exuberant triangle, in *Design for Living* (1933); Petruchio in 1935; Harry Van, the seedy song and dance man, in *Idiot's Delight♦* (1936); Jupiter, come to earth as a mortal to woo a young lady, in *Amphitryon 38* (1937); Trigorin in *The Seagull* (1938); Dr. Valkonen, the scientist caught in the Finno-Russian War, in *There Shall Be No Night♦* (1940); and Serafin, the strolling player who blackmails a buccaneer, in *The Pirate* (1942). The Lunts spent the rest of the war years playing in England. After the war they returned to America, but appeared largely in a series of competent, but indifferent comedies: *O Mistress Mine* (1946), *I Know My Love* (1949), *Quadrille* (1954), and *The Great Sebastians* (1956). Only with their farewell play did they again find a worthy drama, with Lunt portraying Anton Schill, who is destroyed by the woman he once rejected, in *The Visit* (1958). Lunt occasionally directed plays, such as *Candle in the Wind* (1941) and *Ondine* (1954). In her autobiography, Theresa Helburn♦ suggested that there was "always something tortured" in his manner, that, in effect, he never totally stopped playing the timorous, befuddled Clarence, while Billie Burke♦ in her memoirs recalled "his distinguished voice . . . and his luminous brown eyes, with their always-startled expression." John Mason Brown♦ wrote of the Lunts' teamwork, "They are shrewd judges of what to underscore and what to throw away. They realize that the very act of seeming to throw a phrase or a word away is in itself a form of emphasis. They are no less adroit in altering the tempo of their separate scenes than they are in changing the pace of their single sentences. What is more, their watches are always synchronized."

Biography: *The Fabulous Lunts*, Jared Brown, New York, 1986.

Luv, a comedy in two acts by Murray Schisgal. Produced at the Booth Theatre. November 11, 1964. 901 performances.

When Milt Manville (Eli Wallach♦) comes across his old college buddy, Harry Berlin (Alan Arkin), about to commit suicide by jumping off a bridge, he is so casual and courteous that Harry changes his mind, climbs down, and throws away his suicide note. It turns out that Milt, locked in a seemingly hopeless marriage and anxious to wed another girl, is as unhappy as Harry. In a moment of inspiration Milt decides to solve all their problems by foisting his wife, Ellen (Anne Jackson♦), on his friend. His plan works at first. Harry and Ellen wed, and so do Milt and his young girlfriend. However, after a few months Milt decides he wants Ellen back. To achieve this he plans to murder Harry. The plan misfires but Milt and Ellen are reunited. Harry is left to climb a lamppost to escape a vicious dog.

Another of the many small-cast (three performers) plays of the era, this comedy was funnier and filled with more imaginative turns of plot than most. Schisgal (b. 1926) was born in Brooklyn and graduated from Brooklyn Law School. He earned recognition when his double bill *The Typists* and *The Tiger* (1963) was presented off-Broadway. None of his works to reach Broadway after *Luv* matched its popularity. They include *Jimmy Shine* (1968), *The Chinese* and *Dr. Fish* (1970), *All Over Town* (1974), and *Twice Around the Park* (1982).

Lyceum Theatre Although a number of New York playhouses have been called the Lyceum, two are of great historical importance and both at some time were associated with Daniel Frohman.♦ The earliest was built on the west side of Fourth Avenue between 23rd and 24th streets in 1885 by Steele MacKaye,♦ who had recently been forced out of his brilliantly conceived Madison Square Theatre.♦ The new theatre incorporated many of the innovations of the older auditorium and was the first theatre erected with electrical lighting throughout the building. The lighting was supervised by MacKaye's friend Thomas Edison. However, once again MacKaye quickly lost the theatre, and within a year Frohman was in charge. Under his aegis the theatre saw the premieres of many of the best David Belasco♦-H. C. de Mille♦ collaborations as well as *The Prisoner of Zenda*♦ and the New York premiere of *Trelawny of the Wells*. Unfortunately, the theatre district was moving away and although one paper observed in 1899, "A dozen or more years have passed but no playhouse of later construction has come up to the Lyceum in excellence and beauty," the building was demolished in 1902. A year later Frohman opened his new Lyceum, still standing, on 45th Street, just east of Broadway. The auditorium had a long series of hits, which did not save it from the threat of demolition in 1939. Luckily it was spared and continued on its prosperous career. Its longest run has been *Born Yesterday.*♦ The former offices and apartment of Frohman, which sit above the auditorium, are now the home of the Shubert♦ Archive.

Lyceum Theatre School of Acting, see *American Academy of Dramatic Arts*

LYTTON, Edward George Earle Lytton Bulwer- (1803–73) The English novelist and dramatist wrote three plays which became among the most popular and enduring in American theatrical history. The first two were romantic melodramas, *The Lady of Lyons*♦ (1837), whose heroine falls in love with the man she is tricked into marrying, and *Richelieu*♦ (1839), recounting the machinations of the 17th-century French cardinal. Both were performed regularly well into the early years of the 20th century. The last and least successful, although it too was revived throughout the century, was his comedy *Money* (1841). Several of his novels, including *Eugene Aram,* were dramatized at various times by other hands.

M

MacARTHUR, CHARLES (1895–1956) Born in Scranton, Penn., the son of a clergyman, he became a respected, if antic, figure in Chicago journalism, working for the Hearst papers. Typical of the stories about him is one recounting the time he was sent to interview the famous philanthropist Otto Kahn. Kept waiting in the library, he pulled ancient classics from the shelf, entered appropriate inscriptions and signed them with the names of the long-dead authors. Broadway first knew him when he collaborated with Edward Sheldon♦ on *Lulu Belle*♦ (1926), the story of the downfall of a black prostitute. With Sidney Howard♦ he wrote a thinly veiled exposé of evangelist Aimee Semple McPherson, *Salvation* (1928), but the play was short-lived. That same year, however, he joined for the first time with another Chicago newsman, Ben Hecht,♦ to write a marvelous comedy about the jungle-like world of reporting, *The Front Page*♦ (1928). Two more successes followed for the team: *Twentieth Century*♦ (1932), centering on a failing Hollywood producer's desperate attempt at a comeback; and the book for the musical, *Jumbo*♦ (1935). However, the pair came a cropper when they wrote a vehicle for MacArthur's wife, Helen Hayes.♦ The play, *Ladies and Gentlemen* (1939), told of a romance on a murder trial jury. On his own MacArthur next wrote a failed political satire, *Johnny on a Spot* (1942), in which a political campaign manager attempts to conceal the news that his candidate has dropped dead in a bordello. He rejoined Hecht for a final play, *Swan Song* (1946), in which a pianist attempts to murder a young rival. He also had a successful career as a screen writer.

Biography: *Charlie: The Improbable Life and Times of Charles MacArthur,* Ben Hecht, New York, 1957.

Macbeth Shakespeare's shortest tragedy, but one of his best, was first done in Philadelphia in 1759 with the younger Hallam♦ in the title role. Subsequently the play has enlisted almost every great American and visiting tragedian but has rarely been a major commercial success for any of them and has come to be considered something of an actor's jinx. Notable Macbeths have ranged from the formal Thomas Abthorpe Cooper♦ to the gruff Edwin Forrest♦ to the poetic Edwin Booth.♦ Despite the succinct brevity of the work and its excellence as drama each great artist could, apparently, meet only some of the requirements of this deceptively simple-seeming role. Thus, one reviewer noted of Booth's 1870 mounting, "The costumes are primitive almost to savagery, the scenery has a vague and shadowy look, well in keeping with the solemn mystery of the action, even the music has an elementary or aboriginal structure which is equally harmonious with the details that meet the eye. The only thing in truth that seems to suggest incongruity is the figure of Mr. Booth himself. There is something in his person and bearing quite foreign to the military or heroic ideals." Outstanding Lady Macbeths have included Charlotte Cushman,♦ Fanny Janauschek,♦ and Emma Waller.♦ Among the more successful 20th-century revivals was the 1941 offering, starring Maurice Evans♦ and Judith Anderson.♦ The work remains a favorite with collegiate and festival groups.

McCARTHY, JOSEPH (1885–1943) The lyricist was born in Somerville, Mass., and began interpolating his songs into Broadway shows shortly before World War I. Among his early hits was "You Made Me Love You" (music by Jimmy Monaco), which was introduced by Al Jolson♦ in *The Honeymoon Express* (1913). In 1918 he wrote the lyrics to Harry Carroll's melodies for *Oh, Look!,* including the still-popular "I'm Always Chasing Rainbows." Thereafter his work on Broadway was done solely with Harry Tierney.♦ Three of their seven shows were major hits: *Irene*♦ (1919), which offered "Alice Blue Gown" and its title song; *Kid Boots* (1923); and *Rio Rita*♦ (1927), remembered for "The Rangers' Song" and its title song. Their last show was *Cross My Heart* (1928).

McCAULL, JOHN A. (d. 1894) Often called "The Father of American Comic Opera," he settled down in his native Baltimore to practice law after fighting as a colonel for the Confederacy. While handling a case for John Ford♦ (some sources say for Emily Melville,♦ the singer), he found the theatre so attractive that he first specialized in theatrical cases, then entered the producing ranks. He established the McCaull Opera Comique Company, which became a leading importer of foreign comic operas (mostly now forgotten German and Viennese works) and was so successful that several branches were soon organized. Although he was sufficiently commercial to cater to the insistent demand for European material, he also attempted to develop a native school of writing and performing. To this end he was the first important producer to mount the comic operas of John Philip Sousa♦ and gave major breaks to such entertainers as De Wolf Hopper♦ and Francis Wilson.♦ With Rudolf Aronson♦ he built the Casino Theatre,♦ the first legitimate playhouse erected in America expressly for the purpose of offering musicals. Wilson recalled him as "A proud man, he was swift to take offense; he could be a firm friend and a bitter enemy. His impulsiveness often warped his judgment."

McCLENDON, ROSE (1885–1936) The most distinguished black actress of her generation, she was a mature woman before critics in her native New York began to take notice of her. She first attracted attention when she played opposite Charles Gilpin♦ in a touring production of *Roseanne* (1924), then won high praise for her performance as a wise, aged quadroon in the musical *Deep River* (1926). Her three most memorable portrayals followed in short order: Goldie McAllister, the friend of the doomed hero, in *In Abraham's Bosom♦* (1926); the compassionate Serena in *Porgy♦* (1927); and Big Sue, the old sybil, in *The House of Connelly* (1931). In 1935 she helped organize the Negro People's Theatre. She found another great role as Cora Lewis, the black housekeeper whose master has fathered her children, in *Mulatto♦* (1935), but the illness that led to her early death forced her to relinquish the part after a short time. In reviewing the play Brooks Atkinson♦ called her "an artist with a sensitive personality and a bell-like voice," continuing, "It is always a privilege to see her adding fineness of perception to the parts she takes."

McCLINTIC, GUTHRIE (1893–1961) The Seattle-born director and producer studied at the University of Washington and the American Academy of Dramatic Arts♦ before making his acting debut in 1913. He first played for New York audiences a year later, appearing in several shows until 1918, when he joined Jessie Bonstelle's♦ stock company. His directing career began after he left Miss Bonstelle to become Winthrop Ames's♦ assistant. He embarked on his own when he produced and directed *The Dover Road* (1921). Subsequently he directed, and

frequently produced, such popular plays as *The Shanghai Gesture♦* (1926), *Saturday's Children♦* (1927), *Brief Moment♦* (1931), *Winterset♦* (1935), *Ethan Frome♦* (1936), John Gielgud's♦ *Hamlet♦* (1936), *High Tor♦* (1937), *The Star Wagon♦* (1937), *Mamba's Daughters* (1939), and *Key Largo♦* (1939). However, he is most often associated in playgoers' minds with the work he did in conjunction with his wife, Katharine Cornell.♦ He directed her in *The Green Hat* (1925) and *Dishonored Lady* (1930), then beginning with *The Barretts of Wimpole Street♦* (1931), both directed her in and co-produced with her all her later plays. Although he was a sensitive, knowing director, he was a prissy, volatile man, who was deftly parodied as Carleton Fitzgerald in Moss Hart's♦ *Light Up the Sky.♦*

Autobiography: *Me and Kit,* Boston, 1955.

McCLOSKEY, JAMES J. (1825–1913) Born in Canada, he came to America at the age of sixteen in search of employment. In 1849 he joined the trek to California's gold fields, but finding no riches, turned to acting. For three decades he performed with almost all of the great actors of his day. He also wrote dozens of plays, many recounting his California experiences, among them: *Daring Dick* (1870), *Rory of the Hills* (1870), *The Far West* (1870), *The Trail of the Serpent* (1871), *Poverty Flat* (1873), *For Lack of Gold* (1873), *Life or Death* (1874), *Arabs of New York* (1875), *Buff and Blue* (1876), *Nuggets* (1880), and *The Bowery Boys* (1881). His plays were largely melodramatic and unsuccessful; his only truly popular work was *Across the Continent♦* (1871), a saga of vengeance that moved from generation to generation and coast to coast, and on which he made no money, having sold the rights to Oliver Doud Byron.♦ Typical of his melodramas about city life, and typical of the cheaper sort of melodrama of the period, was his *Through by Daylight* (1871). *The Stage* described its plot thus: "There is a condemned but innocent fellow, and a reprieve at the last moment. There are scenes in the Bowery, including the poverty-stricken chambers of working girls and concert saloons. A young woman is saved from the wheels of a rail car; another one falls from a stupendous cliff, and hangs by a branch; counterfeiters are displayed at work; a girl is poisoned and dies; somebody dances a jig; a 'nest of love' is exhibited, and a 'viper' shows up; a man gets whaled with a rope; a rock is rent by lightning; the hero makes a perilous descent upon a cord, saves a young woman, and then marries her; villainy is defeated, and virtue rewarded." McCloskey also tried his hand at theatre management, and for brief periods managed the Marysville Theatre in California and the Park Theatre in Brooklyn. He spent his last years as a court clerk in New York.

McCULLOUGH, JOHN [EWARD] (1832–85) Born in Ireland, he was sent to live with relatives in Philadelphia after the death of his mother when he was fifteen. He soon took an active interest in amateur theatricals, including the local Boothenian Dramatic Association, then made his professional debut at that city's Arch Street Theatre. ◆ He came to the attention of Edwin Forrest, ◆ who adopted him as a protégé. The result of this apprenticeship was that McCullough's repertory and acting style were very much those of the older actor. He played many second leads to Forrest, and after Forrest's death assumed the principal roles in such old Forrest stand-bys as *The Gladiator,* ◆ *Virginius, Jack Cade,* ◆ and *King Lear.* ◆ He left Forrest to assume the management of San Francisco's California Theatre ◆ in conjunction with Lawrence Barrett, ◆ and continued to run the house after Barrett's departure. Financial difficulties forced him to relinquish the post in the late 1870s, so he resumed touring in his best-known roles. His last appearance was in Chicago in 1884, after which his growing mental instability forced his commitment to an institution, from which he was released shortly before his death. A large, rugged, masculinely handsome man, he was highly admired for his fairness in an often selfish profession, although his acting was seen to belong to a passing tradition. For example, J. Rankin Towse ◆ wrote, "His Othello was an imposing and martial figure, with authority in voice and mien and all the external indications of the 'frank and noble nature' with which Iago credited him. And his 'waked wrath' was terrible. . . . But it was only in storm and stress that it was remarkable. In detail it was crude, unimaginative, unfinished, a bold freehand sketch rather than a completed study."

Biography: *John McCullough as Man, Actor and Spirit,* Susie Champney Clark, Boston, 1905.

McCULLOUGH, PAUL, see *Clark, Bobby*

MacDONALD, CHRISTIE (1875–1962) The blonde beauty with one of the finest soprano voices of her generation, she was born in Pictou, Nova Scotia, and was given her start in New York by Francis Wilson, ◆ who featured her in his 1893 revival of *Erminie.* ◆ Between then and her retirement in 1920 she was the leading lady in a score of musicals, most notably *The Spring Maid* (1910) and an operetta written with her in mind by Victor Herbert, ◆ *Sweethearts* ◆ (1913),

in which she introduced the title song. Among her other assignments were the heroines of *The Belle of Mayfair* (1906) and *Miss Hook of Holland* (1908). A critic described her as "dainty as a moss rose" and as one of the few operetta stars "worth fussing over."

MacDONOUGH, GLEN (1870–1924) The Brooklyn-born writer began his career as an actor and author of farces but became best known as a librettist and lyricist. Although he worked with such composers as John Philip Sousa ◆ (the 1900 *Chris and the Wonderful Lamp*) and Raymond Hubbell, ◆ he is best remembered for his collaborations with Victor Herbert. ◆ These included *Babes in Toyland* ◆ (1903), which offered his lyrics to "I Can't Do That Sum" and "Toyland," and *It Happened in Nordland* (1904), in which he put words to "Absinthe Frappé." He was also the American adapter of Johann Strauss's ◆ last work, *Vienna Life* (1901), and of Franz Lehar's ◆ *The Count of Luxembourg* (1912). In all he was associated with over two dozen musicals.

McElfatrick, J. B., and Company The leading firm of theatrical architects at the turn of the century, its New York houses included the Broadway, Empire, ◆ Hudson, Music Hall (later the New York), Lyric (later the Criterion), Republic, Victoria, and Wallack's. In all the firm is said to have designed more than 100 theatres across the country. The firm's founder, John Bailey McElfatrick (1829–1906), was born in Harrisburg, Penn., and practiced for many years in St. Louis before coming to New York in the 1880s.

McEVOY, J. P., see *Potters, The*

McGLYNN, FRANK (1866–1951) A San Franciscan who practiced law for a time before making his theatrical debut in 1896, he had a long, generally undistinguished career except for one role—the title part in John Drinkwater's ◆ *Abraham Lincoln* (1919). His interpretation won high praise, with Alexander Woollcott ◆ observing, "The stature, the patience, the quizzical humor, the homespun benignancy, something of the sweetness, something of the glory of Lincoln, are in this authentic and impressive performance." He returned to it several times during the next dozen years.

McGOWAN, JOHN (1892–1977) A native of Muskegon, Mich., he began his career as a vaudeville song and dance man, then became a leading man in musical comedy, often under the name Jack Mc-

Gowan. He introduced "The Love Nest" in *Mary*♦ (1920) and "I'll Build a Stairway to Paradise" in *George White's Scandals of 1922.*♦ He next turned to play-writing, with his most successful endeavor being *Excess Baggage*♦ (1927), dealing with a failing vaudeville act. Subsequently he collaborated on the books for such musicals as *Hold Everything!*♦ (1928), *Flying High*♦ (1930), and *Girl Crazy*♦ (1930).

MacGOWAN, KENNETH (1888–1963) Born in Winthrop, Mass., and educated at Harvard, he was assistant drama critic for the Boston *Evening Transcript* and critic for the Philadelphia *Evening Ledger* before serving in a similar position on the New York *Globe* from 1919 to 1923. At the same time he was drama critic for both *Vogue* and *Theatre Arts.*♦ With Robert Edmond Jones♦ and Eugene O'Neill♦ he took over the Provincetown Playhouse in New York in 1924 and later that same year also joined the Greenwich Village Theatre. At both houses he helped produce a number of interesting revivals, notably one of *Fashion*♦ as well as several of O'Neill's plays, such as *All God's Chillun Got Wings*♦ (1924), *Desire Under the Elms*♦ (1924), *The Fountain* (1925), and *The Great God Brown*♦ (1926). Although O'Neill had begun to move away from traditional realism in *The Emperor Jones*♦ (1920) before he met MacGowan, it was his meeting and ensuing friendship with MacGowan that confirmed and strengthened this drift, which was aimed at creating a theatre that would be at once both professional and idealistic and which, as MacGowan wrote, would "attempt to transfer to dramatic art the illumination of those deep and vigorous and eternal processes of the human soul." Ironically, when MacGowan later moved to Broadway and mounted more commercial ventures he was less successful. He was also the author of several books on the theatre, including *The Theatre of Tomorrow* (1921); *Continental Stagecraft* (1922), written with Jones; *Masks and Demons* (1923); and *Footlights Across America* (1929). In later years he served as editor-in-chief and associate producer for RKO Pictures.

MacGREGOR, EDGAR (1879–1957) For thirty years the Rochester-born director was one of the most successful stagers on Broadway. Early in his career he served as assistant to William Gillette♦ and Jane Cowl.♦ Although he later occasionally worked on straight plays, he was best known for his sharp direction of musical comedy. His numerous credits included *The Kiss Burglar* (1918); *The Gingham Girl*

(1922), for which he also wrote the book; *Queen High*♦ (1926); *Honeymoon Lane* (1926); *The Desert Song*♦ (1926); *Good News!*♦ (1927); *Funny Face*♦ (1927); *The New Moon*♦ (1928); *DuBarry Was a Lady*♦ (1939); *Panama Hattie*♦ (1940); and *Louisiana Lady* (1947).

McGUIRE, WILLIAM ANTHONY (1885–1940) The Chicago-born playwright began his working career as a journalist, but started writing plays while in his teens. However, all his major successes came in the 1920s. These included his plays *Six Cylinder Love*♦ (1921), in which a passion for automobiles forces a young couple to live beyond their means; and *Twelve Miles Out* (1925), a melodrama about rival bootlegging gangs. In the musical theatre he wrote the librettos or sketches for nine of Florenz Ziegfeld's♦ shows. The most memorable of these were *Rosalie* (1928), *The Three Musketeers*♦ (1928), and *Whoopee*♦ (1929). On occasion McGuire also served as director and producer.

MacHUGH, AUGUSTIN, see *Officer 666*

McHUGH, [JAMES FRANCIS] JIMMY (1894–1969) The Boston-born composer scored a major hit with his first Broadway score for *Blackbirds of 1928,*♦ remembered for "Diga Diga Doo," "I Can't Give You Anything But Love," and "I Must Have That Man." His lyricist was Dorothy Fields,♦ with whom he next wrote the scores for *Hello, Daddy* (1928) and the *International Revue* (1930). From the latter show came "Exactly Like You" and "On the Sunny Side of the Street." He did not return to Broadway until 1939, when his score for *The Streets of Paris* included "South American Way." In 1940 he wrote the music for *Keep Off the Grass.* His last score was for *As the Girls Go* (1948), whose superb songs are undeservedly neglected. His long Hollywood career between 1930 and 1947 produced such memorable songs as "I'm in the Mood for Love" and "A Lovely Way To Spend an Evening."

McINTYRE, FRANK (1879–1949) The bulky comedian, a native of Ann Arbor, Mich., made his debut in 1901 and for many years was a favorite in both musicals and straight plays. His best known roles were the title part in *The Traveling Salesman*♦ (1908) and in the musical *Queen High*♦ (1926).

McINTYRE, [JAMES] (1857–1937) **and HEATH,** [THOMAS] (1852–1938) The longest-lived of any major two-man act, this famous blackface team, who played together for sixty years, was equally famous for a life-long quarrel. Neither man spoke to the other, except in performances. Although McIntyre was born in Kenosha, Wisc., and Heath in Philadelphia, they are said to have spent most of their formative years in the South, where they soon learned to mimic both blacks and stereotypical imitations of them. In their act Heath, with a pillow-stuffed belly, portrayed a shabbily genteel know-it-all who was always able to lure the thin, believing, whiny-voiced McIntyre into preposterous enterprises. They first performed together in 1874, and rapidly became stars in waning minstrelsy and burgeoning vaudeville. They appeared in several Broadway shows written especially for them, most notably in *The Ham Tree* (1905), but also in *In Hayti* (1909), *The Show of Wonders* (1916), and *Hello, Alexander* (1919).

MacKAYE, Percy [Wallace] (1875–1956) One of the most curious figures in American dramaturgy, he was the son of Steele MacKaye♦ and was born in New York. Upon graduating from Harvard he began teaching as well as writing poetry and plays. Scholars have long admired his work. Quinn♦ devotes an extended, essentially laudatory chapter to him in his *History of the American Drama*. But with one exception his plays have never found a public. The exception is *The Scarecrow*♦ (1911), a fantasy based on a tale by Nathaniel Hawthorne in which a New England scarecrow is brought to life by a Mephistophelean figure and a wicked blacksmith, only to turn upon them before destroying itself. The rest of his work ranges from historical drama through political satire and spectacle. Such important theatrical figures as E. H. Sothern♦ and Walter Hampden♦ saw fit to mount a few of these, always without success. Shortly before his death he completed a tetralogy, *The Mystery of Hamlet, King of Denmark; or, What We Will* (1949), which purports to show the events leading up to Shakespeare's play. His books, such as *The Playhouse and the Play* (1909), *The Civic Theatre* (1912), and *Community Drama* (1917), argue for a subsidized, non-commercial theatre and suggest why his theatre pieces today seem more like closet drama.

MacKAYE, [James Morrison] Steele (1842–94) One of the most important innovators in late 19th-century American theatre, he was born in Buffalo, where his father was a respected lawyer and art connoisseur. While still in his teens the younger MacKaye studied art with William Hunt and then sailed for Paris to continue his studies with Gérôme at the École des Beaux Arts. He returned home to fight in the Civil War and rose to the rank of Major before illness forced him to resign. Once again in Paris, he became the disciple of François Delsarte, who was advocating a naturalistic style of theatre. When he came back he promoted the Delsartean school in lectures. In 1872 his first play, *Monaldi,* an adaptation of Washington Allston's novel, dramatized in collaboration with Francis Durivage, won some critical approval, but failed commercially. He then spent time acting and writing in London. On his return to America he offered his well-received comedy-drama, *Won at Last* (1877), in which misunderstandings jeopardize the marriage of an innocent young woman to a man-of-the-world. Afterwards he took over the old Fifth Avenue Theatre♦ and remodeled it with the most modern, elaborate equipment ever seen in an American playhouse, including overhead and indirect lighting and a double, moving stage that allowed rapid scene changes. He reopened the house as the Madison Square Theatre♦ with his play *Hazel Kirke*♦ (1880). In both writing and performance the play was an attempt to move toward the newer principals he was espousing. Centering on a father's rejection of a daughter who refuses his choice of a husband for her, it established a long-run record for a non-musical play. Despite the work's success, MacKaye's mismanagement cost him his theatre, so in 1885 he opened another technically inventive theatre, the Lyceum.♦ Here he established a school of acting that eventually became the American Academy of Dramatic Arts.♦ In time he lost this theatre, too, but continued to write plays. His last durable work was *Paul Kauvar; or, Anarchy*♦ (1887), a romantic drama of the French Revolution focusing on a Republican who is dismayed by the excesses of his associates, and who switches garments with a royalist to save that man's life. In all, 19 plays by MacKaye were produced in New York. Some, such as *Rose Michel*♦ (1875), were translations of foreign works; some were adaptations of novels; and others, original. One, *The Drama of Civilization* (1887), was a patriotic pageant written for "Buffalo Bill" Cody. ♦ Nearly all his plays enjoyed some commercial success. However, only *Won at Last, Hazel Kirke,* and *Paul Kauvar* were regularly revived into the early 20th century. Shortly before his death, MacKaye planned a huge, technically progressive auditorium for the Chicago Columbian Exposition, but it was never built. Otis Skinner♦ remembered him as "tall, spare, emotional and eloquent, looking like a more stalwart Edgar Allan Poe, holding forth to a knot of listeners on some theory destined never to be realized, some dream never to become articulate. He was always magnetic and compelling."

MacKaye was a prime mover both in the modernization of playhouses and in the drift away from the artificialities of older play-writing and acting conventions. He was not, by our contemporary standards, totally successful. His plays today seem as much of the older school as of the newer one he fought for, and they are no longer revived.

Biography: *Epoch,* Percy MacKaye,♦ New York, 1927.

McKenna's Flirtation, a farce in three acts by Edgar Selden. Produced at the Park Theatre. September 2, 1889. 104 performances.

Timothy McKenna (William Barry), a newly rich contractor who is building tenements in the squatter area known as goat town, receives by mistake a letter apparently signed by the wife of his best friend, Michael Ryan (Hugh Fay), a milkman. Thinking she is suggesting a tryst, he starts out to pursue her, getting himself and everyone else in hot water before the mistake is brought to light.

Essentially a farce-comedy♦ replete with scattered vaudeville turns and songs, it was one of many such pieces that straddled the fence at the time between the newly emerging musical comedy and traditional farce. Barry and Fay had long been a popular two-a-day team. Selden was an actor and author of vaudeville sketches.

MACKINTOSH, Cameron (b. 1946) A native of Enfield, England, he studied acting then took work as a stagehand to familiarize himself with all aspects of theatre. He began producing shows for the British provinces before truly hitting the big time in London with *Cats,* ♦ which he brought to Broadway in 1982. Slightly earlier he had co-produced *Tomfoolery* (1981) and *Little Shop of Horrors*♦ (1982) off-Broadway. Alone or with others he subsequently gave New York *Song and Dance* (1985), *Les Misérables*♦ (1987), and *The Phantom of the Opera*♦ (1988). In 1990 he made headlines when he engaged in a brouhaha with Actors' Equity♦ over his right to cast his forthcoming production of *Miss Saigon* as he saw fit. He cancelled the production until the union capitulated. How much of this disagreement was genuine and how much clever publicity is uncertain.

MACLEISH, Archibald, see *J. B.*

McLELLAN, C[harles] M. S. (1865–1916) Born in Bath, Maine, he was a newspaperman before turning his hand to the theatre, although he continued in the literary world and eventually became editor of *Town Topics.* His earliest theatre work was as a librettist and lyricist, and was done under the name Hugh Morton. Beginning in 1896 with *In Gay New York* he created the dialogue and rhymes for some fifteen Broadway musicals, the most notable of which were *The Belle of New York*♦ (1897) and *The Pink Lady*♦ (1911). He also attempted more serious play-writing, scoring a major success with his study of the reformation of a woman criminal, *Leah Kleschna*♦ (1904). Among his other dramas were *The Jury of Fate* (1906), *Judith Zaraine* (1911), and *The Fountain* (1914).

McNALLY, John J. (1852?–1931) Born in Charlestown, Mass., he studied law at Harvard but soon abandoned his practice to become a drama critic on the Charlestown *Chronicle,* the Boston *Times,* and finally the Boston *Herald.* His first theatre work appears to be *Revels* (1880), a farce-comedy♦ (the name given to the prototypical musical comedies of the period), and a revised libretto for E. E. Rice's♦ *Evangeline.* ♦ His entire early stage career was given over to writing additional farce-comedies, and next to Charles Hoyt,♦ he was probably the best in the field. Among his better works were *A Mad Bargain* (1892); *A Country Sport* (1893); and several of May Irwin's♦ vehicles, *The Widow Jones* (1895) and *Courted into Court* (1896). From 1896 to 1905 he was associated with the Rogers Brothers, who were the principal rivals to Weber♦ and Fields,♦ writing for the brothers the books for all their musicals. He withdrew from the stage after writing the McIntyre♦ and Heath♦ vehicle, *In Hayti* (1909).

McNALLY, Terrence (b. 1939) A native of St. Petersburg, Florida, and raised in Corpus Christi, Texas, he studied at Columbia. His early plays included *Next* (1969), *Where Has Tommy Flowers Gone* (1971), and *Bad Habits* (1973), but it was *The Ritz*♦ (1975) that most firmly established him. In 1984 he was librettist for *The Rink. The Lisbon Traviata* (1985) dealt hilariously—until its final moments—with a deteriorating homosexual liaison, while *Frankie and Johnny and the Clair de Lune* (1987), which enjoyed a long off-Broadway run, told of two fortyish heterosexual lovers struggling to reach an accommodation.

McRAE, Bruce (1867–1927) The India-born actor, a nephew of the famed British star Charles Wyndham, supposedly came to America intent on becoming a rancher but soon made his acting debut in 1891 in

Thermidor. In 1899 he was the original Dr. Watson in *Sherlock Holmes,* ◆ then portrayed Charles Brandon, who loves Mary Tudor, in *When Knighthood Was in Flower* ◆ (1901). He was Ethel Barrymore's ◆ leading man in, among others, *Cousin Kate* (1904), *A Doll's House* (1905), *Alice Sit-by-the-Fire* (1905), and *His Excellency the Governor* (1907). He then played John Rosmer opposite Mrs. Fiske ◆ in *Rosmersholm* (1907). Subsequently he was the leading man in such successes as *Nobody's Widow* ◆ (1910), *Come Out of the Kitchen* ◆ (1916), *Daddies* ◆ (1918). *The Gold Diggers* ◆ (1919), and *The Awful Truth* (1922). A highly accomplished actor, he was perhaps better described as attractive than handsome.

McVICKER, J[AMES] H. (1822–96) Born in New York, he began his acting career in New Orleans. Within a short while he developed a reputation as a superior interpreter of Yankee roles. T. Allston Brown ◆ recalled, "He was a good actor, a comedian of the purest and most acceptable type; he united unctuous humour with a gentle dignity that never forsook him, even in the broadest phases of his art." However, he is best remembered for his work in Chicago, where he moved in 1857 and built his own theatre. He became both a leading performer and producer in the city. Although he retained his Chicago base, his success was such that he eventually ran theatres in several major cities. In 1876 he added New York's Lyceum Theatre to his chain, opening it with Edwin Booth ◆ in *Hamlet* ◆ and assuming himself the role of the First Grave-digger.

Ma Rainey's Black Bottom, a play in two acts by August Wilson ◆. Produced at the Cort Theatre. October 11, 1984. 275 performances. NYDCCA.
    Ma Rainey (Theresa Merritt), a black blues-singer, is difficult at the best of times. But these are not the best of times. When she arrives for a recording session, she has had a run-in with the police after an automobile accident, the producer is demanding she use a new arrangment by a cocky young musician, and the equipment either is not functioning or has been sabotaged. Bitter arguments ensue, often leading the participants to dredge up bitter memories of mistreatment by whites and even fellow blacks. By the time Ma Rainey stomps out, the atmosphere is so charged that a slight misstep provokes one black to knife another.
    A collection of superbly delineated character studies rather than a fully realized drama, it nonetheless made for compelling theatre.

Mabou Mines A determinedly avant-garde ensemble founded in 1970 by JoAnne Akalaitis, Lee Breuer, Philip Glass, Ruth Maleczech, and David Warrilow, it specializes in original works which frequently and imaginatively employ mixed media. It is also known for its interpretations of plays by Samuel Beckett. Among its productions have been *Dressed Like an Egg* (1977), *A Prelude to Death in Venice* (1979), *Dead End Kids: A History of Nuclear Power* (1980), and *Cold Harbor* (1983). Music for the productions often has been provided by Glass. The group has traveled widely.

Machinal, a play in two parts by Sophie Treadwell. Produced by Arthur Hopkins ◆ at the Plymouth Theatre. September 7, 1928. 91 performances.
    A Young Woman (Zita Johann), a stenographer, is a cog in the machinery at the Jones Company. Her world is coldly impersonal, moved along by mechanical repetition and ritual.

> Telephone—Mr. J. wants you.
> Young Woman—Me?
> Telephone—You.
> Young Woman—Mr. J.?
> Stenographer—Mr. J.

In her desperate search to find "somebody"—somebody to love her—she takes as a Husband (George Stillwell) a vacuous man who brings her neither change nor real love. After her marriage she meets a Young Man (Hal K. Dawson) and believes she has finally found relief from the unthinking sameness around her. She asks her husband to release her, but he refuses. She kills him. She is tried, convicted, and executed. As she dies she cries out for "somebody."
    The staccato dialogue and rapidly changing scenes were played out against Robert Edmond Jones's ◆ expressionistic settings. Brooks Atkinson ◆ wrote, "Subdued, monotonous, episodic, occasionally eccentric, 'Machinal' is fraught with a beauty unfamiliar to the stage." The play was revived off-Broadway in 1960. A 1990 off-Broadway revival was highly praised.
    The California-born Treadwell (1890–1970) had been an actress and protégé of Helena Modjeska ◆ before attempting to write plays. Half a dozen of her works reached Broadway, but this was her only success.

MACK, ANDREW [né WILLIAM ANDREW McALOON] (1863–1931) The Boston-born actor and singer began his career in vaudeville in 1876, using the name Andrew Williams. He found his greatest success in the 1890s and early years of the 20th century playing romantic leads in Irish plays with music such as *Myles Aroon* and *The Last of the Rohans*. His last important assignment was as a replacement in the role of Patrick Murphy, the father, in *Abie's Irish Rose*. ◆

"Mack Sennett Ballet" Featured in the 1947 musical *High Button Shoes,* it was devised by Jerome Robbins◆ to music by Jule Styne◆ and memorably satirized the classic Sennett comedies, culminating in a wild chase that included the principals, bathing beauties, Sennett cops, and a bear. It remains the finest comic ballet conceived for the popular musical stage. It was restaged in *Jerome Robbins' Broadway* (1989).

MACK, WILLARD [né CHARLES WILLARD MCLAUGHLIN] (1878–1934) The Canadian-born actor and playwright performed in vaudeville for many years before joining a stock company in San Francisco. He came to New York in 1913 with a vaudeville sketch, which the following year he expanded into his first hit play, *Kick In,* ◆ the story of a criminal's attempt at reformation. Among his subsequent successes were such melodramas as *Tiger Rose*◆ (1917), centering on a French-Canadian girl who must hide her lover from a vengeful Mountie; *High Stakes* (1924), in which a writer exposes his sister-in-law as a blackmailer; *The Dove* (1925), the story of two rough men clashing over a cabaret singer; *The Noose* (1926), depicting the plight of a young man who murders to keep his parentage secret; and *A Free Soul* (1928), focusing on a girl who falls in love with her attorney-father's criminal client. Among his many acting assignments he created the part of Captain Bartlett in Eugene O'Neill's◆ *Gold* (1921). He also frequently served as a director and producer.

MACREADY, WILLIAM CHARLES (1793–1873) A great, if controversial, English tragedian, he was lauded for his forceful, albeit somewhat formal acting, and despised for his arrogance and explosive temper. His American debut came at the Park Theatre◆ in 1826 in one of his greatest roles, Virginius, and prompted the *Mirror* to remark, "It is said there is no actor living who unites as much power and original genius with correct taste and cultivated talents as Macready. He has all that nature can give, with all that taste and talent can acquire. His person is tall and commanding—his carriage noble—his face, though not technically a

first rate stage face, is wonderfully expressive, and his voice peculiarly fine, deep and mellow." He followed his Roman with his Damon, William Tell, Macbeth, and Coriolanus. When he returned in 1843, he added such roles as Othello, King Lear, and Richelieu to his American repertory. From the start, elements of the press had attacked him personally, and his open contempt for American actors exacerbated matters. These problems came to a head on his third trip, which began in 1848. His rivalry with Edwin Forrest,◆ as much a national and class rivalry as a personal one, exploded in May 1849 with the Astor Place Riots.◆ Immediately thereafter he sailed for England, never to return. Whatever the culpability of Forrest in the turmoil, Macready must share some of the blame. Mrs. John Drew,◆ who was a young woman when she acted with him, recalled, "Macready was a dreadful man to act with; you had the pleasant sensation of knowing that you were doing nothing that he wanted you to do, though following strictly his instructions. He would press you down with his hand, and tell you in an undertone to stand up! Mr. Macready was a terribly nervous actor; any little thing which happened unexpectedly irritated him beyond endurance."

Biography: *The Eminent Tragedian: William Charles Macready,* Alan S. Downer, Cambridge, 1966.

Madame Butterfly, a play in one act by David Belasco◆ and John Luther Long.◆ Produced by Belasco at the Herald Square Theatre. March 5, 1900. 24 performances.

Cho-Cho-San (Blanche Bates◆), a geisha, falls in love with an American naval officer, Lieutenant Pinkerton (Frank Worthing). When he leaves for home, he promises to be true and to return. The American consul, Mr. Sharpless (Claude Gillingwater), later informs her that Pinkerton has remarried. She refuses to believe it. However, when the fleet returns and the Consul's story is confirmed, she kills herself.

Most historians suggest the dramatization was entirely the work of Belasco, who used Long's short story as his source. Whether or not this was the case, their subsequent joint efforts appear to have been more genuine collaborations. Added as an afterpiece during the run of Belasco's farce *Naughty Anthony,* the play was looked on as static and talky, but nevertheless a theatrically effective character study. It might well have been totally forgotten had not Puccini later created an opera from it.

Madame Sherry, a "musical vaudeville" in three acts. Book and lyrics by Otto Harbach. ♦ Music by Karl Hoschna. ♦ Produced by A. H. Woods, ♦ H. H. Frazee, ♦ and George Lederer ♦ at the New Amsterdam Theatre. ♦ August 30, 1910. 231 performances.

Edward Sherry (Jack Gardner) and his Sherry School of Aesthetic Dancing, where pupils are taught "Every Little Movement" has a meaning all its own, have long been supported by Edward's archaeologist uncle, Theophilus (Ralph Herz). To please his uncle, who spends most of his time in Greece, Edward has pretended to marry and have children. When the uncle suddenly appears, Edward is forced to draft his housekeeper and some of his young pupils into acting as his wife and offspring. Although Theophilus assures them that a wife's smile, "The Smile She Means for You," is the best smile of all, he is not fooled, so he takes everyone out to sea in his yacht and threatens not to return to port until he discovers the truth. Luckily, Theophilus's niece, Yvonne (Lina Abarbanell ♦), appears on the scene. When Edward kisses her "The Birth of Passion" is assured. Before long they agree to marry. Only then does Theophilus consent to return to port.

Other principal song: Put Your Arms Around Me, Honey (interpolation by Junie McCree and Albert Von Tilzer)

A curious combination of musical comedy, operetta and, in the last act, when the plot was all but over, vaudeville turns, this was one of the most memorable and delightful musicals of the era. The hit song, "Every Little Movement," while first sung as part of the dancing lesson, was reprised throughout the show in different tempos and with altered harmonies to suggest the progress of several romances.

Madison Square Theatre In 1879 Steele MacKaye ♦ gutted what had been Augustin Daly's ♦ first Fifth Avenue Theatre ♦ and which had been restored only two years before after a disastrous fire in 1873. He redesigned the playhouse into one of the world's most ingenious theatres, with a moving stage that allowed rapid scene changes, with the orchestra playing from a box above the proscenium and with the first attempt at a primitive air-conditioning system. The house seated only about 700 playgoers and was so arranged as to give the impression of a drawing room. Odell ♦ recalled, "The exquisite interior, in which no color seemed to prevail at the expense of others . . . gave an effect of rich, simple elegance hitherto unknown in New York theatres."

MacKaye's intention was to form a stock company on the order of the Comédie Française. Although the theatre housed *Hazel Kirke,* ♦ the longest-running drama up to its time under MacKaye, its actual owners, the Mallory brothers, editors of a religious publication, squeezed out the often impractical playwright during *Hazel Kirke's* run. It then came under the management first of Daniel Frohman, ♦ then of Albert M. Palmer, ♦ and later of Charles Hoyt, ♦ who temporarily called it Hoyt's Theatre. By the time of Hoyt's death the theatre district had moved away from the area and, though the original name had been restored, bookings became difficult. The building was demolished in 1908.

MAEDER, C. F., see *Fisher, Clara*

MAEDER, FREDERICK G[EORGE] (1840–91) Son of the once popular actress, Clara Fisher, ♦ he was born in New York and made his acting debut in Portland (Maine) in 1859, playing Bernardo in *Hamlet.* ♦ He was considered a good eccentric comedian, but was best known in his own day as a prolific, if undistinguished, playwright. Many of his works seem to have been written to order for particular performers or companies. Typical of his pieces were *Help* and *Lola,* which opened a few weeks apart in 1871. In the former the hero dons numerous disguises to prevent his fiancée's being murdered by her brother-in-law; in the latter the heroine dons numerous disguises to win her man. Among his other works were *Red Riding Hood; or Wolf's at the Door* (1868), *Buffalo Bill* (1872), *Life's Peril; or, The Drunkard's Wife* (1872), written with E. Z. C. Judson (Ned Buntline), and *Nip, the Pretty Flower* (1873).

Magic Show, The, a musical (performed without intermission). Book by Bob Randall. Lyrics and music by Stephen Schwartz. ♦ Produced at the Cort Theatre. May 28, 1974. 1920 performances.

When the Passaic Top Hat, a minor New Jersey night club, hires a young magician, Doug (Doug Henning), to replace a tired old act, it gets more than it bargained for.

The slim plot was merely an excuse for Henning's spectacular feats of magic, which turned the show into a long-running hit.

MAGUIRE, THOMAS (1820?–96) Called in his own day the "Napoleon" of San Francisco theatre, he was believed to have been born in New York to poor immigrant parents. As a young man he was a cab driver who favored hacking in the theatrical area. Using Tammany connections, he served as a bartender in playhouses and then opened his own bar near City Hall. He joined the westward trek of the 49ers, but preferred working in gambling saloons and bars to panning for gold. In 1850 he opened the tiny Jenny Lind Theatre on the second floor of the Parker House, a hotel and casino he ran. The theatre was the first of three to bear the same name, all of which he operated before building Maguire's Opera House, which opened in 1854 and long was San Francisco's leading theatre. He pioneered in encouraging great New York performers to come west and also established the famous San Francisco Minstrels. ♦ For the next quarter-century he dominated San Francisco theatre, building or managing several other playhouses and largely determining what local audiences saw. Many historians believe his decline actually began with the erection of the Academy of Music in 1862, but he remained in San Francisco until 1878. His last important position was as manager of the Baldwin Theatre. ♦ He then returned to New York, where he tried unsuccessfully to enter the theatrical scene. When he died in poverty he was buried by the Actors' Fund. ♦

MAINBOCHER [né MAIN ROUSSEAU BOCHER] (1890–1976) Celebrated Chicago-born designer of high fashion, he studied not only art, but voice and piano in leading world cultural centers before embarking on his career. His first theatrical designs were created in Paris. He almost never designed all the costumes for a show, merely those for its star. Among the women whom he decorated were Mary Martin♦ (*One Touch of Venus*♦ and *The Sound of Music*♦), Ruth Gordon♦ (*Over 21*♦), Tallulah Bankhead♦ (*Private Lives*♦), Ethel Merman♦ (*Call Me Madam*♦), Katharine Cornell♦ (*The Prescott Proposals*), Rosalind Russell♦ (*Wonderful Town*♦), and Lynn Fontanne♦ (*The Great Sebastians*).

MAJOR, CLARE TREE (1880–1954) An actress in England before she emigrated to America, almost immediately upon her arrival in 1914 she began to take an interest in children's theatre. She performed with the Washington Square Players♦ and other groups briefly, then devoted all her attention to the juvenile stage, with which her name became synonymous. She prepared most of her scripts herself and handled their direction. In 1948 she had six companies touring at once.

Majority of One, A, a comedy in three acts by Leonard Spigelgass. Produced by the Theatre Guild♦ and Dore Schary♦ at the Shubert Theatre. February 16, 1959. 556 peformances.

Mrs. Jacoby (Gertrude Berg♦), a Brooklyn housewife who lost a son fighting the Japanese, and Koichi Asano (Cedric Hardwicke), a businessman who lost a daughter at Hiroshima, meet on shipboard. At first they turn their larger, national resentments against each other, but with time they overcome their prejudices to reach perhaps more than an affectionate understanding.

A warmhearted comedy, helped to success by the ebullient Miss Berg, who had been famous as radio's Molly Goldberg, and the distinguished British actor, Hardwicke. The New-York born Spigelgass, who wrote several other less successful plays, was better known as a Hollywood screenwriter and producer.

Male Animal, The, a comedy in three acts by James Thurber and Elliot Nugent. ♦ Produced by Herman Shumlin♦ at the Cort Theatre. January 9, 1940. 243 performances.

Tommy Turner (Nugent), a professor of English, suddenly finds himself confronted by two problems. The first is the return to the campus of Joe Ferguson (Leon Ames), a former college football star and old flame of Turner's wife Ellen (Ruth Matteson). The second is an editorial in the campus paper protesting Turner's reading of a letter sent by the anarchist Vanzetti to Vanzetti's daughter before his execution. Turner's edginess about Joe leads to getting them both drunk and engaging in fisticuffs. The letter proves reasonably harmless, and Joe soon returns home to his own wife.

Richard Watts, Jr.,♦ of the *Herald Tribune* saw the play as "A singularly happy combination of Thurber's comic brilliance and Nugent's gift for human and likeable characters." A 1952 revival, with Nugent as Turner, Robert Preston♦ as Ferguson, and Martha Scott as Ellen, outran the original production.

Thurber (1894–1961), a native of Columbus, Ohio, was best known as a cartoonist and humorist.

Mame, see *Auntie Mame*

MAMET, DAVID (b. 1947) Born in Flossmore, Ill., he studied at Goddard College, then settled in Chicago, where he helped found the St. Nicholas Theatre Company, which produced many of his early plays. To the extent that many of his subsequent works were also first offered to Chicago before being presented in New York, he represents a throwback to a bygone, healthier theatrical era when Chicago, as well as other cities, enjoyed a relative theatrical independence and often originated many major productions. New Yorkers first saw his work off-Broadway in 1975. His *Sexual Perversity in Chicago,* dealing with a failed marriage, and *Duck Variations,* a rambling conversation between two old men, were produced off-Broadway the following year. His best-known works have been *American Buffalo* ◆ (1977), which told of a bungled burglary and which won the New York Drama Critics Circle Award, ◆ *A Life in the Theater* (1977), in which a young, optimistic actor and a disillusioned old timer exchange thoughts, *Glengarry Glen Ross* ◆ (1984), a study of greed and cynicism in the real estate business and winner of a Pulitzer Prize, ◆ and *Speed-the-Plow* (1988), a brief look at behind-the-scenes finagling in the film industry. He also has adapted Chekhov ◆ plays for regional playhouses.

MAMOULIAN, ROUBEN (1897–1987) Born in Russia, the son of an actress, and educated in Paris and Moscow, he worked at the Eastman School of Music before coming to New York to take employment with the Theatre Guild. ◆ For the Guild he staged highly praised mountings of *Porgy* ◆ (1927), *Marco Millions* ◆ (1928), and *Wings over Europe* (1928). All his subsequent important theatrical work was with musicals: *Porgy and Bess* ◆ (1935), *Oklahoma!* ◆ (1943), *Carousel* ◆ (1945), and *Lost in the Stars* ◆ (1949). He was known for his excellent handling of crowd scenes and for an overall sense of theatrically rhythmic movement. He was also highly admired as a film director.

Biography: *Mamoulian,* Tom Milne, London, 1969.

Man and Superman Shaw's ◆ epic look at the battle of the sexes was first presented here by Charles Dillingham ◆ in 1905 with Robert Loraine ◆ as John Tanner and Clara Bloodgood ◆ as Violet Robinson. One of the biggest hits of the season, it ran for six months. The production omitted the long act known as "Don Juan in Hell," a policy followed by most subsequent stagings. Loraine also headed the cast of a 1912 revival. In 1947 Maurice Evans ◆ headed a highly praised revival which chalked up a remarkable run of 294 performances, while "Don Juan in Hell" was given an all-star reading with tremendous success in 1951. The cast included Charles Boyer, ◆ Charles Laughton, ◆ Cedric Hardwicke, and Agnes Moorehead. The full-length work was mounted by the Phoenix Theatre ◆ in 1964 with Ellis Rabb ◆ as Tanner, Rosemary Harris ◆ as Violet, and Nancy Marchand as Anna Whitefield.

Man From Home, *The,* a play in four acts by Booth Tarkington ◆ and Harry Leon Wilson. ◆ Produced by Liebler and Co. ◆ at the Astor Theatre. August 17, 1908. 496 performances.

When Daniel Voorhees Pike (William Hodge ◆), a straightforward, likable lawyer from Kokomo, Indiana, comes to Italy to visit his ward, Ethel Granger-Simpson (Madeline Louis), he finds her engaged to Almeric St. Aubyn (Echlin P. Gayner), the spoiled son of the Earl of Hawcastle (Hassard Short ◆). Pike discovers that the Earl himself is more worthless than his son, downright treacherous, in fact. In exposing them, Pike wins the hand of Ethel. He also frees Ethel's brother Horace (George Le Guere) from an equally unsavory alliance. The three agree to return home to Kokomo.

Although many critics viewed the play as excessively jingoistic, the public disagreed. Walter Prichard Eaton ◆ seemingly summed up both sides when he observed, "We think it a pleasant and popular piece of extremely parochial jingo. We should call it as an excellent bad play." It held the stage for six consecutive seasons and was regularly revived thereafter.

Man of La Mancha, a musical [performed without intermission]. Book by Dale Wasserman. Lyrics by Joe Darion. Music by Mitch Leigh. Produced at the ANTA ◆ Washington Square Playhouse. November 22, 1965. 2,328 performances.

As he reads his story to his fellow prisoners, Cervantes (Richard Kiley ◆) takes on the aspect of his hero, Don Quixote. The unworldly, idealistic Don and his servant Sancho (Irving Jacobson) set out on the impossible dream of ridding Spain of its ills. But the Don cannot distinguish fantasy from reality or good from evil. He even honors a sluttish serving wench, Aldonza (Joan Deiner), by treating her as a lady and rechristening her Dulcinea. In the end the Inquisition forces Cervantes to recognize his illusory world. The realization destroys him.

Principal songs: Dulcinea · The Impossible Dream

An unflinching musicalization of Cervantes's great classic, it was derived from Wasserman's television version. Its success quickly moved it to Broadway and it has enjoyed several important revivals. "The Impossible Dream" was one of the last theatre songs to enjoy widespread popularity.

Leigh and Darion are both New Yorkers. Leigh (né Irwin Mitchnick] (b. 1928) studied under Paul Hindemith at Yale and wrote as his earliest work for Broadway the background music for a 1963 revival of *Too True To Be Good. Man of La Mancha* has been his only Broadway success. Darion (b. 1917) was also lyricist for the musical *Ilya Darling* (1967).

Man of the Hour, The, a play in four acts by George Broadhurst. ◆ Produced by William A. Brady◆ and Joseph Grismer◆ at the Savoy Theatre. December 4, 1906. 479 performances.

Alwyn Bennett (Frederick Perry) is a rich, idealistic young man who has gotten himself elected mayor on a reform ticket. Charles Wainwright (James E. Wilson), a rapacious financier, and Richard Horigan (Frank MacVicars), the local political boss, set out to obtain a perpetual monopoly on the city's public transportation. When Bennett refuses to grant the franchise and announces he will fight it, the men determine to use every means to destroy him. Bennett's problem is compounded by the fact that he loves Wainwright's niece, Dallas (Lillian Kemble), whose fortune is tied to the success of the franchise. On Bennett's side are James Phelan (George Fawcett◆), an alderman who has long opposed Horigan, and Henry Thompson (Geoffrey Stein), Wainwright's private secretary, who unbeknownst to Wainwright is the son of a man Wainwright drove to suicide. Together they succeed in frustrating the monopolists while saving Dallas's money.

The "virile melodrama" was one of the big muckraking hits of its day, on the order of *The Lion and the Mouse*◆ although more careful not to pattern its characters after specific, well-known figures. One critic found it was "less subtle in respect to its conflict of character than 'The Lion and the Mouse,' and observes no such mental development as that which gives Mr. Klein's play much of its vitality." He nevertheless concluded the play performed "a valuable service to the community" in exposing political greed and corruption.

Man on the Box, The, a play in three acts by Grace Livingston Furniss. Produced at the Madison Square Theatre.◆ October 3, 1905. 111 performances.

Lt. Robert Worburton (Henry E. Dixey◆) returning from a long tour of duty, decides to surprise his sister by substituting for her coachman when she leaves an embassy ball. By mistake he picks up the wrong lady, and comic complications ensue.

Mrs. Furniss, who was also co-author of *The Pride of Jennico*,◆ adapted the play from a novel by Harold MacGrath. It owed its success largely to Dixey and one young actress, Carlotta Nillson.

Man Who Came Back, The, a play in four [in some versions five] acts by Jules Eckert Goodman.◆

Produced by William A. Brady◆ at the Playhouse. September 2, 1916. 457 performances.

Wealthy Thomas Potter (Edward Emery) is so disgusted with his dissolute son, Henry (Henry Hull◆), that he disowns him and orders him out of the house. Henry takes to wandering the world, living a life of increasing dissipation. Along the way he meets Marcelle (Mary Nash◆), a dance hall hostess, who becomes his companion in his boozy revels. The pair sink lower and lower until they hit bottom in a Shanghai opium den. Just at this point emissaries from his dying father locate him and beg him to return to his father for a final visit. But they insist he must leave Marcelle behind. He refuses to desert her. Merely making this simple decision, with its moral and ethical implications, somehow revitalizes Henry. In the end he does return, with an equally reformed Marcelle, who is welcomed into the Potter household.

The *Times,* comparing the play to serials then common in many popular magazines, called it "A little lurid, at times intensely theatrical, but interesting all the way through." The play was based on a story by John Fleming Wilson. Brady later claimed the production "made millions" for him.

Man Who Came to Dinner, The, a comedy in three acts by Moss Hart◆ and George S. Kaufman.◆ Produced by Sam H. Harris◆ at the Music Box Theatre. October 16, 1939. 739 performances.

Having slipped on the ice on the Stanleys' doorstep, the celebrated but cantankerous writer Sheridan Whiteside (Monty Woolley◆) is forced to convalesce at the Stanleys' home. He is unhappy about it and determined to see the Stanleys are as unhappy as he is. Even so innocuous a courtesy as an inquiry about his health brings the reply, "I may vomit." He alienates the Stanley children from their parents, and turns his nurse, Miss Preen (Mary Wickes), so misanthropic that she takes a job at a munitions factory in hopes of destroying the human race. When his secretary, Maggie Cutler (Edith Atwater), falls in love with a local newsman, Bert Jefferson (Theodore Newton), he invites a glamorous actress, Lorraine Sheldon (Carol Goodner), to lure the newsman away. And after the actress bungles her assignment he sends her off locked in a mummy case. He even blackmails the Stanleys by threatening to disclose that Mr. Stanley's sister was once acquitted of a celebrated ax murder. Everyone is relieved when he is finally well enough to leave. As he departs he slips on the ice again. He is brought back into the house bellowing his threats to initiate another six weeks of despotism.

The authors made little secret that Whiteside was patterned after their friend, Alexander Woollcott. ◆ Many felt the character of Lorraine Sheldon was modeled after Gertrude Lawrence, ◆ while two other supporting figures, the suave Beverly Carlton and the madcap Banjo, were suggested by Noel Coward ◆ and Harpo Marx ◆ respectively. John Anderson wrote in the *Journal-American* that no such richly Falstaffian character as Whiteside had heretofore been created in American literature, "No one so full of the carbolic acid of human kindness; no one with the enthusiasm, the ruthless wit, the wayward taste, disarming prejudice, and relentless sentimentality of the man so carefully undisguised as the hero." The play remains one of the most frequently revived of all American comedies.

Managers' Protective Association, see *Producing Managers' Association*

MANDEL, FRANK (1884–1958) Although the San Francisco-born writer and producer translated or collaborated on a number of straight plays early in his career, it was his work in the musical theatre for which he is largely remembered. He was co-librettist of, among others, *Mary* ◆ (1920), *The O'Brien Girl* (1921), and *No, No, Nanette* ◆ (1925), before he joined with Laurence Schwab ◆ to form a new production company. Their first offering, in conjunction with Horace Liveright, was the drama *The Firebrand* ◆ (1924). Mandel afterwards collaborated on the books for their productions of *The Desert Song* ◆ (1926) and *The New Moon* ◆ (1928). With Schwab he also produced *Good News!* ◆ (1927), *Follow Thru* ◆ (1929), and several less successful shows. The partnership was dissolved in 1932. Mandel later produced on his own, but his mountings were short-lived.

MANEY, RICHARD (1891–1968) Born in Chinook, Mont., he received his first exposure to theatre when his family moved to Seattle. After settling in New York he became press agent for a 1920 revue that failed, but he soon went on to be the most famous agent of his day. He helped publicize many successes, from the *Greenwich Village Follies* ◆ to *My Fair Lady* ◆ as well as such leading figures as Tallulah Bankhead, ◆ Katharine Cornell, ◆ and producer Billy Rose. ◆ He was also skilled at publicizing himself, thus making his profession better known and understood by playgoers. In 1957 he published an interesting autobiography, *Fanfare*.

Manhattan Theatre Club Founded in 1970 by A. E. Jeffcoat and other New York East Side residents to provide an alternative to commercial theatre, it is situated in the old Bohemian National Hall on East 73rd Street in a complex that includes three major stages as well as rooms for rehearsals, readings, and other events. Lynne Meadow has been its artistic and executive director for many years. Among its productions which were later moved to Broadway were *Ain't Misbehavin'*, ◆ *Crimes of the Heart*, ◆ and *Mass Appeal. Frankie and Johnny in the Clair de Lune* transferred profitably to off-Broadway.

MANHOFF, BILL, see *Owl and the Pussycat, The*

MANN, LOUIS (1865–1931) The New York-born actor made his debut in German-language theatricals while still a child, then withdrew from the stage to complete his education. He performed with such notables as Lawrence Barrett, ◆ John McCullough, ◆ and Tommaso Salvini ◆ and created the role of Dick Winters, one of three look-alikes, in *Incog* (1892), before recognizing that his true métier was in dialect roles. His most famous part was Karl Pfeifer, whose loyalty to the fatherland was tested, in *Friendly Enemies* ◆ (1918). He often appeared in conjunction with his wife, Clara Lipman.

MANN, THEODORE (b. 1924) Born in Brooklyn, he studied law and was a practicing lawyer prior to co-founding the Circle in the Square ◆ in 1950. He has frequently directed that group's warmly received productions. On occasion he has served as co-producer on Broadway, including *Long Day's Journey into Night* ◆ (1956), *Hughie* (1964), and *The Royal Hunt of the Sun* (1965).

MANNERING, MARY [née FLORENCE FRIEND] (1876–1953) The handsome, round-faced, dark-haired actress performed for several seasons in her native England before Daniel Frohman ◆ brought her to America in 1896. She made her first appearance for him in *The Courtship of Leonie*. Shortly thereafter she married James K. Hackett ◆ and scored a major success playing opposite him as Fay Zuliani, the romantic niece of a social butterfly, in *The Princess and the Butterfly* (1897). Two of her best roles came in 1900 when she played Rose in a revival of *Trelawny of the Wells* and as the heroine who loves a fugitive Revolutionary patriot, the title part in *Janice Meredith*. She continued to play leading roles in similar romantic comedies and dramas for the next decade. Her last appearance was as Domini, who loves a renegade monk, in *The Garden of Allah*♦ (1911), after which she retired at the height of her popularity.

MANNERS, J[OHN] HARTLEY (1870–1928) Born in London, he began his theatrical career as an actor, and continued to perform for a time even after he turned to play-writing. He came to America in 1902 as a member of the cast of his own play, *The Crossways,* which he had written as a vehicle for Lillie Langtry.♦ He enjoyed a modest success with *Zira* (1905), which he wrote with Henry Miller♦ and in which a poor girl passes herself off as an heiress. The play was written for Margaret Anglin.♦ Many of his subsequent works were created as vehicles for his wife, Laurette Taylor.♦ By far the most successful was *Peg o' My Heart*♦ (1912), which centered on a poor Irish girl who inherits wealth and goes to live with haughty relatives. *The Harp of Life* (1916) told of a mother's attempt to deal with her daughter's sexual innocence. *Out There* (1917) described how a Cockney drudge finds value in life as a Red Cross war nurse. The play toured with an "all-star" cast for the benefit of the Red Cross. *Happiness* (1917), based on a 1914 one-act play, allowed a poor girl to show a rich one how to enjoy life. The English heroine of *One Night in Rome* (1919) masquerades as an Italian fortune teller to win her sweetheart. In *The National Anthem* (1922) a drunken husband drives his wife to drink. Manners always professed to have serious ambitions as a playwright, but his work was usually bathed in a roseate glow and tailored to the talents of his wife. He seems never to have fully appreciated her abilities as a serious actress, or perhaps was incapable of writing the best dramas for them.

MANSFIELD, RICHARD (1854–1907) The famous, but controversial American actor was born in Berlin. His mother, Erminia Rudersdorff, was a well-known prima donna; his father, an English merchant. He was educated in England and on the Continent. First brought to America in 1872 by his mother, he appeared in amateur theatricals before returning to London. He came back to America in 1882 and made his professional New York debut singing the part of Dromez in the comic opera *Les Manteaux Noirs.* He first won recognition a year later when he assumed the role of Baron Chevrial, the sensual, brutal roué, in A. M. Palmer's♦ production of *A Parisian Romance.* Much to his chagrin, several seasons elapsed before he enjoyed another hit. More lasting success came as the impecunious nobleman who marries for money, only

to learn his wife's fortune is really his, the title part in *Prince Karl*♦ (1886). This was followed by his widely popular version of *Dr. Jekyll and Mr. Hyde* (1887). In 1889 he offered his *Richard III,*♦ then starred in a specially written vehicle, Clyde Fitch's♦ *Beau Brummel*♦ (1890). A string of failures ensued. Realizing the changing nature of his theatre, he turned to G. B. Shaw,♦ who had never been professionaly produced in America, and offered himself as Bluntschli in *Arms and the Man* (1894). However, the offering failed, and he was forced to resort to revivals of his former successes. He had better luck when he mounted *The Devil's Disciple*♦ (1897), playing Dick Dudgeon. One of his biggest triumphs was in the title role of *Cyrano de Bergerac*♦ (1898). In 1903 he first played Prince Karl Heinrich, who must abandon his beloved beer garden waitress, Kathie, for the call of duty, in *Old Heidelberg.* The remainder of his career interspersed revivals of his more popular roles with failed attempts in new vehicles. Shortly before his death, however, he defied the wrath of conservative reviewers by appearing in the title role of *Peer Gynt.*

He was an extremely short man with a pale, square-cut face and thinning brown hair, who was sensitive about his appearance. Many critics and playgoers admired his work as an exemplar of a passing romantic school, but others strongly dissented. Among the dissenters was Channing Pollock,♦ who observed, "As an actor I think he was over-rated. Mansfield had authority, intelligence and a hard, brittle surface that shone in some kinds of comedy. Not even as Beau Brummel did he enlist my ready sympathies, and though I had sat moist eyed through the German performance of *Old Heidelberg,* the American left me admiring but unmoved." He was generally detested by his fellow actors because of his arrogance, short temper, and treachery. With the appearance of the Theatrical Syndicate or Trust♦ he professed to join the other stars of his era in fighting the monopoly, only to quickly sign on with it. He also promised Edward Harrigan,♦ when he leased Harrigan's Theatre, to retain the name, then immediately renamed it the Garrick. His vanity was such that shortly before his death, he commissioned William Winter♦ to write a monumental biography of him. The work was issued in two volumes in 1910 as *The Life and Art of Richard Mansfield.*

MANTELL, ROBERT B[RUCE] (1854–1928) Born in Irvine, Scotland, he first acted in England under the name Robert Hudson. He reverted to his real name when he came to America in 1878 to play in support of Helena Modjeska.♦ After a brief return to England, he came back to the United States to become Fanny Davenport's♦ leading man, most notably as Loris Ipanoff in *Fedora* (1883). His initial appearance as a star came when he played Raymond Garth, who loves one woman but seems inextricably tied to another, in *Tangled Lives* (1886). Subsequently he played the leading roles in similar romantic melodramas such as *The Marble Heart*♦ (1887) and *The Corsican Brothers*♦ (1890). After the turn of the century he appeared almost solely in Shakespearean roles, among them Hamlet, Richard III, Othello, and King John. His performances in these parts divided the critics, many of whom saw his "thundering," "roaring" style as outmoded. Nevertheless, he won huge audiences, especially on the road. He continued to perform until shortly before his death.

Biography: *Robert Mantell's Romance,* Clarence Joseph Bulliet, Boston, 1918.

MANTLE, [Robert] Burns (1873–1948) Born in Watertown, N. Y., he became a drama critic in 1898, serving on Denver and Chicago newspapers before coming to New York in 1911 as critic for the *Evening Mail.* In 1922 he moved to the *Daily News,* where he remained until 1944. Although he was the author of *American Playwrights of To-day* (1929) and *Contemporary American Playwrights* (1938), he is best remembered as the originator and editor of the *Best Plays*♦ series, an annual anthology of plays and statistics, which he continued to edit from 1920 until shortly before his death. His writings were warm and reasonable, without any of the ostentation of some of his fellow critics.

MAPES, Victor (1870–1943) The New York-born author, critic, and manager studied at Columbia and worked in Paris before becoming a stage manager for Daniel Frohman♦ in 1897. At the same time he assumed the post of drama critic for the *World,* writing under the name Sidney Sharp. He had begun writing plays while in Paris and resigned his post as critic when his first American play, *The Flower of Yeddo,* was produced in 1899. More than a dozen of his plays reached Broadway, including *Don Caesar's Return* (1901) and *Captain Barrington* (1903), but he is recalled primarily for three collaborations: *The New Henrietta,* a 1913 updating of *The Henrietta,*♦ written with Winchell Smith♦; *The Boomerang*♦ (1915), also with Smith, which told how a doctor's attempt to cure a patient's jealousy backfires; and *The Hottentot* (1920), written with William Collier,♦ and centering on a man who is afraid of horses but

must serve as a jockey in a steeplechase. During his years as an active playwright he continued to manage theatres in New York and elsewhere.

MARBLE, Dan[forth] (1810–49) Although he entered the theatre relatively late and died young, he was for well over a decade one of the most respected and popular interpreters of Yankee-dialect characters. He was born in East Windsor, Conn., and had been a silversmith before paying $20 for the privilege of making his acting debut at the Chatham Theatre in 1831. Within a short time he was starring in such vehicles as *The Backwoodsman, The Forest Rose,*♦ *Sam Patch, the Jumper, The Stage-Struck Yankee,* and *The Vermont Wool Dealer.* Contemporary critics suggested his characterizations had a more Western tinge and were more romantic and exaggerated than those of Hackett♦ or Hill.♦ He was not a particularly handsome man, having a large-nosed and rough-hewn square face, but his popularity and financial husbanding were such that when he died he left a then not inconsiderable estate of $25,000.

Biography: *Dan Marble,* Falconbridge (Jonathan F. Kelly), New York, 1851.

MARBLE, Scott (1845?–1919) A New York native, he began his career as an actor at Barnum's Museum♦ in 1865 and continued to perform until the late 1880s, when he turned to play-writing. He specialized in action-packed melodramas such as *The Police Patrol* (1892), *The Diamond Breaker* (1893), *Tennessee's Pardner* (1894), *The Sidewalks of New York* (1895), *The Great Train Robbery* (1896), *The Cotton Spinner* (1897), and *The Heart of The Klondike* (1897). His works, like similar ones by other authors, were rarely played in New York and then only at minor houses. But he wrote and had his plays produced around the country until the end of the first decade of the 20th century. By then films had usurped the market for his sort of entertainment, so he became one of the earliest writers of film scenarios.

MARBURY, Elisabeth (1856–1933) The daughter of a famous New York attorney, she was encouraged by Daniel Frohman♦ to become an author's agent. Most of her early clients were such foreign playwrights as Victorien Sardou,♦ Oscar Wilde,♦ Somerset Maugham,♦ and Sir James Barrie.♦ She is believed to have been the first agent to negotiate a percentage of box office receipts for her clients. She later began to represent important American figures, including Clyde Fitch,♦ Rachel Crothers,♦

and Jerome Kern. ◆ In connection with Kern, it was she who apparently suggested to Ray Comstock◆ that the small Princess Theatre◆ be turned into a house for intimate musicals, thus creating the stage for the Princess Theatre Musicals that helped make Kern, Guy Bolton,◆ and P. G. Wodehouse◆ famous.

Autobiography: *My Crystal Ball*, New York, 1924.

MARCH, FREDRIC [né FREDERICK McINTYRE BICKEL] (1897–1975) Born in Racine, and educated at the University of Wisconsin, he made his stage debut under his real name as the Prompter in *Deburau* in 1920. Within a few seasons he had adopted his new stage name and had risen to leading man in several short-lived dramas. He then became a star in films and did not return to Broadway until 1938, when he appeared opposite his wife, Florence Eldridge,◆ in the quick failure, *Yr. Obedient Husband*. Further failures followed before he won praise as the allegorical Mr. Antrobus in *The Skin of Our Teeth*◆ (1942). He subsequently distinguished himself as Major Victor Joppolo, who understands the problems of the conquered Italians, in *A Bell for Adano*◆ (1944); Clinton Jones, the father of a would-be actress, in *Years Ago* (1946); Nicholas Denery, the meddling, self-important artist, in *The Autumn Garden* (1951); James Tyrone, the famous but bitter, tight-fisted actor, in *Long Day's Journey into Night*◆ (1956); and the Angel of God, who confronts and directs the hero, in *Gideon*◆ (1961). His performance as Tyrone won him numerous honors, including a Tony Award.◆ Brooks Atkinson◆ called the performance, "masterful . . . a character portrait of grandeur." It was made all the more believable because, like the figure he was playing, he had a touch of the ham in him and the aura of an earlier-day matinee idol, handsome, but stern-looking.

MARCIN, MAX (1879–1948) Born in Germany but educated in America, this journalist-turned-playwright scored his first success with *The House of Glass*◆ (1915), in which a railroad executive who is determined to pursue an employee he believes guilty of a crime learns that his own wife was once a convicted criminal. He also scored a success with his comedy, *Cheating Cheaters*◆ (1916), in which a woman detective poses as a crook. His biggest hit came a year later when he collaborated with Charles Guernon on *Eyes of Youth*◆ (1917), a story of a girl who is given a choice of paths in life. Among his subsequent hits were *The Woman in Room 13* (1919), written with Samuel Shipman◆ and focusing

on a woman composer accused of murdering a singer; *Silence* (1924), centering on a crook who risks the electric chair rather than hurt his daughter, whom he believes really committed the crime for which he has been sentenced; and *Badges* (1924), written with Edward Hammond and telling of a meek hotel clerk who absolves his girl of a crime of which she is suspected. A skillful contriver of theatrically effective pieces, he often wrote to order, such as his vehicle for the boxer Jack Dempsey, *The Big Fight* (1928). In all some two dozen of his plays reached the boards.

Marco Millions, a play in a prologue, three acts, and an epilogue by Eugene O'Neill. ◆ Produced by the Theatre Guild◆ at the Guild Theatre. January 9, 1928. 92 performances.

As a young man Marco Polo (Alfred Lunt◆) is sent to China on business in the company of his father and uncle. He is so determined to succeed in business that he has no conception of the deep love Kukachin (Margalo Gillmore◆), the Kaan's granddaughter, holds for him. He piles commercial success upon commercial success until he eventually returns to Venice, where he lives in ostentatious luxury, unaware that Kukachin has pined for his love and died for lack of it. Marco, after all, is the eternal merchant. So eternal, in fact, that as the houselights come back on and the audience prepares to leave, there is Marco, the tired businessman, rising from a front row seat and heading for the limousine that awaits him outside.

Although many critics agreed with Brooks Atkinson◆ of the *Times* that this "satiric pageant" was "an original, powerful and searching drama," the play's attack on pervasive, obsessive commercialism had little appeal for the tired businessmen it mocked. Revivals in 1930 and 1964 were no more successful.

Margaret Fleming, a play in five acts by James A. Herne. ◆ Produced at Palmer's Theatre. December 9, 1891. 1 performance.

Philip Fleming (E. M. Bell), a successful and seemingly happily married manufacturer, is dismayed to learn that he has fathered a child by one of his mill girls. He resolves to keep the knowledge from his wife, Margaret (Katherine C. Herne), who is threatened with blindness from her own recent pregnancy. Margaret's maid, Maria (Mattie Earle), has a sister who has just had a child and is apparently dying after a troubled birth. She begs Margaret to visit the sister, and Margaret agrees. There she learns of her husband's infidelity, for the sister is Fleming's mill girl. The shock brings on the blindness that had been threatening. The baby dies despite Margaret's attempt to rear it, and this further shock sends Margaret fleeing. Her apparent desertion is the beginning of hard times for Fleming. They meet by coincidence years later when Margaret stumbles on her own child, who is being raised by Maria. A squabble ensues, and they are hauled into the police station. There Margaret resolves to raise her own child, but never more to see Fleming.

The first important American play to demonstrate Ibsen's♦ influence, it remains a significant milestone in American dramaturgy. Because no New York producer or theatre owner would mount or book the play, the performance at Palmer's was a special matinee. Critics were sharply divided, with the Ibsenites strongly in favor and the anti-Ibsenites vigorously opposed. Herne later revised the play, cutting it to four acts and giving it a happier ending. Although it was afterwards given several important revivals, it never won over either the public or the more traditional critics. Modern critics object not to its debt to Ibsen, but to its vestiges of traditional melodrama.

Margin for Error, a play in two acts by Clare Boothe.♦ Produced by Richard Aldrich♦ and Richard Myers♦ at the Plymouth Theatre. November 3, 1939. 264 performances.

Karl Baumer (Otto Preminger) is a blackmailer, a thief, and a double-crosser. He is also the Nazi consul in New York. Baumer has only contempt for America, a contempt which explodes into a fervent wish to break relations with the country after a Jewish policeman, Officer Finkelstein (Sam Levene♦), is assigned to guard him. Despite Finkelstein's precautions, Baumer is murdered. The murder is especially embarrassing to Finkelstein since he could have had several chances to stop it—for Baumer was poisoned, and stabbed, and shot. Finkelstein is eventually able to pin the poisoning on a young American Nazi, and finds reasons for looking the other way when he learns who the stabber and shooter were. He has just cleared up matters when his captain appears. Finkelstein tells him of the poisoning, the stabbing, and the shooting. The captain, who has known and disliked the consul, can only ask, "Did it kill him?"

Burns Mantle♦ called the work "the first successful anti-Nazi play to reach the stage, a rare combination of melodrama and comedy."

MARION, GEORGE (1860–1945) Born in San Francisco, where he made his debut as an actor in a local stock company, he later toured with Lew Dockstader's♦ Minstrels before settling in New York. He soon turned primarily to directing, staging many of Anna Held's♦ early vehicles for her husband, Florenz Ziegfeld.♦ Joining Henry W. Savage♦ he directed the producer's mountings of such successes as *The Prince of Pilsen♦* (1903), *The County Chairman♦* (1903), *The College Widow♦* (1904), *The Merry Widow♦* (1907), and *Sari* (1914). Although he continued to direct until the end of the 1920s, he insisted that acting was his first love, and after 1919 he regularly returned to the footlights, most notably when he created the role of Chris Christopherson in *Anna Christie♦* (1921).

Mark Taper Forum, THE (Los Angeles) Founded in 1967 by members of UCLA's The Theatre Group on the premise that "a creative theater makes its mark with new material," it first performed at a small theatre in the downtown district. Although its repertory has included classics and popular contemporary works, more than half of its major productions have been world premieres. Several of these afterwards won acclaim on Broadway, including *The Shadow Box,♦ I Ought To Be in Pictures, Children of a Lesser God,♦* and *Burn This*. It now operates out of the 760-seat Mark Taper Theatre at the Los Angeles Music Center and at the 99-seat Taper, Too in the John Anson Ford Cultural Center in Hollywood. It also offers such special projects as the ITP (Improvisational Theatre Project) and tours local schools and community centers.

MARKOE, PETER (1752–1792) Born in Santa Cruz in the West Indies, and educated at Oxford, he settled in Philadelphia in 1783, where he spent his few remaining years. There he wrote not only a novel and poetry, but two theatre pieces. *The Patriot Chief* (1784) tells of a rebellion against a Lydian king, who is saved by his long-lost son. Markoe professed to have written the play "to call attention to the dangers of aristocracy." His stilted comic opera, *The Reconciliation* (1790), is interesting because it represents an early instance of a practice later common in our musical theatre, the musicalization of a straight play, in this case the German play, *Erastus*. Neither work was produced in the author's lifetime, although *The Reconciliation* was scheduled for production by the American Company,♦ but abruptly dropped without any reason being given.

MARLOWE, JULIA [née SARAH FRANCES FROST] (1866–1950) Born in England, at the age of four she was brought by her mother to America, where they joined her father, who had been forced to flee England after apparently injuring a neighbor in a whipping. In America the family assumed the name of Brough, and it was as Fanny Brough that she made her stage debut in 1879 in one of the many juvenile troupes of H.M.S. Pinafore♦ which were the rage of the day. She continued to sing in comic opera for several seasons before playing Heinrich in a touring company of *Rip Van Winkle*♦ in 1882. After studying with Ada Dow and performing in a dramatic company run by Colonel R. E. J. Miles, she made her New York debut as Parthenia in *Ingomar*♦ (1887). She rose rapidly in public esteem, offering over the next few seasons her Viola, Rosalind, and Julia (in *The Hunchback*♦). In 1896 she was Lydia Languish in the all-star revival of *The Rivals,* whose cast included Joseph Jefferson♦ and Mrs. John Drew.♦ For several years she played Shakespearean heroines opposite her first husband, Richard Taber. Following their separation she created the title role in *Barbara Frietchie*♦ (1899), then portrayed Mary Tudor in *When Knighthood Was in Flower*♦ (1901). She assumed these roles at the behest of the Theatrical Syndicate or Trust♦ which wanted her to gain a larger following and also to cover the financial losses her Shakespearean tours had incurred. Most of her later career was again in Shakespearean roles, this time opposite her second husband, E. H. Sothern.♦ Illness forced a temporary retirement in 1915, but after she was hurt in an accident she retired permanently in 1924. An early biographer described her as "of medium height, slender and frail of aspect, with a pale and rather sallow face, great, dark, and wistful eyes, a head that seemed too big for her body, beautiful, dark-brown hair." Many critics remarked on her prominent cleft chin. Her recording of Juliet suggests a lush, musical, and fruity delivery that would be too artificial for modern tastes.

Biography: *Julia Marlowe's Story,* E. H. Sothern, edited by Fairfax Downey, New York, 1954.

MARQUIS, Don, see *Old Soak, The*

MARRE, Albert [né Moshinski] (b. 1925) A native New Yorker, he studied at Oberlin and Harvard. Shortly after World War II he directed the Allied Repertory Theatre in Berlin, then became managing director of the Brattle Theatre Company in Cambridge (Mass.). As artistic director of the New York City Center Drama Company♦ for the 1952–53 season, he staged highly praised mountings of *Love's Labours Lost* and *Misalliance.* Subsequent successes included the musical *Kismet*♦ (1953), *The*

Chalk Garden (1955), *Time Remembered* (1957), *Milk and Honey* (1961), and *Man of La Mancha*♦ (1965), for which he won a Tony Award.♦

MARSDEN, Fred [né William A. Silver] (1842–88) The son of a Baltimore storekeeper, he studied law and practiced in Philadelphia before changing both his profession and his name. From 1872 on he was in constant demand as a creator of vehicles for popular stars. His work ranged from melodrama to farce. Among his plays were *Zip*♦ (1874) and *Musette* (1876) for Charlotte Crabtree♦; *Kerry Gow* (1880) and *Shaun Rhue* (1886) for the well-liked portrayer of Irishmen, Joseph Murphy; *Cheek* (1883) and *Humbug* (1886) for the comedian Roland Reed; and *The Irish Minstrel* (1886) for another Irish delineator, W. J. Scanlan.♦ At the time of his highly publicized suicide, he was said to hold $30,000 in contracts for new plays.

MARSH, Howard [Warren] (d. 1969) The handsome, if stiff-necked tenor was born in Bluffton, Ind., and appeared in a number of Broadway musicals between 1917 and 1930. He is best remembered for three roles: Baron Schober in *Blossom Time*♦ (1921), in which he sang Schubert's "Serenade"; Karl Franz in *The Student Prince*♦ (1924), in which he introduced "Deep in My Heart, Dear," "Golden Days," and "Serenade"; and Gaylord Ravenal in *Show Boat*♦ (1927), in which he sang "Make Believe," "Why Do I Love You?," and "You Are Love."

Marsh Juvenile Troupe A band of youngsters who toured under the aegis of R. G. Marsh, they were extremely popular in the late 1850s when they offered a bill of plays intermingled with song and dance. Their repertory included *Beauty and the Beast, The Rough Diamond,* and *The Loan of a Lover.* Although their vogue faded almost as quickly as it had bloomed, they could be seen as forerunners of the all-children casts of Gilbert♦ and Sullivan♦ operettas some twenty or more years later.

MARSTON, Richard (1847–1917) The son of a noted English Shakespearean actor, Henry Marston, he was born in Brighton, England, and began his career as a performer. However, after coming to America in 1867 he devoted himself primarily to set design. One of his first assignments was creating new scenery for the long-running *The Black Crook.*♦ Shortly thereafter he drew the sets for that spectacle's failed successor, *The White Fawn* (1868), as well as for plays by John Brougham♦ and offerings of the

San Francisco Minstrels. ♦ For many years he served as house designer first at the Union Square Theatre♦ and later at the Madison Square Theatre. ♦ Among the plays which featured his work there were *Rose Michel*♦ (1875) and *A Parisian Romance* (1883). Throughout his subsequent career much of his work was for musicals, including *The Devil's Deputy* (1894), *Fleur-de-Lis* (1895), *Half a King* (1896), and *A Little Bit of Everything* (1904), but he continued designing settings for straight plays such as *The Great Diamond Robbery* (1895) and Richard Mansfield's♦ first American mounting of *Cyrano de Bergerac*♦ (1898). Contemporaries felt he excelled at the designing and painting of outdoor scenes.

MARTIN, ERNEST, see *Feuer and Martin*

MARTIN, JOHN (1770–1807) Although Dunlap♦ calls him the first native American to become a professional actor, he was probably deprived of that honor by the young Princeton graduate known only as Greville. ♦ However, he almost certainly was the first American to have an extended career on his native stages. Dunlap wrote of him, "He was of fair complexion, middle height, light figure, and played the youthful characters of many tragedies and comedies in a style called respectable . . . He laboured hard, lived poor, and died young." He made his debut as Young Norval in *Douglas*♦ at the John Street Theatre♦ in 1791. He later played such roles as Mendoza in Sheridan's♦ *The Duenna;* Octavius in *Julius Caesar*♦; and Malcolm in *Macbeth.* ♦ In 1794 he created the role of Ferdinand in *Tammany.*♦ On occasion he left New York to perform in Annapolis and Philadelphia.

MARTIN, MARY [VIRGINIA] (1913–90) One of the most popular of all contemporary performers, she was born in Weatherford, Texas, and worked as a dance instructor and night-club entertainer before making her show-stopping New York debut singing "My Heart Belongs to Daddy" in *Leave It to Me!*♦ (1938). After a successful career in films she returned to Broadway in *One Touch of Venus*♦ (1943), in which she introduced "Speak Low," and *Lute Song* (1946). One of her most memorable roles was Ensign Nellie Forbush in *South Pacific*♦ (1949), in which she sang "I'm Gonna Wash That Man Right Outa My Hair" and "A Wonderful Guy." In his *Broadway,* Brooks Atkinson♦ recalled, "Miss Martin acted . . . with insight and relish; and as a musical-stage virtuoso she made the songs express the subtle qualities of a disarming human being." Turning to comedy, she played Jane Kimball, an

actress who sets out to win a banker, in *Kind Sir* (1953). She next won applause in a musical version of *Peter Pan*♦ (1954). Another major success came when she played Maria in *The Sound of Music*♦ (1959), singing such songs as "Do-Re-Mi," "My Favorite Things," and the title number. After touring in *Hello, Dolly!*♦ she played in the musical *I Do! I Do!* (1966). Her last Broadway appearance was as Lidya Vasilyevna, a middle-aged woman who has a romance with her doctor, in a failed comedy, *Do You Turn Somersaults?* (1978). In 1986 she toured with Carol Channing♦ in *Legends*. Theatre historian Stanley Green♦ wrote that the attractive, wholesome performer "combined naive charm and buoyant enthusiasm with a warm and rangy soprano."

Autobiography: *My Heart Belongs*, New York, 1976.

MARTINOT, [SARAH] SADIE (1861–1923) The beautiful New Yorker began her stage career at the age of fifteen. She spent several years at the Boston Museum, ♦ where she was the first American Hebe in *H.M.S. Pinafore*♦ in 1878. In New York she played prominent roles both in musicals and straight plays, her biggest success coming in the title role of the operetta *Nanon* (1895). She was also noted for her fiery temperament and as a clothes horse, and in an 1896 revival of *Patience,* in which she played Lady Angela to Lillian Russell's♦ heroine, she gained notoriety by wearing the first strapless gown seen on Broadway.

Marx Brothers, THE A riotous comedy team consisting of five brothers: Chico (né Leonard] (1887?–1961); Harpo [né Adolph] (1888?–1964); Groucho [né Julius] (1890?–1977); Gummo [né Milton] (1895?–1977); and Zeppo [né Herbert] (1901?–79). Gummo left the act early on, and Zeppo joined the act in the teens. Their maternal grandparents had been performers in Germany, while their mother was the sister of comedian Al Shean, of Gallagher♦ and Shean♦ fame. Pushed by their classic stage-mother, they appeared in vaudeville in 1909 as "The Three (or Four) Nightingales." Later Shean wrote a skit for them called "Fun in Hi Skool," and later still a second called "Home Again." During the 1920s they played in three successful musicals: *I'll Say She Is* (1924), *The Cocoanuts* (1925), and *Animal Crackers* (1928). Chico portrayed a high-strung, fast-dealing Sicilian. Harpo, forever mute, hurried across the stage in a red wig, battered hat, and tattered, ill-fitting clothes, chasing girls and stealing everything he could. Groucho, dressed in a poorly tailored morning suit, walking with a deep-kneed crouch, and flourishing his cigar and a painted-on mustache and boxy eyebrows, was at the ready with a wisecrack. Zeppo, the handsomest of the group, was its straight man. Both Chico and Harpo had musical talents which they incorporated into their routines, Chico playing the piano with his singular method of seemingly shooting his fingers at the keys, and Harpo performing, appropriately but often with surprising seriousness, on the harp. The team regularly disconcerted both authors and fellow players by departing from rehearsed texts to ad lib through a scene. In the 1930s they enjoyed an immensely popular film career, returning to the stage only rarely and then usually not as a team but as single performers. Groucho also had a popular radio and television quiz program.

Biography: *The Marx Brothers,* Kyle Crichton, New York, 1950.

Mary, a musical comedy in two acts. Book and lyrics by Otto Harbach♦ and Frank Mandel. ♦ Music by Louis A. Hirsch. ♦ Produced by George M. Cohan♦ at the Knickerbocker Theatre. October 18, 1920. 220 performances.

Mary Howells (Janet Velie) is secretary to rich Mrs. Keene (Georgia Caine) and in love with Mrs. Keene's son Jack (Jack McGowan♦). But Jack seems totally unaware of Mary. He is determined to go West and build low-priced portable homes that young married couples can afford. He calls them "love nests." However, while digging foundations he strikes oil instead. With his newfound wealth he returns home and realizes that he does, indeed, love Mary.

Principal songs: The Love Nest · Mary · We'll Have a Wonderful Party

Although *Mary's* story was not one of rags-to-riches, playgoers and critics of the day lumped the show with *Irene*♦ and *Sally,* ♦ and saw all three as initiating the vogue for such stories in musicals of the time, so that the era from 1921 to 1924 became known as "The Cinderella Era" on Broadway. The show's relatively short run was attributed to the number of road companies Cohan sent out, one of which was playing before the main company opened in New York.

Mary, Mary, a play in three acts by Jean Kerr.♦ Produced by Roger L. Stevens♦ at the Helen Hayes Theatre. March 8, 1961. 1,572 performances.

When Bob McKellaway (Barry Nelson♦) shows his fiancée, Tiffany Richards (Betsy von Furstenberg), reviews of his latest work, he is reminded that his ex-wife used to ask him why his books were so good that "a hundred thousand people wouldn't read them." It was an incessant fusillade of such barbed comments that led him to leave her. Now he must meet with her again to straighten out some income tax problems. When Mary (Barbara Bel Geddes♦) appears, she is as caustic as ever. At the same time, an old friend, Dirk Winsten (Michael Rennie), arrives. He is a fading film star who is deserting Hollywood—"the sinking ship leaving the rats." Dirk's romantic advances make Mary and Bob see that they still love each other. Mary even succeeds in stopping her latest verbal dart in mid-sentence.

Welcomed by Thomas Dash of *Women's Wear Daily* as "urbane, witty and sophisticated," this long-run hit skillfully blended a standard, syrupy plot with consistently brittle, impertinent dialogue.

Mary of Scotland, a play in three acts by Maxwell Anderson. ♦ Produced by the Theatre Guild♦ at the Alvin Theatre. November 27, 1933. 248 performances.

Because Catholic Mary Stuart of Scotland (Helen Hayes♦) represents a genuine political threat to England's Protestant Queen Elizabeth (Helen Menken♦), Elizabeth conspires with disaffected Scottish nobles to overthrow her. Mary is forced to flee to England, where she is captured and imprisoned. The Queens confront each other. Although she realizes that Elizabeth will have her killed, Mary is triumphant, pointing to her son and heir, and to the rich life she has led, while noting that Elizabeth is an unloved, bitter woman.

John Mason Brown, ♦ writing in the *Evening Post,* hailed this blank-verse tragedy as "the best historical drama that has been written by an American—a script which brings the full, flooding beauty of the English language back to a theatre in which its beauties are but seldom heard."

Mary the Third, a comedy in a prologue and three acts by Rachel Crothers. ♦ Produced by Lee Shubert♦ at the 39th Street Theatre. February 5, 1923. 163 performances.

In a double prologue brief glimpses are seen of the first and second Marys (Louise Huff), mother and daughter, as they are courted by their future husbands, William and Robert (Ben Lyon). Now the granddaughter and daughter of those girls, who is also named Mary (Huff), is courted by Lynn (Lyon). However, this third Mary is an ardent flapper who is dismayed to learn that her parents are contemplating divorce and that her grandparents' marriage was not all it seemed to be, either. She determines to "live in sin" rather than repeat their mistakes, but in the end bows to social pressures and her own feelings for her suitor. She can only ask lamely, "It *is* one of those great eternal passions that will last through the ages—isn't it, dear?"

Another of Miss Crothers's woman's-eye views of mores and relationships, the play was welcomed for its wit and shrewd observation, although many critics were uncertain about the precise nature of its philosophic bent.

Mask and Wig Club, THE An organization founded at the University of Pennsylvania in 1889, it has ever since produced comic musicals with an all-male student cast, much on the order of Harvard's Hasty Pudding Club♦ and Princeton's Triangle Club. ♦

MASON, JOHN [BECHER] (1857–1919) Born in Orange, N.J., he was scion to a musical family and the grandson of Lowell Mason, who wrote "Nearer My God to Thee." He made his acting debut in 1878, then served an apprenticeship briefly at Philadelphia's Walnut Street Theatre♦ and for seven years at the Boston Museum. ♦ In 1886 he played Laertes to Edwin Booth's♦ Hamlet. Afterwards he spent time in London before joining Daniel Frohman's♦ company in 1900. He scored some of his greatest successes playing opposite Mrs. Fiske,♦ including Lovberg in *Hedda Gabler* (1904); Paul Sylvaine, who reforms a lady burglar, in *Leah Kleschna*♦ (1904); and John Karslake, who wins back his ex-wife, in *The New York Idea*♦ (1906). In 1907 he won high praise as Jack Brookfield, who uses the powers of the occult to clear a man wrongly charged with murder, in *The Witching Hour.* ♦ Of his performance as Dr. Seelig, the sympathetic Jewish physician who sets straight an erring wife, in *As a Man Thinks* (1911), Walter Prichard Eaton♦ wrote, "Mr. Mason has the power of clearcut, fine and sincere speech . . . With his long and sound training behind him, he projects the ideal of a character worth knowing and listening to." Turning villain, he portrayed the lustful Baron Stephen Audrey in *The Yellow Ticket* (1914). His last memorable role was Judge Filson, who discovers a defendant is his long-lost daughter, in *Common Clay*♦ (1915). George Arliss,♦ who frequently played opposite the paternally dignified actor, remarked after his death, "John Mason would, in my opinion, have been the greatest actor in America if his private character had been as well balanced as his public performances. He had personality, great ability, and a magnificent

voice. But he had no control over the frailties of his nature."

MASON, MRS. (1780–1835) The English actress had made a small name for herself in Dublin and Edinburgh before her American debut at the Park Theatre♦ in 1809. Her initial appearance was a failure, but she soon gained celebrity as a brilliant comedienne, both in classics and contemporary comedies. Much married, she was also known as Mrs. Entwistle and Mrs. Crooke. She spent several highly profitable seasons at Philadelphia's Chestnut Street Theatre♦ and in New Orleans.

MASSEY, RAYMOND [HART] (1896–1983) The tall, gaunt, Canadian-born actor, who brought a singular brooding intensity to many of his best interpretations, made his professional debut in London in 1922. His first New York appearance was in 1931 as Hamlet. He next appeared in a quick failure, *The Shining Hour* (1934), but later enjoyed a major success in the title role of *Ethan Frome*♦ (1936). His most famous role was unquestionably in *Abe Lincoln in Illinois*♦ (1938). Brooks Atkinson♦ observed that he played the President "with an artless honesty that is completely overwhelming in the end." Opposite Katharine Cornell♦ he was Sir Colenso Ridgeon in *The Doctor's Dilemma* (1941); James Morell in *Candida*♦ (1942); and Rodney Boswell, the married lawyer who loves a scheming young girl, in *Lovers and Friends* (1943). After the show closed he toured the war zones playing the Stage Manager in a USO production of *Our Town.* ♦ He next appeared on Broadway playing Professor Higgins to Gertrude Lawrence's♦ Liza Doolittle in *Pygmalion*♦ (1946), then played The Captain in Strindberg's♦ *The Father* (1949). Later he toured in a reading of *John Brown's Body,* before essaying Brutus and Prospero at the American Shakespeare Festival. ♦ His last important New York appearance was as Mr. Zuss, the God-figure, in *J.B.* ♦ (1958).

Master Juba, see *Lane, William Henry*

Matchmaker, The, a comedy in two acts by Thornton Wilder. ♦ Produced by the Theatre Guild♦ and David Merrick♦ at the Royale Theatre. December 5, 1955. 486 performances.

Dolly Levi (Ruth Gordon♦), who is supposedly helping the rich, smug, and pompous merchant Horace Vandergelder (Loring Smith) save his niece from an elopement with an artist, is also supposedly helping the widowed Vandergelder find a new wife. To this end she has a pair of candidates she is pushing. But what Dolly is pushing most is Dolly, for she is determined that she will wed Vandergelder. She arranges for all the figures—the lovers, the candidates, Vandergelder's clerks, and, of course, Vandergelder and herself—to come together at a New York night spot. By the end of the evening she has paired everyone off to her satisfaction—which means she has gotten Vandergelder.

Originally produced as *The Merchant of Yonkers* in 1938, the play was based loosely on Johann Nestroy's 1842 farce *Einen Jux Will Er Sich Machen,* whose central figure was one of the clerks. The 1938 version, which starred Jane Cowl,♦ failed. But Tyrone Guthrie's♦ madcap direction turned the revised farce into a major success. The play served as the basis for the musical *Hello, Dolly!.* ♦

MATHER, MARGARET [née FINLAYSON] (1862?–98) Born in Canada, but raised in Detroit in dire poverty, she came to New York and was encouraged and promoted by J. M. Hill of the Union Square Theatre.♦ He starred her in revivals of *Romeo and Juliet*♦ (1885) and *Leah the Forsaken*♦ (1886). An emotionally disturbed if beautiful young actress, she soon broke with Hill and toured in her own company, then retired. In 1897 she emerged from retirement to play her old roles as well as Imogene in *Cymbeline,* but died while on tour. Otis Skinner,♦ for a time her leading man, said she "had impulse, power, intensity, but it was all unrestrained." Some sources give her birth as 1859.

MATHEWS, CHARLES (1776–1835) The great English mimic and comedian made two trips to America—in 1822 and shortly before his death, when he was ailing. He played first in Baltimore, then appeared in New York in November 1822. Although he performed in numerous popular comedies and farces of the time, he was also known for his "At Homes," one-man shows that could be perceived as precursors to later revues. James E. Murdoch♦ recalled, "By tying a handkerchief over his head in different ways, drawing up his coat-collar behind, or by brushing his hair back from his face or up in what was termed the 'cock's-comb style,' he presented a laughable portraiture without the assistance of vocal idiosyncracies. A working of the brows, a wink of the eye, a twist of the mouth, or dropping of the chin—each and any of these tricks, variously adapted to his ever-changing modes and qualities of voice, was sure to start a laugh upon a stony face; and when all this was added to his exquisite wit, no one could withstand the fun." Biography: *The Life and Correspondence of*

Charles Mathews, the Elder, Comedian, Anne Mathews, London, 1860.

MATHEWS, CORNELIUS (1817–1889) Although he was highly respected in New York as an editor, novelist, and poet, his plays were never well received there. His earliest known work, *The Politicians* (1840), was an attack on local corruption and was never produced, possibly because of local pressure. As a result, he took his later plays to Philadelphia for their premieres. In *Witchcraft; or, The Martyrs of Salem*♦ (1846), a son goes to his death in his unsuccessful attempt to save his mother from a false charge of being a witch. The play was highly praised in all major theatrical centers, except New York. A similar fate befell his historical drama, *Jacob Leisler* (1848), centering on the 17th century New York governor who is executed for defying his successor. His satire, *False Pretenses; or, Both Sides of Good Society* (1855), contrasted the shallowness of both sincere and insincere social sets. It proved the least popular of his produced works.

MATTHAU, WALTER [né MATUSCHANSKAVASHY] (b. 1920) In the late 1940s and early 1950s the sour-faced New Yorker won laughs in a dismaying number of flops. His first major hit came as Michael Freeman, the once successful "playwrote," in *Will Success Spoil Rock Hunter?* (1955). He also scored as Maxwell Archer, a great conductor's sarcastic manager, in *Once More with Feeling* (1958), and as Benjamin Beaurevers, the bored aristocrat, in *A Shot in the Dark* (1961). However, his greatest success came as Oscar Madison, the hopeless slob whose roommate is demanding neat, in *The Odd Couple*♦ (1965). His later career has been in films.

MATTHEWS, [JAMES] BRANDER (1852–1929) Born in New Orleans, he graduated from Columbia and turned to teaching and writing after his family lost its fortune. He taught at his alma mater from 1891 to 1924, and for his last 24 years there was its first Professor of Dramatic Literature. Before that he had written, alone or with collaborators, several popular if now forgotten comedies: *Margery's Lovers* (1884), *A Gold Mine* (1889), and *On Probation* (1889). In 1886 he worked with Laurence Hutton♦ to compile the five-volume *Actors and Actresses of Great Britain and the United States.* Among his subsequent works on the theatre were *The Development of the Drama* (1903), *A Book About the Theater* (1916), *Principles of Playmaking* (1919), and *Rip Van Winkle Goes to the Play* (1926). His writings were warm and thoughtful, giving marked evidence of his wide-ranging interests and travels. He was a founder of The Players. ◆

Autobiography: *These Many Years,* New York, 1917.

MAUGHAM, [William] Somerset (1874–1965) The English novelist and dramatist was one of his era's finest writers of high comedy. His first play to reach America was *Jack Straw,* which Charles Frohman ◆ presented in 1908 at the Empire Theatre ◆ with John Drew ◆ as star. The producer's high reputation coupled with the great stars he cast in the plays gave a special, added cachet to such early works as *Lady Frederick* (1908), *Mrs. Dot* (1910), and *Smith* (1910). However, Maugham's four best works are generally considered to be *Our Betters* (1917), a biting look at American social climbers in England; *Too Many Husbands* (1919), which is known as *Home and Beauty* in England and which can be described loosely as a comic variation of the Enoch Arden theme; *The Circle* (1921), a high comedy examining the past and present infidelities of two generations; and *The Constant Wife* (1926), a witty, observant look at social double standards. His melodrama, *The Letter* (1927), centering on a woman who murders her lover, was also a major success. While his works are revived regularly in England, the only important American revival has been Katharine Cornell's ◆ 1951 production of *The Constant Wife.* One of the great hits of the 1920s, *Rain,* ◆ was dramatized by other writers from one of his short stories.

Mavourneen, a play in four acts by George H. Jessop ◆ and Horace Townsend. Produced at the 14th Street Theatre. September 28, 1891. 102 performances.

Terence Dwyer (W. J. Scanlan ◆) rescues his beloved Kate (Grace Thorne) from abductors, only to have her mean sister, Lady Caroline Dwyer (Helen Tracy), who is also Terence's sister-in-law, contrive to separate the pair and have Terence sent away. But not before the young lovers promise to remain true. After ten years, during which he has made a fortune in America, Terence returns to Ireland to find Kate about to marry another man in order to save the family from bankruptcy. Terence sets matters right and takes Kate for himself.

Only Scanlan's increasingly obvious insanity forced the show to end its initial run. His part was taken over on tour by Chauncey Olcott, ◆ who played the role afterwards for many years. Both men inserted numerous Irish-style ballads into the play.

May Blossom, a play in four acts by David Belasco. ◆ Produced at the Madison Square Theatre. ◆ April 12, 1884. 169 performances.

When Richard Ashcroft (Walden Ramsay) is arrested as a spy during the Civil War he begs his friend, Steve Harland (Joseph Wheelock), to tell his fiancée, May Blossom (Georgia Cayvan ◆), what has happened. But Steve, who covets May for himself, lets her believe that Richard has deserted her. She marries Steve and has a child by him. Richard reappears and Steve's perfidy is revealed, but though Richard asks May to elope with him she refuses. She confronts Steve, who confesses and then goes off to war. Richard is killed in battle, while Steve does not return until long after the war is over. By then May has decided she loves him.

Belasco's first New York success, it was a reworking of his earlier adaptation of a novel, *Sylvia's Lovers,* and very similar in theme to his collaboration with James A. Herne, ◆ *Hearts of Oak.*

MAY [Pettie or Petty], Edna (1878–1948) A native of Syracuse, she began her career in one of the many children's companies of Gilbert ◆ and Sullivan ◆ operetta. She became a star and won international celebrity when she played the lead in *The Belle of New York* ◆ (1897). Although she later appeared in *The Girl from Up There* (1901), most of her subsequent career was in England.

MAYER, Edwin Justus (1896–1960) A New York native, he was a newspaperman for many years and briefly an actor before writing what appeared to be his only success, *The Firebrand* ◆ (1924), which recounted the love of Benvenuto Cellini for a duke's wife. In 1930 he wrote *Children of Darkness,* in which a jailor's daughter falls in love with a debtor and attempts to keep him prisoner. The original production was a failure, but a 1958 revival by the Circle in the Square ◆ was a major success and forced a re-evaluation of the play. His remaining works are of negligible interest. He was long active as a screenwriter.

MAYO, Frank (1839–96) The Boston-born actor made his professional debut in San Francisco in 1856. Within a few years he had earned an excellent reputation, especially in Shakespearean roles. His first major New York appearance was as Ferdinand in an 1869 production of *The Tempest.* ◆ By that time his fame was such that he received billing and pay second only to E. L. Davenport, ◆ who played Prospero. Apparently feeling he could not be certain of a steady income in Shakespearean roles, he soon turned to popular new plays, achieving his greatest success in the title role of *Davy Crockett*♦ (1873). Laurence Hutton♦ wrote, "Mr. Frank Mayo's performance . . . is a gem in its way. He is quiet and subdued, he looks and walks and talks the trapper to the life, never overacts and never forgets the character he represents." He played the part for the remainder of his career, only occasionally essaying other new roles or returning to his old Shakespearean repertory.

MAYO, Margaret [née Lilian Clatten] (1882–1951) Born in Brownsville, Ill., she was an actress from 1896 to 1903, when she retired from performing to devote herself to play-writing. Her earliest successes were adaptations of novels: *The Marriage of William Ashe* (1905) and *The Jungle* (1907). However, she is best remembered as the author of more original plays such as *Polly of the Circus*♦ (1907), centering on the romance of an acrobat and a minister; *Baby Mine*♦ (1910), a story of a wife who reclaims a roving husband by pretending to have a baby; *Twin Beds*♦ (1914), in which a young married couple are pestered by a lecherous neighbor; and *Seeing Things* (1920), written with Aubrey Kennedy and telling of a kooky wife who disguises herself as a ghost to spy on her husband.

Maytime, an operetta in four acts. Book and lyrics by Rida Johnson Young.♦ Music by Sigmund Romberg.♦ Produced by the Messrs. Shubert♦ at the Shubert Theatre. August 16, 1917. 492 performances.

The romance of rich Ottillie Van Zandt (Peggy Wood♦) and the poor workman, Richard Wayne (Charles Purcell♦), is broken up by Ottillie's snobbish father, who forces her to marry her worthless cousin. As the decades pass Richard becomes wealthy and respected, while the cousin succeeds in bankrupting Ottillie. When her estate is put up for auction, Richard appears, buys it all, and gives it back to her. After they are long dead, their grandchildren ignore family opposition and marry.

Principal songs: Jump Jim Crow · The Road to Paradise · Will You Remember?

The bittersweet romance was the biggest musical success of its season. It was said to be the favorite selection of American troops heading for Europe. The play was able to buck the perception that operetta was a German, and therefore enemy, genre. Ironically, it was based on the German musical, *Wie einst im Mai,* but animosity toward the Central Powers forced the Shuberts to jettison Walter Kollo's score and reset the book in America.

They also billed it as a "musical play," not an operetta.

M. Butterfly, a play in three acts by David Henry Hwang. Produced at the Eugene O'Neill Theatre. March 20, 1988. 777 performances.

Sitting in a French prison, René Gallimard (John Lithgow♦) looks back on how he destroyed his marriage and his promising diplomatic carer. A lover of Puccini's *Madame Butterfly,* he long thought of Cio-Cio-San as his "feminine ideal." This created problems when he was stationed in Beijing. There he fell madly in love with a beautiful actress, Soong Liling (B. D. Wong). Somehow, throughout their long relationship, he never realized that Soong was actually a spy and a man.

Although the question of how a supposedly intelligent man could be so staggeringly deceived was never answered satisfactorily, fine writing, superb acting, and a colorful, fluid mounting glossed over the difficulty, at least in the theatre.

Hwang (b. 1957) was the son of parents who emigrated from China to California, where he studied at Stanford, and then attended the Yale School of Drama.♦ His *FOB* (1980) won an Obie Award,♦ and his *The Dance and the Railroad* (1981) also received praise off-Broadway.

Me and My Girl This story of a cockney who inherits an earldom had book and lyrics by L. Arthur Rose and Douglas Furber, and music by Noel Gay. Its original London production in 1937 ran four years; an enlarged, revised version began an even longer run in 1985. The first American production opened at the new Marquis Theatre on August 10, 1986, with Robert Lindsay, star of the West End remounting, in the lead. Its catchy songs, including "The Lambeth Walk," and its outrageous clowning marked a refreshing change from the solemn pretentiousness of many contemporary musicals; it chalked up a run of 1,420 performances.

MEDCRAFT, Russell, see *Cradle Snatchers*

Medea, a tragedy freely adapted by Robinson Jeffers♦ from the play of Euripides. Produced by Robert Whitehead♦ and Oliver Rea at the National Theatre. October 20, 1947. 214 performances.

Medea (Judith Anderson♦) has helped Jason (John Gielgud♦) achieve his goals only to be deserted by him. She revenges his faithlessness by killing her children and the woman he would now marry.

Although dramatizations of the Medea legend had been popular on American stages during the mid-19th century, they were generally the works of French or German writers. Attempts at presenting Euripides' version had been rare and short-lived. Unless one includes *Mourning Becomes Electra,* ◆ Eugene O'Neill's ◆ very free-wheeling adaptation of the *Oresteia,* Jeffers's work has been by far the most successful rendering of a Greek tragedy in American theatrical history and, of course, was much closer to the original than the O'Neill play. Miss Anderson revived it on several occasions, while in 1982 Zoë Caldwell ◆ played the leading role and Miss Anderson was the nurse.

Medicine Shows As offerings of itinerant vendors of patent medicines, these variable mixtures of magic acts, songs, skits, and small-time spectacle allowed peddlers to attract sufficient audiences before beginning their sales pitch. Quack doctors and mountebank players who accompanied them had long trafficked on European byways, but did not spring up in this country in any real number until the early years of the 19th century. At first they were often one-man shows, but soon were enlarged. One especially popular branch, the Indian or kickapoo show, delighted American backwaters and occasional city slums after the Civil War. The heyday of these medicine shows ran from about the 1840s until the beginning of the 20th century, when the Pure Food and Drug Laws, the spread of better medical practices, easier communications, and the coming of films swept them aside. A few stragglers remained active as late as the 1940s. The best study of these wandering entertainments is Brooks McNamara's *Step Right Up: An Illustrated History of the American Medicine Show.*

MEDINA, Louisa H., see *Nick of the Woods*

MEDOFF, Mark, see *Children of a Lesser God*

MEGRUE, Roi Cooper (1883–1927) The New York-born dramatist served as assistant to Elisabeth Marbury ◆ before turning his hand to play-writing. Skilled at both superficial, if theatrically effective melodrama and lightweight comedy, he enjoyed long runs with *Under Cover* ◆ (1914), in which a young lady suddenly finds herself involved with smugglers; *It Pays To Advertise* ◆ (1914), written with Walter Hackett and relating a story of a business rivalry between father and son; *Under Fire* (1915), a behind-enemy-lines spy thriller; *Potash and Perlmutter in Society* (1915), written with

Montague Glass ◆ and telling of two Jewish businessmen who attempt to crash society; *Seven Chances* (1916), in which a young man must marry within a day in order to collect an inheritance; and *Tea for Three* ◆ (1918), a story of a man's attempt to cure his friend's jealousy by flirting with the friend's wife. On occasion he directed other men's plays, most notably the first Pulitzer Prize ◆ winner, *Why Marry?* ◆ (1917), which he co-produced.

MEILHAC, Henri, see *Halevy, Ludovic*

MELMOTH, Mrs. [Charlotte] (1749–1823) The "grande dame" of tragedy on the early American stage, her maiden surname is unknown. She was said to be the daughter of an English farmer and to have run away from school to marry an English actor, Samuel Jackson Pratt, who used the stage name Courtney Melmoth. They quickly separated, but she retained his name professionally. After performing for many years in England and Ireland, she came to America in 1793. She offered readings before making her acting debut as Euphrasia in *The Grecian Daughter.* Although she was past her prime and growing exceedingly corpulent, she won applause for her characterization of the heroines in contemporary drama and for Shakespearean figures such as Lady Macbeth and Constance. She was also skilled in comedy, offering, among others, her portrait of Mrs. Malaprop. Her fiery temper caused occasional problems. She temporarily alienated audiences by refusing to read a patriotic epilogue to *Tammany* ◆ in 1794, and for a time withdrew from the Park Theatre ◆ after fighting with Dunlap. ◆ She retired many years before her death to run a seminary for girls and a dairy farm.

MELVILLE, Emily [also spelled Emilie and Emelie] (1850–1932) Only five years old when she played the Duke of York to Edwin Forrest's ◆ Richard III in Providence (R. I.), the Philadelphian was a popular child star in Louisville and elsewhere on what was called the "Western" circuit. She moved to San Francisco in 1868 and for the next sixty years remained one of its most beloved actresses. Much of her early success was as the prima donna of contemporary comic operas, but she also earned acclaim for her Ophelia and other dramatic interpretations. As late as the 1920s she played important older parts with the Alcazar Theatre's famous stock company and at other local playhouses.

MELVILLE, Rose (1873–1946) An actress born in Terre Haute, Ind., she made her debut in 1889. She scored a major success in a touring play called *Zeb,* in which she appeared as the hayseed Sis Hopkins. She played the part so well that it was elaborated for her, and when the play closed she developed a vaudeville sketch around the same yokel. In her Broadway appearances in such musicals as *Litle Christopher Columbus* (1894) and *By the Sad Sea Waves* (1899) she invariably portrayed Sis. She played little else until she retired some time in the 1920s.

Member of the Wedding, The, a play in three acts by Carson McCullers. Produced by Robert Whitehead♦ and others at the Empire Theatre.♦ January 5, 1950. 501 performances. NYDCCA.

Frankie Addams (Julie Harris♦), a lonely, sensitive 12-year-old girl, lives in a small Southern town with a widowed father, who ignores her, and Berenice Sadie Brown (Ethel Waters♦), the warm, understanding, thrice-married black cook. Only Berenice and Frankie's bespectacled six-year-old cousin John Henry West (Brandon de Wilde) make life bearable for Frankie until her brother Jarvis (James Holden) returns from the army and asks her to be a member of his wedding. Frankie is shattered when she realizes that she cannot accompany them on their honeymoon, as she had expected to do. Although John Henry dies of meningitis and Berenice leaves to get married again, the first stirrings of adolescent romance promise better days for Frankie.

The play was adapted by the playwright from her novel of the same name. Although most critics had initially held serious reservations about the work, praising its luminous performances, especially those of Miss Harris and Miss Waters, but questioning the play's construction, the performances made it a surprise hit and launched Miss Harris into stardom. Miss McCullers (1917–67) was a novelist best known for her sensitive depiction of Southern life.

Men and Women, a play in four acts by David Belasco♦ and Henry C. de Mille.♦ Produced by Charles Frohman♦ at Proctor's 23rd Street Theatre. October 21, 1890. 204 performances.

A panic brings the Jefferson National Bank to the brink of collapse. Its difficulties are aggravated by the discovery that bonds kept in its vault are missing. Suspicion falls on young Edward Seabury (Orrin Johnson), just as Edward is to announce his engagement to Dora Prescott (Maude Adams♦), sister of his best friend and fellow cashier, William Prescott (William Morris♦). Will, too, has just become engaged, to Agnes Rodman (Sydney Armstrong), daughter of Arizona's governor, Stephen Rodman (Frank Mordaunt). Calvin Stedman (R. A. Roberts), who loves Dora, determines to pin the theft on Edward, and when Governor Rodman comes to Edward's defense Stedman reveals that the Governor has a criminal record. This revelation forces Will Prescott to disclose that he stole the bonds. Although he is not prosecuted, he loses his job and cannot find work. Finally the sympathetic bank president, dismissing Will's actions as a youthful mistake, finds him another position. The lovers are all happily paired.

Based on a then recent and celebrated case, the play was the last collaboration of Belasco and de Mille. The New York *Star* praised it as the "best they have ever written." Except for the *Herald,* most critics agreed, even if some saw little purpose in the weak ending.

Men in White, a play in three acts by Sidney Kingsley.♦ Produced by the Group Theatre♦ and others at the Broadhurst Theatre. September 26, 1933. 351 performances. PP.

George Ferguson (Alexander Kirkland) is a young, idealistic intern whose rich fiancée, Laura Hudson (Margaret Barker), cannot understand his self-sacrificing dedication. She is willing to buy his advancement in his profession if he will spend more time with her. But their disagreement comes to a head when Laura discovers that George has had an affair with Barbara Dennin (Phoebe Brand) and that Barbara has died following an abortion. George leaves to study surgery in Vienna.

The first success for both Kingsley and the Group Theatre, much of its success was attributed to the often graphically realistic production and to the then fresh theme. Percy Hammond♦ of the *Herald Tribune* called it "an honest, tricky, and propaganda show that can be attended without a sacrifice of intelligence."

MENCKEN, H[ENRY] L[OUIS] (1880–1956) The crusty Baltimore journalist was best known to theatregoers for his association with the famed critic George Jean Nathan,♦ with whom he edited *The Smart Set* and *The American Merciery,* and with whom he wrote two plays which never reached New York: *The Artist* (1912) and *Heliogabulus* (1920). The character of E. K. Hornbeck in *Inherit the Wind*♦ was modeled after him.

MENKEN, ADAH ISAACS (1835–69) Although her real name was later given variously as Ada McCord, Adelaide McCord, and Dolores Adios Fuertes, this flamboyant, controversial actress, who was the most famous of all American Mazeppas, actually was born in the living quarters of her family's general store in Milneburg, La., and christened Ada Bertha Theodore. After her father's death the family moved to New Orleans, where she was obliged to help support her ailing mother. Her earliest attempts to go on stage led nowhere, so she married Isaac Menken, the son of a Cincinnati manufacturer, and converted to Judaism. Her husband helped her secure a place in a small traveling company. She thereupon adopted her stage name, adding the letter "s" to Isaac apparently for euphonic reasons, and made her debut in 1858 in Shrevesport as Pauline in *The Lady of Lyons.* ♦ A year later she made her New York debut, but finding roles hard to secure, became an assistant to the famous acrobat Blondin, and also tried her hand at a vaudeville act. It was James Murdoch♦ who, on learning of her riding skills, suggested that she attempt *Mazeppa,* with its famous scene in which the hero (a trouser role), tied to his horse and supposedly nude, is sent on a wild ride into the hills. She first played the part in 1861 and performed in little else thereafter. Although her performance was one of the sensations of the era, not all critics were overwhelmed. The *Tribune* wrote, "Her talent is like gold in quartz veins—all in the rough." She later toured in the play and took it to London and Paris, where she died. Away from the stage the small but amply proportioned, dark-haired actress was a fascinating figure. Not only was she a fine rider but an excellent shot. She was one of the first women to smoke in public and loved to gamble. She was much married, but her poetry and scintillating conversation won her such friends as Walt Whitman, Swinburne, and the elder Dumas.

Biography: *Mazeppa,* Wolf Mankowitz, New York, 1982.

MENKEN, HELEN (1901–66) Only five years old when she made her debut as a fairy in a 1906 production of *A Midsummer Night's Dream,* ♦ the attractive, New York-born actress continued her career by appearing in contemporary musicals. She then spent several years in stock before playing opposite John Drew♦ in *Major Pendennis* (1916). She first attained major recognition when she played Miss Fairchild, a young lady whose late mother was adored by *Three Wise Fools*♦ (1918). She won further acclaim as Diane, the poor girl who loves a sewer cleaner even after he is blinded in the war, in *Seventh Heaven*♦ (1922). In 1926 she portrayed the 300-year-old Emilia Marty, who has the formula for eternal youth, in *The Makropoulos Secret,* and the unyielding lesbian, Irene De Montcel, in *The Captive.* She next played Dorinda in a 1928 revival of *The Beaux' Stratagem.* During the 1930s she acted Queen Elizabeth to the Mary of Helen Hayes♦ in *Mary of Scotland*♦ (1933), and Charlotte Lovell, the spinster who cannot reveal to her daughter that she is the young woman's real mother, in *The Old Maid*♦ (1935).

MENOTTI, GIAN-CARLO (b. 1911) The Italian-born composer of opera studied at the Curtis Institute of Music and helped popularize modern opera with Broadway playgoers when several of his works were mounted at legitimate theatres instead of in opera houses. The first of these productions was a double bill known as *The Medium* and *The Telephone* (1947). The latter was merely a trite vaudeville sketch set to music, but the former was a powerful drama centering on a deranged medium, who is ultimately driven to murder. *The Consul* (1950) depicted the cruel, impersonal red tape which prevents would-be refugees from fleeing to freedom. *The Saint of Bleecker Street* (1954) described the tragic attempt of a young Italian-American to take the veil. His last opera to be presented on Broadway, *Maria Golovin* (1958), told the love story of a blinded veteran and the wife of a war prisoner. It failed, but later entered traditional opera repertory. Menotti's music is modern, but unadventuresome and not especially memorable. However, it is dramatically effective, and this, coupled with his ability to tell a story in striking theatrical terms, has accounted for his success.

Merchant of Venice, The Shakespeare's comedy was first done at Williamsburg, Va., in 1752 and marked the debut of the elder Hallam's♦ company in America. The play held the stage actively all through the 19th century, although it was regularly performed in a truncated version, usually ending with the trial scene. Edwin Booth♦ and other notable performers essayed the role of Shylock, many of the more tragically inclined players, such as Booth himself, emphasizing the dark undercurrents in Shylock's story rather than the lighter elements of the play. There was also sharp disagreement on how to portray Shylock, with many performers seeing him simply as a stereotypical villain and Jew. Numerous critics and playgoers suggested the finest of all 19th-century productions was that offered on their visits by Henry Irving♦ and Ellen Terry. ♦

Irving's attempt at injecting sympathy into his portrayal of Shylock and Miss Terry's richly warm and feminine reading of Portia redressed the balance to a large extent. In the 20th century a number of distinguished Jewish actors, including Jacob Adler,♦ David Warfield,♦ Morris Carnovsky,♦ and Dustin Hoffman,♦ essayed the role of Shylock in order to show that Shakespeare was drawing a human figure and not a caricatured Jewish villain, but the role of Portia has again generally been relegated to a secondary place.

Mercury Theatre, The Founded by Orson Welles♦ and John Houseman♦ as a repertory company in 1937, its chief aim was to offer "classical plays excitingly produced." To this end the small, slightly out-of-the-way Comedy Theatre on 41st Street was leased and renamed, and an ensemble formed, which included such later famous performers as Hiram Sherman, Joseph Cotten,♦ and Martin Gabel. During its brief but noteworthy history the group produced a highly-praised modern-dress version of *Julius Caesar*, with the conspirators garbed in uniforms resembling those of German and Italian fascists to suggest a contemporary political parallel. Its other mountings, also generally well received, were *The Shoemaker's Holiday, Heartbreak House,* and *Danton's Death*. In the last of these a backdrop of hundreds of sinister faces helped create a uniquely macabre, threatening atmosphere. Away from its main playhouse the group produced Marc Blitzstein's♦ controversial *The Cradle Will Rock.*♦ By the end of 1938, a combination of financial problems, the desertion of leading players, and pressing demands on others from radio and films caused the group's collapse. Some historians consider the film *Citizen Kane* as the troupe's last and most enduring achievement.

MEREDITH, Burgess (b. 1908) The short, somewhat fey actor and director was born in Cleveland and served a theatrical apprenticeship with the Civic Repertory Theatre♦ in 1930. Although he remained active in the theatre for half a century, he is best remembered for three early roles: Mio, the young man who seeks death after his father is executed, in *Winterset*♦ (1935); Van Van Dorn, who flees civilization for a night, in *High Tor*♦ (1937); and Stephen Minch, who is allowed to return to the days of his youth, in *The Star Wagon*♦ (1937). He also has enjoyed long careers in films, radio, and television.

MERIVALE, Philip (1886–1946) The lanky, suave, slightly haughty leading man was born in India and spent several seasons acting in London before he came to America in 1914 with Mrs. Patrick Campbell. ♦ He made his debut playing Professor Higgins to her Liza Doolittle in *Pygmalion.* ♦ Thereafter he moved back and forth between the West End and Broadway. Among his notable American performances were Prince Albert, who loses a princess to a commoner, in *The Swan,* (1923); Maurice Sorbier, the neglectful husband taught loyalty by his wife, in *Grounds for Divorce* (1924); Hannibal, who spares his enemy at the behest of a beautiful woman, in *The Road to Rome*♦ (1928); His Serene Highness, the personification of Death, who falls in love with a beautiful young girl, in *Death Takes a Holiday* (1929); Jim Warlock, the barrister whose seemingly casual affair leads to tragedy, in *Cynara* (1931); and the Earl of Bothwell in *Mary of Scotland*♦ (1933). In 1935 he appeared with his wife, Gladys Cooper, playing the title roles in *Othello*♦ and *Macbeth.* ♦

MERMAN, Ethel [née Zimmermann] (1908–84) The leading musical comedy queen of her era, she was born in Astoria, N.Y., and performed in cabarets and in vaudeville before making her Broadway debut in *Girl Crazy*♦ (1930). Her singing of "I Got Rhythm"♦ stopped the show and catapulted her to fame. Thereafter she appeared in *George White's Scandals of 1931,* ♦ singing "Life Is Just a Bowl of Cherries"; *Take a Chance* (1932), in which she introduced "Eadie Was a Lady" and "Rise 'n' Shine"; *Anything Goes*♦ (1934), the first of several Cole Porter♦ shows with which she was to be identified and where her hits included "Blow, Gabriel, Blow," "I Get a Kick Out of You," and "You're the Top"; *Red, Hot and Blue!* (1936), remembered for her singing of "It's De-Lovely" and "Ridin' High"; *Stars in Your Eyes* (1939); *Du Barry Was a Lady*♦ (1939), in which she offered "Do I Love You?" and "Friendship"; *Panama Hattie*♦ (1940); and *Something for the Boys* (1943). One of her greatest successes came with *Annie Get Your Gun*♦ (1946), in which she introduced "Doin' What Comes Natur'lly," "I Got the Sun in the Morning," "There's No Business Like Show Business," and "They Say It's Wonderful." She next appeared in *Call Me Madam*♦ (1950), first singing "You're Just in Love," and in *Happy Hunting* (1956). Another major success was *Gypsy*♦ (1959), in which she sang "Everything's Coming Up Roses," "You'll Never Get Away from Me," and the show-stopping soliloquy, "Rose's Turn." Walter Kerr♦ described her in this musical as a "brassy, brazen witch on a mortgaged broomstick, a steamroller with cleats, the very mastodon of all stage mothers." Her last appearances were in a 1966 revival of *Annie Get Your Gun* and as a replacement in the lead of *Hello, Dolly!.* ♦ Prior to her time, Broadway's leading ladies usually had been demure innocents. The dark-haired, brassy performer with perfect projection and impeccable diction changed the nature of heroines for many musicals, usually playing tougher, more knowing, and cynical figures.

Autobiography: *Merman,* with George Eells, New York, 1978.

MERRICK, DAVID [né MARGULOIS] (b. 1911) One of Broadway's busiest, most successful, and most controversial producers, he was born in St. Louis. He practiced law and served under Herman Shumlin♦ before producing his first success, *Fanny,* ♦ in 1954. Among his many subsequent successes were *The Matchmaker*♦ (1955), *Look Back in Anger*♦ (1957), *The Entertainer* (1958), *The World of Susie Wong*♦ (1958), *La Plume de Ma Tante*♦ (1958), *Gypsy*♦ (1959), *Take Me Along*♦ (1959), *A Taste of Honey* (1960), *Becket* (1960), *Irma La Douce* (1960), *Carnival* (1961), *Stop the World!—I Want To Get Off* (1962), *Oliver!* (1963), *Hello, Dolly!*♦ (1964), *Cactus Flower*♦ (1965), *The Persecution of Marat . . . De Sade* (1965); *Promises, Promises*♦ (1968), *Play It Again, Sam*♦ (1969), and *42nd Street*♦ (1981). In all he has produced over seventy plays, many, as the above selection suggests, importations of foreign hits. His methods of publicizing his plays often made front-page news. During the run of *Look Back in Anger* he paid a woman to climb on stage and slap an actor. For an advertisement of one of his musicals to which the critics had been lukewarm, he found a group of men with the same names as the leading Broadway theatre critics and printed the non-professionals' more favorable remarks with their names subscribed.

Merrily We Roll Along, a play in three acts by George S. Kaufman♦ and Moss Hart. ♦ Produced by Sam H. Harris♦ at the Music Box Theatre. September 29, 1934. 155 performances.

At a 1934 houseparty on his Long Island estate, the successful playwright Richard Niles (Kenneth MacKenna) has gathered together his friends and associates, many of whom are as successful as he is. The bracing air and the free-flowing whiskey somehow prove a lethally truth-inducing combination, so before long the principals are reliving the important moments of the past and realizing how bit by bit they sacrificed their integrity to achieve their goals.

In a relentless, backward-moving chronology—into 1927, 1926, right through to 1916—they return to their college years, when Richard admonished them in chapel to be true to themselves. They have not been.

Although Brooks Atkinson♦ saw the work as a "resolute, mature-minded drama," many critics found it more noble in purpose than in execution. After a modest run in New York the play was taken on the road, where it quickly folded. In 1981 Stephen Sondheim♦ offered a musical version, which updated the action and used a cast of exceptionally young unknowns. The musical failed.

MERRY, MRS. [née ANNE BRUNTON] (1769?–1808) The daughter of the English actor, John Brunton, she came to America in 1796, after her husband, Robert Merry, was adjudged a bankrupt and threatened with debtor's prison. She made her debut under Wignell's♦ management in Philadelphia's Chestnut Street Theatre, ♦ playing Juliet. She immediately became the leading actress in that city, then extended her fame to New York when she first performed there a year later as Belvidera in *Venice Preserved.* Among her other great roles were such Shakespearean ladies as Katharine, Constance, and Imogen. Mr. Merry died in 1798. In 1803 she married Wignell, who died a few weeks later. She married the first William Warren♦ in 1806. Ireland♦ wrote of her, "Her person was rather under size, but her figure was elegant, and her action and deportment graceful and easy. Without possessing great beauty of countenance, she had highly expressive features, and, with a fine, clear articulation, her sweetness of voice struck every ear like a charm. Entirely devoid of stage rant, she read with perfect ease and freedom, laying her accent and emphasis naturally, and with critical exactness." The dates of her American career virtually parallel those of her principal rival, Mrs. Melmoth. ♦

Merry Widow, The Operetta had all but passed from the American scene after the earlier great epochs of French opéra bouffe, English comic opera, and Middle-European operetta had died out in the late 1880s and early 1890s. Almost singlehandedly, this Franz Lehar♦ operetta rekindled the mode for Viennese musicals, a vogue that lasted until World War I. Moreover, it set the fashion for operettas of the period, telling stories placed in real, contemporary locales and dealing with modern mores. Heretofore, as well as in later times, most operettas were set in distant eras and exotic, often imaginary lands. Contemporaries perceived the best of the new school as more artful and mature than new American offerings of the time. Even more important was the softer, free-flowing music of this new school. From *The Merry Widow* came such perennial favorites as "Maxim's," "Vilja," and "The Merry Widow Waltz" ("I Love You So"). This last song is frequently credited with initiating the vogue for ballroom dancing that soon became known as "the dancing craze." The original New York stars of *The Merry Widow,* presented at the New Amsterdam Theatre♦ on October 21, 1907, were Donald Brian♦ and Ethel Jackson.♦ Revivals followed regularly, with the most notable coming in 1943 with Jan Kiepura and Marta Eggerth in the leading roles. Recently the work has entered the repertory of several American opera companies.

Merry Wives of Windsor, The Shakespeare's comedy about Falstaff's misadventures seems to have been offered to Americans first at Philadelphia's Southwark Theatre♦ in 1770. Later it became one of J.H. Hackett's♦ showcases. It has remained fairly popular ever since, although recent major mountings have been confined to festival and regional theatres.

Merton of the Movies, a comedy in four acts by George S. Kaufman♦ and Marc Connelly.♦ Produced by George Tyler♦ and Hugh Ford♦ at the Cort Theatre. November 13, 1922. 398 performances.

Merton Gill (Glenn Hunter♦) is so film-struck that he has become the joke of the tiny Illinois town of Simsbury. His preoccupation causes him to neglect his duties as clerk in Amos Gashwiler's general store, so Gashwiler fires him. Gill immediately heads for Hollywood, where he is befriended by "Flips" Montague (Florence Nash), a bathing beauty in a famous slapstick series. She lands him a small part in a film. He is disillusioned by the crassness and deception all about him—why, Beulah Baxter (Gladys Feldman), who has publicly sworn she never uses a double, uses a double—but he plods on. He is finally cast in a slapstick comedy, which he plays with such serious intensity that he becomes a star, and marries "Flips."

Based on Harry Leon Wilson's♦ series in the *Saturday Evening Post,* the play was generally acknowledged to be the 1920s' best spoof of Hollywood.

Metamora; or, The Last of the Wampanoags, a play in five acts by John Augustus Stone.♦ Produced by

Edwin Forrest♦ at the Park Theatre.♦ December 15, 1829. In repertory.

The great Indian chief Metamora (Forrest) is determined not to forsake the land of his forebears, but knows he fights a losing battle. He tells his wife, Nahmeokee (Mrs. Sharpe), "The power of dreams has been on me, and the shadows of things that are to be have passed over me. When our fires are no longer red, on the high places of our fathers; when the bones of our kindred make fruitful the fields of the stranger . . . then will the stranger spare, for we will be too small for his eye to see." Yet he is willing to save the life of a white woman, Oceana (Mrs. Hilson), and help her romance with Horatio [in some texts, Walter] (Mr. Barry♦). In the end, however, the white adversaries prove too much for the Indian, and Metamora dies fighting and cursing them.

Written in response to Forrest's offer of a prize for a new American play, the drama proved one of Forrest's most enduring vehicles and was scarcely ever out of his repertory. After his death numerous other actors attempted the part, with only small success.

Mexican-American War, see *Wars in American Drama*

Middle of the Night, a play in two acts by Paddy Chayevsky.♦ Produced by Joshua Logan♦ at the ANTA Theatre. February 8, 1956. 477 performances.

When a rich, aging, and widowed Manufacturer (Edward G. Robinson♦) falls in love with his young, newly divorced receptionist, their liaison is opposed on both sides: by the Mother (June Walker♦) of the Girl (Gena Rowlands), and by the Manufacturer's Daughter (Anne Jackson♦). Only his Son-in-Law (Martin Balsam) seems sympathetic. The Girl returns briefly to her former Husband (Lee Philips), a coarse, over-sexed musician. Finally the Manufacturer and the Girl reach their own understanding.

Originally produced as a shorter television play, the work was expanded into a drama that divided the New York critics, some seeing it as a sensitive character study, others as soap opera. The magnificent, understated performance of Robinson was the main reason for the play's success.

MIDDLETON, GEORGE (1880–1967) Born in Paterson, N.J., he was the author of some twenty produced plays, the best remembered of which are

Polly with a Past♦ (1917), written with Guy Bolton♦ and telling of a minister's daughter who pretends to be a French adventuress; and *Adam and Eva*♦ (1919), also with Bolton and describing how a spoiled family is taught industry and frugality. Before these he wrote *Hit-the-Trail Holliday*♦ with Bolton in 1915, although George M. Cohan♦ substantially rewrote it and took full credit when the play was produced. He was a founder of the Dramatists Guild.♦

Autobiography: *These Things Are Mine,* New York, 1947.

Midsummer Night's Dream, A Shakespeare's fantastic comedy was first offered at the Park Theatre♦ in 1826. Its popularity in the 19th century was abetted by two landmark revivals. William Burton♦ scored a huge success with his sumptuous production in 1854, with himself as Bottom, while in 1888 Daly♦ staged the first of several mountings by him of the work. His cast included Ada Rehan,♦ John Drew,♦ Virginia Dreher, and Otis Skinner♦ as the lovers, and James Lewis♦ as Bottom. As with Burton's production this revival was mounted with Victorian opulence, its elaborate settings the work of Henry Hoyt.♦ Many of the most memorable 20th-century presentations have been importations. The lavish Old Vic♦ revival in 1954 was on such a scale that it was presented not at a regular playhouse but at the Metropolitan Opera House. The noted dancers Robert Helpmann and Moira Shearer were Oberon and Titania, and Stanley Holloway was an engaging Bottom. By contrast the Royal Shakespeare Company♦ offered Peter Brook's♦ austere and modern interpretation in 1971. One commentator noted, "The fairy tale was no longer ethereal, no more spirits with gauzy wings, but an intensely *physical* magic. Against Sally Jacobs's glaring white three-walled setting, the actors in their orange and purple robes were psychedelically present." An American musical version, *Swingin' the Dream* (1939), had a Jimmy Van Heusen score and an all-black cast that included Louis Armstrong as Bottom, but it was a quick failure.

MIELZINER, Jo (1901–76) The leading set designer of his era, he was born in Paris, but studied in America at the Pennsylvania Academy of Fine Arts and the National Academy of Design. His first professional work in the theatre was as both an actor and designer for Jessie Bonstelle♦ in Detroit. He next served as an actor and stage manager for the Theatre Guild♦ before creating the sets for their 1924 production of *The Guardsman.* Between then and his death he designed the sets, and usually the lighting, for more than 400 Broadway plays. The word most often employed to describe his best work was "poetic." He abandoned, especially in his later years, the detailed realism that was still in vogue when he began, as well as the fashionable expressionistic turn of men such as Robert Edmond Jones. ♦ Instead, he perfected the art of suggestive, skeletonized settings, evocatively lit. A complete list of even his finest work would include virtually all the best plays and some of the most successful musicals for the fifty years he was active, particularly after 1930. Representative of his work were his settings for *Strange Interlude*♦ (1928); *Street Scene*♦ (1929), one of his great realistic recreations; *Of Thee I Sing*♦ (1931); *Winterset*♦ (1935); *On Your Toes*♦ (1936); *Abe Lincoln in Illinois*♦ (1938); *Pal Joey*♦ (1940); *The Glass Menagerie*♦ (1945); *Annie Get Your Gun*♦ (1946); *A Streetcar Named Desire*♦ (1947); *Mister Roberts*♦ (1948); *Death of a Salesman*♦ (1949); *South Pacific*♦ (1949); *Guys and Dolls*♦ (1950); *The King and I*♦ (1951); *Tea and Sympathy*♦ (1953); *Cat on a Hot Tin Roof*♦ (1955); *Gypsy*♦ (1959); and *1776*♦ (1969). Writing of his work for *Winterset,* John Mason Brown♦ noted, "In his visualization of the bridge, Mr. Mielziner has provided *Winterset* with one of the finest backgrounds our contemporary theatre has seen. It is a setting of great majesty and beauty, and alive with a poetry of its own . . . simple, direct and impressive."

Mighty Dollar, The, a play in four acts by Benjamin E. Woolf. ♦ Produced at the Park Theatre. September 6, 1875. 104 performances.

The most famous salon in Washington is appropriately named Grabmoor, for it is here that the leading wheelers and dealers come to contrive arrangements that will allow them to pile up the mighty dollar. They will stop their greedy machinations for a few moments to help a newly married lady, Clara Dart (Maude Granger♦), when she is bothered by a former suitor, but the money grubbing continues the moment she leaves. Prominent among the figures at Grabmoor are the not particularly ethical Congressman, the Hon. Bardwell Slote (W. J. Florence♦), and Mrs. General Gilflory (Mrs. Florence). Slote is given to qualifying his statements with "not by a large majority," and dropping such abbreviations as B.O.T. and P.D.Q., which he later explains mean "bully old time" and "pretty darn quick." The upstart Mrs. Gilflory has her own pet phrases to show off her learning, most notably "from Alpha to Omaha."

Assailed by critics as vulgar and formless, the comedy nevertheless gave the Florences their most enduring success and added the colorful character of Slote to our dramatic literature.

Mikado, *The* Gilbert♦ and Sullivan's♦ comic opera about the preposterous carryings-on in the mythical Japanese village of Titipu won favor with Americans from its first major New York performance at the Fifth Avenue Theatre♦ on August 19, 1885, when it began a run of 250 performances. The cast included Courtice Pounds as Nanki-Poo and Geraldine Ulmar as Yum-Yum. Actually, the New York premiere had taken place on July 20, in an unauthorized production at the Union Square Theatre♦ by Sydney Rosenfeld.♦ An injunction was obtained and the mounting was withdrawn after its initial performance. It has been revived a number of times, including a fine resurrection by Winthrop Ames♦ in 1927, which ran 150 performances. The work is also a favorite with amateur theatre groups. In 1939 it was the source of two jazzy black versions: *The Swing Mikado* and *The Hot Mikado.*

MILES, George Henry (1824–71) A Baltimore lawyer and teacher, he was versatile enough to win praise for his religious novels and poetry, as well as for plays which achieved some popularity in his day and have been admired by later theatrical scholars. The earliest of his plays to be produced was *Mohammed, the Arabian Prophet* (1851). It depicted Mohammed as a warrior against idolatry. A year before its production it was awarded a $1000 prize by Edwin Forrest,♦ who elected not to mount it. It remained for J. A. J. Neafie♦ to offer it to New York. *De Soto* [sometimes called *Hernando de Soto*] (1852) was first offered by James E. Murdoch♦ at Philadelphia's Chestnut Street Theatre♦ and later produced in New York by E. L. Davenport.♦ It centered on the love of a supposed Indian princess, actually a kidnapped white woman, for the explorer. His *Mary's Birthday; or, The Cynic* (1857) was a social comedy focusing on a prodigal daughter. A second comedy, *Senor Valiente* (1859), was well received in Baltimore but failed in New York, despite the presence of Edward Eddy♦ and Julia Dean♦ in the leading roles.

MILLER, Arthur (b. 1915) The New York-born dramatist studied at the University of Michigan, where he was a winner of the Avery Hopwood Award for play-writing. His first play to be produced was *The Man Who Had All the Luck* (1944), the story of a man who attributed his success to hard work. It ran less than a week. *All My Sons♦* (1947), which told of a veteran who learns that his father sold defective airplane parts to the government, won the New York Drama Critics Circle Award. ♦ Both that award and the Pulitzer Prize♦ went to what is generally considered his best play, *Death of a Salesman♦* (1949), which centered on the degeneration and suicide of an aging commercial traveler. Following the production of his translation of *An Enemy of the People* (1950), he offered his tale of a Salem witch hunt, *The Crucible♦* (1953), which many saw as a thinly veiled indictment of McCarthyism and which may yet prove his most durable work. He was next represented by a double bill: *A View from the Bridge♦* (1955), which told of the murderous jealousy of a longshoreman, and which was presented in conjunction with a shorter play, *A Memory of Two Mondays,* a picture of workaday life in a Manhattan warehouse. Nine years elapsed before he had two full-length plays ready in 1964: *After the Fall,* ♦ a semi-autobiographical play based on his marriage to film star Marilyn Monroe; and *Incident at Vichy,* describing the reactions of a group of French arrested by the Nazis. The *Price* (1968) detailed the bitter enmity of two brothers. *The Creation of the World and Other Business* (1972) used Adam and Eve to reflect man's relation to good and evil. The play was a quick failure, as was *The American Clock* (1980), which set the problems of one family against a background of the Depression. Miller was a firmly committed leftist, whose political philosophizing sometimes got the better of his dramaturgy. However, at his best he is a remarkably powerful playwright.

Autobiography: *Timebends,* New York, 1987.

MILLER, Gilbert [Heron] (1884–1969) The son of Henry Miller,♦ he was born in New York and worked for some years as an actor before turning producer. His first productions were in London, where in short order he became as active and important as he soon was to be in New York. Curiously, with a few exceptions, he rarely produced the same plays in both theatre centers. His New York offerings included: *The Constant Wife* (1926), *Journey's End* (1929), *Berkeley Square♦* (1929), *Tomorrow and Tomorrow♦* (1931), *The Animal Kingdom♦* (1932), *The Petrified Forest♦* (1935), *Victoria Regina* (1935), *Tovarich* (1936), *Harriet♦* (1943), *Edward, My Son* (1948), *The Cocktail Party♦* (1950), the 1951 Olivier♦-Leigh double bill of *Antony and Cleopatra♦* and *Caesar and Cleopatra,* ♦ and *Witness for the Prosecution* (1954).

478

MILLER, [JOHN] HENRY (1859–1926) Born in England, he was brought to Canada at the age of fourteen and determined to become an actor shortly thereafter, when he witnessed a performance of *Across the Continent*♦ with Oliver Doud Byron.♦ Joining a stock company in Toronto he made his debut in a bit part in *Amy Robsart* in 1877. His first New York appearance came three years later as Arviragus opposite Adelaide Neilson♦ in *Cymbeline*. He soon rose to leading roles first under Daniel Frohman♦ and then with Charles Frohman♦ at the Empire Theatre.♦ He left the Empire in 1897 to become a star in his own right as Eric Temple, the brilliant composer whose great work is stolen by a jealous rival, in *Heartsease*. Subsequent successes came as Sidney Carton in a dramatization of Dickens's *A Tale of Two Cities*, renamed *The Only Way* (1899); in the title role of *Richard Savage* (1901); and as Dick Dudgeon in *The Devil's Disciple*♦ (1903). In 1905 he took over the Princess Theatre, where he produced and directed *Zira*,♦ which he co-authored with J. Hartley Manners.♦ The next year he presented *The Great Divide*,♦ assuming the role of Stephen Ghent, the Western ruffian who is civilized by the woman he forces to marry him. In 1910 he produced, directed, and starred in *The Faith Healer*,♦ portraying the leading role of Ulrich Michaelis, who struggles to retain his divine curative powers. Among his most important later roles were Neil Summer, whose daughter must save his faltering marriage, in *The Rainbow* (1912); and Jeffrey Fair, whose modern wife nearly destroys their home, in *The Famous Mrs. Fair*♦ (1919). He produced and directed numerous other popular successes, notably *The Servant in the House*♦ (1908), *Daddy Long Legs*♦ (1914), and *Come Out of the Kitchen*♦ (1916), frequently assuming leading roles in these productions during their runs. In 1918 he built Henry Miller's Theatre in New York. He was a handsome, slightly stocky man, much respected for his versatility, but also feared for his famous explosive temper.

Biography: *Backstage with Henry Miller*, Frank P. Morse, New York, 1938.

MILLER, JASON, see *That Championship Season*

MILLER, JOAQUIN, see *Danites, The*

MILLER, MARILYN [née MARILYNN REYNOLDS] (1898–1936) The unquestioned queen of Broadway musical comedy in the 1920s, the tiny, delicate-featured blonde beauty was only five years old when she became a member of her family's vaudeville act.

She toured the world in variety for ten years before Lee Shubert♦ discovered her in London in 1913. She appeared for the Shuberts in the 1914 and 1915 editions of *The Passing Show*♦ as well as in *The Show of Wonders* (1916) and *Fancy Free* (1918), but it was Florenz Ziegfeld♦ who made her a star after she performed in his *Ziegfeld Follies of 1918.*♦ Except for a brief, unsuccessful attempt at *Peter Pan*♦ (1924), under the aegis of Charles Dillingham,♦ she spent the entire decade of the twenties starring in Ziegfeld or Dillingham musicals: *Sally*♦ (1920), in which she introduced "Look For the Silver Lining," "Whip-Poor-Will," and "Wild Rose"; *Sunny*♦ (1925), in which she sang "Who?" and danced to the title song; and *Rosalie* (1928). She later appeared in *Smiles* (1930), before making her farewell in *As Thousands Cheer*♦ (1933), in which she sang "Easter Parade" and "Not for All the Rice in China." A competent actress and singer, she was most admired for her Dresden china beauty and for her airy, traditional dancing. Her biographer disputes the generally accepted idea that her real name was Mary Ellen and insists that her given name, with its spelling modified, was the first use of a name which has since become common.

Biography: *The Other Marilyn,* Warren G. Harris, New York, 1985.

MILLS, FLORENCE (1895–1927) The charismatic black performer who became almost a legend in her own short life, with her sparkling eyes, torchy voice, and graceful stepping, was born in Washington and began performing at the age of four. Her Broadway appearances were in *Shuffle Along*♦ (1921), *Plantation Revue* (1922), *Greenwich Village Follies*♦ (1923), and *Dixie to Broadway* (1924), in which she sang "I'm a Little Blackbird Looking for a Bluebird."

MILTON [DAVIDOR], ROBERT (1885–1956) Born in Russia, but brought to America while still a child, he started his theatrical career as an actor and eventually as assistant director with Richard Mansfield,♦ then worked for a time under Mrs. Fiske♦ and William Harris.♦ Among the shows he later directed were *The Cinderella Man* (1916); *Oh, Lady! Lady!!*♦ (1918); *Friendly Enemies*♦ (1918); *The Charm School* (1920), for which he was co-author; *He Who Gets Slapped* (1922); *You and I*♦ (1923); *The Youngest* (1924); *Outward Bound* (1924); *The Enemy*♦ (1925); *Bride of the Lamb* (1926); *Peggy-Ann*♦ (1926); and *Here Come the Clowns* (1938). He was an early advocate of the Stanislavsky method, and when staging non-musicals insisted his performers create their own imaginary biographies for the characters they were playing.

Mime in American Theatre Mime has never played an important role in the mainstream of American theatre, and virtually all the successful mime presentations on Broadway or in other major theatrical centers have emanated from Europe. Notable examples have been Max Reinhardt's♦ German spectacle, *Sumurun* (1912); the visits, beginning in the 1950s, of Marcel Marceau; and the 1326-performance run of a Swiss mime troupe *Mummenschanz,* between 1977 and 1980. Mime in these instances should not be confused with English-style pantomime, which flourished in this country only during the lifetime of G. L. Fox.♦

MINER, HENRY CLAY (1842–1900) The son of a noted New York civil engineer, he studied to be a pharmacist, but after serving in the Civil War chose instead careers in the theatre and politics. He became an advance agent for several performers, notably William "Buffalo Bill" Cody,♦ and then in 1875 began to lease and build vaudeville houses. In 1895 he attempted unsuccessfully to form a national syndicate with J. H. McVicker♦ and others. He is credited with originating "amateur nights," and his son Tom is thought to have been the first to use a hook to pull recalcitrant performers off the stage. Besides his theatres and political interests, he owned a chain of drug stores, a theatrical cosmetics firm, and was a partner in mining endeavors. He served briefly as head of the Actors' Fund.♦

MINNELLI, LIZA [MAY] (b. 1946) The daughter of Vincente Minnelli♦ and film star Judy Garland, she was born in Los Angeles and made her New York debut in a 1963 off-Broadway revival of *Best Foot Forward.* She later starred in *Flora, the Red Menace* (1965), a one-woman show, *Liza* (1974), *The Act* (1977), and *The Rink* (1984). During the run of *The Act* it was said that she was not actually singing one song on stage but mouthing the words to a recording. She is popular in films.

MINNELLI, VINCENTE (1903–86) For a brief time in the 1930s, the Chicago-born director and designer was one of Broadway's most imaginative artists. His first designs were seen in the 1931 edition of the *Earl Carroll Vanities*♦ and *The Du Barry* (1932). Subsequently he both designed and staged *At Home Abroad* (1935), *The Show Is On* (1936), *Hooray for What!* (1937), and *Very Warm for May* (1939). He also designed, but did not direct, the *Ziegfeld Follies*

of 1936.♦ His designs were known for their tasteful, if slightly exaggerated use of color. He later became a major director of musical films. The performer Liza Minnelli♦ is his daughter.

Autobiography: *I Remember It Well,* New York, 1974.

MINSKY, ABRAHAM (1881–1949) and MICHAEL WILLIAM ["BILLY"] (1891?–1932) The sons of an immigrant who had made a small mark for himself in New York business and politics, they started their theatrical careers by running nickelodeons. When their father built the National Theatre at Second Avenue and Houston Street, no tenant could be found for the small auditorium on the building's roof. The brothers turned it into another film house, but had even greater success when they introduced burlesque. Theirs was not the classic, satiric burlesque, but essentially the modern form of skin show with strippers and low comedians who featured off-color routines. By the 1930s they had been joined by their brothers, Herbert Kay (1892?–1959) and Morton (1902–87), and their chain of burlesque houses numbered over a dozen and reached beyond New York. Although their shows had been raided and sometimes temporarily closed on various occasions, their operation was finally brought to a halt by the laws passed under the aegis of Mayor LaGuardia in 1937. The Minskys have been credited with importantly boosting the careers of Gypsy Rose Lee,♦ Phil Silvers,♦ Abbott and Costello, and others. Morton gave his side of the picture in *Minsky's Burlesque* (1986).

Minstrel Shows Although blackface performers, often billed as "Ethiopian" entertainers, had been growing in popularity for a decade, it was the appearance on February 6, 1843, at the Bowery Amphitheatre of Dan Emmett,♦ Billy Whitlock, Frank Pelham, and Frank Brower as the Virginia Minstrels♦ that is generally allowed to have ushered in the era of American minstrelsy. The popularity of this new form of entertainment was so quick to sweep the nation that within a year a band called the Ethiopian Serenaders was performing at the White House, and other groups followed them there through succeeding administrations until shortly before the Civil War. These early groups were small, usually four to eight men, and their entertainment essentially musical. They were also in marked contrast to the formal, often imported attractions at regular theatres. In his excellent study of minstrelsy, *Blacking Up* (1974), Robert C. Toll noted that for the first time "the vitality and vigor of the folk" was brought into popular culture, adding, "It was immediate, unpretentious, and direct. It had no characterization to develop, no plot to evolve, no musical score, no set speeches, no subsidiary dialogue—indeed, no fixed script at all. Each act—song, dance, joke, or skit—was a self-contained performance that strived to be a highlight of the show." Toll also credits minstrelsy with introducing a sense of fast pacing hitherto unknown on the American stage, and which played no small part in the later development of musical theatre. Yet he recorded as well that minstrelsy "became a sedentary, urban form."

Of course evolution was inevitable. A certain formality soon crept in so that early minstrel shows quickly displayed a somewhat standard two-part form, the first offering the minstrels' celebrated semi-circle, with one end manned by a comic called Mr. Bones clacking an appropriate set of bones, and the other end manned by another comic called Mr. Tambo, wielding a tambourine. At the center was a master of ceremonies known as the interlocutor. For many the great attraction of this section was the balladeer. The second part was a free-wheeling olio, much like a prototypical vaudeville. Stump speeches constituted a popular part of this segment. Comedy sketches, often of plantation life or spoofing contemporary events and plays, were another feature of this part and with time became so important that many students see them as a third, separate section.

From the start minstrelsy helped perpetuate the stereotype of the American black—lazy, dumbly guileful, noisy, flashily garbed, but essentially happy. Make-up exaggerated the stereotype.

As minstrel competition developed, the intimacy of the first shows gave way to gargantuan spectacles often featuring dozens of performers. By this time, however, the popularity of minstrelsy was waning, with vaudeville, comic opera, and musical comedy coming to replace it in the public's affection.

While the shows moved away from their original emphasis on music toward an emphasis on comedy they gave Americans the first enduring songs to come from our theatre. Emmett's "Dixie"♦ jumps to mind at once, but it should be remembered that Stephen Foster♦ was one of many contemporary popular composers to write actively for the minstrel stage. Laurence Hutton♦ suggests that while minstrels did not invent the banjo, they were the prime developers of it and were responsible for its long popularity.

Among the great names of minstrelsy were Dan Bryant,♦ Emmett, E. P.♦ and George N. Christy,♦ Lew Dockstader,♦ "Honey Boy" Evans,♦ J. H. Haverly,♦ Eph Horn,♦ Francis Leon,♦ and Eddie Leonard♦ and such bands as Buckley's Serenaders,♦ Bryant's Minstrels,♦ [the original] Christy Minstrels,♦ Ordway's Aeolians,♦ the San Francisco Minstrels,♦ and Wood's Minstrels.♦ By the 1880s the vogue of minstrelsy had largely disappeared. It remained alive only in a few cities, notably Philadelphia, where Sanford's Minstrels,♦ John L. Carncross,♦ and Dumont's Minstrels kept the tradition alive well into the 20th century. Many great performers, such as Francis Wilson♦ and Al Jolson,♦ spent part of their early careers with minstrel companies, although their fame came elsewhere.

Miracle Worker, The, a play in three acts by William Gibson. ♦ Produced at the Playhouse. October 19, 1959. 719 performances.

Having graduated from Boston's Perkins Institute for the Blind, Annie Sullivan (Anne Bancroft♦) arrives at the Alabama home of Captain Keller (Torin Thatcher) to become a teacher-companion for his daughter Helen (Patty Duke). Helen, who is deaf, dumb, and blind, is an undisciplined but iron-willed youngster. It requires all of Annie's persistence, and sometimes a touch of savagery, to begin to bring the girl around. Not until Helen is purposely drenched and manages to spell out the word "water" does Annie realize she has reached the girl. A friendship slowly develops which will in part release Helen from her lonely, dark world.

The play was based on Gibson's earlier television version, which in turn had been derived from the true story of the Sullivan-Keller relationship. Robert Coleman of the *Daily Mirror* wrote, "Gibson's words are terse and eloquent, highly dramatic, but it is the frightening, harrowing, physical conflicts of his drama that terrify and grip you."

Miss Lulu Bett, a play in three acts by Zona Gale. ♦ Produced by Brock Pemberton♦ at the Belmont Theatre. December 27, 1920. 201 performances. PP.

Lulu Bett (Carroll McComas) is a drudge in the home of her sister Ina (Catherine Calhoun Doucet) and brother-in-law, Dwight Deacon (William E. Holden). When Dwight's brother Ninian (Brigham Royce) visits, he jokingly flirts with Lulu. Dwight reads the civil marriage ceremony, and Lulu and Ninian respond accordingly, before Dwight realizes that he has inadvertently married them. The newlyweds go off on a honeymoon, from which Lulu returns after she learns that Ninian is already married. But Ninian follows her with assurances that his first wife has died.

Based by the author on her own novel of the same name, the play was perceived as an observant, warmly written drama of Midwestern life of the time.

Mister Roberts, a play in two acts by Thomas Heggen and Joshua Logan.◆ Produced by Leland Hayward◆ at the Alvin Theatre. February 18, 1948. 1,157 performances.

Lt. Douglas Roberts (Henry Fonda◆) has long served the bored, unhappy crewmen of a navy cargo ship as a buffer between themselves and the cantankerous, unsympathetic Captain Morton (William Harrigan). The Captain seems more interested in his palm trees than in his men, and Roberts's task is difficult, since the crew so often releases its frustrations in mischief, such as the time Ensign Pulver (David Wayne◆) attempts to blow up the Captain's quarters but blows up the laundry instead. The Captain has regularly refused Roberts's plea for a transfer, but Roberts finally succeeds, only to be killed in action. News of his death prompts the crew to move more forcefully against the Captain. Taking his own action, Ensign Pulver knocks on the Captain's door and announces, "I just threw your palm trees overboard. Now what's all this crap about no movie tonight?"

Based on Heggen's novel, the play was one of the most popular works about World War II. Heggen (1919–49), a native of Fort Dodge, Iowa, however, died a year after the opening.

Mistress Nell, a play in four acts by George C. Hazelton. Produced at the Bijou Theatre. October 9, 1900. 104 performances.

Jealous of the new-found power of Nell Gwynne (Henrietta Crosman◆), the orange-vendor-turned actress who has become the mistress of Charles II (Aubrey Boucicault◆), the Duke of Buckingham (Geoffrey Stein), the king's rival for Nell's favors, and the Duchess of Portsmouth (Adelaide Fitz Allan), Nell's rival for the King's attentions, conspire to destroy her at the same time they attempt to put England under French dominion. To foil their treachery Nell disguises herself as a man.

The show was another example of the romantic swashbucklers so tremendously popular at the turn of the century. Born in Boscobel, Wis., Hazelton (1868?–1921) was an actor and playwright, perhaps best remembered for his collaboration on *The Yellow Jacket.* ◆ His middle name was Cochrane.

MITCHELL, GRANT (1874–1957) Born in Columbus, Ohio, he studied at Yale and at Harvard Law School, then both practiced law and served as a newspaperman before making a late decision to become an actor. After attending the American Academy of Dramatic Arts,◆ he made his debut in 1902 playing opposite Richard Mansfield◆ in *Julius Caesar.* ◆ He soon became a popular performer, most admired for his work in fast-paced comedies of the time. At his height, the actor, who bore a resemblance to the later James Cagney, won applause for such parts as Rodney Martin, who becomes his father's business rival, in *It Pays To Advertise* ◆ (1914); and John Paul Bart, who proves clothes make the man, in *A Tailor-Made Man* ◆ (1917). Within a few years, however, he was reduced to prominent supporting roles, so with the coming of sound films he left for Hollywood.

MITCHELL, JULIAN (1854–1926) Probably the most prolific director of musicals in Broadway's history, he started his career as a dancer at Niblo's Garden.◆ In 1884 he became Charles Hoyt's◆ principal director and staged many of Hoyt's last plays, including *A Trip to Chinatown* ◆ (1891). With Hoyt he learned the art of fast, fluid pacing that characterized his best work. He then moved to Weber◆ and Fields,◆ where he was often credited with establishing that team's celebrated chorus line of beauties. He also did work for others, among them Alice Nielsen's◆ mounting of *The Fortune Teller* ◆ (1898). In 1903 he directed two of the year's biggest musical hits, *The Wizard of Oz* ◆ and *Babes in Toyland.* ◆ Florenz Ziegfeld◆ hired him to help stage the first *Ziegfeld Follies* ◆ in 1907, and he eventually helped mount eight more of them. His work was also seen in *The Pink Lady* ◆ (1911); *Mary* ◆ (1920); *The Perfect Fool* (1921); and *Sunny* ◆ (1925). In all he staged over eighty musicals, although in his later years he was virtually deaf. He was the nephew of Maggie Mitchell. ◆

MITCHELL, LANGDON [ELWYN] (1862–1935) The son of the famous Philadelphia physician and novelist, S. Weir Mitchell, he received much of his education abroad, but returned to study law at Harvard and Columbia and in 1886 was admitted to the New York bar. A year later his first play, *Sylvian,* a romantic tragedy, had been produced and failed. Most of his subsequent writings for the theatre were dramatizations of novels, such as *Becky Sharp* ◆ (1899), which he adapted from *Vanity Fair* for Mrs. Fiske◆; *The Adventures of François* (1900), taken from his father's novel; *The Kreutzer Sonata* (1906), translated from Jacob Gordin's◆ play; and *Major Pendennis* (1916), which he reworked from Thackeray for John Drew. ♦ Only one of his original plays is important, but it remains one of the classic social satires of American stage literature, *The New York Idea*♦ (1906), centering on the uncertain feelings of a newly divorced couple. In 1928 he became the first Professor of Playwriting at the University of Pennsylvania, a post he held for two years.

MITCHELL, [Margaret Julia] Maggie (1832–1918) Although the tiny, curly-haired, sprite-like New Yorker is said to have been on stage from the time she was a child, the earliest record of her performing is as Julia in *The Soldier's Daughter* in 1851. She subsequently became a favorite at the Bowery, where she played the title role of *Oliver Twist*, and at Burton's. However, her greatest success came in 1862 when she appeared in the title role of *Fanchon, the Cricket*,♦ a dramatization of George Sand's *La Petite Fadette*. Her acting of the piquant country girl, including her famous shadow dance, made her an overnight star. Although critics were later to praise her Jane Eyre, Mignon, Pauline (in *The Lady of Lyons*♦), and Parthenia (in *Ingomar*♦), it was her Fanchon which the public demanded and which she continually returned to for the next twenty-five years. Her nephew was Julian Mitchell. ♦

MITCHELL, Norma, see *Cradle Snatchers*

MITCHELL, Thomas (1895–1962) Born in Elizabeth, N.J., he made his debut in Ben Greet's♦ company in 1913 and then played more Shakespeare under the aegis of Charles Coburn. ♦ His best early roles were Charles Bemis, who dreams of a better life, in *The Wisdom Tooth*♦ (1926) and Norman Overback, who decides he is happy having to marry his childhood sweetheart, in *Little Accident*♦ (1928), which he co-authored. After a long career in films he enjoyed success in the title role of *An Inspector Calls* (1947), as Willy Loman in the road company of *Death of a Salesman*, ♦ and in the musical *Hazel Flagg* (1953).

MITCHELL, William (1798–1856) In the 1840s, the leading producer and performer in burlesque, he was brought to America in 1836 by Henry Willard of the National Theatre. In 1839 he took over the tiny Olympic Theatre and made it the home of his delightfully absurd musical travesties. He saw to it that the fun began even before the play began by providing humorously written posters and programs. His pieces had such titles as *Buy-it-Dear, 'Tis Made of Cashmere*, which was a spoof of the ballet *Bayadere, the Maid of Cashmere*. Among his famous impersonations were those of ballerina Fanny Elssler,♦ of Hamlet, and of Dickens's Vincent Crummles. A tall, thin man with striking eyes, he was forced by ill health to retire at the height of his fame.

MITZI, see *Hajos, Mitzi*

MIZNER, Wilson (1876–1933) The once famous, if controversial wit, who was born in Bernicia, Calif., and who had at one time or another hustled for a medicine show, been a professional cardsharp, and managed a celebrated prizefighter, made his playwriting debut with *The Only Law* (1909), written with George Bronson Howard, which told of the private lives of certain low Broadway types. The play failed, but he later enjoyed some success when he collaborated with Paul Armstrong♦ on *The Deep Purple* (1911), in which the hero exposes a vicious badger game; and *The Greyhound* (1912), a story of professional shipboard gamblers and a reflection of Mizner's own participation in such games. Mizner also claimed to have been Armstrong's collaborator on *Alias Jimmy Valentine*♦ (1910), and his biographer states he did receive some program credit.
Biography: *Rogue's Progress*, John Burke, New York, 1975.

M'liss, a play in four acts by Clay Greene.♦ Produced at Niblo's Garden. ♦ September 23, 1878. 16 performances.
M'liss (Kate Mayhew) is "the waif of the Sierras," a bright, attractive young hoyden who has been neglected by her drunken miner father. She is spunky enough to fight off ruffians who would attack the young man she loves, and also to win him away from a more sophisticated lady—"the pink and white thing"—in whom he seems all too interested.
The play, based on a Bret Harte story, was produced in New York after Miss Mayhew won an injunction preventing Annie Pixley♦ from presenting her production of the work. The victory was short-lived, for the injunction was soon lifted and it was Miss Pixley who afterward was identified with the part and toured in it for many years. There is some question as to whether Greene wrote the version Miss Mayhew employed. Miss Pixley's version was sometimes billed as *M'liss, the Child of the Sierras*.

Mlle. Modiste, an operetta in two acts. Book and lyrics by Henry Blossom. ♦ Music by Victor Herbert. ♦ Produced by Charles Dillingham♦ at the

Knickerbocker Theatre. December 25, 1905. 202 performances.

Fifi (Fritzi Scheff♦), a salesgirl in a hat shop, loves Capt. Etienne de Bouvray (Walter Percival), who loves her and is certain "The Time and the Place and the Girl" will all come happily together. The romance is opposed by both Fifi's employer and by Etienne's rich, determined uncle, the Compte de St. Mar (William Pruette). An American, Hiram Bent (Claude Gillingwater), stumbles into the shop and takes a liking to the girl. She tells him of her ambition to become a singer and shows how she would perform "If I Were on the Stage" (an extended piece which includes the song "Kiss Me Again"), so he agrees to pay for her schooling. A year later the stubborn Count, who announces "I Want What I Want When I Want It," holds a fete at which one Mme. Bellini wins applause for her fine singing. When the count learns she is none other than Fifi, he withdraws his objections to the match.

Other principal song: The Mascot of the Troop

Many critics considered this the finest American musical written up to its time, admiring its solidly constructed, humorous book and its superb score, which "fit the story like a glove."

MODJESKA, HELENA [née OPID] (1840–1909) Born in Cracow, she was the daughter of a humble teacher and musician. At an early age she became an actress in her native city, where her half-brother was already a popular performer. Shortly thereafter she married a man twenty years her senior and whose name she gave as Gustave S. Modjeski, but whose full name was actually Gustave Sinnmayer Modrejewski. The marriage was short-lived, although it served, with slight respelling, to give her her stage name. She next married a Polish aristocrat, Karol Bozenta Chlapowski, and fled with him to America when their radical political views became known. They settled in California. A need for funds forced the actress to master English quickly and return to the stage. Her debut at San Francisco's California Theatre in 1877 as Adrienne Lecouvreur marked her as an important newcomer, and she quickly consolidated her reputation with her performances as Ophelia, Juliet, and Camille. She returned to Adrienne Lecouvreur for her New York debut later the same year. For the next twenty-eight seasons, despite a slight paralytic stroke in 1897, her career was a series of triumphs, and she became one of the most respected and beloved of all American performers. Among her greatest roles, besides those already mentioned, were Magda, Frou-Frou, Mary Stuart, and such Shakespearean ladies as Rosalind, Viola,

Lady Macbeth, and Isabella. William Winter♦ admired her for "her slender, graceful figure, her pensive countenance, her sympathetic voice, her air of soft bewilderment, and her handsome dress." Otis Skinner♦ sounded a different note, recollecting, "The dominant characteristics of her acting were eagerness and joy . . . a joy restrained and admirable in execution; the great joy of artistry." She also was respected for the warm encouragement she gave to promising young talent.

Autobiography: *Memories and Impressions of Helena Modjeska,* New York, 1910.

MOELLER, PHILIP (1880–1958) The New York-born producer and director was educated at New York University and Columbia. He was a founder of and director for the Washington Square Players,♦ and after that group disbanded served in similar capacities for the Theatre Guild. ♦ Among the many plays he staged for the Guild were *The Guardsman* (1924), *They Knew What They Wanted♦* (1924), *Ned McCobb's Daughter♦* (1926), *The Second Man♦* (1927), *Strange Interlude♦* (1928), *Dynamo♦* (1929), *Hotel Universe♦* (1930), *Elizabeth the Queen♦* (1930), *Mourning Becomes Electra♦* (1931), *Biography♦* (1932), *Ah, Wilderness!♦* (1933), and *End of Summer♦* (1936). He called himself an "inspirational" director, preferring to let himself and his actors improvise as they rehearsed. Theresa Helburn♦ has written, "His timing was brilliant and in comedy he was unequalled. But he had his blind spots. We used to say rather wistfully that it would be nice if Phil would read a play before he produced it."

MOGULESKO, [ZELIG] SIGMUND (1858?–1914) The bantam, droll comedian was born in Romania and was established as a popular favorite there and on other European Yiddish stages before he arrived in America in 1886. He immediately became the premier Yiddish comedian of his generation. Typical of his virtuosity was his New York debut in what could be translated as *Coquettish Ladies.* In this piece he played a different part in each act: a young pimp in Act One; an old drunk in Act Two; and a gossipy lady matchmaker in the last act. His acting was scarcely realistic, but exaggerated in the fashion of the Yiddish stage. Nonetheless, Abraham Cahan, the well-known Jewish publisher and historian, wrote, "A born genius he was, and his personality was as marvelous as his art. His talent and charm lit that foolish play with rays of divine fire. He bewitched us with his singing and his acting alike."

MOLINEUX, ROLAND BURNHAM (1866–1917) Possibly the only American convicted of murder to have a play produced on Broadway, he was convicted of having sent a bottle of poisoned Bromo-Seltzer to the manager of the Knickerbocker Athletic Club after an argument. The manager's cousin took some and died. After two mistrials Molineux was found guilty, but the verdict was appealed; he was acquitted in a retrial after three years in prison. He then wrote books as well as a play, *The Man Inside* (1913), which told of a district attorney's undercover investigation of political connections to the drug trade. The play was produced by David Belasco,♦ but was only moderately successful. Tensions related to the production apparently proved too much for the author. Shortly after the play closed he was committed to an insane asylum, where he died four years later.

MOLNAR, FERENC (1878–1952) The versatile Hungarian playwright, as skilled at romantic fantasy as at high comedy, came to American playgoers' attention when his early play, *The Devil* (1908), opened at two Broadway theatres on the same night. The production with George Arliss♦ was by far the more successful. Unlike many foreign dramatists, Molnar was exceptionally fortunate in the excellent translations and mountings given his plays in America. Leo Ditrichstein♦ starred in Belasco's version of *The Phantom Lover* (1914); Eva Le Gallienne♦ and Joseph Schildkraut♦ were the leading players in the Theatre Guild's♦ production of *Liliom*♦ (1921); Miss Le Gallienne also took the central role in *The Swan* (1923); the Guild staged *The Guardsman* (1924) with the Lunts♦ as stars; while Holbrook Blinn♦ headed a fine cast in *The Play's the Thing* (1926). Many other of his plays were also well received, and several of his best have had major revivals, notably a 1948 return of *The Play's the Thing*. His works have also lent themselves to musicalization, *The Phantom Lover* becoming *The Love Letter* (1921) and *Liliom* being made into *Carousel*♦ (1945).

MONKS, JOHN, JR., see *Brother Rat*

MONTAGUE, H[ENRY] J[AMES] [né MANN] (1844–78) This late 19th-century Valentino (or James Dean) was born in England and had made a name for himself in Robertson♦ comedies in London before Lester Wallack♦ brought him to America in 1874 to serve as leading man with Wallack's ensemble. Odell♦ has noted, "Montague became at once the accepted matinée idol; he was handsome, gentle and gentlemanly—a perfect specimen of refined English manhood. New York had seen nothing like him before; he had the faculty of making most other leading men seem boorish, ill-dressed, and possibly a bit vulgar . . . His photographs by Mora and Sarony were soon on every dressing-table." He played Captain Molineux in the premiere of *The Shaughraun*♦ and later earned praise for his performances in such contemporary successes as *Caste*, ♦ *Diplomacy,* ♦ and *The Overland Route*. As popular with his confreres as he was with the public, he is often reputed to have suggested the founding of the club that became The Lambs. ♦

MONTEZ, LOLA [née MARIE DOLORES ELIZA ROSANNA GILBERT] (1818?–61) The famous Irish-born beauty was a notorious courtesan who had been mistress to both Franz Liszt and King Ludwig I of Bavaria before coming to America in 1851. Walter Leman♦ long recalled her "face full of expression, fine eyes, and hair that a mermaid might envy." At first her attempts to traffic in her notoriety were commercially successful, although they met with little encouragement from critics. She offered herself as a dancer and an actress, including an appearance in the title role of a specially written vehicle, which purported to recount her European amours, *Lola Montez in Bavaria* (1852). During a long stay in California she helped give Charlotte Crabtree♦ some of her earliest training. When her allure began to wane she endeavored to conquer the lecture circuit, but was less successful. She died in comparative poverty on Long Island (N.Y.), but her legend remains richly alive.

MONTGOMERY, DAVE, see *Stone, Fred*

MONTGOMERY, JAMES (1882–1966) An actor turned playwright, he scored his biggest non-musical success with *Nothing But the Truth*♦ (1916), a farce in which the hero can tell no lies for twenty-four hours. However, he enjoyed a number of hits when he wrote the librettos for musicals based on some of his less popular comedies. Thus, *Oh, Look!* (1918) was derived from his 1912 *Ready Money,* and *Irene*♦ (1919) from his failed 1916 play, *Irene O'Dare*. His plays also served as a source for other librettists, most notably when Otto Harbach♦ turned his 1910 *The Aviator* into *Going Up!* (1917).

MOODY, WILLIAM VAUGHN (1869–1910) The son of a Mississippi river boat captain, he was born in Spencer, Ind., and educated at Harvard, where he became the class poet. He later taught both at

Harvard and at the University of Chicago before retiring to devote himself to writing poetry and plays. His earliest theatrical works were blank-verse dramas, *The Masque of Judgment* (1900) and *The Fire Bringer* (1904). Neither was produced during his lifetime, although scholars have found merit in both. The first ranged from the Incarnation to the Day of Judgment and employed Raphael as its protagonist. The second dealt with Jesus' life. Only two of his plays were produced while he was alive. The earlier of these, *The Great Divide*♦ (1906), was one of the milestones in the history of American theatre. Its story of a puritanical heroine's reconciliation with her more liberated husband was seen as an examination of a fundamental native conflict, and was an early instance of what Quinn♦ has called the "Drama of Revolt." *The Faith Healer*♦ (1909), which centered on a man's attempt to regain divine curative powers, failed, possibly because Moody was too ill to make the requisite revisions. His early death is believed by many scholars to have deprived the theatre of a major voice and to have left it for Eugene O'Neill♦ to bring American drama to maturity a decade later.

Biography: *Estranging Dawn,* Maurice F. Brown, Carbondale, Ill., 1973.

Moon for the Misbegotten, *A,* a play in four acts by Eugene O'Neill.♦ Produced at the Bijou Theatre. May 2, 1957. 68 performances.

Having buried his mother, the hopelessly dissipated James Tyrone, Jr. (Franchot Tone♦) wanders aimlessly in search of a mother figure. He comes to the wretched Connecticut farm of a seedy Irishman, Phil Hogan (Cyril Cusack), where he discovers Hogan's homely, but warm-hearted daughter, Josie (Wendy Hiller). Josie falls in love with James but he is unable to respond fully. He can accept her only as the mother figure he seeks. Leaving Josie in despair, he wanders off on his path toward self-destruction.

The play originally failed in a 1947 tryout and was coolly received when it opened on Broadway ten years later. Not until a fine revival by the Circle in the Square♦ in 1968 were its merits fully perceived. The revival featured Mitchell Ryan as Tyrone, W. B. Brydon as Hogan, and Salome Jens as his daughter. A later revival in 1973, directed by José Quintero♦ and starring Jason Robards, Jr.♦ and Colleen Dewhurst,♦ is recognized as the touchstone performances of the work. A 1984 revival could not find an audience. While not quite top rank O'Neill, it remains a powerfully moving drama and is closely linked to the even more autobiographical *Long*

Day's Journey into Night♦ by the importance of the Tyrone figure to both works.

Moon Is Blue, The, a comedy in three acts by F. Hugh Herbert. ♦ Produced by Richard Aldrich,♦ Richard Myers, and others at Henry Miller's Theatre. March 8, 1951. 924 performances.

After meeting on the observation tower of the Empire State Building, Donald Gresham (Barry Nelson♦), a rising architect, and Patty O'Neill (Barbara Bel Geddes♦) saunter off to his apartment where, on the telephone, he attempts to break off his engagement to a girl he had met earlier. This does not sit well with that girl's father, David Slater (Donald Cook), who is something of a cavalier libertine and who quickly seeks to make a conquest of Patty for himself. Nor does all of this sit well with Patty's father, who arrives to lecture the young couple and then give Donald a solid punch in the jaw. The next day the young couple again meet on the observation tower to decide their future.

This small-cast, light-as-air comedy was one of the long-run hits of the 1950s.

Moon of the Caribbees, The, a play in one act by Eugene O'Neill. ♦ Produced by the Provincetown Players♦ at the Provincetown Theatre (N.Y.). December 20, 1918.

At anchor off a West Indies island, the crew of the *S.S. Glencairn* await the arrival of Bella (Jean Robb), with her girls and her smuggled rum. When the girls arrive, one of them, Pearl (Ruth Collins Allen), flits teasingly between Yank (Harry Winston) and the more reticent Smitty (Charles Ellis). Eventually a fight ensues and one sailor is stabbed to death. The women are finally made to leave the ship, and the sailors, alone on the deck, have nothing to do but listen to the lonely singing coming from the island.

One of four plays eventually incorporated in a full bill of one-actors called *S.S. Glencairn,* ♦ it was the least interesting of the group.

Moonchildren, a play in two acts by Michael Weller.♦ Produced by David Merrick♦ and others at the Royale Theatre. February 21, 1972. 16 performances.

A group of college students worry about a cat soon to give birth, plan to participate in a protest demonstration, deal with the police who have been called to their apartment after the youngsters have been seen parading naked before a window, and react to a parent's death.

Originally presented as *Cancer* in London, this

version was first produced at the Arena Stage.♦ After its Broadway failure it was later revived off-Broadway, where it enjoyed a long run. The play makes excessive use of profanity, but remains sympathetically observant and theatrically effective.

MOORE, CARLYLE, see *Unknown Purple, The*

MOORE, GRACE (1901–47) A native of Del Rio, Tenn., the beautiful blonde singer, who is better known for her later work in films and opera, made her Broadway debut in *Hitchy-Koo, 1920*. After appearing in *Up in the Clouds* (1922), she introduced "What'll I Do?" in the 1923 edition of the *Music Box Revue*♦ and "All Alone" in the 1924 edition. Her last appearance was in *The Du Barry* (1933). In 1944 she wrote an autobiography, *You're Only Human Once*.

MOORE, ROBERT (d. 1984) The director, whose place and date of birth have been given variously as Detroit in 1927 or Washington, D.C., in 1929, began his career as an actor in the late 1940s, initially using the name of Brennan Moore. For a decade he acted and directed at numerous regional theatres. His first New York directorial assignment was a 1961 off-Broadway revival of *The Ticket-of-Leave Man.*♦ However, he did not gain major recognition until he staged *The Boys in the Band*♦ (1968). His subsequent successes were *Promises, Promises*♦ (1968), *The Last of the Red Hot Lovers*♦ (1969), *The Gingerbread Lady* (1970), *Lorelei* (1974), *Deathtrap*♦ (1978), *They're Playing Our Song*♦ (1979), and *Woman of the Year* (1981).

MOORE, VICTOR [FREDERICK] (1876–1962) A popular comedian, whose style was a singular amalgam of wistfulness and toughness, he was a pudgy man with a bleating voice. He was born in Hammonton, N.J., and made his stage debut while in his teens. Success did not come until he entered vaudeville in 1901 and created a skit called "Change Your Act," which he performed with his wife, Emma Littlefield. In the act they played a pair of struggling young vaudevillians. Arthur Hopkins♦ recalled, "The timid Moore, who even in those days, was mostly hips, would waddle to the footlights and beseech the spotlight man in the gallery, as though reluctant to remind him, 'Mister, hey, mister, spotlight, you know, mister, you know like we rehearsed—spotlight.' Moore's ingratiating, supplicating smile withered with the spotlight man's loud retort: 'Ah, take her back to the farm and let the sun shine on her.' " Moore continued to perform the act when-

ever major Broadway bookings were not available. Those bookings began when he played Kid Burns in *Forty-five Minutes from Broadway*♦ (1906), introducing the title song. He subsequently appeared in, among others, *The Talk of New York* (1907); *Oh, Kay!*♦ (1926); and *Funny Face*♦ (1927). In 1931 he created the role of Alexander Throttlebottom in *Of Thee I Sing,*♦ playing opposite William Gaxton.♦ Gaxton's suave, brash style complemented Moore's diffident manner and so they were coupled afterwards in *Let 'Em Eat Cake* (1933), *Anything Goes*♦ (1934), *Leave It to Me!*♦ (1938), *Louisiana Purchase*♦ (1940), *Hollywood Pinafore* (1945), and *Nellie Bly* (1946). His last appearances were as Gramps in a 1953 revival of *On Borrowed Time*♦ and as the Starkeeper in a 1957 revival of *Carousel.*♦

MORANT, FANNY (1821–1900) The attractive, if somewhat mouse-faced, actress was born in England and performed at Drury Lane before settling in America in 1853. From 1860 to 1868 she appeared with Wallack's♦ great company, which she apparently left because she was not being assigned choice roles. She then joined Augustin Daly's♦ new ensemble. With the group she played such diverse parts as the scorned Clothilde in *Fernande;* the motherly, matchmaking Mrs. Ten Eyck in *Divorce*♦; Mistress Page; and Mrs. Candour. Despite her seeming success she left Daly's for the Union Square Theatre,♦ where, willingly or no, she became one of its leading character actresses. Odell♦ has written, "No one ever surpassed her grand old ladies of comedy and drama."

MOREHOUSE, WARD (1899–1966) Born in Savannah, Ga., he was a student at North Georgia College when he joined a professional Shakespearean reader on tour. He subsequently worked for several Southern newspapers and for the New York *Tribune* before joining the New York *Sun*. His "Broadway After Dark" column became one of that paper's most popular features, and in 1943 he was appointed its drama critic. He held that position until the paper, by then called the *World-Telegram and Sun,* folded. Afterwards, he was critic and columnist for the Newhouse papers. He was also the author of one successful play, *Gentlemen of the Press* (1928), and of several eminently readable theatrical histories: *Forty-five Minutes Past Eight* (1939); *George M. Cohan—Prince of the American Theatre* (1943); *Matinee Tomorrow* (1949); and *Just the Other Day* (1953).

MORGAN, FRANK [né FRANCIS PHILIP WUPPERMAN] (1890–1949) The son of a well-to-do New Yorker, he studied at the American Academy of Dramatic Arts♦ before making his professional debut in 1914. Despite his suave appearance he excelled at befuddled characters, playing variations of them in, among others, the musical *Rock-a-Bye Baby* (1918), *Seventh Heaven♦* (1922), *The Firebrand♦* (1924), *Gentlemen Prefer Blondes♦* (1926), the musical *Rosalie* (1928), *Topaze* (1930), and the revue *The Band Wagon♦* (1931). His last years were spent in films. Ralph Morgan♦ was his brother.

MORGAN, HELEN (1900–1941) The tiny, seemingly fragile torch singer was born in Danville, Ill., and first called attention to herself in the 1926 revue *Americana.* Although she appeared in several other shows, she is remembered largely for her performances as Julie in *Show Boat♦* (1927 and 1932), in which she introduced "Bill" and "Can't Help Lovin' Dat Man"; and as Addie in *Sweet Adeline♦* (1929), in which she sang "Don't Ever Leave Me" and "Why Was I Born?." Her voice was higher than modern-day torch singers, actually a soprano voice. Chicago's often acerbic Claudia Cassidy♦ said of it, "She had in her voice the note of heartbreak—authentic heartbreak, worth its weight in theater gold."

Biography: *Helen Morgan: Her Life and Legend,* Gilbert Maxwell, New York, 1975.

MORGAN, RALPH [né WUPPERMAN] (1883–1956) Brother of Frank, he was less well known, although he was a more versatile performer. Originally a lawyer, he took to the stage in 1908. Among his early hits were *Fair and Warmer♦* (1915), in which he played the gadabout Jack Wheeler, and *Lightnin'♦* (1918), in which he was John Marvin, the young man helped in his troubles with speculators by an old boozer. His biggest success in the 1920s came as Tony Dorning, who discovers his wife was unfaithful, in *Cobra* (1924). After replacing Tom Powers as Charles Marsden in *Strange Interlude,♦* he spent many years in films. He returned much later to play a number of supporting roles without much success.

Mormons in American Theatre and Drama Unlike other Christian sects the Mormons embraced and encouraged theatre almost from their very beginnings. Even during their precarious sojourn in Illinois their leader, Joseph Smith, promoted a "Fun House" at the Nauvoo settlement. Mormon missionaries frequently accepted work as actors, ignoring the disdain in which performers were held by many clerics. When they established a permanent home in Salt Lake City they quickly erected a Bowery that served both for religious services and as a playhouse. The first play, *The Triumph of Innocence,* was given in 1848. Brigham Young, who had succeeded Smith as head of the church and who had led the great trek from Illinois to Utah, was himself a lover of theatre and continually urged his followers to perform in and even write plays. Young's children were among the regular performers. He oversaw the erection of several later playhouses, including the Salt Lake Theatre in 1862, a theatre long considered the finest between the Mississippi and California. Curiously, though these playhouses offered a wide-ranging dramatic fare, including religious works, Young is said to have been a special advocate of clean, homespun comedy—a genre designed to divert members from their frequently hard, harassed lives.

Yet the Mormons' affection and respect for theatre counted for little among non-Mormon playwrights, actors, and producers, who either shared or pandered to the contempt in which the sect was held by most Americans of the time. In 1858 both Burton♦ and Wallack♦ offered plays centering on the group. Burton's production, *The Mormons: or, Life in Salt Lake City,* by Dr. Thomas Dunn English, took its hero, a New York alderman, to the Mormon center, where he tries to teach them his views of politics and morality, but finds they are better instructors than he. He leaves with a gift of thirteen wives. At Wallack's in *Deseret Deserted: or, The Last Days of Brigham Young,* two New Yorkers head west to reclaim their mates and wind up in the "paradise of Mahomet," which is presided over by Young. Although both plays were comedies or farces they both clearly displayed an underlying distrust or dislike. Thus, the gratuitous connection with polygamous Islam and the seeming wish to be rid of the very much alive Young suggest an iron fist beneath the velvet glove.

The best known work about the Mormons made no attempt at donning a glove. *The Danites: or, The Heart of the Sierras♦* (1877) was written by Alexander Fitzgerald and Joaquin Miller, and was based on one of the latter's stories. It told of a tale of relentless religious vengeance. In reviewing the play the *Times* described the sect as "an organized body [who] combine religion, murder, and rapine in their every-day life"—a view obviously held by many playgoers. When one of the earliest American comic operas, *Deseret: or, The Saint's Difficulties* (1880), took a tongue-in-cheek look at the group, the *Times* wailed that Mormon polygamy was deserving only of scorn and not of laughter. Typical of later plays was *The Mormon Wife* (1901), which portrayed the downfall of a convert when he attempts a reconciliation with his Gentile spouse. Mormons continued to be portrayed as the blackest villains for many years and when this characterization disappeared, they long continued as disreputable, if comic figures or at least as the butt of essentially derogatory jokes. For example, the comic villain in *The Girl from Utah*♦ (1914) was a Mormon who pursued the heroine, determined to add her to his flock of wives. Poking fun at Mormons remained a not uncommon practice in comedies and musicals into the 1930s.

Morning's at Seven, a comedy in three acts by Paul Osborn.♦ Produced by Dwight Deere Wiman♦ at the Longacre Theatre. November 30, 1939. 44 performances.

The Swansons and the Boltons have lived side by side in a small American town for over fifty years. Cora Swanson (Jean Adair) and Ida Bolton (Kate McComb) are sisters, so there is particular reason for excitement when the youngster of the clans, 40-year-old Homer Bolton (John Alexander), decides to marry his 39-year-old sweetheart, Myrtle Brown (Enid Markey), to whom he has been engaged for many years. The excitement, however, is not all to the good. It makes old Carl Bolton (Russell Collins) more aware of his "spells" of introspection; causes Esther Crampton (Effie Shannon♦), Cora and Ida's sister, to have a falling out with her husband David (Herbert Yost); and prompts Cora to ask yet another sister, Aaronetta Gibbs (Dorothy Gish♦), a spinster who has been living with the Swansons, to move out. By the time Homer and Myrtle are ready to settle down, everything has been happily resolved. Aaronetta is to move across the yard and live with the Boltons.

Although the play opened to excellent reviews, it found only a small public. Burns Mantle♦ attributed the failure to the spate of fine comedies which had preceded it that season—*Skylark,*♦ *The Man Who Came to Dinner,*♦ *The Time of Your Life,*♦ *Margin for Error,*♦ and *Life with Father.*♦ A 1980 revival confirmed the play's merits and ran over a year.

MOROSCO, OLIVER [né MITCHELL] (1876–1945) Born in Logan, Utah, but raised in San Francisco, he began his theatrical career there as an acrobat in a troupe headed by Walter Morosco, whose name he adopted professionally. When the elder Morosco became the lessee of several San Francisco theatres, he made his young protégé his manager. On his own he leased the Burbank Theatre in Los Angeles, and within a few years ran no fewer than six Los Angeles playhouses. To keep his theatres lit he began producing shows in 1909. Among his straight play hits were *The Bird of Paradise*♦ (1912), *Peg o' My Heart*♦ (1912), *The Unchastened Woman*♦ (1915), *The Cinderella Man* (1916), *Upstairs and Down*♦ (1916), *The Brat* (1917), *Lombardi, Ltd.*♦ (1917), and *Cappy Ricks* (1919). His musical successes, for which he often collaborated on the book and songs, included *The Tik Tok Man of Oz* (1912); *Canary Cottage* (1917), which gave Eddie Cantor♦ his first big break; and several shows starring Charlotte Greenwood♦: *So Long, Letty* (1916), *Linger Longer, Letty* (1919), and *Letty Pepper* (1922). He also wrote a number of straight plays. Because of his close association with the Shuberts,♦ they joined him in building the Morosco Theatre in New York and opened it in 1917 with his *Canary Cottage.*

Biography: *The Oracle of Broadway,* edited by Helen M. Morosco and Leonard Paul Dugger, Caldwell, Idaho, 1944.

MORRIS, CLARA [née MORRISON] (1848–1925) Born in Toronto, she spent her early impoverished years there and in Cleveland, where John Ellsler gave her her start as a child ballerina. She soon graduated to larger and larger acting roles, often playing opposite the great actors of her time. She next moved on to Cincinnati before being hired by Augustin Daly♦ for his New York company. She won instant acclaim as the betrayed Anne Sylvester in *Man and Wife* (1870); as the Creole, Cora, who gets revenge on the lover who disfigured her, in *Article 47* (1872); and as the neglected, tragic heroine of *Alixe* (1873). Dissatisfied with Daly's ensemble system, which often had the principal actress in one play perform a minor role in the next offering, she left to become a star in her own right. She scored major successes in such emotional roles as the title parts of *Camille*♦ (1874) and *Miss Multon* (1876), but was less well received when she attempted such tragic assignments as Lady Macbeth and Julia in *The Hunchback.*♦ Yet Modjeska recalled her as "a born actress, genuine, admirable, spontaneous, and powerful in her tragic moments, tender and gentle in the touching scenes, and always true to nature." Failing health forced her to appear less frequently after the 1880s, though she occasionally tried new plays, revived old ones, and played in vaudeville. In 1901 she published a rather self-defensive autobiography, *Life on the Stage,* as well as a curious book of reminiscences, *Stage Confidences.*

MORRIS, GEORGE P., see *Briar Cliff*

MORRIS, Owen (1719?–1809) Virtually nothing is known of the early years of this actor, or of the two Mrs. Owen Morrises with whom he performed. He and his first wife made their debuts with the American Company♦ in 1759. He specialized in comic old men, including Oliver Surface and Polonius. Retiring from the stage in 1790, he died at the age of either 84 or 90. The first Mrs. Owen Morris (d. 1767) was our earliest Ophelia and, if we exclude a performance by British troops during the Revolutionary War, our earliest Lady Teazle. The second Mrs. Owen Morris (1753–1826) was a strikingly tall woman, whose acting ability divided the chroniclers of her time. Nevertheless she proved a popular comedienne with the public, much admired for her Lady Teazle and her Beatrice, as well as her Ophelia. Her eccentricities were notorious, and she went to absurd lengths not to expose herself to daylight. Following the advent of Mrs. Merry,♦ her popularity waned rapidly.

MORRIS, William (1861–1936) The Bostonian began his career at the Boston Museum,♦ then performed for Augustin Daly♦ and toured with Modjeska♦ and Mrs. Fiske.♦ He was William Prescott, the bank thief, in *Men and Women*♦ (1890); Reuben Warner, the idealistic plant manager, in *The Lost Paradise*♦ (1891), and Lt. Hawksworth, who must prove he is not a coward, in *The Girl I Left Behind Me*♦ (1893). Subsequently he toured for over a decade as leading man in several shows. In later years he was a prominent character actor, who remained active until the early 1930s.

MORRIS, William [né Wilhelm Moses] (1873–1932) Eulogized as "the dean of the Golden Age of Vaudeville" and as "the greatest independent [vaudeville] showman of our time," he was born in Germany and arrived in this country as a young man. He worked at various odd jobs to help support his family. When his attempt to become a theatre owner failed in the mid-1890s, he became a performer's agent and by 1900 ran the leading booking agency for two-a-day. Although the United Booking Office♦ eventually hurt him, he remained a major figure until the demise of vaudeville. He was considered a gentleman in a profession crowded with vultures. Among his clients were Nora Bayes,♦ the Dolly Sisters,♦ Walter C. Kelly,♦ and Harry Lauder. ♦

MORSE, Robert [Alan] (b. 1931) The perennially impish boy, he was born in Newton, Mass., and made his Broadway debut as Barnaby Tucker in *The Matchmaker*♦ (1955). His subsequent appearances were in musicals: *Say, Darling* (1958), *Take Me Along* (1959), *How To Succeed in Business Without Really Trying*♦ (1961), *Sugar* (1972), *So Long, 174th Street* (1976), and the non-musical *Tru* (1989), for which he won a Tony Award. ♦ He also briefly headed a road company of *Sugar Babies*♦ in 1980.

MORSE, [Henry] Woolson (1858–1897) Born in Charlestown, Mass., he was educated at the best private schools and at the Boston Conservatory. He then trained abroad. Returning home, he wrote the music, and apparently the book and lyrics, for *Cinderella at School,* but was unable to find a producer, so mounted it with his own money. The production came to the attention of Augustin Daly,♦ who brought it to New York in 1881. Before his early death he wrote the scores for seven other Broadway musicals, among them such once popular, if now forgotten, successes as *The Merry Monarch* (1890); *Wang*♦ (1891), his biggest hit; *Dr. Syntax* (1894), a revision of his first musical; and *Lost, Strayed or Stolen* (1896). While some of his songs were widely sung in their day, none remains popular.

MORTON, Hugh, see *McLellan, C. M. S.*

MORTON, James J. (1862–1938) Often called vaudeville's "first master of ceremonies," the lanky, cadaverous-looking comic became celebrated for his comments about other acts on the bill and for the "confidential" information about those acts, which he proffered to the audience. As a result he was soon called upon to host entire bills. His turn also included his dead-pan attempts to popularize patently dreadful songs he claimed to have written. One of his few Broadway appearances was in the revue *The Merry-Go-Round* (1908).

MORTON, Martha (1865–1925) From the late 1880s until shortly before World War I this New York-born playwright produced a steady stream of essentially romantic, comic stage pieces that were almost always welcome by both critics and audiences. She was an admirer of the German school of play-writing and one of her first successes, *His Wife's Father* (1895), was merely a translation of a German success. Among her subsequent, more original works were *The Fool of Fortune* (1896), in which a failing Wall Street broker suddenly strikes it rich; *A Bachelor's Romance* (1897), telling of a middle-aged city editor who finds love in the country; and *Her Lord and Master* (1902), which pitted a free-spirited American wife against her staid

English husband. She was the sister of Michael Morton. ◆

MORTON, MICHAEL (1864–1931) Brother of Martha Morton, ◆ he was born in England but spent most of his earliest years in America. After going back to England to finish his education, he returned to New York in the 1880s. He soon found work as an actor at Daniel Frohman's ◆ Madison Square Theatre. ◆ He began his prolific career as playwright in 1897 when Frohman mounted his *Miss Francis of Yale,* a farce in which a man is believed to be a woman masquerading as a man. Morton himself staged the play, but it was a failure. He next adapted a German play for William H. Crane ◆ as *A Rich Man's Son* (1899), then dramatized F. Hopkinson Smith's novel, *Caleb West* (1900). In 1902 he moved permanently to London, although he returned on occasion to direct American versions of his London successes.

Moscow Art Theatre Founded in 1898 by Stanislavsky ◆ and Nemirovich-Danchenko, its visit to America during the 1922–23 season, under the aegis of F. Ray Comstock ◆ and Morris Gest, ◆ created an excitement rarely paralleled in American theatre annals. Its repertoy consisted of Tolstoy's *Tsar Fyodor Ivanovitch,* Gorky's *The Lower Depths,* Chekhov's *The Cherry Orchard* and *The Three Sisters,* and Turgenieff's *The Lady from the Provinces,* coupled with excerpts from Dostoevski's *The Brothers Karamazoff.* Additional plays, including *Uncle Vanya,* were offered the next season. The troupe's remarkable ensemble playing according to one critic raised "spiritual realism" to new heights of perfection. Its example also gave rise to another in the many recurrent movements to establish a permanent repertory company in America and played no small part in the early impetus behind the founding of the Civic Repertory Theatre. ◆ Perhaps more importantly and enduringly, these tours gave most American playgoers their first exposure to the works of Chekhov. The company again visited America in 1965, offering *The Cherry Orchard, The Three Sisters,* a dramatization of Gogol's *Dead Souls,* and a piece of political propaganda, *Kremlin Chimes.* The troupe was still admired for its realism and fine ensemble playing, but political considerations tempered the response.

MOSEL, [GEORGE AULT, JR.] TAD (b. 1922) A native of Steubenville, Ohio, he studied at Amherst, Yale School of Drama, ◆ and Columbia. His *All the Way Home* ◆ (1960), a dramatization of James

Agee's novel *A Death in the Family,* earned him both the Pulitzer Prize ◆ and the New York Drama Critics Circle Award. ◆ Eighteen years later he collaborated with Gertrude Macy on *Leading Lady,* the definitive biography of Katharine Cornell. ◆

MOSES, MONTROSE J[ONAS] (1878–1934) A critic and scholar of world drama, the native New Yorker wrote numerous still valuable studies of American theatre. These works include *Famous Actor-Families in America* (1906); *The American Dramatist* (1910); *Representative Plays by American Dramatists* (3 vols.: 1918–25); *The Fabulous Forrest* (1929); and, with John Mason Brown, ◆ *The American Theatre as Seen By Its Critics* (1934).

MOSES, THOMAS G[IBBS] (1856–1934) Possibly the most prolific and important of Midwestern set designers in the late 19th and early 20th century, he was born in Liverpool, England, on the ship of his father, an American sea captain. In his teens he moved to Chicago and began painting scenery at the McVicker Theatre. About the same time he also enrolled at the Chicago Art Institute for further training. In 1880 he joined the newly formed Sosman and Landis Scene Painting Studio, which eventually became the Midwest's leading set builders and of which he was appointed president in 1915. He designed scenery for hundreds of productions, not only in Chicago but for Modjeska ◆ in California and occasional New York productions as well. His forte was said to be "freely rendered rugged landscapes and woodland scenes." Unfortunately, the autobiography on which he was known to have worked for many years, *Sixty Years Back of the Curtain Line,* has yet to be published.

Most Happy Fella, The, a musical in three acts by Frank Loesser. ◆ Produced by Kermit Bloomgarden ◆ and Lynn Loesser at the Imperial Theatre. May 3, 1956. 676 performances.

Rosabella (Jo Sullivan) comes to the Napa Valley expecting to marry a handsome young man who has sent her his picture and proposed by mail. She is certain that she has at last found "Somebody, Somewhere" to really love her. But she soon discovers the handsome man, Joe (Art Lund), is merely a hired hand, and that the man who proposed is actually an aging Italian vintner, Tony (Robert Weede). He had sent her Joe's picture, fearing one of himself would have disheartened her. He believes that she will quickly become reconciled and make him "The Most Happy Fella" in all of the valley. The shock, however, drives Rosabella into

Joe's arms. Eventually she realizes that Tony is an honorable, loving man. Bit by bit, she and Tony admit that they are "Happy To Make Your Acquaintance." When he offers to accept not only her but the baby she is now pregnant with, she comes to love him.

Other principal songs: Big 'D' · Standing on the Corner

Based on Sidney Howard's *They Knew What They Wanted,* ♦ the musical struck many critics as a not altogether successful amalgam of musical play, musical comedy, and opera. The most operatic music was given to Tony; Rosabella and Joe were given songs typical of modern operetta or musical play; while the lighter songs, such as "Big 'D'," were assigned to the secondary, comic roles. Since the show offered something for everyone, it succeeded. A fine 1979 revival failed.

MOSTEL, [Samuel Joel] Zero (1915–77) The hefty, cocky comedian was born in New York where he studied art at New York University. His earliest professional performances were given in small Greenwich Village night clubs. Afterwards he played in several Broadway shows before calling attention to himself as Leopold Bloom in an off-Broadway♦ production of *Ulysses in Nighttown* (1958). He consolidated his reputation with his playing of John, the clerk who turns into a wild animal, in *Rhinoceros* (1961). Moving to musicals, he starred in *A Funny Thing Happened on the Way to the Forum*♦ (1962) and *Fiddler on the Roof*♦ (1964). His performance in the latter as Tevye, the poor Jew who is determined to marry off his daughters, was generally recognized as the high point of his career, and he returned to it for several revivals. *Newsweek* wrote that from his performance "there radiates so supple, luminous, and wide a light as to transform the stage into a scene of high, compelling art. When he sings 'If I were a rich man . . .' he follows these words with a sighing, dream-tasting spiral of Yiddish scat-syllables which become the anthem of yearning for poor men everywhere." He was on tryout tour with a new play at the time of his death.

Motley The name of a firm of costume designers founded in the early 1930s in London by Audrey Sophia Harris, Margaret F. Harris, and Elizabeth Montgomery. The company designed clothes for West End shows for a decade before beginning to offer their work to Americans in 1941. Among the plays which featured their costume designs were *A Bell for Adano*♦ (1944), *Anne of the Thousand Days*♦ (1948), *South Pacific*♦ (1949), *Can-Can*♦ (1953), *Peter Pan*♦ (1954), *Middle of the Night*♦ (1956), *The Most Happy Fella*♦ (1956), and *Long Day's Journey into Night*♦ (1956).

MOULAN, Frank (1875–1939) The New York-born comedian had worked with several prominent comic opera companies before scoring a huge success and becoming a star in *The Sultan of Sulu*♦ (1902). He later played in such musicals as *The Grand Mogul* (1907), *The Arcadians* (1910), *The Siren* (1911), *The Count of Luxembourg* (1912), *Her Regiment* (1917), and *Just Because* (1922). In after years he was popular in the Gilbert♦ and Sullivan♦ repertory.

Mourning Becomes Electra, a trilogy by Eugene O'Neill.♦ Produced by the Theatre Guild♦ at the Guild Theatre. October 26, 1931. 157 performances.

Homecoming—While her husband, Brigadier-General Ezra Mannon (Lee Baker), is away fighting in the Civil War, Christine (Alla Nazimova♦) has an affair with his long-disowned cousin, born out of wedlock, Captain Adam Brant (Thomas Chalmers). Christine's daughter, Lavinia (Alice Brady♦), who hates her mother and secretly loves Brant, suspects the truth and wheedles a confession from him. The Mannons' son, Orin, has always been more favored by his mother than his father has been. When the General returns home he reveals his resentment of this mother-and-son attachment. The revelation, as well as Christine's affair with Brant, leads Christine to poison her husband. She attempts to make the death look natural, but Lavinia discovers the poison. She pleads to her beloved dead father, "Don't leave me alone! Come back to me! Tell me what to do!"

The Hunted—When Orin (Earle Larimore♦) returns from the war, Lavinia describes what has happened and convinces her brother that they must be revenged on their mother. They follow Christine to a rendezvous she has with Brant. When Christine departs, Orin kills Brant. Christine, on learning of Brant's death, commits suicide.

The Haunted—A year later Orin is plagued with a growing sense of guilt. He has come to blame himself for all the family deaths, and not even a long trip with Lavinia has assuaged his doubt or grief. Indeed, he has come to suspect that the love he had for his mother was not entirely natural and that it has been transferred to his sister. Unable to conciliate the furies that hound him, he kills himself. Lavinia once again must don her mourning. She orders the house shut up, knowing she will live there alone for the rest of her life. "It takes the Mannons to punish themselves for being born," she concludes.

O'Neill's five-hour resetting of the classic *Oresteia* was performed in a single evening, with a dinner intermission between the first and second plays. Robert Benchley, ♦ writing in the *New Yorker,* called it "a hundred times better than *Electra* because O'Neill has a God-given inheritance of melodramatic sense." It was revived in 1971 by the American Shakespeare Festival♦ and in 1972 by the Circle in the Square. ♦

MOWATT, ANNA CORA [née OGDEN] (1819–70) The daughter of a prosperous New York merchant, she was born in France and came to live in America when she was seven. At fifteen she was married to a well-known lawyer. Her often poor health restricted her to her rooms, where she took to writing to pass the time. Besides writing poetry and novels, she wrote several unproduced plays. Her first play to see the Broadway stage was the one by which she is remembered, *Fashion*♦ (1845), centering on the social pretensions of a parvenu. The success of the piece allowed her to recruit her strength, although she was always to claim that mesmerism permitted her to master her physical problems. She took advantage of her newfound health and fame to test her skills at acting. Her debut was as Pauline in *The Lady of Lyons*♦ in June 1845. Her success was such that she spent the next two seasons touring, the second season with E. L. Davenport♦ as her leading man. Among her roles were Mrs. Haller in *The Stranger,*♦ Beatrice in *Much Ado About Nothing,*♦ Lady Teazle, and Gertrude in her own *Fashion.* Edgar Allan Poe♦ wrote of the auburn-haired actress, "Her figure is slight—even fragile—but eminently graceful. Her face is a remarkably fine one, and of that precise character best adapted to the stage . . . The eyes are grey, brilliant and expressive . . . The mouth is somewhat large with brilliant and even teeth and flexible lips capable of the most effective variations of expression . . . Her manner on the stage is distinguished by an ease and self-possession . . . Her voice is rich and voluminous." Her second play to be produced was *Armand* (1847), in which the determined hero wins his betrothed away from the French king who covets her. Mr. Mowatt died while touring with his wife in England in 1851. She returned to America to attempt another tour, but her health gave out. She made her farewell at Niblo's Garden♦ in 1854. Three days later she remarried. Her last decade was spent largely in England. Although *Fashion* often has been revived and remains one of the best 19th-

century American comedies, Mrs. Mowatt's real importance may rest with the respectability that she, as a gentlewoman, gave to acting as a profession.

Autobiography: *Autobiography of an Actress; or, Eight Years on the Stage,* Boston, 1854.

Mr. Wilkinson's Widows, a farce in three acts by William Gillette. ♦ Produced at Proctor's 23rd Street Theatre. March 30, 1891. 140 performances.

Mrs. Dickerson (Henrietta Crosman♦) and Mrs. Perrin (Louise Thorndyke Boucicault) are two recently remarried widows who live in the same apartment house and strike up a friendship, which leads to the horrifying discovery that both had the very same husband and that both had married him on the very same day. When Major P. Ferguson Mallory (Thomas Burns) enters the picture to try to clear up the problem, he only succeeds in adding to the confusion.

Based on Alexandre Bisson's *Feu Toupinel,* Gillette's Americanization laundered out many of the more risqué aspects of the original.

Mrs. Bumpstead-Leigh, a comedy in three acts by Harry James Smith. ♦ Produced by Harrison Grey Fiske♦ at the Lyceum Theatre. ♦ April 3, 1911. 64 performances.

Mrs. Bumpstead-Leigh (Mrs. Fiske♦) returns from a long sojourn in England to continue her triumphant social rise. What many of her fawning friends do not know is that she is an imposter, none other than Della Sales of Missionary Loop, Indiana, and the daughter of a man who made his fortune selling quack medicines. She travels with her mother, who is now called Mrs. de Salle (Florine Arnold), and her sister, Viola (Kathlene MacDonell), for whom she is determined to make a proper match. Her world is threatened by the appearance of bumptious Peter Swallow (Henry E. Dixey♦), who had been her suitor years before. But Mrs. Bumpstead-Leigh had not come all this way for nothing. She convinces Peter he is mistaken, and finds the right man for Viola.

This delightfully contrived farce was one of the versatile Mrs. Fiske's biggest successes.

Mrs. Leffingwell's Boots, a comedy in three acts by Augustus Thomas. ♦ Produced by Charles Frohman♦ at the Savoy Theatre. January 11, 1905. 123 performances.

Mrs. Leffingwell (Margaret Illington♦) is a perfectly respectable married woman, and Walter Corbin (William Courtenay♦) is a proper young man-about-town, who loves the equally decorous Mabel

Ainslee (Fay Davis). So imagine the shock waves that rumble through society when Mrs. Leffingwell's quilted blue silk boots are discovered in Corbin's rooms. No one is more shocked than the explosively jealous Mr. Leffingwell (Louis Payne). Matters look dark for the lady and even darker for young Corbin, until it is learned that Mabel's demented brother stole the boots and planted them in the apartment.

This gay, French-like farce was considered too risqué by some of New York's stodgier critics, but the public adored it.

Mrs. Wiggs of the Cabbage Patch, a play in three acts by Anne Crawford Flexner. Produced by Liebler and Co.♦ at the Savoy Theatre. September 3, 1904. 150 performances.

Mrs. Wiggs (Madge Carr Cook) is an eternally optimistic country lady who loves nothing better than helping others. She helps Bob (Thurston Hall♦), a newspaper editor, persuade Lucy (Nora Shelby) to marry him, though it means Lucy must leave her beloved home and head for the big city. She helps her son Billy (Argyle Campbell) in his courtship of the orphaned Lovey Mary (Mabel Taliaferro♦). She even helps her boozy, roving husband, Mr. Wiggs (Oscar Eagle) when he suddenly reappears in her life.

The Kentucky-born Mrs. Flexner (1874–1955) saw a half-dozen more of her plays produced on Broadway between 1901 and 1936, but none was as popular as this, which she drew from the stories of Alice Hegan Rice. The play had toured successfully for a year before reaching New York and continued to tour for many years thereafter. Mrs. Cook (1856–1933), who was born in England but spent most of her acting career here, was long identified with this role. She was the mother of Eleanor Robson.♦

Much Ado About Nothing When first acted at the Southwark Theatre♦ in 1789 Shakespeare's comedy featured the younger Hallam♦ as Benedick and Mrs. Morris as Beatrice. The play proved especially congenial to Victorian temperaments, so Benedick and Beatrice found their way into the repertory of many leading performers of the era. J. W. Wallack♦ used Benedick for his farewell performance in 1859. Other noted artists who appeared in major revivals were Charles and Ellen Kean,♦ Henry Irving♦ and Ellen Terry,♦ and E. H. Sothern♦ and Julia Marlowe.♦ Ada Rehan♦ was also admired for her Beatrice, although her Benedick, Charles Richman,♦ received meager praise. Numbered among the better 20th-century revivals, when the piece has lost some favor, were a 1959 rendering with John

Gielgud♦ and Margaret Leighton,♦ and a 1972 New York Shakespeare Festival♦ production, set in pre-World War I America.

Mulatto, a play in two acts by Langston Hughes. Produced at the Vanderbilt Theatre. October 24, 1935. 373 performances.

Colonel Thomas Norwood (Stuart Beebe) is a rich Georgia plantation owner who has fathered several children by his black housekeeper, Cora Lewis (Rose McClendon♦). Two of these mulatto children, Sally (Jeanne Greene) and Robert (Hurst Amyx), seem exceptional enough that they are sent north to be educated. Sally returns home and is seduced by Norwood's vicious overseer, Talbot (John Boyd). Robert demands to be treated as a white, and when his father threatens to shoot him, he strangles Norwood. A lynch mob is thwarted by Robert's suicide.

Although the play was criticized as diffuse and contrived, its basic drama and Rose McClendon's fine performance (her last) gave the work a substantial run.

[James] Langston Hughes (1902–67) wrote several other plays, none of which was successful. Apart from this drama his best work for Broadway was his lyrics for Kurt Weill's♦ musicalization of *Street Scene.*♦

Mulligan Guards' Ball, The, a play with music in two acts. Book and lyrics by Edward Harrigan.♦ Music by David Braham.♦ Produced by Harrigan and Tony Hart♦ at the Theatre Comique. January 13, 1879. 138 performances.

The Mulligan Guards, led by Dan Mulligan (Harrigan), plan a ball. But Dan is also concerned about the romance between his son Tommy (Hart) and Katy Lochmuller (Nellie Jones). Dan does not approve of the Irish marrying Germans, while Dan's wife, Cordelia (Annie Yeamans♦), detests Katy's mother. The Guards discover a black organization, the Skidmore Guards, has booked the same ballroom. The blacks are forced to take the second floor facilities. But they stomp so wildly the floor gives way, and they come tumbling down upon the Irish. In the confusion Tommy and Katy elope.

Principal songs: The Babies on Our Block · The Mulligan Guard

Originally conceived as a short vaudeville sketch, the piece was enlarged on several occasions and exists in several versions. It is sometimes called simply *The Mulligan Guard.* Its arrival in the 1878–79 season, along with *H.M.S. Pinafore*♦ and *The*

Brook, ♦ signaled the beginnings of modern musical theatre in America.

Mummenschanz, see *Pantomime*

MUNFORD, COLONEL ROBERT (1730?–1784) A Virginia planter who was a major in the Revolutionary War and served as a member of the state's House of Burgesses, he was the author of two intriguing plays which were apparently never produced in his lifetime, but were later published by his son. *The Candidates* (written 1770?) was a satire on local election methods and was set rather drolly at a race course. The minor character of Ralpho is said to be the earliest depiction of a black in American drama. *The Patriots* (written 1775?) attempted a balanced, essentially pacifist view, decrying the extremism of both Torys and Whigs. Quinn ♦ believed that the inclusion of a prologue in the printed text suggested that some sort of production had been offered.

MUNI, PAUL [né FREDERICH WEISENFREUND] (1895–1967) Born in Austria but raised in Chicago, he made his stage debut in Yiddish theatre in 1908. His first work on professional English-speaking stages came in 1926. However, he did not gain prominence until 1931 when he played George Simon, the Jewish lawyer whose world seems to fall apart, in *Counsellor-at-Law.* ♦ In 1939 he portrayed King McCloud, the wartime deserter who attempts to atone for his cowardice, in *Key Largo.* ♦ His last important appearance was as Henry Drummond, the attorney who defends a man accused of teaching evolution, in *Inherit the Wind* ♦ (1955). Muni was a superb technician, although some playgoers felt he wore his technique on his sleeve. He also enjoyed a distinguished career in Hollywood, where he won two Oscars.

    Biography: *Actor: The Life and Times of Paul Muni,* Jerome Lawrence, New York, 1974.

Murder in the Cathedral T. S. Eliot's ♦ 1935 drama about the martyrdom of Thomas à Becket was first presented in America that same year at Yale. The Federal Theatre Project ♦ offered it to New York in 1936. Since then it has remained popular with collegiate and other groups, who often mount it in suitable churches rather than in regular theatres.

MURDOCH, FRANK H. [né HITCHCOCK] (1843–72) Son of a sister of James E. Murdoch, ♦ whose name he adopted for stage purposes, he began acting and writing while still in his teens. His first play, *The Keeper of Lighthouse Cliff* (also called simply *Light House Cliff*), was apparently produced in California in the 1870s and may have influenced James A. Herne's ♦ *Shore Acres.* ♦ His most famous play was *Davy Crockett,* ♦ which he wrote as a vehicle for Frank Mayo. ♦ At the time of its production he was too ill to attend to revisions and by the time New York first saw it in June 1873, seven months after his death, it had been substantially revised by Mayo. Another play produced immediately before his death was his satire on drama critics, *Bohemia; or, The Lottery of Art* (1872). Its Philadelphia premiere was a failure, as was the Boston production of his posthumously mounted sentimental comedy *Only a Jew* (1873). Clara Morris ♦ observed, "He had good height, a good figure, and an air of gentle breeding; otherwise he was unattractive," adding that his sensitivity about his looks often led to petulance.

MURDOCH, JAMES E[DWARD] (1811?–93) The son of a prominent Philadelphia family, he is variously supposed to have been born in 1811, 1812, and 1813. He made his debut at the Arch Street Theatre ♦ in 1829, playing Frederick in *Lovers' Vows.* He quickly attained a national reputation, even though he performed far more frequently in his native city than elsewhere. As the result of accidental arsenic poisoning in 1832, which led to recurring problems, he retired temporarily from the stage on several occasions—in 1842, in 1861, and in 1879—but always returned within a few seasons and did not give his final performances until 1889. He won acclaim for his Claude Melnotte in *The Lady of Lyons* ♦ and his Hamlet. Many contemporaries considered his Hamlet the finest on the American stage until the advent of Edwin Booth. ♦ The *Spirit of the Times* ♦ wrote of his Dane, "The pervading quality of the performance was grace and propriety of conception and delivery: relieved by electrical flashes on passages of a more elevated character." However, he was even more admired as a comedian. Among his best comic interpretations were Rover (in *Wild Oats*), Charles Surface, Orlando, and Benedick. Playgoers and critics both praised his superb elocution and unostentatious manliness. In 1880 he published a semi-autobiographical collection of recollections, *The Stage.*

MURDOCK, JOHN, see *Triumphs of Love, The*

MURRAY, J. HAROLD (1891–1940) A native of South Berwick, Maine, he was a professional singer from childhood, and had appeared in vaudeville before making his Broadway debut in *The Passing Show of 1921.* ♦ Among his subsequent appearances were those in *Caroline* (1923); *China Rose* (1924); *Captain Jinks* (1925); *Castles in the Air* (1926); *Rio Rita* ♦ (1927), in which he introduced "The Rangers' Song" and the title number; *East Wind* (1931); *Face the Music* (1932), in which he sang "Let's Have Another Cup o' Coffee" and "Soft Lights and Sweet Music"; and *Thumbs Up!* (1934), in which he sang "Autumn in New York." He has been described as a "sandy-haired, strong-featured baritone."

MURRAY, JOHN, see *Room Service*

MURRAY, WALTER (fl. mid-18th century) An actor-manager who, with his partner Thomas Kean, ♦ led a band of traveling players around the Eastern seaboard in the early 1750s. At one time their aggregation was known as the Virginia Company of Comedians. Their repertory consisted entirely of the English plays then most popular in London.

Museum of Costume Art Founded in 1937 by Irene Lewisohn, Aline Bernstein, ♦ and Lee Simonson ♦ to house their collections of costumes and their libraries on costume design, the museum grew and moved several times before being absorbed in 1946 by the Metropolitan Museum of Art.

Music Box Revues A series of revues mounted by Sam H. Harris ♦ and Irving Berlin ♦ at their new Music Box Theatre in 1921, 1922, 1923, and 1924. Among the Berlin hits to emerge from the series were "All Alone," "Crinoline Days," "Everybody Step," "Lady of the Evening," and "What'll I Do?" as well as the series' theme song, "Say It with Music." The series featured elaborate sets and costumes on a Ziegfeldian order but also intimate musical numbers and sketches, thus forming a bridge between the waning extravaganzas and the smaller, more intellectually witty revues of the late 1920s and 1930s. Among its famous comic moments were two from the 1923–24 edition, Robert Benchley's ♦ "Treasurer's Report" and George S. Kaufman's ♦ "If Men Played Cards as Women Do."

Music in the Air, an operetta in two acts. Book and lyrics by Oscar Hammerstein II. ♦ Music by Jerome Kern. ♦ Produced at the Alvin Theatre. November 8, 1932. 342 performances.

When Karl Reder (Walter Slezak ♦) writes a song called "I've Told Ev'ry Little Star," he and his fellow Bavarian villagers trek to Munich to have it published. Although "There's a Hill Beyond a Hill," the long march does not daunt them. In Munich, Karl is pursued by a flirtatious prima donna, Frieda Hatzfeld (Natalie Hall ♦), while a composer, Bruno Mahler (Tullio Carminati ♦), falls in love with Karl's sweetheart, Sieglinde (Katherine Carrington). Bruno writes an operetta especially for Sieglinde, including a song called "One More Dance," but she is only happy "When Spring Is in the Air." Her indifference fuels Bruno's ardor, and he confesses to her that no matter what sort of melody he creates, "The Song Is You." The romances and high hopes come to naught, so Karl, Sieglinde, and the villagers head home, concluding "We Belong Together."

Like *The Cat and the Fiddle* ♦ before it, the musical was Kern's attempt to write a modern operetta without resorting to excessive European mannerisms. Many critics consider this his finest, most unified work, citing not only the beauty of the melodies but their prevailing appropriateness of tone. A 1951 revival failed.

Music Man, The, a musical in two acts by Meredith Willson. ♦ Produced by Kermit Bloomgarden ♦ and others at the Majestic Theatre. December 19, 1957. 1,375 performances.

Harold Hill (Robert Preston ♦) is a "con" man who specializes in selling band instruments and the promise of music lessons to small town schools, then disappearing before the instruments can arrive. But when he comes to River City, he comes up against Marion Paroo (Barbara Cook ♦), the town librarian, who has a sharp eye for swindlers. She threatens to unmask him, so Harold is forced to stay on to await the arrival of the instruments and give lessons, although he cannot read a note of music. One result is a horribly cacophonous band concert—which the children's doting parents think masterful. A second result is that Harold and Marion fall in love.

Principal songs: Goodnight, My Someone · Seventy-Six Trombones · Till There Was You · Trouble

Louis Kronenberger ♦ wrote, "If *The Music Man* was not cream, but only nice fresh half-and-half, it did catch the jubilant old-time energy of a small-town jamboree." The musical was drawn from Willson's recollections of his Iowa boyhood. For this apple-pie American work Willson employed numerous clever devices. He used the same basic melody in Hill's rousing "Seventy-Six Trombones" and Marion's tender "Goodnight, My Someone" to suggest a common bond. "Rock Island" mimicked the rhythm of a moving train, while the tongue-in-cheek sermonizing of "Trouble" was turned into a modern-day patter song.

Music Master, The, a play in three acts by Charles Klein.♦ Produced by David Belasco♦ at the Belasco Theatre. September 26, 1904. 627 performances.

For sixteen years, a once successful Viennese conductor, Anton von Barwig (David Warfield♦), has searched for his daughter, who was taken from him by his wife when she deserted him for an American bounder. The search has taken him to New York, where he struggles to make a living by teaching music. His reputation as a teacher brings to his door young society girls, one of whom is Helen Stanton (Minnie Dupree♦). In time von Barwig comes to realize that Helen is his long-lost child, but when he confronts her father, Henry A. Stanton (Campbell Golan), Stanton warns him that exposing the truth would destroy Helen's chances of marrying the wealthy Beverly Cruger (J. Carrington Yates). Reluctantly von Barwig prepares to leave for Vienna, but Helen has discovered who he is and welcomes him into her home.

Most critics dismissed the work as shallow and excessively sentimental. Arthur Hornblow♦ wrote in *Theatre Magazine,*♦ "In the hands of another stage manager [read producer] and with another actor as the music master, we might have had theatricalism and unreality in place of genuineness of character and emotion." Warfield played the role for three years and returned to it at intervals as late as 1916.

My Fair Lady, an operetta in two acts. Book and lyrics by Alan Jay Lerner.♦ Music by Frederick Loewe.♦ Produced by Herman Levin♦ at the Mark Hellinger Theatre. March 15, 1956. 2,717 performances.

Coming from a performance at Covent Garden, Professor Henry Higgins (Rex Harrison♦) meets a fellow scholar, Colonel Pickering (Robert Coote), and a somewhat raucous Cockney flower girl, Liza Doolittle (Julie Andrews♦). Higgins casually mentions to Pickering that given a little time he could turn a flower girl into a lady, so when Liza appears later at his residence asking him to make good on his boast, Higgins accepts Pickering's wager on the affair. It is a long, hard struggle, but by the time Liza can properly enunciate "The Rain in Spain" and Higgins takes her to Ascot, her pronunciation is perfect—even if her conversation is not. Later she is successfully passed off as a lady at a ball, and she is so pleased that she confesses, "I Could Have Danced All Night." At one point Higgins must bribe Liza's father, Alfred P. Doolittle (Stanley Holloway), to stay out of the girl's life. With his newfound wealth Doolittle recognizes that he must subscribe to middle class morality by marrying, so he urges his friends to "Get Me to the Church on Time." But Higgins has no objections to rich, lovesick Freddy Eynsford-Hill (John Michael King) courting Liza. So lovesick is Freddy he is happy merely to be "On the Street Where You Live." Nevertheless, Liza recognizes she is too intelligent for the charming but vacuous young man, so casts her lot with the reluctant Higgins, who is appalled but admits "I've Grown Accustomed to Her Face." When Liza returns Higgins can only respond, "Where the devil are my slippers?"

Considered by many the finest of all American musicals, this show was a triumph not only for its performers and writers, but for its director, Moss Hart,♦ its set designer, Oliver Smith,♦ and its costume designer, Cecil Beaton.♦ Unlike *The Chocolate Soldier,* an earlier musicalization of Shaw's♦ *Arms and the Man,* this lyric version of *Pygmalion*♦ managed to retain all of Shaw's irreverence, wit, and intellectuality while maintaining an unerring sense of style and tone in its own contributions. Its most recent revival was in 1981, with Harrison and Cathleen Nesbitt♦ (as Mrs. Higgins) re-creating their original roles.

My Heart's in the Highlands, a play, performed without intermission, by William Saroyan.♦ Produced by the Group Theatre♦ at the Guild Theatre. April 13, 1939. 44 performances.

Ben Alexander (Philip Loeb), a failed poet, lives from hand-to-mouth with his son Johnny (Sidney Lumet) and his mother-in-law (Hester Sondergaard), who speaks no English. Although they are liked by many of their neighbors and are visited by Jasper MacGregor (Art Smith), an old tragedian who plays music on a golden bugle, they are eventually forced to abandon their humble shack and move on.

Originally slated for only five performances, the play managed a longer run, although most critics were baffled by it.

My Maryland, see *Barbara Frietchie*

My Partner, a play in four acts by Bartley Campbell.♦ Produced at the Union Square Theatre.♦ September 16, 1879. 39 performances.

Although their characters are totally disparate, warm, idealistic Joe Saunders (Louis Aldrich♦) and cynical, self-serving Ned Singleton (Henry Crisp) are the closest of friends. Both love Mary Brandon (Maude Granger♦). When Ned violates Mary, Joe demands that Ned marry her. But Ned is murdered by Josiah Scragg (J. W. Hague), who makes it seem that Joe is the killer. Joe is tried and convicted. Before he is to be executed he and Mary agree to wed. Joe is saved from the gallows when Wing Lee (Charles T. Parsloe♦) discovers Scragg's blood-stained cuff.

Set in California as civilization was brushing away gold rush crudities, the play was not as popular with the public as Campbell's *The White Slave*. ♦ Critics, however, were in virtual agreement that this was his best work. The *Tribune* noted, "It is a very strong piece. The effort has been made to deal with elemental passions and real persons, and to paint a picture of tragedy and heroism upon the tumultuous background of a turbulent semi-civilization; and the object has been accomplished with startling force and unusual, if not even skill . . . It is a better piece of its class than has hitherto been produced in America." The play held first class stages for nearly a decade.

My Sister Eileen, a comedy in three acts by Joseph A. Fields♦ and Jerome Chodorov. ♦ Produced by Max Gordon♦ at the Biltmore Theatre. December 26, 1940. 864 performances.

Two Ohio sisters, Ruth (Shirley Booth♦) and Eileen (Jo Ann Sayers) Sherwood, take a basement apartment in Greenwich Village. The acerbic Ruth is determined to become a famous writer, while her sweeter sister seeks to become an actress. Their apartment, which is constantly jolted by blasts from subway construction, is invaded by "The Wreck" (Gordon Jones), an ex-football player fleeing his mistress's mother. For a time Eileen, though she quickly has dozens of suitors, cannot find work, and Ruth's attempts to persuade Robert Baker (William Post, Jr.), editor of "Manhatter" magazine, to publish her work come to naught. Finally Chick Clark (Bruce MacFarlane), a newspaper reporter, gets Ruth an assignment welcoming a Brazilian naval ship. Ruth invites the sailors home, where a fight ensues, the police arrive, and Eileen punches a policeman. The melee lands Eileen on the front page and also gets her an acting job. Ruth and Baker fall in love.

Based on Ruth McKenney's *New Yorker* stories, the play was hailed by the *Post* as "the giddiest delight to be seen here-abouts since *You Can't Take It with You.*" The comedy served as the basis for the successful musical *Wonderful Town*. ♦

MYERS, RICHARD [SON] (1901–77) A Philadelphian, between 1925 and 1934 he contributed songs or whole scores to a dozen Broadway musicals, including the 1925 and 1926 editions of the *Greenwich Village Follies*♦ and the 1934 edition of the *Ziegfeld Follies*. ♦ He also wrote incidental music for several dramas. Subsequently he turned to producing, and in association with others mounted such offerings as *Margin for Error*♦ (1939); *Goodbye, My Fancy*♦ (1948); 1949 and 1950 revivals of *Caesar and Cleopatra*♦ and *The Devil's Disciple*♦ respectively; *The Moon Is Blue*♦ (1951); *The Love of Four Colonels* (1953); and *Hotel Paradiso* (1957).

N

NASH, MARY (1885–1976) A native of Troy, N.Y., she studied at the American Academy of Dramatic Arts♦ before making her debut in a 1904 musical. From 1905 through 1907 she played important supporting roles opposite Ethel Barrymore♦ at the Empire.♦ She scored major successes as Cecily Rand, who unknowingly marries her own brother, in *The City*♦ (1909) and as Wanda Kelly, the alert telephone operator whose discretion saves the hero, in *The Woman*♦ (1911). Another important assignment was as Marcelle, the hero's partner in degradation, in *The Man Who Came Back*♦ (1916). She continued in leading assignments throughout the 1920s, in such plays as *Captain Applejack* (1921), *The Lady* (1923), and *A Lady's Virtue* (1925), and was Henrietta in a 1926 revival of *The Two Orphans.*♦ Her sister, Florence (1888–1950), was also a popular performer.

NASH, N. RICHARD, see *Rainmaker, The*

NATHAN, GEORGE JEAN (1882–1958) Probably the most famous and respected drama critic of his day, he was born in Fort Wayne, Ind., and educated at Cornell and the University of Bologna. His interest in theatre began while he was still a youngster, and he later claimed to have written plays at the age of eleven. His uncle, the critic and playwright Charles Frederic Nirdlinger, obtained a post for him on the New York *Herald* in 1905, but Nathan soon quit to become critic for two magazines, *Outing* and *The Bohemian.* Two years later he moved to *The Smart Set,* where his name was first associated with that of H. L. Mencken,♦ the pair becoming its co-editors in 1914. From the start, Nathan railed against the shallowness and hollowness of the theatre of his day. Although the battle for a drama of ideas and for the plays of such men as Ibsen,♦ Strindberg,♦ and Shaw♦ had already been joined, he quickly became an eloquent voice in the fray. Recognizing that foreign works with foreign settings could only occasionally have widespread appeal, he turned his attention to native writers. He was the first important critic to extol the genius of Eugene O'Neill♦ and published O'Neill's early work in *The Smart Set.* In later years he championed the plays of Sean O'Casey♦ and William Saroyan.♦ But he also understood that the theatre thrived by being entertaining, so he endorsed many a flippant comedy and light-hearted musical. Indeed, as the American musical became more pretentiously artful, he was one of the few critics to maintain affection for the older style of lyric entertainment. He wrote in 1947, "Me, I'll take the old sentimental shows, however imbecile and lacking in sense." After leaving *The Smart Set,* he founded *The American Mercury* with Mencken in 1924 and co-edited it with him until 1930. He also founded *The American Spectator* in 1932 with O'Neill and others. His criticisms appeared in numerous other magazines and papers, including *Puck, Judge, Vanity Fair,* and *The Saturday Review of Literature.* Among his notable books devoted to the theatre were *Mr. George Jean Nathan Presents* (1917), *The Popular Theatre* (1918), *Comedians All* (1919), *The Theatre, The Drama, The Girls* (1921), *The Critic and the Drama* (1922), *The Testament of the Critic* (1931), *Since Ibsen* (1933), *The Theatre of the Moment* (1936), and *Encyclopedia of the Theatre* (1940). From 1943 until shortly before his death he edited *The Theatre Book of the Year.* Late in life he married actress Julie Haydon.♦ His will established the George Jean Nathan Award "to encourage and assist in developing the art of drama criticism and the stimulation of intelligent theatre going."

National Association of Theatrical Producing Managers, see *Producing Managers' Association*

National Critics Institute, THE Founded in 1968 as a project of the Eugene O'Neill Theater Center,♦ this work/study program offers a four-week summer schedule that combines writing workshops with lectures and seminars on all aspects of theatre. Its principal aim is to assist in the development of knowledgeable and responsible critics.

National Playwrights Conference, THE Another branch of the Eugene O'Neill Theater Center,♦ it was first convened in 1965. Its purpose is to create "a situation in which, without commercial pressures, young dramatists can see their plays presented in staged readings by professional actors and directors before an audience of sympathetic critics and fellow-writers, and can discuss their comments and make revisions on the spot for a less 'provisional' performance." Among the playwrights whose early works were offered there were John Guare,♦ Lanford Wilson,♦ Lee Blessing, and August Wilson.♦

National Theatre (Washington, D.C.) Shortly after a visit by Fanny Kemble,♦ during which she complained about the shameful quality of playhouses in the nation's capital, several Washington civic leaders, led by William W. Corcoran, decided to erect a proper theatre. A site was selected on E Street, not far from the White House, and the new theatre, called the National, opened on December 7, 1835. The auditorium was converted briefly to a circus in 1844, but, after serving as the scene of President Polk's inaugural ball, burned to the ground in 1845. Since then five other theatres, all called the National, have occupied approximately the same lot. Like the first, the next three burned—in 1857, 1873, and 1885. The fifth house, designed by J. B. McElfatrick,♦ opened in 1885 and closed in 1922, when the present theatre was erected. Virtually all the great performers of the American stage have appeared at one or another of these Nationals, and all American Presidents from Jackson through Bush, except for Eisenhower, have attended performances there. Apart from a stint as the circus in 1844 and service as a film house from 1947 to 1952, during which time Actors' Equity♦ refused to allow its members to perform there because of the house's policy of not selling tickets to blacks, the property and the theatres built on it have accumulated a record of theatrical continuity almost unparalleled in American history.

National Theatre Conference, THE An organization composed largely of collegiate and community theatres and devoted primarily to the promotion of non-profit theatre in America, its roots go back to meetings held in the mid-1920s. It was formally founded in 1930 at the University of Iowa, although it was later dissolved and then reorganized under a grant from the Rockefeller Foundation.

National Theatre of England, THE Opened in 1963 as the successor to the Old Vic,♦ the company as such has never made an American tour. However, its offshoot, The Young Vic, presented a diverse repertory of three plays in 1974. A number of important or interesting contemporary English plays, first presented by the National, have later been produced on Broadway, sometimes with players who performed in the original English produc-

tions. Among these shows have been *Rosencrantz and Guildenstern Are Dead* (1967), *The National Health* (1974), *No Man's Land* (1976), *Bedroom Farce* (1979), *Amadeus*♦ (1980), *Plenty* (1983), and *Wild Honey* (1986).

National Theatre of the Deaf, THE A professional touring ensemble of deaf performers, the idea for such a troupe was first discussed in the 1950s but did not become a working reality until the Eugene O'Neill Theater Center♦ took it under its aegis in 1966. The group employs an effectively dramatized version of traditional deaf sign language, but also generally includes a few non-deaf performers who serve as "speakers" and elaborate on the action. The company has made numerous national tours, offering both classic and original plays. It no longer is affiliated with the O'Neill Center.

National Vaudeville Artists An in-house or company union promoted by E. F. Albee♦ to forestall the spread of the independent White Rats.♦ Opponents insisted the initials stood for "Never Vex Albee," but conceded that Albee took good care of its members. He bought and furnished a comfortable clubhouse on 46th Street for them, assured them the best bookings, and occasionally even extended charity to troubled members. However, with the waning of vaudeville he eventually lost interest, although the association continued in a watered-down form after his death.

Native Son, a play in ten scenes by Paul Green♦ and Richard Wright. Produced by Orson Welles♦ and John Houseman♦ at the St. James Theatre. March 24, 1941. 114 performances.
    Bigger Thomas (Canada Lee♦) is a black man with a long record of trouble. He has grown up both frightened by and hateful of the white society he knows he is not a part of. Despite his record, a rich white man hires him as chauffeur. By accident Bigger kills the man's daughter. In a panic, he burns her body and flees. He is captured, tried, and sentenced to death. While awaiting execution, his fears disappear and he becomes convinced he has played a small, but noteworthy role in destroying the security of the white world.
    Based on Wright's novel and performed without intermission, the work, according to Burns Mantle,♦ "builds steadily through a series of theatrical climaxes, and though it may be argued that theoretically these are the common climaxes of a conventional melodrama concerned with the career of a tough Negro, criminally inclined, they take on a new

stature in this particular case." Despite similarly exultant notices by most other critics, as well as Lee's bravura performance and Welles's brilliant direction, the play found a relatively limited audience.

Naturalism A theatrical style sometimes called "realism," it began as a rebellion against the romantic artificialities of much 19th-century theatre. Initially it was conceived by early exponents such as Zola as simply offering an unadulterated slice of life with all theatrical glossing over of hard facts removed and with only limited concern, if any, about the necessity of presenting such views in "well-made" plays. However, it soon came to be perceived, at least popularly, as unswerving portrayals of the seamiest side of existence. Gorky's *The Lower Depths* is often cited as the classic example. Those who separate realism from naturalism often suggest that the former is more selective and therefore has to be more carefully contrived, and they offer the best plays of Ibsen♦ as instances. Obviously both terms are resistant to precise definition. American examples might be O'Neill's♦ sea plays or his *The Iceman Cometh♦;* some of the "living newspapers" of the 1930s; and numerous modern plays.

NATWICK, MILDRED (b. 1908) The Baltimorean made her stage debut in her home town in 1929 and first appeared in New York in 1932 in *Carry Nation*. A versatile performer, she was active for nearly forty years and is best remembered for two comic roles: Madame Arcati, the outlandish medium, in *Blithe Spirit* (1941), and Mrs. Banks, the harassed mother of the bride, in *Barefoot in the Park♦* (1963).

Naughty Marietta, an operetta in two acts. Book and lyrics by Rida Johnson Young.♦ Music by Victor Herbert.♦ Produced by Oscar Hammerstein♦ at the New York Theatre. November 7, 1910. 136 performances.

　　Marietta (Emma Trentini♦) is an independent young lady of noble origin who has fled to America to escape an unwanted marriage. Coming to Louisiana, she meets Captain Dick (Orville Harrold) who, singing "Tramp, Tramp, Tramp," leads his rangers against local troublemakers. At the moment he and his men are seeking a villainous pirate, Bras Priqué. Although no one knows it, the pirate is actually Etienne Grandet (Edward Martindel), son of the lieut. governor. Etienne's ardor for the quadroon Adah (Marie Duchene) has recently cooled, so he casts his attentions on Marietta. Adah laments the fickleness of love " 'Neath the Southern Moon,"

after which Marietta, who has disguised herself as a girl of low birth, pretends to recall the fervor of an "Italian Street Song" of her youth. To win her hand Etienne threatens to reveal her true identity and have her sent back home. Fortunately his own double identity is exposed. Captain Dick confesses to Marietta, "I'm Falling in Love with Someone," but Marietta insists she will only marry the man who can finish a snatch of song she has sung since childhood. When Dick does just that in "Ah, Sweet Mystery of Life" the last bar to marriage falls away.

　　As in the two other major American musical successes of its season, *Madame Sherry♦* and *The Pink Lady,* ♦ this operetta employed its best melody as a sort of motif throughout the evening, although it was not fully sung until just before the finale. The American setting might be seen to have given the musical a certain, special pertinence, but was, after all, set in a distant, romantic time when New Orleans was under foreign rule, so essentially it bowed to operetta's penchant for the long ago and far away. The work is generally acknowledged as Herbert's best. It is still revived on occasion and has entered the repertory of the New York City Opera.

NAZIMOVA, ALLA (1879–1945) The dark, intense Russian-born actress studied in Switzerland and in her homeland, where she soon became a leading lady in St. Petersburg. She came to America in 1905 and was performing at Orlenoff's Russian Lyceum on Third Street when she was spotted by Henry Miller,♦ who convinced her to learn English and to star in his production of *Hedda Gabler*. Walter Prichard Eaton♦ wrote, "Her *Hedda Gabler* was a high-born exotic, an orchid of a woman, baleful, fascinating—and to some of us not at all like Ibsen's heroine." After seeing her in several other plays, he concluded, "We may say that Nazimova is 'insincere,' that her art consists of cleverly handled tricks; but the fact remains that she has brought something to our stage it did not possess before, something modern, subtle, exciting, the power to suggest finer shades of meaning, symbols in the dialogue." Although she subsequently appeared in a number of contemporary plays, with one exception she was best known for her acting in such works as *A Doll's House, The Master Builder, Little Eyolf, The Cherry Orchard, A Month in the Country,* and *Ghosts*. The one great exception was her creation of the role of Christine Mannon, the murderous wife, in Eugene O'Neill's♦ *Mourning Becomes Electra♦* (1931).

NEAFIE, J[OHN] A[NDREW] J[ACKSON] (1815–92) Born in New York, he worked as a joiner before turning to acting. He is said to have paid Edmund Simpson♦ $300 for the privilege of making his debut as Othello at the Park Theatre♦ in 1838. That same season he also offered his Shylock and Richard III. For a time he toured with Edwin Forrest,♦ as principal male support to the older actor. Although he served as leading man at the Bowery♦ in the mid-1840s and regularly returned to New York, the tall, strong-voiced actor spent most of his career touring the South and what was the West of his day.

Ned McCobb's Daughter, a play in three acts by Sidney Howard.♦ Produced by the Theatre Guild♦ at the John Golden Theatre. November 29, 1926. 132 performances.

Carrie (Clare Eames♦), daughter of Captain Ned McCobb (Albert Perry), has married into the good-for-nothing Callahan family. Her faithless husband, George (Earle Larimore♦), has forced McCobb to mortgage his farm to pay for an abortion for George's mistress. George has also been stealing money from the local ferry company. When he is arrested, his bootlegger brother, Babe (Alfred Lunt♦), offers Carrie the money to pay off the mortgage and to provide George's legal fees in return for allowing him to store his whiskey in her barn. Carrie accepts the money, but then cooperates with the authorities to rid herself of both brothers.

Sharply etched character studies elevated this work above the run of contemporary melodramas. The figures of Carrie and Babe allowed Miss Eames and Lunt to give two of their finest, most off-beat performances.

NEDERLANDER, JAMES [MORTON] (b. 1922) The son of Detroit theatre owner David Nederlander (1886–1965), he has enlarged the family holdings until they are second nationally only to those of the Shubert Organization.♦ Among his theatres are the New York Palace♦ and the new Marquis.

Needles and Pins, a "comedy of the present" in four acts by Augustin Daly.♦ Produced by Daly at Daly's Theatre. November 9, 1880. 79 performances.

The pushy Mrs. Vandusen (Fanny Morant♦) is determined to marry off her weak son, Kit (John Brand), to a rich lady, although Kit loves a poor piano teacher, Mary Forrest (May Fielding). She is also determined to marry off her aging, Baby-Jane sister, Dosie Heffron (Mrs. G. H. Gilbert♦), to anybody who will have her so that Silena Vandusen (Ada Rehan♦), Mrs. Vandusen's daughter, may then be free to wed. In revealing her plans to Mr. Vandusen (Charles Fisher♦) she lets slip that she

knows he himself once loved a poor piano teacher named Silena and later persuaded his wife to name their daughter after his lost love. Miss Forrest comes into a huge inheritance and decides to do good deeds with her new wealth. She, too, has learned of the old romance and instructs her young lawyer, Tom Versus (John Drew♦), to make Silena and Vandusen rich enough to marry, not realizing that both have long since married others. Because young Kit had been named for his father, a series of mistaken identities transpires, made all the more complicated when the characters meet at a masked ball. In the end, of course, everything is happily resolved when Mrs. Vandusen learns that Mary is now quite eligible to marry Kit. Tom marries Silena; Dosie seems to snare an elderly collector of bric-a-brac, Nicholas Geagle (James Lewis♦); and Mr. and Mrs. Vandusen can finally look forward to some wedded bliss after long married years of living on needles and pins.

The comedy was loosely adapted from J. Rosen's *Starke Mitteln.* Daly's biographer brother, who claimed the original run was one hundred nights, though it actually tallied 103 performances in two separate engagements during its premiere season, noted that it was this play "in which Miss Rehan, Mr. Drew, Mrs. Gilbert, and Mr. Lewis were first recognized as the famous quartet which for so many seasons endeared Daly's Theatre to the public."

Negro Ensemble Company, Inc., THE With a substantial financial contribution from the Ford Foundation, the group was organized in 1967 by Robert Hooks, a black actor, Douglas Turner Ward, a black playwright, actor, and director, and Gerald Krone, a white theatre manager. Their aim was to establish "a place wherein Black theatrical talent could be continuously presented—without regard to the whims of commercial theatre." Since its inception the company has won numerous awards and additional grants. Among its many notable productions have been *The River Niger♦* (1973) and *A Soldier's Play♦* (1981). In 1988 the group initiated its mounting of Charles Fuller's four-play cycle *We.*

Neighborhood Playhouse Built on Grand Street in 1915 by Alice and Irene Lewisohn, it housed an amateur repertory company until 1920, when the ensemble turned professional. The new troupe offered plays by Shaw,♦ O'Neill,♦ and other contemporary dramatists, as well as a series of popular revues known as *The Grand Street Follies.* The company was disbanded in 1927. The surviving corporation occasionally mounted plays in later years. However, the most important offshoot of the company was the Neighborhood Playhouse School of Theatre, which survives.

NEILSON, [LILIAN] ADELAIDE (1848–80) The English actress, whose own life was as tragic as some of the heroines she portrayed, was of illegitimate birth. Her real name may have been Elizabeth Ann Bland or Brown. A great beauty, she had slightly irregular features, which only added a certain piquancy to her dark eyes and chestnut hair, the latter sometimes dyed with a gold tinge. Her voice was described as musical. She made several American tours between 1872 and 1879. William Winter♦ summed up the general assessment of her when he called her "the best representative of Shakespeare's *Juliet, Viola,* and *Imogen* who had appeared on the stage in our time." He wrote, "The subtlety of [her Juliet] was equalled only by its intensity, and neither was surpassed except by its reality." Her other American offering included Rosalind, Beatrice, Pauline (*The Lady of Lyons*♦), and Lady Teazle.

Biography: *Adelaide Neilson,* Laura Holloway Langford, New York, 1885.

NELSON, BARRY [né ROBERT NIELSON] (b. 1920) The stocky, rather beady-eyed leading man was born in Oakland, Calif., and made his debut in *Winged Victory* (1943). He was Peter Sloan, the aspiring playwright, in *Light Up the Sky*♦ (1948) and scored a major success as Donald Gresham, the romantically inclined architect, in *The Moon Is Blue*♦ (1951). His other long runs came as Bob McKellaway, the writer who can't help loving his exasperating ex-wife, in *Mary, Mary*♦ (1961), and Julian, the philandering dentist, in *Cactus Flower*♦ (1965). In 1983 he headed a road company of *42nd Street* and in 1990 led a tour of *Lend Me a Tenor.*

Nervous Wreck, The, a comedy in three acts by Owen Davis.♦ Produced at the Sam H. Harris Theatre. October 9, 1923. 279 performances.

When timid, hypochondriacal Henry Williams (Otto Kruger♦), recovering on an Arizona ranch from his latest nervous attack, helps Sally Morgan (June Walker♦) escape an unwanted marriage, he finds himself in a heap of trouble. The pair are pursued by a posse. They run out of gas and Henry is forced to hold up a passing motorist to get additional fuel. They then hide in a neighboring ranch, posing as a cook and waitress. By the time Sally's father agrees not to force her to marry the man of his choice, Sally is prepared to nurse Henry through sickness and health indefinitely.

Davis had based his comedy on E. J. Rath's

magazine serial, *The Wreck.* Welcomed by John Corbin♦ of the *Times* as "a really funny farce," the play later became the source for the musical *Whoopee.* ♦

NESBITT, CATHLEEN [MARY] (1888–1982) The beautiful, worldly English actress, once reputed mistress of Rupert Brooke, made her American debut in 1911 with the Irish Players of the Abbey Theatre. ♦ She reappeared regularly thereafter, but is best remembered for several later roles: Julia in *The Cocktail Party*♦ (1950), the kindly, knowing dowager Alicia de St. Ephlam in *Gigi* (1951), Mrs. Larrabee in *Sabrina Fair*♦ (1953), and Mrs. Higgins in *My Fair Lady*♦ (1956). At the age of 92, shortly before her death, she repeated this last role in a 1981 revival.

NETHERSOLE, OLGA [ISABEL] (1866–1951) The Latin-miened English actress, famous for her torrid love scenes, made her American debut in 1894 in *The Transgressor* and then toured playing the leading feminine roles in *Camille,* ♦ *Romeo and Juliet,* ♦ and *Frou-Frou.* ♦ She made several other American tours before winning notoriety by creating the role of Fanny Legrand, the French courtesan, in Clyde Fitch's♦ *Sapho* (1900). Outraged editorials led to her arrest for indecency, but she was acquitted after many notables, including the archly conservative William Winter,♦ appeared in her defense. In later years she played in *Magda, The Labyrinth,* and *Adrienne Lecouvreur,* as well as taking the title role in the New Theatre's♦ mounting of *Mary Magdalene.* Her last American appearances were in vaudeville in 1913, where she offered a truncated version of *Sapho.*

Never Too Late, a comedy in three acts by Sumner Arthur Long. Produced at the Playhouse. November 27, 1962. 1,007 performances.

Although Harry Lambert (Paul Ford♦) and his wife Grace (Maureen O'Sullivan) are well into middle age and have a grown daughter and son-in-law, they are also expectant parents. Harry is a crusty, if somewhat perturbed codger, the sort who replies to his wife's asking if he likes her new hat— "Keep it, anyway." His response to the news that he is to be a father again is one sustained howl. His family's attempts to comfort him all seem to backfire.

This slight comedy was enhanced immeasurably by Ford's dourly droll performance. Not all critics felt that its humor was derived from the main situation, Henry Hewes♦ noting in the *Best Plays*♦

series, "The fun of the play turned out to be the running battle between the parsimonious father and his dependent but frustratedly defiant son-in-law."

Long (b. 1921), a Boston native, is better known as a writer of television comedy.

New Amsterdam Theatre Built in 1903 as the flagship of the Erlanger♦ empire from designs by Herts♦ and Tallant, this ornate house helped establish 42nd Street as New York's principal theatrical thoroughfare. Although the theatre opened with *A Midsummer Night's Dream*♦ and left the legitimate fold after Walter Huston's♦ 1937 *Othello,*♦ it was known primarily as a musical house. Most of the *Ziegfeld Follies*♦ played there, as did *The Merry Widow,*♦ *Sally,*♦ *The Band Wagon,*♦ and other great musical hits. For many years its enclosed roofgarden housed a popular cabaret, which in later times served as a rehearsal space. Plans are currently in the works to restore the house for live theatre.

New Faces This was a series of revues presented by Leonard [Dexter] Sillman (1908–82), a Detroit-born actor-turned-producer, as a showcase for young talent. Editions were offered in 1934, 1936, 1942, 1952, 1956, 1962, and 1968. Players who made early appearances in the show included Imogene Coca, Henry Fonda,♦ Van Johnson, Eartha Kitt, Paul Lynde, Maggie Smith, T. C. Jones, Madeline Kahn, and Robert Klein. The 1952 edition was the most successful and probably the best of the series, offering such memorable comic numbers as "Boston Beguine," sung by Alice Ghostley, and "Monotonous," sung by Miss Kitt. Among its best sketches were "Oedipus Goes South," in which Ronny Graham, lolling in a hammock, spoofed a pouting Truman Capote,♦ and "Tour of the Month," in which a bandaged Paul Lynde, on crutches, described his recent African safari with his late wife. The edition opened at the Royale Theatre on May 16, 1952, and ran for 365 performances.

New Girl in Town, see *Anna Christie*

New Moon, The, an operetta in two acts. Book by Oscar Hammerstein II,♦ Frank Mandel,♦ and Laurence Schwab.♦ Lyrics by Hammerstein. Music by Sigmund Romberg.♦ Produced by Mandel and Schwab at the Imperial Theatre. September 19, 1928. 509 performances.

Robert Misson (Robert Halliday♦) is a French nobleman, whose revolutionary sympathies have forced him to flee to New Orleans, where he is disguised as a servant. He falls in love with his employer's daughter, Marianne (Evelyn Herbert♦). When his friend Philippe (William O'Neal) warns him that love that steals in "Softly, as in a Morning Sunrise" often is betrayed, he will not listen. Robert is convinced not only that he can win Marianne, but that given a band of "Stouthearted Men" he can defeat the royalists. Marianne, determined to love just one man, promises to save her "One Kiss" for him. Before long she and Robert are confessing they have spent many hours "Wanting You." However, when his cover is exposed, he believes Marianne has broken faith. Robert is put on a ship returning to France. Marianne follows him aboard. Misson's men, disguised as pirates, attack the ship and take him and Marianne to a settlement on the Isle of Pines. Robert studiously ignores Marianne, who pleads "Lover, Come Back to Me." There they learn of the Revolution. Robert also learns of Marianne's innocence.

Hailed by St. John Ervine of the *World* as "the most charming and fragrant entertainment of its sort that I have seen in a long time," the musical was the last traditional operetta of its era to enjoy a long run. It was revived by the New York City Opera in 1986.

New Orleans (Louisiana) The first plays presented in New Orleans were apparently those given by a company of French performers who had fled from what is now Haiti after the black revolution there and who set up in the city in 1791. Drama in English began in 1806 when a Mr. Rannie presented a double bill at Moore's Large Building. Thereafter for many years French and English theatre flourished side by side. In 1807 the first real theatre, Théâtre St. Pierre, was erected but survived only three seasons. Noah Ludlow's♦ visits encouraged the growth of English plays, although the city did not become a significant theatrical center until the arrival there of James Caldwell. ♦ He erected several playhouses, including the long famous St. Charles Theatre. These early years are covered in detail in Nelle Smither's *A History of the English Theatre in New Orleans* (1944). Subsequently the city remained an important stop for all great visiting players and supported several local stock companies. It was less affected by the Civil War than most Southern cities and continued to offer lively theatre well into the 20th century. However, today it has become a minor touring town.

New Theatre Underwritten by leading New York citizens, including J. P. Morgan and Otto Kahn, and designed by Carrère♦ and Hastings,♦ the theatre was opened in 1909 with the hope that it would provide a home for a permanent repertory company offering the greatest in classic and new plays. The first attraction was *Antony and Cleopatra,* ♦ with E. H. Sothern ♦ and Julia Marlowe ♦ in the title roles. The opening productions proved disappointing, and this, coupled with the theatre's out-of-the-way location, facing Central Park, discouraged playgoers. Because the huge, elaborate house had large operating costs, the poor attendance forced quick abandonment of repertory plans. For a time the theatre was called the Century and served to house sumptuous Ziegfeld ♦ and Dillingham ♦ musicals, and later was used by Max Reinhardt ♦ for his gigantic mountings. The theatre was demolished in 1930.

New York Clipper, see *Clipper*

New York Drama Critics Circle While discussions about forming an association of local critics were initiated as early as 1927, the group was not officially organized until October 1935. No small part of the impetus at that time came from dissatisfaction with the drama selections of the Pulitzer Prize ♦ committee. The first winner of the New York Drama Critics Circle Award was *Winterset.* ♦ In later years the group added other awards, including those for best foreign play and best musical. The Circle also holds regular meetings to examine problems of contemporary theatre. Among other notable American works to win either the overall best play award or the award for the best American drama or musical were *High Tor* ♦ (1937), *Of Mice and Men* ♦ (1938), *The Time of Your Life* ♦ (1940), *Watch on the Rhine* ♦ (1941), *The Patriots* ♦ (1943), *Jacobowsky and the Colonel* (1944), *The Glass Menagerie* ♦ (1945), *Carousel* ♦ (1946), *All My Sons* ♦ and *Brigadoon* ♦ (1947), *A Streetcar Named Desire* ♦ (1948), *Death of a Salesman* ♦ and *South Pacific* ♦ (1949), *The Member of the Wedding* ♦ and *The Consul* (1950), *Darkness at Noon* and *Guys and Dolls* ♦ (1951), *I Am a Camera* ♦ and *Pal Joey* ♦ (1952), *Picnic* ♦ and *Wonderful Town* ♦ (1953), *Teahouse of the August Moon* ♦ and *The Golden Apple* ♦ (1954), *Cat on a Hot Tin Roof* ♦ and *The Saint of Bleecker Street* (1955), *The Diary of Anne Frank* ♦ and *My Fair Lady* ♦ (1956), *Long Day's Journey into Night* ♦ and *The Most Happy Fella* ♦ (1957), *Look Homeward, Angel* ♦ and *The Music Man* ♦ (1958), *A Raisin in the Sun* ♦ (1959), *Toys in the Attic* ♦ and *Fiorello!* ♦ (1960), *All the Way Home* ♦ and *Carnival!* (1961), *The Night of the Iguana* and *How To Succeed in Business Without Really Trying* ♦ (1962), *Who's*

Afraid of Virginia Woolf? ♦ (1963), *Hello, Dolly!* ♦ (1964), *The Subject Was Roses* ♦ and *Fiddler on the Roof* ♦ (1965), *Man of La Mancha* ♦ (1966), *Cabaret* ♦ (1967), *Your Own Thing* (1968), *The Great White Hope* ♦ and *1776* (1969), *The Effect of Gamma Rays on Man-in-the-Moon Marigolds* ♦ and *Company* ♦ (1970), *The House of Blue Leaves* ♦ and *Follies* ♦ (1971), *That Championship Season* ♦ (1972), *The Hot l Baltimore* ♦ and *A Little Night Music* ♦ (1973), *Candide* ♦ (1974), *A Chorus Line* ♦ (1975), *Streamers* ♦ and *Pacific Overtures* ♦ (1976), *American Buffalo* ♦ and *Annie* ♦ (1977), *Ain't Misbehavin'* (1978), *Sweeney Todd* ♦ (1979), *Talley's Folly* ♦ (1980), *Crimes of the Heart* ♦ (1981), *A Soldier's Play* ♦ (1982), *Brighton Beach Memoirs* ♦ (1983), *Glengarry Glen Ross* ♦ (1984), *Ma Rainey's Black Bottom* ♦ (1985), *A Lie of the Mind* ♦ (1986), *Fences* ♦ (1987), *Joe Turner's Come and Gone* ♦ (1988), *The Heidi Chronicles* ♦ (1989), *The Piano Lesson* ♦ (1990). It should be noted that in many years a foreign play was selected as the overall best play and that some of the American entries listed above won awards only after a clear majority could not decide and so a "weighted" ballot was taken.

New York Dramatic Mirror, see *Dramatic Mirror*

New York Idea, The, a play in four acts by Langdon Mitchell. ♦ Produced by Harrison Grey Fiske ♦ at the Lyric Theatre. November 19, 1906. 66 performances.

Since Cynthia Karslake (Mrs. Fiske ♦) and John Karslake (John Mason ♦) are divorced, there seems to be no reason why Cynthia should not marry Judge Phillip Phillimore (Charles Harbury), who himself has been divorced recently. After all, "Marry for whim! That's the New York idea of marriage." The news prompts the ex-Mrs. Phillimore, Vida (Marion Lea), to set her sights on John. Before long it is announced that John and Vida will marry at the same time as Cynthia and Phillip. Enter an English roué, Sir Wilfred Cates-Darby (George Arliss ♦), who would win both ladies away from their new amours. On the day of the wedding he invites Cynthia, an ardent horsewoman, to the races. She accepts and telegraphs Phillip that she will be late for the nuptials. The delay and Phillip's reaction to it convince Cynthia she has made a mistake. She rushes to John's home, only to learn that the wedding has taken place. Her dismay turns to relief when she discovers the bride and groom are Vida and Wilfred. She returns to John, who has kept her wedding ring just in case.

Theatrical historian Edwin J. Bronner has called

the work "a play of wit and substance, one of the outstanding high comedies of the American theatre." It has enjoyed numerous revivals.

New York School of Acting, see *American Academy of Dramatic Arts*

New York Shakespeare Festival Founded in 1954 by Joseph Papp,♦ it was chartered by the State of New York Educational Department to "encourage and cultivate interest in poetic drama with emphasis on the works of William Shakespeare and his Elizabethan contemporaries, and to establish an annual summer Shakespeare Festival." Performances were given in various locations before the company acquired a permanent home at the Delacorte Theatre in Central Park in 1962. The productions were often refreshingly experimental and sometimes featured such notable players as George C. Scott,♦ Colleen Dewhurst,♦ and James Earle Jones.♦ In 1966 the organization took over the old Astor Library, not far from Washington Square, and converted it into an off-Broadway theatre center. The first of the theatres in the building opened in 1967 with the musical *Hair.* ♦ Although the summer outdoor productions, which were offered free to the public except for some reserved seats, continued to emphasize Shakespearean mountings, the off-Broadway center presented a wide-ranging program of revivals and new plays. The large number of productions, their variety and striking percentage of successes made the New York Shakespeare Festival probably the most exciting producing organization since the heyday of the Theatre Guild.♦ However, many of the plays wallowed in gratuitous profanity and nudity, took aggressively confrontational stances, and displayed an excessive concern with minority problems, so that for all its great values and virtues the Festival also served for many as an unfortunate exemplar of the degeneration of both modern drama and modern society. Of course, the Theatre Guild was subject to much the same charges in the 1920s, so that time may prove detractors unduly alarmed. Among the Festival's notable offerings, besides *Hair,* were *The Basic Training of Pavlo Hummel*♦ (1971); a musical version of *Two Gentlemen of Verona* (1971); *Sticks and Bones*♦ (1971); *That Championship Season*♦ (1972); *A Chorus Line*♦ (1975), an off-beat, modernized version of *The Pirates of Penzance*♦ (1980), and *The Mystery of Edwin Drood* (1985). An attempt by the organization to manage the repertory theatre at Lincoln Center♦ in 1973 was short-lived.

New York Society for Prevention of Cruelty to Children, see *Gerry Society*

New York Star A trade sheet, sometimes known as *Vaudeville News* or as *Vaudeville News and the New York Star,* it was published between 1920 and 1930 as a house organ of the National Vaudeville Artists. ♦ Despite its promotion of Keith and Albee interests, it was often interesting and remains useful as a research tool for vaudeville historians.

Niblo's Garden In 1828 William Niblo (1790?–1878), an entrepreneur who had made his money as a caterer and running a stagecoach line between Boston and New York, built the small Sans Souci Theatre on the grounds of the Columbia Garden at Broadway and Prince Street. Offering light, vaudeville-like entertainments to summer patrons out for fresh air and cool drinks, it proved so successful that a year later he built a larger, more permanent structure. The whole complex was renamed Niblo's Garden and Theatre, which New Yorkers quickly abbreviated to Niblo's Garden. To increase patronage at what was then virtually a northern suburb, Niblo ran stagecoaches from the Battery to the theatre. As the town steadily moved toward his playhouse and older theatres burned or were demolished, Niblo's became a major stage for drama and spectacle. Niblo retired when his own theatre burned in 1846, but was persuaded to rebuild it in 1849. In 1852 he prompted the erection of the Metropolitan Hotel on the site of the garden, and the auditorium thereafter was entered through the hotel lobby. After Niblo retired permanently in 1861, William Wheatley♦ took over management. It was under Wheatley's auspices that *The Black Crook*♦ was produced there in 1866. The extravaganza's success established the theatre as New York's leading home for musical and dramatic spectacle. It was rebuilt after another fire in 1872, but never again enjoyed its former prominence since the theatrical center had continued to move still further north. When it was demolished in 1895 it was New York's oldest playhouse.

Nice People, a play in three acts by Rachel Crothers. ♦ Produced by Sam H. Harris♦ at the Klaw Theatre. March 2, 1921. 247 performances.

Teddy Gloucester (Francine Larrimore♦) and her friends Hallie Livingston (Tallulah Bankhead♦) and Eileen Baxter Jones (Katharine Cornell♦) are hedonistic flappers. Over the objections of her father and aunt, Teddy spends the night partying with the equally high-living Scottie Wilbur (Hugh Huntley).

Teddy and Scottie later find themselves stranded at the Gloucester country cottage. This brings down the wrath of Teddy's father. But during that rainy night at the cottage the youngsters' idyll had been intruded upon by a stranded motorist, young Billy Wade (Robert Ames♦). The serious, proper Wade wins Teddy's affections, much to her father's pleasure. Hallie and Eileen are dismayed to realize that Teddy will be marrying and settling down. They will do no such thing, not when so many attractive men and lively parties beckon.

Although many critics felt the play collapsed in the last act, with its contrived happy ending, the public found it an excellent study of contemporary mores.

NICHOLS, ANNE (1891–1966) Although she is remembered solely for her comedy about two families' opposition to an interreligious marriage, *Abie's Irish Rose♦* (1922), she was actually a highly versatile, if undistinguished theatrical figure. She was born in Dales Mills, Ga., and her earliest stage experience was as an actress. Later she spent several seasons churning out touring plays for Augustus Pitou.♦ She also tried her hand successfully as a librettist, most notably for *Linger Longer Letty* (1919). With her earnings from *Abie's Irish Rose* she turned to producing and directing, although only one of her productions had a modest run.

NICHOLS, MIKE [né MICHAEL IGOR PESCHKOWSKY] (b. 1931) Born in Berlin, but educated at the University of Chicago, he made his New York debut in 1960 in *An Evening with Mike Nichols and Elaine May*. Their humor, often improvised or seemingly improvised, put a velvet glove on an iron fist as they ridiculed the foibles and frustrations of everyday life, such as PTA meetings, dealing with telephone operators, and two youngsters trying to make love and appear sophisticated in an auto. Thereafter Nichols worked primarily as a director of comedies, staging such hits as *Barefoot in the Park♦* (1963), *Luv♦* (1964), *The Odd Couple♦* (1965), *Plaza Suite♦* (1968), *The Prisoner of Second Avenue♦* (1971) and *Social Security* (1986). He also directed such more serious plays as the 1967 revival of *The Little Foxes♦* and a 1973 revival of *Uncle Vanya*. In 1977 he co-produced the musical *Annie.♦*

NICHOLSON, KENYON (b. 1894) Born in Crawfordsville, Ind., he studied play-writing at Columbia University before braving Broadway with his first collaboration, *Honor Bright* (1921). Although most of his plays were written in conjunction with other playwrights, including two with S. N. Behrman,♦ his first success was a solo effort, *The Barker* (1927), in which a carnival pitchman determines his son shall not follow in his footsteps. His biggest hit was *Sailor, Beware!♦* (1933), written with Charles Robinson and telling of a seemingly irresistible seaman who courts an immovable bar-girl. With Robinson he later wrote two other plays that enjoyed modest runs, *Swing Your Lady!* (1936), in which a wrestler falls in love with his lady opponent; and *Apple of His Eye* (1946), a story of a May-December romance.

Nick of the Woods; or, The Jibbenainosay, a play in three acts by Louisa H. Medina. Produced at the New Bowery Theatre. May 6, 1839. 12 performances.

After his family has been massacred by the Indians, Reginald Ashburn (Joseph Proctor♦) adopts the disguise of a pacifist Quaker and travels the wilderness seeking revenge. He becomes known by a number of names—including Bloody Nathan, Nick, and Jibbenainosay, the last meaning an avenging devil. In his wanderings he is accompanied by Telie Doe (Mrs. Shaw♦), a white girl who has been kidnapped and raised by Indians and who turns out to be Ashburn's long-lost cousin. With time he kills numerous Indians, including Wenonga (H. Lewis), the chief who had engineered the murder of Ashburn's family. But this last battle also costs Nick and Telie Doe their lives.

Based on the novel of the same name by Robert M. Bird,♦ the work was often viewed as a corrective to the romantic notions of the Indian then in vogue. First produced a year earlier at the Old Bowery,♦ it failed to catch on until this revival. It remained popular for several decades. Mrs. Medina (d. 1838) was an active playwright of the time, many of whose works were dramatizations of contemporary novels, especially those of Bulwer-Lytton.♦ She was the wife of Thomas S. Hamblin.♦

NICKINSON, ISABELLA, see *Walcot, Charles M.*

NIELSEN, ALICE (1876–1943) Born in Nashville, she decided to become a professional singer after the break-up of her first marriage. Her earliest appearance was as Yum-Yum in an 1893 Oakland (Calif.) production of *The Mikado.♦* She was immediately hired to be the leading lady at San Francisco's Tivoli Opera House.♦ There Henry Clay Barnabee♦ heard her sing and signed her on as a member of the Bostonians♦ in 1896. She scored a major success with the company in Victor Herbert's♦ *The Serenade* (1897). To capitalize on her acclaim, she promptly deserted the Bostonians to form her own company, taking several prominent members with her. Her desertion proved the beginning of the end for the long-popular troupe. Her first solo venture was her greatest triumph, *The Fortune Teller*♦ (1898), which Herbert composed for her and in which she introduced "Romany Life" and "Always Do as People Say You Should." Another Herbert operetta, *The Singing Girl* (1899), proved somewhat less successful. Shortly thereafter she left the legitimate stage for a career in grand opera. By the time she returned to Broadway in 1917 in *Kitty Darlin',* her small, pure voice and her youthful charm had faded; she quietly retired a short time later.

Nigger, The, a play in three acts by Edward Sheldon. ♦ Produced at the New Theatre. ♦ December 4, 1909. In repertory.

Philip Morrow (Guy Bates Post) is a patrician, dedicated Southern governor who has long advocated white supremacy. However, when he hesitates to veto a prohibition bill opposed by his cousin, Clifton Noyes (Ben Johnson), a distiller, Noyes discloses an old letter which reveals that Philip is the grandson of a Negro slave. Urged on by his fiancée, Georgiana (Annie Russell♦), Philip vetoes the bill and prepares to face the voters with the truth about his past.

The only American play to be produced in its first season by the highly touted, but short-lived repertory company at the New Theatre, it was also one of that group's few successes. Although some strident objections were raised to the title, and several critics felt the whole racial problem was subsidiary in the play to the romantic interest, the work was so successful that two road companies were quickly sent out.

'Night, Mother, a play by Marsha Norman. ♦ Produced by the Shubert♦ Organization and others at the John Golden Theatre. March 31, 1983. 388 performances. PP.

Thelma Cates (Anne Pitoniak), a widow, lives with her divorced daughter Jessie (Kathy Bates) in a small, snug country house. They would seem to lead a quiet but satisfactory life. Yet Jessie, an overweight epileptic whose husband has walked out on her and whose son has turned out badly, is so unhappy that on one seemingly normal evening she announces to her mother her intention of committing suicide. At first her mother is disbelieving, but later, recognizing that Jessie has given much thought to the matter and is very much in earnest, she tries,

despite her growing terror, to dissuade her. She cannot.

Essentially a long—90-minute—one-act play, it was honestly if harrowingly written. Its unrelieved rush toward death, its use of only two actors (an all too common bow to modern theatrical economics), and its brevity (while no concession was made in the price of tickets) seem to have displeased many playgoers and apparently given it some unfortunate word-of-mouth. However, it was able to achieve a very respectable run because of its tiny cast, high prices, and the attention the Pulitzer Prize♦ earned it.

Night of January 16, a play in three acts by Ayn Rand. Produced by A. H. Woods♦ at the Ambassador Theatre. September 16, 1935. 232 performances.

At the trial of Karen André (Doris Nolan) for murder it is revealed that she loved her millionaire employer, Bjorn Faulkner, and apparently murdered him after she learned he was bankrupt and had married another woman in return for a large loan. A sense of shock pervades the courtroom when it is announced that the body in question was not Faulkner's after all, and that Faulkner is probably hiding in South America. Karen confesses that she knew Faulkner was preparing to flee. In fact, she was going to join him. But she insists that she knew nothing about the murder. The jury is asked to reach a decision.

The jury was selected each night from members of the audience. Two endings had been rehearsed, one if the jury found Karen guilty, the other if she was acquitted. While many critics dismissed the work as claptrap, audiences were seemingly intrigued by the novel way of handling the decision.

Ayn Rand (1905–82) was a Russian-born author who came to this country in 1926 and who was best known for her novels advocating the most extreme rights of the individual, notably *The Fountainhead.* Her only other play to reach Broadway was *The Unconquered* (1940), an anti-Communist tract.

Nine, a musical comedy in two acts. Book by Arthur Kopit. ♦ Lyrics and music by Maury Yeston. Produced at the 46th Street Theatre. May 9, 1982. 732 performances.

Having reached a point in life where he feels he is both creatively and emotionally exhausted, the great Italian director, Guido Contini (Raul Julia), attempts to recruit his strengths by re-examining his past, especially his relationships with the many women in his life. These women included his mother

(Taina Elg); Saraghina (Kathi Moss), who first taught him about sex; Liliane LaFleur (Liliane Montevecchi), his producer; Luisa (Karen Akers), his unhappy wife; and Carla (Anita Morris), his mistress. His retrospections lead to a happy ending.

Based on Federico Fellini's film, *8½* this pleasantly melodic, lightweight musical was enhanced by Tommy Tune's♦ imaginative staging.

Ninety and Nine, The, a play in four acts by Ramsay Morris. Produced at the Academy of Music. October 7, 1902. 128 performances.

Refugees from a fast-spreading forest fire are huddled at a railroad station, hoping a train will come to their rescue before the fire reaches them. But no engineer can be found to run the only nearby train. Ruth Blake (Katherine Grey), whose family is among those at the station, has long loved Tom Silverton (Edwin Arden), though he appears to most people to be a drunken ne'er-do-well. She knows he can run an engine and she has confidence he is really brave enough to do it. She proves right.

Although the play was looked upon as preposterously dated for most chic audiences, it played at an aging theatre and at low prices, thereby attracting a less sophisticated audience. Morris, who was the author of other melodramas and of Irish romances, claimed the basis for the plot was a hymn of the same name.

NIXON-NIRDLINGER, Samuel F. (1848–1918) Born in Fort Wayne, Ind., and educated at Notre Dame Academy, he spent his early years in a mercantile business in South Bend, then became a traveling salesman for a notions house. In Philadelphia he met George K. Goodwin, the lessee of the Walnut Street Theatre.♦ Goodwin appointed him business manager. Before long Nixon-Nirdlinger owned a chain of theatres, always using Philadelphia as a home office. He is reputed to have been one of the organizers of the Theatrical Syndicate or Trust. ♦

No, No, Nanette, a musical comedy in three acts. Book by Otto Harbach♦ and Frank Mandel. ♦ Lyrics by Harbach and Irving Caesar. ♦ Music by Vincent Youmans. ♦ Produced by H. H. Frazee♦ at the Globe Theatre. September 16, 1925. 321 performances.

Balking at the restraints imposed upon her by her Uncle Jimmy (Charles Winninger♦) and her Aunt Sue (Eleanor Dawn), Nanette (Louis Groody♦) runs off to Atlantic City. By coincidence Jimmy, who is a Bible publisher and a philanderer, has arranged to meet several of his girlfriends at the same resort.

Jimmy's philosophy, as he tells both Nanette and his lady friends, is simple. He insists "I Want To Be Happy," but that he will not be until he can make others happy. Sue and Tom Trainor (Jack Barker), Nanette's beau, have followed in pursuit. Tom paints a lovely verbal picture of the dream house he hopes to share someday with Nanette—a snuggery where they can enjoy "Tea for Two." By the end of the evening, a chastened Jimmy is back with Sue, while Tom and Nanette are planning a home of their own.

The musical was based on a 1920 comedy success, *His Lady Friends.* Despite its relatively short run in New York, the musical had several road companies and internationally was the biggest American musical comedy hit of the 1920s. For many years, "Tea for Two" remained the top American "standard" (a song that retains its popularity after fifteen years). A fairly faithful 1971 revival was a huge success. Its cast included Ruby Keeler, Patsy Kelly, Jack Gilford, Bobby Van, Helen Gallagher and, as Nanette, Susan Watson.

No Place To Be Somebody, a play in three acts by Charles Gordone. Produced by the New York Shakespeare Festival♦ at the Public Theatre. May 4, 1969. 250 performances. PP.

Johnny Williams (Nathan George) is a black racketeer in a seedy world dominated by whites, whom he resents. Johnny hopes that when his old buddy, Sweets Crane (Walter Jones), is released from prison they can take on the Mafia together. But Crane is a drained, disillusioned man when he reappears. Johnny recognizes he must go it alone. His attempt fails, so he persuades Gabe Gabriel, a part-black, effeminate would-be playwright, to kill him. Alone and dressed as a woman, Gabe is left to observe, "My black anguish will fall on deaf ears."

The first off-Broadway play to win a Pulitzer Prize,♦ it was also the first play by a black to earn the award. Gordone (b. 1925) was born in Cleveland but raised in Elkhart, Ind. He served as an actor and director before this, his only successful play to date, was produced. A 1970 revival outran the original production.

No Strings, a musical in two acts. Book by Samuel Taylor. ♦ Lyrics and music by Richard Rodgers. ♦ Produced by Rodgers and Taylor at the 54th Street Theatre. March 15, 1962. 580 performances.

In Paris, David Jordan (Richard Kiley♦), a prize-winning writer who has been suffering a long dry spell, meets a black model, Barbara Woodruff (Diahann Carroll). Their budding romance wilts when David learns that Barbara has been kept by a wealthy admirer. Later they resume their affair, but after recognizing that an interracial marriage would be doomed, they go their separate ways.

Principal songs: No Strings · The Sweetest Sounds

Rodgers's first musical following the death of his long-time partner, Oscar Hammerstein II,♦ it offered one of his best scores as well as some excellent lyrics.

No Time for Comedy, a play in three acts by S. N. Behrman.♦ Produced by the Playwrights' Company♦ at the Ethel Barrymore Theatre. April 17, 1939. 185 performances.

With the world plunging toward war, meddling, pushy Amanda Smith (Margalo Gillmore♦) convinces her friend Gaylord Esterbrook (Laurence Olivier♦) that he should abandon his writing of frivolous comedies and turn to more serious dramatic works. This suggestion infuriates Gaylord's wife, Linda (Katharine Cornell♦), who has been the star of his plays. She snaps at Amanda, "Sleep with him if you must, but don't spoil his style." Gaylord and Amanda decide to leave their respective spouses. Linda finds Gaylord packing and slyly suggests that the situation would make a good play. Gaylord agrees, except that he cannot think of how to end the play. When Amanda calls, impatiently demanding to know what is taking him so long to pack, Gaylord realizes the perfect ending for just such a play. He hangs up on her.

The play was Miss Cornell's first attempt at modern comedy. Richard Watts, Jr.,♦ wrote in the *Herald Tribune* of the author, "His prose style is so graceful, his wit so sprightly, his mind so tolerant and his viewpoint so modest that he becomes the most winning of the drama's counselors."

No Time for Sergeants, a comedy in two acts by Ira Levin.♦ Produced by Maurice Evans♦ at the Alvin Theatre. October 20, 1955. 796 performances.

Will Stockdale (Andy Griffith) is a garrulous, innocent hillbilly who is drafted into the Air Force. Crotchety Sergeant King (Myron McCormick) takes an instant dislike to Will and determines to make his life miserable. He orders him to clean latrines, telling him their captain is especially fond of clean latrines. Will makes the latrines sparkle, but also blurts out King's comments to the captain. Deciding he must get Will out of his squad, King gives him the answers to a classification test, only to have Will mate the answers with the wrong questions. Later Will is presumed lost when his plane flies into an atomic test. At a ceremony awarding him a posthu-

mous medal, Will blithely turns up. He is given a second medal to keep his mouth shut.

Based on Mac Hyman's novel, the play was praised by Brooks Atkinson♦ as "ludicrous, intimate and refreshing."

NOAH, Mordecai Manuel (1785–1851) The son of a Portuguese Jew, he was born in Philadelphia, where he became an avid theatregoer while still a young man. He subsequently moved to Charleston, studying law there and becoming editor of the *City Gazette.* His strongly anti-British stance led him to fight several duels, but also came to the attention of President Monroe, who appointed him consul in Tunis. His first play, *Paul and Alexis* (1812), was an adaptation of Pixerecourt's *Le Pelerin Blanc; ou, les Orphelins du Hameau,* and was mounted in Charleston before his departure. On his return he settled in New York, advancing in local politics until he was appointed Supreme Court Commissioner, and actively contributing to numerous New York newspapers. He also became a leading advocate of establishing a special homeland for his fellow Jews, attempting at one point to convert an island near Buffalo into a Jewish city to be called Ararat. Despite these varied occupations he found time to continue playwriting. His produced works included *The Siege of Tripoli* (1820), *Marion; or, The Hero of Lake George* (1821), *The Grecian Captive* (1822), and *The Siege of Yorktown* (1824). All these plays were essentially patriotic spectacles, even his history of Greco-Turkish conflict seen in terms of its similarity to America's fight for independence. His best-known work, depicting a then-recent incident, was *She Would Be a Soldier; or, The Plains of Chippewa*♦ (1819), in which the heroine disguises herself as a soldier to visit her sweetheart. In the preface to his published plays he offers interesting pictures of the contemporary American theatre and discusses the problems confronting an American playwright in the face of the popularity of English comedies and dramas.

Nobody Home, a musical comedy in two acts. Book by Guy Bolton.♦ Lyrics by various writers. Music mostly by Jerome Kern.♦ Produced by F. Ray Comstock♦ at the Princess Theatre.♦ April 20, 1915. 135 performances.

Vernon Popple (George Anderson) loves Violet (Alice Dovey) but cannot marry her without her aunt's consent. The aunt (Maude Odell), however, refuses, since she has heard that Vernon has been seen about town with the Winter Garden star, Tony Miller (Adele Rowland). Vernon's brother, Freddy

(Lawrence Grossmith♦), arrives in town and Tony, who expects to go out on tour, leases her apartment to him. The tour is cancelled, and all the characters meet at Tony's apartment, where misunderstandings lead to complications that are cleared up only in time for a happy ending.

The show was originally to have been merely an Americanization of the English musical, *Mr. Popple of Ippleton,* but was drastically revised after a preview showed the early adaptation would not work. The new musical, while not without its faults, pioneered in presenting intimate, stylish shows at the tiny Princess and launched the series that became known as the Princess Theatre musicals, and which included *Very Good Eddie,* ♦ *Oh, Boy!,* ♦ and *Oh, Lady! Lady!!.* ♦

Nobody's Widow, a comedy in three acts by Avery Hopwood.♦ Produced by David Belasco♦ at the Hudson Theatre. November 15, 1910. 215 performances.

When newlywed Roxana Clayton (Blanche Bates♦) finds her husband (Bruce McRae♦) kissing another woman, she storms out and announces to her friends that her husband has died suddenly. But wherever she goes there is her "dead" husband quietly trying for a reconciliation. Each time she is about to melt another incident pops up to fuel her anger. The husband's persistence finally wins the day.

Mounted by Belasco because Miss Bates insisted on trying her hand at drawing room comedy, the play won critical and public acceptance, but widened the breach that saw Miss Bates leave the producer after the show closed.

NORMAN, MARSHA [née WILLIAMS] (b. 1947) A native of Louisville, she was educated at Agnes Scott College and at the University of Louisville. After spending time as a schoolteacher and a journalist she wrote her first play, *Getting Out,* ♦ a study of a woman ex-convict, for the Actors' Theatre of Louisville.♦ It was presented there in 1977 and a year later in New York. She also directed for the Actors' Theatre, which subsequently produced her plays *Third and Oak* and *The Circus Valentine.* Her one-acter, *The Laundromat,* was presented off-off Broadway in 1979. She won a Pulitzer Prize♦ for *'Night, Mother*♦ (1983), in which a mother and daughter examine the daughter's wish to kill herself.

NORTON, [WILLIAM] ELLIOT (b. 1903) A Bostonian who was educated at Harvard, he became a drama critic on the Boston *Post* in 1934. In 1956 he moved to the *Record American,* remaining with it after it became the *Herald American* in 1972. His almost fifty years as a major critic is one of the longest stints in American theatrical annals, and gave him a renown and prestige accorded to few critics outside New York. Probably only Claudia Cassidy♦ and Richard Coe♦ were as well known and respected among their generation of non-New York critics.

NORWORTH, JACK [né JOHN KNAUFF] (1879–1959) The bantam song-and-dance man ran away from his Philadelphia home to join a minstrel show, but soon switched to vaudeville. His heyday was probably between 1907 and 1913, when he performed with his second wife, Nora Bayes.♦ Their billing was famous:

NORA BAYES
Assisted and Admired by Jack Norworth.

They appeared in vaudeville and in several Broadway shows, including the [*Ziegfeld*] *Follies of 1908,* ♦ in which they sang his most famous song, "Shine On, Harvest Moon." He also composed a number of other once-popular songs, many of them depending on clever tongue-twisting lyrics for their appeal, such as "Sister Susie's Sewing Shirts for Soldiers." Another major success was "Take Me Out to the Ball Game," for which he wrote the lyric. He continued to appear in vaudeville throughout the 1920s, and after his popularity waned accepted smaller parts in some Broadway plays.

Notable Names in the American Theatre First published in 1966 as *The Biographical Encyclopaedia and Who's Who of the American Theatre,* and revised under its present title in 1976, it includes not only detailed biographies of all major, living American theatrical figures, but excellent lists of New York productions from 1900 on, premieres in America, premieres of American plays abroad, histories of noted theatrical groups, details of all major theatres in New York, complete lists of important awards, a biographical bibliography, and a necrology. In its accuracy and thoroughness it often surpasses the older *Who's Who in the Theatre*♦ and is an essential tool for all theatrical researchers.

Nothing But the Truth, a comedy in three acts by James Montgomery.♦ Produced by H. H. Frazee♦ at the Longacre Theatre. September 14, 1916. 332 performances.

Because Robert Bennett (William Collier♦) is so insistent that honesty is the best policy, his brokerage firm partners bet him $10,000 that he cannot tell nothing but the truth for twenty-four hours. He takes the bet—and nearly loses the firm all its clients. He also nearly loses his lady friend, Gwendolyn Ralston (Margaret Brainerd), when he is forced to confess that she is not the first love of his life. She forgives him when she discovers his other hearthrob has been Maude Adams. At the end of the twenty-four hours he is a richer man, but so on edge that all he can do is tell a string of lies.

Based on a novel by Fred Isham, the comedy served as the source for several later musicals: *Yes, Yes, Yvette* (1927) and *Tell Her the Truth* (1932).

Novels Dramatized on American Stages Novels and short stories have long been the source for much popular theatre. One might even suggest that since Shakespeare and other early playwrights used forerunners of these modern forms as models for their plots, examples have been seen in the American theatre from the start. By the late 18th century fresh theatricalizations of such popular novels as Walpole's *The Castle of Otranto* were offered to American playgoers. Indeed, the romantic movement lent itself handsomely to dramatization. The first major American novel to be transferred to the stage with noted success was *The Spy*♦ (1821). Other Cooper novels followed, as did many of the works of Sir Walter Scott. His *Guy Mannering,* for example, was the source for *Meg Merrilies,* long a standby of Charlotte Cushman♦ and others. But the more obvious examples of romantic writings were not the only works seized upon by contemporary playwrights. Traditional stories of love and adventure were also popular, as witnessed by *Briar Cliff*♦ (1826), George P. Morris's version of *Whigs and Tories.*

After the decline of romanticism's vogue newer styles of novels were adapted in turn. With one exception, none matched the popularity of plays drawn from Dickens's works. *Oliver Twist* was a favorite in several versions, and great American actresses from Miss Cushman on won special applause for their interpretations of Nancy. William E. Burton♦ mounted a number of highly esteemed adaptations, including *Nicholas Nickleby* and *Dombey and Son,* with his Captain Cuttle from the latter rating as one of his most memorable achievements. The great American novelists of this period such as Hawthorne and Melville were ignored, but such now virtually forgotten writers as Mrs. E.D.E.N. Southworth♦ saw many of their works rewritten for the stage. However, by far the most successful and influential dramatizations were those of Harriet

Beecher Stowe's militantly anti-slavery *Uncle Tom's Cabin,* ♦ the version by George L. Aiken♦ establishing a number of contemporary records.

Many of the most popular plays of the last half of the 19th century were also taken from novels, although again the source was generally European. They ranged widely in subject matter and treatment. Among the best known were *Fanchon the Cricket*♦ (1862), suggested by George Sand's tale of rural life, *La Petite Fadette;* the various versions of Dumas père's *Le Comte de Monte Cristo,* especially the 1872 Charles Fechter♦-James O'Neill♦ redaction; *Dr. Jekyll and Mr. Hyde* (1887), from the story by Robert Louis Stevenson; *Trilby* (1895), adapted from DuMaurier's novel; and *Sherlock Holmes*♦ (1899), suggested by the famous Conan Doyle mysteries. Of plays derived from American stories the most beloved was the Dion Boucicault♦-Joseph Jefferson♦ retelling of Washington Irving's♦ *Rip Van Winkle*♦ (1866).

The coming of the 20th century, which saw a tremendous expansion of America as a world power and a consequent rise in its self-confidence, also saw the theatre turn increasingly to native fiction for inspiration, even if it continued to ignore the more literary or masterful writers and to prefer more broadly read authors. Thus, Stephen Crane was totally passed over, and, whereas men such as Henry James♦ and William Dean Howells♦ tried their hands at original dramas, their novels were not yet theatricalized. Instead successful plays were made from the likes of Lew Wallace's *Ben-Hur*♦ (1899) and Edward Noyes Westcott's *David Harum*♦ (1900). The rarer attempts to handle somewhat more thoughtful works, such as Frank Norris's muck-raking *The Pit* (1904), encountered indifferent receptions.

Not until after World War I did Broadway turn with some regularity to more important authors, although it retained its preference for less literary but widely known best-sellers. One of the earliest winners of the Pulitzer Prize♦ was Zona Gale's♦ dramatization of her own *Miss Lulu Bett*♦ (1920). Subsequent winners included *The Green Pastures*♦ (1930), taken from stories by Roark Bradford; *The Old Maid*♦ (1935), derived from an Edith Wharton novel; *The Teahouse of the August Moon*♦ (1953), from Vern Sneider's novel; *Look Homeward, Angel*♦ (1957), taken from Thomas Wolfe; and *All the Way Home*♦ (1960), adapted from James Agee's *A Death in the Family.* Parenthetically, another winner was *The Diary of Anne Frank*♦ (1955), which was based on the writings of a young Jewish girl who died in World War II. While some interesting plays such as *The Heiress*♦ (1947), from James's *Washington Square,* and *Billy Budd* (1951), from Melville, were based on older works by acknowledged masters, most dramatizations still had recourse to contemporary efforts. To cite but a few longer-running examples: *Tobacco Road*♦ (1933), from an Erskine Caldwell novel; *Life with Father*♦ (1939), from Clarence Day's short stories; *Mister Roberts*♦ (1948), from Thomas Heggen's book; *The Member of the Wedding*♦ (1950), adapted by Carson McCullers from her own novel; *No Time for Sergeants*♦ (1955), from Mac Hyman's novel; and *Auntie Mame*♦ (1956), from Patrick Dennis's bestseller. A two-evening version of *Nicholas Nickleby* was hugely successful in 1986, but a much lauded dramatization of *The Grapes of Wrath* failed three years later.

Musicals, too, used novels and short stories for inspiration. One of the earliest successes in the American theatre was *Tom and Jerry; or, Life in London* (1823), taken from the work of Pierce Egan. However, it was not until much later that the musical stage followed the practice more commonly. Three notable early examples were *The Wizard of Oz*♦ (1903), adapted from L. Frank Baum's children's stories; *Show Boat*♦ (1927), from an Edna Ferber♦ novel; and *Porgy and Bess*♦ (1935), taken from Dubose Heyward's novel *Porgy,* by way of the 1927 play of the same name. Both *South Pacific*♦ (1949), taken from James Michener's Pulitzer Prize♦-winning *Tales of the South Pacific,* and *How To Succeed in Business Without Really Trying*♦ (1961), taken from Shepherd Mead's book, went on to garner their own Pulitzer Prizes. Other long-running adaptations included *Guys and Dolls*♦ (1950), which employed some of Damon Runyon's♦ short stories; *The King and I*♦ (1951), from Margaret Landon's *Anna and the King of Siam; The Pajama Game*♦ (1954), based on Richard Bissell's *7 1/2 Cents; Damn Yankees*♦ (1955), from Douglass Wallop's *The Year the Yankees Lost the Pennant; Fiddler on the Roof*♦ (1964), based on short stories by Sholom Aleichem; *Man of La Mancha*♦ (1965), which musicalized *Don Quixote; Mame* (1966), a lyric version of *Auntie Mame;* and *The Wiz* (1975), another version of *The Wizard of Oz.* In more recent years foreign musicals based on novels have enjoyed considerable vogue, notably *Les Misérables*♦ (1981), *The Phantom of the Opera*♦ *(1988),* and *Aspects of Love* (1990).

With rare exceptions, even the most successful stage versions of novels could not offer the depth of characterization or the range of incidents found in their sources, but on their own level of theatrical immediacy they sometimes were among the finest and most enduring works of their epochs.

NUGENT, ELLIOTT [JOHN] (1899–1980) A theatrical jack-of-all-trades, he was the son of vaudevillians and made his debut in Los Angeles two-a-day at the age of four. Born in Dover, Ohio, he temporarily abandoned the stage to study at Ohio State University. His first New York appearance was in a minor role in *Dulcy*♦ (1921). He won fame the next year when he collaborated with his father, J. C. Nugent, on *Kempy*♦ and assumed the title role of the naive plumber who is almost bamboozled into the wrong marriage. The Nugents wrote another hit in 1925, *The Poor Nut,* in which Elliott played John Miller, a shy student who suddenly finds himself an important campus figure. A number of his other plays and appearances in the twenties were unsuccessful. After some time in films he scored another major hit with his collaboration with James Thurber, *The Male Animal*♦ (1940). In the play he portrayed Tommy Turner, a professor who determines to fight for freedom of speech. He won additional applause when he played Bill Page, the soldier on a weekend pass, in John van Druten's♦ *The Voice of the Turtle*♦ (1943). That same year he staged the hit play, *Tomorrow the World.*♦ His last important success came when he re-created the role of Tommy Turner in a 1952 revival of *The Male Animal.*

Autobiography: *Events Leading Up to the Comedy,* New York, 1965.

Nunsense, a musical in two acts. Book, lyrics, and music by Dan Goggin. Produced at the Cherry Lane Theatre. December 12, 1985. Still running at press time.

Five nuns, the only survivors among their order of an epidemic of food poisoning in their school's cafeteria, put on an amateur show to raise money for their sisters' burials.

Undistinguished, and sometimes more amateurish than it was pretending to be, this intimate musical nonetheless proved appealing to a widespread audience. Its low nut also helped it achieve a remarkable run not only off-Broadway, but in numerous local productions around the country and overseas.

Nym Crinkle, see *Wheeler, A. C.*

O

OAKLEY, ANNIE [née PHOEBE ANN MOSES] (1860–1926) Having learned to handle a gun as a child in Ohio, she was offering sharpshooting exhibitions by the time she was in her teens. After beating a renowned sharpshooter, Frank Butler, in a match, she married him, and they toured with a circus before joining Buffalo Bill's♦ Wild West Show. She could shoot a cigarette out of Butler's mouth while he stood behind her and she glanced at him in a mirror, or could shoot holes in every one of a handful of tickets thrown in the air. This last feat caused her name to become attached to punched tickets used as passes and eventually to all free tickets. With the passing of the Wild West Show she retired. For all her skill with guns she was reputed to be a shy woman and a homebody, but this side of her was ignored when her life was musicalized in *Annie Get Your Gun*♦ (1946).

Biography: *Annie Oakley of the Wild West,* Walter Havighurst, New York, 1954.

OATES, ALICE [née MERRITT] (1849–87) One of the notable pioneers of the American musical stage, she was born in Nashville, and studied for a career in opera in Louisville and New Orleans. However, after her marriage to James A. Oates, a prominent actor at Wood's Theatre in Cincinnati, she made her stage debut in supporting roles under his aegis. She toured the Midwest and West, playing increasingly more important assignments. Following the huge success of Lydia Thompson♦ and her English musical burlesques, she organized her own burlesque troupe, touring successfully for several seasons. Within a short while this troupe evolved into the Alice Oates New English Opera Company, which specialized in presenting French opéra bouffe in English. Quick to appreciate the potential of *H.M.S. Pinafore,*♦ she added it to her repertory before it had even been presented to New York. Her appearances in the East were relatively rare, but she remained a star west of the Mississippi for many years.

Obie Awards The Village Voice Off-Broadway Awards, known popularly as Obies, have been presented by the New York publication *The Village Voice* since the 1955–56 season. They are deter-mined by a panel of judges picked annually and cover a wide range of categories, including best new play, best production, and best performers. In 1969 specific categories were largely eliminated, but later were reinstated.

O'CASEY, SEAN [né SEAN O'CATHASAIGH or JOHN CASEY] (1880–1964) The Irish playwright who moved from grimly realistic works into symbolism and expressionism♦ was most successful in America with his earlier plays of troubled Dublin life: *Juno and the Paycock* (1926), which featured Louise Randolph and Augustin Duncan,♦ who also directed, and *The Plough and the Stars* (1927), in an Abbey Theatre♦ production. He began to move away from his earlier style in *Within the Gates* (1934). Although his *Red Roses for Me* (1955), centering on a pre-World War I Dublin strike, was a *succès d'estime* on Broadway with a cast that included Kevin McCarthy, Eileen Crowe, and E. G. Marshall, his later plays were rarely mounted there and found a better welcome off-Broadway and at regional theatres.

Octoroon, The, a play in five acts by Dion Boucicault. ♦ Produced at the Winter Garden Theatre. December 6, 1859. 48 performances.

George Peyton (A. H. Davenport) will inherit Terrebonne, a Southern plantation, on the death of his aunt, Mrs. Peyton (Mrs. W. R. Blake), if his late uncle's mismanagement does not cause his aunt to lose her property. He would like to settle on the estate, where he has met and fallen in love with the regal octoroon Zoe (Agnes Robertson♦). But the villainous Yankee overseer, Jacob McClosky (T. B. Johnston), murders the slave who is sent to pick up a letter bringing Mrs. Peyton assurances of the money she needs to save her land. McClosky also learns that on a technicality Zoe was never legally freed, and he demands she be put up for sale. Dora Sunnyside (Mrs. J. H. Allen), who loves George but understands his feelings for Zoe, offers to buy Zoe's freedom, as does a kindly overseer, Salem Scudder (Joseph Jefferson♦). They are outbid by McClosky. Zoe takes poison rather than become McClosky's property. At the same time McClosky's murder of the slave is unmasked and he is forced to flee. George and Dora rush to Zoe's side. She tells George as she dies, "O! George, you may, without a blush, confess your love for the Octoroon."

Boucicault derived the main story from Mayne Reid's novel, *The Quadroon,* and the incidents relating to the murder of the slave from Albany Fonblanque's novel, *The Filibuster.* For theatrical effect he added a spectacular scene in which a river boat burns. Although Boucicault emphasized the absurdity of Southern racial laws by making Zoe an octoroon instead of a quadroon (that is, one-eighth instead of one-quarter black), he basically attempted to balance the rights and wrongs of sectional division. As Jefferson noted of the play, "The truth of the matter is, it was non-committal. The dialogue and the characters of the play made one feel for the South, but the action proclaimed against slavery and called loudly for its abolition." The play has enjoyed successful revivals, including a fine 1961 mounting by the Phoenix Theatre. ◆

Odd Couple, The, a comedy in three acts by Neil Simon. ◆ Produced at the Plymouth Theatre. March 10, 1965. 964 performances.

Felix Unger (Art Carney◆), having broken up his marriage, arrives bag and baggage at the apartment of his divorced friend Oscar Madison (Walter Matthau◆). Within a short while, the obsessively neat Felix has driven the slovenly Oscar up all four walls, and appears on the verge of destroying Oscar's regular poker game. But after a seemingly disastrous double date with a pair of neighboring sisters, Felix announces he will move in with one of the girls. His stay, however, has not been without its effect. As Oscar resumes his poker game he warns his fellow players not to flick ashes on the floor.

Howard Taubman observed of Simon in the *Times,* "His skill—and it is not only great but constantly growing—lies in his gift for the deliciously surprising line and attitude. His instinct for incongruity is faultless. It nearly always operates on the basis of character." A successful 1985 revival featured women in the principal roles.

ODELL, GEORGE C[LINTON] D[ENSMORE] (1866–1949) Born in Newburgh, N.Y., he was educated at Columbia, where he succeeded Brander Matthews◆ as Professor of Dramatic Literature in 1924. He is best remembered for his *Annals of the New York Stage*◆ (1927–49), a fifteen-volume set covering the history of New York theatre from its beginnings to mid-1894. The work is detailed, accurate, and written with great personal warmth and remains the definitive study of the 18th- and 19th-century New York stage.

ODETS, CLIFFORD (1906–63) The leading playwright of left-wing social protest in the 1930s, he was born in Philadelphia, but raised in New York. His earliest professional work in the theatre was as an actor, including several seasons with the Group Theatre,◆ whose theories of drama and staging he shared. When the Group mounted a special benefit performance of his multiscened, one-act play about a taxi drivers' union strike, *Waiting for Lefty,* ◆ its reception made him famous overnight. However, before the troupe brought the play to Broadway it first produced his drama dealing with a troubled, poor Jewish family, *Awake and Sing!*◆ (1935). The company offered *Waiting for Lefty* a month later as part of a double bill which also included another of his one-act plays, *Till the Day I Die,* centering on the anti-Nazi underground. Although all these plays confirmed Odets in his proletarian sentiments, the contemptuous reception of *Waiting for Lefty* by some Communist groups stemmed his drift to the far left. A confused indictment of the emptiness of the middle class, *Paradise Lost* (1935), was so coldly received that he temporarily abandoned Broadway for Hollywood. On his return he offered what many have considered his best play, *Golden Boy*◆ (1937), whose Italian-American hero elects a dubious if lucrative career as a prizefighter over a career as a violinist. A falling away of his dramatic abilities became evident with *Rocket to the Moon*◆ (1938), in which a dentist attempts to escape from an unhappy marriage to a shrewish wife by having an affair. A symbolic, confused love story, *Night Music* (1940), was assailed by most critics and ran less than three weeks. Nor did *Clash by Night* (1941), focusing on a sleazy, ultimately tragic domestic triangle fare much better. Eight years passed before Odets returned to Broadway with a highly colored attack on Hollywood, *The Big Knife* (1949). His last two plays suggested that the dramatist could still recover some of his earlier sureness. *The Country Girl*◆ (1950) told of an alcoholic actor's attempt at a comeback, while *The Flowering Peach* (1954) was a charming, albeit somewhat languid recounting of the legend of Noah.

At his best Odets was a powerful dramatist with a gift for sympathetic, memorable characterization, but his frequent rejections and returns to Broadway hint that his approach to writing was beset by the very conflict between commercialism and preachy idealism that was the essence of many of his works.

Biography: *Clifford Odets—American Playwright,* Margaret Brenman-Gibson, New York, 1982.

OENSLAGER, Donald [Mitchell] (1902–75) Born in Harrisburg, Penn., he studied at Harvard under George Pierce Baker,♦ then began his theatrical career as an actor. He turned to set design in 1924. Among the memorable shows for which he created sets were *Good News!*♦ (1927), *The New Moon*♦ (1928), *Follow Thru*♦ (1928), *Girl Crazy*♦ (1930), *The Farmer Takes a Wife*♦ (1934), *Anything Goes*♦ (1934), *Stage Door*♦ (1936), *Johnny Johnson*♦ (1936), *You Can't Take It with You*♦ (1936), *Of Mice and Men*♦ (1937), *The Man Who Came to Dinner*♦ (1939), *Margin for Error*♦ (1939), *My Sister Eileen*♦ (1940), *Claudia*♦ (1941), *Born Yesterday*♦ (1946), *Goodbye, My Fancy*♦ (1948), *Sabrina Fair*♦ (1953), *Coriolanus* (1954), *Janus*♦ (1955), *A Majority of One*♦ (1959), for which he won a Tony Award,♦ and *A Far Country*♦ (1961). Although much of his work for the commercial theatre was traditional, he is generally linked with Robert Edmond Jones,♦ Norman Bel Geddes,♦ Lee Simonson,♦ and Jo Mielziner♦ as one of the major developers of modern American stage design. He was for many years on the faculty of the Yale School of Drama♦ and was the author of *Scenery Then and Now* (1936).

Of Mice and Men, a play in three acts by John Steinbeck.♦ Produced by Sam H. Harris♦ at the Music Box Theatre. November 23, 1937. 207 performances. NYDCCA.

Lennie (Broderick Crawford) is a loving but infantile giant who has often killed pets accidentally with his crushing embrace. His buddy and fellow migrant worker, George (Wallace Ford), has warned him to be careful, since one day it might not be an animal that he kills. Their boss's sluttish daughter-in-law (Claire Luce) finds Lennie in a barn, weeping over a dead puppy. When Lennie attempts to embrace her, she screams. In a panic, Lennie breaks her neck. George finds out where Lennie has run to hide and shoots him before the other men can get to him.

Steinbeck based the play on his own novel, which appeared to have been written with a play in mind.

Of Thee I Sing, a musical in two acts. Book by George S. Kaufman♦ and Morrie Ryskind.♦ Lyrics by Ira Gershwin.♦ Music by George Gershwin.♦ Produced by Sam H. Harris♦ at the Music Box Theatre. December 26, 1931. 441 performances. PP.

While loyalists parade, singing "Wintergreen for President," John P. Wintergreen (William Gaxton♦)

recognizes that he has no real issue to run on, so makes his rallying cry "Love Is Sweeping the Country." To that end he agrees to hold a contest and marry the winner. The winner turns out to be a Southern belle, Diana Devereaux (Grace Brinkley), but by the time the contest is over Wintergreen has fallen in love with his secretary, Mary Turner (Lois Moran). As election returns come in he tells Mary "Of Thee I Sing, Baby." His ditching of Miss Devereaux brings a strong protest from the French Ambassador (Florenz Ames), who protests that France has been defamed since Miss Devereaux is "The Illegitimate Daughter" of an illegitimate son of an illegitimate nephew of Napoleon. Wintergreen's response is "Who Cares?" The Supreme Court is eventually called in to pronounce on the case. With Mary pregnant by that time, the Court concludes that anyone who is a daddy cannot be a baddy. The problem of what to do with Miss Devereaux is solved by awarding her to a man whom everyone has ignored and whose name no one recalls, the vice president, Alexander Throttlebottom (Victor Moore♦).

The first musical to win a Pulitzer Prize,♦ it was hailed by George Jean Nathan♦ as "the happiest and most successful native music-stage lampoon that has thus far come the way of the American theatre. With it, further, I believe that American musical comedy enters at length upon a new, original and independent lease on life." A 1952 revival with Jack Carson as Wintergreen and Paul Hartman as Throttlebottom failed.

Off-Broadway The term applied to a widely dispersed group of small theatres away from the principal commercial theatre center near Times Square. Many of these playhouses were established in basements, lofts, converted churches, and elsewhere, and regularly produced plays deemed too risky for commercial production. Although such playhouses existed throughout the century (witness the Provincetown,♦ Greenwich Village, and Neighborhood♦ playhouses), the designation did not take hold until after World War II. Many of the plays first presented in these theatres were later moved to traditional Broadway houses, while others, such as *Threepenny Opera*♦ or *The Fantasticks,*♦ remained in their original playhouses for their entire long runs. By the 1960s off-Broadway theatres were often providing much of the most exciting theatre in New York. Among the notable producing groups were the Circle in the Square,♦ La Mama,♦ the Living Theatre Company,♦ the Negro Ensemble Company,♦ the Phoenix Theatre,♦ and the New York Shakespeare Festival.♦ Many playwrights, such as

Beckett,♦ Genet,♦ and the American Sam Shepard,♦ have been presented in New York almost solely in off-Broadway houses, and several playwrights, such as Tennessee Williams,♦ announced a preference for off-Broadway after their later plays were not well received uptown. The off-Broadway theatre has its own prestigious award, the Obies.♦ Smaller theatres, usually offering even more experimental fare and cheaper productions, have lately been considered off-off-Broadway.

OFFENBACH, JACQUES (1819–80) Although born in Cologne, he achieved his fame in Paris, where he became France's finest and best-known composer of opéra bouffe.♦ In September 1867 his five-month-old *The Grand Duchess of Gerolstein*♦ was presented in New York and initiated the American rage for the genre. Among his other works popular here were *La Belle Hélène* (1868), *Orpheus in the Underworld* (1868), *Barbe Bleue* (1868), *La Perichole* (1869), *La Vie Parisienne* (1869), and *The Princess of Trebizonde* (1871). This rash of premieres came at the same time as the success of *The Black Crook,*♦ *Humpty Dumpty,*♦ and the semi-musical *Fritz, Our Cousin German*♦ and thus helped open American stages to musical theatre.

Officer 666, a farce in three acts by Augustin MacHugh. Produced by Cohan♦ and Harris♦ at the Gaiety Theatre. January 29, 1912. 291 performances.

Travers Gladwin (Wallace Eddinger♦) returns from Europe to learn that someone is posing as him in order to steal both his famous art collection and his girl, Helen Burton (Ruth Maycliffe). To catch the thief, he borrows the uniform of Officer 666 (Francis D. McGinn) and enters his own mansion in disguise. Misunderstandings and mistaken identities ensue, and for a moment Gladwin is even arrested for attempting to steal his own art.

The play was heavily rewritten by Winchell Smith.♦ MacHugh (1877–1925) was an actor and vaudevillian, who wrote numerous vaudeville sketches and several other Broadway plays. His only other success was *The Meanest Man in the World* (1920), telling of a kind-hearted lawyer who decides the best way to rise in the world is to be nasty.

Oh, Boy!, a musical comedy in two acts. Book by Guy Bolton♦ and P. G. Wodehouse.♦ Lyrics by Wodehouse.♦ Music by Jerome Kern.♦ Produced by William Elliot and F. Ray Comstock♦ at the Princess Theatre.♦ February 20, 1917. 463 performances.

Although George Budd (Tom Powers♦) has just married Lou Ellen (Marie Carroll), his problems have only begun. First of all, his guardian-aunt, Penelope (Edna May Oliver), who holds the family purse strings, knows nothing of the marriage and will almost certainly disapprove. Moreover, a young lady named Jackie (Anna Wheaton) has invaded his apartment and has been encouraged to remain there by his sporting friend, Jim Marvin (Hal Forde). Before all the complications have been resolved Jackie has had to pose both as Mrs. Budd and as Penelope.

Principal songs: Nesting Time · An Old-Fashioned Wife · A Pal Like You · Till the Clouds Roll By

This was the best and most successful of the Princess Theatre musicals. It had a solidly constructed, believable, and literate book, and both its humor and songs derived from situations and characters. It was adventuresome in making its heroine not totally likable and in assigning love songs to comics and comic numbers to the lovers. The critic for the *Sun* typified reviewers' reactions when he exclaimed, "If there be such things as masterpieces of musical comedy, one reached the Princess last night."

Oh, Calcutta!, a revue in two acts devised by Kenneth Tynan,♦ with contributions by, among others, Samuel Beckett,♦ Jules Feiffer,♦ John Lennon, and Sam Shepard.♦ Produced at the Eden Theatre. June 17, 1969. 1,314 performances.

A review which trafficked largely in the then-faddish nudity, its nature was summed up by Otis L. Guernsey, Jr.,♦ who noted, "Its clinkers of unredeemed vulgarity in a couple of unfortunate skits [including one in which a naked couple offer themselves for sexual experiment] were somewhat redeemed by the gracefulness of the dancers, in groups and pairs, in poetic movements of the naked and well-formed male and female bodies. The show had a point of view (blithely hetero) and found some humor in the image of a man and a woman, stark naked and fully lit, copulating."

The show, with some changes, was revived off-Broadway on September 24, 1976, and ran for 5,969 performances at the small house.

Oh, Dad, Poor Dad, Mamma's Hung You in the Closet and I'm Feelin' So Sad, "a pseudoclassical tragifarce" in three scenes by Arthur Kopit.♦ Produced at the Phoenix Theatre. February 26, 1962. 454 performances.

Madame Rosepettle (Jo Van Fleet) arrives at a Caribbean hotel accompanied by her usual ménage—the stuffed corpse of her husband, her pet piranha, and her stammering, neurotic son, Jonathan (Austin Pendleton). Into their peripatetic world comes a wide-eyed, determined professional babysitter, Rosalie (Barbara Harris), who quickly determines that the baby she would most like to sit with is Jonathan. But her advances throw Jonathan into a panic, and he smothers her to death. Entering the disordered bedroom, Mamma looks around in dismay and asks, "What is the meaning of this?"

This choice American example of the theatre of the absurd was the off-Broadway sensation of its season.

Oh, Kay!, a musical comedy in two acts. Book by Guy Bolton♦ and P. G. Wodehouse.♦ Lyrics by Ira Gershwin.♦ Music by George Gershwin.♦ Produced by Alex A. Aarons♦ and Vinton Freedley♦ at the Imperial Theatre. November 8, 1926. 256 performances.

Because Jimmy Winter (Oscar Shaw♦) spends so little time on his Long Island estate, Kay (Gertrude Lawrence♦) helps her rum-running brother cache his illegal booze there. When Jimmy returns unexpectedly, he and Kay fall in love. As a result he helps Kay guy the revenue agents and, after renouncing his numerous other promises of marriage, agrees to marry Kay.

Principal songs: Clap Yo' Hands · Do, Do, Do · Maybe · Someone To Watch Over Me

The musical was Miss Lawrence's first starring role, and was said to have been written with her in mind. Her singing of "Someone To Watch Over Me" while cuddled up on a sofa with a small, raggedy doll was one of the era's most memorable musical moments. The show was revived successfully off-Broadway in 1960, but a 1978 mounting, slated for Broadway, folded on the road. In 1990 a revised version, with a black cast, did reach Broadway.

Oh, Lady! Lady!!, a musical comedy in two acts. Book by Guy Bolton♦ and P. G. Wodehouse.♦ Lyrics by Wodehouse. Music by Jerome Kern.♦ Produced by F. Ray Comstock♦ and William Elliot at the Princess Theatre.♦ February 1, 1918. 219 performances.

Just before Willoughby Finch (Carl Randall) is to marry Mollie Farrington (Vivienne Segal♦), the Farrington jewels are stolen. This presents an awkward situation for Willoughby, since it is known that his valet, Spike (Edward Abeles♦), was once a jewel thief. However, Spike proves loyal to his master and recovers the jewels, allowing the wedding to proceed.

Principal songs: Greenwich Village · Not Yet · When the Ships Come Home (Kern wrote "Bill" for this show but the song was dropped before the New York opening.)

Although its authors considered this the best of the Princess Theatre series, critics and the public disagreed, so the trio broke up and the series came to an end.

Oh, Men! Oh, Women!, a comedy in three acts by Edward Chodorov.♦ Produced by Cheryl Crawford♦ at Henry Miller's Theatre. December 17, 1953. 382 performances.

Just as Alan Coles (Franchot Tone♦), a successful society psychoanalyst, is about to marry Myra Hagerman (Betsy von Furstenberg), he learns from one of his patients that his bride-to-be has had a very active and not too selective sex life. He also discovers that the handsome movie-star husband of another patient intends to seduce Myra before the wedding, just to see if Coles "can take it as well as dish it out." Coles quickly realizes he must analyze his own reactions to this news. He does, in time for a happy ending.

Although most critics agreed with Louis Kronenberger,♦ who wrote, "Despite what is fresh and funny, the play cannot maintain a really high level of farce," the public clearly enjoyed the play.

"Oh, Promise Me!" A song with music by Reginald De Koven♦ and lyric by Clement Scott, it was added early on to the score of *Robin Hood*♦ (1891) at the insistence of Jessie Bartlett Davis,♦ who sang it as part of her trouser role of Alan-a-Dale. It is one of the earliest songs from the American musical theatre to retain popularity and for many years was performed at most American weddings.

O'HORGAN, Tom (b. 1926) The Chicago-born director and composer began to be active off-Broadway in 1959. He was long associated with the La Mama Experimental Theatre.♦ However, he is best recalled for his free-wheeling staging of two musicals, *Hair*♦ (1968) and *Jesus Christ Superstar* (1971). He won a Tony Award♦ for his work on the former.

Oklahoma!, a musical in two acts. Book and lyrics by Oscar Hammerstein II.♦ Music by Richard Rodgers.♦ Produced by the Theatre Guild♦ at the St. James Theatre. March 31, 1943. 2,212 performances.

Rejoicing "Oh, What a Beautiful Mornin'," Curly (Alfred Drake♦), a handsome young cowboy, comes to ask Laurey (Joan Roberts) to ride with him in "The Surrey with the Fringe on Top" to the local box social. Since the pair has been quarreling Curly is not surprised to learn that Laurey may go with someone else, but his affection for her is betrayed by his alarm when he learns that her escort may be Jud Fry (Howard da Silva), a farmhand for Laurey's Aunt Eller (Betty Garde). Although farmers and cowboys are not always on the best of terms, Jud is, to Curly, a particularly untrustworthy "bullet-colored, growly man." Laurey has another reason for accepting Jud's invitation. She knows neighbors have been talking about her and Curly. If they are seen clinging together at the social, she tells him, "People Will Say We're in Love." Laurey dreams that Curly and Jud have a fight over her and that Curly is bested. Fearing for Curly, she accepts Jud's invitation. At the social Curly outbids Jud for Laurey's box lunch, so Jud stalks off, muttering threats. When the men do fight later, Curly kills Jud. Curly is acquitted in time for Laurey and him to ride off on their honeymoon, while all their neighbors celebrate the joy of living in "Oklahoma." In a subplot, the flirtatious, oversexed Ado Annie (Celeste Holm♦) gives Will Parker (Lee Dixon) a hard time before agreeing to marry him.

Based on Lynn Riggs's 1931 play *Green Grow the Lilacs,* this breakaway musical, Rodgers and Hammerstein's first professional collaboration, revolutionized American operetta. It set new high standards for integration of song and story, and also was one of the first musicals to integrate narrative, dramatic ballet into the action. Agnes de Mille's♦ ballet, depicting Laurey's dream, played a part in advancing the narrative far more than any other earlier ballet in musical theatre. The show began not only a vogue for ballet, but for musicals unfolding in historic American settings. When it closed, it was the longest running musical in Broadway history. To distinguish this and subsequent American operettas from the Viennese school the term "musical play" came into fashion.

OLCOTT, [CHANCELLOR JOHN] CHAUNCEY (1860?–1932) The handsome singer and actor was born in Buffalo and made his stage debut in 1880 as a ballad singer in a minstrel show. He spent several seasons in minstrelsy before turning to straight plays and comic opera, including an appearance as Lillian Russell's♦ leading man in *Pepita; or, The Girl with the Glass Eyes* (1886). However, he found his true niche after the death of W. J. Scanlan,♦ starring in the sort of romantic musical plays that Scanlan had helped popularize. Among his great successes were

Mavourneen♦ (1892), *The Irish Artist* (1894), *The Minstrel of Clare* (1896), *Sweet Inniscarra*♦ (1897), *A Romance of Athlone* (1899), *Old Limerick Town* (1902), *Eileen Asthore* (1906), *Macushla* (1912), and *The Isle o' Dreams* (1913). Songs he introduced included "Mother Macree," "Macushla," and "When Irish Eyes Are Smiling." His last New York appearance was as Sir Lucius O'Trigger in an all-star production of *The Rivals* mounted by the Players. ♦

Biography: *Song in His Heart,* Rita Olcott, New York, 1939.

Old American Company, see *American Company*

Old Homestead, The, a play in four acts by Denman Thompson♦ [and George W. Ryer, uncredited]. Produced at the 14th Street Theatre. January 10, 1887. 160 performances.

Joshua Whitcomb (Thompson) is a New Hampshire farmer who always has a friendly welcome for neighbors and strangers alike. But he also has a problem that worries him. His son, Reuben (T. D. Frawley), has gone to New York and has not been heard from for nearly a year. Joshua decides to go to New York to seek out Reuben. Joshua's old schoolmate, Henry Hopkins (Walter Lennox), has become a millionaire and owns a mansion in the city, so Joshua stays with his friend. They discover that Reuben has hit the skids and become a derelict. Joshua helps rehabilitate Reuben and makes him promise that he will return home for the holidays. When the holidays come, Reuben does return, a reformed man. Joshua welcomes him and all his friends, admonishing them, "Now don't let this be your last visit to the Old Homestead. Come up in June when all natur' is at her best—come on, all of you, and let the scarlet runners chase you back to childhood."

Called by Odell♦ "certainly the most famous of all rural plays," it grew out of a vaudeville sketch, "Joshua Whitcomb," which Thompson first wrote and performed in 1875. Three years later he expanded it into a full-length play of the same name. The play and the character proved so popular that this second play was written around the figure of the kindly farmer. Thompson played it regularly until shortly before his death in 1911.

Old Maid, The, a play in three acts by Zoë Akins.♦ Produced at the Empire Theatre.♦ January 7, 1935. 305 performances. PP.

When Charlotte Lovell (Helen Menken♦) has an illegitimate daughter, her married cousin, Delia Ralston (Judith Anderson♦), agrees to raise her as her own. Delia also prevents Charlotte from marrying her brother-in-law. Years pass. After Mr. Ralston's death, Charlotte moves in with her cousin. The child, Tina (Margaret Anderson), has grown into an attractive woman who loves her supposed mother and has little time for her prim, dour maiden aunt. At Tina's wedding to rich Lanning Halsey (John Cromwell♦), Charlotte decides to reveal the true story, but finds she cannot summon up the courage to do so. Understanding her agony, Delia quietly tells Tina to give her last kiss to Cousin Charlotte.

Based on Edith Wharton's novel, the play divided New York's critics. But their division turned to unity in their dismay at the play's being awarded the Pulitzer Prize.♦ This dissatisfaction, coupled with the Pulitzer Prize committee's bypassing *Winterset*♦ the next season, led to the establishment of the New York Drama Critics Circle♦ and its own award.

Old Soak, The, a comedy in three acts by Don Marquis. Produced by Arthur Hopkins♦ at the Plymouth Theatre. August 22, 1922. 325 performances.

Clem Halsey (Harry Beresford) is the village drunk and the bane of his wife Matilda (Minnie Dupree♦). She scolds him for having no will power, but he responds, "What do you think kept me drinkin' if twasn't my will power?" When the stocks that his wife has hidden disappear, that is the final straw. She accuses Clem of stealing them and orders him out of the house. Clem learns that his playboy son, Clem Jr. (George Le Guere), actually is the thief, and that he sold the stock at a discount to the Hawleys' cousin, Webster Parsons. Clem sees a way to right matters. Parsons is a snobbish, prissy man. He is also the town's banker, a teetotaler—and the money behind the local bootleggers. So Clem quietly blackmails Parsons into paying him the full price for the stocks.

Alexander Woollcott♦ welcomed the comedy as "a likeable and amusing and mighty cheerful piece."

Don[ald Robert Perry] Marquis (1879–1937) was an Illinois native best known as a humorous columnist. Both this play and his most famous work, *archy and mehitabel,* grew out of figures which originally appeared in his newspaper columns.

Old Vic, THE England's finest and most historic acting company, until it was superseded in 1963 by the National Theatre,♦ it paid a highly praised visit to New York in 1946. Its repertory was *Henry IV, Parts I and II,♦ Uncle Vanya, Oedipus,* and *The Critic.* The company included Laurence Olivier,♦

who offered his memorable Oedipus, Hotspur, and Justice Shallow; Ralph Richardson,♦ praised for his Falstaff; Joyce Redman; and Margaret Leighton.♦ Many critics felt that the company at the time was at its artistic height and that the ensemble playing had not been matched by any troupe since the visit of the Moscow Art Theatre♦ more than two decades before. In 1956 and 1958 the company returned to offer two series of Shakespearean revivals (*Richard II,♦ Romeo and Juliet,♦ Macbeth,♦* and *Troilus and Cressida* in 1956; *Twelfth Night,♦ Hamlet,♦ Henry V* in 1958), and in its final visit in 1962 presented Shaw's *Saint Joan♦* along with two more Shakespearean offerings. Although the roster of performers on these last visits included several distinguished performers, such as Rosemary Harris,♦ Barbara Jefford, John Neville, and Jeremy Brett, the consensus was that the acting lacked the glittering finish and intensity seen in 1946.

OLDMIXON, MRS. [née GEORGINA SIDUS] (1763?–1836) Using the stage name Miss George she made a great impression on London playgoers on her debut at the Haymarket in 1783. She remained a London favorite for ten years before coming to America, shortly after her marriage, to play under the aegis of Wignell♦ at Philadelphia's Chestnut Street Theatre.♦ Critics readily hailed her as the best singing actress of the time, although her remarkably broad talents allowed her to succeed not only in contemporary ballad operas but in wide-ranging roles such as Ophelia, Juliet's Nurse, and Mrs. Candour (in *The School for Scandal).* Ireland♦ recalled that she "was the most brilliant and scientific vocalist in America. She had neither youth nor personal beauty to recommend her; in fact, a peculiar twist in the position of her mouth gave her face a ludicrous appearance, but she possessed great skill as a comic actress, and a thorough musical education, and, with these aids, ranked as one of the most popular *artistes* of the time." Portraits suggest that the "peculiar twist" may have been an exaggeratedly cupid's bow mouth, of the sort so popular in the 1920s. Whatever her shortcomings, she was reputed to be the highest paid performer at the Chestnut Street Theatre. After the opening of the Park Theatre♦ in New York she made numerous appearances there and in other cities, as well. But she remained primarily a Philadelphia actress. She seems to have retired in 1814, although she gave concerts occasionally in later seasons.

OLIVIER, LAURENCE [KERR] (1907–89) The most acclaimed English actor of his generation, he made early New York appearances in *Murder on the Second Floor* (1929), *Private Lives*◆ (1931), and *The Green Bay Tree* (1933). His last pre-World War II appearance was opposite Katharine Cornell◆ as Gaylord Esterbrook, the playwright with serious ambitions, in *No Time for Comedy*◆ (1939). In all these appearances the dark, handsome actor had been looked upon mainly as a promising leading man. By the time he returned after the war in 1946 with the Old Vic,◆ he had earned an international reputation as a versatile performer. With the Old Vic he played Hotspur, Justice Shallow, Oedipus, Puff (*The Critic*), and Astrov (*Uncle Vanya*). He returned in 1951 with Vivien Leigh, his wife at the time, to offer his Caesar and Marc Antony to her Cleopatras. His next major American appearance was to portray Archie Rice, the small-time music-hall song and dance man, in *The Entertainer* (1958). Brooks Atkinson◆ noted of his performance, "He tap-dances, he sings in the nasal tones that are usual in the lower ranks of the profession; he tells blue jokes in a cheap accent and throws the usual insults at the orchestra leader. His shoulders swivel with a kind of spurious bravado. Wearing his hat at a flashy angle, swinging his stick smartly, Mr. Olivier is the very model of the worn-out, untalented music-hall performer who is on the downgrade." For his final American appearances he played the title role of *Becket* (1960) in New York, then assumed the part of Henry II on tour. Some critics have found him excessively mannered, the studied mannerisms growing with the years.

Autobiography: *Confessions of an Actor,* New York, 1982.

OLSEN, [JOHN SIGUARD] OLE (1892–1963) **and JOHNSON,** [HAROLD OGDEN] CHIC (1891–1962) This zany comedy pair first joined forces in 1914 and had established themselves as a popular vaudeville team before touring in *Take a Chance* in 1933. Their greatest success was their madcap revue, *Hellzapoppin*◆ (1938). The show was the longest run musical in Broadway history at the time of its close. The pair met with increasingly less success in their subsequent revues, *Sons o' Fun* (1941), *Laffing Room Only* (1944), and *Pardon Our French* (1950). Unlike most comedy teams, in which one of the pair was essentially a stooge who set up laughs for his or her partner, both Olsen and Johnson participated actively in the gagging. Many felt that Johnson's shrill, high-pitched laughter made him the more outrageous of the pair. They customarily closed their act or their shows with Olsen, who was a native of Peru, Ind., stating, "May you live as long as you like," and

Johnson, a Chicagoan, concluding, "May you laugh as long as you live."

On Borrowed Time, a play in two acts by Paul Osborne.◆ Produced by Dwight Deere Wiman◆ at the Longacre Theatre. February 3, 1938. 321 performances.

Gramps Northrup (Dudley Digges◆) is fearful that after his death his young, orphaned grandson, Pud (Peter Miner), will be placed in the care of his cranky, moralizing Aunt Demetria (Jean Adair). So when the Angel of Death, in the form of Mr. Brink (Frank Conroy), comes for Gramps, the old man chases him up an apple tree and fences him in. Gramps's careless description of the incident convinces Demetria and Dr. Evans (Clyde Franklin) that Gramps has become senile, leading the doctor to certify that Demetria will thereafter be Pud's guardian. In despair, Pud runs away and climbs up the apple tree, from which he slips and falls. Gramps, seeing the lifeless Pud, releases Mr. Brink and joins his beloved grandson in death.

Based on Lawrence Edward Watkin's novel, the work was described by Robert Benchley◆ as a "heart-warming, delightful play." A well-received 1953 revival featured Victor Moore◆ as Gramps.

On Golden Pond, a play in two acts by Ernest Thompson. Produced at the New Apollo Theatre. February 28, 1979. 156 performances.

Ethel (Frances Sternhagen) and Norman Thayer (Tom Aldredge) have been spending their summers in their Maine cottage ever since they have been married. Norman has always been a little crotchety and something of a hypochondriac, but now he is sure he is dying. Nevertheless this summer is a pleasant one, with lots of fishing and visits from friends, family, and neighbors. Yet for once Ethel is reluctantly brought around to Norman's way of thinking, since "practically everyone from the old days on Golden Pond [is] dead. I've seen death, and touched death, and feared it. But today was the first time I've felt it." So as they leave, they take what may well be their final farewells of the summer home.

This quiet idyll reopened the old Apollo Theatre on 42nd Street, initiating a hoped-for rebirth of the street that had once been New York City's main theatrical block and long had been given over to grind movies. The play originally had been produced off-Broadway earlier in the season, and later became a popular film starring Katharine Hepburn◆ and Henry Fonda.◆

Thompson (b. 1949) was born in Vermont, but

studied theatre at various universities around the country before becoming an actor and writing plays. *On Golden Pond* was his first full-length work to be mounted professionally, although an earlier play, *The Westside Waltz,* was revised and used as a vehicle by Miss Hepburn, first on tour and then in New York during the 1981–82 season.

On the Quiet, a comedy in three acts by Augustus Thomas.♦ Produced at the Madison Square Theatre.♦ February 11, 1901. 160 performances.

Robert Ridgeway [in some texts, Treadway] (William Collier♦) has married Agnes Colt (Louise Allen) secretly, since Robert is still a student at Yale. Their attempts to keep the secret lead to the inevitable misunderstandings and mistaken identities, especially in the hands of a dotty English duke and Agnes's interfering brother.

On the Town, a musical comedy in two acts. Book and lyrics by Betty Comden♦ and Adolph Green.♦ Music by Leonard Bernstein.♦ Produced by Oliver Smith♦ and Paul Feigay at the Adelphi Theatre. December 28, 1944. 463 performances.

Three sailors, the romantic Gaby (John Battles), the down-to-earth but vain Chip (Cris Alexander), and the clownish Ozzie (Green) are on leave in New York. During a subway ride Gaby falls in love with a picture of "Miss Turnstiles" (Sono Osato), so the boys set out to find her. Roaming as far as the Museum of Natural History and Coney Island, Chip and Ozzie also find romance, Chip with an outspoken lady cab driver, Hildy (Nancy Walker♦), and Ozzie with an anthropology student, Claire de Loon (Comden).

Principal songs: Lucky To Be Me · New York, New York

Derived from the Bernstein-Jerome Robbins♦ ballet *Fancy Free,* this musical made its authors and choreographer Robbins important figures in the popular musical theatre. An inferior 1971 revival failed.

On Trial, a play in four acts by Elmer Rice♦ [then billed as Elmer L. Reizenstein]. Produced by George M. Cohan♦ and Sam H. Harris♦ in association with Arthur Hopkins♦ at the Candler Theatre. August 19, 1914. 365 performances.

Robert Strickland (Frederick Perry) is accused of murdering Gerald Trask (Frederick Truesdell). According to the prosecution Strickland repaid a loan of $10,000 to Trask, then later that evening returned to the Trask home to steal the money, killing Trask when he caught Strickland in the act. The defense is

not helped by Strickland's silence or by the strange disappearance of Strickland's wife (Mary Ryan). When she is finally found, she confesses that she had years before been seduced by Trask and had gone to his house the night of his murder to plead with him not to reveal her past. But she insists she did not murder him. The defense lawyer catches Trask's secretary, Glover (J. Wallace Clinton), in some damaging contradictions and gets Glover to admit he stole the money. But Glover also insists he did not commit the murder. The jury acquits Strickland.

The play is often said to be the first important drama to make use of the cinematic technique of flashbacks and one of the earliest which, in effect, recounted a trial from beginning to end. Its novelty and expense scared off numerous major producers, but when it finally opened Louis Sherwin of the *Globe* hailed it as "the most striking novelty that has been seen for years," adding correctly, "undoubtedly it will bring about important changes in the technique of the theatre."

On the Twentieth Century, see *Twentieth Century*

On Your Toes, a musical comedy in two acts. Book by Richard Rodgers,♦ Lorenz Hart,♦ and George Abbott.♦ Lyrics by Hart. Music by Rodgers. Produced by Dwight Deere Wiman♦ at the Imperial Theatre. April 11, 1936. 315 performances.

Junior Dolan (Ray Bolger♦), the son of old vaudevillians, becomes a music professor and helps a struggling Russian ballet company. Complications force him to go on in place of the lead dancer and perform opposite Vera Barnova (Tamara Geva♦). Gangsters try to shoot him during the ballet, but they are apprehended in time for a happy ending, which includes his proposal of marriage to sweet Frankie Frayne (Doris Carson).

Principal songs: Slaughter on Tenth Avenue (ballet)♦ · There's a Small Hotel · Too Good for the Average Man

An innovative musical, innovative in no small measure because of the fine Ballanchine♦ ballets, it featured Monty Woolley♦ and Luella Gear♦ in secondary roles. A major revival in 1954 featured Vera Zorina and Bobby Van, while a more successful 1983 revival starred Natalia Makarova.

Once in a Lifetime, a comedy in three acts by Moss Hart♦ and George S. Kaufman.♦ Produced by Sam H. Harris♦ at the Music Box Theatre. September 24, 1930. 406 performances.

The fading of vaudeville and the coming of sound films create turmoil in the entertainment industry.

The two-a-day team of Jerry Hyland (Grant Mills), May Daniels (Jean Dixon), and George Lewis (Hugh O'Connell) find themselves out of work, so head west to give elocution lessons to the terrified actors at the Glogauer film studio. At the studio they discover uniformed pages circulating with signs announcing Mr. Glogauer's whereabouts and roomfuls of dejected playwrights who have been brought to Hollywood en masse, and who now seem likely to have nervous breakdowns from underwork. George is made a film director. He shoots the wrong script, forgets to order the lights turned on, and audibly cracks nuts during the shooting. But the film is hailed as a masterpiece and George as a genius. He is made Glogauer's second-in-command. Glogauer, having nothing better to do, orders the studio demolished and a bigger one built in its place.

In this first of the great Hart-Kaufman collaborations, Kaufman himself assumed the role of the most depressed, articulate playwright. Although *Merton of the Movies* ♦ had earlier used a not dissimilar story to spoof Hollywood, it was this play which initiated a rash of satires on the film industry. A 1979 revival at the Circle in the Square ♦ had only a short run.

One of Our Girls, a comedy in four acts by Bronson Howard. ♦ Produced at the Lyceum Theatre. ♦ November 10, 1885. 200 performances.

Kate Shipley (Helen Dauvray) is the daughter of an American father and French mother. Her mother's family had planned a marriage of convenience for their daughter and had rejected her after she refused to bow to their dictates. They accepted the Shipleys only after Mr. Shipley made his fortune. Now Kate comes to France to visit her mother's family and finds history repeating itself. Her cousin, Julie Fonblanque (Enid Leslie), is refusing to marry the Comte de Crebillon (F. F. Mackay) and has arranged to elope with the man she loves, Henri Saint-Hilaire (Vincent Sternroyd). Kate follows her to her rendezvous and, to avoid problems for Julie, claims it is she Henri is meeting. The situation leads to a duel in which Henri is wounded, but it also brings the Fonblanques to their senses. Julie is allowed to marry Henri, while Kate agrees to marry Capt. John Gregory (E. H. Sothern ♦), who has stood by her.

Many critics, who felt the play was inferior to Howard's *Young Mrs. Winthrop,* ♦ also accused him of stealing the crucial scene in which Kate risks her reputation from Sardou's ♦ *Les Pattes de mouche.* However, Howard insisted he was not familiar with the French play.

One Sunday Afternoon, a play in a prologue, two acts and an epilogue by James S. Hagan. Produced at the Little Theatre. February 15, 1933. 322 performances.

When Biff Grimes (Lloyd Nolan), a dentist, is asked to perform an emergency extraction for Hugo Barnstead (Rankin Mansfield), he plans to kill him with an overdose of gas. Years before Barnstead had framed Grimes and sent him to prison. To make matters worse, Barnstead had then run off with Grimes's attractive girlfriend, Virginia Brush (Mary Holsman). But Grimes discovers that the intervening years have turned Virginia into an overbearing shrew and that Barnstead is a miserably unhappy and troubled man. Grimes himself has long since made a good marriage. So when Barnstead arrives at his office, Grimes does not kill him. He merely extracts the tooth—without any gas whatsoever.

Richard Lockridge of the *Evening Sun* wrote, "It is simple-hearted, and that disarms criticism. Mr. Hagan has, by the sincerity and frequent delicacy of his writing, made the story real and affecting." The day after the play opened Roosevelt declared a national bank holiday. Without funds the play was forced to close for a week until money could be found. It was later reported to have come within a single vote of winning the Pulitzer Prize. ♦

Hagan (1882–1947), a San Diego native, had been a newspaperman, actor, and stage manager before becoming a playwright. Although several of his other works reached Broadway, this was his only success.

One Thousand Milliners Wanted for the Gold Diggins in California An American version of Joseph Sterling Coyne's one-act afterpiece, *One Thousand Spirited Milliners Wanted for the Gold Diggings in Australia,* which had premiered at London's Royal Olympic Theatre in October 1852, it was first presented to New York just over a month later on November 8 by William Burton ♦ at Burton's Theatre. It told of two mischievous young men, Joe Baggs (Burton), a lawyer's clerk, and Tom Tipton (T. B. Johnston), a medical student, who decide to look over a large cross-section of local young ladies by luring them to the office of Baggs's employer, Mr. Singleton (Mr. Gourlay), with promises of lucrative work out West. They trick Singleton into visiting a distant client, then dress up as two kindly spinsters. The girls jam the office, but the ruse is exposed when the men are caught smoking and wearing boots under their frocks. The angry women tie the men to chairs just as a furious Singleton returns. To keep the ladies from broadcasting what has passed the lawyer is forced to offer a champagne party. The play gave Burton one of his biggest hits. Other versions sprang up at competing houses with almost equal success under such simpler titles as *One Thousand Milliners*, *One Thousand Milliners Wanted*, and *Wanted: One Thousand Milliners*. Ben De Bar♦ toured as Baggs for many seasons, and the play held the boards as long as afterpieces remained part of bills.

One Touch of Venus, a musical comedy in two acts. Book by S. J. Perelman♦ and Ogden Nash.♦ Lyrics by Nash. Music by Kurt Weill.♦ Produced by Cheryl Crawford♦ and John Wildberg at the Imperial Theatre. October 7, 1943. 567 performances.

When Whitelaw Savory (John Boles) tells his barber, Rodney Hatch (Kenny Baker), that Savory's statue of Venus is the most beautiful woman in the world, Hatch disagrees. After all, he is engaged to the most beautiful woman in the world, Gloria Kramer (Ruth Bond). To prove his point, he places Gloria's engagement ring on the marble, which promptly comes to life. The escapades of Venus (Mary Martin♦) and Hatch turn Manhattan upside down, with Savory, Gloria and her mother, and a mad Anatolian all in pursuit. The fling destroys the Hatch-Kramer romance, so Hatch is especially disconsolate after Venus returns to stone. But just as he is about to walk away from Savory's art school, a young girl appears. She is the image of Venus, and Hatch is certain he has an engagement ring to fit her finger.

Principal songs: Speak Low · That's Him · The Trouble with Women

With a book and lyrics among the most literate and witty of any American musical comedy, the show was also the first musical comedy to use the briefly voguish Agnes de Mille♦ ballets that *Oklahoma!*♦ had popularized less than seven months before. As with *Oklahoma!*'s dream ballet, the second act "Venus in Ozone Heights" contained material that shaped and furthered the action, in this instance convincing Venus that she would be unhappy remaining earthbound.

O'NEAL, ZELMA [née SCHROEDER] (b. 1907) The vivacious blonde singer and dancer was born in Rock Falls, Ind., and appeared in vaudeville before making her debut in *Good News!*♦ (1927), in which she introduced "The Varsity Drag." She next appeared in *Follow Thru* (1929), in which she sang "Button Up Your Overcoat," and finally in *The Gang's All Here* (1931). The rest of her career was in England.

O'NEILL, EUGENE [GLADSTONE] (1888–1953) Generally acknowledged as the greatest of all American playwrights, he was the son of the celebrated actor James O'Neill.♦ He was born in New York on October 16, 1888, but spent most of his first seven years accompanying his mother and older brother as they followed the actor from city to city. Six years of Catholic schooling were succeeded by four at the Betts Academy and a year as a member of Princeton's Class of 1910. He left the University to accept work in a mail-order house, then spent time prospecting in Honduras. An attack of malaria forced his return to the United States, where he became assistant manager of a theatrical touring company. His desire to escape from his first marriage, coupled with happier memories of boyhood summers in New London, turned him to the sea, so he spent the next several years on a variety of ships, traveling as far as South America. He gave up sailing to accept a small role in his father's company, when the actor was performing a cut-down version of *Monte Cristo* in vaudeville. About the same time he attempted suicide after being seen naked in bed with a prostitute in order to create evidence that would allow his first wife to divorce him. Coincidental with this were his earliest apparent thoughts about becoming a playwright. The relationship on tour with his father was not entirely satisfactory, so the elder O'Neill secretly helped him secure work on a newspaper. However, with the onset of tuberculosis he entered a sanitarium and there more purposefully began writing plays. On his release he continued his writing. In time he enrolled in Professor George Pierce Baker's♦ classes on play-writing at Harvard. The following season was spent writing and holding odd jobs in Greenwich Village, after which he joined the Provincetown Players♦ in the summer of 1916. It was with this ensemble that his professional career began.

The first two one-acters to be mounted by the group were *Bound East for Cardiff*♦ (1916), depicting the death of a seaman aboard a tramp steamer, and *Thirst* (1916), a story of three shipwrecked people on a raft. Later the same year the company produced *Before Breakfast*, in which a nagging wife drives her husband to suicide. In 1917 the players offered five more of his one-acters: *Fog*, focusing on passengers adrift in a lifeboat; *The Sniper*, a bitter anti-war piece telling of a peasant's avenging the deaths of his son and his wife; *The Long Voyage Home*,♦ centering on a shanghaied seaman who longs to return to his farm in Sweden; *Ile*, whose principal figure is a whaling captain threatened with mutiny and madness; and *The Rope*, in which a senile man hangs a noose in his barn in the hope his son will hang himself. During the same year, the Washington Square Players♦ presented *In the Zone,*♦ a story of sailors who believe their mate is a spy. The Provincetown troupe offered two more one-acters in 1918: *Where the Cross Is Made,* a tale of a mad sea captain's obsession with lost treasure; and *The Moon of the Caribbees,*♦ a picture of seamen's squabbles and friendships. The latter play was afterwards combined with *Bound East for Cardiff, The Long Voyage Home,* and *In the Zone* as a full evening under the title *S. S. Glencairn.*♦ *The Dreamy Kid* (1919) recounted the attempts of a black killer to flee from white justice. By 1920 O'Neill's one-acters had clearly stamped him as the most promising of young American playwrights, a promise he moved toward fulfilling that year when his first full-length play to be produced on Broadway, *Beyond the Horizon,*♦ earned a Pulitzer Prize.♦ The play revolved around the star-crossed lives of two brothers, one who goes to sea and the other who remains home to tend the family farm. *The Emperor Jones,*♦ which was produced later that year, was essentially an extended one-act play which employed expressionistic and symbolistic techniques to recount the downfall of a primitive black dictator. Less successful were two one-acters: *Exorcism,* whose hero finds sustenance in his failed attempt at suicide, and *Diff'rent,* detailing the degeneration of an embittered spinster. *Gold* (1921) was a full-length redaction of *Where the Cross Is Made,* while *Anna Christie*♦ (1921), the story of the possible reclamation of a prostitute, was a rewriting of *Chris Christopherson,* which had failed on tryout. O'Neill's other 1921 drama, *The Straw,* dealt with the romance of two patients at a tuberculosis sanitarium. *The First Man* (1922) was an unsuccessful effort to deal with a couple's reaction to an unwanted pregnancy, but its failure was forgotten with the premiere five nights later of his expressionistic study of a brutish stoker's search for the meaning of his existence, *The Hairy Ape.*♦ *Welded* (1924) spotlighted the rigid bonds linking a moody playwright and a mercurial actress. For the Provincetown Players he dramatized Coleridge's *The Ancient Mariner* (1924), employing masks to tell his story. *All God's Chillun Got Wings*♦ examined miscegenation and racial hatred. His best play of 1924 was one of his masterpieces, *Desire Under the Elms,*♦ centering on a cruel, aging farmer whose young wife is seduced by his son. *The Fountain* (1925) recreated the futile search of Ponce de Leon for eternal youth. O'Neill returned to the use of masks for one of his most intriguing, if not entirely

successful plays, *The Great God Brown*♦ (1926), in which a man's relationships to his family, friends, and to his own inner self are explored. The barest suggestion that O'Neill could handle comedy was evident in his study of the timeless businessman, *Marco Millions*♦ (1928), but the work was overshadowed by his five-hour-long probing of the minds of a woman and the men in her life, *Strange Interlude*♦ (1928). The play made extensive use of a long discarded theatrical device, the aside. No Broadway producer would risk mounting his elaborate, philosophical treatise of man's triumph over death, *Lazarus Laughed,* so the work was given its only major production by the Pasadena Community Playhouse♦ in 1928. Once again, O'Neill returned to the use of masks to exemplify the essentially impersonal aspects of mankind. *Dynamo*♦ (1929), exploring America's fascination with the machine age, was intended to be the first of a trilogy, but its failure discouraged the author and he temporarily retired from the theatre. When he returned in 1931, it was with one of his greatest works, *Mourning Becomes Electra,*♦ a resetting of *The Oresteia* in terms of Civil War America. Writing thereafter at a slower pace, he offered Broadway his first comedy in 1933. The play, *Ah, Wilderness!,*♦ was an affectionate look at growing up in America at the turn of the century. However, his reaction to the failure of *Days Without End*♦ (1934), his "modern miracle play" centering on a man redeemed by his acceptance of his religion, coupled with the onset of a debilitating illness, Parkinson's disease, prompted him to retire from the theatrical arena for many years. Nevertheless, in 1936 he was awarded the Nobel Prize for Literature. New York did not see another new O'Neill play until the premiere of *The Iceman Cometh*♦ (1946), in which a traveling salesman who has murdered his wife attempts to convince a group of regulars at a sleazy bar that they cannot live without their illusions. For a brief time afterwards O'Neill's star seemed in decline. However, a brilliant 1956 revival of this play at the Circle in the Square,♦ with Jason Robards, Jr.,♦ as the salesman began a positive re-evaluation of his art. As a result, his widow released other works, which O'Neill had hoped would not be produced for several decades. Many critics consider *Long Day's Journey into Night*♦ (1956) the playwright's finest work. The drama is a thinly disguised autobiography, centering on a famous but mean and tight-fisted actor, his drug-addicted wife, and their two sons. During his illness O'Neill had worked on a projected cycle of eleven plays tracing the history of a single American family. Before his death he had destroyed most of the material for these plays, but two survived. The first to be produced was *A Touch of the Poet*♦ (1957), focusing on a boozy, illusion-riddled innkeeper. The second, *More Stately Mansions* (1967), was concerned with the battle for dominance over a man by his mother and his wife. In 1982 Donald Gallup, curator of Yale's Collection of American Literature, announced that sufficient notes concerning a third play from the series had been found to allow its reconstruction and that it was to be published as *The Calms of Capricorn.* Meanwhile, 1957 saw the posthumous production of another play, *A Moon for the Misbegotten.* ♦ Like *Long Day's Journey into Night,* this work was semi-autobiographical, depicting the search of O'Neill's elder brother (here called James Tyrone, Jr.) for a mother figure. In 1959 two youthful plays which O'Neill had long since rejected and which had been published without his permission in 1950 as part of a volume called *Lost Plays of Eugene O'Neill* were produced. *Abortion* told of the suicide of a young man who believes his girlfriend has died in an illegal operation, while *The Movie Man,* his earliest known attempt at comedy, satirized a still silent Hollywood. Both were written in 1914. The 1950 volume also contained a 1913 skit called *A Wife for Life,* and the 1914 three-act look at marital life, *Servitude.* Another O'Neill play to be offered posthumously to Broadway was *Hughie* (1964), a long one-act play that was essentially a monologue in which a small-time gambler spins self-deluding yarns about himself.

Although O'Neill was perceived early on as a master of stark, realistic tragedy, time has suggested that much of the power and beauty of his work came from its fundamental romanticism and even from a tinge of sentimentality that colored his tragic vision. These aspects, often touching on the supernatural, could be seen from the very start in such examples as the apparition of death as "the pretty lady dressed in black" that beckons to Yank at the end of *Bound East for Cardiff* or the discovery by the rescuing sailors who have been guided to the lifeboat by a child's voice in *Fog* that the child had been dead for a day. But an intellectual or instinctive sureness usually allowed O'Neill to restrain his romantic impulses and weave them effectively into the basically realistic fabric of his stories. O'Neill was almost always at his best when he had a good story to tell and allowed its transcendental implications to simply speak for themselves. His understanding of the dark, labyrinthine side of human nature and of its limitations were unmatched by any other American dramatist and, whether he realized it or not, sufficed

to assure him pre-eminence. When O'Neill attempted to analyze and expound upon his tragic vision, his theatrical acumen sometimes deserted him, so as a rule the most profoundly philosophic of his plays have been among the least actable and therefore the least commercially successful. Nor was he always comfortable when he departed from traditional dramatic structuring and essayed experiments in symbolism, expressionism, ♦ or other more or less novel forms. Curiously, as has long been noted, his plays rarely read well. On the printed page they often seem prolix and turgid. But O'Neill was such a natural child of the theatre that all but a handful of his works come irresistibly alive on stage.

Biography: *O'Neill—Son and Playwright* and *O'Neill—Son and Artist,* Louis Sheaffer, Boston, 1968 and 1973.

O'NEILL, James (1847–1920) Born in Kilkenny, Ireland, he was brought to this country at about the age of five and raised in Buffalo and Cincinnati. He gave up work in a clothing store to become a super at a Cincinnati theatre during an engagement there by Edwin Forrest♦ in 1868. After barnstorming for several seasons he became a leading man first at McVicker's, then at Hooley's Theatre in Chicago. In 1875 he began a two-year stint in New York under the aegis of A. M. Palmer,♦ then left for San Francisco. During his three seasons there he played numerous parts, including that of Jesus Christ in the controversial *Passion Play.* ♦ In 1883 he first appeared in New York in the role with which he was identified ever afterward, Edmund Dantes in *The Count of Monte Cristo.* ♦ Although he subsequently played such roles as D'Artagnan in *The Musketeers* (1899) and the title part in a revival of *Virginius* (1907), his public demanded only his *Monte Cristo* and as a rule he obliged. He was a florid, emotive actor of a supercharged romantic school. His adherence to this older, passing style led to problems when he was called in to direct the American premiere of *Before Breakfast,* an early work by his son Eugene,♦ who later portrayed him affectionately in *Ah, Wilderness!*♦ and more savagely, as a mean pinch-penny, in *Long Day's Journey into Night.* ♦

O'NEILL, Nance [née Gertrude Lamson] (1874–1965) A major turn-of-the-century touring star, she was born in Oakland, Calif., and made her stage debut in San Francisco in 1893 under the aegis of McKee Rankin.♦ She played for several seasons in New York, including a stint as leading lady with the Murray Hill stock company, before embarking on a tour as a star, again under Rankin's aegis. Her repertory reflected those of the great 19th-century actresses, including as it did Juliet, Rosalind, Viola, Parthenia (in *Ingomar*♦), Magda, Fedora, Camille, and Nancy (in *Oliver Twist*). One of her few major New York triumphs was as Odette, the self-sacrificing sister, in David Belasco's♦ 1909 production of *The Lily.* With the coming of films, the road began to fade and so did her popularity. However, she remained active, often in important supporting roles, well into the 1940s.

Open Theatre, see *Chalkin, Joseph*

Opéra Bouffe in America The rage for opéra bouffe exploded on American stages in 1867 with the presentation of such Offenbach operettas as *La Grande Duchesse de Gérolstein*♦ and *La Belle Hélène.* The initial productions were done in French with imported casts, and since they could be understood by few American playgoers, to whom their satire of French politics and society would have meaningless in any case, they relied for their appeal on the color of the mountings, the elan of the performance, and their gorgeous melodies, which ranged from soaringly lyrical to rousing (including most Americans' introduction to can-can music). A reaction set in when they were performed in English, at which time our Victorian morality caused many critics and theatre patrons to condemn their seeming salaciousness. Nevertheless the vogue continued for many years, abetted by the arrival of a later school of more romantic French works such as Audran's *Olivette.* In the 20th century, revivals of these works on Broadway have been sporadic but many of the better operettas have entered the repertories of opera companies.

Oralloossa; or, The Last of the Incas, a tragedy in five acts by Robert Montgomery Bird.♦ Produced at the Arch Street Theatre,♦ Philadelphia. October 10, 1832. 5 performances.

Having slain the Inca leader, Atahualpa, Francisco Pizarro (Daniel Redd) feels free to tighten his stranglehold on Peru. But Pizarro has not reckoned with Atahualpa's son, Oralloossa (Edwin Forrest♦). The treacherous Diego de Almagro (John R. Scott♦) urges Oralloossa on, hoping to supplant Pizarro. However, after Oralloossa kills the Spanish conquistador, Almagro turns Oralloossa's fellow Incas against him. Oralloossa is slain and his sister, Orallie (Miss Eliza Riddle), is buried alive. The new Viceroy, Vaca de Castro (Mr. Quinn), orders Almagro put to death.

This blank-verse drama won one of several prizes Forrest offered for a new American play. Bird later stated he had two purposes in writing the play, "first, the portraiture of a barbarian in which is concentred all those qualities of good and evil which are most strikingly characteristic of savage life; the second, to show how the noblest designs of a great man and the brightest destinies of a nation could be interrupted and destroyed by the unprincipled ambition of a single individual." Forrest met with only indifferent success in the title role, though he continued to revive it on occasion. It also proved a popular vehicle for Edwin Adams♦ until his early death.

ORBACH, [JEROME] JERRY (b. 1935) The swarthy, lanky actor was born in the Bronx and after graduating from Northwestern University studied with such notables as Herbert Berghof♦ and Lee Strasberg.♦ He made his New York debut as a replacement in the role of Macheath in the long-running *Threepenny Opera*♦ in 1958, then called attention to himself when he created the part of El Gallo in *The Fantasticks*♦ (1960), introducing "Try To Remember." Leading men's roles followed in *Carnival* (1961) and *Promises, Promises*♦ (1968). Before assuming his role in the latter he demonstrated his ability in straight comedy by creating the role of Harold Wonder, the put-upon Jewish husband, in *Scuba Duba*♦ (1967). He enjoyed success in another comedy when he portrayed Paul Friedman, the apartment hunter who has a brief liaison with another would-be renter, in *6 Rms Riv Vu* (1972). In 1975 he co-starred with Gwen Verdon♦ and Chita Rivera♦ in the musical *Chicago,*♦ then played a major role in *42nd Street*♦ (1980).

Ordway's Aeolians A mid-19th-century touring minstrel ensemble founded by John B. Ordway. Never quite in the first rank of such organizations, it was nonetheless one of the most innovative. It is generally credited with conceiving the practice of a colorful street parade to announce the troupe's arrival, a practice that soon became common. It apparently was also one of the first to employ more elaborate settings and costumes, and to have attempted to popularize the notion of whiteface minstrel entertainments.

Oregon Shakesperian Festival Association Founded in Ashland, Ore., in 1935 by Angus Bowmer, it had as its original intention to present the complete canon of Shakespeare's plays over a series of summer seasons. Except for a shut-down during World War II, the festival has operated continually since its inception and enlarged both its vision and its program. It now operates three theatres, the 1200-seat, open-air Elizabethan, the 500-seat Bowmer, and the 150-seat Black Swan. While nearly half its repertory remains Shakespearean, its programs today include the full range of classic drama as well as new plays of interest, offered during a season that generally runs from February through October. Since 1988 the group performs in late fall and during the winter at the Portland Center for the Performing Arts. Upon Bowmer's retirement in 1971, Jerry Turner became producing director. Bowmer later wrote a history of the festival, *As I Remember, Adam* (1975).

Oriental Drama in America Oriental (Chinese and Japanese) drama and other aspects of Oriental theatre have never been more than curiosities in America. Language barriers and the marked dissimilarity of Eastern music to Western modes have, of course, been major obstacles, but the whole approach of Chinese and Japanese theatricals has been counter to the fundamentally realistic styles of Occidental writing and playing. As early as the late 18th century, shadow plays, billed as "Chinese Shades" or "Chinese Shadows," were offered briefly, apparently by performers who were relying on descriptions of travelers. In the 1830s and 1840s a woman named Afong May enjoyed some vogue presenting Chinese songs and dances. The first major Oriental company to visit America was the Hook Took Tong, an ensemble of 123 artists, which enjoyed a huge success in San Francisco in 1852 and later played in New York and other Eastern cities. However, the novelty soon wore off, and those Chinese players who elected to remain in America were relegated to dingy playhouses in the Chinese quarters of San Francisco. Some more venturesome American players, such as Mary Anderson♦ and Joseph Jefferson,♦ attended performances there and elsewhere and have left behind graphic descriptions. Miss Anderson wrote, "We visited the Chinese theatre, which is built far underground. In what we know as the green-room we found many Chinamen crowded together . . . the whole atmosphere stifling with the odor of opium smoke and frying food. I was introduced to the great attraction of the Chinese stage, a favorite impersonator of women, who had been paid an immense sum by his countrymen in San Francisco to leave China . . . It was impossible, on seeing him with his delicate features and shining black wig, to believe him to be a man . . . We witnessed the play from the stage (they have no wings or curtain), in full sight of the audience. We

saw but little of it, though we remained a long time, for the Chinese often take a year to act a single play. But we had the good-fortune to see several artists come from behind a door at the back of the stage, go through a scene in which one of them was killed, and the corpse, after lying rigid for a moment, spring up suddenly, bow, smile, and make his exit through the same door, all to the melancholy scraping of a one-stringed instrument and the dismal howl of a human voice." In 1889 the Royal Company of Hong Kong toured major American cities. There have been occasional visits since, including troupes of Chinese acrobats and the Peking Opera after the thaw in relations between the United States and Communist China. The play *The Yellow Jacket*♦ (1912) has been the only successful American drama to consciously employ Chinese techniques, although some writers have suggested that Thornton Wilder's♦ *Our Town*♦ (1938) is indebted to Oriental theatrical mannerisms. The Chinese classic *Pi-Pa-Ki* had some success as *Lute Song* (1946).

Following the opening of Japan to the West, Japanese performers began appearing in American theatres in the late 1860s. They flourished as vaudeville performers, primarily as acrobats, for the next two decades along with the rage for everything Japanese. However, it was not until after World War II that regular Japanese dramatic companies, including the Grand Kabuki, made American tours. The Grand Kabuki first visited America in 1969. The exotic nature of these entertainments again prevented their having a major influence on the mainstream of American play-writing or presentation. Stephen Sondheim's♦ *Pacific Overtures*♦ (1973) employed suggestions of Kabuki style, while the earlier *Rashomon* (1959) was a dramatization of a Japanese film.

Of course, China, Japan, and other Oriental countries have been the settings of numerous American plays and musicals, but despite these backgrounds they have told essentially Occidental-type stories in Occidental terms.

Origin of the Cake Walk, The, see *Clorindy*

Original Cast Recordings From the very beginnings of recorded sound in the late 19th century, prominent American theatrical figures have stood before microphones and left their voices and interpretations for posterity. However sketchily and faintly, such notables as Edwin Booth, ♦ Joseph Jefferson,♦ and early musical stars such as Jessie Bartlett Davis♦ and Eugene Cowles♦ have offered examples of the readings that made them famous. As records grew more commonplace and sophisticated, increasing numbers of artists, especially from our musical stages, made recordings. Usually these were merely the best received songs from a show and were customarily recorded with a studio orchestra. Both Victor and Columbia for many years issued "Gems," medleys of songs from a show on a single side of a large record. The term "original cast recording," on the other hand, came to mean a virtually complete recording of a musical with its original cast and theatre orchestra. In this respect England was far ahead of America, presenting remarkable examples as far back as the turn of the century. One ironic result is that many of the great American musicals of the 1910s, 1920s, and 1930s are available only with their original London casts. The vogue for recording American casts of American shows unquestionably began when Jack Kapp♦ recorded the opening night cast of *Oklahoma!*♦ for Decca in 1943. For about the next quarter of a century every major American musical received a practically complete original cast recording. After Kapp's death, Goddard Lieberson♦ at Columbia Records was in the vanguard of responsible record makers, issuing not only the material from new shows but often going back in time to re-create earlier unrecorded works. The original cast recording of *My Fair Lady*♦ is said to have sold over six million copies, a record in its field. With the decline of the American musical in the 1970s and 1980s, and changes in record company policies, such recordings became fewer. However, in recent years a few specialty houses are reconstructing even Broadway failures and issuing them in limited pressings for what may be perceived as a "cult" market.

Orpheum Theatre Chain A chain of vaudeville theatres founded in the late 19th century by Morris Meyerfield, who was a partner in the Orpheum Theatre in San Francisco, and Martin Lehman, who owned a vaudeville house in Los Angeles. Lehman eventually moved his office to Chicago, where he hired Martin Beck. ♦ With these three men at the helm the chain quickly became dominant between Chicago and the West Coast. It was later merged with B. F. Keith's♦ chain and, after the demise of vaudeville, became part of RKO.

OSBORN, PAUL (1901–88) Born in Evansville, Ind., the son of a minister, he earned B.A. and M.A. degrees at the University of Michigan, then studied with Professor George Pierce Baker♦ at Yale. He taught at both schools before seeing the premiere of his first play, *Hotbed* (1928), a story of hatred and

dishonesty on a college campus. *A Ledge* (1929) was a melodrama centering on a young businessman accused of theft. He scored his first hit when he turned to comedy with *The Vinegar Tree* (1930), in which a middle-aged, married woman dreams of recapturing an old flame. After the failure of *Oliver Oliver* (1934), a story of a mother's attempt to marry off her worthless son, he enjoyed another success with the fantasy *On Borrowed Time*♦ (1938), in which an old man wards off death. *Morning's at Seven*♦ (1939), was a warmly observed look at the lives of a large family. All of his remaining works to reach Broadway were, like *On Borrowed Time,* adaptations of novels. *The Innocent Voyage* (1943), a failure, was derived from Richard Hughes's *A High Wind in Jamaica. A Bell for Adano*♦ (1944), *Point of No Return* (1951), and *The World of Suzie Wong*♦ (1958) were all commercial successes. The diversity of his writing makes it difficult to characterize Osborn, but his best original works were filled with sharply and affectionately drawn figures.

OSBORNE, JOHN (b. 1929) The British dramatist whose *Look Back in Anger*♦ (1957), centering on a poor, unhappy husband, served as America's introduction to the postwar school of "angry young men" subsequently found success with *The Entertainer* (1958), which offered Laurence Olivier♦ as a seedy vaudevillian; *Epitaph for George Dillon* (1958), written with Anthony Creighton and telling of an unhappy, unprincipled playwright; *Luther* (1963), in which Albert Finney portrayed the great religious figure; and *Inadmissible Evidence* (1965), depicting a middle-aged man plagued by self-doubt and self-hatred. Thereafter his gifts seemingly waned and, except for the failed *A Patriot for Me* (1969), none of his plays was given a major Broadway presentation.

Othello First performed in America in 1751 by Robert Upton,♦ this tragedy was, along with *Hamlet*♦ and *Richard III,*♦ one of the three Shakespeare plays most favored by 19th-century classic American tragedians. One special reason for the favor seems to have been that they could alternate in the roles of Iago and Othello. For many early 19th-century Americans Edmund Kean's♦ dignified but volatile Moor served as an exemplar, challenged only by the more ferocious, stentorian Moor of Edwin Forrest. ♦ Both Junius Brutus Booth♦ and Edwin Booth♦ met marked success in either role, with the younger actor's interpretations marked by subtleties apparently foreign to his father. Among the other notable interpreters of one or both parts were Thomas Abthorpe Cooper,♦

G. F. Cooke♦ (whose Iago won praise for not being too theatrically villainous), A. A. Addams,♦ James Fennell,♦ E. L. Davenport,♦ Lawrence Barrett,♦ James Murdoch,♦ John McCullough,♦ and Robert Mantell.♦ Most, but not all of these actors performed the Moor in black or swarthy make-up. A notable Moor was Tommaso Salvini,♦ who emphasized the figure's Mediterranean emotionalism. In modern times Walter Huston♦ suffered a major failure when he essayed the Moor, but Alfred Drake,♦ better known for starring in musicals, won high praise when he offered an insinuating but carefully controlled Iago at the American Shakespearean Festival.♦ However, the most memorable modern revivals have both offered black men as the Moor. In 1943 Paul Robeson♦ gave a richly humane performance to the Iago of José Ferrer♦ and the notable Desdemona of Uta Hagen,♦ while a 1982 production offered James Earl Jones♦ as Othello and Christopher Plummer♦ as Iago.

Other Girl, The, a comedy in three acts by Augustus Thomas.♦ Produced by Charles Frohman♦ at the Criterion Theatre. December 29, 1903. 160 performances.

When "The Kid" (Lionel Barrymore♦), the world boxing champion, is taken under the wing of a fight-mad minister, Dr. Bradford (Frank Worthing), he decides he would like to marry into society and live the good life. The girl he decides to marry is Catherine Fulton (Drina De Wolfe), ignoring the fact that she is engaged to Reginald Lumley (Joseph Wheelock, Jr.). Catherine proves so susceptible to his magnificent physique and rough charms that she agrees to elope. Recognizing that such a match would be a disaster, Catherine's brash friend, Estelle Kitteridge (Elsie De Wolfe), contrives to take her place. In their haste the young couple accidentally run over Reginald. Good sense prevails in the end.

This broad, somewhat preposterous farce owed much of its success to its performances and to what one critic called Thomas's ability to inject "a wealth of accurately observed and truly felt character." Elsie De Wolfe (1865–1950) became for a time a leading set designer in her native New York, after which, as Lady Mendl, she was a well-known author and interior decorator.

Other People's Money, a play in two acts by Jerry Sterner. Produced at the Minetta Lane Theatre. February 16, 1989. Still running at press time.

Lawrence Garfinkle (Kevin Conway) is a smug, uncouth corporate raider, who has set out to take over the conservatively managed, somewhat de-

crepit New England Wire and Cable Company. The company's chairman, Andrew Jorgenson (Arch Johnson), determines to resist. But the cunning, persistent Garfinkle slowly wins over not only many stockholders, he even convinces the company's president (James Murtaugh) to sell to him. Far more surprisingly, he gains the affection of Kate Sullivan (Mercedes Ruehl), who is not only the daughter of Jorgenson's longtime assistant (Scotty Bloch) but a sharp Wall Street lawyer brought in to fend off Garfinkle.

While this incisively written drama succeeded handsomely off-Broadway, a highly praised road company quickly folded. But the play has met further success in regional theatres. It is virtually the only drama to deal with a major economic problem of the decade.

Sterner (b. 1938) is a Bronx native and college dropout. He spent many years in the real estate business before abandoning it to work full time at playwriting. His first produced play was a quick failure; this was his second work to reach the footlights.

Our American Cousin A comedy by Tom Taylor,♦ it originally centered on a rather bumptious Yankee, Asa Trenchard, who arrives in England, where he rescues his virtually impoverished English relatives from the treacherous financial machinations of a supposed family counselor and also marries the young girl whom he himself had inadvertently deprived of an inheritance. The play was initially offered to J. W. Wallack,♦ who rejected it and suggested it be submitted to Laura Keene.♦ She, too, at first was cool to the play. However, when she produced it at her theatre on October 18, 1858, with Joseph Jefferson♦ as Asa, and E. A. Sothern♦ as the silly, lisping Lord Dundreary, the play became one of the biggest comedy hits of its era and helped both actors on the way to stardom. With time Sothern expanded his role until it was the most important part in the play. A comparison of an 1869 printed version and an 1870 manuscript used by Sothern shows markedly different dialogue. The play did not reach its author's native England until 1861. It held the stage in both countries for several decades and was revived with some regularity until the turn of the century. Most Americans know the play as the one being performed at the time of President Lincoln's♦ assassination.

Our Boarding House, a comedy in four acts by Leonard Grover. Produced at the Park Theatre. January 29, 1877. 104 performances.

When her supposed brother-in-law, Joseph Fioretti (W. E. Sheridan♦), informs Beatrice Manheim (Maud Harrison) that her marriage has no legal standing, the other roomers in the Chicago boarding house where she stays are thrown into an uproar. Some are for evicting her, others sympathize. The most prominent among the boarders are Professor Gregarious Gillypod (Stuart Robson♦), the inventor of "The Great Flying Machine," and Colonel M. T. Elevator (W. H. Crane♦), an expert in the ups and downs of the grain market. The pair are friendly enemies, but they share in the general joy when Miss Manheim discovers that not only was her marriage legal after all, but that her late husband has left her a fortune.

The frame device of Miss Manheim's marital problems was merely an excuse to offer a comic selection of boarders. The show was the first to couple Crane and Robson, whose success was so great that they immediately became one of the theatre's leading comedy teams.

Grover (1835–1926) was born on a farm in Livingston County, N.Y., and began his career as an actor, but soon switched to producing and managing theatres. Among the noted theatres he ran were Philadelphia's Chestnut Street Theatre,♦ Washington's National Theatre,♦ and New York's Olympic. This was his only successful play.

Our Town, a play in three acts by Thornton Wilder. ♦ Produced by Jed Harris♦ at Henry Miller's Theatre. February 4, 1938. 336 performances. PP.

The Stage Manager (Frank Craven♦) walks onto a bare, uncurtained stage, with only a few chairs and tables as props, and addresses the audience. He narrates the events of a typical American small town—Grover's Corner, N.H.—in the years 1901–13. The town is going about its leisurely, traditional business. Professor Willard (Arthur Allen) and Editor Webb (Thomas W. Ross) describe the town's scientific and social backgrounds, and much of the drama centers in the families of Webb and Dr. Gibbs (Jay Fassett). The first act, "Daily Life," focuses on the ordinary pursuits of the town on a May day in 1901. The second act, "Love and Marriage," describes the courtship and marriage of Emily Webb (Martha Scott) and George Gibbs (John Craven). The third act, "Death," presents the funeral of Emily, who has died in childbirth. Offered a chance to return to relive any one special day in her life, she selects her twelfth birthday. But the return is painful, for she realizes that the living cannot appreciate how precious life's small moments really are. Moving back to the cemetery, where she finds George crying at her grave, she muses to her mother-in-law, beside whom she is buried, "They don't understand very much, do they?" "No, dear, not very much," Mrs. Gibbs responds. With that, the Stage Manager sends the audience home.

One of the most original and popular of all American plays, it was praised by Richard Lockridge of the *Evening Sun* for its "rare simplicity and truth." Its vibrant humanity—its expression of a sense of "something way down deep that's eternal about every human being"—has helped establish it as an American classic, while its continued appeal can be attributed in good part to its moving depiction of simpler times and simple values. Largely because of its basic sets and optimistic message, it has long been popular with amateur theatrical groups.

Outer Critics Circle The group was formed in 1950 by critics John Gassner, ♦ Charles Freeman, and Joseph Kaye as an "organization of writers on the New York theatre for out-of-town newspapers, national publications and other media beyond Broadway." Its main purpose was "to recognize distinctive achievement in the professional New York theatre by the awarding of medallions and scrolls to selected theatrical participants at an annual awards event" as well as to promote the exchange of ideas and friendships among widely dispersed critics.

Over There Theatre League A group formed during World War I to entertain American troops overseas, much as the USO did in the next war, it was underwritten by producers and other members of the theatrical fraternity and sent out full productions of popular plays and vaudeville bills.

Over 21, a comedy in three acts by Ruth Gordon. ♦ Produced by Max Gordon♦ at the Music Box Theatre. January 3, 1944. 221 performances.

When Max Wharton (Harvey Stephens), a newspaper editor who is barely young enough to be accepted by the armed forces, enters officers' candidate school, his wife, Paula (Miss Gordon), throws up her successful career as novelist and screenwriter to be with him. Army rules and regulations sometimes make things difficult, but not nearly as much as Joel Nixon (Philip Loeb), a Hollywood producer insisting on revisions in Paula's latest script, or Robert Drexel Gow (Loring Smith), Max's demanding publisher, who attempts to get Max out of the army. By the time Max is transferred to Arkansas, Paula has understood that they will have to wait until the war is over to live properly again. She accepts Gow's offer to replace Max as editor.

Ward Morehouse♦ of the *Sun* insisted, "The jokes are better than the story," only to add, "But as entertainment the piece is immense." With this, her first play, Miss Gordon displayed a competency and versatility rare among leading actresses.

OWENS, JOHN E[DMOND] (1823–86) One of the most popular of 19th-century character actors, he was born in Liverpool and brought to America at the age of five. His family settled in Philadelphia, where he made his stage debut in 1841 under the aegis of William Burton. ♦ John Brougham♦ brought him to New York in 1850. Although his rise was comparatively slow, he established himself in the public affection with his characterizations of Dr. Pangloss, Caleb Plummer, Paul Pry, Aminadab Sleek, and Timothy Toodle, many of which Burton had popularized earlier. However, his most famous role was that of Solon Shingle, the cracker-barrel Yankee who forever talks of his "applesass," in the play known both as *Solon Shingle* and *The People's Lawyer.* ♦ He first played the role during the 1856–57 season. Others had played the part before him, but theatregoers and critics generally agreed that his interpretation was the best. He continued to essay new parts until his retirement in 1885, but it was his country bumpkin that his public demanded he keep returning to. Joseph Jefferson♦ considered him "the handsomest low comedian I had ever seen. He had a neat, dapper little figure, and a face full of lively expression. His audience was with him from first to last, his effective style and great flow of animal spirits capturing them." Clara Morris♦ was more graphic when she noted, "Mr. Owens was of medium height and very brisk in all his movements, walking with a short and quick little step. He had a wide mouth, good teeth, and a funny pair of eyes. The eyeballs were very large and round, and he showed an astonishing amount of their whites, which were of an unusual brilliancy and lustre; this, added to his power of rolling them wildly about in their sockets, made them very funny." Owens's wife noted his versatility when she wrote, "In *Solon Shingle* his voice ruralized into eccentricity, and in *Caleb Plummer* it sobered into pathos."

Biography: *Memories of the Professional and Social Life of John E. Owens,* Mrs. John E. Owens, Baltimore, 1892.

Owl and the Pussycat, The, a play in three acts by Bill Manhoff. Produced at the ANTA Theatre. November 18, 1964. 427 performances.

Doris (Diana Sands), a semi-literate prostitute, is evicted from her apartment after her neighbor, Felix Sherman (Alan Alda), complains about her behavior to the landlord. She knocks on Felix's door in the middle of the night, accusing him of being a homosexual informer. The encounter leads to a stormy romance.

Typical of the many absurdly small-cast, relatively actionless plays that theatrical economics had forced upon the theatre, it was dismissed by Howard Taubman of the *Times* as "slick comic writing." Many playgoers nevertheless found it possessed an attractive charm and verve.

Wilton Manhoff (1918?–1974) was a Newark-born radio and television writer, represented on Broadway only by this play.

P

PAGE, GERALDINE [SUE] (1924–87) Born in Kirksville, Mo., she studied at the Goodman Theatre School♦ and with Uta Hagen♦ before coming to playgoers' attention as Alma Winemiller, the frustrated spinster driven to promiscuity, in a 1952 revival of *Summer and Smoke*♦ at the Circle in the Square.♦ Subsequent successes included her Lily, the illiterate wife of a day-dreaming husband, in *Midsummer* (1953); Marcelline, the wife of a homosexual, in *The Immoralist* (1954); Lizzy Curry, the homely spinster whose life is transformed by a brash con man, in *The Rainmaker*♦ (1954); Princess Kosmonopolis, the decaying film star, in *Sweet Bird of Youth*♦ (1959); the possessive Nina Leeds in a 1963 revival of *Strange Interlude*♦; several roles in the double bill *White Lies* and *Black Comedy* (1967); Marion, the aristocratic wife at a series of misbegotten Christmas Eve parties, in *Absurd Person Singular* (1974); and Mother Miriam Ruth, who defends a young nun accused of manslaughter, in *Agnes of God* (1982). She was co-starring in a 1986 revival of *Blithe Spirit* at the time of her death. Although she at first seemed to subscribe to the mannerisms of the Method School, she proved a versatile, wide-ranging actress.

Paid in Full, a play in four acts by Eugene Walter.♦ Produced by Wagenhals♦ and Kemper♦ at the Astor Theatre. February 25, 1908. 167 performances.

Joseph Brooks (Tully Marshall) is an attractive but basically worthless young man who has been lucky enough to marry above his station. His wife Emma (Lillian Albertson), deeply in love with him, is blind to his failings. Not even the warnings of her mother Mrs. Harris (Hattie Russell), her sister Beth (Oza Waldrop), or of James Smith (Ben Johnson), a loyal family friend who has loved Emma for many years, can open her eyes. When Brooks is caught embezzling company funds he demands that Emma plead for him with his boss, Captain Williams (Frank Sheridan), who had once been a partner of Emma's father. In fact, Brooks hints that Emma should be willing to prostitute herself if that is what it takes to exonerate him. Emma dutifully visits Williams. The old man recognizes the shamefulness of Brooks's ploy, writes a letter exculpating Brooks, then reads

Emma the riot act. When Emma returns home Brooks demands a full accounting of what occurred, ready to condemn Emma for doing what he sent her to do. His baseness now is evident even to his wife, who walks out on him.

Although he felt that Walter was not always steadfast in his seriousness of purpose, suggesting, for example, that Mrs. Harris and Beth were farcically exaggerated, Walter Prichard Eaton♦ nevertheless agreed that the play "has a purpose above the mere trickle of a story, the rehashing of conventional situations—that is searching for truth." For all its comic interludes, many playgoers found its grimness too unrelieved.

PAINTER, ELEANOR (1890–1947) A native of Walkerville, Iowa, she had sung leads in opera in Germany and across the United States before making her Broadway debut in *The Lilac Domino* (1914). Her most famous role was the title part in Victor Herbert's *Princess Pat* (1915), in which she introduced "Love Is the Best of All." She later starred in *Glorianna* (1918), a 1920 revival of *Florodora,*♦ *The Last Waltz* (1921), *The Chiffon Girl* (1924), and *The Nightingale* (1927).

Pair of Sixes, A, a farce in three acts by Edward Peple.♦ Produced by H. H. Frazee♦ at the Longacre Theatre. March 20, 1914. 207 performances.

George H. Nettleton (George Parson) and T. Boggs Johns (Hale Hamilton) are partners in a pharmaceutical business that has made a fortune with a "pill [that] will fill the bill." But their success has not kept them from constantly feuding. So their lawyer, Thomas J. Vanderholt (Fritz Williams), arranges for them to play a game of poker, with the loser forfeiting his say in the business for a whole year and serving during that time as the winner's butler. Vanderholt's ploy is not entirely disinterested, since he is Johns's rival for the affections of Florence Cole (Ann Murdock). Vanderholt contrives to have Johns lose. Since Johns will have to give up entirely his share of the company if he fails to keep his part of the bargain, all sorts of obstacles are thrown in the way, including Nettleton's aging, amorous maid, Coddles (Maude Eburne). In the end, however, Johns proves he is a very good loser indeed.

This rollicking, fast-paced farce was turned into the 1926 musical hit, *Queen High,* featuring Charles Ruggles as John, Frank McIntyre♦ as Nettleton, and Luella Gear♦ as Florence, with book by Laurence Schwab♦ and B. G. De Sylva,♦ lyrics by De Sylva and music by Lewis Gensler. The show's hit tune was "Cross Your Heart."

Pajama Game, The, a musical comedy in two acts. Book by George Abbott♦ and Richard Bissell. Lyrics and music by Richard Adler♦ and Jerry Ross.♦ Produced by Frederick Brisson,♦ Robert E. Griffith,♦ and Harold Prince♦ at the St. James Theatre. May 13, 1954. 1,063 performances.

Babe Williams (Janis Paige), head of the union grievance committee at the Sleep-Tite Pajama Factory, refuses to date the factory's new superintendent, Sid Sorokin (John Raitt♦), because he sits on the opposite side of the bargaining table. However, when Sid convinces the company president to give the employees a seven-and-a-half-cent raise, she relents. A subplot centers on the antics of the company's production manager (Eddie Foy, Jr.♦) and the bookkeeper (Carol Haney).

Principal songs: Hernando's Hideaway · Hey, There · Steam Heat

Based on Bissell's novel, *7 1/2 Cents,* the musical was melodic and comic, but also mirrored the persistent liberal, pro-union stance of many Broadway shows. In his first choreographic assignment, Bob Fosse♦ showed the wit and imagination that led him to become a major name in American musicals. A 1973 revival failed.

Pal Joey, a musical comedy in two acts. Book by John O'Hara. Lyrics by Lorenz Hart.♦ Music by Richard Rodgers.♦ Produced by George Abbott♦ at the Ethel Barrymore Theatre. December 25, 1940. 374 performances.

Joey (Gene Kelly), a handsome, small-time dancer, begins his courtship of innocent Linda English (Leila Ernst) by proclaiming about her virtues, "I Could Write a Book." Joey himself is notably short on virtues, so when Vera Simpson (Vivienne Segal♦), a rich, callous, past-her-prime matron, finds herself "Bewitched" by him and offers to set him up in luxury with his own night club, he all but drops Linda. In time Joey's selfishness and egotism pall even for the tolerant Vera. Matters come to a head when Linda tells Vera of a plan to blackmail her by threatening to tell Mr. Simpson of the liaison. The women agree that as far as Joey is

concerned they no longer want him, and the other can "Take Him." Having lost both women Joey wanders off into the night to find another romance.

Other principal songs: Do It the Hard Way · You Mustn't Kick It Around · Zip

Innovative in its no-punches-pulled look at bought love, this became a landmark American musical comedy. Not all critics accepted it at first. While Louis Kronenberger♦ hailed it as "The most unhackneyed musical show since *Of Thee I Sing,*" Brooks Atkinson♦ moaned, "If it is possible to make an entertaining musical comedy out of an odious story, 'Pal Joey' is it . . . [but] . . . can you draw sweet water from a foul well?" Although its initial production was highly successful, an excellent 1952 revival, prompted by the popularity that year of "Bewitched" and an increasingly open moral climate, was more popular. Miss Segal again headed the cast, with Harold Lang as Joey. There have been several subsequent revivals. Kelly was rushed to Hollywood after his appearance in the show, but when the musical was finally filmed years later the lead was assigned to Frank Sinatra.

Palace Theatre Built by Martin Beck♦ on Broadway between 46th and 47th streets, the house was opened in early 1913. By that time, however, Beck had lost it. It quickly became the flagship of the Keith♦ circuit and America's leading vaudeville house. "To play the Palace" was the ambition of all two-a-day performers. With the coming of sound films and the demise of vaudeville, it became a film house in the 1930s. A policy of vaudeville was reinstated briefly in the early 1950s. In 1965 the house was extensively renovated and became a major home to Broadway musicals.

PALMER, A[LBERT] M[ARSHALL] (1838?–1905) Born in North Stonington, Conn., he graduated from New York University Law School, but never practiced law. Instead he became active in politics, where he met Sheridan Shook, Collector of Internal Revenue for New York, and became Shook's righthand man. He worked as a librarian and an accountant, but had little connection with the theatre, until Shook made him head bookkeeper at the Union Square Theatre,♦ which Shook had opened as a variety house in 1871. When a policy of vaudeville failed, Shook appointed Palmer manager in 1872. Palmer quickly assembled a first-rate company and turned the theatre into a legitimate playhouse that rivaled Wallack's as well as Daly's♦ flourishing new troupe. Among his successes were *The Two Orphans*♦ (1874), *A Celebrated Case*

(1878), *The Lights o' London* (1881), and *A Parisian Romance* (1883). After a fight with Shook he left the Union Square in spring 1883, and a year later took over the Madison Square Theatre. ♦ Heretofore his success had come largely from imported plays and from recruiting established actors from other companies, but with growing confidence he now began to give hearings to new works by American authors and to employ untested actors. In 1888 he also took over Wallack's, renaming it Palmer's. His successes in this period included *Beau Brummell* ♦ (1890), *Alabama* ♦ (1891), *Lady Windermere's Fan* (1893), and *Trilby* ♦ (1895), while performers whose careers he furthered included Maurice Barrymore, ♦ John Drew, ♦ Richard Mansfield. ♦ and Clara Morris. ♦ Just before the turn of the century both his health and his theatrical judgment began to fail. His final years were spent first as Mansfield's manager and then as manager of the Herald Square Theatre for Charles Frohman. ♦ He served as president of the Actors' Fund ♦ from 1885 to 1897. His middle name is sometimes given as Marshman.

PALMER, MINNIE (1857–1936) The Philadelphia-born actress and singer made her debut in 1874. She scored her biggest success as Tina, the good girl who must overcome the wiles of a wicked woman, in *My Sweetheart* (1882). The show was even more popular in England than in America, so she remained there for much of her subsequent career. Her last appearance was in a supporting role in *Lightnin'* ♦ (1918).

Panama Hattie, a musical comedy in two acts. Book by Herbert Fields ♦ and B. G. De Sylva. ♦ Lyrics and music by Cole Porter. ♦ Produced by De Sylva at the 46th Street Theatre. October 30, 1940. 501 performances.

Hattie Maloney (Ethel Merman ♦) is a bar girl in the Canal Zone, where she meets and falls in love with a Philadelphia socialite, Nick Bullett (James Dunn). When they agree to marry it is with the understanding that Hattie can win the affection of Nick's young daughter from a former marriage. So Hattie sets about wooing little Geraldine (Jean Carroll) and eventually succeeds.

Principal songs: I've Still Got My Health · Let's Be Buddies · Make It Another Old Fashioned, Please

A brash, brassy musical, without a truly top-drawer Porter score, its excellent production, Miss Merman's appeal, and improving economic times made it the first book musical since the Depression to run more than 500 performances.

PANTAGES, [PERICLES] ALEXANDER (1871(?)–1936) The Greek-born vaudeville magnate reputedly entered the business with profits he made during the Klondike gold rush and from a small produce store he owned next to a theatre in Seattle. He opened a tiny dime vaudeville theatre there in 1902 and quickly expanded. In short order he became the major competition to the Sullivan and Considine ♦ vaudeville circuit in the Northwest. His next move was to expand into Orpheum ♦ territory in California. At his height he controlled the largest independently owned vaudeville chain in the nation and reached as far East as Alabama. With the coming of sound films he sold out to RKO, although he lost considerable monies when the RKO bonds he was given went into default. His age at his death was listed variously as somewhere between sixty-five and seventy-two.

PAPP, JOSEPH [né PAPIROFSKY] (b. 1921) The Brooklyn-born producer and director studied at Hollywood's Actors Laboratory, where he then served as managing director from 1948 to 1950. After understudying both sons in a touring company of *Death of a Salesman,* ♦ for which he was also stage manager, he returned to New York. There he directed and sometimes produced a number of off-Broadway mountings. In 1954 he founded the Shakespearean Theatre Workshop which in time evolved into the New York Shakespeare Festival. ♦ Since then his career has been inextricably tied to that organization.

Biography: *Enter Joseph Papp,* Stuart W. Little, New York, 1974.

Paris Bound, a comedy in three acts by Philip Barry. ♦ Produced by Arthur Hopkins ♦ at the Music Box Theatre. December 27, 1927. 234 performances.

For six years Mary (Madge Kennedy ♦) and Jim Hutton (Donald Cook ♦) have seemed the ideal young couple. Then Mary discovers that Jim has not been totally faithful to her. On their wedding day, Jim's divorced father, James, Sr. (Gilbert Emery ♦), had warned them to overlook occasional strayings, lest it ruin their marriage as it had destroyed his. At first Mary is bitter and determined on divorce. But when she realizes that Jim has ignored her own flirtation with a handsome young composer, Richard Parrish (Donald MacDonald), she decides to live and let live.

Brooks Atkinson ♦ of the *Times* hailed the work as "a comedy of manners, rich in quality, true in temper and buoyant in its social criticism."

Park Theatre Opened in 1798 at the New Theatre by Lewis Hallam♦ and John Hodgkinson♦ to replace the John Street Theatre,♦ it served as New York's only playhouse for a quarter of a century, and for several decades thereafter remained a prestigious auditorium. Subsequent managers included William Dunlap,♦ Thomas Abthorpe Cooper,♦ Stephen Price,♦ Edmund Shaw Simpson,♦ and, briefly, Thomas Hamblin.♦ Under its earliest managers it boasted a fine stock company, probably surpassed only by those in Philadelphia and Boston. Matters changed during Price's thirty-one-year tenure, which began in 1808. It was in his time that New York became the largest American city and thus America's theatrical capital. Probably unwittingly, Price initiated the decline of the stock company by importing foreign celebrities and increasingly emphasizing the star system. Because the growing population required more performances of successes, Price also began to abandon the repertory policy. However, it was not until a year after his death that the three-week stand of Boucicault's♦ *London Assurance♦* (1841) gave New York its earliest "long run." The first American play to enjoy a similar engagement was *Fashion♦* in 1845. The theatre had been reconstructed after several fires, but when it burned to the ground in 1848, shortly after Hamblin had taken over, it was not rebuilt, since by then the theatre district had moved northwards.

The first permanent theatre to be built in Brooklyn was also called the Park. It was opened in 1863 and enjoyed many years of prosperity under the Conways.♦

PARKE, John (1754–89) A Delaware soldier in the Continental Army, he wrote poetry and a biography of Horace as well as *Virginia, A Pastoral Drama on the Birth-Day of an Illustrious Personage and the Return of Peace, February 11, 1784.* In it, Washington appears as the silent Daphnis and is saluted by nymphs and shepherds. Although no record survives of a professional performance, Quinn♦ believed it may have been mounted by some amateur group.

PARKER, Dorothy [née Rothschild] (1893–1967) Born in West End, N.J., the writer and wit occasionally served as a drama critic, most notably for the *New Yorker* during Robert Benchley's♦ vacations. She became famous for her poisonously caustic dismissal of plays and performers. She wrote in one review, "*The House Beautiful* is the play lousy," and elsewhere accused Katharine Hepburn♦ of running a gamut of emotions "from A to B." She also created highly praised sketches for the 1922 revue, *The*

49ers, but only two of her full-length plays reached New York, where both failed. *Close Harmony* (1924), written with Elmer Rice,♦ dealt with neighbors who decided to desert their spouses and elope, but think better of it; while *Ladies of the Corridor* (1953), written with Arnaud d'Usseau, centered on the lonely tenants of a hotel catering to widows. In 1956 she contributed lyrics to *Candide.♦*

Biography: *You Might as Well Live,* John Keats, New York, 1970.

PARKER, Henry Taylor (1867–1934) The Boston-born drama critic, known for many years largely by his initials H.T.P., was said to have left Harvard because it failed to offer sufficient courses in drama and literature. He worked as a correspondent for several papers before becoming drama and music critic for the New York *Globe* in 1900. In 1905 he returned to Boston to assume a similar position with the *Transcript,* remaining with the paper until his death. He was one of the most distinguished critics of his era, respected for his long, thoughtful, and open-minded reviews. John Mason Brown♦ recalled, "This remarkable little man of fine perceptions, with his dark eyes burning quizzically in a head bent forward with a sleuthing thrust and emphatic in its nods, was a giant among critics."

Biography: *H.T.P.: Portrait of a Critic,* David McCord, New York, 1935.

PARKER, Lottie Blair, see *Way Down East*

Parlor, Bedroom and Bath, a farce in three acts by C. W. Bell and Mark Swan. Produced by A. H. Woods♦ at the Republic Theatre. December 24, 1917. 232 performances.

Although Reggie Irving (John Cumberland♦) is shy and harmless, his wife Angelica (Sydney Shields) is convinced he has had a lurid past. So that she won't be disappointed, Reggie writes himself love letters which he signs "Tootles" and which he allows Angie to find. When this ploy seems likely to be exposed, a friend arranges for Reggie to be discovered in a hotel room with another woman. The plan almost backfires when Reggie is discovered with several women, as well as a scandal-sheet columnist and a husband who believes Reggie has alienated the affections of his wife. At least Angie is duly impressed.

This fast-paced, uproarious farce was considered highly "suggestive" in its day. Mark Elbert Swan (1871–1942), a native of Louisville, had a brief career as an actor before turning playwright. Over a dozen of his plays or librettos reached Broadway.

This was his most successful. Bell (1876–1938), a Canadian, who was a lawyer and eventually a member of Parliament, also wrote several other plays and librettos that were produced in the 1910s and early 1920s.

Parlor Match, A, a farce-comedy♦ in three acts by Charles H. Hoyt.♦ Produced at Tony Pastor's Theatre. September 22, 1884. 16 performances.

I. McCorker (Charles E. Evans♦), a not-too-principled book agent, and Old Hoss (William F. Hoey♦), a tramp who was once an auctioneer's assistant, combine their dubious talents to gull Capt. William Kidd (Daniel Hart) into believing he is a natural medium at séances. With the help of Kidd's mischievous daughter, Innocent (Jennie Yeamans), they call back from the dead a motley assortment of figures, who sing and dance for them, and who also speak up in McCorker and Innocent's interests. Old Hoss finds time to rummage through the Kidd household in search of items for an auction, and once, fearing detection, hides in a drawer.

This typical late farce-comedy used its elementary plot as an excuse for an evening of songs, dances, and specialty acts. It toured for many years and during its tour Hoey introduced "The Man Who Broke the Bank at Monte Carlo." An 1896 revival served as Anna Held's♦ American debut.

PARSLOE, Charles Thomas, Jr. (1836–98) The son of a famous actor and theatrical agent, he was born in New York and began his theatrical career as a call boy at Burton's.♦ He later performed in important juvenile roles at Wallack's♦ and elsewhere. His small build and youthful countenance allowed him to continue in such parts well into middle age, although he also became known for his Chinese portrayals. Among the roles he created or became well known for were Bermudas in *Under the Gaslight*♦ (1867), Wishee-Washee in *The Danites*♦ (1877), the title part in *Ah Sin*♦ (1877), and Wing Lee in *My Partner*♦ (1879).

PARSONS, Estelle (b. 1927) Born in Lynn, Mass., she made her debut in the musical *Happy Hunting* (1956). She has since come to exemplify the skilled and admired performer who remains loyal to the theatre but who cannot find successful vehicles for her talents. She has been highly praised for her acting of the leading roles in such short-lived plays as *The Seven Descents of Myrtle* (1968), *And Miss Reardon Drinks a Little* (1971), and *Miss Margarida's Way* (1977). She had enjoyed somewhat longer stands as Sarah in the three plays that constituted *The Norman Conquests* (1975) and as Ruth in the hugely successful 1981 revival of *The Pirates of Penzance.* ♦

Pasadena Community Playhouse Founded in 1918 by Gilmor Brown♦ as a semi-professional troupe, the group prospered, built a fine new theatre, and for many years was Southern California's most exciting playhouse. Besides reviving classics it regularly offered new plays by unknown playwrights at its Laboratory Theatre and conducted a highly praised acting school. Among its outstanding productions was the first mounting of Eugene O'Neill's♦ *Lazarus Laughed* in 1928. The organization later fell on hard times, and its properties were auctioned off in 1970. The theatre reopened in 1986.

Passing Regiment, The, a comedy in five acts by Augustin Daly.♦ Produced by Daly at Daly's Theatre. November 10, 1881. 103 performances.

When members of the Excelsior Regiment of the National Guard of New York are billetted briefly at the Narragansett Pier, a number of romances blossom, including that of Telka Essipoff (Ada Rehan♦), a Russian heiress, and Adjutant Paul Dexter (John Drew♦).

Daly adapted this slight comedy from Von Moser and F. von Schoenthan's comedy *Krieg im Frieden.* One of Daly's biographers, Marvin Felheim, has suggested that the success of the comedy, coming on the heels of *Needles and Pins,* ♦ confirmed the producer in his policy of emphasizing such light entertainment.

Passing Show, The A revue presented by George Lederer♦ at the Casino Theatre♦ on May 12, 1894. A few other prototypical, tentative revues had been presented earlier by John Brougham♦ and others, but this was really the first American revue to employ the generic term (although it spelled it "review") and is generally acknowledged to have started the fashion for such shows. The original production, in keeping with most subsequent turn-of-the-century revues, used a thin storyline to tie together its songs and sketches. In 1912 the Shuberts♦ revived the name *The Passing Show* and offered it as the title of a series of elaborate revues designed to buck the popularity of the *Ziegfeld Follies.* ♦ Editions were presented yearly, excepting 1920, until 1924. The mountings were popular and not without merit, yet it was widely perceived that they fell short of the *Follies* in virtually every aspect. Willie and Eugene Howard♦ were the most regularly featured performers in the series. Charlotte

Greenwood,◆ Marilyn Miller,◆ Ed Wynn,◆ De Wolf Hopper,◆ Jefferson De Angelis◆ (who had appeared in the 1894 production), Fred and Adele Astaire,◆ Marie Dressler,◆ and Fred Allen◆ all appeared in one or more years. Among the enduring songs first sung in the series were "Pretty Baby" (1916), "Good-bye Broadway, Hello, France!" (1917), "Smiles" (1918), and "I'm Forever Blowing Bubbles" (1918). An attempt was made to revive the series in the 1940s, but the production closed on tryout.

Passion Play, The [also known simply as *The Passion*] A play by a Jewish playwright, Salmi Morse, recounting the major events in the New Testament, it was produced in San Francisco in 1879 by Tom Maguire,◆ directed by David Belasco,◆ and starred James O'Neill◆ as Christ. The play divided local critics, most of whom felt it was exceedingly dull, but who nevertheless attested to the emotional fervor with which many in the audience responded. Some Protestant clergy, however, were offended and succeeded in having the producer, the playwright, and the actors hauled into court and fined for violating an ordinance prohibiting the "personation of any scriptural character upon the stage." In 1883, after much protest, the play was produced in New York, where the response was much the same. The New York *Times* stated that the full play consisted of 24 acts, but that only an abridged version of six acts was presented. The abridged version ran nearly four hours, and failed. Shortly thereafter Morse committed suicide by drowning in the Hudson River. Described by one San Francisco paper as a "tall, rabbinical-looking Hebrew, scrupulously dressed in black, with reverent gray hairs, mild, benignant eyes and somewhat heavily molded features," Morse claimed to have spent twenty years in the Middle East doing research for the work.

PASTOR, TONY [ANTONIO] (1837–1908) Often considered the father of modern American vaudeville, he was born in New York, where his father was a theatre violinist. While still a youngster he sang on the temperance circuit, then gave his first professional performance as a child prodigy at Barnum's Museum◆ in 1846. He later played in minstrel shows and with circuses. His debut in contemporary variety was in 1861. At the time, variety still had a certain bad odor attached to it. Most theatres had bars that actively pushed the sale of liquor and attracted a relatively rough order of patrons. An ambitious, highly moral young man, Pastor set out to change all that and quickly succeeded. He opened his first

theatre in 1865. He discouraged serving of drinks, attempted to clean up sometimes off-color acts, and solicited family trade. His methods proved so popular that he opened a larger theatre in 1875, then in 1881 opened the theatre on 14th Street which was afterwards identified with him and where he achieved his greatest success. A small, stocky, moustachioed man, he regularly appeared on his own bills, not merely to introduce the acts, but also to sing his "Rhymes for the Times," comic, topical songs twitting current events and celebrities. Among the stars whose early careers he assisted were Neil Burgess,◆ Emma Carus,◆ Maggie Cline,◆ the Four Cohans, May Irwin,◆ Nat Goodwin,◆ McIntyre◆ and Heath,◆ Lillian Russell,◆ Denman Thompson,◆ and Weber◆ and Fields.◆ Curiously, he is said never to have approved of the term "vaudeville" and to have called it "sissy and Frenchy." Virtually his only failure was his attempt to approach the legitimate stage with extended pieces of a sort that Harrigan◆ and Hart◆ had popularized. Toward the end of his career, despite his fame, he was rudely pushed aside by newer figures who were attempting to set up national chains and monopolize vaudeville.

Biography: *Tony Pastor: Dean of the Vaudeville Stage,* Parker Zellers, Ypsilanti, 1971.

PATRICK, JOHN, see *Teahouse of the August Moon, The*

Patriots, The, a play in a prologue and three acts by Sidney Kingsley.◆ Produced by the Playwrights Company◆ and Rowland Stebbins at the National Theatre. January 29, 1943. 172 performances. NYDCCA.

Thomas Jefferson (Raymond Edward Johnson) returns from France hoping to settle with his daughters at his Monticello retreat. But George Washington (Cecil Humphreys), buffetted by rough political opposition and particularly fearful of rising monarchist strength, urges Jefferson to become his secretary of state. Jefferson accepts reluctantly. Before long he is locked in battle with his arch-rival, the Federalist, Hamilton (House Jameson). Jefferson runs for President in 1800 and wins.

A solidly written chronicle play, it was produced when World War II gave Jefferson's fight for democratic ideals added meaning. Kingsley was a sergeant in the army at the time of the production.

Paul Kauvar; or, Anarchy, a play in five acts by Steele Mackaye.◆ Produced at the Standard Theatre. December 24, 1887. Approx. 100 performances.

Paul Kauvar (Joseph Haworth), a commoner who has risen to high rank in the French Revolution, is repelled by its swift drift into terrorism and he attempts to harbor, under aliases, the Duc de Beaumont (Edwin Varrey) and his daughter, Diane (Annie Robe), whom he secretly marries. The notorious and duplicitous Gouroc (Wilton Lackaye♦), formerly the Marquis de Vaux, betrays the Duc and makes it seem that Kauvar wittingly issued the death warrant. To show his innocence Paul prepares to take the Duc's place at the guillotine. Both the Duc and Paul escape, but Paul is later captured by royalists. After disguising himself as the royalist general, whom he allows to escape, he is reunited with Diane just as news arrives of Robespierre's death and the end of the reign of terror.

This summary only hints at the complications of plot in this gripping if far-fetched melodrama. To some extent the play was inspired by what Mackaye perceived as the unfair trial and execution of the Chicago anarchists in 1887. It was tried out as *Anarchy,* but the title was changed to avoid charges that Mackaye was trading on headlines. Odell♦ recalled, "Its reworking of old material, lovers in danger, villains, sansculottes, swirling, shouting mobs led by the customary mad woman revolutionist, fascinated the public for the best part of the season and came back, later, into the friendly domain of the combination houses. It is the remarkable handling of the mob scenes, with Lillie Eldridge as the shouting terror, Scarlotte, that I chiefly remember."

Paul Pry A comedy by John Poole, it was first produced in New York in 1826, a year after its London premiere. Its story centered on a comically mischievous snooper and busybody who turns hero when he rescues from a well papers that incriminate more serious troublemakers. Thomas Hilson♦ created the part at the Park Theatre,♦ while subsequent interpreters included J. H. Hackett,♦ William E. Burton,♦ the younger William Warren,♦ and John Brougham.♦ The comedy retained its popularity until the early 1870s.

PAULDING, JAMES KIRKE (1778–1860) Famed New York state writer and friend of Washington Irving,♦ his diverse works cover a range of subject matter and genres. Playgoers remember him largely for his comedy about a backwoodsman, *The Lion of the West♦* (1830). In 1847 he published *American Comedies,* which contained four plays by his son, William Irving Paulding, and his own earlier work, *The Bucktails; or, Americans in England.* This comedy, which dealt with the courtship of an American girl by various caricatured English types and which ended with her choosing a "man from home," seems never to have been given a professional mounting.

PAYNE, B[EN] IDEN (1881–1976) After a distinguished career in England, associated largely with Shakespearean productions, he came to America in 1913. He worked as artistic director for little theatres in both Philadelphia and Chicago, but also occasionally directed for Broadway, including the 1916 productions of Langdon Mitchell's♦ *Major Pendennis* and John Galsworthy's♦ *Justice.* From 1919 to 1934 he was professor of drama at the Carnegie Institute of Technology. He then returned to England until 1943, when he came back permanently to America. Although he taught at several major universities, including the University of Texas, he continued in rare instances to direct Broadway plays, among them the Ethel Barrymore♦ vehicle *Embezzled Heaven* (1944).

PAYNE, JOHN HOWARD (1791–1852) Remembered today primarily as the lyricist of "Home, Sweet Home," which was part of *Clari, the Maid of Milan♦* (1823), an operetta he wrote with Henry Bishop, he was a versatile and intriguing figure on our early stages. He was born either in East Hampton or New York, about the time his family moved from the former to the latter, but was raised mostly in Boston, where his father was a schoolmaster. Fascinated by accounts of the English child prodigy Master Betty, he pressed his family to allow him to go on the stage. They demurred and sent him instead to serve an apprenticeship in a New York mercantile house. While there, at the age of fourteen, he began the publication of one of the earliest American theatrical journals, *Thespian Mirror* (Dec. 1805–March 1806). At the same time he wrote his first play, a melodramatic comedy, *Julia; or, The Wanderer.* Its language shocked many critics and playgoers. He made his stage debut in 1809 at the Park Theatre♦ as Young Norval in *Douglas.♦* Dunlap♦ later noted of the small, but still thin and handsome young man, "he performed Young Norval with credit, and his succeeding characters with an increased display of talent." Those characters included Hamlet, Rolla in *Pizarro,♦* and Palmyra in *Mahomet.* In Boston his leading lady was Elizabeth Poe, mother of the poet. But he soon found it difficult to obtain roles and blamed the problem on a jealous cabal headed by Thomas Abthorpe Cooper. ♦ In the year of his debut he also wrote *Lovers' Vows,* a comedy derived from Kotzebue's ♦ *Das Kind der Liebe.* He based his text on various translations, culling the best parts of each. This would be the practice he observed in much of his later writings. When work continued to elude him he left for England, where he spent the remainder of his theatrical career. The London success of many of his works, though he realized little financial gain from them, prompted American mountings, so that by 1831 the Boston *Transcript* could record that an average of twenty-five of his plays were presented there each season. His best known works included *Brutus* ♦ (1819); *Thérèse* (1821), an adaptation from the French; and *Charles the Second* ♦ (1824). He is believed to have written between fifty and sixty plays. He returned to America in 1832, and ten years later was appointed by President Tyler as consul at Tunis. He was serving there when he died. Quinn ♦ has written, "Payne's position in our dramatic history is a peculiar one. His most significant work was done abroad and his direct inspiration was foreign." Payne would probably not have been bothered by this assessment, since he was at heart a pragmatist who once noted, "It seems almost hopeless to look to the stage as a vehicle for permanent literary distinction . . . an *actable* play seems to derive its value from what is *done,* rather than from what is *said.*"

Biography: *America's First Hamlet,* Grace Overmyer, New York, 1957.

PAYTON, CORSE (1867–1934) Self-advertised as "The World's Best Bad Actor," he was born in Centreville, Iowa, and at the age of sixteen organized a traveling company composed largely of members of his family. After trouping the West and Midwest for many years, he opened Corse Payton's Theatre in Brooklyn, where for nearly two decades he headed a stock company that offered a variety of plays each season at a scale of 10, 20, and 30 cents. Among the performers who served some apprenticeship with him were Fay Bainter, ♦ Richard Bennett, ♦ the Gish ♦ sisters Lillian and Dorothy, and Ernest Truex. ♦

PEABODY, JOSEPHINE PRESTON (1874–1922) The New York-born playwright entered Radcliffe with the intention of becoming a poet, but after studying with William Vaughn Moody ♦ decided to write for the stage as well. Her plays, which were often written in blank verse and set in romantic lands, had little appeal to commercial producers, although they were long popular with small "art" theatres. One brief exception was *The Piper* (1911), which she based on Browning's poem of the Pied Piper and in which she went beyond the poem and the legend to have the Piper return to Hamelin and repent his actions. The play won a special award given by Stratford-on-Avon and was later one of the few American works added to the repertory of the short-lived New Theatre. ♦ Her other plays included *The Wayfarers* (1898), *Marlowe* (1901), *The Wolf of Gubbio* (1913), and *Portrait of Mrs. W.* (1922), as well as several one-act pieces.

PEARMAN, [WILLIAM] MR. (1792–1829?) Little is known about this singer who was briefly the darling of New York playgoers and critics. He is said to have been born in Manchester, England, and to have made appearances at London's Lyceum as early as 1817. After his New York debut in 1823 as Count Belino in *The Devil's Bridge,* the *Albion* noted that he "possesses an exquisitely sweet and melodious voice, with fine science and correct taste. The clearness, softness and beauty of his voice we have scarcely ever heard equalled." When he sang Jocoso in the American premiere of *Clari, the Maid of Milan* ♦ he "drew down rapturous encores." He remained in America for only one year, then returned to London. New York saw him again in 1828, after which he is said to have sailed for the West Indies and to have died there.

Peck's Bad Boy, a play in four acts by Charles Pidgin. Produced at Haverly's New York Comedy Theatre. March 10, 1884. 40 performances.

Young Henry Peck (William Carroll) is the bane of his neighborhood, creating mayhem wherever he might be, whether that is his own home, the local grocery and drug stores, or out on a picnic. Accompanying him on his havoc-making escapades are his "chum," Jimmy (Mollie Fuller) and his little girl friend (Florence Bates).

Advertised as "Without plot, but with a purpose—to make people laugh," the play was viewed by the *Clipper* ♦ as indeed "*sans* plot and *sans* motif," but "Though the piece is the veriest nonsense, it is irresistible in its humor." Based on George Peck's "The Bad Boy Sketches," which had originally appeared in the Milwaukee *Sun,* the comedy remained a popular touring attraction for thirty years. Among the many performers who headed road companies and later went on to stardom were George M. Cohan ♦ and Frank Daniels. ♦

Peg o' My Heart, a comedy in three acts by J. Hartley Manners. ◆ Produced by Oliver Morosco ◆ at the Cort Theatre. December 20, 1912. 603 performances.

No sooner do the Chichesters learn they are bankrupt than a small silver lining appears. The late brother of Mrs. Chichester (Emily Melville ◆) has offered her a handsome annuity if she will look after his teenage daughter Margaret (Laurette Taylor ◆). She reluctantly agrees. Peg arrives just as her cousin Ethel (Christine Norman) and a young philanderer, Christian Brant (Reginald Mason), are locked in a secret embrace. The family is appalled at Peg's dowdy dress and at the homely mutt she carries with her. Peg is equally taken aback by her relatives' haughty, unloving nature. Her only real friend would appear to be a young neighboring farmer, Jerry (H. Reeves-Smith ◆). Only after Peg prevents Ethel from foolishly eloping with Brant does the family begin to soften toward her. Before long Jerry reveals he is actually Sir Gerald Adair, her legal guardian. To his proposal of marriage the delighted Peg replies, "My father always said: 'Sure there's nothing half so sweet in life as love's young dream.' "

One of the best loved of all American plays, it is reputed to have had eight road companies which were kept busy for three years. When it closed in New York, it was the longest run non-musical play in Broadway history. Henry Miller's ◆ biographer states that Miller and Manners originally devised the basic story in 1909 as a possible vehicle for Blanche Ring, ◆ who rejected it in favor of a musical comedy.

Peggy Ann, a musical comedy in two acts. Book by Herbert Fields. ◆ Lyrics by Lorenz Hart. ◆ Music by Richard Rodgers. ◆ Produced by Lew Fields ◆ and Lyle D. Andrews at the Vanderbilt Theatre. December 27, 1926. 333 performances.

Peggy Ann (Helen Ford ◆) drudges along helping her mother run a boarding house, hoping to marry Guy Pendleton (Lester Cole), and spending much of her waking time daydreaming of a better life. She dreams of all sorts of riches and adventures, from shopping on Fifth Avenue to fending off pirates. Only Guy's proposal brings her back to reality.

Principal songs: A Tree in the Park · Where's That Rainbow?

The musical used the same basic story that Fields had employed in *Tillie's Nightmare,* a musical he had mounted in 1910 as a vehicle for Marie Dressler. ◆ But the new treatment was unusually adventurous for 1926, with no splashy opening, a quiet finale with only Peggy on stage, much use of Freudian symbolism, and sets changed as the audience watched.

PEMBERTON, BROCK (1885–1950) Born in Leavenworth, and educated at the University of Kansas, he was a newspaperman and drama editor for the New York *Mail* and the New York *World* before becoming assistant to Arthur Hopkins ◆ in 1917. Three years later he produced his first play, *Enter Madame* ◆ (1920). Subsequent successes included *Miss Lulu Bett* ◆ (1920), *Six Characters in Search of an Author* (1922), *Loose Ankles* (1926), *The Ladder* ◆ (1926), *Strictly Dishonorable* ◆ (1929), *Personal Appearance* ◆ (1934), *Kiss the Boys Goodbye* ◆ (1938), *Janie* ◆ (1942), and *Harvey* ◆ (1944).

PENN, ARTHUR (b. 1922) The Philadelphia-born director worked largely in television and films, but is recalled for his staging of such plays as *Two for the Seesaw* ◆ (1958), *The Miracle Worker* ◆ (1959), and *Toys in the Attic* ◆ (1960).

PENNINGTON, ANN (1894?–1971) Both the birthplace and birthdate of the 4'11½", dimpled-kneed dancer are open to question, with Camden, N.J., Philadelphia, and Wilmington all offered as native cities while her birth year is sometimes given as 1892. She appeared in amateur performances in Philadelphia before making her professional debut in the chorus of *The Red Widow* (1911). Subsequently she appeared in seven editions of the *Ziegfeld Follies* ◆ between 1913 and 1924, and five editions of *George White's Scandals.* ◆ In the 1926 version of the latter she introduced "Black Bottom." She also performed in *Miss 1917, Jack and Jill* (1923), *The New Yorkers* (1930), and *Everybody's Welcome* (1931). During the 1940s she danced in tawdry touring companies of *The Student Prince* ◆ and *Blossom Time.* ◆

People's Lawyer, The, a play in two acts by Joseph S. Jones. ◆ Produced at the Park Theatre. ◆ December 12, 1842. 1 performance.

Winslow (Mr. Bellamy), an unscrupulous merchant, fires his clerk, Charles Otis (Mr. Lovell), after Charles refuses to perjure himself for Winslow's benefit. He also persuades another clerk, John Ellsley (Mr. A. Andrews), to plant a watch in Charles's pocket and to accuse Charles of theft. At his trial, Charles is defended by Robert Howard (Mr. Clarke), a crusading attorney who is known as "The People's Lawyer," and who has a special interest in this case, since he loves Charles's sister Grace (Miss Buloid). The trial is thrown into confusion by the testimony of the kindly but fuzzy Yankee, Solon Shingle (George H. Hill♦), who seems to think he is to testify about his lost "barrel of apple-sarse." Pangs of guilt prompt Ellsley to confess the truth.

The play was originally presented in Boston in 1839 and quickly became one of Hill's most popular vehicles. It was also an important vehicle for Charles Burke,♦ who first performed it at Philadelphia's Arch Street Theatre.♦ In 1857 John E. Owens♦ attempted the part and met with such success that he rewrote the play to expand the role of Shingle and under the title of *Solon Shingle* toured with it for a quarter of a century.

PEPLE, EDWARD [HENRY] (1867–1924) Born in Richmond, Va., he turned to play-writing after a long career in railroading. Although well over a dozen of his plays were produced, only two were major successes: *The Prince Chap*♦ (1904), in which a young man is jilted by his fiancée who refuses to believe that the baby in his care is not his, and *A Pair of Sixes*♦ (1914), in which feuding business partners agree to allow a card game to decide who shall be boss. Two other less successful plays are of passing interest: *The Littlest Rebel* (1911), whose story of a young girl's visit to President Lincoln to save her prisoner father later became the basis of a Shirley Temple film, and *The Charity Girl* (1912), a musical about an heiress determined to do good deeds in the slums. The musical, for which Peple supplied book and lyrics, was shut down by the police in one city because of objections to the lyric for "I'd Rather Be a Chippie Than a Charity Bum."

PERELMAN, S[IDNEY] J[OSEPH] (1904–79) The noted Brooklyn-born humorist rarely had good luck on Broadway. His first efforts were sketches for the revues *The Third Little Show*♦ (1931) and *Walk a Little Faster* (1932). With his wife, Laura, he wrote *All Good Americans* (1933), in which an expatriate must choose between love and money, and *The Night Before Christmas* (1941), in which a gang of crooks buys a shop in order to dig a tunnel into the bank next door. Both plays failed. His most successful work was his collaboration with Ogden Nash♦ on the book for *One Touch of Venus*♦ (1943). A loose-jointed comedy about a young man attempting to make his way up in a materialistic world, *The Beauty Part* (1962) was turned into a zany evening by Bert Lahr♦ in a series of roles, but it opened in the midst of a newspaper strike and failed.

PERKINS, ANTHONY (b. 1932) The son of Osgood Perkins,♦ he was born in New York. After playing on summer circuits he made his debut as a replacement in the role of Tom Lee in *Tea and Sympathy*♦ in 1954. Later he appeared as Eugene Gant, the Thomas Wolfe-like figure, in *Look Homeward, Angel*♦ (1957); the leading man in the musical *Greenwillow* (1960); the awkward young man who attempts to crash society, the title role in *Harold* (1962); Andy Hobart, the left-wing magazine writer in love with a right-wing super-patriot, in *The Star-Spangled Girl* (1966); and Jason Carmichael, the haughty playwright who marries one woman and courts another, in *Romantic Comedy* (1979). He has also enjoyed a successful screen career.

PERKINS, OSGOOD (1892–1937) Born in West Newton, Mass., he was educated at Harvard, fought in World War I, and worked in films before making his late debut in a small part in *Beggar on Horseback*♦ (1924). For a time thereafter he drifted between larger roles in short-run plays and supporting roles in minor hits, among them Joe Cobb, who abets his boss's attempts to foment revolution, in *Spread Eagle* (1927). Play and performer came together when he created the role of Walter Burns, the cynical, gimlet-eyed newspaper editor, in *The Front Page*♦ (1928). Twelve years after the play closed Brooks Atkinson♦ wrote that he could still see Perkins "cutting through the uproar like a bright, sharp penknife, and peeling off the layers of the plot as he went along." Subsequent successes came as Michael Astroff in *Uncle Vanya* (1930); as Samuel Gillespie, the acid-tongued secretary, in *Tomorrow and Tomorrow*♦ (1931); as Kenneth Bixby, a famous novelist courted by an old flame, in *Goodbye Again*♦ (1932); as Sganarelle in *The School for Husbands* (1933); as Jake Lee, the pilot who watches his fellow aviators die, in *Ceiling Zero* (1935); and the fortune-hunting Kenneth Rice in *End of Summer.*♦ He was appearing in the tryout of *Susan and God*♦ at the time of his death. He was the father of Anthony Perkins.♦

PERRY, ANTOINETTE (1888–1946) Born in Denver, she began her career as an actress in 1905. After her marriage to Frank Wheatcroft Freauff in 1909 she retired from the stage until 1924. She abandoned performing when she became a director for Brock Pemberton,♦ and often his silent partner in production. Among the plays she staged were *Strictly Dishonorable*♦ (1929), *Personal Appearance*♦ (1934), *Ceiling Zero* (1935), *Kiss the Boys Goodbye*♦ (1938), *Janie*♦ (1942), and *Harvey*♦ (1944).

With Rachel Crothers♦ and Jane Cowl♦ she helped organize the New York Stage Door Canteen♦ and also served as chairman of the board and secretary of the American Theatre Wing. ♦ In 1947 the Antoinette Perry Awards, popularly known as the Tonys, were named after her and given for distinguished achievement in the theatre.

Personal Appearance, a comedy in three acts by Lawrence Riley. Produced by Brock Pemberton♦ at Henry Miller's Theatre. October 17, 1934. 501 performances.

While touring to promote her latest film, *Drifting Lady,* the glamorous, susceptible screen star Carole Arden (Gladys George) develops car trouble near Wilkes-Barre. A handsome young gas-station attendant, Chester Norton (Philip Ober), helps fix the car and also puts her up for the night at the home of his fiancée's parents. Carole falls madly in love with Chester and when he mentions he has an invention to improve sound films she prepares to take him back to Hollywood with her. Fearing the consequences of her behavior, her press agent, Gene Tuttle (Otto Hulette), scuttles the arrangement and leaves Chester in the arms of his local girlfriend.

A basically minor comedy, it was turned into a success largely because of Gladys George's comic playing. It later became the source of Mae West's film *Go West, Young Man.* Riley (1891–1975) was born in Bradford, Penn. His only other play to reach Broadway was a quick failure, *Return Engagement* (1940).

Peter Pan, Barrie's♦ whimsical tale of a boy who refuses to grow up and who takes other children to his special never-land was first offered to American playgoers in 1905 with Maude Adams, ♦ for whom it was written, in the title role. To no small extent because it is a play to which children can be taken it has never lost its appeal. Later Peter Pans have included Marilyn Miller, ♦ Eva Le Gallienne, ♦ and Jean Arthur. Leonard Bernstein♦ composed incidental music for this last production. A musical version with music by Mark Charlap and Jule Styne♦ and lyrics by Carolyn Leigh, Betty Comden, ♦ and Adolph Green♦ was offered in 1954 with Mary Martin♦ as Peter. The musical was revived in 1979 with Sandy Duncan as star and in 1990 with Cathy Rigby.

PETERS, BERNADETTE [née LAZZARA] (b. 1948) The gamine, baby-voiced actress was born in Ozone Park, N.Y. She was not quite eleven which she made her first professional appearance in a City Center♦

revival of *The Most Happy Fella.* ♦ Two years later she played in a touring company of *Gypsy.* ♦ Fame came when she portrayed Ruby (read Ruby Keeler) in *Dames at Sea* (1968), a hugely successful off-Broadway spoof of 1930s film musicals. Although she has appeared in non-musicals, she is best known for her work in lyric entertainments such as *George M* (1968), *Mack and Mabel* (1974), *Sunday in the Park with George♦* (1984), *Song and Dance* (1985), and *Into the Woods* (1987).

PETERS [III], [CHARLES] ROLLO (1892–1967) The son of the California painter Charles Rollo Peters, he was born in Paris but raised in California. He later studied art in Europe. When he returned to America he served as designer and performer with the Washington Square Players, ♦ and after that group was disbanded joined the young Theatre Guild. ♦ He designed many of their early productions, using only odds and ends and materials from closed shows. His designs were seen in *Bonds of Interest* (1919), in which he played Leander, and in *John Ferguson* (1919), in which he portrayed Andrew Ferguson. Among his subsequent roles were Romeo to Jane Cowl's Juliet (he also designed the sets for the 1923 production); Antony to her Cleopatra (again designing the sets); Tom Wrench in *Trelawny of the Wells* (1927); Julian Beauclerc in *Diplomacy♦* (1928); Newland Archer in *The Age of Innocence* (1928); and Jack Absolute in *The Rivals* (1930). Later he appeared in and designed the sets for revivals of *The Streets of New York* (1931) and *The Pillars of Society* (1931).

Petrified Forest, The, a play in two acts by Robert Sherwood. ♦ Produced by Gilbert Miller♦ and Leslie Howard♦ in association with Arthur Hopkins♦ at the Broadhurst Theatre. January 7, 1935. 197 performances.

Alan Squire (Howard) is a world-weary idealist whose wanderings have brought him to the Black Mesa Bar-B-Q in Arizona. This combination of gas station and lunchroom sits near the petrified forest that seems to represent an inevitable and much-desired death to Squire. The owner's daughter, Gabby Maple (Peggy Conklin♦), is an attractive young girl who dreams of romance and of studying art in Paris. She reads some early French poetry to Squire, who is intrigued and not a little smitten. But their idyll is interrupted by the arrival of Duke Mantee (Humphrey Bogart) and his gang, who have decided to use the lunchroom as a hideout. Seeing some hope for the future in Gabby and feeling his own wanderings have reached the end of the road,

Squire signs over his life insurance policy to the girl and goads Mantee into killing him.

Historian William Torbert Leonard has written, "The desperation of the depressed thirties is reflected in Sherwood's drama of [a] lost intellectual, Squire, and the death of his era." Although Percy Hammond♦ of the *Herald Tribune* called the work "a delightful improbability," he concluded it was "made probable by Mr. Howard and his accomplices." When he repeated his role in Hollywood, Bogart's career was launched and for many years he was typecast in gangster roles.

Pfaff's Opened by Charles Pfaff at 647 Broadway in either 1858 or 1859, it was originally a small saloon that soon attracted leading intellectuals and theatrical figures. Its popularity was such that in 1864 Pfaff enlarged the premises into a full-service restaurant. As the theatre district moved northward, the restaurant relocated at 9 West 24th Street. It closed in 1887.

Phantom of the Opera, The A musical based on Gaston Leroux's famous novel, it has a book by Richard Stilgoe and Andrew Lloyd Webber,♦ lyrics by Charles Hart, and music by Webber. This London smash hit was quickly brought to America, where it opened at the Majestic Theatre on January 26, 1988, and repeated its London success. Michael Crawford played the disfigured man who haunts the Paris Opera House, and Sarah Brightman (Mrs. Webber) was Christine, the singer he adores and promotes. It is still playing to packed houses at this writing three years later and has sent out several road companies.

Philadelphia The first important American theatre centre, it was the site of performances in 1749 by Thomas Kean♦ and Walter Murray,♦ possibly at the warehouse of William Plumstead and certainly in the face of stern Quaker and other puritanical opposition. Indeed, the early years were a constant struggle between players and anti-theatrical authorities. This, despite the fact that Plumstead was a magistrate, councilman, and three times mayor. Plumstead's building, which stood on the waterfront between Pine and Lombard streets and which remained standing for another hundred years, was also home to the elder Hallam♦ when he brought his company there in 1754. Douglass♦ and the American Company♦ began regular seasons in the city in 1759. In 1766 he opened the first permanent American theatre there, the Southwark.♦ It was at this playhouse he gave the first professional performance of a native play, *The Prince of Parthia,*♦ in 1767. Three later playhouses figured importantly in the city's history: the Chestnut Street♦ (opened in 1793); the Walnut Street,♦ built as a circus in 1809, converted to drama in 1811, and still in use as the oldest theatre in America; and the Arch Street♦ (opened in 1828). Thomas Wignell♦ was a major figure in the city's early theatricals, while Edwin Forrest♦ used the city as his base throughout most of his career. In the first half of the 19th century the city was also home to the Philadelphia School of Dramatists,♦ many of whose plays were premiered there. Although by the first third of the century the city had lost its primacy to New York, it continued to be a flourishing center. Its most famous ensemble was that run during the last half of the 19th century at the Arch Street Theatre by Mrs. John Drew.♦ About the same time the Philadelphia School of Comic Opera♦ enjoyed a heyday which lasted almost until World War I. The city was also the last important bastion of traditional minstrelsy. Although as many as ten theatres were lit during the 1920s, the city had become largely a tryout and touring town. It sunk to only three occasionally used theatres in the Depression, enjoyed a small revival beginning with World War II, but in recent years has languished again. While much of its present difficulties reflect general problems in contemporary theatre, an interesting case might be made to couple its sharp drop with the decline and eventual demise of its greatest newspaper, *The Evening Bulletin.* The paper's closing left the city without a drama critic comparable in knowledgeability and acuity to its noted reviewer, Ernest Schier.

Philadelphia School of Comic Opera This was the name given, largely in derision by the New York press, to musicals written and produced in Philadelphia in the late 19th century. Many of the more successful musicals toured the country, where they were often well received except by New York. The school is best exemplified by the works of Willard Spenser♦ and by his most successful musical, *The Little Tycoon*♦ (1886).

Philadelphia School of Dramatists This was the name given to a group of playwrights who flourished in Philadelphia in the first half of the 19th century when the city was still the largest or second largest metropolis in the country and when Edwin Forrest,♦ with whom most were associated, made his home there. The group included Robert Montgomery Bird,♦ George H. Boker,♦ Robert T. Conrad,♦ Robert Penn Smith,♦ and John Augustus

Stone.♦ Their best plays were usually blank-verse romantic tragedies.

Philadelphia Story, The, a comedy in three acts by Philip Barry.♦ Produced by the Theatre Guild♦ at the Shubert Theatre. March 28, 1939. 417 performances.

Because the marriage of the socially prominent "virgin goddess" Tracy Lord (Katharine Hepburn♦) to the self-made, priggish George Kitteredge (Frank Fenton) is news, *Destiny* magazine assigns Mike Connor (Van Heflin), a tough special reporter, and Elizabeth Imbrie (Shirley Booth♦), a wisecracking photographer, to cover the event. The pre-wedding festivities are made all the more interesting by the arrival of Tracy's first husband, C. K. Dexter Haven (Joseph Cotten♦). Dexter's subtle baiting of Tracy exacerbates her private doubts about the marriage. She drinks too much and winds up swimming nude in the family pool with Mike. This proves more than George can take, but after he leaves the wedding goes on—with Dexter once again the groom.

The play was written with Miss Hepburn in mind. Although many critics felt it was inferior to some of Barry's earlier works, the public disagreed. It was Barry's biggest commercial success. Miss Hepburn, Cary Grant, and James Stewart starred in a hugely successful film version.

PHILIPPS, Thomas (1802?–41) The distinguished English singer made two extended visits to America. The first was from 1817 to 1819, the second from 1821 to 1823. He appeared largely in the ballad operas and other musicals of the period, such as *The Devil's Bridge* and *Love in a Village,* and in concerts. On his debut the New York *Post* observed, "In the lower notes Mr. Philipps shows great force and rotundity, while his *altissimo* is marked with the utmost sweetness, resembling in clearness and strength the tones of the clarionet." His surname has been spelled as Phillips and Phillipps.

PHISTER, Montgomery [sometimes spelled Physter] (1851–1917) An important 19th-century drama critic, he was born in Maysville, Ky., and was educated at Yale. For most of his newspaper career he was associated with the Cincinnati *Commercial Tribune,* where his thoughtful and fair criticisms were examined seriously by major performers and writers. He is said to have refused several offers to move to New York.

Phoenix Theatre Organized in 1953 by T. Edward Hambleton and Norris Houghton, the group took over the old Yiddish Art Theatre on Second Avenue, which it renamed and where it remained for eight years. Among its notable productions were Sidney Howard's♦ *Madam, Will You Walk* (1953), *Coriolanus* (1954), *The Golden Apple♦* (1954), *Phoenix '55, A Month in the Country* (1956), *The Littlest Revue* (1956), *The Duchess of Malfi* (1957), *Once Upon a Mattress* (1959), *The Great God Brown♦* (1959), and *The Octoroon♦* (1961). Financial problems forced the company to find a smaller house in 1961, where its biggest hit was *Oh, Dad, Poor Dad* etc.♦ (1962). For five years beginning in 1964 the organization joined with Ellis Rabb♦ and the Association of Producing Artists,♦ during which time its successful mountings included revivals of *You Can't Take It with You♦* (1966) and *The Show-Off♦* (1967). Thereafter the group continued to produce off-Broadway until its dissolution in 1982.

PHYSIOC, Joseph A[llen] (1865–1951) Born in Richmond, Va. and raised in Columbia, S.C., he began his career as a set designer in small theatres in Alabama, later moving to New York and taking a job as an assistant scene painter at the Metropolitan Opera. He also briefly tried his skills at acting. In 1894 he joined with Henry E. Hoyt♦ to design the sets for De Koven's♦ comic opera *Rob Roy.* Among the many later successes for which he created the scenery were Mansfield's♦ *Richard III♦* (1896), *Courted into Court* (1896), *Beau Brummell♦* (1900), *The Climbers♦* (1901), *The Lion and the Mouse♦* (1905), *The Traveling Salesman♦* (1908), *Within the Law♦* (1912), *Peg o' My Heart♦* (1912), *Lightnin'♦* (1918), *Seventh Heaven♦* (1922), and *Dracula* (1927). A formal, carefully detailed painter of the old school, he found himself at odds with the more stylized set designs that began to come into vogue shortly before World War I. Rather than adapt, he retired and spent his last years painting pictures for exhibitions.

Piano Lesson, The, a play in two acts by August Wilson.♦ Produced at the Walter Kerr Theatre. April 16, 1990. 329 performances. PP, NYDCCA.

Boy Willie (Charles S. Dutton) drives a load of watermelon from his Mississippi home to the Pittsburgh house of his sister, Berniece (S. Epatha Merkerson). He hopes to sell the melons and also his sister's piano to purchase land his family has worked since slave days. Although she hasn't played the piano in the years following her husband's death, she adamantly opposes selling an instrument built and carved with family portraits by her grandfather. Making Boy Willie's task more difficult, Berniece and others start to see the ghost of a man Boy Willie may have killed. Berniece's suitor (Tommy Hollis) holds an exorcism which brings Berniece back to the piano and brings Boy Willie to the realization that he probably must look elsewhere for his money.

This drama was the first to win a Pulitzer Prize♦ before it actually opened in New York.

Picnic, a play in three acts by William Inge.♦ Produced by the Theatre Guild♦ and Joshua Logan♦ at the Music Box. February 19, 1953. 477 performances. PP, NYDCCA.

On a hot Labor Day morning in a small Kansas town, a cocky, muscle-bound vagrant, Hal Carter (Ralph Meeker), strays into the Owens's backyard and changes the lives of the family. He breaks the heart of the tomboy younger daughter, Millie (Kim Stanley♦), goads Mrs. Owens's (Peggy Conklin♦) spinster sister Rosemary (Eileen Heckart♦) into forcing her reluctant gentleman friend to marry her, and prompts the older daughter, Madge (Janice Rule), to give up her rich boyfriend, Alan (Paul Newman), and to run away with him.

Louis Kronenberger♦ noted, "Mr. Inge's naturalistic round dance of frustrated, unfulfilled, life-hungry women catches something of the mischance and misbegottenness of life itself."

PICON, Molly (b. 1898) Although the tiny, impish, New York-born performer, who was raised in Philadelphia, made her first appearance there in an English-language vaudeville act at a nickelodeon in 1904, most of her early career was spent on the Yiddish stage, where she became a major comic star. She also appeared at the Palace♦ in the late 1920s. With the decline of Yiddish theatre, she turned increasingly to Broadway. Her most successful role was as the American widow looking for a husband in Israel, in the musical *Milk and Honey* (1961).

Autobiography: *So Laugh a Little,* New York, 1962.

PILGRIM, James (1825–77) A minor English-born actor and prolific playwright, he dashed off numerous once-popular plays, many of which dealt with Irish themes or Irish heroes and heroines. Among them were *Ireland and America* (1851), *Robert Emmet* (1853), *Irish Assurance and Yankee Modesty* (1853), and *Katy O'Shiel* (1857). He also wrote a popular drama about the Revolutionary War, *Harry Burnham♦* (1851).

PINERO, Arthur Wing (1855–1934) The English dramatist earned his earliest recognition with several excellent farces, most memorably *The Magistrate* (1885) and *Dandy Dick* (1887), both of which were originally produced in America by Augustin Daly.♦ He later won fame with a more serious "problem play," *The Second Mrs. Tanqueray* (1893), and with the sentimental *Trelawny of the Wells* (1898). Among his other plays to find favor were *The Amazons* (1894), *The Gay Lord Quex* (1900), *Mid-Channel* (1910), and *The "Mind-the-Paint" Girl* (1912).

Pink Lady, The, a musical in three acts. Book and lyrics by C. M. S. McLellan.♦ Music by Ivan Caryll.♦ Produced by Klaw♦ and Erlanger♦ at the New Amsterdam Theatre.♦ March 13, 1911. 312 performances.

Before his marriage to Angele (Alice Dovey), Lucien Garidel (William Elliot) decides to have one last fling with his old flame from the demi-monde, Claudine (Hazel Dawn♦). The fling is complicated by the fact that someone has been stealing kisses from attractive girls in the Forest of Compiègne. The satyr is unmasked, Lucien and Claudine enjoy their time together, then Lucien returns to Angele.

Principal songs: By the Saskatchewan · Donny Didn't, Donny Did · The Kiss Waltz · Love is Divine · My Beautiful Lady (same melody as The Kiss Waltz)

Although Miss Dawn was the lead in this musical, she did not keep the hero in the end, because the mores of the time would not allow a member of her class to win in musical comedy. The show was based on *Le Satyre,* a French farce by Georges Berr and Marcel Guillemand.

Pins and Needles, a musical revue in two acts. Sketches by various authors. Lyrics and music by Harold Rome.♦ Produced by the International Ladies Garment Workers' Union at the Labor Stage. November 27, 1937. 1,108 performances.

Originally mounted as a union lark on weekends, with a cast recruited entirely from union members, this sometimes lighthearted but generally propagandistic revue quickly attracted a large audience and settled down for a run. It poked fun at most of the expected left-wing bêtes noires. When it closed it was, briefly, the longest run musical in Broadway history. However, too much should not be made of the length of the run since it was played initially at the 299-seat Labor Stage (once the Princess Theatre♦) and later at the 849-seat Windsor. Moreover, revisions enticed many playgoers to make return visits. Its most popular musical numbers were

"Sing Me a Song with Social Significance" and "Sunday in the Park."

PINTER, Harold (b. 1930) The English actor-playwright, whose elusive, elliptical tragi-comedies are seen to reflect the influence of Beckett♦ and Ionesco,♦ received his first American mounting when *The Birthday Party,* detailing an uneasy party for a lodger in a boarding house, was produced in San Francisco in 1960 by the Actor's Workshop.♦ It was produced on Broadway in 1967. Other major New York stagings of his works have included *The Caretaker* (1961), centering on a vagrant and two neurotic brothers; *The Homecoming* (1967), in which a woman agrees to sleep with the father and brothers of her husband, and which won the New York Drama Critics Circle Award♦; *No Man's Land* (1976), which focused on the meeting of two aging poets and which starred John Gielgud♦ and Ralph Richardson♦; and *Betrayal* (1980), a study of infidelity told in reverse chronology. Several other of his works have been offered successfully off-Broadway and at regional playhouses.

PINZA, Ezio (1892–1957) The great Metropolitan Opera basso came to Broadway only after his career in opera had ended, but his voice was still superior to almost any other heard in the legitimate theatre and his good looks and personal charm overcame some minor difficulties in his pronunciation of English. He made only two appearances: *South Pacific♦* (1949), in which he introduced "Some Enchanted Evening" and "This Nearly Was Mine"; and *Fanny♦* (1954).

Pippin, a musical (performed without intermission). Book by Roger O. Hirson. Music and lyrics by Stephen Schwartz.♦ Produced at the Imperial Theatre. October 23, 1972. 1,944 performances.

The life of Charlemagne's son, here called Pippin (John Rubinstein♦), is played out in a series of vaudeville-like sketches performed largely by a group of commedia dell'arte-style clowns, who were headed by the Leading Performer (Ben Vereen). Pippin seeks greatness, but settles for compromise and reality.

Principal songs: Magic To Do · No Time At All

Originally written by Schwartz while he was still in college, the show was produced on Broadway after the success of his *Godspell.♦* Otis L. Guernsey, Jr.♦ noted, "In a year of little experiment and less musical appeal . . . *Pippin* was a standout entertainment and stand-in for the dormant avant garde." Bob Fosse's♦ stylized staging was a major factor in the show's success. Another reason was that the musical was one of the first to employ a large television advertising campaign to promote business.

Pique, a play "of today" in five acts by Augustin Daly.♦ Produced by Daly at the Fifth Avenue Theatre.♦ December 14, 1875. 237 performances.

In a moment of anger, Mabel Renfrew (Fanny Davenport♦) renounces her fiancé, Raymond Lessing (Maurice Barrymore♦), and marries Captain Arthur Standish (D. H. Hawkins), son of the puritanical Matthew Standish (Charles Fisher♦). The young couple go to live with the elder Standish. Arthur quickly realizes that Mabel does not love him, and his father's rigid code of behavior further exacerbates difficulties. Arthur finally leaves. Immediately thereafter the Renfrews' young child is kidnapped. The search for the stolen youngster reunites the couple and shows the elder Standish's basic valor. When Raymond weds Mabel's widowed stepmother, Mabel understands that the decision made in pique was the right one after all. With the little boy recovered, she acknowledges, "A happiness that begins tonight for me . . . will endure while heart can beat, or life can last."

The first three acts were based on Florence Lean's novel, *Her Lord and Master,* while the remaining two acts were suggested by the then recent kidnapping, never solved, of Charley Ross. Scenes in the kidnapper's den borrowed heavily from *Les Miserables.* Critics were sharply divided on the merits of the play. The *Tribune* took a middle ground, calling it "not of a high order, either in literary attributes or dramatic construction," but concluding correctly that it combined "comedy, sentiment, and sensation in a way that will not fail to please the average tastes." A road company, one of the first so organized, was quickly sent on tour.

PIRANDELLO, Luigi (1867–1936) The greatest of modern Italian playwrights is best remembered in America for two surrealistic plays which question the nature of truth: *Six Characters in Search of an Author* (1922) and *Right You Are (If You Think You Are)* (1927). Both works are regularly revived by collegiate and regional playhouses and occasionally on and off Broadway. Many of his other works have been produced, but none of these has found enduring favor with American playgoers.

Pirate, The, a comedy in three acts by S. N. Behrman.♦ Produced by the Playwrights' Company♦

and the Theatre Guild♦ at the Martin Beck Theatre. November 25, 1942. 177 performances.

When a troupe of traveling performers comes to a small West Indies town it is refused a license to play by the mayor. However, the license is quickly granted when the leader of the troupe, Serafin (Alfred Lunt♦), lets the mayor know he has recognized him as a long-sought pirate. In short order, romance blossoms between Serafin and the mayor's wife, Manuela (Lynn Fontanne♦). The romance is tempestuous, with Serafin at one point walking a tightrope to enter Manuela's boudoir. Finally the actor hypnotizes Manuela into publicly revealing the truth about her husband, who is carted off to jail.

Suggested by Ludwig Fulda's German play, *The Sea Robber,* the comedy was, as Brooks Atkinson♦ suggested, "not out of Mr. Behrman's usual drawer." Nevertheless, a capital production and the performances of the Lunts turned it into engaging theatre.

Pirates of Penzance, The Gilbert♦ and Sullivan's♦ comic opera about law and order, love, misplaced children, and the difficulties of being born on the extra day of leap year was unusual among Savoyard works in that, in order to protect American copyrights, it was given its world premiere in America at New York's Fifth Avenue Theatre♦ on December 31, 1879. The D'Oyly Carte♦ cast included Hugh Talbot as Frederick, Blanche Roosevelt as Mabel, and J. H. Ryley as the Major General. It ran just over two months. Since then it has been given numerous revivals. Memorable were that of Winthrop Ames♦ in 1926 and that of the New York Shakespeare Festival♦ in 1981. The latter mounting did not employ Sullivan's orchestrations, added material from other shows, and was staged in a freewheeling, untraditional manner, with rock stars Rex Smith and Linda Ronstadt in the romantic leads and George Rose♦ as the Major General. As a result it displeased the purists but won the support of the critics and the public, and enjoyed by far the longest American run of any Gilbert and Sullivan comic opera.

PITOU, AUGUSTUS (1843–1915) Often called "King of the One Night Stands," he began his career in his native New York as an actor in a minor role in Edwin Booth's♦ *Hamlet*♦ in 1867. He remained with Booth for several years before abandoning performing in favor of managing theatres and actors. At one time or another he ran such New York theatres as Booth's, the Fifth Avenue,♦ and the Grand Opera House, and guided the careers of performers such as Rose Coghlan,♦ Chauncey Olcott,♦ and W. J. Scanlan.♦ He was not merely Olcott's agent but his producer and playwright as well, creating the books for and mounting such Olcott romantic musical dramas as *Sweet Inniscarra*♦ (1897), *A Romance of Athlone* (1899), and *Old Limerick Town* (1902). However, most of the plays he produced were designed as touring shows and, without a star of Olcott's attraction, never played major New York houses. After his death his son, Augustus, Jr., continued his policies for nearly a decade.

Pittsburgh Playhouse In 1933 a group of noted local residents joined forces to establish a playhouse to offer a more wide-ranging repertory than was available at the surviving legitimate theatre. At first it used the stage of a school, then performed in a converted speakeasy before opening its own complex of three theatres. When financial problems loomed in the late 1960s, the playhouse became affiliated with Point Park College. Besides its regular season of dramas, it now presents dance programs and plays for children.

PIXLEY, ANNIE [née ANNIE SHEA] (1858–98) The dark-haired, plump but gamin actress was born in Brooklyn and raised in California, where she took her stepfather's name when she began a stage career. She scored successes in *The Danites*♦ and in the title role of an 1876 version of *Snow White and the Seven Dwarfs* called *Snowflake.* Coming to the attention of Joseph Jefferson,♦ she played opposite him in *Rip Van Winkle*♦ before enjoying her most memorable hit as the hoydenish waif who was the title figure of *M'liss.*♦ She bleached her hair blonde to fight off villains in two vehicles Fred Marsden♦ wrote for her, *Zara* (1883) and *Eily* (1885). Later successes included the stage-struck heroine of A. C. Gunter's♦ *The Deacon's Daughter* (1887) and the girl who helps her sweetheart fight in the Civil War, the title part in *Kate* (1890). Most of her vehicles offered her an opportunity to sing and dance, so many critics saw her as an imitator of Charlotte Crabtree.♦ However, as one obituary noted, "There has been no greater favorite with American play-goers."

PIXLEY, FRANK (1867–1919) Born in Richfield, Ohio, he turned to newspaper work on leaving college. After writing a few unsuccessful plays he began a collaboration with composer Gustav Luders♦ which resulted in some of the most popular turn-of-the-century musicals: *The Burgomaster*

(1901), *King Dodo* (1902), *The Prince of Pilsen*◆ (1903), *Woodland* (1904), *The Grand Mogul* (1907), and *Marcelle* (1908). Following Luders's death he retired from the stage and spent his last years writing film scenarios.

Pizarro Richard Brinsley Sheridan's◆ long-popular tragedy of a noble Inca's doomed battle against the Spanish invader, its most famous scene depicted the hero, Rolla, leaping over a chasm with a young child in one hand and his defending sword in another. Sheridan had based his play on a German drama by Kotzebue.◆ When it was first played at the Park Theatre◆ in America in 1800, a year after its Drury Lane premiere, it was further revised by William Dunlap◆ and offered as *Pizarro in Peru; or, The Death of Rolla.* In one version or the other it remained a major attraction for seventy years. Among the notable Rollas who followed John Hodgkinson◆ were James Fennell,◆ Thomas Abthorpe Cooper,◆ Edwin Forrest,◆ William B. Wood,◆ and Edward Eddy.◆

PLACIDE, ALEXANDRE (d. 1812) A rope dancer at the French court, he was forced to flee during the French Revolution and settled for a time in England. He came to America in 1791, landing at Charleston and then performing up and down the coast to great acclaim. Ireland◆ later wrote that he was "the most graceful rope-dancer and the finest gymnast that had yet to reach America." Besides performing he wrote many of the pieces in which he appeared and also managed the French Theatre in Charleston and the Richmond Theatre in Richmond, Va. He fathered a large family, all of whom became known to American playgoers, but most notably his son Henry◆ and daughter Jane.◆

PLACIDE, HENRY (1799–1870) The son of Alexandre Placide,◆ he began performing in his father's shows while still a youngster. His debut as an adult was as Zekiel Homespun in *The Heir-at-Law* at the Park Theatre◆ in 1823. He rapidly grew to be the most polished and celebrated comedian of his day. His most famous roles included Bob Acres, Sir Anthony Absolute, Sir Peter Teazle, and Sir Harcourt Courtly, as well as major parts in now forgotten contemporary pieces. In 1866 Ireland◆ wrote of him, "He is the only one who ever trod the American stage perfectly irresistible in humor, and yet entirely free from grimace and buffoonery . . . no other actor has ever so completely exemplified our idea of what a genuine comedian should be."

PLACIDE, JANE (1804–35) The daughter of Alexandre Placide,◆ she was hailed as the "Queen of the Drama in New Orleans." Her debut took place in Norfolk, Va., in 1820 and her first New Orleans appearance three years later. She remained there, except for brief tours, until 1833, excelling in such tragic roles as Lady Macbeth and Cordelia but also demonstrating skill at comedy. In 1833 she left for a visit to England, and died soon after her return, still at the height of her powers and popularity.

Plain and Fancy, a musical comedy in two acts. Book by Joseph Stein◆ and Will Glickman. Lyrics by Arnold B. Horwitt. Music by Albert Hague. Produced by Richard Kollmar◆ and others at the Mark Hellinger Theatre. January 27, 1955. 461 performances.

Two New Yorkers (Shirl Conway and Richard Derr) come to the Pennsylvania Dutch country of Lancaster County, where they encounter stern Papa Yoder (Stefan Schnabel) as well as two young lovers, Katie Yoder (Gloria Marlowe) and Peter Reber (David Daniels). Problems arise because Peter has left the tight community and is therefore "shunned." But all ends happily.

Principal songs: It Wonders Me · Plenty of Pennysylvania · Why Not Katie? · Young and Foolish

The show was unusual not because of a basically trite love story but because its setting, the Amish country, was one Broadway musicals had heretofore ignored, and which was now treated with a careful respect and affection. One major scene depicted a traditional Amish barn-raising. Curiously, many playgoers who saw the show remember it best for Barbara Cook's◆ performance in a secondary role.

PLATT, LIVINGSTON (1874–1933?) Born in Plattsburg, N.Y., he studied art abroad and began to design for the stage at a theatre in Bruges. He returned to America in 1911 to accept a position as set and costume designer for Mrs. Lyman Gale's Toy Theatre in Boston. His work there came to the attention of Margaret Anglin,◆ who assigned him the task of creating sets and clothing for four 1914 Shakespearean revivals: *The Taming of the Shrew,*◆ *Twelfth Night,*◆ *Antony and Cleopatra,*◆ and *As You Like It.*◆ He eschewed the cumbersome, pseudo-realistic settings then fashionable and instead designed stylized settings whose use of a double proscenium allowed virtually instant changes. These sets were lit by him with striking imagination. He himself noted that his aim was "to see that every space of light and shadow which surrounds the action shall heighten and amplify the significance of the action," and he added, "Too much detail often ruins a play because it distracts attention from the action of the drama itself." Among his highly praised early settings were those for *East Is West*♦ (1918) and *Shakuntala* (1919). In later seasons his fine designs were seen in such less imaginative mountings as *Daisy Mayme*♦ (1926), *The Racket*♦ (1927), *Behold the Bridegroom*♦ (1927), *The First Mrs. Fraser* (1929), *Dinner at Eight*♦ (1932), and *The Pursuit of Happiness*♦ (1933). He disappeared after being detained on moral charges, but whether he committed suicide or lived somewhere obscurely cannot be determined.

Play It Again, Sam, a comedy in three acts by Woody Allen. Produced by David Merrick♦ and others at the Broadhurst Theatre. February 12, 1969. 453 performances.

Having been left by his wife, who wants livelier company, mousy film critic Allen Felix (Allen) is so stupified that he can only suck on undefrosted TV dinners and turn to a fantasy world. But even in his wildest fantasies, in which no less than Humphrey Bogart (Jerry Lacy) comes to his assistance, he keeps striking out with women. His best friend Dick (Anthony Roberts), a hustling businessman, tries to help, as does Dick's wife Linda (Diane Keaton). When the mouse finally roars, he does so by stealing a page out of Bogart's *Casablanca*.

One of the best comic views of the modern anti-hero, the play marked Allen's only Broadway appearance. Allen (né Allen Stewart Konigsberg, b. 1935) is a Brooklyn-born humorist who wrote sketches for the revue *From A to Z* (1960) and a hit comedy about a family mistaken for spies behind the Iron Curtain, *Don't Drink the Water* (1966). He is better known for his witty, zany films.

Playbill In 1884 Frank Vance Strauss founded a company to print theatrical "programmes" in a magazine format that included considerable advertising. Older programs had generally consisted of only four pages, which offered only basic credits and perhaps minimal advertising. In 1911 the founder began to call his publication the *Strauss Magazine Theatre Program*. Each playhouse was given a special full-color cover, but the rest of the playbill varied little. The program's name underwent several later changes, finally adopting *The Playbill* in 1934. Four years earlier sepia had replaced colored covers and the programs' covers began to feature photographs of stars or scenes from the play in question. The organization has also undergone numerous

changes of management. Today's programs, besides credits and advertising, contain numerous articles of interest to playgoers. Since 1982 the company has also published *Playbill—The National Theatre Magazine,* a monthly.

Players, THE The most distinguished of American theatrical clubs, it was incorporated on January 7, 1888. Noteworthy theatrical figures such as Lawrence Barrett,♦ Edwin Booth,♦ Augustin Daly,♦ John Drew,♦ Joseph Jefferson,♦ and A. M. Palmer♦ were among the charter members, but founding members also included Mark Twain♦ and General William Tecumseh Sherman, since the group, which was patterned after London's Garrick Club, was aiming to bring together not only professionals but others interested in the theatre. Booth purchased a large house on Gramercy Park in which he retained a small apartment until his death—and bequeathed the building to the club. He served as its first president and was succeeded by Jefferson, Drew, Walter Hampden,♦ Howard Lindsay,♦ Dennis King,♦ Alfred Drake,♦ Roland Winters, and José Ferrer.♦ The club possesses a fine collection of theatrical memorabilia and a superb library, named for Hampden. For many years its members mounted an annual revival of a classic play, which was presented in a regular Broadway house. Although that policy has been discontinued, the club still offers productions for members on its own small stage and at frequent intervals has black-tie "Pipe Nights" in honor of some celebrated theatrical figure.

Players Equal Suffrage League Formed in late 1913 or early 1914 by the actress Mary Shaw,♦ it was designed to promote women's right to vote. Margaret Anglin,♦ Billie Burke,♦ and Jane Cowl♦ were among its most prominent members. When the League came to Boston to spread its advocacy, Charlotte Crabtree♦ gave them a huge reception and was elected vice president. A few of its members made speeches on its behalf during curtain calls, but most simply spoke at regular meetings or helped underwrite advertisements and campaign literature. The group disbanded after women were enfranchised.

Playwrights' Company, THE A producing company, it was founded in 1938 by Maxwell Anderson,♦ S. N. Behrman,♦ Sidney Howard,♦ Elmer Rice,♦ and Robert E. Sherwood.♦ Although Anderson suggested the organization was begun "to make a center for ourselves within the theatre, and possibly rally the theatre as a whole to new levels by setting a high standard of writing and production," the founders were all established writers who had long since set high standards and whose real reason for embarking on their own was their displeasure with the policies of the Theatre Guild, ◆ which had been their principal producer. In later years Kurt Weill, ◆ Robert Anderson, ◆ lawyer John Wharton, and producer Roger L. Stevens ◆ became members. Among the company's memorable productions were *Abe Lincoln in Illinois* ◆ (1938), *Knickerbocker Holiday* ◆ (1938), *No Time for Comedy* ◆ (1939), *Key Largo* ◆ (1939), *There Shall Be No Night* ◆ (1940), *The Eve of St. Mark* ◆ (1942), *The Pirate* ◆ (1942), *The Patriots* ◆ (1943), *Dream Girl* ◆ (1945), *Anne of the Thousand Days* ◆ (1948), *Tea and Sympathy* ◆ (1953), *Sabrina Fair* ◆ (1953), *Cat on a Hot Tin Roof* ◆ (1955), *The Pleasure of His Company* ◆ (1958), and *The Best Man* ◆ (1960). By 1960 the only founders still alive were Behrman, who had left the group, and Rice, and with few new playwrights on the horizon promising a constant and worthy output, the organization was dissolved. Wharton's *Life Among the Playwrights* (1974) provides an interesting insider's view of the group.

Plaza Suite, a bill of three one-act plays by Neil Simon. ◆ Produced at the Plymouth Theatre. February 14, 1968. 1,097 performances.

Visitor from Mamaroneck: While their suburban house is being painted, Karen (Maureen Stapleton ◆) and Sam Nash (George C. Scott ◆) take the same suite at the Plaza that they had on their honeymoon 24 years before. But Karen discovers that Sam's secretary is his mistress, and when he leaves for a rendezvous with the girl, she is left alone with a bottle of champagne and two glasses.

Visitor from Hollywood: Jesse Kiplinger (Scott) and Muriel Tate (Stapleton) were high school sweethearts. Now Jesse is a successful Hollywood producer, while Muriel, a suburban matron, has followed his career with interest. So when he comes to New York and invites her to his hotel room, she accepts. Before long the old ardor is rekindled.

Visitor from Forest Hills: Minutes before her wedding, Mimsey Hubley (Claudette Nevis) has locked herself in her hotel bathroom and has refused to come out. The frantic attempts of her mother, Norma (Stapleton), and father, Roy (Scott), are unavailing. Roy even tries breaking the door and climbing out on a ledge to enter by the bathroom window. After all Roy's hectic, futile efforts, the groom's quiet "Cool it" succeeds where Roy has failed.

The play prompted Otis L. Guernsey, Jr., ◆ to write of Simon, "He is the Molière of the high-rise era; he knows his contemporaries intimately and he treats them affectionately, but never too gently."

Pleasure of His Company, The, a comedy in two acts by Samuel Taylor ◆ and Cornelia Otis Skinner. ◆ Produced by Frederick Brisson ◆ and the Playwrights' Company ◆ at the Longacre Theatre. October 22, 1958. 474 performances.

Jessica Poole's world is thrown into confusion just before her marriage to Roger Henderson (George Peppard), the son of a rich rancher. Jessica (Dolores Hart) has been raised by her mother, Katherine Dougherty (Skinner) and step-father, Jim Dougherty (Walter Abel). Now her roving, sybaritic father, Biddeford Poole (Cyril Ritchard ◆), suddenly reappears after a 15-year absence. He makes Jessica's life and fiancé seem hopelessly stolid. When he begs her to give up her wedding plans and travel with him she finally agrees—but only for a year.

The play was one of the last literate high-comedies to achieve success in New York.

PLUMMER, [ARTHUR] CHRISTOPHER [ORME] (b. 1929) The Canadian actor has appeared in numerous Shakespearean roles with Shakespearean festivals in Canada and abroad, and won praise for his Iago in a 1981 Broadway revival of *Othello.* ◆ Among his other memorable assignments have been the Earl of Warwick in *The Lark* (1955), the satanic Nickles in *J.B.* ◆ (1958), and Pizarro in *The Royal Hunt of the Sun* (1965). In 1988 he starred in *Macbeth.* ◆ He was married for a time to Tammy Grimes, ◆ and their daughter Amanda Plummer has been featured in off-Broadway and Broadway productions.

PLYMPTON, EBEN (1853–1915) The handsome, virile actor was born and educated in Boston, where he took a job as bookkeeper on the Boston *Post* until a breakdown in his health forced him to leave for California. There he recuperated and then made his stage debut in Stockton in 1871. He came to New York when he was offered a position at Wallack's. ◆ Although he won increasing notice it was not until he moved to the Madison Square Theatre ◆ and portrayed André, the lover whose marriage plans are jeopardized by a murder, in *Rose Michel* ◆ (1875) that his reputation was assured. Important Shakespearean assignments followed as Sebastian and Romeo in 1877, then in 1878 he won applause as Walter Dalrymple, one of the boarders, in *Our Boarding House.* ◆ He enjoyed major successes as

Lord Travers, who wins the heroine, in *Hazel Kirke*♦ (1880), and Dave Hardy, the rugged farmer who wins the heroine, in *Esmeralda*♦ (1881). He later spent several seasons playing leads opposite Mary Anderson♦ and supporting Edwin Booth♦ in several productions, including Laertes in an all-star performance of *Hamlet.*♦ Among his subsequent roles were King Philip II in *In the Palace of the King*♦ (1901); Sir Harcourt Courtly in a 1905 revival of *London Assurance*♦*;* and the Bishop, who is suffering from mental and emotional exhaustion, in *The Duel* (1906). Otis Skinner♦ remembered him as "talented, forceful, but extremely temperamental and egotistical."

Pocahontas; or, The Gentle Savage, a musical burlesque in two acts. Libretto by John Brougham.♦ Music (largely borrowed) adapted by James G. Maeder. Produced by Brougham at Wallack's♦ Lyceum. December 24, 1855. Performances (see note below).

Coming to the court of the Tuscaroras, Captain John Smith (Charles M. Walcot♦) spots the Indian Princess, Pocahontas (Georgina Hodson), at the Tuscarora Finishing Institution. He falls in love with her, and she with him. But Pocahontas's father, King H. J. Pow-ha-tan (Brougham), has promised his daughter to the Dutchman, Mynheer Rolff (Charles Peters). A game of cards settles the matter in Smith's favor.

Filled with doggerel and the outlandish puns beloved of the era, this musical burlesque was offered as an afterpiece. It continued on the bill regularly until January 9th, then frequently reappeared thereafter. For the next thirty years, until both this sort of burlesque and afterpieces went out of style, it was by far the most popular example of its genre. Maeder was the husband of Clara Fisher♦ and the father of Frederick G. Maeder.♦

POE, EDGAR ALLAN (1809–49) The famed American poet and short-story writer was the son of actors, although he was not raised by them. In 1835 he published sections of an unfinished blank-verse drama, *Politian,* which was based on the celebrated Kentucky Tragedy but which he reset in 16th-century Italy. Later he occasionally wrote theatrical criticism for the *Broadway Journal,* of which he became owner, and other publications. As with much of his critical writings, he argued against what he deemed superficial and foreign, this last point ironic in view of his resetting of *Politian.* However, he was a perceptive enough playgoer to quickly, and largely correctly, evaluate the merits of an American

effort such as *Fashion*♦ (see that entry for part of his review).

POLI, S. Z. [né ZEFFERINO SYLVESTRO POLI] (1860–1937) Born in Lucca, Italy, where his father was a church organist, he served a theatrical apprenticeship in Paris before coming to the United States and taking employment at the Eden Musee in 1881. He next became an itinerant peddler until 1892, when he built his first small vaudeville house. By the time he sold out to film interests in the late 1920s he had put together one of the largest chains of vaudeville theatres in the country, most of which were located in New England and the Middle Atlantic states. For public purposes he used only the initials of his given names and reversed them, apparently out of euphonic considerations.

POLLOCK, CHANNING (1880–1946) Born in Washington, D.C., but raised in Omaha and Salt Lake City, his theatrical career began when he returned to his birthplace to become a drama critic for the Washington *Post* and for the *Times*. He also served a stint with the *Dramatic Mirror.*♦ After working as a publicist for Ziegfeld,♦ Brady,♦ and the Shuberts♦ he turned to play-writing. His first play, *The Game of Hearts* (1903), was a quick failure, but later that year he scored his initial success with his dramatization of Frank Norris's muckraking novel *The Pit*. Alone or with collaborators he wrote about thirty shows that saw the footlights, ranging from sketches for several *Ziegfeld Follies*♦ and the books of musical comedies to farce and melodrama. Among his early works were *Clothes*♦ (1906), written with Avery Hopwood,♦ and telling of problems that arise when a young lady attempts to dress beyond her means; *Such a Little Queen* (1909), in which a queen abdicates so that her husband may continue to rule; *The Crowded Hour* (1918), written with Edgar Selwyn, and focusing on a telephone operator, now a wartime entertainer, who uses her old skills to save soldiers; *Roads of Destiny* (1918), telling of a young man who cannot escape his fate no matter which path he takes; and *The Sign on the Door* (1919), centering on a wife wrongly accused of killing her paramour. During this period he continued to write drama criticism, some of which so antagonized his former employers, the Shuberts, that they barred him from their theatres. His career took a marked turn in 1922 with *The Fool,*♦ a story of a modern man who attempts to live by Christ's precepts. The play was assailed by most critics, but Pollock began his own aggressive publicity campaign which eventually made the show a success. His remaining works could all be perceived as contemporary morality plays: *The Enemy*♦ (1925), an anti-war tract depicting the price of hatred; *Mr. Moneypenny* (1928), in which a man strikes a bargain with the devil in return for unlimited wealth; and *The House Beautiful* (1931), a tale of a wife who fantasizes that her husband is a crusader against evil. Critics were increasingly put off by the preachiness of his last plays and grew steadily unkinder. It was of his final work that Dorothy Parker♦ wrote, *"The House Beautiful* is the play lousy." This and other less pithy responses prompted Pollock to retire.

Autobiography: *Harvest of My Years,* Indianapolis, 1943.

Polly of the Circus, a play in three acts by Margaret Mayo.♦ Produced at the Liberty Theatre. December 23, 1907. 160 performances.

Polly (Mabel Taliaferro♦) is a circus rider who is injured in a fall and taken to the home of the local minister, the Reverend John Douglass (Malcolm Williams), to recuperate. The two grow fond of each other, but Polly leaves as soon as she has recovered. She not only feels that a romance with the minister would hurt his standing in his small town, but she wants to continue in the circus tradition that runs far back in her family. The minister has other ideas. He comes after her and persuades her to marry him.

Broadway scuttlebutt of the day said that Frederic Thompson, who was both the show's producer and the star's husband, had a major share in the writing, but others suggested Winchell Smith♦ was a silent collaborator. The circus scenes accounted as much for the show's popularity as did the romantic story.

Polly with a Past, a comedy in three acts by George Middleton♦ and Guy Bolton.♦ Produced by David Belasco♦ at the Belasco Theatre. September 6, 1917. 315 performances.

Rex Van Zile (Herbert Yost) is madly in love with a young lady who is more enamored of doing good deeds than she is of Rex. His friends persuade him to allow himself to go to seed so that the young lady can save him. To this end the friends enlist the aid of the comely Polly (Ina Claire♦), a minister's daughter from East Gilead, Ohio, who has come to New York to study for a concert career and who has taken a job as their maid to help pay her expenses. Polly agrees to pose as Paulette Bady, a French adventuress, and to "vamp" Rex. By the time the ruse has been played out, Rex and Polly are in love.

This pleasant comedy launched Miss Claire on her career as a high comedienne.

PONISI, Mme. [née Elizabeth Hanson] (1818–99) Born in England, she went on stage while still in her teens and shortly afterward married a fellow actor, James Ponisi. In 1850 they came to America, where she made her debut in Philadelphia's Walnut Street Theatre♦ as Mariana in *The Wife,* then played Lady Teazle for her first New York appearance. She rapidly earned a reputation as a fine and versatile performer, playing Cleopatra to Edward Eddy's♦ Antony, and Lady Macbeth, Desdemona, and Cordelia opposite Edwin Forrest.♦ In 1855 she created the title role in *Francesca da Rimini.♦* She joined Wallack's♦ great ensemble in 1871, replacing the famed Mrs. Vernon♦ as the company's leading portrayer of old women, and remained with the troupe until it was dissolved. Her Mrs. Hardcastle and Mrs. Malaprop were numbered among her finest interpretations, but she also continued to create new roles such as Widow O'Kelly in *Shaughraun♦* (1874). She had an expressive, attractive, though not beautiful face, with large, alert eyes.

Ponteach; or, The Savages of America, a tragedy in five acts by Major Robert Rogers. Published in 1766.

The English who come to America are an unpleasant mixture of indifference, callousness, and greed in their treatment of the native Indians. Some, like the hunters Honnyman and Orsbourn, shoot the redskins for sport. The English Governors, Sharp, Gripe, and Catchum, ignore instructions to make peace with the Indians. Sharp says, "Must mind that good old Rule, Take care of One," while Gripe agrees, "Ay, Christian Charity begins at home; / I think it's in the Bible, I know I've read it." The result is the destruction of the well-meaning, even noble Indians, led by Ponteach [pronounced Pontiac]. Grieving over the death of his loved ones, the chief exhorts the elements to . . . "witness for me to your new base Lords, / That my unconquer'd Mind defies them still."

The first tragedy to be written with a basically American theme and to feature Indians, this mediocre blank-verse drama appears never to have been performed.

Rogers (1731?–95) was a Massachusetts native who fought in the French and Indian wars, but who was noted for his sympathies for the redmen. He spent much of his life in England, where he also published his *Journal of the French and Indian War* and *A Concise Account of North America* (1765).

Poor of New York, The, a play in five acts by Dion Boucicault. ♦ Produced by J. W. Wallack♦ at Wallack's Theatre. December 8, 1857. 42 performances.

After depositing $100,000 with the banker Gideon Bloodgood (W. H. Norton), Captain Fairweather (W. R. Blake♦) learns that Bloodgood's bank is shaky, so he returns to give back Bloodgood the receipt and reclaim his money. An argument ensues in which Fairweather dies. Bloodgood keeps the money, but the receipt falls into the hands of the banker's equally treacherous clerk Badger (Lester Wallack♦). Years pass. Fairweather's family is living in dire poverty in the slums, in a room next door to one kept by Badger. Badger attempts to blackmail Bloodgood with the old receipt, but the tenement is set afire. The handsome Mark Livingstone (A. H. Sothern), who is nearly tricked into marrying Bloodgood's haughty daughter, Alida (Mrs. Hoey♦), helps rescue the Fairweathers and the all-important paper. He confronts Bloodgood with the evidence of his crime and wins the hand of the dead captain's daughter Lucy (Mrs. J. H. Allen).

Basing his work on Edouard Brisebarre and Eugène Nus's *Les Pauvres de Paris,* Boucicault added the climactic fire scene to accommodate contemporary demands for a spectacular denouement. The play was revived frequently, usually with the title *The Streets of New York,* and was a major success in England, too, where it was known as *The Streets of Liverpool* or *The Streets of London.*

Porgy, a play in four acts by Dorothy and Dubose Heyward. ♦ Produced by the Theatre Guild♦ at the Guild Theatre. October 10, 1927. 217 performances.

Porgy (Frank Wilson♦) is a crippled black beggar who lives and works in the Charleston tenement called Catfish Row, and who loves the beautiful but weak-willed Bess (Evelyn Ellis). Bess is the mistress of the vicious Crown (Jack Carter), but when Crown flees after murdering a man, she goes to live with Porgy. On Crown's return Porgy fights with him and kills him. He is taken to jail, and while he is there Bess is lured away by the drug peddler, Sporting Life (Percy Verwayne). Porgy leaves Catfish Row to seek her.

Based on Heyward's novel, the play remains one of the greatest of all American folk dramas. It was the source of *Porgy and Bess.* ♦

Porgy and Bess, a "folk opera" in three acts. Book and lyrics by Dubose Heyward♦ and Ira Gershwin. ♦ Music by George Gershwin. ♦ Produced by The Theatre Guild♦ at the Alvin Theatre. October 10, 1935. 124 performances.

When Clara (Abbie Mitchell) fails to lull her baby to sleep with a lullaby about the languorous virtues of "Summertime," her husband, Jake (Edward Matthews), tries with "A Woman Is a Sometime Thing." One reason the baby has trouble sleeping is that Catfish Row is a noisy, dangerous place, where the menfolk are drinking and gambling. The men tease the crippled Porgy (Todd Duncan♦), who rides around in a goat-cart, about his love for Crown's girl, Bess (Anne Brown). Crown (Warren Coleman) himself gets into a fight with his fellow gambler, Robbins (Henry), and stabs Robbins to death. Robbins's wife, Serena (Ruby Elzy), is left to wail "My Man's Gone Now." Crown flees, leaving Porgy, who has been content to boast "I Got Plenty o' Nuttin'," free to court Bess. Arranging for her to get a divorce, he tells her, "Bess, You Is My Woman Now." The neighbors all go on a picnic where a glib drug peddler, Sportin' Life (John W. Bubbles) tells them of his cynical ideas about the Bible, insisting, "It Ain't Necessarily So." Crown suddenly appears, and he and Porgy fight, with Porgy killing Crown with Crown's own knife. Porgy is sent to jail. When he is released he learns that Sportin' Life has taken Bess to New York, so he sets out in his goat-cart to retrieve her.

One of the towering achievements of the American musical theatre, the original production was not a commercial success. A major 1942 revival by Cheryl Crawford, ♦ in which Duncan and Miss Brown re-created their original roles, began to turn the tide. Later, Metropolitan Opera soprano Leontyne Price headed a 1953 revival. The Houston Grand Opera's production toured successfully and reached Broadway in 1976. In 1983 the Radio City Music Hall produced a gigantic mounting which subsequently toured. There have been other lesser revivals, a film version, and in the 1984–85 season it entered the repertoire of the Metropolitan Opera. Hollis Alpert's *The Life and Times of Porgy and Bess* (1990) gives a detailed history of the work.

PORTER, Cole [Albert] (1891–1964) Born into great wealth in Peru, Ind., he was educated at Yale and Harvard. Although he interpolated a few songs into earlier musicals, Broadway heard its first complete Porter score in the short-lived *See America First* (1915). His songs for *Hitchy-Koo 1919* included his earliest success, "Old-Fashioned Garden." Apart from submitting some numbers for the *Greenwich Village Follies of 1924,* ♦ he spent most of the 1920s in Europe, where he studied briefly with Vincent d'Indy. Returning to America he created the songs for *Paris* (1928), whose hit was "Let's Do It." This was followed by *Fifty Million Frenchmen*♦ (1929), remembered for "You Do Something to Me"; *Wake Up and Dream!* (1929), which offered "What Is This Thing Called Love?"; *The New Yorkers* (1930); *Gay Divorce*♦ (1932), which produced "Night and Day"; *Anything Goes*♦ (1934), whose score included "All Through the Night," "Anything Goes," "Blow, Gabriel, Blow," "I Get a Kick Out of You," and "You're the Top"; *Jubilee*♦ (1935), from which came "Begin the Beguine" and "Just One of Those Things"; *Red, Hot and Blue!* (1936), which included "Down in the Depths," "It's De-Lovely," and "Ridin' High"; *You Never Know* (1938); *Leave It to Me!*♦ (1938), which gave us "My Heart Belongs to Daddy"; *Du Barry Was a Lady*♦ (1939); *Panama Hattie*♦ (1940); *Let's Face It!*♦ (1941); *Something for the Boys* (1943); *Mexican Hayride* (1944), whose hit was "I Love You"; *Seven Lively Arts* (1944), recalled for "Ev'rytime We Say Goodbye"; *Around the World in Eighty Days* (1946); *Kiss Me, Kate*♦ (1948), his masterpiece, which included "Always True to You in My Fashion," "Another Op'nin', Another Show," "Brush Up Your Shakespeare," "So in Love," and "Wunderbar"; *Out of This World* (1950); *Can-Can*♦ (1953), which included "Allez-vous En," "C'est Magnifique," "I Love Paris," and "It's All Right with Me"; and *Silk Stockings* (1955).

Porter's songs trafficked in a knowing, sometimes showy, sophistication. His generally silken melodies were combined with his lyrics which ranged from suave and blasé to sexually obsessive and even raunchy. More than any other major song-writer, his songs seemed, except for some of his last musicals, to have a cavalier detachment from their shows.

Biography: *The Life That Late He Led*, George Eells, New York, 1967.

Potash and Perlmutter, a comedy in three acts by Montague Glass♦ [and Charles Klein,♦ uncredited]. Produced by A. H. Woods♦ at the Cohan Theatre. August 16, 1913. 441 performances.

Mawruss Perlmutter (Alexander Carr) and Abe Potash (Barney Bernard♦) are partners in the garment trade. And, oy, have they got problems! Like the customer who says, "I can send a check, but you'll have to wait for the money," to which they can only retort, "Send the money and we'll wait for the check." They also must find a new designer and a new salesman. But their biggest woe comes with the news that an employee, wanted by the Russian government on a murder charge, seemingly has reneged on the $20,000 bail Abe has paid and brought them close to bankruptcy. They put aside their perpetual bickering and finagling to save their

firm. As a bonus, the new designer, Ruth Snyder (Louise Dresser♦), proves so wonderful that Mawruss marries her.

Based on Glass's short stories in the *Saturday Evening Post*, the work was hailed in a *Times* headline as "Indescribably Enjoyable Entertainment." It was a big enough hit to prompt sequels, several of which were also successes.

POTTER, JOHN S. (1809–69) A Philadelphian who began a career as an actor while still in his teens, he abandoned performing to build and manage theatres. Rarely staying long in one place he moved about the entire country often erecting a community's first playhouse. Many of these were primitive wooden theatres, soon superseded. But he is said to have built more theatres than any other single man in American theatrical history, thus becoming a sort of theatrical "Johnny Appleseed." Among the various cities, then sometimes small towns or villages, where he constructed theatres were Natchez, Vicksburg, and Jackson, Miss.; Dubuque, Iowa; Rochester, N.Y.; Cleveland, Ohio; Little Rock, Ark.; and numerous unspecified towns in California and Oregon.

POTTER, PAUL [MEREDITH] [né WALTER McEWEN or McLEAN] (1853–1921) Born in England, he spent time there as a journalist before a scandal forced him to change his name and leave for America. He settled first in Chicago and continued his newspaper work, then took up play-writing. His earliest plays included *The City Director* (1890), which derived its humor from the confusion over eight men named John Smith, and *The Ugly Duckling* (1890), a romantic play written with A. D. Gordon as a vehicle for Mrs. Carter.♦ He scored his greatest success with his dramatization of George Du Maurier's *Trilby*♦ (1895). Virtually all of his later hits were also dramatizations, notably *The Conquerors*♦ (1898), derived from de Maupassant's *Mademoiselle Fifi; Under Two Flags*♦ (1901), taken from Ouida's novel; and *The Honor of the Family* (1908), translated from Emile Fabre's version of Balzac's *La Rabouilleuse*.

POTTER-BROWN, MRS. J., or **POTTER,** MRS. J. B. see *Brown-Potter, Mrs. J.*

Potters, The, a comedy in three acts by J. P. McEvoy. Produced by Richard Herndon♦ at the Plymouth Theatre. December 8, 1923. 245 performances.

According to Ma Potter (Catharine Calhoun

Doucet), Pa Potter (Donald Meek) is "the ablest man in his office, except on payday." She so nags her bumbling, timid husband that he invests in a speculative oil deal in an effort to make the fortune she feels is her due. The oil deal apparently goes sour at the same time their daughter, Mamie (Mary Carroll), elopes. Ma would make Pa's life totally miserable, but a surprise gusher in the oil fields finally gives Pa the upper hand.

The play was welcomed by Burns Mantle♦ as "a life-like study of American family life." Joseph Patrick McEvoy (1894–1958) was born in New York and studied at Notre Dame. He was a newspaperman before turning to the theatre with this, his first produced play. Most of his theatre work was done writing sketches for revues, notably the series known as *Americana* (1926, 1927, 1932). He was also a novelist, and his novel *Show Girl* became the source of Ziegfeld's♦ 1929 musical of the same name.

POWER, Tyrone (1797–1841) Born in Kilmacthomas, Ireland, he established himself as London's greatest delineator of Irish characters before coming to America in 1833. London's appraisal was quickly confirmed by American audiences. He was a tall, handsome, if slightly stocky man with light hair and striking blue eyes. T. Allston Brown♦ praised the "clearness and melodious softness" of his voice. Power was lost at sea in the sinking of the *President* while returning to England.

Autobiography: *Impressions of America,* London, 1836 (reissued, New York, 1969).

POWER, [Frederick] Tyrone (1869–1931) Grandson of the first Tyrone Power,♦ his parents were performers in London, where he was born. He came to America in 1886 and made his debut in St. Augustine, Fla. He then spent time with Augustin Daly's♦ famous ensemble. Later he played the Marquis of Steyne in Mrs. Fiske's♦ *Becky Sharp*♦ (1899); Judas Iscariot in her production of *Mary of Magdala* (1902); the title role in *Ulysses* (1903); Arkissus, the loyal barbarian, in *Adrea*♦ (1905); and Robert, the black sheep brother, in *The Servant in the House*♦ (1908). One of his major assignments was the title role in the musical *Chu Chin Chow* (1917). In his later career he performed largely in prominent supporting roles in Shakespearean revivals. Although he was starred only intermittently he formed an important link between his grandfather and grandson.

Biography: *Tyrone Power,* William Winter, New York, 1913.

POWER, Tyrone (1913–58) The last in a long line of actors bearing his name, he was born in Cincinnati and made his professional debut in 1931 in Chicago, where he continued to perform for several seasons. New York first saw him as Benvolio in Katharine Cornell's♦ *Romeo and Juliet*♦ (1935) and as Bertrand de Poulengy in her *Saint Joan*♦ (1936). After a long career in films he returned to Broadway in a dramatic reading of *John Brown's Body.* He later again played opposite Miss Cornell as the evil Richard Gettner in *The Dark Is Light Enough* (1955), then shortly before his death assumed a series of roles in a 1958 revival of *Back to Methuselah.*

POWERS, James T. [né McGovern] (1862–1943) The small, red-headed, rubber-faced comedian was born in New York and spent time in vaudeville and with circuses before calling attention to himself in a series of farce-comedies♦: *Dreams* (1882), *A Bunch of Keys* (1883), and *A Tin Soldier* (1886). One critic called him "a thorough genius run wild, with a face quite as grotesque as a gargoyle," and added, "This clever actor, in addition to his natural *vis comica,* has a broad sense of humor which animates both his features and his gestures." For several years he was a comedian with the Casino Theatre♦ company, then returned to farce-comedy in *A Straight Tip* (1891), *A Mad Bargain* (1892), *The New Boy* (1894), and *Gentleman Joe* (1896). With the coming to America of the English Gaiety musical comedies he became the principal comedian in many of the best importations, including *The Circus Girl* (1897), *The Geisha* (1897), *A Runaway Girl* (1898), *San Toy* (1900), *The Messenger Boy* (1901), and *Havana* (1909). Thereafter his career began to fade, although he appeared in a number of all-star revivals such as *The Rivals* (1922, 1923, 1930), *Henry IV, Part I*♦ (1926), and *The Beaux' Stratagem* (1928).

Autobiography: *Twinkle Little Star,* New York, 1939.

POWERS, Tom (1890–1955) The handsome, versatile actor was born in Owensboro, Ky., and studied at the American Academy of Dramatic Arts. ♦ He made his debut in Lancaster, Penn., as Dave in *In Mizzoura*♦ in 1911. He came to New York in 1915, and the following year scored personal successes in two short-lived plays, *Mr. Lazarus* and *Mile-a-Minute Kendall,* playing the title role in the latter. Turning to musical comedy, he enjoyed a long run as George Budd in *Oh, Boy!*♦ (1917), in which he introduced "Till the Clouds Roll By." Another success came as Leonard Chadwick, whose attempts at mate-switching backfire, in *Why Not?* (1922). Shortly thereafter he joined the Theatre Guild,♦ performing for them such roles as Gregers Werle in *The Wild Duck* (1925), the Captain in *Androcles and the Lion* (1925); Napoleon in *The Man of Destiny* (1926); and Bluntschli in *Arms and the Man* (1926). He then played Archie Inch, the dedicated street cleaner, in *White Wings*♦ (1926). In 1928 he created the role of Charles Marsden, the novelist still tied to his mother's apron strings, in *Strange Interlude.*♦ He next played King Magnus in *The Apple Cart* (1930). While he remained active until the mid-1940s, the rest of his career was occupied largely either with failures, with road companies, or in replacing other performers, including Orson Welles,♦ whom he succeeded as Brutus in the Mercury Theatre♦ mounting of *Julius Caesar*♦ in 1938.

PRESBREY, Eugene W[yley] (1853–1931) Born in Williamsburg, Mass., he made his debut as an actor in Boston in 1874. He came to New York in 1880, and from 1883 to 1896 served as a director for A. M. Palmer.♦ Late in his career with Palmer he began to write plays. These ranged from light farces to romantic dramas. Many were written in collaboration with other writers or were dramatizations of novels and short stories. They included *The Courtship of Miles Standish* (1895), *A Ward of France* (1897), *A Virginia Courtship* (1898), *New England Folks* (1901), and *Mary, Mary, Quite Contrary* (1905). His biggest success was *Raffles*♦ (1903), written with E. W. Hornung, on whose stories it was based, and centering on a gallant rich man who steals for sport. As a rule, Presbrey directed all his own plays and frequently staged works by other authors as well. About the time of World War I he recognized that his sort of theatre was passing from the scene, so he became a silent film screenwriter.

PRESTON [Meservey], Robert (1918–87) Born in Newton Highlands, Mass., he was raised in California and studied at the theatre school of the Pasadena Community Playhouse.♦ He made occasional West Coast appearances while becoming a film star who specialized in tough men and Western villains. In New York, his versatility was displayed when he succeeded José Ferrer♦ in 1951 in the revival of *Twentieth Century*♦ and when he next portrayed Joe Ferguson in a 1952 revival of *The Male Animal.*♦ After a series of failures he scored a hit as Gil, who learns his wife is not totally faithful, in *Janus*♦ (1955). His major success came when he created the role of the likable con man, Harold Hill, in the musical *The Music Man*♦ (1957), in which he introduced "Seventy-Six Trombones." He later played the title role in the musical *Ben Franklin in Paris* (1964), then played Henry II in the drama *The Lion in Winter*♦ (1966). Returning to song and dance he portrayed the husband in the two-character musical, *I Do! I Do!* (1966).

PRICE, Fanny B[ayard] (1847–97) A niece of William Warren,♦ she was born in Vicksburg, Miss., and made her debut in Chicago while still virtually an infant as the Child to James E. Murdoch's♦ Rolla in *Pizarro.*♦ In 1864 she became leading lady in stock in Louisville, then toured for many years as a star. She almost never appeared in New York, but was popular on the road as the heroine of numerous contemporary plays.

PRICE, Stephen (1783–1840) One of the earliest major theatre managers in America, he was the first not to be an actor or playwright as well. In 1808, when the Park Theatre♦ was having financial difficulties, he bought some of Thomas Abthorpe Cooper's♦ shares in the theatre and assumed joint management with him. He later purchased full control. His careful fiscal husbanding began to turn the ledgers around, but his master stroke was to import London stars, beginning with George Frederick Cooke♦ and Edmund Kean.♦ Scholars such as Odell♦ have seen the destruction of the traditional stock company stemming from this practice, but, in fact, stock companies continued to flourish until the late 19th century. Nevertheless Price's policies did signal the start of purely business interests dominating the American theatre. His penchant for spectacle, however artless it might seem, also demonstrated that he knew what his public most wanted. The Park's heyday virtually coincided with Price's tenure, since at the time of his death the first important competition and the movement northward of New York's theatre district were taking their toll. Price was the scion of an old New York family which had distinguished itself in business, law, and politics.

Pride of Jennico, The, a play in four acts by Abby Sage Richardson and Grace Livingston Furniss. Produced by Charles Frohman♦ at the Criterion Theatre. March 6, 1900. 111 performances.

Princess Marie Ottilie (Bertha Galland) and her maid, who is also named Marie (Gertrude Rivers), come to the Bohemian castle of Basil Jennico (James K. Hackett♦). The women agree to switch places so that Marie Ottilie can see if Jennico will love her even though he thinks her a commoner. He does, despite the evil plotting of Eugen von Rothenberg (Brigham Royce) and the gypsy, Michel (Grace Reals).

The play was based on incidents in a novel by Agnes and Egerton Castle. Alone or together, Mrs. Richardson and Mrs. Furniss wrote several other plays produced in New York at the turn of the century.

PRIMROSE, GEORGE H. (1852–1919) Born in London, Ontario, he began his minstrel career at the age of fifteen when he joined MacFarland's Minstrels, a Detroit company. A few years later he met William H. West, and after spending several seasons together performing in other men's groups, he and West founded Primrose and West's Minstrels. ◆ When the ensemble disbanded in 1898 he joined Lew Dockstader◆ until 1903, then performed for several years in vaudeville before his retirement. He is often credited with originating the soft shoe dance.

Primrose and West's Minstrels A minstrel ensemble formed in 1877 by George Primrose◆ and Billy West, it quickly became one of the most popular of all blackface bands. The company lasted until 1898, although for nine years in the 1880s George Thatcher was a partner and the group was known as Thatcher, Primrose and West's Minstrels. Both Primrose and West had worked for J. H. Haverly◆ and, like Haverly, they emphasized the spectacular aspects of their shows and minimized many of the older, traditional routines. They even experimented with whiteface minstrelsy. "We were looking for novelty," Thatcher was later to say. Minstrel historian Robert C. Toll noted "they brought minstrelsy to a stage where it was distinguished from other entertainment only by its name."

Prince Chap, The, a play in three acts by Edward Peple. ◆ Produced at the Madison Square Theatre. ◆ September 4, 1905. 106 performances.

When a dying model leaves her small daughter with a young sculptor, William Payton (Cyril Scott), Payton's fiancée, Alice Travers (Grace Kimball), assumes the child is his and breaks off their engagement. Years pass. Payton has raised the girl, Claudia, into womanhood, while Alice has married another man and since become a widow. She has learned that Payton had told her the truth and, still loving him, hopes for a reconciliation. Payton is willing to be her friend but has recognized that it is Claudia he truly loves.

The play, Peple's first, opened on the same night

as plays by Augustus Thomas,◆ Clyde Fitch,◆ Hall Caine,◆ and Shaw's◆ *Man and Superman,* ◆ and so was reviewed by critics far down in the pecking order. Nonetheless, it was recognized as a superior work. Two weeks later in its Sunday canvas of recent openings the *Times* called it "the most satisfying offering of the early season." The play toured for several years and returned to New York in 1907. The role of Claudia was played by a different actress in each act in order to convey her growth.

PRINCE, HAL [né HAROLD SMITH PRINCE] (b. 1928) Born in New York and educated at the University of Pennsylvania, he began his theatrical career as a stage manager, then joined Frederick Brisson◆ and Robert E. Griffith◆ with whom he co-produced *The Pajama Game*◆ (1954), *Damn Yankees*◆ (1955), and *New Girl in Town*◆ (1957). With Griffith he produced *West Side Story*◆ (1957) and *Fiorello!*◆ (1959), among others. On his own he next produced *Take Her, She's Mine*◆ (1961) and *A Funny Thing Happened on the Way to the Forum*◆ (1962). After directing and co-producing *She Loves Me*◆ (1963), he produced *Fiddler on the Roof*◆ (1964). Later musicals with which he was associated as producer and director were *Cabaret*◆ (1966), *Company*◆ (1970), *Follies*◆ (1971), and *A Little Night Music*◆ (1973). He subsequently staged *Sweeney Todd*◆ (1979), a musical version of *Merrily We Roll Along*◆ (1981), *A Doll's Life* (1982), *Grind* (1985), *Roza* (1987), and *The Phantom of the Opera*◆ (1988).

Prince has been one of the master directors of modern musicals, making effective crowds out of the understaffed contemporary choruses, giving dramatic movement to the most static scripts, and knowingly underscoring with his staging the meanings and moods of his texts. Along with his frequent associate, Stephen Sondheim,◆ he has been the leading advocate of the "conceptualized musical"—a musical in which text and production are conceived from the start as an integral totality.

Autobiography: *Contradictions,* New York, 1974.

Prince Karl, a play in four acts by A. C. Gunter. ◆ Produced at the Madison Square Theatre. ◆ May 3, 1886. 122 performances.

Impecunious Prince Karl (Richard Mansfield◆) has promised to marry a rich old woman, but changes his mind when he falls in love with Mrs. Florence Lowell (Maida Craigin), a beautiful widow slated to inherit an even larger fortune. Karl feigns suicide and reappears as his own "foster brother," offering to serve Mrs. Lowell as a courier. She learns of his trick but mischievously pretends to be ignorant of it. Eventually she falls in love with him and reveals that her inheritance was that left her by Karl's long-lost uncle and actually belongs to him.

Written as a serious romance and first presented with Mansfield at the Boston Museum,♦ it was quickly turned by the star into an amiable farce.

Prince of Parthia, The, a tragedy in five acts by Thomas Godfrey.♦ Produced by the American Company♦ at the Southwark Theatre♦ (Philadelphia). April 24, 1767. 1 performance (see below).

Vardanes (Mr. Tomlinson) plots to turn his father, King Artabanus (David Douglass♦), against his brother, Arsaces (Lewis Hallam, Jr.♦). Vardanes resents Arsaces's success in war and even more his brother's winning the affection of Evanthe (Miss Cheer♦), a captive maiden whom both Vardanes and the king covet. Vardanes succeeds in having the king imprison Arsaces, but their third brother, Gotarzes (Mr. Wall), leads an army to free him. A battle ensues. Evanthe hears that Arsaces has been killed, so she poisons herself. But the news of his death was only a rumor. Arsaces rushes to the dying girl, and when she expires he kills himself. His last words are "Out, out vile cares, from your distress'd abode." Gotarzes is left to restore order.

The first play by an American author to be professionally produced in America, its dramatic and theatrical values are modest. It was not performed until after Godfrey's death. The incomplete records of the period make it uncertain whether more than one performance was given, and the cast listed above is the one postulated by Seilhamer and generally accepted by later scholars.

Prince of Pilsen, The, a musical in two acts. Book and lyrics by Frank Pixley.♦ Music by Gustav Luders.♦ Produced by Henry W. Savage♦ at the Broadway Theatre. March 17, 1903. 143 performances.

Hans Wagner (John W. Ransome), a Cincinnati brewer, arrives in Nice with his daughter, Nellie (Lillian Coleman), to visit his son Tom (Albert Parr), who is serving there with the American navy. Prince Carl Otto of Pilsen (Arthur Donaldson) is booked into the same hotel. When Hans is confused for the prince, the prince takes advantage of the confusion to go out on the town incognito. He meets and falls in love with Nellie. By the end of the evening Nellie is on her way to becoming a princess, while both her father and brother have also made romantic attachments.

Principal songs: The Heidelberg Stein Song · The Message of the Violet

The best of the many Pixley-Luders collaborations, it continued to tour successfully for over a decade. Part of its popularity may have stemmed from the fact that while it was an operetta it essentially employed the American-in-foreign-lands theme that had only recently become the rage of musical comedy.

Princess Theatre A small 299-seat playhouse built by the Shuberts♦ and others on 39th Street, between Broadway and Sixth Avenue, it was designed by William A. Swasey,♦ who also designed the Shubert flagship, the Winter Garden. ♦ The theatre opened in 1913 as the home for one-act plays, but when this policy failed the playhouse was turned over to intimate musical comedies in 1915. These Kern♦ musicals—*Nobody Home*♦ (1915), *Very Good Eddie*♦ (1915), *Oh, Boy!*♦ (1917), and *Oh, Lady! Lady!!*♦ (1918), along with two others written for the house but presented elsewhere—established new standards for musical comedy. They offered fundamentally believable characters in tight-knit, fundamentally believable situations; they allowed both humor and songs to derive from these characters and situations and sometimes advance the action or character development; and they mounted these singularly literate, witty, and melodic works with grace and charm. The shows became known as the Princess Theatre musicals. The theatre continued to offer experimental plays in the 1920s. With the coming of the Depression it became a film house, but was later rechristened the Labor Stage and served as the original home of *Pins and Needles*♦ (1937). It then became a film house again, and was demolished in 1955.

Prisoner of Second Avenue, The, a comedy in two acts by Neil Simon.♦ Produced at the Eugene O'Neill Theatre. November 11, 1971. 780 performances.

Mel Edison (Peter Falk) and his wife Edna (Lee Grant) have lived in their 14th-floor apartment for six years. Now New York and its high pressure way of life are beginning to tell on Mel. He can hear not only the music the German airline stewardesses keep playing next door, but he can even hear "one car driving around in Jackson Heights." When he loses his job he goes to pieces, wandering about the apartment unshaven and in his pajamas. Visits from his brother and sisters, and visits to a doctor all seem to be of little help. He refuses his family's offer of $25,000 to set up his own summer camp. But somehow their confidence begins to give him the confidence he needs to make a recovery.

Simon's ninth successive hit, it made a warm, human comedy out of the brutal, small materials of everyday life and even out of the seeds of tragedy.

Prisoner of Zenda, The, a play in a prologue and four acts by Edward E. Rose. ♦ Produced by Daniel Frohman ♦ at the Lyceum Theatre. ♦ September 4, 1895. 112 performances.

Years ago, Gilbert, Earl of Rassendyll (Howard Gould) and Prince Rudolf of Ruritania (E. H. Sothern ♦) fought a bitter duel. Now, decades later, the families' paths cross again under different circumstances. The current Prince Rudolf (Sothern) is about to be crowned king, but his brother, Michael, Duke of Streslau (Arthur R. Lawrence) and Rupert of Hentzau (Morton Selten) drug him to prevent the ceremony. Rudolf Rassendyll (Sothern), who is the image of the new king, is hastily enlisted to take the king's place. In doing so he falls in love with Princess Flavia (Grace Kimball), who is to be queen. Rassendyll eventually discovers that the king is being held prisoner at the castle of Zenda and there confronts the conspirators, who are quarrelling over a woman. Rupert kills Michael, then flees. Rassendyll restores Rudolf to his rightful place and reluctantly renounces Flavia, who with equal reluctance accepts her destiny.

Based on Anthony Hope's famous novel, the play was such a huge hit that when prior commitments required Sothern to end his New York engagement, Frohman brought in a second company. The play toured regularly for many seasons, including a company headed by James K. Hackett. ♦ Hackett himself mounted a major revival in 1908, and in 1913 he starred in the first film version. The work served as the basis for the 1925 Sigmund Romberg ♦ operetta *Princess Flavia* and for a failed Vernon Duke ♦ musical, *Zenda,* in 1963.

Private Lives A 1930 English comedy by Noel Coward, ♦ it was presented in New York on January 27, 1931, with Coward and Gertrude Lawrence ♦ recreating their original London roles of a divorced couple who have married new mates, and who meet by chance on their respective honeymoons and rekindle their old romance. Few contemporary comedies have retained such on-going popularity. Major Broadway revivals have included those in 1948 with Tallulah Bankhead ♦ and Donald Cook, ♦ in 1969 with Tammy Grimes ♦ and Brian Bedford, ♦ and in 1983 with film star Elizabeth Taylor and her ex-husband Richard Burton. ♦

PROCTOR, FREDERICK FREEMAN (1851–1929) Born in Dexter, Maine, he began his theatrical career as part of an acrobatic act. A frugal teetotaler, he used his savings to purchase a small theatre in Albany, where he abandoned the policy of serving drinks, cleaned up the acts, and offered the sort of family vaudeville that Tony Pastor ♦ had initiated in New York. By 1890, with a partner named Henry Jacobs, he owned dozens of theatres playing cut-price vaudeville. When the partnership was dissolved in that year, he moved to New York and opened the 23rd Street Theatre. He later joined his arch-rival, B. F. Keith, ♦ to form a large chain, selling out shortly before his death. His middle name was sometimes given as Francis.

Biography: *F. F. Proctor: Vaudeville Pioneer,* William Moulton Marston and John Henry Feller, New York, 1943.

PROCTOR, JOSEPH (1816–97) Although the stern-faced Philadelphia-born tragedian was praised for his performances in such roles as Macbeth (opposite Charlotte Cushman ♦), Marc Antony, and Damon, he elected, like several other important contemporaries, to assure his financial security by relying on a single part with which he was largely identified. That part was the title role in *Nick of the Woods,* ♦ which he first played in 1839 and returned to regularly until he retired. Otis Skinner ♦ characterized him as "stately, formal, of the Forrest School."

Producing Managers' Association A group apparently founded to deal with growing unionism in the theatre, it was long headed by Sam H. Harris ♦ and listed virtually every major producer and theatre owner as a member. It may have been superseded by the Managers' Protective Association, although the latter may represent simply a name change. Arthur Hammerstein ♦ was president. A similar group, the National Association of Theatrical Producing Managers, seems to have had a broader membership, including many figures in burlesque and other theatre forms, and possibly a broader scope as well. Surviving correspondence in the Shubert ♦ Archive shows it dealt with unions, but more often with local and national legal matters and outside pressure groups. William A. Brady ♦ is listed as president. This organization may have given way to the United Managers' Protective Association, which was headed for a time by Marc Klaw. ♦ Both the Producing Managers' Association and the United Managers' Protective Association are listed in newspaper articles dealing with events related to the 1919 strike by Actors' Equity. ♦ More research is required to clarify the history and purpose of these associations.

Professional Players, THE This was a subscription group organized in the late 1920s in major try-out towns to promote better productions and an audience for them. The onset of the Depression and better organized subscription series, such as those offered by the Theatre Guild,♦ led to its quick disbanding.

Professor, The, a play in four acts by William Gillette.♦ Produced at the Madison Square Theatre.♦ June 1, 1881. 151 performances.

Professor Hopkins (Gillette) is a handsome but unworldly pedant who finds himself pursued by a bevy of young girls, a pursuit which infuriates the Yale students who have been courting the girls. He must also confront a kidnapper and the girl he kidnapped, and a long-lost brother and sister.

Called "a character study" by the author, the play was accepted by the public for what it was—a lighthearted summer comedy.

Promises, Promises, a musical comedy in two acts. Book by Neil Simon.♦ Lyrics by Hal David. Music by Burt Bacharach. Produced by David Merrick♦ at the Shubert Theatre. December 1, 1968. 1,281 performances.

Chuck Baxter (Jerry Orbach♦) is a young executive who is willing to help his rise to the top by lending his boss his apartment for trysts. Complications develop when one of his boss's dates attempts to commit suicide in the flat. The girl is Fran Kubelik (Jill O'Hara), and Chuck's careful nursing of her leads to a romance between the two.

Principal songs: I'll Never Fall in Love Again · Promises, Promises

Based on the film *The Apartment,* the clever collaboration of Simon with the popular songwriting team of Bacharach and David gave Broadway one of its brightest musical comedies. This was Bacharach's only Broadway score.

Protective Alliance of Scene Painters, see *United Scenic Artists of America*

Provincetown Players Founded in 1915 in Provincetown, Mass., by a group of theatre lovers headed by Susan Glaspell♦ and her husband George Cram Cook,♦ it gave its first performances that same summer in a small theatre on a wharf in the city. Robert Edmond Jones♦ designed the sets. The second summer the program was much enlarged and

included two plays, *Bound East for Cardiff*♦ and *Thirst,* by Eugene O'Neill.♦ The season was so successful that the group took over a small playhouse in New York's Greenwich Village (later moving to another one) and began the first of over a decade of seasons that would continue until 1929, with a major reorganization after 1921 that left Jones, O'Neill, and Kenneth MacGowan♦ in charge. At first the company offered largely one-act plays, but later included full-length works. Among the major or interesting works offered by the group were John Reed's *Freedom* (1916); O'Neill's *Before Breakfast* (1916); *Fog* (1917); *The Sniper* (1917); *The Long Voyage Home*♦ (1917); *Ile* (1917); Maxwell Bodenheim's *Knot Holes* (1917), written with William Saphir, and *The Gentle Furniture Shop* (1917); O'Neill's *The Rope* (1918); *Where the Cross Is Made* (1918); *The Moon of the Caribbees*♦ (1918); *The Dreamy Kid* (1919); Edna St. Vincent Millay's *Aria da Capo* (1919); Edna Ferber's♦ *The Eldest* (1920); O'Neill's *Exorcism* (1920); *The Emperor Jones*♦ (1920); *Diff'rent* (1920); Glaspell's *Inheritors* (1921); O'Neill's *The Hairy Ape*♦ (1922); a revival of *Fashion*♦ (1924); O'Neill's *The Ancient Mariner* (1924); *All God's Chillun Got Wings*♦ (1924); Edmund Wilson's *The Crime in the Whistler Room* (1924); O'Neill's *Desire Under the Elms*♦ (1924); and Paul Green's *In Abraham's Bosom*♦ (1926). During its hey-day the troupe ran the Greenwich Village Theatre as well as the Provincetown Playhouse. In their excellent history of the company, *The Provincetown: A Story of a Theatre* (1931), Helen Deutsch and Stella Hanau concluded simply, "The Provincetown was more a laboratory than a theater . . . To it belonged the task of developing playwrights, of taking risks with unknown actors and designers."

Pulitzer Prize The most prestigious of all drama awards, it was created by Joseph Pulitzer to honor "the original American play performed in New York which shall best represent the educational value and power of the stage in raising the standards of good morals and good manners." The awards have often been criticized, and displeasure with them prompted the founding of the New York Drama Critics Circle♦ and its awards. Winners (most of which have separate entries in this volume) have been: 1918—*Why Marry?;* 1919—no award; 1920—*Beyond the Horizon;* 1921—*Miss Lulu Bett;* 1922—*Anna Christie;* 1923—*Icebound;* 1924—*Hell-Bent fer Heaven;* 1925—*They Knew What They Wanted;* 1926—*Craig's Wife;* 1927—*In Abraham's Bosom;* 1928—*Strange Interlude;* 1929—*Street Scene;* 1930—*The*

Green Pastures; 1931—*Alison's House;* 1932—*Of Thee I Sing;* 1933—*Both Your Houses;* 1934—*Men in White;* 1935—*The Old Maid;* 1936—*Idiot's Delight;* 1937—*You Can't Take It with You;* 1938—*Our Town;* 1939—*Abe Lincoln in Illinois;* 1940—*The Time of Your Life;* 1941—*There Shall Be No Night;* 1942—no award; 1943—*The Skin of Our Teeth;* 1944—no award; 1945—*Harvey;* 1946—*State of the Union;* 1947—no award; 1948—*A Streetcar Named Desire;* 1949—*Death of a Salesman;* 1950—*South Pacific;* 1951—no award; 1952—*The Shrike;* 1953—*Picnic;* 1954—*The Teahouse of the August Moon;* 1955—*Cat on a Hot Tin Roof;* 1956—*The Diary of Anne Frank;* 1957—*Long Day's Journey into Night;* 1958—*Look Homeward, Angel;* 1959—*J.B.;* 1960—*Fiorello!;* 1961—*All the Way Home;* 1962—*How To Succeed in Business Without Really Trying;* 1963—no award; 1964—no award; 1965—*The Subject Was Roses;* 1966—no award; 1967—*A Delicate Balance;* 1968—no award; 1969—*The Great White Hope;* 1970—*No Place To Be Somebody;* 1971—*The Effects of Gamma Rays on Man-in-the-Moon Marigolds;* 1972—no award; 1973—*That Championship Season;* 1974—no award; 1975—*Seascape;* 1976—*A Chorus Line;* 1977—*The Shadow Box;* 1978—*The Gin Game;* 1979—*Buried Child;* 1980—*Talley's Folly;* 1981—*Crimes of the Heart;* 1982—*A Soldier's Play;* 1983—*'Night, Mother;* 1984—*Glengarry Glen Ross;* 1985—*Sunday in the Park with George;* 1986—no award; 1987—*Fences;* 1988—*Driving Miss Daisy;* 1989—*The Heidi Chronicles;* and 1990—*The Piano Lesson.*

PURCELL, CHARLES (1883–1962) The Chattanooga-born singing actor made his Broadway debut in 1908 and became a popular leading man in the teens and twenties. His best-known roles were in *Maytime*♦ (1917), in which he introduced "Will You Remember?," *Dearest Enemy*♦ (1925), in which he sang "Bye and Bye" and "Here in My Arms," and *Oh, Please!* (1926), in which he introduced "I Know That You Know."

Purlie Victorious, a comedy in three acts by Ossie Davis. Produced at the Cort Theatre. September 28, 1961. 261 performances.

Purlie Victorious Judson (Davis), an exuberant young black man, returns to his home in a small Georgia town hoping to acquire Big Bethel church and convert it into an integrated house of worship. His plans are opposed by the hidebound, unreconstructed Ol' Cap'n Cotchipee (Sorrell Brooke). Cotchipee resents all modern innovations, such as colleges that teach students to pronounce "nigger"

as if it were spelled "negro," as well as the political leanings of his son Charley (Alan Alda), who is "too friendly to the Supreme Court." But Purlie's middle name was not Victorious for nothing.

A delightfully funny comedy, it turned many stereotypes inside out and upside down. Davis was born in Cogdell, Ga., in 1917. He acted in numerous Broadway shows. Although he wrote several other plays, this was his only one to earn a major Broadway mounting. In 1970 it served as the basis for the musical *Purlie,* for which he collaborated on the book.

Pursuit of Happiness, The, a comedy in three acts by Alan Child and Isabelle Louden [pen names for Lawrence Langner♦ and Armina Marshall]. Produced at the Avon Theatre. October 9, 1933. 252 performances.

When Max Christmann (Tonio Selwart), a Hessian soldier in hiding, takes refuge on the Connecticut farm of Captain Aaron Kirkland (Charles Waldron♦), he falls in love with Kirkland's daughter Prudence (Peggy Conklin♦). Prudence is engaged to Thaddeus Jennings (Raymond Walburn), the local sheriff. A Puritan precept states, "Since in a bed a man and maid may bundle and be chaste, it does no good to burn our wood," so it does not seem untoward for Prudence to invite Max to bundle with her. Jennings catches them and demands the local minister denounce the practice of bundling. He agrees, forcing Max and Prudence to wed. Max happily realizes he has enjoyed the American right to "Life, Liberty and the Pursuit of Happiness."

The only successful collaboration by Langner and Miss Marshall, who was actually Mrs. Langner, the play served as the source for the 1950 musical *Arms and the Girl.*

Pygmalion This modern retelling of the Pygmalion-Galatea legend was first seen in America in 1914, with Shaw's♦ original Eliza Doolittle, Mrs. Patrick Campbell,♦ repeating her role. Most critics kindly overlooked the fact that she was far too old for the part. Her transition from street waif to lady was highly praised, with one critic adding, "with the deftest touch she suggests the old Eliza is not so far below the surface after all." Her Higgins was a younger Philip Merivale.♦ Although some critics were disturbed by her American accent, Lynn Fontanne♦ dominated a 1926 Theatre Guild♦ revival in which Reginald Mason was Higgins. The play enjoyed its longest American run when it was revived in 1945 for Gertrude Lawrence,♦ with Raymond Massey♦ as Higgins. Several reviewers suggested Miss Lawrence did not always seem believable, although again they refrained from mentioning that she, too, was old for the part. A 1987 revival starred Peter O'Toole and Amanda Plummer, but Ivar Brogger won applause when he took over during O'Toole's all too frequent indispositions. The play also served as the basis for the most literate of all American operettas, *My Fair Lady*♦ (1956). To many who saw the original production the youthful Julie Andrews♦ and more especially the reptilian Rex Harrison♦ will probably remain the definitive interpreters of the roles.

Q

Queen High, see *Pair of Sixes, A*

QUINN, ARTHUR HOBSON (1875–1960) The Philadelphia-born scholar studied at the University of Pennsylvania and later taught English and Drama there from 1895 to 1945. His books on theatre include *Representative American Plays* (1917), *The Early Drama* (1917), *History of the American Drama from the Beginning to the Civil War* (1923), *Contemporary American Plays* (1923), and *History of the American Drama from the Civil War to the Present Day* (1927). He also served as editor for *Harper's Plays and Playwrights Series.* His two histories of American drama, which like several others of his books were brought up to date after the first publication, remain the most complete and best study of our dramatic literature. While some of his views naturally reflect the thinking of his era, his long exposure to drama and careful training make him a generally reliable guide.

QUINTERO, JOSÉ [BENJAMIN] (b. 1924) Born in Panama, he studied at the University of Southern California and directed summer stock before calling attention to himself with his sensitive stagings at the Circle in the Square,♦ including a 1952 revival of *Summer and Smoke*♦ and a 1958 revival of *Children of Darkness.* However, it was his work on Eugene O'Neill♦ plays for which he is best remembered. These include the celebrated 1956 revival of *The Iceman Cometh*♦ at the Circle in the Square, the original Broadway production of *Long Day's Journey into Night*♦ (1956), *Hughie* (1964), *More Stately Mansions* (1967), a 1973 revival of *A Moon for the Misbegotten,* ♦ and the lauded but commercially unsuccessful 1988 revival of *Long Day's Journey.*

Autobiography: *If You Don't Dance, They Beat You,* Boston, 1972.

R

RABE, DAVID (b. 1940) Born in Dubuque, Iowa, he was educated at Loras College and at Villanova University, then served for a brief time as a newspaperman. His first play to be produced was *The Basic Training of Pavlo Hummel*◆ (1971), which described the disillusionment and death of a soldier in the Viet Nam War. It was produced by Joseph Papp's◆ New York Shakespeare Festival,◆ which mounted all his plays in the 1970s. *Sticks and Bones*◆ (1971) told a similar story of a Viet Nam veteran in slightly absurdist terms. His preoccupation with the war surfaced again with *The Orphan* (1973), which was presented only off-Broadway and which centered on a farm family that had lost a son in battle. *Boom Boom Room* (1973), later called *In the Boom Boom Room,* painted a grim picture of a seedy night-club performer, the type known as a "go-go girl." He returned to army life when he offered *Streamers*◆ (1976), which purported to show an army barracks as a microcosm of troubled American life in the 1960s. *Hurlyburly* (1984) depicted drug-addicted show business hangers-on. He has served as playwright in residence at Villanova University. Despite the relative narrowness of his subject matter, his plays have profited from his basic sense of construction, his pungent comments on American life and human foibles, and his skillful employment and intermingling of expressionism, absurdism, and realism.

RACHEL [née ELISA FELIX] (1820–58) Usually considered the greatest of French classical tragediennes, she made her American debut in 1855 as Camille in Corneille's *Horace.* The *Albion* reported, "There came in a severe classic figure, a polychrome statue, gliding past the columns, and breathing rather than articulating . . . So deep, vibrant and magnetic were the first tones of [her] voice that they sent a thrill through the vast assembly, a thrill which at once opened communication between the genius of Rachel and her new hearers." On later evenings she presented her Phèdre, Adrienne Lecouvreur, and Andromaque, among others. Historians have long disputed the success of her tour, T. Allston Brown,◆ for example, saying she often played to empty houses, while others point to huge salaries and grosses. The figures may have been inflated by the fact that tickets at first were three times going prices, but Brown may be correct, since prices were eventually reduced. Nor can historians agree just where on her tour she took ill; apparently she caught a cold that aggravated her tubercular condition. Her last performance was in Charleston, where she was barely able to perform. She then sailed for France, where she died just over two years afterwards.

Biography: *Rachel,* Joanna Richardson, London, 1956.

Racket, *The,* a play in three acts by Bartlett Cormack. Produced at the Ambassador Theatre. November 22, 1927. 119 performances.

When the reporters who cover an outlying Chicago police station taunt Captain McQuigg (John Cromwell◆) about whether an honest, dedicated police officer would be exiled to a relatively unimportant post if he attempts to buck both political corruption and gangland boss Nick Scarsi, McQuigg evades their barbs. McQuigg knows full well that has been his own history and that Scarsi has now opened a brewery in his district. After he arrests Scarsi's younger brother he also knows he has joined battle. Under an assumed name, Scarsi (Edward G. Robinson◆) appears, demanding to see his brother's girl, Irene (Marion Coakley), who he fears can cause trouble for his brother. A policeman refuses, so Scarsi shoots him. Scarsi escapes, but he is caught and brought back to the station, where McQuigg declines to release him despite a judge's order. In an argument in front of State Attorney Welsh (Romaine Callender), Irene gets Scarsi inadvertently to admit the killing, but Scarsi threatens to destroy Welsh and the whole Chicago political machine if he is prosecuted. Pulling a gun, Scarsi attempts to shoot McQuigg, only to be shot instead.

The play was hailed by Burns Mantle◆ as one that "bears unmistakeably the stamp of authenticity in character, scene and speech and reflects vividly a phase of civic life in America." This was the first time Robinson played a gangster, and the only time on Broadway. Attempts were made by Chicago authorities to ban the play there, in the light of the success of *Chicago*◆ and other similar plays and the bad image of Chicago that resulted.

Cormack (1898?–1942) was born in Hammond,

Indiana, and studied at the University of Chicago before becoming a newspaperman and working with the little theatre movement.♦ This was his only successful play. He later served as a press agent.

Raffles, the Amateur Cracksman, a play in four acts by E. W. Hornung and Eugene Presbrey.♦ Produced by Liebler and Co.♦ at the Princess Theatre. October 27, 1903. 168 performances.

A. J. Raffles (Kyrle Bellew♦) is a highly educated, chivalrous English gentleman. For the fun of it, he is also a jewel thief. Invited to the home of a friendly lord, he thinks nothing of stealing the family diamonds, but his exquisite scruples demand he reject the advances of his host's wife and daughter. Captain Bedford (E. M. Holland) is an amateur sleuth who is determined to catch Raffles. He almost does. Yet after learning that Raffles has returned the lord's jewels and escaped, he can only sigh, "I'm glad of it."

This superb comedy-thriller was based on Hornung's popular stories. It was revived regularly for more than a decade.

Railroad of Love, The, a comedy in four acts by Augustin Daly.♦ Produced by Daly at Daly's Theatre. November 1, 1887. 108 performances.

According to Phenix Scuttleby (James Lewis♦), an aging man-about-town, the pace of modern courtship has become too rapid: "Man alive! it's railroad time with the women nowadays. If you are loaded with millions, you may court on way-freight time, or a particularly fascinating fellow may jog along on accommodation schedule. But the daredevil in love will flash across the switches, through the tunnels, and around curves with a strong heart and no flinching." In this high-speed society Lieutenant Howell Everett (John Drew♦) pursues Viva Van Riker (Phoebe Russell) until he recognizes that she prefers the impecunious artist Benny Demaresq (Otis Skinner♦). Even then he might have pressed his suit but for the appearance of a beautiful, rich widow, Mrs. Valentine Osprey (Ada Rehan♦). A clause in her late husband's will diverts his estate to old Scuttleby if she remarries, unless by some wild chance Scuttleby marries first. Events and friends conspire to marry Scuttleby to Eutycia Laburnam (Mrs. G. H. Gilbert♦), a country dowager who longs for "a change from the eternal birds and crickets" and for air with "not a trace of ozone." So all the couples are happily paired.

Odell♦ recalled, "The Railroad of Love was the most exquisite modern comedy I ever saw at Daly's." Daly took the play from Schoenthan and

Kadelburg's *Goldfische,* adapting it freely and totally Americanizing it. Although it was one of his biggest successes and was revived, its runs were inevitably curtailed by the producer's practice of prior schedulings. Curiously, despite praise from such respected British figures as Ellen Terry♦ and Charles Dickens, it failed in London when Daly produced it there.

Rain, a play in three acts by John Colton♦ and Clemence Randolph. Produced by Sam H. Harris♦ at Maxine Elliott's Theatre. November 7, 1922. 648 performances.

Trade Joe Horn (Rapley Holmes) is a former American who has left his homeland because of Prohibition and similar puritanical ways, and who has established a hotel in Pago Pago that caters to sailors, beachcombers, and others seeking a good time. Into this hedonist band come two disparate figures: the flamboyant Sadie Thompson (Jeanne Eagels♦), an American prostitute fleeing the law in Chicago, and the Reverend Alfred Davidson (Robert Kelly), who is determined to teach the depraved natives the meaning of sin and to save one and all from the devil. The pair soon lock horns, but it is not a fair fight since the missionary is brought to realize that his own motives are not entirely pure, at least where the voluptuous Sadie is concerned. In the end, Davidson commits suicide, and Sadie, preparing to leave for Australia, can only muse, "I guess I'm sorry for everybody in the world."

In his review for the *Times,* John Corbin♦ noted of this dramatization of a Somerset Maugham♦ short story known variously as "Rain" and "Sadie Thompson," " 'Rain' is not a 'pleasant' play . . . but it is strikingly original in theme, true in characterization, vigorous in drama and richly colored." For most playgoers, Miss Eagels's electrifying performance was the evening's high point. A musical version, *Sadie Thompson* (1944), originally conceived for Ethel Merman♦ but finally starring June Havoc, failed.

Rainmaker, The, a play in three acts by N. Richard Nash. Produced at the Cort Theatre. October 28, 1954. 124 performances.

The Currys have two problems: their farm is threatened by a severe, prolonged drought, and they have been unable to marry off plain, outspoken Lizzie Curry (Geraldine Page♦). Into their midst swaggers a handsome con man, Bill Starbuck (Darren McGavin), who promises to bring rain for a fee of $100 and who courts Lizzie. Nature finally brings the rain, but by the time Starbuck leaves he has given Lizzie sufficient confidence and poise for her to win a husband.

Although he felt it became too cluttered with symbolism near the end, Louis Kronenberger♦ praised the work as having "a bright, brisk air and an engagingly humorous smack." It was later made into the long-running musical *110 in the Shade* (1963). Nash did the book, Tom Jones and Harvey Schmidt the songs, while Inga Swenson assumed the leading role. The musical ran 331 performances.

Nash [né Nathaniel Richard Nusbaum] (b. 1913) was born in Philadelphia and educated at the University of Pennsylvania. He wrote a number of unsuccessful plays as well as the books for *Wildcat* (1960) and *The Happy Time*♦ (1968).

Raisin in the Sun, A, a play in three acts by Lorraine Hansberry. Produced at the Ethel Barrymore Theatre. March 11, 1959. 530 performances. NYDCCA.

Lena Younger (Claudia McNeil) hopes to use the $10,000 she will receive from her late husband's life insurance policy to move her family out of the black ghetto. But her son, Walter (Sidney Poitier), takes the money and invests it in a liquor store. Before long his partner absconds with the funds. The Youngers decide to move anyway.

The play was later made into the musical *Raisin* (1973). This was the only Broadway success of the Chicago-born Hansberry (1930–65). Her *The Sign in Sidney Brustein's Window* (1964) had a short run.

RAITT, John [Emmet] (b. 1917) A native of Santa Ana, Calif., the husky, virile singer was Curly in the Chicago company of *Oklahoma!,*♦ but is remembered primarily as leading man in *Carousel*♦ (1945), in which he introduced "If I Loved You," and *The Pajama Game*♦ (1954), in which he sang "Hey, There."

Rajah, The; or, Wyncot's Ward, a comedy in four acts by William Young.♦ Produced by Daniel Frohman♦ at the Madison Square Theatre.♦ June 5, 1883. 190 performances.

Harold Wyncot (George Clarke), an imperious but seemingly indolent and worthless young man, has served in India where his fellow officers contemptuously nicknamed him "The Rajah." On his uncle's death, Wyncott is made his heir as well as the guardian of his uncle's adopted daughter Gladys (Rillie Deaves). He takes over the estate and at first seems to alienate Gladys by his stern rules and pomposity. However, Gladys realizes she loves him after he puts some labor agitators—one of whom is

an escaped convict—in their places and mollifies the other workmen.

Originally meant as a light summer filler, the comedy suceeded beyond everyone's expectations, including those of most reviewers, the majority of whom had dismissed the play. Its popularity was increased by excellent publicity, especially the fame of its third act setting, which included a real waterfall. Frohman sent pictures of this set, taken by B. J. Falk,♦ to papers and magazines around the country.

RAMBEAU, Marjorie (1889–1970) The San Francisco-born actress spent many seasons with stock companies in her home town and in Los Angeles before braving New York. Her first success came in the title role of *Sadie Love* (1915), in which she portrayed a girl who marries a prince, only to learn he is already wed. She scored an even bigger hit as Nan Carey, a detective who poses as a crook, in *Cheating Cheaters*♦ (1916). Her most memorable role followed when she portrayed Gina Ashland, who is given a choice of futures, in *Eyes of Youth*♦ (1917). A major mistake was her rejection of the role of Sadie Thompson in *Rain*♦ (1922), and her career soon began to fade, although she enjoyed minor successes as Edith Fields, who leaves her irresponsible husband, in *Daddy's Gone A-Hunting* (1921), and Jenney, the ambitious divorcée, in *The Goldfish* (1922). George Middleton,♦ who had a bitter experience with her in one of his plays, *The Road Together* (1924), wrote, "Though she lacked soul, she could assume its trappings. Beautiful, too, and eye-arresting, she impressed by the commanding way she moved about. Mistress of stage strategy, gained from hard years in stock, she could handle resourcefully almost any demand of emotion or comedy. With vitality and a perfectly controlled voice she had become so popular that her presence in a play guaranteed it a public." In later years she was well known as a character actress in films.

RAND, Ayn, see *Night of January 16*

RAND, Sally [née Hazel Beck] (1904–79) Born in Missouri, she was a minor figure in films and vaudeville until she created a sensation by dancing nude, with only two ostrich fans to cover her, at a Chicago night club in 1932. From then until her retirement shortly before her death she was a headliner in burlesque with her fan dance. She also appeared in night clubs, including Billy Rose's♦ revue, *Let's Play Fair,* at his Casa Mañana, and she replaced Ann Corio♦ briefly on Broadway in 1965 in *This Was Burlesque*.

RANKIN, [Arthur] McKee (1841–1914) The slim, handsome actor, who grew somewhat portly with time, was born in Sandwich, Canada, and began his acting career in 1861 in Rochester, N.Y., using the name of George Henley. After spending several seasons in London he returned to make his New York debut in 1866 as Hugh de Brass in *A Regular Fix*. In 1872 he became a leading man at the Union Square Theatre,♦ where his roles included Phyllon in W. S. Gilbert's♦ *The Wicked World* (1873); George de Lesparre in *Led Astray*♦ (1873); Armand in *Camille*♦ (1874); and Jacques Frochard in *The Two Orphans*♦ (1874). His greatest success came when he produced and starred as Alexander McGee, who defeats the Mormons and wins the heroine, in *The Danites*♦ (1877). He returned to the play frequently for the next dozen years. Later he appeared in a variety of plays from popular contemporary melodrama to classic comedy. He also was active as a producer and theatre manager. In his last years he toured with his protégé Nance O'Neill. ♦

RAPHAELSON, Samson (1896–1983) Born in New York and educated at the University of Illinois, he was a journalist and short-story writer before turning to the theatre. His first play, *The Jazz Singer*♦ (1925), told of a young man caught between his religious upbringing and his wish to be an entertainer. *Young Love* (1928) centered on a bored couple who attempt mate-switching. It failed, as did *The Wooden Slipper* (1934), in which a would-be actress must choose between marriage and a career. His popular comedy, *Accent on Youth*♦ (1934), revolved around an egotistical playwright who wins his young secretary away from a youthful competitor. He had no success with *White Man* (1936), in which a black man attempts to hide his color, but found favor with *Skylark* (1939), a story of a neglected wife's attempt at a fling. *Jason* (1942) depicted the predicament of a critic who must review a play by a man who tried to seduce his wife. *The Perfect Marriage* (1944) focused on a marriage that was anything but perfect. *Hilda Crane* (1950) was a story of a woman whose unhappiness leads to her suicide. In 1954 Margo Jones♦ produced his *The Heel,* a play about an unscrupulous actor, at her Texas theatre, but it never reached New York. He was also a successful film writer, working closely with Ernst Lubitsch.

RASCH, Albertina (1896–1967) Born and trained in Vienna, she came to this country to dance in the Hippodrome♦ spectacles in 1911. After appearing in a few productions she worked with several opera companies and toured in vaudeville. She staged numbers for *George White's Scandals of 1925,* ♦ but first attracted major attention with her ballets in *Rio Rita*♦ (1927). Her work, largely balletic, was seen in over two dozen subsequent offerings, including *The Three Musketeers*♦ (1928), *Three's a Crowd* (1930), *The Band Wagon*♦ (1931), *The Cat and the Fiddle*♦ (1931), *The Great Waltz* (1934), *Jubilee*♦ (1935), and *Lady in the Dark*♦ (1941).

RATHBONE, Basil (1892–1967) The slim, suave, somewhat hawk-faced actor was born in Johannesburg, and spent over a decade on English stages before making his debut as Count Alexei Czerny opposite Doris Keane♦ in *The Czarina* (1922). Among his subsequent roles were Dr. Agi opposite Eva Le Gallienne♦ in *The Swan* (1923), and Jacques Virieu, who pretends to be a lesbian's fiancé, in the controversial *The Captive* (1926). In later years his best remembered roles were Romeo to Katharine Cornell's♦ Juliet in 1934, and Dr. Sloper, the tyrannical father, in *The Heiress*♦ (1947). Although he is largely recalled as the Sherlock Holmes of many films, his attempt to portray Holmes on stage in 1953 was unsuccessful.

Autobiography: *In and Out of Character,* Garden City, 1962.

RATTIGAN, Terence (1911–82) The English playwright, whose best works were literate and dramatically effective, albeit sometimes superficial, scored his first American success in 1937 with *French Without Tears*. Numbered among his later American successes were *O Mistress Mine* (1946), which starred the Lunts♦; *The Winslow Boy* (1947); *The Browning Version* (1948), with Maurice Evans♦ in the lead; *The Deep Blue Sea* (1952), in which Margaret Sullavan♦ starred; *The Sleeping Prince* (1953); *Separate Tables* (1956); *Ross* (1961); and *In Praise of Love* (1974), with Rex Harrison♦ and Julie Harris♦ heading the cast.

Ravel Family A family of French rope dancers, acrobats, and pantomimists, they first appeared at the Park Theatre♦ in 1832. The leading figure of the group was one son, Gabriel, who was said to be about twenty-two at the time of his American debut. Together or individually they continued to perform, with occasional returns to Europe, until the mid-1860s.

RAYMOND, JOHN T. [né O'BRIEN] (1836–87) Born in Buffalo, N. Y., he ran away from home and made his debut in Rochester in 1853. Afterwards he played in Philadelphia and Baltimore, then toured the South before joining Laura Keene's♦ ensemble in 1861. There he called attention to himself when he replaced Joseph Jefferson♦ as Asa Trenchard in *Our American Cousin.*♦ He gained stardom in 1874 as the daydreaming Colonel Sellers in *The Gilded Age,* so stealing the play that it was rewritten and retitled *Colonel Sellers.*♦ He continued to return to the role regularly until his death. Among his other noteworthy portrayals were Ichabod Crane in *Wolfert's Roost* (1879); Ferdinand Fresh, who steals an odalisque from a harem, in *Fresh, the American*♦ (1881); and General Limber, the wheeling-dealing politician, in *For Congress* (1884). He was a slim, long-faced actor, of whom William Winter♦ wrote, "His humor was rich and jocund. He had an exceptional command over composure of countenance. He could deceive an observer by the sapient gravity of his visage, and he exerted that facial faculty with extraordinary comic effect."

Rebecca of Sunnybrook Farm, a play in four acts by Kate Douglas Wiggin and Charlotte Thompson. Produced by Klaw♦ and Erlanger♦ at the Republic Theatre. October 3, 1910. 216 performances.

Prospects look bleak when ten-year-old Rebecca Rowena Randall (Edith Taliaferro♦) is sent to live with her seemingly crotchety Aunt Miranda (Marie L. Day), but everything turns out joyously.

Adapted from Miss Wiggin's 1903 best-seller, the play was especially popular with children.

Red Mill, The, a musical comedy in two acts. Book and lyrics by Henry Blossom.♦ Music by Victor Herbert.♦ Produced by Charles Dillingham♦ at the Knickerbocker Theatre. September 24, 1906. 274 performances.

Kid Conner (David Montgomery♦) and Con Kidder (Fred Stone♦) are two Americans who find themselves without cash in a small Dutch village. The town's strict burgomaster wants his daughter Gretchen (Augusta Greenleaf) to marry the Governor of Zeeland (Neal McCay), so he locks her in a mill to prevent her eloping with a sea captain, Doris Van Damm (Joseph M. Ratliff). The Americans climb into the mill and help Gretchen escape on the mill's sail. The Governor decides to marry Gretchen's aunt, Bertha (Allene Crater). With the small change they have garnered, Kid and Con head for a boat to take them home.

Principal songs: Because You're You · Every Day Is Ladies' Day with Me · The Isle of Our Dreams · Moonbeams · The Streets of New York

The basic plot—Americans plunked down in an exotic land—was the favorite musical comedy device of its era, but Blossom's fine book and lyrics and Herbert's melodic score made it the best and most beloved of its ilk. It was successfully revived in 1945 with Michael O'Shea, Eddie Foy, Jr.,♦ and Dorothy Stone heading the cast. The revival outran the original, compiling 531 performances.

REED, FLORENCE (1883–1967) The small, dark actress was the daughter of a minor actor-manager, Roland [Lewis] Reed (1852–1901). Born in Philadelphia, she began a long apprenticeship with New York's Fifth Avenue Theatre♦ stock company in 1901, then toured as E. H. Sothern's♦ leading lady, playing Katherine de Vaucelles in *If I Were King*♦ and Ophelia. She later appeared in such successes as *Seven Days*♦ (1909), *The Typhoon* (1912), and *The Master of the House* (1912), before scoring a major success as Marya Varenka, the Russian prostitute pursued by a lustful nobleman, in *The Yellow Ticket* (1914). After turning to musicals with *Chu Chin Chow* (1917), she enjoyed a run as Mrs. Moreland, a small-town girl who has married for money, in *The Mirage* (1920). Her greatest success came as Mother Goddam, the whorehouse proprietor determined to destroy the man who wronged her, in *The Shanghai Gesture*♦ (1926). Looking back, Ward Morehouse♦ recalled, "Miss Reed's recitation of the 'I survived' speech, in which she told of pebbles being sewn into the soles of her feet and of the other tortures she received at the hands of the junkmen, remains one of the most vivid tirades ever to be delivered in the history of melodrama." She never again created so noteworthy a role, although she headed touring companies of *Mourning Becomes Electra*♦ and *Elizabeth the Queen.*♦ In 1942 she was the Fortune Teller in the original production of *The Skin of Our Teeth.*♦ She continued to act until shortly before her death. Her grandfather, John "Pop" Reed, was for many decades the gas man at Philadelphia's Walnut Street Theatre♦ and gained a small foothold in American theatrical legend by bequeathing the theatre his skull to be used in performances of *Hamlet.*

REED, MARK, see *Yes, My Darling Daughter*

REEVES-SMITH, H[ARRY] (1862–1938) The English actor first came to America in 1887 to tour with John Sleeper Clarke♦ and in later years served on tours as leading man to Henrietta Crosman♦ and

Grace George. ◆ His memorable roles on Broadway included the title part of *Captain Jinks of the Horse Marines* ◆ (1901); Peter Mottram, who attempts with disastrous results to reunite a feuding couple, in *Mid-Channel* (1910); Jerry, the heroine's only real friend, in *Peg o' My Heart* ◆ (1912); Hubert Knolys, who is saddled with a selfish wife, in *The Unchastened Woman* ◆ (1915); and the knowing Prentice Van Zile in *Polly with a Past* ◆ (1917). His last major appearance was as the elder Johann Strauss in *The Great Waltz* (1934).

REGAN, SYLVIA , see *Fifth Season, The*

Regina, see *Little Foxes, The*

REHAN, ADA [née ADA CREHAN] (1860–1916) A regal beauty and one of America's greatest actresses, she was born in Limerick, Ireland, but brought to America at the age of five. Her family settled in Brooklyn, where she watched her older sisters adopt stage careers. It was her brother-in-law, Oliver Doud Byron, ◆ who helped her make her debut in 1873 as Clara in his once-famous vehicle, *Across the Continent.* ◆ She then joined Mrs. Drew's ◆ celebrated ensemble at Philadelphia's Arch Street Theatre. ◆ A typographical error in an early program there dropped the first letter of her surname, giving her the stage name she afterwards employed. She left Mrs. Drew to spend seasons with companies in Louisville and Albany. In 1879 she played Mary Standish in a revival of Augustin Daly's ◆ *Pique* ◆ and then played in his *L'Assommoir*. Her performances so impressed Daly that he invited her to join his great company. She made her first appearance with it that September as Nelly Beers in *Love's Young Dream*. Under his guidance she quickly became the finest and probably the most beloved of all younger comediennes. She excelled at classic comedy including such Shakespearean roles as Mrs. Ford, Katherine, Helena, Rosalind, Viola, and Beatrice, as well as Sheridan's Lady Teazle. But she was also at home in the newer comedies Daly presented, among them the American premieres of Pinero's ◆ *The Magistrate* (1885) and *Dandy Dick* (1887), in which she played Mrs. Posket and Georgiana Tidman respectively. Along with Mrs. Gilbert, ◆ John Drew, ◆ and James Lewis, ◆ she was a mainstay of Daly's ensemble. William Winter ◆ wrote, "Her physical beauty was of the kind that appears in portraits of women by Romney and Gainsborough—ample, opulent, and bewitching— and it was enriched by the enchantment of superb animal spirits. She had gray-blue eyes and brown hair." He added, "Her acting, if closely scrutinized, was seen to have been studied; yet it always seemed spontaneous; her handsome, ingenuous, winning countenance informed it with sympathy, while her voice—copious, tender, and wonderfully musical— filled it with emotion, speaking always from the heart." After Daly's death she continued to appear largely in the roles in which he had cast her, but despite her skill and popularity, success eluded her. She retired in 1905.

Biography: *Ada Rehan: A Study,* William Winter, New York, 1891.

Rehearsal Club A residence club founded in New York in 1913 to provide inexpensive, home-style food and lodgings for young actresses. Losses were underwritten by a philanthropic board of directors. The club was bruited to have inspired the background for several plays, most notably *Stage Door* ◆ (1936). The inflation of the 1970s, combined with a changing canon of conduct, prompted its closing in 1980.

REID, [JAMES] HAL[LECK] (1873?–1920) Apparently born in Minneapolis, he started his career as an actor. In short order he turned to playwriting, though he remained an actor virtually until his death. He soon became one of the most prolific authors of such cheap-priced touring melodramas as *Alone in the World, In Convict Stripes, A Midnight Marriage, A Millionaire's Revenge,* and *A Wife's Secret*. He remained active in the field until films destroyed the market, after which he himself became a screenplay writer and a player in silent movies. His son, Wallace Reid, briefly was a Hollywood star. One notice of the elder Reid claimed his real name was actually Harry Preston and that under that name he had served a prison term for an unspecified offense.

Reilly and the Four Hundred, a play with music in three acts by Edward Harrigan. ◆ Lyrics by Harrigan. Music by David Braham. ◆ Produced by Harrigan at Harrigan's Theatre. December 29, 1890. 202 performances.

Wiley Reilly (Harrigan), an immigrant pawnbroker, has watched his lawyer son Ned (Harry Davenport) rise in society and successfully court a socially acceptable lady. But all his plans and dreams could be shattered by Herman Smeltz (Harry Fisher), a sausage tycoon who has somehow wheedled his way into the "400." Wiley knows a dark, long-kept secret about Smeltz and uses it to see that everything ends happily.

Principal song: Maggie Murphy's Home

The first show to play Harrigan's own new theatre, it enjoyed the longest run of any of his plays, but was virtually his last success. The play propelled Ada Lewis,◆ who portrayed a roughneck girl, to fame.

REINAGLE, ALEXANDER (1756–1809) The son of an Austrian musician, he was born and raised in Portsmouth, England. At eighteen he moved to Edinburgh where he studied with Raynor Taylor.◆ He came to America in 1786 and settled in Philadelphia. By 1791 he was a respected composer and teacher with strong ties to local theatre and so found substantial support among Philadelphians when he joined with the actor Thomas Wignell◆ to build what became the Chestnut Street Theatre.◆ The house was opened in 1794 and for the remainder of his career he was active in its management. He also adopted many English ballad operas for local audiences, composed incidental music for other plays, and wrote the score for several light operas, notably *The Sicilian Romance* (1795). The theatre's company regularly visited Baltimore, where Reinagle spent much time in his last years. In a 1983 study, Victor Fell Yellin offers interesting evidence, including a death notice in the *United States Gazette,* suggesting that the accepted date of Reinagle's birth may be wrong and that he may actually have been born as early as 1747.

REINHARDT, MAX [né GOLDMANN] (1873–1943) The famed Austro-German producer first came to the attention of most American playgoers in 1912 when Winthop Ames◆ imported his mounting of the Oriental pantomime *Sumurun.* In 1924 Reinhardt visited New York to re-create his production of *The Miracle,* and then in 1927 brought over his German company for a season of repertory. Following the rise of the Nazis he moved permanently to America, where he staged his version of *A Midsummer Night's Dream*◆ in Hollywood in 1934 and *The Eternal Road* in New York in 1937. Other Broadway directorial credits included Thornton Wilder's◆ *The Merchant of Yonkers* (1938) and Irwin Shaw's◆ *Sons and Soldiers* (1943). His version of *Die Fledermaus* was offered to Broadway as *Rosalinda* (1942) by his son Gottfried shortly before the elder Reinhardt's death.

RÉJANE, GABRIELLE [CHARLOTTE] [née RÉJU] (1857–1920) The fine French comedienne, who was also competent in more serious roles, made two extended American tours, the first in 1895 and the second in 1904. She scored a huge success in her first appearance, as Catherine Hübscher, the outspoken laundress who is not afraid to remind Napoleon that his laundry bill is long overdue, in *Mme. Sans-Gêne.* The Times reported she was "a woman of medium height, lithe and graceful, certainly not young or handsome. Her small nose, round eyes, high brows, and large mouth impress spectators grotesquely . . . Her facial play is inimitable and unique. Her motions are so swift that one can scarcely follow her." Her repertory also included such once popular French works as *Zaza, Divorçons,* ◆ and *Sapho,* as well as a French version of *A Doll's House.* While by no means the failure of her compatriot, Mounet-Sully,◆ she was never the raging success that Bernhardt◆ and Coquelin◆ were.

Religious Drama in America Perhaps because significant religious bodies had early on succeeded in preventing the opening of theatres in colonial America and later, after playhouses had begun to appear, remained a potent source of possible repression, the separation of church and theatre was long a part of the American scene much as the separation of church and state. Very little of what might be termed religious drama was offered to playgoers until late in the 19th century. Dramatizations of Biblical stories were virtually unheard of in the professional theatre and even the portrayal of figures such as ministers was generally restrained and infrequent. Non-Protestant clerics were sometimes characters in tales of Renaissance Italy, but these figures often seemed to derive more from Elizabethan and Jacobean traditions than from genuine observation. (For further material on religious groups see *Jews in American Theatre and Drama* and *Mormons in American Theatre and Drama.*) It may be telling that the first 19th-century success centering on a major religious figure was Bulwer-Lytton's◆ English drama *Richelieu*◆ (1839), which dealt not directly with religious matters but rather with the Cardinal's attempts to influence affairs of state and of the heart. Depicting such meddlesomeness may have appealed to the strong anti-Catholic sentiments of many playgoers, although the real reason for the play's long popularity was undoubtedly the performances of Forrest,◆ Macready,◆ and Booth◆ in the title role. Quite possibly the play's English stamp of approval was also a factor in its success, since so many late 19th- and early 20th-century London hits helped open the American theatre to religious themes.

One of the first important American religious plays of national interest was a version of the classic passion play, known either as *The Passion Play*◆ (1879) or as *The Passion*. However, this dramatization of the New Testament story by a Jewish playwright offended many Christian clergy, who lobbied for its suppression.

The later arrival of such English plays as Henry Arthur Jones's◆ *Saints and Sinners* (1895) and Jerome K. Jerome's *The Passing of the Third Floor Back* (1909) further increased acceptance of religiously oriented works. At the same time native drama began to employ religious and Biblical figures and themes with increasing success. The most notable from a commercial standpoint were the dramatizations of Lew Wallace's famous novel, *Ben-Hur*◆ (1899), which attracted huge audiences as much by their spectacle, including a celebrated chariot race, as by their religious message. Charles Rann Kennedy's simple and more thoughtful *The Servant in the House*◆ (1908), in which Christ returns in the guise of a servant to bring order and love back into a vicar's home, met with great critical acclaim but found only small audiences. The disillusionment and cynicism which followed World War I led to few religious works being attemped during the 1920s. The best known was Channing Pollock's◆ *The Fool*◆ (1922), the theme of which was not unlike that of Kennedy's play, although in this instance a minister destroys himself by attempting to abide by Christ's precepts. Given the tenor of the age, it may be significant that Eugene O'Neill's◆ Dionysian study of a Biblical story in *Lazarus Laughed* (1927) was the playwright's only major effort not to be given a Broadway hearing. Another major success of the period was the 1924 presentation of Max Reinhardt's◆ decade-old pageant *The Miracle*. Of tangential religious interest were such works as Shaw's◆ *St. Joan*◆ (1923), which depicted religious fervor employed for political ends, and *The Ladder*◆ (1926), the curious play by J. Frank Davis which attempted to promote the Eastern idea of reincarnation.

If the hedonism and cynicism of the 1920s offered relatively infertile fields for the growth of commercial religious drama, the political and economic preoccupations of the 1930s proved equally discouraging, especially since the theatre and other arts were dominated by the often irreligious left. Such major playwrights as O'Neill and Philip Barry◆ were given short shrift when they presented their religious questions in theatrical terms—O'Neill in *Days Without End*◆ (1934) and Barry in *Bright Star* (1935) and *Here Come the Clowns* (1938). Yet the most successful and memorable of all American Biblical plays was a product of this era, the Pulitzer

Prize◆ winning *The Green Pastures*◆ (1930), which recounted the Old Testament stories as seen through the eyes of poor, unlettered blacks. It was in this period that T. S. Eliot◆ wrote the first of his religious dramas, *Murder in the Cathedral*◆ (1936). His later works with religious themes included *A Family Reunion* (1947) and *The Cocktail Party*◆ (1950).

By contrast with the bitter, disbelieving response to the failure of "the war to end all wars" to achieve its aim, the prosperous decades which followed World War II and which encompassed the Cold War, the McCarthy era, and several dismaying, brutal hot wars, saw a variety of responses, including a reexamination of religious values and the importance of religion in private lives, and an ill-defined, sometimes wavering fascination with mysticism. The shock of the Nazi extermination of European Jewry brought forth a number of intriguing works dealing with the subject. *The Diary of Anne Frank*◆ (1955), the importation *The Deputy* (1964), and Arthur Miller's◆ *Incident at Vichy* (1964) were among the more interesting of such plays. Plays treating Biblical subjects directly included Robinson Jeffers's◆ curious, failed *Dear Judas* (1947), which attempted to argue that Judas betrayed Jesus in order to ensure Jesus immortality; Archibald MacLeish's◆ *J.B.*◆ (1958), which recounted the Job legend in modern terms; and Clifford Odets's◆ slightly earlier *The Flowering Peach* (1954) and Paddy Chayefsky's◆ *Gideon*◆ (1961), which used the stories of Noah and Gideon respectively to argue for compliance with God's commands. The Odets play was later made into the long-running musical, *Two by Two* (1970). Chayefsky's was the more philosophical and mystical of the pair, although his movement toward religious mysticism was displayed to better advantage in his earlier *The Tenth Man*◆ (1959), a look at Jewish exorcism. Besides *Two by Two,* the musical stage turned to religious themes of one sort or another with great success in this era, offering even longer running works such as *Fiddler on the Roof*◆ (1964), which recounted the oppression of Russian Jews, and two works retelling the New Testament story: *Godspell*◆ (1971) and the English *Jesus Christ Superstar* (1971). English dramas of the era included *Becket* (1960), *A Man for All Seasons* (1961), and *Luther* (1963).

In the late 1970s and early 1980s a number of Catholic playwrights evinced a resurgent interest in their religion. However, such plays as *The Runner Stumbles* (1976), *Do Black Patent Leather Shoes Reflect Up?* (1981), *Sister Mary Ignatius Explains It All for You* (1981), *Mass Appeal* (1981), *Agnes of*

God (1982), and *Nunsense*♦ (1985), while sometimes set in religious institutions and featuring religious figures, more often dealt with the interaction of society and religion than with religion itself or wholly religious problems. One of the most successful of all contemporary plays, *Amadeus*♦ (1980), had the pious Salieri demanding to know why God gave the impious Mozart such genius.

Repertory Theatre of Lincoln Center, THE Founded in 1960 under the auspices of the Lincoln Center for the Performing Arts, it was planned as a non-profit theatre designed to offer a permanent company in seasons of classic and new plays. Robert Whitehead♦ and Elia Kazan♦ were appointed its codirectors. The group's regular homes were to be at what came to be called the Vivian Beaumont Theatre and at the smaller Forum (later called the Mitzi Newhouse) in the Center, but while the houses were still in the final planning stages and under construction, a training program for a core of performers was initiated in 1962. In 1964 the company offered its first production, Arthur Miller's♦ *After the Fall,*♦ at a temporary playhouse, the ANTA–Washington Square Theatre. The first two regular seasons offered a balance between new American plays and European and American classics, but the critical response was cool so by the end of 1964 both Kazan and Whitehead had resigned and were replaced by Herbert Blau and Jules Irving from the Actor's Workshop♦ of San Francisco. A continued lack of striking success prompted Blau's resignation in 1967 and Irving's in 1972. For a time Joseph Papp♦ and his New York Shakespeare Festival♦ attempted to run the theatres. When he and his company threw in the towel, Richmond Crinkley briefly took over management. After several dark seasons, the two playhouses were relit in 1986, but the idea of a repertory ensemble has been abandoned by the new director, Gregory Mosher.

Return of Peter Grimm, The, a play in three acts by David Belasco.♦ Produced by Belasco at the Belasco Theatre. October 17, 1911. 231 performances.

Peter Grimm (David Warfield♦) is a kindly old man who persuades his orphan ward Katrien (Janet Dunbar) to marry his nephew Frederick (John Sainpolis) so that the Grimm line may continue. Katrien agrees out of fondness for Peter, although she loves another man and does not care for Frederick. Peter and his friend Dr. MacPherson (Joseph Brennan) have made a compact—that whoever dies first will attempt to come back to earth with a message from the dead. Peter dies and keeps his promise. In death he has realized that he made a great mistake in pressing Katrien to marry Frederick, but on his return he is unable to "get across" to the living. Only Wilhelm (Percy Helton), the ailing little son of his former housekeeper, is able to see and hear him. The others are skeptical of Wilhelm's visions, so Peter has Wilhelm reveal the ugly truth learned in death—that Wilhelm's father is Frederick. The news frees Katrien to marry the man of her choice. Little Wilhelm dies, and Peter takes him on his shoulder and carries him to the realm of the dead, to the accompaniment of the circus music the boy so loved.

Although Walter Prichard Eaton♦ insisted the "play degenerates into mawkishness and loses its potential poetry," most critics and playgoers agreed with Adoph Klauber♦ of the *Times,* who called the work "a big play, and one which, more than anything its author has done, proclaims him an astonishing genius of the theatre." Warfield toured with the play for two years and revived it successfully in 1921.

Reunion in Vienna, a comedy in three acts by Robert Sherwood.♦ Produced by the Theatre Guild♦ at the Martin Beck Theatre. November 16, 1931. 264 performances.

Ever since her marriage, Elena Krug (Lynn Fontanne♦) has been measuring her psychoanalyst husband Anton (Minor Watson) in terms of her first love—the one that got away, Rudolf Maximilian Von Hapsburg (Alfred Lunt♦). Prince Rudolf had been forced into exile and into driving a cab in Nice after the downfall of the Austro-Hungarian Empire. When Anton learns that Rudolf has returned secretly to Vienna for a reunion of old aristocrats at the Hotel Lucher [read Sacher], he encourages Elena to visit Rudolf in hopes that a fresh perspective will break the spell. The former lovers meet and take up their romance where they left off, but only for a while. The romance is so heavy that Rudolf consults Anton. Finally Rudolf and Elena accept reality. Rudolf returns to France and Elena to Anton.

Although many critics complained that the play did not come alive until Rudolf first appears and the lovers meet in the second act, the scintillating dialogue and the brilliant acting of the Lunts was ample compensation.

Reverend Griffith Davenport, The, a play in five acts by James A. Herne.♦ Produced at the Herald Square Theatre. January 31, 1899. 20 performances.

Although the Reverend Griffith Davenport (Herne) belongs to an old, prestigious Virginia family, he opposes its practice of slave-holding on moral and religious grounds. His wife (Mrs. Herne) and his son Beverly (Sidney Booth) disagree, so only his son Roy rejoices when Davenport frees his own slaves. The war breaks out. Beverly joins the Confederate forces, Roy the Union army. Needing someone to guide troops through Confederate lines in Virginia, Lincoln sends an emissary to ask Davenport's help, and the minister agrees. He is captured by his son, who allows him a brief reunion with his wife before sending him to prison.

The play was based on Helen H. Gardener's novel, *An Unofficial Patriot.* William Dean Howells♦ called the play "the only new thing of importance," ranking it above the then new *Cyrano de Bergerac*♦ and *Trelawny of the Wells.* Most critics and playgoers disagreed, prompting Quinn♦ to suggest, "Perhaps the failure of that play to win popular success may have been due to a subconscious feeling that a man should remain true to his own people, as the universal hero worship of Robert E. Lee has indicated."

Revolutionary War, see *Wars in American Drama*

Revue in America Precursors of the modern revue, while not unknown, were few and far between. Some 18th- and early 19th-century patriotic spectacles may be seen to foreshadow the opulence of later revue tableaux, while the skits and songs of minstrelsy and the mixed vaudeville bills of the later 19th century, as well as such one-man shows of skits as those produced by Charles Mathews, ♦ all pointed unwittingly toward the future genre. Perhaps the most interesting precursor was John Brougham's♦ *Dramatic Review for 1868,*♦ a loosely tied together assemblage of songs and sketches. Like the earliest "reviews" a quarter of a century later, it used an English spelling for the term, the French spelling not coming into vogue until the second decade of the 20th century. Indeed, although revues were an important feature of Parisian theatre for much of the late 19th century, French influence seems to have been small.

The show that unquestionably began the American fashion for revues was *The Passing Show,*♦ which opened at the Casino Theatre♦ on May 12, 1894. It was produced by George Lederer, ♦ had a book and lyrics by Sydney Rosenfeld, ♦ and music by Ludwig Englander, ♦ and a cast that included Jefferson De Angelis, ♦ John Henshaw, Madge Lessing, and Adele Ritchie. ♦ That Rosenfeld was

credited with a "book" instead of with sketches is significant, since virtually all early revues sewed together their songs and skits by means of some elementary plot. The sketches satirized mostly plays of the day, famous figures, and celebrated local incidents. Songs also tended to be largely topical, with love songs added only gradually. Not until shortly before World War I did revues abandon the idea of employing a story line. For several seasons the Casino produced a revue each summer, and for many seasons revues were considered primarily summer fill-ins. Other theatres also housed occasional revues.

The vogue for revues began to grow in earnest with the production by Florenz Ziegfeld♦ of his *Follies of 1907*♦ (he did not add his own name to the series until the 1911 edition). His revues soon came to feature not only better, more important stars than had heretofore been seen in these shows, but offered better, more enduring music, a new standard of extravagant yet tasteful opulence, and a line of chorus beauties that became requisite. Within a few seasons his own editions had to compete with such other annuals as the Shubert♦ *Passing Shows*♦ (which had no connection with the 1894 revue), *George White's Scandals,* ♦ the *Music Box Revues,* ♦ the *Earl Carroll Vanities,* ♦ and others. George M. Cohan♦ was among the important figures who produced occasional revues, and he is often credited with dropping plots from these shows. The heyday of the extravagant revue lasted from just before World War I until shortly after the war. By the mid-1920s these lavish shows began to be considered too heavy and dated. A vogue for lighter, more literate revues took their place. Although American offerings such as *The 49ers* (1922) helped kindle the new fashion, many students see the arrival of *Charlot's Revue*♦ (1924) as signaling the crucial turning point.

American revues of the very late 1920s and the 1930s in this newer style included *The Little Shows,* ♦ *Three's a Crowd* (1930), *The Band Wagon*♦ (1931), *As Thousands Cheer*♦ (1933), *Life Begins at 8:40* (1934), and *At Home Abroad* (1935). Other notable revues of the 1930s included the union-mounted *Pins and Needles*♦ (1937) and the first and most successful of Olsen♦ and Johnson's♦ zany fracases, *Hellzapoppin*♦ (1938). In the 1940s the revue began to fade away, although the decade produced such memorable examples as Irving Berlin's♦ *This Is the Army*♦ (1942); a revue featuring a cast primarily of war veterans, *Call Me Mister* (1946); and the last great revue, the uproariously funny if unmelodic *Lend an Ear* (1948). Thereafter some possible internal exhaustion, coupled with the rise of television and the popularity of the supposedly more purposeful, integrated musical play, swept revues from American stages. In very recent years a peculiar form of revue flourished briefly. These shows had no skits, but instead made an entire evening out of the music of an old or dead composer. Ironically, none of these shows used the music of the giants of the revue field or even of the American musical theatre. Rather they relied on important composers whose connections with Broadway had generally been brief and unsuccessful. The major successes of this form of revue have been *Ain't Misbehavin'* ♦ (1978), *Eubie* (1978), and *Sophisticated Ladies* (1981) which featured the music of Fats Waller, Eubie Blake, ♦ and Duke Ellington respectively, and *Black and Blue* (1989), a potpourri of jazz age material.

At its height the revue gave important starts to many composers and songwriters, such as George Gershwin ♦; De Sylva, Brown, and Henderson ♦; and Harold Rome. ♦ Virtually all of Arthur Schwartz's ♦ great songs have come from revues, while for many years Irving Berlin wrote for little else on Broadway. The form allowed many performers not adept at handling the dialogue or characterization required by book shows to shine. Perhaps the most noteworthy example was Ed Wynn, ♦ whose revues were among the most popular of the 1920s, but who generally failed when caught in book musicals. Many historians look on Al Jolson's ♦ so-called book shows as glorified revues and insist that he, too, shone best as a solo performer. Fanny Brice ♦ gave her best performances in revues. Other notable stars who moved with more ease from one form to the other included Bert Williams, ♦ Eddie Cantor, ♦ Beatrice Lillie, ♦ and Bert Lahr. ♦

REYNOLDS, JAMES (1892–1957) Born in Warrenton, Va., the set and costume designer was given his first opportunities on Broadway by John Murray Anderson, ♦ for whom he created many of the stage pictures for *What's in a Name?* (1920) and the 1920, 1921, 1922, and 1923 editions of the *Greenwich Village Follies.* ♦ Concurrently he helped design the 1921, 1922, and 1923 editions of the *Ziegfeld Follies.* ♦ He also worked on the 1924 edition of the *Music Box Revue.* ♦ In the mid-1920s he was Dillingham's ♦ chief designer, providing sets and costumes for, among others, *Sunny* ♦ (1925), *Criss-Cross* (1926), and *Oh, Please!* (1926). In 1925 he created designs for *The Vagabond King.* ♦ His later work was seen in *The Royal Family* ♦ (1927), *Fifty Million Frenchmen* ♦ (1929), *Life Begins at 8:40* (1934), and *Jumbo* ♦ (1935). His work was admired

for its sumptuous beauty and skillful color coordination. He retired in the mid-1930s to devote himself to writing, painting, and lecturing.

Rialto, THE The name, taken from a famous district in Venice, seems to have caught hold as an expression denoting New York's theatre district in the 1870s when the principal theatres were located between Union Square and Madison Square. It remained a common term well into the 20th century. One newspaper had a regular Sunday section called "News and Gossip of the Rialto." The expression is rarely applied today, however.

RICE, DAN (1823–1900) America's first great circus clown, he was born in New York but grew up largely in frontier towns. By the age of ten he was a jockey, but when increasing weight forced him to abandon riding he joined a circus in Pittsburgh. His brand of low, homespun clowning contrasted markedly with the polished wit of the then reigning favorite, William Wallett. The two men merged forces in 1848, by which time Rice was traveling with his own circus. Wallett would recite a Shakespearean speech in the emotive style of Edwin Forrest, ♦ then Rice would offer a parody such as, "Is this a beefsteak I see before me/With the burnt side toward my hand?" As a rule Rice performed in regular street clothes or in an Uncle Sam costume, generally sporting a conspicuous dark Uncle Sam beard. In after years his drinking caused problems, but as late as the early 1890s he was offering his "One-Ring Circus" in vaudeville and elsewhere.

Biography: *The Life of Dan Rice,* Maria Ward Brown, Long Branch, N.J., 1901.

RICE, E[DWARD] E[VERETT] (1848–1924) Born into a poor family in Brighton, Mass., he left home while still in his teens to become an itinerant actor. He abandoned the theatre to work as a printer and copywriter in Boston, where he married the daughter of an important theatrical manager. Soon afterward he joined forces with J. Cheever Goodwin ♦ to write *Evangeline* ♦ (1874). Following its success he plunged actively into producing, and on rare occasions writing, for the musical theatre of his day. He quickly became one of our musical theatre's most important pioneers. His Rice's Surprise Party was probably the most popular band performing those prototypical musical comedies called farce-comedies. ♦ In 1884 he produced *Adonis,* ♦ the first musical to run over 500 performances in New York. With the coming of English musical comedy he established himself as one of its principal American importers, but he also continued to explore new possibilities with native talents. His 1898 mounting of *The Origin of the Cake Walk; or, Clorindy*♦ on the roof garden of the Casino Theatre♦ was the first time a musical written by blacks and featuring a cast of black actors had been offered to white audiences. Among the major figures he either discovered or gave important boosts to were Henry E. Dixey,♦ Lillian Russell,♦ Fay Templeton,♦ Julian Eltinge,♦ and Jerome Kern.♦

RICE, ELMER [LEOPOLD] [né REIZENSTEIN] (1892–1967) The New York-born playwright studied law and began to practice before switching to the theatre. In a career that lasted over forty years he had no fewer than 24 plays produced on Broadway, ranging from starkly realistic drama to comic fantasy. His earliest work leaned heavily on his experience as a lawyer, and his first drama, *On Trial*♦ (1914), which employed flashbacks to elaborate on courtroom testimony, provided one of the most sensational first nights in theatre history. *For the Defense* (1919) and *It Is the Law* (1922) followed, as did a vehicle for Mrs. Fiske♦ written with Hatcher Hughes,♦ *Wake Up, Jonathan!* (1921). *The Adding Machine*♦ (1923) was an expressionistic fantasy centering on an office drudge trapped by technological regimentation. His comedy about a henpecked man who attempts to flee the roost, *Close Harmony* (1924), written with Dorothy Parker,♦ was well received but failed, while his mystery about an actor murdered during a performance, *Cock Robin* (1928), written with Philip Barry,♦ enjoyed a modest run. He earned a Pulitzer Prize♦ for his unflinching slice of New York life, *Street Scene*♦ (1929), but two other plays the same year, *The Subway,* an expressionistic drama focusing on a frustrated filing clerk, and *See Naples and Die,* telling of the complicatons set in motion by a romantic heiress, were unsuccessful. He deftly probed American expatriates in Paris in *The Left Bank*♦ (1931), then a month later returned to the legal world with *Counsellor-at-Law,*♦ a story of a lawyer whose early indiscretion returns to haunt him. For the rest of the 1930s he wrote largely well-intentioned propaganda pieces which failed to please critics and playgoers: *We, the People* (1932), *Judgment Day* (1934), *Between Two Worlds* (1934), and *American Landscape* (1938). A light show-business comedy, *Two on an Island* (1940), had a modest run. Somewhat more successful was his tale

of people fleeing Europe, *Flight to the West* (1940). His only other success was a frothy comedy about a saleslady who lives in a fantasy world, *Dream Girl*♦ (1945), a work written for his wife, Betty Field. Other late plays included *A New Life* (1943), *The Grand Tour* (1951), *Not for Children* (1951), *The Winner* (1954), and *Cue for Passion* (1958). Rice directed most of his own plays, as well as those by others, including *Abe Lincoln in Illinois*♦ (1938). He served as a regional director of the Federal Theatre Project♦ and was a founder of the Playwrights' Company.♦

Autobiography: *Minority Report,* New York, 1963.

RICE, T[HOMAS] D[ARTMOUTH] (1808–60) The tall, slim entertainer is usually considered the first blackface performer to gain international renown. He was born in New York, where his earliest theatrical work was as a supernumerary at the Park Theatre.♦ A short time later he joined Noah Ludlow.♦ Various accounts exist claiming to offer the origin of his famous "Jim Crow" song and the shuffling dance that accompanied it. The most commonly told is that he saw a crippled black stablehand in Louisville singing a similar song and walking with a similar gait. Rice added his own words, which ran in part:

> Wheel about, turn about
> Do jes so,
> An' ebery time I wheel about
> I jump Jim Crow.

He first performed his routine as an entr'acte in 1828 and brought it to New York in 1832. His success was instant and widespread. Later he incorporated the song and dance into such entertainments as *Bone Squash, The Virginia Mummy,* and *Jim Crow in London.* Although an eccentric, reclusive man, refusing to join the burgeoning minstrel ensembles, he retained his popularity until his death.

RICH, FRANK (b. 1949) A native of Washington, D.C., he studied at Harvard. For many years he was a film critic with several notable publications, including *Time* and the New York *Post.* He joined the New York *Times* in April 1980 and was appointed its drama critic the following September. His reviews have been marked by a sometimes showy erudition, and by so unnecessarily brutal attacks on plays not meeting with his approval that he had been called "The Butcher of Broadway." The cast of a musical he alone panned is said to have taken to wearing buttons reading "Get Rich,

Quick." He has even begun to attack critics who disagree with him, in one case dismissing them as "pompous" and suggesting the play "went right over [their] heads."

Richard Carvel, a play in four acts by Edward E. Rose.♦ Produced by Charles Frohman♦ at the Empire Theatre.♦ September 11, 1900. 128 performances.

Richard Carvel (John Drew♦) overcomes the machinations of a wicked uncle, kidnapping by pirates, and a spell in debtors' prison to fight alongside John Paul Jones (George Le Soir) and win the affection of Dorothy Manners (Ida Conquest).

Based on Winston Churchill's popular novel, the play gave Drew a rare chance to play a swashbuckling role instead of the drawing room sophisticates that he usually portrayed. Though his performance was lauded, it was acknowledged he was really too old for the part.

Richard III The first Shakespeare♦ play to be produced in America, it was offered by Thomas Kean♦ in New York on March 5, 1750. (There is reason to believe he might have presented it in Philadelphia even earlier.) It remained a favorite of virtually all the great 19th-century tragedians, no doubt in large measure because the title part is one of the juiciest villain-heroes in all dramatic literature. Junius Brutus Booth,♦ George Frederick Cooke,♦ and Edmund Kean♦ all made their American debuts in the role, which was also identified with Edwin Forrest,♦ William Macready,♦ and Edwin Booth♦ among others. Perhaps because the role was so meaty most great performers associated with it seem to have eschewed unnecessary histrionics, although by modern standards they would probably be judged overly emotive. Thus, when the elder Booth first offered his interpretation, the *National Advocate* noted, "In the conception of the character of the crooked back tyrant, Mr. Booth seems to be perfect. He exhibited none of those stage tricks, which many, who undertake the part, substitute for their lack of judgment. From his first entrance in which he delivered the soliloquy, 'Now is the winter of our discontent,' to the moment he expired, there was nothing to be recognized but the ambitious, tyrannical, hypocritical and daring Richard." Although the play has fallen somewhat out of favor, it was superbly revived in 1920 with John Barrymore♦ in the lead and remains part of the repertory of all festival theatres.

RICHARDS, Lloyd [George] (b. 1921?) Born in Toronto, Canada, he graduated from Wayne State University and began his career as an actor. Turning to direction, he worked with regional houses, then staged *A Raisin in the Sun*♦ (1959) and the musical *I Had a Ball* (1964) on Broadway. Since 1969 he has been artistic director of the National Playwrights Conference♦ and also served as artistic director of the Yale Repertory Theatre♦ from 1979 to 1991. In recent years he has staged all the plays of August Wilson♦ that have been brought to Broadway, beginning with *Ma Rainey's Black Bottom*♦ (1984).

RICHARDSON, Howard, see *Dark of the Moon*

RICHARDSON, Ralph [David] (1902–83) The excellent, if somewhat stiffly mannered English actor made his American debut as Mercutio and the Chorus in Katharine Cornell's♦ *Romeo and Juliet*♦ in 1935. He returned in 1946 as a member of the Old Vic♦ to offer his Falstaff in *Henry IV, Part I,*♦ Voynitsky in *Uncle Vanya,* Tiresias in *Oedipus,* and Lord Burleigh in *The Critic.* His later appearances have been in three modern plays: *The Waltz of the Toreadors* (1957), *No Man's Land* (1976), in which he co-starred with John Gielgud,♦ and *Early Days* (1981), and in one classic role, Sir Peter Teazle, in a 1963 revival of *The School for Scandal.*

Biography: *Ralph Richardson: An Actor's Life,* Garry O'Connor, Boston, 1982.

Richelieu; or, The Conspiracy The play by Bulwer-Lytton♦ centered on the 17th-century French cardinal who uses his spies and his native skills to thwart attempts to assassinate him. He also brings about an alliance with Spain and helps his ward defy the king and marry the man she loves. Edwin Forrest♦ was the first American Richelieu in 1839. Later Macready♦ and Edwin Booth♦ were known for their interpretations. While Booth was considered the Richelieu par excellence, the play continued to be revived for many seasons after his death. Walter Hampden♦ staged a notable revival in 1929.

RICHINGS, [Mary] Caroline [née Reynoldson] (d. 1882) The adopted daughter of Peter Richings,♦ she was born in England and brought to America while still a child. She made her professional debut as a pianist in 1847, but in 1852 turned to the lyric stage when she sang Marie in the Seguin Opera Company's mounting of *The Daughter of the Regiment.* She later formed her own company and continued to perform until shortly before her death. Although she sang roles that today would be largely confined to opera houses, opera in her day was part of many legitimate theatres' programs. Her repertory included a number of primitive American comic operas, such as *The Doctor of Alcantara.*♦ T. Allston Brown♦ wrote that she was "a thoroughly schooled and most conscientious singer, but she was mechanical and unsympathetic."

RICHINGS, PETER [né PUGET] (1797–1871) Born in Kensington, England, he was the son of a naval captain who sent him to Oxford to prepare for a career in law. His family's opposition to his decision to go on the stage prompted him to emigrate to America in 1821. He made his debut at the Park Theatre♦ as Henry Bertram in *Guy Mannering* that year, but was primarily known as a comedian who excelled at playing fops. Among his best roles were Osric, Sparkish, Captain Absolute, and Sir Benjamin Backbite. In the 1840s he also served as manager for the National Theatre, Walnut Street Theatre,♦ and Chestnut Street Theatre♦ in Philadelphia and the Holliday Street Theatre♦ in Baltimore. He retired in 1868. Clara Morris,♦ who worked with him late in his life, remembered him as "Six feet tall, high-featured, Roman nosed, elegantly dressed; a term from bygone days . . . describes him perfectly: he was an 'old Buck!' "

RICHMAN, CHARLES J. (1870–1940) The Chicagoan made his debut in 1894 and two years later became leading man for Augustin Daly,♦ playing such roles as Orlando and Benedick as well as the heroes of contemporary pieces. Among his subsequent leads were Kearney, who pacifies the troublemakers and wins the heroine, in *The Rose of the Rancho*♦ (1906); Burton Temple, who falls in love with a woman who is attempting to incriminate him, in *The Fighting Hope*♦ (1908); and Robert Stafford, who looks on a wife as property, in *Bought and Paid For*♦ (1911). In after years he was a fine supporting actor in such plays as *Strictly Dishonorable*♦ (1930) and *Biography*♦ (1932).

RICHMAN, HARRY [né REICHMAN] (1895–1972) The brash, jaunty singer was born in Cincinnati, and began his career in vaudeville as a pianist for Mae West,♦ the Dolly Sisters,♦ and Nora Bayes.♦ Striking out on his own he gave imitations of Al Jolson♦ and David Warfield♦ but soon developed a turn in which he sang dressed either in white tie and tails or a straw hat and blazer. His Broadway appearances were almost always in revues, notably *George White's Scandals of 1926,*♦ in which he introduced "The Birth of the Blues" and "Lucky

Day," and *International Revue* (1930), in which he performed "Exactly Like You" and "On the Sunny Side of the Street." Much of his later career was confined to night clubs.

Autobiography: *A Hell of a Life,* written with Richard Gehman, New York, 1966.

RICKETTS, JOHN BILL (1760?–99) The English-born equestrian, whom Odell♦ called "incomparably the greatest circus-man of his day; the finest rider New York had seen," came to America in 1792 and a year later established his circuses and amphitheatres in Philadelphia and New York. He thus became the father of the American circus tradition. Among his advertised feats were "a summerset from a horse in full speed, and a-light on his feet" and "a summerset over thirty men's heads." His success was such that he shortly had to build larger arenas and took his troupe through New England and into Canada. Fires destroyed both his establishments in 1799, so he set sail for England but was lost at sea.

RIGL, EMILY Coming to America with her then better known sister, Betty, to dance in the original production of *The Black Crook*♦ (1866), she gave up dancing to learn elocution and acting, and soon entered Augustin Daly's♦ company, where she became a respected supporting player. She won applause in such contemporary hits as *The Big Bonanza*♦ *(1875), Saratoga*♦ (1875), and *Pique*♦ (1875), as well as for such classic roles as Olivia in *Twelfth Night.*♦ Leaving Daly briefly, she created the role of Francesca, the deserted wife, in *The Galley Slave*♦ (1879). She remained active as late as 1907. Never a major star, she was still considered one of the best actresses of her day.

RILEY, LAWRENCE, see *Personal Appearance*

RINEHART, MARY ROBERTS (1876–1958) The Pittsburgh-born author best known for her mystery novels was also a successful playwright. Her first play, written under the pen name Rinehart Roberts, was *The Double Life* (1906), in which a young man attempts to make a normal life for himself after an injury prevents him from remembering his past. She scored her first hit when she collaborated with Avery Hopwood♦ on a comedy about a mixed group of people thrown together by a quarantine, *Seven Days*♦ (1909). *Cheer Up* (1912) centered on an imposter who tries to run a mental institution. In 1920 she rejoined Hopwood to write two huge successes, *Spanish Love,* which told of two men pursuing the same girl, and *The Bat,* ♦ a mystery based on her novel *The Circular Staircase.* Her last play, an adaptation of another of her books, was *The Breaking Point* (1923). It dealt with a man who must live with the memory of a murder he committed years before.

Autobiography: *My Story,* New York, 1931.

RING, BLANCHE (1876?–1961) The Boston-born daughter and granddaughter of performers, the tiny blonde belter of songs made her first appearance in a small role opposite Richard Mansfield♦ in *A Parisian Romance* in 1892, and later played in companies headed by Nat Goodwin♦ and Chauncey Olcott.♦ She attained stardom overnight after introducing "In the Good Old Summertime" in *The Defender* (1902). She sang "The Belle of Avenue A" in *Tommy Rot* (1902), "Bedelia" in *The Jersey Lily* (1903), and "I've Got Rings on My Fingers" in *The Midnight Sons* (1909). In all, she appeared in two dozen musicals between 1902 and 1938, as well as in several non-musical plays. She was also a great favorite in vaudeville, where she was one of the first to get audiences to sing along with her and where her mimicry was as celebrated as her singing. Among the other songs she made famous were "Come, Josephine, in My Flying Machine," "Waltz Me Around Again, Willie," and "Yip-I-Addy-I-Ay."

RINGLING, ALFRED T. (1863–1919) Born to German immigrant parents in McGregor, Iowa, he was sixteen when he saw Dan Rice♦ perform in a circus. He soon taught himself to be an acrobat, juggler, and clown and began to perform in the rear of his father's harness shop. His four brothers—Albert, Charles, John, and Otto—joined him in 1882 to form Ringling Brothers Classic and Comic Concert Company. Within two years their outfit had grown into a major circus. At the time of World War I they merged with the Barnum and Bailey Circus.

Rio Rita, a musical in two acts. Book by Guy Bolton♦ and Fred Thompson.♦ Lyrics by Joseph McCarthy.♦ Music by Harry Tierney.♦ Produced by Florenz Ziegfeld♦ at the Ziegfeld Theatre.♦ February 2, 1927. 494 performances.

Jim (J. Harold Murray♦), a captain in the Texas Rangers, falls in love with Rio Rita (Ethelind Terry), knowing full well that she is also courted by the unsavory Mexican, General Esteban (Vincent Serrano). Since Jim is searching for the bandit called "The Kinkajou," Esteban tells Rita that Jim's prime suspect is her brother Roberto (George Baxter).

This cools the romance between Jim and Rita until Jim proves "The Kinkajou" is none other than Esteban himself.

Principal songs: The Kinkajou · The Rangers' Song · Rio Rita · If You're in Love, You'll Waltz

Although the plot seemed merely a rewriting of the story of *Naughty Marietta,* ♦ the fine score and sumptuous Ziegfeld production made this musical, which opened the Ziegfeld Theatre, one of the most memorable of its era.

Rip Van Winkle, a play in four acts by Dion Boucicault♦ [and Joseph Jefferson, ♦ uncredited]. Produced at the Olympic Theatre. September 3, 1866. 35 performances.

Rip Van Winkle (Jefferson) is a dissolute, ne'er-do-well, with no illusions about his worthlessness. He tells his daughter Meenie (Marie Le Brun), "Why, don't you know, Meenie, all the houses and lands in the village was mine—they would all have been yours when you grew up? Where they gone now? I gone drunk 'em up, that's where they gone." His guilty unhappiness is not assuaged by his scold of a wife Gretchen (Mrs. Saunders), who finally drives him from his home. With his dog Schneider, he retreats to a cove in the Kaatskill Mountains. There, beset by demons, he drinks himself into a stupor. When he wakes years later, he returns home. No one recognizes him. Gretchen thinks him a beggar, gives him a penny, and takes pity on him. Not until his daughter realizes who he is do matters change. Rip promises to stay sober and Gretchen to be a good wife.

Jefferson had played in earlier dramatizations of the story. While in London he had Boucicault write him a new version, which he first offered there in 1865. The initial American reception was lukewarm, but Jefferson quickly made changes in Boucicault's text and polished his own performance. The play served him as a vehicle and remained one of the most popular American stage pieces for the rest of the century.

RISTORI, ADELAIDE (1822–1906) The great Italian tragedienne was usually perceived as the successor to Rachel♦ on international stages. She began the first of several American tours in 1866 as Medea, and continued her season in such roles as Mary Stuart, Phèdre, Adrienne Lecouvreur, Francesca da Rimini, and Lady Macbeth. However, her greatest role in American eyes was unquestionably her Queen Elizabeth in Giacometti's play about the English monarch. J. Ranken Towse♦ wrote of this interpretation, "The haughty carriage, imperious address, fierce temper, blunt humor, petty vanity, masculine sagacity, and feminine jealousy, were all indicated with surpassing skill and blended into a consistent whole with finished artistry." By no means a beautiful woman—the kindest critics called her handsome—she had little delicacy or poetry in her style, excelling instead in power and grandeur. On her last visit, during the 1884–85 season, she attempted to perform in English with disastrous results.

Autobiography: *Memoirs and Artistic Studies,* trans. G. Mantellini, New York, 1907.

RITCHARD, Cyril [né Cyril Trimnell-Ritchard] (1897–1977) His era's consummate portrayer of fops, he was born in Sydney, Australia, and made his first American appearance in *Puzzles of 1925.* However, he did not call attention to himself with American playgoers until he returned with John Gielgud's♦ company in 1947 to play Tattle in *Love for Love.* Among his later notable roles were the effeminate Georgie Pillson in *Make Way for Lucia* (1948); Lord Foppington in *The Relapse* (1950); Captain Hook in the 1954 musical version of *Peter Pan*♦; Kreton, the man from outer space, in *Visit to a Small Planet*♦ (1957); Biddeford Poole, the incorrigible playboy, in *The Pleasure of His Company*♦ (1958); and Sir in the musical *The Roar of the Greasepaint—The Smell of the Crowd* (1965). Although his wide, humorous eyes and curiously bleating delivery made him irresistible on stage, he was also a sought-after director. His stagings included *John Murray Anderson's Almanac* (1953), *The Reluctant Debutante* (1956), *Visit to a Small Planet,* and *The Pleasure of His Company.*

RITCHIE, Adele [née Pultz] (1874–1930) Born in Philadelphia, the beautiful but now totally forgotten musical comedy star made such a hit in her debut in *The Isle of Champagne* (1893) that she was given a major part in the first American revue, *The Passing Show*♦ (1894). She enjoyed her biggest success in *A Chinese Honeymoon* (1902). In all she was featured or starred in twenty musicals, including the title roles in *Glittering Gloria* (1904) and *Fascinating Flora* (1907).

Ritz, The, a comedy in two acts by Terrence McNally.♦ Produced at the Longacre Theatre. January 20, 1975. 400 performances.

The Ritz is a steam bath catering to homosexuals. To it come Gaetano Proclo (Jack Weston), a garbage man who signs himself in as Carmine Vespucci, the murderous brother-in-law he is attempting to hide

from; Michael Brick (Stephen Collins), a detective hired by the real Vespucci to follow Proclo; and the real Vespucci (Jerry Stiller), bent on killing Proclo. While pursuing their own ends they are pursued by a collection of homosexuals all out for an hour's fun. By the end of the evening Proclo has gotten Carmine gagged and bound, and has left him to be fought over by a policeman and a pervert whose special delight is fat men.

This uproarious farce makes an interesting comparison with a farce of a half century before, *Ladies' Night in a Turkish Bath.*♦ The pieces vividly demonstrate the remarkable change in mores that has occurred, while suggesting that well-made theatrical bedlam can find a home in any social climate.

River Niger, The, a play in three acts by Joseph A. Walker. Produced by the Negro Ensemble Company♦ at the Brooks Atkinson Theatre. March 27, 1973. 280 performances.

Johnny Williams (Douglas Turner Ward), a black man, is a house-painter and poet who has failed as both. His pride and joy is his son Jeff (Les Roberts) who has become an officer in the air force. But when Johnny learns that Jeff is unhappy with his career and will abandon it, he goes on a bender. Sobering up, he writes a long poem which attempts to find meaning in the whole of the black experience.

Originally produced off-Broadway, the play later received a Tony Award♦ as the best play of the season. Walker (b. 1935) was born in Washington and educated at Catholic University. He has taught at several colleges. This has been his only commercial success.

RIVERA, Chita [née Dolores Conchita Figueroa Del Rivero] (b. 1933) The vivacious Latin-miened dancer was born in Washington and studied at the American School of Ballet. She appeared in the choruses of *Guys and Dolls,*♦ *Call Me Madam,*♦ and *Can-Can*♦ before garnering attention in *Shoestring Revue*♦ (1955). Roles followed in *Seventh Heaven* (1955) and *Mr. Wonderful* (1956), after which she created the part of Anita in *West Side Story*♦ (1957). Starring assignments followed in *Bye Bye Birdie*♦ (1960), *Bajour* (1964), a touring company of *Sweet Charity*♦ (1967), *Chicago*♦ (1975), *Merlin* (1983), *The Rink* (1984), and *Jerry's Girls* (1985).

RIVES, Amélie (1863–1945) The Virginia-born playwright, poet, and novelist, who married the Russian Prince Troubetzkoy, wrote a number of blank-verse tragedies at the turn of the century, including *Herod and Miriamne* (1888), *Athelwold* (1893), and *Augustine the Man* (1906). At the same time she also dramatized her novelette, *The Quick or the Dead?* (1888). With her husband she wrote *Allegiance* (1918), in which German-Americans find their loyalties are torn. Her later works were a dramatization of *The Prince and the Pauper* (1920); a recounting of an old Irish legend, *The Sea-Woman's Cloak* (1925); and a light triangle comedy, written with Gilbert Emery,♦ *Love in a Mist* (1926).

Road to Rome, The, a play in three acts by Robert Sherwood.♦ Produced by William A. Brady, Jr.♦ and Dwight Deere Wiman♦ at the Playhouse. January 31, 1927. 392 performances.

Fabius Maximus (Richie Ling) cannot understand why his wife, Amytis (Jane Cowl♦), is not excited over his being declared Dictator of Rome, or why she seems so intrigued by their enemy, the Carthaginian Hannibal (Philip Merivale♦), whose army is pushing toward the city. When news arrives of a Roman defeat and of Hannibal's presence nearby, Amytis pretends to flee. Instead she goes to Hannibal's camp, where she does something the Roman army cannot do. She talks to him, lets him make love to her, and convinces him to withdraw.

Described by Charles Brackett of *The New Yorker* as "A hymn of hate against militarism—disguised, ever so gaily, as a love song," it was rejected by most major producers. Its success established Sherwood as a new playwright of importance.

Road to Yesterday, The, a play in four acts by Beulah Marie Dix♦ and E. G. Sutherland.♦ Produced by Lee Shubert♦ at the Herald Square Theatre. December 31, 1906. 216 performances.

An impressionable American girl, Elspeth Tyrrell (Minnie Dupree♦), comes to London for a hectic tour. One night she falls asleep and dreams she is living in Elizabethan times and is kidnapped by a handsome ruffian. When she awakes she realizes that the ruffian resembles a friend of a friend. She had never before considered marrying the man, but now she does.

The play, which mixed a satirical look at reincarnation and a swashbuckling tale, was the source of Victor Herbert's♦ last musical, *The Dream Girl* (1924).

ROBARDS, JASON, JR. (b. 1922) The dark, somewhat weather-beaten-looking actor was the son of another famous actor. Born in Chicago, he studied at the American Academy of Dramatic Arts♦ and with Uta Hagen,♦ and began appearing profession-

ally in the late 1940s. However, acclaim first came only with his performance as Hickey in a 1956 Circle in the Square♦ revival of *The Iceman Cometh.*♦ Brooks Atkinson♦ wrote, "His unction, condescension and piety introduce an element of moral affectation that clarifies the perspective of the drama." He subsequently distinguished himself in other Eugene O'Neill♦ roles, including James Tyrone, Jr. in the original Broadway production of *Long Day's Journey into Night♦* (1956), Smith in *Hughie* (1964), and James Tyrone, Jr. in a 1973 revival of *A Moon for the Misbegotten.*♦ He displayed his versatility in such other roles as the ne'er-do-well Julian Berniers in *Toys in the Attic♦* (1960); William Baker, who seems to live for his hanger-on friends, in *Big Fish, Little Fish♦* (1961); Murray Burns, the non-conforming father, in *A Thousand Clowns♦* (1962); and Quentin, who marries a celebrated actress, in *After the Fall♦* (1964). In 1983 he scored as Martin Vanderhof in a revival of *You Can't Take It with You.*♦ He re-created the role of Hickey in a 1985 revival of *The Iceman Cometh,*♦ then played James Tyrone, Sr. and Nat Miller in 1988 revivals of *Long Day's Journey into Night♦* and *Ah, Wilderness!*♦

ROBBINS, JEROME [né RABINOWITZ] (b. 1918) Born in New York, he studied ballet with Anthony Tudor and other famous dancers. In the late 1930s he appeared in several Broadway musicals, but it was only after he attained success as a choreographer and dancer with the Ballet Theatre that he returned to the musical comedy stage to devise the dances for *On the Town♦* (1944), which had been inspired by his ballet *Fancy Free.* His "Mack Sennett Ballet"♦ for *High Button Shoes* (1947) remains the comic masterpiece among all dances created for Broadway musical comedies. His work for this show was followed by his dances for *Look, Ma, I'm Dancin'* (1948), *Miss Liberty* (1949), *Call Me Madam♦* (1950), and *The King and I♦* (1951). In 1954 he co-directed *The Pajama Game.*♦ Starting with *Peter Pan♦* (1954) he served as director for all the shows he choreographed: *Bells Are Ringing* (1956), *West Side Story♦* (1957), *Gypsy♦* (1959), and *Fiddler on the Roof♦* (1964). He also staged *Oh Dad, Poor Dad,* etc.♦ (1962), a non-musical. If he was often the wittiest of choreographers he was also brilliantly adept at creating the starkest of dance dramas, as witnessed by his work for *West Side Story.* Other examples of his great variety included the imaginatively stylized "Small House of Uncle Thomas" ballet in *The King and I,* and the folkloristic Jewish dances in *Fiddler on the Roof.* In recent years he has devoted himself largely to creating works for major ballet companies, but returned to the theatre for the retrospective *Jerome Robbins' Broadway* (1989).

Roberta, a musical comedy in two acts. Book and lyrics by Otto Harbach. ♦ Music by Jerome Kern. ♦ Produced by Max Gordon♦ at the New Amsterdam Theatre. ♦ November 18, 1933. 295 performances.

When his Aunt Minnie (Fay Templeton♦) dies, John Kent (Ray Middleton), an all-American fullback, inherits the exclusive dress shop she runs in Paris under the name of Roberta. He allows his aunt's young assistant, Stephanie (Tamara), to run the shop, and soon a romance blossoms between the two. The appearance of John's old flame, Sophie (Helen Gray), nearly destroys the affair. But John recollects that Sophie deserted him before and could do it again. He settles for Stephanie, who turns out to be a Russian princess.

Principal songs: Smoke Gets in Your Eyes · The Touch of Your Hand · Yesterdays · You're Devastating

Derived from Alice Duer Miller's novel, *Gowns by Roberta,* the musical exemplifies the ability a single hit song once had to turn a potential failure into a success. Critics lambasted the show, especially its deadeningly dull book, but the raging popularity of "Smoke Gets in Your Eyes" turned its fate around.

ROBERTS, Florence (1871–1927) Although born in the East, she was raised in California and made her debut at San Francisco's Baldwin Theatre♦ in 1889. Shortly thereafter she became the leading lady at the Alcazar Theatre when its stock company was the finest in the state and played classic roles such as Juliet, Ophelia, Portia, Rosalind, Parthenia (*Ingomar*♦), Camille, and La Tosca, as well as leads in many now forgotten plays. She also made successful star tours of the West but played New York rarely. After World War I she toured South Africa, played in a few silent films, and then retired.

ROBERTS, James (1835–92) Born in Bath, England, he learned his trade as a scene painter in London theatres before coming to America in 1860. A meeting with Augustin Daly♦ in 1869 led to his becoming Daly's chief set designer, and his work was seen in such memorable productions as *Man and Wife* (1870), *Saratoga*♦ (1870), and the 1872 revival of *The Merry Wives of Windsor.* Injuries sustained in the burning of Daly's Fifth Avenue Theatre♦ left his hearing permanently impaired and his health weakened. He thereafter usually created only one or two

sets for a production. Nevertheless he continued to be Daly's house set designer until his death, so that he had a hand in all of Daly's triumphs of the time. His specialty was realistic interiors.

ROBERTS, J[AMES] B[OOTH] (1818–1901) The squat, heavy-set, stern-faced actor was born in Newcastle, Del. and made his debut at Philadelphia's Walnut Street Theatre♦ playing Richmond to Junius Booth's♦ Richard III in 1836. Critics were laudatory. When he played Sir Giles Overreach in New York in 1857 the *Tribune* wrote, "Mr. Roberts may be cited as a fine actor, with an ever-present intellectuality coloring and shaping his delineations. We have seen no such *Sir Giles Overreach* since the time of the elder Booth, and, indeed, we imagine that Mr. Roberts has some merits to which older actors were strangers. We mean particularly his ability to speak naturally. Without being positively graceful, he is easy; without a commanding stature, he commands universal attention." Nevertheless, he found but small favor with New York audiences, although he remained an important star on the road. Among his major roles were Richard, Lear, Othello, Iago, and Jaffier.

ROBERTSON, Agnes (1833–1916) Born in Edinburgh, she began to perform when she was thirteen, and soon became the ward of the famous English actor Charles Kean. After marrying Dion Boucicault, ♦ she traveled with him to America, where she made her debut in 1853 as Maria in his *The Young Actress.* Her American career was tied inextricably with his. Among her important roles were Grace in several revivals of *London Assurance*♦; Violet, the Rachel-like figure, in the 1856 play of the same name; Jessie Brown, who helps save beleagured townsmen, in *Jessie Brown; or, The Siege of Lucknow*♦ (1858); Dot, the title role in a 1859 dramatization of *The Cricket on the Hearth;* Zoe, the doomed heroine of *The Octoroon*♦ (1859); and Eily O'Connor, the secretly wed heroine of *The Colleen Bawn*♦ (1860). In late 1860 she returned to England and thereafter appeared in America only on rare occasions. Odell♦ described her as 'one of the most simple, artless and captivating artistes ever seen on our stage; in guileless Scotch and Irish peasant girls she has probably never been surpassed." Although most of her American career was confined to seven years, Odell concluded, "America had had the best of her career."

ROBERTSON, T[HOMAS] W[ILLIAM] (1829–71) The English playwright, whose quiet, restrained examinations of middle-class domesticity were known popularly as "cup and saucer plays," was, as far as most Americans were concerned, caviar to the general public. In New York his best plays were offered by Lester Wallack♦ and were usually produced by the elite organizations in other cities. Wallack's productions included *Society* (1866), *Ours* (1866), *Caste*♦ (1867), *School* (1869), and *Progress* (1869). Revivals of Robertson's plays were long a mainstay at Wallack's, but his American imitators as a rule had small success anywhere.

ROBESON, PAUL (1898–1976) Born in Princeton, N.J., and educated at Rutgers and Columbia, the black singer and actor made a number of noteworthy appearances on Broadway, including the roles of Jim Harris, the black lawyer who marries a white woman, in *All God's Chillun Got Wings*♦ (1924), and Brutus Jones in a 1925 revival of *The Emperor Jones.*♦ Jerome Kern♦ and Oscar Hammerstein II♦ are said to have written the role of Joe in *Show Boat*♦ with him in mind, but he did not sing it until the London premiere and played it in America only in the 1932 revival. His greatest success came when he played Othello to José Ferrer's♦ Iago in 1943. The production became the longest-running Shakespearean revival in history. Nevertheless, despite his success, his Communist sympathies led him to spend many of his last years in Russia.

Autobiography: *Here I Stand,* Boston, 1971.

Robin Hood, a comic opera in three acts. Libretto by Harry B. Smith.♦ Music by Reginald De Koven.♦ Produced by The Bostonians♦ at the Standard Theatre. September 28, 1891. 40 performances.

The Sheriff of Nottingham (Henry Clay Barnabee♦) wrongfully deprives Robert, Earl of Huntington (Tom Karl), of his lands. He gives them and the Earl's fiancée, Maid Marian (Caroline Hamilton), to his own friend, Guy of Gisbourne (Peter Lang). Robert becomes an outlaw and assumes the name of Robin Hood. He is captured through treachery. The Sheriff intends to force him to witness the marriages of Marian to Guy, and of Annabel (Lea Van Dyke), the betrothed of Alan-a-Dale (Jessie Bartlett Davis♦), to the Sheriff himself. But before the wedding can take place Robin Hood is rescued by his band, who carry a pardon from the king.

Principal songs: Brown October Ale · Oh, Promise Me♦

Generally acknowledged as the first great masterpiece of the American musical stage, the work was revived regularly for nearly half a century. The reasons for its early success were varied and proba-

bly did not include the re-used scenery and costumes initially employed by the Bostonians.♦ Indeed, Smith recalled that the first mounting, because of the re-used material, cost just over one hundred dollars. But the solid and, for the time, witty libretto, the songs, which were among the earliest classics of the American musical theatre, and the excellent singing and acting of the company all played a part. Smith has suggested an additional reason, noting most contemporary comic operas were created as show pieces for prima donnas while this operetta carefully balanced the men's and women's roles.

ROBINSON, BILL (1878–1949) The beguiling black tap dancer, known affectionately as "Bojangles," began his career by performing for pennies on street corners while still a child in his native Richmond, Va. At seventeen he became part of a vaudeville act. Within a few seasons he was doing a solo turn, featuring his relaxed, self-assured stepping. His Broadway appearances were in *Blackbirds of 1928,*♦ *Brown Buddies* (1930), *Blackbirds of 1933, The Hot Mikado* (1939), *All in Fun* (1940), and *Memphis Bound* (1945).

Biography: *Mr. Bojangles,* James Haskins, New York, 1988.

ROBINSON, CHARLES, see *Sailor, Beware!*

ROBINSON, DAVID G. (fl. mid-19th century) Known affectionately as "Doc" or "Yankee" Robinson, but not to be confused with Fayette Lodawick Robinson,♦ who was also addressed as "Yankee," he was born between 1805 and 1809 in East Monmouth, Maine. He is said to have attended Yale and to have been graduated as a physician in the early 1830s. Later he toured with his family in his own temperance play, *A Reformed Drunkard,* before moving to San Francisco around 1847. He set himself up as a doctor and also opened a drug store. In 1850 he built one of the city's first playhouses, the 280-seat Dramatic Museum on California Street, and began to present his own burlesques, including *Seeing the Elephant,* a spoof of gold-rush prospectors, and *Who's Got the Countess?,* a send-up of Lola Montez.♦ At the same time he wrote and performed in satires on local politics. These proved so popular that when he ran for alderman, he was elected. After the Museum burned, he erected and managed several other theatres. He also guided the career of his young daughter, Sue Robinson, who was briefly acclaimed as a child prodigy or "fairy star."♦ However, by the mid-1850s his luck and popularity deserted him. Some historians have suggested he died of fever in 1856 in Mobile, Ala., but Walter Leman♦ wrote in his autobiography that he encountered Robinson living in obscure poverty in the 1870s. He has been described as a "tall, angular man with hawklike eyes and an acid wit."

ROBINSON, EDWARD G. [né EMANUEL GOLDEN-BERG] (1893–1973) The stocky, gruff actor was born in Bucharest, but was raised in New York. He studied at City College of New York, Columbia, and the American Academy of Dramatic Arts♦ before making his professional debut in Binghamton, N.Y., in 1913. Ten years later he joined the Theatre Guild's♦ acting ensemble, appearing with them in such plays as *Peer Gynt* (1923), *The Adding Machine♦* (1923), *Androcles and the Lion* (1925), and *Ned McCobb's Daughter♦* (1926). He was considered an actor of great range, depth, and promise, but shortly after creating the role of the gangster, Nick Scarsi, in *The Racket♦* (1927), he left for a long career in Hollywood and returned only to tour in *Darkness at Noon* in 1951 and to create the role of The Manufacturer in *Middle of the Night♦* (1956).

Autobiography: *All My Yesterdays,* with Leonard Spigelgass, New York, 1973.

ROBINSON, FAYETTE LODAWICK (1818–84) Known popularly as "Yankee" Robinson, but not to be confused with San Francisco's David G. Robinson,♦ who often was given the same nickname, he was born near Avon Mineral Springs, N.Y., and was a decendant of Dr. Robinson, a minister who came to America on the *Mayflower.* He began his career in 1835 when he joined a small traveling tent show. Although he made a few failed attempts at becoming a regular actor, he gained fame only after he established his own traveling tent show which he called Robinson's Athenaeum. His versions of *The Drunkard* and similar shows proved exceedingly popular with rural and small-town audiences. He also established a circus with which, according to his obituaries, he "gained a reputation second only to Barnum." He was a rather homely, balding man with a huge goatee.

ROBSON, ELEANOR [ELISE] (1879–1979) Born in England, she was brought to America as a child by her mother, who had remarried after her father's death and who acted under the name of Madge Carr Cook.♦ After graduating from a seminary on Staten Island in 1897, she went to join her mother, who was playing in San Francisco, and found herself thrust on stage to replace an ailing performer in *Men and Women.♦* She played in stock for several seasons before creating the role of Bonita in the original Chicago production of *Arizona♦* in 1899, a role she also later played in the New York production. Impressed by her great beauty and fine acting, George C. Tyler♦ cast her as Constance in Browning's *In a Balcony* (1900). She remained under Tyler's aegis for the rest of her career. Among her memorable interpretations were her Juliet in 1903 and her Kate Hardcastle in 1905, but she is best recalled for her playing of Mary Ann, the sweet-natured, innocent drudge who wins the hand of a rich composer, in *Merely Mary Ann* (1903). She retired after her marriage to August Belmont III, becoming a celebrated socialite and philanthropist. In the latter capacity she was long associated with the Metropolitan Opera.

Autobiography: *The Fabric of Memory,* New York, 1957.

ROBSON, STUART [né HENRY ROBSON STUART] (1836–1903) Born in Annapolis, the comedian made his acting debut in Baltimore in 1852. He gained experience in numerous stock companies, then joined Laura Keene's♦ New York company in 1862. Later he spent time with Mrs. Drew♦ at the Arch Street Theatre♦ in Philadelphia and with William Warren♦ in Boston. The height of his career came when he teamed with W. H. Crane♦ in *Our Boarding House♦* (1877). The pair quickly became the most popular team in the theatre, appearing together in, among others, *Our Bachelors* (1878), *The Comedy of Errors* (1878), *Sharps and Flats* (1880), and *The Henrietta♦* (1887). After the team broke up in 1889 Robson continued to appear in some of the plays that had made them famous, as well as playing Tony Lumpkin in an 1893 mounting of *She Stoops To Conquer* and in such specially written vehicles as *The Meddler* (1898) and *The Gadfly* (1899). Of Robson's acting in *The Meddler* one critic wrote, "His prodigious comic personality, his wooden countenance, his staccato utterance, and his long-familiar squeak inevitably give an extravagant turn to the fun." At a time when many clergy regularly railed at theatre people, Robson was known among fellow actors for his odd pastime of maintaining a scrapbook filled with published accounts of erring ministers.

Rocket to the Moon, a play in three acts by Clifford Odets.♦ Produced by the Group Theatre♦ at the Belasco Theatre. November 24, 1938. 131 performances.

Ben Stark (Morris Carnovsky♦) is a young dentist badgered by his pushy, shrewish wife, Belle (Ruth Nelson), who believes he can make more money for himself and have more celebrity as a specialist. Belle's rich father, Mr. Prince (Luther Adler♦), is caught in the middle. He wants the best for his daughter and has offered to set his son-in-law up as a specialist, but he himself was unhappily married and lives longing for the life he never had. He suggests that Ben have an affair with his dental secretary, Cleo Singer (Eleanor Lynn). Ben does, but the affair turns out badly and Ben returns to his wife.

When many critics assailed the play for its weak last act, Odets rewrote the work, but despite much fine dialogue and character observation the play never fully succeeded.

RODGERS, RICHARD [CHARLES] (1902–79) One of the greatest of American theatrical composers, he was born in New York and educated at Columbia, where he wrote music for college shows. His career as a stage composer can be divided into three parts. The earliest was his collaboration with lyricist Lorenz Hart♦ on the songs and occasionally the books of imaginative musical comedies. Their work for Broadway was heard initially in *Poor Little Ritz Girl* (1920), but success did not begin to come until they wrote "Manhattan" for the first *Garrick Gaieties*♦ (1925). Other show and song successes included *Dearest Enemy*♦ (1925), remembered for "Bye and Bye" and "Here in My Arms"; *Garrick Gaieties of 1926,* with its "Mountain Greenery"; *The Girl Friend* (1926), which offered "The Blue Room" and its title song; *A Connecticut Yankee*♦ (1927), from which came "My Heart Stood Still" and "Thou Swell"; *Present Arms* (1928), whose score contained "You Took Advantage of Me"; *Spring Is Here* (1929), recalled for "With a Song in My Heart"; *Simple Simon* (1930), which included "Ten Cents a Dance"; *Jumbo*♦ (1935), among whose melodies were "Little Girl Blue," "The Most Beautiful Girl in the World," and "My Romance"; *On Your Toes*♦ (1936), which offered "There's a Small Hotel" and the ballet "Slaughter on Tenth Avenue"♦; *Babes in Arms*♦ (1937), with a score that contained "Johnny One Note," "The Lady Is a Tramp," "My Funny Valentine" and "Where or When"; *I'd Rather Be Right*♦ (1937); *I Married an Angel*♦ (1938), remembered for its title song and "Spring Is Here"; *The Boys from Syracuse*♦ (1938), from which came "Falling in Love with Love" and "This Can't Be Love"; and *Pal Joey*♦ (1940), whose hit was "Bewitched." After breaking with Hart he joined Oscar Hammerstein II♦ and largely abandoned musical comedy. Their *Oklahoma!*♦ (1943) revolutionized American operetta writing. Among its great songs were "Oh, What a Beautiful Mornin'," the title song, "People Will Say We're in Love," and "The Surrey with the Fringe on Top." Its success was followed by, among others, *Carousel*♦ (1945), from which came "If I Loved You" and "June Is Bustin' Out All Over"; *South Pacific*♦ (1949), which offered "Bali Ha'i," "I'm Gonna Wash That Man Right Outa My Hair," "Some Enchanted Evening," and "A Wonderful Guy"; *The King and I*♦ (1951), whose score included "I Have Dreamed," "Getting To Know You," "Hello, Young Lovers," and "Shall We Dance?"; and *The Sound of Music*♦ (1959), remembered for "Climb Ev'ry Mountain," "Do-Re-Mi," "My Favorite Things," and the title song. After Hammerstein's death, Rodgers's luck soured although he continued to compose fine music, most notably when he set his own lyrics to his melodies for *No Strings*♦ (1962), which included the title song and "The Sweetest Sounds." Besides writing some librettos with Hart, with Hammerstein he also produced many of his later shows as well as those by others, including *I Remember Mama*♦ (1944), *Annie Get Your Gun*♦ (1946), *Happy Birthday*♦ (1946), and *John Loves Mary*♦ (1947).

Other scores, besides those mentioned above, were for *Peggy-Ann*♦ (1926), *Betsy* (1926), *She's My Baby* (1928), *Chee-Chee* (1928), *Heads Up!* (1929), *America's Sweetheart* (1931), *Too Many Girls* (1939), *Higher and Higher* (1940), *By Jupiter* (1942), *Allegro* (1947), *Me and Juliet* (1953), *Pipe Dream* (1955), *Flower Drum Song* (1958), *Do I Hear a Waltz?* (1965), *Two by Two* (1970), *Rex* (1976), and *I Remember Mama* (1979).

From the start Rodgers's music was both traditional and inventive. One notable point was his steady return to the waltz at a time when many composers neglected it. Perhaps his most remarkable effort in this style was "The Carousel Waltz." Because of the shows he was writing for and because of his lyricist, his material with Hart tended to be lighter and jauntier. Working with Hammerstein, both his sentimental and humorous moments tended to become more heavy-handed. But his gift for incomparable melody never deserted him, nor did his willingness to attempt musicals on fresh, challenging themes.

Autobiography: *Musical Stages,* New York, 1975.

ROGERS, MAJOR ROBERT, see *Ponteach*

ROGERS, WILL[IAM PENN ADAIR] (1879–1935) The famed cowboy humorist was born in Olagah, in

Indian Territory, and began his theatrical career with a traveling Wild West Show. He turned to vaudeville in 1904 and made his New York debut a year later. In 1912 he made his first appearance in a Broadway show, *The Wall Street Girl*. However, playgoers recall him best for his appearances in the 1916, 1917, 1918, 1922, and 1924 editions of the *Ziegfeld Follies,* ♦ where he spun out his witty, homey philosophy and comments while toying with a lariat. His last Broadway appearance was in *Three Cheers* (1928). In the same year, at the instigation of Robert Sherwood♦ and *Life,* he made an only half-serious run for the presidency on the Anti-Bunk Ticket, using a slogan Sherwood devised as a send-up of Calvin Coolidge, "He chews to run." Shortly before his death in a plane crash he had appeared as Nat Miller in a 1934 West Coast production of *Ah, Wilderness!.* ♦ He was also popular in films and on radio.

Autobiography: *Autobiography of Will Rogers,* ed. Donald Day, Boston, 1949.

Rogers Brothers, THE [né GUS (1869–1908) and MAX (1873–1932) SOLOMON] The brothers, both of whom were born in New York, began to perform together in 1885 and soon became favorites at Tony Pastor's, ♦ with their "Dutch" dialect routines. When Weber♦ and Fields♦ rose to popularity but refused to cooperate with the Theatrical Syndicate or Trust, ♦ Abe Erlanger♦ set out to make the Rogers Brothers their rivals. They were starred in *A Reign of Error* (1899) and then in an annual series of musicals with such titles at *The Rogers Brothers in Wall Street* (1899) and *The Rogers Brothers in Washington* (1901). The series continued until Gus died. Although Gus was considered the lesser of the pair, Max's career quickly faltered.

Rollo's Wild Oat, a comedy in two acts and an interlude by Clare Kummer. ♦ Produced at the Punch and Judy Theatre. November 23, 1920. 228 performances.

Rollo Webster (Roland Young♦), the amiable heir to an air brake fortune, has no real interest in running the business. His only ambition is to play Hamlet. He uses his money to mount his own production of the play. For Ophelia he casts a pretty young lady named Goldie MacDuff (Lotus Robb) who has taken to the stage solely to support herself and who has lost out on a chance for a part in The Midnight Frolics because she cannot stay awake that late. At the first performance Goldie–Ophelia interrupts Rollo–Hamlet to tell him his grandfather is dying. Rollo rushes offstage to be with his

grandfather, and leaves his stage manager to come before the audience to ask if there is another Hamlet in the house. Finally, Rollo's dresser is hurried into costume, only to discover the costumes have not been properly sewn. At home Rollo makes another discovery: his grandfather is very much alive and had resorted to a ruse to keep Rollo from making a fool of himself. All that is left for Rollo to do is to propose to Goldie, which he does.

Alexander Woollcott♦ hailed the comedy as "a kind of airy and capricious nonsense which was familiar enough in the best of Oscar Wilde." The play remained popular with amateur groups for several decades.

Romance, a play in three acts by Edward Sheldon. ♦ Produced at Maxine Elliott's Theatre. February 10, 1913. 160 performances.

Harry Putnam (George Le Soir), who is reluctant to tell his grandfather, Bishop Armstrong (William Courtenay♦), that he is engaged to an artist, is surprised when the bishop tells him his own history. The bishop recounts how, many years before, the rage of New York had been the great diva Margherita Cavallini (Doris Keane♦), and how, as the new rector of St. Giles, he had been invited to meet her at a fashionable soiree. Strait-laced enough to have reservations about such a meeting and wondering if Cavallini were a proper lady, he told a beautiful young woman at the affair of his doubts. She was, of course, Cavallini. He fell in love instantly. Later he was revolted to learn she had been a man's mistress, but his love was such that he forced himself to overlook her past. Cavallini, however, realized their worlds were far apart, and though she loved him, walked out of his life to allow him to continue his calling. As the bishop finishes his story, he is brought the evening paper, which announces Cavallini's death. After Harry has gone, he pulls from his pocket some faded violets and a woman's handkerchief.

One of the greatest successes of its decade, it held the stage with some regularity for over a dozen years. A musical version, *My Romance* (1948), failed, despite a pleasing Sigmund Romberg♦ score.

ROMBERG, SIGMUND (1887–1951) The Hungarian-born composer was slated to become an engineer, but when sent to Vienna he took work at the Theatre-an-der-Wien and studied with Richard Heuberger. Coming to America in 1909, he accepted odd jobs until he could establish his own small dance band and publish some songs. These songs came to the attention of the Messrs. Shubert, ♦ who signed him as their house composer in 1914. In 1916 alone he wrote music for at least six of their shows. Most of the songs were tinny ragtime melodies. A year earlier he had enjoyed his first enduring success with "Auf Wiedersehn," which was one of his additions to Eysler's score for *The Blue Paradise,* but he did not begin to gain real recognition until he was allowed to compose a score entirely in his own middle-European idiom for *Maytime*♦ (1917), from which came "The Road to Paradise" and "Will You Remember?" He returned to hack work but scored a major success with his redactions of Schubert melodies for *Blossom Time*♦ (1921), including "Song of Love." Four huge successes followed later in the 1920s: *The Student Prince*♦ (1924), whose score included "Deep in My Heart, Dear," "Drinking Song," "Golden Days," and "Serenade"; *The Desert Song*♦ (1926), from which came the title song as well as "One Alone" and "The Riff Song"; *My Maryland*♦ (1927), which gave us "Mother," "Silver Moon," "Will You Marry Me?," and "Your Land and My Land"; and *The New Moon*♦ (1928), recalled for "Lover, Come Back to Me," "One Kiss," "Softly, as in a Morning Sunrise," and "Stouthearted Men." With the coming of the Depression and the rise of Nazism the vogue for German-style operettas waned, and Romberg had little success in the 1930s. However, he scored a final success in 1945 with a bit of nostalgic Americana, *Up in Central Park,* ♦ whose hit was "Close as Pages in a Book." After his death his underrated score for *The Girl in Pink Tights* (1954) was offered to Broadway. In all he composed songs for nearly sixty Broadway musicals.

Romberg was often accused of borrowing themes from classic compositions and his music often seems less original and less passionate than that of his principal rival, Rudolf Friml.♦ Nevertheless, the pair was almost solely responsible for the great outpouring of gorgeous, memorable melodies in the final American heyday of traditional operetta.

Biography: *Deep in My Heart,* Elliott Arnold, New York, 1949.

ROME, Harold [Jacob] (b. 1908) Born in Hartford, Conn., he studied both law and architecture at Yale, then accepted work as a draftsman. He quit that job to work at a summer camp, where he began composing songs for camp shows. His first Broadway score was for the union revue *Pins and Needles*♦ (1937) and included "Sing Me a Song with Social Significance." Later shows have included *Sing Out the News* (1938), from which came "FDR Jones"; *Call Me Mister* (1946), which offered "South

America, Take It Away"; *Wish You Were Here* (1952), remembered for "Where Did the Night Go?" and the title song; *Fanny*♦ (1954), whose biggest hit was its title song; *Destry Rides Again* (1959); and *I Can Get It for You Wholesale* (1962). Rome served as his own lyricist. Stanley Green♦ has written, "The ability to express in songs honest emotions of those who are least articulate has been one of his most distinguishing characteristics. For Rome is, essentially, a people's composer and lyricist who . . . provides the common man with uncommon musical expressions."

Romeo and Juliet Shakespeare's♦ greatest love story was first unveiled for New Yorkers in 1754 with Mr. Rigby and Mrs. Hallam♦ heading the cast. It has retained its popularity ever since. Although the leading 19th-century actors often played Romeo, the fashion for "trouser roles" at the time allowed Charlotte Cushman♦ and other celebrated actresses to assume the part as well. Adelaide Neilson♦ and Julia Marlowe♦ were among the most admired Juliets. Curiously, a rare old recording made by Miss Marlowe and E. H. Sothern♦ of their reading of the balcony scene suggests that performances of the period might have been too lush for modern tastes. In more recent years Ethel Barrymore,♦ Jane Cowl,♦ and Katharine Cornell♦ have found varying luck in the part. One reason for Miss Barrymore's failure may have been that she assigned the part of Romeo to a minor actor, McKay Morris, thus turning the play into a one-star vehicle and upsetting its balance. Miss Cowl and Miss Cornell were craftier, hiring Rollo Peters♦ and Basil Rathbone♦ respectively. All these artists were no longer truly young, so that they incorporated a change, begun by Ellen Terry,♦ of making Juliet eighteen or nineteen years old instead of fourteen. As his wife's director, Guthrie McClintic♦ also restored many important cuts, including the "Gallop apace, you fiery-footed steeds" speech which had been dropped at least since Miss Neilson's day. Laurence Olivier♦ and Vivian Leigh presented their version in 1940. The musical *West Side Story*♦ (1957) was suggested by the play, but set its action in contemporary New York and had the lovers associated not with rival families but with rival street gangs.

Room Service, a farce in three acts by John Murray and Allen Boretz. Produced by George Abbott♦ at the Cort Theatre. May 19, 1937. 500 performances.

Gordon Miller (Sam Levene♦), a penny-ante producer, has a play, a director named Harry Binion (Philip Loeb), a cast of twenty-two actors, and the promise of a theatre but no money. He sells a 10 percent interest in the show to Joseph Gribble (Cliff Dunstan), the manager of the White Way Hotel, in return for lodging his entire entourage. But when the bills mount the hotel attempts to oust the company. Miller has his not very bright playwright, Leo Davis (Eddie Albert◆), pretend he is too ill to move. The ploy is threatened with exposure, so Miller and Binion announce Davis has committed suicide, and they stall for time by claiming they must attend to the funeral. In desperation the hotel helps finance the play, which becomes a smash hit.

The play was originally produced by Sam H. Harris,◆ who withdrew it on tryout. Abbott took over, helped rewrite it, and directed it. Richard Watts, Jr.,◆ of the *Post* welcomed it as "the funniest play that New York has seen in years and years." The play was later made into a Marx Brothers◆ film. A 1983 revival closed before reaching New York. In 1985 an off-Broadway revival was well received. Boretz (1900–1986) was a New Yorker who wrote material for several revues and also wrote several failed plays. Murray [né Pfeferstein] (1906–84) was also a New Yorker and also wrote revue material. This was their only successful play.

ROONEY, Pat[rick James], Jr. (1880–1962) The tiny, pixieish performer, a native New Yorker, was the son of another famous vaudevillian, the first Pat Rooney (1844–92), who was also known for his song and dance routines. The younger Rooney and his wife, Marion Bent (1879–1940), became one of vaudeville's most popular teams. Among his most applauded numbers was "The Daughter of Rosie O'Grady," to which he did a clog dance while nonchalantly keeping his hands in his pockets. He also appeared with his wife in musical comedy and revue, notably in *Love Birds* (1921). After arthritis forced his wife to retire, he continued to perform alone. One of his memorable appearances was in *Guys and Dolls*◆ (1950), in which he introduced "More I Cannot Wish You." His son, Pat Rooney III (1909–79), occasionally performed with him and sometimes did a solo song and dance act.

ROOSEVELT, Franklin Delano When George M. Cohan◆ portrayed Roosevelt as the central figure in the musical *I'd Rather Be Right* (1937), it marked the first time an incumbent President had been so featured. The George S. Kaufman◆-Moss Hart◆ libretto treated him affectionately. The major work to treat of him after his death has been *Sunrise at Campobello*◆ (1958), which looked at his struggle

with polio. He also was an important character in the musical *Annie*◆ (1977).

ROSE, [William Samuel] Billy [né Rosenberg] (1899–1966) The feisty, bantam, theatrical jack-of-many-trades was born in New York. He began his theatrical career as a lyricist writing the words for such hits as "A Cup of Coffee, a Sandwich, and You" for *Charlot's Revue of 1926* and the title song for *Great Day* (1929). Turning producer, he brought to Broadway *Sweet and Low* (1930) and a reworked version, *Billy Rose's Crazy Quilt* (1931), *The Great Magoo* (1932), *Jumbo*◆ (1935), *Carmen Jones*◆ (1943), and *Seven Lively Arts* (1944). He also owned the National Theatre, which he renamed the Billy Rose, and the Ziegfeld Theatre,◆ which he eventually sold to developers. Besides regular theatre work he ran "Aquacades" at the New York and San Francisco World's Fairs and several popular night clubs. For a time he was married to Fanny Brice.◆

Biography: *Only a Paper Moon: The Theatre of Billy Rose,* Stephen Nelson, Ann Arbor, 1987.

ROSE, Edward E[verett] (1862–1939) Born in Stanstead, Quebec, and educated at Harvard, he became at the turn of the century the most prolific and respected adapter of novels for the stage. He was less successful as a rule when he tried his hand at original drama. Among his most successful redactions were *The Prisoner of Zenda*◆ (1895), *Under the Red Robe*◆ (1896), *David Harum*◆ (1900), *Richard Carvel*◆ (1900), *Janice Meredith* (1900), *Alice of Old Vincennes* (1901), and *Penrod* (1918). Nearly fifty of his works reached the boards. He also was successful at direction, his hits including *The Pride of Jennico*◆ (1900) and *Alias Jimmy Valentine*◆ (1910).

ROSE, George [Walter] (1920–88) The English actor made his American debut with the Old Vic◆ in 1946, but first gained major attention when he portrayed The Common Man in *A Man for All Seasons* (1961). Among his later roles were Martin Ruiz, the conquistador-narrator, in *The Royal Hunt of the Sun* (1965), Alfred P. Doolittle in 1968 and 1972 revivals of *My Fair Lady,*◆ the effeminate Henry in *My Fat Friend* (1974), Hawkins, the knowing servant, in *The Kingfisher* (1978), Captain Hook in a 1979 revival of *Peter Pan,* ◆ and Major-General Stanley in a 1981 revival of *The Pirates of Penzance.* ◆ In 1985 he was co-starred as the Reverend Ernest Lynton in a revival of *Aren't We All?,* and later the same year was co-starred in the musical *The Mystery of Edwin Drood.*

Rose-Marie, a musical in two acts. Book and lyrics by Otto Harbach♦ and Oscar Hammerstein II.♦ Music by Rudolf Friml♦ and Herbert Stothart.♦ Produced by Arthur Hammerstein♦ at the Imperial Theatre. September 2, 1924. 557 performances.

Rose-Marie La Flamme (Mary Ellis) works at Lady Jane's, a small hotel in the Canadian Rockies. She is courted by both Jim Kenyon (Dennis King♦) and the villainous Ed Hawley (Frank Greene), who manages to throw blame for the murder of the Indian Black Eagle (Arthur Ludwig) on his rival. The truth was that Black Eagle had found his wife Wanda (Pearl Regay) with Hawley, and Wanda had killed her husband when he attacked Hawley. A clever trader, Hard-Boiled Herman (William Kent), tricks Wanda into a confession, so Rose-Marie and Jim are free to wed.

Principal songs: Indian Love Call · The Mounties · Rose-Marie

The musical sparked the revival of traditional operetta after World War I. The war had made operetta, which many perceived as German and therefore enemy entertainment, unwelcome, and shortly after the war the era of Cinderella musical comedies had taken over. However, the excellence of the writing and the freshness of the setting coupled with the long-dormant appeal of operetta allowed this musical a singular success. It was the biggest international musical hit of the decade, offering not only several American road companies but running 851 performances in London and establishing a Paris long-run record of 1,250 performances.

Rose Michel Steele MacKaye's♦ adaptation of Ernest Blum's French drama was first played at the Union Square Theatre♦ in 1875. The story told of the dilemma of the heroine who must choose between revealing that her husband is a murderer and destroying the happiness and forthcoming marriage of her daughter. Rose Eytinge♦ played the title role. The play was one of the biggest hits of its decade and was revived occasionally for the rest of the century.

Rose of the Rancho, The, a play in three acts by David Belasco♦ and Richard Walton Tully.♦ Produced by Belasco at the Belasco Theatre. November 27, 1906. 327 performances.

Lawless Americans are seizing Spanish land in California and, if necessary, killing the Spaniards who own the land and have developed it. A young man named Kearney (Charles Richman♦) has been sent from Washington to investigate matters and has

fallen in love with Juanita (Frances Starr♦), the half-American daughter of one of the old Spanish landowners. She falls in love with Kearney, rejecting family pleas to marry a Spaniard. Her family's property is being menaced by the vicious Kinkaid (John W. Cope), who succeeds in making it appear that Kearney is helping him seize the land. This turns Juanita against Kearney for the moment, but when the truth comes out she is free to marry him.

The production was one of Belasco's many triumphs of theatricality—that is, of brilliantly detailed production and clever appeal to immediate emotion—over form and substance.

Rose Tattoo, The, a play in three acts by Tennessee Williams.♦ Produced by Cheryl Crawford♦ at the Martin Beck Theatre. February 3, 1951. 306 performances.

In a small village on the Gulf Coast, the passionate and devout Sicilian-American, Serafina della Rosa (Maureen Stapleton♦), lives with an idealized memory of her late husband, a truck driver. But, for all the defenses she builds, the truth about her husband's many infidelities are eventually brought home to her and threaten to destroy her until Alvaro Mangiacavallo (Eli Wallach♦) comes into her life. He too is a truck driver, and his warmth and ebullience help restore Serafina's zest for life. Happy again, she even encourages a budding romance between her daughter Rosa (Phyllis Love) and a young sailor, Jack Hunter (Don Murray).

The play had been written with Italian film star Anna Magnani in mind, but she refused to play it on stage, though she eventually made the film version. Many critics were disturbed by Williams's growing penchant for symbolism, which was woven through the work.

Rosedale; or, The Rifle Ball, a play in five acts by Lester Wallack.♦ Produced at Wallack's Theatre. September 30, 1863. 125 performances.

Lady Florence May (Mrs. Hoey♦) is a widow whose late husband stipulated in his will that if she remarry without the consent of his uncle, Col. Cavendish May (H. F. Daly), she would forfeit her inheritance, half of which would go to her young son and half to the Colonel. The Colonel plots to kill the child and either to push Florence into remarrying without his consent or to break her heart. To this end he connives with the blackguard Miles McKenna (John Gilbert♦). Meanwhile, Elliot Grey (Wallack), a former suitor of Lady Florence, returns to the village. He has become a soldier of fortune since being rejected, but remains loyal and loving.

Matthew Leigh (Charles Fisher♦), a local doctor, also loves Florence. Years before, Matthew's baby brother had been stolen by gypsies, so when McKenna tells him he is that same younger brother and now has a criminal record, Matthew breaks off his suit. McKenna and the Colonel then kidnap Florence's son. But Elliot Grey retrieves the child and reveals that he, Elliot, is Matthew's real lost brother. Matthew and Florence are free to wed.

This complicated, often preposterous and action-filled melodrama was one of Wallack's biggest successes, remaining in the company's repertory until the end. That such a piece could have so vast an appeal to audiences in New York's most elite playhouse suggests that the difference between Bowery melodrama and many of Wallack's plays was one of degree not kind. Even after Wallack's company disbanded, the play was revived regularly for the rest of the century. Based on a novel called *Lady Lee's Widowhood,* the authorship of the dramatization was sometimes questioned, but it is now generally conceded to have been Wallack's own.

ROSENFELD, SYDNEY (1855–1931) A curious figure in Broadway theatrical history, he was born in Richmond, Va., and later claimed he was smuggled through enemy lines during the Civil War so that he might attend school in New York. He apparently began his theatrical career by adapting foreign plays but soon turned his hand to any sort of writing that might turn a profit. Alone or with collaborators he wrote such diverse fare as the burlesque *Well-Fed Dora* (1884); W. H. Crane's♦ vehicle *The Senator*♦ (1890); the libretto for the first major revue, *The Passing Show*♦ (1894); the book and lyrics for the operetta *The Mocking Bird* (1902); and the book for the popular Elsie Janis♦ musical, *The Vanderbilt Cup* (1906). He was often accused of plagiarism and in one celebrated case was stopped from mounting a pirated production of *The Mikado*♦ in 1885. He continued to produce and write actively until the end of World War I. In all, about fifty of his works reached Broadway. He was also editor of the popular humor periodical *Puck.* A rival adapter and librettist, Harry B. Smith,♦ noted, "His distinguishing physical feature is an umbrageous hirsute thatch worn à la Pompadour."

ROSS, JERRY, see *Adler, Richard*

ROSTAND, EDMOND (1868–1918) The romantic French dramatist is known in this country almost entirely for one work, his masterpiece, *Cyrano de Bergerac*♦ (1898). His *L'Aiglon* is recalled largely as a vehicle for Sarah Bernhardt,♦ who included it in her American tours. Much was expected of his *Chantecler,* which Charles Frohman♦ offered in 1911 with Maude Adams♦ as star, but the production was a costly failure.

Round Up, The, a drama in four acts by Edmund Day. Produced by Klaw♦ and Erlanger♦ at the New Amsterdam Theatre.♦ August 26, 1907. 155 performances.

When guilt at having stolen his best friend's wife becomes too much for Jack Payson (Orme Caldara♦), he heads out into the desert to seek that former buddy, Dick Lane (Wright Kramer). Lane is a mining engineer who has sought to forget his bitterness by accepting work in dangerous and forsaken places. Just as the men meet, a band of Apaches attacks the encampment. The two men fight side by side until Lane is killed and the Indians routed, after which Payson can return home with a somewhat clearer conscience.

A rather strange story, since the man who comes out best was the less likable of the two and since the woman in question never appears, the play found much of its appeal from the performance of Maclyn Arbuckle♦ as Sheriff "Slim" Hoover, who is resigned that "nobody can love a fat man."

Day (1866–1923), a New Yorker, was an actor-turned-playwright whose works included a farce-comedy, *The Head-Waiters* (1902); a melodramatic vehicle for boxer Jim Corbett, *Pals* (1905); and a comedy for Lillian Russell,♦ *The Widow's Might* (1909).

Roundabout Theatre Company Founded in 1965 by Gene Feist to present seasons of revivals of notable plays, the group first performed in a church, then in the basement of a supermarket before finding a home in a converted cinema. In 1984 the company moved to the old Tammany Hall building off Union Square. Jane Alexander, Jim Dale,♦ Anthony Hopkins, and Irene Worth♦ are among the distinguished performers who have appeared in a broad range of plays including Shakespeare and classical Greek drama, but emphasizing 19th- and 20th-century British works. The company takes pride in having the largest list of regular subscribers in New York.

ROUVEROL, AURANIA, see *Skidding*

Row at the Lyceum, A; or, Green Room Secrets, a play in one act by John Brougham.♦ Produced by

Brougham at Brougham's Lyceum. April 22, 1851. 21 performances.

As the audience enters it finds actors and others associated with the blank-verse tragedy, *Horror on Horror's Head; or, The Liar and the Slave,* about to begin a rehearsal. Just as the session starts one of the performers (Mrs. Brougham) objects to the smallness of her part. Her complaint brings her to the attention of a man in the audience (Brougham), who jumps up, claims she is his wife, and demands she leave the stage. From the gallery come the shouts of a fireman (W. J. Florence♦) who threatens to whip the protester if he touches his wife. A ruckus ensues, stopping the rehearsal. Both the supposed husband and fireman run on stage, where they are grabbed by the police. At this point all the performers turn to the audience, while one of them recites an epilogue confessing that the row at the Lyceum was all a joke.

A refreshing bit of zany nonsense, quite untypical of the theatre of its day, it was, however, typical of the adventurous, wide-ranging, and free-spirited Brougham, who was also a pioneer of musical revue.

ROWE, GEORGE FAWCETT (1834–89) Little is known about the early years of this actor and playwright, who was advertised as being "from the London and Australian theatres" when he made his New York debut in 1866. As a performer his most successful roles were as the comic upstart Digby Grant in *Two Roses* (1872); Wilkins Micawber in *Little Em'ly* (1874); and Hawkeye in his own dramatization of Cooper's *Leatherstocking; or, The Last of the Mohicans* (1874). His other writings ranged from his burlesque for Lydia Thompson,♦ *Mephisto and the Four Sensations* (1873) to his adaptation of Feuillet's♦ melodrama *The Sphinx* (1874) for Clara Morris.♦

Royal Family, The, a comedy in three acts by George S. Kaufman♦ and Edna Ferber.♦ Produced by Jed Harris♦ at the Selwyn Theatre. December 28, 1927. 343 performances.

The Cavendishes are the greatest acting family in America, presided over by the aging Fanny Cavendish (Haidee Wright). Her daughter Julie (Ann Andrews) is the leading contemporary actress, while Julie's daughter Gwen (Sylvia Field) is a promising ingenue. Both Julie and Gwen are toying with marriage and with abandoning the theatre. Fanny's dashingly handsome son Tony (Otto Kruger♦) could have been the greatest performer of all, but he prefers the celebrity that comes with being a film star and wild affairs with women. His escapades keep him perpetually on the run. Fanny's brother

Herbert Dean (Orlando Daly) is a fine farceur and former matinee idol who is fighting the ravages of age and of a faltering career. Hovering over the family is the great producer Oscar Wolfe (Jefferson De Angelis♦). For all their complaints about their lives, the call of the theatre is irresistible, so Julie leaves her own problems to rush off to meet a curtain and Fanny dies while planning yet another tour.

This uproarious send-up of the Barrymores♦ and the Drews♦ infuriated Ethel Barrymore,♦ but Brooks Atkinson♦ of the *Times* felt the authors had "toyed entertainingly and absorbingly with the madness of show folk and the fatal glamour of the footlights." The play has enjoyed numerous revivals.

Royal Shakespeare Company, THE An outgrowth of the Shakespearean theatre at Stratford-on-Avon in England, it expanded its repertory to include non-Shakespearean classics and modern plays when it opened a branch theatre in London. It has since come to be considered by many critics as the finest contemporary English acting ensemble. Although it has occasionally offered American playgoers examples of its Shakespearean productions since the mid-1960s, its most successful offerings here have been non-Shakespearean works. The most notable have been *Marat/Sade* (1965), a gymnastic, almost psychedelic *A Midsummer Night's Dream♦* (1971), *Sherlock Holmes♦* (1974), and *Nicholas Nickleby* (1981). These large-cast productions were striking for the skillful fluidity and dramatic effectiveness with which numbers of people were moved and testified to the excellence of such modern British directors as Peter Brook♦ and Trevor Nunn. Among the rising performers seen in these mountings were Glenda Jackson, Patrick Magee, Ian Richardson, Ben Kingsley, and John Wood.♦ *Nicholas Nickleby* occupied two evenings and charged $100 per ticket for the complete entertainment. Nevertheless it was its season's biggest hit. Other productions seen here, though not necessarily with their London casts, included *Old Times* (1972), *London Assurance♦* (1974), and *Piaf* (1981). In 1984 it offered mountings of *Cyrano de Bergerac♦* and *Much Ado About Nothing,♦* then in 1987 brought over its highly praised *Les Liaisons Dangereuses.*

ROYAL [DEWAR], TED (1904–81) The noted orchestrator was born in Skedee, Okla. and after attending the University of Kansas continued his musical studies in Houston and New York. His orchestrations were first heard by Broadway playgoers in *Too*

Many Girls (1939), and later in such shows as *Du Barry Was a Lady*♦ (1939), *Panama Hattie*♦ (1940), *Pal Joey*♦ (1940), *Mexican Hayride* (1944), *Annie Get Your Gun*♦ (1946), *Brigadoon*♦ (1947), *Where's Charley?*♦ (1948), *Guys and Dolls*♦ (1950), *House of Flowers*♦ (1954), and *Mr. Wonderful* (1956).

ROYCE, EDWARD (1870–1964) Born in Bath, England, he began his theatrical career as a set designer, but later took up dancing and became a choreographer, then finally turned to directing musical comedies. He was brought to this country at the suggestion of his friend Jerome Kern,♦ and his first New York assignment was creating the dances for *The Doll Girl* (1913), for which Kern supplied interpolations. His many subsequent successes, as director and sometimes also as choreographer, included *Oh, Boy!*♦ (1917), *Leave It to Jane*♦ (1917), *Going Up* (1917), *Oh, Lady! Lady!!*♦ (1918), *Apple Blossoms*♦ (1919), *Irene*♦ (1919), *Sally*♦ (1920), *Good Morning, Dearie* (1921), *Orange Blossoms* (1922), for which he was also co-producer, *Kid Boots* (1923), and *The Merry Malones* (1927).

ROYE, RUTH [née BECKER] (1895?–1960) Although she now appears to be totally forgotten, the tiny singer with the turned-up nose was one of vaudeville's most popular attractions, establishing a record of six consecutive weeks at the Palace—the longest for any woman single. Vaudeville historians Charles and Louise Samuels noted, "She created excitement with everything she sang. She delivered ballads well but her explosive delivery of such comic numbers as 'Mooching Along' and 'He's a Devil in His Own Home Town,' were what made her a sensation." She introduced "Abba Dabba Honeymoon" and was always associated with "Waiting for the Robert E. Lee," although she was not the first to sing it.

ROYLE, EDWIN MILTON (1862–1942) Born in Lexington, Mo., and educated at Salt Lake City's Collegiate Institute, Princeton, the University of Edinburgh, and Columbia Law School, he abandoned law to become an actor. His first play, *Friends* (1892), told of two men in love with the same girl and starred him and his wife, Selma Fetter Royle (1860–1955). In his later works he displayed a wide variety of skills, writing farce—*My Wife's Husbands* (1903); musical comedy—*Marrying Mary* (1906), the lyric version of *My Wife's Husbands;* and poetic tragedy—*Launcelot and Elaine* (1921). However, he is remembered largely for one melodrama, *The Squaw Man*♦ (1905), a story of an exiled Englishman in America and his tragic love for an Indian girl. In all, more than thirty of his plays were produced.

RUBINSTEIN, JOHN [ARTHUR] (b. 1946) Son of the famous pianist Arthur Rubinstein, he was born and educated in Los Angeles. He first called attention to himself on Broadway when he played the title role in the musical *Pippin*♦ (1972). Later he won applause as James Leeds, a teacher who falls in love with his deaf student, in *Children of a Lesser God*♦ (1980), and as Lt. Barney Greenwalt, the prosecutor, in a 1983 revival of *The Caine Mutiny Court-Martial*. He subsequently played leads off-Broadway and in replacement casts on Broadway.

RUBY, HARRY [né RUBINSTEIN] (1895–1974) The New York-born composer began his career as a vaudeville pianist. Later he joined with lyricist Bert Kalmar♦ to form one of the most successful songwriting teams in the decade or so after World War I. Beginning with *Helen of Troy, New York* (1923), he composed the scores and often collaborated on the librettos for eleven Broadway musicals, the most notable of which were: *The Ramblers* (1926), whose hit song was "All Alone Monday"; *The Five O'Clock Girl* (1927), remembered for "Thinking of You"; *Good Boy* (1928), from which came "I Wanna Be Loved by You"; and *Animal Crackers* (1928), which included Groucho Marx's♦ famous entrance number, "Hooray for Captain Spaulding."

RUNYON, [ALFRED] DAMON (1884–1946) Born in Manhattan, Kansas, the writer was long admired for his columns depicting raffish Broadway life for the Hearst papers and for his short stories of the same demi-monde. In 1935 he collaborated with Howard Lindsay♦ on *A Slight Case of Murder*, in which a gangster who is determined to reform finds the dead bodies of four other gangsters on his own property. However, playgoers will probably recall him longest as the author of the short stories which provided the basis for *Guys and Dolls.* ♦

Biography: *The Men Who Invented Broadway: Damon Runyon, Walter Winchell and Their World,* John Mosedale, New York, 1981.

RUSSELL, ANNIE (1864–1936) Born in Liverpool but raised in Canada, she made her first appearance in Montreal, playing opposite Rose Eytinge♦ in *Miss Multon* in 1872. Her New York debut was in 1879 as Josephine in a traveling juvenile company of *H.M.S. Pinafore.* ♦ She continued to play with various tours, including one that took her to South America and Australia, before scoring a major success as the girl whose newly rich parents would prevent her making a love match, the title role of *Esmeralda*♦ (1881). Among her later roles were the title part in a dramatization of Tennyson's *Lancelot and Elaine,* called simply *Elaine* (1887), and, after a long retirement because of illness, the role of the girl who marries a man she does not love to escape from her brutal father, the title part in Bret Harte's *Sue* (1896). She also played Winifred, the daugher of a kleptomaniac, in Fitch's♦ *The Girl and the Judge*♦ (1901). In her final active years she organized the Old English Comedy Company, in which she assumed such roles as Kate Hardcastle, Beatrice, Lydia Languish, and Lady Teazle. She retired in 1918. Odell♦ later wrote of this frail, darkish woman, with a slightly lugubrious face, "All who saw Miss Russell know how sweet she was either in comedy or in pathetic plays, and will recall gratefully her charm, her grace, her exquisite voice, her genuine dramatic power."

RUSSELL, LILLIAN [née HELEN LOUISE LEONARD] (1861–1922) The first great prima donna of the modern American musical stage, known to her admirers and the press as "Airy Fairy Lillian," she was born in Clinton, Iowa, where her father was the owner and editor of the local newspaper. She grew up in Chicago and then New York, taken there after her parents' divorce by her mother, a famous early advocate of women's rights. In New York she studied singing with Leopold Damrosch. Her professional debut came when she accepted a position in the chorus of E. E. Rice's♦ 1879 production of *H.M.S. Pinafore.*♦ One year later Tony Pastor♦ hired her, gave her her stage name, and featured her in his vaudeville. It was in his travesties of *Olivette, The Pirates of Penzance,*♦ and *Patience* that she caught the eyes and ears of New York's critics and playgoers. Her performance in the *Patience* parody led to her being cast in the Bijou Theatre's regular 1881 production of the comic opera, although her first major assignment had come several months earlier when she played the leading feminine role in Audran's *The Grand Mogul* (also known as *The Snake Charmer*). Between then and 1899 she appeared as the star of no fewer than 24 musicals, many of them written expressly for her. These included *Polly* (1885), *Pepita* (1886), *Dorothy* (1887), *The Grand Duchess*♦ (1889), *La Cigale* (1891), *Princess Nicotine* (1893), *La Périchole* (1895), *The Tzigane* (1895), *An American Beauty* (1896), and *The Wedding Day* (1897). In her prime

she was a gorgeous, well-proportioned, if ample, blue-eyed blonde. "Her voice," wrote her biographer, "while never rich, was at least a clear, full-throated, lyric soprano of true pitch and impressive quality." At the same time she was notorious for not paying bills, for not honoring contracts, for walking out both on her shows and her several husbands, and even for the callousness displayed in refusing to attend her father's funeral. When her popularity began to wane slightly she joined Weber♦ and Fields♦ in their famous music hall, remaining with them until 1903. It was in their 1902 production *Twirly-Whirly* that she sang "Come Down, Ma Evenin' Star," the only song she was ever to record. A musical version of *The School for Scandal* was written for her in 1904 and called *Lady Teazle.* Except for an appearance in the 1912 Weber and Fields reunion with *Hokey Pokey* it marked her last performance in a musical. She continued to act in vaudeville and in straight plays until shortly before her death, but it was commonly accepted that she was living on her reputation.

Biography: *Lillian Russell,* Parker Morell, New York, 1940.

RUSSELL, SOL SMITH (1848–1902) The lanky, bright-eyed comedian was born in Brunswick, Mo. and made his stage debut at the age of twelve in Jacksonville, Ill. He toured for many years both as an actor and as a monologist, whose most celebrated turn was the spoof of a European lecturer. He spent some time with Augustin Daly's♦ ensemble beginning in 1874, but was best known for three roles which he played around the country for many years: Tom Dilloway, the seeming ne'er-do-well, in *Edgewood Folks*♦ (1880); Noah Vale, the inventive, itinerant begger, in E. E. Kidder's♦ *A Poor Relation* (1889); and David Holmes, the dedicated bookworm who finds romance and fresh air with his young ward, in Martha Morton's♦ *A Bachelor's Romance* (1897).

RUSSELL, ROSALIND (1912–76) The glamorous comedienne was born in Waterbury, Conn. She studied at the American Academy of Dramatic Arts,♦ then played in stock before making her New York debut in the 1930 edition of the *Garrick Gaieties.*♦ Minor roles followed, after which she went to Hollywood, where she became a major film star. She returned to the stage in 1951 to tour as Gillian, the love-struck witch, in *Bell, Book and Candle.*♦ Her two major Broadway assignments were the lead in the musical *Wonderful Town*♦

(1953) and as the wildly unconventional guardian of a young boy, the title role in *Auntie Mame*♦ (1956).

RYAN, DENNIS (d. 1786) Virtually nothing is known about this early actor-manager. With his wife he performed in New York in 1783, then later that year headed a company that played in Baltimore and toured the South. In keeping with the times he played everything from Iago and Falstaff and Young Marlow in *She Stoops To Conquer* to numerous roles in long forgotten contemporary works.

RYERSON, FLORENCE, see *Harriet*

RYSKIND, MORRIE (1895–1985) Born in New York, where he studied at Columbia, he began his theatrical career by writing sketches and lyrics for *The 49ers* (1922) and *Merry-Go-Round* (1927). With George S. Kaufman♦ he wrote the book for *Animal Crackers* (1928), then helped revise Kaufman's book for *Strike Up the Band*♦ (1930). He shared a Pulitzer Prize♦ with Kaufman and Ira Gershwin♦ for his work on *Of Thee I Sing*♦ (1931) and afterwards rejoined them for *Let 'Em Eat Cake* (1933). In 1940 he wrote the book for *Louisiana Purchase*. His other theatre work was all for failed musicals. He was also a writer of screenplays.

S

Sabrina Fair, a comedy in two acts by Samuel Taylor.♦ Produced by the Playwrights' Company♦ at the National Theatre. November 11, 1953. 318 performances.

The Larrabees are extremely rich Long Islanders with two eligible sons, the wayward David (Scott McKay) and the misanthropic Linus, Jr. (Joseph Cotten♦). They also have a chauffeur, Fairchild (Russell Collins), whose brilliant daughter Sabrina (Margaret Sullavan♦) has just returned from a stint in Paris. David and several other local boys court her, but she recalls that as a child it was Linus, Jr., whom she loved. Now Linus seems unreceptive. However, he has not bargained on Sabrina's charm and insinuating ways. Whether he wins her or she wins him is moot. To add icing to the cake, Linus, Sr. (John Cromwell♦) discovers that Fairchild has been quietly playing the stock market and is a very rich man in his own right.

Brooks Atkinson♦ welcomed the work as one written "with taste and good humor about agreeable people."

SACKLER, HOWARD, see *Great White Hope, The*

SADDLER, FRANK (d. 1921) The Pennsylvania-born, Munich-educated orchestrator was one of the first in his field who was not also an active composer or conductor although early in his career he led pit bands at burlesque theatres. George Gershwin♦ called him "the father of modern arranging." He is credited with bringing to the musical comedy orchestra pit the elegant, polished sound that had usually been heard only in the best operettas. Up to the time of his death he orchestrated almost all of Jerome Kern's♦ shows, including *Very Good Eddie*♦ (1915), *Oh, Boy!*♦ (1917), *Oh, Lady! Lady!!*♦ (1918), *The Night Boat* (1920), and *Sally*♦ (1920). He also arranged the music for the Hippodrome♦ extravaganzas presented by Dillingham♦ as well as such other Dillingham shows as *Watch Your Step*♦ (1914), *Stop! Look! Listen!* (1915), *Jack o' Lantern* (1917), and *Tip Top* (1920).

Sag Harbor, a play in four acts by James A. Herne.♦ Produced by Liebler and Co.♦ at the Republic Theatre. September 27, 1900. 76 performances.

Two brothers, Ben (Forrest Robinson) and Frank Turner (Lionel Barrymore♦), both love Martha Reese (Julie A. Herne). Although she loves Frank, she marries the older Ben out of a sense of obligation. Two years later Frank reappears and almost persuades Martha to elope with him. Only the intervention of Captain Dan Marble (Herne), who recounts the disastrous results of a similar elopement, dissuades the couple.

Herne's last play, it was deemed by many to be merely a rewriting of his early *Hearts of Oak,* albeit Herne publicly denied this. Critics admired Herne's warm performance but were sharply divided on the merits of the drama. The *Commercial Advertiser,* speaking for the majority who rejected the work, noted, "It looks as if he had set about the construction of a popular drama with a certain local atmosphere, without having a story to tell, a character to present, or one strong mood to create; in short, without having anything to say."

Sailor, Beware!, a comedy in two acts by Kenyon Nicholson♦ and Charles Robinson. Produced by Courtney Burr at the Lyceum Theatre. ♦ September 28, 1933. 500 performances.

When the crew of the *U.S.S. Dakota* arrives in the Canal Zone, the men decide to see if their leading man with the ladies, Chester "Dynamite" Jones (Bruce MacFarlane), can win the cold heart of Billie "Stonewall" Jackson (Audrey Christie), the celebrated night-club hostess at the Idle Hour Cafe. Bets are placed both by the sailors and the girls at the night club, and "Dynamite" and "Stonewall" are brought together. For a while an immovable object confronts an irresistible force, until Billie learns that the sailors have called off their bets.

Despite a large cast and an elaborate, expensive-to-run production, this rowdy but funny comedy became one of the most profitable successes of the Depression. Charles Knox Robinson (1909–80), a New Yorker, had several other plays produced, the most successful of which was a Walter Huston♦ vehicle, *Apple of His Eye* (1946).

Saint Joan Winifred Lenihan♦ was the first American Joan in the Theatre Guild's♦ 1923 production of Shaw's♦ play. Although some critics felt her performance was too undisciplined and frenetic to be totally satisfying, Lawrence Langner,♦ looking back over several decades, insisted her "courage, fervor and youth" made her the best Joan he had ever seen. Prior commitments had forced Katharine Cornell♦ to refuse to read for the part in 1923, when she was said to have been the leading candidate. However, she headed the cast of her own 1936 revival, whose supporting players included Brian Aherne,♦ Tyrone Power,♦ Arthur Byron,♦ Charles Waldron,♦ and Kent Smith. John Anderson of the *Journal* observed, "Her performance is enkindled by the spiritual exaltation of a transcendent heroine." In 1951 Uta Hagen♦ starred as the Maid, giving a determined, totally believable performance which paid only small attention to the mystic aspects behind the story. Less successful was a 1956 Phoenix Theatre♦ revival in which Siobhan McKenna made Joan into a fanatic, not very intelligent Irish serving girl.

St. Louis Municipal Outdoor Theatre Known locally as "The Muny," it was opened in a huge amphitheatre in the city's Forest Park in 1919 with a production of *Robin Hood.*♦ Since then it has mounted an annual summer season of revivals, with occasional new musicals on the bill. Major stars have often appeared with the group. Since 1982 it has sponsored a "Broadway Series" which offers touring musicals, during the colder months, at the Fox, a converted film house.

SAKS, GENE [JEAN MICHAEL] (b. 1921) A native New Yorker, he was graduated from Cornell then spent several years studying acting. He performed on and off-Broadway for more than a decade before turning to directing in the early 1960s. Among his major directorial assignments have been *Enter Laughing* (1963), *Half a Sixpence* (1965), *Generation* 1965), *Mame*♦ (1966), *Same Time, Next Year*♦ (1975), *California Suite* (1976), *I Love My Wife* (1977), *Brighton Beach Memoirs*♦ (1983), *Biloxi Blues*♦ (1985), *Broadway Bound*♦ (1986), and *Rumors* (1988). He is probably the best stager of comedies of his generation.

Sally, a musical comedy in three acts. Book by Guy Bolton.♦ Lyrics mostly by Clifford Grey. Music by Jerome Kern.♦ Produced by Florenz Ziegfeld♦ at the New Amsterdam Theatre.♦ December 21, 1920. 570 performances.

Sally Rhinelander (Marilyn Miller♦), an orphan and a dishwasher at the Elm Tree Alley Inn, is befriended by her co-worker "Connie" (Leon Errol♦), the exiled Duke Constantine of Czechogovinia, and by the rich young bachelor Blair Farquar (Irving Fisher). She later substitutes for a dancer at a party Blair has thrown. This leads to a fight between her and Blair, but also to a contract to dance in the *Ziegfeld Follies*. She becomes a big hit, and she and Blair are reconciled.

Principal songs: Look For the Silver Lining · Whip-Poor-Will · Wild Rose

Hailed by Charles Darnton of the *World* as "nothing less than idealized musical comedy," the show was one of its era's biggest and most beloved successes and established the beautiful, light-footed Miss Miller as the leading female musical star of her era. A 1948 revival, without Miss Miller, Ziegfeld's flair, and Joseph Urban's♦ great designs, failed.

Salomy Jane [also known as *Salomy Jane's Kiss*], a play in four acts by Paul Armstrong.♦ Produced by Liebler and Co.♦ at the Liberty Theatre. January 19, 1907. 122 performances.

When Salomy (Eleanor Robson♦) is molested by an insistent suitor, a stranger (H. B. Warner♦) shoots the man. Although she learns that the stranger shot the molester for personal reasons, she helps him escape a lynch mob.

Armstrong based the play on a Bret Harte story.

Salvation Nell, a play in three acts by Edward Sheldon.♦ Produced by Harrison Grey Fiske♦ at the Hackett Theatre. November 17, 1908. 71 performances.

Nell Saunders (Mrs. Fiske♦) is a scrubwoman at Sid McGovern's seedy bar on Tenth Avenue. She is loved by the ne'er-do-well Jim Platt (Holbrook Blinn♦). When Al McGovern (John Dillon) makes advances to Nell, a fight ensues and Jim kills Al. After Jim is taken away by the police, Myrtle Odell (Hope Latham), a prostitute who is a habituée of the bar, attempts to persuade Nell to adopt her trade. Nell refuses the offer, and instead comes under the guidance of Major Williams (David Glassford) of the Salvation Army. With her newfound fervor she awaits Jim's release from prison. At first Jim is appalled and offended by Nell's attempts to reform him, but her goodness and perseverance finally win him over. When he confesses, "I need yer help!," she answers, "I want ye to take me home."

Sheldon's first success and one of Mrs. Fiske's most memorable vehicles, *Theatre Magazine* wrote of it, " 'Salvation Nell' is from the heart of the times . . . The intent is not to entertain us with the disagreeable or to make us acquainted with vice for our amusement. It is all incidental to the pity and sympathy which it should evoke."

SALVINI, Tommaso (1829–1916) The distinguished Italian tragedian made five American visits between 1873 and 1889. He had a majestic figure and a mobile face with a large forehead, dark, striking eyes, and an aquiline nose. His voice has been described as "one of the most powerful, flexible, and mellifluous organs ever implanted in a human throat." He made his debut in his greatest role, Othello. Critics were laudatory, even ecstatic, all the while recognizing that his was no traditional Moor. However, Henry Austin Clapp♦ observed, "It seemed to me that his Othello was Shakespeare orientalized and supersensualized, at the cost of some of the Master's heroic conception, and of much of the Poet's beautiful thought. Salvini knew that Othello was a Moor, and a Moor he would have him in body, soul and spirit . . . a tawny barbarian, exuberant with the qualities assigned to his race . . . in the fierce savagery of his jealous rage, during the last half of the play, the imaginative grace and beauty of many passages were smothered and lost." His performance was so violent that when he later played opposite American performers many actresses refused to be his Desdemona. Those later performances, in which he continued to speak in Italian while the others played in English, were nonetheless notable evenings. The most memorable of these bilingual productions were several in which he co-starred with Edwin Booth,♦ playing Othello and the Ghost to Booth's Iago and Hamlet. Among his other roles were Hamlet, Macbeth, King Lear, Coriolanus, Ingomar, and Paolo. His son Alessandro (1860–96) enjoyed some American success.

Autobiography: *Leaves from the Autobiography of T. Salvini,* New York, 1893.

Same Time, Next Year, a comedy in two acts by Bernard Slade.♦ Produced at the Brooks Atkinson Theatre. March 13, 1975. 1,453 performances.

In 1951 George (Charles Grodin), a businessman from New Jersey, and Doris (Ellen Burstyn♦), a California housewife, meet while George is on a trip. They soon are in bed together in a motel. Although both are married, they find the affair so pleasant that they agree to meet each year in February for a brief tryst. During each annual rendezvous they grow to know each other better, exchange confidences and even fall in love, but never, apparently, seriously consider divorce and

marriage. The meetings keep up for twenty-four years, and promise to go on indefinitely.

The comedy was recognized as one of the better of the many one-set, two-character plays forced on the theatre by the crushing economics of the day.

Sam'l of Posen; or, The Commercial Drummer, a play in four acts by George H. Jessop. ♦ Produced at Haverly's Fourteenth Street Theatre. May 16, 1881. 96 performances.

Samuel Plastrick (M. B. Curtis) is a Polish immigrant who would like to give up his work as a traveling salesman and settle down, especially after he meets Rebecca Heyman [in some programs Dreyfus] (Gertie Granville), whose uncle was a friend of his father back in the old country. Rebecca and her friend Jack Cheviot (Nelson Decker) obtain work for him at Mr. Winslow's jewelry store. Jack is Mr. Winslow's nephew and leads a dissipated life but wants to reform and marry Ellen (Carrie Wyatt). Unfortunately, another nephew of Winslow's, Frank Kilday (Frank Losee), implicates Jack in a crime of which Jack is really innocent. Winslow (Welsh Edwards) fires Jack, Rebecca, and Samuel. The determined Samuel sets out to get the goods on the real criminal, Frank. He does, in time for a happy ending.

Curtis is said to have commissioned Jessop to write a play in which the central figure was a good Jew. With Edward Marble, Curtis later rewrote the play and took credit for it. He continued to play the title role for over a dozen years.

Samuel French, Inc. For many decades the leading licenser of plays to amateur theatres, it was founded in the early 1850s by Samuel French (1821–98), who was born in Randolph, Mass. His early years are obscure, but by the late 1830s he was peddling cheap editions and pulp literature. Sometime between 1846 and 1854 he began publishing plays. In 1854 he initiated the series known as French's American Drama and shortly thereafter bought out his major competitor, William Taylor and Co., for whom he had served briefly as an agent. He moved to England in 1872 to open a London branch, leaving his sons in charge of his American enterprises. The company eventually had branches in all major English-speaking theatrical centers. For many years it offered services in allied fields, such as make-up and costuming, but they have long since been abandoned. In recent times the company has begun to license musicals as well as straight plays. Its "acting editions" provide detailed stage directions as well as helpful information on scenery, props, and other matters.

San Francisco (California) While the city did not join the theatrical ranks until relatively late, it soon became an exciting and major center. Shortly after the 1849 Gold Rush eccentric impresarios such as "Doc" Robinson♦ came to the fore, but they were quickly replaced by more durable figures. Thomas Maguire♦ was a major manager; Mrs. Judah♦ a popular actress. Lawrence Barrett♦ and John McCullough♦ also spent significant portions of their careers there, while David Belasco♦ received his earliest training in the city's playhouses. Among the famous theatres were the raffish Bella Union,♦ the Tivoli Opera House,♦ the Baldwin,♦ and the California.♦ New theatres were quickly built after the 1906 earthquake. Among the important figures and organizations to emerge were Homer Curran,♦ Edwin Lester,♦ and their San Francisco Light Opera Company. After World War II the city saw the rise of the Actor's Workshop♦ and the American Conservatory Theatre♦ as well as numerous interesting off-Broadway style groups.

San Francisco Minstrels Founded in San Francisco in the early 1850s by Charley Backus,♦ Billy Birch,♦ and others under the sponsorship of Thomas Maguire,♦ the troupe went to New York in 1865. It became that city's longest-lived and last permanent minstrel company, surviving until it was absorbed by J. H. Haverly♦ in 1883. Backus and Birch remained its headliners virtually until the end. Minstrel historian Robert C. Toll noted that the troupe was "considered unrivaled masters of the freewheeling, spontaneous ad lib" and compared its often zany art to that of the Marx Brothers.♦ Typical of its skits was "Pleasant Companions," which was set in an insane asylum and whose characters included a demented, flag-waving politician, a lunatic lover, and a mad kleptomaniac. When a burglar enters he is preached to by the politician, kissed by the lothario, and has his clothes and tools stolen by the nutty thief.

SANDERSON, Julia [née Julia Sackett] (1887–1975) The doll-faced beauty, who was the leading musical star between the heydays of Lillian Russell♦ and Marilyn Miller,♦ was born in Springfield, Mass., and was the daughter of a popular actor, Albert Sackett. She was a child when she made her debut in Philadelphia with Forepaugh's Stock Company. After serving a five-year apprenticeship there she appeared in the chorus of several musicals. Her big break came when De Wolf Hopper♦ cast her as his leading lady in a 1904 revival of *Wang.*♦ Important roles followed in both New York and London before she achieved stardom with her performance in *The Arcadians* (1910). Her successs included *The Siren* (1911); *The Sunshine Girl* (1913); *The Girl from Utah*♦ (1914), in which she introduced "They Didn't Believe Me"♦; *Sybil* (1916); *Rambler Rose* (1917); and *The Canary* (1918). In many of these shows she was co-starred with Donald Brian♦ and Joseph Cawthorn.♦ So popular was the trio that George M. Cohan♦ saluted them with the song "Julia, Donald and Joe" in *The Cohan Revue of 1916.* After playing in *Hitchy Koo, 1920* she joined her husband Frank Crumit in her last Broadway success, *Tangerine* (1921). She later toured in prominent roles in *No, No, Nanette*♦ (1925) and *Oh, Kay!*♦ (1927), then played with Crumit in vaudeville before retiring from the stage. Although she had a fine voice and was exceptionally comely, she lacked the verve and exploitive sex appeal of either Miss Russell or Miss Miller.

SANDOW, Eugene (1867–1925) The German-born strong man was brought to America in 1893 by Rudolph Aronson♦ to perform in a vaudeville bill at the Casino Theatre.♦ The act caused little stir, but was caught by young Florenz Ziegfeld,♦ who bought out Sandow's contract and whose promotion of the performer launched the producer on his career. Ziegfeld had Sandow lift a piano and also a platform holding three horses. After the two men had a falling out, Sandow continued to perform in vaudeville until his vogue waned. He retired to England, where he died after attempting to lift an automobile out of a ditch.

Sanford's Minstrels The troupe was founded by Sam S. Sanford (1821–1905), who in 1853 had erected the first theatre in Philadelphia designed especially for minstrel entertainments. The theatre burned a few months later, and it was not until April 1855 that Sanford's Minstrels began a seven-year stand at Philadelphia's Eleventh Street Opera House. The company was famous for its "Happy Uncle Tom," a take-off of *Uncle Tom's Cabin,* ♦ which purported to show how content blacks were in the South. The troupe was also known for its elaborate patriotic tableaux, such as "The Pilgrim Fathers" and "The Signing of the Declaration of Independence," which moved away from traditional minstrel material and foreshadowed the tableaux vivants of later revues.

Saratoga; or, Pistols for Seven, a comedy in five acts by Bronson Howard.♦ Produced by Augustin Daly♦ at the Fifth Avenue Theatre.♦ December 21, 1870. 101 performances.

Bob Sackett (James Lewis♦) is engaged to the lovely belle, Effie Remington (Fanny Davenport♦). That would be just fine with everyone, except that Bob has, in one manner or another, promised himself to the widow Olivia Alston (Fanny Morant♦), the newly wed Lucy Carter (Clara Morris♦), and the popular little flirt Virginia Vanderpool (Linda Dietz). Attempting to escape from the mess he has gotten himself into he takes off for Saratoga, where, to his horror, he is confronted by the women as well as by Lucy's wildly jealous husband, Frederick (J. Burnett), and the elder Vanderpools (W. Davidge♦ and Mrs. Gilbert♦).

One of the finest of all American 19th-century comedies, this broadly farcical piece was also one of the first American works to achieve widespread international popularity. It was done in England as *Brighton* and in Germany as *Seine erste und einzige Liebe.*

Sardi's Long the favorite restaurant in New York theatrical circles, it was founded in 1921 by Eugenia and Vincent Sardi in the basement of a brownstone on 44th Street. The brownstone was torn down in 1926 to make way for what is now the St. James Theatre, so the Shuberts♦ built the Sardis a new restaurant slightly to the east on the same street. The walls of the eatery are covered with celebrated caricatures of theatrical figures and were done first by Alex Gard, and, after his death in 1947, by Don Bevan♦ and Richard Baratz. It has become a traditional gathering place where actors and others associated with a new show await the early reviews. Vincent Sardi, Jr., sold the restaurant in 1986. It closed briefly in 1990, then reopened, but its future is now in some doubt.

SARDOU, Victorien (1831–1908) One of the most successful French dramatists of his day and an exponent, like Scribe♦ before him, of the "well-made" play, he saw many of his most successful Parisian works find a welcome in America. Among the best received were *Ferreol* (1876), *Diplomacy♦* (1878), *A Scrap of Paper* (1879), *Divorçons♦* (1882), *Fedora* (1883), *La Tosca* (1888), *Gismonda* (1894), and *Madame Sans-Gêne* (1895). Most closely identified with his work in America was Fanny Davenport,♦ who re-created here many of the roles written for Bernhardt.♦ One curious play of his was *L'Oncle Sam,* which the French government at-

tempted to ban, surprisingly as too derogatory of Americans. Augustin Daly♦ agreed to produce it in New York. The story was exceptionally complicated but included as major figures the Hon. Samuel Tapplebot (Uncle Sam), "a perfect type of the American whom nothing discourages, always at the front, his eyes fixed upon his three beacons—wealth for an end, cunning for the means, and as for morals—success," and a comic widow whose house straddles a state line and who finds in the respective state courts that she has won her living room but lost her dining room. The play was not a success, but since no Americans took serious offense, a Parisian mounting followed the 1873 New York premiere.

SARGENT, Epes (1813–80) The Boston journalist, novelist, and author of tracts on spiritualism was also for a brief time a successful playwright. His best known work was *Velasco* (1837), which was first performed by James E. Murdoch♦ in Boston and later produced in New York, Philadelphia, and London. Its story, which Sargent said was based on the career of Rodrigo Diaz (El Cid), told of star-crossed lovers whose romance is destroyed by a jealous rival, by the death of the girl's father at the hands of her lover, and by a vengeful brother. His other tragedies were *The Bride of Genoa* (1837), which was published as *The Genoese,* and *The Priestess* (1855). His comedies included *The Candid Critic, The Lampoon,* and *Change Makes Change* (1845). From 1839 to 1847 he lived in New York, where he was an editor of the *Mirror.* During this time he befriended Anna Cora Mowatt,♦ and it was at his suggestion that she wrote her famous comedy *Fashion.* ♦ He also aided her in lauching her career as an actress.

SARGENT, Epes Winthrop (1872–1938) The acerbic critic, who wrote under the names "Chicot" and "Chic," was born in Nassau in the Bahamas. He began his American career as a music critic but soon took an interest in vaudeville, becoming the first major critic to devote his attention almost exclusively to the genre. He was often vicious in attacking poor-quality acts, excessive sentimentality, and foreign performers he felt were trading on their overseas reputations and their exotic appeal. But he also berated greedy managers who overworked and underpaid performers, and who forced them to endure shameful working conditions. Explaining his harshness, he remarked late in his life, "The average actor was too dumb to appreciate the niceties of language. I could not say he was a bad actor. I had to tell him he was a damned bad actor." After serving on several papers he became one of the original staff members of *Variety*. ♦ Vaudeville historian Douglas Gilbert noted, "Chicot's influence on the development of vaudeville can hardly be overestimated."

SARONY, NAPOLEON (1821–96) The most famous of 19th-century theatrical photographers, said to have photographed over 30,000 actors or actresses, he was born in Quebec, where he studied lithography under his father. Coming to New York in 1833, he eventually co-founded the lithographic film of Sarony and Major, which pioneered in the modern theatrical poster. He sold out after his wife's death and went to Europe to study painting, but soon found an even greater interest in the new art of photography. While in England he photographed Adah Isaacs Menken♦ in scenes from *Mazeppa*. The popularity of these photographs established him in his new career. He returned to America in 1865, and quickly became by far the leading figure in his field. He did not like to photograph actual productions, preferring that performers pose formally in his studios.

SAROYAN, WILLIAM (1908–81) The eccentric playwright was born in Fresno, Calif., where his Armenian parents were fruit farmers and where he worked at odd jobs before gaining fame as a short-story writer. He came to playgoers' attention with *My Heart's in the Highlands*♦ (1939), which centered on a poor poet, his young son, and a dying Shakespearean actor who becomes their guest. His next play, *The Time of Your Life*♦ (1939), which focused on the habitués of a seedy San Francisco bar, won both the New York Drama Critics Circle Award♦ and the Pulitzer Prize,♦ although Saroyan noisily rejected the latter. A play about the romance of a con man and a befuddled spinster, *Love's Old Sweet Song* (1940), met no success, and several subsequent plays were tried out in summer stock but failed to reach New York. *The Beautiful People*♦ (1941), which did play New York, was a saga of an unusual family, and was followed by a failed double bill, *Across the Board on Tomorrow Morning* and *Talking to You* (1942). *Hello, Out There* (1942) dealt with an unjustly imprisoned gambler, while *Get Away Old Man* (1943) depicted the struggle between a power-mad film executive and a brazen writer. The play closed quickly, and for many years Saroyan could not obtain another Broadway hearing, although many of his plays were produced elsewhere or by small houses off-Broadway. Only one other work achieved an important mounting, *The Cave Dwellers* (1957), in which a collection of misfits take

refuge in an abandoned playhouse. Saroyan directed and produced a number of his own plays, often working in collaboration with Eddie Dowling. ♦ Wollcott Gibbs♦ called the writer "the most completely undisciplined talent in American letters," and Brooks Atkinson,♦ in a preface to Saroyan's published plays, noted, "when he writes out of general relish, usually in isolated scenes, [he] is at his best and made a definite contribution to the mood of these times, [but] when he permits himself to discuss ideas he can write some of the worst nonsense that ever clattered out of a typewriter."

Biography: *William Saroyan,* Howard R. Floan, New York, 1966.

Saturday's Children, a play in three acts by Maxwell Anderson.♦ Produced at the Booth Theatre. January 26, 1927. 310 performances.

After Bobby Halevy (Ruth Gordon♦) nabs the man of her dreams, Rims O'Neill (Roger Pryor), she quickly realizes how unrealistic her ideas of married life were. Financial problems, family interference, and a certain immaturity all converge to destroy the marriage. Bobby leaves Rims and takes a room in a boarding house which forbids men to call on lady tenants. Rims, still deeply in love, climbs a fire escape to visit Bobby and convince her that though Saturday's child must struggle for a living, life is worthless without love.

Percy Hammond♦ of the *Herald Tribune* called the work a "hushed little comedy" and admired "the quiet speed with which it tells its story."

SAVAGE, HENRY W[ILSON] (1859–1927) Born in New Durham, N.H., he was educated at Harvard and had become a prosperous Boston realtor until a client who ran the Castle Square Opera House failed and he was forced to assume its management. He turned it into one of the nation's most successful stock companies, eventually sending out several branch companies. Moving to New York he produced a series of notable turn-of-the-century hits, including *The Sultan of Sulu*♦ (1902), *The County Chairman*♦ (1903), *The Prince of Pilsen*♦ (1903), *The College Widow*♦ (1904), *The Merry Widow*♦ (1907), *Madame X* (1909), *Excuse Me* (1911), and *Sari* (1914). He often prefaced his name with Colonel, although his claim to that distinction was a matter of dispute.

SAVOY [BERT, né EVERETT MCKENZIE] (1888?–1923) **and BRENNAN,** JAY (1883?–1961) The Boston-born Savoy performed in carnivals and as a chorus boy prior to becoming a female impersonator. His style was in marked contrast to the maiden aunt absurdities of many predecessors or to the elegant manners of Julian Eltinge. ♦ Savoy was probably the first of the outrageous, wildly swishy drag queens. Much of his act involved stories about his friend Margie. He also popularized such phrases as "You don't know the half of it, dearie" and "You must come over." His costume consisted of a flaming red wig, curvaceous gowns, and huge picture hats. Several theatrical historians have suggested that Mae West♦ copied much of her style from him. In 1913 he joined with Brennan, a Baltimorean, who played his handsome, dapper, eye-fluttering straight man. The pair were quickly headliners, appearing not only at the Palace♦ but in such Broadway shows as *Miss 1917* and two editions of the *Greenwich Village Follies.* ♦ After Savoy was killed in 1923, Brennan tried other partners and a solo act, continuing to perform until his retirement in 1945.

SCANLAN, W[ILLIAM] J[AMES] (1856–1898) A puckish performer with a fine Irish tenor voice, he was born into a poor family in Springfield, Mass., and while still in his teens formed a vaudeville act with William Cronin. After the act disbanded in 1877 he toured for some time with Minnie Palmer. ♦ His first major success came when he portrayed Carroll Moore, an Irishman whom the Germans arrest as a French spy, in Bartley Campbell's♦ *Friend and Foe* (1882). The role brought him to the attention of Augustus Pitou, ♦ under whose aegis he starred in similar parts in such plays of Gaelic romance as *Shane-Na-Lawn* (1885), *The Irish Minstrel* (1886), *Myles Aroon* (1888), and *Mavourneen*♦ (1891). He composed many of the songs he introduced, including "Peek-A-Boo," which was one of the most popular songs of its era. Like several great stars of his day he had to be forcibly removed from the stage when he became insane as the result of paresis.

SCARBOROUGH, GEORGE [MOORE] (1875–1951) Born in Mount Carmel, Texas, he was educated at Baylor University and the University of Texas. He was slated to follow in his father's footsteps as a lawyer but elected instead to become a playwright. While waiting to find a producer he served as a newspaperman and as a federal Secret Service agent, later putting his experience to use in several of his melodramas. Over a dozen of his plays reached Broadway, his most notable successes including: *The Lure* (1913), a saga of white slavery; *At Bay* (1913), in which an amateur sleuth rescues a district attorney's daughter from a blackmailer; *The*

Heart of Wetona (1916), a story of an Indian maid in the clutches of treacherous white men; *Moonlight and Honeysuckle* (1919), a comedy in which a girl tests her suitors with fictitious tales about her past; and *The Son-Daughter* (1919), written with David Belasco, ♦ telling of a Chinese girl sold by her father.

Scarecrow, The, a play in four acts by Percy MacKaye. ♦ Produced by Henry B. Harris♦ at the Garrick Theatre. January 17, 1911. 23 performances.

With the aid of a Yankee version of the Devil known as Dickon (Edmund Breese♦), the 17th-century witch Goody Rickby (Alice Fisher) turns a scarecrow into a man she names Lord Ravensbane (Frank Reicher). To be revenged on Justice Merton (Brigham Royce), who once had been her lover, she sends Ravensbane to Merton's home, where the young man becomes betrothed to Merton's niece Rachel (Beatrice Irwin). Rachel's former fiancé, Richard Talbot (Earle Brown), exposes Ravensbane. At the same time, however, Ravensbane has developed a heart and a conscience. Realizing the damage he has done, he purposely destroys the brimstone-burning pipe that has kept him alive. His dying lament is, "Oh, Rachel, could I have been a man—!"

Based on Hawthorne's tale "Feathertop," the play was first presented by the Harvard Dramatic Club♦ in 1909. Its commercial production by Harris was a failure, but it remains popular with collegiate and amateur groups. It was given a fine off-Broadway revival in the 1953–54 season.

Scene Design in American Theatre Although the decorative aspects of theatre are essential to the complete enjoyment of a play and to the understanding of our theatre's history, no full-scale study of American set design and set designers, along with costumes, lighting, and their creators, has yet been published. Until such a history appears only a cursory outline of developments can be offered, and this must of necessity neglect the almost wholly unchartered developments and figures away from New York.

Virtually nothing is known about the scenery employed in the very earliest American theatricals, although it can be assumed that it was a possibly primitive version of the wing-and-drop or wing-and-shutter variety used in English playhouses. The first relatively sophisticated settings probably appeared when Lewis Hallam♦ and his company sailed from England to establish a traveling company in the colonies. There is reason to believe that Hallam brought much of his scenery with him and that it had previously been used at London's Goodman's Fields Theatre. A notice printed in the *Virginia Gazette* at the time of Hallam's arrival nonetheless claimed "the Scenes, Cloaths, and Decorations, are entirely new, extremely rich, [and] being painted by the best Hands in London, are excelled by none in Beauty and Elegance." Despite the period settings of some of the plays Hallam offered, his costumes were undoubtedly contemporary, in the fashion of the time, and his generalized settings, which had to be used in various plays, lit by candlelight.

If we cannot be certain of the quality of Hallam's scenery, we can be even less certain of what it represented. Within a few decades most playhouses retained at least five basic settings—a rich interior, a simple interior, a garden, a woodland scene, and a street scene—but whether the limited space available to Hallam and the exigencies of frequent travel allowed him the luxury of even these few settings is unknown. Certainly after the revolution, when Lewis Hallam, Jr.,♦ headed the Old American Company,♦ a temporary decline in quality may have become evident. In 1787 the New York *Advertiser* complained, "Frequently where the author intended a handsome street or beautiful landscape, we only see a dirty piece of canvas . . . nor is it uncommon to see the back of the stage represent a street while the side scenes represent a wood."

Yet the final years of the 18th century saw the emergence of the first great American set designers with the work of the European-trained Charles Ciceri♦ in Philadelphia and New York, and Monsieur Audin♦ in Charleston. Indeed Ciceri, who worked in Paris and London before coming to America, is credited with bringing here the first transparent scrim. At the same time, so far as American theatre was concerned, the hesitant introduction of architecturally conceived scenery, as opposed to mere painted flats, may have occurred in Boston in 1797 with the production there of John Daly Burk's♦ *Bunker Hill,* in which the hill was "raised gradually by boards extended from the stage to a bench."

The English-born John Joseph Holland,♦ long connected with New York's Park Theatre,♦ is sometimes credited with being the first American set designer to attempt historical accuracy in his work, but it was not until two decades after his death that a burgeoning movement toward realism ushered in two major developments. The first was the box set, which allowed playgoers to imagine themselves as viewing a room from an invisible fourth wall. This new treatment of interiors received instant and widespread attention because it was introduced in conjunction with the most successful play of the era, Dion Boucicault's♦ *London Assurance*♦ (1841). Five years later the visit of Charles Kean,♦ far more than Holland's tentative efforts, established the notion that theatrical period pieces should be accurately set. The older tradition of standard settings built in the wing-and-drop style received a further blow with the erection of Edwin Booth's♦ ill-fated theatre in 1869. Booth dispensed with the exaggeratedly raked stage, which made realism difficult; with proscenium doors, which had been used for entrances and exits made difficult or at least artificial by the wing-and-drop designs; and with the huge apron in front of the proscenium. None of these changes originated with Booth, but the actor's distinguished reputation gained them immediate acceptance.

The 19th century also saw the two major basic changes in lighting come about. The introduction of gas lighting is believed to have taken place at Philadelphia's Chestnut Street Theatre♦ in 1816, although the expense of installing the gas works, which required an elaborate distillation of coal, prevented gas from becoming commonplace for nearly two decades. For example, the first New York house to convert was the Chatham in 1825. The first practical spotlight, known as the limelight, the calcium light, the oxyhydrogen light, or the Drummond light, while perfected in Europe in the 1840s, came into general usage here only about the time of the Civil War. There is reason to believe it was first employed in New York in the 1866 production of *The Black Crook.*♦ Primitive electric lighting began to gain a foothold in the 1880s and grew into a standard method of illumination far more rapidly than gas had. These brighter methods of lighting gradually helped eliminate the exaggerated make-up and acting which darker stages had required.

Although architecturally conceived scenery became increasingly frequent throughout the 19th century and into the early 20th century, most scenic effects were achieved by careful painting, and set designers were therefore usually known as scene painters, a term not necessarily demeaning. A partial list of the great American scene painters during these years would include Ernest Albert,♦ D. Frank Dodge,♦ Philip Goatcher,♦ the Grain family,♦ Ernest Gros,♦ George Heilge,♦ George Heister,♦ Henry E. Hoyt,♦ Richard Marston,♦ Thomas G. Moses,♦ Joseph Physioc,♦ James Roberts,♦ Russell Smith,♦ Edward G. Unitt,♦ Charles Witham,♦ and William Voegtlin.♦ That these men worked largely in New York, Chicago, and Philadelphia suggests not that these cities excelled in set design but that our knowledge of scenery and scene painters elsewhere is sadly scant.

The movement away from realistically painted flats and toward more stylized, suggestive, and architecturally conceived sets, usually enhanced by imaginative lighting, began to gain prominence around the time of World War I. Many historians agree that it was the work of Robert Edmond Jones♦ for the 1915 production of *The Man Who Married a Dumb Wife* which "sounded the note that began the American revolution in stage scenery." Other modern designers of distinction have included Boris Aronson,♦ Norman Bel Geddes,♦ Stewart Chaney,♦ Frederick Fox,♦ Jo Mielziner,♦ Livingston Platt,♦ Oliver Smith,♦ and Joseph Urban.♦ Their work has often been made even more attractive by the artistry of modern lighting designers, though some of these men created their own lighting effects. Indeed, with the increasing use of transparent scrims and skeletonized settings, lighting frequently became an integral part of the stage picture rather than serving merely to illuminate it. In a few avant-garde instances lighting served as the primary scenery. Recent seasons have seen such technically elaborate scenery, especially in imported English musicals, that computers have been needed to control it.

SCHEFF, [FRIEDRIKE JAEGER] FRITZI (1879–1954) The tiny, fiery prima donna with the hourglass figure was born in Vienna, where her mother was a leading singer with the Imperial Opera. She studied and sang in Europe before being brought to the Metropolitan Opera House in 1901. Two years later Charles Dillingham♦ persuaded her to leave the opera stage and starred her in Victor Herbert's♦ *Babette.* She subsquently played the principal roles in five other musicals, the most famous being Herbert's *Mlle. Modiste♦* (1905), in which she introduced "Kiss Me Again." After several seasons in vaudeville her career began to fade, although she remained on stage virtually until her death. Except for occasional revivals of *Mlle. Modiste* and a 1908 Herbert operetta, *The Prima Donna,* she thereafter played mostly supporting roles.

SCHENCK, [JOSEPH T.] JOE, see *Van and Schenck*

SCHILDKRAUT, JOSEPH (1896–1964) The swarthy, dashingly handsome son of the famous German and Yiddish actor Rudolf Schildkraut, he was born in Vienna and studied for the stage both in Germany

and at the American Academy of Dramatic Arts.♦ His first American appearances were under his father's aegis in German-language performances at the Irving Place Theatre in 1910. Shortly afterward he returned to Europe, where he acted for Max Reinhardt♦ and other famous producers. Coming back to America in 1920, he scored his first great success here in the role of the feckless carnival barker, the title part in *Liliom♦* (1921). Another major triumph came as Benvenuto Cellini, the roguish artist-lover, in *The Firebrand♦* (1924). For a time, beginning in 1932, he was an important member of Eva Le Gallienne's♦ Civic Repertory Theatre. ♦ After many years in films he enjoyed a long run as the mild-mannered murderer, the title role in *Uncle Harry♦* (1942). His last major role was as Mr. Frank, the father of the doomed Jewish girl, in *The Diary of Anne Frank♦* (1955).

Autobiography: *My Father and I,* New York, 1959.

SCHISGAL, MURRAY, *see Luv*

SCHMIDT, HARVEY, see *Fantasticks, The*

SCHNEIDER, [ABRAM LEOPOLDOVICH] ALAN (1917–84) Born in Karkov, Russia, but raised and educated in America, where he studied at the University of Wisconsin and Cornell, and with Lee Strasberg,♦ he first directed on Broadway in 1948 with *A Long Way from Home.* Among his other Broadway assignments have been *The Remarkable Mr. Pennypacker* (1953), *Anastasia* (1954), *Who's Afraid of Virginia Woolf?♦* (1962), *The Ballad of the Sad Café* (1963), *Tiny Alice♦* (1964), *A Delicate Balance♦* (1967), *Moonchildren♦* (1972), *A Texas Trilogy♦* (1976) and *Loose Ends♦* (1979). Because much of the most exciting and responsible contemporary theatre is on regional stages, he spent a large part of his career directing at college theatres and other important playhouses away from Manhattan. He mounted many productions for Washington's Arena Stage,♦ ranging from Shakespeare and Chekhov to world premieres, and was made an associate director of the organization in 1971. He was also a director of John Houseman's♦ Acting Company. Off-Broadway he figured importantly in staging many of Samuel Beckett's♦ plays.

Autobiography: *Entrances,* New York, 1986.

SCHOENFELD, GERALD, see *Shubert, Lee, Sam S., and J.J.*

SCHWAB, LAURENCE (1893–1951) The Boston-born, Harvard-educated producer and writer enjoyed his first hit when he co-produced the musical *The Gingham Girl* (1922). Subsequent productions, often mounted in collaboration with Frank Mandel,♦ included *Captain Jinks* (1925), *Queen High♦* (1926), *The Desert Song♦* (1926), *Good News!♦* (1927), *The New Moon♦* (1928), *Follow Thru♦* (1929), *Take a Chance* (1932), and *May Wine* (1935). Except for *The Gingham Girl, The Desert Song,* and *May Wine,* he served as co-librettist for these musicals.

SCHWARTZ, ARTHUR (1900–1984) The Brooklyn-born composer studied piano and music over his lawyer-father's strenuous objections. He wrote songs for vaudeville performers and occasional numbers for revues before joining with Howard Dietz♦ to create the songs for *The Little Show♦* (1929), which included "I Guess I'll Have To Change My Plan." They followed this with *The Grand Street Follies* (1929); *The Second Little Show* (1930); *Three's a Crowd* (1930), whose score contained "Something To Remember You By"; *The Band Wagon♦* (1931), from which came "Dancing in the Dark," "I Love Louisa," and "New Sun in the Sky"; *Flying Colors* (1932), recalled for "Louisiana Hayride"; *Revenge with Music* (1934), whose hits were "If There Is Someone Lovelier Than You" and "You and the Night and the Music"; and *At Home Abroad* (1935). With other lyricists he wrote *Virginia* (1937), remembered for "You and I Know"; then he worked again with Dietz on *Between the Devil* (1937), from which came "By Myself" and "I See Your Face Before Me." Dorothy Fields♦ served as his collaborator for *Stars in Your Eyes* (1939), while Ira Gershwin♦ was his lyricist for *Park Avenue* (1946). Working with Dietz again, he also served as co-producer of *Inside U.S.A.* (1948), which included "Haunted Heart." One of his finest scores, to Fields's lyrics, was for *A Tree Grows in Brooklyn♦* (1951), whose songs included "I'll Buy You a Star" and "Look Who's Dancing." With Fields he also wrote *By the Beautiful Sea* (1954). Dietz rejoined him for *The Gay Life* (1961) and *Jennie* (1963). One of the most underrated of Broadway's great composers, his music ranged from moody ballads to sprightly rhythm numbers. Curiously, all his book shows were commercial failures, and only the revues for which he wrote made money.

SCHWARTZ, JEAN (1878–1956) Born in Budapest, but brought to America at the age of ten, he began his musical career as a song-plugger for a sheet-music firm. Like most composers of the time he heard his earliest songs sung as interpolations in other men's scores. These songs included "Rip Van Winkle Was a Lucky Man" from *The Sleeping Beauty and the Beast* (1901); "Mr. Dooley" from *A Chinese Honeymoon* (1902); and "Bedelia" from *The Jersey Lily* (1903). Between 1904 and 1928 he wrote the greater part or the entire score for about thirty Broadway musicals, including many of *The Passing Shows.* ♦ His 1910 revue *Up and Down Broadway* left behind "Chinatown, My Chinatown." Almost all of these songs were written with lyricist William Jerome (1865–1932), but his most enduring hit was an interpolation in the 1918 Jolson♦ extravaganza, *Sinbad,* "Rock-A-Bye Your Baby with a Dixie Melody," for which Joe Young and Sam Lewis provided words.

SCHWARTZ, MAURICE (1890–1960) Born in Sedikor, Russia, he came to America in 1901 and four years later gave his first professional performance with a Yiddish theatre in Baltimore. He acted in various cities before joining David Kessler♦ in New York in 1912. When World War I made German-language plays unpopular, he took over the Irving Place Theatre and turned it into the Yiddish Art Theatre, an organization he headed with occasional intermissions and reorganizations until 1950. Called the "John Barrymore of the Yiddish Theatre," he was an actor of the old school. Dark-haired and with piercing eyes, he had a flamboyant style, a rumbling voice, and, according to Yiddish theatre historian Nahma Sandrow, "distinctive rapid gabbling inflections." Although he made infrequent appearances on English-language stages, it was largely for his work in Yiddish that he was admired. Among his most noted roles were his Shylock and his aging Hassidic rabbi, the title part in his dramatization of I. J. Singer's *Yoshe Kalb.*

SCHWARTZ, STEPHEN (b. 1948) A New Yorker who was educated at Julliard and Carnegie Tech. His songs have not enjoyed widespread or enduring popularity. Nevertheless he wrote the music and lyrics for three exceptionally long-run successes: *Godspell♦* (1971), *Pippin♦* (1972), and *The Magic Show♦* (1974). In 1986 he served solely as lyricist for the short-lived musical *Rags.*

SCOFIELD, [DAVID] PAUL (b. 1922) One of the finest of contemporary English actors, he has made only two American appearances, first as Sir Thomas More in the role he created in England in *A Man for All Seasons* (1961) and later touring briefly in the title role of the Royal Shakespeare Company's♦ *King Lear*♦ in 1964.

SCOTT, GEORGE C[AMPBELL] (b. 1927) Born in Wise, Va., and educated at the University of Missouri, he first gained prominence as an imprisoned nobleman in the Circle in the Square's♦ 1958 revival of *Children of Darkness*. Among his subsequent assignments were Lt. Col. Chapman, the Judge Advocate, in *The Andersonville Trial* (1959); Ben Hubbard in a 1967 revival of *The Little Foxes*♦; all the leading men's parts in the triple bill *Plaza Suite*♦ (1968); Dr. Astrov in a 1973 Circle in the Square revival of *Uncle Vanya;* Willy Loman in the same group's 1975 revival of *Death of a Salesman*♦; Foxwell J. Sly in a 1976 rewriting of *Volpone* called *Sly Fox;* and Garry Essendine in the 1982 Circle in the Square revival of *Present Laughter*. For the New York Shakespeare Festival♦ he has offered his Antony and Shylock. Although the hard-faced actor is often perceived as a serious dramatic performer, and he has shown great skill in such parts, much of his success has come from his often overlooked abilities as a comedian. He has also enjoyed a fine film career.

SCOTT, JOHN R. (1808–56) Born in Philadelphia, where he was active in amateur theatricals, he made his professional debut at New York's Park Theatre♦ in 1829 playing Malcolm to J. B. Booth's♦ Macbeth. He rose quickly to become a favorite both at Philadelphia's Arch Street Theatre♦ and at the Bowery♦ in New York. Although he essayed such classic tragic parts as Othello, Hamlet, and Sir Giles Overreach, he was most admired for his romantic leads in the new melodramas of the day, but he never won favor at the most prestigious houses. Ireland♦ wrote of him, "Possessing a fine personal appearance and great natural abilities, he might, with proper caution in personal habits and a closer application to study, have ranked among the very highest of our actors. His school was that of Forrest, but he was not a servile imitator and, like [J. B.] Booth, in the latter part of his career he was apt to disappoint his audiences by his sudden disappearances."

SCRIBE, [AUGUSTIN] EUGÈNE (1791–1861) The leading French dramatist of the first half of the 19th century, he reacted to the overblown, romantic melodramas of his day by devising the "well-made" play, in which essentially middle-class problems were presented in neat, economically contrived plots and with prosaic, commonplace dialogue. While these plays were theatrically effective, many detractors felt they merely substituted taut construction for vitality and depth. Although a number of his works were translated and met with varying success in America, he was best known and largely remembered here for a single drama, *Adrienne Lecouvreur*. Almost without exception, however, the heroine's greatest interpreters in America were either foreigners or foreign-born actresses, from Rachel♦ through Ristori♦ and Modjeska♦ to Bernhardt.♦

Scuba Duba, a comedy in two acts by Bruce Jay Friedman. Produced at the New Theatre. October 10, 1967. 692 performances.

Harold Wonder (Jerry Orbach♦) is an ultraliberal Jewish intellectual whose liberalism is sorely tested when his wife, Jean (Jennifer Warren), runs off with "a spade frogman," Foxtrot (Cleavon Little). Harold seeks reassurance by lugging around his version of a personal security blanket, a scythe; by inviting over an attractive bikinied neighbor; and by conversations with his psychiatrist, Dr. Schoenfeld (Ken Olfson), and his very Jewish mother (Stella Longo). When Jean brings Foxtrot home Harold storms out, telling his wife that he is going shell-hunting with some girls, and that if he enjoys it she is through.

One of the best off-Broadway comedies of its era, its author, the Bronx-born Friedman (b. 1930), was better known as a novelist. This was his only successful play.

SEABROOKE, THOMAS Q. [né THOMAS JAMES QUIGLEY] (1860–1913) A native of Mount Vernon, N.Y., he made his debut in 1880 and for the next several years appeared in dramas and a few comedies. He won popularity as star of such musicals as *The Isle of Champagne* (1894) and *Tabasco* (1895). His greatest success came in the imported English musical, *A Chinese Honeymoon* (1902). Thereafter his vogue waned, although he remained a headliner in vaudeville.

Season in the Sun, a comedy in three acts by Wolcott Gibbs.♦ Produced at the Cort Theatre. September 28, 1950. 367 performances.

Tired of writing glib articles for *The New Yorker,* George Crane (Richard Whorf♦) flees with his wife Emily (Nancy Kelly) to the supposed quiet and privacy of Fire Island, where George proposes to dedicate himself to becoming a serious novelist. But quiet and privacy are not what George finds. Instead, his summer cottage turns into a waystation for a motley assortment of kooks and bores. In desperation, George returns to the relative sanity of New York City.

The comedy was one of the rare successful attempts by a modern critic at play-writing.

Second Man, The, a comedy in three acts by S. H. Behrman. ◆ Produced by the Theatre Guild ◆ at the Guild Theatre. April 11, 1927. 178 performances.

Clark Story (Alfred Lunt ◆), a novelist and carefree hedonist, proposes to marry the rich, understanding Mrs. Kendall Frayne (Lynn Fontanne ◆), but his plans are sidetracked when Monica Grey (Margalo Gillmore ◆) tells him she is pregnant. Seeming to accept his fate, he ruefully tells Monica's disappointed suitor, Alistin Lowe (Earle Larimore ◆), how dreary the prospect of marriage to Monica appears to him—"Her talk is not small. It is infinitesimal." Inevitably Monica and Clark recognize they are wrong for each other. She is reconciled with Alistin, while Clark agrees to let Mrs. Kendall keep him in luxury.

Although many critics complained about the slight plot, most agreed with John Mason Brown, ◆ who hailed the play's "shimmering dialogue."

Secret Service, a play in four acts by William Gillette. ◆ Produced by Charles Frohman ◆ at the Garrick Theatre. October 5, 1896. 176 performances.

Lewis Dumont (Gillette), a Northern agent posing as the Confederate officer Captain Thorne, comes to Richmond, where he wins the affection of a loyal Virginian, Edith Varney (Amy Busby). She obtains a commission for him as a major, which he, of course, must refuse. Benton Arrelsford (Campbell Gollan) of the War Office suspects that Thorne is a spy, but Thorne cleverly confounds all Arrelsford's attempts to expose him. However, Edith has come to realize Thorne's real position, so she offers him a means of escape. He rejects the chance, yet he is sufficiently shamed that he revokes forged orders which he has telegraphed to Confederate lines and which would have prompted an unnecessary retreat. He is arrested and sent to prison. Edith promises to wait for his release.

A gripping, soundly constructed melodrama, in which, as Quinn ◆ noted, "Not a word is wasted and not an action," it was originally tried out with Maurice Barrymore ◆ as Dumont. Withdrawn for revisions, it later gave Gillette one of his greatest successes.

SEDLEY-SMITH, W. H., see *Drunkard, The*

SEELEY, BLOSSOM (1892?–1974) The pert, blonde "Queen of Syncopation" was born in San Francisco, where she made her vaudeville debut at the age of ten as "The Little Blossom." Between 1911 and 1915 she appeared in a number of Broadway revues, and made her Palace Theatre ◆ debut in 1913. With her was her husband, Rube Marquard, a well-known baseball player. She later divorced him and married the Milwaukee-born Benny Fields (1894–1959) in 1922, and the pair became one of vaudeville's most popular song and dance teams. Among the songs she was associated with were "Way Down Yonder in New Orleans," "I Cried for You," and "A New Kind of Man with a New Kind of Love for Me." She retired in 1936, but after a film biography brought her back into the limelight, returned for a time in 1952.

Seesaw, see *Two for the Seesaw*

SEGAL, VIVIENNE (b. 1897) The petite, chubby-faced beauty was born in Philadelphia, where she studied for a career in opera and appeared with local opera companies. Her father, a prominent Philadelphia physician, bought her the leading role in *The Blue Paradise* (1915), in which she introduced "Auf Wiedersehn." Paying for entry into the theatre was nothing new, but most performers who bought their way in had little talent and soon disappeared. Miss Segal was not only lovely to look at and listen to, but proved a good actress and superb comedienne, so she remained at the top for her entire career. Among the musicals in which she played leading roles were *Miss 1917; Oh, Lady! Lady!!* ◆ (1918); *The Little Whopper* (1919); *The Yankee Princess* (1922); *The Desert Song* ◆ (1926), in which she sang "Romance"; *The Three Musketeers* ◆ (1928); a 1931 revival of *The Chocolate Soldier; I Married an Angel* ◆ (1938); *Pal Joey* ◆ (1940 and 1952), in which she sang "Bewitched"; and a 1943 revival of *A Connecticut Yankee.* ◆

SELDES, GILBERT (1893–1970) The distinguished author and critic was born in Alliance, N.J., and was graduated from Harvard. He earned widespread recognition with his book *The Seven Lively Arts* (1924), which was one of the earliest serious studies of popular entertainment and in which he insisted that Al Jolson ◆ and Fanny Brice ◆ were the equal of more traditional stars such as John ◆ and Ethel Barrymore. ◆ He also wrote numerous articles and reviews, as well as several plays, including an adaptation of *Lysistrata,* which was produced on Broadway in 1930. In his later years he became more interested in radio and television, and served as professor and dean at the University of Pennsylvania's Annenberg School of Communication. He was the father of actress Marion Seldes.

Self, a comedy in three acts by Mrs. Sidney F. Bateman.♦ Produced by William Burton♦ at Burton's Chambers Street Theatre. October 27, 1856. 18 performances.

Mrs. Apex (Mrs. A. Parker) lives far beyond her means, as does her unscrupulous son by her first marriage, Charles Sanford (Mr. Morton). Mary (Mrs. E. Davenport), her stepdaughter, has, on the other hand, lived prudently and saved $15,000. Charles forges Mary's name to a check of that amount, and when Mr. Apex (Charles Fisher♦) later attempts to cash a check Mary has given him, the check bounces. Mary realizes what has happened, but refuses to betray her stepbrother. Furious, Mr. Apex orders her out of the house. It requires the thoughtful ministrations of her uncle, the retired banker John Unit (Burton), to bring the family to its senses. His philosophy takes into account that "after all, our labours are prompted by that great motive power of human nature—*Self!*"

The comedy, which owed a clear debt to the earlier *Fashion,*♦ was filled with clever minor characters, who sported such names as Cypher Cynosure and Mr. Promptcash, but it was the character of Unit, not unlike that of Trueman in *Fashion,* which stole the show. After Burton relinquished the role, John E. Owens♦ toured in it for many years.

SELWYN, ARCH[IBALD] (1877?–1959) The famous producer's early history is obscure. He appears to have been the son of a Polish-Jewish immigrant whose surname was actually Simon, and he was probably born in Toronto. He came to New York after his older brother Edgar♦ had made a success as an actor. He held a series of odd jobs before his brother obtained a position for him in the box office of the Herald Square Theatre. Later he formed a play brokerage business with Edgar, and then the brothers merged with Elisabeth Marbury♦ and John Ramsay to form the larger American Play Company.♦ The brothers' other firm, Selwyn and Company, was a major producer whose hits included *Within the Law*♦ (1912), *Under Cover*♦ (1914), *Fair and Warmer,*♦ (1915), *Why Marry?*♦ (1917), *Tea for Three*♦ (1918), *Wedding Bells* (1919), *Smilin' Through* (1919), *The Circle* (1921), Jane Cowl's♦ *Romeo and Juliet*♦ (1923), *Charlot's Revue*♦ (1924), and *Dancing Mothers*♦ (1924). After splitting with

his brother he continued to produce alone, although whatever success he had was with importations such as *This Year of Grace* (1928) and, with Florenz Ziegfeld, ♦ *Bitter Sweet*♦ (1929). He also built three New York theatres with his brother—the Apollo, the Selwyn, and the Times Square—as well as two bandbox playhouses in Chicago.

SELWYN, EDGAR (1875–1944) A theatrical jack-of-all-trades, he was born in Cincinnati to a poor, peripatetic Jewish family whose last name apparently was Simon. He made his stage debut in 1896 in *Secret Service,* ♦ then played several years in stock. With his swarthy good looks he began to rise, but not fast enough to suit him. He turned his hand to play-writing to create his own romantic vehicles, among them *Pierre of the Plains* (1908) and *The Arab* (1911). Then he abruptly abandoned acting, although he continued to write. By this time, however, he was joined by his brother Arch, ♦ and the pair entered into a career of play brokerage, producing, and theatre building (see entry above for Arch Selwyn). After their company was dissolved he went his own way, producing alone or with others, such hits as *Gentlemen Prefer Blondes*♦ (1926), *The Barker* (1927), and *Strike Up the Band*♦ (1930). He retired in 1941.

Senator, The, a play in four acts by David D. Lloyd and Sydney Rosenfeld.♦ Produced at the Star Theatre. January 13, 1890. 119 performances.

Silas Denman (J. G. Padgett) and his daughter Mabel (Lizzie Hudson Collier) come to Washington to press a claim dating back to the War of 1812. Sympathetic Senator Hannibal Rivers (W. H. Crane♦) agrees to help, since the money will allow Mabel to wed the Austrian diplomat Count Ernst von Strahl (Henry Bergman). Rivers soon learns that von Strahl is a faithless philanderer. With the help of a rich, coquettish widow, Mrs. Hilary (Georgiana Drew Barrymore♦), he exposes the Count. Mrs. Hilary also lures away a crucial senator who would stop the claim. Winning the claim proves too much for old Denman, who suffers a fatal stroke. But Rivers's actions earn him Mabel's hand, while Mrs. Hilary is rewarded with the hand of an officer she has had her eye on.

Lloyd died before completing this play, so Rosenfeld was called in to finish it. The role of Rivers was one of Crane's best interpretations. Contemporaries ranked the character with Barnwell Slote of *The Mighty Dollar*♦ and Colonel Sellers as one of the great pieces of American comic writing.

Separate Rooms, a comedy in three acts by Joseph Carole, Alan Dinehart, Alex Gottlieb, and Edmund Joseph. Produced at Maxine Elliott's Theatre. March 23, 1940. 613 performances.

When gossip columnist Jim Stackhouse (Dinehart) learns that Pam (Glenda Farrell) has been reluctant to fulfill her marriage obligations to his brother Don (Lyle Talbot), he blackmails her into becoming a more loving wife.

Although dismissed by most critics as a negligible work, the play used cut-rate tickets and a sexually exploitive ad campaign to become one of the biggest hits in a season of hits. Dinehart (1890–1944), a native of St. Paul, was a popular performer on vaudeville and legitimate stages, and in films. Gottlieb (1906–88), born in Russia and raised in Kansas, subsequently became a film and television producer.

Serious Family, The Morris Barnett's free English adaptation of the French comedy *Un Mari en Champaigne* was first presented by William E. Burton♦ in 1849 and immediately became one of his greatest hits. Burton portrayed Aminadab Sleek, a comic, cowardly spouter of pious sentiments who is finally routed by young love. The play remained in his repertory for the rest of his career. Although William Davidge♦ and others later played the role with some success, by the 1880s the play was rarely mounted.

Servant in the House, The, a play in five acts by Charles Rann Kennedy.♦ Produced by Henry Miller♦ at the Savoy Theatre. March 23, 1908. 80 performances.

Everyone in the home of the Reverend William Smythe (Charles Dalton), including his snobbish wife "Auntie" (Edith Wynne Matthison) and his niece Mary (Mabel Moore), believe they have seen their new butler, Manson (Walter Hampden♦), somewhere before, but they cannot actually place him. Manson is a strange man, singularly humble and wise, and dressed in ancient Eastern garb. But the vicar has more pressing problems. Not only is he attempting to repair his dilapidated church, but on this very day he expects visits from three people he has not seen in many years. One is his wife's brother, the Bishop of Lancashire (Arthur Lewis), who is virtually deaf and blind and whom the vicar despises because of the Bishop's preoccupation with worldly success. The Bishop has consented to come after learning that the vicar's brother Joshua, long out of touch and now supposedly in charge of a large, but very distant see, will also be there. The third arrival

is to be another long-lost brother, Robert (Tyrone Power♦), who took to drink after his wife's death and is now a common laborer. The vicar and his wife have had nothing to do with him, but have raised his daughter Mary in ignorance of her father's history. It remains for Manson's quiet charity and sense to bring the family closer together and teach them the true meaning of their religion. In the end it is suggested that Manson is Joshua, but the vicar is not sure he may not also be someone else. He asks Manson, "In God's name, who are you?" Manson replies, "In God's Name—your brother."

Despite its division into five acts, the action of this modern morality play was continuous. Walter Prichard Eaton♦ called it "not a sermon or a tract, but a statement of applied or ethical religion in terms of the drama, a play with its own dramatic appeal and human significance." Almost inevitably, a play such as this had little broad appeal.

Seven Days, a comedy in three acts by Mary Roberts Rinehart♦ and Avery Hopwood.♦ Produced by Wagenhals♦ and Kemper♦ at the Astor Theatre. November 10, 1909. 397 performances.

James Wilson (Herbert Corthell) has not told his rich Aunt Selina (Lucille La Verne) about his divorce from his wife Bella (Hope Latham), so when Selina suddenly appears he is forced to palm off his friend Anne Brown (Florence Reed♦) as his wife. Anne is an odd girl, a psychic who is convinced—correctly as it turns out—that there is a burglar in the house. Suddenly a policeman appears and announces that James's cook is in the hospital with a communicable disease. Therefore, everyone in the house is under a seven-day quarantine. Bella suddenly arrives and she, too, is confined. For the next week the group attempts to do household chores and learn to cook. They get to know each other all too well.

This slight farce was one of the biggest hits of its era and was later made into the musical *Tumble In* (1919).

Seven Keys to Baldpate, a comedy in a prologue, two acts, and an epilogue by George M. Cohan.♦ Produced by Cohan and Sam H. Harris♦ at the Astor Theatre. September 22, 1913. 320 performances.

Baldpate is a summer hotel, normally closed in the winter. But when a writer, William Hallowell Magee (Wallace Eddinger♦), bets the owner that he can write a work in twenty-four hours if left alone there, the owner agrees to open the closed hotel for him. As he starts to write, Magee finds he is not alone. Come to the hotel are a gun-toting man, a pretty young newspaper reporter, with whom Magee falls in love at first sight, an adventuress, and some politicians and a railroad magnate looking to make a secret deal. Shots and screams galore seem to interrupt Magee's work. But when the twenty-four hours are up, Magee has finished his piece. Were the interruptions a joke staged by the owner of the hotel, or were they simply the story that Magee was writing?

Based on the novel by Earl Derr Biggers, the play has remained a favorite with summer stock and other similar groups.

7-20-8; or, Casting the Boomerang, a "comedy of To-Day" in four acts by Augustin Daly.♦ Produced by Daly at Daly's Theatre. February 24, 1883. 49 performances.

"Portrait of a Lady," picture #728 at the annual Academy exhibition, so lovingly depicts a beautiful woman and her huge dog that both Courtney Corliss (John Drew♦), a handsome young man-about-town, and the remote Lord Lawntennis decide to seek her out. The Englishman sends an effervescent Italian opera impresario, Signor Tamborini (William Gilbert), to do his legwork. Corliss's and Tamborini's search brings them to the country estate of Launcelot Bargiss (James Lewis♦), whose daughter Flos (Ada Rehan♦) is indeed the lady of the picture. Flos, who fears she will "die of the blues" if she cannot escape her dreary isolation and live in New York City, is immediately taken by Courtney. He suggests she not be afraid of a little adventure, that the follies of youth are the happy memories of old age, and that we all cast little boomerangs that come home to haunt us and eventually amuse us. At the same time Mrs. Bargiss (Mrs. G. H. Gilbert♦) has submitted to a shady publisher all the love poems her husband had sent her when they were courting, unaware that he lifted them from Shakespeare and other great poets. Courtney persuades the family to spend a season in New York, where Bargiss is eventually caught having a fling on the town and where he must buy up all copies of his supposed works to save his reputation. When it turns out that Lord Lawntennis is actually seeking to purchase the dog in the painting, Flos and Courtney are free to wed.

Based loosely on Schoenthan's *Die Schwabenstreich,* the play was the first major success of Daly's second troupe and saved the company from probable bankruptcy. Although prior commitments shortened the original run, Daly revived and toured the work regularly. The title was derived from the small

theatre at 728 Broadway (by then Harrigan♦ and Hart's♦ Theatre Comique), which Daly had use briefly after his Fifth Avenue Theatre♦ had burned.

Seven Year Itch, *The,* a comedy in three acts by George Axelrod. Produced by Courtney Burr and Elliott Nugent♦ at the Fulton Theatre. November 20, 1952. 1,141 performances.

Richard Sherman (Tom Ewell♦) is a nervous, wildly imaginative paperback publisher who finds that his wild imagination leads to thoughts of infidelity when he becomes a summer bachelor. These thoughts are given a nudge by a flower pot that nearly lands on him from a balcony above his. The flower pot belongs to the girl (Vanessa Brown) upstairs and serves as an excuse for their meeting. Despite Richard's Walter Mittyish dreams of conquest, the voice of his conscience and his own comic apprehensions keep him on the straight and narrow.

Brooks Atkinson♦ hailed the play as "original and funny." The New Yorn-born Axelrod (b. 1922) wrote only one other popular play, *Will Success Spoil Rock Hunter?* (1955), a spoof of Hollywood told in terms of the *Faust* legend. He was also co-producer of *Visit to a Small Planet*♦ (1957) and later directed several comedies.

Seventeen, a play in four acts by Hugh Stanislaus Stange and Stannard Mears. Produced by Stuart Walker♦ at the Booth Theatre. January 22, 1918. 225 performances.

Young Willie Baxter (Gregory Kelly♦) is not above stealing his father's evening clothes in order to court baby-talking Lola Pratt (Ruth Gordon♦).

The play was based on Booth Tarkington's♦ famous novel of puppy love.

1776, a musical (performed without intermission). Book by Peter Stone. Lyrics and music by Sherman Edwards. Produced at the 46th Street Theatre. March 16, 1969. 1,217 performances.

In the spring and summer of 1776, delegates have gathered in Philadelphia to work on a Declaration of Independence. Much of the give and take is seen through the eyes of the waspish John Adams (William Daniels), who writes about it to his beloved Abigail (Virginia Vestoff). Jefferson (Ken Howard) and Franklin (Howard Da Silva) also play prominent roles. By the time the Declaration is signed, they and their associates have all had to compromise a bit.

With no memorable songs or lively dance numbers, this unusual musical relied on the intelligence of its book and lyrics, fine acting and elegant mounting to please audiences. It remains popular with amateur and collegiate groups.

Seventh Heaven, a play in three acts by Austin Strong. Produced by John Golden♦ at the Booth Theatre. October 30, 1922. 704 performances.

Diane (Helen Menken♦) is saved from her brutal sister Nana (Marian Kerby), who would force her into prostitution, by the sympathetic sewer cleaner Chico (George Gaul). He takes her to his shabby seventh floor walk-up—his seventh heaven—where the youngsters quickly fall in love. When war breaks out and Chico is called into the army, they pledge their loyalty. Diane goes to work in a munitions factory. As the war ends, she is led to believe that Chico has been killed, so she takes up with another man, Brissac (Frank Morgan♦). Chico returns, but since he has been blinded, he does not see Brissac. The lovers are reunited, and Diane can only agree with Chico's assessment of himself—that he is "a most remarkable fellow."

Many critics felt this highly sentimental drama was immeasurably strengthened by Helen Menken's performance, but the show toured successfully for several seasons without her. Janet Gaynor and Charles Farrell headed a successful film version in 1927, but a musical version failed on Broadway in 1955.

Strong (1881–1952) was born in San Francisco but was raised in Samoa (his step-grandfather was Robert Louis Stevenson). Nearly a dozen of his plays reached Broadway, most notably *A Good Little Devil* (1913), in which a blind girl's sight is restored by fairies; and *Three Wise Fools*♦ (1918), in which three aging bachelors are rejuvenated by the daughter of a woman they all had loved.

Sex, a play in three acts by Jane Mast. Produced at Daly's Theatre. April 26, 1926. 375 performances.

Margie LaMont (Mae West♦) shares her apartment with a blackmailing gigolo. When he drugs a rich socialite, Margie rescues her. But the woman, fearing for her reputation, accuses Margie of theft. Margie gets even by seducing the woman's son.

Not only was the show panned by critics, but many newspapers refused to accept its advertisements. As a result the producer flooded New York with posters boldly plugging the title. The show was still playing to good business when it was raided by the police. Miss West was hauled into court and sentenced to ten days in the workhouse. Jane Mast was reputed to have been Miss West's pen name.

SEYMOUR, WILLIAM [GORMAN] (1850?–1933) Born in New York City to actor parents, he began performing while still a child and subsequently acted with most of the great players of the last half of the 19th century. He also served an apprenticeship in other aspects of theatre. He started to direct while serving a stint at the Boston Museum♦ late in the century, then moved on to become a principal stager for Charles Frohman♦ and for Liebler and Company.♦ His courtesy to actors and his willngness to follow a playwright's ideas won him wide respect. At the time of his death he was called "the dean" of Broadway's directors.

Shadow Box, The, a play in two acts by Michael Cristofer. Produced at the Morosco Theatre. March 31, 1977. 315 performances. PP.

At a hospital for the terminally ill, three patients await death in separate cottages. Joe (Simon Oakland) is a family man who is determined that he and his wife and son enjoy their last weeks together. Brian (Laurence Luckinbill) is a bisexual author who would like to reach an understanding with his ex-wife and his lover. Felicity (Geraldine Fitzgerald) is an aging woman who finds solace in pretending that a long-dead daughter is still alive.

Like many of the best modern works, this play was presented at important regional theatres—the Mark Taper Forum♦ and the Long Wharf Theatre♦ —before reaching New York. Otis L. Guernsey, Jr.,♦ observed that the work was "remarkable more for texture and tone than momentum," adding, "Cristofer handled his subject—not death itself, but life before death—with emotional maturity, with a touch of gallows humor but no trace of morbidity."

Cristofer [né Michael Procaccion] (b. 1946) was born in Trenton, N.J., and raised there and in Princeton. He dropped out of Catholic University to become an actor. This has been his only noteworthy play.

SHAFFER, PETER [LEVIN] (b. 1926) An English playwright whose works have often met with remarkable success in America, he has been represented on Broadway by *Five Finger Exercise* (1959), a story of a British family; a double bill, *The Private Ear* and *The Public Eye* (1963); *The Royal Hunt of the Sun* (1965), telling of the Spanish conquest of Peru; a second double bill, *Black Comedy* and *White Lies; Equus*♦ (1974), centering on a mentally disturbed young man; and *Amadeus*♦ (1981), dealing with the relationship of Salieri and Mozart. *Lettice and Lovage* (1990) dealt with a kooky tour guide and her stern, refugee supervisor. His twin brother Anthony, was the author of the popular thriller, *Sleuth*◆ (1970).

SHAKESPEARE, WILLIAM (1564–1616) Shakespeare came to American stages relatively early, although there have since been notable peaks and valleys in his popularity with playgoers and producers. The first Shakspearean play performed on an American stage was probably *Richard III,*◆ which Thomas Kean◆ acted in New York on March 5, 1750, and may have played earlier in Philadelphia. Kean and his partner Walter Murray◆ did not use Shakespeare's actual text but rather Colley Cibber's version. Indeed, the use of Restoration and 18th-century redactions of virtually all Shakespeare's plays was a commonplace as much in America as in London until well into the last half of the 19th-century.

For the remainder of the 18th century and the very early years of the next the Shakespearean repertory of the time was presented as part of the regular season by the stock companies that dominated the various American theatrical centers. However, with the appearance of noted tragedians such as Cooper,◆ Cooke,◆ and Edmund Kean,◆ and the rise of the star system, the great actors began to tour. They generally toured alone, accepting whatever supporting casts and scenery local playhouses offered. Not until after the Civil War did great tragedians such as Edwin Booth◆ and Lawrence Barrett◆ begin to travel with specially selected companies and their own scenery. These touring ensembles peaked at the turn of the century, notably with the company headed by Julia Marlowe◆ and E. H. Sothern. ◆ A few touring tragedians such as Fritz Leiber,◆ who continued to trek into the 1930s, were looked upon as anachronisms. The productions of the great itinerant ensembles, as well as those mountings by distinguished stock companies from Burton's◆ through Daly's◆ were, according to modern standards, top-heavy with elaborate scenery.

In the 20th century the rise of a more blatant commercialism on Broadway, the growth of an audience not steeped in older traditions, and perhaps simply a surfeit of Shakespeare caused a gradual dropping off of productions. Thereafter most noted productions were mounted as occasional vehicles for special stars. To some extent collegiate playhouses compensated for this falling away.

About the time of World War I Shakespearean productions also discarded their sumptuous settings, relying thereafter primarily on more suggestive sets and imaginative lighting. These changes came about as much for aesthetic reasons as for commercial ones. In the 1930s and thereafter Shakespearean festivals were established from Oregon to Connecticut, and many of the rarely performed works, no longer deemed profitable in mainstream theatres, were offered here along with more famous plays.

The following is a thumbnail history of the Shakespearean canon in America. Plays followed by ◆ are given individual entries:

All's Well That Ends Well Although the play had been performed on rare occasions by collegiate and regional theatres, The New York Shakespeare Festival◆ gave it its professional premiere, as far as the city was concerned, when it included it in the 1966 season in Central Park. In 1983 the Royal Shakespeare Company◆ offered a critically acclaimed mounting, set at the time of World War I, but the public would not accept it.

Antony and Cleopatra◆

As You Like It◆

Comedy of Errors, The First done at the Park Theatre◆ in 1804, its most memorable American revival was the free-wheeling version offered with W. H. Crane◆ and Stuart Robson◆ in 1878 and again in 1885. It has been performed intermittently since, but is probably most familiar to playgoers through the Rodgers◆ and Hart◆ musical version, *The Boys from Syracuse*◆ (1938), which employed only a single line of the text.

Coriolanus Done initially at Philadelphia's Southwark Theatre◆ in 1767, it remained popular with all the classic tragedians, including Edwin Forrest◆ and John McCullough,◆ and is still revived with some regularity.

Cymbeline Its American premiere was at the Southwark Theatre in 1767 with Mrs. Cheer◆ as Imogen and the younger Hallam◆ as Posthumus. Never very popular, it nonetheless provided successful vehicles for Adelaide Neilson◆ and Viola Allen,◆ but has rarely been revived in modern times.

Hamlet◆

Henry IV◆

Henry V Cooper was apparently the first American Henry at the Park in 1804. One of the least popular of the plays, it is best known through Olivier's◆ postwar film version.

Henry VI The three parts of the history have been presented in America only on collegiate and festival stages.

Henry VIII This pageant play was first offered to New York in 1799. Although infrequently done, it was part of the season mounted in 1946 by the American Repertory Theatre. ◆ Principals in that production included Victor Jory as Henry, Eva Le Gallienne♦ as Katharine of Aragon, and Walter Hampden♦ as Cardinal Wolsey.

Julius Caesar♦

King John First mounted at the Southwark Theatre in 1768 with Douglass♦ in the title role, it has never been popular with American playgoers, although such celebrated performers as McCullough and Modjeska♦ have starred in revivals.

King Lear♦

Love's Labours Lost Not produced in New York until Daly's celebrated 1874 mounting, it continues as one of the plays least often resurrected.

Macbeth♦

Measure for Measure The New York performances by Mr. and Mrs. Barnes♦ in 1818 are the earliest known American presentation of this comedy, which has since occupied a sort of middle ground, neither as neglected as such comedies as *Love's Labours Lost* nor as popular as *As You Like It* or *Twelfth Night*. Adelaide Neilson♦ headed a memorable 1880 mounting, although critical reaction to the play itself as "repulsively immoral" may explain the relative infrequency of Victorian stagings. The changing moral climate in the 1950s and 1960s was probably a factor in the increasing revivals, especially at Canada's Shakespeare Festival.

Merchant of Venice, The♦

Merry Wives of Windsor, The♦

Midsummer Night's Dream, A♦

Much Ado About Nothing♦

Othello♦

Pericles Stagings of this play have been confined to collegiate and festival theatres.

Richard II First offered to New York by J. W. Wallack♦ in 1819, it is one of the rare Shakespearean plays which has proved far more popular in the 20th century than it was earlier. Noteworthy among contemporary revivals was Maurice Evans's♦ 1937 production, to which he returned on several later occasions.

Richard III♦

Romeo and Juliet♦

Taming of the Shrew, The♦

Tempest, The First offered in 1770 at the Southwark Theatre in Dryden's redaction, it was many years before a faithful rendering was presented. A movement toward textual accuracy was seen in one of the great 19th-century productions, that of William E. Burton♦ in 1854 with Charles Fisher♦ as Prospero and Burton as Caliban. Besides restoring much, although not all, of the original text, Burton employed music by Arne, Purcell and, somewhat anachronistically, Halévy, and empha-

sized pictorial spectacle. By contrast, a notable modern version, staged by Margaret Webster♦ in 1945 with Arnold Moss as Prospero and Canada Lee♦ as Caliban, while rearranging the original text at some major points, offered relatively lean, suggestive settings and costumes and employed modern music by David Diamond.

Timon of Athens

Titus Andronicus

Troilus and Cressida Productions of these three works have been almost wholly in collegiate and festival theatres, although the Old Vic♦ offered the last named in its 1956 visit.

Twelfth Night♦

Two Gentlemen of Verona Charles and Ellen Kean♦ were the first performers to offer Americans this play, which they acted during their 1846 visit. Daly staged a major revival in 1895. While rarely mounted since, except at collegiate and festival productions, it provided the source of a successful musical of the same name in 1971. Produced by the New York Shakespeare Festival, it employed rock music, some highly objectionable, scatological lyrics, and a mixture of modern, skeletonized settings with period costuming.

Winter's Tale, The First offered in 1795 in a version called *Florizel and Perdita,* the play's most successful 19th-century revival was that of Mary Anderson,♦ who assumed the roles of both Hermione and Perdita. A 1946 Theatre Guild♦ revival was short-lived.

Shame Woman, *The* a play in nine scenes by Lula Vollmer. ♦ Produced at the Greenwich Village Theatre. October 16, 1923. 276 performances.

For twenty years, ever since she was seduced by Craig Anson (Edward Pawley), Lize Burns (Florence Rittenhouse) has been shunned by her North Carolina hillbilly neighbors as a "shame woman." She has lived in an isolated cabin with only her adopted daughter Lily (Thelma Paige) for company. Lonely and heartsick, she has never had the courage to tell Lily of her past or to warn her not to wander carelessly among the hills. However, learning that Lily has been meeting a man at night, Lize finally forces herself to tell Lily her history. Lily runs from the room and kills herself, and Lize realizes what has taken place. When Anson calls at the cabin Lize finds out he was Lily's seducer. She kills him with a potato knife to prevent him from boasting of his latest conquest and from disclosing that Lily, too, had become a "shame woman."

John Corbin♦ of the *Times* saw the work as "an exposition, truly epic in its length and its dead seriousness, of the wrongs women suffer at the hands of predacious men."

Shanghai Gesture, The, a melodrama in four acts by John Colton.♦ Produced by A. H. Woods♦ at the Martin Beck Theatre. February 1, 1926. 331 performances.

At the "Far-Famed House of Mother Goddam," a Shanghai brothel, the proprietress entertains the head of the British-China Trading Company, Sir Guy Charteris (McKay Morris). Mother Goddam (Florence Reed♦) reminds Sir Guy of several things he has forgotten—that they were once lovers, that he had promised to marry her, and that he had sold her to some cruel Chinese junkmen when he fell in love with an English girl. As Sir Guy and his friends look on, Mother Goddam now sells a young girl to similar junkmen, then reveals that the girl was a daughter she had had by Guy. When the daughter, Poppy (Mary Duncan), returns to the brothel as a dope addict and a prostitute Mother Goddam strangles her.

Originally written as a vehicle for Mrs. Fiske,♦ who was dismissed by director Guthrie McClintic♦ during the tryout, the play was lambasted by many critics. George Jean Nathan♦ called it "a pâté of box-office drivel." But its lurid story and Miss Reed's memorable performance made it a major hit.

SHANNON, EFFIE (1867–1954) Born in Cambridge, Mass., she began a stage career that was to span 70 years when she appeared as an extra in John McCullough's♦ production of *Coriolanus* in Boston in the early 1870s. Her first important assignment followed shortly, when she portrayed Eva in *Uncle Tom's Cabin.* ♦ Billed as La Petite Shannon, she grew up to be a tall, slim beauty. Her first New York assignment came in 1886 in *Tangled Lives.* She played for a time for Augustin Daly,♦ including Titania in his 1888 mounting of *A Midsummer Night's Dream.* ♦ A year later she created the role of Jenny Buckthorn in *Shenandoah.* ♦ In the 1890s she supported Rose Coghlan♦ and Lillie Langtry.♦ Stardom came when she played opposite her husband, Herbert Kelcey,♦ in Clyde Fitch's♦ *The Moth and the Flame* (1898), appearing as the innocent yet self-willed Marion Wolton. She enjoyed another success as Indiana Stillwater, the American bride of a thoughtless Englishman, in *Her Lord and Master* (1902). In 1907 she was Blanche in the first American performance of *Widowers' Houses,* after which she toured for two years as Marie-Louise, a role Margaret Illington♦ had created in *The Thief.* She was Miss Harrington, the stern maiden aunt, in

Pollyanna (1916), then won major acclaim for the dual roles of the German and American wives in the war play *Under Orders* (1918). During the 1920s she played in such revivals as *She Stoops To Conquer* (1924) and *Trelawny of the Wells* (1927), appearing as Mrs. Hardcastle and Miss Trafalgar Gower, but she was also the first American Hesione Hushabye in *Heartbreak House* (1920) and Mrs. Winslow, whose last son was inadvertently left out of his father's will, in Philip Barry's♦ *The Youngest* (1924). She created the part of Esther Crampton, one of the sisters in a closely knit family, in *Morning's at Seven♦* (1939). In 1942 she replaced Jean Adair as Martha Brewster, one of two sweet, but murderous old ladies, in *Arsenic and Old Lace,* ♦ and played the role until her retirement two years later.

SHARAFF, IRENE (b. 1910?) The Boston-born costume designer studied in America and in Paris before serving as assistant to Aline Bernstein♦ at the Civic Repertory Theatre. ♦ Working alone or with distinguished collaborators, she later created the stylish, color-splashed costumes for such shows as *As Thousands Cheer♦* (1933), *Life Begins at 8:40* (1934), *Jubilee♦* (1935), *Idiot's Delight♦* (1936), *On Your Toes♦* (1936), *The Boys from Syracuse♦* (1938), *Lady in the Dark♦* (1941), *The King and I♦* (1952), *Candide♦* (1956), *West Side Story♦* (1957), *Funny Girl♦* (1964), *Sweet Charity♦* (1966), and the 1973 revival of *Irene.* ♦

Shaughraun, The, a play in three acts by Dion Boucicault.♦ Produced by Lester Wallack♦ at Wallack's Theatre. November 14, 1874. 143 performances.

Robert Ffolliott (J. B. Polk) is a rich young Irishman who is under sentence of death for his Fenian sympathies. His fiancée, Arte O'Neal (Jeffreys Lewis), lives on one of his estates with his sister Claire Ffolliott (Ada Dyas). Corry Kinchela (Edward Arnott), who hopes to win Ffolliott's lands, plots to have him captured. His plans are momentarily frustrated when Captain Molyneaux (H. J. Montague♦), the British officer sent to arrest Robert, falls in love with Claire. But Robert is eventually arrested. However, Kinchela learns that a pardon is in the offing, so he suggests to Robert that he flee, planning to kill him during his escape. Robert's best friend, Conn, the Shaughraun (Boucicault)—"the soul of every fair, the life of every funeral, the first fiddle at all weddings and parties"—helps Robert make good his escape. Kinchela shoots Conn, leaving him for dead, and takes Arte and Claire captive. Playing dead, Conn learns the girls' whereabouts. They are rescued and

Kinchela arrested. Robert and Arte, and Molyneux and Claire, are free to wed.

Called by Odell♦ "that best of all Boucicault Irish plays," it was also his most financially successful and enjoyed the longest run of any play at Wallack's in the 1870s. Boucicault and others revived it regularly. Historian Jack A. Vaughn has written, "It is skillfully structured to provide its implausible, sensational situations with a maximum of credibility, and it contains several scenes of genuine humor and Gaelic charm. The role of Conn is one of the better acting parts of the period." A shaughraun was a wanderer or vagabond. The show was revived with tremendous success in London in 1988 by the National Theatre. ♦

SHAW, George Bernard (1856–1950) The most famous and possibly the most controversial of 20th-century English playwrights was described by the *Times* in its review of the first major American production of one of his plays as "the eccentric and able London socialist, essayist, music critic, Ibsenite, and wearer of gray flannel clothes." That first production was Richard Mansfield's♦ 1894 mounting of *Arms and the Man* and was seen by the same paper as "unrelieved satire." With occasional shadings of difference, critical opinion of Shaw in America has remained much the same ever since. His plays are often perceived to minimize the importance of dramatic construction and depth of characterization, and to rely on effective debates for their theatrical attraction. Especially in early years his subjects offended many playgoers and critics, dealing as they did with such matters as prostitution, religious hypocrisy, slum landlordism, profiteering, and, of course, socialism. In these early years his most noted exponents included Mansfield and Arnold Daly,♦ while in after seasons the Theatre Guild♦ regularly offered even his minor plays. The last several decades have witnessed a marked waning of interest in his works, although he will undoubtedly undergo reassessment.

Below is a thumbnail history of some of his plays in America. *Caesar and Cleopatra, Candida, The Devil's Disciple, Man and Superman, Pygmalion,* and *Saint Joan* will be found under separate entries.

Androcles and the Lion A short comedy twitting early Christians, it was hissed at its 1913 London premiere, but received a cordial welcome when Harley Granville-Barker♦ presented it in New York in 1915 with O. P. Heggie♦ as Androcles. The major American revivals occurred in 1925, when the Theatre Guild presented it with Henry Travers as the hero and such superior players as Romney

Brent, Clare Eames,♦ Tom Powers,♦ and Edward G. Robinson♦ in supporting roles, and in 1946 when the American Repertory Theatre♦ offered it with Ernest Truex♦ in the lead. Because of its relative brevity it has almost always been given as part of a double bill.

Arms and the Man This beguiling spoof of militarism was, as mentioned earlier, the first Shaw play presented in America. Although he often had little time for Shaw, William Winter♦ saw the comedy as one "that causes thought as well as mirth," and called Mansfield's performance "a delicious piece of mystification, crisp in speech and diversified by airy nonchalance and whimsical humor." The major revival was in 1925 when the Theatre Guild presented Lunt♦ and Fontanne♦ in the leads. Howard Lindsay♦ recalled Lunt's Bluntschli as "cold, precise, hard and . . . probably one of the greatest high-comedy performances any actor, American or British, has given in our time." Many Americans know the play best through its musical version, the Viennese operetta *The Chocolate Soldier.*

The Doctor's Dilemma A comedy about egocentricity and medical ethics, it was first presented in New York by Arnold Daly in 1915. The first major revival was that by the Theatre Guild in 1927 with a remarkable cast that included Helen Westley,♦ Dudley Digges,♦ Earle Larimore,♦ Lynn Fontanne, and Alfred Lunt as Dubedat. Many critics felt the acting was superior to the play. A change in emphasis came in 1941 when Katharine Cornell♦ revived the work with herself as Jennifer Dubedat and Raymond Massey♦ as Sir Colenso. Bramwell Fletcher was Dubedat. The Phoenix Theatre♦ mounted the play in 1955 with Roddy MacDowell as the doomed artist.

Heartbreak House First presented in America by the Theatre Guild in 1920 with a cast that included Helen Westley, Dudley Digges, and Effie Shannon,♦ and with Albert Perry as Shotover, this look at a modern Armageddon seems to have spoken eloquently to a world where a major war is always looming and so has been offered a number of fine revivals. Orson Welles,♦ dressed to resemble Shaw, played Shotover in the Mercury Theatre's♦ 1938 mounting, while Maurice Evans♦ assumed the role in a 1959 production. Rex Harrison♦ played the part in a 1983 revival, with Rosemary Harris♦ in support.

Major Barbara Grace George♦ presented and starred in the 1915 American premiere of this play about big business and warmongering, offering a notable cast of then-famous or up-and-coming theatrical names, including Clarence Derwent, ♦ Guthrie McClintic, ♦ Ernest Lawford, John Cromwell, ♦ Mary Nash, ♦ and Conway Tearle. It was welcomed at the time as "a provocative, often richly amusing and continuously stimulating comedy." Major revivals have included a 1928 Theatre Guild presentation with Winifred Lenihan ♦ as Barbara and Dudley Digges as Undershaft and an exceptionally successful 1956 production, which ran seven months, with Glynis Johns and Charles Laughton ♦ in the leads.

Mrs. Warren's Profession This play about prostitution prompted court action in 1905, both during its New Haven tryout and in New York. Its stars, Arnold Daly, who was also the producer, and Mary Shaw, ♦ were arrested but were acquitted of charges of presenting an immoral play. However, the work proved more sensational than durable, revivals being infrequent and short-lived. Uta Hagen ♦ headed a fine 1985 revival.

As the fate of *Mrs. Warren's Profession* suggests, the initial success or notoriety of a Shaw play was no reliable indicator of its future vogue. Several plays that were huge successes at their first American presentation since have been largely neglected, while other works, often branded as minor, have enjoyed tremendous success later on, thanks on occasion to an unusual production or the appearance of a major star. An example of one would be *Fanny's First Play,* which ran eight months in New York when it was premiered there in 1912—an exceptional run for the time—but which has never had a major revival. By contrast such plays as *The Apple Cart* and *The Millionairess,* dismissed or totally ignored at first, enjoyed newsworthy and relatively successful mountings when produced with Maurice Evans (1956) and Katharine Hepburn ♦ (1952) respectively. Other plays have been produced occasionally, but rarely with much success, although many remain popular with collegiate and festival theatres, and sometimes with summer stock.

SHAW, IRWIN (1913–84) Born in New York and educated at Brooklyn College, the writer briefly gave promise of becoming an important playwright. That promise came from two of his first three plays: *Bury the Dead* ♦ (1936), an anti-war piece, and *The Gentle People* ♦ (1939), a tale of two put-upon old men. His other plays were *Siege* (1937), a story of trapped Loyalists in the Spanish Civil War; *Retreat to Pleasure* (1941), in which two politically disparate men court the same woman; *Sons and Soldiers* (1943), in which a pregnant woman must choose between saving herself or her baby; *The Assassin* (1945), a dramatization of the killing of the French

Admiral Darlan; *Patate* (1958), a translation of a French play; and *Children from Their Games* (1963), in which a disillusioned veteran attempts to persuade an old friend to shoot him. Although Shaw's sympathies fell in line with the leftish sentiments of many playgoers and critics, apart from *Bury the Dead* and *The Gentle People* his later writings were wanting in terms of theatrical effectiveness. He finally abandoned the theatre to become a popular novelist.

SHAW, MARY (1860–1929) The Boston-born scion of an old New Hampshire family, she made her debut at the Boston Museum ♦ in 1878 and afterward performed in important supporting roles with Modjeska, ♦ Mrs. Fiske, ♦ Julia Marlowe, ♦ and many other major stars. However, she is remembered largely for her early advocacy of Ibsen ♦ and Shaw. ♦ She was the first American Mrs. Warren in *Mrs. Warren's Profession* (1905) and won critical acclaim for her Hedda Gabler and Mrs. Alving. Her playing of Mrs. Warren led to her arrest and subsequent acquittal on morals charges. She was also a celebrated lecturer on theatre. That she never achieved widespread popularity despite critical praise may have been because the public was daunted by her intellectual approach to theatre. Some sources give her birthdate as 1854.

SHAW, OSCAR [né SCHWARTZ] (1889–1967) Born in Philadelphia and educated at the University of Pennsylvania, the pleasant-looking song-and-dance man, with the slicked-down black hair and the toothy grin, began his theatrical career as a chorus boy in *The Mimic World* (1908). During the next four years he appeared in important secondary roles in musicals, then left to spend time in England. On his return in 1915 he won the second male lead in *Very Good Eddie,* ♦ in which he introduced "Some Sort of Somebody." He was rarely idle for the next seventeen years, his hits including *Leave It to Jane* ♦ (1917); *Two Little Girls in Blue* (1920), in which he introduced "Oh Me! Oh My!" and "Dolly"; *Good Morning Dearie* (1920), in which he sang "Ka-lu-a"; *Music Box Revue* ♦ (1924); *Oh, Kay!* ♦ (1926), with "Do, Do, Do" and "Maybe" among his numbers; *The Five O'Clock Girl* (1927), where his big hit was "Thinking of You"; and *Flying High* ♦ (1930), in which he performed "Thank Your Father." In 1932 he toured as John T. Wintergreen in the road company of *Of Thee I Sing,* ♦ after which his career faded away. His last roles were in non-musicals, the most important being his replacement of Dennis King ♦ as the lead in *Petticoat Fever* (1935).

She Loves Me, a musical in two acts. Book by Joe Masteroff. Lyrics by Sheldon Harnick. ♦ Music by Jerry Bock. ♦ Produced by Hal Prince ♦ and others at the Eugene O'Neill Theatre. April 23, 1963. 301 performances.

Georg Novack (Daniel Massey), a clerk at Maraczek's Parfumerie, has been writing to a girl he knows only as "Dear Friend," so when Amalia Belash (Barbara Cook ♦) obtains employment in the same shop he has no reason to suspect she is his correspondent. He discovers the truth after they arrange a rendezvous at the Café Imperiale. But since his relations with Amalia have not been the best, he leaves the restaurant without disclosing his identity. When she reports in sick he appears at her apartment. At first she is furious, thinking he is checking on her excuse, but a gift of ice cream alters matters. She also tells him how much she loves her unseen, unknown correspondent. By Christmas Eve Georg has identified himself to her and they walk away from the store in a happy embrace.

Principal songs: Dear Friend · Ice Cream · She Loves Me

A musical version of Ernst Lubitsch's film *The Shop Around the Corner* and the play on which that film was based, Miklos Laszlo's *Parfumerie,* the show failed despite almost universally glowing notices. Stanley Green ♦ suggested that the reason for the failure may have been that this charming bonbon was "too gentle, too intimate, and too free from Broadway razzle-dazzle to attract the customers." The musical has since become a "cult" show among aficianados.

She Loves Me Not, a comedy in two acts by Howard Lindsay. ♦ Produced by Dwight Deere Wiman ♦ and Tom Weatherly at the 46th Street Theatre. November 20, 1933. 360 performances.

Escaping from the police after witnessing a gangland murder, the night-club dancer Curley Flagg (Polly Waters) seeks refuge in the Princeton dorm room of Paul Lawton (John Beal). Paul and his friends cut Curley's hair, give her men's clothes, and introduce her as a younger brother. They even try to get Curley work—in films. The result is that the campus is invaded by the press, film crews, and an odd assortment of curiosity seekers. College authorities look askance at this and almost expel the students. When order is restored, the boys are allowed to continue their education, Curley lands a major movie contract, and Paul finds romance with the dean's daughter.

Based on a novel by Edward Hope, the play was greeted by Richard Lockridge of the *Sun* as "a jovial

six-ring circus." Many critics felt the performance of Burgess Meredith ♦ as Buzz Jones, Paul's buddy, was the highlight of the evening.

She Would Be a Soldier; or, The Plains of Chippewa, a play in three acts by Mordecai M. Noah. ♦ Produced at the Park Theatre. ♦ June 21, 1819. In repertory.

When her father insists she marry the bumpkin farmer Jerry Mayflower (John Barnes ♦), Christine (Catharine Leesugg) disguises herself as a man and runs away to be with her fiancé, Lenox (James Pritchard), who is fighting with the American army in the War of 1812. Entering the army camp she is seized as a spy and condemned to death. She is blindfolded and placed in front of a firing squad before Lenox recognizes her and stops the execution. Jerry rushes in, but realizing the lengths Christine has gone to to be with Lenox, accepts the inevitable. He adds, "Miss Crissy, you look very pretty in pantaloons, and make a fine solger, but after all, I'm glad to have escaped a wife who wears the breeches before marriage."

Written with Miss Leesugg in mind, the play remained popular for many years. It was performed in a regular commercial production in New York as late as 1848, and its modern editor, Richard Moody, records no fewer than 31 performances in New Orleans between 1825 and 1842. He concludes, "For its sincerity of tone, its brightness and charm, its democratic spirit, and its praise of the Indian, Noah's play ranks a full step above . . . other dramas dealing with similar historical events."

SHEAN, AL, see *Gallagher and Shean*

SHELDON, EDWARD [BREWSTER] (1886–1946) The son of wealthy Chicagoans, he was educated at Harvard, where he was one of the first important pupils of Professor George Pierce Baker. ♦ He submitted an early play, *A Family Affair,* to Alice Kauser, ♦ who rejected it. But after a meeting with the young playwright, she encouraged him to develop another idea he spoke of. That idea became his first success, *Salvation Nell* ♦ (1908), in which a scrubwoman reforms her ne'er-do-well lover. In *The Nigger* ♦ (1909), a segregationist governor discovers he has Negro blood. *The Boss* ♦ (1911) told of a corrupt politician reformed by the daughter of a man he determined to destroy. With his next play, *Princess Zim-Zim* (1911), a comedy about a Coney Island snake-charmer, he began moving away from the hard-hitting realism that had given him his reputation. *Egypt* (1912) was a preposterous melodrama about gypsies. He returned to his earlier style with *The High Road* (1912), in which a presidential candidate suddenly discovers his wife has a blemished history. His greatest success was *Romance*♦ (1913), the story of the doomed love affair of an opera singer and a minister. In 1914 he dramatized Sudermann's *Song of Songs*, and Hans Christian Andersen's *The Little Mermaid* as *The Garden of Paradise*. Two subsequent successes were also translations: *The Jest* (1919), from an Italian play, and *The Czarina* (1922), from a Hungarian drama. With the onset of the illness that left him blind and hopelessly paralyzed for the rest of his life, he resorted to collaborations for his final works. The three most successful were *Lulu Belle*♦ (1926), written with Charles MacArthur♦ and centering on a New York prostitute, and two written with Margaret Ayer Barnes: *Jenny* (1929), a comedy about a stuffy businessman and a glamorous actress, and *Dishonored Lady* (1930), in which the heroine poisons one lover to be free to love another. Although throughout his career Sheldon willingly sacrificed depth for theatrical effectiveness, his best plays remain gripping theatre and would probably still be stageworthy if prejudices against his apparent clap-trap could be set aside.

Biography: *The Man Who Lived Twice*, Eric Wollencott Barnes, New York, 1956.

Shenandoah, a play in four acts by Bronson Howard.♦ Produced by Charles Frohman♦ at the Star Theatre. September 9, 1889. 250 performances.

The outbreak of the Civil War means that two West Point friends, Kerchival West (Henry Miller♦) of New York and Robert Ellingham (Lucius Henderson) of Virginia, must take opposing sides. Both men become colonels in their respective armies. Until the outbreak of hostilities, the men have loved each other's sisters, Madeline West (Nanette Comstock) and Gertrude Ellingham (Viola Allen.♦). Robert is taken prisoner and Gertrude is arrested as a spy. They are brought before West, who finds Gertrude surprisingly hostile. But West is stabbed by another Confederate, Thornton (John E. Kellerd♦), who, in order to save himself, tells General Haverhill (Wilton Lackaye♦) that West has been the lover of Haverhill's wife. Since West has a locket with Mrs. Haverhill's picture the charge seems believable, but West reveals he obtained the locket from a young soldier, Lt. Bedloe (G. W. Bailey). Bedloe turns out to be Haverhill's son, fighting under an assumed name. Taken prisoner, he is exchanged for Robert. The men go back to fighting, and not until the war is over are the lovers reunited.

This summary gives some indication of the complexity of the plot, which many critics assailed. Nevertheless, the play was a major hit. Much of it was derived from an earlier, unproduced Howard comedy, *Drum Taps,* which Howard had offered to Lester Wallack.♦ The anglophilic Wallack demanded the play be reset in the Crimea, and Howard refused. The play was also the first major success for its producer, Frohman, and launched his long, distinguished career.

Shenandoah, a musical in two acts. Book by James Lee Barrett, Peter Udell, and Philip Rose. Lyrics by Udell. Music by Gary Geld. Produced at the Alvin Theatre. January 7, 1975. 1,050 performances.

The Anderson family has determined to stay out of the Civil War, preferring their good life on a farm in Virginia's Shenandoah Valley. But after the youngest son Robert (Joseph Shapiro) is kidnapped by soldiers, Charlie Anderson (John Cullum) and his other sons decide they have no choice but to join the bloody struggle.

Principal songs: Next to Lovin' · Violets and Silverbells

The musical was based on a film of the same name. After opening to divided notices, the show resorted to cut-rate tickets. Although it rarely enjoyed a sell-out week, the low-priced seats and good word-of-mouth helped it to enjoy a long run and even send out a road company. It was revived briefly in 1989.

SHEPARD, SAM (né SAMUEL SHEPARD ROGERS, JR.) (b. 1943) Born in Fort Sheridan, Ill., and reared in California Shepard is one of the most prolific of late 20th-century playwrights. He began to have his works produced off-Broadway in 1964 and has since written over 30 plays which have been offered either off-Broadway or at regional theatres. Several of his plays have earned special Obie Awards♦ for distinguished writing: *Icarus's Mother* (1965); *Chicago* (1966); *Red Cross* (1967), a play with a pure white set in which a man is plagued by crabs and a woman fantasizes about splitting her head open; *La Turista* (1967), in which a sunburned American couple vacationing in Mexico are treated by witch-doctors for intestinal distress in a bright yellow hotel room; *Forensic and the Navigators* (1967); and *Action* (1975). *Buried Child*♦ (1978), a blackly humorous play in which a couple who have buried a child that is a product of incest do not recognize their grandson on his return to their decaying farm, was awarded a Pulitzer Prize.♦ *Fool for Love*♦ (1983) described the futile love-hate relationship of a half-brother and half-sister. *A Lie of the Mind*♦ (1985), telling of problems following a young husband's brutal beating of his wife, won the New York Drama Critics Circle Award. ♦ His other plays include *The Tooth of the Crime* (1973), *The Curse of the Starving Class* (1979), and *True West* (1980). In Shepard's plays, an imaginative language composed of slang, scientific jargon, B-movie dialogue, and rock and roll idioms, and a stage peopled with farmers, devils, and witchdoctors, rock stars, space men, cowboys, gangsters, and other American stereotypes demonstrate his interest in popular American culture and the folklore of the American Southwest. Shepard has also had a successful career as a film actor.

SHEPARD, THOMAS Z[ACHARY] (b. 1936) A native of Orange, N.J., he studied at Juilliard, Oberlin, and Yale Graduate School of Music. He worked for many years at Columbia Records, where he made re-creations of such old shows as *Lady in the Dark*♦ and later supervised original cast recordings of newer musicals such as *Company*♦ and the revivals of *No, No, Nanette*♦ and *Irene.*♦ Moving to RCA, he put on disk, among others, *Sweeney Todd,*♦ the complete *Porgy and Bess,*♦ and *Ain't Misbehavin'.*♦ His aim is "to create a theatrical illusion while in the context of the best musical performance possible."

SHERIDAN, RICHARD BRINSLEY (1751–1816) He was the earliest English playwright whose works were presented in America while they were still new to the London stage and that have retained their popularity ever since. The initial representations of his most enduring works, *The Rivals* and *The School for Scandal,* were given here during the Revolutionary War by British soldiers and their friends in 1778 and 1782 respectively. Professional productions followed shortly thereafter. Throughout the 19th century the plays remained special favorites with the great ensemble houses such as Wallack's♦ and Daly's♦ in New York, Mrs. Drew's♦ in Philadelphia, and the Boston Museum. ♦ Late in the century Mrs. Drew and Joseph Jefferson♦ toured in a famous all-star company of *The Rivals.* In the early years of the 20th century major professional revivals, including those headed by Kyrle Bellew♦ and Ada Rehan,♦ were far-between and short-lived. Later The Players♦ briefly mounted several all-star productions. Curiously, important back-to-back revivals of *The School for Scandal* were offered in 1962 and 1963 by the APA♦ and an English troupe headed by John Gielgud♦ and Ralph Richardson. ♦ *The Duenna* and *The Critic* keep a fitful hold on

American stages, the latter having a memorable revival by the Old Vic♦ on its 1946 visit.

One of Sheridan's most popular works in his lifetime was his adaptation of Kotzebue's♦ *Die Spanier in Peru* as *Pizarro.* ♦ It was frequently performed in America, either in Sheridan's actual version or Dunlap's♦ redaction for many decades, but has long since faded from view.

SHERIDAN, W[ILLIAM] E[DWARD] (1840?–87) Born in Boston, where he made his debut at the Howard Athenaeum♦ in 1858, he became a leading portrayer of villains and tragic figures in Cincinnati until the outbreak of the Civil War. After the war, despite a badly injured arm, he continued to be an important actor in Cincinnati, St. Louis, and at the Chestnut Street Theatre♦ in Philadelphia. Among his notable roles were Othello, Shylock, and Sir Giles Overreach. He also was the first American Beamish McCloud in *Arrah-Na-Pogue*♦ (1865). Following a long San Francisco engagement, he left for a tour of Australia, where he died. Otis Skinner♦ remembered the virile, deep-set and dark-eyed actor as "a man of splendid power, with one of the most intriguing voices I ever listened to." Others remarked on his voice's striking resonance.

Sherlock Holmes, a play in four acts by William Gillette. ♦ Produced by Charles Frohman♦ at the Garrick Theatre. November 6, 1899. 256 performances.

Alice Faulkner (Katherine Florence) holds letters written to her late sister by a member of royalty. She believes that her sister died of a broken heart from the man's faithlessness and is determined to use the letters against him. But Madge (Judith Berolde) and James Larrabee (Ralph Delmore), two blackmailers, also want the letters and are holding Alice prisoner. Sherlock Holmes (Gillette) is called into the case and by arranging a fake fire manages to discover the whereabouts of the letters and to free Alice. But the Larrabees have called in Professor Moriarty (George Wessells) to aid them. One by one Holmes foils his designs, although it seems that when he lures Alice and the detective to a shabby, gloomy gas works, he has caught them in his vise. Holmes throws the place into darkness and tricks the villains as to his whereabouts with a lighted cigar. He convinces Alice to give up the letters to the proper authorities, and Alice finds herself falling in love with Holmes.

Based on short stories of Sir Arthur Conan Doyle (whom some early programs listed as co-author), the play was Gillette's greatest success. For many years he alone was identified with the role, which he returned to regularly as late as 1931. A richly Victorian revival by the Royal Shakespeare Company, ♦ with John Wood ♦ in the title role, ran for 471 performances in 1974.

SHERWOOD, ROBERT E[MMET] (1896–1955) Born in New Rochelle, N.Y., he studied at Harvard, where he was active on the *Lampoon,* of which his father had been a founder, and with the Hasty Pudding Club. ♦ Although he took Professor George Pierce Baker's ♦ course in the history of the theatre, he did not, as sometimes has been reported, take his celebrated course in play-writing. He spent World War I with the Canadian Black Watch, for whom his 6'6" height presented no problems, but came out of the war disillusioned with the governments that had brought it about. After serving in various capacities at *Vanity Fair, Life,* and *Scribner's* and earning a reputation as one of the earliest serious critics of film, he found success with his first play, *The Road to Rome* ♦ (1927), an anti-war comedy set in ancient times. This was followed by the failure of *The Love Nest* (1927), a comedy based on a story by Ring Lardner ♦ and centering on a woman dismayed at Hollywood. He scored a modest success with a comedy about a henpecked king, *The Queen's Husband* (1928). However, his story of an American soldier and an English prostitute, *Waterloo Bridge* (1930), found a better reception in London than in New York, while his comic study of a reactionary Senator, *This Is New York* (1930), won little favor. Nevertheless, the rest of the 1930s proved his heyday. *Reunion in Vienna* ♦ (1931) recounted the meeting of an exiled prince and his former mistress. *The Petrified Forest* ♦ (1935) told of a world-weary wanderer's search for death. His Pulitzer Prize ♦-winning *Idiot's Delight* ♦ (1936) focused on a group of assorted figures awaiting the next war. He received his second Pulitzer Prize for *Abe Lincoln in Illinois* ♦ (1938), recounting the years leading up to Lincoln's presidency. During this same period his translation of a French comedy, *Tovarich* (1936), was also popular. His biographer has suggested that with his Lincoln play he purged himself of his war-bred disillusionment and a negative streak that had heretofore run through his works. How this purgation affected his writing is moot, but he wrote only one other play of lasting merit, *There Shall Be No Night* ♦ (1940), a story of a Finnish scientist and his American wife during the Finno-Russian War. It earned him a third Pulitzer Prize. His last works were *The Rugged Path* (1945), a story of a liberal newspaperman serving in the navy; the book for the musical *Miss Liberty* (1949); and the revision of Philip Barry's ♦ unfinished play, *Second Threshold* (1951). One of the founders of the Playwrights' Company, ♦ he turned to politics in his last active years, serving as a speechwriter for President Roosevelt and writing a history of Roosevelt's relations with Harry Hopkins.

Biography: *The Worlds of Robert E. Sherwood,* 1965, and *The Ordeal of a Playwright,* John Mason Brown, ♦ New York, 1970.

SHIPMAN, SAMUEL [né SHIFFMAN] (1883–1937) The New York-born playwright began his career by translating Jacob Gordin's ♦ *The Kreutzer Sonata* for English-language production in 1904. Over the next thirty-three years he had a hand, usually as collaborator, in some thirty plays to reach the boards. The most successful were *Elevating a Husband* (1912), a comedy written with Clara Lipman in which an arty wife finds a way to make her businessman husband share her interests; *Friendly Enemies* ♦ (1918), written with Aaron Hoffman ♦ and telling of friends with conflicting wartime loyalties; *East Is West* ♦ (1918), written with John B. Hymer and centering on the problems of a young Chinese woman; *The Woman in Room 13* (1919), written with Max Marcin ♦ and recounting the plight of a lady composer suspected of murder; *Lawful Larceny* (1922), his biggest solo success, which told of a wife's revenge on her husband's greedy mistress; *Crime* (1927), written with Hymer and depicting how a criminal mastermind uses two young innocents; and *Behind Red Lights* (1937), written with Beth Brown and telling of a murder in a brothel.

Shoestring Revue Produced in 1955 and 1957 by Ben Bagley, ♦ these off-Broadway productions lacked memorable melodies but were among the wittiest revues ever offered to Broadway and gave important boosts to the careers of Beatrice Arthur, Dody Goodman, Arte Johnson, Chita Rivera, ♦ and one great comedienne who was to die very young, Dorothy Greener.

Shore Acres, a play in four acts by James A. Herne. ♦ Produced at the Fifth Avenue Theatre. ♦ October 30, 1893. 244 performances.

Nathan'l Berry or Uncle Nat (Herne) is a kindly old man who has largely let life pass him by. The property he inherited with his brother Martin (Charles G. Craig) now belongs entirely to Martin. And Martin also long ago wed the girl Nat had courted. Unlike Nat, Martin is narrow-minded, unsentimental, and greedy. He would even sell to developers the piece of land on which their mother is buried. Martin's daughter Helen (Katherine Grey) loves a young physician, Sam Warren (David M. Murray). While Martin opposes a marriage, Nat can see nothing wrong in encouraging the youngsters to elope. They do, on the *Liddy Ann.* A storm arises and the ship is in danger of being wrecked on the nearby rocks. Martin is the keeper of Berry Light but is so angry at the youngsters that he refuses to light the beacon. After a fight, Nat succeeds in lighting it and saving the ship. When the newlyweds are safely home Nat offers his pension money to keep the property in the family. Martin is shamed into admitting how wrong he has been. With the others gone, Nat slowly turns out all the lights at Shore Acres and puts the house to bed.

Written as *The Hawthornes* and tried out as *Shore Acres Subdivision* and *Uncle Nat,* the work did not succeed until it played a long run at the Boston Museum♦ before coming to New York. Except for William Winter,♦ New York critics extolled the play. The *Mercury* observed, "Mr. Herne's play marks an epoch in the drama of the American stage." Herne toured in the play for five years. For many playgoers and reviewers the high moment of the drama was at the end, with Herne's quiet, five-minute pantomime of making the house safe for the night. Several modern scholars have noted that Chekhov's♦ use of a similar conclusion for *The Cherry Orchard* was twelve years later.

SHORT, [Hubert] Hassard (1877–1956) Born in England, he began his theatrical career as an actor in 1895 and came to America in 1901. Here he continued to perform until 1919, his roles including important parts in *Peg o' My Heart*♦ (1912) and *East Is West*♦ (1918). He abandoned acting to try his skill at directing and designing, quickly becoming an important figure behind the scenes of many Broadway musicals. He made innovative use of moving stages (including elevators), mirrors, perfume sent through the auditorium, and colored lights. He was sometimes credited with replacing footlights with lights hung from the auditorium. Among the forty musicals on which he worked were the *Music Box Revue*♦ (1921, 1922, 1923), *Sunny*♦ (1925), *Three's a Crowd* (1930), *The Band Wagon*♦ (1931), *As Thousands Cheer*♦ (1933), *Roberta*♦ (1933), *The Great Waltz* (1934), *Jubilee*♦ (1935), *Lady in the Dark*♦ (1941), *Mexican Hayride* (1944), *Make Mine Manhattan* (1948), and his last show, *My Darlin' Aida* (1952).

Show Boat, a musical in two acts. Book and lyrics by Oscar Hammerstein II.♦ Music by Jerome Kern.♦ Produced by Florenz Ziegfeld♦ at the Ziegfeld Theatre.♦ December 27, 1927. 575 performances.

When Cap'n Andy (Charles Winninger♦) and his wife Parthy Ann (Edna May Oliver) bring their show boat *Cotton Blossom* into town for a performance, their daughter Magnolia (Norma Terris) meets a handsome professional gambler, Gaylord Ravenal (Howard Marsh♦). The youngsters fall in love at first sight, although they profess it is "Make Believe." Magnolia seeks advice on what to do from a black workhand, Joe (Jules Bledsoe♦), who tells her probably "Ol' Man River" alone can answer her but that the river "don't say nothin'." The ship's leading lady, Julie (Helen Morgan♦), begins to understand Magnolia's situation and, recalling an old folk song, tells her how she too "Can't Help Lovin' Dat Man" of hers. But when Julie is accused of having Negro blood she is forced to leave the boat, taking the leading man with her. Magnolia and Gaylord are pressed into assuming the leads. Soon enough they are telling each other "You Are Love." They marry and head off. Years pass. At the Chicago World's Fair they seem amazed not only at the sights but at how their love has grown, and ask, "Why Do I Love You?" But eventually Gaylord's gambling costs him all his money, so he deserts Magnolia. She applies for a job singing at a night club where Julie, now a drunkard, is rehearsing her "Bill" number. Julie recognizes Magnolia and sacrifices what is left of her own career to help Magnolia begin hers. When Cap'n Andy finds his daughter there he persuades her to return to the *Cotton Blossom.* More years pass. One day an aging Gaylord returns. To his relief he is welcomed by Magnolia.

One of the greatest and best loved of all American operettas, the musical was based on Edna Ferber's popular novel. It was recognized at once as a masterpiece. The 1932 revival included Paul Robeson,♦ for whom the part of Joe was originally intended. A 1946 revival, which opened just after Kern's death, included the composer's last new song. Several other revivals followed, including one in 1983. There have also been three film versions. With hindsight, it has become obvious that this show was the precursor of the modern American "musical play," the American operetta genre which resorted to the American past for its material and employed American musical idioms in its songs.

Show Boats Although their origins are uncertain, these floating playhouses which brought theatre to towns along the great rivers of the United States are a singularly American phenomenon. Possibly the earliest figure of note in their development was Samuel Drake,♦ who in 1815 took his family of actors and other performers from Pittsburgh to Kentucky by means of the Allegheny. However, while Drake's band gave performances along the way, he seems not to have actually used his small boat for these theatricals but rather selected sites ashore. It remained for a young actor-manager who had first worked and traveled with Drake to take a flat-bottomed boat with a small enclosed space at one end to travel down the Cumberland and Mississippi rivers offering plays on board in 1817. He was Noah Ludlow,♦ and he too preferred where possible to give his plays on land.

Credit for conceiving and running a boat specifically designed to present plays seemingly goes to William B. Chapman, Sr.♦ He launched his earliest venture, apparently called the *Floating Theatre,* around 1831. It was described by Ludlow, who saw it at that time and who had long since established himself as a regular theatre manager, as "a large flat-boat with a rude kind of house built upon it, having a ridge-roof, above which projected a staff with a flag attached, upon which was plainly visible the word Theatre." The boat, or at least the enclosed structure on it, was about 100 feet long and 14 feet wide. The enclosure had a shallow stage at one end and benches running the width of the auditorium. Like Drake before him, the core of Chapman's company was his own family. They traveled annually from Pittsburgh to New Orleans, stopping mainly at smaller towns and plantations which lacked even the semblance of a permanent playhouse. As a rule, stands were for one night only. When the ship reached New Orleans, Chapman would sell it rather than attempt the difficult northward passage and, returning north, commission another ship for use the following season. After Chapman's death, his widow sold the latest boat to Sol Smith,♦ who operated it briefly and then joined Ludlow in a famous managerial partnership.

By the time of Chapman's death in 1839, show boats had spread to other waterways and sometimes presented more than melodramas, comedies, and primitive olios. In the late 1830s and early 1840s one Henry Butler plied the Erie Canal with his combination museum and theatre. Not surprisingly, his repertory leaned heavily toward nautical comedies and dramas, such as *Black-Eyed Susan.* In 1845 New Yorkers and Brooklynites could enjoy entertainments on a vessel at first called the Great North River Opera House, which was moored at the foot

of Spring Street and which was described as "a floating dramatic temple,—with galleries, boxes, pit, scenes, and machinery, as well as with commodious cabins, for the dressing rooms of the artistes." It was said to have been a large, converted "Man-of-War Built Steamship" and to have seated 2000 playgoers. When Manhattan drama buffs tired of it, it was moved to a pier at Fulton Street in Brooklyn. Spaulding and Rodgers' Floating Circus Palace, built in Cincinnati in 1851, featured clowns and equestrians and other animal acts on an unusually short, wide vessel. The offerings were done in arena style and presented olios and dramas as well as circuses.

The Civil War disrupted the spread of this entertainment form, but after the conflict it made a quick comeback. One of the first was the *Will S. Hays,* built in 1869 by the famous clown, Dan Rice.♦ Even more elaborate and enduring were the five vessels known as French's New Sensation, all constructed and operated by Captain Augustus Byron French. The first was launched in 1878 and the second a few years later. Since Mrs. French was the only woman on the Mississippi to hold both a pilot's and a master's license, the couple was able to run two ships concurrently. Despite French's celebrated flamboyance, he maintained a strict discipline among his small company and presented no play capable of provoking controversy or offense. This, combined with the relative luxury of his boats, gave these crafts a new cachet and respectability. Two other celebrated Mississippi captains were E. A. Price and E. E. Eisenbarth, who later became curiously linked in the romantic story of these boats. Eisenbarth was believed to be the first to name a boat the *Cotton Blossom* and the first to attempt an opera aboard ship. Prince built the long popular *Water Queen* in 1885. It was his boat which was used in the famous 1936 film version of *Show Boat,* ♦ although Edna Ferber had called the boat in her story the *Cotton Blossom.* The Bryant family were also well-known owners and captains, and Billy Bryant's *Children of Ol' Man River* (1936) provides one of the most interesting stories of life on these vessels.

The romanticized picture of show boats with huge side or rear paddle wheels and towering smokestacks is historically inaccurate, since most show boats were not self-propelled but were pushed along by small tug boats. The show boats themselves were customarily three decks high, the first two decks being enclosed and containing not only the long, narrow auditorium, but living quarters for the company. The top deck was open except for a sort of cupola which served various functions on different vessels.

The repertory remained conservative and with time came to appear absurdly out of date to more sophisticated city theatregoers. However, admissions more or less matched those of small-town theatres with a 50-cent top ticket prevailing until the Civil War and many charging $1.00 thereafter. The quality of acting in these plays undoubtedly left much to be desired, and the boats, unlike minstrel shows,♦ vaudeville,♦ or burlesque,♦ seem not to have produced any great stars of their own or even have served as a training ground for stars in other fields. However, the frequent employment of an olio between the acts or before and after the main attraction remains unexplored as a possible source for the later burgeoning of variety or vaudeville.

The boats began to go into a sharp decline with the development of larger cities and, even more so, with the coming of films. The coup de grâce came with the Depression. A few surviving boats remain moored at city docks, where they serve as dinner theatres or more or less as living museums.

Show-Off, The, a play in three acts by George Kelly.♦ Produced at the Playhouse. February 5, 1924. 571 performances.

The Fishers, a lower-middle-class Philadelphia family, are dismayed that their daughter Amy (Regina Wallace) is in love with the likes of Aubrey Piper (Louis John Bartels). They think he is not only a nut but crazy as well. Of course Aubrey sees matters differently. With his patent leather shoes, his cheap, slick toupee, and a carnation in his buttonhole he is convinced he is "The pride of old West Philly!" When Amy marries him despite the grumbling of her father (C. W. Goodrich) and the barbed warnings of her mother (Helen Lowell♦), she learns quickly that he is not the good provider he boasted of being. Matters come to a head when Aubrey, in a borrowed car, hits both a trolley and a policeman. His brother-in-law Frank (Guy d'Ennery) is forced to bail him out and later pay his fine. At the same time Mr. Fisher dies of a stroke. Just as the future looks bleak Amy's brother Joe (Lee Tracy♦) is awarded $100,000 for a rust-proofing invention. He acknowledges that Aubrey inadvertently gave him the lead that made the invention possible. Moreover, the family is amazed to learn that Aubrey secretly confronted the people with whom Joe was dealing and bulldozed them into doubling their offer. To his awed wife, Aubrey remarks, "A little bluff goes a long way sometimes."

Mrs. Fisher, however, is not awed. She can only exclaim, "God help me, from now on."

Expanded from a vaudeville sketch which Kelly had created, the play was the biggest hit of its season and was hailed by Heywood Broun♦ as "the best comedy which has yet been written by an American." The Pulitzer Prize jury selected it for their annual award, but, to virtually everyone's surprise, was overridden by Columbia University officials who gave the award to *Hell-Bent fer Heaven.♦* The comedy was revived with Helen Hayes♦ as star in 1967.

Show Shop, The, a play in four acts by James Forbes.♦ Produced by Selwyn and Co.♦ at the Hudson Theatre. December 31, 1914. 156 performances.

Max Rosenbaum (George Sidney), a shoestring but eternally optimistic Broadway producer, learns that his leading lady and leading man have walked out on him on the eve of the dress rehearsal for his new play. He hastily signs Bettina Dean (Patricia Collinge♦) as his leading lady, even though his sour-tongued director Wilbur Tompkins (Ned A. Sparks) warns him that Bettina's notorious mother, Mrs. Dean (Zelda Sears♦), will always be on hand. Jerome Belden (Douglas Fairbanks♦), a handsome young man-about-town, loves Bettina, but Mrs. Dean, recalling that marriage destroyed her chance to become a star, will not hear of it for her daughter. To be with Bettina, Jerry offers to underwrite the play and assume the role of leading man. The play is so bad it folds out of town, but Mrs. Dean insists that there will be no marriage until her daughter becomes a star on Broadway. Jerry then pays Rosenbaum $5000 to produce another play, with the stipulation that it must flop but also that it must play at least one night in New York with Bettina as star. To make certain it fails Rosenbaum again casts Jerry as his leading man. The play is called *A Drop of Poison,* but Mrs. Dean orders it renamed *Dora's Dilemma* after Bettina's role. Although Jerry's performance is as bad as the play, the critics love it. Taking the bull by the horns, however, Bettina and Jerry announce they are leaving the show and marrying. Since Mrs. Dean has realized her wish, a compromise is reached which allows the youngsters to marry, but to stay with the play for its run.

Called by Walter Prichard Eaton♦ "the most pungent, amusing, and yet the most kindly satire of stage life and the shams of theatrical production, yet written by an American," this neglected gem is a superbly written comedy, rich in backstage lore and especially in its marvelous portrait of the classic stage mother.

Shrike, The, a play in two acts by Joseph Kramm. Produced by José Ferrer♦ and others at the Cort Theatre. January 15, 1952. 161 performances. PP.

Despondent over his failure to obtain work as a theatrical director, Jim Downs (Ferrer) attempts to kill himself. He is committed to the psychiatric ward of a local hospital. Taking advantage of her legal status, his vicious, estranged wife Ann (Judith Evelyn) determines to keep him there until he comes back to her. She quietly turns the doctors against him and agrees to his release only after he promises to abandon a warm, loving girl with whom he has been having an affair. Trapped, he reluctantly accepts Ann's terms.

Although the play seems to be largely forgotten, it was a gripping melodrama and superbly acted. Kramm (b. 1907), a Philadelphian who attended the University of Pennsylvania, served as a newspaperman before turning to acting and directing. This was his only successful play.

SHUBERT, [Levi] Lee (1873?–1953), Sam[uel] S. (1876?–1905), and J[acob] J. (1878?–1963) [nés Szemanski] The brothers, who were born in Shervient, Lithuania, were brought to America by their father, an unsuccessful and alcoholic peddler, in 1882 and settled in Syracuse, N.Y. Lee and Sam soon had odd jobs at local theatres, and Sam shortly became box-office treasurer at one. When Sam purchased the area touring rights to the Charles Hoyt♦ play *A Texas Steer* in 1894, the brothers' career was really under way. By 1900 Sam and Lee were ready to tackle New York, although this meant bucking the Theatrical Syndicate or Trust♦ and its boss Abe Erlanger.♦ They leased the old Herald Square Theatre, made a precarious agreement with Erlanger, and booked in *Arizona*♦ (1900). The play's success put their house on a firm footing. Within a few years, joined by J. J., they would break Erlanger's monopoly, and become the largest theatre owners in New York and elsewhere, as well as the most active producers in America. When Sam was killed in a train wreck, Lee took over management. Many had felt that Sam was the driving force behind the brothers, but Lee proved as good an executive. From the start J. J. was the least of the trio, left to attend to the staging of productions and to import his beloved operettas. Their first production, *The Brixton Burglary* (1901), was not a success, but their second, the musical *A Chinese Honeymoon* (1902), was, and between then and 1954 "The

Messrs Shubert," as their billing read, produced 520 plays on Broadway. Their emphasis was largely on musicals, since, if successful, they promised the greatest return. A brief sampling of their productions, musical and non-musical, includes *Heidelberg* (1902), *Widowers' Houses* (1907), *The Passing of the 3rd Floor Back* (1909), *The City*♦ (1909), *Little Eyolf* (1910), *The Passing Show*♦ (first edition, 1912), *Ruggles of Red Gap* (1915), *Peter Ibbetson* (1917), *Maytime*♦ (1917), *Sinbad* (1918), *He and She*♦ (1920), *Blossom Time*♦ (1921), *Bombo* (1921), *The Student Prince*♦ (1924), *Countess Maritza* (1926), *Life Begins at 8:40* (1934), *At Home Abroad* (1935), *The Show Is On* (1936), *Hellzapoppin*♦ (1938), and *Dark of the Moon*♦ (1945). Among their principal New York houses were the Shubert, the Winter Garden,♦ and the Princess.♦ Although the brothers' tactics were often deemed crass and ruthless, they could be seen as responding to the tactics of the Trust and other unethical managers. Typically, in later years, they often gave substantially reduced rents to struggling, worthwhile attractions and kept many theatres in the legitimate fold that might otherwise have been lost to it. The vast collection of records, manuscripts, and other materials left behind by the brothers has been reorganized into the Shubert Archive, housed in the Lyceum Theatre. ♦ The brothers' various companies were restructured in 1973 as the Shubert Organization. The new company has been headed by two native New Yorkers, Bernard B. Jacobs (b. 1916), a graduate of New York University and Columbia Law School, and Gerald Schoenfeld (b. 1924), a graduate of the University of Illinois and New York University Law School.

Biography: *The Shuberts of Broadway,* Brooks McNamara, New York, 1990.

Shubert Alley A famous theatrical throughfare between 44th and 45th Streets, just west of Broadway, it was created by the space between the back of the Astor Hotel and the Shubert and Booth Theatres. After the demolition of the hotel and the erection of a skyscraper in its place, the alley remained. It is popular with playgoing pedestrians and is not open to vehicular traffic.

SHUE, Larry (1946–85) Born in New Orleans but raised in the Midwest in an academic environment, he began writing plays while still at Illinois Wesleyan. His three best-known works are *The Foreigner* (1984), in which an embarrassingly shy Englishman creates turmoil at a Georgia fishing lodge by pretending he can't speak English; *The*

Nerd (1987), telling of an oddball whose visit upsets his old "buddy"; and *Wenceslas Square* (1988), in which a professor returns to look at Prague after a long absence. Shue was also an actor. His early death ended speculation about his potential.

Shuffle Along, a musical comedy in two acts. Book by Flournoy Miller and Aubrey Lyles. Lyrics by Noble Sissle. Music by Eubie Blake.♦ Produced at the 63rd Street Theatre. May 23, 1921. 504 performances.

Two partners in a Jimtown grocery store, Steve Jenkins (Miller) and Sam Peck (Lyles), become opposition candidates for mayor. Each promises the other that if elected he will make his partner chief of police. Jenkins wins and keeps his word, but Peck soon realizes he has nothing to do. Noisy fights and public charges of corruption follow, so before long Harry Walton (Roger Matthews) announces he will run as a reform candidate. He ousts the partners, who ramble off seeking new worlds to conquer.

Principal songs: I'm Just Wild About Harry · Love Will Find a Way

Although there had been a number of turn-of-the-century black musicals, most starring Bert Williams♦ and his partner George Walker, the vogue for black shows had died off until the raging popularity of this show set off a new boom which survived into the 1930s. Its superb, rhythmic dancing was a major attraction and set a pattern that caused most black musicals of the decade to be looked on primarily as dancing shows. Except for *Blackbirds of 1928,*♦ none of the period's black musicals matched its success.

SHUMLIN, HERMAN (1898–1979) Born in Atwood, Colo., he worked in New York for the *Clipper*♦ and *Billboard,*♦ then served with Schwab♦ and Mandel♦ and with Jed Harris♦ before embarking on an independent career as producer and director. Among his notable productions were *The Last Mile*♦ (1930), *Grand Hotel* (1930), *The Children's Hour*♦ (1934), *The Little Foxes*♦ (1939), *The Male Animal*♦ (1940), *The Corn Is Green* (1940), *Watch on the Rhine*♦ (1941), *The Searching Wind* (1944), *Inherit the Wind*♦ (1955), in which he shared direction with Margo Jones,♦ and *The Deputy* (1964). Lillian Hellman,♦ whose plays he produced, wrote of him, "When a director is as good as Mr. Shumlin, his work is very important indeed . . . Mr. Shumlin has made many an actor into a star, and many a star into a decent actor. The theatre, for him, is not a place to show off . . . He is one of the few directors who believes in the *play;* he is one of

the very few who has the sharp clarity, the sensitivity, the understanding, which should be the director's gift to the play."

Siberia, a play in six acts by Bartley Campbell,♦ Produced at Haverly's 14th Street Theatre. February 26, 1883. 40 performances.

After the assassination of Czar Alexander II, radicals and Jews come under attack in Russia. Sara (Georgia Cayvan♦) and Marie (Blanche Mortimer) are the daughters of a Christian mother, but since their father is Jewish they find it prudent to flee. They wander across Russia, encountering both friendship and betrayal.

Although most critics agreed that the play's complicated plot forbade retelling, they were divided on the work's merits. Among those who approved, the *Tribune* observed that Campbell "handled [his] materials so as to arouse and maintain interest in a story that is extravagant and [in] persons who are radically commonplace." Each act built to a melodramatic climax. This and its topicality kept the work on the boards for a quarter of a century.

SIEDLE, MRS. CAROLINE (1867?–1907) Probably the first woman in America to receive widespread recognition as a costume designer, she was born in England, but little is known of her early history. She began to call attention to her work in the mid-1890s and until her early death specialized in creating the colorful costumes for the period's musicals. She designed many of Lillian Russell's♦ productions as well as such successes as *El Capitan*♦ (1896), *The Wizard of Oz*♦ (1903), *Babes in Toyland*♦ (1903), *It Happened in Nordland* (1904), *The Red Mill*♦ (1906), *The Rich Mr. Hoggenheimer* (1906), and *A Parisian Model* (1906). On her death, Julian Mitchell♦ remarked, "Without her assistance I should never have been able to carry out the musical comedy color schemes which have made beautiful stage pictures. Her taste was always good, and her ability to design amounted to genius."

SILLMAN, LEONARD, see *New Faces*

SILSBEE, JOSHUA (1813–55) Little is known about the early life of this famous comedian. Sources disagree as to whether he was born somewhere in New York State or in Litchfield, Conn. He did not turn to acting until 1839, when he made his debut in Natchez, Miss. For several years he played in towns along the Mississippi and in Cincinnati, specializing in juveniles and fops. However, his greatest success came when he began portraying Yankee characters much like those played by G. H. Hill♦ and Dan Marble.♦ He made his New York debut in 1843. By that time his Lot Sapsago, Deuteronomy Dutiful, Jonathan Ploughboy, and other similar roles were his stock in trade. In 1850 he went to England, where for a brief time he became the most popular exponent of stage Yankees. One critic noted, "Faithfully as he performs the Yankee character, his performances are permeated with the natural humor of the man. His looks, gestures, and action—even the arch twinkle of his eye—impress the spectator with ludicrous emotions, and his inflexible countenance, rigidly innocent of fun while his audience are in roars of laughter, gives an additional zest to the humor." He returned to America in 1853, but died in California while on a transcontinental tour.

Silver Cord, The, a play in three acts by Sidney Howard.♦ Produced by the Theatre Guild♦ at the John Golden Theatre. December 20, 1926. 112 performances.

Mrs. Phelps (Laura Hope Crews♦) is a pathologically possessive mother determined to destroy the engagement of her son Robert (Earle Larimore♦) to Hester (Margalo Gillmore♦), as well as the marriage of her son David (Eliot Cabot♦) and his wife Christina (Elizabeth Risdon). When Christina accuses her of being little more than a civilized cannibal, she responds, "I would cut off my hands and burn out my eyes to rid my son of you." She succeeds in driving Hester to suicide and cowing Robert, but with Christina's encouragement David breaks his mother's "silver cord."

Gilbert Gabriel of the *Sun* called the work, "A play for the mature, the unafraid; and to them it guarantees an evening of excitive truths and rare dramatic instinct." While many critics compared the piece favorably to George Kelly's♦ study of a selfish spouse, *Craig's Wife,*♦ it failed to find the large public of the earlier play.

Silver Spoon, The, a comedy in four acts by Joseph Stevens Jones.♦ Produced at the Boston Museum.♦ February 16, 1852. In repertory.

Having been elected by his "feller townsmen" to represent Cranberry Center in the "Gineral" assembly, Jefferson S. Batkins (William Warren♦) comes to the state capital to assume his post and fight for his country neighbors against the big city "klinks"—his reading of "cliques." He decides to stay with Ezra Austin (W. H. Smith♦), whose aunt, Hannah Partridge (Mrs. Thoman), he had courted long ago and whom he proposes to court again. At the same time young Glandon King has returned from Europe

for the reading of his father's will. The will announces that since Glandon has been given everything he wanted in life, his father's money goes to establish a college, and Glandon's sole reward is a silver spoon. A shady lawyer, Simon Feedle (Mr. Curtis), attempts to break the will and establish his law clerk, Tom Pinfeather (C. H. Saunders), as a second son of the late Mr. King. The ploy is exposed and a later will is discovered in which King announces that if Glandon has made no effort to break the first will, then the entire estate is his. Glandon's proposal of marriage is accepted by Austin's daughter Sarah (Mrs. Wulf Fries), while Hannah agrees to become Mrs. Batkins.

Despite its title this most popular of all Boston 19th-century comedies really centered on Batkins, whose gaffes cause endless embarrassment and whose innocence gets him into several awkward situations. Much of the comedy came from a confused speech Batkins hopes to make to the assembly and which he tries out on anyone who will listen. The play remained in Warren's and the Boston Museum's repertory until Warren's death, and was popular in stock until shortly before World War I.

SILVERMAN, Sime (1873–1933) Born in Cortland, N.Y., but raised in Syracuse, he was the son of a banker who tried unsuccessfully to have his son follow in his footsteps. Instead, young Silverman went to New York, where he became a critic first on the *Daily American* and later on the *Morning Telegraph*. He wrote as "The Man in the Third Row" for the former and as "Robert Speare" for the latter. After being fired when a vaudeville act he had panned canceled its annual Christmas ad, he borrowed $1500 and in 1905 started his own theatrical paper, *Variety.*♦ Under his guidance as editor and publisher it soon became the most important American theatrical trade journal. He demanded absolute impartiality and attempted to report news as fully as possible. He also originated much of the curious slang for which the paper became known. Later he founded *The Times Square Daily,* an extended gossip sheet, which led to the *Daily Variety* around the time of his death.

Biography: *Lord Broadway: Variety's Sime,* Dayton Stoddart, New York, 1941.

SILVERS, Phil[ip] [né Silver] (1911–85) The Brooklyn-born comedian who specialized in smart-alecky bunglers began performing as a child and had appeared in vaudeville and burlesque before making his Broadway debut in *Yokel Boy* (1939). By the time he returned to the theatre in *High Button Shoes* (1947), he had won recognition in films. He later starred in *Top Banana* (1951), *Do Re Mi* (1960), and a 1972 revival of *A Funny Thing Happened on the Way to the Forum.* ◆ He was also famous for his Sgt. Bilko in the long-run television series of that name.

SIMON [JOVAN IVAN], JOHN (b. 1925) A native of Yugoslavia, he was educated at Harvard. Subsequently he has served as drama critic for such periodicals as the *Hudson Review* and *New York* magazine. He has also taught at several universities and has published numerous books, although most of these have been about films. He is often perceived as the most vitriolic of contemporary critics.

SIMON, [MARVIN] NEIL (b. 1927) The most successful playwright of his era, he was born in the Bronx and educated at New York University. Early in his career he was a radio and television script writer, then turned to the stage by writing sketches for summer camp revues. His sketches were also seen in *Catch a Star* (1955) and *New Faces of 1956.* ◆ With his first full-length play, *Come Blow Your Horn* ◆ (1961), centering on a businessman with two rebellious sons, he initiated a string of hits unparalleled in American stage history. After writing the book for *Little Me* (1962), he offered *Barefoot in the Park* ◆ (1963), which focused on the problems of a young married couple. *The Odd Couple* ◆ (1965) dealt with two disparate divorced men attempting to live together, and was followed by the book for *Sweet Charity* ◆ (1966). Later that same year his *The Star-Spangled Girl* pitted an ultra-conservative girl against two ultra-liberal boys. *Plaza Suite* ◆ (1968) was a triple bill of one-act plays. His book for *Promises, Promises* ◆ (1968) and his comedy, *Last of the Red Hot Lovers* ◆ (1968), a look at a would-be lothario, contined his streak of long runs, which *The Gingerbread Lady* (1970), a study of an alcoholic singer, barely maintained. The streak moved ahead with *The Prisoner of Second Avenue* ◆ (1971), which focused on a man's fight against an overcrowded, impersonal civilization, and *The Sunshine Boys* ◆ (1972), depicting the reunion of an old vaudeville team. Neither *The Good Doctor* (1973), a dramatization of Russian stories, nor *God's Favorite* (1974), a retelling of the Job story in modern terms, won universal approval, and both had only modest runs. But Simon was back in form with *California Suite* (1976), a bill of four playlets; *Chapter Two* ◆ (1977), telling of a widower's problems with a second marriage; the book of *They're Playing Our Song* ◆

(1979); and *I Ought To Be in Pictures* (1980), a story of a screen writer and the daughter he meets after a sixteen-year separation. His tale of a schoolteacher in old Russia, *Fools* (1981), was coldly received and it quickly closed. His *Brighton Beach Memoirs* ◆ (1983) began a semi-autobiographical look at an intellectual Jewish boy growing up. *Biloxi Blues* ◆ (1985) and *Broadway Bound* (1986) completed the trilogy. *Rumors* (1988) was a farce in which party guests try to conceal their host's attempted suicide. Simon, a shrewd observer of human foibles and a master of the surprise one-line joke, often makes remarkably effective comedies out of potentially unpleasant themes. Much of his success depends on these qualities, since his plays rarely offer major plot twists. Many of his plays have been made into popular films, often with his own screenplays.

SIMONSON, LEE (1888–1967) The New York-born designer, who studied at Harvard under Professor George Pierce Baker, ◆ did his earliest commercial set designs for the Washington Square Players. ◆ After serving in World War I he became one of the founders of the Theatre Guild ◆ and did many of the Guild's most noteworthy sets. He also usually lit his own sets and often created the costumes for the same productions. Among his memorable achievements were his designs for *Liliom* ◆ (1921), *He Who Gets Slapped* (1922), *R.U.R.* (1922), *Peer Gynt* (1923), *The Adding Machine* ◆ (1923), *The Road to Rome* ◆ (1927), *Marco Millions* ◆ (1928), *Dynamo* ◆ (1929), *Hotel Universe* ◆ (1930), *Elizabeth the Queen* ◆ (1930), *End of Summer* ◆ (1936), *Idiot's Delight* ◆ (1936), and *Joan of Lorraine* (1946). His associate, Theresa Helburn, ◆ wrote, "He could perform miracles with light and he has produced some of the most interesting experimental sets seen on the American stage." His creations ranged from the expressionistic settings for *The Adding Machine* and the realistic dynamo for the play of the same name to the virtually bare stage for *Joan of Lorraine.* He also wrote *The Stage Is Set* (1932) and *The Art of Scenic Design* (1950) as well as the autobiographical *Part of a Lifetime* (1943).

SIMPSON, EDMUND SHAW (1784–1848) Born in England, where he was expected to follow his father into the family's business, he elected instead to go on the stage. His debut occurred at Towchester in 1806 in *The Stranger.* ◆ While performing in Dublin three years later he was signed by Cooper ◆ and Price ◆ to appear at the Park Theatre. ◆ His American debut took place in October 1809 in *The Road to Ruin.* He was greeted with "the warmest approbation" and quickly established himself as a versatile performer. Among his early roles were Charles Teazle, Jaffier, and Richmond, which he played to the Richards of both Kean♦ and J. B. Booth.♦ In 1812 he was appointed acting manager of the Park, and in 1815 he became Price's partner in the theatre. He was injured during a performance in 1828. While permanently crippled he continued to perform until 1833, after which he played only on special occasions. Following Price's death in 1840, he attempted to run the theatre alone, but the theatre district had moved northward and the Park encountered continual financial problems. Shortly before his own death he sold out to Hamblin. ♦ Whatever the failures of his last years—and they were overcome briefly by the successful premieres of *London Assurance*♦ and *Fashion*♦—he remained a popular and respected figure with New York playgoers and critics.

Singer's Midgets A vaudeville act comprising about twenty Austro-Hungarian midgets who were brought to this country in the 1910s by Leo Singer, they rapidly become one of two-a-day's most popular attractions. The act featured baby animals, a Lady Godiva skit, and a musical playlet. Within a short time its popularity led to the formation of a second company. After the demise of vaudeville the midgets performed in carnivals and circuses until about the time of World War II. The only midget company to equal its popularity was The Liliputians,♦ but that group performed largely in legitimate musicals in the 1890s and early 20th century.

SINN, Colonel William E. (1834?–99) A leading 19th-century theatre manager, he was born in the Georgetown section of Washington, D.C., and spent several years as a traveling salesman before changing professions. It was his sister's husband, Leonard B. Grover,♦ the author of *Our Boarding House*♦ and a successful theatre operator, who took him into partnership in Washington in 1861. Within a few years they had several theatres in the area as well as in Cincinnati. On his own he took over Philadelphia's Chestnut Street Theatre♦ in 1864 and the Front Street Theatre in Baltimore in 1869. However, he was most successful after moving his base to Brooklyn in 1875. He quickly turned the Park Theatre there into the city's leading house and later ran several other auditoriums. Although he never served in any army, he was made a Colonel in the Confederate forces for his help in enlisting men during the Civil War.

Sinners, a play in four acts by Owen Davis.♦ Produced by William A. Brady♦ at the Playhouse. January 7, 1915. 220 performances.

Mary Horton (Alice Brady♦) leaves her small New Hampshire town and her widowed mother (Emma Dunn) to seek her fortune in New York. She quickly falls in with the wrong company and accepts their immoral ways. Learning that her mother is dying, she returns home, where she is determined to keep from her simple, pious mother the truth about her behavior. The arrival of some of her big city friends does not help matters.

Although many critics considered the play little better than the cheap melodramas Davis had written for Al Woods,♦ Davis himself felt it was one of the dramas that marked his emergence as a more serious writer.

Six-Cylinder Love, a comedy in three acts by William Anthony McGuire. ♦ Produced by Sam H. Harris♦ at the Sam H. Harris Theatre. August 25, 1921. 430 performances.

Having lived beyond their means, Richard Burton (Donald Meek) and his wife Geraldine (Eleanor Gordon) are facing eviction. To pay moving costs they will have to sell their new car. But they don't have to look far for a buyer as there are newlyweds next door. In no time Marilyn Sterling (June Walker♦) is convinced that she wants nothing more than a new car, so her doting husband Gilbert (Ernest Truex♦) buys the Burtons' auto. Before long the Sterlings are living wildly beyond their means, and when Mr. Stapleton (Burton Churchill), Gilbert's staid boss, pays a sudden visit, his unfavorable impression of their mode of living costs Gilbert his job. Gilbert sells the car and convinces Mr. Stapleton to give him back his job. But Gilbert suddenly finds a new expense item in his ledgers: Marilyn will soon need a baby carriage.

Burns Mantle♦ noted, "Somewhat extravagant as to story, its characters are purposely exaggerated to give it a farcical trimming, and thus punctuate its proceedings with laughter. The basic dramatic situations, however, and the impelling motives that inspire its principal characters, are sincerely and convincingly human." The play was one of the most popular comedies of its era.

SKELLY, Hal [né Joseph Harold Skelley] (1891–1934) Born in Allegheny, Penn., he performed in circuses before joining the original Chicago production of *The Time, the Place and the Girl*♦ in 1908. Further appearances followed in circuses, musical comedy touring troupes, and with Lew Dockstader's♦ minstrels. After playing the lead in the road tour of *So Long, Letty,* he made his New York debut in *Fiddlers Three* (1918). Throughout the twenties he was a leading comedian in other musicals, but he is best recalled for his role in a non-musical play, when he portrayed Skid, the failing performer, in *Burlesque*♦ (1927).

Skidding, a comedy in three acts by Aurania Rouverol. Produced at the Bijou Theatre. May 21, 1928. 448 performances.

Marion Hardy (Marguerite Churchill) decides to break off her engagement and begin a political career by helping her father, Judge Hardy (Carleton Macy), in his own campaign. The campaign is a success, but so is Judge Hardy when he makes Marion realize she will be happy in marriage.

Largely dismissed by the critics, the comedy far outran many better plays in an excellent season. It served as the basis for the Andy Hardy movies so long popular in Hollywood, with Lewis Stone as the Judge and Mickey Rooney as Andy. Mrs. Rouverol (1886?–1955), a Californian, wrote several less successful plays and also worked as a film writer.

Skin of Our Teeth, The, a play in three acts by Thornton Wilder.♦ Produced at the Plymouth Theatre. November 18, 1942. 359 performances. PP.

Mr. and Mrs. Antrobus (Fredric March♦ and Florence Eldridge♦) live in a modern home in Excelsior, New Jersey, with their malevolent son Henry (Montgomery Clift♦) and their giddy daughter Gladys (Frances Heflin). Their pets are a mammoth and a dinosaur. But the advancing Ice Age is threatening to destroy their home and world. Moreover, nature's blind menace is exacerbated by human rapacity. The Antrobuses survive to no small extent because Mr. Antrobus is inventive enough to create the wheel and the alphabet (while his wife discovers sewing and cooking), and he is enlightened enough to encourage art and learning. Nor can he be seduced by their aggressive maid Sabina (Tallulah Bankhead♦). Millennia pass. At an Atlantic City convention of the Ancient and Honorable Order of Mammals Mr. Antrobus is elected president. A cassandric fortune-teller (Florence Reed♦) spouts gloom and doom as the murderous Henry continues to attack those he hates; Sabina, made a beauty queen, still determines to lure Mr. Antrobus away from his wife; and a deluge arises to engulf the world. Mr. Antrobus manages to get pairs of animals aboard an ark before the waters destroy them. Yet the flood has scarcely passed when a great war decimates civilization. Not even this can discourage

Mr. Antrobus, who determines to build a better new world. At this point Sabina begins the same scene she had at the play's opening, only to stop and add, "This is where you came in. We have to go on for ages and ages. You go home. The end of the play isn't written yet."

Wilder's modern allegory, which juxtaposed biblical events with such modern phenomena as the Miss America Pageant, baffled many tryout critics but was an instant success in New York. Students have seen in it strong influences not only of expressionist and epic theatre but also of James Joyce's *Finnegans Wake.* The original production was aided immeasurably by Miss Bankhead's tour-de-force performance, which allowed her to be both siren and liaison with the audience, by Elia Kazan's♦ fluid direction, and by Albert Johnson's♦ surrealistic settings and his use of projection screens. The play remains one of the few effective stage allegories and is still revived with some regularity. Major mountings have included a 1945 English production, a 1955 New York production, and in 1961 an international tour assisted by the State Department.

SKINNER, Cornelia Otis (1901–79) The regal-looking daughter of Otis Skinner♦ was born in Chicago and began to act while a student at Bryn Mawr. She made her professional debut in her father's production of *Blood and Sand* (1921). After appearing in several other plays she first presented her bill of one-woman character sketches in 1925, then toured with it for several seasons. She returned to these sketches at frequent intervals throughout her career. Among her noteworthy regular roles were the embittered actress, Julia Lambert, in *Theatre* (1941); Emily Hazen, the wife of a fence-straddling diplomat, in *The Searching Wind* (1944); Mrs. Erlynne in a 1946 revival of *Lady Windermere's Fan;* and Katherine Dougherty, whose ex-husband suddenly reappears at their daughter's wedding, in *The Pleasure of His Company*♦ (1958). She was also the author of a number of plays and books.

SKINNER, Otis (1858–1942) The son of a Cambridge, Mass., minister, he made his debut at the Philadelphia Museum in 1877, then played with the stock company at that city's Walnut Street Theatre♦ for two seasons. It was as a member of this ensemble that he made his first Manhattan appearance when the troupe visited New York. After playing small roles opposite Edwin Booth♦ and Lawrence Barrett♦ he spent four seasons with the famous company of Augustin Daly.♦ In 1889 he joined Helena Modjeska♦ and Booth to play such roles as Claudio,

Bassanio, Laertes, and Macduff, later touring with Modjeska as her leading man. He embarked on a career as star in 1894 and played such notable parts as the Count of Grammont, who falls in love with a girl he is supposed to woo for his king, in *His Grace de Grammont* (1894); Lanciotto, in his celebrated 1901 revival of *Francesca da Rimini♦;* Colonel Philippe Bridau, the swaggering bully who must restore his family's good name, in *The Honor of the Family* (1908); the scampish, conniving beggar, Hajj, in *Kismet♦* (1911); Antonio Camaradonio, the fun-loving Italian whose ways shock small-town Pennsylvanians, in *Mister Antonio* (1916); and Juan Gallardo, the doomed bullfighter, in *Blood and Sand* (1921). Writing of Skinner's acting in his most famous part, Hajj, Walter Prichard Eaton♦ noted, "Mr. Skinner is, in this country, the man of destiny for the part—abounding energy, triumphant clarity of speech, romantic swagger, physical picturesqueness, all are his . . . that slight note of unreality in his acting which sometimes mars his impersonations of seriously romantic roles or roles in modern plays, here admirably blends with the glamour of dreamlike fantasy." George Middleton♦ characterized him as "flamboyant and scene-filling, like rich claret running over everything." In his later years he frequently returned to his older hits, besides starring in a number of classic revivals. Alone or with his wife, Maud, he was also the author of numerous books on theatre, including *Mad Folk of the Theatre* (1928), *One Man in His Time* (1938), and *The Last Tragedian* (1939), as well as the autobiographical *Footlights and Spotlights* (1924). He was the father of Cornelia Otis Skinner. ♦

SKULNICK, Menasha (1892?–1970) The diminutive, doleful-looking comedian, famous for his ludicrous shrugs, was born in Warsaw and spent many years on European Yiddish stages before coming to America in 1930. Long a favorite of Yiddish audiences here, he made his English-language stage debut as Max Pincus, the harassed executive, in *The Fifth Season♦* (1953), then scored another success as the biblical Noah in *The Flowering Peach* (1954). He later toured in several successes, but his subsequent Broadway appearances were all in failures.

SLADE, Bernard (b. 1930) Born in St. Catharines, Canada, he was raised in England, but returned as a teenager to work in stock and television. He is the author of three successive Broadway hits: *Same Time, Next Year♦* (1975), a history of a couple's annual trysts; *Tribute♦* (1978), in which a terminally ill man must come to terms with himself and his son;

and *A Romantic Comedy* (1979), focusing on the love life of a vain playwright.

"Slaughter on Tenth Avenue" A ballet in *On Your Toes♦* (1936), it was one of the first ballets in musical comedy to have both a story and a connection with the plot of the show. Its story told of a hoofer, danced by Ray Bolger,♦ who loves a stripper, danced by Tamara Geva.♦ His rival, the boss, attempts to kill him, but shoots the girl instead. The hoofer then kills the boss. In the play the dancer was supposedly pursued by gangsters and was forced to keep on dancing until the police could arrest the thugs. Balanchine♦ was the choreographer. The ballet's music by Richard Rodgers♦ has retained its popularity. Bobby Van and Vera Zorina danced it in a 1954 revival, while Lara Teeter and Natalia Makarova, later succeeded by Galina Panova, performed in the 1983 mounting.

Sleuth Anthony Shaffer's♦ two-character thriller, in which a husband confronts his wife's lover, was presented on Broadway in November 1970, nine months after its London premiere. Anthony Quayle and Keith Baxter were the leads. Although it ran only half as long as the London original, its 1,217 performances made it the second longest stand of any London play in New York.

SLEZAK, Walter [Leo] (1902–83) The son of the famed opera singer Leo Slezak, he was born in Vienna and had a successful career there in musicals before being brought to this country to appear in the musical *Meet My Sister* (1930). Actually, Lee Shubert♦ had seen Oscar Karlweis in a show, but when an emissary was sent to engage him, Slezak was substituting and was signed by mistake. The pudgy, beady-eyed actor proved a surprise success and was seen in numerous plays, the most memorable being *Music in the Air♦* (1932), in which he introduced "I've Told Every Little Star"; *I Married an Angel♦* (1938); *My Three Angels* (1953), in which he played the conniving Joseph; and *Fanny♦* (1954). He was long popular in films.

Autobiography: *What Time's the Next Swan?*, Garden City, 1962.

SLOANE, A[lfred] Baldwin (1872–1925) The most prolific composer of musical comedy at the turn of the century, he wrote the scores for no fewer than two dozen Broadway musicals between 1896 and 1912. He was born in Baltimore, where his songs were first heard in amateur productions. Coming to New York he began interpolating melodies in other men's scores and soon was invited to create his own scores. His biggest hit was "Heaven Will Protect the Working Girl," which Marie Dressler♦ introduced in *Tillie's Nightmare* (1910), but none of his songs found enduring popularity. Among his shows were *The Mocking Bird* (1902), *The Wizard of Oz♦* (1903), *Lady Teazle* (1904), and *The Summer Widowers* (1910). He composed only rarely after 1912, but he did provide much of the music for the 1919 and 1920 *Greenwich Village Follies.♦* His last score, for *China Rose* (1925), was heard after his death.

SMITH, C[HARLES] AUBREY (1863–1948) The British actor, who in his last years personified English gentlemen in films, had a long career on American stages. His many appearances included supporting or leading roles in *The Light That Failed* (1903), *The Morals of Marcus* (1907), *The Runaway* (1911), and *The Constant Wife* (1926), but his most successful appearance came as Basil Winterton, who brings together all his illegitimate children, in *The Bachelor Father* (1928).

SMITH, CECIL (1906–56) After studying at Harvard he served for many years on the faculty of the University of Chicago. At the same time he was music critic and sometime drama critic for the Chicago *Tribune.* He was also associated with other publications, including *Theatre Arts Monthly,♦* of which he was associate editor and for which he generally wrote on musicals. His *Musical Comedy in America* (1950) was the first serious study of the whole history of our musical theatre and remains a perceptive, eminently readable work. It was brought up to date by Glenn Litton in 1981.

SMITH, EDGAR [McPHAIL] (1857–1938) The Brooklyn-born playwright, librettist, and lyricist was the author of some 150 works to reach Broadway. He began his career as an actor, then briefly turned playwright, including several collaborations with Augustus Thomas.♦ However, he found his true métier when he was hired by the Casino Theatre♦ in 1886 to translate and adapt foreign musicals the theatre was importing. In 1897 he moved to Weber and Fields,♦ where he wrote many of their celebrated burlesques, among them *The Con-Curers* and *Cyranose de Bric-a-Brac* in 1898. Two of his biggest hits were introduced by Fay Templeton♦ in *Fiddle-Dee-Dee* (1900): "I'm a Respectable Working Girl" and "Ma Blushin' Rosie," both with music by John Stromberg. He also wrote or adapted *Old Dutch* (1909), *Tillie's Nightmare* (1910), *La Belle Paree* (1911), *The Blue Paradise* (1915), and *Hello, Paris* (1930), his last show.

SMITH, DR. ELIHU HUBBARD (1771–98) The New England-born physician and author wrote one of the earliest American comic operas, *Edwin and Angelina; or, The Banditti* (1796), a musical dramatization of Oliver Goldsmith's "The Hermit." He also wrote several admired theatrical prologues. However, his promising career was cut short when he died while attending his patients in a yellow fever epidemic.

SMITH, HARRY B[ACHE] (1860–1936) The most prolific librettist and lyricist in the history of the American theatre, he was, by his own count, the author of some 300 librettos and 6000 lyrics. Broadway saw 123 of his shows, while many others were mounted in Chicago and elsewhere. He was born in Buffalo, but grew up in Chicago. He spent many years in a variety of capacities with Chicago newspapers and magazines, although he also gained some acting experience as a member of the Chicago Church Choir Opera Company. His friendship with Reginald De Koven♦ led the pair to conclude they could write American comic operas the equal of Gilbert♦ and Sullivan's.♦ Their initial effort, *The Begum* (1887), had only small success, but with *Robin Hood♦* (1891) they created the first enduring work of our lyric stage, although, oddly, Smith did not write the lyric for "Oh, Promise Me,"♦ that operetta's biggest success. He later provided the books and often the lyrics to such musicals as *The Serenade* (1897); *The Fortune Teller♦* (1898), which included "Gypsy Love Song"; *The Singing Girl* (1899); *The Casino Girl* (1900); *The Little Duchess* (1901); *The Office Boy* (1903); *Babette* (1903); *The Free Lance* (1906); *The Rich Mr. Hoggenheimer* (1906); the [*Ziegfeld*] *Follies♦* (1907–10, 1912); *The Girl from Utah♦* (1914); *Watch Your Step♦* (1914); *Stop! Look! Listen!* (1915); *Angel Face* (1919); *Countess Maritza* (1926), which offered his American lyric for "Play Gypsies—Dance Gypsies"; and his last, *Marching By* (1932). Although his work seems lackluster and often stilted when compared with later writers, he was a pioneer who was respected by his contemporaries for his excellent humor and style. He was the earliest American lyricist to be honored with a published collection of his lyrics.

Autobiography: *First Nights and First Editions,* Boston, 1931.

SMITH, Harry James (1880–1918) Born in New Britain, Conn., he studied biology at Williams College and Harvard, then taught at Oberlin. He abandoned teaching in 1906 to become an associate editor at the *Atlantic Monthly.* At the same time he started to write plays. His first to be produced was *Mrs. Bumpstead-Leigh*♦ (1911), the story of a social-climbing American. It marked him as a writer of great promise, but his second play, *Blackbirds* (1913), which dealt with the romance of two crooks who meet on an ocean liner, was a quick failure. His reputation was restored with the huge success of *A Tailor Made Man*♦ (1917), in which a humble tailor sets out to prove that clothes make the man, and with *The Little Teacher* (1918), a story of a schoolmarm who befriends two abused children. Smith was killed in an accident while serving with the Canadian Red Cross.

SMITH, Oliver [Lemuel] (b. 1918) Born in Waupaun, Wisc., and educated at Penn State, he first designed sets for Broadway in 1942 with *Rosalinda.* Since then his work has been seen in such shows as *On the Town*♦ (1944), which he co-produced; *Brigadoon*♦ (1947); *High Button Shoes* (1947), *Gentlemen Prefer Blondes*♦ (1949), which he co-produced; the 1952 revival of *Pal Joey*♦; *In the Summer House*♦ (1953), again co-producing; *My Fair Lady*♦ (1956); *Auntie Mame*♦ (1956); *Candide*♦ (1956); *Visit to a Small Planet*♦ (1957); *West Side Story*♦ (1957); *The Sound of Music*♦ (1959); *Camelot*♦ (1960); *Mary, Mary*♦ (1961); *Barefoot in the Park*♦ (1963); *Hello, Dolly!*♦ (1964); *The Odd Couple*♦ (1965); *Plaza Suite*♦ (1968); *The Last of the Red Hot Lovers*♦ (1969); the 1975 revival of *The Royal Family,*♦ and *Lunch Hour* (1980). As the list suggests, his creations covered a wide range of periods and plays, all done with style and imagination. He has won numerous honors, including seven Tony Awards.♦

SMITH, Queenie (1902–78) A native New Yorker, the petite, bouncy performer was trained for ballet and had danced at the Metropolitan Opera before making her Broadway debut in *Roly-Boly Eyes* (1919). Between 1922 and 1932 she played major supporting roles or leads in eleven musicals. Her most notable role was the title part in *Tip-Toes*♦ (1925), in which she introduced "Looking for a Boy," "That Certain Feeling," and "These Charming People."

SMITH, Richard Penn (1799–1854) The grandson of Provost William Smith of the University of Pennsylvania and the son of a noted minister, he was a distinguished Philadelphia lawyer and the most active of the gentlemen playwrights who comprised the Philadelphia School of Dramatists. ♦ His playwriting covered the period 1825–36. *The Pelican,* a one-act farce, and *The Divorce,* a romantic comedy, were his earliest efforts. Neither was produced. His first play to reach the boards was *Quite Correct,* which was played at the Chestnut Street Theatre♦ in 1828. Based on Theodore Hook's story, *Doubts and Fears,* it told of a hotel keeper who determines to remain "quite correct" while abetting several romances. His next play, *The Eighth of January*♦ (1829), was a celebration of Jackson's victory at New Orleans. *The Disowned; or, The Prodigals* (1829) was a redaction of a French melodrama. *A Wife at a Venture* (1929) was a comedy about Bagdad citizens offered a choice of marriage or conscription. Another adaptation from the French, *The Sentinels; or, The Two Sergeants* (1829), was followed by a patriotic drama, *William Penn* (1829). Many students consider his *The Triumph at Plattsburg*♦ (1830) the best play about the War of 1812, although it seems not to have been a success. He next used his unproduced *The Divorce* to provide a subplot for his Elizabethan-like comedy about a jealous husband, *The Deformed; or, Woman's Trial*♦ (1830). *The Water Witch* (1830) dramatized James Fenimore Cooper's romance. Contemporaries felt his best play was *Caius Marius*♦ (1831), a study of power in the hands of an idealistic if embittered upstart. Following the production of a short afterpiece, *My Uncle's Wedding* (1832), he offered his last comedy, *Is She a Brigand?* (1833), which tooks its fun from mistaken identities. His final dramas, *The Daughter* (1836) and *The Actress of Padua* (1836), were both derived from the French. Scraps of at least five other unproduced plays remain in manuscript. Although he was highly respected by contemporaries, even the discovery of the complete text of *Caius Marius* cannot change the judgment of his modern editors, Ralph H. Ware and H. W. Schoenberger, who concluded, "Smith was a practical playwright who always wrote with a view to stage presentation. A fairly competent craftsman, he had little originality, for thirteen of his plays are based upon either native or foreign inspiration."

Biography: *The Life and Writings of Richard Penn Smith,* Bruce W. McCullough, Menasha, Wisc., 1917.

SMITH, Robert B[ache] (1875–1951) The younger brother of Harry B. Smith,♦ he followed in his brother's footsteps to become a successful librettist and lyricist. Born in Chicago, he served a brief apprenticeship with Weber♦ and Fields,♦ where he wrote the lyric for "Come Down, Ma Evenin' Star" in *Twirly-Whirly* (1902). Then alone or with collaborators, he worked on such shows as *Fantana* (1905); *The Spring Maid* (1910); *Sweethearts*♦ (1913), which included his lyrics for "Every Lover Must Meet His Fate, " "Pretty as a Picture," and the title song; *Angel Face* (1919), remembered for "I Might Be Your Once-in-a-While"; and his last show, *The Girl in the Spotlight* (1920).

SMITH, Russell (1812–96) The most famous Philadelphia set designer of the 19th century, he was born in Glasgow, and brought to America in 1819 after his parents' political views made them unwelcome in Scotland. He spent much of his childhood in Pittsburgh, where he began his theatrical career as an actor. However, he soon recognized that painting was his major interest and began to create sets as well as study painting under James R. Lamdin. When Wemyss♦ opened the Pittsburgh Theatre in 1833 the young artist was appointed set designer. Two years later he followed Wemyss to Philadelphia's Walnut Street Theatre.♦ Although he later worked occasionally for Mrs. John Wood♦ and Boucicault♦ in New York, at the Boston Museum,♦ and in Baltimore and Washington, most of his work was done in Philadelphia. In his long career he supplied scenery, drop curtains, and some interior decoration not only for the Walnut, but for the Chestnut Street Theatre♦ under William Wood,♦ for the Academy of Music, and for Mrs. Drew♦ at the Arch Street Theatre. ♦ He excelled at painting atmospheric outdoor sets, although he designed many other types of settings as well. One Philadelphia paper wrote of his efforts for the 1837 production of *Thalaba,* "In examining some of the scenes, we were particularly struck wth the sepulchre of Zeniah, which has a gloomy and melancholy appearance, in admirable keeping with the play. The scene of the Arabian Tombs is also worthy of commendation. The effect of twilight, and the harmony of light and shade, are conceived and executed in masterly fashion. The beautiful Isles near the rock of Babelmandel, forcibly arrested our attention. Tumultuous clouds are seen dashing over high mountains in the distance; these, with the deep blue of the sea, contrasted with a rich, warm foreground, produce, altogether, a truly magnificent effect."

Biography: *Russell Smith, Romantic Realist,* Virginia E. Lewis, Pittsburgh, 1956.

SMITH, Sol[omon Franklin] (1801–69) The son of a farmer, who as a boy had played the fife for troops at the Battle of Bunker's Hill, he was born in Norwich, N.Y., but raised in nearby Solon. Because his family was large and poor, he was hired out to another, distant farmer when he was eight years old. At the age of twelve he ran away, walking 300 miles to join his brothers in business in Boston. In 1814 he was sent to be a clerk at their Albany store and there first attended the theatre. Lured by its attractions, he left to enlist in a theatrical company, but was forced to return to his brothers. His real career began with performances in Vincennes, Ind., in 1819. By 1823 he had his own company, which financial difficulties forced him to disband four years later. At that time he joined the company of J. H. Caldwell,♦ who was offering plays in cities along the Mississippi. He also performed at the Park Theatre♦ in New York and in Philadelphia under Wemyss. ♦ In 1835 he entered into partnership with Noah Ludlow. ♦ For the next 16 years they dominated what was then the western extremes of the American theatre, building the first major theatre in St. Louis and offering plays up and down the Mississippi. The partnership was dissolved in 1853. As an actor he excelled at low comedy and was especially admired for his Mawworm in *The Hypocrite.* He made only rare appearances after 1853, declining Burton's♦ invitation to act in New York and another manager's offer of $10,000 to tour for a year as Mawworm and other similar figures. He became a lawyer and was elected to the State Convention of Missouri, which was designed to bring about that state's secession from the Union. His son, Mark (1829–74), was a popular actor, specializing in old men's parts.

Autobiography: *Theatrical Management in the West and South for Thirty Years,* New York, 1868.

SMITH, Winchell (1872–1933) The brilliant theatrical jack-of-all-trades was born in Hartford, Conn. He was an usher at the Herald Square Theatre when Richard Mansfield♦ urged him to become an actor. After making his debut in 1896 as Lt. Foray, the telegraph operator, in *Secret Service,* ♦ he continued to act for a decade. In 1903 he was Arnold Daly's♦ silent partner in the first American production of *Candida.* ♦ However, he was best known as a playwright, almost always in collaboration with others, and as a director. His only important solo venture was *The Fortune Hunter*♦ (1909), the story of a city boy who seeks to marry a rich small-town girl. Among his other credits were *Brewster's Millions*♦ (1906), written with Byron Ongley and telling of a man who must spend a million dollars in order to inherit more; *Polly of the Circus* ♦ (1907), written with Margaret Mayo ♦ and recounting the romance of an acrobat and a minister; *The Boomerang* ♦ (1915), written with Victor Mapes ♦ and depicting how a doctor's treatment of jealousy backfires; *Turn to the Right* ♦ (1916), written with John E. Hazard and describing the efforts of former convicts to save an old lady from a swindler; and *Lightnin'* ♦ (1918), written with Frank Bacon ♦ and centering on a likable ne'er-do-well. Besides directing many of his own plays he staged such works as *The Last of Mrs. Cheyney* (1925), *The Wisdom Tooth* ♦ (1926), and *The Vinegar Tree* (1930). Although he continued to direct until shortly before his death, he had long since abandoned play-writing, recognizing, "The theater's gone on ahead of me . . . I'm out of date." Ward Morehouse ♦ called him "a shrewd showman . . . with an extraordinary sense of the theater, an actor-director-playwright who became the most astute play-fixer of the stage for the period of two decades."

SMITH, W. H., see *Drunkard, The*

Smith and Dale, see *Avon Comedy Four*

SOBEL, Bernard (1887–1964) Born in Attica, Ind., he earned degrees from several universities and taught before turning to the theatre. Although he wrote plays and served as drama critic for the New York *Mirror* in the early 1930s, he was better known as the publicist for such leading theatrical figures as Florenz Ziegfeld, ♦ Charles Dillingham, ♦ Abe Erlanger, ♦ and the Shuberts, ♦ and for writing numerous books on the theatre. Among his works were *Burleycue—A History of Burlesque* (1931), *The Theatre Handbook* (1940), *Broadway Heartbeat* (1953), and *A Pictorial History of Vaudeville* (1961).

Society of American Dramatists and Composers An organization founded in 1890 by Bronson Howard, ♦ David Belasco, ♦ and others to assure authors fair treatment from producers, to attempt to set a standard for royalties, and to fight play and song piracy. The group had only small success in dealing with producers, but it lobbied effectively in Congress and in state legislatures for better copyright laws. Play piracy largely disappeared as a result of its efforts and the new laws. Its other aims were later achieved by the Dramatists' Guild. ♦

Society of Stage Directors and Choreographers With actors, authors, and almost all other theatrical branches formed into unions it was only a matter of time before the stagers of plays and musicals banded together. This group was founded in 1959 and in 1962 was recognized by the League of American Theatres and Producers. ♦

Soldier's Play, A, a play in two acts by Charles Fuller. Produced by the Negro Ensemble Company ♦ at the Theater Four. November 20, 1981. 468 performances. PP.

When black Sergeant Vernon C. Waters (Adolph Caesar) is shot dead at a Louisiana army base, the Ku Klux Klan is suspected of the killing. To the resentment of some white officers, a black officer, Capt. Richard Davenport (Charles Brown) is sent to investigate. His investigation shows that more than the Klan had motives for gunning down the sergeant. The white officers resented Waters as much as they resent Davenport, while the black troops Waters commanded hated him because he considered most of them ill-behaved inferiors. "I'm the kinda colored man," Waters proclaimed, "that don't like lazy, shiftless Negroes!" Davenport determines that it was, indeed, one of the black soldiers who killed the sergeant. The officers dismiss the incident as "the usual, common violence any commander faces in Negro military units." But Davenport warns the whites to change their thinking and accept the fact that someday they will have to take orders from blacks.

Fuller (b. 1939) was born in Philadelphia. Several of his other plays have been produced off-Broadway, including the Obie Award ♦-winning *Zooman and the Sign* (1981), in which a father seeks retribution for his murdered daughter.

Solid Gold Cadillac, The, a comedy in two acts by Howard Teichmann and George S. Kaufman. ♦ Produced by Max Gordon ♦ at the Belasco Theatre. November 5, 1953. 526 performances.

When a sweet little old lady named Laura Partridge (Josephine Hull ♦) turns up at a huge corporation's stockholders' meeting and begins to ask embarrassing questions, the executives try to shut her up by giving her a job writing letters to other stockholders. Her letters are so warm and homey that by the next meeting she has enough proxies to take over the company. She does, first quietly firing the corrupt officials who had hoped to silence her.

Most critics felt the play was held together by Miss Hull's beguiling performance. Kaufman's biographer, Malcolm Goldstein, observed of the play, "No one could deny that this was a slim plot and that it resounded with echoes of a score of plots concocted by Kaufman in the past." One notable moment occurred when Laura was seemingly caught in a scandalous situation with a cabinet member. A drop curtain was lowered to show the front pages of New York's papers. All but one splashed the story across the first page. It made no mention of the scandal, apparently concluding that international, political, and economic crises were all the news fit to print. The play marked the farewells to Broadway of Gordon and Miss Hull, and was also Kaufman's last produced play. Howard Miles Teichmann (1916–87), a Chicagoan who began his theatrical career with the Mercury Theatre,♦ wrote several other plays after this, all of which failed. He also wrote biographies of Kaufman and Alexander Woollcott. ♦

Solon Shingle, see *People's Lawyer, The*

SONDHEIM, STEPHEN [JOSHUA] (b. 1930) The most daring and often controversial composer-lyricist of his era, he was born in New York and given his pre-college education at the George School in Newtown, Penn. There he met James Hammerstein, who introduced him to his father, Oscar II.♦ The elder Hammerstein became a sort of mentor to Sondheim. After majoring in music at Williams College he continued his studies with Milton Babbitt. His lyrics were first heard in *West Side Story*♦ (1957), including those for "I Feel Pretty," "Maria," and "Tonight." For *Gypsy*♦ (1959) he wrote the words to such hits as "Everything's Coming Up Roses," "Small World," "Together," and "You'll Never Get Away from Me." With *A Funny Thing Happened on the Way to the Forum*♦ (1962) he began writing both words and music. The show presented such songs as "Lovely" and the comic "Everybody Ought to Have a Maid" and "Free." After the failure of *Anyone Can Whistle* (1964), an offbeat musical about an insane asylum and a fake miracle, which he wrote with librettist Arthur Laurents♦ and which had Lee Remick, Harry Guardino, and Angela Lansbury♦ in the cast, he wrote lyrics to Richard Rodgers's♦ music for *Do I Hear a Waltz?* (1965). Many critics considered *Company*♦ (1970) one of the most innovative musicals of its generation. Among its Sondheim songs were "The Ladies Who Lunch" and "Side by Side by Side." *Follies*♦ (1971) offered "I'm Still Here" and "Losing My Mind." Turning to operetta he offered a score written in 3/4 time for *A Little Night Music*♦ (1973). From that score came his most popular song, "Send in the Clowns," as well as the witty "Liaisons." The failure of *Pacific Overtures*♦ (1973) was followed by another oper-

etta, *Sweeney Todd*♦ (1979). In 1981 his *Merrily We Roll Along*♦ was harshly received and had a brief run. *Sunday in the Park with George*♦ (1984) won a Pulitzer Prize. ♦ His somber version of beloved fairy tales, *Into the Woods* (1987), enjoyed a long run. Although many of his songs have become "cult" favorites, few have enjoyed wide-ranging popularity. Nevertheless, he is one of the most musicianly of contemporary composers. His forte, however, is his brilliant lyric-writing, and only the most elegant, decorous work of Alan Jay Lerner♦ equals it among contemporaries. Sondheim is an exceedingly clever rhymer and a superb, if misanthropic, wit. This wit and misanthropy have combined with his musicianship to make his musical comedies unique while they have given his operettas a style and tone closer to the comic opera masterpieces of Gilbert♦ and Sullivan♦ than anything since the heyday of the Savoyard works.

Biography: *Sondheim and Co.*, Craig Zadan, New York, 1974.

Song of Norway, an operetta in two acts. Book by Milton Lazarus. Lyrics and music (based on themes by Edvard Grieg) by Robert Wright♦ and George Forrest.♦ Produced by Edwin Lester♦ at the Imperial Theatre. August 21, 1944. 860 performances.

Grieg (Lawrence Brooks) dreams of being a great composer. His dreams are shared by his friend Rickard (Robert Shafer) and his sweetheart Nina (Helena Bliss). He is lured to Italy by the great prima donna Louisa Giovanni (Irra Petina), but finds he cannot create amid all the glitter and excitement and so returns to Norway and his beloved to write his music.

Principal songs: Freddy and His Fiddle · Now · Strange Music

The last successful pseudo-biography in the tradition of *Blossom Time*♦ (1921), the work was revived in 1981 by the New York City Opera.

SONNECK, OSCAR [GEORGE THEODORE] (1873–1928) One of the most important figures in initiating studies of early American musical stages, he was born in Jersey City, N.J., but was raised by his widowed mother in Germany. He returned to America at the turn of the century and in 1902 was appointed the first chief of the music division of the Library of Congress. His *Early Opera in America* (1915) offered much valuable material on 18th-century American comic opera, while additional material could occasionally be gleaned from his other books.

Sonneck Society, THE Founded in 1975 at the instigation of Irving Lowens, who became its first president, the organization is devoted to the promotion of American music. The group was named after Oscar Sonneck. ♦ Its publications include a Society newsletter. Several of its members have contributed important studies in the field of musical theatre, the results of which have been offered as papers at the Society's meetings and sometimes published in the newsletter or elsewhere.

SOTHERN, E[DWARD] A[SKEW] (1826–81) The tall, lanky actor, one of the best eccentric comedians of his era, was born in Liverpool. Using the name Douglas Stewart, he had appeared on English stages before making his American debut in Boston in 1852 as Dr. Pangloss in *The Heir-at-Law*. He joined Wallack's ♦ celebrated ensemble in 1854 and began using his real name. However, success and fame did not come until 1858 when he grudgingly accepted the part of Lord Dundreary in Laura Keene's ♦ mounting of *Our American Cousin.* ♦ The critic Henry Austin Clapp ♦ later recalled, "I think the funniest small thing I ever noted at a theatrical performance was his delivery of one of Dundreary's speeches in connection with Sam's 'letter from America.' The passage began, 'Dear Bwother,' Mr. Sothern reading the opening words of the epistle; then he made one of his pauses, and with a characteristic click and hitch in his voice, commented—'Sam always calls me his bwother—because neither of us ever had a sister." . . . on the words 'because neither of us ever had a sister' the actor's voice became instantly saturated with mock pathos, and the sudden absurd demand for sympathy reached the amazed auditor with soul-tingling effect." Sothern soon expanded the role until it virtually dominated the play. Among his other notable parts were the title roles in a play about Dundreary's relative, *Brother Sam* (1862) and in *David Garrick* (1864), as well as Fitzaltamont, the failed actor, in *The Crushed Tragedian* (1877). Critics were divided on the merits of his acting in the last two, both more or less serious plays, but many felt that his Brother Sam and not his Dundreary was his finest achievement. His public thought otherwise.

Biography: *A Memoir of Edward Askew Sothern,* Thomas Edgar Pemberton, London, 1889.

SOTHERN, E[DWARD] H[UGH] (1859–1933) Smaller and more handsome than his father, E. A. Sothern, ♦ he proved a more versatile actor and became one of the great Shakespeareans of his day.

He was born in New Orleans and educated in England, where he planned a career as a painter. However, deciding to follow his father's profession, he made his debut in New York in 1879 as a cabman in his father's *Brother Sam*. He then toured with John McCullough ♦ before becoming a member of Daniel Frohman's ♦ Lyceum Theatre ♦ company. He remained there for ten years until 1898. Among his many successes were Jack Hammerston, the befuddled auctioneer who loves a baronet's daughter and must buy back her bankrupt father's estate, in *The Highest Bidder* (1887), and the title role in *Lord Chumley* (1888), but his greatest success came in the dual roles of the real Prince Rudolf and his look-alike impostor, in *The Prisoner of Zenda* ♦ (1895). While at the Lyceum he married Virginia Harned, ♦ and the two played together for many years, including his first important Shakespearean production, *Hamlet* ♦ (1900). However, his fame reached its pinnacle when he co-starred with his second wife, Julia Marlowe, ♦ in a series of Shakespearean seasons, beginning in 1904 with *Romeo and Juliet.* ♦ His major roles included Benedick, Shylock, Antony, and the one numerous critics felt was his best, Malvolio. He continued to act occasionally after Miss Marlowe retired in 1924. While Ludwig Lewisohn wrote, "He speaks the verse as verse and yet as authentic human speech. He conveys an impression of complete naturalness while never slurring the iambic pattern of his text," a surviving recording of the balcony scene from *Romeo and Juliet* suggests a lush, formal style which would not be popular today.

Autobiography: *The Melancholy Tale of "Me,"* New York, 1916.

Sound of Music, The, an operetta in two acts. Book by Howard Lindsay and Russel Crouse. ♦ Lyrics by Oscar Hammerstein II. ♦ Music by Richard Rodgers. ♦ Produced by Leland Hayward, ♦ Richard Halliday, Rodgers, and Hammerstein at the Lunt-Fontanne Theatre. November 16, 1959. 1,443 performances.

Maria (Mary Martin ♦), a postulant at an Austrian convent, prefers to sit in the fields listening to "The Sound of Music" than to attend to her duties. Although the Mother Abbess (Patricia Neway) can affectionately agree with many of the items on Maria's list of "My Favorite Things," she reluctantly decides to send her to serve as governess at the home of a stern, widowed naval officer, Captain Georg von Trapp (Theodore Bickel). Maria wins the children's love by showing them that singing is as simple as "Do-Re-Mi." Trapp is opposed to the

Nazis, so when they order him to report for duty, he and Maria agree to flee with the children to the safety of the West. They can summon their courage because Maria remembers that the Mother Abbess had often advised her not to cringe in life but to "Climb Ev'ry Mountain."

Other principal songs: Edelweiss · Sixteen Going on Seventeen

Written shortly before Hammerstein's death and thus this great partnership's last work, the musical, which was based on Maria von Trapp's autobiographical *The Trapp Family Singers,* was condemned by such staunch detractors of operetta as Brooks Atkinson.♦ The public, however, adored it. A film version (1965), with Julie Andrews♦ in the lead, broke records for its time.

SOUSA, JOHN PHILIP (1854–1932) Born in Washington, D.C., to a Portuguese father and Bavarian mother, he began his musical training while still in grammar school. At the age of thirteen he ran away from home to join a circus, but was soon brought back and made to enlist as an apprentice in the U.S. Marine Band. He remained with the band for seven years, all the while furthering his studies with George Felix Benkert. He next worked with various theatre orchestras, primarily in Philadelphia. It was there he began to compose comic opera scores. In 1880 he became the bandmaster for the Marine Band and gained his greatest fame as a bandleader and composer of marches. His first musicals, mounted by John McCaull,♦ never played New York. His best known works, for which he sometimes served as librettist and lyricist, were *El Capitan*♦ (1896), remembered for "El Capitan's Song"; *The Bride Elect* (1898), from whose second act finale he later drew "The Bride Elect March"; *The Charlatan* (1898); *Chris and the Wonderful Lamp* (1900); and *The Free Lance* (1906). He also occasionally orchestrated other men's scores, offered interpolations to other shows, and in 1915 appeared with his band in the Hippodrome♦ extravaganza, *Hip Hip Hooray.* Although he sometimes had difficulty writing music for singers, his work was eminently theatrical and often memorably melodic. He is probably the only composer of his era, aside from Victor Herbert,♦ who could enjoy a major revival.

Autobiography: *Marching Along,* Boston, 1928.

South Pacific, a musical in two acts. Book by Oscar Hammerstein II♦ and Joshua Logan.♦ Lyrics by Hammerstein. Music by Richard Rodgers.♦ Produced by the authors and Leland Hayward♦ at the Majestic Theatre. April 7, 1949. 1,925 performances. PP.

Nellie Forbush (Mary Martin♦), an American nurse serving in the Pacific in World War II, is told by the rich French planter, Emile de Becque (Ezio Pinza♦), that "Some Enchanted Evening" she will fall in love. But it seems unlikely she will fall for any of the brazen servicemen who sing of and tease "Bloody Mary" (Juanita Hall) and who insist "There Is Nothin' Like a Dame." Mary would like her daughter Liat (Betta St. John) to marry Lt. Joseph Cable (William Tabbert), and in order to promote their romance extols the virtues of a magical isle called "Bali Ha'i." Meanwhile Nellie is falling for de Becque, although when she learns he has fathered some Eurasian children she swears, "I'm Gonna Wash That Man Right Outa My Hair." Later she changes her mind and acknowledges that she is in love with "A Wonderful Guy." Cable tells Liat she is "Younger than Springtime," but also admits that he is opposed to inter-racial marriages. Cable and de Becque go off together on a dangerous mission. Cable is killed, but the planter returns to embrace a welcoming Nellie.

Based on James A. Michener's *Tales of the South Pacific,* this was one of the greatest and most successful of modern operettas. However, its plea for racial understanding caused problems when it attempted to tour the South.

Southwark Theatre (Philadelphia) Sometimes called the South Street Theatre, it was the first permanent playhouse erected in America. Because of prejudices against theatricals it was built just outside what was then the center of the city. The structure, largely of brick, was painted red and was lit by oil. Opened in 1766 by Douglass♦ and his American Company♦ and later managed by his successors, Lewis Hallam, Jr.,♦ and John Henry,♦ it housed the first performance of a professionally produced American play, *The Prince of Parthia,* ♦ in 1767. It remained in use as a playhouse until 1821. The building had served for many years as a distillery before it was demolished in 1912.

SOUTHWORTH, E[MMA] D[OROTHY] E[LIZA] N[EVITTE] (1819–99) She was once a popular writer of sentimental and melodramatic novels usually set in the South. Her works lent themselves to dramatizations that became for a short while the rage of lesser theatres. The most successful was *The Hidden Hand* (1859), but others included *The Bride of Evening* (1858), *The Doom of Deville* (1859), and *Rose Elmer, or; A Divided Heart* (1860).

SOVEY, RAYMOND (1897–1966) Born in Torrington, Conn., and educated at Columbia, he began his theatrical career as an actor, but soon switched to set-designing. His designs were seen in such shows as *The Butter and Egg Man*♦ (1925), *Gentlemen Prefer Blondes*♦ (1926), *Coquette*♦ (1927), *The Ladder*♦ (1928), *The Front Page*♦ (1928), *Little Accident*♦ (1928), *Strictly Dishonorable*♦ (1929), *Strike Up the Band*♦ (1930), *Green Grow the Lilacs* (1931), *Counsellor-at-Law*♦ (1931), *Her Master's Voice*♦ (1933), *The Petrified Forest*♦ (1935), *Yes, My Darling Daughter*♦ (1937), *Our Town*♦ (1938), *Tomorrow the World*♦ (1943), *Over 21*♦ (1944), *State of the Union*♦ (1945), *Gigi* (1951), *Witness for the Prosecution* (1954), and *The Great Sebastians* (1956). A versatile artist, he was noted for his elegant interiors.

Spelvin, George The name given to a character or an actor in a play to hide his real identity. It was employed as early as 1886 by Charles A. Gardner in his *Karl, the Peddler.* William Collier jokingly credited Spelvin as co-author of *Hoss and Hoss* (1893). Its use was most widely popularized by Winchell Smith,♦ who first employed the name for a performer in *Brewster's Millions*♦ (1906). The success of the play prompted Smith to revive the name in many of his subsequent shows. John Golden♦ also used the name in several of his productions. At one time *Theatre Arts*♦ (*Monthly*) gave the name to a critic who wrote on other critics. The name Harry Selby has sometimes been similarly employed.

SPENSER, WILLARD (1852–1933) A native of Cooperstown, N.Y., he settled after his marriage in a suburb of Philadelphia and soon became the leader of what was called the Philadelphia School of Comic Opera.♦ His comic operas *The Little Tycoon*♦ (1886) and *Princess Bonnie* (1895) were among the most popular musicals of the late 19th century. None of his subsequent shows reached New York, but several were major hits in Philadelphia. These later works included *Miss Bob White* (1901), *Rosalie* (1906), and *The Wild Goose* (1912).

SPEWACK, SAMUEL (1899–1971) and BELLA [CO-HEN] (1899–1990) Samuel was born in Russia but raised in America. After attending Columbia he served for several years as a journalist. Bella was born in Bucharest and raised in New York. She became a journalist and worked on several New York papers and as a theatrical press agent before joining with her husband to write approximately a dozen plays or musicals that reached Broadway. Most successful were *Boy Meets Girl*♦ (1935), a spoof of Hollywood; librettos for *Leave It to Me!*♦ (1938)—based on their 1932 comedy *Clear All Wires*—and *Kiss Me, Kate*♦ (1948); and *My Three Angels* (1953), their adaptation of a French play about three good-natured criminals. On his own, Samuel wrote *Two Blind Mice* (1949), a satire on bureaucracy in which two old ladies continue to run a government office that Congress has long since abolished. Samuel also directed many of their plays.

Squall, The, a play in three acts by Jean Bart. Produced at the 48th Street Theatre. November 11, 1926. 444 performances.

Fleeing from her gypsy band, Nubi (Suzanne Caubet) takes refuge in the home of Juan Mendez (Horace Braham), pleading, "Me Nubi. Nubi good girl. Nubi stay." With the gypsies gone, she goes about seducing all the men at the Mendez home.

The show was propelled into a long run with major assistance from Leblang's Ticket Office Agency♦ and from Richard Maney's♦ excellent press work. Maney had a field day with critic Robert Benchley's♦ response: "Me Benchley. Benchley bad boy. Benchley go." Bart later wrote several less successful plays.

Squaw Man, The, a play in four acts by Edwin Milton Royle.♦ Produced by Liebler and Co.♦ at Wallack's Theatre. October 23, 1905. 222 performances.

Captain James Wynnegate (William Faversham♦) loves Diana (Selene Johnson), his cousin's wife. Yet, when it is learned his cousin has stolen funds from a charity, James agrees to emigrate to America so that it will appear he is the culprit. He settles in the West, takes the name Jim Carston, and soon falls in love with and marries an Indian, Nat-u-ritch (Mabel Morrison), who once saved his life. But when Lady Diana comes to America to tell Wynnegate that his innocence has been recognized and that he is now Earl of Kerhill, Nat-u-ritch understands that she is in his way. She kills herself to give her husband and their young son a chance for a better life.

One of the major successes of its day, it was revived with some frequency as late as 1921. It served as the source for an important early silent film and afterwards was made into the unsuccessful musical *The White Eagle* (1927).

SPIALEK, HANS (1894–1983) Born in Vienna, he studied music there and also in Russia while he was a prisoner of war. He later composed and conducted before coming to America in 1924. He soon became one of Broadway's most distinguished orchestrators. Among the 147 shows he worked on were *The New Moon*♦ (1928), *Fifty Million Frenchmen*♦ (1929), *The New Yorkers* (1930), *On Your Toes*♦ (1936), *Babes in Arms*♦ (1937), *The Boys from Syracuse*♦ (1938), *Du Barry Was a Lady*♦ (1939), *Pal Joey*♦ (1940), *Panama Hattie*♦ (1940), and *Something for the Boys* (1943). His elegant arrangements were heightened by what he called his attempt to convey the exciting "atmosphere of being in a theatre." When he reconstructed his orchestrations for the 1983 revival of *On Your Toes,* his work was widely hailed for its disarming simplicity and appropriateness to the music.

Spirit of the Times, The A weekly, founded in 1831 as *The Spirit of the Times and Life in New York,* it soon shortened its name and was billed as "A Chronicle of Turf, Agriculture, Field Sports, Literature and the Stage." While offering detailed accounts of New York theatricals, it also maintained correspondents in other important theatrical centers. Publication ceased in 1861. A similar periodical, *Wilkes' Spirit of the Times,* was issued from 1859 to 1902.

Spy, The; A Tale of the Neutral Ground, a play in three acts by Charles Powell Clinch.♦ Produced at the Park Theatre.♦ March 1, 1822. In repertory.

The itinerant peddler Harvey Birch (R. C. Maywood) is believed by many to be a Loyalist spy, although he is actually serving secretly in Washington's intelligence. Out of his good nature he performs acts of kindness for many friends he knows to have Loyalist sympathies and even helps the British captain Henry Wharton (Jacob Woodhull) escape execution. In the end Birch is shot, but before he dies a letter signed by Washington is found on him and his true position is recognized.

Based on James Fenimore Cooper's then popular novel, the play was probably the very first successful American dramatization of an American novel. It held the stage for several decades. Clinch remained faithful to the original, except for the dramatic ending which he added. Its success prompted the dramatization of more Cooper novels, as well as other authors' works.

S.S. Glencairn, see *Bound East for Cardiff; In the Zone; Long Voyage Home, The; Moon of the Caribbees, The*

Stage Door, a play in three acts by George S. Kaufman♦ and Edna Ferber.♦ Produced by Sam H. Harris♦ at the Music Box Theatre. October 22, 1936. 159 performances.

While boarding at the Footlights Club, a home for aspiring young actresses, Terry Randall (Margaret Sullavan♦) finds her loyalty to the theatre sorely tested. Her fiancé, the radical playwright Keith Burgess (Richard Kendrick), tired of living "on bread and cocoa for days at a time," abandons her and the stage for a lucrative film offer, as does a sexy but untalented fellow resident. Another girl commits suicide after being fired from a part. But it is a motion picture scout, David Kingsley (Onslow Stevens), who urges her to have the courage of her convictions. She does, thereby winning a juicy role and David as well.

Most critics compared the play unfavorably with earlier Kaufman-Ferber collaborations, *The Royal Family*♦ and *Dinner at Eight,*♦ but enjoyed reading certain parts as identifiable caricatures—such as Keith Burgess's mirroring the history of Clifford Odets.♦

Stage Door Canteen A cabaret and dining room designed during World War II to entertain soldiers free of charge. It was founded by the American Theatre Wing♦ and the USO (United Service Organization). The first and principal one was established in the basement of the 44th Street Theatre. Broadway performers and others passing through New York offered their services gratis, not merely entertaining but often serving as waiters and dishwashers. Irving Berlin♦ saluted it in his all-soldier show, *This Is the Army*♦ (1942), with the song "I Left My Heart at the Stage Door Canteen." Similar, smaller establishments were opened in other major theatrical centers. The USO also sent shows to service camps. Both the canteens and the USO were disbanded after the war.

Stage Women's War Relief An organization founded during World War I by Rachel Crothers,♦ Jane Cowl,♦ and others to allow actresses and other women of the theatre to assist in the war effort. It provided free tickets for soldiers and made similar charitable contributions. The group disbanded at the end of the war.

STAGG, CHARLES and MARY (fl. early 18th century) A husband and wife, they were listed as "actors" on a 1716 petition to erect a theatre in Williamsburg, Va. Nothing is known of their origins, if they did in fact perform in Williamsburg, or what happened to them afterwards. If they were professionals, their appearance on the American theatrical scene little more than a decade after Anthony Aston♦ marks them as two of America's earliest recorded performers.

STAHL, Rose (1870–1955) A thin-faced, nasal-voiced actress, with tangled blonde hair and hazel eyes, won huge acclaim in two roles, then faded from the scene. She was born in Montreal and made her acting debut with a Philadelphia stock company. She continued with various stock groups and in minor roles on Broadway before turning to vaudeville, where she caused a stir in a playlet called "The Chorus Girl." Its author, James Forbes,♦ expanded the work into a full-length play, *The Chorus Lady*♦ (1906). For nearly five years she played Patricia O'Brien, a feisty, slangy chorine who saves her sister's virtue. Her only other success was the title role in *Maggie Pepper* (1911), in which she portrayed a salesgirl who wins both a promotion and the store's boss after she unwittingly tells him how to run his store.

Stair and Havlin A large chain of theatres extending from the East Coast to Kansas City and situated primarily in smaller cities and towns, it was run by E. D. Stair, J. H. Havlin, and their silent partner George H. Nicolai. The chain, which flourished in the early years of the 20th century, specialized in offering action-packed melodrama and knock-about farce. Many of their attractions were proprietary, although they often bought out Broadway hits after the plays had toured major theatrical centers.

Stalag 17, a play in three acts by Donald Bevan and Edmund Trzcinski. Produced by José Ferrer♦ at the 48th Street Theatre. May 8, 1951. 472 performances.

A close camaraderie develops among the American soldiers held as prisoners of war in a German camp. Only one soldier, Sefton (John Ericson), remains aloof. So when the Germans foil an escape, Sefton is suspected of being the informer and is treated roughly. But it remains for Sefton to trap the real spy, Price (Laurence Hugo). Price attempts to flee but is gunned down by the Germans.

William Hawkins of the *World-Telegram* wrote that the play "hits the top as gripping drama." The suspense grows close to unbearable." Both authors had been prisoners of war. [Joseph] Donald Bevan (b. 1920), a native of Holyoke, Mass., is better known as an artist whose caricatures are mounted at Sardi's.♦ Trzcinski (b. 1921) is a New Yorker who has served as an actor and director. This has been their only successful play. The thriller became an award-winning film starring William Holden and

later was the basis of the television series *Hogan's Heroes.*

STANGE, Stanislaus (1862–1917) Born in Liverpool, he came to America in 1881. Here he embarked on a career of acting and play-writing. His biggest straight play success was his dramatization of the novel *Quo Vadis?* (1900). However, he was most in demand as a lyricist and librettist, working often with Julian Edwards.♦ At least eighteen of his musicals reached New York. Among the more successful were *Madeleine* (1895), *Brian Boru* (1896), *The Wedding Day* (1897), *The Jolly Musketeer* (1898), and his best work, *When Johnny Comes Marching Home*♦ (1902). He enjoyed his longest run with his adaptation of Oscar Straus's♦ Viennese favorite, *The Chocolate Soldier* (1909), which he also directed.

STANISLAVSKY, Konstantin (1863–1938) The famous Russian director co-founded the Moscow Art Theatre♦ and used his position to promote his theories of realistic, psychologically probing ensemble acting and to discard seemingly artificial conventions. He came to the United States in 1923 with his company and offered not merely a superb example of his theory put to practice but employed interviews that accompanied his visit as a further platform. The acting of several ensembles in the 1930s, such as the Group Theatre,♦ and the later "Method" technique advocated by Lee Strasberg♦ were clearly and often admittedly influenced by Stanislavsky's ideas. Frequently overlooked was the fact that Stanislavsky rose to prominence just as sophisticated electric lighting was making stages brighter and thus minimizing the need for the heavy make-up and exaggerated gestures that had prevailed until then. While many great performers have been raised on these newer methods, the emphasis on understanding a character rather than on theatrical discipline has sometimes led to sloppy or eccentric performances and has not necessarily improved and meshed ensemble playing.

Autobiography: *My Life in Art,* trans. by J. J. Robbins, Boston, 1924.

STANLEY, [Patricia Kimberly] Kim [née Reid] (b. 1925) The tall, attractive blonde, whose somewhat high voice and jittery mannerisms exemplified the modern "method school" of acting, was born in Tularosa, N.M. She attended the universities of New Mexico and Texas before studying acting at the Pasadena Community Playhouse♦ and at the Actors Studio.♦ She acted in several off-Broadway productions and then replaced Julie Harris♦ in *Monserrat* (1949), but scored her first major success as Millie, the lovesick tomboy sister, in *Picnic*♦ (1953). Among her important later roles were Cherie, the flashy night-club singer, in *Bus Stop*♦ (1955); Sara Melody, the daughter who rebels against her drunken innkeeper father, in *A Touch of the Poet*♦ (1958); Elizabeth von Ritter, Freud's first important patient, in *A Far Country*♦ (1961), and Masha in a 1964 revival of *The Three Sisters*. She retired from the stage to teach acting.

STAPLETON, [LOIS] MAUREEN (b. 1925) The actress, with what *Vogue* described as "big show-girl eyes, a small mouth, the skill of a Japanese tumbler, a radiance, and a voice that combines harridan and chamber music with layers of 'cello and violin," was born in Troy, N.Y., and studied acting with Herbert Berghof.♦ She made her New York debut in 1946 in *The Playboy of the Western World* but rose to stardom as Serafina, the emotional widow, in *The Rose Tattoo*♦ (1951). Subsequent notable roles included Lady Torrance, the sex-starved storekeeper, in *Orpheus Descending* (1957); Carrie Berniers, the possessive sister, in *Toys in the Attic*♦ (1960); three different characters in the triple bill *Plaza Suite*♦ (1968); and Eva Mears, the alcoholic singer trying to stay away from drink, in *The Gingerbread Lady* (1970). She also assumed leading parts in several revivals, among them Lady Anne in *Richard III*♦ (1953), Masha in *The Seagull* (1954), and Amanda in *The Glass Menagerie*♦ (1965, 1975). Later she replaced Jessica Tandy♦ in *The Gin Game*♦ (1978) and then played Birdie to Elizabeth Taylor's Regina in a 1981 revival of *The Little Foxes.* ♦

Star Wagon, The, a play in three acts by Maxwell Anderson. ♦ Produced by Guthrie McClintic♦ at the Empire Theatre. ♦ September 29, 1937. 223 performances.

When Martha Minch (Lillian Gish♦) berates her husband of 35 years, Stephen (Burgess Meredith♦), for not making enough money, Stephen shrugs off her complaint. Stephen is a fine inventor whose boss, Duffy (Kent Smith), is ready to fire him for inventing a tire that will not wear out. But Stephen also has a more interesting invention—a time machine he calls his star wagon. He uses the machine to go back into his youth with Martha and re-live the chance he had to marry a rich girl, Hallie Arlington (Jane Buchanan). The visit convinces Martha and him that they made the right decisions.

After all, look at the man who married Hallie—none other than crotchety old Duffy!

This likable Anderson fantasy was assessed by Mary McCarthy in the *Partisan Review* as "richer in period comedy than in metaphysics. It is entertaining and quite harmless."

STARR, FRANCES [GRANT] (1881–1973) The soft-eyed beauty, probably the loveliest of David Belasco's♦ great stars, was born in Oneonta, N.Y. She spent many years in stock after making her debut in 1901. Spotting her in a minor comedy, Belasco hired her as a replacement for Minnie Dupree♦ in the leading feminine role in *The Music Master,* ♦ then raised her to stardom as Juanita, who saves her family's land from ruthless speculators, in *The Rose of the Rancho*♦ (1906). Her most memorable role was Laura Murdock, the kept woman who can find no escape from her lot, in *The Easiest Way*♦ (1909). Of her performance, one critic wrote, "The suggestion of abject hopelessness at the end is indescribably affecting, and its impressiveness is embodied in the frail personality and remarkably sensitive playing of Miss Frances Starr, whose performance has a tremendous emotional depth hardly to be expected in so delicate an organism." Subsequent roles for Belasco included Dorothy, the girl with a dual personality, in *The Case of Becky* (1911); the title role of the unworldly nun who becomes pregnant, in *Marie-Odile* (1915); Anne Churchill, the governess who reforms a wastrel, in *Little Lady in Blue* (1916); Sally, the poor girl who refuses to become the mistress of a member of Parliament, in *Tiger! Tiger!* (1918); and Connie Martin, the seamstress who loves a sailor, in *Shore Leave* (1922). After she left Belasco her career faltered, although she kept busy until she retired in the early 1950s. Her most important role in that period was Mrs. Brown, the heroine's dying mother, in *Claudia*♦ (1942).

State of the Union, a comedy in three acts by Howard Lindsay♦ and Russel Crouse. ♦ Produced by Leland Hayward♦ at the Hudson Theatre. November 14, 1945. 765 performances. PP.

Having been out of power for so long, the Republicans are desperate to find a candidate who will win the White House for them. Led by James Conover (Minor Watson), they pick an idealistic industrialist, Grant Matthews (Ralph Bellamy♦). For him to win it will be necessary for his wife Mary (Ruth Hussey) to campaign with him, since rumors are rife that Grant has been having an affair with the publisher Kay Thorndyke (Kay Johnson). Conover is quick to assure Mary that there will be no problems. After all, there is only one fundamental difference between the Democrats and the Republicans, "They're in—and we're out!" But a problem does arise. Grant's idealism is too much for the political bosses, and rather than compromise his beliefs, Grant withdraws.

The comedy was said to have been suggested loosely by the career of Wendell Willkie. To keep the play up to the minute, especially when certain headlines had to be read, the authors nightly wired all companies minor changes in the script.

STEIN, GERTRUDE (1874–1946) The eccentric, expatriate author was best known to playgoers as the librettist for Virgil Thomson's opera, *Four Saints in Three Acts*♦ (1934). Burns Mantle♦ noted, "A perfectly mad text has been supplied by Gertrude Stein, who flatters herself she writes perfectly by ear, even though no one can make sense of what she writes." Three of her plays were presented in New York after her death: *Yes Is for a Very Young Man* (1949), telling of life in Nazi-occupied France; *Doctor Faustus Lights the Lights* (1951), a modern retelling of the old legend which included in her version an actress playing a dog who kept repeating "Thank you"; and *In Circles* (1967), another plotless jumble of words. She was also the subject of a well-received one-woman play at the Circle Repertory,♦ *Gertrude Stein, Gertrude Stein, Gertrude Stein* (1979).

STEIN, JOSEPH (b. 1912) The New York native studied at City College of New York and began his career by contributing sketches to Broadway revues in 1948. Alone or with collaborators he later wrote the books for such musicals as *Plain and Fancy*♦ (1955), *Mr. Wonderful* (1956), *Take Me Along*♦ (1959), and *Fiddler on the Roof*♦ (1964). He also successfully dramatized Carl Reiner's comic novel *Enter Laughing* (1963).

STEINBECK, JOHN (1902–68) Born in Salinas, Calif., and educated at Stanford, the popular novelist first wrote for the stage by dramatizing his novel about the doomed friendship of two migrant workers, *Of Mice and Men*♦ (1937). His subsequent plays all failed. Like his first they were dramatizations of his stories. *The Moon Is Down* (1942) told of life in Nazi-occupied Norway. *Burning Bright* (1950) told of a sterile husband whose wife has a child by another man. His novel, *East of Eden,* served as the basis for the unsuccessful musical, *Here's Where I Belong* (1968).

Steppenwolf Theatre Company This Chicago-based ensemble was founded in 1976 by Jeff Perry, Terry Kinney, and Gary Sinise. Its repertory mixes European classics, older American plays, and new works. The quality of its productions and the success of some of its premieres have brought national recognition both to the group and to such rising young performers and directors as Glenne Headly, John Malkovich, and Mr. Sinise.

STETSON, JOHN (1836–96) The impresario was born in Charlestown, Mass., and gained early fame as an athlete who soon began to run and do acrobatics for money. Later he became the publisher of a controversial Boston magazine. Turning to the theatre he took over numerous playhouses including the Howard Athenaeum,♦ the Olympic, the Globe and the Park in Boston, and the Globe, Booth's, the Fifth Avenue,♦ the Standard, and the Star in New York. He worked closely with Harrigan♦ and Hart♦ in their first years as a team and afterwards managed such stars as Tommaso Salvini,♦ Mrs. Langtry,♦ Modjeska,♦ and James O'Neill.♦ He also produced shows, including several of the original importations of Gilbert♦ and Sullivan.♦ Writing of the "big, bass, blustering" impresario, Otis Skinner♦ remarked, "His usual manner was that of a war tank—he went through things as if they stood in his way. One look at his aggressive face, square jaw, and clouded *dead* eye was enough to cause timid ones to step aside. Perhaps many stories of his 'malapropisms' were apocryphal, but he unquestionably had a penchant for big-sounding words. Once upon his return from Europe he expressed his satisfaction in being again on *terra cotta.*" Unlike many other noted theatrical producers and theatre owners who made and lost fortunes, he died a very wealthy man.

STEVENS, ASHTON (1872–1951) Born in San Francisco, he began his career as a drama critic there in 1894 with the *News-Letter.* He worked on several other local papers until 1907, when he began a three-year stint on the New York *Evening Journal.* However, most of his career was spent in Chicago, with the *Herald* and *Examiner* from 1910 to 1932, then on the *Herald-American* until his death. An outspoken, often acerbic critic, he fought "dullness" not only in plays but in drama criticism and among audiences as well, once writing that "dull people don't like Mrs. Fiske's acting."

STEVENS, EMILY (1882–1928) The talented niece of Mrs. Fiske♦ was born in New York and made her stage debut in a small role in her aunt's mounting of

Becky Sharp♦ in 1900. She continued with Mrs. Fiske for nearly a decade, playing such increasingly important roles as Claire Berton in *Leah Kleschna*♦ (1904) and Grace Phillimore in *The New York Idea*♦ (1906). Among her later roles were Emily Griswold, who reforms her corrupt, power-hungry husband, in *The Boss*♦ (1911); Lily Wagner, the spoiled wife who takes to prostitution, in *Today*♦ (1913); Caroline Knolys, the selfish wife who would steal another woman's husband, in *The Unchastened Woman*♦ (1915); Mathilde Fay, the hedonistic wife who seduces and deserts her young nephew, in *Fata Morgana* (1924); and the title role in a 1926 revival of *Hedda Gabler*. Although she specialized in neurotic, disagreeable women, the theatre world was shocked when the beautiful actress committed suicide at the height of a brilliant career.

STEVENS, Roger L. (b. 1910) One of Broadway's most distinguished producers, he was born in Detroit and studied for a time at the University of Michigan. Having made a considerable fortune in real estate he entered the producing lists in 1949 with a mounting of *Twelfth Night.*♦ In 1951 he became a member of the Playwrights' Company,♦ and in 1954 formed the Producers Theatre. That same year he was a co-founder of the American Shakespeare Festival.♦ He was also associated with the Phoenix Theatre♦ for many years. In 1971 he became the head of the John F. Kennedy Center for the Performing Arts♦ in Washington. Besides the plays produced with the groups mentioned above he has co-produced such plays as *Bus Stop*♦ (1955), *A View from the Bridge*♦ (1955), *West Side Story*♦ (1957), *Under the Yum Yum Tree* (1960), *Mary, Mary*♦ (1961), and *Finishing Touches*♦ (1973).

STEWART, Grant, see *Caught in the Rain*

STEWART [Rubin], Michael (1929–87) The Yale-educated New Yorker came to playgoers' attention with sketches for revues in the 1950s. He subsequently wrote the books for such musicals as *Bye Bye Birdie*♦ (1960), *Carnival!* (1961), *Hello, Dolly!*♦ (1964), and *George M!* (1968). In 1977 he provided the book and lyrics for *I Love My Wife*. With Mark Bramble he created the book for the stage version of the film *42nd Street*♦ (1980).

Sticks and Bones, a play in two acts by David Rabe.♦ Produced by the New York Shakespeare Festival♦ at the Public Theatre. November 7, 1971. 366 performances (including Broadway run).

Ozzie (Tom Aldredge) and Harriet (Elizabeth Wilson) are typical Americans with two typical American sons, David (David Selby) and Rick (Cliff De Young). However, David goes off to the Vietnam War, and when he returns he is no longer typical. Instead he talks with a Vietnamese girl who he insists follows him around but whom no one else can see, and his conversation dwells on bloody horrors. Not knowing what else to do with David, Ozzie and Harriet convince him to commit suicide. Rick lends him a razor and even helps his brother cut his wrists. Then Rick rushes to take one last photograph of David for the family album.

The play was praised by Douglas Watt♦ of the *Daily News* as a "serious and strikingly original anti-war play . . . a powerful human document." Ozzie and Harriet Nelson and their sons Rick and David were performers in an early television series about an apple-pie American family.

Still Alarm, The, a play in four acts by Joseph Arthur.♦ Produced at the 14th Street Theatre. August 30, 1887. 16 performances.

The romance between Jack Manley (Harry Lacy) and Elinore Fordham (Blanche Thorne) is looked at askance by the villainous John Bird (Nelson Wheatcroft), who is not above trying to burn the lovers alive. The New York fire department comes to their rescue.

The play was supposedly written with the help of A. C. Wheeler.♦ Its famous scene of horses and engines setting out from the firehouse and of the rescue from a burning building made it one of the most popular plays of the era, especially with backwater audiences. Although New York critics sneered, the play chalked up a run of 104 performances when it returned to Manhattan in March 1888.

Stock Companies in America In the sense that they were more or less permanent companies of players, the first American troupes, such as those of Douglass♦ and Hallam,♦ and possibly even the players associated with Thomas Kean♦ and Walter Murray,♦ could loosely be called stock companies, as could the ensembles attached to the earliest established theatres. However, for a number of decades all these companies, because of the relative smallness of American cities and therefore the limited coterie of playgoers, had to perform in repertory fashion, giving a different play with each successive performance and only returning to a play once several others had been mounted. By later definition a stock company was an organized group of players who would perform a single play for a limited run before proceeding to the next work. Thus stock companies in this sense could develop only after the growth of larger cities and a notable increase in the number of playgoers. As such, traditional stock ensembles did not really begin to develop until the 1840s, with William Mitchell's♦ band of burlesque artists an interesting early example. Burton♦ soon established noteworthy troupes in Philadelphia and New York. The heyday of American stock companies may be said to have begun when the Wallack♦ family established their first ensemble and opened their first New York theatre in 1852. Augustin Daly,♦ A. M. Palmer,♦ and, for a time, the old Lyceum Theatre♦ under Daniel Frohman♦ followed over the next several decades. Whether Wallack's or Daly's marked the apogee is moot, but time has been kinder to the memory of Daly's great players such as John Drew,♦ Mrs. Gilbert,♦ James Lewis,♦ and Ada Rehan.♦ All these companies offered schedules of new plays interspersed with mountings of major revivals of older classics, but the emphasis was generally on comedy or romantic escapist drama, and very few of the more innovative, significant serious plays of the time first premiered at their houses, although there were notable exceptions. Away from New York, great companies flourished in larger cities such as Philadelphia, most notably at the Arch Street Theatre♦ under Mrs. Drew,♦ and in Boston at the great Boston Museum.♦ With the growing practice of open casting for each new mounting, a practice pushed by the Frohman♦ brothers and many of their contemporaries, and the increasing emphasis on stars relied on by many of these same producers, the great stock companies began to fade away in the 1890s. A few fine stock troupes continued to thrive briefly away from New York in the early years of the 20th century. These included the companies headed by George Fawcett♦ in Baltimore and by Henry Jewett♦ in Boston. However, by the 1910s stock companies were no longer in the first rank of American theatrical organizations. Nevertheless, many continued to thrive in outlying parts of New York City and elsewhere in America. They usually offered troupes of second-class actors and newcomers anxious to learn the trade. Their bills consisted largely of plays which had been popular a season or two before in "first-class" houses, although some more venturesome groups regularly tried out new plays. An excellent example of this sort of stock company was run for many years by Jessie Bonstelle♦ in Buffalo and Detroit. The Depression and sound films dealt the final death blow to such ensembles, although in later years summer stock♦ troupes have flourished seasonally.

STODDART, J[AMES] H[ENRY] (1827–1907) Born in Yorkshire, England, he was the son of a moderately popular actor, and first played children's roles opposite his father. He performed mainly in Scotland and the north of England before coming to America, where he made his debut with Wallack's♦ company in 1854 as Mr. Sowerberry in *A Phenomenon in a Smock Frock.* The slim, handsome, if somewhat gaunt-faced actor was immediately recognized as a superior low comedian. His performance of Don Whiskerandos in *The Critic* was hailed by the English comedian Charles Mathews as the best he had ever seen. A fiery temperament allowed him to stay at Wallack's only two years, after which he moved to Laura Keene's. ♦ Despite occasional angry departures he remained there nearly ten years before returning to Wallack's. By 1875 he was playing under Palmer's♦ aegis at the Union Square.♦ His performance as the rascally innkeeper Pierre in *Rose Michel*♦ was so successful that he largely abandoned comic roles for more villainous ones. It was his refusal to play the Baron Chevrial in *A Parisian Romance* (1883) that gave Richard Mansfield♦ his start. Although his prominence later diminished, Stoddart continued to act until he was struck down by a train, ending an American career of over half a century.

Autobiography: *Recollections of a Player,* New York, 1902.

STONE, [VAL] FRED [ANDREW] (1873–1959) Born in Valmont, Colo., he was raised in Topeka. With his brother he joined a circus and continued to perform as an acrobat in tents for several years. He then moved briefly to the legitimate stage before enlisting in one of Haverly's minstrel companies. There he met Dave [David Craig] Montgomery (1870–1917), a native of St. Joseph, Mo. When the minstrel troupe was disbanded, the pair went into vaudeville as grotesquely made-up acrobatic clowns. Their first Broadway appearance was in *The Girl from Up There* (1901). Subsequently they starred in *The Wizard of Oz*♦ (1903); *The Red Mill*♦ (1906), in which they introduced "The Streets of New York"; *The Old Town* (1910); *The Lady of the Slipper* (1912); and *Chin-Chin*♦ (1914). By the time of Montgomery's death they were indisputably the most popular musical comedy team. After his partner's death, Stone appeared in *Jack o' Lantern* (1917), *Tip Top* (1920), *Stepping Stones* (1923), *Criss-Cross* (1926), *Ripples* (1930), and *Smiling*

Faces (1932). All but the last two were huge hits. Later he appeared with only small success in a number of straight plays. Whether alone or with Montgomery, much of Stone's humor came from his comic acrobatics. The rest was often equally child-like. In *Jack o' Lantern* he announced his real name was Tony Chestnut, and to make people remember it he pointed to his toe, knee, chest, and head. Then he added his real name did not matter, since he was so light in the head that he was known as Jack o' Lantern. His wife Allene Crater and daughter Dorothy were also popular performers.

Autobiography: *Rolling Stone,* New York, 1945.

STONE, JOHN AUGUSTUS (1800–34) This once admired playwright was born in Concord, Mass. He made his debut as an actor in Boston in 1821 as Old Norval in *Douglas* ♦ and despite his youth thereafter specialized in old men's parts. Without ever becoming a star he played in New York regularly from 1822 to 1831, and then moved to Philadelphia. However, his fame rests not with his acting but with his response to Edwin Forrest's ♦ 1828 offer of a $500 prize for "the best tragedy, in five acts, of which the hero, or principal character, shall be an aboriginal of this country." That response was the prize-winning *Metamora; or, The Last of the Wampanoags* ♦ (1829), which gave Forrest one of his greatest successes. His other plays include *Tancred; or, The Siege of Antioch,* which was published in 1827 but seems not to have been performed; *Tancred, King of Sicily; or, The Archives of Palermo* (1831), a different play from the previous one and telling of fraternal hatred; *The Demoniac; or, The Prophet's Bride* (1831); a revision of J. K. Paulding's ♦ *The Lion of the West* ♦ (1831); *The Ancient Briton* (1833); and *The Knight of the Golden Fleece; or, The Yankee of Spain* (1834), which served as a vehicle for G. H. Hill. ♦ Several other plays are said to have been performed, but only the scantiest records of them survive. In ill health and despondent, he committed suicide by drowning in the Schuylkill River. Although one obituary noted, "Mr. Stone has contributed more, both as author and performer, to raise the character of the stage, than any other native American," his work retains only historical interest.

STOPPARD, TOM [né THOMAS STRAUSSLER] (b. 1937) One of the more brilliant and accessible modern English playwrights, he was first represented on Broadway by *Rosencrantz and Guildenstern Are Dead* (1967). His later works to reach New York included *Jumpers* (1974), *Travesties* (1976), *Dirty Linen* and *New-Found-Land* (1977), *Night and Day* (1980), and *The Real Thing* (1984). Several of his other plays have been popular with little theatres and elsewhere, although they have been denied the benefit of Broadway's approval. His best plays show a marked influence of the theatre of the absurd, but unlike most examples of the school, also manifest a traditional theatrical construction, superior character development, and pithy, witty dialogue.

STOTHART, HERBERT (1885–1949) The Milwaukee-born composer wrote part or all of the scores for a dozen Broadway musicals in the 1920s. However, the only memorable songs to come from these shows were those by his collaborators. His work included *Always You* (1920); *Tickle Me* (1920); *Wildflower* (1923), written with Vincent Youmans; *Rose-Marie* ♦ (1924), written with Rudolf Friml ♦; *Song of the Flame* (1925), written with George Gershwin ♦; *Golden Dawn* (1927), written with Emmerich Kalman ♦; and *Good Boy* (1928), written with Kalmar ♦ and Ruby. ♦ He also served as a conductor and orchestrator, before leaving for Hollywood.

STRANG, LEWIS C[LINTON] (1869–1935) Born in Westfield, Mass., and educated at Boston University, he took work at the Boston *Journal* where he eventually became its drama critic. Later he held a similar position on the Washington *Times*. At the turn of the century he churned out a spate of books that still hold interest for theatrical historians: *Famous Actresses of the Day* (2 vols., 1899 and 1902); *Famous Actors of the Day* (2 vols., 1899 and 1901); *Prima Donnas and Soubrettes of Light Opera and Musical Comedy in America* (1900); *Celebrated Comedians of Light Opera and Musical Comedy in America* (1901); and *Players and Plays of the Last Quarter Century* (1902).

Strange Interlude, a play in nine acts by Eugene O'Neill. ♦ Produced by the Theatre Guild ♦ at the John Golden Theatre. January 30, 1928. 426 performances. PP.

Nina Leeds (Lynn Fontanne ♦) has turned against her father, Professor Leeds (Philip Leigh), for persuading her fiancé not to marry her until the war was over. The young man was killed in the war. Nina becomes a nurse in a soldiers' hospital, where three men fall in love with her. Charles Marsden (Tom Powers ♦) is a writer who is too shy and too attached to his mother's apron strings to confess his affection openly. Dr. Edmund Darrell (Glenn Anders ♦) is fond of Nina, but recognizes her curious emotional problems and prefers the safety of his career. He does, however, press her to marry Sam Evans (Earle Larimore♦), a weak man for whom she has little feeling. She consents and soon is pregnant, but when her mother-in-law, Mrs. Evans (Helen Westley♦), reveals that the family has had a tendency toward insanity, Nina has an abortion. She keeps this a secret from Sam and shortly afterward has a child by Edmund, who asks her to divorce Sam and marry him, but she refuses. Eleven years pass. Her son, Gordon (played by Charles Walters in early scenes and John J. Burns in later ones), grows up preferring Sam to his real father or his increasingly possessive mother. Realizing she has lost both Edmund and Gordon, she is stunned when Sam's death removes him, too, from her life. Only the loyal Charles remains, so she marries him. Charles urges her to regard the past as an interlude. She agrees, concluding, "our lives are merely strange dark interludes in the electrical display of God the Father!," and she congratulates Charles, "who, passed beyond desire, has all the luck at last."

The action of the play, in which O'Neill consciously drew on Freud, frequently stopped to allow the characters to probe their inner thoughts in extended soliloquies. "The effect," wrote Joseph Wood Krutch,♦ "is to combine to a remarkable extent the vivid directness of the drama with the more intricate texture of the modern novel, and, indeed, the play brought to the stage certain subtleties which only the novel hitherto seemed capable of suggesting." Because the drama was four hours long, the producers raised the curtain at 5:15 and had a long intermission for dinner at seven o'clock. Although it quickly became the season's conversation piece and won the Pulitzer Prize,♦ it was banned in several important cities, most notably in Boston. A major revival was mounted in 1963.

Stranger, The William Dunlap's♦ adaptation of Kotzebue's♦ *Menschenhass und Reue* was first presented at the Park Theatre♦ on December 10, 1798, and initiated the popularity of the German playwright in America. Its air of melancholy and mystery provided American playgoers with their introduction to theatrical romanticism. The story recounted the heroic actions of a Stranger who comes to a castle where a Mrs. Haller is staying. Mrs. Haller has been unfaithful to her husband, and they have long been separated. Although she is courted by Baron de Steinfort, she refuses all offers of marriage. The Stranger turns out to be Mrs. Haller's husband. At first he is reluctant to be reunited with her, but the entreaties of their children eventually prevail. Thomas Abthorpe Cooper♦ was

the first American Stranger. The play remained in favor until the Civil War era. Later actors who essayed the title role included J. W. Wallack,♦ Thomas Barry,♦ and James Murdoch.♦

STRASBERG, LEE [né ISRAEL STRASSBERG] (1901–82) Born in Poland, he was brought to America at the age of seven. He soon developed an interest in theatre, working at a settlement playhouse and later studying at the American Laboratory Theatre.♦ After a time as an actor with the Theatre Guild♦ he joined Harold Clurman♦ and Cheryl Crawford♦ in founding the Group Theatre.♦ However, for many his main influence was his work at the Actors Studio.♦ He came to the organization in 1948, a year after its inception, and quickly became its guiding force. There he advocated the "method school" of acting, a style influenced by Stanislavsky's♦ theories and which encouraged performers to respond as much to their own inner feelings as to the requirements of the text or dramatic effectiveness. Although the result was that the American theatre was beset with much undisciplined and inelegant acting, a number of fine performers emerged from his classes. These included Anne Bancroft,♦ Julie Harris,♦ Geraldine Page,♦ Kim Stanley,♦ and Maureen Stapleton.♦ His daughter Susan became an actress.

STRAUSS, JOHANN (the younger) (1825–99) Son of the famous "Waltz King," he became the leading composer of late 19th-century Viennese operetta.♦ Although he is best known today for *Die Fledermaus* and *The Gypsy Baron,* these were not the works which captured the fancy of the period's playgoers. Rather it was such now relatively forgotten pieces as *The Merry War* (1882); *The Queen's Lace Handkerchief* (1882), selected to open the Casino Theatre♦; and *Prince Methusalem* (1883), which drew enthusiastic crowds. Even *A Night in Venice* (1884) had only a short run. However, under a number of titles such as *Champagne Sec* and *Rosalinda, Die Fledermaus* enjoyed Broadway revivals throughout the first half of the 20th century.

Straw-hat Theatre, see *Summer Stock*

Streamers, a play in two acts by David Rabe.♦ Produced by the New York Shakespeare Festival♦ at the Mitzi E. Newhouse Theatre (Lincoln Center). April 21, 1976. 478 performances. NYDCCA.

An army barracks seems like a microcosm of 1965 America. Among the soldiers are Billy (Paul Rudd), an idealist who sees himself as a typical American;

Roger (Terry Alexander), a black man who has made a precarious peace with an alien society; Richie (Peter Evans), a young man disturbed by homosexual problems; and Martin (Michael Kell), a boy so upset with army life he is prepared to commit suicide. Into their midst comes Carlyle (Dorian Harewood), a bitter, vicious, trouble-making black man. The others recognize they must purge him to save their society, but they fail. Carlyle goes on a murderous rampage, and Billy is one of his victims.

This play was perceived as an allegory of the American scene of the time, when large areas of American cities were subject to burning, rioting, and looting and of the dilemma this presented for many Americans.

Street Scene, a play in three acts by Elmer Rice. ◆ Produced by William A. Brady◆ at the Playhouse. January 10, 1929. 601 performances. PP.

A row of old New York brownstones has become a street of tenements housing a wide variety of people. Among them are an Irish couple Frank (Robert Kelly) and Anna Maurrant (Mary Servoss), their daughter Rose (Erin O'Brien-Moore), and younger son Willie (Russell Griffin). Rose is attractive and is courted by two men, the flashy, prosperous Harry Easter (Glenn Coulter) and her serious but affectionate Jewish neighbor, Sam Kaplan (Horace Braham). When Frank discovers his wife having an affair with the milkman Steve Sankey (Joseph Baird), he kills them both. Left alone with a brother to raise, Rose rejects proposals from Harry and from Sam—whom she prefers. She is determined to bring up Willie so that he can be freed from the life she and her parents have known.

John Anderson of the *Evening Journal* wrote, "It is a play which builds engrossing trivialities into a drama that is rich and compelling and catches in the wide reaches of its curbside panorama the comedy and heartbreak that lie a few steps up from the sidewalks of New York." In 1947 a superb opera version, with music by Kurt Weill, ◆ lyrics by the poet Langston Hughes, ◆ and a cast headed by Anne Jeffreys, Brian Sullivan, and Polyna Stoska, failed on Broadway, but later became part of several opera companies' repertories.

Streetcar Named Desire, A, a play in three acts by Tennessee Williams. ◆ Produced at the Ethel Barrymore Theatre. December 3, 1947. 855 performances. PP, NYDCCA.

Blanche Du Bois (Jessica Tandy ◆), who lives with illusions of past elegances, comes to visit her sister Stella (Kim Hunter) and brother-in-law, the coarse,

brutish Stanley Kowalski (Marlon Brando). She is appalled at the way they live. What small consolation she can draw from the visit derives from Stanley's lonely, kindly friend, Harold "Mitch" Mitchell (Karl Malden), whom she begins to dream of marrying. Learning that her sister is pregnant, Blanche disgustedly tells her she will live like the local streetcar that travels only through the seediest, most narrow of streets. Stanley, furious, discloses to Mitch that Blanche's husband committed suicide after she discovered he was a homosexual, that Blanche has been fired as a teacher for attempting to seduce a student and is now a nymphomaniac. Later Stanley rapes Blanche, but when she tells Stella this on Stella's return from having her baby, Stella is disbelieving and has Blanche committed to an insane asylum. To the doctor who comes for her, Blanche remarks, "Whoever you are—I have always depended on the kindness of strangers."

Brooks Atkinson◆ wrote of Williams and his drama, "Out of poetic imagination and ordinary compassion, he has spun a poignant and luminous story." The original production was made especially memorable by Jo Mielziner's◆ glowingly imaginative setting, Elia Kazan's◆ taut yet sympathetic direction, and the tender, understanding performance of Miss Tandy. But for many playgoers the evening's high point was Brando's rough-hewn strength. Brando (b. 1924), a native of Omaha, had appeared in *I Remember Mama*◆ (1944), *Truckline Café* (1946), and *Candida*◆ *(1946),* among other plays, before making this, his final stage appearance. Since then his work has been confined to films. The play was revived in 1988, but the production lacked fire and failed.

Streets of New York, The, see *Poor of New York, The*

STREISAND, Barbra, see *Funny Girl*

Strictly Dishonorable, a comedy in three acts by Preston Sturges. Produced by Brock Pemberton◆ at the Avon Theatre. September 18, 1929. 557 performances.

When Isabelle Parry (Muriel Kirkland), a sweet Southern belle, is deserted by her churlish escort, Henry Greene (Louis Jean Heydt), at a New York speakeasy, she finds herself there with only two other men, Count Di Ruvo (Tullio Carminati◆), a Metropolitan Opera star known affectionately as Gus, and the avuncular Judge Dempsey (Carl Anthony), who lives above the night club. Anxious for some fun, she accepts Gus's offer to spend the evening with him, even though he assures her his intentions are strictly dishonorable. But as the evening progresses Gus finds himself falling in love. When Henry returns contritely, he is asked to wait in the car. Isabelle tells Gus that she, too, is in love. Not willing to miss his opportunity, Gus says his only condition is that he wants four sons and seven daughters. The Judge offers to tell Henry not to wait any longer.

This charming, graceful comedy was Sturges's only Broadway success, although many critics had admired his *The Guinea Pig* (1929). After two more failures, *Rapture* (1930) and *Child of Manhattan* (1932), Sturges [né Edmond P. Biden] (1898–1959) became a famous Hollywood writer and director. He returned to the theatre in the 1950s with two unsuccessful musicals, *Make a Wish* (1951) and *Carnival in Flanders* (1953).

Strike Up the Band, a musical comedy in two acts. Book by Morrie Ryskind♦ and George S. Kaufman.♦ Lyrics by Ira Gershwin.♦ Music by George Gershwin.♦ Produced by Edgar Selwyn♦ at the Times Square Theatre. January 14, 1930. 191 performances.

Horace J. Fletcher (Dudley Clements) wants his country to go to war over a Swiss tariff on chocolates. He is even willing to underwrite the war, so long as it is called the Horace J. Fletcher Memorial War. But when his daughter's fiancé, Jim Townsend (Jerry Goff), threatens to reveal that Fletcher uses Grade B milk in his chocolates, Fletcher becomes an ardent pacifist. However, his change takes place too late. The war is out of control and only won when the Americans decode the Swiss yodeling signals. Delighted with the outcome, the Americans decide to go to war with Russia over a tariff on caviar.

Principal songs: I've Got a Crush on You · Soon · Strike Up the Band

Originally produced in 1927, the musical was withdrawn after its tryout. Ryskind rewrote Kaufman's original book, softening many of Kaufman's sharpest barbs and framing the story as a dream. Much of the fun came from the antics of Bobby Clark♦ and his sidekick, Paul McCullough, although their roles were not crucial to the main plot.

STRINDBERG, [JOHANN] AUGUST (1849–1912) Although the Swedish dramatist's plays have never been popular in our commercial theatre, they have been performed with some frequency by experimental and collegiate playhouses. The best known are probably *Miss Julie* and *The Father,* which, despite a paucity of notable American productions, have

exerted a major influence on American dramaturgy. His use of both realism and later of expressionism had a notable effect on the writings of Eugene O'Neill♦ and other American dramatists.

STRITCH, ELAINE (b. 1925) The "gritty-voiced blonde" from Detroit had appeared in a number of straight plays before calling attention to herself when she sang "Civilization" in the 1947 revue *Angel in the Wings.* After singing "Zip" in a 1952 revival of *Pal Joey,* ♦ she toured in the Ethel Merman♦ role in *Call Me Madam.* ♦ She was later seen in the 1954 revival of *On Your Toes*♦; as Grace, the hard-nosed operator of a road house, in *Bus Stop*♦ (1955); in Noel Coward's♦ *Sail Away* (1961), in which she sang "Why Do the Wrong People Travel?"; and in *Company*♦ (1970), in which she introduced "The Ladies Who Lunch." Much of her subsequent career has been in England.

STRONG, AUSTIN, see *Seventh Heaven*

STROUSE, CHARLES [LOUIS] (b. 1928) The New York-born composer studied at the Eastman School of Music and then with Aaron Copland and Nadia Boulanger. Deciding to emphasize show music, he became a rehearsal pianist. He wrote for resort and off-Broadway revues before scoring a major success with his first musical, *Bye Bye Birdie*♦ (1960), remembered for "Baby, Talk to Me," "A Lot of Livin' To Do," and "Put On a Happy Face"; *All American* (1962), which included "Once Upon a Time"; *Golden Boy* (1964); *It's a Bird It's a Plane It's Superman* (1966); *Applause* (1970); and *Annie*♦ (1977), whose hit was "Tomorrow." Three subsequent shows, *A Broadway Musical* (1978), *Bring Back Birdie* (1981), and *Dance a Little Closer* (1983), were all fast flops. He scored a minor success off-Broadway with *Mayor* (1985), a musical version of Mayor Koch's autobiography, then suffered another failure on Broadway with *Rags* (1986). While fundamentally traditional, his music has been wide-ranging and inventive.

Student Prince, The, an operetta in four acts. Book and lyrics by Dorothy Donnelly.♦ Music by Sigmund Romberg.♦ Produced by the Messrs. Shubert♦ at the Jolson Theatre. December 2, 1924. 608 performances.

When Dr. Engel (Greek Evans) is assigned to accompany Prince Karl Franz (Howard Marsh♦) to Heidelberg, he recalls for the Prince his own "Golden Days" there. The Prince readily joins the other students in the camaraderie of their "Drinking Song," at the same time falling in love with a beer-garden waitress, Kathie (Ilse Marvenga). They pledge that "Deep in My Heart, Dear" they will always love each other. Before long he is under her window singing a "Serenade." But after Karl Franz's grandfather dies, he knows he must assume the throne and marry the girl who has been selected for him, Princess Margaret (Roberta Beatty), although she, too, loves someone else. Karl Franz returns briefly to Heidelberg to say farewell to Kathie and to promise to remember forever their happy times together.

Although the title was correctly *The Student Prince in Heidelberg,* hardly anyone called it that. The show was Romberg's biggest success and the quintessential example of both his work and period operetta. Along with *Rose-Marie,* ♦ which had opened earlier in the same season, it sparked a five-year revival of traditional operetta. The musical continued to tour season after season until the late 1940s and has been revived occasionally since.

STUDLEY, J[OHN] B. (1831–1910) The Bostonian made his professional debut in Columbia, S.C., in 1848. Thereafter he played seasons as leading man in many important companies around the country before becoming leading man to Charlotte Cushman♦ and essaying a memorable Bill Sykes in her mounting of *Oliver Twist.* A melodramatic actor of what was increasingly perceived as an old school, he proved absolutely right as the villainous Byke in *Under the Gaslight♦* (1867) and as the drunken Wolf in *Horizon♦* (1871). His later career typified that of many admired second-rankers, with major supporting parts and occasional leads in first class New York houses and starring roles in touring shows and at minor New York theatres.

STURGES, PRESTON, see *Strictly Dishonorable*

STYNE, JULE [né JULIUS KERWIN STEIN] (b. 1905) Born in London but brought to America at the age of eight, he proved a child prodigy on the piano, giving recitals with the Chicago and Detroit symphonies and entering the Chicago College of Music at thirteen. He later abandoned classical music in favor of becoming a pianist in a dance band and eventually organized his own band. After many years of composing for Hollywood films, he turned to Broadway and enjoyed a smash hit with his second try, *High Button Shoes* (1947), whose score included "I Still Get Jealous" and "Papa, Won't You Dance with Me?" Among his subsequent long runs were *Gentlemen Prefer Blondes♦* (1949), remembered for "Bye, Bye, Baby." "Diamonds Are a Girl's Best

Friend," and "A Little Girl from Little Rock"; *Two on the Aisle* (1951); *Hazel Flagg* (1953); part of the score for *Peter Pan♦* (1954), including "Never Never Land"; *Bells Are Ringing* (1956), which offered "Just in Time" and "The Party's Over"; *Say, Darling* (1958); *Gypsy♦* (1959), his finest work, from which came "Everything's Coming Up Roses," "Small World," "Together," and "You'll Never Get Away from Me"; *Do Re Mi* (1960), recalled for "Make Someone Happy"; *Subways Are for Sleeping* (1961); *Funny Girl♦* (1964), whose hit was "People"; *Fade In—Fade Out* (1964); *Hallelujah, Baby!* (1967); and *Sugar* (1972). Styne's traditional but melodic and eminently theatrical music will probably be seen as the last set squarely in the school of great American composers that began with the musical comedy songs of Irving Berlin♦ and Jerome Kern.♦ He was unquestionably the most prolific and successful of composers to appear on Broadway just after World War II.

Subject Was Roses, The, a play in two acts by Frank D. Gilroy. Produced at the Royale Theatre. May 25, 1964. 832 performances. PP, NYDCCA.

When Timmy Cleary (Martin Sheen) returns from the war, his father John (Jack Albertson) and his mother Nettie (Irene Dailey) find themselves fighting each other to win his love and respect. Nettie, for example, makes his favorite breakfast of waffles, but at first Timmy seems not to notice. After two days together, Timmy tells his parents that he is leaving to strike out on his own. Scarred from the family infighting, John and Nettie grudgingly agree.

A small-cast, largely actionless play typical of its day, its winning so many awards, especially after two seasons in which no Pulitzer♦ award was given, testified to the hollowness of contemporary American play-writing.

Gilroy (b. 1925) was born in 1925 and educated at Dartmouth and Yale. His early play, *Who'll Save the Ploughboy?* (1962), won an Obie.♦ However, all the plays which followed *The Subject Was Roses* were failures.

Subway Circuit This was the name given to a group of theatres, some within Manhattan but most of them in the other boroughs, that regularly offered touring shows after their Broadway runs and on rare occasions served as tryout theatres. They had disappeared by the 1950s.

Sugar Babies, a musical revue in two acts by Ralph G. Allen. Produced at the Mark Hellinger Theatre. October 8, 1979. 1,208 performances.

A collection of traditional burlesque skits and musical numbers, the show was an affectionate look back at the raunchy glories of the Minsky♦ era. It starred two popular film performers, Mickey Rooney and Ann Miller. That the stars may have been a bigger attraction than the burlesque material was suggested by the quick failure of a road company headed by two top Broadway figures, Carol Channing♦ and Robert Morse.♦ When Rooney and Miss Miller took the show on the road it was remarkably successful. Allen (b. 1934) was born in Philadelphia and has taught theatre at important universities. This is his first Broadway show.

SULLAVAN, MARGARET (1911–60) The throaty-voiced blonde beauty was born in Norfolk, Va., and after several years in amateur and stock productions made her Broadway debut in 1931 in *A Modern Virgin*. She is best remembered for four roles: Terry Randall, the aspiring actress, in *Stage Door*♦ (1936); Sally Middleton, the actress who finds love with a soldier on wartime leave, in *The Voice of the Turtle*♦ (1943); Hester Collyer, a woman in love with an unloving man, in *The Deep Blue Sea* (1952); and Sabrina Fairchild, the chauffeur's daughter who lands her father's boss's rich son, in *Sabrina Fair*♦ (1953). She was trying out in what promised to be another success when she committed suicide. She was also popular in films. *Haywire*, a book by her daughter Brooke Hayward about her and Brooke's father, producer Leland Hayward,♦ was published in 1977.

SULLIVAN, ARTHUR, see *Gilbert and Sullivan*

Sullivan-Considine Circuit A vaudeville chain founded in 1902 by John Considine, who had made his money in Seattle catering to prospectors leaving for the Yukon gold rush. He brought in Big Tim Sullivan, a political boss, for his political connections. Within a few years the chain was one of the largest on the West Coast and extended as far east as Louisville. Considine and his chain had the reputation of being one of the most ethical in the business. He is said never to have cancelled an act.

Sullivan, Harris and Woods A firm founded in 1899 by P. H. "Paddy" Sullivan, who provided the financing, Al Woods,♦ and Sam H. Harris,♦ it was for a number of years a principal producer of cheap, touring melodramas. The firm disbanded after both Woods and Harris elected to pursue independent careers on Broadway.

Sultan of Sulu, The, a musical comedy in two acts. Book and lyrics by George Ade.♦ Music by Alfred G. Wathall. Produced at Wallack's Theatre. December 29, 1902. 192 performances.

Ki-Ram (Frank Moulan♦) leads an idyllic life as the Sultan of Sulu until sailors from the American navy arrive to claim the island for Uncle Sam. Determined to maintain his trouble-free ways, Ki-Ram courts the lady judge-advocate whom the American government has sent. But when the judge realizes that Ki-Ram is merely offering her a place in his harem, she issues several decrees which assure an end to Ki-Ram's bliss. Luckily a legal technicality is discovered that allows Ki-Ram to resume his own lackadaisical ways.

Principal songs: Since I First Met You · The Smiling Isle

One of the few Chicago-originated musicals to win acclaim in New York, it initiated the rage, which lasted for several seasons and culminated with *The Red Mill,*♦ for musical comedies centering on the contrast between American and foreign ways of life. Other examples included *The Isle of Spice, The Yankee Consul, The Sho-Gun, It Happened in Nordland,* and *Fantana.*

Summer and Smoke, a play in a prologue and two acts by Tennessee Williams.♦ Produced by Margo Jones♦ at the Music Box Theatre. October 6, 1948. 100 performances.

Alma Winemiller (Margaret Phillips), the prim daughter of the local minister, is at once repelled and fascinated by her handsome, amoral neighbor, Dr. John Buchanan, Jr. (Tod Andrews). She sets about to give him higher moral standards, while he takes it upon himself to teach her the realities of life and sex. Both are all too successful, for John becomes high-minded and spiritual, while Alma dwindles into the town prostitute.

One of Williams's best constructed and imaginative plays, it was coolly received at first hearing and failed. A 1952 revival by the Circle in the Square,♦ with Geraldine Page♦ as Alma, prompted a critical re-evaluation. The revival ran nearly a year.

Summer Stock As early as the first half of the 19th century, summer playhouses on the outskirts of growing American cities began to attract playgoers seeking entertainment as they escaped from city heat and crowds. Many began as parks or gardens where citizens came for light refreshment and cooling breezes. In New York, Chatham Garden had a popular theatre in the 1820s, and a decade later Niblo's Garden♦ offered shows as well as food and drink. The theatre at Chatham Garden soon bowed to the encroaching city, but as New York moved northward the theatre at Niblo's was incorporated into a new hotel and remained a major playhouse, for a time in the heart of the theatre district, until late in the 19th century. The oldest summer playhouse still operating, Elitch's Gardens Theatre,◆ was founded in Denver in 1890. Almost all these theatres were opened with the idea of presenting light olios for summer, but several of the more successful soon started to offer regular plays, particularly comedies. Although their development was assisted by the spread of trolley-car lines to outlying reaches around the turn of the century, it was really the arrival of the automobile several years later that spurred the greatest growth.

One of the earliest summer theatres to gain widespread recognition was the Provincetown Playhouse,◆ which opened on a wharf in Provincetown, Mass., during World World I. However, it was atypical in many ways. Most notably, it was dedicated to serious new drama and not to the rehashed escapist material that soon came to characterize most summer stock. Second, it soon opened a New York branch for winter seasons. Third, it was built on a wharf. Many early summer stock theatres were begun in converted barns or mills and often self-consciously retained a distinct rustic ambiance for many years. One result was the name popularly given to summer stock—straw-hat theatre—which reflected its barn-like origins as much as it did the fashion of wearing straw hats in summer. Other examples, atypical in their dedication to serious theatre, were the Hedgerow Theatre◆ in Moylan, Penn., and the playhouse at Williamstown, Mass.

Far more on the order of what the public came to think of as summer theatres were such long successful operations as the Bucks County Playhouse in New Hope, Penn.; the Westport Country Playhouse in Westport, Conn.; the Cape Playhouse in Dennis, Mass.; the North Shore Players in Marblehead, Mass.; and the Boothbay Playhouse in Boothbay, Maine.

Even if much of their fare consisted of frothy comedies, most of the better straw-hats offered occasional serious drama and tryouts of new plays. Many also lured stars, either Broadway stars in between major assignments or Hollywood names who did not want to commit themselves to a full New York season or feared the more demanding standards of New York critics. Other houses did not use stars but employed a genuine, if seasonal stock company. These theatres were built on essentially traditional lines, but huge open-air amphitheatres

such as the one at Jones Beach, near New York, and that of the St. Louis Municipal Opera Company,◆ also thrived, although they specialized in musicals. The Paper Mill Playhouse, a regular enclosed conversion in Milburn, N.J., because of its proximity to New York, was able to extend its seasons, usually of musicals, to an almost year-round operation.

The heyday of the straw-hats was between the two World Wars and for a short period thereafter. One postwar development was the rise of tents, generally offering musicals in-the-round. Economic and other considerations then began to affect playhouses, closing some and forcing others to rely on packaged tours, usually featuring high-priced names. Most of the tents gave way to permanent structures, with large concrete parking lots that retained little of the bucolic atmosphere once so carefully fostered. However, a number of the old, traditional playhouses still flourish.

Sunday in the Park with George, a musical in two acts. Book by James Lapine◆. Music and lyrics by Stephen Sondheim.◆ Produced by the Shubert Organization◆ and others at the Booth Theatre. May 2, 1984. 604 performances. PP.

Georges Seurat (Mandy Patinkin) is determined to finish his painting, "A Sunday Afternoon on the Island of La Grande Jatte," even if it means his friends and associates will ridicule him and even if in the process he must neglect and lose his mistress, Dot (Bernadette Peters). Years later his American great-grandson, George (Mr. Patinkin), is also an artist, hoping to find meaning and purpose working on a multimedia "Chromolume." He is encouraged by his grandmother, Marie (Miss Peters). Visiting the drearily overdeveloped Grande Jatte after her death, he finds solace in her memory and in notes once scribbled by his great-grandfather.

Principal songs: Sunday in the Park with George · Color and Light · Children and Art.

Although the show was something more than a *succès d' estime,* it was deemed too esoteric to tour after its Broadway run. A high point was the replication of the Seurat painting at the end of the first act.

Sunny, a musical comedy in two acts. Book and lyrics by Otto Harbach◆ and Oscar Hammerstein II. ◆ Music by Jerome Kern. ◆ Produced by Charles Dillingham◆ at the New Amsterdam Theatre. ◆ September 22, 1925. 517 performances.

Sunny Peters (Marilyn Miller◆) is a circus performer working in England, where she meets and falls in love with a fellow American, Tom Warren

(Paul Frawley). When Tom has to return to the States, Sunny decides to follow him but realizes she cannot afford the fare. Her ex-husband, the circus owner Jim Deming (Jack Donahue♦), suggests they remarry, sail back together, then get a divorce. Sunny prefers to stow away. She is caught but everything ends happily.

Principal songs: D'ye Love Me? · Sunny · Who?

One of the best and most successful 1920s musical comedies, it marked Kern's first association with Harbach and Hammerstein, who would become his principal collaborators.

Sunrise at Campobello, a play in three acts by Dore Schary. Produced by Schary and the Theatre Guild♦ at the Cort Theatre. January 30, 1958. 558 performances.

Franklin D. Roosevelt (Ralph Bellamy♦) has taken a swim that has left him tired and achy. Within a few hours he can no longer move parts of his body. His wife Eleanor (Mary Fickett), his mother Anna (Roni Dengel), and his long-time political associate Louis McHenry Howe (Henry Jones), all recognize that he has polio. They gather together to help Roosevelt, who is depressed and even terrified when he thinks of his helplessness should a fire break out. Although Anna wants him to retire, for three years she and the others persist in their encouragement and aid until Roosevelt has so recruited both his strength and his spirit that he is able to go to New York to nominate Al Smith (Alan Bunce) at the 1924 Democratic convention.

One of the many contemporary plays centering on the problems of a cripple, it gained added interest from its portraits of historical figures. Schary (1905–80), a native of Newark, N.J., had been a newspaperman and a Hollywood executive before embarking on a theatre career. He also produced *A Majority of One*♦ (1959) and co-produced and directed *The Unsinkable Molly Brown* (1960), among others.

Sunshine Boys, The, a comedy in two acts by Neil Simon.♦ Produced at the Broadhurst Theatre. December 20, 1972. 538 performances.

Willie Clark (Jack Albertson) and Al Lewis (Sam Levene♦) were an old vaudeville team who fought and separated many years earlier. Willie now lives alone, largely in pajamas, in a small New York hotel. Al lives with his daughter in New Jersey. CBS wants to do a nostalgic program about the history of comedy and wants to reunite Lewis and Clark. It falls to Al's nephew, Ben Silverman (Lewis J. Stadlen), to persuade the old men to forget their animosities and perform together again. This proves

a hard task but Ben finally succeeds. After the broadcast Willie takes sick. At the same time he learns he must move to the Actors' Home. Al pays him a visit and announces that since his daughter is to have another baby, he, too, must move to the Home. They sit together and reminisce about old performers they once knew.

Hailed by T. E. Kalem of *Time* magazine as "a cripplingly funny show," this affectionately savage comedy was Simon's tenth consecutive success. Walter Matthau♦ and George Burns headed the film version.

Sun-Up, a play in three acts by Lula Vollmer.♦ Produced at the Provincetown Theatre. May 25, 1923. 356 performances.

Widow Cagle (Lucille LaVerne), a North Carolina mountain woman whose son is fighting in World War I, discovers that the stranger (Eliot Cabot♦) she has been harboring is not only a deserter but is the son of the man who killed her moonshining husband. When she learns that her son has died in the war, she determines to kill the deserter. However, as she is about to pull the trigger, the voice of her son warns her that his own death came from such blind hatred and that killing The Stranger will serve no purpose. She changes her mind and even refuses to turn the man over to the sheriff. Instead she will spend her remaining years alone, but in peace. She tells her son's voice, "I'm a knowin' God A'mighty is a takin' keer of ye."

Although Miss Vollmer worked for the Theatre Guild,♦ she was unable to get that company to produce the play. Minor producers finally took a chance with it, but its fine reviews and immediate success prompted Lee Shubert♦ to move it to the Princess Theatre. ♦

Superstition, a tragedy in five acts by James Nelson Barker. ♦ Produced by William Wood♦ at the Chestnut Street Theatre♦ (Philadelphia). March 12, 1824. In repertory.

In a duel to protect the honor of Mary Ravensworth (Mrs. Duff♦) from the unwanted attentions of George Egerton (F. C. Wemyss♦), Charles Fitzroy (Wood) wounds Egerton but walks aways unscathed. Rather than pleasing Mary's father, the Reverend Ravensworth (Mr. Darley), the news angers him, since Charles and his mother Isabella (Mrs. Wood) have not shown the proper respect for his clerical office. Matters are made worse when the village is attacked by Indians. Charles and a man called The Unknown (Mr. Duff♦) lead the attack against them, defeat them, and again walk away unharmed. Charles and his mother are then perceived as devils and at their trial Ravensworth testifies against them. Charles is executed and his mother dies of grief. The Unknown turns out to be William Goffe—one of the men who had sentenced Charles I to death—and also to be Isabella's father and Charles's grandfather. Mary is left to denounce her father for his cruelty.

One of the first important American plays based on domestic history, the blank-verse drama skillfully wove together the various events, all conspiring inexorably against the hero. One student of American drama, W. J. Meserve, has called the work "the single outstanding American play written during the first quarter of the nineteenth century." It sometimes was given the subtitle *The Fanatic Father*.

Susan and God, a play in three acts by Rachel Crothers. ♦ Produced by John Golden♦ at the Plymouth Theatre. ♦ October 7, 1937. 288 performances.

Selfish, vain Susan Trexel (Gertrude Lawrence♦) becomes a convert to the Oxford movement and sets about to reform the world. She arrives as a guest at the home of Irene Burroughs (Vera Allen), promptly crimping Irene's affair with Michael O'Hara (Douglas Gilmore). She then sets to work on her own alcoholic husband Barrie (Paul McGrath) and her "girl scout gone wrong" daughter Blossom (Nancy Kelly). For a time she does succeed in keeping Barrie on the wagon, but when she accuses him of having an affair with another woman, he slips off. Susan is made to recognize that being meddlesome is not being religious, and that real faith comes from within.

Although many critics felt there was not sufficient story line and that Miss Lawrence was left to carry the play, Richard Lockridge wrote in the *Evening Sun,* "It doesn't need proving that Miss Crothers, theme or no theme, can write dialogue that humor glints on, and handle her situations and characters with a suave dexterity enchanting to watch." The author returned to the theatre for this, her last play, after five years of writing for films.

SUTHERLAND, EVELYN GREENLEAF [née BAKER] (1855–1908) Born in Boston, and educated there and in Europe, she married Dr. John Preston Sutherland in 1879 after her return home. (He afterward became dean of the Boston University School of Medicine.) She began to write for the stage comparatively late in life, first attempting some one-act plays. Several were produced in Boston before the Theatre of Arts and Letters♦

mounted *Drifting,* her collaboration with Emma Sheridan Fry, in New York in 1892. Of her full-length plays, the three best-known were *Beaucaire*♦ (1901), written with Booth Tarkington♦ and based on his novel about a duke masquerading as a barber; *A Rose o' Plymouth Town* (1902), written with Beulah Marie Dix♦ and recounting the story of Priscilla Alden; and her biggest hit, again with Miss Dix, *The Road to Yesterday*♦ (1906), in which the heroine's dreams take her back to adventurous times 300 years earlier.

SWAN, MARK, see *Parlor, Bedroom and Bath*

SWASEY, WILLIAM A. An architect who designed several important New York theatres, including the 48th Street, 44th Street, Princess,♦ 39th Street, and Winter Garden. ♦

Sweeney Todd, the Demon Barber of Fleet Street, a musical in two acts. Book by Hugh Wheeler. ♦ Lyrics and music by Stephen Sondheim. ♦ Produced at the Uris Theatre. March 1, 1979. 557 performances.

Bitter at his imprisonment and at the world in general, Sweeney Todd (Len Cariou♦) returns to London and sets up as a barber. But he is no ordinary barber. He slits his customers' throats and turns their bodies over to his friend, Mrs. Lovett (Angela Lansbury♦), who bakes them into pies. He even succeeds in murdering the venal judge who sent him to prison, but when he learns he has also inadvertently murdered his long-lost wife his mind snaps completely and he pushes Mrs. Lovett into her own oven. He in turn is murdered by a young boy Mrs. Lovett had befriended.

Principal songs: The Ballad of Sweeney Todd · Johanna · A Little Priest · Not While I'm Around

The musical was based on Christopher Bond's 1973 play, *Sweeney Todd,* which in turn was derived from George Dibdin Pitt's 1847 melodrama, *The String of Pearls,* long a favorite at the Bowery Theatre. ♦ Both critics and playgoers were sharply divided over the musical's merits: some considering it a superbly artful, venturesome work; others, a pretentious, even offensive bore. Its subsequent road tour was not especially successful. A highly praised 1989 revival also proved disappointing at the box office.

Sweet Adeline, a musical in fifteen scenes. Book and lyrics by Oscar Hammerstein II. ♦ Music by Jerome Kern. ♦ Produced by Arthur Hammerstein♦ at the

Hammerstein Theatre. September 3, 1929. 234 performances.

When Addie Schmidt (Helen Morgan♦), who sings at her father's Hoboken beer garden, loses her beloved Tom Martin (Max Hoffman, Jr.) to her own sister Nellie (Caryl Bergman), she leaves New Jersey to seek a stage career. Her climb is aided by James Day (Robert Chisholm), who also makes her forget Tom.

Principal songs: Don't Ever Leave Me · Here Am I · 'Twas Not So Long Ago · Why Was I Born?

Written as a vehicle for Miss Morgan after her success in *Show Boat,* ♦ the show started out as a smash hit only to have its run curtailed by the onset of the Depression.

Sweet Bird of Youth, a play in three acts by Tennessee Williams. ♦ Produced by Cheryl Crawford♦ at the Martin Beck Theatre. March 10, 1959. 375 performances.

Under the name of Princess Kosmonopolis, the boozy, drug-addicted, fading screen star, Alexandre Del Lago (Geraldine Page♦), comes to a small Gulf Coast town with her handsome gigolo, Chance Wayne (Paul Newman). Wayne had grown up in the town and had left after giving the political boss's daughter a case of venereal disease. Boss Finley (Sidney Blackmer♦) has not forgotten and has determined to be avenged. Suddenly Alexandre discovers she has made a huge success in a new film and appears on the verge of a major comeback. She walks out on Chance, telling him, "You've gone past something you couldn't afford to go past; your time, your youth, you've passed it. It's all you had, and you've had it." Recognizing the truth of what she has said, Chance decides not to follow her, but to stay and await the men coming to castrate him.

Louis Kronenberger♦ recorded, "At its best, *Sweet Bird of Youth* has force and fascination. But far too often everything seems excessive, with a fuming and rioting depravity." Apart from *The Night of the Iguana* (1961), the play was Williams's last commercial success and signaled the victory of his preoccupation with degeneracy over his gifts as a playwright.

Sweet Charity, a musical comedy in two acts. Book by Neil Simon. ♦ Lyrics by Dorothy Fields. ♦ Music by Cy Coleman. ♦ Produced at the Palace Theatre. ♦ January 29, 1966. 608 performances.

Charity (Gwen Verdon♦) is a dance hall hostess at the Fandango Ballroom. She longs to settle down with a man, but the men in her life simply love her and leave her—when they bother loving her at all.

One steals her purse and throws her in a lake; another, jilted by his date, shoves her in a closet when his date returns. Finally, she is trapped in an elevator with Oscar (John McMartin), who looks to her to be the man she has waited for. But when he learns what she does, he, too, walks out on her.

Principal songs: Baby, Dream Your Dream · Big Spender · If My Friends Could See Me Now

Based on Fellini's film, *Nights of Cabiria,* the musical served as the first attraction when the Palace was turned into a legitimate theatre. Curiously, although the show had a better book and more memorable songs than many musicals of the time, with Miss Verdon performing the dynamic choreography of her husband Bob Fosse, ♦ it was often perceived as essentially a dancing show. A successful 1986 revival starred Debbie Allen.

Sweet Inniscarra, a play in four acts by Augustus Pitou. ♦ Produced by Pitou at the 14th Street Theatre. January 24, 1897. 104 performances.

Gerald O'Carroll (Chauncey Olcott♦), an Irishman raised in London, comes to the small Irish town of Inniscarra, where he falls in love with the local schoolteacher, Kate O'Donoghue (Georgia Busby). Her father objects to their romance and attempts to have Gerald shanghaied. Gerald escapes and returns to Inniscarra in time to prevent Kate from being forced into an unwanted marriage.

This play, interlarded with a few Irish-style songs, was typical of the romantic dramas in which Olcott and his competitors trafficked so profitably for many years. As the working-class Irish deserted the theatre for films, this sort of play disappeared.

Sweet Kitty Bellairs, a play in four acts by David Belasco. ♦ Produced by Belasco at the Belasco Theatre. December 9, 1903. 206 performances.

Kitty Bellairs (Henrietta Crosman♦) is an Irish lass determined to rise to the top of society in 18th-century Bath. When she and her arch rival, a former queen of Bath society (Edith Crane), are both forced to hide behind the bed curtains in the room of Kitty's soldier sweetheart (Charles Hammond), it is Kitty who comes forth to disclose herself, thereby saving her rival from scandal. Calculation or selflessness, it wins Kitty both acceptance and a man.

Derived from Agnes and Edgerton Castle's *The Bath Comedy,* the play was later turned into a 1917 Rudolf Friml♦ operetta, *Kitty Darlin'.*

Sweethearts, an operetta in two acts. Book by Harry B. Smith♦ and Fred de Gresac. ♦ Lyrics by Robert B. Smith. ♦ Music by Victor Herbert. ♦ Produced at the New Amsterdam Theatre. ♦ September 8, 1913. 136 performances.

Sylvia (Christie MacDonald ♦) was found as a baby by the laundress Dame Paula (Ethel De Fre Houston), who raised her as one of her daughters. While traveling incognito, Franz (Thomas Conkey), the heir-presumptive to the throne of Zilania, meets Sylvia and falls in love with her. But his hopes seem thwarted when Lieutenant Karl (Edwin Wilson) comes courting. Karl, however, proves to be a lothario, and so is rejected. At the same time, a search has been going on for a long-lost Zilanian princess. She turns out to be Sylvia. Franz and Sylvia wed and promise to rule Zilania fairly together.

Principal songs: Angelus · The Cricket on the Hearth · Every Lover Must Meet His Fate · Jeannette and Her Little Wooden Shoes · Pretty as a Picture · Sweethearts

One of the best of Herbert's operettas, it was successfully revived in 1947 with Bobby Clark♦ as the principal comedian.

SWOPE, Martha The leading contemporary theatrical photographer, she was born in Tyler, Texas, and studied dance with George Balanchine♦ at the School of American Ballet. However, her photographs of her fellow dancers were remarkable enough to compel her to change her career. In the late 1960s she began photographing Broadway plays and performers. Her work is distinguished by its candor and theatrical immediacy.

SYDNEY, Basil (1894–1968) The distinguished English actor first came to America with Granville Barker♦ in 1914. He made several other trips in the twenties and thirties, but is remembered in America for his Hamlet, which he played in 1926 in modern dress.

T

Tab Shows The name given to traveling shows, often drastically cut-down versions of Broadway musical comedies or revues, but just as often original compilations. They toured in the smallest towns and frequently played carnivals. The name was later applied to live shows given in conjunction with film showings.

Tailor Made Man, A, a comedy in four acts by Harry James Smith.♦ Produced by George M. Cohan♦ and Sam H. Harris♦ at the Cohan and Harris Theatre. August 27, 1917. 398 performances.

John Paul Bart (Grant Mitchell♦), a drudge in a tailor's shop, dreams of marrying Tanya Huber (Helen MacKellar), his boss's daughter, and of becoming a great and famous man. Tanya's fiancé is an arrogant, snobbish man who has written a book in which he says that with proper clothes and charm any man can reach the top. John appropriates some evening clothes that the man has left at the shop and heads out to conquer society. He is soon lionized, courted by an heiress, and given a cushy Wall Street job. Of course, he is eventually exposed and sent back to the tailor shop. By that time, however, Tanya has fallen in love with him, so his future is not totally unpromising.

Although Smith, Cohan, and Harris openly acknowledged that the play was based on a German work by Gabriel Dregley, the adaptation and production were good enough to overcome wartime prejudices against almost anything German.

Take Me Along, see *Ah, Wilderness!*

TALIAFERRO, Edith (1893–1958) Born in Richmond, Va., the daughter of theatre people, she made her debut at the age of three in *Shore Acres.*♦ She was active on the stage for over forty years, scoring by far her biggest success in 1910 in the title role of *Rebecca of Sunnybrook Farm.*♦ She played the role for three years. Her sister Mabel (1887–1979) had an even longer career, making her debut at the age of two in *Blue Jeans*♦ and continuing to act regularly into the 1950s. Her greatest hit was the role of the dainty acrobat who falls in love with a minister, the title part of *Polly of the Circus*♦ (1907).

Talley's Folly, a play in one act by Lanford Wilson.♦ Produced at the Brooks Atkinson Theatre. February 20, 1980. 277 performances. PP, NYDCCA.

After a year's absence Matt Friedman (Judd Hirsch) comes calling again on Sally Talley (Trish Hawkins). Her bigoted family has told Friedman that since he is a Jew he is not welcome, and one member of the family has even threatened to shoot him. Moreover, they have hinted at some dark secret in Sally's past. Sally confesses to Matt that the secret is simply her inability to have children, the result of an earlier disease. Unconcerned, Matt asks Sally to elope, and she agrees.

The brief, two-character play was one in a series about the Talley family, which also included *The 5th of July*♦ (1978). It was originally presented off-Broadway in 1979 but won its awards only after its Broadway presentation.

TAMIRIS, Helen [née Becker] (1905–66) The New York-born choreographer studied with Michael Fokine and came to the Broadway stage late in her career. She scored a major success with her "Currier and Ives Ballet" in *Up in Central Park*♦ (1945). Her later work was seen in such musicals as the 1946 revival of *Show Boat*♦; *Annie Get Your Gun*♦ (1946); *Inside U.S.A.* (1948); *Touch and Go* (1949), for which she earned a Tony Award♦; *Fanny*♦ (1954); and *Plain and Fancy*♦ (1955).

Taming of the Shrew, The Initially offered in Garrick's version, *Catherine and Petruchio,* at Philadelphia's Southwark Theatre♦ in 1766 with Miss Cheer♦ and the younger Hallam♦ in the title roles, Shakespeare's♦ comedy continued to be offered in this and similar versions, and usually with similar titles, for over a hundred years. Later casts included Mrs. Mason and Thomas Abthorpe Cooper,♦ Mrs. Darley and William Macready,♦ Mrs. Sharpe and W. B. Wood,♦ and Ada Clifton and Edwin Booth.♦ Augustin Daly♦ presented the first more or less faithful version, under its correct title, in 1887 with John Drew♦ and Ada Rehan♦ in the leading roles. He offered the play as high comedy, not farce, and mounted it with sets of carefully painted realism and opulence. Julia Marlowe♦ and E. H. Sothern,♦ and Lunt♦ and Fontanne♦ were later hailed as the dueling lovers. The great American musical *Kiss Me, Kate*♦ (1948) was derived from the comedy, offering brief snatches of it as well as using lines in its lyrics, especially its finale, but framing it as a play within a play and setting the frame, which told a similar story, in modern times. Alfred Drake♦ and Patricia Morison were the original leads.

Tammany; or, The Indian Chief, a musical in two acts. Libretto by Mrs. [Anne Kemble] Hatton. Music by James Hewitt. Produced at the John Street Theatre.♦ March 3, 1794. In repertory.

The Indian Chief Tammany (John Hodgkinson♦) loves an Indian maiden (Mrs. Hodgkinson). After she is kidnapped by the invading Spaniards led by Ferdinand (John Martin♦), Tammany rescues her. Pursued by the Spaniards, they take refuge in a cabin, which the Spaniards set afire, killing the lovers.

The earliest produced stage work about American Indians, it reached the boards at the time of widespread sympathy for the French Revolution. According to Odell,♦ "The piece was consequently turned into a symbol of republicanism, and as such was patronised by the hot-heads of New York, to the utter rout of the aristocrats."

Mrs. Hatton (1757?–96?) was the sister of the famous English performers John Philip Kemble and Mrs. Siddons. She was also the official poet of New York's Tammany Society. James Hewitt (1770–1827) was a violinist, composer, conductor of the orchestras at the John Street Theatre and later at the Park Theatre,♦ and in later years one of the first important music publishers in America.

TAMS-WITMARK, see *Aborn, Milton*

TANDY, Jessica (b. 1909) The slim, sharp-voiced actress was born in England and first appeared on Broadway in *The Matriarch* (1930). She made only occasional appearances thereafter until she won wide acclaim for her performance as Blanche Du-Bois, a woman living with illusions of gentility, in *A Streetcar Named Desire*♦ (1947). Among her subsequent roles were the suicidal divorcée, the title role in *Hilda Crane* (1950); Agnes, the loyal, loving wife in a long-lived marriage, in *The Fourposter* (1951); Mary Doyle, the shy woman who is courted by the Devil, in *Madam, Will You Walk?* (1953); Agnes, the wife in a vaguely menaced household, in *A Delicate Balance*♦ (1966); Fonsia Dorsey, the card-playing inmate at a home for the aged, in *The Gin Game*♦ (1977); Annie Nations, an elderly widow who can commune with her dead husband, in *Foxfire*

(1982); and Lady Elizabeth Milne, whose liberalism shocks her husband, in *The Petition* (1984). *Variety*♦ wrote of her performance in *Foxfire,* which earned her a Tony Award,♦ "Everything about the character, her confusion, simplicity, love of her husband and son, pride in her offstage grandchildren, is played with crystalline expressiveness and excitingly precise detail." She appeared with her husband, Hume Cronyn,♦ in the last six plays. Without Cronyn, she essayed Amanda in an unsuccessful 1983 revival of *The Glass Menagerie.*♦ The couple performed regularly at major regional playhouses, most notably the Tyrone Guthrie Theatre,♦ where she assumed such diverse roles as Queen Gertrude, Madam Ranevskaya, and Linda, the wife in *Death of a Salesman.*♦

TANGUAY, Eva (1878–1947) The highest-paid performer in the heyday of vaudeville, she was known as the "I Don't Care Girl," after her most famous song. Born in Marbleton, Canada, she appeared in stock and in Broadway plays before turning to two-a-day in the early 1900s. She was a hoydenish, frizzy-haired blonde, celebrated for her animated delivery and her outlandish, often wildly feathered costumes. Although Percy Hammond♦ once compared her brassy singing to "the wail of the prehistoric diplodocus," her public clamored for more. The *Dramatic Mirror*♦ insisted she was "Vaudeville's Greatest Box Office Attraction." Indeed, her popularity was such that Albee♦ and Keith♦ were rarely able to restrain her from singing risqué songs that other stars could not get away with. Her numbers had such titles as "It's Been Done Before but Never the Way I Do It," "Go as Far as You Like," and "I Want Somebody To Go Wild with Me." When vaudeville died in the 1930s she retired. She lived a virtual recluse, all but blind by the time she died in obscurity.

TANNEN, Julius (1881–1965) One of vaudeville's leading stand-up comedians, he was placed in an orphanage in his native New York while still a youngster. He proved an intractable youth and even in his teens could not hold a job. Stability came only when the slim, dour-faced performer found a niche in two-a-day and became one of its most noted wits. Some idea of his humor can be gleaned from such remarks as "Those paper cups give me a sensation of drinking out of an envelope" and "A lady has the right to be as homely as she pleases—but this one abuses the privilege." His often acrid comedy delighted New Yorkers, but he rarely found a welcome in smaller cities.

TARKINGTON, [Newton] Booth (1869–1946) The famed Indiana novelist first achieved theatrical success when he dramatized his novel, *Monsieur Beaucaire,* in collaboration with Evelyn Greenleaf Sutherland♦ in 1901. The play was sometimes known simply as *Beaucaire♦* and told of a duke who poses as a barber. With Harry Leon Wilson♦ he wrote *The Man from Home♦* (1908), in which an American saves his ward from a disastrous foreign marriage, and *Cameo Kirby* (1909), a story of a riverboat gambler. For Otis Skinner♦ he wrote *Mister Antonio* (1916), telling of a carefree Italian in a stodgy Pennsylvania town. *The Country Cousin* (1917), written with Julian Street, centered on a country girl who finds love with a big city millionaire. *Clarence♦* (1919) depicted how a meek ex-soldier reforms a disorganized family. In *Intimate Strangers* (1921) a young lawyer prefers a charming spinster to her pretty niece, while *Tweedles* (1923), written with Wilson, dealt with the romance of a waitress and a wealthy man. His last play to reach New York, *Colonel Satan* (1931), recounted some imaginary escapades of Aaron Burr. Several of his novels were dramatized by other authors, including *Seventeen♦* (1918), *Penrod* (1918), and *The Plutocrat* (1930). He was much admired for his warm, homey humor. But Arthur Hobson Quinn♦ noted, "He is best in drama when he gives rein to [his] fancy, abandons [the] effort to deal with ordinary conditions, and frankly takes his characters and situations into another time and place where he is freed from the limitations of accuracy."

Tavern, The, a play in two acts by George M. Cohan.♦ Produced by Cohan at the Cohan Theatre. September 27, 1920. 252 performances.

The quiet of a small country inn is disrupted by the arrival of several people who report bandits are active at a nearby crossroads. The arrivals include a Vagabond (Arnold Daly♦), a Woman (Elsie Rizer), and a Governor (Morgan Wallace) and his family. The Woman and the Governor's daughter (Alberta Burton) fall in love with the dashing Vagabond. But the evening becomes increasingly menacing until a sheriff and an attendant from a local asylum come to claim some escapees, including the Vagabond.

Cohan based his farcical spoof of melodrama on a turgid, seriously conceived play by Cora Dick Gantt, whom he gave credit for his own work in early playbills. Alexander Woollcott♦ noted, "Something of the still echoing laughter started by the hermit in 'Seven Keys to Baldpate' is recalled by the fun he brings to 'The Tavern.' " Cohan assumed the leading role in several revivals, and the piece continues to find some favor in summer stock and with amateur groups.

TAYLEURE, Clifton W. (1831–87) Best known for his long-popular dramatization of *East Lynne♦* (1863), for which he was reputedly paid a mere $100, he began his career as an actor who specialized in playing old men. Much of his earliest career seems to have been spent at Baltimore's Holliday Street Theatre,♦ where he continued to serve as the house's dramatist after his retirement from performing in 1856. Among his works from this period was his version of *Horseshoe Robinson♦* (1856). By the late 1860s he managed several important Broadway theatres, including the Olympic and the Grand Opera House. He also wrote numerous undistinguished melodramas, with such titles as *A Woman's Wrongs* (1874), *Rube; or, The Wall Street Undertow* (1875), and *Parted* (1876).

TAYLOR, Charles A[lonzo] (1864?–1942) Born in South Hadley, Mass., he is said to have run away from home after reading a life of P. T Barnum. ♦ He tried a number of odd jobs before writing his first play. Within a short time he was a successful turn-of-the-century producer and author of cheap touring blood-and-thunder melodramas, many of which were written for his wife, Laurette Taylor.♦ His titles included *The Escape from Chinatown, Escape from the Harem, From Rags to Riches,* and *Stolen by Gypsies.*

Biography: *Blood and Thunder,* Dwight Taylor, New York, 1962.

TAYLOR, [Joseph] Deems (1885–1966) The distinguished New York-born composer and music critic was known to playgoers for his score to the musical *The Echo* (1910), as well as his incidental music to such works as *Liliom♦* (1921), *The Adding Machine♦* (1922), and *Beggar on Horseback♦* (1924). He also wrote opera, including *Peter Ibbetson,* which was commissioned by the Metropolitan Opera.

TAYLOR, Laurette [née Loretta Cooney] (1884–1946) One of the greatest, yet, in a way, most tragic of all American actresses, she was born in New York and began her theatrical career as a child in vaudeville, where she was billed as "La Belle Laurette." She later played many years in various stock companies as well as touring in plays by her first husband, Charles A. Taylor.♦ Her earliest success came when she portrayed Luana, the Hawaiian princess who commits suicide after her American lover deserts her, in *The Bird of Paradise*♦ (1912). Even greater acclaim fell to the slim redhead with wide hazel-blue eyes for her winsome performance as the girl sent to live with snobbish relatives, the title part of *Peg o' My Heart*♦ (1912). The play was written by her second husband, J. Hartley Manners.♦ Afterwards she wasted her enormous, if sometimes undisciplined talent, starring in minor vehicles he wrote for her. Following his death she virtually retired from the stage, becoming reclusive and alcoholic, but returned for occasional revivals. The most notable was a 1938 mounting of *Outward Bound,* in which she played Mrs. Midgit. Her last Broadway appearance was generally acknowledged as not only her greatest but as one of the most memorable performances of her generation. This was the role of Amanda Wingfield, the mother who resolutely lives in dreams of past glories, in *The Glass Menagerie*♦ (1945). She continued in the role until shortly before her death. Stark Young♦ wrote in the *New Republic* of her performance, "Hers is naturalistic acting of the most profound, spontaneous, unbroken continuity and moving life. There is an inexplicable rightness, moment by moment, phrase by phrase, endlessly varied in transitions." Theresa Helburn♦ summed up the actress's unique aura, observing, "Her inner radiance fell like moonlight on an audience without the use of any stage tricks that I could detect. In my day there has been no such radiant personality as hers." She was 5′ 5″, with large brown eyes and high eyebrows.

Biography: *Laurette,* Marguerite Courtney, New York, 1955.

TAYLOR, Mary [Cecilia] (1836–66) "Our Mary," as she was known affectionately to her admirers, was born in New York, where her father played in the Park Theatre♦ orchestra. If the birth date customarily given for her is correct, she was about two years old when she made her debut at the National Theatre as Cupid in *Zazezizozu.* By the mid-1840s she was a popular performer at both the Olympic and the Bowery.♦ Her notable roles included Prince Ahmed in *The Magic Arrow* (1844) and Eliza Stebbins in *A Glance at New York*♦ (1848). She retired at the time of her marriage in 1851. The buxom beauty, who must be considered the Shirley Temple of her day, did not totally delight all her audiences. Joseph N. Ireland,♦ who saw her, recalled, "Miss Taylor's two great and unfailing charms were her delicious voice and the perfect ease with which she went through every work allotted her. As a vocalist, she was lacking in feeling and expression; as an actress, she had been so thor-

oughly drilled into pert sauciness of manner in the Olympic burlesques, that it clung to her in every character."

TAYLOR, Raynor (1747?–1825) The English-born composer and occasional actor came to America in 1792. He settled in Philadelphia, where, according to his biographer, "As a specialty he cultivated burlesque olios or 'extravaganzas' which came dangerously near being music hall skits." Among his works were his "mock Italian opera," *Capocchio and Dorinna,* and his "comic burletta," *Old Woman of Eighty Three,* both from 1793. His most important theatrical work was his music for the "New Grand Romantick Drama," *The Ethiop; or, The Child of the Desert* (1814). One scholar, Victor Fell Yellin, has written, "His overture to *The Ethiop* is perhaps the finest theatrical overture that has survived from the Federal period." In a 1983 study Yellin noted that Taylor apparently spelled his given name Rayner and that the accepted modern spelling perpetuates a late-19th-century error.

TAYLOR, Samuel (b. 1912) Although born in Chicago, he was raised in San Francisco and attended the University of California. He was a writer for radio and a play reader before *The Happy Time*♦ (1950), his dramatization of Robert Fontaine's novel, gave him his first success. His other memorable comedies were *Sabrina Fair*♦ (1953), the story of a chauffeur's daughter and a rich man; and *The Pleasure of His Company*♦ (1958), in which a playboy father returns home to complicate his daughter's wedding plans. He also wrote the book for the musical *No Strings*♦ (1962).

TAYLOR, Tom (1817–80) The English playwright and journalist enjoyed tremendous success in America with both his domestic comedies and exciting melodramas. His biggest hits included: *Still Waters Run Deep* (1855), a play which treated sex with an openness uncommon for its day; *Our American Cousin*♦ (1858), long one of the most popular of imported comedies, although it is largely remembered today as the play Lincoln was watching when he was assassinated; *The Overland Route* (1860); and *The Ticket-of-Leave Man*♦ (1863), one of the earliest detective plays. *Our American Cousin* and *The Ticket-of-Leave Man* are still occasionally revived at colleges and off-Broadway, but merely as period curiosities.

Tea and Sympathy, a play in three acts by Robert Anderson.♦ Produced by the Playwrights' Company♦ and others at the Ethel Barrymore Theatre. September 30, 1953. 712 performances.

At the New England boys' school he attends, Tom Lee (John Kerr) is considered an "off horse," a boy whose shyness sets him apart from others and even leads to suspicion of homosexuality. Neither the sanctimonious, aggressively masculine headmaster, Bill Reynolds (Leif Erickson), nor his own father, Herbert Lee (John McGovern), helps matters. Tom's problems are brought to a head when he is cast as a girl in a school play. The only person who understands Tom and is willing to provide more than the customary tea and sympathy is Reynolds's wife Laura (Deborah Kerr). She berates Reynolds for persecuting Tom to hide his doubts about his own masculinity, then discreetly offers herself to the boy, remarking, "Years from now—when you talk about this—and you will!—be kind."

Louis Kronenberger♦ saw the play as "a full-fashioned theatre piece, a thoroughly effective matinee drama."

Tea for Three, a comedy in three acts by Roi Cooper Megrue. ♦ Produced by Selwyn and Co.,♦ at Maxine Elliott's Theatre. September 19, 1918. 300 performances.

Because he knows so many men find The Wife (Margaret Lawrence) attractive, The Husband (Frederick Perry) becomes unreasonably jealous. Aware of this, The Wife and The Friend (Arthur Bryon♦) meet for lunch and determine to teach The Husband a lesson. They arrange for The Husband to catch them in a compromising, but actually innocent situation. The Husband demands that he and The Friend draw lots, the loser to commit suicide. The Friend loses. Only after he believes The Friend dead does The Husband recognize the absurdity of his jealousy. When The Friend reappears, very much alive, The Husband invites him to continue his harmless tête-à-têtes with The Wife at will.

The *Times,* while acknowledging the play was not of great substance, concluded, "It has a very rare virtue of doing what it intends with neatness and a certain finality of skill which keeps the attention of the audience throughout and insures an evening of genuine entertainment."

Teahouse of the August Moon, The, a comedy in three acts by John Patrick. Produced by Maurice Evans♦ and others at the Martin Beck Theatre. October 15, 1953. 1,027 performances. PP, NYDCCA.

Captain Fisby (John Forsythe) is under orders to bring democracy to an Okinawan village, whether the villagers want it or not. He attempts to establish some free enterprise, but the only thing the islanders can produce are cricket cages, for which there is no export market. When one wily local, Sakini (David Wayne♦), transforms Fisby's plans for a schoolhouse into a teahouse, where some stronger spirits may also be served, all hell breaks loose. Fisby's frightened, befuddled superior, Col. Wainwright Purdy III (Paul Ford♦), arrests Fisby and orders the teahouse destroyed. The demolition is no sooner complete than Purdy discovers the teahouse has been hailed in Washington as a shining example of "American 'get-up-and-go.' " Luckily, Sakini and his friends have only dismantled and hidden the building materials, so the edifice is hastily reassembled to await the visit of the Congressmen and news photographers.

Based on a novel by Vern Sneider, this ingratiating comedy, which some felt was really held together by Wayne's superb characterization, nonetheless walked away with the season's awards. It was the source of the failed musical *Lovely Ladies, Kind Gentlemen* (1970).

Patrick (b. 1907) was born in Louisville, and attended both Columbia and Harvard. Although he had several other plays produced on Broadway, his only other success was *The Hasty Heart* (1945), a story of a soldier who learns he is dying. However, several of his less successful plays remain popular with amateur and summer stock groups.

TEAL, BEN (1857?–1917) The San Francisco-born director served an apprenticeship in his home town as actor and assistant director under young David Belasco. ♦ In 1889 he wrote *The Great Metropolis* with George H. Jessop,♦ which he also staged. This was the first play to be produced by A. L. Erlanger,♦ and shortly thereafter Teal became the head staff director for Klaw♦ and Erlanger. He staged many of the firm's musical extravaganzas as well as the series of musical comedies the organization produced for the Rogers brothers. ♦ His most memorable non-musical success was *Ben Hur*♦ (1899), but he also directed many other works including *Sweet Nell of Drury Lane* (1900) and *The Wanderer* (1917).

Tears and Smiles, a comedy in three acts by James Nelson Barker. ♦ Produced at the Chestnut Street Theatre♦ (Philadelphia). March 4, 1807. In repertory.

When Sydney Osbert returns to Philadelphia from

his victories over Mediterranean pirates, he prepares to finish wooing Louisa Campdon. To his dismay she is being actively courted by the foppish Fluttermore, who is disdainful of everything American and believes what is not French is not good. Sydney finally succeeds with a little help from the all-American Nathan Yank and from Widow Freegrace, although she is busier wooing and winning Yank's master, the ladies' man, Rangely.

Barker's first produced play and first success was clearly influenced by *The Contrast.* ◆ It has, unfortunately, little enduring merit.

TEICHMANN, HOWARD, see *Solid Gold Cadillac, The*

TELLEGEN, LOU (also billed as LOU-TELLEGEN) [né ISIDOR LOUIS BERNARD VAN DAMMELER] (1881–1934) The Dutch-born matinee idol played for many seasons on European stages before making his American debut opposite Sarah Bernhardt ◆ on her 1910 tour. He settled permanently in America in 1914. For the next seven years he played in numerous romantically melodramatic vehicles, often having a hand in their writing. After a career in films he made several unsuccessful attempts at a comeback on stage, then committed suicide.

Autobiography: *Women Have Been Kind,* New York, 1931.

TEMPEST, MARIE [née MARY SUSAN ETHERINGTON] (1864–1942) The London-born singer and comedienne was a West End favorite for over fifty years. A small, lithe, and graceful woman, with a cute turned-up nose, she starred in many important late 19th-century English musicals. Her American debut in 1890 was in one of these, *The Red Hussar.* For the next five years she played largely in America, appearing in the American premiere of *Der Vogelhändler,* known here as *The Tyrolean* (1891), and in two comic operas written for her by Reginald De Koven, ◆ *The Fencing Master* (1892) and *The Algerian* (1893). She also toured in several other of her English roles. In 1900 she abandoned the musical stage to concentrate on straight comedy. Her subsequent American appearances were rare, most notably in *The Marriage of Kitty* (1903) and as Becky Sharp in *Vanity Fair* (1911).

Biography: *Marie Tempest,* Hector Bolitho, London, 1936.

TEMPLETON, FAY (1865–1939) She was one of the most beloved of all American performers, her career spanning 64 years from her 1869 appearance as

Cupid in vaudeville to her portrayal of Aunt Minnie, the aged shop owner, in *Roberta* ◆ (1933), in which she introduced "Yesterdays." (Some sources say she appeared first as a child in *East Lynne* ◆ in 1868.) Her New York debut was as Puck in Augustin Daly's ◆ 1873 mounting of *A Midsummer Night's Dream.* ◆ She was born in Little Rock, Ark., the daughter of a singer and a theatrical manager and editor. Following her debut she rarely left the stage and by the 1880s was featured in a succession of comic operas. She later starred in such musicals as *Hendrik Hudson* (1890) and *Excelsior, Jr.* (1895). She had grown a little plump by the time she added her exuberant clowning and throaty-voiced singing to Weber ◆ and Fields's ◆ burlesques in 1898. She remained with them for five seasons, in 1900 introducing "Ma Blushin' Rosie" in their *Fiddle-Dee-Dee.* One of her greatest successes came in George M. Cohan's ◆ *Forty-Five Minutes from Broadway* ◆ (1906), in which she sang "Mary's a Grand Old Name" and "So Long, Mary." Although she ostensibly retired in 1910, she returned on occasion to play in the Weber and Fields 1912 reunion, as Buttercup in several revivals of *H.M.S. Pinafore,* ◆ and in vaudeville.

Ten Nights in a Barroom, a play in five acts by William W. Pratt. Produced at the National Theatre. August 23, 1858. 7 performances.

Joe Morgan, the village drunkard, is encouraged in his boozing and other irresponsible ways by Simon Slade, the evil owner of the "Sickle and Sheaf." Even the plea of his little daughter Mary— "Father, dear father, come home"—cannot drag Morgan away for long. In a barroom brawl Mary is acidentally struck by a glass thrown at her father. The shock helps Morgan reform. Slade is killed by his own son, and the village votes to close the saloon.

This prohibitionist drama, based on a story by T. S. Arthur, was never popular in major cities, but was second only to *Uncle Tom's Cabin* ◆ on rural circuits. Some contemporary programs divide the play into four or six acts.

Tent Shows In the early 19th century entertainment in tents began to appear in regions which could not support full-time playhouses. The trend was given widespread popularity when it was taken up by religious groups, including the Millerites in the 1840s and, far more importantly, the Chautauqua Movement in the 1870s and thereafter. The latter interwove vaudeville turns and didactic plays with the group's lectures and preachings. But numerous other troupes, unaffiliated with any religious sect and usually totally secular, toured the country, especially Southern, Midwestern, and Western regions, offering minstrel shows, vaudeville, drama, comedy, and musicals. These groups did not use the circular seating arrangements common to circuses but built stages at one end of the tent and seated audiences in traditional fashion. It was because of their popularity that performers such as Sarah Bernhardt♦ had no difficulty obtaining tents or audiences when they defied the Trust♦ and were denied regular stages. There were as many as 400 tent companies touring when the practice peaked around 1920. Something of the nature of many of their plays can be deduced from the most popular character in them, a redheaded young country bumpkin named Toby, who seemed stupid and lazy but often proved surprisingly sly.

Tenth Man, The, a play in three acts by Paddy Chayefsky.♦ Produced at the Booth Theatre. November 5, 1959. 623 performances.

About to banish demons from Evelyn Foreman (Risa Schwartz), the granddaughter of one of their members, the old men who belong to a shabby orthodox synagogue find they have only nine worshippers in attendance. Jewish religious law requires a minyon, or quorum of ten. So they convince a clean-cut young man who happens to be passing by to join them. He is Arthur Brooks (Donald Harron), who turns out to be possibly even more troubled than Evelyn. The exorcism expels his devils, but not the girl's. Arthur, however, has fallen in love and believes his love will cure Evelyn.

Some critics felt the play's ending was contrived, but Brooks Atkinson♦ noted, "Although 'The Tenth Man' aspires to lofty areas of mysticism, it always has its feet on the ground." A 1989 revival failed.

Ten-Twent'-Thirt' The name given to popular-priced theatres and touring companies in the late 19th and very early 20th century. These companies toured small towns and poorer large city neighborhoods, offering shows for which the best seats were thirty cents and the cheapest were a dime. Many important theatrical figures and ardent playgoers got their first taste of theatre from these outfits, which were also a training ground for future stars.

TERRY, ELLEN [ALICE] (1848–1928) A highly polished performer whose regal beauty and radiant personality overcame whatever shortcomings she possessed as an actress, she made her American debut in 1883, playing Queen Henrietta opposite Henry Irving♦ in *Charles I*. Among the other roles she essayed on this and several subsequent tours with Irving were Jeanette (*The Lyons Mail*), Ophelia, Beatrice, Viola, and her most famous portrayal, Portia. William Winter♦ wrote, "Ellen Terry embodied Portia . . . the essential womanliness of that character was for the first time in the modern theatre adequately interpreted and portrayed. Upon many play-going observers indeed the wonderful wealth of beauty that is in the part—its winsome grace, its incessant sparkle, its alluring because piquant as well as luscious sweetness, its impetuous ardour, its enchantment of physical equally with emotional condition, its august morality, its perfect candour, and its noble passion—came like a surprise." After leaving Irving she later toured most successfully in 1907 as Lady Cecily Wayneflete in *Captain Brassbound's Conversion*. In after years she traveled as a lecturer on Shakespeare. She wrote an autobiography, *The Heart of Ellen Terry* (1928), and following her death her correspondence with G. B. Shaw♦ was published.

That Championship Season, a play in three acts by Jason Miller. Produced by the New York Shakespeare Festival♦ at the Public Theatre. May 2, 1972. 844 performances (including Broadway run). PP, NYDCCA.

Four former players have come to the home of their old coach (Richard A. Dysart) for a reunion. Their championship basketball season would seem to have been but the beginning of successful careers for them, but appearances are deceiving. George Sikowski (Charles Durning) has become a corrupt politician; Tom Daley (Walter McGinn), a cynical alcoholic; Phil Romano (Paul Sorvino), a ruthless, lecherous strip miner; and James Daley (Michael McGuire), a failed high school principal with dreams of success in politics. The coach, despite his vacuous winning-is-all philosophy, has abandoned basketball because it is no longer a sport for whites.

The play was a mordant, unflinching look at middle-American life.

Miller (b. 1940) was born in Scranton, Penn., and is an actor as well as a playwright. This has been his only major Broadway success.

THAYER, MRS. [EDWARD] [née AGNES DIAMOND] (d. 1873) The English-born actress made her debut under the name of Mrs. Palmer Fisher in Kentucky theatres in 1820 and shortly thereafter moved to Philadelphia, where she married Thayer. She rarely played New York, but until her retirement in 1865 was a favorite at Philadelphia's Chestnut Street♦ and Arch Street♦ theatres. Both T. Allston Brown♦ and her obituaries referred to her as "the Clive of the American stage," and Brown added that she "is the *beau ideal* of comedy . . . and wears Thalia's mask with infinite glee and grace." Mr. Thayer (1798–1870) was a Bostonian who was said to have been university educated and to have served in the navy and as a lawyer before becoming an actor in 1821. He played opposite his wife with distinction until their retirement.

TheaterWeek A magazine founded in 1988 by Charles Ortleb to cover commercial theatre on Broadway and elsewhere, including overseas, it thus seemed to fill a long-needed gap, especially since *American Theatre*♦ emphasized non-profit stages. Unfortunately, it has suffered frequent staff changes and has increasingly promoted leftist and homosexual matters. Moreover, it has employed too many younger writers with little real sense of theatrical history. Its future is uncertain.

Theatre Arts A magazine founded in Detroit in 1916 with Sheldon Cheney♦ as editor, it was first issued as a quarterly. It later became a monthly, edited first by Edith J. R. Isaacs♦ and then by Rosamond Gilder.♦ In its heyday it featured erudite yet popular articles on all aspects of theatre, and avoided the more gossipy commonplaces of other such magazines. It also regularly offered superbly reproduced photographs. In 1948 it combined with *The Stage* (a magazine that had grown out of a Theatre Guild♦ house organ). Publication was discontinued in 1964.

Theatre Collections Although American collections of theatrical or "performing arts" materials have proliferated in recent years—at least on a major public scale—they appear to have existed for almost as long as the American theatre itself. However, most early collections were those of amateurs. Many of these were dispersed on the deaths of the collectors, but a handful of relatively late ones were bequeathed to public collections that began to take important shape at the beginning of the present century. One older, semi-public collection of note is the library at The Players.♦ By the 1930s between sixty and seventy significant collections were acknowledged.

The first major collegiate theatrical collection may well have been that at Harvard, founded in 1901 at the urging of Professor George Pierce Baker.♦ Developing over the years, it remains probably the most important academic collection. Other important academic collections include the William Seymour Theatre Collection at Princeton, the Hoblitzelle Theatre Arts Library at the University of Texas at Austin, and the Wisconsin Center for Film and Theatre Research at the University of Wisconsin at Madison.

By far the greatest collection at a public library is that of the Research Library of the New York Public Library, located in the Museum of the Performing Arts at Lincoln Center. The Library of Congress also has an outstanding collection. An example of a small, but nonetheless notable collection is that at the Free Library in Philadelphia.

Another outstanding assemblage is The Shubert♦ Archive, housing the vast collection of the Shubert brothers and located at the Lyceum Theatre♦ in New York.

A 1981 publication, *Theatre and Performing Arts Collections*, edited by Louis A. Rachow, offers detailed discussions of several important collections and a long, but necessarily incomplete list of others.

Much significant material remains in the hands of private collectors, some of whom have opened their holdings to scholars on a quasi-public basis.

Theatre Communications Group Calling itself "the national organization for the nonprofit professional theatre," it was founded in 1961 to serve the needs of the growing regional theatre movement. It assists with casting, job placement, management, and research problems, and also issues numerous publications. Among its publications are its lively magazine, *American Theatre* (which despite its title, however, gives short shrift to Broadway), reissues of out-of-print plays, and other works covering a wide range of theatrical matters.

Theatre Development Fund A non-profit corporation founded in 1967 "to stimulate the production of worthwhile plays in the commercial theatre." The most visible manifestation of this stimulus is the TKTS♦ booth on Times Square, at which cut-rate tickets are sold. Through other ticket distribution programs the group aids off-Broadway productions. It also helps in costume rentals to non-profit and educational organizations and offers a "Theatre Access Program" to help handicapped playgoers obtain transportation and special seating.

Theatre Guild, THE The most exciting and responsible producing organization of the 1920s and 1930s, it began as an outgrowth of the defunct Washington

Square Players. ♦ The group was formally organized in 1919 with a board consisting of, among others, Lawrence Langner, ♦ Philip Moeller, ♦ Rollo Peters, ♦ Lee Simonson, ♦ and Helen Westley. ♦ Later important additions to the board were Dudley Digges ♦ and Theresa Helburn. ♦ The first production was *Bonds of Interest* (1919), but the group's success was signaled by its second mounting, *John Ferguson* (1919). Other early productions included *Jane Clegg* (1920), *Heartbreak House* (1920), *Mr. Pim Passes By* (1921), *Liliom* ♦ (1921), *He Who Gets Slapped* (1922), *Back to Methuselah* (1922), and *R.U.R.* (1922), all of which were foreign works. Not until its production of Elmer Rice's ♦ *The Adding Machine* ♦ (1923) did the group begin to mount American works as aggressively as it had mounted imported ones. Among its subsequent productions, both American and European, were *Saint Joan* ♦ (1923), *The Guardsman* (1924), *They Knew What They Wanted* ♦ (1924), *The Garrick Gaieties* ♦ (1925), *Ned McCobb's Daughter* ♦ (1926), *The Silver Cord* ♦ (1926), *The Second Man* ♦ (1927), *Porgy* ♦ (1927), *Marco Millions* ♦ (1928), *Strange Interlude* ♦ (1928), *Dynamo* ♦ (1929), *Hotel Universe* ♦ (1930), *Elizabeth the Queen* ♦ (1930), *Mourning Becomes Electra* ♦ (1931), *Reunion in Vienna* ♦ (1931), *Biography* ♦ (1932), *Both Your Houses* ♦ (1933), *Ah, Wilderness!* ♦ (1933), *Mary of Scotland* ♦ (1933), *Days Without End* ♦ (1934), *Valley Forge* ♦ (1934), *Porgy and Bess* ♦ (1935), *End of Summer* ♦ (1936), and *Idiot's Delight* ♦ (1936). By the mid-1930s political, artistic, and financial disagreements had resulted in the formation of two major breakaway organizations, the Group Theatre ♦ and the Playwrights' Company. ♦ Thereafter both the Guild's daring and its success waned, although over the next few years it produced *The Philadelphia Story* ♦ (1939), *The Time of Your Life* ♦ (1939), *There Shall Be No Night* ♦ (1940), and *The Pirate* ♦ (1942). It was on the verge of financial collapse when the success of *Oklahoma!* ♦ (1943) saved it, but it was never again so important a producer. Its later offerings included the Robeson ♦-Ferrer ♦ *Othello* ♦ (1943), *Carousel* ♦ (1945), *The Iceman Cometh* ♦ (1946), *Come Back, Little Sheba* ♦ (1950), and *Sunrise at Campobello* ♦ (1958), as well as several other hits. In its heyday the Guild was the principal producer of such playwrights as George Bernard Shaw, ♦ O'Neill, ♦ Anderson, ♦ and Sherwood, ♦ and greatly advanced the careers of such players as the Lunts. ♦ Its pioneering subscription plan guaranteed audiences in New York and elsewhere the best in modern theatre, and in turn assured the Guild a loyal, knowledgeable group of playgoers.

Theatre-in-the-round, see *Arena Style Theatre*

Theatre Library Association Founded in 1937 as an affiliate of the American Library Association, its purpose is "to further the interests of gathering, preserving, and making available through libraries [and] museums . . . records (books, photographs, playbills, etc.) of theatre in all its forms." The group holds regular meetings as well as publishing its quarterly *Broadside* and annual *Performing Arts Resources*.

Theatre Magazine Founded in 1900 as a pictorial quarterly called *Our Players*, it changed its name to *The Theatre* in May 1901, when it became a monthly edited by Arthur Hornblow. ♦ Subsequently it was known as *Theatre Magazine* or simply *Theatre*. It became the finest of popular monthlies devoted to the theatre, as opposed to the more intellectual *Theatre Arts,* ♦ and survived for exactly thirty years, closing after its April 1931 issue.

Theatre of Arts and Letters, THE An attempt during the 1892–93 season by a group of minor authors, headed by Henry Burton McDowell, to establish subscription audiences in New York, Boston, Washington, and Baltimore, and to present plays of literary merit, it folded after its first season.

Theatre Row A group of small theatres on the south side of 42nd Street between Ninth and Tenth Avenues, they were established in the mid-1970s with the loose idea of creating a convenient complex of non-profit off-Broadway playhouses. Although the idea of being totally non-profit has not been adhered to strictly, the playhouses constitute the largest cluster of off-Broadway theatres in New York and are situated just below the main theatre area and two blocks west of what was once the main theatrical thoroughfare. Names of some of the playhouses have changed occasionally. Among the current ones are the Samuel Beckett Theatre, the Harold Clurman Theatre, and the Douglas Fairbanks Theatre. Other theatres are named for the organization running them, such as the Manhattan Punch Line Theatre and Playwrights Horizon.

Theatre Union, THE A non-profit producing company formed in 1932 to mount plays of social significance at popular prices, its largely left-wing dramas were offered primarily at the Civic Repertory Theatre. It disbanded in 1937 following the failure of its last production, John Howard Lawson's ♦ *Marching Song*.

Theatre World An annual survey of plays produced in New York and elsewhere, it was first issued for the 1944–45 season. Daniel Blum was the original editor. Since his death, John Willis, who was his assistant, has been editor. Unlike the *Best Plays*♦ series, it does not offer synopses of plots or detailed excerpts from any works. Instead it provides at least one photograph of each major production. It also features biographies and has continued to present useful obituaries, a feature *Best Plays* unfortunately has long since dropped. Some librarians suggest it is less unwieldy and therefore easier to use than *Best Plays,* even if in some respects it is not as thorough.

Theatrical Commonwealth, THE This was the name first given themselves by a group of actors and other theatre figures who banded together in 1805 after William Dunlap's♦ failure and attempted to assure themselves an income. The group apparently fell apart with the resumption of production at the Park Theatre.♦ In 1812 a group of Philadelphia performers, unhappy with conditions in theatres there, used the name in their attempt to mount their own productions, but they failed. A year later in New York still another band of disgruntled actors, who were displeased with policies at the Park or who could not even get work there, appropriated the term. They took over an old circus building, converted it into a theatre, and began offering their own attractions in the fall of 1813. For a brief time their excellent mountings gave the Park serious competition, but the company disbanded in early 1814, shortly after the death of Mrs. Twaits, one of its leading actresses and the wife of its manager.

Theatrical Syndicate, THE [also known as THE THEATRICAL TRUST] Formed in 1895 at a secret meeting which included A. L. Erlanger,♦ Charles Frohman,♦ William Harris,♦ Al Hayman,♦ Marc Klaw,♦ Fred Nixon-Nirdlinger,♦ and Fred Zimmerman,♦ its ostensible purpose was to bring order to the chaotic booking practices then prevalent in the theatre. Within a short time, however, the group monopolized virtually all major American playhouses and dictated terms to producers, actors, and other theatrical figures. A few stalwart opponents, notably Mr. and Mrs. Fiske♦ and Sarah Bernhardt,♦ bucked the group, and were often reduced to playing in rundown auditoriums and in tents. David Belasco♦ later joined its adversaries. However, despite often violent opposition in the national press, the group maintained a practical stranglehold on the American theatre until its monopoly was broken by the organization built by the Shubert

brothers♦ in the early years of the 20th century. By the time of World War I, the Shuberts had supplanted the Syndicate as the dominant force in American theatre.

There Shall Be No Night, a play in three acts by Robert E. Sherwood.♦ Produced by the Playwrights' Company♦ in association with the Theatre Guild♦ at the Alvin Theatre. April 29, 1940. 181 performances. PP.

The Nobel Prize-winning scientist, Dr. Kaarlo Valkonen (Alfred Lunt♦), and his American-born wife, Miranda (Lynn Fontanne♦), are reluctant to believe that the Russians will invade his beloved Finland. Nor can they see much purpose in resistance, should the Russians make war. But when war breaks out and their son Erik (Montgomery Clift♦) enters the army, Kaarlo joins the medical corps. He concludes that this war will not be the end of civilization, but rather "the long deferred death rattle of the primordial beast."

While many critics felt the acting turned a thin but well-meant play into an exciting evening, John Mason Brown♦ wrote, "No one can complain about the theatre's being an escapist institution when it conducts a class in current events at once as touching, intelligent and compassionate as *There Shall Be No Night.*" After the Russian defeat of the Finns, Sherwood changed the locale of the play to Greece and made the Germans the villains.

Thespian Oracle, The The earliest known American periodical devoted to theatre was first published in Philadelphia in January 1798 and seems to have survived only for a single issue. Not until 1805 did two somewhat longer-lived journals appear: *The Theatrical Censor* in Philadelphia and John Howard Payne's♦ *The Thespian Mirror* in New York.

"They Didn't Believe Me" A song with music by Jerome Kern♦ and lyric by Herbert Reynolds, it was one of several Kern melodies interpolated into the 1914 English importation, *The Girl from Utah,*♦ where it was sung by Julia Sanderson♦ and Donald Brian. ♦ Its success and novelty were such that it set the model for future ballad writing in the musical theatre and signaled the end of the primacy of the waltz, which for many years had been the designated form for musicals' "hit" songs.

They Knew What They Wanted, a play in three acts by Sidney Howard. ♦ Produced by the Theatre Guild♦ at the Garrick Theatre. November 24, 1924. 192 performances. PP.

Tony (Richard Bennett◆), an aging Italian winegrower in the Napa Valley, proposes by mail to a San Francisco waitress, Amy (Pauline Lord◆). Fearing she would consider him too old and too ugly, he sends her a photograph of his hired hand Joe (Glenn Anders◆). When Amy arrives she is shocked to learn the truth, and soon finds herself having an affair with Joe. Tony is forgiving, even offering to adopt the baby Amy will have. His goodness melts Amy's disdain, and she agrees to marry him.

This drama, given what were generally acknowledged as some of the finest performances of the era, was made into the successful musical *The Most Happy Fella*◆ (1956).

They're Playing Our Song, a musical comedy in two acts. Book by Neil Simon. ◆ Lyrics by Carole Bayer Sager. Music by Marvin Hamlisch. ◆ Produced at the Imperial Theatre. February 11, 1979. 1,082 performances.

Vernon Gersch (Robert Klein) is a successful young composer, and Sonia Walsk (Lucie Arnaz), an equally successful young lyricist. When they are thrown together for a projected collaboration a romance starts to blossom. However, its course is anything but smooth. First of all, Sonia is still trying to break off an old romance, and her former lover phones her at odd hours with his problems. Then, on an idyllic trip to Long Island, Vernon's car breaks down, and they wind up sleeping in the wrong house. Finally, though he must head for Hollywood and she for London, they promise to take up again.

Principal songs: If He Really Knew Me · They're Playing Our Song

This musical carried Broadway's slimming process to an almost anorexic extreme with only two principals and a chorus of six who acted as the principal's alter egos. Even the score, of only nine songs, many regularly reprised, was smaller than customary.

Third Degree, The, a play in four acts by Charles Klein. ◆ Produced by Henry B. Harris◆ at the Hudson Theatre. February 1, 1909. 168 performances.

A bogus art collector commits suicide after his old, long-married flame refuses to visit him. The woman's alcoholic son, Howard Jeffries, Jr. (Wallace Eddinger◆), is seen coming from the house, and the police, after a brutal interrogation, force a confession of murder from the innocent young man. His parents, whom he alienated by marrying a poor girl, will not come to his aid, but his loyal wife,

Annie (Helen Ware), secures a leading attorney, Richard Brewster (Edmund Breese◆), who unearths the suicide note and forces the police to make their error public.

As he had with *The Lion and the Mouse,* ◆ Klein successfully mingled social commentary derived from the muckraking of the time, in this instance the campaign against wanton police brutality, with gripping theatre.

Thirteenth Chair, The, a play in three acts by Bayard Veiller. ◆ Produced by William Harris, Sr.,◆ and Jr.,◆ at the 48th Street Theatre. November 20, 1916. 328 performances.

Mrs. Crosby (Martha Mayo) is pleased when her son Will (Calvin Thomas) announces his engagement to Helen O'Neill (Katherine La Salle), although Helen is reluctant to talk about her own mother. Only Edward Wales (S. K. Gardner) expresses any reservations about the betrothal. But the matter is put aside since Mrs. Crosby has engaged a medium, Rosalie La Grange (Margaret Wycherly◆), to hold a séance in which it is hoped a murdered friend will identify his murderer. During the séance Wales is stabbed to death, although no knife can be found. Suspicion falls on Helen, especially after it becomes known that she is actually Rosalie's daughter. Rosalie then traps the real murderer in a second séance.

Thirty years after its premiere, John Chapman◆ noted that the play "remains the best of all the shriek-in-the-dark dramas," adding, "Who will ever forget the first spine-curling thrill of seeing that nasty skewer stuck in the ceiling, or the chunk with which it fell down and stuck, quivering, in the tabletop?" Margaret Wycherly was Mrs. Bayard Veiller.

This Is the Army Proceeds from this 1942 revue with an all-soldier cast and with songs by Irving Berlin◆ went to service charities. Berlin's new songs for the show included "American Eagles," "I Left My Heart at the Stage Door Canteen," "I'm Getting Tired So I Can Sleep," and "This Is the Army, Mr. Jones," while Berlin himself toured with the show to sing "Oh, How I Hate To Get Up in the Morning." He had first sung the song in a similar all-soldier revue of World War I, *Yip, Yip, Yaphank* (1918), whose score had also included his "Mandy." Other services mounted shows during both wars, but without the enormous success of these two army revues.

THOMAS, A[LBERT] E[LLSWORTH] (1872–1947) Born in Chester, Mass., and educated at Brown, he served with several New York newspapers before becoming a playwright. Thirty of his plays were produced, beginning with *Her Husband's Wife* (1910), in which a wife, believing she is dying, sets out to choose her successor. His longest runs included *Come Out of the Kitchen*♦ (1916), based on a story by Alice Duer Miller and telling of an impoverished Southern family who rent their mansion and themselves out to rich Yankees; *Just Suppose* (1920), in which the Prince of Wales falls in love with an American girl; *The Champion* (1921), written with Thomas Louden, and recounting a prizefighter's problems with his snobbish father; *The French Doll* (1922), an adaptation of a Parisian hit in which a French lady must choose between two American suitors, one old and rich, the other young and handsome; and *No More Ladies* (1934), in which a wife takes to flirting with other men to save her marriage.

THOMAS, AUGUSTUS (1857–1934) Born in St. Louis, he flirted briefly with becoming a lawyer, but later worked on the railroad and was active in journalism. His first produced play, *Editha's Burglar,* was an adaptation of a novel by Mrs. F. Hodgson Burnett♦ and was originally mounted by an amateur dramatic company in his home town. Rewritten with the help of Edgar Smith,♦ it was done successfully on Broadway in 1889. Shortly thereafter Thomas supplanted Dion Boucicault♦ as the play doctor and adapter for the Madison Square Theatre.♦ His first totally original success was *Alabama*♦ (1891), which focused on the relationship between an unregenerate old Confederate and his more nationalistic son, and which signaled Thomas's interest in plays based on American themes. Among his more notable achievements were *In Mizzoura*♦ (1893), which centered on the love of a kindly sheriff for a thoughtless girl; *Arizona*♦ (1900), a saga of love and treachery among soldiers in Arizona Territory; *The Witching Hour*♦ (1907), in which the occult is employed to solve a murder; *As a Man Thinks* (1911), in which a doctor can reconcile feuding spouses, but cannot prevent his own daughter's elopement.; and *The Copperhead*♦ (1918), dealing with a Northerner supposed to have Southern sympathies. Besides these more-or-less realistic dramas, he also wrote several popular comedies, the best of which were *The Earl of Pawtucket*♦ (1903), in which an English nobleman tries to pass himself off as a Yankee; and *Mrs. Leffingwell's Boots*♦ (1905), recounting the comic complications follow-

ing the discovery of a lady's silk slippers in a bachelor's apartment. Thomas served as president of the Society of American Dramatists♦ for many years, and after the death of Charles Frohman♦ became active in the firm that the producer left behind. Not counting his early translations and adaptations, some three dozen of his plays were produced. As a writer he was sometimes criticized for working too hastily and unevenly, but was lauded for his determination to make American drama reflect American themes and interests. Quinn♦ concluded, "A more searching analysis of Thomas's work reveals a basic interest in those situations in which a human being becomes the center of a struggle between the intense desire for personal liberty and the circumstances which obstruct that desire in its fulfillment. The roots of all significant drama have, of course, lain in the struggle of the individual against fate or his surroundings. But the importance of Thomas's contribution lies in the distinctly American way he has treated that theme."

Autobiography: *The Print of My Remembrance,* New York, 1922.

THOMAS, JOHN CHARLES (1891?–1960) Although better known for his later career in opera and on radio, the stocky baritone from Meyersdale, Penn., made his Broadway debut in *The Passing Show of 1913,*♦ and later played leads in *The Peasant Girl* (1915), *Step This Way* (1916), *Her Soldier Boy* (1916), and *The Star Gazer* (1917). After heading a road company of *Maytime,*♦ he scored his biggest hit in *Apple Blossoms*♦ (1919), in which he introduced "You Are Free."

THOMASHEFSKY, [BARUCH] BORIS (1868–1939) Born in Kiev, Russia, he came to America with his parents in 1881, after his father was expelled for anti-government leanings. He worked in a shirt factory before starting out in the budding Yiddish theatre of the time. Within a few years he had developed into a handsome young man and a matinee idol. Besides winning fame as a performer, he eventually ran his own theatre, wrote plays, and produced his own shows. He was less inclined than Jacob Adler♦ and other contemporaries to the loftiest theatre, often preferring claptrap, romantic operettas. Even as an old man he insisted on playing young lovers. His attempts to perform in English on regular Broadway stages met with no success.

Autobiography: *My Life* (in Yiddish), New York, 1937.

THOMPSON, [Henry] Denman (1833–1911) One of many 19th-century actors who made a career largely of a single role, he was born in Beechwood, Penn., but raised in New England. He performed as a circus acrobat and in stock before creating a vaudeville sketch about a kindly country man named Joshua Whitcomb, whom he first portrayed in the mid-1870s. His success was such that a play, *Joshua Whitcomb* (1878), was written around the character. He toured with it for about a decade. In 1887 he wrote a second play, this time with George W. Ryer, centering on the New Hampshire farmer. The play was *The Old Homestead*♦ (1887), which told how Josh goes to the big city to save his son. It quickly became one of the most popular plays of its era. Thompson played the leading role until just before his death. On rare occasions he essayed other parts, sometimes in plays he was credited with writing, but none was the least successful, so he soon returned to playing Josh. Thompson was a stocky, red-haired (if balding), slightly jowly man with a friendly, avuncular face, who performed Josh in baggy pants, an ill-fitting vest, thick glasses, and a large straw hat.

THOMPSON, Ernest, see *On Golden Pond*

THOMPSON, Fred (1884–1949) Between 1913 and 1944 the London-born librettist, working alone or with collaborators, wrote some fifty musicals. Most were for the West End, but in the 1920s he had a hand in eleven Broadway offerings, including *Lady, Be Good!*♦ (1924), *Tip-Toes*♦ (1925), *Rio Rita*♦ (1927), *The Five o'Clock Girl* (1927), and *Funny Face*♦ (1927). All but the last were written with Guy Bolton.♦ Shortly before his death he worked with Bolton on *Follow the Girls*♦ (1944).

THOMPSON, Lydia (1836–1908) A yellow-haired beauty whose ample proportions pleased an over-stuffed era, she caused a sensation in New York in 1868 when she arrived from her native London with her troupe of British blondes to perform a series of burlesque musicals such as *Ixion; or, The Man at the Wheel* and *The Forty Thieves*. The most shapely of the girls, including Miss Thompson, regularly assumed the trouser roles in these offerings, so as to show off their legs. Although the more prudish and finicky critics found some of her entertainments salacious, most observers admired her comic flair and graceful, dainty movements. Her success initiated the rage for extended burlesques that flourished in America until the retirement fifty years later of Weber♦ and Fields.♦ Miss Thompson continued to make regular trips between the West End and Broadway, her last American appearance coming in 1894 in *The Crust of Society*.

THOMPSON, Woodman (1889?–1955) The Pittsburgh-born set designer created the scenery for some seventy shows, and is best remembered for his colorful work on Winthrop Ames's♦ revivals of Gilbert and Sullivan♦ operettas in the 1920s, including *Iolanthe* (1926) and *The Pirates of Penzance*♦ (1926). However, he also designed other important productions such as *Beggar on Horseback*♦ (1924), *What Price Glory?*♦ (1924), *The Firebrand*♦ (1924), *The Cocoanuts* (1925), *The Wisdom Tooth*♦ (1926), *The Desert Song*♦ (1926), *The Barretts of Wimpole Street*♦ (1931), Katharine Cornell's♦ production of *Romeo and Juliet*♦ (1934), and *The Magnificent Yankee* (1946). He taught set design at Columbia for many years until shortly before his death.

THOMSON, Virgil, see *Four Saints in Three Acts*

THORNE, Charles R[obert] (1814?–93) The son of a New York merchant, he made his acting debut at the Park Theatre♦ in 1829 and continued to perform for fifty years. He was also active in management, on various occasions running not only the Chatham Garden and National Theatre in New York and the Baldwin Theatre♦ in San Francisco, but touring with his wife, Ann Maria Mestayer Thorne (d. 1881), and his company through South and Central America. For a time he managed a troupe which performed along the Erie Canal.

THORNE, Charles R[obert], Jr. (1840–83) He began performing while still a child in his parents' company [see preceding entry]. On reaching maturity his good looks and dashing personality prompted producers to cast him in such roles as Hawkshaw, the detective, in *The Ticket-of-Leave Man*♦ (1873); Armand, opposite Clara Morris,♦ in *Camille*♦ (1875); and Raphael in *The Marble Heart*♦ (1877). These were established roles in well-known plays. Among the important parts he created on the American stage were the tight-lipped, virtuous Chevalier de Vaudrey in *The Two Orphans*♦ (1874) and John Strebelow, who teaches his reluctant wife to love him, in *The Banker's Daughter*♦ (1880). The illness that led to his death forced him to retire while still much in demand.

THORNTON, James (1861–1938) Famed off-stage as a prodigious drinker, the gloomy looking performer and composer was born in Liverpool, but brought to Boston while still a youngster. He soon turned to both songwriting and comedy. At first he performed in vaudeville with a partner, often his wife Bonnie, but later became one of the best monologuists in the field. He would walk on stage carrying a newspaper, read imaginary headlines through his pince-nez, and then comment dourly on them. By contrast, his songs, many of which are still popular, belonged to the school of unabashed sentimentality and included "My Sweetheart's the Man in the Moon," "She May Have Seen Better Days," and "When You Were Sweet Sixteen."

Three Faces East, a play in three acts by Anthony Paul Kelly. Produced by Cohan♦ and Harris♦ at the Cohan and Harris Theatre. August 13, 1918. 335 performances.

German espionage headquarters enlists the aid of a beautiful girl known as Fraulein Helene (Violet Heming) to take the place of a murdered English-woman and go by U-boat to make contact with the mysterious Franz Boelke (Emmett Corrigan), who hopes to blow up the cabinet during a meeting. The Germans' plans are thwarted and Boelke exposed after it is revealed Helene is actually an English counterspy. She even finds time for a romantic fling.

Cohan's extensive rewriting and swift-paced direction, coupled with wartime prosperity, accounted in large measure for the success of this thriller. The Chicago-born Kelly (1895–1932) was primarily a screenwriter, whose only other Broadway play was *The Phantom Legion* (1919), another war drama.

Three Men on a Horse, a farce in three acts by John Cecil Holm and George Abbott.♦ Produced at the Playhouse. January 30, 1935. 835 performances.

Having had a tiff with his wife Audrey (Joyce Arling), the meek-mannered greeting-card writer, Erwin Trowbridge (William Lynn), finds solace at a bar where he happens to mention that, while he does not bet, he invariably picks winners at the races. Three small-time racketeers latch onto him and win one race after another. Since Erwin's inspiration comes only when riding on a bus, this means they do a lot of traveling. But after they become doubtful of one of his choices and force him to place a bet, his inspiration deserts him. So do the racketeers. He returns to his wife and to writing corny couplets.

Robert Benchley♦ said the play was "distinctly low in tone, broad in method, and ostensibly mad in design, but there is an underlying comic truth running through it, even in minor roles, which made it consistently funny to me, and sometimes more than funny." One of the best modern American

farces, it was the basis for two musicals, *Banjo Eyes* (1941) and *Let It Ride!* (1961).

John Cecil Holm (1904–81) was a Philadelphia-born actor, director, and playwright. His biggest success, apart from this play, was his book for the musical *Best Foot Forward* (1941).

Three Musketeers, The, an operetta in two acts. Book by William Anthony McGuire.♦ Lyrics by P. G. Wodehouse♦ and Clifford Grey. Music by Rudolf Friml.♦ Produced by Florenz Ziegfeld♦ at the Lyric Theatre. March 13, 1928. 319 performances.

With his friends Aramis (Joseph Macaulay), Athos (Douglass R. Dumbrille), and Porthos (Detmar Poppen), the dashing D'Artagnan (Dennis King♦) comes to Paris, where he soon falls in love with Constance Bonacieux (Vivienne Segal♦). However, when the villainous Richelieu (Reginald Owen) threatens to expose the fact that Queen Anne of France (Yvonne D'Arle) has given some precious jewels to the Duke of Buckingham (John Clark), D'Artagnan makes a hurried trip to England to recover them. Once they are safely in the Queen's hands, he can resume his love-making and dueling.

Principal songs: Ma Belle · March of the Musketeers · My Sword and I · Your Eyes

Friml's last success was sumptuously mounted by Ziegfeld, with superb Joseph Urban♦ settings. It has enjoyed intermittent revivals. A clumsily revised and ineptly mounted 1984 revival was short-lived.

Three of Us, The, a play in four acts by Rachel Crothers.♦ Produced at the Madison Square Theatre.♦ October 17, 1906. 227 performances.

Rhy Macchesney (Carlotta Nillson) and her two younger brothers own "The Three of Us" mine. Rhy's fiancé, Stephen Townley (Frederic Truesdell), learns of an even richer lode and passes on the information to Rhy. The older of Rhy's two brothers, Clem (John Westley), who has no love for mining and wants to go East, overhears the conversation. He sells the scuttlebutt to a speculator, Louis Berresford (Henry Kolker), who quickly buys the property. For a time Stephen thinks Rhy betrayed him, but he later learns better.

Of this, her first success, one critic noted, "Miss Crothers has gone straight ahead without any resort to the commonplace trickery of the stage. Her people have hearts, and she gets to these hearts. They have brains and minds; they act on natural and not fictitious impulse. . . ."

Three Wise Fools, a play in three acts by Austin Strong. Produced by Winchell Smith♦ and John Golden♦ at the Criterion Theatre. October 31, 1918. 316 performances.

Judge James Trumbull (William Ingersoll), Dr. Richard Gaunt (Harry Davenport), and the banker Thomas Findley (Claude Gillingwater) are three middle-aged bachelors who share a Washington Square home. They also share memories of a sweetheart now dead who rejected them in favor of a man later convicted of a crime he did not commit. Into their lives comes Miss Fairchild (Helen Menken♦), daughter of their old flame. She appears to rejuvenate their humdrum existence until some escaped convicts appear on the scene and the girl attempts to take the blame for the crime her father supposedly committed. The men are shattered and turn against the girl, before Gordon Schuyler (Charles Laite), a nephew of one of the men, sets matters aright. Gordon proposes to Miss Fairchild. After all, he may be wise but he is no fool.

The show opened to divided notices and was ready to close until Golden erected one of Broadway's first huge signs in front of the theatre and turned unsold seats over to Leblang's Ticket Agency. ♦ Within a week or two the show became a sellout. Strong acknowledged that the play was heavily rewritten by Smith. For a mini-biography of Strong, see *Seventh Heaven.*

Threepenny Opera, The A modern, markedly satiric redaction of John Gay's *The Beggar's Opera,* it had a libretto by Bertolt Brecht♦ and music by Kurt Weill. ♦ The story centered on the outlaw Macheath, his wooing of Polly Peachum, his betrayal, near-execution, and reprieve. Originally presented in Berlin in 1928 as *Die Dreigroschenoper,* an adaptation by Gifford Cochran and Jerrold Krimsky failed on Broadway in 1933. A second adaptation, this time by Marc Blitzstein, ♦ was offered off-Broadway at the Theatre de Lys on March 10, 1954. When this acclaimed production closed after a limited engagement of 95 performances, the critical cry for its return was such that it was revived on September 20, 1955, at the same theatre and ran for 2,611 performances, an off-Broadway record at the time. The cast included Lotte Lenya, ♦ Weill's wife, as the prostitute Jenny, in a role she had created in the original German production, as well as Scott Merrill as Macheath, Jo Sullivan as Polly Peachum, and Beatrice Arthur as Lucy Brown. The action was transferred from the 18th century to Victorian times. This production helped rekindle an interest in the works of both Weill and Brecht. The play's best-

known song, "The Ballad of Mack the Knife," remains widely sung. Weill's curious, jazz-influenced melodies and orchestrations prompted similar instrumentation in later musicals, most notably in *Cabaret.* ♦ A third translation, one by Ralph Manheim and John Willett, was offered by the New York Shakespeare Festival♦ in 1976. A major 1990 revival, in yet another translation, was poorly received.

Three's a Family, a comedy in three acts by Phoebe and Henry Ephron. Produced by John Golden♦ at the Longacre Theatre. May 5, 1943. 497 performances.

After quarreling with her husband Eugene (Francis de Sales), Kitty Mitchell (Katherine Bard) moves with her new baby into her parents' small apartment. She is barely unpacked when her brother, Archie Whitaker (Edwin Philips), appears with his pregnant wife. Since the Whitakers are already bedding down Mrs. Whitaker's sister and two live-in maids, the place becomes awkwardly crowded. It takes aged Doctor Bartell (William Wadsworth), who is partially blind and totally befuddled, and who has resumed his practice because of the wartime shortage of doctors, to bring some order out of the chaos.

Although most critics dismissed the show as trite and unoriginal, wartime prosperity and the public's search for escape turned it into a major hit.

Phoebe [née Wolkind] (1916–71) and Henry Ephron (b. 1912) were a New York husband and wife team whose only other success was *Take Her, She's Mine* (1961).

THROCKMORTON, CLEON (1897–1965) Born in Atlantic City, he studied at Carnegie Institute of Technology and at George Washington University. He then embarked on a career as a landscape and figure painter, but after a few years turned to the theatre. He worked on the designs for *The Emperor Jones*♦ (1920) and later created the sets of *All God's Chillun Got Wings*♦ (1924), *S. S. Glencairn*♦ (1924), *In Abraham's Bosom*♦ (1926), *Burlesque*♦ (1927), *Porgy*♦ (1927), *Another Language*♦ (1932), and *Alien Corn*♦ (1933). By his retirement in the early 1950s he had designed sets for over 150 plays. He also drew up architectural plans for such summer theatres as the Cape Playhouse in Dennis, Mass., and the Westport (Conn.) Country Playhouse.

THUMB, TOM [né CHARLES SHERWOOD STRATTON] (1838–83) Although the term "Tom Thumb" had been given for centuries to dwarfish people, it is largely associated in Americans' minds with the 25-inch-tall midget whom P. T. Barnum♦ first exhibited at his museum in 1843. The boy was then five years old, but Barnum attempted to make him more interesting by claiming he was eleven and this has led some sources to conclude that he was born in 1832. He eventually grew to a height of 40 inches. His hair was flaxen, his eyes dark, and he always offered the impression of pink-cheeked good health. Barnum gave him the rank of general and bedecked him in all sorts of fancy regalia. The producer also gave him an elaborate miniature carriage with tiny ponies in which to ride down Broadway. Under Barnum's management he toured not only as a curiosity, but performed in specially written playlets as well. In 1863 he married 32-inch-tall Lavinia Warren, and the couple appeared together for many years.

THURBER, JAMES, see *Male Animal, The*

THURSTON, HOWARD (1869–1936) The famous magician was born in Columbus, Ohio, and was performing in a small Western theatre when Herrmann the Great♦ caught his act and was baffled by Thurston's trick of a mysteriously rising and falling playing card. Thurston explained that the card was attached to a thin black thread and manipulated by two stagehands from the wings. Herrmann helped Thurston obtain better bookings and the younger performer soon developed an extremely showy act that always featured the celebrated card trick. He was a somewhat haughty performer, who never really won his audiences' affection, but his skill kept him a headliner throughout the world.

Ticket-of-Leave Man, The Tom Taylor's♦ play about a parolee whose trusting disposition leads to misadventures was first played in New York in November 1863, six months after its London premiere. The play was a huge success, with W. J. Florence♦ in the principal role of Bob Brierly. Numerous revivals followed for the rest of the century.

TIERNEY, HARRY [AUSTIN] (1890–1965) Born into a musical family in Perth Amboy, N.J., the composer pursued his studies at the Virgil Conservatory of Music in New York before embarking on a career as a concert pianist. His growing interest in popular music, however, led him to sail for England in 1913. There he worked for a London music publisher, interpolated songs into West End shows, and eventually wrote his first score. Returning to America, he

again began by interpolating songs, most notably "M-I-S-S-I-S-S-I-P-P-I" in Ziegfeld's♦ 1916 *Midnight Frolics*. He also wrote the music for *What Next?* (1917), which never reached New York. His first complete score heard on Broadway was for the most successful musical up to its day, *Irene*♦ (1919), recalled for "Alice Blue Gown" and its title song. Six more Broadway shows followed in the 1920s, with the longest runs going to *Kid Boots* (1923), and *Rio Rita*♦ (1927), from which came "The Rangers' Song" and the title number. In the 1930s he composed several operettas, but none reached New York. The lyricist for Tierney's Broadway shows was Joseph McCarthy.♦

Tiger Rose, a play in three acts by Willard Mack.♦ Produced by David Belasco♦ at the Lyceum Theatre.♦ October 3, 1917. 384 performances.
   Rose Bocion (Lenore Ulric♦) is a French-Canadian "hellcat." She is loved by all the men in the neighborhood, including the moony Pierre Le Bey (Pedro De Cordoba) and the villainous mountie, Constable Devlin (Mack). But she loves only Bruce Norton (Calvin Thomas). When Bruce commits a murder, actually justifiable, he becomes a fugitive, hunted by Devlin, who would use the circumstances to have his way with Rose. She, however, resists, and helps hide Bruce until all the facts can be brought to light.
   A good, if unexceptional melodrama, the play was made into a long-running hit by Belasco's spectacular staging, which offered a frightening on-stage thunderstorm.

TILLER, JOHN (1852?–1925) The famed British dancer and choreographer was born in Manchester, England, and at an early age established a celebrated British dancing school. He sent many bands of "Tiller Girls" to dance in American musicals, especially in the 1910s and 1920s. In these years in particular they specialized in precision routines that many critics dismissed as glorified acrobatics. His girls appeared in the 1922 and 1924 editions of the *Ziegfeld Follies,*♦ in *George White's Scandals of 1923,*♦ and in several musical comedies produced by Charles Dillingham.♦ After Tiller's death his associate Mary Read continued his policies.

Time of the Cuckoo, The, a play in two acts by Arthur Laurents.♦ Produced by Robert Whitehead♦ and Walter Fried at the Empire Theatre.♦ October 15, 1952. 263 performances.
   A lonely American spinster, Leona Samish (Shirley Booth♦), comes to Venice to look at the sights of

the old world and, not incidentally, to look for romance. She finds it with a suave, handsome Italian, Renato de Rossi (Dino Di Luca). But the idyll is shattered when Renato proves both a sponger and a married man.

Louis Kronenberger♦ saw this small but delicately made play as "one with shrewd comments and effective scenes, one where, in terms of love, there is much to be said on both sides; or where—in line with Hebbel's requirement for sound drama—*all* the people seem in the right." The play was later made into the musical *Do I Hear a Waltz?* (1965) by Laurents, with music by Richard Rodgers♦ (the title song is one of his most memorable waltzes) and lyrics by Stephen Sondheim. ♦ The lack of an actress of the quality of Miss Booth or Katharine Hepburn♦ (who played the part in the film version, *Summertime*), and the inexplicably slack production kept the musical from duplicating the play's success.

Time of Your Life, The, a play in three acts by William Saroyan. ♦ Produced by the Theatre Guild♦ in association with Eddie Dowling♦ at the Booth Theatre. October 25, 1939. 185 performances. PP, NYDCCA.

At a run-down San Francisco bar, the openhearted, openhanded Joe (Dowling) encourages one and all to be their own eccentric selves. He finds employment for a would-be dancer, Harry (Gene Kelly), and fosters the romance between his sidekick Tom (Edward Andrews) and Kitty Duval (Julie Haydon♦), a prostitute. An old Indian fighter, Kit Carson (Len Doyle), spins wild yarns of his imaginary past and kills the vicious detective, Blick (Grover Burgess). After a pinball addict, Willie (Will Lee), strikes the jackpot, Joe muses, "In the time of your life, live, so that in that good time there shall be no ugliness or death for yourself or for any life your life touches."

John Mason Brown♦ called the work "at once gleeful and heartbreaking, tender and hilarious, probing and elusive." It was the first play to win both major drama awards.

Time, the Place and the Girl, The, a musical comedy in three acts. Book and lyrics by Will M. Hough♦ and Frank R. Adams. ♦ Music by Joe Howard.♦ Produced at Wallack's Theatre. August 5, 1907. 32 performances.

After a drunken brawl Tom Cunningham (George Anderson) and Johnny Hicks (Arthur Deagon) are forced to take refuge in a sanitorium, where Tom discovers an old flame, Margaret Simpson (Violet McMillan), and Johnny finds a new one, Molly Kelly

(Elene Foster). An infectious outbreak forces the authorities to quarantine the sanatorium and the enforced stay gives Tom and Johnny time to pursue their courtships successfully.

Principal songs: Blow the Smoke Away · Waning Honeymoon

This musical was a Chicago show which had established a new long-run record of over 400 performances in that city and had toured the country profitably. Its short New York run typified the city's response to most Midwestern shows.

Times, The; or, Life in New York, a comedy in three acts by "a gentleman of this city." Produced at the Park Theatre. ♦ December 10, 1829. In repertory.

This apparently lost play was written as a vehicle for J. H. Hackett, ♦ giving him the popular character of Industrious Doolittle. According to the *Mirror,* the comedy consisted of "a dozen or so of scenes thrown cleverly though loosely together, exhibiting the manners and habits of the worthy inhabitants of this city . . . There is a pretended English baronet . . . a Frenchman, two Broadway dandies (a black and a white), a plain merchant and his fashionable wife, a talking speculating Yankee, and a brace of young ladies and young gentlemen." Odell♦ viewed it as an important precursor to plays such as *A Glance at New York*♦ and the later Harrigan and Hart♦ shows, while Quinn♦ saw it as foreshadowing *Fashion.* ♦ It was, most certainly, in the tradition of *Tom and Jerry,*♦ which had been offered at the same theatre six years earlier.

Tin Pan Alley This term, said to have been coined by composer Monroe H. Rosenfeld, described the cluster of publishing houses on two blocks of 28th Street between Fifth Avenue, Broadway, and Sixth Avenue. Many younger composers, who later became important to the American musical theatre, received their start there, often as song-pluggers. A not too subtle distinction developed between a "Tin Pan Alley composer" and a "Broadway composer." The former largely wrote songs published separately or designed for vaudeville singers, while the latter offered whole scores for musicals.

TINNEY, FRANK (1878–1940) The diminutive, babyfaced comedian was born in Philadelphia, where he made his first appearance at the age of four, performing in blackface. Although he rarely used a dialect, he continued to employ blackface for much of his career. He became a favorite in vaudeville, where his act consisted of patently corny jokes, confidences to the audiences, and joking with the conductor. His turn had a carefully contrived loose-ness and ingenuousness. He also appeared in such musicals as the 1910 and 1913 editions of the *Ziegfeld Follies,*♦ *Watch Your Step*♦ (1914), *The Century Girl* (1916), *Tickle Me* (1920), *Daffy Dill* (1922), and the 1923 edition of the *Music Box Revue.*♦ In 1923 he was involved in a notorious scandal and two years later suffered the mental breakdown that prompted his retirement from the stage.

Tiny Alice, a play in three acts by Edward Albee.♦ Produced at the Billy Rose Theatre. December 29, 1964. 167 performances.

The world's richest woman, Miss Alice (Irene Worth♦), bequeaths two billion dollars to the Catholic Church with the stipulation that the strange lay brother Julian (John Gielgud♦) be sent to her home to accept the money. Julian, who confesses he has spent six years in a mental institution, is seduced by Alice, and dies, exclaiming, "God, Alice . . . I accept thy will."

Although Albee remarked that the play "is an examination of how much false illusion we need to get through life," most critics were baffled by the work. It provoked acrimonious discussion, and still does when the play is revived.

Tip-Toes, a musical comedy in two acts. Book by Guy Bolton♦ and Fred Thompson.♦ Lyrics by Ira Gershwin.♦ Music by George Gershwin.♦ Pro-duced by Alex A. Aarons♦ and Vinton Freedley♦ at the Liberty Theatre. December 28, 1925. 194 performances.

When Al (Andrew Tombes) and Hen Kaye (Harry Watson, Jr.) of the vaudeville act, The Three K's, are stranded in Palm Beach with the girl in their act, Tip-Toes (Queenie Smith♦), they wangle some money and set Tip-Toes up in local society. She is wooed and won by a handsome young glue magnate, Steve Burton (Allen Kearns♦).

Principal songs: Looking for a Boy · Sweet and Low-Down · That Certain Feeling · These Charming People · When Do We Dance?

Although Ira Gershwin was later to claim this was the first show in which he honed his skills as a lyricist, Alexander Woollcott♦ concluded, "It was of course [George] Gershwin's evening, so sweet and sassy were the melodies . . . so fresh and unstinted the gay, young blood of his invention."

Tivoli Opera House (San Francisco) Sometime be-tween 1872 and 1875 Joseph Kreling converted an old mansion into a beer garden offering musical entertainment. The enterprise was so successful that in 1878 he built a larger, more formal café and theatre, changing the name from the Tivoli Beer Garden to the Tivoli Opera House. The main floor, however, remained for many years given over to tables and service of beverages, so technically this could not be considered the first legitimate theatre designed exclusively for the performance of musi-cals. (That honor belongs to New York's Casino Theatre.♦) Nevertheless, for most of its history the Tivoli was the principal producer of musicals west of the Mississippi. It mounted not only East Coast successes but also a number of importations not seen in the East, as well as original musicals. Although some of its artists, such as composer-conductor William Furst,♦ comedian Edwin Stevens, and soprano Alice Nielsen♦ went on to national fame, many favorites, such as Ferris Hartman, Annie Meyers, and Arthur Cunningham remained merely local stars. By the turn of the century the theatre's vogue had passed, and, like so many other houses, it was destroyed in the 1906 fire.

TKTS This is the name given to the box offices set up by the Theatre Development Fund♦ in a large trailer in Times Square to offer cut-rate tickets to Broadway shows. The arrangement began in 1973 and quickly became a major factor in increasing theatre attendance in New York. Shows generally turn over unsold tickets for sale on the day of the performance. The arrangement is highly reminiscent of that run for many decades by Leblang's Ticket Office.♦ Some grumbling has surfaced to suggest that the seemingly high prices of contemporary Broadway tickets have purposely been pegged that way with the sale of these lower priced seats in mind, and that by generally lowering prices, especially for balcony seats, the same end could be achieved. However, most producers and theatre owners have been reluctant to argue with success, and the arrangement, under various names, has spread to other theatrical centers.

To the Ladies, a comedy in three acts by George S. Kaufman♦ and Marc Connelly.♦ Produced by George C. Tyler♦ and A. L. Erlanger♦ at the Liberty Theatre. February 20, 1922. 128 perfor-mances.

Leonard Beebe (Otto Kruger♦) is a salesman for the Kincaid Piano Company. He is something of a dreamy visionary, unlike his quiet, down-to-earth wife Elsie (Helen Hayes♦). When Mr. and Mrs. Kincaid (George Howell and Isabel Irving) visit the Beebes they are most impressed with Elsie, who arranges with Mrs. Kincaid to wangle Leonard a promotion. The plan is to have him speak at a company banquet, but when he becomes tongue-tied, Elsie must make the speech for him. It wins him the promotion.

Despite generally welcoming notices the play was only a modest success in New York, and proved somehow too arcane to have any appeal on the road.

Tobacco Road, a play in three acts by Jack Kirkland. Produced at the Masque Theatre. December 4, 1933. 3,182 performances.

The Lesters are a shabby, worthless family of sharecroppers who have lost the land their ancestors had long farmed in a desultory fashion. Jeeter Lester (Henry Hull♦) is the shiftless head of the family. He has sold his oldest daughter for seven dollars, and when her husband, Lov Besney (Dean Jagger), comes to complain that she will not consummate the marriage, allows his other daughter Ellie May (Ruth Hunter), to run off with Lov. His son, Dude (Sam Byrd), marries a neighbor who has enough money to let him buy an old car. When Dude's mother, Ada (Margaret Wycherly♦), berates her son, he runs her over and kills her. Jeeter seems indifferent to all this, just sitting on his stoop and rubbing dirt with his hand.

Based on the novel by Erskine Caldwell, the play was assailed by almost every critic. Richard Lockridge of the *Sun* typified much of the revulsion when he referred to the work as "A play that achieves the repulsive and seldom falls below the faintly sickening." To the surprise of the show-wise, the play became the longest running drama up to its time.

Kirkland (1902–69) was born in St. Louis and was represented on Broadway as author and/or producer of ten plays. His only other success was *I Must Love Someone* (1939), a fictionalized account of the famous Florodora girls, written with Leyle Georgie.

TOBIN, GENEVIEVE (b. 1902) The New York-born actress began her career in 1912 and within a few seasons was being touted by many critics as a successor to Maude Adams.♦ Although her career never lived up to its earliest promises, she won praise as Patricia O'Day, the immigrant who wins over her guardian, in *Little Old New York* (1920); Polly Brown, the chorus girl who becomes a film star, in *Polly Preferred* (1923); Cordelia in a 1923 special staging of *King Lear♦*; Nancy Blake, who encourages the hero to assert himself, in *The Youngest* (1924); and in the musical *Fifty Million Frenchmen♦* (1929).

Today, a play in four acts by George Broadhurst♦ and Abraham S. Schomer. Produced at the 48th Street Theatre. October 6, 1913. 280 performances.

When Frederick Wagner (Edwin Arden) fails in business, his spoiled, spendthrift wife Lily (Emily Stevens♦) cannot accept the fact that she must give up the luxuries she has enjoyed. To ensure that she need not, she secretly goes to work in a fashionable brothel. Her husband has become the agent for the landlord who owns the building in which the brothel is located, and when he arrives there on a professional visit he discovers his wife's wiles. A confrontation follows, after which he leaves her.

While many critics agreed with Adolph Klauber♦ of the *Times,* who dismissed the work as "an indecent, vicious play," enough of the play-going public was titilated to turn the work into a major success.

TODD, MICHAEL [né AVROM GOLDBOGEN] (1907–58) The flamboyant producer was born in Minneapolis and first called attention to himself with his productions at the 1933 Chicago World's Fair. His first Broadway offering, *Call Me Ziggy* (1937), was a three-performance failure, and he did not begin to make a name until his mounting in 1939 of *The Hot Mikado.* He enjoyed a long run with *Star and Garter* (1942) and with such subsequent musicals as *Something for the Boys* (1943), *Mexican Hayride* (1944), *Up in Central Park♦* (1945), *As the Girls Go* (1948), and *Michael Todd's Peep Show* (1950). Most of his musical productions were perceived as glorified burlesque, with an emphasis on scantily clad, beautiful girls and gaudy sets and costumes. Among his non-musical offerings were *Pick-Up Girl* (1944); Mae West's♦ vehicle, *Catherine Was Great* (1944); and Maurice Evans's♦ *Hamlet♦* (1945).

Biography: *A Valuable Property,* Michael Todd, Jr., and Susan McCarthy Todd, New York, 1983.

Tom and Jerry; or, Life in London W. T. Moncrieff's dramatization of Pierce Egan's story was first played at the Park Theatre♦ in 1823. The play took its leading figures on a tour of the city, interspersed with song and dance. Its popularity gave rise to numerous similar, loosely constructed entertainments, but more importantly, in the opinion of many students, it planted the seeds for later musical comedy and revue.

Tomorrow and Tomorow, a play in three acts by Philip Barry.♦ Produced by Gilbert Miller♦ at the Henry Miller Theatre. January 13, 1931. 206 performances.

Gail (Harvey Stephens) and Eve Redman (Zita

Johann) live in a small American town where Gail's father had founded a college. They are childless. When a noted doctor comes to teach at the school, the college authorities ask the Redmans to house him. Before long, Eve has had not only an affair with Dr. Hay (Herbert Marshall) but his child, although she leads Gail to believe the baby is his. Years later, the boy suffers an emotional trauma after an accident, and Eve summons Hay. He manages to cure the boy, something other doctors had failed to do. Hay begs Eve to come with the boy and live with him, but she remains true to her faithful, uncomprehending husband.

Burns Mantle♦ hailed the play as "sensitively and delicately wrought in both character and situation."

Tomorrow the World, a play in three acts by James Gow and Arnaud d'Usseau. Produced at the Ethel Barrymore Theatre. April 14, 1943. 500 performances.

Emil Bruchner (Skippy Homeier) is a young boy whose liberal father was killed by the Nazis, who then raised and thoroughly indoctrinated him. He is brought to America by his uncle, Michael Frame (Ralph Bellamy♦), a university professor. Emil spews hatred, tries naïvely to spy for the Germans, and in a particularly vicious moment slashes an old family portrait. But Frame, his sister Jessie (Dorothy Sands), and, most of all, a compassionate schoolteacher, Leona Richards (Shirley Booth♦), eventually make him see the error of his ways.

This was one of the war's more literate propaganda pieces. Gow (1907–52), who was born in Creston, Iowa, and d'Usseau (1916–90), who was born in Los Angeles, were primarily film writers. Their only other success was *Deep Are the Roots*♦ (1945).

TONE, FRANCHOT (1905–68) Born in Niagara Falls, N.Y., the lanky, somewhat swarthy actor studied at Cornell, then made his professional acting debut with a stock company in Buffalo. Broadway first saw him in *The Belt* (1927). Among his major roles were Tom Ames, the young, unhappy publisher, in *Hotel Universe*♦ (1930); Curly McClain, the cowboy who must kill a farm hand before he can marry his sweetheart, in *Green Grow the Lilacs* (1931); Will Connelly, the aristocrat who marries the daughter of a tenant farmer, in *The House of Connelly* (1931); Harold Goff, the racketeer who is killed by the kindly folk he preys on, in *The Gentle People*♦ (1939); Alan Coles, the psychoanalyst who discovers his bride-to-be is no virgin, in *Oh, Men! Oh, Women!*♦ (1953); and James Tyrone, the dissipated

young man in search of a mother-figure, in *A Moon for the Misbegotten*♦ (1957). He was long popular in films.

Tony Awards Officially known as the Antoinette Perry Awards, they were established by the American Theatre Wing♦ in 1947, a year after the death of Miss Perry,♦ and have been offered ever since for "distinguished achievement" in the theatre. There are numerous categories, including best play, best musical, best actor, best actress, best supporting actor, best supporting actress, best actor in a musical, best actress in a musical, set designer, costume designer, director, director of a musical, composer, choreographer, etc. Special awards are also given regularly. Apart from the Pulitzer Prize♦ and the New York Drama Critics Circle Award♦ for best plays, these are the most respected of all theatrical honors.

Too Many Cooks, a comedy in three acts by Frank Craven.♦ Produced by William A. Brady♦ at the 39th Street Theatre. February 24, 1914. 223 performances.

After Alice Cook (Inez Plummer), a pretty Irish stenographer, agrees to marry Albert Bennett (Craven), a genial young clerk, they decide to build a cozy home on a plot Albert has bought with his savings. However, the youngsters make one horrendous error—they invite their families and friends to watch the bungalow rise. Alice's mother, father, two aunts, an uncle, two brothers, and two sisters all put in appearances, suggesting ways to change the house plans. So do Albert's uncle and friend. The suggestions lead the young couple into arguments and eventually into breaking off the engagement. As if that is not enough, the carpenters go on strike, so that Albert must finish the shingling alone. With no wife to share his home, he puts the crookedly shingled cottage up for sale. As he is about to leave he looks longingly at a single rose blooming on the small bush Alice had planted. Just then, Alice returns. The pair is reconciled, and they conclude they will live happily ever after with all the comforts of home but with relatives allowed only on rare occasions.

Walter Prichard Eaton♦ noted the play was written "in the bald vernacular" and concluded that it "is funny, it is wholesome, it is true—and, best of all, it is unconsciously and thoroughly American." The comedy was the source of the hit 1922 musical, *Up She Goes,* which Craven adapted from his own play, with music by the *Irene*♦ team of Joseph

McCarthy♦ and Harry Tierney,♦ starring Donald Brian♦ and Gloria Fay.

Too Much Johnson, a comedy in three acts by William Gillette. ♦ Produced by Charles Frohman♦ at the Standard Theatre. November 26, 1894. 216 performances.

Whenever the philandering Augustus Billings (Gillette) entertains his French mistress in New York, he tells his wife (Maud Haslam) and his suspicious mother-in-law, Mrs. S. Upton Batterson (Kate Meek), that he is going to inspect his plantation in Cuba. Of course, he has no plantation. But the ladies insist on joining him on one of his trips. They also find an incriminating letter in his coat pocket. Luckily, it's addressed to one Mr. Johnson, who, Billings quickly remarks, is his overseer. In Cuba, Billings manages to "borrow" a friend's hacienda and the party even meets a cantankerous man named Johnson (Ralph Delmore). By the final curtain Billings has squirmed his way out of a series of uncomfortable situations.

Based on a French play, *La Plantation Thomasin,* the work was one of Gillette's biggest hits and one of his few attempts at comedy.

Toodles, The, a play in one act by William E. Burton. ♦ Produced by Burton at Burton's Chambers Street Theatre. October 2, 1848. In repertory.

Timothy Toodle (Burton) is a lovable, easy-going man with a peculiar wife (Mrs. Vernon♦). She has a penchant for buying useless things at auctions in the belief that she will sometime find a use for them. For example, she brings home a doorplate with the name of Thompson on it, suggesting that if they ever have a daughter and if that daughter marries a man named Thompson and he spells his name with a "p," then the doorplate will come in handy. Determined to put an end to such wasteful expense, Toodle attends an auction and brings home a coffin, in case his wife dies before he does.

Based on a sentimental old play, *The Broken Heart; or, the Farmer's Daughter,* it took that piece's comic relief for its main theme and made the principal story of the old play its subplot. It gave Burton one of his greatest successes, which he continued to play in until his death. Other comedians also found applause with the work, notably John Sleeper Clarke. ♦

Topsy and Eva, a musical comedy in three acts. Book by Catherine Chisholm Cushing. ♦ Lyrics and music mostly by the Duncan Sisters. ♦ Produced at the

Sam H. Harris Theatre. December 23, 1924. 165 performances.

This lighthearted song and dance version of *Uncle Tom's Cabin,* ♦ with the emphasis, as the title suggested, on Topsy (Rosetta Duncan) and Eva (Vivian Duncan), opened in Chicago, where it was a surprise hit and ran 46 weeks before coming to New York. Despite its relatively short New York run it was exceptionally popular on the road and toured for much of the rest of the decade. The sisters revived it as late as the 1940s. Its hit song was "Rememb'ring."

Torch-Bearers, The, a comedy in three acts by George Kelly. ♦ Produced at the 48th Street Theatre. August 30, 1922. 135 performances.

Paula Ritter (Mary Boland♦) is a devotee of the rising little theatre movement, and so is delighted to be cast at the last minute to replace another amateur whose husband died of a heart attack after watching his wife try to act. Paula's own husband Fred (Arthur Shaw) is none too happy with his wife's obsession. Nor does he care for the director, a haughty, dictatorial, frustrated actress named Mrs. J. Duro Pompinelli (Alison Skipworth), who has never gotten over the small success of her book, "Method in Acting as Distinguished from Technique." During the performance everything goes wrong, so Paula reluctantly agrees to Fred's request that she abandon the stage.

Stark Young♦ called it a play "of real wit," prophesying, "The chances are that Mr. Kelly, if he remembers what is joyous, will be our best writer of comedy." Despite its merits and excellent notices, the play had only a modest run, but it long remained a favorite of the very groups it satirized.

Torch Song Trilogy, a bill of three one-act plays by Harvey Fierstein. Produced at the Actors Playhouse. January 15, 1982. 1,222 performances.

The International Stud—Arnold (Fierstein), a female impersonator, thinks that with Ed (Joel Crothers), a man he picks up in a homosexual bar, he may have found the love he has been looking for.

Fugue in a Nursery—Ed is now engaged to Laurel (Diane Tarleton), who invites Arnold and his new lover, Alan (Paul Joynt), to Ed's farm, where things do not quite work out.

Widows and Children First!—Several years later Ed's marriage is on the rocks and he seeks to reestablish his relationship with Arnold, who, in turn, has taken up with David (Matthew Broderick), a teen-ager he plans to adopt. The arrival of Arnold's mother, Mrs. Beckoff (Estelle Getty), complicates matters for everyone.

Essentially a compassionate, if darkly funny, view of the various aspects of male homosexuality, this long evening was successful enough to be transferred to Broadway at the end of its first season, and later to win a Tony Award♦ as the season's best play. Fierstein (b. 1954), a native of Brooklyn, became a female impersonator at fifteen. He wrote several other plays before this, his first major success. He later wrote the book for *La Cage aux Folles*♦ (1983).

Tortesa, the Usurer, a play in five acts by Nathaniel Parker Willis. ♦ Produced at the National Theatre. April 8, 1839. 6 performances.

The usurer Tortesa (James W. Wallack♦) so loves Isabella (Virginia Monier), the daughter of Count Falcone (Mr. T. Matthews), that he buys up and gives Falcone all the mortgages on the Count's lands. But Isabella loves a young painter, Angelo (E. S. Conner), and plays dead rather than marry Tortesa. Impressed, Tortesa relinquishes his claim on her, stating, "She's taught me that the high-born may be true."

Although Odell♦ dismissed this blank-verse as "a very silly tragi-comedy," it remained popular for about a decade.

Touch of the Poet, A, a play in four acts by Eugene O'Neill. ♦ Produced at the Helen Hayes Theatre. October 2, 1958. 284 performances.

Cornelius Melody (Eric Portman), who keeps an inn near Boston, is a tyrannical, boozy Irishman living off memories of his past importance. As a young soldier he fought with Wellington at Waterloo. He dominates his submissive wife Nora (Helen Hayes♦) and even his more forthright, aggressive daughter Sara (Kim Stanley♦). Melody regards his neighboring Yankees as beneath contempt, so when Sara is spurned by the son of a rich New Englander, he sets out to avenge the slight. Instead, he is beaten and humiliated. Returning home, he shoots his beloved old mare, thereby severing a last small link with his past.

Destined as part of the eleven-play cycle which O'Neill never finished, the play "has substance, a point of view, human principle and theatre," as Brooks Atkinson♦ observed.

Tower Beyond Tragedy, The, a poetic drama in two acts by Robinson Jeffers. ♦ Produced by the American National Theatre and Academy♦ at the ANTA Theatre. November 26, 1950. 32 performances.

Clytemnestra (Judith Anderson♦) has long hated her husband Agamemnon (Frederic Tozere). While he is away at war she falls in love with Aegisthus (Philip Ruston). On Agamemnon's return, Clytemnestra and Aegisthus murder him. She, in turn, is slain by her son, Orestes (Alfred Ryder), to avenge his father's death.

The play, which was based on Aeschylus' *Oresteia,* had first been staged a year earlier in California. Despite many glowing notices, it failed to find a public.

TOWSE, J[OHN] RANKIN (1854–1933) Born in Streatham, England, and educated at Cambridge, he began his theatrical career as a spear-carrier in London productions. He came to America in 1869, taking a job with the New York *Evening Post.* Five years later he was made the paper's drama critic. He held the position for 54 years, until his retirement in 1927. Like his close friend William Winter, ♦ he was an arch-conservative and highly pedantic. Although he leaned over backwards to be fair, it became clear with the passing years that he found less and less sympathy with modern theatre. On his retirement he issued a violent denunciation of what he considered the theatre's descent into immorality and cheapness. His memoirs, *Sixty Years of the Theatre* (1916), extolled the palmy days of Edwin Booth♦ and the Wallacks.

Toys in the Attic, a play in three acts by Lillian Hellman. ♦ Produced by Kermit Bloomgarden♦ at the Hudson Theatre. February 25, 1960. 556 performances. NYDCCA.

Carrie (Maureen Stapleton♦) and Anna Berniers (Anne Revere) are two spinsters who live in genteel poverty and who have few pleasures in life except their ne'er-do-well brother Julian (Jason Robards, Jr.♦). When he marries and seems on the verge of making an illicit fortune, the sisters become frightened of losing him. The battle between the sisters and Julian's wife, Lily (Rochelle Oliver), drives the sisters apart, destroys Julian's scheme to get rich, and destroys Julian as well. No one gives any credence to his promise to start again.

The play was Miss Hellman's last hit before she abandoned the theatre. It displayed her knife-sharp insight into human rapacity and sexual longing.

TRACY, LEE (1898–1968) The exuberant, red-headed actor was born in Atlanta, Ga., and made his debut as Joe in *The Show-Off*♦ (1924). He is best remembered for two early roles, Roy Lane, the spunky hoofer, in *Broadway*♦ (1926), and Hildy Johnson, the even spunkier newsman, in *The Front*

Page♦ (1928). His last important assignment was as Arthur Hockstader, the sharp-tongued ex-President, in *The Best Man*♦ (1960).

TRACY, SPENCER, see *Last Mile, The*

Traveling Salesman, The, a comedy in four acts by James Forbes. ♦ Produced by Henry B. Harris♦ at the Liberty Theatre. August 10, 1908. 280 performances.

Beth Elliott (Gertrude Coghlan) runs the depot at Grand Crossing. Although the local citizenry thinks she is "jest as smart as a steel trap," she is naïve enough to hope that no one will bid against her when her family property is auctioned off for back taxes. Bob Blake (Frank McIntyre♦), a traveling salesman, arrives in town. He is immediately taken with Beth, and she with him. But a group of sharpies who are determined to buy the Elliott property make it appear that Bob has cheated Beth out of the land. By the time she realizes Bob is innocent, she has accepted the crooks' check, thereby apparently sealing a deal. Bob advises her to give the crooks a dose of their own medicine, but she refuses. However, when Bob learns that no married woman in the state can execute a deed without her husband's signature, an obvious and happy way out is found.

Much of the earlier acts of the play were devoted to vignettes of contemporary small-town life, and developed the plot at what today would seem an unacceptably leisurely pace. Yet the charm of the piece and an excellent production made it one of the major successes of its time.

TREADWELL, SOPHIE, see *Machinal*

Treasure Island, a play in four acts by Jules Eckert Goodman. ♦ Produced at the Punch and Judy Theatre. December 1, 1915. 205 performances.

Young Jim Hawkins (Mrs. Charles Hopkins) finds himself sailing to a far away island in search of buried treasure.

Mounted at a bandbox theatre as a Christmas treat for children, the adaptation of Robert Louis Stevenson's famous novel proved a huge success.

TREE, ELLEN (1805–80) The romantic English actress made her American debut at the Park Theatre♦ in 1836 as Rosalind. Many considered her a great beauty, albeit some, such as Ireland,♦ complained of her elongated neck and slightly stooped shoulders. Similarly, her acting divided critics, many considering her art not yet fully

developed. Nevertheless, in the three years she remained here she proved a major attraction for playgoers. Among her roles were Lady Teazle, Letitia Hardy (*The Lyons Mail*), Julia (*The Hunchback*♦), and Marianna (*The Wife*). After marrying Charles Kean♦ she made two later visits, in 1845 and 1864. Whatever beauty she had possessed had faded, but her acting had noticeably matured. On these returns she offered her Beatrice, Ophelia, and Portia, as well as playing leading roles in numerous popular contemporary pieces.

TREE, HERBERT BEERBOHM [né HERBERT DRAPER BEERBOHM] (1853–1917) The esteemed English actor-manager made several American visits, the first in 1895 and the last in 1916. However, he never won the admiration accorded him in London. Here his productions were seen as overblown, and his acting as shallow. He thought Americans and especially American drama critics savagely rude, and he despised American unions. With something of the wit of his brother, Max, he remarked, "The man of property is subject to the will of the property-man."

Biography: *Beerbohm Tree: His Life and Laughter,* Hesketh Pearson, London, 1956.

Tree Grows in Brooklyn, A, a musical in two acts. Book by Betty Smith and George Abbott. ♦ Lyrics by Dorothy Fields. ♦ Music by Arthur Schwartz.♦ Produced by Abbott at the Alvin Theatre. April 19, 1951. 267 performances.

Handsome Johnny Nolan (Johnny Johnston) is a ne'er-do-well whose marriage to sweet, adoring Katie (Marcia Van Dyke) can only come to an unhappy end. At the same time, Aunt Cissy (Shirley Booth♦) keeps dreaming of her long-lost love, a gentleman of singular refinement. But when she encounters him again after many years, her dreams, too, are shattered.

Principal songs: He Had Refinement · I'll Buy You a Star · I'm Like a New Broom · Look Who's Dancing · Make the Man Love Me

The musical version of Miss Smith's novel had uncommonly fine songs and a brilliant, wistfully comic performance by Miss Booth, who stopped the show nightly with "He Had Refinement." But it also had a long, tedious, and unnecessary ballet, and the misfortune to open in a season of stronger than usual competition.

TRENTINI, EMMA (1881?–1959) The petite, fiery singer was reputedly born in the slums of Mantua and was singing in a Milanese cabaret when Oscar

Hammerstein♦ discovered her. He signed her to appear with his Manhattan Opera Company, where she performed from 1906 until Hammerstein sold out in 1910. He then starred her in his mounting of Victor Herbert's♦ *Naughty Marietta*♦ (1910), in which she introduced "Ah, Sweet Mystery of Life" and "Italian Street Song." Herbert's biographer, Edward N. Waters, using, in part, comments of contemporary critics, noted "her vocalization was 'uncommonly brilliant,' her high notes were clear and birdlike, and her manner was 'sprightly, magnetic and vivacious.' " However, her success made her so arrogant and difficult to deal with that Herbert refused to write another operetta for her. That assignment fell to young Rudolf Friml,♦ in whose *The Firefly*♦ (1912) she sang "Giannina Mia" and "Love Is Like a Firefly." She later appeared in *The Peasant Girl* (1915) and in vaudeville, but having alienated virtually everyone who might help her, she left for London and then her homeland, where she died in relative poverty.

Trial of Mary Dugan, The, a play in three acts by Bayard Veiller.♦ Produced by A. H. Woods♦ at the National Theatre. September 19, 1927. 437 performances.

A *Follies* beauty, Mary Dugan (Ann Harding), is on trial for the murder of millionaire Edgar Rice. Her defense seems to be faltering until her young brother Jimmy (Rex Cherryman), a lawyer just beginning his career, insists he himself replace her present lawyer, Edward West (Cyril Keightley). Mary admits to affairs with several men, but wins favor with the jury when she reveals that the money she received was used to provide Jimmy's education. After it is determined that Rice was stabbed to death by a powerful, left-handed man, Jimmy provides the reason for her initially weak defense. Rice, it seems, was murdered by attorney West, who loved Mary and who was furious at Mary's preferring the millionaire.

Time remarked that the play "moves more swiftly than the law with all its ruthless directness. Its plot has the fascinating features of a front-page murder story."

Triangle Club This theatrical organization was founded at Princeton University in 1888 as the Princeton Dramatic Association. Its first musical was *The Honorable Julius Caesar* (1890), on which Booth Tarkington♦ collaborated. It adopted its present name in 1893. Since then it has specialized in all-student musicals, many of which have toured. It is the only one of such collegiate groups whose musicals have produced a song of widespread, lasting popularity. "East of the Sun (and West of the Moon)," with words and music by Brooks Bowman, came from its 1934 production, *Stags at Bay*. Among the group's members who later went on to theatrical renown are José Ferrer♦ and Joshua Logan. ♦

Tribute, a play in two acts by Bernard Slade. ♦ Produced at the Brooks Atkinson Theatre. June 1, 1978. 212 performances.

Friends have gathered at a theatre for a tribute to Scottie Templeton (Jack Lemmon) and to help him relive his best days. Scottie is a screenwriter, more interested in getting a laugh than in getting ahead. Somehow he has not even found time to have a proper relationship with his young son Jud (Robert Picardo). Now Scottie is dying of cancer. If he can do nothing else he determines he will at least come to emotional terms with the boy. He succeeds, and he and Jud hug each other as the tribute ends.

In the *Best Plays*♦ series, editor Otis L. Guernsey, Jr.,♦ noted that the "flawed script" was turned into a fine theatre piece by Lemmon's "towering performance."

Trilby, a play in four acts by Paul M. Potter.♦ Produced by A. M. Palmer♦ at the Garden Theatre. April 15, 1895. 208 performances.

Three artists, known as The Laird (John Glendinning), Taffy (Burr McIntosh), and Little Billee (Alfred Hickman), use a pretty model, Trilby O'Ferrall (Virginia Harned♦), for work in their Latin Quarter atelier. But after a fight with Billee, Trilby leaves and is befriended by the strange genius Svengali (Wilton Lackaye♦). Using his hypnotic powers, he turns the girl into a great opera singer. Billee recognizes her at a performance and asks her to abandon Svengali and marry him, but she refuses. However, when Svengali suddenly dies, Trilby's voice deserts her. She is reunited with Billee briefly. Unfortunately, her exertions under Svengali's influence coupled with the traumatic release from them prove too much. She withers and dies.

Based on the novel by George du Maurier, the adaptation was one of the greatest and more memorable successes of its era. The play still is revived, including a notable restaging in 1938 by Walter Hampden. ♦ It also provided the source for a musical which closed during its tryout, *The Studio Girl* (1927).

TRIMBLE, JOHN (1803?–67) A leading mid-19th-century architect and builder of theatres, he was born in New York and turned to the theatre only after brief stints in the navy and as a carpenter. It was as a carpenter that he took work at the Bowery Theatre♦ and later at the National. When the National burned he found himself unemployed, so began to design and erect playhouses. He built thirty-four auditoriums as far south as Charleston, S.C., and as far west as Buffalo. His New York City theatres included the Olympic, the Broadway, the 1845 rebuilding of the burned-out Bowery, Brougham's Lyceum, Laura Keene's, and Christy and Wood's. He continued to work until shortly before his death, although in his last years he was beset by increasing blindness.

Trinity Square Repertory Company (Providence, R.I.) One of the nation's leading regional theatres, it was founded in 1964 and performed for many years in a converted church before opening two new stages at a renovated film house during the 1973–74 season. It presents a varied bill of classics and new plays, with which it has also toured both nationally and in Europe. Since the departure of Adrian Hall♦ in 1989, it has suffered from a quick turnover of artistic directors. Its future is uncertain.

Trip to Chinatown, A; or, An Idyl of San Francisco, a musical in three acts. Book and most lyrics by Charles H. Hoyt.♦ Music by Percy Gaunt.♦ Produced by Hoyt at the Madison Square Theatre.♦ November 9, 1891. 657 performances.

To assuage the concern of their guardian Uncle Ben (George A. Beane), a group of youngsters who really plan a night on the city tell him they are going sightseeing in Chinatown. They have enlisted the aid of a chaperone, Mrs. Guyer (Anna Boyd), but her letter of acceptance reaches Ben, who thinks she is inviting him to an assignation. He goes to the restaurant which she has mentioned and at which the youngsters have booked a table. There he gets drunk, finds he has forgotten his wallet, but luckily misses the couples and Mrs. Guyer. When he would scold them for deceiving him, they let him know they are aware of his own little escapade.

Principal songs: After the Ball (an interpolation by Charles K. Harris) · The Bowery · Reuben and Cynthia

For nearly thirty years, until *Irene,*♦ this held the record as Broadway's longest-run musical. Its loose construction allowed for frequent changes in songs and minor principals. Loie Fuller,♦ for example, danced in it for a time. The immense success of "After the Ball," which was added by the manager of a road company playing in Milwaukee, furthered the musical's success. With this show, more than any

other, farce-comedy♦imperceptibly became musical comedy.

Trip to Niagara, A; or, Travellers in America, a play in three acts by William Dunlap.♦ Produced at the Bowery Theatre.♦ November 28, 1828. In repertory (see note below).

Two English visitors, Mr. Wentworth (John Fisher) and his sister Amelia (Mrs. Hughes), come to America on a visit with a fellow Englishman, John Bull (W. B. Chapman♦), and an Irishman, Dennis Dougherty (Henry Wallack♦). Wentworth likes nothing he sees, but his sister seems delighted by both the land and its citizens. Bull would like to marry Amelia, and she agrees provided he can get her brother to stop being critical. Bull succeeds and Wentworth proclaims, "When the film of prejudice is removed from the eye, man sees his fellow man of every clime a brother . . . we shall have reason to bless our Trip to Niagara."

The play was one of the first to give credit in its programs and advertisements to its designers. In a way, though not common practice at the time, this was only natural since even Dunlap confessed he had written the work as a "running accompaniment to the more important product of the Scene-painter." The panoramic effects made this one of the earliest important American spectacles and gave Dunlap, ironically, his biggest commercial success. The piece was played almost continually from its premiere until January 14, 1829, but thereafter only rarely. The theatre, however, reused the panoramas for other plays.

Triumph at Plattsburg, The, a play in two acts by Richard Penn Smith.♦ Produced at the Chestnut Street Theatre♦ (Philadelphia). January 8, 1830. In repertory.

In order both to elude the British and to find his missing daughter Elinor (Mrs. Roper), Major McCrea (Mr. Foot) dons the clothes of André Macklegraith (Mr. Maywood) and poses as the half-wit son of Mrs. Macklegraith (Mrs. Turner). Elinor has fled after marrying British Captain Stanley (Mr. Rowbotham), whom she now believes has deserted her. Her arrival at the mill threatens to expose her father, but he escapes. He encounters Stanley, who proves his affections for Elinor are genuine.

Set against the background of the War of 1812, this well-constructed but extremely short comedy-drama was turned into a full evening's entertainment by the inclusion of such spectacular scenes as "a view of the Arrival and Capture of the British Fleet." For all its brevity, many scholars consider it the best of Smith's historical plays.

Triumphs of Love, The; or, Happy Reconciliation, a four-act comedy by John Murdock (1749–1834), who was said to be a Philadelphia barber. The play was produced at the New Theatre in that city on May 22, 1795. Set loosely against the background of the Whiskey Rebellion and the troubles with Algiers, it directed much of its social satire against the inbreeding of the Quakers, as exemplified by the Friendly family. The play has miminal literary merit. Its importance rests with its being the first professionally produced play in America to deal with the Society of Friends as well as the first to have an American Negro in its cast of characters. This figure was Sambo, a slave whom George Friendly frees during the story. As was the practice at the time, the character was portrayed by a white actor in blackface. If Murdock was in fact a barber he must have been a fairly affluent and versatile one, since he had published at his own expense not only this play but two others which he wrote: *The Politicians; or, A State of Things* (1798), a plea for strong government, and *The Beau Metamorphized* (1800), a farce.

TRUEX, ERNEST (1889–1973) The small, raspy-voiced actor whose stage career spanned over seventy years was born in Rich Hill, Mo., where he made his first appearance as a child prodigy in 1894. He played many years in stock before his New York debut in 1908. His small stature and youthful looks were responsible for his being cast in young boy roles even when he was in his twenties. Among his notable roles were Charles MacLance, whom fairies rescue from a wicked aunt, in *A Good Little Devil* (1913); Barney Cook, the boy detective who solves a kidnapping, in *The Dummy*♦ (1914); the musical *Very Good Eddie*♦ (1915), in which he introduced "Babes in the Wood" and "Size Thirteen Collar"; Gilbert Sterling, the young husband pressured into living beyond his means, in *Six-Cylinder Love*♦ (1921); Johnny Quinlan, the title role in *The Fall Guy*♦ (1925); Kinesias in a 1930 revival of *Lysistrata;* Wallace Porter, the mystery writer forced to concoct a perfect alibi for his kidnappers, in *Whistling in the Dark* (1932); and Newton Fuller, a city man who attempts to move to the country, in *George Washington Slept Here*♦ (1940). Although he continued acting for another quarter-century, including roles with the American Repertory Theatre♦ in 1946, he never again was in a long-run success.

TRZCINSKI, EDMUND, see *Stalag 17*

TUCKER, SOPHIE [née SONIA KALISH] (1884–1966) Long billed as "The Last of the Red-Hot Mamas," the buxom, brash, blonde singer gave her birthplace as either Russia or Poland. She was still a babe in arms when her parents brought her to America. Within a few years she was singing for customers in her parents' Hartford, Conn., restaurant. By 1906 she was performing in vaudeville. She played in the [*Ziegfeld*] *Follies of 1909*♦ and reached the Palace♦ in 1914. Among the songs she made famous were "After You've Gone," "My Yiddishe Mama," and "Some of These Days," which became her theme number. Vaudeville historians Charles and Louise Samuels wrote that she "had the biggest, brassiest voice of all. The beat in her voice made your heart pound with it, and in syncopated time. With the same gusto she sang everything from the sentimental ballad 'Mammy's Little Coal Black Rose' to her cathouse special, 'There's Company in the Parlor, Girls, Come On Down.' " From 1919 to 1941 she appeared in half a dozen Broadway musicals, most notably *Leave It to Me!*♦ (1938). She continued to perform until her death, playing mostly night clubs in her last years.

Autobiography: *Some of These Days,* Garden City, 1945.

TULLY, RICHARD WALTON (1877–1945) The playwright was born in Nevada City, Calif., and educated at the University of California. His first work, *The Strenuous Life,* was mounted briefly in Los Angeles by Oliver Morosco,♦ but never brought East. However, the men later combined again to score a major success with *The Bird of Paradise*♦ (1912), a story of a Hawaiian girl who commits suicide after her American lover deserts her. Its popularity prompted one of the most famous lawsuits in American theatrical history. A schoolteacher, Grace Fendler, sued, claiming the drama was plagiarized from her *In Hawaii.* She was awarded $608,000, but an appellate court reversed the decision and made her pay all legal costs. Tully's other successes were *The Rose of the Rancho*♦ (1906), dealing with the American takeover of the Southwest; *Omar the Tentmaker* (1914), recounting the adventures of the poet; and *The Flame* (1916), telling of Americans stranded among a barbarous Yucatan tribe. Tully directed some of his own plays, as well as directing and occasionally producing other men's works, notably *Poor Little Rich Girl* (1913), *The Masquerader* (1917), and *Keep Her Smiling* (1918). A few later works met with little success.

Recognizing that his brand of melodramatic romance had lost its appeal to playgoers, Tully worked for a while in films and became a noted rancher and breeder of horses.

TUNE, TOMMY (b. 1939) A native of Wichita Falls, Texas, the lanky, attractive if slightly effete actor, director, and choreographer made his Broadway debut in the chorus of *Baker Street* (1965). In 1973 he won a Tony Award♦ for his supporting performance in *Seesaw*. He was a choreographer and co-director for *The Best Little Whorehouse in Texas*♦ (1978), then won another Tony for his choreography of *A Day in Hollywood/A Night in the Ukraine* (1980), which he also directed. He directed *Nine*♦ (1982), and later served as co-star, co-choreographer, and co-director of *My One and Only* (1983). He subsequently staged and choreographed *Stepping Out* (1987) and *Grand Hotel* (1989). Off-Broadway♦ he staged such long-running plays as *The Club* (1976) and *Cloud 9* (1981).

TUNICK, JONATHAN (b. 1938) A New Yorker who studied at Julliard, he has, usually alone but sometimes with others, orchestrated such shows as *Promises, Promises*♦ (1968), *A Little Night Music*♦ (1973), *A Chorus Line*♦ (1975), *Pacific Overtures*♦ (1976), *Sweeney Todd*♦ (1979), *Nine*♦ (1982), *Baby* (1983), and *Into the Woods* (1987). His work exemplifies the best in the modern Broadway sound, using not only contemporary harmonies and instrumentation, but also electronics, which have pervaded the musical theatre during the last several decades.

Turn to the Right!, a play in three acts by Winchell Smith♦ and John E. Hazzard. Produced by Smith and John Golden♦ at the Gaiety Theatre. August 18, 1916. 435 performances.

When Joe Bascom (Forrest Winant) is released from prison after serving time for a crime he did not commit, he returns to the peach farm owned by his widowed mother (Ruth Chester). He does not tell his family where he has passed the last year, nor does he tell them the truth about the two friends he brings with him—his prison-mates Muggs (William E. Meehan) and Gilly (Frank Nelson). Although one was an expert at opening safes and the other was a pickpocket, both are determined to go straight. However, when they learn that the devious Deacon Tillinger (Samuel Reed) is using legal technicalities to take the farm from Mrs. Bascom, they resort to their old ways for one final time. They open the deacon's safe, take precisely the money he is

demanding, pay it to him, pick his pocket, then return the money to the safe. Mrs. Bascom is shown how to make enough income from her fruit jams to remain solvent, and Joe and his buddies all win the hands of local girls. Everything is just peachy.

This clean, homey comedy was one of the biggest hits of its era. It was John Golden's first success, and he noted in his 1930 autobiography that it "has been playing continuously for 15 years." A 1981 musical version failed on the West Coast despite President Ronald Reagan's attempt to have a Los Angeles critic promote it.

Hazzard (1881–1935) was a New Yorker. Although better known as a comedian, he also wrote several other less successful plays and musical comedy books.

Twain, Mark, see *Ah Sin*

Twelfth Night Shakespeare's barbed attack on prudery and hypocrisy apparently was first presented to Americans in Boston in 1794. The work did not always sit well with Victorian morality, but there were notable productions in the 19th century. These included Ellen Tree's♦ 1837 revival, her 1845 revival with her husband Charles Kean,♦ William Burton's♦ 1851 mounting, and several productions at Wallack's♦ and Daly's.♦ Among the important 20th-century productions were those in 1905 with Julia Marlowe♦ and E. H. Sothern♦ (with many critics considering his unctuous Malvolio a high point of his career), and in 1940 with Helen Hayes♦ and Maurice Evans.♦ The successful rock musical, *Your Own Thing* (1968), was a skillful lyric version.

Twentieth Century, a play in three acts by Ben Hecht♦ and Charles MacArthur.♦ Produced by George Abbott♦ and Philip Dunning♦ at the Broadhurst Theatre. December 29, 1932. 152 performances.

In desperate need of a success to recoup both his fortune and his reputation, the flamboyant, egomaniacial producer, Oscar Jaffe (Moffatt Johnston), books a compartment on the famous train the Twentieth Century Limited. He hopes not only to elude his persistent creditors, but also to sign the fading screen star, Lily Garland (Eugenie Leontovich), who has booked a neighboring compartment. Lily, he feels, owes him one, since he had taken her when she was merely Mildred Plotka and made her his star and his mistress. His plan is to have her play Mary Magdalene in his production of *The Passion Play*. A check from a fanatically religious millionaire, Matthew Clark (Etienne Girardot◆), would seem to assure his production. Although the check proves worthless when Clark is shown to be a harmless mental case, Jaffe manages to sign Lily in the midst of one of their tempestuous battles.

Percy Hammond◆ wrote, "Show business gets a cruel razzing from *20th Century* . . . in which those impish bad boys of the Drama kick it urgently on its pants and inspire, thereby, much hilarity." The play was a reworking of Charles Bruce Millholland's unproduced comedy, *The Napoleon of Broadway.* Millholland had worked for Morris Gest,◆ and his play's central figure satirized both Gest and Gest's father-in-law, David Belasco.◆ When Hecht and MacArthur took over they added some touches of Jed Harris◆ to their leading figure. John Barrymore◆ and Carole Lombard headed the film cast. The play was successfully revived in 1950 with Gloria Swanson and José Ferrer.◆ Later it became the basis of the musical *On the Twentieth Century* (1978), written by Betty Comden◆ and Adolph Green,◆ with music by Cy Coleman,◆ and with John Cullum and Madeleine Kahn as Jaffe and Lily. A high point of the evening was Robin Wagner's set re-creating the famous old train, which led *Variety*◆ to begin its notice, "It's ominous when an audience leaves a musical whistling the scenery"—only partly true, for the score was tuneful and the evening good fun. A 1987 revival of the musical folded on the road.

Twin Beds, a farce in three acts by Salisbury Field and Margaret Mayo.◆ Produced by William Harris, Jr.,◆ at the Fulton Theatre. August 14, 1914. 411 performances.

Complications begin when an intoxicated Italian tenor, Signor Monti (Charles Judels), wanders by mistake into the room of Blanche (Madge Kennedy◆) and Harry Hawkins (John Westley), a floor below his own. By the time Blanche comes home Signor Monti is all but undressed. She persuades him to put his clothes back on, only to find the all-too-efficient maid Norah (Georgie Lawrence) has removed them for cleaning. Naturally, Harry arrives and is furious. But when he warns Monti that a scandal could follow and Monti's picture appear in the paper, the befuddled tenor can only thank him for offering him some much-needed publicity. Signora Monti (Ray Cox), an Amazonian harridan, also enters and also misunderstands. They are screaming at each other when the curtain falls.

Greeted as one of the best comedies in years, the play was threatened with bad business by the outbreak of the war. Harris arranged one of the wildest publicity campaigns Broadway had ever known, including dray wagons and trucks with the name of the show plastered on their sides, which conveniently broke down at well-travelled intersections. The play soon caught on and became one of the era's most popular comedies.

Two for the Seesaw, a play in three acts by William Gibson.◆ Produced at the Booth Theatre. January 16, 1958. 750 performances.

Having had a falling out with his wife in Omaha, Jerry Ryan (Henry Fonda◆) finds himself lonely and adrift in New York. He calls a young girl for a date. She turns out to be a warmhearted but aggressively bohemian Jewish girl, Gittel Mosca (Anne Bancroft◆). A romance ensues, but in the end different backgrounds and different interests send them on their separate ways.

One of the best of the many two-character plays that inundated Broadway in this period, it combined, as Louis Kronenberger◆ noted, "the capacities of an author with the mere commonplaces of a situation; and though it did not falsify its ending, it oversentimentalized it." The play later became the source of the musical *Seesaw* (1973), adapted by Michael Bennett◆ and with Cy Coleman's◆ music and Dorothy Fields's◆ lyrics. Ken Howard and Michele Lee played the leads.

Two Mrs. Carrolls, The, a play in two acts by Martin Vale. Produced at the Booth Theatre. August 3, 1943. 585 performances.

Geoffrey Carroll (Victor Jory) is a psychopathic artist living with his wife Sally (Elizabeth Bergner◆) in the south of France. While Sally mysteriously weakens, the unfaithful Geoffrey has an affair with Cecily Harden (Irene Worth◆). Geoffrey's first wife, Harriet (Marjory Clark), visits Sally and warns her that Geoffrey had once tried to kill her with a slow-working poison. Sally alerts her friend, Guy Pennington (Richard Stapley), who locks Geoffrey in the house and calls the police. Geoffrey takes a lethal dose of his own poison.

Martin Vale was the pen name for Marguerite Vale Veiller, the widow of Bayard Veiller.◆ The play was first produced in England, but failed when the English version was tried out in America. Seven years later this rewritten version succeeded.

Two Orphans, The Called by Odell◆ "one of the greatest theatrical successes of all time in America," Hart Jackson's translation of Cormon and D'Ennery's◆ *Les Deux Orphelines* was first performed at the Union Square Theatre◆ in 1874. The work centered on two ladies, one blind, who come to Paris where they are accidentally separated. The blind girl falls into the clutches of a vicious harridan, while her sister is carted off by a lecherous nobleman. They suffer a variety of harrowing experiences before they are happily reunited. Kate Claxton♦ and Kitty Blanchard played the title roles. The work held the boards almost continually for the rest of the century and was given a major revival as late as 1926, when Fay Bainter♦ and Mary Nash♦ assumed the leading roles.

TYLER, Geoʀɢᴇ C[ʀᴏᴜsᴇ] (1867–1946) One of the American theatre's busiest producers, he was born near Chillicothe, Ohio, and had served as a reporter and editor for several Ohio newspapers before becoming the manager of James O'Neill.♦ In 1897 he joined with Theodore Liebler♦ to form Liebler and Co., which was soon one of the leading turn-of-the-century producers. Among its many notable productions were *The Christian*♦ (1898), *Sag Harbor*♦ (1900), *The Squaw Man*♦ (1905), *The Man from Home*♦ (1908), *Alias Jimmy Valentine*♦ (1910), and *The Garden of Allah*♦ (1911). The firm also brought to this country Mrs. Patrick Campbell,♦ Duse,♦ and Réjane.♦ A series of failures at the time of World War I brought about the dissolution of the company. For a time Tyler was associated with Klaw and Erlanger,♦ then in 1919 embarked on a career as an independent producer. His productions included *Clarence*♦ (1919), *Dulcy*♦ (1921), *To the Ladies*♦ (1922), *Merton of the Movies*♦ (1922), *Young Woodley* (1925), and *The Plough and the Stars* (1927). In the middle and late 1920s he mounted a series of important revivals, including, in 1928 alone, *She Stoops To Conquer, Diplomacy,*♦ *The Beaux' Stratagem, Jim the Penman,*♦ and *Macbeth.*♦ These were well received for the most part, but they were coupled with his presentations of unsuccessful new plays. Shortly thereafter he retired from the theatre. In just short of forty years he had mounted over 200 plays, but like so many other producers of his era, he died insolvent.

Autobiography: *Whatever Goes Up,* Indianapolis, 1934.

TYLER, Roʏᴀʟʟ (1757–1826) Born in Boston, he read for the law at Harvard, then served in the army before being admitted to the bar. On a visit to New York he saw a performance of *The School for Scandal* and, encouraged by Thomas Wignell,♦ wrote the first humorous American play to be professionally produced, *The Contrast*♦ (1787). A comedy of manners pitting American openness against foreign pretensions, it was followed a month later by the now lost *May Day in Town; or, New York in an Uproar.* This was a comic opera satirizing the annual practice of spring cleaning and moving. A much later comedy, *The Georgia Spec; or, Land in the Moon* (1797), is also lost, but is said to have spoofed the Yazoo frauds. He wrote a number of other plays which have left behind no record of production. These include *The Farm House; or, the Female Duellists,* which seems to have been an adaptation of an English comedy; *The Doctor in Spite of Himself,* apparently a translation of Molière; *The Island of Barrataria,* derived from *Don Quixote* and telling of Sancho Panza's comic attempts to be a governor; and three "sacred dramas," *The Origin of the Feast of Purim; or, The Destinies of Haman and Mordecai, Joseph and His Brethren,* and *The Judgement of Solomon.* In after years, he moved to Vermont, where he became that state's Chief Justice from 1807 to 1813 and also taught law at the University of Vermont. Although Tyler was clearly one of the most adept of contemporary gentlemen playwrights—*The Contrast* can still be performed effectively—his importance remains fundamentally historical.

TYNAN, Kᴇɴɴᴇᴛʜ [Pᴇᴀᴄᴏᴄᴋ] (1927–80) The noted English drama critic served as critic for the *New Yorker* from 1958 to 1960 and also was co-author of the long-running *Oh, Calcutta!*♦ (1969). Although generally perceived as an ardent modernist, he often worked quietly behind the scenes, especially in England, to restore neglected classics to the stage.

U

UHRY, ALFRED, see *Driving Miss Daisy*

ULRIC, LENORE [née LEONORA ULRICH] (1892–1970) A dark, volatile actress, at her best conveying sultry, impassioned women, she was born in New Ulm, Minn., and learned her trade in stock in Milwaukee, Chicago, and elsewhere. She first called national attention to herself when she toured in 1914 as the doomed Hawaiian princess in *The Bird of Paradise.* ◆ Her New York debut came a year later in *The Mark of the Beast* (1915). Although the play was a quick failure, her performances brought her to the notice of David Belasco. ◆ For the next fourteen years she appeared under his aegis, playing Wetona, the cruelly deceived Indian maiden, in *The Heart of Wetona* (1916); Rose Bocion, who saves her lover from a villainous policeman, in *Tiger Rose* ◆ (1917); Lien Wha, who strangles the man her father has sold her to, in *The Son-Daughter* (1919); and the saucy chorus girl who wins the hand of her producer, the title part in *Kiki* (1921). Alexander Woollcott ◆ said of her performance, "The relish and the fire and the comic spirit with which she undertakes the embodiment of the naive, ignorant, aspiring, ardent little Parisian chorus girl is a joy to behold." By now a full-fledged star, she continued under Belasco as Carla, who disguises herself as a Turkish princess to test her husband's loyalty, in *The Harem* (1924); as the doomed Harlem prostitute, the title role in *Lulu Belle* ◆ (1926); and the title role of the destructive siren in *Mima* (1928). After leaving Belasco she enjoyed one last success as Dot Hunter, the harlot who seduces a minister's son, in *Pagan Lady* (1930). Thereafter she continued to be busy, but was never again a star. Among her later roles were Anita, the Moorish whore, in *The Fifth Column* ◆ (1940) and Charmian to Katharine Cornell's ◆ Cleopatra in 1947.

Umpire, The, a musical comedy in two acts. Book and lyrics by Will M. Hough ◆ and Frank R. Adams. ◆ Music by Joseph Howard. ◆ Produced at the LaSalle Theatre (Chicago). December 2, 1905. 300 performances.

Johnny Nolan (Cecil Lean ◆) is an umpire who makes such an outrageous call in a crucial game that he is forced to flee. He runs all the way to Morocco. There he participates in a football game, where he not only redeems himself but wins the hand of the center, who turns out to be a young lady, Maribel Lewton (Florence Holbrook).

Principal songs: Cross Your Heart · I Want a Girl Like You · You Look Awful Good to Father

The first American musical to deal with baseball and football, the show established a Chicago long-run record (broken the next year by *The Time, the Place and the Girl* ◆). In fact, its run was longer than that of any musical in New York the same season, except for the Hippodrome ◆ extravaganza. More than any other musical it established the primacy of the tiny LaSalle as Chicago's principal home for locally written musicals, a primacy that lasted nearly a decade. The show apparently never played New York.

Unchastened Woman, The, a play in three acts by Louis Kaufman Anspacher. ◆ Produced by Oliver Morosco ◆ at the 39th Street Theatre. October 9, 1915. 193 performances.

Caroline Knollys (Emily Stevens ◆) is a selfish and unscrupulous woman. Caught making a false declaration at customs, she attempts to bribe Emily Madden (Willette Kershaw), a woman official, whom she knows to have once been the mistress of her husband Hubert (H. Reeves-Smith ◆). When she fails, she makes public the illicit liaison. She would also attempt to steal a young artist, Lawrence Sanbury (Hassard Short ◆), from his wife Hildegarde (Christine Norman). Although Hildegarde wins back Lawrence, and Hubert and Emily force Caroline to issue a statement recanting her charges, Caroline gives no hint that she is remorseful or will change her ways.

The success of this uncompromising look at a despicable woman surprised many. Walter Prichard Eaton ◆ saw the work as "a character study of a frivolous and selfish woman, gaining its appeal from that study rather than from mere narrative excitement, or farcical situation, or machine-made slang . . . it gives the players a chance to act, not to show off a few pretty personal tricks."

Uncle Harry, a play in three acts by Thomas Job. Produced at the Broadhurst Theatre. May 20, 1942. 430 performances.

Harry Quincey (Joseph Schildkraut♦) is a mild-mannered bachelor, dominated by his two spinster sisters, Lettie (Eva Le Gallienne♦) and Hester (Adelaide Klein), who call him "Uncle" Harry. Furious at their destroying his chance to marry Lucy Forrest (Beverly Roberts), he tricks Lettie into buying some poison and then has her serve it unwittingly to Hester in some cocoa. Lettie is sentenced to die for the murder. To Harry's dismay, Lucy will now have nothing to do with him. Remorsefully, he confesses the crime, but the authorities believe he is merely trying to save his sister. He visits Lettie in prison, where she refuses to reveal the truth. Harry thus is doomed to a life of loneliness and disgrace.

Richard Lockridge of the *Sun* called the work, "An admirably sinister murder play, slightly diabolical in its ingenuity and warranted to make the timid look hereafter with uneasy suspicion on all quiet little men." The Welsh-born Job (1900–1947) spent most of his career teaching drama at Yale, Carnegie Tech, and elsewhere. Although several other of his plays were produced, this was his only success.

Uncle Tom's Cabin, a play in six acts by George L. Aiken. ♦ Produced at Purdy's National Theatre. July 18, 1853. 325 performances.

George Harris (J. J. Prior) tells Eliza (Mrs. J. J. Prior) he is fleeing to Canada. Eliza then learns that she and her young son are to be put up for sale, so she informs Uncle Tom (J. Lingard) that she, too, must run away. She escapes by crossing an icy river. St. Clare (J. B. Howe) has bought Uncle Tom, who had saved the life of little Eva (Cordelia Howard♦). Eva is brought up with a small black girl, Topsy (Mrs. G. C. Howard), who has no conception of her origins and insists, "I 'spect I growed." The kindly Uncle Tom warns St. Clare that his drinking will cause problems, but St. Clare does not heed his advice. Although Harris and Eliza are reunited, St. Clare is stabbed to death by Simon Legree (N. B. Clare) before he can sign the papers freeing Uncle Tom and his other slaves. Legree proves a cruel master, but he is shot dead while resisting arrest for St. Clare's murder. Little Eva dies and is carried to heaven on the back of a milk-white dove.

Although numerous dramatizations of Harriet Beecher Stowe's famous novel were offered, all unauthorized, this was by far the most popular, and had established a long-run record of 100 nights in Troy, N.Y., before coming to Broadway. One modern editor, Richard Moody, dismissed the tendency of many writers and critics to look on the work disdainfully, noting, "The forces of right and wrong on the slavery issue—not the struggle between North and South—are clearly and vigorously exposed. The language has an irresistible strength and vitality, and the rich panorama compels us to sense the magnitude of a vicious and pervasive evil." The most popular theatre work of its era, it played a major role, along with the original novel, in stoking the fires of abolition. Aiken's version was said to be the first play offered on Broadway as an entire evening, without an afterpiece or any other entertainment. In one version or another it continued to tour the country for decades. There were forty-nine troupes in 1879 and no fewer than a dozen companies still active in 1927! The first year not to see a full tour is believed to be 1930. Many actors and families made careers of the play. They were known as "tommers" and their trade as "tomming."

Under Cover, a play in four acts by Roi Cooper Megrue. ♦ Produced by Selwyn and Co. ♦ at the Cort Theatre. August 26, 1914. 349 performances.

A man known as Steven Denby (William Courtenay♦) has smuggled a valuable necklace into the country. He hides it in his room at the home of friends he is visiting. Inspector Daniel Taylor (De Witt C. Jennings) is determined to retrieve the jewels and threatens to jail the sister of Denby's fiancée, Ethel Cartwright (Lily Cahill), for a crime the sister inadvertently committed, if Ethel does not help trap Denby. Denby appears to walk into the trap, but turns the tables by disclosing his real identity and the significance of the jewels.

A tautly made thriller, it used the then novel device of having much of the action of the last act take place while the action of the third act was supposedly going on.

Under the Gaslight, a play in five acts by Augustin Daly. ♦ Produced at the New York Theatre. August 13, 1867. 47 performances.

Laura Cortlandt (Rose Eytinge♦) is jilted by her lover, Captain Ray Trafford (A. H. Davenport), when he discovers she is merely an adopted daughter and actually of humble parentage. Laura runs away from home but is hauled into court, where the villainous Byke (J. B. Studley♦) claims she is his child and so is given custody of her. He attempts to take her to New Jersey, but is stopped by a one-armed ex-soldier, Snorkey (J. K. Mortimer), and the recreant Trafford. In the tussle Byke throws Laura into the river. She swims to safety, then returns to the family who adopted her. The furious Byke decides to rob the Cortlandt home. Snorkey overhears his plans, but Byke catches him and ties him to the railroad tracks, knowing an express train will pass by shortly. Laura happens on the tethered man and releases him just as the train comes. She returns home to settle down with Trafford.

The famous railroad track scene was said to have been borrowed by Daly from an 1865 English play, *The Engineer.* Although Daly was able to patent the effect, it soon became a staple of cheap melodrama and later of early films.

Under the Red Robe, a play in four acts by Edward E. Rose. ♦ Produced by Charles Frohman ♦ at the Empire Theatre. ♦ December 28, 1896. 216 performances.

When Gil de Berault (William Faversham ♦) twice violates the strictures against dueling imposed by Cardinal Richelieu (J. E. Dodson), the Cardinal demands that either he betray the brother of his sweetheart, Renée de Cochefort (Viola Allen ♦), or forfeit his life. The clever Berault manages to get the best of the Cardinal and live.

Based on a novel by Stanley Weyman, the play was offered by Frohman in London before he brought it to New York. It was the source of the 1928 musical *The Red Robe.*

Under Two Flags, a play in five acts by Paul M. Potter. ♦ Produced by Charles Frohman ♦ and David Belasco ♦ at the Garden Theatre. February 5, 1901. 135 performances.

Cigarette (Blanche Bates ♦) is a spunky camp follower, or *vivandière,* in the bleak, French-occupied mountains of North Africa. To defend her country and win her man, she will even fight off a host of Bedouins or ride her horse, Cochise, through a duststorm in the Chellelah Gorge. Needless to say, she wins her man.

Although other dramatizations of Ouida's novel had been touring the country for several years, this was the first to play in a major New York house.

Union Square Theatre Briefly one of the most famous of New York theatres, it was situated in the middle of the block between Broadway and Fourth Avenue, on 14th Street, part of the old Morton House. It was designed by H. M. Sims for Sheridan Shook, who opened it in 1871 as a variety theatre. When vaudeville failed to attract, he turned over management to A. M. Palmer ♦ in 1872. Palmer established a fine stock company there, and for the next eleven years the house vied with those of

Daly ♦ and Wallack ♦ in prestige. While the other two were best known for comedy, the Union Square enjoyed most of its great successes with the romantic dramas of the time. Among the theatre's major hits, all French in origin, were Sardou's *Agnes,* Clara Morris ♦ in *Camille,* and *The Two Orphans.* After Palmer moved his company further north in 1883 the house's reputation began to fade. Destroyed by fire in 1888, the theatre was rebuilt, but the heart of the theatre district had moved away and before long the theatre was again a vaudeville house. It was later home to burlesque and to films. The shell of the old theatre, complete with stagehouse, remains on the site.

United Booking Office Founded at the turn of the century by B. F. Keith ♦ and E. F. Albee, ♦ and manipulated largely by the latter, it soon had a virtual stranglehold on major vaudeville bookings. Performers and theatres who resisted often found themselves out in the cold. When, for example, S. Z. Poli ♦ refused to join, Albee sent letters to banks in all towns where Poli had important theatres, advising them that Keith would soon be considering a theatre there which would undoubtedly ruin the existing vaudeville house. Banks called in Poli's loans, so he was forced to join the UBO. *Variety,* ♦ William Morris, ♦ and the White Rats ♦ were among the UBO's most formidable opponents, but it was not until the demise of vaudeville that the office's monopoly was really destroyed.

United Managers' Protective Association, see *Producing Managers' Association*

United Scenic Artists of America On September 11, 1885, the Protective Alliance of Scenic Painters of America was organized with Harley Merry as president and Richard Marston ♦ as chairman. The history of this group is obscure but it may have given rise to the United Scenic Artists of America, whose New York local was founded September 20, 1912, with the stated purpose "to promote fraternal feeling among its members, regulate working hours, obtain just compensation for the working day and for overtime and to cope with such other problems of mutual interest to its members as may from time to time arise." In 1918 it became affiliated with the Brotherhood of Painters, Decorators and Paperhangers of America (now the Brotherhood of Painters and Allied Trades). Membership is available not only to set designers but to costume and lighting designers as well.

United States Amusement Company A short-lived merger in 1907 of Erlanger♦ and the Shuberts,♦ supposedly designed to create their own vaudeville empire and buck the Keith♦ interests and the United Booking Office.♦ They sold out to their rivals, apparently their real intention, within the year.

UNITT, EDWARD G. (fl. late 19th and early 20th century) One of the busiest set designers of his day and a favorite of both Daniel♦ and Charles Frohman,♦ he kept a studio for many years in the former's Lyceum Theatre.♦ His work was extremely versatile but harder to characterize than that of many of his contemporaries. Among the plays for which he created sets were Bronson Howard's♦ *Aristocracy* (1892), *Under the Red Robe♦* (1896), *The Little Minister* (1897), *The Conquerors♦* (1898), *The Liars* (1898), *Barbara Frietchie♦* (1899), E. H. Sothern's♦ 1900 revival of *Hamlet,♦ David Harum♦* (1900), *Captain Jinks of the Horse Marines♦* (1901), *If I Were King♦* (1901), *Quality Street* (1901), *The Girl with Green Eyes♦* (1902), *The Red Mill♦* (1906), *A Grand Army Man♦* (1907), and *The Blue Bird* (1910).

University Players This was a group founded by Bretaigne Windust♦ and Charles Leatherbee in 1928 as the University Players Guild. Productions, mostly revivals, were given each summer through 1932 at Falmouth, Mass. In its last year the company changed its name to the Theatre Unit, Inc., and after a season at Falmouth played briefly in Baltimore. Among its many young figures who afterwards became famous were Henry Fonda,♦ Joshua Logan,♦ Myron McCormick, Mildred Natwick,♦ Kent Smith, James Stewart, and Margaret Sullavan.♦ Norris Houghton later wrote the history of the company in *But Not Forgotten.*

Unknown Purple, The, a play in a prologue and three acts by Roland West and Carlyle Moore. Produced by West at the Lyric Theatre. September 14, 1918. 273 performances.

A brilliant but socially naïve inventor, Peter Marchmont (Richard Bennett♦), spends years in prison after his unfaithful wife (Helen MacKellar) and her lover, James Dawson (Earle Brown), steal his latest invention and frame him for a crime he did not commit. On his release he determines not only to be revenged but to reclaim his young son, whom his wife has kept from him. To this end he invents a device that makes him invisible when pressed in his hand, leaving only an eerie purple light to suggest his whereabouts. Under the purple cloak of invisibility he wins retribution.

Apart from Bennett's superb performance, which delicately balanced both the gently loving and cruelly vindictive aspects of the hero, most critics were intrigued by the curious nature of the play. It profitably combined the universally popular "crook play" with a then much rarer element of science fiction, and added to these the suddenly voguish flashback device. Critics named various older plays and went as far back as Jules Verne for the inspiration of the science fiction portions of the play, but to a man they credited *On Trial♦* as the source for the flashbacks. *On Trial* had also been perceived as the model for *Forever After,♦* which had opened a week earlier, thus suggesting how striking and fresh was its employment of flashback technique. Moore (1875–1924), a native of Oakland, Calif., was an actor and playwright whose only other success was *Stop, Thief* (1912), in which crooks crash a wedding.

Up in Central Park, a musical in two acts. Book by Herbert♦ and Dorothy Fields.♦ Lyrics by Miss Fields. Music by Sigmund Romberg.♦ Produced by Michael Todd♦ at the Century Theatre. January 27, 1945. 504 performances.

Rosie Moore (Maureen Cannon), the daughter of a Tweed Ring politician, loves the muckraking reporter, John Matthews (Wilbur Evans), but after he writes an article exposing Mr. Moore and his cronies, Rosie breaks off their romance. She marries another man. Luckily, when she comes to her senses, she learns her new spouse is a bigamist, so she can still marry John.

Principal songs: April Snow · The Big Back Yard · Close as Pages in a Book

A solid Romberg score and Helen Tamiris's♦ memorable "Currier and Ives Ballet" helped make this show a smash hit. However, it returned to New York just as Brooks Atkinson♦ returned to his post on the *Times*. Atkinson perceived it as superannuated operetta and led a virulent attack on it, after which it fell out of favor.

Up in Mabel's Room, a farce in three acts by Wilson Collison and Otto Harbach.♦ Produced by A. H. Woods♦ at the Eltinge Theatre. January 15, 1919. 229 performances.

As a shy, worrying newlywed, Garry Ainsworth (John Cumberland♦) is loath to have anything disturb his bride, so when he remembers that he once gave a silk undergarment to an old flame, Mabel Essington (Hazel Dawn♦), he decides he must get it back immediately. He visits Mabel in her room, but has no sooner arrived than just about everybody he does not want to see appears.

"An amusing farce of the lingerie genre," as one critic put it, the comedy was one of a number of similar pieces that Woods mounted in these years.

Up She Goes, see *Too Many Cooks*

Upstairs and Down, a comedy in three acts by Frederic and Fanny Hatton.♦ Produced by Oliver Morosco♦ at the Cort Theatre. September 25, 1916. 320 performances.

At a giddy Long Island weekend party the hostess, Nancy Ives (Christine Norman), begins to wonder about the amorality and immorality of her social set. Her guests are petty, selfish, and self-deceiving. Two of them, sisters, Elizabeth and Alice Chesterton (Mary Servoss and Juliet Day), are good examples—lying and backbiting each other in their efforts to attract the same man, Terrence O'Keefe (Courtney Foote). Deciding she would be happier in a blue collar world, Nancy heads for the servant quarters. But there she finds the same meanness and backstabbing among the staff headed by the Ives's valet, Louis (Leo Carrillo). At least the rich people upstairs have the advantages of comfort and elegance.

Although the play vacillated between social satire and standard Broadway farce, it delighted playgoers not troubled by a sense of tone.

UPTON, Robert (fl. mid-18th century) Although he has been called "the first advance agent and business manager in America," little is known about his history. He was sent by the elder Hallam♦ to America in 1751 to prepare for the coming of the Hallam troupe. Instead he set up his own company, with himself and his wife as leading performers, and in 1751–52 gave a brief New York season. The repertory included the first known American mounting of *Othello,* ♦ as well as *Venice Preserved, Richard III,* ♦ and *The Provoked Husband.* The season failed, so rather than confront Hallam he sailed for England in February 1752. Thereupon he disappears from the records.

URBAN, Joseph (1872–1933) One of the greatest of all set designers, he was born in Vienna, where he later studied at the Art Academy under Baron Carl Hassauer and at the Polytechnicum. He first came to America to create the Austrian Pavilion for the 1904 St. Louis Fair. The Boston Opera Company brought him back in 1911 to design its sets, but it was his work on *The Garden of Paradise* (1914) that brought him to the attention of Florenz Ziegfeld♦ and launched his Broadway career. Although he designed sets for James K. Hackett's♦ Shakespearean revivals and other straight plays, it was his work on musicals for which he became famous. He created the sets for all the *Ziegfeld Follies* ♦ from 1915 to 1931 as well as such other shows as *Sally* ♦ (1920), *Sunny* ♦ (1925), *Rio Rita* ♦ (1927) *Show Boat* ♦ (1927), *The Three Musketeers* ♦ (1928), *Whoopee* ♦ (1928), and *Music in the Air* ♦ (1932). He was the first major designer to carefully coordinate colors and to employ subtle lighting to enhance his color schemes. Typical of the work of "Unfailing Urban" was his opening set for *Rosalie* (1928), in which a brown arch framed a brown village rising to a bluish-brown sea. His favorite color, and Ziegfeld's, was blue, and he gained fame for what became known as "Urban blue." He also designed several theatres, most notably the egg-shaped, boxless Ziegfeld Theatre,♦ with its magnificent murals and gilt stage. Away from the theatre he served as architect for numerous homes and buildings and also earned a reputation as an illustrator of children's books.

U.S.O., see *Stage Door Canteen*

V

Vagabond King, *The,* an operetta in four acts. Book by Brian Hooker,♦ W. H. Post, and Russell Janney. Lyrics by Hooker. Music by Rudolf Friml.♦ Produced by Janney at the Casino Theatre.♦ September 21, 1925. 511 performances.

When the disguised Louis XI (Max Figman) encounters the scoundrelly, silky-tongued poet, François Villon (Dennis King♦), he is at once so amused and annoyed by the man that he makes him "king for a day." In that one day the poet must woo and win Katherine de Vaucelles (Carolyn Thomson), or lose his head. Villon leads the Parisian rabble against the Burgundians and routs them to save Louis's kingdom. Huguette (Jane Carroll), a prostitute who has loved the poet, commits suicide so as not to stand in Villon's way. The king is moved, recognizing that none of his subjects would willingly make such a sacrifice for him. He allows Katherine and Villon to wed.

Principal Songs: Huguette Waltz · Only a Rose · Some Day · Song of the Vagabonds

A musicalization of Justin Huntly McCarthy's *If I Were King,*♦ the operetta was one of the most memorable of its era. It has been revived occasionally.

Valley Forge, a play in three acts by Maxwell Anderson.♦ Produced by the Theatre Guild♦ at the Guild Theatre. December 10, 1934. 58 performances.

Washington (Philip Merivale♦) has grown short-tempered watching his men starve and die in the cruel winter at Valley Forge and receiving no real aid from a narrow-minded, greedy Congress. When his old sweetheart, Mary Philipse (Margalo Gillmore♦), braves the storms to visit him, he agrees to a meeting with British General Howe (Reginald Mason) to arrange for a surrender. But when Howe arrives, Washington recognizes that the bravery of his own men demands he fight to the finish.

Supposedly written after several critics had complained that Anderson was more interested in English Elizabethan history than in his own, the play won generally laudatory notices, but could not find a public. Its imaginary meeting of Washington and Howe paralleled a similarly fictitious meeting of Mary and Elizabeth in *Mary of Scotland.*♦

VAN [Gus, né August Van Glone] (1888–1968) **and SCHENCK** [Joe, né Joseph T.] (1891?–1930) Childhood friends in their native Brooklyn, they served together as trolley-car conductor and motorman before entering vaudeville in 1910. Schenck played the piano and sang with his tenor voice in close harmony with Van, who excelled at dialect numbers. They were generally acknowledged as the best two-man "piano act" in vaudeville. The team also appeared in Broadway musicals, including *The Century Girl* (1916) and the 1919, 1920, and 1921 *Ziegfeld Follies.*♦ In their first *Follies* appearance they sang "Mandy," with which they were thereafter identified. Following Schenck's death, Van continued with a solo act.

VAN DAM, Rip (1660?–1749) He was the proprietor of what was possibly the first New York theatre. According to a newspaper account, dated December 11, 1732, "On the 6th instant, the *New Theatre* in the buildings of the Hon. Rip Van Dam, Esq. was opened with the comedy of the *Recruiting Officer.*" He served for a time as Governor of the Province of New York and had conducted a city census a year before this playhouse opened. His building was still used for occasional theatrical purposes as late as 1750.

VANDAMM, Florence (1883?–1966) The London-born photographer married an American photographer, George R. Thomas, in 1918. The pair came to New York in the early 1920s and quickly became leaders in theatrical photography, using the name Vandamm. Mr. Thomas specialized in on-stage pictures until his death in 1944, while Mrs. Thomas handled studio portraits. From 1944 until her retirement in 1950 she worked both at theatres and in her studio. The couple is said to have photographed nearly 2000 shows.

VANDENHOFF, George (1820–84) The son of John Vandenhoff,♦ he performed in England before making his American debut at the Park Theatre♦ in 1842 as Hamlet. A tall, manly actor, he remained a popular performer, largely in Shakespearean roles, until his retirement in 1856. Ireland♦ noted, "Although lacking the passion and intensity requisite for the loftiest assumptions of drama, Mr. Vandenhoff possessed all the accomplishments and elegances of mind and person demanded for the highest grades of genteel comedy and a wide range of serious parts somewhat subordinate to the standard of Shakespeare's subtlest creations. As a studied work of art, his Hamlet was nearly perfection in action, attitude and elocution, and his Claude Melnotte and Alfred Evelyn have been held in the esteem of many critics, as superior to any others seen on the American stage." He was also admired for his Hotspur, Falconbridge, and Benedick. After his retirement he practiced law for a time.

Autobiography: *An Actor's Notebook; or the Green-Room and Stage,* London, 1865.

VANDENHOFF, JOHN M. (1790–1861) The striking, deep-voiced tragedian was considered a major rival to Macready♦ when he made his American debut in 1837 as Coriolanus. Significantly, he was the first important foreigner not to first appear at the Park Theatre,♦ his debut coming at Wallack's♦ National. Among his other noteworthy roles were Macbeth, Pierre (*Venice Preserved*), Shylock, Brutus, and Hamlet. Although the *Knickerbocker* complained of his "over-weening desire to impress his audience with the astonishing consequence of every movement portrayed, and every syllable expressed," he found general acceptance during his several visits between his debut and 1844. James Murdoch♦ felt he was "the finest tragedian of the classic school of acting ever seen on the American stage" and observed of his Coriolanus, "There was a sharp ring in his voice and an incisive stroke in his utterance of command and rebuke that rung the words like a shot . . . while in his declamatory and deeply contemplative tones there were the stately pace of quantity and the measured flow of rhythm, which gave to his recitations a grace and dignity."

VAN DRUTEN, JOHN (1901–57) The London-born playwright originally planned a career in law, which he practiced and taught for a time. He was well known for such plays as *Young Woodley* (1925), *There's Always Juliet* (1932), and *The Distaff Side* (1934) prior to his coming to America. His best-received American works were *The Voice of the Turtle*♦ (1943), centering on the romance of a soldier on leave and an actress; *I Remember Mama*♦ (1944), a dramatization of Kathryn Forbes's stories of growing up in turn-of-the-century San Francisco; *Bell, Book and Candle*♦ (1950), a tale of a beautiful young witch who makes a publisher fall in love with her; and *I Am a Camera*♦ (1951), a dramatization of

Christopher Isherwood's *Berlin Stories,* which focused on an amoral young girl in early Nazi Germany. He was at his best as a witty, urbane observer of modern society.

Autobiography: *The Widening Circle,* New York, 1957.

Variety The leading contemporary theatrical journal, it was founded in 1905 by Sime Silverman♦ and has been published weekly ever since. As its title indicated, its original emphasis was on vaudeville, but it rapidly branched out to cover all aspects of what it called "show biz." It publishes weekly reports on the grosses and attendance at all major stage productions and devotes several pages to news of legitimate theatre, albeit in recent decades it has had to give far more coverage to films and television. Its theatrical reviews have generally been the most accurate in predicting the success or failure of shows, and at the end of each theatrical season it offers a detailed record of the year's statistics. It has long since become famous for such headlines as "Wall Street Lays An Egg" and "Stix Nix Hix Pix," the latter reflecting its distinctive verbal shorthand which also included such terms as "legits," "filmusicals," and "b.o." for box office figures. A *Daily Variety* is published on the West Coast. In 1987 the trade sheet was purchased by England's Cahners Publishing Co.

Vaudeville Comedy Club This was an attempt about 1901 by Percy G. Williams♦ to form an organization consisting largely of leading vaudeville comedians and to circumvent the policies of Keith♦ and Albee.♦ It was quickly quashed.

Vaudeville in America The term "vaudeville" in America has almost never had the same connotation as it had in the original French. Instead, it was borrowed rather late to indicate an entertainment consisting of short, variegated acts, some musical, some comic, all offered on the same bill. Small olios—another term for this sort of entertainment—appeared early in American stage history, usually as divertissements on the extended bills offered in the late 18th and the first half of the 19th century even in the best legitimate theatres. Nonetheless, most students see the real seeds of modern vaudeville in the "free concert saloons," "free-and-easies," and Western "honky-tonks" that sprang up in the years just before the Civil War. To lure customers—almost exclusively male, except for prostitutes—these establishments provided a series of acts whose tilt, both in its comedy and lyrics and in the presentation of its occasional dancing, was rough and often salacious.

In the 1870s and 1880s attempts began to clean up the nature of the bills so as to attract a more widespread, higher class audience. Although several impresarios apparently began to incorporate such changes at about the same time, the most famous was Tony Pastor,♦ who was hailed as the leader in the field and whose vaudeville house in New York was considered to offer the pinnacle in such entertainment. Like others, he banned the sale of intoxicating drinks, discouraged rowdiness, and removed any performer whose act was in any way offensive. About the same time, the term "vaudeville" began replacing the term "variety," which had been accepted for several decades. (A similar transition was occurring concurrently in the British equivalent, the music hall.)

The heyday of American vaudeville was the first quarter of the 20th century. The huge national circuit established by Keith♦ and Albee♦ was paramount in the field. Keith, like Pastor before him, carefully guarded the morals of his patrons, while his partner Albee established an often vicious near monopoly that frequently played havoc with competition and imposed salary and other dictates on performers. Other notable managers included Alexander Pantages,♦ S. Z. Poli,♦ F. F. Proctor,♦ and Martin Beck.♦ Beck built the Palace Theatre♦ in New York, which quickly became two-a-day's most prestigious auditorium.

Historian Don B. Wilmeth has noted that "At its height, ten people attended a vaudeville show to everyone who patronized other forms of entertainment; as many as ten to twenty thousand vaudeville acts were competing for bookings." For many people, vaudeville indicated modes of dress and established certain canons of behavior. Thus, while managers insisted on removing offensive acts, certain religious and racial stereotypes were allowed to persist since they were not perceived as truly offensive. Yet for all its tremendous popularity and despite the enormous salaries paid headliners, vaudeville was never to have quite the cachet that attached to the legitimate stage. As a result, many performers used variety merely as a stepping stone. Lillian Russell♦ and Harrigan♦ and Hart♦ were among the earliest to leave the field to find even greater glory in the theatre. The loose structure of many musical comedies of the period allowed artists who were essentially vaudevillians to find occasional homes there. May Irwin,♦ Marie Cahill,♦ Blanche Ring,♦ and, to a lesser extent, Eva Tanguay♦ were all vaudeville headliners who found a welcome in book

musicals. George M. Cohan♦ moved from vaudeville to exceptional success on Broadway. The growth of the even more loosely structured revue proved a further lure. But traffic was not all one way. With the coming of his children, a leading musical comedy star, Eddie Foy,♦ left book shows to create one of the greatest acts in two-a-day, Eddie Foy and the Seven Little Foys. Other legitimate stars used vaudeville to fill in between shows, while the genre afforded a haven for many fading stars who found the road receptive and loyal after more fickle Broadway audiences had lost interest in them. A few notable vaudevillians, such as Harry Lauder,♦ never ventured afield.

The coming of radio and then sound films, both major family entertainments, precipitated the demise of two-a-day. Most historians generally mark the showing of feature films at the Palace in 1932 as the end of traditional vaudeville, although it persisted, especially as tab shows presented along with feature films throughout the 1930s in some large cities. Attempts to revive big-time vaudeville at the Palace in the 1950s failed.

Vaudeville Managers Protective Association Founded in 1900 by Keith♦ and Albee,♦ it enlisted the support of most owners of major vaudeville circuits and forced performers and others to abide by its terms, which included 5 percent kick-backs on all players' salaries. The White Rats,♦ a union formed by actors attempting to buck the Association, was effectively disarmed.

VEILLER, Bayard (1869–1943) The Brooklyn-born playwright had served as a police reporter and as a theatrical press agent before turning dramatist. Although nearly twenty of his plays were produced, he is best remembered for three superior thrillers: *Within the Law*♦ (1912), telling of the revenge of a girl wrongly convicted of theft; *The Thirteenth Chair*♦ (1916), in which a medium clears her daughter of suspicion of murder; and *The Trial of Mary Dugan*♦ (1927), in which the heroine's lawyer-brother wins her acquittal in court.

Autobiography: *The Fun I've Had,* New York, 1941.

VERDON, [Gwyneth Evelyn] Gwen (b. 1926) The slim redhead, whose performances suggested both sexuality and vulnerability, was born in Culver City, Calif. She learned dancing from her mother Gertrude, as well as several noted dance teachers, including Jack Cole.♦ Her first Broadway assignment was in a musical that failed to reach New York, after which she served as Cole's assistant in choreographing *Magdalena* (1948). She helped him again and also danced in the failed revue, *Alive and Kicking* (1950). Recognition came when she danced in *Can-Can*♦ (1953). Thereafter she was starred in a series of musicals choreographed by Bob Fosse,♦ to whom she was married for a time: *Damn Yankees*♦ (1955), in which she introduced "Whatever Lola Wants (Lola Gets)"; *New Girl in Town*♦ (1957); *Redhead* (1959); *Sweet Charity*♦ (1966); and *Chicago*♦ (1975).

VERNON, Mrs. [née Jane Marchant Fisher] (1796–1869) One of our greatest comediennes, she was born in Brighton, England, and first appeared on stage at London's Drury Lane in 1817. With her brother, John Aubrey Fisher, and her future husband, George Vernon, she made her American debut at the Bowery Theatre♦ in 1827 in *The Heir at Law*. Her sister, Clara Fisher,♦ made her debut the same evening at the Park Theatre. ♦ Shortly thereafter, she married Vernon, who died three years later. For a time she was overshadowed by her sister and brother, but eventually surpassed them both in popularity and achievement. Through the years she moved through a wide range of characterizations, first at the Park and the Broadway, and finally with Burton♦ and with Wallack. ♦ She was a tall woman with a slightly pinched but expressive face. Summing up, late in her career, Ireland♦ wrote, "In early life, Mrs. Vernon was better capable of personating *Lady Teazle,* and *Letitia Hardy,* then many actresses who were recognized as stars, and we have seen her *Mrs. Candour* (which was unmatched in merit) and her *Widow Rackett* (almost equally excellent) throw them in the shade. In dissipated women of fashion . . . her portraitures were inimitable . . . In burlettas and burlesques of any kind, she gave a more heightened effect, a more brilliant and fantastic coloring than any actress we have had the fortune to see . . . For several years past, Mrs. Vernon has had antiquated dowagers, and spinsters in the last stages of desperation, exclusively in her charge, and in that line she still maintains her well-earned position of superiority." She was said to have been an extremely intelligent woman, who often quietly helped direct the plays in which she appeared.

Very Good Eddie, a musical comedy in two acts. Book by Philip Bartholomae and Guy Bolton.♦ Lyrics mainly by Schuyler Greene. Music by Jerome Kern. ♦ Produced by Elisabeth Marbury♦ and Ray Comstock♦ at the Princess Theatre. ♦ December 23, 1915. 341 performances.

Little Eddie Kettle (Ernest Truex♦) and his battle-axe bride, Georgina (Helen Raymond), are about to leave on their honeymoon aboard a Hudson River steamer, as are two other newlyweds, Percy (John Willard) and Elsie Darling (Alice Dovey). Eddie seems resigned to a life of dogged loyalty since he is so tiny he wears only a "Size Thirteen Collar." For different reasons, Percy and Georgina have to go ashore briefly, and the boat sails without them. Eddie is left to look after Elsie not only on board but at an inn where they are to lodge for the night. When a storm arises Eddie tells Elsie they have no reason to fear if they will only be as brave as the "Babes in the Wood." By the time Percy and Georgina rejoin them the next day, Eddie is a changed man and not about to take orders from anyone.

Other Principal Song: Some Sort of Somebody

The first of the Princess Theatre musicals to become a smash hit, it was successfully revived, first at Goodspeed♦ and then on Broadway, in 1975. It ran 304 performances.

VESTRIS, Madame [née Lucia Eliza Bartolozzi] (1797–1856) This early English actress-manager came to America in 1838 with her husband, the younger Charles Mathews. A dark-haired, large-eyed beauty, she made her debut as Gertrude in *The Loan of a Lover.* Her later repertory consisted largely of such ephemeral pieces. Unfortunately, her refusal to mingle with guests at her hotel and her tactless remarks about several popular American performers enflamed opinion, which had already been prejudiced by rumors of scandal. Her American visit was a failure, although Mathews managed to salvage some small personal success.

VIDAL, Gore (b. 1925) Born in West Point, N.Y., the caustic but brilliantly witty writer, while better known as a novelist, has also written several superior comedies. His biggest successes were *Visit to a Small Planet*♦ (1957), based on his earlier television play and recounting the adventures of a wildly militant extra-terrestrial man on earth; and *The Best Man*♦ (1960), a story of the battle for nomination of a presidential candidate. His other plays were *Romulus* (1962), an adaptation of a play by Friedrich Duerrenmatt♦; *Weekend* (1968), centering on a presidential candidate blackmailed by his own son; and a loose-jointed political satire, *An Evening with Richard Nixon and . . .* (1972).

Biography: *The Apostate Angel,* Bernard F. Dick, New York, 1974.

Viennese [and German] Operetta in America One may say, at the risk of some oversimplification, there have been two basic schools of Middle-European operetta which have enjoyed popularity in America. The earliest was exemplified by the works of such composers as von Suppé, Millöcker, and Strauss.♦ The success of Suppé's *Fatinitza* in 1879 inaugurated the era, although it reached its peak as far as most Americans were concerned with the great Strauss operettas. Curiously, most of what today are perceived as Strauss's masterpieces—works such as *Die Fledermaus* and *The Gypsy Baron*—were not the most popular with contemporary audiences, for whom such pieces as *The Merry War, The Queen's Lace Handkerchief,* and *Prince Methusalem* had more appeal. Despite their success their influence on American lyric theatre styles was minimal. *Die Fledermaus* has since been revived on Broadway under a number of titles such as *The Merry Countess* (1912), *A Wonderful Night* (1929), *Champagne, Sec* (1933), and *Rosalinda* (1942), but for the most part revivals of these works have been confined to the repertories of opera companies.

By the turn of the century the initial vogue had died along with its creators. However, in 1907 the widespread success of Lehar's♦ *The Merry Widow*♦ resurrected the demand for operetta, albeit for a less pyrotechnic style given over to eminently danceable ballroom waltzes. Oscar Straus's *A Waltz Dream* and *The Chocolate Soldier,* Lehar's *The Count of Luxembourg,* and Emmerich Kalman's♦ *Sari* were among the notable works from this period, which flourished from 1907 to 1914, when ill feelings stemming from World War I put a sharp but temporary end to it, and which was alive again briefly in the 1920s. Before the war these works were considered the best on the modern musical stage and were copied in such American pieces as *The Pink Lady.*♦ Victor Herbert's♦ great works sometimes betrayed a small debt to these examples as well, although he displayed French, Irish, and other influences alongside the Germanic ones. Victor Jacobi and Fritz Kreisler's *Apple Blossoms*♦ played a large part in reviving interest after the war, as did the works of two naturalized Americans, Sigmund Romberg♦ and Rudolf Friml.♦ The most successful importation of the era was Kalman's *Countess Maritza.* Thereafter, despite occasional revivals, the genre went through a period of disdain, although *The White Horse Inn,* with music by Benatsky and Stolz, was a hit in the 1930s. Recently, especially with some opera companies' addition of operetta to their repertories, interest has again begun to wax, albeit very slowly.

Viet Nam War, see *Wars in American Drama*

View from the Bridge, A, a play in one act by Arthur Miller.♦ Produced by Kermit Bloomgarden,♦ Roger L. Stevens,♦ and Robert Whitehead♦ at the Coronet Theatre. September 29, 1955. 149 performances.

Eddie Carbone (Van Heflin), a Brooklyn longshoreman, is desperately in love with his niece Catherine (Gloria Marlowe). Furious that she prefers Rodolpho (Richard Davalos), a handsome young illegal immigrant, he tries to convince her that the boy is a homosexual. When this ploy fails he informs the immigration authorities, who arrange to deport the boy. Eddie is killed by Rodolpho's vengeful brother.

Originally presented as part of a double bill, with the play *A Memory of Two Mondays,* it was later enlarged and revised by Miller. The revised version was successfully presented off-Broadway in 1965, and far outran the original production. It was also revived in 1983, with Tony Lo Bianco heading the cast.

VINCENT, Mrs. J. R. [née Mary Ann Farley] (1818–87) The most beloved of 19th-century Boston actresses, she was born in Portsmouth, England, where she was orphaned at an early age. A servant of her guardians encouraged her to go on stage. She made her debut in Cowes in 1835 and later that year married comedian James R. Vincent. The couple came to America in 1846 to play at Boston's National Theatre. Vincent died in 1850. Two years afterwards the National burned. Mrs. Vincent then joined the Boston Museum,♦ where she became a favorite and continued to perform until just a few days before her death. The heavy-set, kind-faced actress appeared in 444 different roles at the Museum, including Portia, Gertrude, Mrs. Malaprop, Lady Teazle, Nancy Sykes, Widow Racket (*The Belle's Stratagem*), Widow Melnotte (*The Lady of Lyons*♦), and Helen (*The Hunchback*♦). On her death virtually all Boston papers referred to her as "dear old Mrs. Vincent."

Biography: *Fiftieth Anniversary of the First Appearance on Stage of Mrs. J. R. Vincent . . . Fifty Years of an Actress' Life,* Boston, 1885.

Virginia Company of Comedians, see *Murray, Walter*

Virginia Minstrels Generally acknowledged as the first traditional blackface minstrel troupe in America, it was established in 1843 by Frank Brower, Dan Emmett,♦ R.W. Pelham, and Billy Whitlock. On

February 6th they offered their "novel, grotesque, original and surpassingly melodious ethiopian band" in an evening of song and comedy at New York's Bowery Amphitheatre, and thus ushered in the decades-long ascendancy of minstrel entertainment. All four men had at one time or another appeared separately in blackface acts, often called "ethiopian" turns, but no one had heretofore offered an entire company and entire evening of blackface. They borrowed the term "minstrel" from the Tyrolese Minstrel Family, a group of European singers who had recently been touring America. Thus they not only initiated a new form of entertainment but at the same time gave it the name by which it would be known. The troupe played several short engagements in New York, then left for England, where personal differences prompted the men to disband.

Virginian, The, a play in four acts by Owen Wister and Kirke La Shelle. ◆ Produced by La Shelle at the Manhattan Theatre. January 5, 1904. 138 performances.

In a rough and tumble Wyoming of wild cowpunchers and ruthless cattle thieves, The Virginian (Dustin Farnum◆) is a model of rectitude and courtesy. He can put a foul-mouth ruffian in his place by warning him, "When you call me that, smile!" But he also has a way with the gentler sex, so when he courts Molly (Agnes Ardeck), a schoolteacher come from Vermont, she agrees to marry him.

One of the many dramatizations of the novels popular at the time, the stage version lacked sufficient action and life according to many critics. Its success came largely from Farnum's performance. His collaboration in dramatizing the novel was the only major theatrical venture for the Pennsylvania-born Wister (1860–1938).

Visit to a Small Planet, a comedy in three acts by Gore Vidal. ◆ Produced at the Booth Theatre. February 7, 1957. 388 performances.

Dressed as a proper gentleman of the 1860s, Kreton (Cyril Ritchard◆), a creature from a planet far out in space and whose hobby has been studying little, backward Earth, lands in Manassas, hoping to catch a glimpse of the Civil War. Unfortunately his timing is a bit off, so he arrives at the Manassas home of the celebrated television commentator, Roger Spelding (Philip Coolidge), just as Spelding is hosting his old friend, the bureaucratic, cliché-ridden General Tom Powers (Eddie Mayehoff). Kreton becomes intrigued with civilization's improvements—such as giant battleships and hydro-

gen bombs—and sets about trying to start another world war. To his disappointment, he fails. Heading back home, he decides to see if his time machine will still let him witness the Civil War and promises to return "One bright day in 1861. The Battle of Bull Run . . . Only next time I think it'll be more fun if the South wins."

Brooks Atkinson◆ hailed the comedy as "a topsy-turvy lark that has a lot of humorous vitality."

VOEGTLIN, ARTHUR (1858?–1948) The son of William Voegtlin, ◆ he was born in Chicago and planned to become a more serious painter before deciding to follow his father's profession. His earliest designs were seen in Charles Hoyt's◆ farce-comedies, ◆ including *A Trip to Chinatown*◆ (1891), and in later musicals and dramas. However, he was best remembered for his work at the Hippodrome, ◆ where he designed all that theatre's great spectacles from its opening in 1905 until 1918. He was generally credited with devising the theatre's huge water tank and the underwater tunnel through which performers disappeared.

VOEGTLIN, WILLIAM T. (1835–?) Born in Basle, Switzerland, he came to America in 1850 and began to work as a scene painter in New Orleans. He rapidly made a name for himself there and in San Francisco before coming to New York about 1870. In that year he designed the ornate sets for the first major revival of *The Black Crook,* ◆ and his work established him as a leading creator of extravagant scenery although he often designed less flamboyant productions as well. He spent much of his later career at Niblo's Garden◆ and the Grand Opera House, both then homes to spectacles, and later worked at Booth's Theatre. His work was seen in such offerings as *Heartsease* (1870), *Kit, the Arkansas Traveller*◆ (1871), *Connie Soogah* (1875), *Hiawatha* (1880), and Margaret Mather's◆ *Romeo and Juliet*◆ (1885). He was the father of Arthur Voegtlin. ◆

Voice of the Turtle, The, a comedy in three acts by John van Druten. ◆ Produced by Alfred de Liagre, Jr.,◆ at the Morosco Theatre. December 8, 1943. 1,557 performances.

Olive Lashbrooke (Audrey Christie), an actress with a male friend in every city, stops briefly at the apartment of another actress, Sally Middleton (Margaret Sullavan◆), to await a date that she has asked to meet her there. But just before the date arrives, another male friend calls to ask Olive to go out with him, and she agrees. This leaves Sally to entertain the man Olive has stood up, Bill Page (Elliot Nugent♦), a soldier on leave. Before his weekend pass expires, Bill and Sally have fallen in love.

The first small-cast play—only three characters—to become a smash hit, it set a precedent that later economics forced other playwrights to abuse.

VOKES, Rosina (1854–94) The daughter of a London costumer, she and her brother and sisters—Fred[erick Mortimer] (1846–88), Jessie (1851–84), and Victoria (1853–94)—came to America in 1871 along with Fawdon Vokes, who was not a member of the family and whose real name was Walter Fawdon (?-1904). They made their New York debut in 1872 in *The Belles of the Kitchen,* a loosely structured melange of comedy and music dealing with high life below stairs. Many students see the show as a forerunner of modern musical comedy. During several visits between their debut and 1875, they regaled playgoers with similar shows such as *The Right Man in the Wrong Place* and *Fun in a Fog,* but always returned to their popular *Belles of the Kitchen.* From the first Rosina had been considered "infinitely the cleverest, the most bewitching" of the group, so when she reappeared in America in 1885 with her own company, she was instantly welcome. One paper wrote, "She is still young, agile, slender, and graceful; the piquant prettiness of her face and the droll charm of her manner still exert a strong influence upon the susceptible spectator; her roguish eyes are used with the same old irresistible effect. She still sings a comic song as only Rosina Vokes can sing one, and in her rendering . . . she boldly

challenges comparison (on the part of listeners with long memories) with Mrs. John Wood and Lydia Thompson . . . she dances like a sylph." Until shortly before her early death she continued to tour in made-to-order vehicles with titles such as *The Tinted Venus, My Milliner's Bill, My Uncle's Will,* and *A Lesson in Love.*

VOLLMER, Lula (1898–1955) A pioneer in the American folk-play, she was born in Keyser, N.C., and educated at what later became Asheville College. After graduation she went to New York to try to sell her play *Sun-Up.* ♦ Although she worked for the Theatre Guild♦ as a box-office clerk, the Guild joined other producers in rejecting the work, which was finally mounted by a minor producer in 1923. It told the story of a vengeful mountain woman who eventually makes peace with the world. She waived her royalties for the play, giving them instead to help educate Southern mountaineers. In the same year she also won praise for *The Shame Woman♦* (1923), the tale of a backwoods lady who murders the man who violated her and her daughter. None of her subsequent plays was a commercial success, although several had considerable merit. Among the more noteworthy were *The Dunce Boy* (1925), centering on a mountain woman's futile attempts to better her doomed, retarded son; *Trigger* (1927), in which a fervently religious girl alienates her superstitious neighbors; and *The Hill Between* (1938), a story of a young doctor and his rich wife who visit his backward mountain kinfolk.

WAGENHALS [LINCOLN A. (1869–1931)] **and KEMPER,** [Collin (1870–1955)] The two Ohio men, both of whom had worked briefly as actors, began their partnership in 1893 when they acquired a theatre in Binghamton, N.Y. Within a few seasons they were managing such notables as Arthur Byron,♦ Helena Modjeska,♦ Henry Miller,♦ Annie Russell,♦ and Frederick Warde.♦ In 1906 they became the first lessees of the new Astor Theatre. Among their successful productions in this period were *Clothes*♦ (1906), *Paid in Full*♦ (1908), *Seven Days*♦ (1909), and *The Greyhound* (1912). Shortly after the production of this last play they broke up their organization temporarily, reactivating it in 1918. Wagenhals and Kemper's later successes included *Seeing Things* (1920), *Spanish Love* (1920), *The Bat*♦ (1920), and *Why Men Leave Home* (1922). They retired permanently in the mid-1920s.

WAGNER, ROBIN [SAMUEL ANTON] (b. 1933) The San Francisco native studied at the California School of Fine Arts and created his earliest designs for theatres in his hometown. In New York he worked for a time under Ben Edwards and Oliver Smith,♦ then served as designer for Washington's Arena Stage♦ from 1964 to 1967. Among his Broadway works have been the settings for *Hair*♦ (1968), *The Great White Hope*♦ (1968), *Promises, Promises*♦ (1968), *Jesus Christ Superstar* (1971), *Sugar* (1972), *Seesaw* (1973), *A Chorus Line*♦ (1975), *On the Twentieth Century*♦ (1978), *42nd Street*♦ (1980), *Dreamgirls*♦ (1981), and *Jerome Robbins' Broadway* (1989).

WAINWRIGHT, MARIE (1853–1923) The Paris-trained actress from an old-Philadelphia family, she was the daughter of a navy commodore and grand-daughter of a bishop. She made her debut in New York as Juliet in 1877, then spent several years with the Boston Museum,♦ where she was the first American Josephine in *H.M.S. Pinafore*♦ and the first American Countess Zicka in *Diplomacy.*♦ Thereafter she served as leading lady to Lawrence Barrett,♦ then headed her own company. She continued to act until her death, in later years assuming important secondary roles in such plays as *Marie-Odile* (1915) and *Dear Brutus* (1918).

Waiting for Godot Samuel Beckett's♦ absurdist "tragicomedy" told of two seedy men waiting for a blurry figure they called Godot. When he fails to appear they decide to leave, but stand perfectly still. This baffling play opened at the John Golden Theatre on April 19, 1956, and enjoyed one of the longest runs of any work of the theatre of the absurd—59 performances, thanks in large measure to remarkable acting by Bert Lahr♦ and E. G. Marshall. Lahr's performance was all the more remarkable in that he is reputed never to have understood a word he was speaking, but he had lots of company across the footlights. An off-Broadway revival in 1971 with Paul E. Price and Henderson Forsythe in the leading roles ran for nine months. It was mounted at Lincoln Center♦ for a short run in 1988.

Waiting for Lefty, a play in six scenes by Clifford Odets.♦ Produced by the Group Theatre♦ at the Longacre Theatre. March 26, 1935. 168 performances.

At a meeting of a taxi drivers' union, members await the return of their committeeman, Lefty Costello. The union is addressed by several people who urge them not to strike, but then is harangued by agitators, who depict capitalism as corrupt and dying. When news arrives that Lefty has been killed, the drivers vote to strike.

At a time when many Americans were being polarized politically, this play was one of the most effective propaganda pieces for the left. It was initially offered at a series of special matinees. One of its producers, Cheryl Crawford,♦ noted, "Never before or since have I heard such a tumultuous reaction from an audience. The response was wild, fantastic. It raised the roof." The play was later moved to the Broadway engagement noted above. Although it was tremendously popular for a time with radical groups, it is now perceived as too simplistic to have lasting merit.

WALCOT, CHARLES M[ELTON] (1816–68) One of the most adept and popular of mid-19th-century comedians, he was born in London and trained there as an architect. He came to America in 1837. After marrying an actress he decided to try his own luck on stage. His debut was in the summer of 1842. That fall he joined William Mitchell♦ at the Olympic, displaying his comic flair not only in his acting but in numerous burlesques he wrote for the company. When Mitchell's group disbanded, he played briefly with Burton,♦ then joined Wallack's♦ ensemble. There, from 1852 to 1859, he excelled in such classic roles as Charles Surface and Bob Acres. He also took the title part in his highly successful burlesque, *Hiawatha; or, Ardent Spirits and Laughing Waters* (1856). He was a handsome, blue-eyed man with a conspicuously high forehead. His son, Charles, Jr. (1840–1921), who was born in Boston and who inherited his father's good looks, made his stage debut under the name of Charles Brown. With his wife, the former Isabella Nickinson (1847–1906), he was long a favorite in romantic roles at Philadelphia's Walnut Street Theatre.♦ From 1887 on, the couple played older parts with Daniel Frohman's♦ Lyceum Theatre♦ company.

WALDRON, CHARLES D. (1874–1946) While never a star, this actor from Waterford, N.Y., enjoyed a career of nearly half a century playing both leads and major supporting roles. After making his debut in 1898, he spent almost a decade learning his trade in stock companies from New York to San Francisco. He returned to New York in 1907 as Lt. Burton, the Northerner who loves a Confederate girl, in *The Warrens of Virginia.♦* His biggest hit came in the title role of *Daddy Long Legs♦* (1914). In 1921 he was Gray Meredith, one of an unfortunate triangle, in *A Bill of Divorcement.* Among his later parts were Dr. Besant, father of the doomed flapper, in *Coquette♦* (1927); Edward Moulton-Barrett, father of the poetess, in *The Barretts of Wimpole Street♦* (1931); Aaron Kirkland, the Yankee farmer, in *The Pursuit of Happiness♦* (1933); and Senator Langdon, the conservative Southerner, in *Deep Are the Roots♦* (1945).

WALKER, DON[ALD JOHN] (1907–89) Born in Lambertville, N.J., and educated at the University of Pennsylvania, he orchestrated over 100 Broadway musicals, beginning with *May Wine* (1935). His work was heard in, among others, *Leave It to Me!♦* (1938), *By Jupiter♦* (1942), *Carousel♦* (1945), *Finian's Rainbow♦* (1947), *Gentlemen Prefer Blondes♦* (1949), *Call Me Madam♦* (1950), *Wish You Were Here* (1952), *Wonderful Town♦* (1953), *The Pajama Game♦* (1954), *Damn Yankees♦* (1955), *The Most Happy Fella♦* (1956), *The Music Man♦* (1957), *Fiddler on the Roof♦* (1964), *Cabaret♦* (1966), and *Shenandoah♦* (1975).

WALKER, GEORGE, see *Williams, Bert*

WALKER, JOSEPH A., see *River Niger, The*

WALKER, JUNE (1899?–1966) The petite blonde gave several different birth dates and places in interviews, but was most likely born either in Chicago or New York. Her first Broadway assignment was in the chorus of *Hitchy-Koo, 1918.* Among her notable roles were Marilyn Sterling, who is determined to live beyond her means, in *Six-Cylinder Love♦* (1921); Sally Morgan, who runs away from an unwanted marriage, in *The Nervous Wreck♦* (1923); Lorelei Lee, a gold-digging flapper, in *Gentlemen Prefer Blondes♦* (1926), Antoinette Flagg, the illegitimate American daughter of a rich Englishman, in *The Bachelor Father* (1928); Laurey Williams, an Oklahoma farm girl caught between a young cowboy and a villainous hired hand, in *Green Grow the Lilacs* (1931); and Molly Larkins, the "canawler's" daughter courted by a quiet farmer and a vicious boatman, in *The Farmer Takes a Wife* (1934). Much of her subsequent career was in failures or as a replacement for leading ladies in long-running successes. Her last important original assignment was The Mother, whose daughter loves a much older man, in *Middle of the Night♦* (1956).

WALKER, NANCY [née ANNA MYRTLE SWOYER] (b. 1921) The extremely short, sour-faced comedienne was born in Philadelphia and made her stage debut as the wallflower at a college prom in *Best Foot Forward* (1941). After appearing as a man-hungry taxi driver in *On the Town♦* (1944), she was starred in such musicals as *Barefoot Boy with Cheek* (1947), *Look, Ma, I'm Dancin'* (1948), *Along Fifth Avenue* (1949), *Phoenix '55, Copper and Brass* (1957), and *Do Re Mi* (1960). In non-musicals she scored a major success as Julia Starbuck in a 1956 revival of *Fallen Angels,* and appeared in 1968 with the APA♦ as Charlotte Ivanovna in *The Cherry Orchard* and Julia in *The Cocktail Party.♦* Brooks Atkinson♦ said of her, "Next to Beatrice Lillie, Nancy Walker is the funniest woman in the theatre . . . She can destroy a drawing-room comedy just by walking silently across the stage, her shoulders thrust a little forward, her face drawn and sad. Nothing smart or elegant in style has much dignity left once Miss Walker appears on stage and takes one hopeless look at the properties." Another critic said that when she struck an attitude the attitude struck back. Unfortunately, she was rarely lucky in the choice of vehicles, and so disappeared from the stage while still at the height of her comic powers. Much of her later career was in television.

WALKER, STUART (1888–1941) Born in Augusta, Ky., he began his career in 1909 as an actor but soon became assistant director to David Belasco.♦ Five years later he served a brief tenure with Jessie Bonstelle,♦ then in 1915 established his Portmanteau Theatre. He also ran companies in such cities as Cincinnati, Indianapolis, Chicago, Louisville, and Baltimore. His ensembles were essentially progressive stock companies and he, like Miss Bonstelle, is credited with the solid early training of many later stars. His last years were in films.

WALL, THOMAS (fl. mid-18th century) This actor and sometimes manager first appears in American records when he performed with David Douglass's♦ American Company♦ in Charleston in 1766. He was advertised as being "From the Theatre Royal, Drury Lane and the Haymarket London." He continued to play with the company for many seasons not only in Charleston, but at Philadelphia's Southwark Theatre♦ and New York's John Street Theatre.♦ For the most part he assumed secondary roles. In 1781 he built a theatre in Baltimore in partnership with Adam Lindsay.♦ During his two years as manager he took on such leading roles as Richard III, but he appears to have overreached himself, since after relinquishing the managerial reins to Dennis Ryan♦ he remained to again play lesser parts. Eola Willis, in her *The Charleston Stage in the XVIII Century,* suggests he may have been the same Thomas Llewellyn Lechmere Wall who left behind a valuable collection of playbills covering forty years. George O. Seilhamer, who adds that he may also have used the name John Wall, noted, "Wall was not a great actor, but he was an ambitious one, and to him and his partner, Lindsay, not to Hallam and Henry, as has always been asserted, was due the revival of the drama in the United States when the dark hours of the War for Independence were over."

WALLACH, ELI (b. 1915) The Brooklyn-born actor, who has never lost his borough accent or mannerisms, made his Broadway debut in 1945 and soon afterward acted with the American Repertory Theatre.♦ He first won major attention as Alvaro Mangiacavallo, the passionate truck driver, in *The Rose Tattoo*♦ (1951). In later years he appeared with his wife, Anne Jackson,♦ in such shows as *Rhinoceros* (1961), *The Typists* and *The Tiger* (double bill, 1963), *Luv*♦ (1964), a 1973 revival of *The Waltz of the Toreadors, Twice Around the Park* (1982), a 1988

revival of *Cafe Crown,* and a 1990 tour in *Love Letters.*

WALLACK, HENRY [JOHN] (1790–1870) The eldest son of Mr. and Mrs. William Wallack, who were popular performers at London's Astley's Amphitheatre, he came to America in 1819 and made his debut at Baltimore's Holliday Street Theatre.♦ After time there and at Philadelphia's Chestnut Street Theatre,♦ he moved to New York, where his first appearance was in 1821 as Young Norval at the Anthony Street Theatre. Later he performed both at the Chatham Garden Theatre and at the Bowery,♦ for a time attempting unsuccessfully to manage the former. He returned to Europe in 1829 and did not play again in America until four years later. He performed only briefly before once more returning to England. In 1837 he came back to manage the National Theatre for his brother James.♦ When the Broadway Theatre opened in 1847 with *The School for Scandal,* he played Sir Peter Teazle. He continued to perform, with occasional sojourns to London, until 1854, when he marked his farewell by playing Sir John Falstaff at the National. He was a versatile, accomplished actor, although he was never identified with any special roles and never won the fame accorded to his son James, Jr.,♦ his brother James,♦ or his nephew Lester.♦

WALLACK, JAMES WILLIAM (1794–1864) The younger brother of Henry Wallack,♦ he was slated for the navy but chose to continue his family's acting tradition. He had played opposite Edmund Kean♦ and other leading figures before making his American debut at the Park Theatre♦ in 1818 as Macbeth. Subsequently he offered his Rolla, Coriolanus, Romeo, Hamlet, and Richard III. For the next 33 years he shuttled between America and England. His important American engagements during these years included a successful 1828 season at Philadelphia's Arch Street Theatre,♦ where he competed favorably with Forrest♦ at the Walnut Street Theatre♦ and Cooper♦ at the Chestnut Street Theatre,♦ and his management of New York's National Theatre during the 1837–38 and 1838–39 seasons. It was here that he offered the premiere of *Tortesa, the Usurer*♦ (1839). Odell♦ has written that these seasons "marked the beginning of the end of the Park Theatre. Wallack really first showed New York what was meant by perfect stage-management, with an eye to every detail, however slight." He settled permanently in New York in 1851 and the following year opened his theatre and organized the company that was a leading American ensemble for the next 35 years, first under him, then under his son Lester. ♦ Although his repertory covered a full range of classic and modern, tragic and comic, his forte was comedy. With rare exceptions, he ignored native works, preferring the safety of English and Continental writing. He retired from acting in 1859 but continued to operate his theatre (including a new one built in 1861) until shortly before his death. His contemporary, James H. Hackett, ♦ described him thus: "His figure and bearing . . . were very distingué; his eye was sparkling; his hair dark, curly, and luxuriant; his facial features finely chiselled; and, together with the natural conformation of his head, throat, and chest, Mr. Wallack presented a remarkable specimen of manly beauty."

Biography: *A Sketch of the Life of James William Wallack,* New York, 1865.

WALLACK, JAMES WILLIAM, JR. (1818–73) Despite his name, he was the son of Henry Wallack♦ and was born in London shortly before his parents emigrated to America. In 1822 he made his debut as the child in *Pizarro*♦ at Philadelphia's Chestnut Street Theatre. ♦ His first New York appearance seems to have come ten years later at the Bowery, ♦ as a peasant in *Hofer, the "Tell" of the Tyrol.* For a time he acted in his uncle's company at the National. Although he inherited the Wallacks' good looks, rugged build, and fine, deep voice, he was generally judged as little more than adequate in comedy. Tragedy was his strong point, and he was admired for his Iago, Othello, Macbeth, and Richard III. Besides such classic roles he won applause as Fagin and, shortly before his retirement in 1872, as Mathias in *The Bells.* More than any other member of his family he spent most of his career away from New York, spreading the Wallack name to all the major American theatrical centers. He toured as far west as California, for a time in association with E. L. Davenport. ♦ Ireland♦ remarked on his "elegance of mien, picturesqueness of attitude, and spirited declamation."

WALLACK, [JOHN JOHNSTONE] LESTER (1819–88) The son of James William Wallack, ♦ he was the only major member of the Wallack family born in America. However, despite his birth in New York, he acknowledged his English background by serving his theatrical apprenticeship in England and in Ireland, where he employed the stage names Allan Field and John Lester. His American debut did not occur until 1847 when he appeared at the Broadway Theatre as Sir Charles Coldstream in *Used Up.* Not until some time after this did he adopt the name

Lester Wallack. His contemporary, W. J. Florence, ♦ described him as "tall, straight as an Indian, graceful and distinguished in appearance. Piercing black eyes, an abundance of jet black hair, shapely limbs, small extremities, and, withal, a figure that permitted a perfect fitting of tastefully chosen clothes, were among the advantages that he once possessed and which made him almost Hyperion." For a time he played under Burton, ♦ where he won applause as Sir Andrew Aguecheek and Charles Surface. When his father formed the ensemble that was to be one of America's great companies for over three decades, he joined it and within a few years took over its management. He played nearly 300 roles with the company, including Orlando, Benedick, and Marlow, as well as leading parts in such contemporary works as *Ours, Diplomacy,* ♦ *A Scrap of Paper,* and his own dramatization of *Rosedale.* ♦ His tenure was praised for the excellence of his productions and his actors' performances, but was also criticized for his failure to mount many classics and his dismissal of native American works. He once told Bronson Howard♦ that he might accept an early draft of his Civil War play *Shenandoah*♦ if it were reset in the Crimea. With the rise of Augustin Daly♦ in the 1870s Wallack's star began to fade slightly; however, he remained an honored figure until his retirement in 1887.

Autobiography: *Memories of Fifty Years,* New York, 1889.

Wallack's, see *Wallack, James William,* and *Wallack, Lester*

WALLER, EMMA (1820–99) The English-born tragedienne made her American debut as Ophelia at Philadelphia's Walnut Street Theatre♦ in 1857. The following year her first New York appearance came as Marina in *The Duchess of Malfi.* She excelled at many of the same roles which Charlotte Cushman♦ played so well, and some critics maintained she copied Cushman's style, although she is said never to have seen her fellow actress perform. Her greatest interpretations included Meg Merrilies, Lady Macbeth, Julia (*The Hunchback*♦), and the already mentioned Marina. Like Miss Cushman she also appeared in many men's roles, including Hamlet and Iago. T. Allston Brown♦ noted, "Her Lady Macbeth was a wonderful performance, and I doubt if its equal has ever been seen on the American stage . . . Her delineation of Meg Merrilies was wild, fearful, startling. She gave it all of Charlotte Cushman's powerful impulses, but blended with it a feeling and pathos that lulled the whirlwind of passion and smoothed the ruggedness of its features." Much of her career was spent away from New York, including a season managing a theatre at Troy, N.Y. Winter♦ recalled, "She was a woman of stately presence; her countenance was singularly expressive; she possessed dark, piercing eyes, a pallid expression, and a voice of unusual depth and compass." She retired in 1878, but continued to teach for many years.

Walnut Street Theatre (Philadelphia) The oldest active playhouse in America, it was built as a circus in 1809 and converted to legitimate theatre two years later. Despite occasional dark periods and use as a burlesque house, its history has been distinguished. For many years it was a major rival to the city's Arch Street♦ and Chestnut Street theatres,♦ and for much of the 19th century housed an important stock company. It served as a venue for major tryouts and tours until the 1960s. Thereafter it has been home primarily to local mountings, although some tryouts and road companies have been booked occasionally.

WALSH, BLANCHE (1873–1915) The daughter of a New York politician, the sharp-featured actress was famous as a quick study at very short notice and she replaced the female leads in such shows as *Secret Service♦* and *Trilby.♦* For a time she toured with her own company in a repertory of Sardou♦ plays. Among the roles she created on Broadway were Maslova, the peasant forced into prostitution, in *Resurrection* (1903) and Margaret Rolfe, who clears her husband of a false charge of murder, in *The Woman in the Case* (1905). Her relatively early death left unanswered whether she would have become a major star.

WALTER, EUGENE (1874–1941) The Cleveland-born playwright served as a newsman and theatrical advance agent before writing his first play. In all some two dozen of his works reached Broadway. The best were a pair of melodramas which were perceived as bringing a fresh note of stark realism to the theatre of their time: *Paid in Full♦* (1908), in which a wife saves her worthless, ungrateful husband from jail and then walks out on him, and *The Easiest Way♦* (1909), a story of a kept woman's unsuccessful attempt to find real love and a decent life. Although he never lived up to the promise of these early plays, several later works were not without merit; *The Trail of the Lonesome Pine* (1912), a tale of feuding mountaineers; *Fine Feathers* (1913), in which a man is pushed into dishonest

dealings by his ambitious wife; and *Just a Woman* (1916), centering on a man who has little love for the woman who helped make him a success. He also wrote the book *How To Write a Play* (1925).

WALTON, TONY [ANTHONY JOHN] (b. 1934) The English-born set designer, and sometime costume designer, has enjoyed a successful career on both sides of the Atlantic. On Broadway his work has been seen in such shows as *A Funny Thing Happened on the Way to the Forum♦* (1962), *Pippin♦* (1972), *Chicago♦* (1975), *The Act* (1977), *A Day in Hollywood/A Night in the Ukraine* (1980), *Sophisticated Ladies* (1981), *Woman of the Year* (1981), *The Real Thing* (1984), *I'm Not Rappaport♦* (1985), a 1986 revival of *The House of Blue Leaves,♦ Social Security* (1986), a 1987 revival of *Anything Goes,♦* and *Lend Me a Tenor* (1989).

Wang, a musical in two acts. Book and lyrics by J. Cheever Goodwin. ♦ Music by Woolson Morse.♦ Produced at the Broadway Theatre. May 4, 1891. 151 performances.

Wang (De Wolf Hopper♦) is the conniving Regent of Siam. This scarcely bothers the young prince, Mataya (Della Fox♦), who is more concerned with his own courtship of Gillette (Anna O'Keefe). But Gillette's mother, La Veuve Frimousse (Marion Singer), is convinced that Mataya wants Gillette only for her money since, as the widow of a former French consul, Frimousse has managed to get her hands on the entire treasury of Siam. But the ever resourceful Wang engineers a marriage, not only between Mataya and Gillette, but between himself and the widow, relieving her of the money at the same time.

Principal songs: Ask the Man in the Moon · A Pretty Girl

One of the biggest hits of its time, it owed much of its success to Hopper's broad clowning as well as to the charm and singing of Miss Fox in a typical trouser role of the period.

Wanted: One Thousand Milliners, see *One Thousand Milliners,* etc.

War of 1812, see *Wars in American Drama*

WARDE, FREDERICK [BARKHAM] (1851–1935) A somewhat curious figure in the American theatre, he was born in Oxfordshire, England, and after rejecting his family's plan for him to become a lawyer, made his stage debut in 1867. He came to America in 1874, where he was seen as an actor of great promise and given important assignments opposite John McCullough,♦ Charlotte Cushman,♦ Edwin Booth,♦ Lawrence Barrett,♦ and other leading contemporaries. In 1881 he organized his own company and toured in a repertory of Shakespeare and such other aging favorites as *The Gladiator,*♦ *The Lady of Lyons,*♦ and *Virginius.* He had little interest in modern works. His scholarly bent prompted him to begin lecturing on theatre in 1907, and he continued to lecture after he retired in 1919. He also wrote *The Fools of Shakespeare* (1913) and the autobiographical *Fifty Years of Make-Believe* (1920).

WARFIELD, DAVID [né WOLLFELD or WOHLFELT] (1866–1951) The San Francisco-born actor began his theatrical career as an usher at the city's Bush Street Theatre, later advancing to a super and a bit player. There his path briefly crossed that of David Belasco. ♦ By the 1890s he had moved to New York, where he soon became a favorite of audiences at the Casino Theatre♦ and then at Weber♦ and Fields,♦ portraying comic, usually long-bearded, Jews. He was surprised when Belasco approached him to star in a more serious role, that of Simon Levi, the Lower East Side peddler and auctioneer who inherits money, loses it in a swindle, and later recoups it, the title part in *The Auctioneer*♦ (1901). Still greater success came as Anton von Barwig, who searches for his long-lost daughter, in *The Music Master*♦ (1904). He played the part for three years, then appeared as Wes Bigelow, the aging Civil War veteran who must reform his adopted son, in *A Grand Army Man* (1907). Another major triumph was his portrayal of a man who comes back from the dead to settle family matters, the title role in *The Return of Peter Grimm*♦ (1911). The *Times* hailed the performance of the stocky, square-faced actor as "tremendously appealing, tender, and natural," continuing, "His playing is marked throughout by directness, simplicity, understanding, and the economy of means, which in combination spell the great art of acting." For the next eleven years he played in this and in revivals of his earlier successes, but when he decided to retire at the height of his fame in 1922 he essayed the one last role he was determined to play, Shylock. Critics were divided and though he toured with the work for two seasons, it was one of his rare commercial failures.

WARNER, H[ENRY] B[YRON] [né LICKFOLD] (1876–1958) The slim, suavely handsome actor was born in London and followed his father, who acted under the name of Charles Warner, onto the stage. He was established as a West End leading man when he left for America in 1905 to play leading roles opposite Eleanor Robson. ♦ His greatest success came when he played Lee Randall, who must acknowledge he is a convicted criminal if he is to save a young girl, the title role in *Alias Jimmy Valentine*♦ (1910). His other Broadway runs were as He, the bachelor who pursues a married woman, in *Sleeping Partners* (1918); Maitland White, the businessman who would prefer to be a painter, in *You and I*♦ (1923); and Jim Warren, the accused murderer who must remain mute to save his daughter from blackmail, in *Silence* (1924). His last years were spent in films.

WARREN, MERCY OTIS (1728–1814) The sister of James Otis and the wife of James Warren, who was president of the Provisional Congress of Massachusetts, she did her share for the Revolution by writing two political satires: *The Adulateur*♦ (1773), a send-up of Massachusetts governor Thomas Hutchinson, and *The Group*♦ (1775), which deals with the king's abrogation of the Massachusetts charter. Both were printed and widely read, but neither appears to have been performed. In 1790 she published a pair of blank-verse tragedies, *The Sack of Rome* and *The Ladies of Castile*. Other plays, notably *The Blockheads* (1776), have been attributed to her, though most modern scholarship finds the attributions suspect.

WARREN, WILLIAM (1767–1832) The heavy-set, puffy-faced actor was born in Bath, England, and had been playing some time in the provinces when Wignell♦ hired him to perform with his company at Philadelphia's Chestnut Street Theatre. ♦ He came to America in 1796, but an outbreak of plague in Philadelphia forced him to make his debut in Baltimore. Philadelphia first saw him as Friar Laurence. He quickly established himself as a favorite, later taking over management of the theatre with William Wood. ♦ Among his notable roles were Sir Anthony Absolute, Sir Toby Belch, Brabantio, Sir John Falstaff, and Sir Peter Teazle. Although he excelled at comedy, he was a fine judge of all young talent, comic or serious, and it was he and Wood who gave Forrest♦ his first major opportunity. Warren was married three times, each time to actresses. His first wife, who came to America with him, was Anne Powell; his second, Mrs. Merry♦; and his last was Esther Fortune, sister-in-law of the first Joseph Jefferson. ♦ He had six children, all of whom had careers in the theatre. He retired in 1829, but later made several special appearances.

WARREN, WILLIAM [JR.] (1812–88) Considered by many of his contemporaries to be the greatest 19th-century American comedian, he was the son of the celebrated Philadelphia actor-manager. Shortly after his father's death in 1832 he made his debut at Philadelphia's Arch Street Theatre♦ as Young Norval in *Douglas*. ♦ He then played in various cities over the next fourteen years, including brief engagements in New York and in London. In 1846, tired of a roving life, he settled in Boston and was enlisted as a member of the Howard Atheneum♦ company. A year later he moved to the Boston Museum,♦ where, except for one season, he continued as its leading comedian until his retirement shortly after celebrating his semi-centenary as an actor in 1882. During his stint there he gave over 13,000 performances in nearly 600 plays. His most admired interpretations included Sir Peter Teazle, Sir Lucius O'Trigger, Polonius, Tony Lumpkin, Touchstone, and numerous comic roles in contemporary pieces, including Jefferson Scattering Batkins in *The Silver Spoon*. ♦ He was a large, tall, jowly man, with penetrating, heavy-lidded eyes and a large shock of curly black hair. Although the noted Boston critic, Henry Austin Clapp,♦ complained that "the one fault of his style was a slight excess in the use of stentorian tones," most critics undoubtedly would have agreed with an obituary which noted, "Next to fine precision and justness which characterized Mr. Warren's style, the versatility of his power denoted his distinction as an artist. His range as a comedian was unequalled, and to the interpretation of every variety of character he brought that exquisite sensibility and clearness of insight, that mobility of nature and fulness of understanding which made his work vital, natural and satisfying."

Autobiography: *Life and Memoirs of William Warren,* Boston, 1882.

Warrens of Virginia, The, a play in four acts by William C. de Mille. ♦ Produced by David Belasco♦ at the Belasco Theatre. December 3, 1907. 190 performances.

Although the Civil War has separated Lieutenant Burton (Charles D. Waldron♦) of the Union Army from his Southern fiancée, Agatha Warren (Charlotte Walker), Burton succeeds in wangling permission to visit her. However, his commander requires him to travel with plans purporting to show future Northern movements. Of course, the plans are false and are designed to fall into the hands of the Confederates. The trick works, and the forces led by Agatha's father, General Warren (Frank Keenan), are routed. Agatha learns of the ploy and refuses to

have anything further to do with Burton. The ending of the play only hints that a reconciliation may occur when the war is over.

Typical of the sentimental, romantic, and pro-Southern Civil War dramas of the era, the play owed much of its success to Belasco's staging and to Keenan's performance of the Lee-like general.

Wars in American Drama Given its basic importance in establishing this country, the Revolutionary War has inspired few plays of merit and most of these have found but small acceptance from playgoers. Because of the scant opportunities for production, including the fact that British troops held several of the major theatre centers, contemporary dramas such as *The Adulateur,* ♦ *The Fall of British Tyranny,* ♦ or *The Group*♦ have been classified as "pamphlet plays," although several of them seem to have had some circulation and helped steel patriotic resolve. As the war receded in history certain figures found special appeal for dramatists, among them Ethan Allen, Benjamin Franklin, ♦ Nathan Hale, Francis Marion, and Israel Putnam. But by far the most popular figures were George Washington♦ and two men associated with treasonous behavior, Benedict Arnold and Major André. ♦ As a rule, Washington figured primarily in spectacles and other plays designed to reinforce patriotic sentiment. On the other hand, the real drama, even tragedy, of André's story gave rise early on to Dunlap's♦ *André*♦ (1798). *The Widow's Son*♦ (1825) focused on war-bred hatred and hysteria. Between the turn of the century and the coming of the Civil War dozens of dramas, comedies, and spectacles treating the Revolution were mounted. In his *History of the American Drama,* Quinn♦ offers a partial list of more than 50 plays mounted between 1826 and 1860, most of which have not survived. Among the most interesting are *Briar Cliff*♦ (1828), *Putnam, the Iron Son of '76* (1844), *Love in '76*♦ (1857), and *Horseshoe Robinson*♦ (1858). As a rule, the more famous, successful works did not deal directly with the ramifications of the Revolution nor its more celebrated incidents, which were usually left to spectacles. Indeed, the most popular of such plays tended to be lighthearted pieces merely set against the background of the war. *Putnam,* for example, was the only successful work of Nathaniel H. Bannister (1813–47), an ill-starred Baltimore actor and prolific playwright. It was first mounted at the Bowery, ♦ ran for 78 performances, and was revived regularly there and elsewhere for many years. The basic story, interlarded with substantial comic relief, depicted the hero's dramatic escape from the British and his equally dramatic rescue of an Indian child.

In later years interest in the war waned. Later 19th- and early 20th-century examples include James A. Herne's♦ *The Minute Men of 1774–75* (1886), and two Clyde Fitch♦ efforts, *Nathan Hale* (1898) and *Major André* (1903). Only *Nathan Hale* succeeded, largely because of the popularity of its stars, Nat Goodwin♦ and Maxine Elliot.♦ Subsequently, the war was dealt with in such scattered plays as Maxwell Anderson's♦ serious, but a failure, *Valley Forge♦* (1934) and in the popular comedy, *The Pursuit of Happiness♦* (1933). Significantly the most successful modern treatments have been on the musical stage, notably the fluffy, but melodic *Dearest Enemy♦* (1925) and the more purposeful *1776♦* (1969).

The War of 1812 suggested little to dramatists, the most notable works being Robert Penn Smith's♦ two offerings, *The Eighth of January♦* (1829) and *The Triumph at Plattsburg♦* (1830), while the Mexican-American War produced nothing of interest, unless the plays about Davy Crockett, who figured in the Texas battles that led up to the war, are considered.

By its very nature, the Civil War long remained of supreme interest to American playwrights. Although both Northern and Southern dramatists were prolific during the war, their immediate response produced nothing of lasting value nor even of such contemporary popularity as the novel and its dramatization which many felt was a major factor in polarizing opinions before the war, *Uncle Tom's Cabin.♦* Most plays of the moment were flag-waving affairs. The plays which came directly after the conflict and reflected the continuing interest in the battles were of no lasting significance. Probably the first important Civil War drama was Dion Boucicault's♦ commercially unsuccessful *Belle Lamar* (1874). Its story (a Southern lady—married to a Union officer—who chooses regional loyalty over personal affection) established a pattern for the basic dilemma to be portrayed in many of the dramas which followed, as did its use of a spy as a pivotal figure. In short, slavery, slave economics, and secession—the issues fundamental to the war—were passed over in favor of romantic and melodramatic themes that employed the war itself largely as background. Belasco's♦ *May Blossom* (1884) was a further harbinger of the outpouring of Civil War themes which began with *Held by the Enemy♦* (1886) and continued through the era of the Spanish-American War up to the time of World War I with such works as *Shenandoah♦* (1889), *Secret Service♦*

(1895), *The Heart of Maryland♦* (1895), *The Reverend Griffith Davenport♦* (1899), *Barbara Frietchie♦* (1899), the musical *When Johnny Comes Marching Home♦* (1902), *The Warrens of Virginia♦* (1907), and *The Copperhead♦* (1918). If the fundamental issues behind the war were taken for granted or glossed over in most of these plays, they did receive a somewhat more probing examination in plays dealing with Reconstruction such as *Alabama♦* (1891) and *The New South* (1893). John Drinkwater's *Abraham Lincoln* (1919) touched on several basic war issues, albeit briefly. The most notable of later plays to employ the war was Eugene O'Neill's♦ *Mourning Becomes Electra♦* (1931), which used the conflict as a background for the retelling of the Greek legends. Much of the later theatrical employment of the war was in musicals, including *My Maryland* (1927), which was based on *Barbara Frietchie,* and *Shenandoah♦* (1975) (which was not based on the earlier play of the same name).

During our involvement in World War I American dramatists produced nothing of enduring merit. Our initial response appears to have been confined largely to patriotic tableaux in the extravagant revues of the era and in such entertainments as Irving Berlin's♦ all-soldier revue, *Yip Yap Yaphank* (1918). One of the most popular plays about the war, *Friendly Enemies♦* (1918), appeared several months after the armistice and dealt not with the battlefield but with divisions on the home front. However, most students agree the best American play about the war was Maxwell Anderson♦ and Laurence Stallings's♦ salty, cynical comedy *What Price Glory?♦* (1924). In the 1920s and 1930s the war served as the setting for such pacifist pleas as *The Enemy♦* (1925) and *Johnny Johnson♦* (1936). These plays signaled the unromantic, basically antiwar stance that would underlie much subsequent writing about war. *The Petrified Forest♦* (1935) looked at the world-weariness that grew out of the war and the Depression.

The approach of World War II inspired such interesting plays as *Idiot's Delight♦* (1936), *There Shall Be No Night♦* (1940), Hemingway's *The Fifth Column♦* (1940), and *Watch on the Rhine♦* (1941), but during the war itself most serious drama, such as *The Eve of St. Mark♦* (1942) and *A Bell for Adano♦* (1944), was solid but unexceptional. *Tomorrow the World♦* (1943) looked at the difficulties of eradicating Nazi ideology, while *The Searching Wind* (1944) was more concerned with prewar diplomatic bungling. The most successful wartime works were such fluffy comedies as *The Doughgirls♦* (1942) and *Dear Ruth♦* (1944). Possibly the best American play about the war, *A Sound of Hunting* (1945), appeared shortly after the war and failed. Another late, worthy, but unsuccessful play was Arthur Laurents's♦ *Home of the Brave* (1945). By far the most successful plays about the war came years afterward and lightened their undercurrents of seriousness with comedy or romance. Most notable were *Mister Roberts*♦ (1948) and the musical *South Pacific*♦ (1949). Other memorable plays about the war were *Command Decision*♦ (1947), *The Caine Mutiny Court-Martial* (1954), and *A Soldier's Play*♦ (1982).

If the Korean War promoted nothing of real note, the Viet Nam War, the first war in our history actively opposed by a substantial number of thoughtful citizens, called forth a wealth of provocative theatre. The war coincided with what many saw as breakdowns in our society, with massive protests, with widespread rioting and looting as protests against racism, and by the beginnings of the worst inflation in American history. Dramas relating to the war reflected the turmoil. One of the most successful was the musical *Hair*♦ (1968), which featured nudity and a variety of protest songs and unpleasant themes, such as drug addiction, racism, and sexual promiscuity, in its portrayal of a young man who must decide whether or not to serve in the war. The savagely satiric *MacBird!* (1967) was another interesting work. Probably the most important dramatist to deal with the war was David Rabe,♦ who began writing about it while the conflict continued and followed with more material after the war. His plays included *The Basic Training of Pavlo Hummel*♦ (1971), *Sticks and Bones*♦ (1971), and *Streamers*♦ (1976). Although often not as craftily plotted as earlier war stories, they portrayed in superb theatrical terms the chaos, rage, and disintegration generated by the war.

Washington, George Despite his important place in our history and some seemingly theatrical dilemmas he faced during his life, our first President has generally defied transfer into an interesting stage figure. Dramatists began to employ him as a character as early as 1776, when he appears in *The Fall of British Tyranny.* ♦ While the vicious royalist farce *Battle of Brooklyn*, probably from the same year, subjects the American leader to slander and ridicule, most contemporary works, written by disaffected colonists or later, patriotic citizens, depict him hagiographically. This was especially true of the spectacles that were popular in the late 18th century. Thus, in *Virginia* (1784) he remains a mute "Daphnis," saluted by shepherds and nymphs, while he was presented as "Etherius" in *Americana,* a 1798

Charleston, S.C., mounting. The best delineation came in Dunlap's *André* (1798), where the general is shown as unswerving but compassionate in his refusal to reprieve the hero. Washington regularly reappeared as the central figure in 19th-century plays such as *Washington; or, The Retaliation* (1832) and *George Washington; or, The Traitor Foiled* (1850). In more recent times a number of well-known playwrights have attempted plays centering on various periods of Washington's life but have met with major disappointments. Examples of these might be Augustus Thomas's♦ *Colonel George of Mount Vernon* (1896), several plays by Percy MacKaye,♦ including *Washington, the Man Who Made Us* (1920) and *Wakefield* (1932), and Maxwell Anderson's♦ *Valley Forge*♦ (1934). He figured as an important character in Sidney Kingsley's more successful *The Patriots*♦ (1943). The real Washington was an avid playgoer who often ignored the protests of powerful puritanical interests.

Washington Square Players When, in 1914, an intellectual group known as the Liberal Club rejected the idea of a dramatic branch, several disappointed members banded together to organize their own theatrical company. The founders included Edward Goodman, Lawrence Langner,♦ Philip Moeller,♦ and Helen Westley.♦ They patterned their organization after one founded in Chicago by Maurice Browne♦ and named it for the area in which it originated. In 1915 they began to offer one-act plays at the tiny Bandbox Theatre, a year later moving to the larger Comedy Theatre. They eventually presented a number of full-length plays. Although they attempted to emphasize American writing and did produce such short works as Eugene O'Neill's♦ *In the Zone*♦ and Elmer Rice's♦ *Home of the Free,* many of their most admired mountings were of such foreign offerings as Maeterlinck's♦ *Aglavaine,* Checkhov's♦ *The Seagull,* and Shaw's♦ *Mrs. Warren's Profession.* The group was dissolved in 1918, but during its brief history gave important starts to the careers of such later significant figures as Katharine Cornell,♦ Rollo Peters,♦ and Lee Simonson.♦ Many of its prime movers formed the Theatre Guild♦ shortly afterwards.

WASSERSTEIN, WENDY, see *Heidi Chronicles, The*

Watch on the Rhine, a play in three acts by Lillian Hellman.♦ Produced by Herman Shumlin♦ at the Martin Beck Theatre. April 1, 1941. 378 performances.

The widowed Washington matron, Fanny Farrelly (Lucile Watson), soon will have a crowded household, for not only is she entertaining the Roumanian Count de Brancovis (George Coulouris) and his wife (Helen Trenholme), but she is expecting to welcome her daughter Sarah (Mady Christians♦), Sarah's husband, Kurt Mueller (Paul Lukas), and their children. She has not seen them for many years since Kurt is a German and the Muellers lived in Germany until Kurt's anti-fascist sympathies forced him into exile. The homecoming is marred by the Count, who recognizes Kurt and threatens to blackmail him. Kurt kills him, then decides he must return alone to Germany to continue the fight against Nazism.

Writing in *PM,* Louis Kronenberger♦ observed, "It is a play about human beings and their ideological ghosts; a play dedicated to the deeds they are called upon to perform, not the words they are moved to utter. It is a play whose final crisis, though peculiar to one man's life, is yet central to our own." Lukas won an Academy Award when he repeated his role in the film version opposite Bette Davis.

Watch Your Step, a musical comedy in three acts. Book "(if any)" by Harry B. Smith.♦ Lyrics and music by Irving Berlin.♦ Produced by Charles Dillingham♦ at the New Amsterdam Theatre.♦ December 8, 1914. 175 performances.

The plot, which dealt with the attempts of some heirs to meet the terms of a musical comedy will, was so slight that many critics perceived the show as a revue. Smith acknowledged its slightness in his often quoted credit, "Plot (if any) by." The show's importance rests with its music. Berlin provided a score almost entirely in a ragtime idiom. Coming just four months after Jerome Kern♦ established the pattern for the modern ballad with "They Didn't Believe Me"♦ in *The Girl from Utah,*♦ this score consolidated the vogue for show songs written in a totally American style, most often deriving from black musical tradition. With Irene and Vernon Castle♦ in leading roles it also promoted both the contemporary "dance craze" and show songs created as much for ballroom dancing as for singing.

Principal songs: Simple Melody · Syncopated Walk

WATERS, Ethel (1900?–1977) The warm, versatile performer was born in Chester, Penn., giving both 1900 and, later, 1896 as her birth year. She spent years in both black and white vaudeville before making her Broadway debut in *Africana* (1927), in which she introduced "I'm Coming Virginia." Later musical appearances included *Blackbirds of 1930*♦;

Rhapsody in Black (1931); *As Thousands Cheer*♦ (1933), in which she sang "Heat Wave" and "Suppertime"; and *At Home Abroad* (1935), in which she introduced "The Hottentot Potentate" and "Thief in the Night." She first demonstrated her dramatic skills as Hagar, the vengeful, illiterate mother who kills her child's molester and then herself, in *Mamba's Daughters* (1939). Returning to the musical stage she won applause for her singing of "Taking a Chance on Love" and the title song in *Cabin in the Sky*♦ (1940). In 1945 she played in the revue *Blue Holiday.* For many her most memorable performance came as Berenice Sadie Brown, the surrogate mother to a young tomboy, in *The Member of the Wedding*♦ (1950). Brooks Atkinson♦ wrote, "Miss Waters gives one of those rich and eloquent performances that lay such a deep spell on any audience that sees her . . . it has exalted spirit and great warmth of sympathy." Her last important appearance was in *At Home with Ethel Waters* (1953).

Autobiography: *His Eye Is on the Sparrow,* Garden City, 1951.

WATKINS, Harry (1830?–94) A minor 19th-century playwright and actor, he kept a vivid, gossipy, and eventually embittered journal which he maintained from 1845 to 1863 and which was edited and published in 1938 by Maud and Otis Skinner♦ as *One Man in His Time.* It affords unique glimpses of theatrical life both in backwaters and in New York.

WATKINS, Maurine, see *Chicago*

WATSON, Billy [né Isaac Levie or Levine] (1866–1945) The singer, comic, and burlesque producer was born on New York's Lower East Side and made his debut as an entertainer in New York in 1881. He soon did so well as a "Dutch" comedian in burlesque and vaudeville that he had his own theatres. He rejected David Belasco's♦ offer to head the main road company of *The Music Master,*♦ instead playing for many years in *Krausemeyer's Alley.* In this comedy he played a Jewish father who objects to his son's marrying an Irish girl. When Anne Nichols♦ was sued for plagiarism after the opening of *Abie's Irish Rose,*♦ she used the text of *Krausemeyer's Alley* to prove the basic theme was public property. However, Watson's greatest fame came as the producer of *Billy Watson's Beef Trust,* a comic burlesque show that featured a line of chorus girls all weighing over 190 pounds and dressed in striped tights. He retired from the stage in 1925, returning only for rare revivals of *Krausemeyer's Alley.*

WATTERS, George Manker, see *Burlesque*

WATTS, Richard, Jr. (1898–1981) Born in Parkersburg, W.V., and educated at Columbia, he had long served as the film critic for the *Herald Tribune* before succeeding Percy Hammond♦ as that paper's drama critic in 1936. After spending the war years in China he became the critic for the New York *Post,* a position he held until a few years prior to his death. For the *Post* he also conducted a pithy column called "Random Notes on This and That." The noted press agent, Richard Maney, described him as "urbane, sensitive and waspish."

Way Down East, a play in four acts by Lottie Blair Parker, revised by Joseph R. Grismer.♦ Produced by William A. Brady♦ and Florenz Ziegfeld♦ at the Manhattan Theatre. February 7, 1898. 152 performances.

After being seduced and losing the child of that liaison, Annie Moore (Phoebe Davies) wanders aimlessly until she finds refuge as a servant in the New England farm of Squire Bartlett (Odell Williams). Ignorant of her past, the Bartletts prove sympathetic. But when the Squire learns her history he drives her from his home in the midst of a raging snowstorm. She loses her way and nearly dies before she is rescued by the Bartletts' son David (Howard Kyle). He has come to love her and finally persuades his parents that she is worthy to be his wife.

Although the play was little more than a compilation of settings and motifs popular in melodrama of the period, it was praised for its restraint and honesty. It became one of the greatest successes of the American stage and held the boards for nearly two decades. Miss Davies, who was Mrs. Grismer in private life, played the role over 4000 times.

Lottie Blair Parker (1868–1937) was born in Oswego, N.Y., and began her theatrical career as an actress, eventually playing opposite John McCullough,♦ Mary Anderson,♦ and Dion Boucicault.♦ She wrote about a dozen produced plays, including *White Roses* (1892) and *Under Southern Skies* (1901), but none was as popular as *Way Down East,* which was made into a major silent film.

WAYBURN, [Edward Claudius] Ned (1874–1942) Born in Pittsburgh, he started his theatrical career as an usher at Chicago's Grand Opera House. For a time he turned actor, but in 1901 he began to direct and choreograph Broadway musicals. Over the next thirty years he staged no fewer than sixty shows in New York and Chicago. Except for the *Ziegfeld Follies,* ♦ six of which he staged between 1916 and 1923, few are remembered today. The list includes *Mr. Bluebeard* (1903), *The Ham Tree* (1905), *The Time, the Place and the Girl*♦ (1907), *Old Dutch* (1909), *The Passing Show of 1912,* ♦ *The Century Girl* (1915), *The Night Boat* (1920), *Two Little Girls in Blue* (1921), and his last show, *Smiles* (1930). He is credited with inventing tap-dancing in 1903. Later he founded his own dance school and wrote *The Art of Stage Dancing* (1925). He flourished long before directors were given to conceiving musicals as totally integrated efforts. Rather than concern himself with overall style and tone, he was preoccupied largely with creating stage pictures and with pacing. After he gave Ira Gershwin♦ and Vincent Youmans♦ the tempo and meter he wanted for each song in *Two Little Girls in Blue,* Gershwin concluded, "Obviously to Wayburn neither the play nor the numbers were the thing—only tempo mattered."

WAYNE, David [né Wayne James McMeekan] (b. 1914) The versatile character actor was born in Traverse City, Mich., and made his first professional appearance in Cleveland in a 1936 revival of *As You Like It.* ♦ He played in several major Broadway and touring productions before scoring a huge success as the leprechaun Og in *Finian's Rainbow*♦ (1947), in which he sang "Something Sort of Grandish" and "When I'm Not Near the Girl I Love." He followed this with the roustabout Ensign Pulver in *Mister Roberts*♦ (1948); the wily Sakini in *The Teahouse of the August Moon*♦ (1953); the eccentric Uncle Daniel in *The Ponder Heart* (1956); the unctuous Mr. Finnegan in *The Loud Red Patrick* (1956); the musical *Say, Darling* (1958); the hypochondriacal George Kimball in *Send Me No Flowers* (1960); and Private Meek in *Too True To Be Good* (1963). In 1964 he joined the Lincoln Center Repertory Company♦ and appeared in important roles in *After the Fall,* ♦ *Marco Millions,* ♦ *But for Whom Charlie,* and *Incident at Vichy.* His last major Broadway appearance was in the musical *The Happy Time* (1968).

WEBB, Clifton [né Webb Parmalee Hollenbeck] (1893–1966) The slim, dapper, somewhat epicene performer was born in Indianapolis, and began acting professionally when still a young boy, goaded on by Mrs. Hollenbeck, who was to become one of Broadway's famous stage mothers. He left the theatre to study painting and then to work under Victor Maurel to prepare for an opera career, which was short-lived. By 1911 he was a song and dance man in *The Purple Road*. Later he played in, among others, *Dancing Around* (1914), *See America First* (1916), *Love o' Mike* (1917), *Listen Lester* (1918), and *As You Were* (1920). After a stint in London he returned to create the role of the sporting youngblood, Victor Staunton, in *Meet the Wife* (1923). He played a major supporting role in the musical *Sunny*♦ (1925), but reached stardom only with *The Little Show*♦ (1929), in which he sang "I Guess I'll Have To Change My Plan." In *Three's a Crowd* (1930) he performed "Body and Soul" with Libby Holman. ♦ This was followed by *Flying Colors* (1932) and by *As Thousands Cheer*♦ (1933), in which he introduced "Easter Parade" and "Not for All the Rice in China." His last musical appearance was in *You Never Know* (1938). Two Noel Coward♦ comedies marked his farewell to the stage. In both instances he played the parts Coward had written for himself in London: Charles Condomine, whose dead wife comes back to haunt his new marriage, in *Blithe Spirit* (1941) and Garry Essendine, the egomaniacal actor, in *Present Laughter* (1946). In his later years he was popular in films.

WEBBER, ANDREW LLOYD (b. 1948) The London-born son of musical parents, he first achieved American recognition when his popular recording, *Jesus Christ Superstar,* remembered for its title song and "I Don't Know How To Love Him," was dramatized in 1971. Subsequent shows have included *Joseph and the Amazing Technicolor Dreamcoat,* which was first presented in America in 1977 but which did not settle in for a long Broadway run until 1982; *Evita* (1979), whose hit was "Don't Cry for Me, Argentina"; *Cats*♦ (1982), with its hit song "Memory" ; *Song and Dance* (1985); *Starlight Express* (1987); *The Phantom of the Opera*♦ (1988); and *Aspects of Love* (1990). Most of his more successful shows have relied heavily on spectacle, but he has also been more successful than any of his contemporaries in transferring modern musical idioms, notably rock, to the popular stage.

WEBER, JOSEPH [MORRIS] (1867–1942) The native New Yorker, a child of immigrants, was ten years old when he made his stage debut with his childhood friend and longtime partner, Lew Fields. ♦ Within a few years the pair was touring in vaudeville with their comic "Dutch" turn (see details in entry for Fields). In 1896 they took over the tiny Broadway Music Hall, renaming it Weber and Fields' Music Hall. There they presented double bills which consisted of a short musical comedy and a burlesque

of a current Broadway success. The Music Hall immediately became one of Broadway's most popular attractions and continued so until the pair split up in 1903. For a time Weber by himself attempted to continue the policy at the theatre, but some of the magic was gone and he soon abandoned the attempt. He produced several regular musicals and plays, the most successful of which was *The Climax*♦ (1909). The team was reunited briefly in 1912, after which Weber continued to produce, including such shows as *The Only Girl* (1914), *Eileen* (1917), and his last musical offering, *Honeydew* (1920). Before retiring he mounted a revival of the old play *Caste*♦ in 1927.

Biography: *Weber and Fields,* Felix Inman, New York, 1924.

WEBSTER, JEAN, see *Daddy Long-Legs*

WEBSTER, MARGARET (1905–72) The distinguished actress and director, who was the daughter of two famous players, Ben Webster and Dame May Whitty, was born in New York but spent most of her early years on British stages. American audiences first saw her work when she directed *Richard III*♦ in 1937 and first saw her act when she appeared as Masha in a 1938 revival of *The Sea Gull*. She subsequently directed several American Shakespearean productions, scoring her greatest success in 1943 with her staging of *Othello*. ♦ This production, which starred Paul Robeson♦ and José Ferrer♦ and in which she played Emilia, ran 295 performances, a still unbroken record for a Shakespearean mounting. She staged a highly praised revival of *The Tempest*♦ in 1945. In 1946 she joined Eva Le Gallienne♦ and Cheryl Crawford♦ to found the American Repertory Theatre,♦ directing and performing in several of its offerings during its short career. From 1948 to 1950 she toured with her Shakespearean company. Although her stagings were usually lauded for their understanding of Shakespeare's characters and for their theatrical effectiveness, she regularly caused controversy for tampering with Shakespeare's texts: she eliminated the Clown in *Othello,* while in *The Tempest* she made an epilogue of the famous fourth act speech beginning "Our revels now are ended." Her theories and reminiscences were blended in her book *Shakespeare Without Tears* (1942).

WEILL, KURT (1900–1950) The German composer came to America in 1935 as a refugee from Nazism, accompanied by his wife Lotte Lenya. ♦ American playgoers already had heard his unique, often jittery and staccato, jazz-influenced music in an earlier production of *The Threepenny Opera* (1933). Shortly after his arrival his incidental music for Max Reinhardt's♦ *The Eternal Road* (1937) was played in the New York production of the play. His American works were *Johnny Johnson*♦ (1936); *Knickerbocker Holiday*♦ (1938), recalled for "September Song"; *Lady in the Dark*♦ (1941), whose score included "[The Saga of] Jenny" and "My Ship"; *One Touch of Venus*♦ (1943), which offered "Speak Low"; *The Firebrand of Florence* (1945); a musical version of *Street Scene*♦ (1947); *Love Life* (1948), from which came "Green-Up Time" and "Here I'll Stay"; and *Lost in the Stars*♦ (1949). At the time of his death he was working with Maxwell Anderson♦ on *Raft on the River,* a musicalization of *Huckleberry Finn.* A 1954 revival of *Threepenny Opera* became one of the most successful of all off-Broadway offerings and revived interest in his work, especially after "The Ballad of Mack the Knife" became widely popular. However, attempts to present his other German musicals have not met with success, including a staging at the Metropolitan Opera of *The Rise and Fall of Mahagonny.*

Biography: *The Days Grow Short,* Ronald Sanders, New York, 1980.

WEITZENKORN, Louis, see *Five Star Final*

Welcome Stranger, a comedy in four acts by Aaron Hoffman.♦ Produced by Sam H. Harris♦ at the Cohan and Harris Theatre. September 13, 1920. 309 performances.

When kindly Isidor Solomon (George Sidney) opens a clothing store in a small New England town he finds himself confronted with local anti-Semitism. By his good deeds and thoughtfulness he wins over the townspeople one by one. However, the local mayor remains rabidly against him until Solomon offers his fellow citizens an explanation for the mayor's determined stance. The proofs Solomon offers are written in Yiddish and are the birth notice and other early material about the mayor, who had long hidden his own Jewish background.

One of the earliest attempts to confront American anti-Semitism, it was greeted by Alexander Woollcott♦ as "an almost continuously amusing piece of theatrical entertainment."

WELLER, Michael (b. 1942) The New York-born playwright studied at Windham College and Brandeis. He has written numerous plays which have been well received off-Broadway and at regional playhouses, but has met with little success on Broadway. His best-known plays are *Moon-children*♦ (1972), a free-structured look at student attitudes and styles of life, and *Loose Ends*♦ (1979), a study of a failed romance.

WELLES, [George] Orson (1915–85) Born in Kenosha, Wisc., the exceptionally talented actor, director, producer, and writer began performing while still a child. He called attention to his abilities in 1933 when he performed opposite Katharine Cornell♦ as Mercutio, Marchbanks, and Octavius Moulton-Barrett (*The Barretts of Wimpole Street*♦). For the Federal Theatre Project♦ he staged highly admired productions of many plays, including an all-black *Macbeth,*♦ and *Dr. Faustus,* taking the lead in the latter. In 1937 he founded the Mercury Theatre♦ with John Houseman,♦ directing most of the company's productions, among them a modern-dress *Julius Caesar,*♦ in which he appeared as Brutus. Subsequently, along with many members of the Mercury company, he moved to Hollywood, where he created such memorable films as *Citizen Kane* and *The Magnificent Ambersons.* He also precipitated panic in many quarters with his 1938 radio broadcast, *War of the Worlds.* Thereafter, however, his work on Broadway was intermittent. The best was his production, with Houseman, and direction of *Native Son*♦ (1941). In 1946 he adapted, directed, and played Dick Fix in a musicalization of *Around the World in Eighty Days.* In 1956 he directed and starred in *King Lear.*♦ Few artists of such brilliance and diversity have appeared on the American theatre scene, but he became an example of one who either burnt himself out early on or wasted his talents on futile efforts.

Biography: *Orson Welles,* Joseph McBride, New York, 1972.

WEMYSS, Francis Courtney (1797–1859) The London-born actor and manager, son of a British naval officer, had an American mother. He had appeared on English stages for several years before coming to America in 1822 to join the company at Philadelphia's Chestnut Street Theatre.♦ He was an accomplished, if unexceptional, comedian, who in keeping with the diversity required by the stock companies of the day often assumed dramatic roles. He was acting in one of these, Duncan to Macready's♦ Macbeth, at the time of the Astor Place Riots.♦ He eventually became manager of the Chestnut Street Theatre, and later of houses in Baltimore, Pittsburgh, and New York, including Barnum's♦ American Museum.♦ Much admired for his off-stage courtliness and integrity, he was a secretary of the Dramatic Fund.♦ However, he is best remembered as the author of the autobiographical *Twenty-six Years of the Life of an Actor and Manager* (1847) and as editor of *The Acting American Theatre,* a series of volumes of early American plays published in Philadelphia.

WEST, Mae [Mary Jane] (1892–1980) The blonde, busty, Brooklyn-born actress and playwright, who came to epitomize a bawdy, if somewhat tongue-in-cheek sexuality, began acting in stock at the age of five. From 1911 to 1921 she appeared in a number of Broadway musicals. During those same years she became a headliner in vaudeville. She specialized in leeringly risqué songs, although when one of Albee's♦ agents or the police were known to be in the theatre, she is said to have offered them with a childish innocence which suggested she did not know the meaning of the lyrics. She caused a furor and ultimately was jailed for her performance as Margie LaMont, the prostitute, in her own play *Sex♦* (1926). Her next play, *The Drag* (1927), was considered so off-color that it was banned in New York. She scored a major success as a barroom hostess, the title role of her play *Diamond Lil♦* (1928), which was revived in 1949. Several other plays failed, but she enjoyed one final success, apart from the 1949 revival, when she portrayed the famed Russian empress in her play *Catherine Was Great* (1944). Her curtain speech during its run was "Catherine had 300 lovers. I did the best I could in a couple of hours." Her highly popular films during the 1930s helped lead to a tightening of Hollywood's moral codes.

Autobiography: *Goodness Had Nothing To Do with It,* Englewood Cliffs, N.J., 1959.

West Side Story, a musical in two acts. Book by Arthur Laurents. ♦ Lyrics by Stephen Sondheim. ♦ Music by Leonard Bernstein. ♦ Produced by Robert E. Griffith♦ and Harold S. Prince♦ at the Winter Garden Theatre. ♦ September 26, 1957. 734 performances.

The Sharks and the Jets are rival street gangs in New York City. Tony (Larry Kert), a founder of the Jets, who has more or less drifted away from them, falls in love with Maria (Carol Lawrence), the sister of the Sharks' leader. When Tony tries to stop a fight between the groups, he is caught up in the battle and in a fury kills Maria's brother. He later hears that Maria has been killed by a Shark for her loyalty to him, so he attacks and kills the supposed killer. Tony, in turn, is slain. The story of Maria's death proves untrue, and she is left to follow Tony's mourners at his funeral.

Principal songs: I Feel Pretty · Maria · Tonight

A modern version of the *Romeo and Juliet* story, it was devised at the suggestion of Jerome Robbins,♦ whose direction and choreography caught, as one critic observed, the "tautness and malevolence" of the work. He won an Academy Award when he later transferred his material to the screen. The musical has been revived numerous times and enjoyed a huge success overseas.

WESTERN, [Pauline] Lucille (1843–77) Born in New Orleans, the daughter of performers, she began her stage career in Boston at the age of five, playing alongside her younger sister Helen (1844–68). For many years they toured together as child stars. Helen had barely reached maturity at the time of her death, but although Lucille was to live only nine years more, she became a major attraction in that time. Her most famous role was Lady Isobel Mount Severn, the loving mother and faithless wife, in *East Lynne♦* (1863). She was also admired for the strong, emotional roles she portrayed in such plays as *Green Bushes, Camille,♦ The Stranger,♦* and *Oliver Twist.* Although she had a slightly pinched face and a pointed nose, she was judged a great beauty. Clara Morris♦ wrote of her, "She was a born actress . . . in all she did there was just a touch of extravagance—a hint of lawless, unrestrained passion. There was something tropical about her, she always suggested the scarlet tanager, the jeweled dragon-fly, the pomegranate flower, or the scentless splendor of our wild marshmallow."

Western Managers Vaudeville Association This was an organization founded by Martin Beck♦ as a breakaway from the United Booking Office. ♦ For a time it controlled all major vaudeville houses west of Chicago.

WESTLEY, Helen (1879–1942) The Brooklyn-born actress made her debut in 1897 and acted in stock for many years before becoming a founder first of the Washington Square Players♦ and then of the Theatre Guild. ♦ She was a character actress who never became a star, but continued throughout her career to play important featured roles, among them Mrs. Zero in *The Adding Machine♦* (1923), Aunt Eller in *Green Grow the Lilacs* (1931), and Frau Lucher in *Reunion in Vienna♦* (1931). Theresa Helburn♦ praised her sure instinct in helping the Guild select plays, and noted, "She had a theatrical appearance and manner, and dressed rather like a femme fatale—coal-black hair and black, slinky, dresses, a little like Charles Addams's young witch."

WEXLEY, John, see *Last Mile, The*

What a Life, a comedy in three acts by Clifford Goldsmith. Produced by George Abbott♦ at the Biltmore Theatre. April 13, 1938. 538 performances.

Henry Aldrich (Ezra Stone) is a mischievous, fun-loving high school student who shows no promise of following his father to Princeton. He is nearly expelled after his drawing of a bespectacled whale, labeled Mr. Bradley, falls into the hands of the school's principal—Mr. Bradley (Vaughn Glaser). When his mother promises him money to go to the junior prom if he passes his history test, he blithely copies another student's answers. Later he is falsely accused of stealing the school band's instruments and hocking them. He finally does manage to get to the prom, though he has to borrow the carfare from his date.

Welcomed by John Mason Brown♦ as "a veritable Utopia of farce," it was one of the biggest successes of its day, and later became a popular radio program, with Stone again as Henry Aldrich.

Goldsmith (1900–1971) was born in East Aurora, N.Y., and had worked as a high school nutritionist and lecturer before writing this, his only play.

What Price Glory?, a play in three acts by Maxwell Anderson♦ and Laurence Stallings.♦ Produced by Arthur Hopkins♦ at the Plymouth Theatre. September 5, 1924. 435 performances.

Captain Flagg (Louis Wolheim♦) and First Sergeant Quirt (William Boyd) are career soldiers and long-time friendly enemies. Quirt is put in charge of Flagg's company while the Captain is given a leave in Paris. In Flagg's absence, Quirt has a fling with Charmaine (Leyla Georgie), the local village girl whom Flagg considers his own. When, on Flagg's return, Charmaine's father announces that his daughter has been ruined, Flagg demands Quirt marry the girl. The plans are set aside on orders for the company to return to the front. Quirt is wounded and while convalescing briefly resumes his affair. But a second call comes to head for the front. Flagg leaves, yelling to Charmaine to put her money in real estate, while Quirt, equally unconcerned about the girl, follows, shouting, "Hey, Flagg, wait for baby!"

In its day the play was judged a breakaway landmark in the stage's battle for honesty and genuinely reflected speech. Alexander Woollcott♦ noted in the *Sun,* "No war play written in the English language . . . has been so true, so alive, so salty and so richly satisfying," while Heywood Broun♦ of the *World* called it "far and away the most credible of all war plays." It has remained the finest American drama about World War I, although its outspokenness now seems tame and its realism streaked with a touch of romance.

WHEATLEY, Sarah [née Ross] (1790–1872) The wife of the Irish-born actor, Frederick (d. 1836), she was born in Nova Scotia and made her debut at the Park Theatre♦ in 1805. A comely woman, with large, beautiful eyes, she was not at first deemed a superior actress. With time, however, she endeared herself to playgoers for her portrayals of elderly females. Among her notable parts were Mrs. Malaprop and Juliet's nurse. Insisting she never cared for acting, she retired from the stage in 1843, and was never lured back. Three of her children became prominent: Julia as a singer, Emma (1822–54), an actress, and William,♦ an actor and noted manager.

WHEATLEY, William (1816–76) Born in New York, the son of Frederick and Sarah Wheatley,♦ he made his debut at the age of ten opposite Macready.♦ For many years he acted at Philadelphia's Walnut Street♦ and Chestnut Street♦ theatres, then managed that city's Arch Street Theatre,♦ first with John Drew♦ and later alone. His greatest success came when he took over Niblo's Garden♦ in 1862. The huge returns there from his production of *The Black Crook*♦ permitted him to retire in 1868.

WHEELER, A[ndrew] C[arpenter] (1835–1903) The once famous newspaperman, writer, and drama critic, who wrote under a string of pseudonyms, was born in New York and educated at City College of New York. He began his newspaper career on the staff of the then young New York *Times,* but turned briefly to play-writing when he lived for a time in Kansas and Iowa. After serving with papers in Milwaukee and Chicago he returned to New York shortly after the Civil War and under the name "Trinculo" became drama critic for the New York *Leader.* He then moved to the *World,* where his highly caustic, but widely informed play reviews were printed under the byline "Nym Crinkle." He continued to employ that name when he switched to the *Sun.* After several years he returned to the *World,* continuing there until shortly before his death. He also wrote as "Nym Crinkle" for numerous magazines, but used other names as well. Rumor suggested he was an uncredited collaborator on several famous plays of his era, including *The Still Alarm*♦ (1887) and *Blue Jeans*♦ (1890).

WHEELER, HUGH [CALLINGHAM] (1912–87) The London-born dramatist had been an established novelist before turning to the theatre. His first produced play, *Big Fish, Little Fish* (1961), was a highly praised study of the parasitic people surrounding an easy-going man. He had less success with his examination of the relationship of a shy girl and a homosexual, *Look, We've Come Through* (1961), or his adaptation of Shirley Jackson's novel about a young woman suspected of murder, *We Have Always Lived in the Castle* (1966). Turning to musicals, he wrote the book for *A Little Night Music*◆ (1973) and revised the book for the 1973 revival of *Candide.*◆ After helping with the book for *Pacific Overtures*◆ (1975), he wrote the book for *Sweeney Todd*◆ (1979).

When Johnny Comes Marching Home, a musical in three acts. Book and lyrics by Stanislaus Stange.◆ Music by Julian Edwards.◆ Produced by F. C. Whitney◆ at the New York Theatre. December 16, 1902. 71 performances.

Although the Southern belle Kate Pemberton (Zetti Kennedy) loves Union colonel John Graham (William G. Stewart), she is not above attempting to steal documents that will help her side. John catches her, but is forgiving. Reconciliation is helped along when it is learned that John is a Southerner's long lost son.

Principal songs: Fairyland · My Own United States

Often cited as Stange and Edwards's best work, it was revived regularly for at least twenty years. Its story is one of many that painted a romanticized picture, quite sympathetic to the Confederacy.

When Knighthood Was in Flower, a play in four acts by Paul Kester. ◆ Produced by Charles Frohman◆ at the Criterion Theatre. January 14, 1901. 176 performances.

The self-willed Mary Tudor (Julia Marlowe◆), sister of Henry VIII (Charles Harbury), is ordered by her brother to marry Louis XII of France. Since she loves a commoner, Charles Brandon (Bruce McRae◆), she refuses. She tells the King's messenger, "Say to the King my brother that I will see him and his Kingdom sunk in hell before I'll marry Louis of France." She then persuades Charles to elope. The pair are captured and Mary is forced to marry the French monarch. Louis soon dies. She flees to England and finally marries Charles, whom Henry creates Duke of Suffolk.

The play was based on Charles Major's popular novel. Miss Marlowe was condemned by many critics for playing in this entertaining hokum, but her Shakespearean tours had often proved unprofitable, and she later wrote, "My first season of *Knighthood* made me a fortune sufficient to render me independent for the rest of my life. The second season I more than doubled it. Freedom [to concentrate on Shakespeare] was mine."

When Ladies Meet, a comedy in three acts by Rachel Crothers.◆ Produced by John Golden◆ at the Royale Theatre. October 6, 1932. 191 performances.

Mary Howard (Frieda Inescort) is a novelist who has written a book about a woman who loves a married man and about what happens when that woman meets the man's wife. Her book turns out to be a preview of her own life, for Mary loves her publisher, Rogers Woodruff (Herbert Rawlinson), and does meet his wife, Claire (Selena Royle), at the home of Bridget Drake (Spring Byington). At first neither woman realizes who the other is, but when the realization finally dawns on them they recognize they have more feelings in common than either of them has with Rogers. Mary quickly falls out of love. Bridget assumes Rogers will now return to Claire. Mary, however, ruefully informs her, "She doesn't want him now. That's what I've done to her. I'll never forget *her eyes—what she saw.*"

The last but one of Miss Crothers's observant studies of women interacting, it was praised by the *Post* for being "as rich in its humor as it is warm in its sympathy."

Where's Charley?, a musical comedy in two acts. Book by George Abbott.◆ Lyrics and music by Frank Loesser.◆ Produced by Cy Feuer◆ and Ernest H. Martin◆ at the St. James Theatre. October 11, 1948. 792 performances.

Jack Chesney (Byron Palmer) and Charley Wykeham (Ray Bolger◆) are two Oxford students who must find a chaperon if they are to entertain their lady friends, Kitty Verdun (Doretta Morrow) and Amy Spettigue (Allyn McLerie). Since they expect a visit from Charley's Brazilian aunt, Donna Lucia (Jane Lawrence), and know that she has been detained, Charley dresses up as the lady to pose as a chaperon. Naturally Donna Lucia makes an untimely appearance. But she is smart and generous enough to understand the situation and even persuades the boys' fathers to approve of wedding plans.

Principal songs: My Darling, My Darling · Once in Love with Amy

Based on *Charley's Aunt,*◆ the musical was

charming, clean entertainment, and gave Bolger his biggest hit. Many commentators have suggested the surprisingly long run the show enjoyed stemmed from its cleanness and its being perceived as "family" entertainment, fit for children. Bolger underscored this with his show-stopper, "Once in Love with Amy," which he regularly persuaded his audience to sing along with him. A revival in 1974, however, met with little success.

WHIFFEN, MRS. THOMAS [née BLANCHE GALTON] (1845–1936) The London-born actress and singer studied voice with her mother, Mary, who was an opera singer, and later completed her education in France. She performed for a time in England before coming to America in 1868 with her aunt's opéra-bouffe company. In 1879 she was the first New York Buttercup in *H.M.S. Pinafore.* ◆ Subsequently she abandoned the musical stage and spent many seasons with the ensembles at the Madison Square Theatre, ◆ Daniel Frohman's ◆ Lyceum, ◆ and Charles Frohman's ◆ Empire Theatre. ◆ Among the roles she created at the Empire were Mrs. Mossop in *Trelawny of the Wells* (1898) and Mrs. Jinks in *Captain Jinks of the Horse Marines* ◆ (1901). After leaving Frohman she played opposite Mary Mannering, ◆ Eleanor Robson, ◆ Margaret Anglin, ◆ and Henry Miller, ◆ including the role of Mrs. Jordan in *The Great Divide* ◆ (1906). She continued to perform actively until she was well into her eighties, one of her last roles again being Mrs. Mossop in a 1928 revival of *Trelawny.* Not unattractive, despite a low forehead, huge eyes, and a prominent chin, she was probably the last in a long line of New York's "dear old ladies"—actresses, sometimes quite young at the start, who specialized in playing lovable or cantankerous old women.

Autobiography: *Keeping Off the Shelf,* New York, 1928.

WHITE, GEORGE [né WEITZ] (1890–1968) A New York native, he ran away from home to become a dancer, appearing in vaudeville and, between 1910 and 1918, in several Broadway musicals, including two editions of the *Ziegfeld Follies.* ◆ In 1919 he launched his own series of revues, *George White's Scandals,* ◆ and mounted 13 editions, the last coming in 1939. He often appeared as a dancer in his own shows, which he regularly directed and wrote material for as well. His other productions included *Runnin' Wild* (1923), which introduced "The Charleston"◆; *Manhattan Mary* (1927); and *Flying High* ◆ (1930).

WHITE, MILES [EDGREN] (b. 1914?) The costume designer was born in Oakland, Calif., and studied at the University of California and several local art schools before creating the clothes for *Right This Way* (1938). His designs were later seen in such shows as *Best Foot Forward* (1941), *The Pirate* ◆ (1942), *Oklahoma!* ◆ (1943), *Bloomer Girl* ◆ (1944), *Carousel* ◆ (1945), *High Button Shoes* (1947), *Gentlemen Prefer Blondes* ◆ (1949), the 1952 revival of *Pal Joey,* ◆ and *Bye Bye Birdie* ◆ (1960). He won a Tony Award ◆ for his costumes for *Bless You All* (1950) and *Hazel Flagg* (1953).

WHITE, ONNA The Nova Scotia-born choreographer performed in several musicals before creating the dances for a 1956 revival of *Carmen Jones.* She has since created the dances for numerous Broadway shows, most notably *The Music Man* ◆ (1957), *Take Me Along* ◆ (1959), *Irma La Douce* (1960), and *Mame* ◆ (1966).

White Cargo, a play in three acts by Leon Gordon. Produced by Earl Carroll ◆ at the Greenwich Village Theatre. November 5, 1923. 702 performances.

Longford (Richard Stevenson) comes to a West African plantation resolved to avoid the boredom, alcoholism, and trafficking with native girls that are rampant among the white overseers there, but with time he falls for a local half-caste, Tondeleyo (Annette Margules). In keeping with his strict code he insists on marrying her. She, however, eventually becomes bored and attempts to poison him. He is forced to return home, just more "white cargo" for the passage north, while his friends make Tondeleyo drink the poison she has prepared.

Dismissed by most critics as turgid and trashy, the play went on to become one of the decade's biggest hits. Some sources give the number of its performances as 864. The English-born Gordon (1895–1960) was an actor and playwright who was later a major film writer and producer. This was his only Broadway success.

White Rats, THE Founded in 1900 by George Fuller Golden as a fraternal order for vaudevillians and named after the British Water Rats, who had helped Golden when he was stranded in London, its early members included Dave Montgomery and Fred Stone. ◆ Although its attempts at union militancy failed—forcing Montgomery and Stone into the legitimate theatre for want of bookings and destroying other vaudevillians' careers—it eventually became prosperous enough to have its own clubhouse and periodical, *The Player.* However, internal disagreements combined with pressure from Keith,♦ Albee,♦ and other major vaudeville magnates led to its bankruptcy in 1917 and dissolution a year later.

White Slave, The, a play in six acts by Bartley Campbell.♦ Produced at Haverly's 14th Street Theatre. April 3, 1882. 40 performances.

At his death Judge Hardin (Welsh Edwards) would free his housekeeper Nance (Etelka Wardell) and her quadroon daughter Lisa (Georgia Cayvan♦). But Hardin's adopted son, Clay Britton (Gus Levick), who has acted as his foster father's manager, has squandered the estate and must reluctantly sell everything and everyone to William Lacy (Frank Roberts). Lacy is a villainous man who boasts, "I never deal in anything except horses and niggers." Lacy has been quietly engineering Britton's downfall, and when the young man becomes aware of the treachery he attempts to rescue Lisa. Lacy sends him to jail. He also warns Lisa that unless she loves him he will reduce her to the lowest of his slaves, with "a hoe in your hand, rags upon your back." Lisa responds, "Rags are royal raiment when worn for virtue's sake." More complications follow before Lisa is shown to be the white child of Judge Hardin's long dead daughter. Lacy is finally sent to prison for a murder he committed, and Lisa and the repentant Britton are free to wed.

Most critics damned the play, seeing it as an inferior rewriting of Boucicault's♦ *The Octoroon,*♦ but also acknowledging that it would undoubtedly appeal to the public. Helped by the almost instant fame of its celebrated line, the work became Campbell's biggest success and was mounted regularly as late as 1918.

White Wings, a comedy in four acts by Philip Barry.♦ Produced by Winthrop Ames♦ at the Booth Theatre. October 15, 1926. 27 performances.

Archie Inch (Tom Powers♦) is proud that he is the latest in a long line of street-cleaners, or white wings, who clean up after horses. He is so proud, in fact, that he threatens to break off his romance with Mary Todd (Winifred Lenihan♦), whose father invented the automobile which is doing away with the need for horses. He vows that he will never take another job until the last horse is gone. Mary has no choice but to shoot the last horse, Joseph (George Ali), whereupon Archie becomes a taxi driver whose first task is to cart off the bodies of Joseph and of his own grandfather, Major Inch (Albert Tavernier).

Although most major critics were delighted with the fantasy, the public stayed away until the closing notice was posted. By then it was too late to move the play to another theatre. George Ali specialized in playing animals.

WHITEHEAD, ROBERT (b. 1916) The noted producer was born in Montreal and educated in Canada. He first came to Broadway's attention when he produced the highly successful mounting of *Medea* in 1947. He subsequently served as managing director for ANTA,♦ as a founder of The Producers' Theatre, and as a director of the Repertory Theatre of Lincoln Center.♦ Sometimes with these groups, sometimes with other partners, and sometimes alone he has offered such memorable evenings as *The Member of the Wedding*♦ (1950), *The Time of the Cuckoo*♦ (1952), *Bus Stop*♦ (1955), *A View from the Bridge*♦ (1955), *The Visit* (1958), *A Touch of the Poet*♦ (1958), *A Man for All Seasons* (1961), *After the Fall*♦ (1964), *Finishing Touches*♦ (1973), *A Texas Trilogy*♦ (1976), and *Lunch Hour* (1980). In 1982 he directed his wife, Zoë Caldwell,♦ in another revival of *Medea*, then staged her one-woman show, *Lillian* (1986). Approximately fifty Broadway productions have borne his stamp.

WHITING, JACK (1901–61) The Philadelphia-born song and dance man made his debut in the *Ziegfeld Follies of 1922.*♦ For more than three decades he played leading men or major supporting figures in two dozen musicals. Among his assignments were *The Ramblers* (1926), in which he introduced "All Alone Monday"; *Hold Everything*♦ (1928), in which he sang "You're the Cream in My Coffee"; *America's Sweetheart* (1931), in which he performed "I've Got Five Dollars"; *Take a Chance* (1932); *Hooray for What!* (1937), in which he sang "Down with Love"; *Very Warm for May* (1939); *Beat the Band* (1942); *Hazel Flagg* (1953), in which he soft-shoed to "Ev'ry Street's a Boulevard in Old New York"; and *The Golden Apple*♦ (1954).

WHITNEY, FRED C. (1865?–1930) The producer grew up in Detroit, where his father was a prominent theatre manager. Although he mounted a number of straight plays, including a 1900 dramatization of *Quo Vadis?*, he was best known for his production of such musicals as *The Fencing Master* (1892), *The Algerian* (1893), *Rob Roy* (1894), *Brian Boru* (1896), *A Normandy Wedding* (1898), *Dolly Varden* (1902), *When Johnny Comes Marching Home*♦ (1902), *Love's Lottery* (1904), which lured Mme. Schumann-Heink from opera, *The Chocolate Soldier* (1909), and *The Spring Maid* (1910).

Whoopee, a musical comedy in two acts. Book by William Anthony McGuire.♦ Lyrics by Gus Kahn. Music by Walter Donaldson. Produced by Florenz Ziegfeld♦ at the New Amsterdam Theatre.♦ December 4, 1928. 407 performances.

Since she loves the Indian Wanenis (Paul Gregory) and does not want to marry Sheriff Wells (Jack Rutherford), Sally Morgan (Frances Upton) runs away with the aid of the hypochondriacal Henry Williams (Eddie Cantor♦). They are pursued by a posse, their car breaks down, and they take refuge on a ranch. When it is learned that Wanenis is really a white man, objections to Sally's marriage disappear. Henry is left with his loyal nurse Mary Custer (Ethel Shutta).

Principal songs: Love Me or Leave Me · Makin' Whoopee

Based on Owen Davis's♦ *The Nervous Wreck,*♦ the play was one of the 1920s' biggest musical successes, but was forced to close when the stock market crashed and Ziegfeld needed money. He sold the rights to film-maker Samuel Goldwyn, who immediately made it into a movie. Donaldson (1898–1947) was a highly popular composer—"My Blue Heaven," "My Buddy"—who rarely wrote for the stage. A 1979 revival, which originated at the Goodspeed Opera House,♦ tampered heavily with the text and tone of the work.

WHORF, RICHARD (1906–66) A sullen-looking but versatile theatrical figure, he was born in Winthrop, Mass., and made his debut in Boston in 1921 as the Artful Dodger in *Oliver Twist.* In the 1930s and early 1940s he was a principal supporting player to the Lunts♦ in such plays as a 1935 revival of *The Taming of the Shrew,*♦ *Idiot's Delight*♦ (1936), *Amphitryon 38* (1937), a 1938 revival of *The Seagull,* and *There Shall Be No Night*♦ (1940). However, he is best remembered as George Crane, the writer looking for a peaceful place to work, in *Season in the Sun*♦ (1950), and Johnny Goodwin, the irresponsible business partner, in *The Fifth Season*♦ (1953). In 1949 he played Richard III, also designing sets and costumes for the production. He designed numerous other productions, winning a Tony Award♦ for his costumes in *Ondine* (1954). Furthermore, he directed several plays, including the musical *Seventeen* (1951).

Who's Afraid of Virginia Woolf?, a play in three acts by Edward Albee.♦ Produced at the Billy Rose Theatre. October 13, 1962. 664 performances. NYDCCA.

Martha (Uta Hagen♦) is a frustrated, foul-mouthed woman married to a quiet college professor, George (Arthur Hill♦). She has long held it against him that he has not been the success her father was. Matters come to a head one night when they invite a young couple new to the college, Nick (George Grizzard♦) and Honey (Melinda Dillon), to stop by for a drink. Under the influence of alcohol and under the guise of "fun and games" the small gathering explodes into a session of mordant sado-masochism. By the time the younger couple is ready to leave, George has publicly destroyed Martha's most cherished illusion—that the childless couple has a son.

Although somewhat baffled by the meaning of this 3½-hour play, Henry Hewes♦ praised the work as "an inexorable emotional contest between two recognizably real and thoroughly intelligent human beings."

Who's Who in the Theatre A basic reference book, it was first published in England in 1912 and updated for many years by its longtime editor, John Parker (1875–1952). It included biographies of living English and American theatrical figures, dates and lengths of long runs in London and New York, as well as other matters of interest. Since Parker's death others have assumed editorship. In 1978 the Gale Research Company of Detroit published a four-volume *Who Was Who in the Theatre,* which included the biographical entries of all figures who had died by 1976 and thus been dropped from the regular series. The company also now publishes the standard *Who's Who in the Theatre.*

Why Marry?, a comedy in three acts by Jesse Lynch Williams.♦ Produced by Selwyn and Co.♦ and Roi Copper Megrue♦ at the Astor Theatre. December 25, 1917. 120 performances. PP.

Ernest Hamilton (Shelly Hull♦) is a brilliant young scientist who does not yet earn enough money to consider marrying. His fiancée Helen (Estelle Winwood♦) is his lab technician. She is a modern woman, willing to wed and work, but she fears marriage would distract Ernest from his research. Goaded on by her unhappily married brother John (Edmund Breese♦), she therefore decides simply to live with Ernest—with no commitments. This does not sit well with her family, especially Uncle Everett (Nat C. Goodwin♦), although Everett's own wife is in Reno getting a divorce. But after his wife agrees to return to him, Everett convinces the young lovers that "bad as marriage is, until we reform it, it is the best we have to offer you."

This witty, epigrammatic comedy, which many

contemporary critics perceived as America's answer to G. B. Shaw,♦ was the first play to win a Pulitzer Prize.♦

Widow Bedott, a comedy in four acts by David Ross Locke [Petroleum Vesuvius Nasby]. Produced at Haverly's Lyceum Theatre. March 15, 1880. 56 performances.

Widow Bedott (Neil Burgess♦) is a small-town busybody, always willing to chat and meddle while she bakes pies in her kitchen. She also is determined to marry again, and to marry the Elder Shadrack Sniffles (George Stoddart). Before he realizes what is happening he is ready to lead her to the altar— much to the annoyance of Widow Jenkins (Nellie Peck).

Supposedly Lincoln's♦ favorite humorist, Locke made this dramatization of his *Widow Bedott Papers* specifically for Burgess, the era's most famous female impersonator. Although others played the role, none surpassed his interpretation, to which he returned regularly for nearly a decade.

Widow's Son, The; or, Which Is the Traitor?, a tragedy in three acts by Samuel Woodworth.♦ Produced at the Park Theatre.♦ November 25, 1825. In repertory.

Furious that his mother has been called a witch and himself branded a traitor, Captain William Darby (John H. Clarke) does in fact betray Fort Montgomery to the British during the Revolutionary War. His mother Margaret (Mrs. Battersby) is shamed by his actions and offers to spy for Washington. Her work proves excellent, and she finally has the bitter satisfaction of knowing that William has been killed by the British, and not by her fellow Americans.

Although the play was apparently a failure, it has remained of interest to students of American drama, even if they cannot agree on its merits. Quinn♦ called it "one of the best conceived and constructed plays of its kind," adding, "The play pictures well the bustle and confusion that marked the irregular warfare of that period of the Revolution, and the constant danger in which the characters move keeps the interest of the auditor stimulated." On the other hand, Odell,♦ while calling it "a harrowing tale," concluded it "is an extremely poor, extravagant, ill-constructed thing."

Wife, The, a play in four acts by David Belasco♦ and Henry C. de Mille.♦ Produced by Daniel Frohman♦ at the Lyceum Theatre.♦ November 1, 1887. 239 performances.

Helen Truman (Georgia Cayvan♦) loves Robert Gray (Henry Miller♦), but rejects him when she learns he has jilted Lucile Ferrant (Grace Henderson). On the rebound, she marries John Rutherford (Herbert Kelcey♦), who is in despair when he discovers the truth. However, he resolves to win her love, and does.

The *Herald* called it "A good play of American life, serious in its purpose, yet with its emotional scenes relieved by pleasant comedy . . . well written and quick in action, the interest never being allowed to flag." Obviously influenced by Bronson Howard's♦ *The Banker's Daughter,*♦ the play was written to order to accommodate the Lyceum ensemble and marked the first in a series of successful collaborations by Belasco and de Mille.

WIGNELL, THOMAS (1753–1803) The English-born actor and manager was brought to America in 1774 by his cousin, the younger Lewis Hallam.♦ However, the outbreak of the Revolution forced him to sail almost immediately for Jamaica, and he did not begin to earn a name for himself until his return in 1785. He soon became a favorite with the Old American Company♦ at the John Street Theatre♦ in such roles as Joseph Surface, Prospero, and Laertes. Dunlap♦ described him as "a man below ordinary height, with a slight stoop of the shoulders; he was athletic, with handsomely formed lower extremities, the knees a little curved inward, and feet remarkably small. His large blue eyes were rich in expression, and his comedy was luxuriant in humour, but always faithful to his author. He was a comic actor, not a buffoon." However, much of his importance rests with his work behind the scenes. He is said to have been the man who encouraged Royall Tyler♦ to write *The Contrast*♦ (and was its first Jonathan). In 1793 Philadelphia's Chestnut Street Theatre♦ was built for a company he recruited. With Alexander Reinagle♦ he ran the theatre until his death. Under his aegis it was the leading playhouse in the city and its ensemble often considered the finest in the country. For a brief time before he died he was married to Mrs. Merry.♦

WILDE, OSCAR [FINGAL O'FLAHERTIE WILLS] (1854– 1900) The Irish playwright and wit was a figure of notoriety and some derision when he first visited America in 1882. His visit coincided with the production here of Gilbert♦ and Sullivan's♦ *Patience,* in which he was satirized, bolstering both the popularity of the musical and his own renown. His early play *Vera* (1883) was mounted during his stay here, but failed. He is best recalled for his *Lady*

Windermere's Fan (1893), which was first presented here with Julia Arthur♦ and Maurice Barrymore♦ in leading roles, and *The Importance of Being Ernest* (1895), whose original American cast included Henry Miller,♦ William Faversham,♦ and Viola Allen.♦ *A Woman of No Importance* (1893) and *An Ideal Husband* (1895) are sometimes resurrected. His controversial *Salome* (1906) was not given a professional performance until after his death. Notable revivals have included Cornelia Otis Skinner's♦ 1946 presentation of *Lady Windermere's Fan* and John Gielgud's♦ 1947 staging of *The Importance of Being Ernest*.

WILDE, PERCIVAL (1887–1953) The prolific playwright and author was born in New York and educated at Columbia. Although few of his works were produced on Broadway and none was a commercial success, he is reputed to have had more plays performed regularly by amateur theatres than any other contemporary dramatist. Among his popular titles were *The Aftermath, The Lady of Dreams,* and *The Reckoning*. Of his many textbooks the best known was probably *The Craftsmanship of the One-Act Play*.

WILDER, THORNTON [NIVEN] (1897–1975) The popular, broad-ranging novelist and playwright was born in Madison, Wisc., and received his B.A. from Yale and an M.A. from Princeton. He had won fame for his excellent novels—especially the popular *The Bridge of San Luis Rey*—before writing some notable one-act plays such as *The Long Christmas Dinner* and *The Happy Journey to Trenton and Camden*. Although an earlier full-length play, *The Trumpet Shall Sound* (1926), dealing with a Christ-like figure in New York, was a failure, as were several later long plays, three of his full-length works are among the most interesting in the modern American theatre. *Our Town♦* (1938) was an affectionate look at village life. It was awarded a Pulitzer Prize,♦ as was *The Skin of Our Teeth♦* (1942), an allegory based on man's fight for survival. *The Matchmaker♦* (1954) told of the wily doings of a conniving woman. It was a rewriting of his earlier *The Merchant of Yonkers* (1938), which in turn had been derived from an old Austrian comedy. He also wrote a 1932 translation of *Lucrèce* for Katharine Cornell,♦ and in 1937 made an adaptation of *A Doll's House* for Ruth Gordon.♦ Despite the diversity of themes and forms, his best plays all offered thoughtful, perceptive views of essentially ordinary people.

Biography: *Thornton Wilder: An Intimate Portrait,* Richard H. Goldstone, New York, 1975.

WILLARD, E[DWARD] S[MITH] (1853–1915) The English actor, celebrated for his portrayal of villains, made his mark in America as the vengeful potter, Cyrus Blenkarn, in *The Middleman* (1890), a role to which he returned on many subsequent visits and offered on his farewell tour in 1905. That he was equally skilled in comedy was demonstrated in 1892 when he played the absent-minded Professor Goodwillie in Barrie's♦ *The Professor's Love Story*. His other popular vehicles included *John Needham's Double* (1892) and *The Cardinal* (1902).

WILLARD, JOHN, see *Cat and the Canary, The*

WILLIAMS, BARNEY [né BERNARD FLAHERTY or O'FLAHERTY] (1823–76) Born in Cork, Ireland, the comedian came to America as a youngster and made his first appearance in New York as a super in 1836. He spent some time in minstrelsy before finding his true métier in roles depicting a lovable, heavy-drinking Irishman. Contemporaries credited his wife, the former Marie Pray (1828–1911), whom he married in 1850, with prompting his change of roles. She usually played pert Yankee women opposite him. Together they toured successfully for many years in such vehicles as *Rory O'More, The Emerald Ring, Connie Soogah,* and *The Fairy Circle*. Ireland♦ noted, ". . . in the conventional stage Irishman of low life, the ranting, roving, blarneying blade, or in the more dull and stupid grade of bogtrotters, he has gained a popularity on our stage unequaled by any rival."

WILLIAMS, [EGBERT AUSTIN] BERT (1874?–1922) The greatest of black American comedians and one of the finest of all comedians, he was born in the West Indies and was brought to the United States while still a youngster. He played for a time in minstrelsy, then in 1895 joined with George Walker (d. 1911) to form an act in which Walker played the sharp-dealing dandy and Williams his downtrodden patsy. Williams dressed shabbily, walked with a slow shuffle, and had a lugubrious delivery that often packed a hidden punch. Together they appeared in four Broadway shows: *The Gold Bug* (1896), *In Dahomey♦* (1903), *Abyssinia* (1906), and *Bandanna Land* (1908). At a time when racial bigotry was rampant even among leading drama critics, *Theatre Magazine♦* proclaimed him "a vastly funnier man than any white comedian now on the American stage." After Walker's death from paresis, Williams appeared in

Mr. Lode of Koal (1909) and in eight editions of the *Ziegfeld Follies,* ♦ beginning in 1910. He was also popular in vaudeville and was identified with such songs as "Nobody" and "The Darktown Poker Club." Although he was an intelligent, handsome, light-skinned man he was forced to black up for his appearances and never permitted to abandon the stereotypical black he portrayed so hilariously.

　Biography: *Nobody: The Story of Bert Williams,* Ann Charters, New York, 1970.

WILLIAMS, HATTIE (1870?–1942) The vivacious Boston beauty made her debut in 1893 and subsequently appeared in several Charles Hoyt♦ farces. She then won applause in *Vivian's Papas* (1903) and *The Girl from Kay's* (1904). Subsequently she starred in such musicals as *The Rollicking Girl* (1905), *The Little Cherub* (1906), *Fluffy Ruffles* (1908), and *The Doll Girl* (1913), as well as in several farces. She retired at the height of her success.

WILLIAMS, HERB [né HERBERT SCHUSSLER BILLER-BECK] (1884?–1936) With his wife, Hilda Woolfus, the Philadelphian formed a vaudeville act in which he would play the piano and she would sing. The act was meant to be serious but on their opening night their terror was such that Williams fell off his stool and his wife knocked over all their music. The audience thought the act was meant to be comic and laughed so much that the couple was forced to turn their routine into a wild farce, which made them internationally famous.

WILLIAMS, HERSCHEL, see *Janie*

WILLIAMS, JESSE LYNCH (1871–1929) Born in Sterling, Ill., and educated at Princeton, he began his career as a writer of short stories. He worked for a time on newspapers and used his experiences to write his first produced play, *The Stolen Story* (1906). Later he won the first Pulitzer Prize♦ for drama for his study of young love, *Why Marry?*♦ (1917). Five years later *Why Not?* (1922) told of two married couples who decide to exchange mates. His last play was *Lovely Lady* (1925), in which an amorous widow attempts to destroy a happy marriage. He also wrote several popular novels.

WILLIAMS, JOHN D. (1886?–1941) The Boston-born producer worked for a time with Erlanger♦ and Charles Frohman.♦ After the latter's death he embarked on an independent, somewhat brief, career which nevertheless established him as one of

our most thoughtful producers. His mountings included *Justice* (1916), *Our Betters* (1917), *The Copperhead*♦ (1918), *Sleeping Partners* (1918), *Beyond the Horizon*♦ (1920), *Gold* (1921), *The Assumption of Hannele* (1924), *L'Aiglon* (1927), and *Pagan Lady* (1930). He also directed plays on occasion, notably *Rain*♦ (1922).

WILLIAMS, PERCY (1857–1923) One of the most colorful and ethical independent vaudeville magnates, he was born in Baltimore and began his career as an actor in touring productions. Later he ran a medicine show. Turning to vaudeville he built up a fair sized chain of theatres and also helped organize the Vaudeville Comedy Club, ♦ to buck Keith♦ and Albee. ♦ After little more than a decade he sold out for over five million dollars. When he died he left his mansion and the rest of his estate to establish a home for aged and poor performers, stating in his will, "I made my money from the actors, I herewith return it to them."

WILLIAMS, TENNESSEE [né THOMAS LANIER WILLIAMS] (1911–83) Considered by many to be the leading playwright of his age, he was born in Columbus, Miss. His father was a violent, aggressive traveling salesman; his mother, the high-minded, puritanical daughter of a clergyman; his elder sister, a young woman beset by mental problems which eventually necessitated that she be institutionalized. His family thus provided him with the seeds for characters who would people so many of his plays. He attended several universities before graduating from the State University of Iowa. During this time several of his early works were produced at regional and collegiate playhouses. He also held numerous odd jobs. His first play to receive a major production was *Battle of Angels* (1940), which folded on the road. Success came with his study of a woman who raises her family on her dreams of past grandeur, *The Glass Menagerie*♦ (1945). Subsequent successes were *A Streetcar Named Desire*♦ (1947), a story of the downfall of another woman living with delusions of grandeur; *Summer and Smoke*♦ (1948), which told of the interactions of an inhibited spinster and a freethinking young doctor; *The Rose Tattoo*♦ (1951), in which a hot-blooded widow finds new romance; *Cat On a Hot Tin Roof*♦ (1955), a tale of a plantation family's in-fighting; *Sweet Bird of Youth*♦ (1959), centering on a fading actress, her gigolo lover, and his doomed return to his roots; *Period of Adjustment* (1960), a comedy about two rocky marriages; and *The Night of the Iguana* (1961), in which a collection of basically failed people attempt to resolve their lives in a seedy Mexican inn. He won the New York Drama Critics Circle Award♦ for *The Glass Menagerie,* and both that and the Pulitzer Prize♦ for *A Streetcar Named Desire* and *Cat on a Hot Tin Roof.* During these years he had a number of failures, including *You Touched Me!* (1945), written with Donald Windham; a surrealistic fantasy, *Camino Real* (1953); and *Orpheus Descending* (1957). Several of his one-act plays were also mounted. Although he continued to write and be produced, the plays which followed *The Night of the Iguana* were neither critical nor commercial successes. His preoccupation with social degeneracy and homosexuality, which had heretofore been contained by his sense of theatre and poetic dialogue, overcame these saving restraints and lost him a public for the newer works.

Biography: *The Kindness of Strangers: The Life of Tennessee Williams,* Donald Spoto, Boston, 1985.

Willie, West and McGinty Although this madcap act did not appear on the scene until after vaudeville's star had begun to set and first played the Palace in 1926, a 1969 poll of critics, producers, and others associated with vaudeville in its heyday listed the turn on more "ideal bills" than any other famous act. Ostensibly a group of laborers erecting a home, they were in reality "demon house-wreckers," whose brilliantly timed slapstick destroyed more than they built.

WILLIS, N[ATHANIEL] P[ARKER] (1806–67) Famous in his own day primarily as a poet, short-story writer, and editor, he was born in Portland, Maine, but raised in Boston and educated at Yale. In 1837 he won a contest held by Josephine Clifton♦ for the best blank-verse tragedy to suit her talents. His play was *Bianca Visconti,*♦ a romantic tale of doomed love. The play remained popular for several decades. However, *The Kentucky Heiress,* a comedy written for Miss Clifton and also presented in 1837, was a failure and now appears lost. His other success was *Tortesa, the Usurer*♦ (1839), written for James Wallack♦ and telling of a moneylender who generously gives up the woman he seeks.

WILLS, NAT M. [né EDWARD MCGREGOR] (1873–1917) Born in Fredericksburg, Va., he was billed as "The Happy Tramp" and played his tramp with several partners before doing a single turn. He dressed in a baggy, patchy suit and wore a tiny cap. His front teeth were blacked out and he used his scruffy beard to light matches. He was said to spend recklessly in acquiring new material. This careless

spending coupled with alimony he was required to pay led to virtual bankruptcy and prompted his suicide while he was still at the height of his fame.

WILLSON, MEREDITH [né ROBERT MEREDITH REINIGER] (1902–84) Born in Mason City, Iowa, the noted composer and musician performed for several seasons as a flutist in the band of John Philip Sousa.♦ Later he was prominent in radio. He turned to the theatre relatively late in life and wrote three hugely successful musicals. For *The Music Man*♦ (1957), which reflected his Iowa boyhood, he wrote not only the music and lyrics but the book as well. Its hit songs included "Seventy-Six Trombones" and "Till There Was You." He created only the lyrics and music for *The Unsinkable Molly Brown* (1960), recalled for "I'll Never Say No," and then offered book and songs for *Here's Love* (1963).

WILSON, AUGUST (b. 1945) The son of working-class blacks, he was born in Pittsburgh and was a high-school dropout. In his twenties he started to write poetry, only later turning to drama. His earliest plays were mounted at regional theatres. Not until the Eugene O'Neill Memorial Theater Center♦ and the Yale Repertory Theatre♦ took an interest in his works did he receive widespread recognition. His subsequent plays attempted to illustrate aspects of Afro-American life in different decades. *Ma Rainey's Black Bottom*♦ (1984) was set in the 1920s; *Fences*♦ (1987), in the late fifties and the sixties; *Joe Turner's Come and Gone*♦ (1988), in 1911; and *The Piano Lesson*♦ (1990), in the 1930s. Each of these plays has won either the Pulitzer Prize♦ or the New York Drama Critics Circle Award♦—or both. *Fences* also won a Tony.♦ This profusion of awards is baffling, for while the plays have powerful scenes or moments, they are basically an unhomogenized melange of styles and techniques. Wilson employs realism, mysticism, some extremely eccentric characters, musical segments and anything else that might work for immediate effect. As a result, the plays, except possibly for *Ma Rainey,* lack a sense of tone and a legitimate, sustained dramatic thrust.

WILSON, FRANCIS (1854–1935) The Philadelphia-born comedian began performing while still a youngster and spent time in minstrelsy before acting in straight plays. However, the pinnacle of his career came when he joined the company of the newly opened Casino Theatre♦ in 1882, scoring his greatest success as Cadeaux in the theatre's 1886 production of *Erminie.*♦ James Huneker♦ wrote of his portrayal of the lovable rogue, "A secondary role became a stellar one, thanks to Mr. Wilson's racy interpretation . . . with a comic force undeniable . . . as full of the joy of life as Sam Weller, and of original sin as the Artful Dodger." Wilson played the part nearly 1300 times, both in the original production and in several revivals. In 1889 he formed his own production company and over the next thirteen years appeared in eleven musicals, including *The Oolah* (1889), *The Lion Tamer* (1891), *Half a King* (1896), *The Strollers* (1901), and *The Toreador* (1902). Except for revivals of *Erminie,* he then abandoned musicals. Most notable among his later successes were his performances as Sir Guy De Vere, who dreams he is a medieval knight, in *When Knights Were Bold* (1907), and Thomas Beach, who becomes his young niece's guardian, in Wilson's own play, *The Bachelor's Baby* (1909). In 1913 he was elected president of Actors' Equity,♦ a post he held until he retired from the stage in 1921. Besides writing other plays, Wilson was the author of numerous books on the theatre, including works on John Wilkes Booth♦ and Joseph Jefferson,♦ and a pleasant autobiography, *Francis Wilson's Life of Himself,* Boston, 1924.

WILSON, FRANK (1886?–1956) One of many actors remembered for a single role, he was born in New York and studied at the American Academy of Dramatic Arts.♦ He had been understudy and replacement to the leads in *All God's Chillun Got Wings*♦ and *In Abraham's Bosom*♦ before creating the part of the kindly cripple, the title role of *Porgy*♦ (1927). He played the role in New York, on tour, and in London for over two years, but thereafter found few important parts and was often reduced to portraying servants.

WILSON, HARRY LEON (1867–1939) Noted as a novelist and as editor of *Puck* from 1892 to 1902, he was born in Oregon, Ill. His most successful play was *The Man from Home*♦ (1908), in which an American saves his ward from making an unfortunate foreign marriage. The play was written with Booth Tarkington,♦ who was his collaborator in a series of less successful works, including *Cameo Kirby* (1909), a story of a riverboat gambler; *Your Humble Servant* (1910), dealing with the tour of a "ham" actor; *Tweedles* (1923), in which a waitress falls in love with a rich man; and *How's Your Health?* (1929), a comedy about a hypochondriac. Several of his stories were dramatized by other playwrights, including *Ruggles of Red Gap* (1915),

His Majesty Bunker Bean (1916), and *Merton of the Movies*♦ (1922).

WILSON, JOHN C[HAPMAN] (1899–1961) Born in New Jersey and educated at Yale, he spent many years as a stockbroker before his friendship with Noel Coward♦ led him into the theatre. With Coward, the Lunts,♦ and the Theatre Guild♦ he co-produced a number of works, including *Design for Living* (1933) and *Tonight at 8:30* (1936), sometimes as a silent partner. Embarking on his own he later produced such works as *Blithe Spirit* (1941), *Lovers and Friends* (1943), *Bloomer Girl*♦ (1944), *O Mistress Mine* (1946), *Present Laughter* (1946), and *The Winslow Boy* (1947). He directed many of his own productions as well as those of other producers, notably *Kiss Me, Kate*♦ (1948) and *Gentlemen Prefer Blondes*♦ (1949).

WILSON, LANFORD (b. 1937) Born in Lebanon, Mo., he began writing plays while attending the University of Chicago. Coming to New York he soon earned attention for his plays presented off-Broadway and off-off-Broadway. His first play to reach a regular playhouse was *The Gingham Dog* (1969), a highly praised but commercially unsuccessful story of a failed interracial marriage. *Lemon Sky* (1970) dealt with a father-son conflict that precipitates a family's disintegration. In 1973 his picture of life in a dingy New York hotel, *The Hot l Baltimore,*♦ began a run of 1,166 performances, an off-Broadway record for a non-musical by an American. He later wrote two plays about the same Southern family, *The 5th of July*♦ (1978) and *Talley's Folly*♦ (1980), the latter winning both the Pulitzer Prize♦ and the New York Drama Critics Circle Award.♦ His 1983 play *Angels Fall*, dealing with people brought together by a nuclear accident, won critical praise, but could not find an audience. *Burn This* (1987) described the stormy romance between a choreographer and the coarse, over-sexed brother of her homosexual roommate, who has recently died. As a rule his best work blends the careful structural formality of older schools of playwriting with the preoccupations of modern authors.

WIMAN, DWIGHT DEERE (1895–1951) Born in Moline, Ill., the heir to a huge manufacturing fortune, he studied drama under Monty Woolley♦ at Yale. After a brief fling in films he joined with William A. Brady, Jr.,♦ to produce such plays as *Lucky Sam McCarver*♦ (1925), 1926 revivals of *Little Eyolf* and *The Two Orphans,*♦ *The Road to Rome*♦ (1927), and *The Little Show*♦ (1929).

Following the partnership's dissolution he produced, occasionally with associates, such memorable plays as *The Vinegar Tree* (1930), *Gay Divorce*♦ (1932), *She Loves Me Not*♦ (1933), *On Your Toes*♦ (1936), *Babes in Arms*♦ (1937), *On Borrowed Time*♦ (1938), *I Married an Angel*♦ (1938), *Morning's at Seven*♦ (1939), *By Jupiter*♦ (1942), and *The Country Girl*♦ (1950).

WINCHELL, WALTER [né WINCHELES] (1897–1972) The most influential Broadway columnist of his day, he was born in New York and received some of his early training as a child vaudevillian. His staccato writing and similar delivery when he went on the air, his often explosive innuendos and curious "Winchellisms," such as "infanticipating" for "pregnant," earned him a huge following, and he was credited with saving a number of Broadway shows, most notably *Hellzapoppin,*♦ from probable failure.

Biography: *Winchell,* Bob Thomas, Garden City, 1971.

WINDUST, BRETAIGNE (1906–60) The director was born in Paris and educated at Princeton, where he was a member of the Theatre Intime. He later served as stage manager for the original production of *Strange Interlude,*♦ then co-founded the University Players♦ in 1928. He spent several years as an actor before directing *Idiot's Delight*♦ (1936). His elegantly stylish, carefully paced mounting earned him numerous subsequent assignments, including *Amphitryon 38* (1937), *Life with Father*♦ (1939), *Arsenic and Old Lace*♦ (1941), *State of the Union*♦ (1945), *Finian's Rainbow*♦ (1947), and *The Great Sebastians* (1956).

Winged Victory, a play in two acts by Moss Hart.♦ Produced by the U.S. Army Air Forces for the benefit of the Army Emergency Relief Fund at the 44th Street Theatre. November 20, 1943. 212 performances.

Centering on the air force career of three men, Allan Ross (Mark Daniels), an Ohio bank teller, Pinky Scariano (Don Taylor), a barber, and Irving Miller (Edmund O'Brien), a young man from Brooklyn, the story follows them through their basic training, to their tour of duty on a bomber they name "Winged Victory," and to their battle in which Pinky is seriously injured, but seems likely to survive.

A stirring propaganda piece with a huge cast, many of whom later went on to stardom, the play earned millions of dollars for the relief fund in its limited engagements around the country.

Wingless Victory, The, a play in three acts by Maxwell Anderson. ♦ Produced by Katharine Cornell♦ at the Empire Theatre. ♦ December 23, 1936. 110 performances.

To the horror of his sanctimonious New England family, Nathaniel McQueston (Walter Abel), captain of the ship *Wingless Victory,* returns to port with a wife, the dark-skinned Malayan princess Oparre (Miss Cornell). She is accepted grudgingly only because Nathaniel is so rich. However, with time she recognizes she will never be truly welcome and that she stands in Nathaniel's way, and so kills herself and her children.

The play, which opened less than a month before Anderson's *High Tor,* ♦ was viewed by many as old-fashioned melodrama in the guise of blank-verse tragedy. Stark Young♦ of the *New Republic* dismissed it as "semitosh from start to finish."

WINNINGER, CHARLES [né KARL WINNINGER] (1884–1969) A native of Athens, Wisc., the heavy-set, outgoing comedian began performing at the age of five and had appeared with circuses, in vaudeville, and on a show boat called the "Cotton Blossom" before he made his Broadway debut in the 1910 musical *The Yankee Girl.* Over the next quarter-century he appeared in a dozen musicals, introducing "I Want To Be Happy" in *No, No, Nanette*♦ (1925) and creating the role of Cap'n Andy in *Show Boat*♦ (1927). After a long career in films he appeared in the 1951 revival of *Music in the Air.* ♦

WINSLOW, HERBERT HALL (1865–1930) Between *Town Lots; or, A Paper City* (1888) and *He Loved the Ladies* (1927), the prolific, wide-ranging dramatist, who was born in Keokuk, Iowa, wrote approximately one hundred produced plays. Most were written as vehicles for lesser touring stars and only a handful of his works ever reached New York. None had lasting merit. Typical of his output was *The Vinegar Buyer,* which was written in 1902 for Ezra Kendall, a popular vaudevillian, and which toured for several seasons. A stereotyped period comedy of rural life, it was immensely popular with small-town audiences, but when it braved New York was waved away as "a series of vaudeville jokes strung out through three acts."

Winter Garden Theatre Opened in 1911 by the Shuberts, ♦ it was built on the east side of Broadway at 50th Street on the site of the old American Horse Exchange. William A. Swasey♦ was the architect. The auditorium was unusually wide and seated proportionately far more in the orchestra than in most Broadway houses. Although the Shubert offices were long located in or near the Sam S. Shubert Theatre, this house was often called the producers' flagship. In the 1910s and 1920s it was home to many Al Jolson♦ musicals, as well as to the annual *Passing Shows.*♦ In the 1930s it housed several superior revues. Among its later hits were *Mexican Hayride* (1944), *Wonderful Town*♦ (1953), *Peter Pan*♦ (1954), *West Side Story*♦ (1957), *Mame*♦ (1966), and *Cats*♦ (1982).

WINTER, WILLIAM (1836–1917) The most influential and widely read critic of his era, he was born in Gloucester, Mass., and educated at Harvard. He came to New York in 1859 to become literary editor of *The Saturday Press,* then served as drama critic for the *Albion.* In 1865 he was appointed the *Tribune*'s critic, a post he held until his retirement in 1909, after which he contributed articles to various magazines. His early criticism was learned, basically sound, and open-minded, but with the rise of realism in the 1880s he became increasingly unaccepting of new theatrical movements and was the often shrill leader of the anti-Ibsenites. He came to conclude that morality was all-important, and that no play, however meritorious, was worthy of patronage if it violated his rigid canons of right and wrong. He continued to promote not only the standards of writing he knew as a young man but also the methods of acting prevalent when he first attended plays. He wrote numerous books on theatre, including *Other Days* (1908), *Old Friends* (1909), and the two-volume *The Wallet of Time* (1913), as well as biographies of David Belasco,♦ Edwin Booth,♦ Joseph Jefferson,♦ Richard Mansfield,♦ and Ada Rehan.♦ His penchant for composing memorial odes to dead actors earned him the nickname "Weeping Willie." Typical both of his style and of his later, crotchety views were his comments in his Mansfield biography, "The Ibsen movement . . . impressed me, from the beginning, as unhealthful and injurious. The province of art, and especially of dramatic art, is beauty, not deformity; the need of the world is to be cheered, not depressed; and the author who avows, as Ibsen did, that he goes down into the sewers,—whatever be the purpose of his descent into those insalubrious regions,—should be left to the enjoyment of them."

Winterset, a play in three acts by Maxwell Anderson.♦ Produced by Guthrie McClintic♦ at the Martin Beck Theatre. September 25, 1935. 195 performances. NYDCCA.

Mio (Burgess Meredith♦) is certain that his anarchist father, Bartolomeo, was unjustly sentenced to death for the murder of a paymaster. He visits Judge Gaunt (Richard Bennett♦), who presided over the trial, but recognizes that the jurist has become mentally deranged. Mio concludes that his best hope for bringing the truth to light is Miriamne (Margo), whose brother witnessed the crime. Mio and Miriamne fall in love and when the gangsters who were the real culprits kill Mio, she threatens to reveal the truth, and she, too, is killed.

Gilbert W. Gabriel exemplified the generally enthusiastic response to this blank-verse play when he wrote in the *American,* "It is, to date, Anderson's masterpiece. This, underneath all its full-flower eloquence, is melodrama, right, tight, trig melodrama, and immensely exciting melodrama, too." The play was Anderson's second attempt to dramatize the Sacco-Vanzetti story. His earlier collaboration with Harold Hickerson, *Gods of the Lightning* (1928), had failed.

WINWOOD, ESTELLE (1883–1984) In a career that spanned seventy years this performer moved from a beautiful leading lady and comedienne to a fine character actress. She was born in Lee, England, made her professional debut in 1898, and came to America in 1916. Her early roles included Helen, who is torn between marriage and living with her fiancé out of wedlock, in *Why Marry?*♦ (1917), as well as leading parts in such Somerset Maugham♦ plays as *Too Many Husbands* (1919) and *The Circle* (1921). She later played important roles in such works as *Ten Little Indians* (1944) and *Lady Windermere's Fan* (1946), then scored one of her most memorable triumphs as the loony Mme. Constance in *The Madwoman of Chaillot* (1948).

Wisdom Tooth, The, a comedy in three acts by Marc Connelly.♦ Produced by John Golden♦ at the Little Theatre. February 15, 1926. 160 performances.

Charley Bemis (Thomas Mitchell♦) is an industrious, frugal senior clerk at the office in which he works, but he is so readily and so often browbeaten by his associates that he comes to look on himself as a carbon copy of a man. After Sally Field (Mary Philips), who also has a room at the house where Charley boards, berates him for his timidity, Charley falls asleep and recalls his youth, including a circus where none other than Barnum and Bailey had praised him. The dream gives him the strength to be the man he long has wanted to be. True, his standing up to his boss costs him his job, but then he may do more than play cribbage with an admiring Sally.

This was Connelly's first solo effort following his split with George S. Kaufman,♦ and the play's comedy delighted critics even if its loose construction did not. After a slow start, it caught on, thanks in no small part to Thomas Mitchell's excellent performance.

WISE, THOMAS A. (1865–1928) The burly character actor was born in Faversham, England, but came to America while still young. He made his debut in Dixon, Calif., and later toured with Joseph Grismer♦ and then with William Gillette. ♦ He is best recalled for such roles as Amos Bloodgood, who pretends to be a Mason, in *Are You a Mason?* (1902); William Langdon, the Senator who fights corruption, in *A Gentleman from Mississippi*♦ (1908), of which he was co-author; and Falstaff in a 1916 revival of *The Merry Wives of Windsor*. With Harrison Rhodes, his collaborator on *A Gentleman from Mississippi*, he wrote several other less successful plays.

Wish You Were Here, see *Having Wonderful Time*

WISTER, OWEN, see *Virginian, The*

Witchcraft; or, the Martyrs of Salem, a play in five acts by Cornelius Mathews. ♦ Produced by James E. Murdoch♦ at the Bowery Theatre. ♦ May 17, 1847. 5 performances.
Gideon Bodish (Murdoch) comes to the defense of his morose, memory-haunted mother, Ambla (Mrs. Wilkinson), when she is placed on trial for witchcraft. The court is heavily influenced by the testimony of Susanna Peache (Mrs. Sergeant), who loves Gideon and who believes that Ambla had used her occult powers to discourage the romance. After Ambla is executed, Susanna realizes she has lost Gideon and so commits suicide. Jarvis Dane (J. A. J. Neafie♦), a rival suitor of Susanna, kills Gideon to avenge her death.
This often poignant and gripping blank-verse tragedy was first presented at Philadelphia's Walnut Street Theatre,♦ where it was a major success. Although it failed in New York, it was popular in other cities across the country, and, apparently, in Europe as well. Whether or not Mathews was familiar with a similar, earlier play, *Superstition,*♦ is unknown.

Witching Hour, The, a play in four acts by Augustus Thomas. ♦ Produced by Sam S. and Lee Shubert♦ at the Hackett Theatre. November 18, 1907. 212 performances.

Although Jack Brookfield (John Mason♦), a professional gambler, was long ago rejected by Helen Whipple (Jennie A. Eustace), he remains loyal and loving enough to help her when her son Clay (Morgan Conan) is convicted of murdering a man who taunted him about his curious fear of cat's-eye jewels. A retrial is arranged. Brookfield knows that Clay has been railroaded by district attorney Frank Hardmuth (George Nash), Clay's rival for the hand of Viola Campbell (Janet Dunbar). Brookfield releases to the newspapers material to show Hardmuth's complicity in a governor's murder. Believing in the powers of telepathy, Brookfield is sure that the sympathy of readers will be passed on to the jury in Clay's retrial. After Clay is acquitted, Hardmuth attempts to shoot Brookfield, who employs hypnosis to force Hardmuth to drop his gun.
The play was hailed by William Winter♦ as "the most interesting drama in years—the play of the century." Despite its somewhat preposterous acceptance of the amazing powers of telepathy and instant hypnosis, this is generally acknowledged as Thomas's best play. His interest in the occult grew out of his association with the celebrated mind-reader Washington Irving Bishop.

WITHAM, CHARLES W. (1842?–1926) One of the leading set designers of the last half of the 19th century, he was born in Portland, Maine. (Some sources give his birth date as 1832.) No records survive showing where he studied, but the technical excellence of his later drawings suggests a thorough schooling. In 1867 Edwin Booth♦ appointed him to design and paint all the architectural scenes for the projected Booth's Theatre. After the playhouse opened two years later Witham's work for such dramas as *Hamlet,* ♦ *Julius Caesar,* ♦ *The Merchant of Venice,* ♦ and *Richelieu*♦ demonstrated a notable historical accuracy. He left Booth in 1873 to work with Augustin Daly,♦ creating primarily modern interiors but also the sets for Dion Boucicault♦ spectacles. Edward Harrigan♦ made him his chief set designer in 1881. Harrigan's plays of New York low-life allowed Witham to move sharply toward realism in his work, which thereafter displayed a marked asymmetry.

Within the Law, a play in four acts by Bayard Veiller.♦ Produced by the American Play Company♦ at the Eltinge Theatre. September 11, 1912. 541 performances.
Falsely accused of theft by her employer, Edward Gilder (Dodson Mitchell), and sentenced to three years in prison, Mary Turner (Jane Cowl♦) warns

Gilder she will be avenged. Four years pass. In her one year of freedom Mary has organized a group of criminals whom she keeps operating just within the law. She also weds Gilder's son Richard (Orme Caldara♦) and advises the elder Gilder, "Four years ago you took away my name and gave me a number. Now I've given up that number and I've got your name." Against her orders, her gang attempts to rob Gilder's home. One is killed, but in confessing the others establish Mary's innocence. Mary and Richard realize they do love each other, and even the elder Gilder is apparently reconciled.

Originally a failure when William A. Brady♦ produced it with his wife, Grace George,♦ as star, it was rewritten, recast, and restaged by Holbrook Blinn.♦ To *Variety*♦ it was "a great big elemental problem play, put before the public so that it cannot fail to be understood."

Wizard of Oz, The, a musical in three acts. Book and most lyrics by Frank Baum. Music by Paul Tietjens and A. Baldwin Sloane. ♦ Produced at the Majestic Theatre. January 20, 1903. 293 performances.

When little Dorothy (Anna Laughlin) and her cow Imogene (Joseph Schrode) are whisked away from her Kansas farm by a wild cyclone and taken to the faraway land of Oz, they are joined by a Scarecrow (Fred Stone♦), a Tin Man (Dave Montgomery♦), and also a Cowardly Lion (Arthur Hill) as they travel to visit the Wizard who will help them return to Earth. Of course, it is all a dream.

Based on the famous children's book by Baum, he was forced to minimize the part of the lion to spotlight its two stars. No major songs emerged from the original score, but two interpolations, "Sammy" (James O'Dea/Edw. Hutchinson) and "Hurrah for Baffins Bay" (Vincent Bryan/Theodore Morse), were briefly popular. In 1975 an original, highly successful all-black musical, *The Wiz,* employed the same story. The two-act musical opened at the Majestic Theatre (not the same Majestic as in 1903) on January 5, 1975, and ran 1,672 performances. It had a book by William F. Brown and lyrics and music by Charlie Smalls. Stephanie Mills played Dorothy; Hinton Battle, the Scarecrow; Tiger Haynes, the Tinman; and Ted Ross, the Lion. Its principal songs were "Believe in Yourself," "Ease On Down the Road," and "Who Do You Think You Are?"

WODEHOUSE, P[ELHAM] G[RANVILLE] (1881–1975) After making a name for himself as a novelist and humorist, the writer, who was born in Guildford, England, came to America and served as drama critic for *Vanity Fair.* In 1916 he wrote lyrics for *Miss Springtime,* then joined composer Jerome Kern♦ and librettist Guy Bolton♦ to work on the book and lyrics for the Princess Theatre♦ shows. His 1917 credits included *Have a Heart; Oh, Boy!,* ♦ recalled for "Till the Clouds Roll By"; *Leave It to Jane,* ♦ remembered for "The Siren's Song"; *The Riviera Girl; Miss 1917;* and *Kitty Darlin'.* Among his later contributions were those as lyricist and co-librettist for *Oh, Lady! Lady!!*♦ (1918), from which came "Bill," not popularized until *Show Boat*♦ (1927); co-librettist for *Oh, Kay!*♦ (1926); co-lyricist for *Rosalie* (1928); and co-librettist for *Anything Goes*♦ (1934), although his work on this had to be jettisoned after the sinking of the *Morro Castle.* Wodehouse may well be considered the first truly great lyricist of the American musical stage, his easy, colloquially flowing rhymes deftly interwoven with a sunny wit.

Biography: *P. G. Wodehouse,* Frances Donaldson, New York, 1982.

WOLHEIM, LOUIS [ROBERT] (1881–1931) Born in New York, he had served as a mining engineer and a teacher at Cornell University before his friends John♦ and Lionel Barrymore♦ persuaded him to join them in *The Jest* (1919). A huge, strapping man with a conspicuous broken nose, he is best remembered for two exceptional portrayals: Yank, the primitive coal stoker who dreams of a better life, in *The Hairy Ape*♦ (1922), and Captain Flagg, the foul-mouthed career soldier, in *What Price Glory?* ♦ (1924).

Woman, The, a play in three acts by William C. de Mille. ♦ Produced by David Belasco♦ at the Republic Theatre. September 19, 1911. 247 performances.

Illinois Representative Jim Blake (John W. Cope) has only contempt for the public he serves—"The public," he snarls, "makes me sick." He also fears that public and what will happen when it wakes up to his corruption. He is especially anxious to push through a bill allowing railroads to inflate their stocks. To this end he feels he must besmirch his idealistic opponent, Matthew Standish (Cuyler Hastings), by disclosing Standish has been unfaithful to his wife. But first he must determine who the woman is. Knowing that when he broaches the matter to Standish, Standish is certain to call the woman, Blake attempts to bribe a telephone operator, Wanda Kelly (Mary Nash♦), to give him the number Standish calls so he can trace it. Wanda has heard Blake tell his scheme to his cronies and is loathe to help. But she plays along by being evasive. Standish does call the woman, but so does another man shortly thereafter. Wanda realizes that the woman is Blake's own daughter. She not only finds a means to keep anyone from being hurt but wins the affection of Blake's more amiable son, Tom (Harold Vosburgh), in the process.

One of the most successful of the muckraking melodramas of its age, it was greatly enhanced by Belasco's brilliantly paced and strikingly realistic production. Adolph Klauber◆ called it "a naturally developed series of situations, curiously well knit, and consistently cumulative in their emotional effect."

Woman's Way, A, a play in three acts by Thompson Buchanan.◆ Produced by William A. Brady◆ at the Hackett Theatre. February 22, 1909. 112 performances.

When Howard Stanton (Frank Worthing) confesses to his wife Marion (Grace George◆) that he is in love with the widowed Mrs. Blakemore (Dorothy Tennant), Marion invites her to a dinner party. There Howard learns that Mrs. Blakemore is not the angel he thought her to be.

This slight but pleasant comedy owed much of its success to Grace George's engaging performance.

Women, The, a comedy in three acts by Clare Boothe.◆ Produced by Max Gordon◆ at the Ethel Barrymore Theatre. December 26, 1936. 657 performances.

Bitchy Sylvia Fowler (Ilka Chase) persuades Mary Haines (Margalo Gillmore◆) to use her gossipy manicurist Olga (Ruth Hammond), knowing full well that Olga will reveal the affair Mary's husband, Stephen, is having. Mary heads for Reno, falling in with a motley crew of would-be divorcées. She is eventually joined by Sylvia, seeking her own divorce. Most of the women are catty, self-serving, and as unfaithful as the men they condemn. Eventually Mary learns that Stephen's remarriage has been unsuccessful. She is prepared to take him back and also prepared to deal with her lady friends, announcing, "I've had two years to sharpen my claws."

Although several important critics disliked the play—Brooks Atkinson◆ complaining of its "stingingly detailed pictures of some of the most odious harpies ever collected in one play"—the play, with an all-female cast, was one of the biggest comedy hits of the decade.

Wonderful Town, a musical comedy in two acts. Book by Joseph Fields◆ and Jerome Chodorov.◆ Lyrics by Betty Comden◆ and Adolph Green.◆ Music by Leonard Bernstein.◆ Produced by Robert Fryer◆ at the Winter Garden Theatre.◆ February 25, 1953. 559 performances.

Just as a tour guide is showing tourists the stagey, bohemian wonders of "Christopher Street," Ruth (Rosalind Russell◆) and Eileen Sherwood (Edith Adams) arrive to find an apartment. The one they rent is in a dingy cellar, close to the explosive subway excavations. The girls quickly become homesick for "Ohio," but are determined to conquer New York. One neighbor, known as The Wreck (Jordan Bentley), is an old football player living on memories of how he could "Pass That Football." Eileen quickly finds dates, but all Ruth can do is recognize that she knows "One Hundred Easy Ways" to lose men. Even a romance with her editor, Robert Baker (George Gaynes), seems to go sour, leaving Baker to insist he prefers "A Quiet Girl." Through Eileen, Ruth gets an assignment to interview some Brazilian sailors. The interview leads to a wild "Conga" and then to a melee which makes headlines. The notoriety lands the girls a job in a night club where they sing a cacophonous salute to New York, "Wrong Note Rag."

Louis Kronenberger◆ observed of this musical version of *My Sister Eileen,*◆ "The libretto is amusing, the lyrics are gay, the score is fresh," and summed up the entertainment as "a bouncy, freewheeling musical." Miss Russell's "droll, sardonic" performance, at once broad and subtle, enhanced the original production. The musical has enjoyed several revivals.

WOOD, AUDREY (1905–86) Considered by many to have been the pre-eminent playwrights' agent of her day. She was born in New York, daughter of the first manager of the Palace Theatre.◆ In 1937 she and her husband, William Liebling (1894–1969), founded Liebling-Wood, Inc., with Mr. Liebling representing actors' interests. Almost immediately their labors for clients bore fruit with *Room Service.*◆ After the agency was dissolved in 1954, Miss Wood worked alone. Among her clients were Tennessee Williams,◆ William Inge,◆ Robert Anderson,◆ and Arthur Kopit.◆

WOOD, JOHN The distinguished English actor, who was educated at Oxford and spent many years with both the Old Vic◆ and the Royal Shakespeare Company,◆ has appeared in several notable presentations on Broadway, including the lead in a 1974 revival of *Sherlock Holmes*♦; Henry Carr, the reminiscing, senilescent British official, in *Travesties* (1975); the title role in a 1977 revival of *Tartuffe*; and Sidney Bruhl, the murderous author, in *Deathtrap*♦ (1978). In 1981 he replaced the original stars Salieri in *Amadeus*.♦

WOOD, Mrs. JOHN [née MATILDA CHARLOTTE VINING] (1831–1915) Born in Liverpool, the comedienne made her American debut in Boston in 1854 and first appeared in New York as Don Leander in *The Invisible Prince* at the Academy of Music in 1856. That same season she scored a popular success as Minnehaha in Charles Melton Walcot's♦ *Hiawatha*.♦ Later she managed a theatre in San Francisco, then took over the Olympic from Laura Keene.♦ She operated it for three years before sailing back to England. However, she returned at intervals into the mid-1870s. She was considered a superb performer in burlesque, although some American critics found her voice thin and her face immobile. She was, nevertheless, a vivacious actress who won over most audiences. American papers continued to follow her English career with interest.

WOOD, Mr. JOSEPH (1801–90) AND Mrs. [née MARY ANN PATON] (1802–63) The English couple were considered among the finest singing actors of their time and were established London favorites when they first visited America in 1833. Although they were at once highly successful, their stays were marred first by a theatre riot stemming from a disagreement they had with the editor of the New York *Courier and Inquirer* in 1833, and later by an altercation over their refusal to appear at a benefit. They never played here after 1841. Most of the works they sang in would today be confined to opera houses, but they also performed in ballad opera such as *Love in a Village* and in *Clari, the Maid of Milan*.♦

WOOD, [MARGARET] PEGGY (1892–1978) The beautiful, versatile performer was born in Brooklyn and made her stage debut as a member of the chorus of *Naughty Marietta*♦ in 1910. She quickly rose to more important assignments, scoring a memorable success in *Maytime*♦ (1917), in which she introduced "Will You Remember?" She starred in several more musicals before playing Portia in a 1928 mounting of *The Merchant of Venice*.♦ After several major roles in London musicals, she returned to New York and appeared in such shows as *Champagne, Sec* (1933); as Mildred Watson Drake, the popular writer whose friendship is threatened, in

Old Acquaintance (1940); and as Ruth Condomine, whose husband's dead first wife comes back as an annoying ghost, in *Blithe Spirit* (1941). She is probably best remembered for her eight-year stint as Mama in the television series *I Remember Mama*.

Autobiography: *How Young You Look,* New York, 1940.

WOOD, WILLIAM [BURKE] (1779–1861) Born in Montreal, he worked as an accountant and as a lawyer's assistant before attempting his own business venture. The venture failed and he spent time in Philadelphia's debtor prison, then made his acting debut in Annapolis in 1798. Later the same year he first performed in Philadelphia. Wignell♦ appointed him treasurer of the city's Chestnut Street Theatre,♦ which, after Wignell's death, he took over in conjunction with the elder William Warren.♦ The pair also managed theatres in Baltimore, Annapolis, and Washington. He left the Chestnut Street Theatre in 1826 and for a time managed the Arch Street Theatre.♦ All this while he continued to act, excelling at comedy, until his retirement in 1846. He later wrote *Personal Reflections of the Stage* (1855), which confirmed his predilection for English drama and English performers.

WOODRUFF, HENRY [INGOTT] (1870–1916) The son of a prosperous New York businessman, he made his debut in the famous 1879 juvenile company of *H.M.S. Pinafore*♦ and subsequently acted with Daniel E. Bandmann,♦ Adelaide Neilson,♦ and other celebrities. In 1893 he was Charley Wykeham in the first American production of *Charley's Aunt*.♦ He then left the stage to attend Harvard. After graduation he resumed his career, displaying his versatility in important roles in Shakespearean revivals, musical comedies, and contemporary farce and drama. His slightly pudgy, boyish good looks and comic skills helped him score his biggest success as the nobly self-sacrificing collegian, the title role in *Brown of Harvard* (1906). In 1909 he starred in the Chicago musical *The Prince of Tonight,* in which he introduced "I Wonder Who's Kissing Her Now." For several years before his early death he toured in a popular vaudeville playlet, "A Regular Businessman."

Wood's Minstrels Founded in 1851 by Henry Wood, brother of New York mayor Fernando Wood, the company survived until 1865 as one of New York's most durable and popular ensembles. George Christy♦ joined the company for a time in its early years and it was known briefly as Christy and

Wood's. The troupe was a pioneer in moving away from traditional minstrel forms by including extended burlesques of famous plays and current events in its productions.

WOODS, A[LBERT] H[ERMAN] [né ALADORE HERMAN] (1870–1951) One of his era's most successful and colorful producers, he was born in Budapest and brought to this country as an infant. After growing up on New York's Lower East Side he tried various odd jobs in the garment trade and then became an advance agent for a traveling show. His first productions were cheap touring melodramas on the order of *The Bowery After Dark* and *Bertha, the Sewing Machine Girl.* ◆ Many of these were mounted by Sullivan, Harris and Woods, ◆ the firm he founded with P. H. Sullivan and S. H. Harris. ◆ In 1909 he braved Broadway with *The Girl from Rectors,* and during the next 34 years produced over 100 shows, including *Potash and Perlmutter* ◆ (1913), *Kick In* ◆ (1914), *Common Clay* ◆ (1915), *Cheating Cheaters* ◆ (1916), *Business Before Pleasure* ◆ (1917), *Eyes of Youth* ◆ (1917), *Parlor, Bedroom and Bath* ◆ (1917), *Friendly Enemies* ◆ (1918), *Up in Mabel's Room* ◆ (1919), *Ladies' Night* ◆ (1920), *Lawful Larceny* (1922), *The Shanghai Gesture* ◆ (1926), *The Trial of Mary Dugan* ◆ (1927), and *Five Star Final* ◆ (1930). He leaned heavily toward the lurid melodrama that had given him his start, as well as to bedroom and ethnic comedy. He also built the Eltinge Theatre and named it after one of his most profitable stars, Julian Eltinge. ◆ In his heyday he was famous for sitting in front of his theatre, smoking his big cigar, and calling all visitors "sweetheart."

WOODWORTH, SAMUEL (1785–1842) The peripatetic editor, publisher, and poet was born into a poor family in Scituate, Mass., and was largely self-taught. He worked on many popular periodicals in Boston, New Haven, Baltimore, and New York, serving as editor of the New York *Mirror* in 1823. It was after this stint that he wrote most of his plays, although he wrote the book of a comic opera, *The Deed of Gift,* in 1822. *Lafayette, or, The Castle of Olmutz* (1824) dealt with its hero's 1792 imprisonment in Germany. His libretto for *The Forest Rose; or, American Farmers* ◆ (1825), which he called a "pastoral opera," was followed by his best play, *The Widow's Son; or, Which Is the Traitor?* ◆ (1825), centering on treason during the Revolutionary War. *The Cannibals; or, The Massacre Islands* (1833) was a spectacular thriller drawn from Capt. Benjamin Morrell's *Narrative of Four Voyages,* while another play of the same year, *Blue Laws; or, Eighty Years*

Ago, was a farce. He is often credited with writing a third play produced about the same time, *King's Bride Cottage.* His last work, *The Foundling of the Sea,* also 1833, was written in response to G. H. Hill's ◆ search for a play containing a prominent Yankee character. In 1836 he abandoned all literary interests and went to work for the navy, but was paralyzed a year later by a stroke. Except possibly for *The Widow's Son* there is little of enduring merit in his plays, and posterity will recall him, if at all, as the lyricist of "The Old Oaken Bucket."

WOOLF, BENJAMIN E[DWARD] (d. 1901) The playwright and librettist was born in England and brought to America at an early age. In his teens he was apprenticed to an engraver. He abandoned that work in favor of becoming a violinist in the orchestra his father conducted at Burton's Theatre. He later moved to Boston where he conducted the orchestra at the Boston Museum. ◆ His poetry was published in book form, and his paintings exhibited at important Boston galleries. Oddly, he seems never to have composed music for public performance. Instead, between 1860 and the mid-1890s he wrote over thirty plays and librettos for Boston production. Playgoers around the country knew him best for two works: his libretto for one of the earliest full-fledged American comic operas, *The Doctor of Alcantara* ◆ (1862), and his comedy about American politics and materialism, *The Mighty Dollar* ◆ (1875). His nephew, Edgar Allen Woolf (1881–1943), was also a playwright and librettist.

WOOLLCOTT, ALEXANDER (1887–1943) Born in Phalanx, N.J., and educated at Hamilton College, he served as a police reporter for the New York *Times* before becoming one of its drama critics in 1914. With time off for World War I, he remained at the paper until 1922. Between then and 1928 he was the critic for the *Herald,* then the *Sun,* and finally the *World.* His fellow critic, John Mason Brown, ◆ called him "a sizzling mixture of arsenic and treacle," and said "he was as warm in his resentments as in his enthusiasms . . . his daily reviews . . . may not have been criticism but they were performances, Woollcott performing so that the emotions of a first night were captured in print with an immediacy unmatched in our time." Describing the reaction of an audience, whom he characterized as "old meanies," to a dismal, unintentionally funny 1925 play Woollcott reported in his review that "two drama critics and four laymen had to be picked up out of the aisle and put back in their seats." He wrote paeans of praise on Mrs. Fiske◆ and the Marx◆ brothers, but detested many of Eugene O'Neill's◆ best plays. His books, often filled with theatrical criticism and reminiscences, included *Mrs. Fiske* (1917), *Mr. Dickens Goes to the Play* (1923), *Enchanted Aisles* (1924), *The Story of Irving Berlin* (1925), *Going to Pieces* (1928), *While Rome Burns* (1934), and *Long, Long Ago* (1943). With George S. Kaufman◆ he wrote two failed plays, *The Channel Road* (1929) and *The Dark Tower* (1933). In his last years he devoted himself largely to radio and to writing magazine articles, but also took time to appear in *Brief Moment*◆ (1931) and *Wine of Choice* (1938), and in 1940 headed the road company of *The Man Who Came to Dinner,*◆ playing Sheridan Whiteside, a character drawn after his own image.

Biography: *Smart Aleck,* Howard Teichmann, New York, 1978.

WOOLLEY, Monty [Edgar Montillion] (1888–1963) Born in New York, he spent many years teaching drama at his alma mater, Yale, before becoming a professional director and actor. He staged several classic revivals, then turned to the musical theatre to direct such shows as *Fifty Million Frenchmen*◆ (1929), *The New Yorkers* (1930), and *Jubilee*◆ (1935). In 1939 he won applause in the musical *On Your Toes,*◆ but, with his pointed beard and sour hauteur, is best recalled as Sheridan Whiteside, the bellowingly cantankerous celebrity, in *The Man Who Came to Dinner*◆ (1939).

Wooster Group, The A small artists' collective which explores alternative, experimental theatrical byways, its genesis was The Performance Group, founded in 1967 by Richard Schechner. A splinter group, working with Spalding Gray and Elizabeth LeCompte, began operating in 1975 and this offshoot has been known as The Wooster Group since 1980. It often performs in a flexible 150-seat space called The Performing Garage. Among its productions have been *Sakonnet Point* (1975), *Point Judith* (1979), and *LSD* (*Just the High Points*) (1984). The ensemble toured Europe in 1986.

World of Susie Wong, The, a play in two acts by Paul Osborn.◆ Produced by David Merrick◆ and others at the Broadhurst Theatre. October 14, 1958. 508 performances.

Robert Lomax (William Shatner), a young artist living in Hong Kong, finds Susie Wong (France Nuyen) very attractive, even after he realizes she is a prostitute. Although Susie is willing to discuss her profession in detail and continue to ply her trade, Lomax prefers to paint her portrait and reform her. Kay Fletcher (Sarah Marshall) would lure Lomax away to a more respectable life, but Lomax will not listen.

Osborn based his work on the novel by Richard Mason. To many critics both the play and its production harked back to such Belasco◆ mountings as *Lulu Belle.*◆ Although they dismissed the work as sophomoric, audiences found it vastly entertaining.

World Wars I and II, see *Wars in American Drama*

WORM, [Conrad Henrik] A[age] Toxen (1866–1922) A native of Denmark, at the turn of the century he was a press agent whose clients included James O'Neill.◆ He served the Shuberts◆ as a manager from 1910 until shortly before his death, but was better known as one of the most imaginative publicists of his era. He originated the once famous "Masked Hostess" who was a greeter in Shubert enterprises, and he created such stunts as having the chorus girls of *The Red Petticoat,* a musical which dealt with a lady who runs a barber shop, offer free manicures to men in the audience.

WORTH, Irene (b. 1916) Born in Nebraska, the actress made her professional debut on tour with Elisabeth Bergner◆ in *Escape Me Never* in 1942. Her New York debut came the folowing year in *The Two Mrs. Carrolls.*◆ Thereafter she spent most of her career in London, although she returned for a number of later appearances. These included Celia Coplestone, the other woman, in *The Cocktail Party*◆ (1950), Albertine Prine, the hero's strange mother-in-law, in *Toys in the Attic*◆ (1960), and the title role of the enigmatic seductress in *Tiny Alice*◆ (1964). In recent years she has appeared more frequently in New York, most notably in revivals, playing the Princess Kosmonopolis in *Sweet Bird of Youth*◆ (1975), for which she won a Tony,◆ Madame Ranevskaya in *The Cherry Orchard* (1977), Winnie in Beckett's◆ *Happy Days* (1979), Ella Rentheim in *John Gabriel Borkman* (1980), Miss Madrigal in *The Chalk Garden* (1982), and Volumnia in *Coriolanus* (1988).

WRIGHT, Robert [Craig] (b. 1914) Born in Daytona Beach, Fla., he attended the University of Miami and worked in various musical capacities before joining with his career-long collaborator, George Forrest [Chichester, Jr.] (b. 1915), a native of Brooklyn. They wrote for films and for West

Coast theatrical productions and then came East to contribute material to the *Ziegfeld Follies of 1943.*♦ Their most successful Broadway efforts have been *Song of Norway*♦ (1944) and *Kismet*♦ (1953), for which they wrote lyrics to their rearrangement of the music of Grieg and Borodin, respectively. Both musicals were first mounted in California. Several of their other musicals, for which they sometimes provided original music, were successful on the West Coast but failed when they were brought East. Then they collaborated on the popular *Grand Hotel* (1989).

WYCHERLY, Margaret [née De Wolfe] (1881–1956) The slim, sad-eyed, slightly Semitic-looking actress was born in London, but raised in Boston. After studying at the American Academy of Dramatic Arts,♦ she made her debut in 1898 opposite Madame Janauschek♦ in *What Dreams May Come.* She spent time with Jessie Bonstelle's♦ stock company and in stock in San Francisco before returning to New York, where she played in several classic revivals and in new plays by Yeats and Shaw.♦ Among her notable later roles were Madame LaGrange, the medium who must solve a murder, in *The Thirteenth Chair*♦ (1916), written by her husband Bayard Veiller♦; the wife who decides to abandon a faithless husband, the title role of *Jane Clegg* (1920); the Mother, who was one of *Six Characters in Search of an Author* (1922); Daisy Devore, who is willing to love a nonentity, in *The Adding Machine*♦ (1923); Mrs. Hallam, the domineering mother, in *Another Language*♦ (1932); and Ada Lester, the downtrodden mother, in *Tobacco Road*♦ (1933). In later years she replaced Laurette Taylor♦ in *The Glass Menagerie,*♦ and shortly before her death played the Dowager Duchess of York in *Richard III.*♦

WYNDHAM, Charles (1837–1919) The great English comedian had had medical training, so served as a doctor for the Confederate Army during the Civil War. He also acted briefly during the war, but caused little stir. In 1869 he returned to America and won applause with Wallack's♦ ensemble in such roles as Charles Surface. Shortly thereafter he organized his own company and toured the country until he sailed for England in 1873. Although he soon became one of London's most popular actor-managers, he made a number of subsequent, if brief, tours in America. A tall, handsome man with a husky voice, he made his last appearance as Tom Kemp in *The Mollusc* (1909). One critic noted, "Sir Charles's mastery of the art of make-up is shown to distinct advantage in the piece. Although he is 72 years of age, he easily deceived the audience into believing that Tom Kemp is under 40. His delivery is remarkable virile, and his personality vigorous."

Biography: *All on Stage: Charles Wyndham and the Alberys,* Wendy Trewin, London, 1980.

WYNN, Ed [né Isaiah Edwin Leopold] (1886–1966) The Philadelphia-born comedian was the son of a well-to-do hat manufacturer who hoped his son would take over the business. Instead he became a professional vaudevillian at the age of fifteen, for several seasons performing in an act known as the Rah Rah Boys. By the time he made his Broadway debut in *The Deacon and the Lady* (1910), he had finely honed the tricks that became his trademarks—the lisp, the fluttering hands and squeaky giggle, the preposterous inventions, the zany clothing, and the outrageous puns (he once appeared as a show boat impresario who had "bred his cast upon the waters"). Among his subsequent shows were the 1914 and 1915 editions of the *Ziegfeld Follies,* ♦ *The Passing Show of 1916,*♦ *Doing Our Bit* (1917), *Sometime* (1918), *The Ed Wynn Carnival* (1920), *The Perfect Fool* (1921), *The Grab Bag* (1924), *Manhattan Mary* (1927), *Simple Simon* (1930), *The Laugh Parade* (1931), *Hooray for What!* (1937), *Boys and Girls Together* (1940), and *Laugh, Town, Laugh* (1942). He directed and produced many of these shows, as well as writing much of their material.

Y–Z

Yale Repertory Theatre AND **Yale School of Drama** The school of drama stemmed from the University's department of drama, which was established in 1924 following the generous grant by Edward S. Harkness and which succeeded in luring Professor George Pierce Baker♦ away from Harvard to become its head. In 1955 it was reorganized as a separate graduate school offering a Master of Fine Arts degree. Courses are given in numerous categories including play-writing, acting and directing, theatrical design, administration, drama criticism, and literature. The repertory theatre was, in turn, an outgrowth of the drama school and was founded in 1966 by Robert Brustein,♦ who remained its director until 1979, when he was followed by Lloyd Richards.♦ Stan Wojewodski, Jr., has been announced to succeed him in 1991. The group attempts to present not only new plays, especially those of young American dramatists, but freshly re-thought versions of classics.

Yankey in England, The, a comedy by David Humphreys. This work was produced by amateurs in 1814 but seems not to have been performed professionally. It deals with an American Whig and a Tory who become an admiral and a general after the Revolution, and who find themselves in London, where they meet a French count and countess. The countess is an adventuress who has a "Yankey," Doolittle, for a servant. He is a typical comic Yankee, bumptious, naïve, and yet cunning. However, when the countess's schemes go awry and she prepares to swallow poison, another, more sensible Yankee, Newman, sets matters to right.

The play is the first to transplant the traditional stage Yankee to foreign parts, a device that was revived with contemporary variations in American musical comedy ninety years later. Humphreys (1752–1818) was a Connecticut-born, Yale-educated gentleman-author who served as Washington's aide-de-camp and later was a Federal official. He wrote essays, poems, and one other known play, the romantic drama *The Widow of Malabar* (1790).

YEAMANS, ANNIE [née GRIFFITHS] (1835–1912) Best remembered as Cordelia Mulligan in the Harrigan♦ and Hart♦ plays, the tiny, small-mouthed actress was born on the Isle of Man. As a child she was taken to Australia, where her parents hoped to find theatrical success. She performed for many years as a bareback rider in a circus and married an American clown who was also a member of the troupe. Together they toured Asia. Coming to San Francisco, her husband died, so she took herself and their children to New York. Although not in the original casts, she performed with G. L. Fox♦ in *Humpty Dumpty,*♦ acted in Augustin Daly's♦ *Under the Gaslight,*♦ and as Aunt Ophelia in *Uncle Tom's Cabin.*♦ She first played opposite Harrigan in 1877 and continued to be his leading lady for eighteen years. Richard Harding Davis♦ wrote of her Cordelia, "We could never replace her coquetry or her brogue or her red wig and her bashful wiggle and shiver of pleasure when she is told how beautiful she is. She makes such an excellent foil to Harrigan with her excited, bustling garrulousness, the opposite at every point to the star's calm, easy confidence." After Harrigan's retirement she appeared in such plays as *The Great Train Robbery* (1895), *Why Smith Left Home* (1899), and *Under Cover* (1903), as well as in several musicals. Her daughters were also popular actresses, especially Jennie Yeamans [née Eugenia Marguerite Yeamans] (1862–1906).

Years Ago, a comedy in three acts by Ruth Gordon.♦ Produced by Max Gordon♦ at the Mansfield Theatre. December 3, 1946. 199 performances.

After watching Hazel Dawn in *The Pink Lady,* Ruth Jones (Patricia Kirkland) decides to become an actress. To the consternation of her father Clinton (Fredric March♦), she rejects his plan for her to become a physical education teacher and also rejects the suit of Harvard student Fred Whitmarsh (Richard Simon). At first only Mrs. Jones (Florence Eldridge♦) encourages her. But when Clinton, an ex-seaman, comes to recognize his daughter's determination, he pawns his prize telescope to help pay her way.

Originally written with a contemporary setting and tried out as *Miss Jones,* this semi-autobiographical comedy was rewritten, recast, and retitled. Of its Broadway version, Ward Morehouse♦ wrote in the *Sun,* "The play has atmosphere and character. It has been written with an understandable affection."

Yellow Jacket, The, a play in three acts by George C. Hazelton and J. Harry Benrimo.♦ Produced by William Harris, Jr.♦ and the Selwyns♦ at the Fulton Theatre. November 4, 1912. 80 performances.

When Chee Moo (Saxone Morland) bears the emperor an ugly baby, both she and her son, Wu Hoo Git, are given to a farmer to be put to death. The farmer spares them, and, while Chee Moo soon dies, Wu Hoo Git (George Relph) grows up to be a handsome young man. Guided by the spirit of his dead mother and by his beloved Suey Sin Fah (Grace A. Barbour), he bests his rival stepbrother and secures the yellow jacket that signifies he is emperor. Much of the story is told by a Chorus (Signor Perugini), while a dour, cigarette-smoking Property Man (Arthur Shaw) moves makeshift scenery about.

Hailed by Walter Prichard Eaton♦ as "a triumph for all concerned," the play was supposedly derived from several real Chinese plays and designed to show American playgoers what Chinese drama was like. Over the next twenty years it was given important revivals, several of which outran the original production. For details on Hazelton see *Mistress Nell.*♦

Yes, My Darling Daughter, a comedy in three acts by Mark Reed. Produced by Alfred de Liagre, Jr.,♦ at the Playhouse. February 9, 1937. 405 performances.

When young Ellen Murray (Peggy Conklin♦) decides to spend a weekend with her handsome fiancé, Douglas Hall (Boyd Crawford), her mother, Ann Whitman Murray (Lucile Watson), is outraged. This comes as a shock to Ellen since her mother was once one of Greenwich Village's most notorious bohemians, an advocate of free-thinking and free love. Ellen spends the weekend with Doug, but she also agrees to marry him, thereby satisfying everyone.

This light, amusing comedy was what the theatre called a "sleeper." Reed (b. 1890) was born in Chelmsford, Mass., and studied at Harvard under George Pierce Baker.♦ His only other success was *Petticoat Fever* (1935), a comedy about a radio operator's attempt to woo a woman pilot in Labrador.

Yiddish Art Theatre Founded in 1918 by Maurice Schwartz♦ at the Irving Place Theatre, it eventually moved to a fine, new theatre built for it on Second Avenue. Yiddish theatre historian Nahma Sandrow,

noting Schwartz's insistent pragmatism, observed that the organization was "as close to traditional Yiddish theatre as to austere revolutionary art theatre principles." One result was that even in its first season a breakaway group called the Jewish Art Theatre was formed by Jacob Ben-Ami♦ and others. But the breakaway group was short-lived while the original organization, by presenting a mixture of classics and trivial material, survived until 1950. The company also toured on occasion.

Yip, Yip, Yaphank, see *This is the Army*

YORDAN, PHILIP, see *Anna Lucasta*

You and I, a comedy in three acts by Philip Barry.♦ Produced by Richard G. Herndon♦ at the Belmont Theatre. February 19, 1923. 174 performances.

Maitland White (H. B. Warner♦) gave up his beloved painting when he married so that he could support his family as a successful businessman. Eventually, however, the urge to return to his art proves too much. He paints a portrait, which turns out to be just good enough to be sold for advertising purposes. He muses, "There is no such hell on earth as that of the man who knows himself doomed to mediocrity in the work he loves." But he can persuade his son, Roderick (Geoffrey Kerr), who is prepared to give up his own dream of becoming an architect in order to marry Veronica Duane (Frieda Inescort), not to repeat his mistake. Maitland does just that.

This Harvard Prize Play, known originally as *The Jilts,* was Barry's first work to receive a professional production. Theatrical historian Edwin J. Bonner has called it "an intriguing tragicomedy studded with epigrammatic wit."

You Can't Take It with You, a comedy in three acts by Moss Hart♦ and George S. Kaufman.♦ Produced by Sam H. Harris♦ at the Booth Theatre. December 14, 1936. 837 performances. PP.

Curmudgeonly, seventy-five-year-old Martin Vanderhof (Henry Travers) is the patriarch of a wacky New York City household. His daughter, Penelope Sycamore (Josephine Hull♦), writes plays that no one will produce, while her husband Paul (Frank Wilcox) manufactures fireworks in the cellar. One of Vanderhof's granddaughters, Essie (Paula Trueman), practices ballet in the living room, the same living room in which her husband Ed (George Heller) plays his xylophone and runs his printing press. Another granddaughter, Alice (Margot Stevenson), invites the parents of her rich fiancé, Tony

Kirby (Jess Barker), to the house for dinner. The Kirbys arrive a night early, and in the middle of the mayhem Paul's fireworks explode. Everyone is hauled off to jail. Vanderhoff has also been hounded by the government for never having paid any income tax, but when the government learns that Vanderhof's wife years before had buried a homeless milkman, using Vanderhof's name, it concludes he is legally dead and not liable.

One of the greatest in all American farces, it has remained a favorite of amateur and summer stock groups, and was given major revivals in 1965 and 1983. This last revival, which emphasized the sentimental aspects of the play, was staged by Ellis Rabb and starred Jason Robards, Jr.,♦ and Colleen Dewhurst.♦

You Know I Can't Hear You When the Water's Running, four one-act plays by Robert Anderson.♦ Produced at the Ambassador Theatre. March 13, 1967. 756 performances.

The Shock of Recognition—Jack Barnstable (George Grizzard♦), a playwright, gets more than he bargained for when he auditions Richard Pawling (Martin Balsam), an overeager actor, for a part that requires nudity.

The Footsteps of Doves—When Harriet (Eileen Heckart♦) tells her husband George (Balsam) that they are switching from a double bed to twin beds, he decides he prefers to sleep with a younger woman.

I'll Be Home for Christmas—Chuck (Balsam) and Edith (Miss Heckart) realize, as they fight over how to raise their children, just how empty their marriage has become.

I'm Herbert—Herbert (Grizzard) and Muriel (Miss Heckart), an elderly couple, try in vain to remember their early love affairs.

A diverse, diverting collection of short plays, it enjoyed one of the longest runs of any such bill.

YOUMANS, VINCENT [MILLIE] (1898–1946) Born in New York, where his father and grandfather were well-known hatters, he originally considered a career in engineering but soon turned to music. A stint in the navy in World War I, during which time John Philip Sousa♦ played at least one of his compositions, confirmed him in his decision. He served as a song-plugger and inserted interpolations into a failed revue before writing much of the score for *Two Little Girls in Blue* (1921), recalled for "Dolly" and "Oh, Me! Oh, My!" In 1923 he collaborated on *Wildflower,* in which his best numbers were "Bambalina" and the title song, and *Mary Jane*

McKane. A year later he wrote his first complete score for *Lollipop,* whose hit was "Tie a String Around Your Finger." The biggest musical comedy success of the 1920s was his *No, No, Nanette*♦ (1925), whose songs included "I Want To Be Happy" and "Tea for Two." *Oh, Please!* (1926) offered "I Know That You Know," while from the far more successful *Hit the Deck!*♦ (1927) came "Hallelujah" and "Sometimes I'm Happy." Thereafter he decided to abandon musical comedy writing and return to operetta. He had also co-produced *Hit the Deck!* and ambitiously attempted to produce other offerings. But his subsequent shows proved failures and drove him to bankruptcy. *Rainbow* (1928) was followed by *Great Day* (1929), which despite its short run left behind its title melody as well as "More Than You Know" and "Without a Song." *Smiles* (1930) offered "Time on My Hands," and *Through the Years* (1932), "Drums in My Heart" and the title song, the composer's own favorite. His last Broadway musical was his collaboration on *Take a Chance* (1932), remembered for his "Rise 'n' Shine." Especially in his early years his identifying signature was his employment of the shortest themes, often two to four notes, repeated with variations in harmony and in tempo. In later years his musical line was frequently longer, but he never fully discarded his early technique. After writing the music for the film *Flying Down to Rio,* he contracted tuberculosis. This, his heavy drinking and partying, coupled with a curious intractability in negotiations, all combined to remove him from the scene and hastened his death. Shortly before he died he produced *Vincent Youmans' Revue* (1943), using other men's music, but it failed to reach New York.

Biography: *Days To Be Happy, Years To Be Sad,* Gerald Bordman, New York, 1982.

YOUNG, JOHN H. (early 1860s–?) The Michigan-born set designer served an apprenticeship under Thomas G. Moses.♦ Coming to New York, he established himself quickly as a versatile artist capable of designing for the whole range of theatrical productions. His sets were seen in such mountings as Daly's♦ 1889 revival of *As You Like It*♦; *The Man Without a Country* (1894); *Under the Polar Star* (1896), which included his highly lauded depiction of an iceberg; *Cymbeline* (1897); *Way Down East*♦ (1898); *The Auctioneer*♦ (1901); and *The Pit* (1904). He was also sought after by producers of musicals, creating the settings for many of Weber♦ and Fields's♦ famous entertainments at their music hall; *Babes in Toyland*♦ (1903); *It Happened in Nordland* (1904); *George Washington, Jr.* (1906); the *Follies of*

1907, the first edition of what became famous as the *Ziegfeld Follies*♦; and *The Candy Shop* (1909).

Young Mrs. Winthrop, a play in four acts by Bronson Howard.♦ Produced at the Madison Square Theatre.♦ October 9, 1882. 190 performances.

Douglas Winthrop (George Clarke) is as preoccupied with business as his wife, Constance (Carrie Turner), is with playing a social game. When Douglas, claiming the call of business, asks his wife not to go to a ball and instead to remain home with their ailing child, she agrees. Then she hears rumors questioning Douglas's fidelity, so she changes her mind. Douglas, in fact, has gone to the home where the ball is being held, but on legitimate matters. While they are away the child dies and this leads to the couple's separation. The kindly family lawyer, Buxton Scott (Thomas Whiffen), brings about a reconciliation and makes both husband and wife see the excessiveness and consequences of their preoccupations.

One of the first important American plays to deal with materialism and social climbing without satire, it was praised by the *Times* as "a play which tells what we understand; which has a genuine purpose, though not a didactic heaviness, and which hoes to its mark simply, directly, and effectively." It remained a favorite in stock at least until World War I.

YOUNG, RIDA JOHNSON (1875?–1926) A beautiful Baltimore society woman, she elected for a time to become an actress and performed with E. H. Sothern♦ and Viola Allen.♦ Later she gave up performing to write plays, librettos, and lyrics. Her best-known works were *Brown of Harvard* (1906), centering on an idealized undergraduate; *The Lottery Man*♦ (1909), in which a handsome young bachelor raffles himself off; *Naughty Marietta*♦ (1910), including her lyrics for "Ah, Sweet Mystery of Life," "I'm Falling in Love with Someone," "Italian Street Song," " 'Neath the Southern Moon," and "Tramp! Tramp! Tramp!"; *Captain Kidd, Jr.* (1916), in which an old New York bookseller seeks the pirate's treasure; *Maytime*♦ (1917), which offered her lyric for "Will You Remember?"; and *Little Old New York* (1920), a period piece telling of an Irish girl who disguises herself as a boy to claim a fortune. Some sources list her birth as early as 1869.

YOUNG, ROLAND (1887–1953) The short, suave, thinly mustached comedian was born in London and had performed for some time on West End stages before making his American debut in 1912. He earned applause in numerous supporting roles, including those in two plays, *Good Gracious Annabelle*♦ (1916) and *A Successful Calamity* (1917), written by his future mother-in-law, Clare Kummer.♦ After he scored a major success in the musical *Buddies* (1919), Mrs. Kummer wrote *Rollo's Wild Oat*♦ (1920) for him. In it he played an incompetent actor who attempts Hamlet. In 1924 he played Neil McRae, the composer who dreams of the consequences of his marriage to a rich girl, in *Beggar on Horseback.*♦ His last success was as Ned Farrar, a would-be singer mistaken for a servant, in Mrs. Kummer's *Her Master's Voice*♦ (1933). He was long popular in films.

YOUNG, STARK (1881–1963) The noted American critic and author was born in Como, Miss., and educated at the University of Mississippi and at Columbia. After teaching English for several years he joined the staff of the *New Republic,* then served as drama critic for the *Times* during the 1924–25 season. He later served on the staff of *Theatre Arts*♦ while continuing to review plays for the *New Republic.* He wrote a number of unsuccessful original plays as well as admired translations of Chekhov. On rare occasions he also directed plays, including Eugene O'Neill's♦ *Welded* (1924). Among his books were *The Flower in Drama* (1923), *The Theatre* (1927), and a highly acclaimed historical novel, *So Red the Rose* (1934).

YOUNG, WILLIAM (1847–1920) Born near Chicago, where he studied and practiced law for a time, he later became an actor with the express intention of learning play-writing from a performer's vantage point. His early blank-verse tragedies, *Pendragon* (1882), dealing with the Arthurian legend, and *Ganelon* (1891), dealing with the son of the man who betrayed Roland at Roncesvalles, were both mounted by Lawrence Barrett.♦ The latter was much esteemed. His most successful plays, however, were his romantic comedy, *The Rajah*♦ (1883), which dealt with an indolent man who has a ward thrust upon him and must make himself seem a hero to her, and his 1899 dramatization of *Ben Hur.*♦ About a dozen of his other plays were mounted, with varying success.

You're a Good Man Charlie Brown, a musical comedy in two acts by Clark Gesner. Produced at Theatre 80 St. Marks. March 7, 1967. 1,597 performances.

A day in the life of Charlie Brown (Gary Burghoff), a very young man "with what you call a failure face," is spent in the company of his dog

Snoopy (Bill Hinnant), who thinks he is the German ace known as The Red Baron; Linus (Bob Balaban), who forever needs his security blanket; Linus's sister Lucy (Reva Rose), a battle-axe in the making; and the musical Schroeder (Skip Hinnant). They deal in their own special ways with such juvenile concerns as baseball and school.

Principal songs: Happiness · You're a Good Man Charlie Brown

Derived from Charles M. Schulz's comic strip, this low-budget musical became one of off-Broadway's biggest successes and remains popular with high school and other amateur theatre groups, as well as in professional stock. Gesner (b. 1938) was born in Augusta, Maine, and graduated from Princeton. He wrote revue, night-club, and television material before this, his only successful show.

ZAKS, JERRY (b. 1946) Born in Stuttgart, Germany, he was educated in America, including Dartmouth and Smith College. He began his career as an actor before turning to directing. After working in off-Broadway and regional houses he called attention to himself with three fine revivals at the Lincoln Center♦: *The House of Blue Leaves*♦ and *The Front Page*♦, both in 1986, and *Anything Goes*♦ in 1987. Among his other successful stagings have been *Wenceslas Square* (1987), *Lend Me a Tenor* (1989), the latter earning him a Tony Award,♦ and *Six Degrees of Separation* (1990).

ZIEGFELD, FLORENZ, JR. (1867–1932) The most famous of all American producers, still synonymous more than a half-century after his death with glamour and opulence, he was born in Chicago, where his father ran a musical conservatory. As director of musical events for the 1893 Columbian Exposition, the elder Ziegfeld sent his son to Europe to secure talent. Instead of hiring distinguished musical figures, the young Ziegfeld signed on music-hall performers and circus acts. In 1893 he also became manager of the strong man Eugene Sandow,♦ and his promotion of Sandow established his own name, too. His first Broadway production was an 1896 revival of *A Parlor Match,*♦ which featured his first wife, Anna Held.♦ His subsequent productions, mostly vehicles for his wife, were *Papa's Wife* (1899), *The Little Duchess* (1901), *The Red Feather* (1903), *Mam'selle Napoleon* (1903), *Higgledy Piggledy* (1904), and *A Parisian Model* (1906). Even in these early productions he began to earn a reputation for offering a chorus line of beautiful girls in sumptuous costumes. His next production was the *Follies of 1907,*♦ which initiated

the famous series. (See details in entry for *Ziegfeld Follies,* below.) His other musical productions were *The Soul Kiss* (1908), *Miss Innocence* (1908), *Over the River* (1912), *A Winsome Widow* (1912), *The Century Girl* (1916), *Miss 1917, Sally*♦ (1920), *Kid Boots* (1923), *Annie Dear* (1924), *Louie the 14th* (1925), *No Foolin'* (1926), *Betsy* (1926), *Rio Rita*♦ (1927), *Show Boat*♦ (1927), *Rosalie* (1928), *The Three Musketeers*♦ (1928), *Whoopee*♦ (1928), *Show Girl* (1929), *Bitter Sweet*♦ (1929), *Simple Simon* (1930), *Smiles* (1930), a 1932 revival of *Show Boat,* and *Hot-Cha!* (1932). Although he was often accused of being indifferent to great comics or great show songs, his roster of brilliant clowns and the numerous still popular melodies that came from his shows belie the accusations. He also produced a number of non-musical plays, including *Rose Briar* (1922) for his second wife, Billie Burke.♦ Ziegfeld's personal extravagances were as well publicized as his shows—among them his penchant for sending long telegrams to people within reach of his phone. His productions were the costliest of their day, and were praised not merely for their richness but for their tasteful visual beauty, especially those designed by Joseph Urban.♦ The producer's excellences so overshadowed those of his associates in contemporary eyes that, for example, the original production of *Show Boat* was hailed by most critics as a Ziegfeld show and not a Kern♦ or Hammerstein♦ show. Writing of the earlier *Sally,* Alexander Woollcott♦ concluded, "It is of none of these, not of Urban, nor Jerome Kern, not of Leon Errol, not even of Marilynn Miller that you think as you rush for the subway at ten minutes to midnight. You think of Mr. Ziegfeld. He is that kind of producer. There are not many of them in the world." Through much of his career he was associated with two of New York's almost legendary theatres, the New Amsterdam,♦ where most of his *Follies* played, and the Ziegfeld,♦ which he opened in 1927. His life was made into a popular film, with William Powell as the producer.

Biography: *Ziegfeld,* Charles Higham, Chicago, 1972.

Ziegfeld Follies The greatest and longest-lived series of extravagant revues, the first edition was mounted by Ziegfeld♦ on a shoestring budget as the *Follies of 1907.* The producer did not add his name to the series until 1911. Annual editions were produced through 1925. From 1922 on the revues were advertised as "Glorifying the American Girl." Ziegfeld himself later offered editions in 1927 and 1931, and also toured the show known on Broadway as *No Foolin'* as the *Ziegfeld Follies of 1926.* Writing during the series' heyday, George Jean Nathan◆ observed, "Out of the vulgar leg-show, Ziegfeld has fashioned a thing of grace and beauty, of loveliness and charm; he knows quality and mood. He has lifted, with sensitive skill, a thing that was mere food for smirking baldheads and downy college boys out of its low estate and into a thing of symmetry and bloom." After his death the Shuberts◆ bought the rights to the name and produced editions in 1934, 1936, and 1943. These editions were successful even though it was conceded they lacked the tasteful, imaginative opulence of Ziegfeld's own mountings. A 1957 edition was a quick, dismal failure.

Among the great stars presented in these revues by Ziegfeld, many of whom he discovered and developed, were Nora Bayes,◆ Fanny Brice,◆ Eddie Cantor,◆ Ray Dooley,◆ Leon Errol,◆ W. C. Fields,◆ Marilyn Miller,◆ Ann Pennington,◆ Will Rogers,◆ and Bert Williams.◆ Song hits from the shows include "Shine On Harvest Moon" (1908), "By the Light of the Silvery Moon" (1909), "Row, Row, Row" (1912), "Hello, Frisco" (1915), "A Pretty Girl Is Like a Melody" (1919), "My Man" and "Second Hand Rose" (1921), "Mr. Gallagher and Mr. Shean" (1922), and "Shaking the Blues Away" (1927). The Shubert versions included "The Last Roundup" and "Wagon Wheels" (1934) and "I Can't Get Started" (1936). From the first the productions were known for their eye-filling costumes and sets, but not until Joseph Urban◆ was signed on, beginning with the 1915 edition, did the series reach its legendary apotheosis. His stylish designs and carefully coordinated colors were instantly recognized as the finest work the American musical stage had yet seen. Settings often depicted exotic, color-rich lands and musical numbers were regularly given themes. Thus, in "A Pretty Girl Is Like a Melody" mannequins paraded dressed as "Barcarolle," "Elegy," and other classic styles. From 1917 through 1925 Ben Ali Haggin's◆ lavish tableaux vivants were also a feature. Among the many great Ziegfeld beauties were Marion Davies, Dolores, Paulette Goddard, Lillian Lorraine, Mae Murray, Drucilla Strain, and Avonne Taylor.

Ziegfeld Theatre Possibly the finest theatre ever built in New York, it was financed by William Randolph Hearst and designed by Joseph Urban◆ and Thomas Lamb.◆ Ziegfeld◆ opened it in February 1927 with his production of *Rio Rita*.◆ The auditorium was egg-shaped, with no boxes but with a gilt, undecorated proscenium and a gilt stage whose apron extended unusually far. Its walls and ceiling, which seemed virtually as one, were covered with Urban's

playful murals done in rich, burnished colors. Public rooms and backstage facilities were exceptionally spacious. Among the shows that played there in Ziegfeld's day were *Show Boat*◆ (1927), *Bitter Sweet*◆ (1929), and the *Ziegfeld Follies of 1931*.◆ After his death the house became a cinema, until Billy Rose◆ restored it to the legitimate fold in 1944. Its notable later offerings included *Brigadoon*◆ (1947), *Gentlemen Prefer Blondes*◆ (1949), and *Kismet*◆ (1953). It was torn down in 1967 to make way for a skyscraper.

ZIMMERMAN, J. FRED (1841?–1925) One of the founders of the notorious Theatrical Syndicate or Trust,◆ he began his career as treasurer of Washington's National Theatre.◆ Later his firm of Nixon◆ and Zimmerman devloped what was then a virtual monopoly of Philadelphia theatres, including the Chestnut Street Opera House, the Broad Street Theatre, the Forrest, and the Garrick. Curiously, the only three major legitimate theatres never controlled, or run only briefly by him, were the city's three most historic houses, the Chestnut Street◆ (which was not the same as the Opera House), the Arch Street,◆ and the Walnut Street.◆

ZINDEL, PAUL, see *Effect of Gamma Rays, . . .*

Zip; or, Point Lynne Light, a play in three acts by Frederick Marsden.◆ Produced at the Park Theatre. January 8, 1877. 8 performances.

Zip (Charlotte Crabtree◆) is a young girl who lives with a lighthouse keeper she believes to be her father. He is murdered by men who are determined to sink a passing ship and who black out the lighthouse and set up a false beacon. Zip foils their plans and learns that one of the passengers whom she has saved is her real mother. She is taken off to England to confirm her inheritance. A new set of villians try to deprive her of it, but once again she triumphs. She even finds a sweetheart.

One of Lotta Crabtree's most popular vehicles, and typical of most of them, the story gave her plenty of opportunities to sing, dance, and play her banjo. It remained in her repertory until she retired.

ZIPPRODT, PATRICIA (b. 1925) Born in Evanston, Ill., she studied at Wellesley College, the Chicago Art Institute, and New York's Fashion Institute. Among the shows for which she has created costumes are *A Visit to a Small Planet*◆ (1957), *Oh Dad, Poor Dad. . .*◆ (1962), *Fiddler on the Roof*◆ (1964), *Cabaret*◆ (1966), *Plaza Suite*◆ (1968), *1776*◆ (1969), *Pippin*◆ (1972), *Chicago*◆ (1975),

Brighton Beach Memoirs♦ (1983), *Sunday in the Park with George*♦ (1984), a 1986 revival of *Sweet Charity*♦ and a 1988 mounting of *Macbeth.*♦

Zira, a play in four acts by J. Hartley Manners♦ and Henry Miller.♦ Produced by Miller at the Princess Theatre. September 21, 1905. 128 performances.

Seeing a chance for a better life, Hester Trent (Margaret Anglin♦) takes the place of a woman she believes has died. This leads to complications, especially when the other woman turns up alive, but also leads to a happy romance.

Based on Wilkie Collins's *The New Magdalen,* which had already been dramatized with marked success in 1873, the new version was reset in contemporary South Africa during the Boer War.

Zoo Story, The, a one-act play by Edward Albee.♦ Produced at the Provincetown Playhouse.♦ January 14, 1960. 582 performances.

In the parlance of the day, Peter (George Maharis) is a beatnik, a shabbily dressed, aggressively hostile young man. He accosts Jerry (William Daniels), a mild-mannered publisher, who is sitting quietly on a park bench, and begins to pour out his history and feelings. This includes telling of a dog at his boarding house whom kindness could not move and with whom cruelty allowed him to establish an impersonal modus vivendi. It soon becomes evident that Peter is determined to die, by his own hand or by someone else's. And his death wish is realized.

Presented earlier in Berlin, this talky, then suddenly dramatic, play established Albee as a promising writer.